A Dictionary of Jewish–Christian Relations

An A to Z companion to 2,000 years of encounter between Judaism and Christianity, *A Dictionary of Jewish–Christian Relations* is a pioneering work which explores and defines the many factors that characterise the historic and ongoing relationship between the two traditions. From Aaron to Zionism, the editors have brought together over 700 entries – including events, institutions, movements, people, places and publications – contributed by more than 100 internationally renowned scholars.

The *Dictionary*, compiled under the auspices of the Cambridge-based Centre for the study of Jewish–Christian Relations, offers a focus for the study and understanding of Jewish–Christian relations internationally, both within and between Judaism and Christianity. It provides a comprehensive single reference to a subject which touches on numerous areas of study such as theology, religious studies, history, Jewish studies, literature and social and political studies, and will also attract the interest of a wide international readership beyond these disciplines.

Edward Kessler is a Founding and Executive Director of the Cambridge Centre for the study of Jewish–Christian Relations. He is the author of several works on Jewish–Christian relations including the acclaimed *Bound by the Bible: Jews, Christians and the Sacrifice of Isaac* (2004).

Neil Wenborn is a full-time writer and publishing consultant. He is the author of several biographies and is co-editor of the highly respected *History Today Companion to British History.*

A Dictionary of
Jewish–Christian Relations

EDITED BY
Edward Kessler
and
Neil Wenborn

CAMBRIDGE
UNIVERSITY PRESS

Cambridge Centre for the study
of Jewish–Christian Relations

CAMBRIDGE UNIVERSITY PRESS
Cambridge, New York, Melbourne, Madrid, Cape Town, Singapore, São Paulo

Cambridge University Press
The Edinburgh Building, Cambridge CB2 2RU, UK

Published in the United States of America by Cambridge University Press, New York

www.cambridge.org
Information on this title: www.cambridge.org/9780521826921

First published 2005

Printed in the United Kingdom at the University Press, Cambridge

A catalogue record for this book is available from the British Library

Library of Congress Cataloguing in Publication data

A dictionary of Jewish-Christian relations / edited by Edward Kessler and Neil Wenborn. – 1st ed.
    p.   cm.
Includes bibliographical references and index.
ISBN 0-521-82692-6 (hardback)
1. Judaism–Relations–Christianity–Dictionaries.   2. Christianity and other religions–Judaism–Dictionaries.   I. Kessler,
Edward, Dr.   II. Wenborn, Neil.   III. Title.
BM535.D487   2005
261.2′6′03–dc22   2005012923

ISBN-13 978 0 521 82692 1 hardback
ISBN-10   0-521-82692-6 hardback

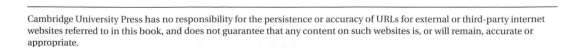

Contents

List of Maps

Contributors

Anna Sapir Abulafia
Vice-President and College Lecturer in History, Lucy Cavendish College, Cambridge, UK

David Abulafia
Professor of Mediterranean History, University of Cambridge, Cambridge, UK

James K. Aitken
Research Fellow, Department of Classics, University of Reading, and Honorary Fellow, Centre for the study of Jewish–Christian Relations, Cambridge, UK

Philip Alexander
Professor of Post-Biblical Jewish Studies, University of Manchester, Manchester, UK

Hamutal Bar-Yosef
Professor Emerita, Ben-Gurion University, Beer-Sheva; Research Fellow, The Hartman Institute, Jerusalem, Israel

Michael Battle
Assistant Professor of Spirituality and Black Church Studies, Duke University, Durham, North Carolina, USA

Anders Bergquist
Vicar of St John's Wood, London; formerly Vice-Principal of Westcott House, Cambridge and Canon Residentary of St Alban's Abbey, St Alban's, UK

Reimund Bieringer
Professor of New Testament Exegesis, Faculty of Theology, Katholieke Universiteit Leuven, Belgium

Barbara E. Bowe
Professor of Biblical Studies, Catholic Theological Union, Chicago, Illinois, USA

Mary C. Boys
Skinner & McAlpin Professor of Practical Theology, Union Theological Seminary, New York, USA

Marcus Braybrooke
President of the World Congress of Faiths, Co-Founder of the Three Faiths Forum, UK

Margaret Brearley
Lecturer/Academic Board member, London Jewish Cultural Centre; formerly Fellow in Jewish–Christian Relations, Selly Oak Colleges and Institute of Jewish Affairs, London, UK

James Carleton Paget
Lecturer in New Testament Studies, University of Cambridge, Fellow and Tutor of Peterhouse, Cambridge, UK

Kenneth Cracknell
Professor of Theology and Global Studies, Brite Divinity School, Fort Worth, Texas, USA

Robert Crotty
Adjunct Professor of Religion and Education, University of South Australia, Adelaide, Australia

Philip Culbertson
School of Theology, Auckland University, Auckland, New Zealand

Philip A. Cunningham
Executive Director, Center for Christian–Jewish Learning, Boston College, Boston, Massachusetts, USA

Alan Detscher
St Catherine of Sienna Parish, Riverside, Connecticut, USA

Audrey Doetzel
Christian–Jewish Relation and Encounter, Sisters of our Lady of Sion, Canada-USA

Alice L. Eckardt
Professor Emerita, Lehigh University, Bethlehem, Pennsylvania, USA

Artem Fedortchouk
St Andrew's Biblical Theological College, Moscow, Russia

Eugene J. Fisher
Associate Director, Secretariat for Ecumenical and Interreligious Affairs, US Conference of Catholic Bishops, Washington, DC, USA

Martin Forward
Helena Wackerlin Professor of Religious Studies and Executive Director of the Wackerlin Center for Faith and Action, Aurora University, Aurora, Illinois, USA

Lawrence E. Frizzell
Director, Institute of Judaeo-Christian Studies, Seton Hall University, South Orange, New Jersey, USA

Helen P. Fry
Honorary Research Fellow, Department of Hebrew and Jewish Studies, University College, London, UK

Petr Fryš
Director, Society of Christians and Jews (ICCJ), Prague, Czech Republic

Ruth Gledhill
Religion Correspondent, *The Times*, London, UK

Deirdre J. Good
Professor of New Testament, The General Theological Seminary, New York City, USA

Sergei Hackel
Formerly Reader in Russian Studies, University of Sussex, Brighton, UK, and Archpriest of the Russian Orthodox Church

Walter Harrelson
Professor Emeritus, Vanderbilt University Divinity School, and Adjunct University Professor, Wake Forest University Divinity School, Southport, North Carolina, USA

C. T. R. Hayward
Professor of Hebrew, Department of Theology, University of Durham, Durham, UK

Hans Hermann Henrix
Director, Bischöfliche Akademie des Bistums Aachen, Aachen, Germany

Michael Hilton
Rabbi, Kol Chai Hatch End Jewish Community, London, UK

K. Hannah Holtschneider
Lecturer in Modern Judaism, New College, Edinburgh, Scotland

Colin Honey
Senior Research Associate, The Lonsdale Centre for Applied Ethics, Melbourne, Australia

Morna D. Hooker
Lady Margaret's Professor Emerita, University of Cambridge, and Fellow of Robinson College, Cambridge, UK

William Horbury
Professor of Jewish and Early Christian Studies, and Fellow of Corpus Christi College, Cambridge, UK

Rebecca J. W. Jefferson
Research Assistant, Taylor-Schechter Genizah Research Unit, University Library, Cambridge, UK

Robin M. Jensen
The Luce Chancellor's Professor of the History of Christian Art and Worship, Vanderbilt University Divinity School, Nashville, Tennessee, USA

Ivor H. Jones
Methodist Minister, resident in Lincoln; formerly Principal of Wesley House, Cambridge, UK

Adam Kamesar
Hebrew Union College, Cincinnati, Ohio, USA

Wolfram Kinzig
Professor of Ecclesiastical History (Patristics), Evangelical Theological Faculty, University of Bonn, Bonn, Germany

William Klassen
Adjunct Professor of Religion, University of Waterloo, Waterloo, Ontario, Canada

Ruth Langer
Associate Professor of Jewish Studies, Theology Department, and Associate Director, Center for Christian–Jewish Learning, Boston College, Boston, Massachusetts, USA

Daniel R. Langton
Centre for Jewish Studies, Department of Religions and Theology, University of Manchester, Manchester, UK

Christopher M. Leighton
Executive Director, Institute for Christian and Jewish Studies, Baltimore, Maryland, USA

Amy-Jill Levine
E. Rhodes and Leona B. Carpenter Professor of New Testament Studies, Vanderbilt Divinity School, Nashville, Tennessee, USA

Lee I. Levine
Professor of Jewish History and Archaeology, Hebrew University, Jerusalem, Israel

Jane Liddell-King
Member of the English Faculty, University of Cambridge, Cambridge, UK

Judith Lieu
Professor of New Testament Studies, King's College, London, UK

Gareth Lloyd Jones
Professor of Theology and Religious Studies, Department of Theology and Religious Studies, University of Wales, Bangor, UK

Andrew Louth
Professor of Patristic and Byzantine Studies, University of Durham, Durham, UK

Rachel McCann
Associate Professor, School of Architecture, Mississippi State University, Mississippi, USA

John McDade
Principal of Heythrop College, University of London, London, UK

Michael McGarry
Rector, Tantur Ecumenical Institute for Theological Studies, Jerusalem, Israel

Bernard McGinn
Naomi Shenstone Donnelley Professor Emeritus of Historical Theology and of the History of Christianity, Divinity School, University of Chicago, Chicago, Illinois, USA

James S. McLaren
Senior Lecturer, School of Theology, Australian Catholic University, Fitzroy, Victoria, Australia

Dennis D. McManus
Senior Adjunct Professor, Department of Theology, Department of Classics, Georgetown University, Washington, DC, USA

Steven J. McMichael
Assistant Professor, Theology Department, University of St Thomas, Saint Paul, Minnesota, USA

Jonathan Magonet
Principal, Leo Baeck College – Centre for Jewish Education, London, UK

Ian Markham
Professor of Theology and Ethics, and Dean, Hartford Seminary, Hartford, Connecticut, USA

Justin J. Meggitt
Staff Tutor in the Study of Religion, Institute of Continuing Education, and Fellow, Hughes Hall, University of Cambridge, Cambridge, UK

John C. Merkle
Professor of Theology, College of Saint Benedict, Saint Joseph, Minnesota, USA

David M. Neuhaus
Pontifical Biblical Institute (Jerusalem), Shalom Hartman Institute (Jerusalem) and Religious Studies Department, Bethlehem University, Bethlehem, Palestinian Autonomy

Judith H. Newman
Associate Professor of Old Testament, Emmanuel College, University of Toronto, Toronto, Canada

Stephen Nicholls
Centre for German–Jewish Studies, University of Sussex, Brighton, UK

Peter Ochs
Edgar Bronfman Professor of Modern Judaic Studies, University of Virginia, Charlottesville, Virginia, USA

John J. O'Keefe
Associate Professor of Theology, Creighton University, Omaha, Nebraska, USA

David Patterson
Emeritus President, Oxford Centre for Hebrew and Jewish Studies, Yarnton, Oxford, UK

John T. Pawlikowski
Professor of Social Ethics and Director, Catholic–Jewish Studies Program, Catholic Theological Union, Chicago, Illinois, USA

Sarah J. K. Pearce
Senior Lecturer and Director of the Parkes Institute for the Study of Jewish/Non-Jewish Relations,

University of Southampton,
Southampton, UK

Peter A. Pettit
Director, Institute for Jewish–Christian
Understanding; Assistant Professor, Department of
Religion, Muhlenberg College, Allentown,
Pennsylvania, USA

Christine Pilkington
Principal Lecturer in Religious Studies, Canterbury
Christ Church University College, Canterbury,
UK

Stephen Plant
Senior Tutor and Director of Studies, Wesley House,
Cambridge, UK

Marcus Plested
Vice-Principal and Director of Studies, Institute for
Orthodox Christian Studies (Cambridge Theological
Federation) and Research Fellow, Faculty of Divinity,
University of Cambridge, Cambridge, UK

Daniel Polish
Rabbi of congregation Shir Chadash, Poughkeepsie,
New York, USA

Didier Pollefeyt
Professor of Catechetics, Religious Education and
Jewish–Christian Dialogue, Faculty of Theology,
Katholieke Universiteit Leuven, Belgium

John D. Rayner
Honorary Life President of Liberal Judaism; Emeritus
Rabbi of the Liberal Jewish Synagogue, London, UK

Stefan C. Reif
Professor of Medieval Hebrew Studies, Faculty of
Oriental Studies; Director, Genizah Research Unit,
University Library; Fellow of St John's College –
University of Cambridge, Cambridge, UK

John Rogerson
Emeritus Professor of Biblical Studies, University of
Sheffield; Canon Emeritus of Sheffield Cathedral,
Sheffield, UK

Jonathan Romain
Minister, Maidenhead Synagogue, Berkshire,
UK

Daniel Rossing
Director, Jerusalem Center for Jewish–Christian
Relations, Jerusalem, Israel

John K. Roth
Edward J. Sexton Professor of Philosophy and
Director of the Center for the Study of the Holocaust,
Genocide, and Human Rights, Claremont McKenna
College, Claremont, California, USA

Miri Rubin
Professor of European History, Queen Mary,
University of London, London, UK

A. James Rudin
Senior Interreligious Advisor, The American Jewish
Committee; Distinguished Visiting Professor of
Religion, Saint Leo University, Saint Leo, Florida,
USA

Marc Saperstein
Charles W. Smith Professor of Jewish History and
Director of the Program in Judaic Studies, The
George Washington University, Washington, DC,
USA.

John F. A. Sawyer
Emeritus Professor, University of Newcastle upon
Tyne, Newcastle upon Tyne, UK

Joachim Schaper
Reader in Old Testament, School of Divinity,
History and Philosophy, University of Aberdeen,
UK

Simon Schoon
Minister of the Reformed Church, Gouda; Professor of
Jewish–Christian Relations, Theological University,
Kampen, Netherlands

Stefan Schreiner
Professor of History of Religions and Jewish Studies
and Director of Institutum Judaicum, University of
Tübingen, Tübingen, Germany

Frank Shaw
Formerly Visiting Assistant Professor of Classics, St
Francis Xavier University, Antigonish, Nova Scotia,
Canada

Franklin Sherman
Founding Director, Institute for Jewish–Christian
Understanding, Muhlenberg College, Allentown,
Pennsylvania, USA

Michael A. Signer
Abrams Professor of Jewish Thought and Culture,
Department of Theology, University of Notre Dame,
Notre Dame, Indiana, USA

David Sim
Senior Lecturer, School of Theology, Australian Catholic University, Victoria, Australia

Norman Solomon
Member of the Oxford University Teaching and Research Centre in Hebrew and Jewish Studies, Yarnton, Oxford, UK

R. Kendall Soulen
Professor of Systematic Theology, Wesley Theological Seminary, Washington, DC, USA

Joann Spillman
Professor of Theology, Rockhurst University, Kansas City, Missouri, USA

Sacha Stern
Reader in Jewish Studies, School of Oriental and African Studies, University of London, London, UK

Kenneth Stow
Professor of Jewish History, University of Haifa, Haifa, Israel

Jesper Svartvik
Docent and Senior Research Fellow, Lund University and the Swedish Research Council, Lund, Sweden

Lucy Thorson
Program Director, Cardinal Bea Centre of Jewish Studies, Gregorian Pontifical University, Rome, Italy

Liam M. Tracey
Professor of Liturgy, St Patrick's College, Maynooth, Ireland

Christine Trevett
Professor, School of Religious and Theological Studies, Cardiff University, Cardiff, UK

Murray Watson
Lecturer in Sacred Scripture, St Peter's Seminary, London, Ontario, Canada

David Weigall
Formerly Head of Department of History, Anglia Polytechnic University, Cambridge, UK

Michael Weisskopf
Lecturer in Russian-Jewish history, Department of Slavic Studies, Hebrew University, Jerusalem, Israel

Susan White
Harold L. and Alberta H. Lunger Professor of Spiritual Resources and Disciplines, Brite Divinity School, Fort Worth, Texas, USA

George R. Wilkes
Lecturer, Centre for the study of Jewish–Christian Relations; Affiliated Lecturer, Divinity Faculty, University of Cambridge, Cambridge, UK

Isabel Wollaston
Senior Lecturer, Department of Theology, University of Birmingham, Birmingham, UK

Abigail Wood
School of Humanities, University of Southampton, Southampton, UK

Melanie J. Wright
Academic Director, Centre for the study of Jewish–Christian Relations, Cambridge, UK

Editors' preface

Since the beginning of the twentieth century the relationship between Judaism and Christianity has changed dramatically and is one of the few pieces of encouraging news that can be reported today about the encounter between religions. The rapprochement in relations and the development of a new way of thinking were pioneered by a small number of scholars and religious leaders in the first half of the century. However, it was the impact of the Holocaust, the creation of the State of Israel, the development of the ecumenical movement and the work of the Second Vatican Council (1962–5) which in combination made the changes more widespread. As a result, Christianity, so long an instigator of violence against Jews, rediscovered a respect and admiration for Judaism, and the once close relationship, which had become a distant memory, has been to a large extent restored. For Jews, the traditional view that they were on their own and that Christianity was an enemy has been replaced by a realisation that partnership with Christianity is possible and that both faiths share a Messianic vision of God's kingdom on earth.

At the same time as gaining a new appreciation of Judaism, Christianity during this period acknowledged its contribution to antisemitism and the detrimental impact of the legacy of the *Adversus Judaeos* (anti-Jewish) literature. It no longer holds that Jewish interpretation of scripture was false or has been replaced by Christian interpretation. This is illustrated by the teaching of the Roman Catholic Church, which now states: 'The Jewish reading of the Bible is a possible one, in continuity with the Jewish Sacred Scriptures . . . a reading analogous to the Christian reading which developed in parallel fashion.' (*The Jewish People and their Sacred Scriptures in the Christian Bible*, 2002). The Churches are also aware of the need to learn about developments in post-biblical Judaism, as demonstrated by the World Lutheran Federation's assertion that 'Christians also need to learn of the rich and varied history of Judaism since New Testament times, and of the Jewish people as a diverse, living community of faith today. Such an encounter with living and faithful Judaism can be profoundly enriching for Christian self-understanding' (*Guidelines for Lutheran–Jewish Relations*, 1998). Consequently, there is today wide recognition within Christianity that the formation of Christian identity is dependent upon a right relationship with Judaism. Every bishop is now commended to 'promote among Christians an attitude of respect towards their "elder brothers" so as to combat the risk of anti-semitism, and . . . should be vigilant that sacred ministers receive an adequate formation regarding the Jewish religion and its relation to Christianity' (*Congregation for Roman Catholic Bishops, Directory for the Pastoral Ministry of Bishops*, 2004).

For their part, many Jews initially responded with distrust to the modern changes in Christian teaching about Judaism; others engaged in dialogue with Christians for defensive reasons, in order to tackle prejudice and antisemitism. There were, of course, individual Jewish figures who promoted a positive view of Christianity, such as Martin Buber who reminded Jews that Jesus was a fellow Jew, their 'elder brother'. But in recent years there have been stirrings of a new and much more widespread interest in Christianity among Jews, illustrated by the publication in 2000 of *Dabru Emet* ('Speak Truth'), a cross-denominational Jewish statement on relations with Christianity which asserts, for example, that 'Jews and Christians seek authority from the same book – the Bible (what Jews call "Tanakh" and Christians call the "Old Testament")'. The eight-paragraph statement demonstrates awareness of a common purpose with Christianity. Furthermore, the impact of the papal visit to Israel, also in 2000, made an indelible mark on the Jewish psyche.

Of course, there continue to be divisions and quarrels over, for example, attitudes towards the State of Israel and its relationship with the Palestinians as well as with its other Arab neighbours. Evidence of increasing antisemitism, particularly in Europe and the Middle East, has also led to a corresponding increase in

Jewish sensitivity to criticism, particularly Christian criticism. In addition, the consequences of 9/11 and the upsurge of violence in the Middle East are causing a strain on relations. Nevertheless, it seems clear that in the mainstream of both traditions many of the principal divisive issues have been either eliminated or taken to the furthest point at which agreement is possible. The efforts of Catholics and Protestants towards respect for Judaism project attitudes that would have been unthinkable a few decades ago. Christian theology has been profoundly revised at the official level: all Churches are now committed to the fight against antisemitism, and the vast majority are actively committed to teaching about the Jewishness of Jesus, and the problem of mission to Jews has been significantly reduced.

Yet it is not only questions of faith that have provided the basis for relations between Judaism and Christianity. Jews and Christians do not exist only in religious communities – they also live in the world. The Jewish–Christian encounter has influenced and been influenced by the evolution of civilisation and culture, both for good and for ill. Take, for example, the record of the German Mennonite community. As Melanie Wright has shown, although core elements of Anabaptist theology – radical Church–state separation and pacifism – should (*if* one assumes that having the right theology leads to right action) have prevented them from participating in Nazism, German Mennonites abandoned their heritage in order to support Hitler. To understand this one needs to turn not to theology, but to the socio-political realm. Many of the Church's members were returnees from the Soviet Union and consequently, in the context of the new ethnic politics, keen to prove their identity as true Germans. They believed that failure to do so would have had negative consequences for the Church.[1]

The *Dictionary of Jewish–Christian Relations* is the first work comprehensively to address not only the theological, but also the philosophical, historical, sociological and political dimensions of the ongoing encounter between Judaism and Christianity. Surprising as it may seem, while the history of that encounter stretches over two millennia, it represents a relatively new subject of study. Although the distinctiveness, even uniqueness, of the relationship between the two faiths has long been noted by Jews and Christians alike, there has until now been no single work that explores and defines the many factors that go to make up this relationship. The dramatic developments of the last half-century have led to a greater degree of mutual respect, as witnessed in the widespread use of such familial terms as 'elder and younger brothers'. Yet these terms remain vague and undefined. They illustrate the fact that the uniqueness of the relationship is far easier to proclaim than to define, let alone explain. The contributors to this *Dictionary*, drawn from a wide range of disciplines, backgrounds and countries, are therefore involved in a ground-breaking endeavour. In uncovering the elements of the long and continuing relationship between Judaism and Christianity, we hope that the *Dictionary* will contribute significantly to the definition of, and will act as a focus for, a new field of study.

That field is by its very nature interdisciplinary, and a key feature of the *Dictionary* is that it not only focuses on subjects – whether historical, theological, political or cultural – within the Jewish–Christian encounter itself, but also reflects broader historical, theological, political or cultural subjects through the prism of that encounter. Thus, it includes not only the sort of entries the reader might expect to see in a work of this kind – baptism, Hebrew Bible, New Testament, Messiah, Holocaust – but also entries on such topics as architecture, abortion, the Ottoman Empire, Russian literature, music. Just as 'Holocaust studies' is accepted today as a field within which people use tools and insights from a range of different disciplines, so Jewish–Christian relations both involves and impacts upon many other fields of study. The entries in the *Dictionary* include *inter alia* events, institutions, movements, people, places, publications and theology, and the extensive network of cross-references between them itself serves to dramatise – and, we hope, tempt the reader to explore – the variety and interconnectedness of the subject's many aspects. For example, it should no longer be possible for a student of English literature to claim an understanding of *The Merchant of Venice* without understanding the perception of Jews and Judaism in sixteenth-century England, or for a biblical scholar to address the development of Christian scriptural interpretation without an examination of Jewish interpretations of scripture. Nor is it possible for a historian to study modern history without

[1] Wright, M. J., *The Nature and Significance of Relations between the Historic Peace Churches and Jews during and after the* Shoah, in Porter, S., and Pearson, B. W. R. (eds), *Christian–Jewish Relations through the Centuries* (Sheffield, Sheffield Academic Press, 2000), 410–12.

taking into consideration the impact of the Holocaust or the creation of the State of Israel. The *Dictionary* will therefore be of interest not only to Christians and Jews, but also to all those who are interested in the contribution to, and continuing influence upon, contemporary society of the encounter between the two traditions.

At the same time, however, the *Dictionary* deliberately avoids offering either a Jewish approach to the relationship or a Christian one; nor, while it necessarily deals with the subject, is its principal focus on dialogue between the two religions – dialogue is a subsection of Jewish–Christian relations but not its equivalent. In other words, the guiding criterion for the choice of entries has not been their significance to the understanding of Judaism or Christianity (or even both); rather, it has been their significance to the encounter *between* Judaism and Christianity. No doubt, as with any work of this kind, there are other subjects we might have included, as well as differences in emphasis and approach between related subjects, but every entry aims to describe and evaluate the importance of its subject to the encounter, and that importance is the touchstone against which both its inclusion and its treatment have been rigorously tested.

In providing a broader basis for a discourse about Judaism and Christianity than has ever been achieved before, the *Dictionary* will, we hope, not only help establish boundaries for the field of study, but will also provide a valuable insight into the relationship between the two traditions. The significant growth of Holocaust studies, as well as growing Christian recognition of Christianity's contribution to antisemitism and the Holocaust, has burdened the study of Jewish–Christian relations with emotion and apologetic. The same burden has increased the general ignorance among adherents of both religions of the historical and theological roots of the contemporary Jewish–Christian encounter. The *Dictionary* seeks to lay bare those roots, as well as to trace their outgrowth in the encounter itself. It is based on the latest scholarly thinking and does not attempt to flatter or to veil unpleasant truths, for only accurate descriptions of the Jewish–Christian encounter can provide a basis for positive relations in the future. It is to be hoped that the *Dictionary* will contribute both to the self-professed need within Christianity to develop a closer and more understanding relationship with Judaism and to the need within Judaism to update its own traditions and make more widely known its teachings about Christianity.

Finally, the transformation of Jewish–Christian relations has significance for the wider interfaith encounter. The contemporary encounter intends not to abolish differences but to develop a partnership – for Jews a *ḥevruta* and for Christians a common mission – to tackle one of the great challenges of the twenty-first century: the encounter between all faiths. The challenge takes place daily not only in the seminary or the place of worship, but also in the classrooms of the primary, secondary and tertiary sectors as well as in popular culture and in the workings of intercommunal and international relations. The establishment of Jewish–Christian relations as a field of study will not lead to consensus or uniformity, nor will it tell us all we want or need to know about the relations between the two traditions. However, a better understanding of the relationship will lead to the realisation that, while Judaism and Christianity are separate, they are also profoundly connected. The *Dictionary of Jewish–Christian Relations* and its bringing together of Jewish and Christian scholars from around the world is one more sign that a new relationship has begun. If this can happen between Judaism and Christianity it can surely happen in the encounter with other religions as well.

Acknowledgements

It will be no surprise that editing a book of this scale has been hard work. That it has also turned out to be so rewarding is due to several institutions and a significant number of people.

We would like to acknowledge the Centre for Advanced Religious and Theological Studies of the Faculty of Divinity of the University of Cambridge, who agreed to support and house the *Dictionary*; the publishers, Cambridge University Press, and especially Kevin Taylor, Kate Brett and Gillian Dadd, each of whom has taken a great deal of care in seeing the project to completion; the Centre for the study of Jewish–Christian Relations, and especially its staff, who have supported us and sustained our morale throughout the three years during which the *Dictionary* was in preparation; Deborah Patterson Jones for helping to get the project off the ground in its early stages; finally, to the British Academy, who generously made a grant to support the research, as did the Posen Foundation, which has always taken an interest in the work of the Centre for the study of Jewish–Christian Relations.

As for individuals, it is no easy task to thank properly everyone who encouraged us from inception. Indeed, if anyone should keep within their word-limit, it should surely be the editors. However, of the many factors that made this work rewarding the most important was our contact with contributors, who were willing to give their time and energy to a project that must often have seemed to consume more of both than they had anticipated. Their patience and willingness to take on board editorial suggestions, on numerous occasions, are greatly appreciated. We particularly thank Professor John Pawlikowski, who read through the manuscript at a draft stage and offered wise advice, and also Petr Fryš, whose ready and efficient help in the final stages of the project, not least with preparing the bibliography, was invaluable. To you all, we thank you.

Abbreviations

b.	Babylonian Talmud		Mal.	Malachi
m.	Mishnah		**New Testament**	
t.	Toseftah		Matt.	Matthew
y.	Jerusalem/Palestinian Talmud		Mark	Mark
Hebrew Bible/Old Testament			Luke	Luke
Gen.	Genesis		John	John
Exod.	Exodus		Acts	Acts
Lev.	Leviticus		Rom.	Romans
Deut.	Deuteronomy		1–2 Cor.	1–2 Corinthians
Josh.	Joshua		Gal.	Galatians
Judg.	Judges		Eph.	Ephesians
Ruth	Ruth		Phil.	Philippians
1–2 Sam.	1–2 Samuel		Col.	Colossians
1–2 Kgs	1–2 Kings		1–2 Thess.	1–2 Thessalonians
1–2 Chr.	1–2 Chronicles		1–2 Tim.	1–2 Timothy
Ezra	Ezra		Titus	Titus
Neh.	Nehemiah		Phlm.	Philemon
Esth.	Esther		Heb.	Hebrews
Job	Job		Jas	James
Ps./Pss	Psalm(s)		1–2 Pet.	1–2 Peter
Prov.	Proverbs		1–2–3 John	1–2–3 John
Eccl.	Ecclesiastes		Jude	Jude
Song	Song of Songs		Rev.	Revelation
Isa.	Isaiah		**Apocrypha**	
Jer.	Jeremiah		Bar.	Baruch
Lam.	Lamentations		1–2 Esd.	1–2 Esdras
Ezek.	Ezekiel		Jdt.	Judith
Dan.	Daniel		1–2 Macc.	1–2 Maccabees
Hos.	Hosea		Sir.	Sirach
Joel	Joel		Tob.	Tobit
Amos	Amos		Wis.	Wisdom of Solomon
Obad.	Obadiah		**Old Testament Pseudepigrapha**	
Jon.	Jonah		*1 En.*	*1 Enoch (Ethiopic Apocalypse)*
Mic.	Micah		*2 En.*	*2 Enoch (Slavonic Apocalypse)*
Nah.	Nahum		*Jub.*	*Jubilees*
Hab.	Habakkuk		*L.A.B.*	*Liber antiquitatum biblicarum*
Zeph.	Zephaniah			*(Pseudo-Philo)*
Hag.	Haggai		*Pss. Sol.*	*Psalms of Solomon*
Zech.	Zechariah		*T. Dan*	*Testament of Dan (Testaments of the Twelve Patriarchs)*

New Testament Pseudepigrapha

Ps.-Clem.	Pseudo-Clementines

Philo

Conf.	De confusione linguarum
Contempl.	De vita contemplativa
Fug.	De fuga et inventione
Leg.	Legum allegoriae
Legat.	Legatio ad Gaium
Migr.	De migratione Abrahami
Mos.	De vita Mosis
Opif.	De opificio mundi

Josephus

Ag. Ap.	Against Apion
Ant.	Jewish Antiquities
J. W.	Jewish War
Life	The Life

Apostolic Fathers

Barn.	Barnabas
Did.	Didache
Diogn.	Diognetus
Herm. Mand.	Shepherd of Hermas, Mandate
Ign. Magn.	Ignatius, To the Magnesians
Ign. Phld.	Ignatius, To the Philadelphians
Ign. Smyrn.	Ignatius, To the Smyrnaeans
Ign. Trall.	Ignatius, To the Trallians
Mart. Pol.	Martyrdom of Polycarp

Greek and Latin Works

Ambrose

Abr.	De Abraham
Enarrat. Ps.	Ennarationes in XII Psalmos davidicos

Aquinas

Summa	Summa Theologica

Augustine

Adv. Jud.	Tractatus adversus Judaeos
Civ.	De civitate Dei
Enarrat. Ps.	Enarrationes in Psalmos

Clement of Alexandria

Paed.	Paedagogus

Cyprian

Dom. or.	De dominica oratione
Test.	Ad Quirinium testimonia adversus Judaeos

Eusebius

Hist. eccl.	Historia Ecclesiastica
Vit. Const.	Vita Constantini

Gregory of Nazianzus

Ep.	Epistulae

Irenaeus

Haer.	Adversus haereses

Jerome

Comm. Gal.	Commentariorium in Epistulam ad Galatas libri III
Comm. Habac.	Commentariorium in Habacuc libri II
Comm. Isa.	Commentariorium in Isaiam libri XVIII
Epist.	Epistulae
Ruf.	Adversus Rufinum
Vir. ill.	De viris illustribus

John Chrysostom

Adv. Jud.	Adversus Judaeos

Justin

1 Apol.	Apologia 1
Dial.	Dialogus cum Tryphone

Origen

Cels.	Contra Celsum
Comm. Jo.	Commentarii in evangelium Joannis
Comm. Rom.	Commentarii in Romanos
Ep. Afr.	Epistula ad Africanum
Fr. 1 Cor.	Fragmenta ex commentariis in epistulam 1 ad Corinthios
Fr. Luc.	Fragmenta in Lucam
Hom. Gen.	Homiliae in Genesim
Hom. Jos.	Homiliae in Josuam
Hom. Num.	Homiliae in Numeros
Princ.	De principiis

Pliny the Elder

Nat.	Naturalis historia

Pliny the Younger

Ep.	Epistulae
Ep. Tra.	Epistulae ad Trajanum

Pseudo-Tertullian

Adv. omn. haer.	Adversus omnes haereses

Quintilian

Decl.	Declamationes

Suetonius

Claud.	Divus Claudius

Tertullian

Adv. Jud.	Adversus Judaeos
Apol.	Apologeticus
Cor.	De corona militis
Marc.	Adversus Marcionem
Paen.	De paenitentia
Pud.	De pudicitia

Maps

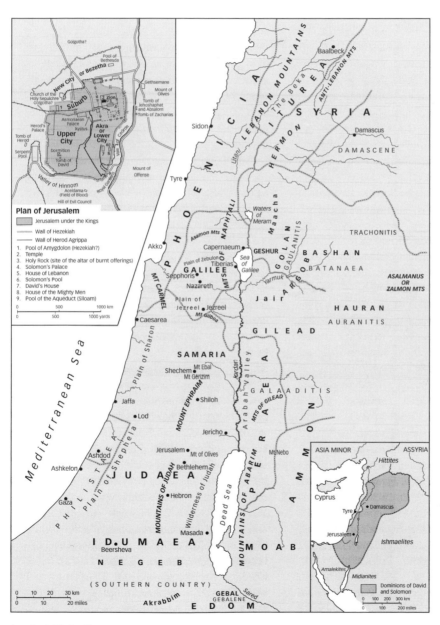

Plan of Jerusalem

- Jerusalem under the Kings
- Wall of Hezekiah
- Wall of Herod Agrippa

1. Pool of Amygdolon (Hezekiah?)
2. Temple
3. Holy Rock (site of the altar of burnt offerings)
4. Solomon's Palace
5. House of Lebanon
6. Solomon's Pool
7. David's House
8. House of the Mighty Men
9. Pool of the Aqueduct (Siloam)

Ancient Palestine

The Roman Empire at the time of greatest expansion, 138 CE

| 0 | 150 | 300 | 450 | 600 km |
| 0 | 50 | 100 | 150 | 200 | 250 | 300 | 350 | 400 miles |

The Roman Empire

The Byzantine Empire

The Ottoman Empire

The Russian Empire

The State of Israel

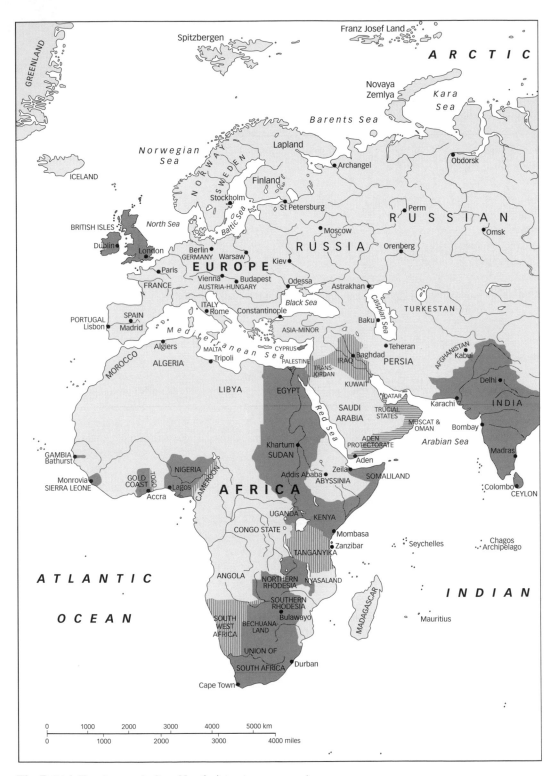

The British Empire, excluding North American possessions

Severnaya
Zemlya

O C E A N

New Siberia

Turukhansk

S I B E R I A

Yakutsk

Okhotsk

Bering Sea

E M P I R E

Krasnoyarsk

*Sea of
Okhotsk*

Irkutsk

MONGOLIA

MANCHURIA

A S I A

Vladivostok

*Sea of
Japan*

JAPAN

CHINESE EMPIRE

Pekin

KOREA

Tokyo

T I B E T

C H I N A

Shanghai

P A C I F I C

Chungking

O C E A N

Canton

Calcutta

Hong Kong

BURMA

*Bay of
Bengal*

ANAM

PHILIPPINE
ISLANDS

Rangoon

SIAM

Manila

Andaman
Is

Bangkok

Saigon

Caroline Is

Marshall Is

Nicobar Is

*South China
Sea*

EAST INDIAN ARCHIPELAGO

Gilbert Is

Singapore

Borneo

Phoenix Is

Cocos Is

NEW
GUINEA

Solomon Is

Ellis Is

O C E A N I A

O C E A N

New
Hebrides

Fiji Is

Samoa

New
Caledonia

Tonga

AUSTRALIA

Kermadec Is

Sydney

British Empire, 1905

British possessions

NEW ZEALAND

British mandated territories

Wellington

British protected territories

Hobart

The structure of the book

A Dictionary of Jewish–Christian Relations is an A to Z companion to 2,000 years of encounter between Judaism and Christianity. From Aaron to Zionism, it consists of entries on theological, historical and cultural topics – including events, institutions, movements, people, places, publications and theology – contributed by more than a hundred scholars worldwide.

As we explain in the Preface (see page xiii), the selection and treatment of every entry has been rigorously tested against the criterion of its significance to the Jewish–Christian encounter. However, while we have tried to ensure that the length of each entry corresponds broadly to the importance to the encounter of the subject of that entry, the very interconnectedness of the entries has led us to remain flexible in our judgement of the internal balance. There can be no doubting, for example, the epoch-making significance of the Second Vatican Council in the history of Jewish–Christian relations. However, the Vatican II entry is connected at so many points to the subjects of other individual entries that we have sought to avoid undue repetition by allowing cross-references to do some of its work for it. Much the same applies, for example, to the entry on Germany, where there would have been little point rehearsing the significance to the encounter of Hitler, Nazism and the Holocaust, all of which form the subject of individual entries and are thus cross-referred to from the Germany entry.

Indeed, it is an index of the interconnectedness of the field of Jewish–Christian relations itself that every entry in the *Dictionary* includes cross-references to other entries. Such cross-references are printed in bold in the text. As with any book of this kind, there is a fine editorial line to be walked between, on the one hand, providing helpful routes of access for the reader from each entry to the body of the work as a whole and, on the other, giving the impression that the truth always lies elsewhere. We hope we have trodden that line as surefootedly as possible. We have aimed to include cross-references only where they may provide readers with additional information to inform their understanding of the subject in hand. We have not, for example, cross-referenced every mention of God or the Bible, even though both are the subject of individual entries. Again, wherever possible without artificiality we have tried to ensure that cross-references fall within the body of the text of an entry and that they take the same form as the heading of the entry to which they cross-refer. In some cases, however, we have included 'See alsos' at the end of an entry for such other entries as the reader may find it particularly helpful to read in conjunction with that entry. We have also permitted some inexact cross-references where it would have been artificial to do otherwise and where following up the inexact cross-reference will anyway take the reader to the same point in the book as would an exact cross-reference: for example, **eschatological** to **eschatology**, or **Pharisaism** to **Pharisees**. We have included what seem to us a minimum of cross-reference headings (e.g. **Christian Zionists** *see* **Zionists, Christian**; **Election** *see* **Chosen People**), and an even smaller minimum of cross-references to cross-reference headings. Again, the watchword has been the avoidance of artificiality: the cross-references are there to enhance the reader's understanding of the subject, not as an exercise in spurious editorial standardisation. The mode we and the contributors have tried to achieve in each entry is perhaps best characterised as resonant economy, and the cross-referencing is intended as an important part of the resonance.

The *Dictionary* includes numerous biographical entries, for people as various as Church Fathers and musicians, artists and popes, rabbis and medieval kings. In selecting whom to include we have again been guided by the relationship of the parts to the whole. We have not, for example, included entries for a wide range of modern scholars whose work has had an impact on Jewish–Christian relations, since there exists an overarching entry on modern scholarship in Jewish–Christian relations which deals thematically with the work of many of these scholars. Similarly, we have not included entries for composers or writers whose relevance is already educed in the entry on music or the various entries on national literatures, unless the work of that composer or writer is of sufficient significance to the encounter to warrant a dedicated entry: Bach, Wagner, Shakespeare and Bialik are examples of individuals who escape the gravitational pull of their generic entries to secure an individual place in the sun. Since it would have been artificial to include cross-reference headings for all those people who are mentioned in other entries but do not have a dedicated entry, we have provided an index of people to enable the reader to find all references to individuals wherever they may fall in the book; where the individual in question has a dedicated entry the page reference for that entry is given in bold in the index. Again, within the limits of artificiality, life and/or regnant dates are given in the text after the first mention of any people not themselves the subject of individual entries.

It is an important part of the intention of the *Dictionary* to act as a springboard for further exploration of the field of Jewish–Christian relations, and a detailed bibliography is crucial to that purpose. Here too we had a choice to make. Many dictionaries of this kind sensibly include short bibliographies at the end of individual entries. In the present dictionary, however, we have again taken into account the interconnectedness of the subject and, rather than court a prohibitive degree of repetition between bibliographical entries, we have included a single bibliography at the end of the whole work, subdivided by the broader theological and historical categories into which the individual entries fall. No bibliography of this kind can be comprehensive, but we hope that it will serve both to support references in the entries and as a helpful source of further reading.

A Dictionary of Jewish–Christian Relations embodies the latest scholarly thinking in the field of Jewish–Christian relations and in the many other disciplines on which it draws. We and the contributors have been at pains to ensure, however, that it remains accessible not only to scholars, but also to anyone interested in the historical and continuing encounter between Judaism and Christianity. We hope the decisions we have made about the structure of the book will have gone some way towards achieving that aim, but we would always be interested to hear suggestions from readers as to how its accessibility might be enhanced in future editions.

AAAA

Aaron

Aaron is a figure represented in both Testaments and referred to typologically in both. His priestly role is the dominant feature shared by Judaism and Christianity, but in the latter this role is appropriated in order to highlight the superiority of the priesthood of **Jesus**. Thereafter, because the Jewish tradition continued to stress his priestly status, he faded out of the Christian tradition.

In the book of Exodus Aaron appears as the brother of **Moses** and **Miriam**, playing a subordinate but important role as spokesperson for Moses before the Pharaoh, although in the earliest literary strata of the **Torah** there is no evidence that he is a **priest**. His priestly role becomes clear only in the later so-called Priestly Document, in the description of the construction of the Tabernacle and the designation of himself and his sons as hereditary priests (Exod. 28–29; Lev. 8). A negative appraisal of Aaron in the Jewish tradition centres on the story of the **Golden Calf** (Exod. 32) and, later, his opposition to Moses in Num. 12. However, in later rabbinic tradition his image is entirely positive. He was praised because of his elevation to the high priesthood and he became the paradigm of the priesthood. Further, as spokesperson for Moses he was lauded as a lover of peace who could reconcile disputes (Hillel in *Avot* 1.12). In the mystical tradition he became one of the seven invisible holy guests (*ushpizin*) whom observant Jews welcomed to their tabernacles on **Sukkot**. The priestly tradition and Chronicles established the principle that he was the necessary ancestor, through Eleazar and Ithamar, of all legitimate priests. The priestly genealogy of Aaron and the confusing narrative tradition, with its pejorative and laudatory elements, would have developed within the post-exilic priestly group rivalry in the late eighth century BCE between Aaronides and Zadokites.

Aaron, as a point of contact between Jews and Christians, was acknowledged in the Letter to the Hebrews as the founder of the Jewish priesthood, who offered acceptable **sacrifice** to God. The anonymous author appropriated the still-developing Jewish tradition and contrasts the once-and-for-all priesthood of Jesus (which was claimed to derive from the priesthood of **Melchizedek**) with the inferior yet legitimate priesthood of Aaron. There is no **polemic** intent against Aaron in Hebrews. Two texts, Ps. 2.7 and 110.4, are used to show that God designated Jesus as the unique Son and High Priest. His self-sacrifice, analogous to the sacrifice of the High Priest on the **Day of Atonement**, is depicted as a covenant-inaugurating event, fulfilling the expectations of the new **covenant** in Jeremiah. In this way, the Levitical priesthood, as subsumed in Aaron, was claimed by Christians to be superseded, as was also the Torah, conceived in cultic terms; since the Levitical priesthood served the Torah, a new priesthood required a new Torah. Written in the **diaspora**, probably in **Alexandria** for a Roman congregation, Hebrews demonstrates the **supersessionist** direction of Christian thinking in the late first century CE.

See also **typology**   ROBERT CROTTY

Abelard, Peter (1079–1142)

French philosopher, theologian, teacher, abbot and poet: he regarded Judaism as philosophically and spiritually inferior to Christianity, yet expressed rare compassion for Jewish suffering. Controversial and influential, Abelard was a supreme dialectician, applying Aristotelian logic by rationally analysing contrasting authorities and emphasising intentions behind deeds. Abelard had personal contact with Jews, knew limited **Hebrew** derived from **Jerome**, and argued (to Heloise, his former beloved, now an abbess) that nuns should learn Hebrew. Although in *Dialogus inter philosophum, Judaeum et Christianum* his fictive Jew empathised with Jewish oppression and envisaged a biblically promised blissful future, Abelard believed that the minutiae of Mosaic **Law** burdened Jews, distracting them from genuine love of God.   *MARGARET BREARLEY*

Abner of Burgos (c.1270–1340)

Apostate and anti-Jewish polemicist. Baptised aged 50 as Alfonso of Valladolid, in his writings Abner urged Jewish **conversion** and intensified existing anti-Jewish **polemics**, becoming a major source for later apostates and Spanish Christian **anti-Judaism**. Following Raymond **Martini**'s *Pugio Fidei*, Abner's tractates attacked Jews, the **Talmud** and Judaism. Abner urged anti-Jewish measures, including conversionist preaching and segregation of Jews from Christians, influencing Alfonso XI of Castile (*r.*1312–50) to outlaw the *Aleinu* prayer (1336). Abner's eclectic theology stressed messianism, predestination and astrological influence, interpreted *aggadah* christologically, and viewed Christians as the 'true Israel'. Joseph ibn Pollegar (Pulgar) (first half of the fourteenth century) and Hasdai **Crescas** wrote texts refuting Abner.   *MARGARET BREARLEY*

Abortion

Both Judaism and Christianity base their understanding of the sacredness of human life on Gen. 1, which has made possible a serious **dialogue** on the issue of abortion in recent years. In 1977, for example, an ongoing dialogue group co-sponsored by the American Jewish Committee, the Board of Rabbis of Southern California and the Roman Catholic Archdiocese of Los Angeles issued a joint statement, *Respect for Life*, while in 1980 the Catholic/Reformed Christian national consultation did the same. Both pointed to the shared understanding of the human person as 'the image and likeness of God' as uniting Christian with Christian and Christian with Jew. Both call on religious groups to work together to contribute what they share 'to influence civil discourse', to promote 'positive alternatives to abortion' such as adoption, and to 'overcome problems of poverty, inequality, and sexual exploitation'. Both view the ideal society as one in which women would see few, if any, abortions to be necessary.

Catholicism, **Evangelical** Protestantism and **Orthodox Judaism** regard the unborn fetus as human. Orthodox Judaism would prohibit most abortions on moral grounds, but, following **Maimonides**, considers abortion to be a right and even a duty when the mother's life or health is seriously threatened. **Roman Catholicism** does not allow for this exception, except on the rare occasions when the principle of double effect applies (i.e. abortion is not the intended outcome, but may happen as an unintended consequence of a procedure to save the mother's life). Like much of Protestant Christianity, on the other hand, Reform and much of Conservative Judaism regard the fetus as potential life, not, until the moment of birth, as an independent entity. While there is a variety of opinion among these Jewish and Protestant authorities, there is general agreement that the life and health of the mother take precedence over the potential life of the fetus.

Both Jews and Christians, while divided on the application of moral principles, base them on biblical revelation. While many Protestant Christians and Jews argue the importance of preserving freedom of choice for women, and thus oppose legal restrictions on abortion as an attempt to impose the religious law of one group upon others in a pluralistic society, many other Christians and Jews argue that the unborn, no less than other 'marginalised', economically or physically disadvantaged groups, deserve legal protection. Catholics see the pro-life struggle as a 'seamless garment' with related issues such as euthanasia, **capital punishment**, nuclear war and life-threatening poverty. Reform Jews and many Protestants see the issue in the context of the right of individual conscience and pluralism itself. Liberal Protestants and progressive Jews, therefore, lobby politically together to ensure the legal right to abortion, while Catholics, Evangelical Christians and Orthodox Jews lobby for legislation to protect the rights of the unborn.

See also **medical ethics**   *EUGENE J. FISHER*

Abraham

The biblical figure of Abraham unites and divides the three great monotheistic religions. Judaism, Christianity and **Islam** all trace their spiritual ancestry to Abraham, viewing him as a paradigm of the human–divine relationship and the consequences of the search to live in the presence of God.

The biblical narrative, from Gen. 11.10–23 to 25.7–11, describes Abraham's life, which is marked by encounters with God and particularly by God's promise of the continuity of his family line, who will inherit the land. This has become a key theme throughout the history of Jewish–Christian relations. The Bible associates Abraham's name with the divine blessing as the progenitor of the Israelites, and **Moses** asks God to remember the 'promises to Abraham, Isaac, and Jacob' when retelling his intervention on behalf of Israel because of their sin at the **Golden Calf** (Deut. 9.27). The promise of the land **covenant** as part of the promise to Abraham, **Isaac** and **Jacob** is mentioned in Deut. 34.4 and Josh. 24.3, and his unique status is repeated by **Isaiah** in his declaration that 'God redeemed Abraham' (29.22 and 41.8, where Abraham is called 'My beloved').

The **New Testament** reveals both continuities and discontinuities with these images. Matthew and Luke affirm that **Jesus** descends from the seed of Abraham but the Gospels introduce a disjunction: in Matt. 3.17 **John the Baptist** says that ancestry from Abraham is not sufficient to avoid the divine wrath. Abraham, Isaac and Jacob will be at the **eschatological** banquet, but those who are children of 'the kingdom' will be thrown into utter darkness (8.11). The dichotomy between the followers of Jesus and those who reject him is reflected in the image of Abraham in the Gospel of John. Some of 'the Jews' (*see* **hoi Ioudaioi**) argue that their ancestor Abraham assures them freedom from sin; however, the Gospel asserts that unbelieving Jews are plotting to kill Jesus. This is not God's work, and they are children of Satan. Jesus ultimately asserts that 'Before Abraham was, I AM' to demonstrate that his identification with God as Father (I AM) surpassed that of Abraham's seed (8.39–58).

Paul's assessment of Abraham has been a significant point of contention in Jewish–Christian relations. In the letters to the Galatians and Romans, he puts Gen. 15.6, where belief in God was 'accounted to him as righteousness', at the foundation of Abraham's covenant that would bring rewards and promises. Subsequent revelations to Abraham, such as the commandment of **circumcision** (Gen. 17) or the revelation of the Law to **Moses** (Exod. 19), were valid until the coming of Jesus, whose death and resurrection brings all people into the covenant of Abraham (Gal. 3.23–29; Rom. 4). Paul associates those who believe in the covenant entered by circumcision with the children of **Hagar** or slavery, while those who enter through Christ are truly descendants of Isaac, children of the promise (Gal. 4.21–30; Rom. 4). Narratives of the **early Church**, such as the *Epistle of Barnabas*

(par. 9), reinforce the division between those who believe in the Christ and are spiritual, and those who adhere to the covenant of circumcision of the flesh.

Philo of Alexandria, a contemporary of Paul, bequeathed an interpretation of Abraham that would find its way into both Christianity and **Rabbinic Judaism**. The Abraham narratives are an **allegory** for the journey of the **soul** towards spiritual and moral perfection. For the Rabbis, like Philo, every detail in the Abraham narratives constitutes a significant part of the divine promise to the Jewish people for all generations. However, the Rabbis, while endorsing the moral and spiritual dimensions of Philonic allegory, emphasise the concrete details in the life of Abraham. They claimed that the **Torah** was revealed for the sake of Abraham (*Gen. Rab.* 12.9). Abraham was greater than **Noah** because he walked with God rather than before him (*Gen. Rab.* 30.10). In an effort to demonstrate the **universalism** of Judaism, Abraham and **Sarah** are depicted as missionaries converting their pagan contemporaries to the God of Israel (*Gen. Rab.* 39.14). Abraham's circumcision at an advanced age is a sign that even proselytes to Judaism should not avoid the commandment (*Gen. Rab.* 46.2). The **binding of Isaac** is concrete evidence that Abraham was obedient to God by his faith as well as actions. These rabbinic views, along with more systematic retelling of the Abraham narratives in midrash *Pirke Rabbi Eliezer*, reveal a response to Christian appropriations of Abraham.

The Koran describes Abraham as the *hanif*, the God-seeker *par excellence*. Muslims revered Abraham as a holy figure, and traced their lineage back to his son Ishmael. Muslim traditions elaborate the biblical narratives, understanding the object of Abraham's sacrifice to be Ishmael rather than Isaac.

Both Jews and Christians claim Abraham as their own spiritual mentor and guide. Throughout most of their history, these traditions have been in contention about the propriety of the inheritance of the promises. These promises for Christians are grounded in the faith Abraham revealed in *Gen.* 15.6, rather than in the concrete acts of obedience to God that led Abraham to be circumcised and ultimately to bear the burden of nearly sacrificing his son Isaac. Jews have continued to look to the entire narrative of Abraham which will ultimately yield the blessings of continuity of the Jewish people and their peaceful dwelling in the **land of Israel**.

The **Vatican II** document *Nostra Aetate* (1965) proclaimed the 'stock of Abraham' as the point of origin for a new relationship between Christians and Jews. This turn to biblical origins was part of a Catholic return to scriptural traditions in Vatican II. Yet Jewish claims to be the inheritors of the land of Israel through the promises of Abraham have been the source of controversy between Jews and Christians as well as with Muslims. However, some Jews, Christians and Muslims seek reconciliation of their differences by appealing to the fact that each tradition harks back to the biblical Abraham. The resolution of their theological and communal differences will depend upon how carefully they negotiate the virtues of Abraham that belong to all three traditions and appreciate the particular claims made by each of them.   *MICHAEL A. SIGNER*

Abrahams, Israel (1858–1925)

Scholar of Rabbinic Judaism, co-founder of the *Jewish Quarterly Review* and leader of Liberal Judaism in England. Abrahams was appointed Senior Tutor at Jews College in 1881 and in 1902 became Reader in Rabbinics at Cambridge University, where he influenced a generation of students, both Jews and Christians. He succeeded in making **Rabbinic Judaism** better understood by Christian students and academics. His *Studies in Pharisaism and the Gospels* (*First Series* 1917, *Second Series* 1924) made an important contribution to contemporary Christian attitudes towards Rabbinic Judaism.

See also **Progressive Judaism**   *EDWARD KESSLER*

Absolution

Absolution is a characteristically Christian category: a **priest**, conditional on a penitent confessing **sins**, vowing immediate reform of life and accepting a **penance**, says to him/her, 'I absolve you from your sins in the name of the Father, and of the Son and of the Holy Spirit'. **Roman Catholic** and **Orthodox Christianity** understand 'the words of the priest as instruments of the divine power because it is the divine power that works inwardly in all the sacramental signs' (Aquinas, *Summa* III, 84.3). In these traditions, the absolving words of the priest are the external sign (**sacrament**) of divine **forgiveness**. Other Christian traditions, less sacramental and resistant to the idea of a distinct priestly ministry

in the Church, view priestly absolution as a usurpation of a role that is God's alone. The Jewish roots of Christian sacramental religion lie in Solomon's prayer of dedication of the **Temple** (2 Chr. 6), when he asks that the Temple rituals may be universally effective in conveying divine mercy and power, and in the **atonement** rituals of Tabernacle and Temple.

Both Jewish and Christian traditions emphasise the reality of divine forgiveness as an experiential moment in the life of Israel and Church, and they both know words of divine absolution linked to rituals of **repentance**. Linked to the **Day of Atonement**, the promise to Israel in Lev. 16.30 ('atonement shall be made for you, to cleanse you; from all your sins you shall be clean before the Lord') is the basis of later beliefs in both traditions: for the Jewish community in post-70 CE it inspires the powerful **liturgy** of the cleansing of Israel's sins on Yom Kippur, and for the Christian community it comes to be applied to Christ's (priestly) self-offering for sins (Heb. 9.24f.). Judaism, permeated by a deep conviction that God forgives all who repent of their sins, does not understand its rituals in relation to divine mercy in the sacramental ways of the Catholic and Orthodox Churches. There, words of absolution spoken by a priest in the name of the Church consciously continue Jesus' ministry towards sinners: the Gospels, recognising that God alone does this, present **Jesus** as declaring that sins are forgiven (Mark 2.5; Luke 7.48; John 5.14), giving the power of 'binding and loosing' to human beings (Matt. 18.18) and bestowing on the apostles a post-resurrection command to forgive sins in his name: 'if you forgive the sins of any, they are forgiven' (John 20.23). Judaism post-70 CE retains a deep religious perception of the reality of divine mercy in relation to Israel: on Yom Kippur the gates of mercy are opened, sins are cleansed and reconciliation achieved with God. So what distinguishes the two traditions is not their comparative appreciation of God's forgiveness, but how this is mediated: Jews do not regard the people of Israel as empowered to convey divine mercy in the way that Christians think that the Church does.   *JOHN MCDADE*

Abulafia, Abraham (1240–after 1290)

Born in Saragossa, Abraham ben Samuel Abulafia was the founder of an influential school of **Kabbalah**, which had a strong impact in southern

Italy and Sicily. While in **Spain** he was condemned as a deluded pseudo-prophet. His contemplative techniques sought to bring the soul of man close to God, and drew on methods and ideas of Spanish and German Jewry, and also, perhaps, on other religions. He had Messianic pretensions, and the most famous episode in his life was a visit in 1280 to Pope Nicholas III (1277–80), to whom he proposed to reveal himself as a prophet and redeemer of the Jews. He was arrested, but the death of the pope led to his release; he went to Sicily and Malta, disappearing around 1291. A prolific author, his work secured a new readership in the **Renaissance**, both among Christians (**Pico della Mirandola** studied his writings closely) and among the mystics of Safed; long dismissed as a false **Messiah**, he was rehabilitated in the twentieth century by Gershom Scholem (1897–1982) and Moshe Idel (b. 1947).   *DAVID ABULAFIA*

AD/BC *see* **CE/BCE**

Adam

The figure of Adam in Jewish–Christian relations serves both to unite and to divide. From a Jewish perspective, Adam becomes the forerunner of the Jewish people as a whole. We read in *Genesis Rabbah* 19.7, commenting on Gen. 3.7, 'When Adam sinned it [the **Shekinah**, God's presence] departed to the first level of the heavens'. It can be argued that Adam's experience in the Garden represents God's relation to **Israel** 'worked out in miniature' (G. A. Anderson, *The Genesis of Perfection* 16). God grieves over the nation's transgression and longs for obedience from the whole people for paradise to be restored. For the Christian, Adam points not to a whole people but uniqely to the figure of Christ. However, Adam is regarded in both Judaism and Christianity as the first human being, and his story, told in the opening chapters of Genesis, is significant theologically. There are two distinct biblical accounts of Adam's origin (1.26–30, in which Adam is the climax of creation, and 2.4a–9). The Hebrew word *adam*, which always appears in the singular, means 'man'. In the first account, the definite article is used (*ha-adam*), suggesting that it is not a proper name here (unlike in 4.25 and 5.1–5, where the definite article is dropped). He comes from the earth (*adamah*), according to Gen. 2.7. Until the nineteenth century, he was generally held to be a historical figure, but most Jews and Christians today read the stories, including the second narrative set in **Eden** (2.15–3.24), as **myth**, expressing important ideas about the human condition. In both **creation narratives**, the emphasis is on the particular responsibility given to human beings, enjoying a unique relationship with God (the phrase 'in God's image' in Gen. 1.27 receives much attention, especially in Christian doctrine), to care for other creatures and the land. In both Jewish and Christian **ethics**, these biblical texts have long been used as the basis of **environmental** concern. It is argued by some modern ethicists that the stress on human 'dominion' over nature has replaced a sense of responsibility, encouraging exploitation of the earth's resources. Even in traditional sources, Adam's behaviour is taken as a paradigm for human conduct in general. So the **Mishnah** (e.g. *Sanhedrin* 4.5) asserts that our descent from one man means that whoever destroys or saves a single life destroys or saves the whole world. The **New Testament** similarly interprets the story as **typology**, viewing Adam as archetypal man who brings **sin** into the world. In Christian thought **Jesus** is seen as the fulfilment of what God intends for humankind. He is the second Adam who is needed to redeem the human condition. This is particularly important in the **Christology** of **Paul**. In Rom. 5.12–21 and 1 Cor. 15.22, 45–49 Adam is described as the source of sin and death. The first man, made from earth or dust, is the prototype of all humanity, since all are of dust and are mortal. Christ, as the second Adam (or 'last' Adam in the sense of 'most complete'), is also mortal and so dies but is then raised by God as the 'first fruits of those who have died'. Paul argues this as the basis of the Christian belief in the **Resurrection**: 'for as all die in Adam, so all will be made alive in Christ'. The **Kabbalah** speaks of Adam's sin creating a cosmic flaw, disturbing God's intended harmony. Adam's descendants must seek to restore cosmic harmony. Jewish sources generally, however, have no concept of **original sin**, but depict human beings as constantly struggling between good and evil impulses. Most of the **Church Fathers**, by contrast, develop Paul's ideas in terms of a 'fall' from grace. Notably **Augustine**, and later **Calvin**, take the story of Adam as implying the innate corruption of human nature. The Rabbis in **Talmud** and **midrash** suggest that Adam encompasses both male and female characteristics and that he was created an androgynous creature, **Eve**, the first created woman, being taken from Adam's 'side' rather than 'rib' (Gen. 2.22). Both

Jewish and Christian writers have variously drawn on this part of the story to emphasise, on the one hand, either male priority/patriarchy (his needs are met in receiving woman as a partner) or, on the other hand, gender equality (man is incomplete without woman).   *CHRISTINE PILKINGTON*

Adenauer, Konrad (1876–1967)

German politician and statesman. Konrad Adenauer is best known for his initiative as the first Chancellor of the Federal Republic of **Germany** to pay reparations to the **State of Israel** and to the Conference on Jewish Material Claims against Germany (Luxemburg 1952). His involvement with Jews dated from at least as early as his years as Mayor of Cologne (1917–33), when he was removed from office by the Nazis and went into hiding at Maria Laach monastery. As Mayor, Adenauer formed good relations with the leaders of the Jewish community. He was also a member of the **Zionist** organisation Pro-Palästina Komitee. As President of the Catholic Church Congress in Germany (Katholikentag) in 1922, Adenauer campaigned for cooperation with the non-Catholic majority. When the Nazis came to power in 1933, antisemitic campaigns in Cologne branded him a *Blutjude* ('blood-Jew') and a representative of the Zionist movement. While hiding, and then without a steady job during the Nazi years, Adenauer and his family were dependent on the financial assistance of Jewish friends, who were among the few to maintain their friendship during this time. Briefly reinstated by the Americans as Mayor of Cologne in 1945, Adenauer encouraged Cologne Jews to return to their city from Theresienstadt. As Chancellor he saw it as his moral duty to offer reparations, recognising that the moral guilt and personal and communal loss could never be repaid.   *K. HANNAH HOLTSCHNEIDER*

Adversus Judaeos literature

The term 'Adversus Judaeos literature' refers to a body of Christian polemical texts specifically directed against the Jews, which were written from the first century to at least the eighteenth century CE. Such literature appears in the form of systematically arranged tracts, or an account of a dialogue or of a public debate. Some would not wish, however, to restrict the term to texts dedicated specifically to this theme, arguing that there is much material *Adversus Judaeos* in Christian writings that ostensibly are concerned with other subjects (so, for instance, many Christian exeget-

ical works contain lengthy anti-Jewish sections; and the voluminous Christian writer **Origen** writes much that could be construed as straightforwardly anti-Jewish, but never wrote a work *Adversus Judaeos*). While we first meet the term *Adversus Judaeos* only in the third century, here as the title of a work by **Tertullian**, literature of this kind predates that period.

There is no book or letter in the **New Testament** devoted to an anti-Jewish subject. In some senses this is not surprising for, in spite of the presence of some texts that speak negatively of people termed '*hoi Ioudaioi*', it is not clear how many of the New Testament's authors would have seen themselves as non-Jews (the term 'Christian' only appears twice in the entire collection). So a figure like **Paul**, subsequently to be seen as a key figure in the separation of Judaism from Christianity, and a man not averse to criticism of non-Christian Jews, could still describe himself as a 'Hebrew of Hebrews' (Rom. 11.1). But however we regard the **identity** of individual early Christian authors, there is a certain amount of material in the New Testament, whatever its original intention, that came subsequently to be exploited for its perceived anti-Jewish content. In this respect one might highlight from many possible examples Paul's negative comments on the **law** (see especially Gal. 3–5); John's harsh comments about '*Ioudaioi*' (see especially John 8.45), Matthew's attack upon the **Pharisees** (Matt. 23) and his clear attribution of blame for the death of **Jesus** to the Jews (Matt. 27.25); and the author of the Epistle to the Hebrews' strong condemnation of the cult (see especially Heb. 10) and his explicit endorsement of the better character of the Christian **covenant**.

Some scholars have argued that the earliest examples of *Adversus Judaeos* literature in the specific sense referred to above would have been in the form of so-called 'testimony books' (*see* **testimonia**), collections of citations from the Hebrew scriptures with some commentary appended, in which the confluence of ancient promise and Christian fulfilment and concomitant rejection of non-Christian Jews was made plain. Such books would have looked somewhat like the third-century work, attributed to **Cyprian** of Carthage, *Testimonia ad Quirinum*, and they would originally have been inspired by the Jewish custom for creating florilegia of texts as witnessed in 4QFlorilegia at Qumran.

Although this theory has been questioned on a number of grounds, not least the absence of any evidence for such anti-Jewish testimony books before Cyprian, the theory is right to highlight the essentially biblical character of *Adversus Judaeos* literature.

Actual extant texts that have a strongly *Adversus Judaeos* character are first witnessed with *Barnabas* (*c*.132 CE) (*see* **Apostolic Fathers**) and then more clearly with **Justin Martyr**'s *Dialogue with Trypho* (*c*.160 CE), ostensibly an account of a discussion between Justin and a named Jew, Trypho, and his companions in Ephesus a little time after the **Bar-Kokhba** revolt (the dialogue form, which was well known in antiquity, may have first been used in an anti-Jewish setting in *The Dialogue of Jason and Papiscus*, now lost, and sometimes dated as early as the 130s CE). This type of writing is then regularly evidenced in Christian literature throughout the patristic and medieval periods and beyond, in a variety of languages and forms, and from the pen of such Christian luminaries as **Chrysostom, Augustine** and **Luther**. Some have sought to posit a change in emphasis after the arrival of **Constantine**, with a sharper, more condemnatory tone now in evidence. This can be overplayed, however, as can the claim that the contents of such literature changed from this time. In fact there is considerable continuity in the themes discussed.

These themes concern the redundancy of the Jewish law, argued for in a variety of ways, either by reference to the law's limited duration, its **particularist** and post-Abrahamic character, its inappropriateness now that the Temple had fallen or, finally, its allegorical intention (see, *inter alia*, *Barn.* 2, 9, 10 and 15; Justin, *Dial.* 18–24; Tertullian, *Adv. Jud.* 3–6; Novatian, *On the Jewish Meats*); the lost status of Jews as the **chosen people** and the corresponding assertion that the Gentiles/Christians are now the chosen people (see, *inter alia*, *Barn.* 13–14; Tertullian, *Adv. Jud.* 12–14; Cyprian, *Test.* 19–23; **Pseudo-Cyprian**, *De Montibus et Sion*) – in such discussions the Christian church was presented as the new **Israel** and the rightful owners of the scriptures, and much was made of the fact that since 70 CE the Jewish **Temple** had been destroyed and their land occupied (in this context we should note the harsh and febrile reaction of Christians to **Julian the Apostate**'s attempts to rebuild the Jewish Temple in Jerusalem *c*.362 CE, exemplified in the writings of Chrysostom, Gregory of Nyssa (330–*c*.395), and **Cyril of Alexandria**); enumeration of biblical evidence for the view that Jesus is rightfully termed the **Messiah** (Justin, *Dial.* 48f.; Cyprian, *Test.* 2.1–7; **Aphrahat**, *Homily* 17); and, connected with the previous theme, a defence of Christian trinitarianism, or, more particularly, the status of Jesus as the **Son of God**, and this often against Jewish accusations that Christians were guilty of **idolatry** in worshipping Christ. While much of this ancient Christian anti-Jewish **polemic** reflected specific Christian concerns and did not seek to pick up on anti-pagan polemic against Jews (often accusations laid against Jews could also be laid against Christians; and the fact that Christians shared part of their Bible with the Jews made their attitude towards Judaism a complex and double-edged one), there were some continuities, not least in aspects of Christian criticism of Jewish laws and in their keenness to play up the Jews' fallen state.

In the western medieval tradition this material was reused and to a certain extent updated. A particular new feature is the increasing use of rabbinic material brought to a climax in the thirteenth century by Raymond **Martini** in his *Pugio Fidei*, where an attempt is made to prove Christianity out of **Talmud** and **midrash**. Soon afterwards we witness a similarly tendentious use of Jewish mystical writings, especially the *Zohar* (*see* **mysticism**).

Scholarly discussion of this literature has made much of the related questions of its purpose and audience. To some scholars, notably **Harnack**, R. Ruether (b. 1936), D. Rokeah (b. 1930) and to a slightly lesser extent H. Schreckenberg (b. 1933), the literature is quite unconcerned with its ostensible aim, the **conversion** of Jews, and gives voice much more clearly to internal Christian needs, many of which were taken up with proving the biblical basis of Christianity. In asserting that Christianity was the fulfilment of promises in the Hebrew scriptures, it was necessary, so the argument goes, to argue against those – that is, the Jews – who would interpret those same scriptures in a contrary way. Christian *Adversus Judaeos* literature simply gives voice to the anti-Jewish tendency of Christian parenesis. In a variation on this argument, some have wanted to assert that a pagan audience might be more appropriate for such literature, not least because pagan critics of Christianity, such as the second-century **Celsus**, as recorded in Origen's *Contra Celsum*, saw Christians as renegades from Judaism, implicitly denying Christian claims to be the true Israel. In positing such views, these scholars have highlighted the repetitive and stereotypical character of the content of *Adversus Judaeos* literature, the unreal representation of both Jews and Jewish opinion (is not Justin's Trypho, for instance, portrayed as a bit too amenable to Christian views when he asserts that he could believe in a suffering Messiah in *Dial.* 90?), a point that becomes clear in those dialogues where Jews end up converting to Christianity. Emphasis is also laid upon the apparent lack of evidence for Jewish–Christian contact and on the fact that material from *Adversus Judaeos* writings can end up in texts that are not of that genre (a famous example here might be the fact that parts of Tertullian's *Adversus Judaeos* end up almost word for word in Book 3 of his *Adversus Marcionem*). Responses to such positions have come from scholars such as Jean Juster (*c.*1886–1916) Marcel Simon (b. 1907) and William Horbury (b. 1942). They have argued that the Jewish community was too large and significant to avoid, that there is in fact more evidence than some would allow for contact between Christians and Jews, that the *Adversus Judaeos* literature is not without variety, and that on occasion it betrays genuine knowledge of the Jewish community and its practices. While admitting that some anti-Jewish statements appear in settings of a strictly parenetic kind and so may be said to assume no Jewish opponent, the fact that there is literature *Adversus Judaeos* should be taken seriously. Such a view comes closer to seeing this literature as evidence for Jewish–Christian contact. In recent times, and broadly in line with this view, some have argued that the same literature is seeking to assert a clear-cut distinction between Jews and Christians, which in fact did not reflect the reality on the ground, where interaction and exchange, as Chrysostom implies in his *Adversus Judaeos*, was much more commonplace.

See also **anti-Judaism**; **antisemitism**

JAMES CARLETON PAGET

African theology

Developed by sub-Saharan black Africans, African theology appears at first glance to demonstrate little awareness of the Jewish–Christian encounter. However, African emphasis on the **Old Testament**, such as the biblical understanding of **creation**, the life cycle, and the family and **community** – expressed, for example, in African **sacrifices** at births, **weddings**, funerals and other religious ceremonies, hand-washing ceremonies and the rite of **circumcision** – provides a natural link between Judaism and Christianity. Western missionaries were in fact reluctant to use the Old Testament in the instruction of converts, fearing that its atmosphere would be too close to indigenous African culture and converts might feel that there was no need to proceed to the **New Testament**.

An African Christian–Jewish consultation took place in Cameroon in 2001, under the auspices of the **World Council of Churches**, and pointed to a number of 'convergences' in African theology and Judaism, other than the centrality of the biblical text and story. These included the similarities between the concept of *shalom* and *Ubuntu* (humaneness or humanity), the role of the word and of *palaver* (discussion, consensus-formation) and the idea of *tikkun* (repair) and the theology of reconstruction.

African theology is unhindered by many of the concerns underlying Jewish–Christian **dialogue** in Europe. An example is the topic of memory, since Jews and Africans have experienced a similar history of exclusion, exploitation and violence (from **antisemitism** and the ***Shoah*** to the slave trade, apartheid and the Rwandan genocide) as well as of survival. In this context, the biblical account of the Exodus and the journey from bondage to freedom plays a central role in African as well as in Jewish theology.

EDWARD KESSLER

Afterlife

Traditionally, Judaism and Christianity both have affirmed belief in an afterlife, and Christian expressions of this belief are, to a large extent, rooted in Judaism. The ancient Israelite belief in *Sheol*, a netherworld abode of the dead – whether they had been righteous or wicked in life – had little influence on either **Rabbinic Judaism** or Christianity. Instead, beliefs in the **resurrection** of the dead, expressed in a few late passages in the Hebrew scriptures (most explicitly in Dan. 12.2), and in the heavenly immortality of the **soul**, found in the apocryphal writings of the Second Temple period, were developed in both traditions. There are a wide variety of traditional Jewish beliefs regarding the soul after **death**, the resurrection of the body and the nature of the 'world to come' (*olam ha-ba*). This makes it virtually impossible to articulate a generally accepted Jewish view of an afterlife. It is clear, however, that the emphasis on the sanctity of this life has always been more important in Judaism than belief in an afterlife, and, therefore, the latter is less central to Judaism than to Christianity, which is based on belief in the resurrection of **Jesus** and on the resurrection of believers to new life in Christ.

In both Judaism and Christianity, resurrection of the body has been understood both literally and metaphorically. When taken metaphorically, it has often been understood in terms of spiritual **immortality**. Even when resurrection of the body has been understood literally, theologians have usually meant not merely the resuscitation of the body but the transformation of it. Also, in both traditions, it has generally been believed that the righteous are rewarded with eternal life while the wicked are punished. But the idea of eternal damnation has not been taught in Judaism as it has been in Christianity, and Judaism has consistently affirmed the belief that the righteous of all nations will be saved, whereas traditional Christianity has taught (though with various interpretations) that there is 'no **salvation** outside the Church'.

Despite traditional Jewish affirmations of an afterlife, one of the ways that Christian apologists of the Middle Ages attempted to demonstrate the superiority of Christianity over Judaism was to contrast what they claimed to be the unambiguous Christian promise of immortality with ambiguous Jewish promises of an afterlife. Some Jewish philosophers responded by claiming that Judaism does contain the unambiguous promise of immortality, while many other Jews have suggested that a preoccupation with and certainty about the hereafter may be indicative of spiritual immaturity: failure to face the finality of death; failure to acknowledge the limits of what can be known; failure to appreciate fully the value of **life** this side of the grave; failure to obey God out of love rather than for the sake of earning eternal reward and avoiding eternal punishment. Even today, in the context of irenic interfaith encounters, many Christians express surprise at how Jews minimise the importance of belief in an afterlife, while many Jews express bewilderment at what they consider a Christian preoccupation with an afterlife.

JOHN C. MERKLE

Aggadah *see* **midrash**

Agobard (779–840)

Archbishop of Lyons, author of several letters criticising the integrationist policy toward Jews of Carolingian Emperor Louis the Pious (778–840) and – with other colleagues – a treatise *On Jewish Superstitions and Errors*. Agobard accused Jews of flaunting their success and reviling Christianity, and called for the enforcement of earlier legislation that consigned them to a status of clear subservience. He was especially scandalised by reports that Christians turned to Jews for **blessings** over their crops and preferred Jewish preachers to their own. His writings reveal a knowledge of post-biblical Jewish literature, which he strongly condemned. Agobard's vigorous efforts to reverse the pro-Jewish imperial policy were not successful. *MARC SAPERSTEIN*

Akedah *see* **binding of Isaac**

Akiba (*c*.40–*c*.135)

An outstanding tannaitic sage, famous for his contribution to both the evolving hermeneutical principles in *halakhah* and the texture of *aggadah*. During the second Jewish revolt he supported Shimon bar Koseba, acclaiming him to be **Bar Kokhba**, 'Son of the Star' (a Messianic title; see Num. 24.17). One of many points of contact between the Jewish and Christian traditions is the statement assigned to Akiba in *Leviticus Rabbah* 1.5, which has a clear-cut parallel in Luke 14.7–11: both these passages illuminate the importance of humility with a **parable** about a guest who, having taken the lowest place at a feast, is invited by the host to move to the table of honour. *JESPER SVARTVIK*

Aleinu

'It is incumbent upon us', the first Hebrew word of an important Jewish prayer. Originally composed for the **liturgy** for the **New Year** (*Rosh Hashanah*), since the late Middle Ages it has been used at the conclusion of all three daily worship services. The first part proclaims the obligation of Jews to praise and extol God, who has made them different from the other nations. A contentious passage follows: 'For they [the nations] bow down before vanity and emptiness (*hevel va-rik*, Isa. 30.7) . . . while we bow down . . . before the King of kings of kings, the Holy One blessed be He'. A medieval apostate claimed that since the numerical equivalent of the letters in *va-rik* equal the value of the letters in *Yeshu* (Hebrew for **Jesus**), the phrase was an encoded slander against Christian worship. Martin **Luther** railed vitriolically against the prayer; Jewish leaders insisted that it referred only to pagan **idolatry**. In 1703 the Prussian government ordered that the offending clause be eliminated, and it was dropped from the Ashkenazi (though not from the Sephardi) liturgy. The remainder of the prayer is a stirring expression of the hope for universal, all-inclusive recognition of the one true God.

MARC SAPERSTEIN

Alexander II (d. 1073)

Pope (1061–73). He wrote that unlike Saracens, who were active enemies, Jews 'were always prepared to be subservient' and should be allowed to live in peace. Citing the precedent of **Gregory the Great**, Alexander's formulation – perhaps elicited by the Jews of Rome, who looked to the bishop of the city as their secular ruler – was incorporated about 1140 into Gratian's legal textbook, the *Decretum*, as the canon *Dispar nimirum est* (23.8.1). Afterwards, the concept of Jewish acquiescence was cited repeatedly, notably by the ex-General of the **Dominicans** Humbert of Romans at the Second Ecumenical Council of Lyons in 1274. *KENNETH STOW*

Alexander III (c.1105–81)

Pope (1159–81). He presided over the Third Lateran Council, 1179, which declared all Christian testimony against Jews valid 'since . . . Jews [must] be subservient', forbade Christian servants in Jewish homes and the erecting of new synagogues. All these laws had antecedents in the canonical collections of Burchard of Worms (*c*.965–1025), Ivo of Chartres (1040–1116) and Gratian (*c*.1140) (*see* **Alexander II**). Alexander III enforced these rules, overcoming opposition from the French kings **Louis VII** and, initially, Philip Augustus (*r*.1180–1223); by 1283, royal charters prohibited Jews from holding Christian servants; before 1179, the opposite was expressly permitted. Following the *Summa Coloniensis* (2.136) – an anonymous collection of canons prepared in Cologne in 1169 – Alexander was possibly seeking to prevent ritual impurity, acquired through 'overfamiliarity', including dining in common, which disqualified Christians from receiving the **Eucharist**. Out of context for a twelfth-century pope, Alexander assumed converts might 'backslide' unopposed into Judaism. *KENNETH STOW*

Alexandria

Founded in 332 BCE by Alexander the Great (d. 323 BCE) on the Mediterranean coast of **Egypt** close to the Nile Delta, Alexandria rapidly emerged as a great city, becoming the capital of the Ptolemaic Empire and retaining its importance under the Romans, under whose sway it passed in 31 BCE. The city fell to the Arabs in 642 and has remained under Muslim control ever since. Alexandria has long been the home of very significant Jewish and Christian communities, both of whom have made a distinctive (and in some respects analogous) contribution to their respective traditions. The Jewish presence in the city dates back to its beginnings. Jews were guaranteed religious freedom, civil rights and a substantial degree of autonomy by Alexander and his successors. The community grew rapidly, numbering perhaps 500,000 by the second century BCE. Alexandria fostered an immensely creative engagement between Jewish and **Greek** culture, witnessed perhaps most iconically in the translation of the **Hebrew Bible** into Greek, the famed **Septuagint** which also became the **Old Testament** of the Christian community. This interaction with the Greek world can also be seen in **Philo**, whose brilliant expression of the Jewish faith using the language and conceptual tools of the Greek philosophical tradition laid the foundations for much subsequent (and mainly Christian) theological endeavour. Relations with the pagan inhabitants of the city deteriorated in the Roman period, as witnessed in the persecution launched under Gaius Caligula (*r*.37–41) and the prominent role of the Jews of Alexandria in the abortive rising of the Jewish **Diaspora** (114–17), after which the community was drastically reduced in size and influence. It is after this time that the Christian community of the city begins to come into focus. A number of early Christian texts, such as the *Epistle of Barnabas* (a text with close affinities to the Jewish tradition; *see* **Apostolic Fathers**), are often associated with Alexandria. Alexandria nurtured some of the key theologians of the early Church. Clement (*c*.150–*c*.215) was certainly familiar with Jewish customs, theology and exegetical traditions, making extensive use of Philo. **Origen** knew the Jewish tradition extremely well and took the trouble to learn **Hebrew**, as witnessed in his famous **Hexapla**. In his lambasting of the pagan philosopher **Celsus**, Origen notes the superiority of the Jewish way of life over that of the pagans – an unusual line of argument. Relations between Jews and Christians appear to have steadily worsened under the Christian Empire. There are reports of clashes during the episcopate of **Athanasius**.

The fiery **polemic** of his later successor, **Cyril of Alexandria**, inflamed an already heated situation. Under Islamic domination, the city lost importance to Cairo, but Jewish and Christian communities remained very visible parts of the city's fabric, albeit rarely in close contact. In recent years the Greek and Jewish communities have almost vanished, largely due to economic pressure exerted by Nasser's Arab socialist government and the promise of a better life in Greece or **Israel**. This has left the **Coptic** Christians as the only significant non-Muslim community in what was once a city famed for its multiplicity of cultures (and, sadly, for the tensions between them).   *MARCUS PLESTED*

Alfonsi, Peter (1062–*c*.1144)

Born in Huesca, Spain, as a Moses HaSefaradi, Peter converted to Christianity in 1106 under the patronage of King Alfonso of Aragon, and moved to England where he served as court physician to King Henry I (*r*. 1100–35). He wrote *The Scholar's Guide*, which transmitted many motifs and themes from Arabic culture into Latin literature. His *Dialogue of Peter named Alfonsi with Moses the Jew* was one of the most widely read anti-Jewish **polemical** works of the medieval period. Written as a 'conversation' between the two personae of the author before and after his conversion, it traces Peter's growing disenchantment with Judaism, his exploration of alternatives and his conclusion that Christianity was the religion that best corresponded to reason (*ratio*) and the laws of nature. While these themes correspond to those of his contemporaries Peter **Abelard** and **Anselm of Canterbury**, Peter offers a more pointed critique of Judaism as based on a literalist **anthropomorphic** concept of God through his translations of aggadic sections from rabbinic literature, which he calls *doctrina*. This attack upon the **Talmud** as a source of Jewish refusal to recognise Jesus as the **Christ** was also used by **Peter the Venerable** and leads to more extensive criticism of rabbinic sources by the mendicant orders in the later Middle Ages. Chapter 6 of the *Dialogue* offers a proof of the **Trinity** utilising the Hebrew letters YHWH and may be early evidence for Christian use of the Jewish **mystical** tradition. Peter's *Dialogue* (ch. 7) presents one of the first systematic critiques of **Islam**.   *MICHAEL A. SIGNER*

Allegory

Allegory (*allegoria*) is a mode of interpretation of a text widely used in antiquity meaning 'speaking one thing and signifying something other than what is said', though it can also be a compositional technique, as for instance in Prudentius's (348–*c*.410) *Psychomachia*, where the virtues are portrayed as biblical figures. Such allegorisation was used to interpret the poets, especially Homer, as a way of distilling a meaning of contemporary relevance from texts (such as poetical texts) deemed to be inspired: the apparent (or 'surface') meaning of the text is either discarded or more commonly regarded as pointing to a deeper meaning. Such a practice is found in both Jewish and Christian **exegesis** from the beginning, though the actual term *allegoria* is not always, or even often, found. Both **halakhah** and **aggadah** are ways of going beyond the apparent significance of the text and finding a meaning relevant to contemporary concerns. In Christian usage, whether called allegory or not (mostly not), interpretation of the Greek **Septuagint** translation of the Hebrew scriptures came to treat the text as, in one way or another, prophetic of the coming of **Jesus** as the **Messiah** or the **Christ**. Initially passages in the prophets were interpreted in this way (which was thought of as identifying the real object of the prophetic words, not as any kind of allegory), but gradually such a process was applied to the whole of what came to be called the '**Old Testament**'. A distinction came to be made between the 'literal meaning', that is what a text meant when correctly construed, and its 'spiritual' meaning; in this context **Paul**'s remark 'The letter kills, but the spirit gives life' (2 Cor. 3.6) was often quoted. The 'spiritual meaning' can clearly be regarded as allegorical, in the strict sense, though other words were more commonly used: *anagoge*, an interpretation that lifts the reader to God, a moral interpretation that derives a moral lesson (in some respects not unlike *halakhah*), or more generally *theoria*, contemplation (leading to a deeper meaning). It has become common in scholarship to distinguish between the Alexandrian school of exegesis (*see* **Alexandria**), which favoured allegory, and the Antiochene school (*see* **Antioch**), which eschewed it. But common to these two schools was the conviction that the meaning of the Old Testament was revealed in Christ, as the fulfilment of the promises made to **Israel**. Christians frequently accused the Jews, who rejected the derivation of such a meaning from their scriptures, of being literal-minded, not seeing beyond the literal meaning of the scriptural text. This is not to be taken as a methodological criticism: it simply means that the Jews rejected a deeper meaning of the scriptures that pointed to Christ and the coming of the messianic age; in their own exegesis 'allegorical' methods were practised. Indeed, the debate (e.g. in the fourth century) about 'allegory' among Christians is scarcely methodological at all, but rather concerned with the way in which **Origen**, in particular, supported heterodox opinions (on **creation**, **eschatology** and the nature of the **soul**) by means of allegory. In seeking a deeper meaning in the scriptures, Christians and Jews were at one, and Christians often borrowed from Jewish exegetical traditions, a striking example of such being the interpretation of the Song of Songs.

See also **typology**   *ANDREW LOUTH*

Alonso de Espina (d. 1469)

Franciscan writer and preacher. Alonso de Espina wrote his *Fortalitium Fidei* around 1460 after spending time as an itinerant preacher. Espina is also known for his activity as a proponent of the Spanish **Inquisition**, which was set up for the eradication of **heresy**, especially heresies associated with Jewish converts (**Conversos** or **Marranos**). Until recently, the supposition has been that Alonso was a Converso, based primarily on elements of Hebrew found in the *Fortalitium Fidei*, but this claim has been found to be false, based primarily on internal evidence gathered from this same text. The text collects and synthesises much of the previous medieval *Adversus Judaeos* literature. Book III of the five-book work, entitled *De bello Judeorum* ('Concerning the war of the Jews'), is made up of 12 chapters or 'considerations' which, viewed in their entirety, constitute an 'encyclopedia' of the different types of **polemics** against the Jews, including in the twelfth consideration the **eschatological** role of the Jews at the end of time and the second coming of Jesus Christ that will result in the **conversion** of the Jews. The *Fortalitium Fidei* was a resource for subsequent preachers and writers in the history of Christian **anti-Judaism**.   *STEVEN J. MCMICHAEL*

Alphonse of Poitiers (1220–71)

Ruler of Poitou, Auvergne and Toulouse. In crusading zeal, Alphonse emulated his brother, **Louis IX** of France, but his **anti-Judaism** was more venal. While on Saint Louis' **Crusade** (1249) he decreed the **expulsion** of Jews from Poitou. To finance his joining the Eighth Crusade (1268) he ordered the arrest of all Jews within his territories, their property to be assessed and a huge ransom imposed. In 1269 he compelled all Jews to wear the Jewish badge (*see* **yellow badge**) on pain of heavy fines. Shortly before his return in 1271, his deputy administrators expelled the Jews of Moissac. Yet, a typical Christian prince, Alphonse summoned a Jewish physician from Spain to cure his failing eyesight.

MARGARET BREARLEY

Altar

As well as being a simple piece of furniture, the altar functions as a multivalent symbol in both Christianity and Judaism. For the early Christian movement it began as a piece of furniture for their table fellowship, in which they remembered the pre- and post-resurrection meals of **Jesus**, especially that meal later remembered as the '**Last Supper**'. The altar developed throughout Christian history a complex set of meanings. Some of these evocations have been drawn from the Hebrew scriptures with their traditions of altars as places of **sacrifice** and **incense**, and have profoundly influenced the Christian understanding and design of the altar. Particularly important in this regard was the image of the stone four-cornered altar in the Temple at **Jerusalem**. The altar grew from being a table of wood set in the midst of the worshipping assembly, on which the gifts of **bread** and **wine** were placed for the celebration of the **eucharist**, to being a place of sacrifice where the unbloody sacrifice of the eucharist re-enacts the bloody sacrifice of the cross of Jesus. These meanings have changed, coexisted and been in conflict over the centuries. One could argue that in Judaism the reverse process happened, with the altar of the **Temple** being replaced with the table of the home, serving as the focal point for sharing meals and performing the rituals of **Shabbat**.   *LIAM M. TRACEY*

American Jewish Committee *see* Jewish–Christian relations, institutions; United States of America

American literature *see* literature, American

Amidah

The *Amidah* is the central component of rabbinic liturgy, recited at every service. The prayer was decreed mandatory by Rabban **Gamaliel** II in the late first century CE. Its recitation compensates for the absence of the **Temple** and its **sacrifices**. Although some of its themes appear elsewhere earlier, there is no evidence that the *Amidah* itself existed or was regularly recited in the Second Temple period. Unlike Jewish table ceremonies, ritual scripture reading or even the **blessings** that accompany the **Shema**, the *Amidah* seems hardly to have influenced the emerging **liturgy** of the Church. A **Greek** version of the prayer's **Sabbath** text apparently underlies a late-fourth-century Christian liturgical compilation, the *Apostolic Constitutions* 7.33–38. Given the close relations now posited between Jews and Christians in these centuries, the very uniqueness of this source suggests that the *Amidah* was not widely recited yet, even by Jews. The significant differences between the texts suggest that the *Amidah*'s text was still very fluid. However, because Christians, after the destruction of the Temple, understood the **eucharist** to replace the Temple sacrifices, they may have felt no desire to adopt this prayer. In addition, its weekday text presents an eschatological vision of a reconstructed Jewish state, complete with Temple and Messianic Davidic rule, which is fundamentally inconsistent with Christian **eschatology**. The extent to which this vision can be understood as a response to Christian claims requires deeper investigation. The angelic liturgies, the Jewish *Kedushah* (which appears, among other places, in the third blessing of the *Amidah*) and the Christian *Sanctus/Trishagion* probably share a common source in Second Temple period **apocalypticism**. The weekday text's twelfth benediction, the *birkat ha-minim*, and occasionally other elements of its Messianic vision, were objects of Christian criticism and **censorship** through the ages. Some contemporary liberal versions of the *Amidah* broaden its horizons to pray not only for the **people Israel** but also for all humanity.   *RUTH LANGER*

Anabaptists

Anabaptism began as a Christian reform movement in Western Europe. The label Anabaptist means 're-baptiser', and dates from 1525, when a group of adults were baptised in Zurich. According to their opponents, the participants (having been baptised as infants) were 're-baptised', whereas the reformers held that only adult 'believers'' **baptism** was valid. Today's descendants of the Anabaptists include the various Mennonite Churches, the Amish and the Hutterites. Excommunicated by the Hutterites in 1990, the Bruderhof, who originated in twentieth-century **Germany** (influenced

by the writings of Martin **Buber** and Gustav Landauer (1870–1919) on Hasidism and anarchism respectively), are also heirs to the Anabaptist tradition.

Despite diverse geographical and theological origins, Anabaptists share common emphases that give their relations with Jews a distinctive character. For example, in sixteenth- and seventeenth-century Europe, Anabaptist radicalisation of the **Reformation** concept of the 'priesthood of all believers' fuelled interest in **biblical interpretation**, fostering encounters with Judaism. Hans Denck and Ludwig Hätzer's 1527 translation of the Prophets depended heavily on Jewish tradition, consciously avoiding **Christological** interpretations of the text. Although most pre-twentieth-century Anabaptists were in some way **supersessionist**, an emphasis on voluntarism and radical **Church and state** separation meant they generally avoided organised **mission** to Jews. The preference for *lebendiger Glaube* ('lived faith'/implicit theology) and exemplary biographies (typically, martyrologies) over systematic articulations of **doctrine** means that there is no extensive **anti-Judaism** within the Anabaptist textual tradition. Moreover, the Anabaptists' history of persecution and suffering at the hands of other Christians led at times to attitudes of relative **tolerance**; **Spinoza** lodged with Mennonites in the seventeenth century.

Anabaptist behaviour during the **Holocaust** varied. Some Mennonites (mostly recent refugees from the Soviet Union, keen to prove their German credentials) rejected their traditional pacifism and supported **Hitler**. Many others in Europe and the Americas were **bystanders**, reluctant to participate in 'worldly' affairs. The Bruderhof, unyielding opponents of **Nazism**, fled to England in 1937. There they sheltered Jewish refugees, whom they taught agricultural skills in preparation for **kibbutz** life. The Bruderhof continue communications and exchange visits with Kibbutzim.

In recent decades, positive contacts between Anabaptists and Jews have developed. Dutch Mennonite Frits Kuiper (1898–1974) founded *Nes Ammim* (now run by Reformed Christians) as a Christian witness and expression of **repentance** in **Israel**. American Mennonite theologian John Howard Yoder (1927–97) studied the parting of the ways extensively, and argued for a reconceptualisation of Anabaptist history – locating what

Anabaptists identify as the 'fall' of Christianity in its schism from Judaism, rather than (as traditionally) in the Constantinian conflation of Church and state. As in other churches, there is disagreement within Anabaptism between those who would Judaise Christianity (*see* **Judaising Christians**), non-Judaisers who affirm Christianity's Jewish roots and Judaism as means of relating with God, and others, who emphasise the need for Jews to convert to Christianity.

Anabaptist–Jewish relations are little studied: historian Franklin Littell (b. 1917) has written on Anabaptists, but does not discuss them in his work on the **Holocaust**. The response of some Christians to the views of Anabaptist **dialogue** participants is characterised by a lack of sympathy. Conversely, modest growth in Anabaptist influence on wider Christianity is exemplified by the **World Council of Churches**' 'Decade to Overcome Violence', and the popular mediation of John Howard Yoder's thought by Protestant theologian Stanley Hauerwas (b. 1940).

See also **Historic Peace Churches**

MELANIE J. WRIGHT

Anacletus II (*c*.1090–1138)

Antipope. Pietro Pierleone was Antipope to Innocent II (*r*.1130–43) from 1130 to 1138. His Jewish grandfather Benedict converted to Christianity and married a Christian woman, and the family became powerful in papal politics. Pierleone was involved in ecclesiastical missions and presided at the councils of Chartres and Beauvais. In the papal election of 1130 he was elected by a small faction of Romans, while his opponent Innocent II was supported by the councils of Reims and Pisa as well as most European royalty, the only exceptions being William X Duke of Aquitaine (1099–1137) and Roger of Sicily (1093–1154), who was Anacletus's brother-in-law. The opposition to Anacletus, which notably included **Bernard of Clairvaux**, focused on his Jewish ancestry and his 'Jewish physiognomy', calling him 'Judaeo-Pontifex'. They accused him of the systematic robbery of chapels and churches with the help of the Jews, as well as of incest. The Jewish community of Rome seems to have supported his office. Eventually, the population of Rome turned against him, and he maintained the papal office until his death only with the help of Roger of Sicily. His pontificate was the source of medieval legends about a **Jewish Pope**. However, modern historians of the Church have written about him with contempt.

MICHAEL A. SIGNER

Ancient authors

Interest in Greek and Roman writers' views on Judaism arose in the nineteenth century when the first collection of sources was produced by T. Reinach (1860–1928). He sought to show that **antisemitism** was 'as old as Judaism' itself, and such views of an eternal antisemitism, bolstered by the ancient evidence, have been influential. They came to be questioned by James **Parkes** and Jules **Isaac**, who recognised the contribution made by Christian teaching to the history of antisemitism and downplayed the hostility in ancient writers. Greeks and Romans display positive and negative attitudes to both Jews and Christians. From the third century BCE Greek writers in **Egypt** (e.g. pseudo-Hecataeus) seem to have expressed hostility to Jews, focused on the figure of **Moses**, and these attitudes perhaps arose from political conflicts. At the same time some writers were impressed by the Jewish belief in one god (e.g. Theophrastus (*c*.371–287 BCE)), comparable to pre-Socratic notions of the one being. Nevertheless, the Jewish way of life did lead to accusations of separateness and unfriendliness. How far these were widely held beliefs is unclear, and it is difficult to detach the political motives from the genuine beliefs of the writers. Whatever the original intentions, the recording of some of these views by Christian writers did lead to their influence later.

The arrival of Christianity also led to some harsh accusations, especially as the Romans considered new cults as suspicious and dangerous (cf. Pliny the Younger (62–*c*.115 CE) and Tacitus (*c*.55–after 117 CE) on Christian *superstitio*). The Greek writer Theophrastus's belief, for example, that Jews committed human sacrifice was adopted by later writers and applied to Christians. **Celsus** in the second century wrote an attack on Christianity that still needed to be refuted nearly a century later by **Origen**, and the Neoplatonic philosopher Porphyry (*c*.232–*c*.304) in the third and the Emperor **Julian** in the fourth century each attacked Christianity. As a result Christians sought to emphasise their own antiquity (e.g. **Justin Martyr**) and the role of Christians in the **Roman Empire** at the expense of Judaism. Many Roman discussions of Christianity reflect issues that became central to Christianity itself. Thus the antiquity of Christianity and its relation to Judaism was raised by Roman writers, as were questions of God in the world, the civil position of Christianity and the divinity of **Jesus**. Galen (129–c.211) was the first to indicate that the view of **creation** had to be altered to take into account Christian views of God, leading to the doctrine of *creatio ex nihilo*.

We have in many ways moved away from the nineteenth-century interest in ancient views of Jews and Christians, which were motivated by social issues of that time, and are beginning to see the complexity of relationships between groups in antiquity. There has been a renewed interest, nonetheless, in the origins of antisemitism, but the political circumstances of the time help to place the ancient statements in their context.   *JAMES K. AITKEN*

Andrew of Crete (c.660–740)

Byzantine Churchman and hymnographer. The first decade of Islamic rule in the Middle East saw a revival of Jewish–Christian tension, manifest in Andrew's sermons in which he bears witness to Emperor Leo III's (r.717–41) persecution of the Jews, and his liturgical poetry which expresses anti-Jewish sentiment against those who had rejected the **Messiah**. A native of Damascus, he was tonsured a monk at the monastery of the Resurrection in **Jerusalem** and spent some time in Constantinople before being consecrated Archbishop of Gortyna and Metropolitan of Crete. He was renowned as a preacher and is one of the earliest composers of the form of liturgical poetry called the 'canon', a series of verses embellishing the biblical canticles at the morning service of matins.   *ANDREW LOUTH*

Andrew of St Victor (d. 1175)

Biblical exegete who provided the most sustained commentaries on the Hebrew Bible since **Jerome**. Andrew was most likely born in England, but entered the Abbey of Saint Victor in Paris where he was influenced by the writings of Master Hugh of St Victor (d. 1142). He later returned to England as abbot of Wigmore in Herefordshire, where he died. Andrew's primary significance as a biblical interpreter was his exclusive focus on the books of the **Hebrew Bible** and their literal sense. He entered into conversations with Jews, most likely in Paris, and recorded their understanding of biblical words and phrases in his own **commentaries**. The information from Jews in Andrew of St Victor's biblical commentaries ranges from translations of biblical words into Old French, paraphrases of passages in the **Talmud** or midrashim that expli-

cate a particular verse, or descriptions of contemporary Jewish **mourning** customs. Many of these passages reflect the explanations given by contemporary Jewish exegetes such as **Rashi**, Rabbi Joseph b. Simeon Kara (1060/70–1130/40) or Rabbi Samuel b. Meir (1085–1174). These Jewish scholars represented the new exegetical trend of *Peshat* or plain meaning as the basis for interpretation, rather than relying exclusively upon explanations transmitted in the name of the Rabbis in the Talmud or **midrash**. Andrew rejected Jewish explanations that asserted the **eschatological** restoration of the Jews, but his **exegesis** marks a significant advance in the development of Christian **biblical interpretation** based on Hebrew and Jewish sources.

See also **Victorines**   *MICHAEL A. SIGNER*

Angels

Angels (*angelos* = **Septuagint** rendering of Hebrew *malakh*, retained by **Jerome** in the **Vulgate** as *angelus*; hence *angel* in common English use) as messengers and agents of divine purpose play an important role in many expressions of Jewish and Christian belief and worship. Texts in the **Hebrew Bible** before the time of the Second Temple already speak of divine beings among whom the Lord sits in judgement (Ps. 82), of those who execute his purposes on earth, and of cherubim, seraphim and 'living creatures' who surround and worship the Lord in glory. Such ideas are greatly developed in the Second Temple period, especially in **apocalyptic** writings and in the **Dead Sea Scrolls**. Some common themes can be traced within a complex of ideas that is too rich and varied to categorise neatly.

Hierarchies of angels become increasingly particular and elaborate, enhancing the sense of divine transcendence, and esoteric knowledge of the angelic hierarchy becomes of advantage to those who can get it. This theme is greatly developed in later writing, both Jewish (e.g. in *heikhalot* **mysticism**) and Christian (e.g. in the *Celestial Hierarchy* of Pseudo-Dionysius the Areopagite (c.500 CE), the most influential early Christian work on angels). The dualistic concept of the world as a moral battleground between opposing forces of good and evil (fallen) angels did not persist in Christian thought, but the transformation of the biblical Satan/*diabolos* ('Interposer') into the leader of the fallen angels and principal power of **evil** in creation has enjoyed a longer career. Again, the action of priests in the earthly Temple copies the liturgy of angelic priests in a heavenly Temple. Enoch and Daniel had looked forward to communion with angels in the final consummation of things; the authors of 1QH 3.19–23 or 4Q400–407 saw themselves as participating in the angelic life now. Such ideas persist in Christian traditions, especially through the use of the *Sanctus* (based on the vision of the seraphim in Isa. 6.3) at the **eucharist**. Angels may also be attached to individual humans as companions and guardians. This idea is developed in the book of Tobit (*c.*200 BCE?) and has flourished in both religions, enjoying an unexpected flowering in the trauma of the First World War. While in popular versions of Kabbalah angels might also be approached through invocations and incantations, there was no corresponding technology for influencing guardian angels in popular Christianity, where intercessions were more likely to be made through **saints** than angels. The role of angels as divine messengers and agents persists through all these developments, and they are thus encountered in the **New Testament** (e.g. Luke 1.26; 2.8–14; Acts 5.19). *ANDERS BERGQUIST*

Anglicanism

Anglican relations with Jews and Judaism vary considerably, partly because the Anglican Communion's 70 million members are widely spread, with individual congregations to be found in 164 countries, and partly because the 38 provinces of the Anglican Communion are self-governing churches, headed by a primate or presiding bishop. In the **United Kingdom** and North America, where there are sizeable Jewish communities, Anglican churches attach considerable importance to Jewish–Christian relations. Statements on the subject by the Anglican Church of **Canada**, for example, date back to 1927. In Africa and Asia, however, there are few Jews, and churches show little interest in Judaism. Indeed, some churches in **India** have suggested that passages from the Hindu scriptures should replace readings from the **Old Testament**. Moreover, Anglicans in Africa and Asia, who struggled against imperialism, identify with the Palestinians in what they see as their liberation struggle and show little sympathy with **Israel**. This is especially true of Anglicans in the Middle East, most of whom are Arabs (*see* **Arab Christianity**). The focus of unity for Anglicans is the Archbishop of Canterbury, with whom all Anglican bish-

ops are in communion. Cohesion is strengthened by the Lambeth Conference, held every ten years and attended by all bishops, and by the Anglican Consultative Council. Recent Archbishops of Canterbury have all been committed to seeking good relations with the Jewish people and supportive of the work of the **Council of Christians and Jews**. The 1988 **Lambeth Conference** issued a detailed statement on Judaism and relations with the Jewish people, entitled *Jews, Christians and Muslims: The Way of Dialogue*. In a different context, the 1988 Lambeth Conference affirmed Israel's right to recognised and secure borders and the Palestinians' right to self-determination. The Anglican Consultative Council sponsors a Network of Inter Faith Concerns for the Anglican Communion (NIFCON). In recent years Anglicans have increasingly rejected traditional anti-Jewish teaching. Several Anglicans, such as Herbert **Danby**, James **Parkes** and Peter Schneider (1928–82), made important contributions to the new approach. The importance of **dialogue** is now widely recognised. Three Anglican–Jewish consultations have been held. Co-chaired by the Chief Rabbi and by either the Archbishop of Canterbury or the Archbishop of York, they concentrated on social and moral issues and avoided theological discussion. In 1980 at Amport House, Andover, the subject was 'Law and Religion in Contemporary Society'; in 1987 at Shallowford House near Stafford discussion centred on the moral issues raised by AIDS and on the report 'Faith in the City'; in 1992 at St George's House, Windsor, there were papers on Israel and on **mission**, and discussion of 'Guidelines on Jewish Christian Relations' which were eventually published by the Council of Churches for Britain and Ireland in 1994. The appropriateness of missionary efforts to convert Jews and attitudes to Israel/Palestine are still matters of strong debate in the Anglican Communion. Anglicans have played a full part in national and international ecumenical bodies in their discussions with Jews, especially through the **World Council of Churches**.

See also **Church of England**

MARCUS BRAYBROOKE

Anointing

Applying vegetable, or specifically olive, oil to persons or objects for healing or blessing has a long history in both the Jewish and Christian traditions. In the Jewish tradition rituals of anointing accompanied the investing of kings and **priests** (e.g.

Exod. 28.41; 30.30; 1 Sam. 10.1; 15.1; 2 Sam. 2.4) and the consecrating of sacred objects like the **altar** and tabernacles (e.g. Num. 7). In the daily life of ancient times the respectable host anointed the head of his guest upon welcoming him to his home. Furthermore, healers employed the soothing and healing qualities of oil to assuage the suffering of the afflicted (Isa. 1.6; Luke 10.34). In Christianity some traditions of both East and West imitate sacramentally the example of **Jesus** (e.g. 'They [the disciples of Jesus] drove out many demons and anointed many sick people with oil and healed them.' Mark 6.13); naturally, Jesus drew upon his own Jewish experience for such a healing gesture.

As with so many dimensions of its life, that parts of the Christian community have adopted and adapted a Jewish practice like anointing reflects the interweaving of Jewish and later Christian practice. Furthermore, that Jesus is honoured as the anointed one – *christos* in Greek, *mašiaḥ* in Hebrew, **Messiah** in English – shows the intimate intersection and disagreement between the communities. While the physical gesture of anointing is secondary, one may note that identifying *who* is the anointed one – has he come or is he only to come in an accompanying future messianic era? – has fuelled **polemics** between the communities for centuries.

As they seek to find less intellectualist, more bodily religious expression, Western Christians are retrieving anointing with oil. This is especially true of religious women with **feminist** sensitivities. For example, women in the Jewish and Christian traditions, bonding in a feminist quest for common religious expression even as they recognise and honour their own traditions, have found in the anointing ritual a meaningful expression of the more holistic, less rationalistic approach to religion. While the Jewish tradition has, like the Protestant tradition, abandoned anointing with oil in its rituals, the feminist enterprise may well provide a new context for retrieving this ancient practice among Jews and all Christians.   *MICHAEL MCGARRY*

Anselm of Canterbury (*c*.1033–1109)

Abbot, Archbishop of Canterbury, reformer, theologian and philosopher, famous primarily for his ontological proof for the existence of God and also his doctrine of the **incarnation** and **atonement** of Christ. He addresses parts of a major treatise on incarnation and atonement (*Cur Deus Homo?*) to the objections of 'unbelievers', including Jews, voiced by a student, Boso. It is highly unlikely that Anselm had substantial contact with Jewish thinkers, and thus these objections are literary devices. They are, however, serious and sophisticated, and Anselm treats them with respect. In this way Anselm differs from most of the authors of the **Adversus Judaeos** tradition, who ridicule the views of their (usually fictive) Jewish opponents.   *JOANN SPILLMAN*

Anthropomorphism

The Jewish–Christian encounter has frequently engaged with the problem of 'anthropomorphism'. Anthropomorphism is the propensity to liken God to a human or to attribute human characteristics to God, and is found often in the Bible. As G. B. Caird (1917–84) noted, the vast majority of the biblical language that refers to God is anthropomorphic (*The Language and Imagery of the Bible*, 174): God displays the whole range of human actions and characteristics, and in terms of occupation, God is everything from a king to a potter (*Language*, 175). As a result, both Judaism and Christianity have strands that make use of these anthropomorphic images in theology and worship, as for example the rabbinic **aggadah** and the mystical tract *Shiur Komah*, and some Christian **music** (especially modern worship songs) and mystical writers (for example St John of the Cross).

When it comes to formal theology, especially in its medieval forms, both Judaism and Christianity found anthropomorphism problematic. **Maimonides** in the twelfth century was a significant influence on the Christian theologian **Aquinas** in the thirteenth (David B. Burrell, *Knowing the Unknowable God*), arguing that the biblical images capture the human experience of God, not how God is in Godself. Both maintained that God is timeless (literally there is no duration in God) and therefore immutable (there is no change in God) and as a result agree that it is impossible for God to resemble the creation. Aquinas took issue with Maimonides about God-talk, however: Maimonides suggested that God-talk should be confined to negative assertions; Aquinas suggested the doctrine of analogy, which attempts to transcend the options of 'univocally' (a word when applied to God has exactly the same meaning as it has in its human context) and equivocally (the word has a different and unrelated meaning) (Eric Mascall, *Existence and Analogy*).

There have been interesting patterns of influence between Christians and Jews in these debates. Christian theologians sympathetic to the classical position find support amongst some Jewish theologians, while those Christians sympathetic to a more dynamic picture of God have an equal number of revisionist theological Jewish supporters. The attraction of anthropomorphic imagery is that the image of God is both intimate and dynamic; the attraction of the classical account of God is that it preserves the perfection of God. Many modern Christians and Jews operate somewhere in between these two poles. The impact of A. N. Whitehead (1861–1947) and the emergence of process thought in Christian theology have had an impact on both Jewish and Christian accounts of God.

IAN MARKHAM

Antichrist

Christian concept of satanic princely ruler as arch-enemy of Christ in the end-times; a recurrent anti-Jewish motif. Rooted in Persian and Babylonian mythology and adapted from Jewish sources (Daniel; Maccabean identification of Antiochus IV Epiphanes as the ultimate wicked king), Christian notions of Antichrist occurring in letters of St John and 2 Thessalonians were first applied to historical enemies of the Church (Nero, **Gnostics**).

While medieval and **Reformation** polemicists intermittently identified political opponents – individual popes, emperors (especially Frederick II *r*.1215–50), even (for sectarians) the clergy – as Antichrist, the Jews were permanently linked to Antichrist. Scholastics (Thomas **Aquinas**, Albertus Magnus (*c*.1200–80)) asserted Antichrist's Jewish identity and ability by magical 'miracles' and rebuilding the Temple to convince all Jews of his Messiahship. Popular imagination envisaged Antichrist as a demonically conceived Jewish bastard. Medieval Christian **art**, drama and sermons consistently identified Jews as Antichrist's followers; his satanic attributes – animality, grossness, cunning, uncleanness, sorcery – were projected onto Jews. Natural disasters, famines, plagues and wars were interpreted as 'signs of the times' heralding Antichrist's imminence; heightened **millenarian** fears of his prophesied Jewish cohorts could erupt in mass violence against Jews. Christian myths of **blood libel** and **host desecration** stemmed partly from perceptions of Jews as worshippers and servants of Antichrist/Satan, inimical to Christ and destined for hell.

Post-Reformation theology de-emphasised Antichrist. While millenarian expectations of malign Jewish/Antichrist alliance occasionally still surface in marginal dispensational/pre-millennial Protestant groups, they are promulgated widely through the *Protocols of the Elders of Zion* and *Protocols*-influenced films and literature.

MARGARET BREARLEY

Anti-Christian Jewish teaching

Although negative assessments of Christianity can be found in **ancient authors**, the first apparent attack came from the second-century pagan **Celsus** in his *True Word*, as recorded in **Origen**'s *Contra Celsum*. There are a number of criticisms of Christianity in rabbinic literature too, ranging from attacks on 'heretics' and **idolatry**, which might in part be aimed at Christians, to negative portrayals of **Jesus**. But the first tract against Christians was the *Toledot Yeshu*, a parody of the Gospels that is attested from the tenth century but probably originates earlier. If the traditions of this text are traceable earlier, it would indicate that there was a current of anti-Christian teaching in the rabbinic period, but probably for many Jews Christians were not an issue at all: references to Christianity in the **Talmud** are very few. The lack of a strong anti-Christian tradition reflects a degree of separation, but where it is found it indicates contact. Jewish opposition would have been a response to Christian teaching and missionary activity, and reflects a similar expression of **identity** and internal education. In the **Byzantine** period such texts tend to be in **Hebrew** (perhaps translations from Arabic originals), implying they were aimed at an internal Jewish audience. After the rise of **Islam** we find many more examples of anti-Christian texts. *The Alphabet of Ben Sira* (probably ninth century) contains the tale of the miraculous birth and prophecy of the ancient writer Ben Sira, intended as a parody of the life of Jesus. Jewish polemical literature appears to have developed in Islamic lands, and its language was Arabic, reflecting the influence of Arabic polemical literature. Where we have Hebrew texts, such as a Genizah fragment (e.g. ENA NS 50 fol. 9), their grammar sometimes reflects an Arabic original. The earliest medieval polemicist was Dāwūd ibn Marwān al-Muqammas (ninth–tenth century), a Jew who converted to Christianity and, upon returning to Judaism, wrote two polemical works against Christianity; he included anti-Christian material in his theological study *'Ishrūn Maqāla*. In the tenth century Saadiah Gaon (882–942) also included anti-Christian arguments in his writings but without composing a separate treatise. One of the most popular works of the time was the *Book of Nestor the Priest*, said to have been written by a Christian priest who had converted to Judaism. The text, whose original date is uncertain, has survived in both an Arabic and a Hebrew version, and in its argument draws extensively from the **New Testament** (particularly the Gospels) and the New Testament **Apocrypha**, quoting sometimes in Hebrew and sometimes in **Greek**. It is quoted by Jacob ben Reuben (southern France) in the twelfth century, and used by Joseph Kimhi (*c.*1105–70) and David **Kimhi**, and Sa'd ibn Mansur ibn Kammuna (Baghdad, 1280). The popularity of such texts ensured a long history for the tradition of anti-Christian **polemic**, and many more texts continued to be written for centuries. Later works include a sixteenth-century Hebrew translation of Matthew's Gospel that negates statements in the New Testament, and the seventeenth-century Italian writer Judah Briel (*c.*1643–1722).   *JAMES K. AITKEN*

Anti-Defamation League *see* **Jewish–Christian relations, institutions; United States of America**

Anti-Judaism

There has been considerable controversy over the use of the terms 'anti-Judaism' and '**antisemitism**'. Some employ them interchangeably. Others prefer to limit 'anti-Judaism' to religious and theological defamation of Jews and Judaism, which might not always translate into personal hatred. Still others have argued that the term 'anti-Judaism' is used by some to soften the impact of actual antisemitism. It is not likely that this controversy will end soon. Certainly, there is some basis for a distinction based on actual experience. We know, for example, that during the **Holocaust** there were Christians who held traditional theological views about Jews and Judaism and yet risked their lives to save Jewish people. Anti-Judaism is here used to refer to the pre-**Enlightenment** period as well as to theological approaches to Jews and Judaism since the beginning of **modernity**.

Considerable discussion has ensued over the years regarding the presence of anti-Judaism in the **New Testament**. No clear consensus has emerged.

Most scholars regard what appears to be anti-Jewish **polemic** in the New Testament as a reflection of deep internal disputes within Judaism at the time of its composition. But these scholars also insist that such polemic became anti-Judaic after Christianity and Judaism had formally separated. They also point to a number of texts in the Gospel of John and the letter to the Hebrews that must be seen as fundamentally anti-Judaic. The noted biblical scholar Raymond Brown (1928–98) argued that such texts cannot remain part of Christian education today, a point subsequently endorsed by Cardinal Joseph **Bernardin**, a major episcopal leader in Christian–Jewish **dialogue**.

Whatever the situation with regard to the New Testament, anti-Judaism clearly becomes a central component of Christian teaching as we enter the time of the **Church Fathers**. A number of Christian scholars, including Robert Wilken (b. 1936), David Efroymson (b. 1931) and Rosemary Radford Ruether (b. 1936), have uncovered a prevailing anti-Judaic bias at the core of patristic literature. While notable exceptions such as Clement of Alexandria (*c.*150–*c.*215) can be found, the great patristic writers such as Bishop Melito of Sardis, Tertullian, Origen, Irenaeus and Eusebius all made anti-Judaism an integral part of their explanation of the Christian faith. In his homily *Peri Pascha* ('Concerning the Pascha') **Melito** compared the celebration of the **Passover** with that of **Easter**. For Melito the events of Jewish history merely served as prototypical models for the great event of Easter; but having fulfilled this role with the coming of Christ they serve no useful spiritual purpose. This is the beginning of the Christian theology of **supersessionism** that regarded Judaism as a religious wasteland. **Tertullian** presented **Jesus** as the **Messiah** whom Jews ought to have recognised but did not, resulting in their subjection to divine wrath. **Origen**'s approach was marked by the claim that Jews refused to believe in Jesus as the Saviour because they lacked a spiritual sense of the scriptures that would allow them to go beyond the literal meaning. **Irenaeus** explained Jewish **law** as necessary for a time because of human sinfulness; but the coming of Jesus and the destruction of **Jerusalem** signalled that the time of the Jews and their law was over. The most important and comprehensive anti-Judaic document was **Justin Martyr**'s *Dialogue with Trypho*. It became a model for discussions about Judaism in the ancient Church and sowed the seeds for an anti-Judaic attitude that would come to dominate the thinking of the churches from the fourth to the twentieth century. Justin's writings were the first real expression of the idea that Jewish social misfortunes are the consequences of divine punishment for the death of Jesus (*see* **deicide, charge of**); as a result, Jews will never be able to escape suffering in human society, remaining confined to a marginal and miserable existence. This theology became the source for the 'wandering Jew' imagery so prevalent in Christian popular thinking and **art**. A final example is **Eusebius**, who in his early fourth-century work *Ecclesiastical History* confines the role of the Jews to that of witnessing to divine justice.

In 323 CE Christianity was granted a special position within the **Roman Empire**. Judaism theoretically continued as a legal religion (*see* ***religio licita***), but this legal status was frequently ignored. By the time Emperor Constantine converted to Christianity in 329, the imperial government had already begun to institute restrictive measures against Jews. By the end of the fourth century the civil status of Jews was in serious danger and their image had greatly deteriorated. The Jew was now viewed as a semi-satanic figure, cursed by God and specially set apart by the civil government. It was in the fourth century that Christian preachers turned upon Judaism with great vehemence. Foremost among these preachers was John **Chrysostom**, whose denunciations of the Jewish people were delivered in eight sermons in which he accused the Jews of all imaginable crimes and vices: the **devil** lived in Jewish homes, the synagogue was an assembly of animals. Chrysostom attributed this to the Jews' assassination of Jesus: God has always hated the Jews and they will forever remain without **Temple** or nation. The Christian picture of Judaism developed in the fourth and fifth centuries gave the churches for centuries a pseudo-religious basis for countless persecutions of the Jews. Misguided Christians considered themselves chosen to assist God in fulfilling the curse upon the Jews and felt they were free to engage in attacking Jews with a divine seal of approval. All was not total darkness for Jews during the ensuing centuries: the **Visigoths** and Lombards basically accepted the protection accorded the Jewish community in the **Theodosian Code**, and several popes, such as **Gregory the Great**, while intent on converting Jews, gave public support to their legal protection. But subsequently the strong anti-Judaic attitude of the Church Fathers returned to dominate Christian societies. St **Agobard** of Lyons reinstituted the harsh language against the Jews begun by John Chrysostom, and the **Crusaders**, on their way to liberate the Holy Land from Muslims, often attacked Jewish communities en route in areas such as the German Rhineland. The notion of Jewish ritual murder (*see* **blood libel**) also arose, charging that each **Holy Week** Jews killed a Christian, usually a child, as a sacrificial offering for Passover. With the establishment of the **Inquisition** in the thirteenth century and the ensuing struggle with heretics, Jewish writings were censored and suppressed (*see* **censorship**). The **Talmud** was condemned and Albertus Magnus (1200–80) ordered the burning of all copies. By the end of the thirteenth century the mass murder of Jews had become a common occurrence in **Germany** and **France**.

The classical anti-Judaic teachings of Christianity combined with new forms of political, cultural and biological antisemitism as we enter the modern era. Classical anti-Judaism came to an end only with the declaration by the **Second Vatican Council** that Jews were to be regarded as still in the **covenant** after Christ, that they could not be held collectively responsible for the death of Christ, and that Jesus and the **early Church** were profoundly impacted by the Jewish teachings of their time. Gregory Baum (b. 1923), who served as an expert at the Council, has termed chapter 4 of the conciliar declaration *Nostra Aetate* the most remarkable about-face in the ordinary teaching of the Church to take place at Vatican II. The example of the Catholic Church was repeated in almost all Protestant denominations, who from the mid-1960s also issued documents repudiating the Church's classic anti-Judaic theology.

There are no developments within **Orthodox Christianity** regarding the legacy of Christian anti-Judaism that parallel what has occurred over the past 40 years in **Roman Catholicism** and mainline **Protestantism**. Some individual Orthodox leaders such as the Patriarchs of Constantinople and Moscow have issued statements against antisemitism in connection with international conferences, and some individual scholars have spoken out as well. But there has been no sustained effort as yet to review educational materials and theological literature as there has been in the two other major branches of Christianity. This is an extremely sensitive issue in Orthodox Christianity given the special status of patristic literature in the Orthodox Christian tradition. **Evangelical** Christian Churches have also not confronted the legacy of Christian anti-Judaism to the same extent as mainline Protestant denominations, though there have been somewhat greater efforts on their part than in the Orthodox Churches. In connection with the controversy over Mel Gibson's **film** *The Passion of the Christ* (2004) some Orthodox Christian scholars and Evangelical Christian publications have acknowledged a need for Christianity to deal with anti-Judaism far more directly than has been the case until now.   *JOHN T. PAWLIKOWSKI*

Antinomianism

Antinomian literally means 'against the law'. For the Jewish–Christian encounter this has principally been a term used by Christians to define a key difference with Judaism. Thus, in Christian theology, the term is used to describe those who believed that God's action in Christ had liberated the Christian from the requirement to observe the moral law. **Paul**, writing in Rom. 3.8, is sensitive to this criticism, describing it as a slander that he is advocating the doing of evil 'that good may come'.

However, some Christian groups adopted a form of antinomianism. Certain forms of **Gnosticism** exercised liberty in respect to sexuality, and in North Africa in the second and third centuries the Adamite sect condemned marriage and worshipped naked. In 1537 to 1540 Martin **Luther** (who coined the term) argued against Johann Agricola's (1494–1566) negative view of the **law**. Luther maintained that the law had three purposes: first, it revealed sin; second, it established fundamental social decency; and third, it provided a rule of life for those who have been redeemed in Christ. For Lutherans, this was confirmed at the Formula of Concord in 1577. Later, in Puritan America, Anne Marbury Hutchinson (1591–1643) was condemned as an antinomian in 1637 for teaching that the 'covenant of **grace**' was set apart from the 'works of the law'. In many of these cases a contrast was drawn with Judaism, as the religion that was 'under law'.

In fact there are also groups within Judaism that have been described as antinomian. The seventeenth-century Sabbetaians, so called after their Messianic leader **Shabbetai Zvi**, had antinomian sympathies. The Sabbetaians gave birth to the Frankist movement, led by Jacob **Frank**, whose mystical festivities were alleged to be accompanied by sexual orgies. And more broadly, **Reform Judaism** is often accused of antinomianism because of its willingness to harmonise the tradition of Judaism with **modernity**.

Of the variety of different ways in which the term has been used, including the view that traditional moral expectations are not binding, the most significant for the Jewish–Christian encounter is the view that the Jewish law is not binding. By this definition, with the exception of **Messianic Jews** and **Seventh-Day Adventists** all Christians are antinomian to some degree, and this antinomianism has sometimes fuelled or been used to justify **antisemitism**. However, arguments in the **New Testament** over the status of the **Torah** are mirrored in contemporary Judaism, where there are heated internal debates about the relationship of the requirements of the Torah to contemporary behaviour.   *IAN MARKHAM*

Antioch

One of the great cities of the Roman Empire, eventually capital of the diocese of the East (*Oriens*). It was, from the early days of Christianity, and remained one of the most important places of encounter between Jews and Christians, for it had a large Jewish community; indeed it was in Antioch that Jewish converts to Christianity were first called 'Christians' (Acts 11.26). An early Christian bishop of Antioch, **Ignatius**, who died a martyr in Rome *c.*107, displays both the influence of Jewish **apocalyptic** traditions and opposition to too deep an attachment to Jewish traditions (even the **Old Testament**) on the part of Christians. As Christianity developed, Antioch became one of the principal sees of the Christian Church, mentioned as such along with Rome and **Alexandria** at the first Ecumenical Council, held in Nicaea (canon 6). The development of a body of Eastern **canon law** in the fourth century seems to have taken place in Antioch. With the establishment of Constantinople as the new capital of the **Roman Empire**, Antioch seems to have become an ally of the new capital rather than a rival, as was the case with Alexandria, and some of the early patriarchs of Constantinople were drawn from Antioch (e.g. John **Chrysostom** and Nestorius (*r.* 428–31)). **Greek** Christianity has often been presented in terms of a rivalry between Antioch and Alexandria, though how genuine this rivalry was may be doubted. Both were, however, centres of learning, and it seems safe to say that while Alexandria, with its magnificent library, was famed for philosophy and scientific achievement, Antioch was famous for its **rhetorical** schools. Its greatest pagan rhetorician was Libanius (314–*c.*393), who lamented that the Christians had prevented his pupil, John Chrysostom, from becoming his successor. The Christian 'Antiochene School', traditionally seen in opposition to the 'Alexandrian School', is often regarded as having been particularly influenced by the Jewish community in Antioch, and although there is little doubt that Antiochene exegetes were aware of Jewish exegetical traditions, it is doubtful if they were as deeply indebted to such traditions as the Alexandrian **Origen**. Theodore (*c.*350–428), later bishop of Mopsuestia, was the most important of the Antiochene exegetes (revered in the later Church of the East as 'the interpreter'); his unwillingness to accept as Christian prophecies many passages traditionally regarded as such by most Christians may well have been due to Jewish sensitivities. The Jewish presence in Antioch was significant, and apparently attractive to members of the Christian community in the latter decades of the fourth century. Such **Judaising** on the part of Christians provoked from Chrysostom, then a priest at the Golden Church, a series of sermons that contain ugly expressions of anti-Jewish sentiment. The Jewish presence in Antioch may well have been strengthened during the short reign of **Julian the Apostate** (361–3), for Julian's attempts to restore traditional religions (which apparently included Judaism and envisaged the restoration of the **Temple** in **Jerusalem**) took place during his long stay in Antioch (May 362–March 363), prior to his fateful expedition against the Persians. It is most likely echoes of this recently restored Jewish confidence that inspired Chrysostom's attack. Antioch retained its importance during the fifth and early sixth centuries, but suffered from an earthquake in 526 and never fully recovered from temporary seizure by the Persians in 540 and its virtually permanent acquisition by the Arabs in 636–7. In 609 there was a massacre of Jews, who seem however to have been caught up in the rivalry between the circus factions fomented by the Emperor Phocas (*r.* 602–10), rather than the victims of any attempt at forcible **baptism**, something that soon became a recurrent feature of Byzantine imperial policy.   *ANDREW LOUTH*

Antisemitism

Antisemitism is here defined as a post-**Enlightenment** phenomenon following upon earlier forms of **anti-Judaism**, though this is not a differentiation all scholars would accept. Antisemitism as used here thus refers to denigration of Jews rooted in a new form of thinking about biology and genetics, as well as in certain political and cultural trends associated with the emergence of **modernity** in Europe. More recent forms of antisemitism have also appeared in certain sectors of the African-American community in the **United States**, as well as in the Arab world and within radical forms of **Islam** in the Western world. But antisemitism in the post-Enlightenment period often still involved a deep-seated disdain for Jews and Judaism based in Christian beliefs. **Passion plays**, which were becoming more commonplace in this era, intensified anti-Jewish attitudes, and even pre-modern forms of anti-Judaism often seemed to portray Jews as evil at the very core of their being, often linking them with Satan. For example, the later writings of Martin **Luther** on the Jews certainly leave the distinct impression of them as a demonic and depraved people in a way similar to more modern forms of antisemitism. While these writings have been specifically repudiated by the Evangelical Lutheran Church in America (1984), as well as **Lutheran** churches in Europe, Argentina and Australia and in a more general way by the Lutheran World Federation, they show that historically speaking no absolutely clear-cut distinction between anti-Judaism and antisemitism is possible.

The coming of the modern era, with its theme of social liberation, did result in a measure of political freedom for individual Jews in certain countries, but not for the Jewish people as a community. So long as Jews identified themselves primarily as individual citizens they were accorded a measure of civil rights in the countries most directly impacted by the Enlightenment, such as France and Germany. But their ability to exist within these societies with a strong sense of communal **identity** was still highly circumscribed. In some countries, such as **Russia**, home to a very substantial Jewish population, the situation worsened for Jews with the appearance in 1905 of the so-called ***Protocols of the Learned Elders of Zion***. Written by Russian antisemites, the *Protocols* claimed the existence of a powerful Jewish cabal that was plotting to take control of global society. The *Protocols* still circulate in some countries today.

In the nineteenth and early twentieth centuries antisemitism took on yet another form in many parts of Christian Europe, such as France, Germany and **Poland**. While not as widespread in North America, this form of antisemitism did surface in the teachings of such groups as the Ku Klux Klan, who identified Jews, along with Catholic and African Americans, as groups perverting authentic Christianity. This new form of antisemitism accused Jews of being supporters both of Communism and of **liberalism**, which many Christians regarded as equally diabolical forces threatening the continued existence of the Church in Europe. Jews were accused of being at the heart of what was termed Freemasonry, a movement that advocated religious freedom, a notion especially repugnant in official Catholic circles where it was roundly condemned by the popes of the period. Jews were also charged with being a major source of social immorality in society as purveyors of pornography. Though Christian leaders generally did not accept the bio-racism advocated by the geneticists of the time, their attack on Jews as a fundamentally corrupting force in society came very close at times to the description of Jews found in biological writings of the day. In Catholic Poland supposed Jewish association with Freemasonry became especially intense, as it did in France. In Poland Freemasonry, which was often regarded as controlled by Jews, infuriated Polish Catholic nationalists, who were concerned that Catholic hegemony over the life of the nation would be severely diminished if Freemasonry expanded its influence in the country. In **France** the new, modern form of antisemitism has its roots in part in the notorious **Dreyfus Affair**, which generated a growing disdain for Jews in French society, Catholic nationalists included. To the French nationalistic and religious right Dreyfus the Jew symbolised all the liberal, alien and de-Christianising pressures on the traditional Christian order in the country. The Catholic Church through its media gave considerable support to the anti-Dreyfus sentiment sweeping France.

Protestant Churches generally shared in the modern antisemitic outlook on Jews and Judaism. Like the Catholic Church, they regarded liberal Jews as a threat to the Christian culture of Europe (though studies on Protestant educational materials undertaken at Yale University in the late 1950s also revealed a strong strain of antisemitism in mainline American **Protestantism**). This was especially the case in **Germany** in the first part of the twentieth century. The German Christian movement during the time of the Third Reich argued for a fundamental coalescence between Christianity and **Nazism**. While this movement was opposed by the so-called **Confessing Church** in Germany, identified with Karl Barth (1886–1968) and Dietrich **Bonhoeffer**, its outlook on the Jews was never specifically repudiated in the Confessing Church's central document called the Barmen Confession. Leading Protestant scholars such as Gerhard **Kittel** and Martin Noth (1902–68) wrote of Judaism as a 'dead' religion after the appearance of Christ. In **Orthodox Christianity** there were strong outbreaks of antisemitism in Russia throughout the nineteenth and early twentieth centuries. Even today, antisemitism is frequent in popular expressions of Orthodox Christianity in Russia, with the few voices speaking out against it often subjected to intense criticism. Antisemitism generally remains an unexamined problem in the Orthodox Churches, where the historic anti-Jewish theology of the patristic writers forms a central source of religious identity. Antisemitism, sometimes in the guise of anti-**Zionism**, has also appeared in the last several decades in Middle East Churches in connection with the Israeli–Palestinian conflict. While **Arab Christians** in the Middle East certainly have the right to critique policies of the **State of Israel** they regard as unjust, such criticisms become highly problematic when they are expressed in the classical antisemitic images of Christianity, such as the depiction of Palestinians as Jesus being crucified by the Jews.

In the last four decades many churches have attempted to confront their legacy of antisemitism. In 1989 the Vatican's Pontifical Commission for Justice and Peace issued a major statement denouncing racism as sinful and clearly placing antisemitism and anti-Zionism high on its list of continuing manifestations of racist ideologies. In fact, it termed antisemitism the most tragic form of such racist outlooks. And Pope **John Paul II** provided decisive leadership in the effort to conscientise the global community regarding the fundamental sinfulness of this social disease. During a visit to Hungary in 1991, conscious of a resurgence of antisemitism in certain parts of post-Communist Europe, he denounced antisemitism and all forms of racism as a sin against God and humanity, a denunciation repeated in his book *Crossing the Threshold of Hope*. To commemorate the hundredth anniversary of the Rome synagogue in 2004, with antisemitism on the rise in many places in Europe, he sent two curial cardinals to the anniversary celebration to read his statement which once more condemned antisemitism in decisive language. In 1998 the Vatican issued its long-awaited statement *We Remember*, which dealt with antisemitism and its role in the **Holocaust**. While the document does clearly acknowledge antisemitic attitudes within Christianity that contributed to the Nazi attack on the Jews, it tended to portray such attitudes as held by people on the fringes of the Church rather than acknowledging that these 'wayward' Christians, as it terms them, took their perspective on Jews from what they heard in sermons and saw in Christian **art**. Many Protestant Church statements have likewise denounced antisemitism as fundamentally immoral. The 2001 comprehensive document on Christian–Jewish relations issued by the Fellowship of Reformation Churches in Europe (*see* **Leuenberg Church Fellowship**) quotes a number of documents from its member churches which clearly condemn antisemitism. The statement from the Synod of the Evangelical Lutheran Church in the Rhineland released in 1980 (*see* **Rhineland Synod**) is highlighted, as is a 1998 declaration of the Evangelical Lutheran Church in **Austria** which insists that the Christian Churches must share responsibility for the Holocaust and are duty-bound to resist any personal or social manifestations of antisemitism. The Churches have yet to come to the point where they see antisemitism as an integral part of the Catholic tradition, something that requires comprehensive spiritual chemotherapy today if Christianity is to retain its moral credibility. As the great Christian pioneer in combating antisemitism James **Parkes** put it, it was 'the Christian Church alone, which turned normal xenophobia and normal good and bad communal relations between two human societies into the unique evil of antisemitism'.

JOHN T. PAWLIKOWSKI

Aphrahat (mid-fourth century CE)

Little is known of the life of Aphrahat 'The Persian Sage'. Coming from the region of Mosul and Nineveh in the upper Tigris valley, he might have had contact with Jews in the area, especially with the rabbinic academy at Nisibis nearby, but his writings reflect no knowledge of rabbinic issues and what he says of Judaism could have been derived from the Bible alone, although there are some traces of Jewish biblical **exegesis**. Apparent credal formulations in Aphrahat could be of Jewish origin, and although some of the contents are biblical, he might have had real knowledge from contact with Jews in the region. In many of the last 12 of his 22 'Demonstrations', replete with biblical and especially **Old Testament** allusions, he presents arguments against Judaism around the themes of **circumcision**, Passover, **Sabbath**, messianism, **dietary laws** and **Zionism**. He sees Judaism as having been supplanted by Christianity, such that Jews are, for example, mistaken in celebrating the **Passover** (Demonstration 12) because in Christ through the **eucharist** lies the true Passover. Chastity too, an important issue for **Syriac Christians**, is advocated and used as a further example of the error of Judaism in its command to propagate life. These anti-Jewish Demonstrations were composed in 344 during the persecution of Christians by the Zoroastrian King Shapur II of Persia (*r.*310–79) in response to the rise of Constantinian Christianity, which might indicate an intention less to persuade Jews of error than to prevent Christians defecting to Judaism as a 'safe' religion free from persecution. A primarily Christian target audience might also account for the only moderate engagement with rabbinic interests in the Demonstrations. *JAMES K. AITKEN*

Apocalypticism

The concept of apocalypticism as a type of religious thought is based on the existence of 'apocalyptic' literature (from Gk. *apokalypsis*, 'unveiling', 'revelation'), 'a genre of revelatory literature with a narrative framework, in which a revelation is mediated by an otherworldly being to a human recipient, disclosing a transcendent reality which is both temporal, insofar as it envisages eschatological salvation, and spatial, insofar as it involves another, supernatural world' (J. J. Collins (ed.), *Apocalypse: The Morphology of a Genre*, 9). There are 'historical' apocalypses 'concerned with the rise and fall of nations and with the end of history and the world' and 'cosmic' or 'mystical' apocalypses which explore 'the eschatology of the individual and the fate of the soul after death' (J. J. Collins (ed.), *The Encyclopedia of Apocalypticism*, vol.1, xiv). Apocalyptic literature was produced, to name just some examples, by ancient and medieval Judaism and Christianity, **Islam** and the Graeco-Roman, Iranian, Mesopotamian and Egyptian religions. Apocalypticism as a religious concept extends beyond these boundaries, since apocalyptic themes also occur in non-apocalyptic genres.

The origins of Jewish apocalypticism are found in post-exilic prophecy. Zech. 1–8 and similar texts afford us some insights into 'proto-apocalyptic' thought. The **Hellenistic** period saw the first flowering of apocalyptic literature. Milestones are the Ethiopic Enoch, in which are found the oldest Jewish apocalypses, and Dan. 7–12, the only biblical witness to apocalypticism proper. The rise of apocalypticism resulted from the loss of a firm theological and political orientation in the post-exilic period and from the experience of religious persecution under Antiochus IV (*r.*175–164 BCE).

Ancient Judaism produced a rich array of apocalyptic works. **Eschatological** expectations were central, but **wisdom literature** and priestly traditions also made profoundly important contributions. Among the Qumran texts (*see* **Dead Sea Scrolls**), particularly the War Scroll and the Damascus Document provide impressions of apocalyptic thought. Early Jewish **mysticism** and **Gnosticism** have points in common with the apocalyptic tradition, and early Christianity, in the first two centuries (before the conscious suppression of apocalypticism in mainstream Christianity), was deeply influenced by Jewish apocalyptic literature. All regional varieties of early Christianity, amongst them those of Syria-Palestine, Asia Minor and Egypt, produced apocalyptic writings, the most famous being the book of Revelation, which inspired later concepts of apocalypticism and the practice of the groups that promoted them.

Whereas the **Talmudim** and the 'classic' **midrashim** are not touched by apocalyptic thought, Judaism in late antiquity and in the early medieval period once again produced apocalyptic literature, which in turn influenced the Kabbalah, leading to an amalgamation of mysticism and apocalypticism (G. Scholem). Outbreaks of religious activity instigated by apocalyptic expectations include those connected with the **expulsion** from **Spain** and the movement of **Shabbetai Zvi**.

The resurgence of apocalyptic ideas in late ancient and medieval Christianity had far-reaching consequences. Thus, the **Crusades** are not least a product of the lively expectation of the eschatological battle in the Holy Land. Apocalyptic thought also inspired some of the great reform movements inside and outside the Church. The teachings of **Joachim of Fiore** systematised apocalyptic thought and fuelled eschatological speculation. Leading figures of the **Reformation** were deeply influenced by apocalypticism, predominantly Thomas Müntzer (*c.*1489–1525), but also **Luther**.

Christian apocalypticism lives on in some nonconformist and pietistic traditions, whereas in Judaism Shabbetai Zvi's heresy and end discouraged further apocalyptic thought and activity.

JOACHIM SCHAPER

Apocrypha

Literally 'hidden away', the apocrypha are books included in the **canon** of the Roman Catholic Church and Orthodox Church but not in the Protestant or Jewish Bible. They consist of 13 works written from the Second Temple period and were included in the **Septuagint**, but by the end of the first century had been rejected by Jews as scripture. The term was first applied by **Jerome**, because the books were not included in the Hebrew canon. Christians have tended to take more interest in the apocrypha than Jews, and only after the sixth century was there occasional Jewish interest in certain books (e.g. Ben Sira) or stories (e.g. Hannah and her seven sons), parts of which found their way into the **Talmud** (cf. *Gittin* 57b). In the sixteenth century there was a revival of Jewish interest in the apocrypha among scholars such as Azariah dei Rossi (*c.*1511– *c.*1578) who translated the *Letter of Aristeas* into Hebrew.

See also **Apocryphal New Testament**; **Pseudepigrapha**   *EDWARD KESSLER*

Apocryphal New Testament

This term points somewhat imprecisely to the existence of books, mainly from the second century CE, although possibly in the case of some parts of the Apocryphal Gospels from the late first century, which were not incorporated in the Christian **canon** but that are later amplifications of or inventions based on or constructions that develop features of the canonical books. This suggests a rough distinction between, on the one hand, Apocryphal books such as Apocryphal gospels, passion, birth or childhood narratives, acts of **Pilate** or of particular **apostles**, and Christian apocalypses, and, on the other hand, **Apostolic** literature such as *1* and *2 Clement*, letters of **Ignatius** and Polycarp and the *Didache*. The parallels between Jewish and Christian apocalypses are evident, particularly where both are concerned with signs and portents in relation to the imminence or otherwise of the last times (*see* **apocalypticism**). Some Apocryphal gospels that amplify the narratives of **Jesus**' death and resurrection, such as the second-century *Gospel of Peter*, increase the responsibility of the Jewish people and of **Herod** for the **crucifixion**. There is, however, one fragmentary gospel, the *Gospel of the Saviour* (known usually by the description 'the unknown Berlin Gospel'), which reveals its friendship to the Jewish people as the Saviour prays that his death may be at the hands of others than the **people of Israel**.

Difficulties arise, however, in evaluating Apocryphal literature in relation to Judaism because of the imprecision of the often used classification 'Jewish-Christian'. Even in the case of the *Gospel of the Nazarenes*, where there is evidence of Nazarenes who observed the **Law** and read scriptures in **Hebrew**, an actual connection between that gospel and a specific group is not proven. Other Apocryphal gospels, particularly those found at Nag Hammadi, such as the *Gospel of Thomas* and the *Gospel of Truth*, betray a strong Gnostic influence. It has been claimed on the basis of the Apocryphal gospels that **Gnosticism** entered Christianity via Judaism. Despite some associations between Gnosticism, **James, brother of Jesus** and 'Jewish Christianity', such a claim overlooks the possibility that Gnosticism did not emerge as a single movement but flourished in many different forms.

IVOR H. JONES

Apologetics

A literary form used particularly by early Christian authors such as **Justin Martyr** and **Origen** to support and explain Christian teaching both to a Christian and to a non-Christian audience. The genre is based on early Jewish apologetical writings such as those of **Philo of Alexandria** (e.g. *Apology on behalf of the Jews*) and **Josephus** (e.g. *Ag. Ap.*). The first Christian apologies appeared under Hadrian (*r*.117–138 CE), influenced by Greek and Roman rules and customs. They demonstrate a move away from Judaism and developed around the same time as the *Adversus Judaeos* literature. Scholars have debated whether there is a relationship between Christian apologetic and anti-Jewish writings. The apologists felt the need to defend Christianity from a variety of different groups, including the state, the philosophers and Christian heretics, as well as Jews. By explaining itself to a society in which Jews belonged and were noticeable (**ancient authors** noted the existence of Jewish custom in Christian teaching and practice) Christians faced the dilemma that Judaism represented the heritage of Christianity and provided its means of access to claims of antiquity, which was crucial to legitimacy in the eyes of the ancient world. The response of the apologists was to differentiate Christianity from Judaism and to counter Jewish teaching, resulting in an association between Christian apologetics and **polemic**.

Apologetic writings also shed light on pagan perceptions of Christianity and Judaism: for example, **Celsus** acknowledges both the origins of Christianity in Judaism and Christians' rejection of these origins, but finds nothing commendable in either (*Cels.* 2.1.4). Although apologetic writings may appear to be written for a non-Christian (or non-Jewish audience), it seems likely that the primary readership comprised Christians (or, in the case of Jewish apologetic, Jews) seeking a clearer understanding of their faith. For Christian apologists Judaism represented an obstacle to Christianity's credibility, and writers attacked Jews as 'barbarians', referring to the rebellions against Rome, such as **Bar Kokhba**'s revolt in 132–5, and for failing to understand their own scriptures and the prophecies they detected therein. Justin Martyr is typical in claiming that true understanding lies with Christians, and that the scriptures therefore belong no longer to Jews but to Christians alone (*Dial.* 29).

EDWARD KESSLER

Apostasy

The Greek term *apostasia* simply means to separate, to stand away from or to rebel, but it has a specifically religious connotation in both Judaism and Christianity.

In Judaism apostasy entails the deliberate forsaking of God and/or his **commandments** in direct contravention of the Sinai **covenant**. The wilful rejection of God was considered to be the definitive act of apostasy (Deut. 32.15; Josh. 22.18–19; 2 Chr. 33.19; Isa. 30.1; Jer. 2.19). The apostasy of the **people of Israel** is a constant theme in the **Hebrew Bible** (Judg. 2.11–15; 3.7; 1 Kgs 12.28–32; 16.30–3; 22.51–3; 2 Chr. 12.1; 28.1–4; 33.1–9, 21–3). God raised up judges and prophets to remind his people of their covenant responsibilities (cf. Judg. 2.16–19; 1 Kgs 18.17–18; Jer. 1.13–16; Ezek. 2.1–7), and he dispensed punishments for continued disobedience. However, the merciful God of Israel was prepared to forgive his people and restore the covenant relationship with them. This could be achieved by true **repentance** characterised by the worship of God alone and the observance of his Law (1 Kgs 8.46–53; Ezek. 18.30–1; Dan. 9.3–19).

In the **New Testament** apostasy (*apostasia*) denotes the deliberate rejection of God (cf. Heb. 3.12), the renunciation of the principles of the Christian faith (Heb. 6.6; cf. 1 John 2.19), and is considered to be a necessary component of the end events (2 Thess. 2.3; 1 Tim. 4.1; cf. Matt. 24.10–12; 2 Tim. 4.3–4). It was an important issue in early Jewish–Christian relations. In Acts 21.21 **Paul of Tarsus** is accused of teaching apostasy from Moses by advising Jews not to observe the (Mosaic) regulations. While this particular charge is seemingly false – Paul taught that Gentile Christians are not bound by the **Torah**, but he accepted the right of **Jewish Christians** to observe the Law if they chose to do so (cf. Rom. 14.1–15.13) – it is true that Paul himself opted not to keep the Mosaic commandments (1 Cor. 9.20–1; Rom. 14.14, 20). On the contemporary Jewish understanding of apostasy, many Jews would have viewed Paul as an apostate. For their part some Christians viewed the Jewish rejection of the Christian message as an act of continuing disobedience to the will of God, and so implicitly as an act of apostasy (e.g. Mark 2.1–12; Matt. 22.1–10). In an important exception to this view, Paul explains the unbelief of his fellow Jews not in terms of their wilful rejection of God, but as a necessary component in the divine plan of **salvation** (Rom. 11.7–12).

At some point in the rabbinic period, the Rabbis inserted the *Birkat ha-minim* into the twelfth benediction of the synagogue service. The reason for the introduction of this malediction against apostates and heretics is not clear, but it may have been a reaction to the rise and success of Christianity. After the time of **Constantine**, Jewish **conversion** to Christianity was often considered by Jews to be an act of apostasy. In turn the Christian emperors and Church councils deemed Christian converts to Judaism as apostates, and laws were enacted and punishments dispensed to prevent such conversions. *DAVID SIM*

Apostle

The Greek *apostolos*, 'one sent out', is occasionally attested in Greek literature, where it refers to a messenger or envoy; it corresponds to the Hebrew *shaliaḥ* ('sent'; sometimes translated 'agent'), such as a High Priest's representative to **Diaspora** communities. The Church appropriated the secular term (see 2 Cor. 8.23) and added to it connotations of missionary work and healing.

For **Paul** (2 Cor. 12.12) an apostle establishes legitimacy through 'signs'; Paul himself claims the title based on his vision of and commission by the risen **Jesus** (1 Cor. 9.1; 15.7–8; Gal. 1.1). For Luke (6.13; see Mark 3.14) 'Apostles' denotes, as a subset of 'disciples', the 12 men Jesus commissions. Matt. 10.2–4, Mark 3.16–19, Luke 6.13–16 and Acts 1.13 list, with variants, the 12 apostles; the number symbolises the 12 tribes of **Israel**. Whether the apostles represent a 'new' or 'true Israel' and so displace the Jewish people, or whether they are to be seen in continuity, remains debated. Discrepancies in the lists indicate that the number was of greater importance than the individuals.

Acts 1.13 includes among qualifications for apostolic office being an eyewitness to Jesus from his baptism by John and thereby limits the apostolic role to Jews. Acts authorises Paul's apostolic role both by depicting Paul's commission by Jesus and by having him approved by the apostles based in **Jerusalem**. By the second century the term ceased to designate an office, although Church documents and leaders continued to speak of direct links to the apostolic authority of that first generation.

AMY-JILL LEVINE

Apostolic Fathers

The designation of a group of writings, dating from approximately the 90s to the mid-second century CE, as 'Apostolic Fathers' is not ancient and probably goes back to the seventeenth century. Normally included in this collection are *1* and *2 Clement*, *Barnabas*, *Polycarp*, the seven epistles of **Ignatius** (the so-called middle recension), *Hermas* and the *Didache*. In some collections we also find fragments attributed to Papias, the *Martyrdom of Polycarp* and *Diognetus*. Amongst other things, this collection provides us with a potentially useful set of documents for our understanding of the developing relationship between Judaism and Christianity, lodged, as they are, between the time of the writing of the last books of the **New Testament** and the work of the early Christian apologists such as **Justin Martyr**.

It is in the writings of the Apostolic Fathers that we first meet the terms 'Judaism' and 'Christianity' used together, implying the existence of two quite separate entities (Ign. *Magn.* 10.3, although we cannot be sure whether Ignatius was the originator of this contrast). But such precise statements of division are only witnessed elsewhere in the *Didache*, where we find the word 'Christian' but not its opposite 'Jew' (*Did.* 12.4), and the probably much later *Diognetus* (*Diogn.* 3f.) and *Martyrdom of Polycarp* (*Mart. Pol.* 12–13) where we find the terms 'Jew' and 'Christian'. No reference to such entities is found in *Barnabas* (here the terms 'them' and 'us' are preferred, although on a number of occasions the probably early third-century Latin translator renders them by 'Jew' and 'Christian'), *Hermas, 1* and *2 Clement*, and *Polycarp*. Some scholars have taken the absence of such designations to imply either that the authors of these texts did not entertain a developed sense of themselves as somehow separate from Judaism (in this reading *Barnabas* gives evidence of inner-Jewish **polemic**) or, particularly in the case of *Hermas* and *1 Clement*, that they regarded Jews and Judaism as of no real concern to them. These remain nothing more than arguments from silence, but the first suggestion at least warns us against the universal adoption of the schema of clear division implied particularly in Ignatius, possibly in the face of an alternative view.

Insofar as these writings refer to Judaism, they are negative in tone. So, for instance, in Ignatius it is explicitly stated that 'it is monstrous to talk about Jesus Christ and practise Judaism' (*Magn.* 10.3) and that 'if anyone interpret Judaism to you, do not listen to him' (*Phld.* 6.1). *Didache* appears to refer to the Jews as hypocrites, exhorting his community not to fast on Mondays and Thursdays 'with the hypocrites', but instead on Wednesdays and Fridays (*Did.* 8.1) (*see* **fasting**), and *Barnabas*, amongst other things, attacks Jewish literal understanding of

sacrifice (*Barn.* 2), **dietary laws** (*Barn.* 10), **Sabbath** (*Barn* 15) and **circumcision** (*Barn.* 9), going so far as to attribute Jewish understanding of the last of these to an evil **angel** (*Barn.* 9.4). According to the same author, the Jewish **covenant** relationship with God was lost as a result of the worship of the **Golden Calf** (*Barn.* 4 and 14). For him it is self-evident, as appears to be the case in some New Testament texts (Matt. 27.25; Acts 2.23), that the Jews are the killers of Christ (*Barn.* 6, 7 and 8; *see* **deicide, charge of**). In the *Martyrdom of Polycarp* the Jews appear as persecutors of the Christians, in this respect imitating their forebears' treatment of Christ as recorded in the Gospels, helping, amongst other things, to stoke the flames of Polycarp's executionary pyre (*Mart. Pol.* 13); and *Diognetus* indulges in a full-scale assault upon the superstitious and ritualised character of Jewish worship, but here, in contrast to *Barnabas*, with no reference to the Hebrew scriptures (*Diogn.* 3 and 4).

To some scholars such polemic should be taken to imply the presence within the Christian community of those who were inclined to follow Jewish practices or even to convert to Judaism. More direct evidence of a **Judaising** influence in the communities addressed comes, for instance, in *Barn.* 3.6, with its reference to being 'shipwrecked' by **conversion** to 'their', i.e. the Jewish, **law**, and from the same work the textually problematic 4.6 where, on one reading, the author appears to refer to those who regard the Christian and Jewish covenants as the same thing. An aggressive attitude on the part of Jews to Christians is less in evidence, although it can again be inferred (cf. in particular Ign. *Phld.* 6.1).

However we understand the polemic of some of these texts, almost all of the Apostolic Fathers betray a strong indebtedness to Judaism in terms of their ideas and the manner in which they express themselves. So, for instance, *1 Clement*, which, as has already been mentioned, does not refer to Jews, can be taken, with its strong reliance upon scripture, its penchant for **Septuagintal** language, and its clear relationship to aspects of **Hellenistic** Jewish culture, to possess a strikingly Jewish character. The also probably Roman *Hermas*, although in a different way, provides evidence of a similarly close relationship to a Jewish ideological world, as also do *Barnabas* and the *Didache*, the former in particular betraying knowledge, whether direct or not, of extra-biblical Jewish traditions and methods of biblical **exegesis** (see in particular chs 7 and 8, where he appears to show knowledge of non-biblical material on the **Day of Atonement**, and ch. 12 with its emphasis upon the coming of the kingdom and the defeat of Amalek, where similar knowledge is betrayed).

The Apostolic Fathers' contribution to our understanding of evolving Jewish–Christian relations is at best fragmentary. Only in some of the texts is the issue of central importance, and we cannot infer from these texts clear conclusions about the subject, in particular on the question of Jewish reaction to Christianity. But already these texts, like those of their predecessors in the New Testament, show up the complex character of Christian interaction with the Jewish tradition, at one and the same time contemptuous of the latter and yet dependent upon it for the expression of its own **identity**.

See also Adversus Judaeos literature; anti-Judaism; **Early Church**   JAMES CARLETON PAGET

Aquila (second century CE)

Supposed to have been a pupil of Rabbi Eliezer and Rabbi Joshua ben Hananiah or of **Akiba** and a relative of the emperor Hadrian (*r*.117–138), Aquila was of 'pagan' stock and joined the Church before he converted to Judaism. He is known as an eminent translator of the **Hebrew Bible**. The old theory that identifies Aquila and **Onkelos**, who produced a **Targum** which is in some respects similar to Aquila's Greek translation, is no longer tenable. Aquila revised an earlier version of the **Greek** Bible, presumably the *kaige* recension. His translation, which is said to have been produced in the first quarter of the second century CE, is characterised by an extremely literalist approach. It served the need of the Jewish community for a more precise rendering of the Hebrew than that offered by the **Septuagint**, and even its *kaige* recension, in order better to refute Christian exegetical claims with regard to the Bible. Since its literalism is so pronounced that only readers with some knowledge of **Hebrew** can have benefited from Aquila's rendering, it seems likely that it was used as a reference work. Aquila's version thus seems to have served as a tool in Jewish–Christian **polemics**. It was, however, praised by such eminent Christian scholars as **Jerome** and **Origen** and has been preserved mainly in the third column of Origen's **Hexapla**, but also in fragments that survive in the **Cairo Genizah** collection.   JOACHIM SCHAPER

Aquinas, Thomas (c.1225–74)

Dominican philosopher, theologian and foremost medieval Scholastic; 'doctor angelicus'; canonised 1323, declared 'Doctor of the Church' 1567. The classic, authoritative exponent of authentic Catholic doctrine (Leo XIII, *Encyclical*, 1879), he discouraged overly harsh anti-Jewish measures. Influenced by Aristotle's newly discovered metaphysical writings, he opposed the teaching of Averroes (1126–98), Aristotle's Muslim interpreter, who asserted the contradictory nature of faith and reason. He systematised theology, grounded in traditional authority and faith, yet flexibly utilised Aristotelian emphasis on reason and knowledge of natural laws. He argued that while certain doctrines (the **Trinity, original sin** etc.) derive primarily from **revelation**, others (God's existence, providence) are ascertainable through natural reason. Aquinas polemically defended the Mendicant orders. In *Summa contra Gentiles*, he created a sophisticated, encyclopedic manual against Muslims and Jews designed for the use of missionaries; Aquinas argued solely from reason, using biblical texts only to confirm arguments, except when justifying specifically Christian doctrines premised on scripture. He read Jewish thinkers sensitively, particularly **Ibn Gabirol** and **Maimonides**. In *De regimene Judaeorum* Aquinas affirmed that since Jews are destined to perpetual slavery due to their sin, sovereigns may regard Jewish goods as their own property, but should use money confiscated from Jewish usurers for pious purposes. Although Aquinas supported imposing the Jewish badge (*see* **yellow badge**), upheld coerced **conversions** and proposed substituting manual labour for money-lending (*see* **usury**), he opposed undue fiscal harshness towards Jews and removal of children from parents as contrary to natural law. Later Jewish 'Thomists', championing Maimonides against Averroes, translated his *Summa Theologia* into Hebrew.   MARGARET BREARLEY

Arab Christianity

Christian Arabs constitute minorities in numerous Arab countries (Lebanon (over 30 per cent), Egypt, Syria, Iraq, Jordan and the Palestinian Territories (2–12 per cent)) and in Israel (2 per cent). Until recently they shared this **minority** status with Jews in the Arab world. Today, relations between Arab

Christians and Jews are difficult because of the political conflict between the Arab world and Israel.

Although Arab civilisation since the seventh century has been intricately connected to **Islam**, Christians and Jews contributed to its flowering. By the seventh century many Arab tribes had converted to Judaism or Christianity, and after the advent of Islam numerous Christians and Jews became Muslims. Muhammad (*c.*570–632) met Christians and Jews and they influenced nascent Islam. When the Muslims invaded the ancient Christian heartland many Jews and 'heterodox' Christians (Monophysites, Nestorians) welcomed them, preferring them to oppressive **Byzantine** or Zoroastrian rule. Gradually reduced to minority status, Jews and Christians were guaranteed protected status (*dhimma*) and a certain degree of autonomy and preserved their places of worship in return for a head tax. Christians and Jews progressively adopted Arabic. By the tenth century Jews and Christians had translated their scriptures into Arabic and begun writing in Arabic. The renowned translation of the **Hebrew Bible** into Arabic by Saadiah Gaon (882–942) was even adopted by the **Coptic Church** in Egypt. However, relations between Christians and Jews were often marked by competition for the favour of the Muslim rulers.

The **Crusades** further divided Christians in Arab lands. Whereas Christians in these lands, together with Muslims and Jews, were often victims of the Crusaders, some Christians sided with the armies from Europe. In later centuries, Christians in Arab lands were further split by the penetration of Christian missionaries from the West: Catholic missionaries created Eastern rite communities in union with the Catholic Church, and Protestant missionaries created local Protestant churches. The Roman Catholic Patriarchate of **Jerusalem** was also revived. Some Western missionaries brought with them strains of European Christian **anti-Judaism**. During the long centuries of **Ottoman** rule, the various Christian and Jewish communities enjoyed internal autonomy.

During the nineteenth century European powers, eager for influence in the area, intervened on behalf of both Christians and Jews. At this time Christian Arab and Jewish emigration from the Middle East began in earnest. The setting up of European-sponsored Christian schools created an educated class of Christians (and also Jews) who played an essential role in the nineteenth-century renaissance of Arab culture. Christian Arabs were also instrumental in promoting Arab nationalism, as a secular and modern movement. Christian Arabs (and some Jews) also played an important role in the formation of the Arab Communist parties. In the cultural domain, especially in **music**, Christians and Jews often worked alongside Muslims.

Zionism and the **State of Israel** deeply affected the denominational mosaic in the Arab world. Certain Israeli leaders sought to win over Christian Arabs by underlining joint Jewish and Christian minority status in a Muslim-dominated region. Israel has actively supported Christian separatist forces in Lebanon and in Sudan. However, Christian Arabs generally remain integrated within the Arab world. Whereas non-Arabs headed most Churches in Arab lands until recently, Arabs have increasingly risen to roles of leadership. Christian Palestinians have also played an important role in the Palestinian resistance movements. The political situation partially explains the opposition of the Arab Catholic representatives at **Vatican II** to the positive changes in Church attitudes to the Jews. Almost no Jews live in the Arab world today, and in Israel/Palestine Jews and Christian Arabs generally find themselves on opposing sides of the political divide. **Palestinian liberation theology** has sought to formulate Christian Arab thinking within this context.

In Israel efforts to create a **dialogue** between Christian Arabs and Jews have met with some success. Certain structures for dialogue focus on the common search for peace and justice, while others seek to promote awareness of shared religious, historical and cultural heritage. The 2000 Synod of the Catholic Churches in the Holy Land published a document on inter-religious dialogue that tackled for the first time the specific agenda for an Israeli Jewish–Arab Christian dialogue. Catholic Patriarch Michel Sabbah (b. 1933), the first Arab in this role, and Lutheran Bishop Munib Younan (b. 1950) have established Church structures for relations with the Jews. Greek Catholic priest Emile Shoufani (b. 1947) has led a movement to promote understanding of the *Shoah* among Arabs in Israel. The uniqueness of Jewish–Christian dialogue in Israel is, of course, that Jews are the dominant majority and Christians are a marginal minority. In addition, almost all dialogue includes Muslims as an essential party (*see* **tria-logue**).   DAVID M. NEUHAUS

Aramaic

One of the (Northwest) Semitic languages that are closely related to **Hebrew**, Aramaic came to be the language spoken by Jews in **Israel** in the Persian period. Although **Greek** gradually replaced it as the *lingua franca* for many Jews, Aramaic was still spoken in the Galilee and was the official language of communication in the Seleucid empire. It was **Jesus**' first language, but it is probable that he also spoke Greek, especially when communicating with non-Jews. Apparent influences of Aramaic in **New Testament** Greek might well be attributable more to such a bilingual situation than to a direct translation from lost Aramaic sources. The Jews in Babylon continued to speak Aramaic, and large portions of rabbinic literature are composed in it. In the time of **Bar Kokhba** (first half of second century CE) Aramaic seems to have been preferred to Hebrew, and although there were attempts to write in Hebrew, these reflect considerable Aramaic influence. Syriac is a dialect of Aramaic spoken by **Syrian Christians**, and to this day (neo-) Aramaic has continued to be spoken by Jews and Christians. As the language of Jesus, and a language common to both Judaism and Christianity throughout their history, Aramaic is a neglected shared heritage of the two faiths.   JAMES K. AITKEN

Archaeology *see* **architecture; Dura Europos; Sardis**

Archisynagogus *see* **leaders of the Jews, externally appointed**

Architecture

Because experience of the sacred transcends the particularities of specific cultures, Jewish and Christian religious architecture shares many characteristics, both with each other and with the architecture of other religions. A vertical spatial axis recalls the connection between the human and divine realms, while a horizontal axis concretises the experience of searching for or approaching God. Communality with God and with others is experienced in centralised spaces, and God's ineffable spirit is alluded to in our experience of light, or the play of light across material surfaces.

The moveable tabernacle and court accommodated the religious experience of the early, nomadic Jewish tribes. Construction of the Jerusalem **Temple** by Solomon, Zerubbabel and **Herod** translated the nomadic tabernacle into durative stone. Each Temple reiterated the arrangement of the tabernacle with its porch, Holy Place and Holy of Holies, concretising a progression through degrees of sacrality to reach the most sacred goal at the end.

The synagogue may have developed as a space of communal Jewish worship as early as the Babylonian exile (586–538 BCE), but the earliest synagogue thus far excavated, in Delos, Greece, dates from the first century BCE. The Christian Church developed in the first century CE, with the earliest excavated example, in **Dura Europos** (Salhiyeh), Syria, dating from the third century CE. Excavations of a single street in Dura Europos have uncovered three separate houses accommodating a Mithran sanctuary, a Jewish synagogue (from 245 CE) and a Christian church (*c.*230 CE). The spatial arrangement and surface articulation of both the synagogue and the church reveal their domestic origins and the adaptation of the domestic building type to accommodate the experience of worship, which often demanded various auxiliary spaces in addition to the main worship hall.

Synagogues developed to accommodate communal prayers and the reading and interpretation of scriptures. They were typically plain on the exterior, both to emulate the Temple and, later, to avoid attracting notice within the larger Christian civic environment. They were also designed to minimise distraction, orienting seating towards the centre. Injunctions against graven images were first adhered to and later relaxed, but synagogues never integrated **art** in the manner of Christian churches.

Early churches allowed worshippers to hear the reading of the mass and to partake in a common meal, the holy **eucharist**, representing acceptance of the sacrifice of Christ's body and blood. Unlike synagogues, where the ark and the bimah (the raised platform from which the **Torah** scrolls were read) could be in either the short or the long walls and the bimah could be centrally located, in the Christian church entry and **altar** generally occupied opposing short walls, emphasising the directionality of the longitudinal axis. The plain exteriors of churches gave way to increasingly resplendent façades as the religion gained power in Europe.

Classical-era synagogues and churches drew architecturally from Roman civic architecture, particularly the basilica or hall of justice. The synagogue at **Sardis**, Turkey (third to fourth centuries CE) is basilican in form with a colonnaded forecourt leading to the Jerusalem-facing entry wall. The arrangement parallels Old St Peter's in Rome (*c*.320–30). Both are axially laid out, with a frontal entrance into the forecourt and a font in the centre of the court – the Jewish font recalling the brazen laver in the Temple's forecourt and the Christian font to accommodate **baptism**. Both the Jewish prayer hall and the Christian nave occupy the central longitudinal space in these buildings, with shallow single side aisles flanking the prayer hall and double side aisles flanking the nave. Each building terminates in a semicircular apse, where Jewish elders sat facing the Jerusalem wall and its two aedicular Torah shrines, and where the Christian pope sat facing eastward towards the altar and the congregants. The primary spatial difference is the church's cross-arm, or transept, which mediates between the nave and the apse, while the mediating space in the synagogue does not project cross-axially. The church's transept arrangement developed into a canonical cruciform plan symbolic of Christ's **cross**. The synagogue contains a bimah in the centre of the prayer hall, while the church features a raised platform, or bema, directly before the apse. In the church, an altar is located on the bema at its juncture with the higher apse. Curiously, the synagogue also contains a decorative stone table reminiscent of an altar, located at the centre of the juncture between the prayer hall and the mediating bay before the apse. This table is unparalleled in other synagogues.

The spatial resemblance between these two houses of worship is remarkable, indicating that the architectural precedent of the Roman basilica was more influential than liturgical differences between the two religions at the end of the classical era. As the power of Christendom increased in Europe, synagogue and church began to diverge architecturally. Churches experimented with both centralised (notably San Vitale in Ravenna, 526–47) and longitudinal forms, with the basilican form remaining predominant, and grew increasingly articulated on the exterior, taking pride of place as freestanding monuments in the civic realm. Synagogues, aware of their precarious position within the dominant Christian culture, adopted relatively inconspicuous exteriors to blend into the urban fabric. The Christian **liturgy**, in which worshippers heard the mass and then filed forward to receive the eucharist, encouraged retention of the longitudinal basilican form, while Jewish worship spaces became increasingly centralised to accommodate communal prayer and the reading of the scrolls. The Ashkenazi synagogue at Worms, Germany (orig. 1175), and Worms Cathedral (1110–81) illustrate the divergence of the two types. The cathedral is a fairly straightforward development of the basilican plan of Old St Peter's, with the omission of the forecourt and axial entry reflecting the German variant of opposing east and west apses and using lateral entries, and stands apart from the urban fabric. The synagogue, in contrast, blends into the streetscape, with the men's prayer hall reached through a courtyard and the women's prayer hall through a simple opening onto the street. Both church and synagogue have vaulted ceilings and arched windows, and their carved column capitals are stylistically similar. But their spatial characters are different, with the axial cathedral displaying the loftiness and grandeur of the architecture of a dominant religion and the more centralised synagogue retaining the scale of Christianity's domestic, civic and religious meeting rooms.

Centralisation was a major preoccupation of **Renaissance** architecture, and churches adapted (but never abandoned) their longitudinal plans to widen at the crossings, thus emphasising the centre, while synagogues evolved to include women's galleries centering on and overlooking the men's prayer halls. The Sefardi Portuguese Synagogue, or Esnoga, in Amsterdam (1671–75) featured the first integral women's gallery, and the neoclassical Bevis Marks Synagogue in London (1701) restated the arrangement of the Esnoga. Churches and synagogues of the Renaissance and neoclassical periods displayed rationally inspired classical columns and orders, with the neoclassical period evolving to emphasise clean lines and restrained ornament. While St Paul's Cathedral (1675–1710) in London, by Sir Christopher Wren, is larger, more spatially articulated and more ornate than the Esnoga and Bevis Marks, all three have spatial commonalities. All are longitudinal buildings with a tall central space and lower side aisles, in the tradition of European Christian churches. The most striking spatial difference is St Paul's great central dome, which marks the crossing of the nave and the transept. The orientation of seats provides another important spatial difference, with the cathedral's seats facing the short wall of the eastern apse while the synagogues' benches run parallel to the long walls, facing inward.

Synagogues and churches in the eighteenth and nineteenth centuries reflect the stylistic revivalism of the era. Both Christianity and Judaism produced examples of Romanesque, Gothic and Moorish revivals. While Romanesque revivalism, with its round arches and relative severity, seemed neutrally neoclassical and therefore suitable for either religion, the Gothic style, exemplified in St Giles in Cheadle, Staffordshire (1841–46) by A. W. N. Pugin, and All Saints, Margaret Street, London (1849–59) by William Butterfield, was enthusiastically appropriated by churches as the truest expression of Christianity. Jewish congregations tended to avoid Gothic revivalism in favour of the Moorish style, which had eastern roots and lacked explicit associations with Christianity, and erected examples such as the Dohány utca synagogue (1854–59) in Budapest by Ludwig von Förster and the Tempio Maggiore (1874–82) in Florence by Falcini, Micheli and Treves. The revivalist churches and synagogues feature pointed or multifoil arches, carved stone, polychromatic brickwork, and patterned interior surfaces. Although they are different in ornamental detail, the overall effect and spatial characteristics are similar.

With the abstracted, simple volumes of modernism, religious architecture returned to its original existential themes of path, centre, vertical axis and light in an attempt to transcend cultural particulars with timeless architectural form. The triple chapels at Brandeis University in Waltham, Massachusetts (1954) by Harrison and Abramowitz perhaps best illustrate the commonalities that underlie Judaism, Christianity and by extension other experiences of the sacred. The three chapels form a cluster of religious buildings, each chapel distinct yet part of the larger whole formed by the Jewish, Protestant and Catholic communities. Each simple, abstract form defines a space of worship distinct from the larger world yet connected to it through light and views to nature. An increasingly close architectural relationship can also be noticed in the Catholic Church's recent revised design guidelines for new churches, which specify a centralised plan that arranges congregational

seats to face inward from all directions towards a central altar, thus moving closer to the synagogue's arrangement around a central bimah. Thus the church has joined the synagogue in an emphasis on experiencing God in our midst rather than as a distant goal symbolised by the axial procession to an altar.   *RACHEL McCANN*

Argentina

At the end of the sixteenth century Portuguese and Spanish Catholics of Jewish descent, primarily **Conversos** but also **Marranos**, established themselves in Argentina. Over the following centuries they almost wholly assimilated into the dominant Catholic community. The bulk of the Jewish immigration occurred from 1880 onwards when **pogroms** in **Russia** forced many Jews to flee. There are presently 230,000 Jews in a country of 37 million, of whom 80 per cent are Catholic.

Jews first established themselves in the interior of the country as farmers, but from 1918 onwards became industrial workers and, together with Italian Catholics, formed the first trade unions. In the 1920s nearly 80,000 immigrants arrived, establishing themselves in Buenos Aires and other major cities. During this time there was significant **antisemitism**, and in response the Jewish community created the Delegation of Jewish-Argentinean Associations (DAIA). Because Argentina was willing to accept high levels of immigration, numerous Nazis settled in the country shortly before and after the Second World War. The Jewish community faced periods of antisemitism as well as of peaceful coexistence with the Catholic majority; the abduction of Adolf Eichmann in 1960 and the consequent trial in Jerusalem a year later aroused anti-Jewish sentiment. Under the Peronista government (1946–68) a registry of non-Catholic cults was established, and Catholic religious instruction in public schools was introduced. Jewish (and Protestant) students were required to take classes in morality, generally taught by a Catholic teacher. Following the introduction of democracy in 1985, the constitution was revised and the president and vice-president no longer needed to be Catholic. The new constitution forbade racial discrimination, but antisemitic attacks have continued to be commonplace: a bomb destroyed the Israeli Embassy in 1992, and two years later the Jewish Community Centre in Buenos Aires was destroyed, killing over 100 people. In 1997 Cardinal O'Connor (1920–2000) of

New York visited Buenos Aires and in a major speech, delivered in Spanish in the Cathedral, denounced antisemitism in the strongest terms.

Dialogue between Argentinian Jews and Catholics began earnestly after *Nostra Aetate* in 1965. Before then the Catholic leadership officially disapproved of an inter-religious relationship, and some indifference to the relationship between Catholics and Jews has remained. Argentinian representatives have participated in the Jewish–Christian meetings organised by the Latin American Council of Bishops (CELAM), the Anti-Defamation League and the Latin American Jewish Congress. The Argentinian Episcopal Conference opened a department for the relationship with Judaism and other faiths. The Latin Rabbinical Seminary in Buenos Aires has organised meetings between rabbinical students and teachers and their counterparts in Christian seminaries (both Catholic and Protestant). The Universidad Austral hosted seminars between Jews and Christians, and one notable meeting in 1999 discussed *Historical Experience: Reckoning of the Soul and Reconciliation*, which focused on reconciliation after the Generals' Junta. However, the country's difficult social and economic situation has made Jewish–Christian relations a low priority for most Argentinians.

See also **South America**   *EDWARD KESSLER*

Arianism

Arianism derives from Arius, a presbyter from **Alexandria** (d. *c*.336), who claimed that the divine Son was not begotten from the Father but created from nothing and was therefore not coeternal with the divine Father. Arius may have been indirectly influenced in certain respects by Jewish or **Jewish-Christian** speculation about God, but also by the theology of **Origen**. Arianism ignited the Trinitarian controversy of the fourth century.

Arius's main opponent was, first, his bishop Alexander (d. 328) and later Alexander's successor **Athanasius of Alexandria**. The controversy escalated to such a degree that in 325 the emperor **Constantine** felt obliged to convene a synod at Nicaea (later called the First Ecumenical Council) in order to pacify the Church. The Creed of Nicaea stated that Father and Son were 'of the same substance' (Greek *homooúsios*) and explicitly rejected Arius's doctrines; Arius was condemned and sent into exile. Constantine's endeavour failed, however, because the decrees of Nicaea were by no means immediately accepted by all bishops and theologians. It was widely felt that the term *homooúsios* was not well suited to describe the relationship between Father and Son, because it was not found in the Holy Scriptures and because it was unclear whether it meant substantial identity or some form of likeness. The period between Nicaea and Constantinople, therefore, saw a very heated and often confusing debate between the defenders of Nicaea (among whom Athanasius) and its opponents (who were by no means all Arians). The hegemony of certain views in this debate largely depended on the religious policies of the ruling emperors.

The dispute continued until it was finally settled in 381 at the Second Ecumenical Council of Constantinople, which took up the distinction between 'substance' (Greek *ousía*) and 'person' (Greek *hypóstasis*, *prósopon*): Father, Son and **Holy Spirit** were described as three persons sharing the same (divine) substance. The Creed of Constantinople (often erroneously called the Nicene creed) subsequently became the most widespread of all creeds. In the West a form of Arianism survived among the Goths (*see* **Visigoths**), and in later centuries Arianism remained an attractive theological position in Christian dissident circles. 'Arian' views (which often had little in common with the ideas of Arius himself) were advocated by radical Reformers in Upper Italy and Eastern Europe (Socinians, Antitrinitarians, Unitarians) in the sixteenth and seventeenth centuries and later by English **Unitarians**.

There has been considerable debate about the extent to which the development of Trinitarian doctrine in the fourth century was not only a reaction against Arianism, but must also be considered anti-Jewish. This is, however, true only insofar as Arius apparently attempted to preserve a strict monotheism, and an attack on this monotheism was therefore by implication also an attack on Jewish ideas of God. Arius himself, however, felt no particular sympathies with Judaism; instead his monotheism was probably primarily motivated by philosophical (Neoplatonist) concerns.

See also **Son of God**; **Trinity**   *WOLFRAM KINZIG*

Art

Throughout their histories, both Judaism and Christianity experienced periods when representational art was either repressed or repudiated.

Because of Christianity's Jewish roots, historians have often assumed that the basis for Christian reticence about graphic and plastic arts was Jewish aniconism and the prohibitive language of the second of the **Ten Commandments**: 'You shall not make for yourself an idol, whether in the form of anything that is in heaven above, or that is on the earth beneath, or that is in the water under the earth' (Exod. 20.4). Christians, in other words, were acting like faithful Jews when they avoided visual imagery. The absence of extant, definitively Christian visual art prior to the beginning of the third century CE has then been taken as evidence of Jewish influence on the earliest centuries of the Church and of Christian observance of this Mosaic injunction.

Based on this assumption, historians often account for the emergence of identifiably Christian iconographic motifs in the early third century as evidence of the estrangement of **Church and synagogue** and of gradual Christian accommodation to pagan practices and popular culture, coupled with growing rejection of Mosaic **Law**. Recent scholarship has challenged these explanations, however, citing other cultural forces that may have originally deterred the development of Christian visual art, in particular the economic and social instability of the emergent Christian community. Nevertheless, certain early Christian writers saw Jewish aniconism as a model for Christian resistance to the **idolatry** of their surrounding culture. The Alexandrian Christian teacher **Origen**, for example, defended the Jews to the pagan critic **Celsus** by comparing polytheism's worship of corruptible images of humans and animals with Jewish prohibition of artists and image-makers of any kind (*Cels.* 4.31).

Further complicating the question of the influence of Jewish aniconism on Christian attitudes to art is the fact that, during the time that identifiable Christian art began to emerge, Jewish representational art was likewise being developed. For example, while most Jewish catacombs of **Rome** were decorated with non-figurative symbols such as the menorah, shofar or Torah ark, the **iconography** found in the catacomb of the Vigna Randanini also featured borrowings from Roman pagan art, including the figure of Fortune, peacocks and small nude boys (*putti*) harvesting grapes. Discoveries of the past century, such as the splendidly decorated third-century synagogue at **Dura Europos**, as well

as figured mosaic pavements in fourth- to sixth-century synagogues in modern-day **Israel** (some of them featuring such pagan motifs as zodiacs, King **David** playing a harp, and traditional personifications of the four seasons), similarly revealed a far from uniform attitude among Jews in various parts of the ancient world toward the production and use of representational and figurative art.

Although from the mid-third century onwards both Jews and Christians produced visual art, Jewish production seems to have been far more limited in quantity and variety than that of Christian artisans. Based on existing evidence, the use of figurative art in Judaism was never widespread, and seems to have disappeared almost completely between the seventh and the thirteenth centuries, a period that coincides with the Iconoclastic Controversy in Christianity. The reappearance of Jewish figurative art in the Middle Ages is supplemented by reports that some rabbis in twelfth- and thirteenth-century Europe permitted paintings and even sculptures of humans and animals, while yet others disapproved of them in religious and even domestic settings. Although some scholars have speculated that the absence of evidence for Jewish art in the intervening centuries suggests deliberate destruction more than religious inhibition, the contrast with Christian output is noteworthy. From the fourth through the thirteenth centuries Christian art forms grew rapidly in both West and East, adding new styles and motifs, decorating churches, sacred books and personal or domestic objects. Despite the most thoroughgoing periods of iconoclastic destruction and repression in the ninth and sixteenth centuries (*see* **iconoclasm**), Christian art has never completely disappeared, even temporarily.

And despite this record of survival, Christian theologians, like their Jewish counterparts, continued to worry about the temptations of artworks placed in a religious context. For example, while Pope **Gregory the Great** insisted on the value of paintings on the walls of churches to instruct those who could not read the lessons in the books, he cautioned against the dangers of these images by insisting that his clergy take care to prohibit anyone from mistakenly worshipping the pictures themselves (*Ep.* 9.105, and *Ep.* 11.13). Similarly, Rabbi Meir ben Barukh (d. 1293) in thirteenth-century

Rothenburg warned against Jewish prayer books that contained images of animals and birds, since those who used those books would turn aside to contemplate the pictures rather than inclining their hearts to God in heaven (Tosafot to *b. Yoma* 54a). Thus, even though they might acknowledge a didactic or pious purpose for visual art, authorities from both religions remained concerned that such art, misunderstood or misused, could become a source of sin rather than edification for those same unsophisticated viewers they were meant to aid.

Because of their common scriptures, Christians and Jews occasionally illustrated the same story, but in different ways with distinct (although related) purposes. For example, most early Christian visual presentations of **Abraham**'s offering of **Isaac** portray the moment when God's voice (shown as a hand descending from the sky) stays Abraham's upraised knife. Based on its common juxtaposition with scenes from Jesus' passion, along with comparison to early **exegesis** of and homilies on the story, scholars have asserted that in these images Isaac is the prototype of **Jesus**, and the sacrifice serves as an artistic reference to (or substitution for) the **crucifixion**. In a roughly contemporary Jewish representation of the **binding of Isaac** (*Akedah*) above the Torah shrine in the Dura Europos synagogue, Isaac is already lying upon the flaming altar. To the viewer's left we see a representation of the (by then destroyed) Temple in Jerusalem.

However, the existence of the Dura Synagogue frescoes, along with the high frequency of scenes or characters from the Hebrew scriptures in Christian iconography, as well as some later midrashic or extra-canonical elements found in the Christian compositions, has led some scholars to posit the existence of Jewish prototypes for much Christian art. J. Strygowsky (1862–1941), at the turn of the twentieth century, was one of the first to argue for such a Jewish source. Since then, a number of art historians, including C. R. Morey (1877–1955) and K. Weitzmann (1904–93), have concluded that the imagery of early Christian illuminated Bibles, and perhaps even the iconography of the Christian catacombs in Rome, were based on artwork that had been produced for illustrated Jewish Bibles or other texts – in particular illustrated versions of the **Pentateuch**, Octateuch, or even an entire copy of

the **Septuagint**. Artisans working in cosmopolitan centres such as **Antioch** or **Alexandria**, where the practice of illustrating classical texts had been well developed, would have crafted such manuscripts. These texts would then have been the source for both early Christian iconography and the artistic programme of the Dura Synagogue.

If these theories were correct, the case would be considerably strengthened for the mutual influence and cooperation between Christian and Jewish artists in the third through sixth centuries. However, certain problems arise with a Jewish source thesis. First, no such prototypical illustrated Jewish Bible has been discovered; furthermore, the links often proposed between the lost originals and later Christian illuminated Bibles are all Christian manuscripts, such as the fifth- or sixth-century Cotton Genesis and the ninth-century Ashburnham Pentateuch. Second, when the frescoes from the Dura Synagogue are compared with early Christian catacomb paintings, or even with later Christian manuscripts, they show marked distinctions in style, content and composition. For example, in the Dura Synagogue the finding of **Moses** by Pharaoh's daughter is represented with a more pointedly Eastern or Persian, and with a far more complex and richly detailed, composition (including showing the princess as naked and in the water with the child) than the same scene in the Via Latina Catacomb. The rare occurrences of midrashic elements in Christian art, such as the representation of **Jacob**'s dream showing him resting his head on three stones (*Genesis Rabbah* 68.11), may point more to Christian familiarity with the rabbinical literature than to an iconographic prototype. Thus, little evidence exists to assert a common Jewish source in antiquity for later Jewish and Christian art. Instead, both religions seem more likely to have developed independent styles and motifs, while yet sharing a set of core stories from their sacred literature and its traditional elaborations.

Nevertheless, a general influence of Christian art upon Jewish (and vice versa) cannot be denied during the Middle Ages, when the two cultures lived in close proximity. Following a long hiatus, Jewish art emerged again with the development of manuscript illumination, beginning in the ninth century with simple geometric and calligraphic forms, including some so-called carpet pages (thus still avoiding figurative art). The oldest known illuminated Hebrew manuscript – a codex of the Prophets – comes from Tiberias; dated to the late ninth century, it was probably produced for the **Karaite** sect. Although illuminated Qur'ans may have influenced these earliest examples, later illuminated Hebrew manuscripts, for example those originating in thirteenth- and fourteenth-century **Spain**, were as often influenced by the Gothic style of Western Christian works.

Passover *haggadoth* were undoubtedly the most important of the Hebrew **illuminated manuscripts**, and many of them contain full-page coloured illustrations of the exodus from Egypt. Meant for private, non-liturgical use, some of these *haggadah* manuscripts may have been luxury items made by Christian workshops for Jewish clients. At the same time, although barred from joining Christian workshops, independent Jewish artists rose to some prominence and produced books of their own, including illuminated Bibles, illustrated commentaries of **Rashi**, *mahzorim*, Passover *haggadoth*, and more secular works (including the writings of **Maimonides** and Hebrew translations of Avicenna's medical textbook). Some scholars have tried to explain the so-called 'bird's head' *haggadoth* as products of a Jewish workshop, made especially for Christian clients, while others interpret them rather as a Jewish attempt at avoiding representation of a human figure.

From the thirteenth century onwards, Christians portrayed Jews in their visual art, usually with some degree of negative stereotyping and often with outright derision. Christian visual art tended to show Jews as having pointed chins, forked beards, distorted facial features (e.g. hooked noses) or physical deformities. Jews were shown wearing peculiar or foreign-looking costumes, peaked or funnel-shaped hats (*Judenhute*) or **yellow badges** of identification. Even biblical patriarchs such as Abraham and Moses were given negative attributes. For example, Christian artists endowed Moses with horns that, although originally meant to suggest his honour and power (probably based on a mistranslation of the **Septuagint** description of Moses' shining face in Exod. 34.29), soon came to signify ignominy and even disrepute. The horns on Michelangelo's (1475–1564) famous monumental sculpture of Moses in Rome's San Pietro in Vincoli may not have been originally intended as derisive, but came to be seen by later viewers as a negative attribute, specifically pointing to his Jewishness.

The visual allegory of **Ecclesia and Synagoga**, probably based on an earlier Christian allegorical reading of Lamentations' personification of **Jerusalem** as a downtrodden widow, was an especially widespread and powerful image from the Carolingian era forward, proclaiming Christian **replacement** of Jews as God's covenanted people. The frequent juxtapositions of the image of the defeated Synagoga and the scene of crucifixion points to another common Christian presentation of Jews as responsible for the death of Christ, a motif that becomes common in Western Christian visual art. Jews as Christ-murderers – **deicides** – and as mockers, torturers or executioners are frequently shown in Christian representations of the Passion. In other images, however, Jews are equally reviled as moneylenders or usurers (*see* **usury**), associates of Satan and the **Antichrist**, or as companions of witches and **demons** engaging in the profaning of Christian sacraments (**host desecration**) or ritual murder – a theme whose literary parallels are the **blood libel** legends. Jews are also shown with a sow, either sucking on her teats or performing other obscene acts. Possibly a reference to the Jewish oath in a medieval court of law, which was taken on a dead sow's skin, this image was particularly degrading, especially to Jews who viewed the pig as an impure animal. Later on, the illustrations of popular literature, including the famous Jewish characters of **Shakespeare** and **Dickens** (Shylock and Fagin), were arguably more **antisemitic** than the texts themselves.

By contrast to these defamatory images of Jews made by Christians, the great Protestant artist Rembrandt van Rijn (1606–69) was known for his unusually sensitive portrayal of Jews, both in portraits and in representations of biblical scenes, based upon Jewish acquaintances he made in his native Amsterdam. Perhaps the most famous of these is his late painting titled 'The Jewish Bride', which represents the bridal couple with both dignity and tenderness. In the twentieth century some Jewish artists also took up Christian themes, including the Russian artist Marc **Chagall**, who included images of Jesus' crucifixion (often showing Jesus wearing a Jewish prayer shawl in place of a loincloth) in some of his paintings reflecting on his childhood in a

Russian Jewish village, and the sculptor Jacob Epstein (1880–1959), who adapted the image of the *pietà* (Mary holding her dead son) and of the risen Christ as war memorials. Epstein also produced a sculpture of Lazarus emerging from his tomb for New College, Oxford.   *ROBIN M. JENSEN*

Asceticism

The Greek word *askesis* originally referred to physical exercise or training. It gradually came to denote a rigorous way of life that forsook worldly comforts for spiritual ends. Asceticism as a permanent lifestyle has never been a prominent feature within the Jewish tradition, which has generally viewed the world and its pleasures as a gift of God to be enjoyed. Yet the Jewish scriptures demand that on certain occasions abstinence was necessary on a temporary basis. For example, **fasting** was an important requirement of the **Day of Atonement** (Lev. 16.29; 23.26–32), while abstention from wine was observed by priests serving at the altar (Lev. 10.8–9). In the late Second Temple period, more permanent ascetic practices began to be observed in some Jewish circles. The Essenes renounced worldly pleasures and embraced **celibacy**, and **John the Baptist** adopted an ascetic lifestyle (Mark 1.6; Matt. 11.18). Asceticism was not an important feature of early Christianity. **Paul of Tarsus** advocated **marriage** for those who desired it (1 Cor. 7.8–9, 25–8), while the Deutero-Pauline literature is critical of Christians who adopt ascetic practices (Col. 2.23; 1 Tim. 4.1–5). In the ensuing centuries, however, an important monastic movement characterised by a rigorously ascetic and celibate lifestyle developed within Christianity. By the late medieval period, some groups of hasidic Jews had embraced certain ascetic observances, almost certainly in imitation of Christian **monasticism**. Yet, in general terms, Judaism and Christianity have different understandings of ascetic practices. In Judaism they are concerned with **atonement**, while in Christianity they serve to strengthen the religious conviction of the believer.   *DAVID SIM*

Asch, Scholem (1880–1957)

Yiddish novelist and dramatist. Asch was born in Poland but spent much of his life in Israel, the UK and the USA, gaining American citizenship in 1920. Many of his works dealt with Christian origins, for example, *The Nazarene* (1949), *The Apostle* (1943) and *Mary* (1949). The focus of these novels, and in particular Asch's depiction of **Jesus** as a **rabbi**, alienated some Jewish readers, who accused him of **apostasy**. However, he influenced later authors, including Isaac Bashevis Singer (1904–91). Asch also explored contemporary Jewish–Christian relations, for example in *East River* (1948), which is about Jews and Catholics in New York. *MELANIE J. WRIGHT*

Asia Minor

Roman province covering the south-west of modern Turkey; the term is often used more loosely for the more extensive area bounded by the Black Sea to the north and the Mediterranean to the west and south, and so including Anatolia. It has been an important area for Jewish–Christian encounters. There were Jewish communities in several of the cities in the region by the third century BCE, and **Josephus** gives a full account of the protected rights allowing them to follow their traditional law and practice in his time. Numerous Jewish inscriptions and remains, including a synagogue at **Sardis** and the record of a charitable organisation at Aphrodisias, witness to the continuing vitality of Judaism through Late Antiquity until the barbarian invasions of the seventh century. These communities appear well integrated within the city, often reflecting contemporary civic values, including potential high status for women, while maintaining their separate **identity** through the centuries. Like most **Diaspora** communities they used only **Greek** and the **Septuagint**, with **Hebrew** beginning to appear later. According to the Acts of the Apostles, the area was evangelised by **Paul of Tarsus**; letters from him and his successors to churches in the area show that they were predominantly Gentile in origin and were the site of conflicts over observation of Jewish **law** (e.g. Galatians). However, the number of other works associated with the region, including the Johannine writings, Revelation and **Ignatius**'s epistles, suggest that Christianity here was both lively and diverse. Further east, Phrygia was the home of Montanism, a prophetic movement founded in the second century CE, claiming to be the place of the descent of the new **Jerusalem**. For the history of Jewish–Christian relations in the early period, other key figures and events associated with Asia Minor include Polycarp (*c.*70–155/160), bishop and martyr of Smyrna (*see* **Apostolic Fathers**), **Justin Martyr**'s encounter with Trypho (traditionally at Ephesus), **Melito of Sardis** and a number of the Apologists. As well as the explicit **polemic** some of these articulate, they also betray a variety of continuing contacts and social interaction, as do **inscriptions** and particularly epitaphs, mainly from the second to the fourth centuries CE: some of these, in their invocations of 'God [or Zeus] most high' and their concerns for **penitence** and **forgiveness**, seem to express a shared piety or religiosity, which defies description as exclusively Jewish or 'pagan' or 'Christian', suggesting patterns of cross-fertilisation between the three.   *JUDITH LIEU*

Asian Christianity

Christianity is a minority religion in Asia, with the exception of the Philippines, and is primarily concerned with its relationship to the major Asian religions rather than with Jewish–Christian relations. However, the significance of **minority** status, as shared by both Asian Christianity and Judaism, and especially the claim of a particular relationship to God in a world of religious pluralism, was explored in a **World Council of Churches** meeting in 1993.

For some Asian theologians, like Sri Lankan S. Wesley Ariarajah (b. 1941), the relationship with Judaism is no different from the Christian relationship with any other faith tradition and Judaism has no role to play in the Church's theological understanding of Jesus' ministry. Ariarajah has described the effort to return **Jesus** to his Jewish context as a 'futile attempt' to create Christian faith expression in a non-European context. He acknowledges Jesus' connections with the Jewish community of his day, but in his view these carry no theological significance. Other Asian thinkers, however, such as Vietnamese–American scholar Peter Phan Van Loi (b. 1951), explore the contextualisation of Christian theology in differing cultural settings and maintain that Jesus' Jewish context remains indispensable for an accurate understanding of his basic teachings. Scholars such as Phan Van Loi, while developing a theology suitable for an Asian context, argue that this cannot succeed without an effort to understand the original message of the **New Testament** and that this in turn is impossible without a deep appreciation of Jewish religious thought at the time of Jesus and of the composition of the New Testament.   *EDWARD KESSLER*

Assimilation

Assimilation – the absorption of a person or group into a surrounding culture – has long been viewed, particularly by critics of Jewish–Christian **dialogue**, as a dangerous consequence of modern Jewish–Christian relations. For example, the fear of Jewish assimilation into Christian society has often led Orthodox leaders to discourage the possibility of close contact between members of the two faiths, while it has also acted as a significant brake on developing interfaith relations even amongst Progressive rabbis. Although it is invariably the Jewish community that has been the **minority** in Christian lands, Church leaders have also worried that their flock may be influenced by Jews in their midst. Their main concern was a lessening of faith and the introduction of heretical ideas. This fear lay behind the fact that the entry of Roman Catholicism into dialogue with Jews and Judaism was delayed until the 1965 publication of ***Nostra Aetate***. With the onset of the **emancipation** and the waning of the sharp religious and social divisions between Jews and Christians that had existed previously, the practical problems of assimilation became particularly acute for Jews. Some converted to Christianity, although primarily as a means of social advancement, while many others let their Jewish **identity** lapse and failed to educate their children Jewishly. The growth of secularism after the Second World War meant that the Church, too, faced a major challenge. Alongside changing Christian attitudes towards and increasing appreciation of Judaism (a process that began in the early twentieth century), and the growth of Jewish–Christian dialogue, the secular challenge led some to call for a 'common mission' and for ministers in both faiths to see each other as allies against a common enemy, and religious indifference as a greater threat than religious differences. These factors combined to lessen the sense of rivalry that characterised past relations and to pave the way for joint study groups or seminars on issues of common interest, both at national leadership level and in local areas.   *JONATHAN ROMAIN*

Association of Saint James *see* **Saint James, Association of**

Athanasius of Alexandria (c.298–373)

Churchman and theologian. Probably a native of **Alexandria** and for nearly half a century Pope or Patriarch of Alexandria, Athanasius's attitude to the Jews can probably be taken as typical of his place and time. Most likely educated among the early Egyptian monks, he is first heard of as one of the deacons of Alexander, Patriarch of Alexandria (c.313–28), in the entourage at the Council of Nicaea

(325). In 328 he succeeded Alexander as Patriarch. He spent the rest of his life fighting for what he, and the later Church, regarded as Christian orthodoxy, provoking the wrath of the Emperor, who exiled him from his see four times. Although in his time Alexandria still had a large Jewish community, there is little evidence of contact with Jews in Athanasius's writings. One of his early works, his apology for Christianity in two parts, *Contra Gentes* and *De Incarnatione*, deals at length with Jewish (and 'Greek', i.e. pagan) objections to Christianity, but whether he is dealing with genuinely contemporary Jewish arguments, or indulging in a literary *topos* inspired by his conception of the work as an *apologia crucis*, 'a scandal to Jews and folly to Gentiles' (1 Cor. 1.24), cannot be decided. He accuses those he called **Arians**, whom he regarded as rejecting Christ's divinity, of '**Judaising**', meaning that, like the Jews, they reject Christian claims for **Christ**. In his interpretation of the **sacrifice of Isaac** in his *Festal Letters* (no. 6), he displays awareness of rabbinic interpretations of the episode, though whether he has derived this directly from the rabbis is again not clear.   *ANDREW LOUTH*

Atheism

In ancient times, pagans called both Christians and Jews atheists because they rejected belief in the official gods of the **Roman Empire** and refused to participate in sacrifices and ceremonies in their honour. Yet the challenge faced by both Judaism and Christianity came from pagan superstition, not godlessness. Even in the Middle Ages when thinkers such as **Aquinas** and **Maimonides** formulated 'proofs' of God's existence, their targets were those who advanced heretical views of **God**, such as denying his unity, or creative power, rather than arguing that he did not exist. In its modern sense of a general denial of the existence of God, Jewish as well as Christian theologians have addressed themselves to the questions raised by atheism. However, unlike in the case of secularism, Jews and Christians have considered the issues separately, even though related concepts such as **death of God theology** have resulted in joint Jewish–Christian reflection.   *DAVID WEIGALL*

Athens *see* **Greek language and culture**

Atonement

Atonement involves the process of reconciliation and the transcending of alienation. The literal sense of the word is of becoming at one with another. The alienation may be between one person and another or between a person and God. This idea plays a central, though very different, role in the beliefs and practices of both the Jewish and Christian religious traditions. The fundamental understandings of both traditions derive from the **Torah**.

In the Torah, people were enjoined to make atonement both for wrong behaviour and for (spiritual) defilement. This atonement is done in two ways. For wrongs done to other people one had to pay reparations and participate in a rite of **sacrifice**. The shedding of blood is clearly an important part of the expiation process, perhaps as an expression of the vicarious exchange of the life of the sacrificial animal for the life of the person making atonement. For wrongs against God, including defilement, sacrifice was sufficient. Implicit in this system is the understanding that in wrongs against another person God is also an aggrieved party, and even while reparations were made to that aggrieved party appropriate atonement to God was required as well. In Leviticus (16.29–34 and 23.27–32) atonement is given concrete expression in the form of the **Day of Atonement**. Later, the literary prophets placed less emphasis on the rituals of sacrifice and more on the reformation of one's behaviour. These fundamental teachings of the Torah played out very differently in the traditions of Judaism and Christianity because of different understandings of two critical issues: the essential nature of human beings and the efficacy of vicarious atonement.

The conventional Jewish understanding of human nature sees people as having two inclinations, one calling people to the good and the other to wrong actions. People, having **free will**, are capable of responding to the one inclination or the other. To such an understanding of human nature '**sin**' is less a condition than a description of wrong actions chosen. The consequences of such actions are not ineradicable. Rather, they can be reversed by what the rabbis came to call *teshuvah*. *Teshuvah* literally means turning: it functions as the equivalent of the English words atonement or **repentance**. The rabbis reiterate the biblical understanding that for wrongs against God this process of atonement is sufficient, but for wrongs against another person atonement is not complete until the wrongdoer has confronted the injured party, made compensation for the wrong and asked for **forgiveness**. In Christian thought the understanding of atonement is conditioned upon a different understanding of human nature. People are understood to be conceived in sin, and held in the bonds of **original sin**, what **Augustine** calls 'inherited corruption'. The death of **Jesus** (born without defilement by original sin) is understood as an atonement necessary to save people in a way that, because of their fallen state, they cannot save themselves.

The second significant issue that divides Jewish and Christian approaches to atonement is the issue of vicarious atonement. The rabbis require the involvement of the individual in their own *teshuvah*. Thus, they note that it is not sufficient to make verbal confession without intending to change one's actions. Rather, the individual has the responsibility for initiating the process of *teshuvah* and of monitoring its effectiveness. *Teshuvah* is the result of the individual's choice and the fruit of the individual's actions. The practice of vicarious atonement came to an end in Judaism with the cessation of sacrificial cult when the **Temple** was destroyed. In Christian teaching, however, the passion of Jesus is often depicted as *the* great act of atonement in human history. Jesus' death becomes, in effect, a vicarious atonement on behalf of all those who believe in him. Indeed, Jesus' death is often depicted as an extension of the sacrificial rites of the Temple, in which one life is offered up on behalf of another. In Matthew (26.28f.), Mark (10.45) and Luke (24.25) – but not in John – Jesus presents himself, or is presented, as an atonement offered on behalf of all humanity. Similar understandings find expression in the epistles in such statements as 'Christ died for us' (Rom. 5.8). **Paul** elaborates on these themes in Rom. 3.24f., Heb. 7.27, 9.11–28 and 10.10–14, and elsewhere. In such a perspective it is not the action of the believer that is significant, but the action taken on the believer's behalf. This means, in effect, that reconciliation with God proceeds independent of any human action. As such it is not a process that takes place within human beings, but is, instead, a condition initiated by God. In this system people cannot initiate the process of reconciliation; all they can do is receive it.

Alongside the emphasis on belief in Jesus as the key to **salvation**, and its implications of vicarious atonement, a contrasting stream of Christian thought emphasised the possibility of making 'satisfaction' to God for our sins. The tension between the polarities of faith and works is articulated in the epistle of James, which emphasises works, in contrast to Paul, who represents the faith end of the continuum. That tension is seen in the doctrinal struggles between the Catholic Church and the various Protestant denominations, and within the various Christian bodies themselves. Certainly, there is no single, definitive position that can be called *the* Christian understanding of atonement or the means of achieving it. Still, the weight of Christian thought is on the faith end of the spectrum, while the weight of Jewish thinking, like James, is clearly and consistently on the 'works' end.

Despite significant differences in ideology between Jewish and Christian traditions, there is considerable agreement in the actual religious practice of the two communities. Words of atonement are found in the **liturgies** of both traditions. Both liturgies offer the faithful the opportunity to confess their sins to God and to seek forgiveness from God for those failures. And, as a practical matter, both Jewish and Christian practice includes a strong emphasis on reconciliation between people and between the individual and God. Both traditions include concrete practices to ritualise the act of atonement: the rite of Confession in the Catholic Church, the various forms of atonement ritual in the Protestant traditions, and the Day of Atonement – along with other ritualisations of confession – in Judaism.

Any discussion of the phenomenon of atonement in the Jewish and Christian traditions would be incomplete without noting the fact that in recent years the issue of atonement and the specific term *teshuvah* have taken on significance in the Jewish–Christian **dialogue** itself. Various Christian bodies have made atonement to the Jewish people for their role in the history of anti-Jewish teaching and actions, culminating in the **Holocaust**. Emblematic of this is a statement by Cardinal Edward **Cassidy**, the use in which of the Hebrew term has continued to resonate in Jewish–Christian relations: 'That anti-Semitism has found a place in Christian thought and practice calls for an act of *Teshuva* and of reconciliation on our part.'   DANIEL POLISH

Augustine of Hippo (354–430)

Bishop and teacher, the most influential thinker on Jews and Judaism amongst the **Church Fathers**. Born in Carthage of a Berber mother and a Roman father, Augustine chose a career of teaching and practising **rhetoric**, eventually at the imperial court at Milan. His conversion to Christianity after years of religious seeking is well documented in his *Confessiones* (*c*.395); his lifelong interest in the refutation of all other religions would mark him as an apologist of Christianity, but as one who saw a unique role for Jews and Judaism in the **salvation** of the Church and the world.

Augustine's notions of Judaism seem to arise principally from the careful study of the **Old Testament**, with little knowledge of but a great desire for **Hebrew** (*De Doctrina Christiana* (*c*.396), 34.cc.15–122), in addition to sporadic acquaintance with rabbinic opinion and limited interaction with Jews of North Africa (cf. *Epistula* 8). His thoughts on Jews and Judaism are scattered throughout his immense corpus of writings, though five compositions are especially focused on this topic: *Epistula* 196, in which he reviews the Abrahamic **covenant** and its relationship to Christians and Jews; the treatise ***Adversus Judaeos*** (429), concerned centrally with '**Judaising**' practices amongst Christians; the *Contra Faustum Manichaeum* (397–8), a debate against the Manichean leader, Faustus (*c*.340–before 400), in which Augustine tries to connect the mark of **Cain** to the Jews in their special relationship to the church; *Sermo* 91, which argues the Messiahship of **Jesus**; and *Sermo* 112, which likens the Jews to the prodigal son of Luke 15.11–32, while at the same time describing them as beloved of God. In addition, there are many other places in Augustine's writings that contain significant references to, or brief discussion of, Jews and Judaism, such as the *De Civitate Dei* 18.46, the *Ennarationes in Psalmos* (392–420) and various letters such as *Epistulae* 40, 75 and 82.

Perhaps the most significant teaching Augustine left to the Latin West about the Jews was his conviction that they serve a threefold, symbiotic role with the Church in the salvation of the world. First, though Jews are understood to be irrevocably in covenant with God, their alleged blindness to the acceptance of Christ as **Messiah** marked them as no longer the principal elect of God. Instead, the Church was to be the new **Israel** by adoption through **Christ**, while Jews were to be put protectively under the 'yoke' of Christian rule, at least for the sake of their possible **conversion**. Second, Augustine taught, along with **Paul** (cf. Rom. 11.26), that Judaism is the vehicle for the salvation of the whole world, though now through the Church. Finally, a synthesis of Augustine's thinking gives rise to what many scholars have accurately called the 'witness doctrine' or belief that the Jews serve as 'witnesses' to the victory of the Church as the true Israel, to the mercy of God who preserves them in spite of all adversity, and to the truth of the Hebrew scriptures as foretelling the coming of Christ.   DENNIS D. MCMANUS

Auschwitz

Auschwitz/Oświęcim, a town in south-east **Poland**, near Kraków, has become the symbol of the murder of Jews by the Nazis during the Second World War. Before this region was newly invested with the Nazi ideology of a 'perfect' 'Germanic' agricultural society and, in the process of engineering this, became the location of the infamous death camp at Birkenau, Oświęcim had a long and varied history of Jewish–non-Jewish interaction. The Jewish centre of present-day Oświęcim tells of a history that encompasses Christian–Jewish hostility as well as cooperation and mutual appreciation. In 1939 the Jewish population of Oświęcim constituted 60 per cent of the town's inhabitants. Under the leadership of Heinrich Himmler (1900–45) the native Polish farming population was deported and Germans from the Reich and the Baltic were 'resettled' there. Industrial workers were retained for the German war effort, but their local leaders and other Poles were imprisoned, tortured and executed in army barracks built partly for the purpose. The Jewish population of the town was deported to **ghettos** in the Łódź region, the synagogue being closed and burned in 1940. From autumn 1941 Auschwitz I (*Stammlager*), located adjacent to Oświęcim, expanded to include the area of the former village of Birkenau where Soviet POWs built the concentration camp (Auschwitz II) and, adjacent to this, the Buna factory of IG-Farben (Auschwitz III). Beginning as a place for the brutal oppression of the Polish population, their torture, murder and use as slave labourers until death at Auschwitz I, Auschwitz II became a place of 'selection' of Jews to be deployed for slave labour, and from 1942 a place of the murder of Jews from many European countries, mainly at Birkenau where incoming transports of Jews were 'selected' to slave labour or murder in one of the five gas chambers with adjacent crematoria. Current figures state that between spring 1942 and November 1944 about 1.1 million Jews were murdered at Auschwitz-Birkenau. The fact that Christians were among both the murdered and the murderers complicates interpretation of the significance of Auschwitz for both communities. Oświęcim as a place of Jewish–Christian coexistence and interaction, and Auschwitz as a place where both Jews and Christians suffered and died, occupies an important place in Jewish and Christian memory, and since the late 1980s has as a result become a focus for conflict in the **Carmelite controversy**.   *K. HANNAH HOLTSCHNEIDER*

Australia

Today about 70 per cent of Australians claim to be Christian and 0.4 per cent Jewish (although the latter figure is undoubtedly an underestimate since some Jews avoid the optional census figure on religious adherence). Originally Jews were, like most Australian Christians, of British stock, but from the 1880s Eastern European Jews came as free settlers and German and Austrian Jews migrated from the 1930s. Prior to 1945 most Jewish–Christian encounters were informal, even ecumenical dialogue between Christian denominations being a rarity at this time. There were exceptions such as the activity of the Melbourne rabbi Hermann Sanger (1910–80), a refugee from Germany, who established Liberal Judaism and fostered personal friendships with Christian clergy. However, after 1945 Australian Christians became more aware of their Jewish neighbours due to reports of the **Holocaust** and the establishment of the **State of Israel**. The Jewish preponderance in Melbourne and Sydney led to these two cities being the natural centre for any **dialogue**. The earliest formal forum was the Fellowship for Biblical Studies, established in Melbourne in 1950. While, as would be expected, more Christian scholars than Jewish have been members, the Fellowship has encouraged Jewish–Christian religious dialogue on an intellectual level. Another decisive factor has been the work of the **Sisters**

of Sion, who established a Centre for Christian–Jewish Relations in Melbourne in 1963 and thenceforward became an active force in forging relations between the two traditions in Melbourne and Sydney. After some abortive attempts, the Victorian Council of Christians and Jews was established in 1985; its most significant achievement has been the publication of *Rightly Explaining the Word of Truth*, guidelines for Christian clergy and teachers in their use of the Christian scriptures' references to Jews and Judaism. Subsequently **Councils of Christians and Jews** were formed in New South Wales, Western Australia, South Australia, the Australian Capital Territory and Queensland. In 1991 the Victorian and New South Wales Councils united to form the Australian Council of Christians and Jews, a member of the International Council of Christians and Jews.   *ROBERT CROTTY*

Austria

The population of Austria, currently around 8 million, is overwhelmingly (78 per cent) Roman Catholic, whether practising or nominally, compared with 5 per cent Protestant. During the **Reformation** deep inroads were made by **Protestantism**, but by the end of the seventeenth century the Counter-Reformation had strongly reasserted **Roman Catholicism**, not least owing to the activities of the **Jesuits** and the continued loyalty of the Habsburg rulers. Although, under the influence of the **Enlightenment**, Emperor **Joseph II** had extended a limited degree of **toleration** to the Jewish population (as well as to **Calvinism** and **Lutheranism**), no synagogue was allowed until 1832, and traditionally Jews were debarred from the legal profession and civil service and from permission to buy land. Only in 1867 did the Austrian constitution guarantee freedom of religion and conscience for all. The number of Jews in Austria (currently about 8,000) increased dramatically from 6,200 in 1860 to 175,000 in 1910, reflecting immigration from other areas of the Austro-Hungarian Empire, notably Bukovina, Galicia and **Hungary**. By the outbreak of the First World War Jews constituted 12 per cent of the population of Vienna, where figures such as Gustav Mahler (1860–1911) and Sigmund **Freud** were making a contribution of global significance to modern culture and thought. Vienna was also home to Theodor **Herzl**, founder of political **Zionism**. The same period saw the marked rise of demagogic **antisemitism**, notably illustrated by the career of Karl Lueger (1844–1910), Mayor of Vienna and leader of the so-called Christian Social Party. The rump state of Austria that emerged from the collapse of the Habsburg Empire in 1918, becoming a republic, was riven by political tensions, often leading to violence, between Socialists on the one hand and Christian Socialist believers in Catholicism, authoritarian government and German nationalism on the other. Supporters of the latter were frequently highly antisemitic, with the animus of clerical antisemites, who tended to be opposed to **modernity** and liberal capitalism, directed primarily against secularised Jews. In the 1930s the Fatherland Front – a movement calling for Austria to be converted into a corporately organised 'Social Christian German state' – steered Catholicism along a right-wing course. There was a counter-current, exemplified by the foundation of a Christian society to combat antisemitism in 1891, the publication in the 1930s of the Catholic magazine *The Fulfilment* which sought to resolve misunderstandings between Christian and Jew, and the writings of the Christian author Hermann Bahr (1863–1934) who derided antisemitism as 'the morphine of little people', but Austrian Jews were too divided and their Christian allies too few to be effective against the antisemitic onslaught. With the Nazi occupation in 1938, the Anschluss, Austria was incorporated into **Germany** as the 'Ostmark', and a train of anti-Jewish violence was unleashed, leading to arrests, emigration, deportation and, in the Second World War, mass extermination. Of those Jews who remained in Austria very few survived the **Holocaust**. Immediately after the Second World War Austria was commonly regarded as 'Hitler's first victim', but this overlooked widespread popular enthusiasm for incorporation into the Third Reich. **Hitler** was an Austrian and, as Chancellor Vranitsky (b. 1937) admitted publicly in his visit to Israel in 1993, Austrians had been not only victims but also 'willing servants of **Nazism**'. This was highlighted by the controversy surrounding Kurt Waldheim (b. 1918), United Nations Secretary-General and then President of Austria (1986–91), who was accused of complicity in Nazi war crimes in Greece and Yugoslavia. His visit to the Vatican in 1986 and the ensuing argument coincided with Pope **John Paul II**'s announcement of a Commission to examine the Holocaust. Unsurprisingly, antisemitism and the Holocaust remain important issues in Jewish–Christian relations in Austria today.

DAVID WEIGALL

Avicebron *see* Ibn Gabirol, Solomon ben Judah

Avodah zarah

Rabbinic, halakhic designation of all non-Jewish religious cults, which are assumed in the **Mishnah** and **Talmud** to be polytheistic and idolatrous (*avodah zarah* means 'foreign worship'). The prohibition of worshipping *avodah zarah* applies also to non-Jews, as it is one of the **Noachide laws**. From the Talmudic period to the present day, halakhists have generally ruled that Christianity is to be categorised as a form of *avodah zarah* (e.g. *b. Avodah Zarah* 6a and 7b; **Maimonides**, *Laws of Avodah Zarah* 9.4). The reason for this ruling is rarely discussed or even spelled out; it would appear, however, that worship of **Jesus** has been interpreted as worship of a human being, or the **Trinity** as polytheistic (as implicit in Albo, *Sefer ha-Ikkarim* 3.25). Few halakhists have argued that Christians are not *avodah zarah* worshippers: **Meiri** (the context and meaning of his argument remain however unclear) and some post-**Emancipation** authorities. By contrast with Christianity, **Islam** is generally categorised as not *avodah zarah* and hence a legitimate non-Jewish religion (Maimonides, *Laws of Forbidden Foods* 11.7). *Avodah Zarah* is also the name of a Mishnaic and Talmudic tractate, which deals not with the actual prohibition of idolatrous worship (which is almost taken for granted in rabbinic literature), but rather with restrictions on drawing benefit from *avodah zarah* through trade and other social relations with non-Jews. These restrictions were partially relaxed in the Middle Ages (especially by the Tosafists of Northern France), when the Jews of Europe had become heavily dependent, for their subsistence, on commercial interaction with Christians. *Avodah zarah* remains a topic for debate among **Orthodox Jews** involved in Jewish–Christian **dialogue** – for example, the vigorous discussion following the refusal of American Orthodox scholar and interfaith activist David Berger (b. 1943) to sign the declaration ***Dabru Emet***.

See also **idolatry** *SACHA STERN*

BBBB

Babylonian Talmud *see* **Talmud**

Bach, Johann Sebastian (1685–1750)

Renowned composer of vocal and instrumental **music**. Bach was self-consciously **Lutheran**, and served for the greater part of his career as organist and choirmaster of Lutheran parishes in various German cities, notably the St Thomas Kirche in Leipzig. In view of this, the question has been raised whether **Luther**'s anti-Jewish views may have been reflected in Bach's music. Particular attention has been given to the *St John Passion*, with its use of the collective term 'the Jews' to designate the enemies of Jesus, although the forceful settings of 'Let him be crucified' and 'His blood be on us and on our children' in the *St Matthew Passion* are also problematic. It is plain, however, that the chief fault lies with the **New Testament** texts themselves, which Bach was not at liberty to alter. As to the non-biblical texts of the chorales and arias, which provide an interpretive commentary on the unfolding story, modern scholarship has revealed that Bach's libretto has a markedly less anti-Jewish tone than his source material, especially the 'Brockes Passion' (B. H. Brockes, *Der für die Sünde der Welt gemarterte und Sterbende Jesus*, Hamburg, 1712). Bach's chief concern was not to blame the Jews but to drive home the guilt of sinful humanity as a whole for Jesus' crucifixion: 'I, I and my sins . . . have brought upon you the sorrow that has struck you' (*St John Passion*, No. 11). To guard against **antisemitic** implications, some performances today include an educational component designed to put the New Testament texts and Bach's treatment of them in historical context, and to remind audiences of the new sensitivities needed in a post-**Holocaust** era.   *FRANKLIN SHERMAN*

Baeck, Leo (1873–1956)

Rabbi and community leader. Educated in Reform Jewish seminaries in Breslau and Berlin, Baeck completed a doctorate on **Spinoza** with Wilhelm Dilthey (1833–1911). In 1905 he published *The Essence of Judaism*, an extended response to **Harnack**'s *The Essence of Christianity* (1900). Baeck confronts Christianity with the charge of being a 'romantic religion', centring on feelings and obliterating the idea of a Jewish ethical imperative according to which human beings need to act in response to the call of faith. Baeck claims that Christianity relies on the idea that, since all **salvation** is accomplished in Jesus Christ, correct **doctrine** overrides the need for right action. Contrasting Christianity with Judaism, Baeck argues that Judaism is the highest form of religion, the **Torah** encapsulating the demands of an ethical life. Teaching at the Hochschule für die **Wissenschaft des Judentums** in Berlin, he also served as a community rabbi, rising to the position of president of the Allgemeiner Deutscher Rabbinerverband. Baeck declined offers of immigration to be deported with his community to Theresienstadt concentration camp in 1943. He survived and emigrated to London where he continued his teaching and rabbinical career. In his later years Baeck became increasingly involved in Jewish–Christian **dialogue** on an academic and community level. Baeck's views of Christianity show the influence of his teachers Heinrich Graetz (1817–91) and Hermann **Cohen**. Since 1954, Leo Baeck Institutes have been founded in the United States and Britain, promoting research on his work and furthering the study of Judaism.   *K. HANNAH HOLTSCHNEIDER*

Balaam

Balaam, who was hired to curse Israel but succumbed to the will of God (Num. 22–24), was portrayed negatively in Jewish writers (**Philo**, **Josephus**, Pseudo-Philo, rabbinic writings) and in the **New Testament** (2 Pet. 2.15–16; Jude 11; Rev. 2.14), even though his oracle (Num. 24.17) foretold the coming of the **Messiah** (a contradiction that **Origen** contended with). Rabbinic literature, possibly in controversy with Christians, sees him as a Gentile seer, symbolic of all that is evil among the nations. In this context, Balaam the seer may on occasion represent a veiled reference to **Jesus**.   *JAMES K. AITKEN*

Balfour Declaration

In a letter dated 2 November 1917 and addressed to Lord Rothschild, a prominent English Jewish Zionist, the British Foreign Secretary Arthur James Balfour (1848–1930) publicly declared the support of the British government for the Jewish claim to Palestine: 'His Majesty's government view with favour the establishment in Palestine of a national home for the Jewish people and will use their best endeavours to facilitate the achievement of this object, it being clearly understood that nothing shall be done which may prejudice the civil and religious rights of existing non-Jewish communities in Palestine or the rights and political status enjoyed by Jews in any other country.' The Declaration gained international legal status when it was incorporated into the provisions for the British Palestine **Mandate** in 1922. Gentile or **Christian Zionism** undoubtedly contributed to the creation of the Declaration. This was founded upon a romanticised, mythologised view of the Jewish people and was encouraged by the piety and popular **millenarianism** of various **Evangelical movements**. Since the time of **Cromwell**'s readmission of the Jews to England in 1655, the English had been fascinated with the idea of the restoration of the Jews to the **Promised Land**. In the twentieth century there were many British politicians and publicists, including Balfour and Prime Minister **Lloyd George**, whose intimate familiarity with scripture allowed them to see their support of **Zionism** as fulfilment of a historical mission. Balfour in particular allowed his religious philosophy to shape his politics and was profoundly impressed by the peculiarity of the Jewish experience down through the centuries, in which he saw a 'deep underlying principle of self-determination' pointing to 'a Zionist policy'. To such men the announcement that signalled their intent to return the Land to the ancient **people of Israel**, an announcement made just as British forces were poised to capture **Jerusalem** from the Ottoman Turks, appealed as a grand symbolic gesture of historic justice. It would be simplistic to regard the Declaration solely or even mainly in terms of religious agendas. Nevertheless, the intersection of religion and politics at this point cannot be ignored in any account of why Britain set aside the interests of the Arab inhabitants of the land, who made up around 90 per cent of the population (10 per cent of whom were **Arab Christians**), and how she sustained her commitment to a national home for the Jewish people throughout the difficult Mandate period. It also partly accounts for why the British government was more receptive than other European powers to the Zionist cause and why they were predisposed to be persuaded by the arguments of Zionist leaders, including Chaim **Weizmann**. Weizmann himself later explained that British statesmen 'believed in the Bible, that to them the return of the Jewish people to Palestine was a reality, so that we Zionists represented to them a great tradition for which they had an enormous respect'.   *DANIEL R. LANGTON*

Balkans

This term refers to both the Balkan Peninsula in south-eastern Europe and the countries of that region bounded by the Adriatic, Aegean and Black Seas. The majority of people are either (Eastern) Orthodox Christians, Roman Catholics or Muslims, with the Eastern Orthodox faith divided into self-governing national churches. Jews have lived in this area from the Hellenistic period onwards. From the fourteenth to the nineteenth centuries the region was under the control of the Turkish **Ottoman Empire**, during which time Jews and Christians both formed recognised **minorities** and shared a similar situation of **toleration** and occasional threats, with Sarajevo, in which the Jewish community was established in the early sixteenth century, generally a good example of happy coexistence between the Abrahamic faiths.

This situation changed radically in the twentieth century, during which the region – always a focus of major international rivalry, internecine ethnic conflict and political fragmentation – was crucially unstable. In 1939 only 0.5 per cent of the population of Yugoslavia were Jewish, and **antisemitism** existed mainly in nationalist Catholic clerical circles in Croatia and pro-fascist populist groups in Serbia. However, the German intervention in Yugoslavia in the Second World War led to massacres of the Jewish population, particularly in Jasenovac concentration camp and by deportation to **Auschwitz**. Less than one fifth of the Jewish population escaped the **Holocaust** – at the end of the war there were only some 15,000 survivors, many of whom emigrated to **Israel**. There was near-total destruction of Greek Jews during the Nazi occupation, especially in Macedonia and Thrace, while in Romania no fewer than 420,000 Jews were killed in this period either as a consequence of **pogroms** in which the Romanian authorities participated or through deportation to the camps. As a result of this decimation, and the historical pre-eminence of the fault-line between Christian and Muslim communities, the savage conflicts of the 1990s as Yugoslavia disintegrated are of more significance to interfaith relations generally (and their vulnerability to political manipulation), than to Jewish–Christian relations in particular.   *DAVID WEIGALL*

Baptism

Baptism is the principal mode by which an individual is initiated into the Christian **community**, and a sign and guarantor of that inclusion. It involves at the very least a water rite, and at one time or another in Christian history declarations of repentance, forms of professions of faith, anointing with oil and the laying on of hands. Christian denominations can be roughly divided between those who baptise babies (with sponsors making the baptismal promises on their behalf) and those who baptise adults upon mature admit of faith. Only two Christian groups, the Society of Friends (*see* **Quakers**) and the Salvation Army, eliminate the water rite altogether from their initiation practice.

Christian baptism traces its roots both to the Jewish practice of proselyte baptism (increasingly common by the first century CE) and to the action of **John the Baptist**, whose preaching in the Judean desert concerning the coming Reign of God called for baptism in the Jordan River as a sign of **repentance** (see Matt. 3; Mark 1.1–11; Luke 3.1–21), as well as to the *mikvah*, the periodic ritual baths for purity. The earliest followers of **Jesus** adopted a similar water rite, probably accompanied by the candidate's acknowledgement of Jesus as **Messiah**, as a way of marking **conversion** and commitment to discipleship. While submersion in water (which is the root meaning of the Greek word *baptizein*) seems to have been the practical norm in the early period, by about the seventh century Christians were commonly using smaller amounts of water in the rite. Already in the earliest period of Christian history questions are being raised about whether anyone other than Jews could be considered candidates for baptism. The apostle Peter is criticised by the Christian community in Jerusalem for associating with the uncircumcised, but he argues that

it has been revealed to him that 'God had given even to the Gentiles the repentance that leads to life' (Acts 11.18). In the early centuries of theological reflection on initiation Christian writers often used the analogy of **circumcision** in interpreting the religious significance of baptism. Like circumcision, baptism signalled inclusion in the **covenant** community, sealed in blood; in the case of baptism, however, the blood was not the blood shed in the rite of circumcision but rather the blood shed by Jesus in his **crucifixion**. Both baptism and circumcision were also thematically linked to the exodus. Just as the blood of circumcision was connected to the blood on the doorposts of the houses of those enslaved in Egypt, so were the waters of baptism connected to God's eternal promise to redeem confirmed in the waters of the Red Sea. By the fifth century, however, these theological ties with Christianity's Jewish past had been largely lost. Baptism was generally understood as the act by which **salvation** was guaranteed, both by assuring the eradication of sin, and particularly what had come to be called '**original sin**' (that is the sin of **Adam** and **Eve** transmitted to every human being at conception), and by inserting the person into the Church, where the salvific work of Jesus Christ was exclusively operative. Because of the fear that a child might die unbaptised, and thus suffer eternal damnation, babies began routinely to be baptised *quam primam* ('as soon as possible'), effectively detaching baptism from the ongoing process of Christian nurture and the life of faith.

The persistent, early link between Christian exclusivism and baptism has had important consequences for the history of the relationship between Christians and Jews. Although the principle of freedom from coercion in religious matters has become quite well established in the modern period, for centuries forced baptisms were not uncommon in the encounter between dominant Christian populations and religious **minorities**. In many periods of the Church's history Jews were baptised against their will both because of the strong and pervasive conviction among Christians that without baptism their souls were doomed to perdition, but also because of the belief that eternal rewards would be granted to those who added to the numbers of the redeemed, by whatever method. The history of these coerced conversions continues to cast a shadow on Christian–Jewish relations, as it does on the wider Christian witness to peace and freedom. Baptism has often had a significant place on the agenda of the various Christian renewal movements. Those who have believed that the scriptural evidence for baptism should be absolutely normative for Christian congregations have called for the rejection of infant baptism, for the restoration of total submersion as the only appropriate mode of baptism, and for the imposition of strict behavioural and doctrinal norms for any persons seeking admission to the Christian community through baptism. In other cases, groups anticipating that God would bring an imminent, apocalyptic end to the world saw baptism as the means by which the righteous would be identified and, thus, spared the inevitable tribulation. While these sectarian approaches to baptism have caused deep divisions within the Church, insistence on firm adherence to specific Christian doctrines or a clearly defined conversion experience has also helped to undermine the theological foundations of forced baptisms.

Baptism continues to be among the most controversial aspects of Christian theology and practice, and it is not always easy for Jews and Christians to talk together about questions of community **identity** and the God–human relationship without these internal debates coming into play. At the same time, the attempt on the part of many Christian thinkers to recover the Jewish antecedents of Christian baptismal theology has meant that some common ground is beginning to be established. Over the past quarter-century, this ancient shared imagery has begun to find a place in newly revised rites of initiation. For example, variations of the sixteenth-century reformer Martin **Luther**'s 'Flood Prayer' now appear as the central prayer of blessing over the water in the baptismal liturgies of many Christian denominations. In this prayer, the whole history of God's use of water in **redemption** is chronicled, beginning with the parting of the waters in **creation**, the delivering of **Noah** and the miracle at the Red Sea. Despite seemingly insurmountable differences of theological opinion, the power of baptism in the religious imaginations of Christian people cannot be overestimated. It seems clear, however, that the place of baptism in the future of Jewish–Christian relations is likely to be determined not only by the variegated patterns of contemporary baptismal theology and practice, but also by the history of the use of baptism as a weapon in relations with people of other faiths. *SUSAN WHITE*

Bar Kokhba (d. 135)

(*Nom de guerre* of Simeon Bar Kosiba.) Messianic claimant and leader of Jewish resistance to Roman rule. Simeon Bar Kosiba headed the disastrous Jewish revolt of 132–5 which, despite some initial successes, was eventually crushed by a concerted and costly Roman military effort. The assumed name Bar Kokhba ('son of the star') appears to derive from a Messianic interpretation of Num. 24.17. Many at the time followed Rabbi **Akiba** in recognising Bar Kokhba as the promised **Messiah** who would deliver Israel from bondage to Rome. Recovered coinage styles Simeon the 'Prince of Israel' and also makes use of the star motif. Later Talmudic sources refer to him, with hindsight, as Bar Koziba ('son of the lie'). The decisive defeat of the revolt effectively put paid to any practical hope for Jewish independence or for the rebuilding of the **Temple**. It also forced large numbers of Jews out of Judea, especially to Babylonia. The then emperor, Hadrian (*r.*117–38), took the opportunity to rebuild **Jerusalem** as the thoroughly Hellenistic Aelia Capitolina and to deny Jews entry to the city – an act of great symbolic importance even if not always rigorously enforced. Bar Kokhba is universally reviled in Christian sources: **Eusebius** treats him as a ludicrous charlatan, while **Justin Martyr**, writing in the years immediately following the revolt, indicts Bar Kokhba with the graver charge that he 'gave orders that Christians alone should be led to cruel punishments unless they would deny Jesus Christ and utter blasphemy' (*1 Apol.* 31). Bar Kokhba's own attitude to Christians, as witnessed in the (very brief) letters discovered in the 1950s and 1960s, provides no positive evidence of any definite **anti-Christian** bias. *MARCUS PLESTED*

Barmitzvah

Term commonly used since the 1560s (*Shulhan Arukh, Orah Hayyim* 55.10) for the coming of age of a Jewish boy on reaching 13. Coming of age ceremonies have been celebrated throughout history in all societies, and barmitzvah began among Jews living in Christian societies. However, the precise nature of the Jewish–Christian encounter that led to barmitzvah remains elusive, and merits further research. The age of 13 is mentioned in various medieval rabbinic sources (*Avot* 5.24; *Genesis Rabbah* 63.10). A curious account by one Hermannus *quondam* Judaeus, a born Jew who became a Christian, appears to describe his bar-mitzvah in Cologne around 1120. Later in life Hermannus came to view his experience as a step on the road to **baptism** into the Church. Apart from this, there is no evidence of any special ceremony to mark the event until the fourteenth century in Provence and Germany. The popular demand for such a ceremony may be connected with new pro-hibitions on children taking part in formal **worship**. In the **early Church** communion was administered to children, but the Fourth **Lateran Council** (1215) limited it to those old enough to understand. Sim-ilarly, there is evidence from the thirteenth cen-tury of boys leading Jewish prayers, but by the fif-teenth century it was frowned upon. Once there was a formal date to begin from, the need for a ceremony grew. Barmitzvah seems to offer a num-ber of parallels with Christian confirmation, but this was and still is celebrated at a younger age by Christians. I. G. Marcus (1996) compares barmitz-vah to the Catholic ceremony of oblation, when boys aged 12–14 entered a religious order. A bat-mitzvah for a girl is an innovation of **Progressive Judaism**, and has been extended in recent years to some Orthodox synagogues. The coming of age ceremonies practised at age 13 in Ameri-can **Unitarian** Churches are clearly influenced by the popularity of barmitzvah in American Jewish culture. *MICHAEL HILTON*

Barnabus, Epistle of *see* Apostolic Fathers

BCE *see* CE/BCE

Bea, Augustin (1881–1968)

Roman Catholic cardinal, biblical scholar, ecu-menist. Born in Germany, Bea worked as a **Jesuit** priest, taught biblical theology at the Gregorian University in Rome and was rector of the Pontifi-cal Biblical Institute (1930–49). One of Pope **Pius XII**'s closest theological advisors, he was named a cardinal by Pope **John XXIII** in 1959. In March 1960, in the wake of Pope John's announcement of **Vati-can II**, he petitioned for the creation of a new Vati-can body to coordinate and promote Catholic ecu-menical efforts; the Secretariat for Christian Unity was formally established in June, with Bea as its first president (its responsibilities were later broadened to include Jewish–Catholic relations). Bea's reputa-tion as churchman and scholar made him one of the most respected voices in the discussions of Vatican II, and he was instrumental in steering many of the more controversial documents through the process

of debate and acceptance. When in 1960 Jules **Isaac** asked Pope John to address the Catholic Church's relationship with the Jews as part of the Council's agenda, the Pope agreed and referred him to Bea for more detailed discussions. Later that year Bea asked Nahum Goldman (1895–1982), the President of the World Jewish Congress, to solicit the input of a cross-section of international Jewish groups toward a memorandum that could inform the Council's discussions. Bea himself strongly advocated such a document, and under his guidance a draft 'Decree on the Jewish People' was prepared. Some con-sidered it politically and theologically unwise, and a storm of protest and threats from Arab states resulted in its being withdrawn; at the instigation of the Pope and Bea, however, the schema was later restored, as part of *Nostra Aetate*. Bea person-ally presented and argued for the relevant sections, which proved to be among the most emotionally and politically charged of the Council's texts, and his interventions were widely seen as decisive in the final outcome. In 1966 Bea published his own com-mentary, *La Chiesa e il popolo ebraico* ('The Church and the Jewish People'), addressing the sensitive issues of '**deicide**' and the claim of Jewish responsi-bility for Christ's death, as well as the spiritual and historical links between the Jewish and Christian peoples. *LUCY THORSON & MURRAY WATSON*

Beatitudes

The beatitudes witness to the common faith tradi-tion of Judaism and Christianity. The word 'beati-tudes', from the Latin, encompasses a body of say-ings with a particular form. The technical term for beatitudes is 'macarism', from the Greek for 'blessed' or 'happy'; the Hebrew parallel is *ashre*. The general meaning of all these terms is 'in a rela-tionship of righteousness with God'. Beatitudes are found in many ancient literatures, including Egyp-tian, Greek and Jewish. The **Hebrew Bible** contains 45 beatitudes, mostly in the **Psalms** and Proverbs. More are found in the **Septuagint**, the Intertesta-mental literature, and the Essene and **Gnostic** cor-pus, so the literary form was familiar to Judaism long before Jesus. The **New Testament** contains 37 beatitudes, though some are repeats. The two most famous collections are Luke 6.20b–23 and its apparent expansion, Matt. 5.3–12. Both are con-nected to the '**Sermon on the Mount**'. Generally, beatitudes in the Hebrew Bible assume that the behaviour's reward is in the present, while the

New Testament beatitudes promise a future, or **eschatological**, reward. Scholars argue whether the beatitudes in the Sermon on the Mount are original to **Jesus** or not.   *PHILIP CULBERTSON*

Begin, Menachem (1913–92)

Israeli statesman. Born in Brest-Litovsk and educated in Warsaw, from 1944 until 1948 Begin was leader of the Jewish Irgun Zvai Leumi which was engaged in armed revolt against the British **Mandate** in Palestine. After the foundation of the **State of Israel** he set up the Herut (Freedom) Party and was subsequently twice elected prime minister, in 1977 and 1981, initiating the widespread settlement of Gaza, Judea and Samaria. His decision to invade Lebanon in 1982 was widely condemned internationally and prejudiced Jewish–Christian relations in the world at large, though the Israeli action also led to the formation of links with Christian groups such as the Christian Falange. He was awarded the Nobel Peace Prize, signing a peace treaty with Egypt in 1979 after the Camp David Accords. The first significant Israeli politician to woo the American Christian right, Begin was instrumental in the rise of **Christian Zionism** in the **United States**.

DAVID WEIGALL

Bell, George (1883–1958)

English clergyman, ecumenist and opponent of **antisemitism**. As Bishop of Chichester (1929–57), Bell's involvement in the ecumenical movement gave him unusually detailed knowledge of **Germany** during the 1930s and 1940s. He was instrumental in persuading international Church opinion as early as 1933 to condemn antisemitic actions by the Nazi government, defending the right in international law to intervene in the internal workings of a state where **human rights** are violated. He campaigned to welcome Jewish refugees from Germany. His interest in German Jews was largely humanitarian and focused chiefly on 'non-Aryan Christians' (i.e. those with Jewish ancestry who were practising Christians). He launched a national appeal in 1936, though it faltered and was replaced by a **Church of England** Committee for 'Non Aryan Christians'.   *STEPHEN PLANT*

Benediction *see* blessings and curses

Berdyaev, Nikolai Aleksandrovich (1874–1948)

Russian philosopher. Berdyaev began his career as a Marxist thinker, but soon reverted to Russian **Orthodox Christianity**, critically assessed. After expulsion from **Russia** (1922), Berdyaev settled in Paris. He was to be widely published in his lifetime. His existentialism shared some concepts with Martin **Buber**, whom he knew. In *The Study of History* (1923; Eng. trans. 1936), Berdyaev devoted a chapter to the unique role of Judaism. This did not prevent his use of borrowed phrases elsewhere on 'the Jews' refusal to accept Christ' (1934). At the same time he insisted that no authentic Christian could permit himself to harbour hatred for the Jews; such racism could only be described as anti-Christian (1938). Though Berdyaev's views on the subject were well known, his European reputation prevented his arrest during the German occupation (1940–44), but several of his closest friends were seized for the support they gave to Jews. Two of them (Mother Maria Skobtsova (1891–1945) and Father Dimitrii Klepinin (1900–44)) are numbered with the **Righteous Gentiles** (1987); both were canonised as **martyrs** by the Orthodox patriarchate of Constantinople (2004).   *SERGEI HACKEL*

Bernard of Clairvaux (1090–1153)

Mystic, theologian, active in ecclesiastical activities, Bernard continued the tradition of ambivalence towards Jews and Judaism that began with **Augustine** and **Gregory the Great**. While preaching the Second **Crusade** (1146), he intervened to protect German Jewry from the monk Randulph. He repudiated the views of **Peter the Venerable** and emphasised the difference between fighting the Muslims, which he regarded as legitimate, and inflicting physical harm on the Jews, which he argued against. Bernard also objected to Peter's desire to strip the Jews of their material possessions, arguing that Jews should only abolish the interest on loans to crusaders. He admonished the Christians with the tale of Peter the Hermit who persecuted the Jews during the First Crusade. However, Bernard intervened in the papal election of 1130 in support of Innocent II (*r*.1130–43) against his rival **Anacletus II** due to the latter's Jewish origins. Bernard's sermons and **mystical** writings reveal the standard **anti-Judaic** motifs that were well established in Christian tradition: he emphasised Jewish carnality, the inability of Jews to exercise proper reason, and their stubborn disbelief. The sermons on the Song of Songs develop the **allegorical** rivalry between Church and synagogue (*see* **Ecclesia/Synagoga**).   *MICHAEL A. SIGNER*

Bernardin, Joseph (1928–96)

Cardinal archbishop of Chicago (1982–96). Committed to human dignity and conciliation,

Bernardin took up *Nostra Aetate*'s call to **dialogue** with the Jews within the structures and programmes of the Archdiocese. A prominent, courageous and credible teacher of the twentieth-century American Catholic Church, he brought Chicago's leading Jewish and Protestant leaders together in an ecumenical council, Religious Leaders of Metropolitan Chicago (which now also has Muslim representation). Through a variety of bilateral efforts he supported the relationship between the two communities with structures of implementation and continuity which involved the relational, pastoral and scholarly dimensions. At his death prominent Jewish leaders offered in the cathedral, as part of the official wake and funeral, *A Jewish Farewell – Words of Tribute and Respect*, in which Bernardin was mourned as the perfectly righteous man, a friend and a brother.

AUDREY DOETZEL

Bialik, Hayyim Nachman (1873–1934)

Perhaps the greatest Hebrew poet in the past 600 years, Bialik also wrote novellas and stories of the highest quality. Born in Radi in the **Ukraine**, he mastered traditional **Hebrew literature** at an early age, and was attracted by the movements of **enlightenment** and early **Zionism**. From 1900 he resided in Odessa, but in 1921 he was allowed to leave Russia for **Germany** through the efforts of Maxim Gorky (1868–1936). In 1924 he settled in British **Mandate** Palestine, where he was revered as the national poet. Following the Kishinev **pogrom** in 1903, inspired by a Christian **blood libel**, Bialik composed a short poem, 'On the Slaughter', and in 1904 a long poem, 'In the City of Slaughter', which represent a shriek of pain and disgust at the bestiality of a mob howling for blood. His description of the cowardice of the victims led to the formation of Jewish self-defence units. Two of his novellas, *Behind the Fence* and *The Shamed Trumpet*, deal specifically with Jewish–Christian relations in **Russia**. The plot of the former is a stereotypical Romeo and Juliet theme transposed to a provincial Russian town. The lovers are children of rival families, but also divided by religious and social class: the son of a small-scale Jewish lumber merchant and a Christian foundling oppressed by a grim and cruel Russian peasant woman. *The Shamed Trumpet* describes the tragic uprooting of a Jewish family from a Volhynian village on the eve of Passover as a result of the promulgation of the notorious **antisemitic** 'temporary May

Laws' in 1882. A third novella, *Big Harry*, also contains elements of Jewish–Christian relations, but in a more humorous vein. A recent English translation of Bialik's novellas has rekindled interest in his work.

DAVID PATTERSON

Bible

Derived from *biblia*, the Greek plural of 'book', the term Bible is used by both Jews and Christians to refer to that collection of books held to be sacred by their respective traditions and, by most, to be inspired by God. In the Jewish tradition this is Tanakh, or the 45 books of the Hebrew scriptures, including the **Torah**, the Prophets and the Writings. In the Christian tradition, the Bible is made up not only of the Old Testament/Tanakh, but also of the New Testament: 27 books which recount the life of **Jesus** of Nazareth and the formation of the **early Church**, and include letters from Church teachers to the new communities in **Asia Minor**. For Christians, both Old and New Testaments are God's **revelation** to humankind, first to the Jewish people (as found in the Hebrew scriptures) and then to the Gentile world through Jesus and his followers and interpreters.

Self-evidently, the Bible has been critically important in Jewish–Christian relations through the ages. Indeed, one might well claim that a major fissure between Jews and Christians has been caused precisely by opposing or mutually exclusive interpretations of scripture. Typically Christians have seen the Hebrew scriptures as simply a prelude to the **New Testament** or as exhausted by their **Christological** meaning. Considering the Old Testament to be mostly a series of foreshadowings and prophecies of Jesus, many Christians concluded that the Jews were either stupid in not understanding their own scriptures or sinful in not recognising Jesus as **Messiah**. Furthermore, **Bible translations**, produced by each community in isolation from the other, have supported the perspective of each. Whether in the Hebrew Tanakh, the Greek **Septuagint**, the Latin **Vulgate** or **Luther**'s German translation, both communities have found different meanings in their different versions. It can accurately be said, therefore, that the Bible has both divided and united Jews and Christians.

Among many issues in the Jewish–Christian encounter with the Bible are the following. First, there is the complex issue of by which name

Christians should refer to that part of their Bible that they share with the Jewish people (*see* **Old Testament**). Second, while the order of books in the Hebrew scriptures differs for Christians and Jews, more important and fundamental are differences in *interpreting* the Old Testament. The overwhelmingly Christological interpretation that Christians bring to it, Jewish scholars say, renders it an almost completely different book. The meaning and interpretation of the Hebrew scriptures can thus be a fruitful subject of **dialogue** between Jews and Christians. Third, twentieth-century Christian scholars have discovered Jewish understandings of their scriptures to be an indispensable component of their meaning. Ignored or derided in the past, this 'surplus of meaning', from the Christian viewpoint, has emerged as a significant enrichment and deepening of the Bible's meaning. Fourth, from the latter half of the twentieth century many Jewish scholars began to explore the New Testament as a fertile resource for understanding Second Temple Judaism of both Palestine and Asia Minor, and conversely insights from Jewish studies of Jesus, **Paul** and religious practices of the Apostolic Age of the Church have deeply enriched Christian studies. Fifth, a promising area for collaboration is the search for the meaning of divine **inspiration** of the Bible and, for some, the issue of its consequent inerrancy. While both issues tend to be emphasised more within the Christian community, in a **postmodern** world some conservative sectors of the Jewish community also wrestle with them. Finally, cooperative projects between Jewish and Christian biblical scholars have helped Christians deal with problematic texts in the New Testament (see, for example, **anti-Judaism**) and have addressed commonly experienced problematic texts in both Testaments (such as those involving violence, sexism, slavery or racism).

Among contemporary expressions of Jewish and Christian dealings with the Bible and the other are two very important documents. ***Dabru Emet****: A Jewish Statement on Christians and Christianity* (2000) affirms, among other things, that 'Jews and Christians seek authority from the same book – the Bible (what Jews call "Tanakh" and Christians call the "Old Testament")'. In 2001, the Vatican's Pontifical Biblical Commission issued the statement *The Jewish People and their Sacred Scriptures in the Christian Bible*, which addresses from the Catholic viewpoint, and primarily from a historical perspective, such major biblical themes as the relationship between the Testaments, the unity of both Testaments and what pastoral implications these might have for Christians. The publication of both documents reflects the maturity to which contemporary Jewish–Christian relations have come, while pointing out the need for future discussion on the Bible's central place in both traditions.

Finally, Jews and Christians have often benefited from sharing their respective community's attitude towards the Bible in the ordinary life of their members. Christians often think that their reading of the Hebrew scriptures is paralleled, both in interpretation and centrality, in the Jewish community. They may ask, for instance, How do Jews understand the '**Suffering Servant**' in the book of Isaiah? Jews, for their part, often are puzzled by some Christians' literalist and fundamentalist readings of the scriptures without the necessary (from the Jewish perspective) interpretation of the **Talmud**. Some ask, for instance, If Christians consider our scriptures to be the Word of God, why do they not observe the **Sabbath**? Such questions suggest that both may benefit from listening to, and learning from, the other on the place and authority of the Bible in their respective traditions.

See also **biblical criticism**; **biblical interpretation**; **biblical theology**   *MICHAEL MCGARRY*

Bible translations, ancient

The earliest extant Christian writings come from **Paul of Tarsus**, and are composed in **Greek**. Their frequent, sometimes lengthy quotations of Jewish scriptures are periodically identical with the **Septuagint** of the texts being cited; but often they diverge from that translation, even quite extensively. The same observation holds true for the rest of the **New Testament**, and the writings of the **Apostolic Fathers** and the Apologists. All these documents raise questions about the identity and character of the Greek versions of scripture they cite, and reveal a complex state of textual affairs. Light is thrown on this by a scroll of the Twelve Prophets translated into Greek found in the *Nahal Hever* scrolls corpus, indicating that already before the fall of the Second Temple Jewish scholars were aware of disorder in Greek translations of the Bible, and had attempted to rectify it. This scroll regularly represents the Hebrew particle *gam*, 'also', as *kaige*, 'and at any rate', and is closely related to another revision of the Septuagint attributed to Theodotion (*fl.* end of second century CE): *kaige*-Theodotion is now the name given to this recension. *Kaige* itself (dated first century BCE) evidently represents an early stage of recensional endeavour which continued into the second century CE. From the early part of that century (*c.*125 CE) comes the revised Greek version of **Aquila**, which was influenced by *kaige*-Theodotion. It was issued in two editions, bears the character of the exegetical school of **Akiba**, and marks a determined attempt to represent the letter and spirit of the original **Hebrew** in Greek in as faithful a way as possible. At this time, Christian use of inaccurate Greek translations was becoming widespread, non-Jews without knowledge of Hebrew making up the overwhelming majority of Church membership. By the middle of the century **Justin Martyr** could use Greek **Testimonia** texts which differed from the Hebrew biblical originals and allege that his Jewish interlocutors had tampered with the text of scripture by omitting important details. A further revision of the Greek Bible at the end of the second or beginning of the third century CE by Symmachus (*fl.* probably late second century CE), possibly an Ebionite, more likely a Jew, sought to preserve the 'literal' approach of Aquila's version in a more elegant and literary style; interestingly, it appeared approximately at the same time as the redaction of the **Mishnah**, which explicitly permits translation of the scriptures into Greek (*Megillah* 1.8).

While the third century witnessed a decline of Jewish interest in Greek translations of the Bible, the Christian scholar **Origen** addressed the serious implications of the Church relying on a 'Septuagint' that poorly reflected the underlying Hebrew and sought to recover the 'original' Greek translation. To this end he acquired some knowledge of Hebrew and collected the Greek witnesses known to him, producing his famous **Hexapla**, indicating in its Septuagint column Greek additions and omissions in respect of the Hebrew. This enterprise brought him into direct and apparently amicable contact with Jews; but the resulting text of his Septuagint, which he also published with the versions of Aquila, Symmachus and Theodotion in his Tetrapla, was only one of a number of Christian recensions of this version known at the end of the fourth century, when **Jerome** in his preface to the **Vulgate** trans-

lation of Chronicles refers to revisions by Lucian (d. 312 CE), Hesychius (*fl. c.*300 CE) and, by implication, other scholars.

The complex and variable relationships between Jews and Christians revealed in respect of the Greek versions is apparent also in the history of the Syriac Bible translation made from the Hebrew called **Peshitta**. Recent research suggests that some books in this version (especially Chronicles) may have been translated into Syriac by Jews whose attachment to rabbinic norms was slender, and that Jewish converts to Christianity may also have had a hand in the production of certain other books. Be that as it may, the translators of **Pentateuch** and Prophets in particular from time to time show affinity with Jewish exegetical tradition extant in **Targum** and the classical **midrashim**, particularly the former. Their dependence on written forms of such tradition is unlikely, but it cannot be denied that they had access to Jewish circles where learned exposition of the Bible was known, and subsequently embodied in the version. The case of Proverbs, however, is remarkable, in that the Targum of that book depends upon the Peshitta; here particularly it would seem that there was some close association between Jews and Christians. In addition, the Syriac translators sometimes had recourse to the Septuagint, although the influence of the Greek varies considerably from book to book. In the **Apocrypha** the translators worked from a Hebrew text of Ben Sira (late third to early second century BCE), but otherwise translated from the Septuagint. Syriac familiarity with and dependence upon Jewish exegetical tradition continued in the work of the early Syriac commentators **Aphrahat** and **Ephrem**; but both these scholars were capable of scathing attacks on the Jews from whom they had derived this learning. Even so, influence of this contact between Jews and **Syriac Christians** may be perceived in other less polemical Christian writers, most notably Eusebius of Emesa (d. *c.*359), whose quotations of 'the Syrian' and 'the Hebrew' in his commentaries often betoken knowledge of a Syriac Bible translation or information derived from a Jewish source.

In the West the first **Latin** versions of the Bible appeared in North Africa and southern Gaul: this Old Latin (*Vetus Latina*) rendering was a translation of the Septuagint, and survives in various forms which themselves may possibly reflect originally distinct versions, although attempts to prove the independence of North African and European translations cannot be judged successful. **Augustine** speaks of the *Itala* as a European form of the Old Latin, apparently distinct from the North African; but the version as a whole is probably best regarded as having developed slowly over a period of time, being often revised in the light of such Septuagint manuscripts as became available. A certain amount of traditional Jewish material appears in the Old Latin, and it has been suggested that the ultimate source of this may be found in the synagogues of North Africa and the oral interpretations of scripture given during the service, taken up and used by Christians. Here, perhaps, we encounter Christian attendance at synagogue worship, something discouraged by the bishops, but which seems to have flourished at popular level.

Particularly in the West, peculiar renderings, or even downright mistranslations of Hebrew words, could produce unfortunate effects. Famous is the Vulgate of Exod. 34.35 describing **Moses**' face as 'horned', a mistaken interpretation of Hebrew *karan*, 'shone brilliantly', as *keren*, 'horn', such that Michelangelo's (1475–1564) famous statue of Moses shows him with horns protruding from his forehead.   *C. T. R. HAYWARD*

Bible translations, modern English

Christian readers of the Bible in English did not move away from the Authorised/King James Version (KJV) (1611) until the late nineteenth century, with the Revised Version (RV) (NT 1881, OT 1885, Apocrypha 1895). Jewish readers had by then been expressing dissatisfaction with the KJV for almost a century, in revisions and **commentaries** intended to remove 'Christian mistranslations' – especially in Gen. 1.2, Isa. 7.14 and Ps. 2.12, which had been points of controversy as far back as **Justin Martyr**'s *Dialogue with Trypho*. Thus we find the KJV corrected by Isaac Delgado (1789), Selig Newman (1839) and Abraham Bemisch (1851–6). Isaac Leeser's 1845 revision was especially influential for the principles it set out: the Jewish Publications Society (JPS) Bible (1917) is a revision of the RV on Leeson's principles. After the Second World War, the JPS sponsored an entirely new version of the Bible, prepared by Jewish scholars from the original text, and quite independent of any Christian version – the New JPS Version (Torah 1962, Prophets 1978, Writings 1982; gathered in a one-volume edi-

tion 1985). Modern Jewish versions of the Bible have therefore been partly directed by a desire to emancipate Jewish scriptures from a burden of Christian **biblical interpretation**.

Modern Christian versions are very numerous, and only the most significant are mentioned here. The mid-twentieth century saw heroic single-translator versions and also revisions in the KJV tradition such as the Revised Standard Version (RSV) (NT 1946, OT 1952, Apocrypha 1956), which was very widely used in the late twentieth century. The New RSV (1989) took account of recent developments in biblical scholarship and tried to be alive to **feminist** concerns in its use of gender-inclusive language for human beings. This has been the policy of most Bible translations since.

Entirely new Christian translations have been made, independent of the KJV/RSV tradition. The New English Bible (NT 1961, OT 1970) was an Anglican venture, overhauled as the Revised English Bible (1990). The Jerusalem Bible (1966) is important as the first English Bible authorised for Roman Catholic use since the Rheims-Douai Bible of 1582/1610. The New International Version (1978) has enjoyed wide popularity especially among evangelical Christians, as have Today's English Version and the Good News Bible. Modern English versions have on the whole been directed by a desire to make the Bible available in English that is idiomatic and accessible, and informed by recent textual scholarship. Questions have recently been raised as to whether it is possible to mitigate the anti-Jewish strain of some customary translations (e.g. whether 'the Judeans' would not be a better rendering than 'the Jews' of **hoi Ioudaioi** in John's narrative of Jesus' death), but these concerns have yet to make their mark on the Christian versions most widely used.   *ANDERS BERGQUIST*

Biblical criticism

A comprehensive term that encompasses a wide variety of scientific methods to analyse biblical texts. These analytical methods can be divided into two broad categories. Historical criticism seeks to situate a biblical writing in its historical context. Historical critical methods study the social, cultural and political milieus in which a text was composed; component sources that may be discernible in the text; precedents in neighbouring societies; archaeological data; and indications of the editing or redacting of the text over time. Literary criticism is concerned with the text as it now stands and how it engages readers. Literary critical methods study the structures and features of the text; the strategies the text employs to persuade readers of its claims; the readers the text proposes to address; and the characteristics of today's readers and their specific questions and concerns.

Since the Christian **Bible** includes the scriptures of ancient Israel and accounts of the birth of the Church within first-century Judaism, its interpretation is a crucial factor in shaping Christian attitudes towards Jews and Judaism. The rise of biblical criticism, therefore, has had enormous consequences – originally negative, but more recently very positive – for Jewish–Christian relations.

Different critical methods have gradually developed since the nineteenth century when the use of biblical criticism blossomed in European Protestant circles. Indeed, biblical criticism only became possible with the appearance after the **Enlightenment** of a historical and a psychological consciousness, which recognises that people's ideas and attitudes are culturally conditioned and shaped by subjective experiences.

Some biblical critics held a rationalist perspective that was very sceptical of transcendent biblical claims that, by definition, were not verifiable by empirical means. Their work was seen as a threat to Christian faith by some Church leaders because it delegitimated the authority of the Bible. This led to the condemnation of biblical criticism by Roman Catholic officials in the late nineteenth and early twentieth centuries and the rise of Protestant **fundamentalists** who insisted that the Bible was the literal and infallible word of God. However, since the 1943 encyclical *Divino Afflante Spiritu* of Pope **Pius XII**, the Roman Catholic Church has mandated the use of all forms of biblical criticism by Catholic scholars. This has led to a dramatic revitalisation of Catholic biblical scholarship. Some fundamentalist Christian communities have moderated earlier views by restricting the Bible's freedom from error to matters of faith and morals and no longer to more scientific or historical assertions. There remains considerable diversity among the various Christian traditions about the use of biblical criticism and the nature of biblical authority.

Rationalist biblical critics in the nineteenth century shared the **supersessionism** of the Christian world. The 'documentary hypothesis' most frequently associated with Julius **Wellhausen** – which holds that the **Pentateuch** is the result of the editing together of four major distinct 'sources' composed over disparate centuries – was used not only to dismiss Jewish claims of Mosaic authorship but also to reinforce the prevalent cultural denigration of Judaism itself. Examination of the presuppositions of the modern interpreter that are characteristic of some forms of literary criticism provides a corrective to such **polemical** use of critical tools.

European Jews thus experienced biblical criticism being hostilely used against their own traditions. This, combined with the differences between the critical and rabbinic thought worlds, caused Jews generally to be wary of biblical criticism. Over time the liberal Jewish movements have more readily utilised biblical critical methods, while more traditional Jews have tended to see biblical criticism as irrelevant for **Torah** study.

The use of critical methodologies is of great significance for Jewish–Christian relations. Greater textual evidence from the Late Second Temple period (*see* **Dead Sea Scrolls**) and critical efforts to determine the social settings of Christian biblical books have shed new light on the **New Testament**'s presentation of Jews as well as on the origins of Christianity and **Rabbinic Judaism**. Historical critical studies have determined that much negative or 'anti-Jewish' speech stems from the rhetorical conventions of the period and from debates occurring among Jews both within the Church and with Jews outside the Church. For example, there is a widespread scholarly consensus that the Gospel of John was composed in a largely Jewish Church that at one point in its history became estranged from the local Jewish community. The anger and argumentative **rhetoric** of this internecine struggle is apparent in the Gospel's frequent negative use of *hoi Ioudaioi* (= 'the Jews') and its exclusivist assertion that only believers in **Jesus** would escape condemnation.

Critical scholarship has also disclosed that the Late Second Temple Period Jewish world was far more diverse than previously thought. The creative interplay of **apocalypticism** and **eschatology** with Temple- and Torah-centred Jewish traditions in the cultural context of **Hellenism** and the political rule of the **Roman Empire** was the setting in which the earliest churches and forebears of the rabbis functioned. Biblical critical research unearths how such ideas as God's rule, **Messiahs**, **resurrection**, election, **redemption**, **incarnation**, **angels** and scriptural interpretation unfolded differently in Rabbinic Judaism and Christianity.

Historical critical studies are also crucial for understanding the four Gospel **passion narratives**. Vulnerable to persecution by the Roman Empire as an illegal sect, the Gospels' authors tend to exonerate Roman officials for Jesus' execution with the result that Jewish characters play a larger role than is historically probable. The results of such critical investigations of the passion narratives have been incorporated into some official Christian teaching documents. It should also be noted that critical research into the ministry of the **historical Jesus**, apart from the circumstances of the **crucifixion**, affects how the Christian religious imagination conceives of his mission and his interactions with Jewish contemporaries.

It should be noted that studies of teaching materials have demonstrated that the use or absence of critical biblical scholarship is the greatest single determinant of whether Jews and Judaism are presented positively or negatively in Christian **textbooks**.

Questions still remain about how to relate biblical critical studies to the Christian doctrinal tradition. The resulting tensions can impact Jewish–Christian relations. This is true both for the pastoral and doctrinal implications of New Testament texts and for the relationship between the two 'testaments' of the Christian Bible (*see* **biblical theology**).   *PHILIP A. CUNNINGHAM*

Biblical interpretation

Jews and Christians may share a significant portion of the **Bible**, but their differing interpretations lie at the heart of the tensions and conflicts between the two communities, as well as within each community. These differences are also the source of mutual enrichment, particularly today when many Jewish and Christian scholars collaborate. The continued vitality of Jewish–Christian relations depends in large measure on each community understanding and appreciating interpretive similarities and dissimilarities, without exaggerating either.

As a classical text of antiquity compiled over many centuries, the Bible invites and requires interpreting. Readers can discern an interpretive process

at work even within its own pages (cf. Exod. 34.28 and Deut. 4.13). Extra-canonical texts, such as the **Dead Sea Scrolls** and the **Pseudepigrapha**, reveal a variety of methods by which interpreters of the Second Temple Period made meaning of ancient texts. In the first century BCE, Hillel synthesised these into seven rules for the exposition of texts; later rabbis expanded these principles to 13 and then to 32.

Methods alone, however, do not determine meaning. Rather, the presuppositions of the interpreting community shape the construal of texts; the way the **New Testament** draws on texts from the **Old Testament** provides a case in point. As Jews, the early followers of **Jesus** looked to the scriptures to articulate and make sense of their emerging beliefs. Later they drew upon these texts in their own writings in accord with Jewish modes of interpretation. Yet they approached the scriptures with a distinctive premise: Jesus was Messiah and Lord. Thus began an intra-familial debate about the right way to interpret **Torah**.

Several generations later, however, this debate intensified into a serious rivalry between Christians, an illicit religious **minority** in the **Roman Empire** until 313, and their sibling Judaism, long established and well respected. Much of the Christian challenge revolved around the scriptures. Christian teachers such as **Justin Martyr**, **Tertullian** and **Origen** argued that the Jews misinterpreted their own scriptures by reading them literally. As a consequence, the Jews were blind to God's ways, unable to read the prophecies correctly, that is, to see the prophets as pointing to Jesus. In the course of argument, Christian apologists levelled charges that proved long-lasting and destructive: Jews were mired in the **Law** and lacked faith. Christians had become the true spiritual **Israel** – *verus Israel* – superseding Jews. Thus they were now the sagacious interpreters of Israel's scriptures: 'For we believe and obey them, whereas you, though you read them, do not grasp their spirit' (Justin Martyr, *Dialogue with Trypho*, *c*.135). Others framed their arguments more abrasively. The *Epistle of Barnabas* portrayed Jews as 'wretched people who went astray' (16.1); therefore, God abolished their rites and practices, establishing instead a **covenant** with the followers of Jesus.

Typology, a widespread mode of reading multiple levels of meaning in texts, became an important tool in the Christian apologetic arsenal. **Augustine's**

aphorism summarises its premise: 'In the Old Testament the New Testament lies hid; in the New Testament the Old Testament becomes clear' (*Questions on the Heptateuch* 2.73). Accordingly, the story of the near-sacrifice of Isaac (Gen. 22) became a type of the **crucifixion** of Jesus, the exodus through the Red Sea a type of **baptism**, and **Noah**'s ark a type of the church. The events and characters of the Old Testament foreshadowed what Christ fulfilled; the prophets predicted his Messianic character. Thus, the **early Church** writers established an enduring theological trajectory that denied legitimacy to Jewish readings of scripture.

Jewish interpreters preserved the Bible for their own community and countered Christian claims by exposition of both the literal meaning of passages (*peshat*) and the ethical and mystical layers (*darash*). The famous dictum attributed to Rabbi Ben Bag-Bag in the **Mishnah** exemplifies the rabbinic genius of attentiveness to every dimension of a text: 'Turn it, and turn it and turn it again, for everything is in it' (*Pirke Avot* 5.22). The **Talmud** and collections of **midrashim** (creative interpretations of both legal and narrative materials) became the principal lenses through which Jews interpreted the Bible. The tragedies of history offered another lens: the twelfth-century liturgical poem structured around the **binding of Isaac** in Gen. 22 (the *Akedah*) laments the massacres unleashed by the **Crusades**. The Late Middle Ages also witnessed the emergence of eminent interpreters such as **Rashi**, Abraham **ibn Ezra** and David **Kimhi**. Their learned biblical commentaries enriched Jewish life and influenced Christian scholars such as Nicholas of **Lyra**, and Hugh and **Andrew of St Victor** to give greater weight to the literal meaning of passages and thereby offset the excesses of typology and **allegory** among Christian exegetes. The **Reformation** extended this emphasis, precipitating the advent of historical criticism in the nineteenth century (*see* **biblical criticism**). Although both Jewish and Christian scholars use historical criticism in its more developed forms today, in its early years it was deeply anti-Jewish in its assumptions about the legalism of post-exilic or 'late' Judaism (*Spätjudentum*) and the Christocentric character of 'salvation history' (*Heilsgeschichte*).

The refinement of critical methods in the twentieth and early twenty-first centuries has made possible remarkable collaboration in every aspect of biblical interpretation, and not only in translation and **exegesis**. Scholars join forces to study topics that have been the source of division (e.g. joint analyses of the **Dead Sea Scrolls**, the concept of the **Messiah**, and **anti-Judaism** in Christian writings). A radical change in attitude toward Jewish interpretation is evident among many scholars and in some Churches. A 2001 document from the Vatican's Pontifical Biblical Commission acknowledges that 'Christians can and ought to admit that the Jewish reading of the Bible is a possible one, in continuity with the Jewish Sacred Scriptures from the Second Temple period, a reading analogous to the Christian reading which developed in parallel fashion' (*The Jewish People and their Sacred Scriptures in the Christian Bible*, II, A, 7). Christians can 'learn much from Jewish exegesis practiced for two thousand years'.

Mutual study cannot (and should not) resolve the differences that shape the particularities of each community. The **canon**, both in content and order, will remain a boundary marker, as will the differing presuppositions each community brings to the interpretive process. Talmud and **commentary** will continue to shape Jewish readings, paralleled to an extent by **Roman Catholic** and **Orthodox** emphasis on **tradition**, but differing from many Protestant readings, especially in **evangelical** and **fundamentalist** circles.

Nonetheless, significant commonalities must be recognised. Both Jews and Christians regard their respective scriptures as a revelatory text. Both read them in a liturgical context. Both interpret the Bible as essential to their **identity** and practice: forming persons in an understanding of who they are and how they are to live as Jews and Christians in the present in anticipation of the fullness of God's reign.

MARY C. BOYS

Biblical theology

Biblical theology is primarily a Christian endeavour to develop an overarching theological framework that encompasses both the **Old Testament** and the **New Testament** of the Christian **Bible**. Although this synthetic effort is sometimes called 'Old Testament theology', it essentially seeks to relate the scriptures of ancient Israel to the Christian New Testament. The project directly impacts Jewish–Christian relations since 'the meeting between the people of God of the Old Covenant, never revoked by God, and that of the New Covenant, is at the same time a dialogue . . . between the first and the second part of [the church's] Bible' (**John Paul II**, 17 November 1980).

The construction of a theological synthesis of the biblical books in the Tanakh has not appealed to Jewish interpreters, but in recent times some Jewish scholars 'have not "moved on" from Bible to Talmud but have remained focused on the Bible, applying their reading of the Bible to everything else they learn' (Tikva Frymer-Kensky, in Bellis and Kaminsky (eds), *Jews, Christians and the Theology of the Hebrew Scriptures*, 113). The significance of this for a Jewish 'biblical theology' remains to be seen.

When **supersessionism** dominated Christian theology, Christians concluded that the Old Testament had religious value only insofar as it prepared for the coming of Christ and the Church. Thus, the 'Old' Testament was – with rare exceptions such as the work of **Andrew of St Victor** – thoroughly subsumed by Christians into New Testament perspectives and categories. However, the rise of historical criticism (*see* **biblical criticism**) in the modern period eventually contributed to a new Christian appreciation of the independent spiritual wealth of the biblical and post-biblical Jewish traditions. The attendant recognition of the multiplicity of not easily harmonised theological perspectives in the Old Testament made the effort to devise an overarching biblical theology even more problematic. In addition, **postmodern** understandings that the meaning of a text derives from a dialectical interaction between a text and its reader(s) undermined the modernist ideal of a univocal textual meaning. Thus, the Church's traditional **Christological** reading of the Old Testament could be described as 'a retrospective perception whose point of departure is not in the text as such, but in the events of the New Testament proclaimed by the apostolic preaching' (Pontifical Biblical Commission (PBC), *The Jewish People and their Sacred Scriptures in the Christian Bible*, §21, 2001). Rabbinic readings of the Tanakh were thus 'parallel' and 'analogous' (PBC, §22) to Christian readings of the Old Testament, raising the question of why a biblical theology developed by looking backwards through New Testament lenses should be automatically superior to alternative readings. The task of relating the two Testaments is so vexing that one scholar has concluded that 'we are as yet nowhere close to knowing how to write an Old Testament theology' (Blenkinsopp, 'Tanakh and New Testament', 113).

The need for a new paradigm is evident in the many attempts to develop different nomenclature than the traditional 'Old Testament' and 'New Testament', but despite the lack of terminological consensus, it may be that some essential components or principles for constructing a **post-supersessionist** Christian biblical theology are now emerging:

1. The independent theological validity of Israel's scriptures in their own ancient contexts must be affirmed. This would seem to be required by the Christian rejection of Marcionism (*see* **Marcion**).

2. There should be a Christian acknowledgement 'that these Scriptures are the Holy Scriptures of Judaism as well as of Christianity' (Rolf Rendtorff, in Bellis & Kaminsky, 144). This means, for example, that Jewish and Christian interpreters need to grapple with the theological consequences of the different orderings of the biblical books in the canons of the Old Testament and the Tanakh.

3. Since 'the New Testament often does no more than resume' the scriptures of ancient Israel (Pontifical Commission for Religious Relations with the Jews, *Notes*, II, 7, 1985), Christians would miss much of great spiritual worth if they were to encounter ancient Israel's scriptures only through the limited New Testament citations of them. A biblical treatment of why the innocent suffer, for example, would be inadequate if only New Testament texts were considered and Job, Ecclesiastes, Isaiah and certain Psalms were ignored.

4. False polarisations, such as supposedly between 'law' and 'gospel', should be avoided. 'The Hebrew Bible is full of gospel, and Christian tradition, not only Catholic but also Protestant, is far from being without law' (Rendtorff, in Bellis and Kaminsky, 149). Dichotomous perspectives inevitably oversimplify the polyvalent richness of the scriptures and the Jewish and Christian traditions.

5. It is futile for a biblical theology to pursue comprehensive substantive themes given the

myriad of perspectives in the scriptures of ancient Israel. Rather, those scriptures should be understood as bearing witness to a continuing theological dialogue and interaction between God and humanity, especially the **people of Israel**. Biblical theologians should resist the temptation to bring either ontological or historical closure to their theologising, but ought to affirm an open-ended, multi-dimensional model (Walter Brueggemann, in Bellis and Kaminsky, 100–5).

Clearly, the work of biblical theology is in a period of transition that holds the promise of significant transformation in the years ahead.

PHILIP A. CUNNINGHAM

Bidding prayers *see* **intercessions**
Billerbeck, Paul *see* **Strack–Billerbeck rabbinic commentary**

Binding of Isaac (*Akedah*)

Abraham's attempted sacrifice of Isaac (Gen. 22) portrays Abraham's relationship with God and how his faith in and commitment to God was demonstrated by his willingness to sacrifice his long-awaited son at God's command. Little attention is given to **Isaac** in the well-known biblical account, which has been important from at least as early as the third century CE when it was read at Rosh ha-Shana and **Easter**; it is also mentioned in the **eucharist** ceremony.

Classical interpretations of the binding of Isaac illustrate exegetical interaction between Christian and Jewish interpreters. The rabbis and **Church Fathers** reflect a great deal on the story. In the rabbinic writings, Isaac is no longer portrayed as a peripheral figure but becomes equal, if not superior, to **Abraham**. The rabbis portray Isaac as the willing martyr who volunteers to give up his life for his people. Indeed, such is the merit of Isaac's action that **Israel** benefits from it in the future. For the Church Fathers, Isaac is interpreted typologically. Beginning with the *Epistle of Barnabas*, Isaac is compared to **Jesus** and is a model of the **Christ** who was going to suffer, a **typology** developed in detail by **Melito** and **Origen**.

The rabbinic portrayal of Isaac parallels a number of aspects of the Christian understanding of Jesus. Most striking is the description of Isaac carrying the wood for the sacrifice on his shoulders as 'a man who carries his cross (*ẓaluv*) on his shoulder'

(*Genesis Rabbah* 56.3), an interpretation clearly influenced by the **New Testament** description of Christ carrying his cross to the **crucifixion**. There are a number of other examples of rabbinic interpretations being influenced by Christian teaching. Like Jesus, Isaac was willing to give up his life; was not forced by human hand to carry the cross but carried it freely; was not forced to offer himself as a sacrifice but willingly gave himself up to his father; was described as weeping bitterly when told by Abraham that he was to be sacrificed. Like Jesus, Isaac shed his blood, and is depicted at the gates of Hell. Finally, the *Akedah* was described as atoning for all, Jew and non-Jew, in a similar way to **Paul**'s concept of **baptism**. Thus, Jewish interpretations of the binding of Isaac cannot be properly understood without reference to the Christian context. The rabbis were not only aware of, but were influenced by, Christian **exegesis**.

For their part, Christian scholars were influenced by rabbinic interpretations. For example, **Romanos Melodos** in his description of Isaac being tied hand and foot uses the same wording as the **Mishnah**'s description of the *tamid* offering. The prevention of movement on the part of Isaac is not repeated elsewhere in the patristic writings and is paralleled only by rabbinic interpretations.

EDWARD KESSLER

Bioethics *see* **medical ethics**

Birkat hamazon

Grace after meals. Christian liturgists searching for the origins of the **eucharist** and its accompanying prayers have frequently looked to the Jewish *birkat hamazon*. The **Last Supper** was a Jewish festive meal. Second Temple period evidence suggests that meals, particularly for holidays, had become an important focus of Jewish ritual life. Some groups gathered regularly as *ḥavurot*, (table) fellowships or associations, with their own distinctive sets of rituals, including **blessings** before and after eating. The earliest rabbinic witness, the **Mishnah**, presumes that when a group eats together they will conclude with a communal grace consisting of an invocation and three blessings. The details of these blessings emerge only in later texts: they praise God for providing sustenance, thank God for covenantal elements including the land, and petition God for mercy, especially the rebuilding of **Jerusalem**. The rabbis date a fourth blessing praising God's fundamental goodness to 135 CE; over the centuries much more was added.

If **Jesus** with his **apostles** and the subsequent gatherings of early **Jewish Christians** considered themselves ḥavurot, it is highly likely that their meal-based rituals adapted this model. One would expect to see traces of this in the emerging eucharistic liturgies of the **early Church**. Leading scholars have suggested parallels between the structures and themes of early Christian eucharistic prayers and the later documentable texts of the *birkat hamazon*. However, there is simply no evidence to prove or disprove their suppositions. We know almost nothing about the variety of Jewish (or Christian) liturgical practices in the period when the eucharist emerged. *RUTH LANGER*

Birkat ha-minim

The **Talmud** (*Berakhot* 28b–29a) records that the *birkat ha-minim* (the malediction of the sectarians/heretics) was established under Rabban **Gamaliel** II's direction in the late first century as an apparent addition to the *Amidah* as its twelfth blessing. The occasion for this enactment and its original object has been the subject of significant scholarly speculation. The suggestion that it was a specific response to Christianity, explaining John's references (9.22; 12.42; 16.2) to the eviction of Christians from the synagogue, is now largely rejected. Epiphanius (*c*.315–403) and **Jerome** are the first **Church Fathers** to refer to it unambiguously, and they know that it curses **Jewish Christians**, calling them *minim* and Nazarenes. No Jewish texts pre-date the ninth century CE, when some, but not all, do indeed specify these categories, among others. One version from the **Cairo Genizah**, likely recited by Jews living under **Islam**, reads: 'May there be no hope for the apostates, and may the arrogant empire be uprooted, smashed, and brought low speedily in our days, and may the *noẓerim* and the *minim* be immediately lost.' The precise application of the blessing's terms depended on the historical realities of the worshippers. *Noẓerim* and *minim* probably originally referred to Jewish Christians, but likely later came to refer to Gentile Christians as well. *Minim* at times seems also to refer not to a specific group, but rather to Jewish heretics in general. For Jews living in Christian lands, whose text did not include the more specific *noẓerim*, *minim* often did designate Christians. From at least as early as the mid-sixteenth century Christian

censors, sensitive also to the blessing's curse of converts to Christianity and its prayers for the downfall of persecuting governments and of Israel's enemies, forced changes to this prayer (*see* **censorship**). Many twentieth-century texts pray for the downfall of 'evil' and of God's enemies and omit all reference to **apostates** and *minim*. *RUTH LANGER*

Black Christian–Jewish relations

Because of the history of slavery in the Americas, Black Christians are aware of a shared narrative with Judaism of oppression and God's deliverance. During the civil rights era in the **United States**, relations between Black Christians and Jews deepened. For example, many of the marchers and Freedom Riders in the 1960s were Jews and Black Christians. The Reverend James Bevel (b. 1936), a leader of the Southern Christian Leadership Conference in Selma, Alabama, wore a *kippah* at several civil rights rallies, and Rev. Martin Luther King (1929–68) supported human and civil rights for Jews, used the Jewish experience in his speeches and called for Baptists to stop trying to convert Jews. When King spoke at the Conservative Rabbinical Assembly's convention in 1968, he was greeted by over a thousand rabbis singing 'We Shall Overcome' in Hebrew. King was planning to join Rabbi Abraham Joshua **Heschel** for a Passover seder in 1968, but was assassinated before such fellowship could occur. These examples provide a glimpse of a positive social relationship between Black Christians and Jews.

There have also been difficulties in the social relationship, however, particularly in the United States, a country in which colour racism is a more profound problem than **antisemitism**. Some Blacks see Jews as robbing them of their **identity** as 'most oppressed group' as a result of the **Holocaust**, and for their part Jews express concerns at the controversial comments of Black Christian leaders such as Rev. Louis Farrakan (b. 1933) and Rev. Jesse Jackson (b. 1941). One of the most influential figures in Black Christian–Jewish relations, Hubert Locke (b. 1934), has written about the similarities between the experiences of Blacks and Jews in Western societies (**diaspora**; legal restriction; post-**emancipation** marginality). Noting German race 'scientists" work on Black people, he has challenged the notion of the Holocaust as a uniquely Jewish experience and argues for solidarity between Black Christians and Jews, urging them to challenge

Western nations to live up to their claims of justice and equality.

From a biblical and theological perspective, there are a number of common themes that are central to both Black Christian and Jewish identities. For example, for an oppressed people faith in God requires the vision to see that God will deliver them out of oppression as God delivered the Israelites from Egypt. Jews and Black Christians have thus found deep similarity through the theme of Exodus. On the one hand they were slaves and yet they are the children of promise. Both Black theology and Judaism assume a spiritual vision about the reconstruction of a new humanity no longer defined by oppression but by liberation. According to Black theology, reflection about God is not only rational discourse about ultimate reality, but practical justice meted out by those oppressed. A similar description can be applied to Jewish theology in its emphasis on the presence of God and the practice of the community in knowing God. Both Black theology and Jewish theology abide by the tenets of **liberation theology**, although divergent attitudes towards the **State of Israel** cause friction. Again, God's election establishes a **covenant**, which imprints upon Israel an obligation to respond in faith and obedience to God. Black Christians came to interpret God's covenant with Israel as creating Israel as a distinct nation, not a distinct *ethnoi*, enabling, for example, Black Jews (such as **Ethiopian** Jews) to be intelligible to Black Christians.

However, just as there are tensions in the social relationship, there are also problems in the theological encounter between Black Christians and Jews. For Black Christians, Blackness is defined as all victims of oppression who realise that the survival of their humanity is bound up with their liberation from whiteness. Blacks live in a society in which Blackness means criminality, subhumanity and anarchy. It is not clear to them to what extent Jewish identity is capable of being white or black, or to what extent Jewish theology claims a theological anthropology similar to that of Black theology. *MICHAEL BATTLE*

Black Death

The wave of disease that ravaged the European population between 1347 and 1351 also marked a period of suffering and destruction for Jewish communities. The Black Death was a plague caused by the *Yersinia pestis*, a bacterium that resides in the stomachs of fleas, and thus spreads through the movement of small mammals, whose furs form their habitat. Spreading from central Asia to the shore of the Black Sea, the epidemic crossed Europe, killing at least a third and probably closer to a half of the European population. The densely settled urban communities – where most Jews lived – were particularly badly struck. Every aspect of life was affected: family life was disrupted, harvest perished in fields, church services all but ceased with the death of priests, political institutions ground to a halt. In the midst of these traumatising events rumours began to circulate about a Jewish plot to poison wells and cause the mortality. One chronicler even supplied the recipe for such a poison, which included crumbs of a consecrated eucharistic wafer. Pope Clement VI (1342–52) attempted to quash these accusations and encouraged urban authorities to protect the Jews, but in hundreds of cities of the Holy Roman Empire and the Low Countries, where most Jews resided in the later Middle Ages, massacres of whole communities resulted, especially in the Rhineland – Frankfurt, Mainz and Cologne – but also further east, notably in Prague. The Mainz *Memorbuch* listed 279 affected communities, and survivors commemorated the dead in **liturgy**. The massacres declined with the virulence of the plague, leaving displaced Jews, who in many cases (like Prague) were eventually allowed to resettle. *MIRI RUBIN*

Black theology *see* **Black Christian–Jewish relations**

Blasphemy

The interpretation of the charge of blasphemy, as proposed in the literary reports of the **trial of Jesus**, has been an obstacle to fruitful Jewish–Christian relations. Misinterpretation has contributed to the charge of **deicide** laid by Christians against Jews.

Basically the term means 'to curse God', in the sense of repudiation or speaking contemptuously of the divinity. The punishment for blasphemy recorded in the **Torah** was stoning (Lev. 24.10–23), while the **Mishnah** confirmed death by stoning but restricted its definition of blasphemy to those cases where the name of YHWH had been pronounced after the accused had been warned by two witnesses (*Sanhedrin* 7.5). In the **Talmud** Rabbi Meir extended the prohibition to include the substitute names of God. The prohibition of blasphemy was also considered incumbent on Gentiles as one of the **Noachide Laws** (*Sanhedrin* 56a, 60a).

The Gospel traditions include instances where, during his ministry, 'Jews' accused **Jesus** of blasphemy. For example, in John 10.33 the Jews (*hoi Ioudaioi*) state: 'It is not for a good work that we are going to stone you but for blasphemy, because you, though only a human being, are making yourself God.' It is unclear what precisely would have been entailed in blasphemy in the first century CE, but it can be assumed that Jesus' statement that he acted *in loco* YHWH would have sufficed. Thus the story in Mark 2.1–12, where Jesus claims to forgive sins and therefore to control the channel of **forgiveness** in society, is an implied claim to divine authority and would have laid Jesus open to the charge. The judicial charge of blasphemy laid against Jesus by the High Priest **Caiaphas** is recounted in Mark (14.61–66). Jesus was accused of claiming to assume the two titles 'Messiah' and 'Son of the Blessed One'. The twin titles would have been derived from a Christian midrashic reading of Ps. 2. Jesus replies obliquely to the charge with the response of 'I am' and 'you will see the **Son of Man** seated at the right hand of the Power'. 'I am' in this context of self-disclosure must refer to the revelation formula connected with the divine name of YHWH. Mark's Jesus thus corrects the two titles in the indictment by substituting 'Son of Man', making clear the Daniel context in which the Son of Man is depicted as the judge of the world at the end of times. Later Gospels had difficulty with the Markan text: Matthew changes the 'Son of the Blessed One' to the more direct '**Son of God**' and paraphrases the ambiguous 'I am'; in Luke the term 'blasphemy' does not appear and the 'I am' is turned into an innocuous statement. However, before **Pilate**, in all Gospels, the charge is based not on the two allegedly blasphemous titles but on Jesus' claim to be 'King of the Jews', which had seditious overtones.

The indictment in the **Sanhedrin** trial is too closely connected with a reading of Ps. 2 to be considered historical. It is more likely the fruit of later Christian reflection on the psalm, which endeavoured to transfer blame for the death of Jesus from the Romans to the Jews; this judicial charge would then have been read back into the Gospel accounts of confrontations between Jesus and Jewish groups during his ministry. Historically, Jesus would not have been condemned for the religious crime of blasphemy, which carried the penalty of stoning and in which the Romans would have had no interest, but for suspected seditious activity against civil order, which carried the penalty of **crucifixion**. However, the Jewish charge of blasphemy and its relationship to the consequent crucifixion continued to be taken as historical fact and provided the basis for the counter-charge that the Jews had killed Jesus and thereby brought down God's judgement on themselves. The literalist reading of the **passion narratives** and the charge of blasphemy in the trial of Jesus have been an ongoing obstacle to Jewish–Christian relations. *ROBERT CROTTY*

Blessings and curses

Jewish and Christian blessing and curse traditions are closely related in origin. Hebrew blessings and apotropaic curse texts are found from the early seventh century BCE onwards, and continue and develop for centuries. From the early centuries CE curse traditions are eclectic, mixing language and imagery from Jewish, Christian and other religious traditions, so that it is not always easy to identify their religious origins. Blessing became a standard part of ancient ritual, and more developed forms, such as the *Amidah*, are well known.

The biblical paradigm of blessing and cursing from Mounts Gerizim and Ebal respectively in Deut. 27–28 on those who follow or disobey the law early on became an image in **disputation**. Likewise, the 'curse of the law' (Gal. 3) has been an issue of discussion in Jewish–Christian relations. As a difficult text it could be seen as implying that Jews are cursed, and therefore contribute to anti-Jewish teaching. The 'curse' in this sense can be seen as referring to the covenantal curses enacted from Mount Ebal, and therefore the expression emphasises the covenantal obligation of the **law**. Positive statements calling for blessing rather than cursing can be found in the **New Testament** itself (e.g. Rom. 12.4 and Ja. 3.8–10) and can be used to counteract any contemporary misunderstanding of such images. *JAMES K. AITKEN*

Blood

Blood in Judaism and Christianity is laden with meaning. Basic to both religions is the **Torah**'s notion that a living being's '**soul** [or life, *nefesh*] is in the blood' (Lev. 17.11; Gen. 9.4): that is, blood is either **life** itself or the seat of life. Bloodshed represents the taking of life, and in sacrificial ritual the victim's spilled blood is vital to the atonement obtained. A key **New Testament** passage here is Heb. 9.22, which ends with the proviso 'without the shedding of blood, no forgiveness occurs', a 'cultic maxim well known in Jewish tradition' (Attridge, *The Epistle to the Hebrews*, 258). Christianity departs from Judaism with the notion that **Jesus**' shed blood serves as a **sacrifice** (propitiatory and/or expiatory) for the **forgiveness** of the world's sins. At Rom. 5.9 Jesus' death is referred to as 'blood' (Tuckett, 'Atonement in the NT'). When the **early Church** was deciding which laws or customs from Judaism should carry over into Christianity, abstention from eating blood was an important inclusion (Acts 15.20–29). Likely here we see an early manifestation of what later came to be called **Noachide laws**, requirements that many ancient Jews felt were binding on Gentiles (or necessary for aliens living among Israelites according to Mosaic **Law**). This prohibition is attested for centuries within the church (Bockmuehl, *Jewish Law in Gentile Churches*, 166–7). Its historically strictest application is among **Jehovah's Witnesses**, who extend it to the sphere of medicine, forbidding whole blood transfusions, though they do permit some blood products and therapies.

See also **blood libel**; **dietary laws**; **eucharist**; **food**   *FRANK SHAW*

Blood libel

Blood libel refers to the accusation that Jews kill a young Christian boy and use his blood in the ritual preparation of unleavened bread or *mazzah* for the **Passover** ritual. Although there is some indication that it may be traced to eleventh-century **Germany**, the earliest direct evidence is the case of **William of Norwich** in 1144. Charges spread from England to **France** (1171) and **Spain** (1182) and throughout Europe by the seventeenth century. Despite official secular and ecclesiastical investigations in the thirteenth century by Emperor Frederick II (*r*.1215–50) and Pope **Innocent IV** that denied any possibility that Jews used human blood, accusations continued against the Jewish community in Western and Eastern Europe into the twentieth century. The Nazis revived the charges that Jews killed children and used their blood. The blood libel has also become part of the arsenal of anti-Jewish agitation in extreme forms of contemporary **Islam**. The origins of blood libel appear in antiquity, where **Josephus** relates that Antiochus Epiphanes (*r*.175–164 BCE) was told that Jews engage in human

sacrifice and cannibalism within the precincts of the **Temple**. Ironically, **Tertullian** reports that early Christians were also accused of eating human flesh. By the Middle Ages the blood libel incorporated the idea that Jews engaged in conspiracy to lure Christian boys; that they used the blood in the preparation of matzah, or to engage in **magic**. By extension of the blood libel, Jews were accused of stealing the consecrated wafer of the **eucharist** and mutilating it until blood flowed. Jews were also accused of poisoning water wells during the period of the **Black Death**. Scholars have been unable to explain the persistence of this perduring invention. It may have its origins in xenophobia, fuelled by the psychology of projection and inversion, where a central principle such as the real presence in Christianity is projected onto the Jewish community, whose scripture provides details of blood **sacrifice** (Leviticus). Irrespective of its origins, the blood libel has served as an explanation for the continuing existence of the Jewish people as enemies of Christ: Jewish success despite persecution is attributed to furtive practices that subvert the truth of Christianity and weaken it.

See also **Hugh of Lincoln; Rozanov, Vasily Vasileyevich; Russia**   *MICHAEL A. SIGNER*

Bonhoeffer, Dietrich (1906–45)

Protestant Pastor and theologian hanged for involvement in an attempt to assassinate **Hitler**. His view of Judaism is controversial. He qualified as a lecturer in 1930 and was ordained in 1931. He helped form the **Confessing Church**, which resisted state interference in Church life. From 1935 he led an illegal seminary and from 1939 worked for German military intelligence while exploiting ecumenical contacts on behalf of the resistance. Arrested in 1943, partly for smuggling Jews to Switzerland, he was hanged at Flossenburg when evidence of complicity in the 1944 plot against Hitler emerged.

Bonhoeffer's 1933 essay 'The Church and the Jewish Question' echoed **Luther** in asserting that the '**chosen people**' crucified Christ and must bear a curse in history. But it admonished the state for failing to protect Jews against persecution, insisted the Church is responsible for victims of persecution irrespective of religious confession, and advocated direct action for victims. Bonhoeffer resisted the trend in German Protestantism theologically to marginalise or abandon the 'Old Testament', manifest at its most extreme in the pro-Nazi 'German Christian' movement. He joined the conspiracy in disillusionment with the Confessing Church's policy to defend only baptised Jews. His wartime writings suggest development in his attitudes to Judaism. He believed expelling Jews from Europe meant expelling Christ, and in his *Ethics* wrote 'the Jew keeps open the question of Christ', suggesting that the continuing existence of Judaism was essential to the continuance of Christianity. Contemporary debate turns on whether he is regarded as part of the problem Jewish–Christian relations must resolve, or is one of the few theologians who made future **dialogue** possible.   *STEPHEN PLANT*

Bread

The staple food of the grain-based cultures of the Middle East, bread achieved symbolic value in the Jewish culture that gave birth to Christianity and Judaism. In the **Temple** cult, daily **sacrifices** included various forms of bread, called the *minḥah*; 12 loaves, renewed weekly, probably representing the 12 tribes, constituted the 'showbread' displayed before God. The Temple cult distinguished between leavened and unleavened bread for various functions. Unleavened bread, *maẓẓah*, is the central ritual food of **Passover**, when all leavened food, *ḥameẓ*, is forbidden, recalling the bread of affliction cooked in haste in the exodus from Egypt (Exod. 12.15–20, 39). In the **Hebrew Bible** 'bread' functions frequently as a synecdoche for **food** in general, its paucity representing poverty (e.g. 1 Kgs 22.27; Isa. 30.20; 2 Chr. 18.26). This meaning echoes in the **Lord's Prayer**, where 'daily bread' alludes to Prov. 30.8–9, the 'allotted bread' of necessary sustenance.

Rabbinic Judaism to today demonstrates substantial continuity with the biblical understanding. While grain sacrifices no longer exist, bakers remove and burn a small portion of the dough, the *ḥallah*, in commemoration (thus the name for the special **Sabbath** and festival loaves). Early modern Yiddish women's prayers (*teḥines*) for discarding the *ḥallah* indicate that women saw this task as distinctly priestly. Eating bread 'establishes a meal' setting; the blessing over bread, unlike other food **blessings**, applies to all kinds of foods consumed during the meal; a meal including bread requires the full grace after meals, *birkat hamazon*.

Jesus' use of bread at the **Last Supper** and its consequent role in the **eucharist** derives from this context. If the Last Supper was a Passover meal, it would have included unleavened bread, as is customary for the eucharist of some churches. Jesus' ritual reference to bread and then **wine** (in all but Luke's institution narrative, i.e. Jesus' directives at the Last Supper for its ongoing observance), reversing the order of rabbinic preprandial rituals, represents either an innovation, an extra-rabbinic Jewish practice or a context including the grace after meals and its cup of wine and not just the meal's beginning. The eucharist's transformation of the meal's bread into a sacrificial element reflects more the role of bread in the Temple than the ceremony's roots in domestic ritual. **Cyril of Jerusalem** (*Mystagogical Catechesis* 4.5) understood the showbread to prefigure the eucharist, requiring similar purity for those consuming it. Thus, the bread, with the wine, become the ultimate elements of Christian ritual sacrifice; it combines the Temple's grain offering symbolically with the animal sacrifices of flesh and blood.

The intertwining of domestic and sacrificial continued in the **early Church** when eucharistic gatherings occurred in domestic settings; with the development of dedicated and elaborated church buildings, the table became increasingly an **altar**, set apart from the greater community as **sacred space**, thus emphasising its sacrificial aspects. Some contemporary liturgical reforms seek to retrieve the domestic roots of the ritual. In contrast, the consumed bread retains a purely domestic role in Judaism. However, the elaborated, often braided forms of the Sabbath and festival loaves, perhaps developed in imitation of festive loaves in Christian milieus in which Jews lived, elevate that bread from the level of the mundane.

RUTH LANGER

Brenner, Joseph Chaim (1881–1921)

Hebrew novelist and critic. A number of Brenner's novels and stories, most of which contain marked autobiographical elements, deal with Jewish–Christian relations. *Shanah Aḥat* ('One Year') reflects his experiences in the Russian army from 1901–3, emphasising the contempt in which Jewish recruits were held by both the Christian officers and their fellow conscripts. Arrested as a deserter at the outbreak of the Russo-Japanese war, Brenner spent many months in a series of prisons, before being physically rescued and smuggled across the border into Germany. His experiences are graphically portrayed in his novel *Me-Aleph ad Mem* ('From A to M'), once again depicting the bitter relationship between Jewish and Christian prisoners and their warders. Proceeding to London in 1904, Brenner lived in the East End Jewish ghetto for three years. Although his works in London are concerned primarily with the degradation of Jewish life, one of his stories, 'Rosh-Hodesh Mai' ('The First of May'), contrasts the miserable Jewish trade unionists unfavourably with their dignified Christian counterparts. Arriving in Palestine in 1909, where he remained until his murder by Arabs in 1921, Brenner experienced harsh conditions worsened still further by the ravages of the First World War. The wretched conditions portrayed in his last three novels are symbolised in the final paragraph of *Mi-Kan u-mi-Kan* ('From Here and There') where the old idealist Aryeh Lapidot and the young boy Amram stand guard in an empty field with their heads crowned with thorns – a clear Christian reference. Brenner preached a simple but powerful message – responsibility for everyone and at all times, and above all compassion.

DAVID PATTERSON

British Israelites

British Israelites hold that the British and American (or 'Anglo-Saxon') peoples are the surviving remnant of the ten 'lost' tribes of **Israel**, the true descendants of **Jacob**, and the rightful inheritors of the biblical covenants between God and the people Israel. There is no single, unified British Israelite **doctrine**, but in general terms, they believe that, following the collapse of the Northern kingdom in 721 BCE, the ten tribes moved northwards and westwards, eventually settling in 'the isles of the seas' (Isa. 11.11; Jer. 31.10), that is, in what is now the **United Kingdom** and **Ireland**. These events, and other prophecies, are enshrined in the Great Pyramid of Giza in Egypt, regarded as the 'temple' in Rev. 11.1.

British Israelites do not constitute a separate Christian denomination, but have influenced the development of a number of groups within conservative **Protestantism**, most notably the Worldwide Church of God. More recently, although British Israelitism did not begin as a hate movement, its **supersessionist** theology has provided a rationale for violently racist Christian Identity churches in the **United States**. Uniting these groups is the view that modern Jews are not genuine Israelites but an apostate people, rejected by God. Some hold that Jews

are descendants of the biblical Judeans, who intermarried with Edomites (*see* **Edom**) and **Samaritans** to the extent that their Israelite 'blood-line' was lost. Others argue that most Jews are European descendants of the **Khazars**, a Turkic people who accepted Judaism in the seventh century CE.

The *Rights of the Kingdom* by John Sadler (1649) foreshadows British Israelitism insofar as it traces links between the constitutions of England and biblical Israel, but the movement's modern forms date from John Wilson's book *Our Israelitish Origin* (1840) and its heyday was in the late nineteenth and early twentieth centuries. The Anglo-Israel Association was formed in 1879, and in 1919 it became the British-Israel World Federation, reflecting the dissemination of British Israelite ideas in North America, where Howard Rand (1889–1991) and William Cameron (1878–1955) were prominent advocates of British Israel ideas. As editor of Henry Ford's newspaper, *The Dearborn Independent*, Cameron authored several **antisemitic** pieces and introduced the *Protocols of the Elders of Zion* to an American readership.

Post-Second World War British Israelite leaders include Texan Baptist John A. Lovell (1907–74), who had an active radio and tract ministry, and Gerald L. K. Smith (1913–70). Born to **Methodist** parents, Smith underwent a powerful conversion experience as a teenager, and became a travelling preacher, pastor and Ku Klux Klansman. His views, informed by modern race 'science', formed a bridge between the older, non-violent British Israelitism of the nineteenth century, and the ultra-right extremism of contemporary Christian Identity movements. Whereas more traditional British Israelites believe that individual Jews may come to share in the **covenant** with God through faith in **Jesus**, Identity movements typically view Jews as a degenerate, mixed race, beyond **salvation**. Moreover, they contend that, as the recipients of God's promises, white 'Aryan' Israelites are mandated to overcome their demonic opponents through violent means.

See also **Judaising Christians**

MELANIE J. WRIGHT

Brother Daniel Affair

In 1962 Daniel Rufeisen (1922–98), a Jewish convert to Christianity, immigrated to **Israel** under the Law of Return. He argued that his **nationality** was Jewish although his religion was Catholic. Complicating the issue was the fact that, according to *halakhah*, as the child of a Jewish mother Brother Daniel was indeed Jewish. The Chief Rabbinate ruled that he should be given citizenship as a Jew, regardless of his faith decisions. The Supreme Court ruled that, despite this and the unusual circumstances (he had saved many Jews during the **Holocaust**), it was not possible to be both a Catholic **priest** and a Jew. While the national term 'Jew' did not necessarily imply the practice of religious Judaism, 'in common parlance' it could not be applied to someone who practised another faith. Although Brother Daniel lost his case, he was later naturalised as an Israeli citizen and lived in a Carmelite monastery in Haifa until his death.   *EDWARD KESSLER*

Bruderhof *see* Anabaptists

Buber, Martin (1878–1965)

Jewish thinker. As a pioneer of dialogic thinking Buber has had a great impact on the Christian world. Against the Orthodox verdict that 'he is already outside (Judaism)', Emmanuel Levinas (1906–95) affirmed the 'obligation to acknowledge Buber's achievement'. Buber helped the churches and Christian theology recognise that God's **covenant** with the Jewish people has not been revoked, and made many Christians aware of the importance of a literal translation of the Bible. Furthermore, without sacrificing his Jewish **identity**, he spoke of having an open, brotherly relationship with **Jesus**.

Born in Vienna, Buber spent his childhood in Lvov, Galicia, with his grandfather Solomon Buber, a recognised expert on the **midrash**. He grew up in a multilingual environment where he encountered Hasidism for the first time; his later writings on Hasidism propagated an individualistically accented piety in a free rendering of the texts. With his *Addresses on Judaism* (1909–11) he exerted considerable influence on the Jewish youth of Central Europe. He promoted the Jewish renaissance of the post-First World War era, and from the perspective of a 'Hebrew **humanism**' understood **Zionism** as a holy way. Buber published his fundamental philosophical treatise *I and Thou* in 1923. In 1925 the first chapters of his German translation of the Bible appeared, a work he began with Franz **Rosenzweig**, continued on his own after Rosenzweig's death in 1929, and completed in 1961. To this day it is widely accepted in the German-speaking Christian world.

In 1923 Buber began lecturing on Jewish philosophy and **ethics** at the University of Frankfurt. Through lectures and publications he actively supported the Jews in **Germany** who were being persecuted by the National Socialists; in 1938 he emigrated to **Jerusalem**, where he was professor of social philosophy at the Hebrew University until 1951. Buber promoted the idea of an Arab-Israeli state, and after the foundation of the **State of Israel** in 1948 lectured extensively in the **United States**, but especially in Germany, establishing his reputation as a leading representative of his generation.

Christian examination of his work, which began during Buber's lifetime, focused on his philosophical thought and his view of the relationship between Judaism and Christianity. In the years following the First World War a number of thinkers – Gabriel Marcel (1889–1973), Eugen **Rosenstock-Huessy**, Rosenzweig and others – had discovered the central importance of encounter for understanding the meaning of truth and human existence, but it was above all Buber in *I and Thou* who propagated the idea. He saw something incomparable in the *I–Thou* relation, which could not be attributed to knowledge or theoretically acquired truth and which establishes the connection between the individual *I* and the eternal *Thou of God*: 'The extended lines of relations meet in the eternal *Thou*. Every particular *Thou* is a glimpse through to the eternal *Thou*' (*I and Thou*, 75).

Christians have been equally attentive to Buber's characterisation of the differences between Christians and Jews. In contrast to Christianity, the immediacy of God in Judaism denotes an 'absence of **incarnation**' with respect to God (*Der Jude und sein Judentum*, 205). Buber discerned a further difference in what he identified as the 'absence of a caesura in the history of humanity' (ibid.). The Church believes in Christ's coming as **redemption**. Judaism is unable to believe this and thus has no knowledge of a caesura; its calendar begins instead with creation. Christian theology has engaged with this twofold objection both by recognising the thread of Buber's arguments and by contradicting them (e.g. Josef Wohlmuth (b. 1938)). Christian reaction to his comparison of Christianity and Judaism in his *Two Types of Faith* (in *Werke 1*, 651–782) has sometimes seemed to reverse Buber's intention: Buber typifies Christianity as faith that accepts facts as true whereas Judaism, in contrast, is faith in the sense of a 'trusting in'; some Christian theologians, however, in their efforts to explain Christian faith as a 'trusting in', have drawn precisely on Buber's criticism of Christianity, interpreting it as a positive insight for their understanding of a Christian 'faith of trust' (Hans Urs von Balthasar (1905–88), Eugen Biser (b. 1918) and others). The following sentences from Buber's preface to *Two Types of Faith* became very popular among Christians: 'Since I was young I have felt that Jesus is my elder brother. That Christianity has seen and sees him as God and redeemer has always been a very serious matter for me which I must try to comprehend for his sake and my sake' (*Werke 1*, 657). Buber's connection of his relationship to Jesus with faithfulness to his Jewish identity has earned him the respect of many Christians.

Buber probably had the most significant impact on Jewish–Christian relations with a statement he made in 1933. In his historic dialogue with the Protestant New Testament scholar Karl Ludwig Schmidt (1891–1956) on 14 January that year he insisted on the following confession, over against the Christian thesis concerning the invalidity of the Old Covenant: 'The Covenant has not been terminated.' His linguistically powerful comparison in particular is quoted again and again: 'The [Christian] cathedral [of Worms] is as it is. The [Jewish] cemetery [of Worms] is as it is. But we have not been rejected' (*Theologische Blätter* 12 (1933), 272f.). Pope **John Paul II** embraced Buber's assertion of the unrevoked nature of God's covenant with the Jewish people: during a pastoral visit to Germany he gave an address to representatives of the Jewish community in Mainz on 17 November 1980 in which he praised Rosenzweig and Buber 'who, through their creative familiarity with the Jewish and German languages, constructed a wonderful bridge for a deeper meeting of both cultural areas'. He also stressed the meaning of **dialogue** as 'the meeting between the people of God of the Old Covenant, never revoked by God (cf. Rom. 11.29), and that of the New Covenant'. John Paul II repeatedly stated his conviction that God's covenant with **Israel** had not been revoked; finally, in the prayer for **forgiveness** he left at the Western Wall of Jerusalem on 26 March 2000, he called the Jewish people simply the 'people of the Covenant'. In this papal recognition one can perhaps see Buber's

effect on Jewish–Christian relations at its most profound.   *HANS HERMANN HENRIX*

Bulgakov, Sergei (1871–1944)

Russian Marxist economist and Orthodox theologian. Born the son of a priest in Livny, Bulgakov abandoned Christianity for Marxism but later returned to the Church. From 1923 he was an Orthodox priest and theologian in Paris's Russian émigré community. Several later essays combine shrewd political commentary on the origins of **antisemitism** and condemnation of racist violence with the disturbing view that 'Jewishness' (*yevreitsvo*) generates its own persecution by remaining distinct from its 'host' community. He understood Bolshevism as a form of secularised 'Jewishness'. His controversial account of 'sophia' sees God's **wisdom** permeating and unifying the whole created order and is indebted to Jewish **mysticism**.   *STEPHEN PLANT*

Burial

Burial is the disposition of a dead body, usually by placing it in a grave or into an above-ground tomb. In both Jewish and Christian traditions burial historically has been the predominant mode of disposal of the dead, and in many cases is the only authorised method. Not only have Jews and Christians made common responses to the various social factors that have influenced the shape of burial practice, with the increasingly common **intermarriage** between Jews and Christians the pastoral questions surrounding the burial of the dead have become more insistent, and **dialogue** at the local level on the construction and leadership of interfaith burial services has been vigorous. But because of significant differences between Jewish and Christian theologies of death, for much of their history the theology and practice of burial in the two communities have taken separate paths.

For the Christian community, burial is an act of faith in the resurrection of the body to eternal life which is promised in the Gospels and prefigured in the disciples' discovery of the empty tomb (Matt. 28; Mark 16; Luke 24; John 20). In all Christian burial rites the prayers and symbolic action point to the hope of resurrection, and to Jesus' own **resurrection** as a model for all Christians. That being said, burial customs among Christians have always been highly diverse, varying according to the social, geographical and denominational circumstances of the deceased. Even today, local and regional traditions remain strong, often superseding the officially sanctioned rites of denominations. Because to be denied a proper burial is understood to be the greatest humiliation one can suffer, both Jews and Christians consider giving each deceased person a 'decent burial' to be of the highest religious importance, and within Judaism it is considered the supreme act of benevolence. Burial societies (*hevrah kaddisha*) were often set up to meet this need in Jewish communities, and among economically and socially disadvantaged Christians similar mechanisms were established to ensure a reverent disposal of the dead.

Scholars have recently worked to uncover the history of mutual influence between Jewish and Christian burial practices. The spread within Judaism of the use of coffins for the encasement of dead bodies and the significance of placing a handful of earth from the Holy Land into a coffin before burial are two possible connections. In the modern period, several social factors have affected the practices of burial for both Jews and Christians alike. In the industrialised West the most important of these was the rise of the funeral trade in the eighteenth and early nineteenth century, which removed many of the rituals of burial from the control of the immediate family of the deceased. With the establishment of the **State of Israel**, the question of exhumation, normally forbidden, has also been debated, and an exception to the general prohibition has been made for those who wish to be reburied there. In recent years the question of the possibility of cremation as an alternative to burial has also been vigorously discussed among both Jewish and Christian theologians. For Christians cremation has traditionally been seen as antithetical to the idea of the resurrection of the body; for Jews it has been seen as a desecration of the body. Although Reformed Jews will occasionally cremate the dead, most Jews still respect rabbinic mandates against cremation, and there remains strong opposition, in both academic theology and pastoral practice, among many Christians. In many heavily urbanised places, however, increasingly limited space for burial has put cremation back on the agenda of both Churches and synagogues. *SUSAN WHITE*

Burning bush

The burning bush has been used symbolically by both Jews and Christians. Its image is drawn from the text of Exod. 3 where **Moses** is confronted by YHWH speaking from a bush that burns but is not consumed. Valiant efforts have been made to identify the bush botanically, but it is now widely accepted that the identification of the bush (Hebrew, *seneh*) is linked to the name of the mountain, Sinai, in the biblical text. As a symbol, the burning bush has been integrated into the badge of the Australian **Council of Christians and Jews**. In the early Christian centuries it was drawn into Christian **iconography**, particularly at St Catherine's monastery at the foot of Sinai where early icons escaped the iconoclasts. There is an icon of Moses removing his sandals before the bush in the Chapel of the Burning Bush. Here, on Saturdays, the monks assemble for the **eucharist**; by custom, those celebrating the eucharist and those visiting the chapel remove their shoes. In the Middle Ages there was a development in Christian understanding of the burning bush. It was used to symbolise the virginal conception of **Jesus**. Just as the bush was said to be not consumed by fire, so too the Virgin **Mary** was penetrated but not consumed by the **Holy Spirit**. Hence there were images of Mary rising from the burning bush. In the fifteenth century Enguerrand Charenton's 'Coronation of the Virgin' (found in the Hospice of Villeneuve les Avignon) made use of this imagery. *ROBERT CROTTY*

Bystanders

Bystanders are persons present at an event who hear or see something, but do not become actively involved in it. The term was applied to the **Holocaust** and it remains particularly important in Jewish–Christian relations, as demonstrated by the following quotation from Yehuda Bauer (b. 1926), historian of the Holocaust: 'Thou shalt not be a victim. Thou shalt not be a perpetrator. Above all, thou shalt not be a bystander.' The perpetrators of the Holocaust constituted a relatively small percentage of a European population that was overwhelmingly Christian, but that population contained millions of bystanders whose detachment, indifference, fear for personal safety, or **antisemitism** aided and abetted – even if unintentionally – the destruction of European Jewry. Few issues vex contemporary Jewish–Christian relations more than how to account for the Holocaust bystanders and how to overcome the widespread phenomenon of bystanding when persons and communities are being treated unjustly. The term has also been applied to the genocide in Rwanda in the 1990s.   *JOHN K. ROTH*

Byzantium/Byzantine Empire

From the reign of Emperor Theodosius I (*r.* 379–95), the Roman Empire, as the Byzantine Empire called itself, adopted as its official religion **Orthodox Christianity**, as defined at the Council of Constantinople (381) and then at later councils called by the emperors. This put on a legal footing opposition between Christians and Jews. Other religions than, and heretical versions of, Christianity were proscribed: sacrifices were forbidden, and ultimately resort was had to persecution. This situation was incorporated in the legal codes of the Byzantine Empire: the **Theodosian Code**, assembled by the authority of Theodosius I's grandson, Theodosius II (408–50), and the *Codex Justinianus*, drawn up by the lawyer Tribonium (late fifth century to 546/7) in the reign of **Justinian I** (527–65). The position of the Jews, however, was special: recognised as belonging to a *religio licita*, Jews were allowed to practise their religion and to continue worshipping in their synagogues; officially persecution was forbidden, and indeed official attitudes were more severe towards Christian **heresy** than Judaism. This status was, however, ambivalent: it was intended to preserve (until the second coming of Christ) the Jews as a standing witness to the truth of the gospel they had rejected; to this end they were to continue in a diminished state, forbidden to have Christian slaves, to proselytise, work for the government, teach in public institutions or serve in the army; nor were they allowed to build new synagogues, or even (in practice) to make major repairs to existing ones. Jewish communities were found throughout the Byzantine Empire, and Jews regularly immigrated from neighbouring Muslim and Western Christian lands. The ban on Jews living in **Jerusalem**, imposed by the Emperor Hadrian (*r.*117–38) after the Jewish revolt of 132 CE, was still held to be in force in the seventh century, on the eve of the Arab Conquest of the Holy Land. The Jews were, however, encouraged by the Emperor **Julian the Apostate** to rebuild the Temple in 362, and their rejoicing at the fall of Jerusalem to the Persians in 614 was deeply resented by Christians. Although persecution was forbidden, the Emperors Herakleios (*r.* 610–41), Leo III (*r.* 717–41), Basil I (*r.*867–86), and Romanos I Lekapenos (*r.*920–44) ordered the forced **baptism** of Jews. This was officially opposed by the Christian Church and condemned by leading theologians, such as Maximus the Confessor (580–662), though individual voluntary **conversions** were welcomed, and indeed encouraged. In the Holy Land the Jewish community, established mainly in Galilee, was ruled by a group of scholars headed by a *nasi*, called in Greek the 'patriarch of the Jews', a position that lasted to the fifth century. In the **Diaspora** Jewish communities tended to live apart, usually near the market and running water, led by rabbis appointed with the consent of the government, enjoying autonomy in religious and social affairs. These communities raised their own taxes and provided various social services: education, care of the sick, burial etc. Part of the communal tax went to the government, though whether there was a special Jewish poll tax is disputed. Jews became prominent as merchants, craftsmen and particularly as physicians. Much valuable light is shed on the Jewish communities of Byzantium, especially in Constantinople, by the account of a journey from **Spain** along the Mediterranean coast to Byzantium in the 1160s by Benjamin of Tudela, who observed that 'the Greeks hate the Jews, whether good or bad, and hold them under a heavy yoke . . . Yet the Jews are rich, kind and charitable.'   *ANDREW LOUTH*

CCCC

Caiaphas (held office 18–37 CE)

Gaining direct rule of Judea in 6 CE, Rome assumed the authority to appoint high priests, whose duties included performing **Temple** rituals, managing the Temple treasury and presiding over the **Sanhedrin**. Son-in-law of the high priest Annas (6–15 CE), Caiaphas was appointed in 18 and held office until 37, when both he and Pontius **Pilate** were dismissed. Although Pilate's subordinate, Caiaphas typically appears in **Passion plays** as his superior and so contributes to the impression that 'Jews' – whom Caiaphas represents – crucified **Jesus** (*see hoi Ioudaioi*). His traditional costuming – luxurious robes, outlandish headgear (sometimes with horns), money in hand – contributes to the stereotype of Jewish cupidity, and his collaboration with **Rome** symbolises Jewish disloyalty to the local population. Ironically, certain Jewish sources support the view of various high priests as rapacious and corrupt. **Josephus** records that the priests of Annas's family were 'heartless when they sit in judgment'.

Historians debate the extent of Caiaphas's involvement in Jesus' death (*see* **trial of Jesus**). Caiaphas's probable relocating of merchants (Matt. 21.12; Mark 11.15; Luke 19.45; John 2.14) from the Mount of Olives to the Temple precincts (*b. Shabbat* 15a; *Sanhedrin* 41a; *Avodah Zarah* 8b) may have prompted Jesus' 'cleansing'; this in turn may have precipitated his arrest. Caiaphas also likely perceived that Jesus, or at least the messianic claims made for him, threatened the peace of **Jerusalem**. This political situation provides the context for Caiaphas's ironic prophecy 'It is better for you to have one man die for the people than that the entire nation perish' (John 11.50; see *Genesis Rabbah* 94.9).   *AMY-JILL LEVINE*

Cain and Abel

According to Gen. 4, Cain and Abel were the first and second sons of **Adam** and **Eve**. Cain killed Abel in a fit of rage because God preferred his brother's offering, thus perpetrating the first murder in biblical history. Christians from earliest times saw this story – along with the stories of two other pairs of brothers, **Isaac** and **Ishmael**, and **Jacob** and Esau – as typifying the relationship between the Jews and the Church, Cain representing the Jews (or, very occasionally, specifically that embodiment of Jewish perfidy, **Judas Iscariot**) and Abel either Christ or the Christian **martyrs**.

Already in Second Temple times Jewish exegetes had identified Abel as the archetype of the righteous man persecuted by the wicked (**Philo**, *On the Sacrifices of Abel and Cain, That the Worse Always Attacks the Better, On the Posterity of Cain*). This idea was taken up in the **New Testament**. Condemning the **Pharisees** for killing God's prophets, Jesus warns: 'On you will come all the righteous blood shed on earth, from the blood of righteous Abel to the blood of Zechariah' (Matt. 23.35). 1 John 3.12 exhorts Christians not to be like Cain who was 'of the evil one, and slew his brother' because 'his works were evil, and his brother's righteous'. Heb. 12.24 contrasts the blood of Abel crying for vengeance from the ground with the blood of Christ which offers **atonement** (cf. Heb. 11.4; Jude 11). These suggestive remarks were elaborated by later Christian writers, and the story of Cain and Abel became a popular subject of Christian **exegesis**, **preaching**, **art** and anti-Jewish **polemics**.

The comparison between **Jesus** and Abel focused mainly on three points. First, Abel as a shepherd foreshadowed Jesus the Good Shepherd (**Isidore of Seville**, *Allegoriae quaedam Script. sac.* 5); Christian art often depicts Abel in Christlike pose holding in his arms or carrying on his shoulders a lamb. Second, both Abel and Christ offered **sacrifices** pleasing to God: the lamb which Abel offered and God accepted prefigured Christ the **Lamb of God** (Ambrose, *Enarrat. Ps.* 12). And third, both were cruelly done to death by their brethren

(**Athanasius**, *Contra Faustum* 12.9–10: 'Abel, the younger brother, was killed by Cain, the elder. So Christ, the head of the younger people, was killed by the elder people, the Jews.')

Once Abel was identified as a type of Christ, or the persecuted Christian, the identification of Cain with the Jews would have seemed obvious to the Christian mind. Christian artists in the Middle Ages express the identity by depicting Cain in a conical Jewish hat. Apart from the fact that Cain was wicked, killed his righteous brother and offered an unacceptable sacrifice, three specific features of the biblical narrative seemed further to confirm the **typology**. First, God was said to have marked Cain with a sign so that no one should kill him. This was interpreted by Christian exegetes in a number of ways: **Augustine** related it to the idea that God had preserved the Jews as a witness to the triumph of the Gospel (*Enarrat. Ps.* 58.1); others linked it with physical marks that the Jew was supposed to carry on his body to show that he was cursed by God. Second, Cain's condemnation to perpetual wandering as an outcast and vagabond was seen as corresponding to the wandering, pariah status of the Jews (*see* **Wandering Jew**). Third, if Eve's mysterious words, 'I have gotten a man with the Lord' (Gen. 4.1) were taken, as by some Christian (and Jewish) interpreters, to mean that Cain was fathered by the **devil** (see already 1 John 3.12), the possibility of a further link with the Jews emerged, for according to one extreme Christian **antisemitic** view the Jews were actually from the seed of Satan.

Curiously, there seems to be little evidence, at least in the classic sources, that Jews attempted to counter directly this Christian use of the Cain and Abel story. Jewish exegetes continued to identify Abel as a type of the righteous and sometimes see Cain as typifying their opponents. Thus **Targum** Pseudo-Jonathan describes Cain as a freethinker who holds that there is 'no judgement, no judge, and no other world'. Whatever group is implicitly attacked here, it is obviously not the Christians (some have suggested the **Sadducees**). But there is no obvious attempt to turn the tables and argue that Abel represents the persecuted Jews and Cain their Christian tormentors. The contrast with Jewish treatments of the Jacob and Esau story, which strongly reflect a knowledge of Christian polemics, could hardly be more pointed.   *PHILIP ALEXANDER*

Cairo Genizah

A depository (from Hebrew and Arabic root *gnz*, 'hide', 'store', 'bury') in the Ben Ezra synagogue of Old Cairo (Fustat) that was used from at least the eleventh until the nineteenth century for worn-out Jewish texts thought to have some sacred element. Over 200,000 fragmentary manuscripts, amounting to as many as 800,000 folios, are housed in numerous libraries around the world, almost 70 per cent at Cambridge University Library in the UK. They were brought there in 1897 by Jewish (e.g. Solomon Schechter (1847–1915)) and Christian scholars (e.g. Margaret Gibson (1843–1920) and Agnes Lewis (1843–1926)) committed to Jewish manuscript research. Their close study demonstrates how the Jewish, Christian and Muslim communities in the eastern Mediterranean in the period of the **Crusades** were socially and economically integrated and exercised mutual religious influences. Religious **conversion** was not uncommon, and the religious texts and notions of the other were mastered and challenged by leading thinkers.   *STEFAN C. REIF*

Calendar

The calendar is an important indicator of how Christianity gradually distinguished itself from Judaism in the early centuries CE. By the fourth century the Christian calendar had adopted festivals, such as **Christmas** and various **martyr** days, that marked it out as clearly distinctive. But the first Christians appear to have kept a fully Jewish calendar, with festivals such as Unleavened Bread (Acts 20.6) and **Pentecost** (Acts 2.1; 20.16); although it is likely that from the very beginning **Passover** was reinterpreted as a commemoration of the **crucifixion**, which would have affected profoundly the character of its observance (see 1 Cor. 5.6–8).

The earliest distinctively Christian day in the calendar appears to have been Sunday or the 'Lord's Day'. Sunday observance is not clearly attested in the **New Testament** (see Acts 20.7; 1 Cor. 16.2), and the meaning of 'Lord's Day' in Rev. 1.10 is open to interpretation. For **Ignatius** (*Magn.* 9), 'Lord's Day' seems to designate the day of the Passion (Easter?); nevertheless, it is clearly conceived as a substitute for the **Sabbath**, which Ignatius condemns. The perhaps contemporary *Epistle of Barnabas* (15.1–9) is more explicit: the Sabbath, now obsolete, must be replaced with the 'eighth day' (Sunday) on which **Jesus** rose. But whilst Sunday was widely observed by the second century, not all Christians considered it as a substitute for the Jewish Sabbath. As late as the fourth century, in Syria, the *Apostolic Constitutions* (7.23 and 30, apparently following the *Didache* 8 and 14) instruct the observance of both the Sabbath (Saturday) and the Lord's Day (Sunday). But the *Didache* (8.1) repudiates the Jewish calendar in other ways, by instructing Christians to fast on Wednesday and Friday, and not with the 'hypocrites' (i.e. Jews or Judaisers) on Monday and Thursday (*see* **fasting**).

Controversies about the date of **Easter**, evident from the late second century, often reflect a concern to distinguish it from the Jewish Passover. Although this was probably not the main issue of the **Quartodeciman controversy**, the observance of Easter on Sunday (rather than on the preceding fourteenth day of the lunar month, the date of Passover) had the effect of drawing it away from its Jewish counterpart. It would appear, however, that Christians in this period still determined the fourteenth of the month (upon which the date of Easter was based) according to when the Jews happened to be celebrating Passover (Eusebius, *Hist. eccl.* 5.24.6). This changed in the third century, when Christians began to determine the date of Easter independently, by calculation (through the use of 'Easter cycles'): the intention, clearly spelled out by **Pseudo-Cyprian** (*De Pascha Computus*), was to break loose from dependency on the Jewish calendar. The Council of Nicaea (325 CE) ruled, furthermore, that the lunar month in which Easter occurred should not be determined according to the Jewish calendar, allegedly always in error (Eusebius, *Vit. Const.* 3.18–9; anti-Jewish invectives are noteworthy in these sources). This led to the adoption of the 'rule of the equinox', whereby Easter should always occur after the vernal equinox (a rule not observed hitherto by Jews); although in many parts of Asia Minor, Syria and the Near East the practice of 'following the Jews' (observing Easter in the same month as Passover) continued for more than one century (*Apostolic Constitutions* 5.17.1–3; John Chrysostom, *Adv. Jud.* 3; Epiphanius, *Panarion* 70.9.13; Socrates, *Ecclesiastical History* 4.28 and 5.21–2). Paradoxically, these changes in the Christian calendar may have had an influence on the Jewish calendar, with the apparent adoption by fourth-century Jews of similarly calculated calendars and also the 'rule of the equinox'.

SACHA STERN

Callixtus II (d. 1124)

Pope (1119–24). A scion of the royal house of Burgundy, Callixtus II oversaw the ending of the quarrel between Rome and the German Empire over the investiture of bishops, and legislated against simony, clerical marriage and concubinage, and ecclesiastical forgery. In 1120 he issued the bull *Sicut Judeis*, forbidding the forced conversion of Jews, upholding their freedom of worship, and maintaining their right to due process of law. Despite many later citations of, and appeals to, this bull, it proved unable to banish anti-Jewish sentiment and activity from the Western Church. *MARCUS PLESTED*

Calvin, John (Jean) (1509–64)

Reformation theologian. John Calvin became a convert to **Protestantism** in 1534 and rapidly rose to a dominant leadership position in the second generation of the **Reformation**. Coming from France, where Jews had been excluded since the fourteenth century, and spending most of his remaining years in Geneva where no Jews lived, he probably had no personal contact with Jews. As one of the more moderate anti-Jewish spokesmen of the Reformation, he never produced writings specifically focused on and against Jews, though he had much to say about them and their faith in many of his writings and particularly in his sermons. Yet he uniquely stressed the unity of the Hebrew scriptures and the **New Testament**, the one **covenant** initiated by **Abraham** and permanently upheld by God, and the continuing importance of the **Law** for Christians. In general, Calvin accepted the Jewish understanding of **Torah** and insisted Christians must learn from Jews in order to understand the **Hebrew Bible**. Through the Law people learned to know the will of God, were restrained from unacceptable behaviour and became aware of sin and their need for God's **redemption**. The Law taught love of God and of neighbours for God's sake, and for Christians it helped them to conform their lives to God's image as shown in **Jesus**. Thus the Mosaic Code remains useful for governing until it is abrogated in the Messianic age; however, he believed Jews wrongly used it as a means of justification. He was very cautious about **Christological** interpretation of the

Old Testament (except for certain passages which he insisted referred to Christ) and he often deviated from traditional Christian interpretation. He insisted that **Israel**'s 'special destiny and mission was to shine forth everywhere' and point the way for others; to Jews alone had God 'bestowed knowledge of his name' (*The Institutes of the Christian Religion* II, 11.11). Calvin was one of the very few voices in the Church speaking against the centuries-old Christian theology of Israel's disinheritance and against seeing the Church as replacing the Jewish people as heir of the covenant. Instead he insisted that God's covenant with the Jewish people is enduring and eternal despite their breaking it. He stressed that the entire reformation confession *sola gratia* (by mercy alone), rooted in God's covenant with Abraham, promises to share Israel's blessing with all people. At times Calvin used 'Israelite' to mean both Jews and Gentiles elected by God as the remnant to be saved. Nevertheless, in his written dialogue with one Jew (*Ad quaestiones et objecta Iudaei cuiusdam*; 'Response to Questions and Objections of a Certain Jew') he affirmed the triumphant Church position, and did not mention God's eternal faithfulness to Israel's covenant. He also cited **Isaiah**'s assertion that when **Messiah** comes 'there will not be full restoration of Israel because a good part will not return to God'. He insisted that the kingdom Christ initiated was a spiritual rather than a materialistic kingdom. To the Jewish objection that Jesus did not initiate the Messianic age with justice, peace and righteousness he replied there could be no peace as long as people were evildoers who did not accept God's redemption in Christ. Calvin could not see Judaism as a viable alternative since 'only Christ is the sole means of salvation'. He never advocated the use of force against Jews, nor attempted to undermine conditions for those moving into Lithuania and Poland (where a goodly number of Reformed Christians also lived), or against Jews still living in parts of Germany. Above all, he looked toward and longed for the new time when Jews and Christians together would praise and worship God with the psalms of David.   *ALICE L. ECKARDT*

Calvinism

Calvinism became a major force in the second stage of the Protestant **Reformation** in France, the Rhine Valley, the Netherlands, Scotland, England and the North American colonies, and a minor force in Poland, Hungary and Bohemia. During

Calvin's extensive correspondence with the spreading Calvinist/Reformed Churches he never revealed hostility to the resident Jewish population in **Poland**. Reformed theology is represented in Presbyterian, Congregational, Puritan and Reformed churches. While these Churches developed their own specific forms under differing local factors and needs, they generally followed Calvin in stressing the pre-eminence of biblical authority including the Old Testament's teachings (**law**) and the ongoing validity of God's **covenant** with **Abraham** and the Jewish community. God's free gift of faith was seen as the undergirding of human responsibility and good works. In worship the singing of the Decalogue (**Ten Commandments**) and **Psalms** played a prominent role, while simplicity of **worship** excluded instrumental **music**, chants, prayers to saints and use of images. Calvinist thought first gave people the idea of ecclesiastical liberty and then of political liberty, and played a major role in the sixteenth-century Dutch revolt, and that of eighteenth-century American colonists. Seventeenth-century Dutch churchmen developed close contact with **rabbis**, along with interest in the meaning of Israel. A Hebrew printing press was founded in Amsterdam in 1626, and the founder's son, **Menasseh ben Israel**, appealed to Oliver **Cromwell** in 1655 for the right of Jews to return to England. Cromwell gave the London **Marrano** Co. informal permission to establish a synagogue and a cemetery. Jews first appeared in the Calvinist Dutch colony of New Amsterdam in 1654 as captives of a French sea captain; the Dutch West India Co. ordered that the 23 Jews be released from prison and given freedom of the colony. Dutch citizens of a Long Island community petitioned that Holland's law of liberty be extended to 'Jews, Turks, and Egyptians'. The relative religious, intellectual and political freedom of Jews in the **Netherlands** cannot all be attributed to Calvinism as the orthodox Calvinists were less tolerant than the prevailing national spirit. In **Italy** the small Waldensian (Calvinist) and Jewish communities developed special links, both espousing biblical **fundamentalism**. Puritan theology in seventeenth-century Holland, Britain and the American colonies came to believe Jews would be restored to their ancient land as a sign of God's impending millennial reign (Restorationism). Calvinists often came to identify their own sufferings, exile and special mission with those of biblical Jews, thus viewing exile less as punishment. New England Puritans based their legal code on the **Old Testament**, respected Jews as living descendants of biblical Israelites, and shared a love of the **Hebrew language**. During the Second World War the Dutch people affirmed their solidarity with their Jewish countrymen and attempted to help them. The Dutch Reformed Church emphasised **Paul**'s teaching that God's election of Israel remains inviolate, and began to rethink its theology regarding **conversion** of Jews. In 1970 it issued a statement that insisted that the **land of Israel** was part of God's lasting election of the Jewish people, and saw the modern 'reunion of people and land' as a sign that it is God's will to be on earth together with man. In some contrast, the Presbyterian Church (USA) in 1987, while affirming that the covenant of Abraham included a promise of land, went on to understand 'land' as a 'biblical metaphor for sustainable life, prosperity, peace, and security' rather than specific property. While affirming God's 'irrevocable' election of the Jewish people and the church as engrafted into Israel's covenant, it reaffirmed its duty to 'bear witness' to all peoples. The Protestant Federation of **France** took a firm stand against the anti-Jewish policies of the Vichy government and the Third Reich. Yet in 1948 its paper to the **World Council of Churches**' first assembly held that the sufferings of the Jewish people were both God's judgement for their unfaithfulness in rejecting **Jesus** and an 'appeal to conversion'. It acknowledged that the aim of general conversion 'cannot be anything less than the spiritual destruction of Israel' (*The Theology of the Churches and the Jewish People*). In 1987 the United Church of Christ (Congregational and Reformed churches) affirmed that God's work in Jesus Christ is a sign of God's continuing affirmation of Israel's covenant and election. Further, it insisted the **deicide** accusation is a theological and historical error.   *ALICE L. ECKARDT*

Canada

Jews who participated in the opening up of the Americas to European settlement were initially legally barred from residence in New France – the areas of northern Canada claimed by the French following their discovery of the St Laurence River in 1534 – where immigration was restricted to Catholics. However, they did settle in the British colonies to the south by 1758 and after the incorporation of New France into the British Empire began also to settle in Lower Canada. A population of 1,000 Jews in 1871 increased to over 100,000 by 1914, primarily as a result of emigration from Eastern Europe in the face of rising **antisemitism**.

Jews also moved north from the **United States**, part of the cross-border migration common in much of Canadian history. Canada, having been a British colony with predominantly British Churches, fostered the same attitudes towards Jews as the **United Kingdom**, ensuring it was less of a 'melting pot' than the United States. In the 1930s the Canadian government responded to the unemployment caused by the Depression by imposing severe restrictions on immigration, and permission for Jews to enter was rarely given. Antisemitism was common, and Canada took in proportionately fewer Jews from Nazi-controlled Europe than any Western country.

Today, however, as a result of significant immigration after the Second World War, Canada sees itself as a multicultural society in which the government supports cultural and religious groups (again a noticeable difference with the United States). Key issues in Jewish–Christian relations in Canada include the significance of the **Holocaust**, the role of the **State of Israel**, and the ongoing violence in the Middle East.

The Canadian **Council of Christians and Jews** (CCCJ) was founded in 1947, and local Christian–Jewish organisations, loosely connected with the CCCJ, exist in Toronto, Montreal and Calgary. In other cities Jewish–Christian **dialogue** is part of wider interreligious conversations. The Canadian Christian–Jewish Consultation organises official dialogue with the Canadian Jewish Congress, the Conference of Catholic Bishops, the United, Anglican, Lutheran and Presbyterian Churches, and one denomination of Baptist Churches.

The United Church of Canada, the largest Protestant body in Canada, published in 1997 an important document called *Bearing Faithful Witness*. It called for **repentance** for theological **anti-Judaism** and political antisemitism and was hailed as a watershed in its acknowledgement that 'the church's rejection of Jews was an act of disobedience to God'. It proposed guidelines for Christians in their relationship with Jews and Judaism, stating that 'the hope of Israel is the Christian hope, too:

Earth under God's rule in peace, prosperity and justice for all'. *EDWARD KESSLER*

Candle

While illumination of indoor ritual spaces probably originated from practical necessity, especially at night, certain elements of that lighting took on symbolic meanings in Judaism and Christianity. Some of these uses share common origins, some are unrelated, and others are later borrowings. In the Second Temple the elaborate seven-branched candelabrum (*menorah*) provided illumination continually. Zech. 4.10 explains these lights as God's eyes 'ranging over the whole earth'. **Hanukkah** celebrates the rededication of this Temple utensil. Depictions and reproductions of this *menorah* became a central Jewish symbol. The idea of its perpetual light generated the synagogue's *ner tamid*, a decorative lamp placed above the Torah ark to represent God's continuous presence. **Sabbath** lights, pragmatic in origin, became the markers of this day's sacred time. Christian use of lamps and candles derives from these Jewish and also pagan origins, infused with **Christological** meanings. Light often marks divine presence, specifically that of Christ, as in the new light of **resurrection** lit at the climax of the **Easter** Vigil, candles placed on or around the altar at the time of mass, or a perpetual sanctuary light placed before the reserved host. Pagan origins lie behind the use of lights in processions to accompany dignitaries, in funerary and memorial settings to honour the dead and as the votive offerings of individuals before shrines of saints or statues. Similar popular usage appears in the Jewish world, particularly at tombs and in conjunction with **mourning**, indicating the ease with which neutral objects like candles have been historically reinterpreted and integrated into new symbolic systems. *RUTH LANGER*

Canon

The canon, in the Jewish–Christian context, is the corpus of scriptural writings considered authoritative and standard for determining religious beliefs and practices (from Greek, *kanon*, 'measuring stick'). The Christian canon includes the Jewish – the Tanakh or Bible, known by the Christians as the **Old Testament** – but not vice versa.

Given the pivotal place of the scriptures in Jewish–Christian relations, it is important to review the history of the formation of the canon of sacred books proper to each tradition. Canonisation is a long process that involves all the stages from composition, editing, archiving (combining texts on a scroll) and collecting scrolls into larger units; it is not a precipitate act. The theory, for example, that the rabbis gathered at **Yavneh** (*m. Sanhedrin* 11.4) around 90 CE and made a conciliar decision regarding the Hebrew canon is discredited. Canonisation came about because believing communities over time accepted certain books as authoritative and not others. By the end of the first century CE there were indications that a Hebrew canon of either 24 books (4 Esd. 14.44–46) or 22 books (**Josephus**, Origen, **Jerome**) was being postulated. The Qumran library indicates that there had been an inherited corpus of authoritative books to which specific groups were adding other texts esteemed by their smaller constituencies. Most likely, the more established collection was decided by the Hasmoneans to confirm the legitimacy of their rule in Judah. The rabbis inherited this inchoative canon and, in the disputed instances (Song of Songs, Ecclesiastes, Ruth and **Esther**), they distinguished between books that did or did not 'defile the hands'; most probably the term designates those books that belonged to what they considered the sphere of **holiness**. The corpus of books gave this community a shape; hence they too were holy and capable of defiling. The physical Torah scrolls lodged in synagogues replaced the Holy of Holies in the Temple of Jerusalem.

By the end of the first century CE the process of determining these books had, for the most part, been achieved. From that point there was a further need to standardise the texts being copied; this would take until the sixth century. However, the process of canonisation of the Hebrew text was being finalised at the very time that Christianity was disengaging itself from the Jewish mainstream, requiring a meticulous sifting of the Jewish textual heritage. (For the first two centuries CE, Christian usage of 'scripture' (Greek, *graphe*) normally signified the Hebrew scriptures.) These early Christians inherited the burgeoning canon, although in common with other **Diaspora** Jewish groups made use of the **Septuagint**, a Greek version of the Hebrew scriptures dating from the third century BCE. The earliest surviving indication of this interaction of Christian scholarship with Jewish is seen in **Justin Martyr**. Justin's *Dialogue with Trypho* is an attempt at Jewish–Christian **dialogue**. While Justin uses the

Septuagint, he limits himself to those writings that would be acceptable to the partner in dialogue, 'those textual passages recognised among your own people' (*Dial.* 7.12). Being used as a source for anti-Jewish **apologetic**, the Septuagint became more and more an exclusively Christian corpus and was given an equal or higher dignity by Christians when compared to the Hebrew text. This was justified by Christian elaboration on the legend of its translation (as recorded in the *Epistle of Aristeas*), which was now used to explain the fact that the text contained allegedly clear references to the coming of the **Messiah** in Jesus and the universal opening of the Torah to all peoples. The Jews were thereby alienated from the Septuagint and relied on the alternative texts of **Aquila** and the **Jewish-Christian** Symmachus (*fl.* probably late second century CE). Thus, Jew and Christian were at an impasse. Christians charged Jews with falsification of their Hebrew texts, since the Septuagint had readings that were either different from the Hebrew or not even contained in the Hebrew. Jews derided Christians for their ignorance in accepting variant readings in a Greek translation which had no counterpart in the Hebrew original. This Jewish–Christian impasse explains the work of **Origen** and his **Hexapla**, a Bible in six parallel columns, which was influential because it clearly indicated to both Christian and Jew which books had not been accepted into the Hebrew canon.

The Christians thus had access to a fluid canon, and there would have been differences from one Christian community to another. A few would have utilised a Hebrew text; most would have used the Septuagint. But they would have been pulled in two directions. In discussion and **polemic** involving mainstream Jews they would have tended to conform their collection to the Hebrew one, acknowledged by their opponents as authoritative. But for their own purposes they would have retained other sacred books even if they were not within the confines of the Hebrew canon. Therefore, while the book of Enoch was esteemed among early Christians, its **Son of Man** traditions being prominent in Mark and the Enochian 'Asa'el being used in Revelation, it was falling into disuse in Jewish circles and was therefore excluded from the Christian canon of the Old Testament. This would explain the fact that certain books within the Christian collection, the **apocrypha**, were regarded as of lesser status, although the fourth to fifth century codices (Alexandrinus, Sinaiticus, Vaticanus) include them. However, specifically Christian writings, which were composed in the first two centuries, also gradually gained esteem. This situation was similar to that conjectured for Qumran. There would have been an inherited collection of Hebrew scriptures, mainly in the Septuagint version. To this corpus there were being added collections of other specifically Christian writings. The Christian determination of a canon of their own writings was made by the fourth century on the criteria that the writings were of apostolic origin, that they were orthodox and that they were generally in use in the churches for teaching and **liturgy**. The earliest collection of Christian writings was probably the letters of **Paul**, followed by the Gospels. By the late second century the four Gospels of Matthew, Mark and Luke (which are related to each other) and John had outstripped other gospels, such as the *Gospel of Thomas*, in general distribution, liturgical usage and common esteem. Further, it was believed (wrongly) that these four Gospels were written by **apostles** or a companion of an apostle. The determination of a fixed canon was accelerated due to a confrontation with **Marcion**, a heretic who was excommunicated in 144 CE. He rejected the Hebrew scriptures *in toto* and accepted only a heavily edited version of Luke and the letters of Paul. Only in the late second century (**Melito of Sardis**, Clement) were the terms 'Old Testament' and '**New Testament**' applied to the separate collections of Hebrew and Christian books in the Christian canon. Prior to that the two terms referred to the covenantal relationship between God and **Israel**, God and Christians.

With the **Renaissance** and the **Reformation** there was a tangible need to translate the 'Old Testament' into the vernacular. But the earliest form of that Old Testament had been Greek not Hebrew, and there was no fixed Greek text and no agreed list of canonical contents. The text that was chosen for the translation was the Hebrew, wherever there was a Hebrew version. Some books that had previously been translated from the Greek were now replaced by the Hebrew. Translations thus reverted from a Christian Bible to a largely Hebrew Bible. While the Council of **Trent** imposed on Roman Catholics the broad canon that included the apocrypha, Protestants in the sixteenth century preferred the Jewish canon. From the nineteenth century English Protestant Bibles were printed minus the apocrypha, but they have been reinstated since **Vatican II**. Luther maintained that the inherent quality of a book attested to its canonicity. He thereby excluded the recognised apocrypha, including parts of Esther and Daniel. These books were acknowledged as useful and good for reading but not scripture. This made Jewish–Christian dialogue over the scriptures more difficult. One of the topics for ongoing Jewish–Christian dialogue has to be the meaning of canonicity and its implications for the texts that will inevitably form the topic for discussion.

See also **Bible**; **Bible translations, ancient**; **Bible translations, modern English**; **Dead Sea Scrolls**; **Hebrew Bible**   *ROBERT CROTTY*

Canon law

In Roman law the Greek term *kanon* (measuring rod) was a synonym for *regula* (rule); later it applied to Church law, with rulings from councils (local or ecumenical, i.e. of the universal Church) or bishops. Christian leaders drew upon their biblical and Jewish heritage, along with principles of natural law and Roman legislation, to structure the spiritual, moral and social order of their communities. Even before the Emperor **Constantine** favoured Christianity, the local Church in Elvira, **Spain** called a council (or synod) about 305 to grapple with current issues. Here and in other European dioceses where Jews lived some conciliar decrees affected them, invariably in ways adverse to their interests. Besides the protection of Roman law, privileges granted to the Jews in the **Roman Empire** by Julius Caesar (100–44 BCE) were respected in principle, so that Jews could maintain synagogues and regulate the details of their community life according to their own laws. However, at times mobs failed to respect these ancient laws, and some synagogues were destroyed or taken over by Christians. Ambrose, bishop of Milan, (*c.*339–97) thwarted the decree of Emperor Theodosius I (*r.*379–95) that the Bishop of Callinicum in **Asia Minor** should make restitution to the Jewish community for the wanton destruction of its synagogue. Christian emperors and other rulers often restricted the initiatives of Jews, for example to build a new synagogue, at the behest of local bishops.

After the demise of the Roman Empire in the West, popes and bishops exerted authority to maintain the basic rights of Jews to practise their faith and prohibited forced **conversion**. The decisions of Pope **Gregory I** regarding Jews on religious liberty, conversion to Christianity and ownership of Christian slaves were included in canonical collections of the *Decretum* of Gratian (about 1140) and the *Decretals* of Pope **Gregory IX**. Local legislation to segregate Jews was applied to the entire Latin Church at the Fourth **Lateran Council** in 1215, importing from Islamic lands the demand that Jews wear clothing that distinguished them from the general population. Pope **Innocent III** based this on the commandment to wear fringes (Num. 15.37–38) but later a sign was sewn onto the outer garment (*see* **yellow badge**). Jews were forbidden to hold public office, and converts were exhorted not to relapse into Jewish practices ('remnants of the former rite').

Canon law and the civil law of the Papal States applied to Jews in many parts of **Italy** until 1870. In 1917 the *Codex Juris Canonici* supplanted all previous legislation; this Code concerns only the life of Catholics of the Roman Rite. In 1983 the new *Code of Canon Law*, the revision initiated by Pope **John XXIII**, was promulgated. The only area of concern to Jews is legislation regarding 'interfaith marriage', which is permitted with a dispensation from the local bishop. The Catholic party should strive to bring children of the **marriage** into the Church but no promise is required of the non-Catholic party.

Raul Hilberg, in *The Destruction of the European Jews*, 4–6, gives a list of canonical measures to which Nazi anti-Jewish legislation corresponds. Although many of the measures were enacted by local councils and did not extend over an area comparable to the Nazi Reich, they did set a precedent for **Hitler** to justify laws that gravely curtailed the civil and human rights of Jews in **Germany** and in occupied countries.   *LAWRENCE E. FRIZZELL*

Canonisation

Canonisation, which presents the holy person as a model and intercessor, has in recent years, and especially with the canonisation of Edith **Stein** in 1998 and the beatification of Pope **Pius IX** in 2000, strained Catholic–Jewish relations.

In the Catholic Church canonisation is effected by the pope; in the Orthodox Churches it occurs through a synodal decision. It establishes that a member of the Church has 'practised heroic virtue and lived in fidelity to God's grace' (*Catechism of the Catholic Church*, no. 828). The **early**

Church – prompted by the extolling of **martyrs** in Maccabees and Daniel – initially venerated only martyrs who had been killed for the sake of their faith. Later the cult was extended to personalities who were already renowned for **holiness** during their lifetimes and whose reputation was confirmed after their deaths by extraordinary signs. Today the veneration of the holy person by the faithful, as well as a procedural examination of his or her heroic virtue and exemplary nature, precede Catholic canonisation. It is reserved to the pope to decide whether a person is to be canonised (i.e. admitted to the list of saints, called the 'canon'). For Catholics the veneration of saints is a meaningful, but in no way central, activity of faith; according to Church teaching it is 'good and profitable' to call on saints for their intercession with God.

Even though the Christian invocation of saints for intercession derived from Jewish traditions like 2 Macc. 15.12ff., and in spite of the fact that the Church later revered 'saints of the Old Covenant' (Abraham, David, Elias and others), the rabbis rejected Christian veneration of saints and insisted that 'there is no Holy one like the Lord' (1 Sam. 2.2). Thus, there is already in the rabbinical name for God, 'the Holy One, praise be to him', a criticism of the Christian cult of the saints (Arthur Marmorstein (1882–1946)).

There is no equivalent to Church canonisation for Jews. However, according to Jewish teaching, it is one's obligation to hallow God's name, even with one's life if the worst comes to the worst. In the synagogal **liturgy** the martyrs – Jews who have adhered to their faith in times of persecution and paid with their lives – are named as models for the living, but also to remind God of their commitment. In addition, Jewish piety is familiar with the 'merits of the fathers' – *zecut avot* – which are called to mind when one stands before God to beg for **forgiveness** or for rescue from distress. The prayer that refers to the 'merits of the fathers', however, is addressed directly to God; the fathers are neither invoked nor asked to intercede with God as in Christian piety.

This is true for the official teaching of the tradition. In the religious customs of Judaism, however, there is no clear-cut dividing line. The graves of outstanding men are revered, for example, and **pilgrimages** are made to them on certain days; the custom is to leave little slips of paper on the graves with petitions. And people who have exhibited great piety, justice and asceticism are presented as models. This proximity of the Christian and Jewish cults is in need of further investigation.

See also **sainthood**   HANS HERMANN HENRIX

Canons of Laodicea

Legal ecclesiastical enactments of fifth-century Laodicean church that became, along with other council or synod documents, the basis for **canon law**. The early Christian struggle with Judaism was most often not with Judaism per se but with Christians who found themselves attracted to Judaism for various reasons. The so-called Canons of Laodicea (dated anywhere from 443 to 481) deal with many problems in the early Christian community, especially the problem of Christian Judaising. At least 7 of the 60 canons deal with this issue: for example, the Canons command that the Gospels are to be read on the **Sabbath** (Saturday) with the other scriptures; strongly encourage Christians not to rest on the Sabbath but to honour the Lord's Day of the Christians (Sunday); and demand that Christians not feast together with Jews nor receive unleavened bread from them. They reveal the desire of Church authorities in this period to prevent Christian social and religious engagement with Jews and Judaism, and reflect the fact that close social relations were going on between certain ordinary Christians and Jews in the fourth and fifth centuries.

See also **Judaising Christians**

STEVEN J. MCMICHAEL

Capital punishment

While capital punishment has been abandoned in much of Western Europe, it remains a hotly debated issue in the **United States**. Frequently, conservative Christian proponents of the practice point to '**Old Testament**' examples to bolster their political arguments, presuming modern Jews would agree with the ancient texts – thus ignoring the fact that Judaism, like Christianity, is a living tradition capable of applying unchanging revealed truths anew as historical situations change. Yet since at least the second century CE, **Rabbinic Judaism** has opposed capital punishment save in the rarest of cases (see *m. Makkot* 1.10), and the modern **State of Israel** has applied it in only one case, that of Adolf Eichmann (1906–62), the architect of the **Holocaust**. Rabbinic tradition did not base its approach on the three citations of the *lex talionis* in the Bible, but progressively limited their application, for example by requiring the testimony of two direct witnesses and that all capital cases be tried twice. Similarly, Catholic and much of Protestant tradition now oppose capital punishment, some entirely, some, like Judaism, reserving it for the rarest of cases. Jews and Christians alike rule it out as a means of revenge or retribution. Pope **John Paul II** opposed the practice on the grounds that society can protect itself without denying criminals the chance to reform (27 January 1999), and a joint 1999 statement of the National Council of Synagogues and the US Conference of Catholic Bishops concluded: 'Both traditions begin with an affirmation of the sanctity of human life. Both . . . acknowledge the theoretical possibility of a justifiable death penalty, since the Scriptures mandate it for certain offenses. Yet both have, over the centuries, narrowed those grounds until, today, we would say together that it is time to cease the practice altogether.' Mainstream Protestant, Catholic and Jewish leaderships work together to lobby politically for the ending of the death penalty in the US. *EUGENE J. FISHER*

Carmelite controversy

The terrain of the concentration camp at **Auschwitz** and the death camp at Birkenau were repeatedly the centre of controversy in the late 1980s and 1990s. A fundraising appeal following the establishment of a Carmelite convent at the site of Auschwitz I in 1984 suggested that the Carmel is intended to be 'a spiritual fortress and guarantee of the conversion of strayed brothers from our countries as well as proof of our desire to erase the outrages so often done to the Vicar of Christ'. This brought forth a wave of protest by Jewish organisations around the world, as it was understood to call for the **conversion** of Jews to Christianity, with this **mission** being engineered at a site of mass Jewish suffering. The protest culminated in a call for the immediate closure of the Carmel, claiming that it was inappropriate for any religious institution to establish a dedicated site of prayer in the grounds of the Auschwitz camps. The ensuing controversy between Jewish protesters and the supporters of the nuns at Auschwitz debated the appropriateness of religious symbolism through a discussion of the 'ownership' of the site of the camps. This controversy continued for almost a decade, with demonstrations by opponents and supporters of the Carmel at the site of the convent, and international delegations of Jews and Catholics meeting repeatedly to resolve the con-

flict. In 1987 agreement was reached to move the Carmel to a site nearby and transform it into a centre for 'information, education, meeting and prayer'. However, it was 1993 before, as a result of a Vatican directive, the nuns moved out of the building.

Religious symbolism had not been foreign to the sites of the concentration camps at Auschwitz. In 1983 Polish youths had erected crosses and **stars of David** on the field of ashes in Birkenau in an effort of commemoration. At one point a church was established in the offices of the commandant at Birkenau, as also in a building in Auschwitz I. Christian symbolism, in particular before 1989, was a feature of the sites of the former concentration camp, which were understood as sites of Polish suffering. Since the Carmelite controversy it is disputed whether Jews are included in the commemoration of all Poles murdered at Auschwitz or need to be mentioned separately.

One result of the controversy is the differentiation of victims into many groups, each finding its own way of commemorating the murders of its members. Yet the struggle over the appropriateness of religious symbolism at Auschwitz remains controversial. While Jewish groups in particular are calling for a halt to all religious symbolism at these sites, the establishment of more or less permanent symbols appears important for Christian commemoration. This was demonstrated in 1998 when the removal of the Papal **Cross**, established at Auschwitz I in 1989 following a mass celebrated by the pope in Birkenau in 1979, and an end to prayer meetings at the site were called for in the wake of the move of the Carmel off the site of Auschwitz I. Crosses were erected in 'support of the Papal Cross' and, while these have since been removed, the controversy about the Papal Cross has not been concluded. *K. HANNAH HOLTSCHNEIDER*

Cassidy, Edward (b. 1924)

Roman Catholic cardinal archbishop and President of the Holy See's Commission for Religious Relations with the Jews (1989–2001), who helped creatively develop the positive heritage of **Vatican II**. When the International Catholic–Jewish Liaison Committee (ILC) was at an impasse, this Australian-born leader made a profound contribution in Prague (1990) with his call to reconciliation. Cassidy was involved in the establishment of diplomatic relations between the Holy See and the **State** of Israel (1994), the publishing of *We Remember: A Reflection on the Shoah* (1998) and the act of pardon in St Peter's Basilica on the first Sunday of Lent, 2000. He accompanied Pope **John Paul II**'s visit to Jerusalem (March 2000) and mediated between the Catholic and Jewish communities in the aftermath of *Dominus Iesus* (September 2000).

AUDREY DOETZEL

Catechesis/catechism

'Catechesis is an *education in the faith* of children, young people and adults which includes especially the teaching of Christian doctrine . . . with a view to initiating the hearers into the fullness of Christian life.' Pope **John Paul II**'s description shows that this Christian term is indistinguishable from the transmission of tradition. Since the sixteenth century the principal texts in this process are authorised catechisms – brief, systematic and accessible summaries of central Christian teaching composed in both the Protestant and Catholic churches. There is little space for anti-Jewish **polemic** in these catechisms because the opponent is usually the other Christian community. Recent Christian catechesis since **Vatican II** deliberately fosters a positive evaluation of Judaism.

The 1992 *Catechism of the Catholic Church* draws upon Vatican II's new approach to Judaism, seeing positive significance in Christ's Jewish birth, **circumcision**, observance of the Law and the Feasts, and respect for the **Temple**, and affirms that nothing in his ministry and teaching annuls the validity of the gifts that God wills to bestow on the Jewish people. Building upon the authoritative *Notes on the Correct Way to Present the Jews and Judaism in Preaching and Catechesis* (1985), it highlights what **Jesus** had in common with **Pharisees**, presents him as a **Torah**-faithful Jew, avoids speaking of 'the Jews' (*see* **hoi Ioudaioi**) as collectively opposed to Jesus, and deliberately counters any attempt to blame the Jewish people for his death. It reaffirms the teaching of the Council of **Trent** (1560) that Christian sinners are more to blame for the death of Jesus than those few Jews who were implicated in it.

The *Notes* (the most authoritative statement on modern Catholic catechesis on Judaism) treat of the Church's relation to Judaism as a concern for 'a still living reality closely related to the Church'. Although they deal with the relation of Jewish and Christian scriptures, the Jewish roots of Christianity, and Jews in the **New Testament**, there is a serious attempt to move away from a purely historical and archaeological approach to Judaism's importance for Christianity. Catechesis on Judaism is to begin by listening to Jews: it encourages Christians to learn 'by what essential traits the Jews define themselves in the light of their own religious experience', thereby encouraging Christians to refrain from telling Jews what their role is. It recognises that the history of Israel flowed into the **Diaspora**, 'which allowed Israel to carry to the whole world a witness – often heroic – of its fidelity to the one God . . . while preserving the memory of the land of their forefathers at the heart of their hope'. It encourages Christians to see 'the permanence' of the Jewish people (their survival from ancient times) as accompanied by 'a continuous spiritual fecundity, in the rabbinical period, in the Middle Ages, and in modern times'. Catechesis on Judaism guided by the *Notes* is intended to prepare Christians for **dialogue** with the Jewish people and for a shared witness to God. *JOHN MCDADE*

CE/BCE

Although often perceived by users as neutral terms, the chronological designations AD ('*anno domini*') and BC ('before Christ') are in origin professions of Christian faith; their international currency is in part a product of colonialism. For these reasons, it is increasingly common, particularly in academic and interfaith circles, to substitute them with CE ('common era') and BCE ('before common era'), the term 'common' referring here to the fact that the system of dating used continues to be the internationally recognised Gregorian **Calendar**. Some people object to CE/BCE on traditionalist grounds, or because they wish to assert the pre-eminence of Christianity. *MELANIE J. WRIGHT*

Celan, Paul (1920–70)

(Born Paul Antschel.) Poet and Holocaust survivor. Romanian-born, Celan lived most of his life in Paris. He married a Catholic (Gisèle de Lestrange) and resisted the epithet 'Jewish author', considering it **antisemitic**. However, much of his work memorialises the **Holocaust** (*Death's-Fugue* is a powerful evocation of the death-camps). Many of his poems (e.g. *Winter* and *Psalm*) draw on Jewish and Christian imagery, suggesting associations between **Jesus**, Christian dogmatism and Jewish suffering. The increasingly fractured nature of his later poetry embodies Celan's own struggle, as a Jew writing in

German, to come to terms with the past. He committed suicide in 1970.

See also **literature, French** *MELANIE J. WRIGHT*

Celibacy

Renunciation of **marriage**, required by bishops in the **Orthodox Churches** and by all priests in the **Roman Catholic** Church but not required in **Protestantism**. Because celibacy is rejected in Judaism, it is often seen as a significant division between the two religions. The value of an unmarried state is emphasised by **Paul** (e.g. 1 Cor. 7.1ff.) and the necessity of marriage is questioned in Matt. 19.12, but the **New Testament** also indicates that some of the disciples were married (1 Cor. 9.5). Celibacy did exist in first-century Judaism, and **Josephus** attributes the practice to the Essenes. Occasionally the rabbinic literature refers to the celibacy of a **rabbi**, such as Simeon ben Azzai (second century CE), who stated he could not marry because his soul was in love with **Torah**. The rabbis accepted that other Jews, on account of 'love of Torah', could follow Ben Azzai's lead and remain unmarried, but they emphasise the first command of the Bible, to be fruitful and multiply (Gen. 1.28). By contrast, the **Church Fathers** demanded clerical celibacy from the fourth century, based on the Levitical prescriptions requiring abstinence from sexual relations for at least a day before the performance of ritual service. Likewise, **priests** were required to maintain a high standard of purity on account of their role as offerers of sacrifice.

See also **sex/sexuality** *EDWARD KESSLER*

Celsus (*fl. c.*180 CE)

'Pagan' philosopher and polemicist against Christianity. In *The True Word* Celsus produced the first extended attack against Christianity, but the work is known to us only from the detailed refutation by **Origen** in *Against Celsus* (*Contra Celsum*), written *c.*235 CE at the request of Origen's patron, Ambrosius. Origen not only summarises but also quotes both individual charges and extended passages of Celsus's arguments, and he claims to have represented the main thrust of the work. As well as exposing what he saw as the philosophical weaknesses of Christian thought, and the disreputable character of its founder and followers, Celsus addresses its relationship with Judaism. He puts a range of arguments in the mouth of 'a Jew', objecting to the Christians' **apostasy** and repeating charges that **Jesus** was born illegitimately and was executed

as a 'magician'; similar charges are known from later rabbinic sources, but it remains uncertain whether Celsus had close contacts with genuine Jewish sources or whether his 'Jew' was his own literary creation to give added weight to his argument. Celsus also repeats many of the traditional Roman charges against the Jews, their suspect origins in Egypt, Moses' deviousness and their antisocial stance, and he directs these against the Christians who claim the same history. Celsus had read the lost *Dialogue of Jason and Papiscus*, and possibly also **Justin Martyr**'s *Apology*. In his refutation, Origen develops the theme of the obduracy of the Jews to explain their rejection of Jesus, but he also takes over and develops a theme of Jewish **apologetic**, that Abraham and Moses were older than Plato and the origins of Greek wisdom. *JUDITH LIEU*

Censorship

Religious and secular authorities from ancient to modern times have deemed it one of their duties to protect their people from literature they believe could corrupt their morals, undermine their loyalty or lead them to err in belief or practice. Their efforts to do so are called censorship. Censorship can be imposed in a variety of ways. There may be an institutional apparatus, an office of the censor, to which books must be submitted to be authorised for circulation. Or censorship may be imposed, and official disapproval signalled, in more informal, indirect ways, e.g. by invoking laws of **blasphemy** or decency. Censorship can range from permitting the offending texts to circulate, but with the objectionable passages excised or blanked out, to destroying the whole book, and imprisoning or putting to death its author or printer.

Censorship in Judaism is documented from late antiquity. By finally closing the **canon** of sacred scripture and issuing the definitive list of the 'holy writings' (*kitvei ha-kodesh*), the rabbis in talmudic times were exercising a form of censorship. In doing so they created a category of 'outside books' (*sefarim hizonim*), including the Gospels and other 'books of the heretics' (*sifrei minim*), which they did not approve of Jews reading. Because they usually lacked the coercive power to prevent such books from circulating, they imposed their censorship by other means. Jews were instructed not to save such works from a burning building, even if they contained the sacred name of God. If such books came into the authorities' hands they might order them to be 'hidden away' (e.g. immured, or put in some other form of *genizah*). Censorship extended in a mild form even to the *Sefer Torah*, where changes were deliberately introduced to avoid possible misunderstanding or to preserve public decency. The **Talmud** records how the translators of the **Septuagint** avoided certain renderings so as not to offend the Ptolemies. The most potent instrument of rabbinical censorship is the *Herem* (the Ban), which relies on social rather than physical coercion: it is effective only if the community consents to implement the boycott pronounced by the authorities. Jewish authors who have been banned include **Spinoza**, Immanuel of Rome (1260–*c*.1328) and Azariah dei Rossi (*c*.1511–*c*.1578). Censorship remains a potent force even today in **Haredi** communities. An attempt was made in 2002 to ban *The Dignity of Difference* by Chief Rabbi Jonathan Sacks (b. 1948).

Christian censorship of books has followed a similar pattern to Jewish, though it has been more thoroughgoing because Christians have been able to exercise more political power. The defining of the Christian canon of scripture was itself an act of censorship. It downgraded certain texts to the status of **apocrypha**: these could be read for edification but could not serve to determine faith or practice. And it excluded a whole swathe of works from either category. Reading these was not explicitly banned, but there was always a strong implication that it was not a spiritually profitable exercise. Christian authorities from time to time seized heretical books and destroyed them. The justification for this was found in the episode at Ephesus recorded in Acts 19.19, where books of **magic** were burned, ignoring the fact that this was a voluntary act by new converts and not one imposed by the authorities. In the Middle Ages copies of the Talmud were burned in Europe (*see* **Talmud trials**). The Talmud barely survived: only one more or less complete manuscript of the whole text (Munich 95) is now extant.

In late medieval and early modern times the censorship of books was institutionalised by the **Roman Catholic** Church. Censors had to certify that books contained nothing objectionable before they could be copied or printed. This had a severe effect on Jewish manuscripts and printed books. The censors were often converted Jews with a good knowledge of **Hebrew** and **Aramaic**, and they did

their work thoroughly. Words and phrases were replaced, if they were thought to be derogatory of Christianity – e.g. *minim*, 'heretics', which was taken as referring to Christians, was changed to *covedei kokhavim*, 'star worshippers'. Words, phrases and even whole passages were blacked out. Complete books were placed on the *Index Librorum Prohibitorum* and banned from circulation. The publication of Jewish books was also tightly controlled in Tsarist and Soviet **Russia** and in other countries. The most spectacular act of censorship in modern times was the Nazis' public burning of books 'infected by the Jewish spirit' on 10 May 1933.

Censorship of Jewish books has left a permanent mark. At the beginnings of Hebrew printing printers themselves removed or altered passages which they thought might offend the censor, to prevent their books appearing mutilated. This internal pre-censorship was supported by a number of rabbinical synods, beginning with Ferrara in 1154. Standard modern prints descended from these early editions bear the scars. Thus the great Vilna edition of the Talmud, still used in many yeshivahs, lacks passages referring to **Jesus**, because they were deleted from the *editio princeps*.   *PHILIP ALEXANDER*

Centre for the study of Jewish–Christian Relations (CJCR) *see* **Jewish–Christian relations, centres for the study of**

Chagall, Marc (1887–1985)

Jewish painter and designer. Chagall was born to hasidic parents in Vitebsk (Belarus), but lived mainly in France. He worked in various media, addressing *shtetl* life and biblical themes in a distinctive style that fuses fantasy, religion and nostalgia. Chagall's belief in the possibility of Jewish–Christian conciliation is manifest in his work for ecclesiastical commissions (e.g. windows for cathedrals at Metz and Rheims). He also depicted **Jesus** as a symbol of Jewish suffering (e.g. in the paintings *White Crucifixion* and *Sacrifice of Isaac*). This tense juxtapositioning of Jewish and Christian **iconography**, and the hostility it provoked, prefigures the Asher Lev novels of Chaim Potok (b. 1929).

See also **art**   *MELANIE J. WRIGHT*

Charity

Charity, from the Latin *caritas*, is one translation of *agape* (the other being '**love**'). While the Bible never intends 'charity' to be translated as giving to the poor, in the English-speaking Jewish and Christian traditions 'charity' as being concerned about, and acting on behalf of, the poor is nonetheless a central religious and human obligation. It is in this sense of caring outreach to the less fortunate that charity is interpreted here.

One finds references to the importance of giving alms throughout the Bible, both in the **Old Testament** (sometimes as *zedhakah*, '**righteousness**'; e.g. Lev. 19.9–10; Deut. 24.10–22) and in the **New Testament** (e.g. Matt. 6.2–3; Acts 9.36). In the **Hebrew Bible** the less fortunate are often itemised as the 'widow, the orphan, and the stranger'. Thus, both Judaism and Christianity encourage similar charitable practices such as hospitality to strangers and assistance to the needy. One difference between traditional Jewish and early Christian understanding of charity is that in **Rabbinic Judaism** charitable acts were often accompanied by a wide range of communal rituals, while in early Christianity charity was sometimes associated with a heroic ethic of self-sacrificing devotion, particularly of an ascetic nature.

Questions of the relation between personal caring for the poor and advocacy of particular programmes of state welfare and social services are areas in which Christians and Jews might fruitfully share biblical and traditional insights about the nature and extent of their religious obligations to the poor, whether of money, time or expertise. Indeed in the recent past projects of common action for the poor, both structural and individual, have marked some of the most powerful moments of Jewish–Christian cooperation, such as in the **United States**, where Jews and Christians from the late 1920s onwards launched common campaigns for racial equality, rights of workers and housing rights. *MICHAEL MCGARRY*

Chosen People

Both Jews and Christians claim to be chosen by God. The **Hebrew Bible** identifies three key features of the people of God. First, the people enter into a relationship with God through God's election, e.g. Deut. 14.1–2, which implies that, although all peoples belong to the Lord, Israel is God's special possession and becomes known as a holy people. Second, God's choice of Israel is associated with the **land of Israel**, which becomes a constitutive element of being a people of God, e.g. Gen. 17.8: 'I will give to you and to your descendants after you the land of your sojournings, all the land of Canaan for an everlasting possession; and I will be their God.' Third, the people of God receive a **mission**, which is often described in terms of 'being a light to the nations' (Isa. 42.6). Israel is not chosen as the people of God out of arbitrary preference for a particular people but in order that God's name be blessed (Gen. 12.2–3). God does not force the people that he chooses and calls *ami* (my people); rather, something is sought in return, and as a result God and the people of God are described as partners in a relationship.

The Bible recounts that the people of God failed to fulfil its obligations, and as a result lost its autonomy and land and went into exile. Nevertheless, there is no suggestion that God rejected the people; rather, the prophets announce a new **covenant** (e.g. Jer. 31.31; Ezek. 36.26) which would be written on the tablets of their hearts. According to the prophets, the covenant is so established on the divine side that it cannot be broken on the human side: the God of Israel is linked to the **people of Israel** in a covenant that is eternal and unbreakable.

In the **Septuagint** the people of God is not translated by *laos*, which is the New Testament's standard translation of *am*; rather, *ekklesia tou Theou*, which corresponds to *kahal ha-shem*, community of God, is adopted. *Ekklesia* becomes an expression of the assembly of the New Covenant in Jesus Christ. This is illustrated in particular by one of the later **New Testament** writings, 1 Pet. 2.9, which, with reference to Exod. 19.5–6, marks the transfer of the features of the *am ha-shem* to the Christian community, which is now *de facto* the *genos ekklethon* (chosen people or race). Christianity thus appropriates Jewish election and is described as a royal priesthood, a dedicated nation and a people claimed by God.

Paul is often viewed as arguing that membership of the true Israel is not determined simply by physical descent from **Abraham**, but rather by spiritual affinity to Abraham's trusting relationship with God. In other words, Israel is simply composed of a combination of Jews and Gentiles. The former, owing to their spiritual past, include those who have extended their trust relationship in God to a dependence upon **Jesus** as Lord; the latter includes those Gentiles who have entered into the covenantal relationship with God by their acceptance of Jesus. This, however, is a facile interpretation of Paul – in fact the New Testament writer who struggles most deeply with the meaning of the election of Israel and the election of the Church – imputing to him as it does simply the view that the old becomes new. The traditional Christian attitude towards Jews is, however, expressed by such a view. For example, **Justin Martyr** makes this equation when he states that 'we [Christians] are the true and spiritual Israelite nation, and the race of Judah and of Jacob, and Isaac and Abraham' (*Dial.* 11.5).

Although Paul's view was influenced by rabbinic teachings, a greater motivation in his case would seem to be embarrassment that the majority of Jews are not part of the new 'people of Israel'. He cannot believe that the Jews as a people and a religion are totally and forever outside the people of God. As a result, he suggests that both Israel and the Church are elect and both participate in the covenant of God. For Paul, therefore, the Church's election derives from that of Israel, but God's covenant with Israel remains unbroken – irrevocably (Rom. 11.29). For Paul the mystery of Israel is that their rejection and their stumbling do not mean that they cease to be accepted by God; rather, they allow the Gentiles to participate in the peoplehood of Israel. This view has become the basis for modern Christian understanding of the chosenness of Israel. For instance, American Greek Orthodox writer Theodore Stylianopoulos (b. 1937) writes that regardless of whether Israel is disobedient (as Christians have been disobedient over the centuries) the faithfulness of God remains: 'As a father to His children, who has deep and unbreakable faithfulness to His children, the election does continue for Jews in the present day as well' ('Faithfulness to the Roots', 156).

From the Jewish perspective no change took place in Israel's covenantal relationship with God: the traditional rabbinic attitude is that Judaism remained a community of faith. As far as Christianity was concerned, however, a radical break had occurred. Christianity had introduced a new covenant, or at the very least a radical transformation of the old covenant. According to the New Testament, the relationship between God and his people was mediated decisively through his Son, Jesus Christ. The question that has absorbed many theologians is whether the appearance of Christianity signifies an end for the role of the Jewish people. There are at least three possible ways in which the relation between the 'old' and 'new' peoples might be understood: first, only one (the

newer) is truly the 'people of God'; second, there are two peoples of God, the Jewish and the Christian; and third, the two peoples are really one people of God – identical in some respects and different in others.

The first position states simply that there is only one 'people of God' – the Christians. In this case either the Jews convert to Christianity or remain as Jews, a remnant destined to suffer, whose lowly position gives witness to the truth of Christ. This position was set forth in great detail by a number of **Church Fathers** and dominated Christian thought until it began to be questioned during and after the **Enlightenment**. Dispersed throughout the earth since the destruction of the **Temple**, Jews were viewed as preserving the original prophecies looking forward to Christ and witnessing to Christian truth. Indeed, according to **Augustine**, they were the 'satchel bearers' of the Church. The Jews had once been the people of God, but the high privileges they earned were now transferred to the Church because of their rejection of Christ. This approach can be described as substitution or **replacement theology**.

The second position argues that there are two peoples of God, the Jewish and the Christian. This view is espoused by theologians such as the Jewish writer Franz **Rosenzweig**, who suggests that both Jews and Christians participate in God's revelation and both are (in different ways) intended by God. Only for God is the truth one; earthly truth remains divided. Modern proponents of this view include James **Parkes**, who was convinced that the revelation in Christ did not replace the covenant at Sinai and as a result Judaism and Christianity were inextricably linked together (*Judaism and Christianity* (1948)).

The third position asserts that Jews and Christians represent one people of God who are identical in some respects and different in others. Although the two groups differ substantially, they nevertheless share sufficient common ground to make it possible for the same covenant to be applied to both. The most comprehensive theological model among Protestant theologians can be seen in the three-volume work by Paul van Buren (1924–98), who argues that the people 'Israel' should be recognised as two connected but distinct branches (*A Theology of Jewish–Christian Reality* (1980–8)). The Christian Church represents the Gentile believers drawn together by the God of the Jewish people in order to make God's love known throughout the world. Through Jesus Gentiles were summoned by God for the first time as full participants in God's ongoing **salvation** of humanity.

Evangelical scholars such as David Holwerda (b. 1932) dismiss many of these arguments. Yet while arguing that other writers have played down the differences between Judaism and Christianity, and in doing so have produced a theology that is not true to the New Testament message, Holwerda nevertheless asserts that 'the category of election still applies to the Jewish people, even those who do not now believe in Jesus' (*Jesus and Israel* (1995), 25). He argues that although the Church is the new Israel, the old Israel remains elect and in God's faithfulness still has a future. In taking this view, Holwerda is clearly dependent upon **Romans 9–11**.

The problem is illustrated by *Nostra Aetate*, perhaps the most influential of the recent church documents on Jewish–Christian relations. On the one hand, the document states that 'the church is the new people of God' while, on the other, 'the Jews remain most dear to God because of their fathers, for He does not repent of the gifts He makes nor of the calls He issues (cf. Rom. 11.28–29)'. Thus Pope **John Paul II**, who addressed the theological bond between Christianity and Judaism far more than any other pope in history, maintained that the Jews are still elect even though the Christians are the new Israel. In his historic visit to the Great Synagogue in Rome (1986) and his pilgrimage to Israel (2000) he stated that the Church discovers the bond of identity between Jews and Christians when it searches into the meaning of its own existence. Indeed, the Church has a relationship with Judaism unlike any other religion because of an 'intrinsic' link through Christ.

The establishment of the State of Israel has also had a significant influence on the understanding of chosenness in Jewish–Christian relations. For instance, the **Rhineland Synod** (1980) referred to the continuing existence of the Jewish people, its return to the land of promise and the creation of the State of Israel as 'signs of the faithfulness of God towards His people'. The dramatic change in thinking is illustrated by the *Notes on the Correct Way to Present Jews and Judaism in Preaching and Catechesis in the Roman Catholic Church* (1985), which repeats John Paul II's widely quoted reference in

1980 to 'the people of God of the Old Covenant, which has never been revoked'. The *Notes* state: 'The permanence of Israel (while so many ancient peoples have disappeared without trace) is a historic fact and a sign to be interpreted within God's design. We must in any case rid ourselves of the traditional idea of a people *punished*, preserved as a *living argument* for Christian apologetic. It remains a chosen people, "the pure olive on which were grafted the branches of the wild olive which are the gentiles" (John Paul II, 6 March 1982, alluding to Rom. 11.17–24).'

See also **Promised Land**; **supersessionism**

EDWARD KESSLER

Chosenness *see* **Chosen People**

Christ and Christology

The understanding of Christ and Christology in the various Christian traditions has always been closely tied to the perception of Jews and Judaism within the churches. The term 'Christ' refers to Jesus' divinely constituted role as **Messiah**, Lord and Saviour of humankind. The terms 'Jesus' and 'Christ' are to a degree interchangeable, although 'Christ' is the preferred one when speaking in a theological or liturgical context.

For centuries, Christianity expressed its self-identity in terms of the fulfilment of Judaism. The understanding has been that **Jesus** was the anticipated Jewish Messiah who had fulfilled the biblical promises and had inaugurated the era of full human **redemption**, even though its completion remained distant. Christology as a theological framework attempted to explain the redemptive impact of Jesus the Christ on all of creation.

The problem that arose as early as the second century CE and which remained with the Churches until the twentieth century was the intimate linkage established by the **Church Fathers** and subsequent theologians between the meaning of Christology and Jewish exclusion from the original covenant because of Jewish failure to recognise Jesus as the Christ. Jews were seen as closely involved with Jesus' execution, thus bringing upon their heads a permanent curse. Jews were called 'blind' with respect to the new revelation in Jesus. They were said to practise a much inferior form of religion rooted in **law**, while Christians based their faith on the experience of **grace** made present through Christ's coming. Jews were described as rejecting belief in Jesus, being replaced as a result in the covenantal relationship with God by the new Christian community.

These negative expressions of the meaning of Christology with regard to Judaism and the Jewish people took time to coalesce in the **early Church**. Though some of them go back to misinterpreted or selective scriptural passages, these beliefs about the Jews are essentially post-biblical. Through the patristic writings they framed Christian **identity** along anti-Jewish lines. In so doing, they created what has been termed the *Adversus Judaeos* ('against the Jews') tradition. In this Christological perspective Jesus the Jew had clearly become a barrier between Jews and Christians rather than a point of bonding. Nearly all Christian Churches have appropriated all or part of this negative vision of the Jews as an integral part of their catechesis, preaching, worship and theology. Rosemary Ruether (b. 1936) has demonstrated in her now classic volume *Faith and Fratricide* that **anti-Judaism** lay at the heart of patristic theology. It became in effect the 'left-hand of Christology'. The great writers of the patristic era, such as **Tertullian, Origen, Irenaeus** and **Eusebius**, all made the *Adversus Judaeos* an integral part of stating the fundamental meaning of Christianity.

In the Catholic Church this *Adversus Judaeos* tradition received its first major challenge at the Second Vatican Council (**Vatican II**). Chapter 4 of the conciliar declaration on non-Christian religions titled *Nostra Aetate* set forth an entirely different theological perspective on the role of the Jewish people after the Christ event. The Catholic theologian Gregory Baum (b. 1923) has termed this change one of the most significant reinterpretations of the ordinary teaching of the Catholic Church by Vatican II.

Most major Protestant denominations have issued statements that follow along the path laid out at Vatican II. Some have even made bolder assertions than the Council itself. The **Rhineland Synod** statement, documents from the United Church of **Canada**, the **Evangelical** Lutheran Church in America and the United **Methodist** Church, as well as the recent document from the Leuenberg Consultation of the Reformation Churches in Europe (*see* **Leuenberg Church Fellowship**), have significantly advanced the fundamental rethinking of Judaism's theological status after the covenant, a rethinking that will have significant impact on Christology.

The process of rethinking Christology in relation to continuing Jewish covenantal exclusion is not as advanced within **Orthodox Christianity**, although there has been some movement by individual theologians.

In these new Christian statements Jews are now seen as integral to the ongoing divine covenant. Jesus and early Christianity are portrayed as deeply rooted in a constructive sense in the faith of Second Temple Judaism. Jews may not be held collectively responsible for the death of Jesus; rather the statements argue that there was no basis for such a charge of **deicide** against the Jews in the first place. In so doing, they undercut the basis of the classical Christian theology of Jewish covenantal displacement, which had its roots in this charge.

The formal process of rethinking theologically the meaning of Christ, Christian identity and the Jewish people is generally regarded as having begun with the historic meeting of Jews and Christians (Catholics, Protestants and Greek Orthodox) at **Seelisberg**, Switzerland in 1947. Subsequently, several prominent Christian scholars in Europe, including Karl Barth (1886–1968), Jean Daniélou (1905–74), the future Cardinal Augustin **Bea**, James **Parkes** and Hans Urs von Balthasar (1905–88), began to speak out on the question. While not agreeing completely on every point, on one critical issue their voices were in unison: Jews must now be regarded as continuing in a covenantal relationship with God, however the Church eventually might interpret the meaning of the Christ event.

Many of the early proponents of a new theological vision of the Jewish–Christian relationship appealed to **Romans 9–11** for justification of their position. **Paul** insists in these chapters that God remains faithful to the original **Chosen People**. They also tended to rely on Romans for a new model for the Christian–Jewish relationship – the 'mystery' approach in which Christians and Jews are both proclaimed members of the covenantal household of God despite the apparent contradiction of such an assertion in purely human terms. In the **United States** Msgr John **Oesterreicher**, who would become a leading figure at Vatican II, introduced the works of some of these pioneering scholars to the Christian theological community via the publication of a multi-volume series called *The Bridge*.

The process of eradicating the *Adversus Judaeos* Christological tradition from Christian theology gained new impetus at Vatican II. The actual composition of the Vatican declaration on the Church and the Jewish people showed the poverty of the Christian **tradition** relative to its understanding of relations with the Jewish people. Every other document issued by Vatican II abounds with references to the tradition of the Church – the Fathers, papal statements, declarations by previous Church councils. Not so Chapter 4 of *Nostra Aetate*. There was simply little, if any, positive material upon which to draw, except to return as a starting point to Romans 9–11, as the Council in fact did.

In other words, the church was finally picking up in the second half of the twentieth century a process that had been short-circuited since the latter stages of St Paul's life. Constructing a new theology of the Church and the Jewish people in light of the Christ event was clearly emerging as a formidable undertaking. Because the effort to reformulate the theology of the Christian–Jewish relationship inevitably touches upon the very nerve centre of Christianity, namely Christology, the pace of change will likely be slow and fraught with controversy. But for the same reason a renewed theological understanding of the Church's linkage with the Jewish people has repercussions for the whole of Christian theology. The theologian Johann-Baptist Metz (b. 1928) has stressed that the restatement of the Church's relationship with the Jewish people is in fact a revision of Christian theology as such.

The process of revising the Church's understanding of the Christ event in light of its new understanding of the Jewish–Christian relationship has been enhanced by the work both of scripture scholars and systematicians. In **New Testament** studies we are now witnessing a remarkable turnabout in the basic understanding of Jesus' relationship to the Jewish community and tradition of his time. The influence of scholars such as Rudolf Bultmann (1884–1976), Ernst Käsemann (1906–98) and Helmut Koester (b. 1926), who universalised Jesus out of his Jewish roots and claimed a totally **Hellenistic** background for Paul, is rapidly waning. Such **exegesis** that harboured the seeds of a theological anti-Judaism is being replaced by new scholarly stress on Jesus and the early Church's strong, continuing attachment to Judaism. Biblical scholars such as Cardinal Carlo Martini (b. 1927), James

Charlesworth (b. 1940), W. D. Davies (1911–2001) and Daniel Harrington (b. 1940) have underscored the fact that without understanding the Judaism of the period we cannot understand Jesus' message, which was deeply imbued with Jewish religious perspectives of his time. Robin Scroggs (1930–2005) and Anthony Saldarini (1941–2001) have shown that for a century or more (and even beyond in some parts of Christianity) many Christians continued to harbour a profound attachment to Judaism which they expressed in part by regular participation in Jewish worship. Hence Christologies that revolve around the notion that through the Christ event Christianity totally fulfilled (and replaced) Judaism can no longer be easily sustained.

Realising the significance of the revolution in biblical scholarship regarding Jesus' relationship to Judaism, a number of Christian theologians have begun to rethink the statement of Christology. Generally speaking, two constructive approaches to stating the relationship between Christians and Jews have emerged in the last half-century. They are usually referred to as the single and double covenant perspectives, though most of the theologians involved in the discussion feel neither fully captures the reality of the linkage.

The question of **covenant** stands at the very heart of the Christological question. The recent document from the ecumenical Christians Scholars Group on Christian–Jewish Relations makes this point very strongly. *A Sacred Obligation* argues that with the recent recognition within the Church of the permanency of God's covenant with the Jewish people there comes the realisation that the redemptive power of God is at work within Judaism. So, if Jews who do not share the Christian faith are indeed in such a saving relationship with God, then Christians require new ways of understanding the universal significance of Christ.

The single-covenant approach assigns Jews and Christians to one continuing covenantal tradition that began with God's revelation to **Moses**. In this perspective the Christ event represents the decisive moment when the Gentile nations entered fully into the special relationship with God that Jews already enjoyed and in which they continue. Monika Hellwig (b. 1929), Paul van Buren (1924–98) and Clemens Thoma (b. 1932), along with most official documents on Jewish–Christian relations, have taken this theological path.

The double-covenant viewpoint generally also begins with a strong affirmation of the continuing bond between **Israel** and the Church. But it prefers to highlight the distinctiveness of the two traditions and communities, especially after their separation, and to emphasise that in the person of Jesus a vision of God emerged that is distinctively new in some of its central features. Such distinctiveness, these scholars underline, does not invalidate Judaism's covenantal status. The Jewish covenant, on the contrary, remains a source of revelation both for Jews and Christians. Franz Mussner (b. 1916), J. Coert Rylaarsdam (1907–98), John Pawlikowski (b. 1940) and Gregory Baum, among others, have argued for this perspective, albeit in considerably different ways.

In recent years a number of scholars have become somewhat dissatisfied with the single and double covenant options. These scholars, both Jewish and Christian, have begun to suggest new images of the relationship. Alan Segal (b. 1945) and Hayim Perelmuter (1915–2001) have proposed 'siblings' as an appropriate model while Mary Boys (b. 1947) has spoken of 'fraternal twins', Clark Williamson (b. 1935) of 'partners in waiting' and Daniel Boyarin (b. 1946) of 'co-emergence'. All of these images stress both linkage and distinctiveness between Christianity and Judaism. They tend to emphasise a more 'parallel' rather than the traditional 'linear' dimensions of the relationship, with Christianity and Judaism, as we know them today, having emerged out of a religious revolution in Second Temple Judaism. Such 'parallel' images render any Christology rooted in a linear understanding of the Jewish–Christian relationship highly problematical.

Some theologians such as Jürgen Moltmann (b. 1926), Franklin Sherman (b. 1928) and John Pawlikowski have explored connections between the **Holocaust** and Christological understanding. For one, they argue, if the notion of God and the divine–human relationship needs restatement in the light of the Holocaust experience, then the perspective on the Christ event also needs reconsideration given its understanding as embodying the divine presence in a special way. Some, such as James Moore (b. 1946), also maintain that the Holocaust forces the Church to proclaim a Christology of witness and resistance within the framework of an overarching theology of discipleship.

Redemption in and through Christ, after the Holocaust, can no longer be understood in merely 'spiritual' terms, but must be tied to the historical experience of people at a particular moment in time. Several of these scholars, especially Sherman and Marcel Dubois (b. 1907), posit a direct link between Jesus' sufferings on the cross and the sufferings of the Jewish people during the Holocaust. But others, such as John Pawlikowski and Alice (b. 1923) and Roy Eckardt (1918–98), find such a comparison very problematical. Jesus' sufferings have always been seen as voluntary and redemptive. This cannot be claimed for Jewish suffering during the Holocaust.

Despite the recognition of some theologians within the Christian community that the recent repudiation of the *Adversus Judaeos* tradition has profound implications for Christological statement, major problems remain. The Vatican document *Dominus Iesus* (September 2000) has argued that all **salvation** ultimately comes through Christ and that those that do not acknowledge that stand in considerable peril in terms of their redemption. While some Catholic leaders have insisted this document does not pertain to the Jews, this is difficult to accept in light of the line of argumentation it advances. The noted theologian Cardinal Walter Kasper (b. 1933), since 2001 head of the Holy See's Commission for Religious Relations with the Jews, has advanced the notion that Jews are an exception to the rule in terms of the universality of salvation in Christ because they are the only non-Christian religious community to have authentic revelation from the Christian perspective. Hence **Torah** is sufficient for Jewish salvation. This thesis remains in its infancy. Its ultimate test will be whether in the light of such affirmation there is clear recognition on the part of the Church that there is no **mission** to the Jews. The Leuenberg document (2001) also rejects the need to actively seek the **conversion** of Jews.

Jewish theology thus far has shown little interest in these Christological developments within the Church. A few Jewish scholars have stressed the importance of understanding Jesus' profound rootage in Judaism and the contribution of the New Testament to the understanding of first-century CE Judaism. The authors of the Jewish document on Christianity **Dabru Emet** hold open some possibility for a new Jewish interest in Christology, as do the writings of Jewish scholars such as Michael Wyschogrod (b. 1928) and Elliot Wolfson (b. 1956). Wyschogrod has spoken of the '**incarnation**' of the Jewish people, while Wolfson has uncovered 'traces' of incarnationalism in the Jewish **apocalyptic** tradition.   *JOHN T. PAWLIKOWSKI*

Christian Hebraists *see* **Hebraists, Christian**

Christian Identity movements *see* **British Israelites**

Christian perspectives on Judaism *see* **Judaism, Christian perspectives on**

Christian Scholars Group on Christian–Jewish Relations (CSG) *see* **Jewish–Christian relations, centres for the study of**

Christian Zionism *see* **Zionism, Christian**

Christianity, Jewish perspectives on

In its original form, Christianity consisted of some Jewish followers of **Jesus** declaring him as the **Messiah**, claiming to represent the true path during the last era of world history, and demanding conversion to their interpretation of Judaism. Christianity was therefore one Jewish group amongst others such as the **Sadducees**, Hellenists, **Zealots**, Essenes and **Pharisees**, but only Christians and the Pharisees survived the destruction of the **Temple** in 70 CE. James Dunn (b. 1939) has correctly pointed out that the separation between Christianity and Judaism consisted of a series of 'partings of the ways', which began when the Jewish followers of Jesus started to attract large numbers of Gentiles. The abolition of Jewish customs such as **circumcision** and *kashrut* (**food** laws) contributed to the rejection of Christianity by most Jews, and Jewish opposition to Christianity was also increased by Christian failure to support Jewish revolts against Rome and the Messianic claims of **Bar Kokhba**. By the time of the completion of the **Talmud** (*c.*500) Judaism and Christianity had fully diverged. It is not coincidental that around the same time **Jewish Christianity** also ceased to exist.

The main theological divide between Jews and Christians concerned Christian claims about the divinity of Jesus. Bitterness between Jews (as well as Gentiles) over the significance of Jesus can be seen in the **New Testament**, where views about Jesus' authority and significance – a major proportion of which developed after his death – were ascribed to Jesus himself. A similar process can be noticed in rabbinic writings, where some **anti-Christian teachings** are ascribed to rabbis who lived before Jesus. By portraying these views as the words of revered religious leaders they become more authoritative.

The rabbinic writings are cautious in their comments on Christianity because of Christian **censorship** and fear of retribution. Nevertheless, it is possible to find implicit, and occasionally explicit, repudiation of Christianity. For example, Rabbi Ishmael (*fl.* second century CE) is reported to have stated that Christians 'inject hatred, jealousy between Israel and their father in heaven'. Rabbi Johanan ben Zakkai (*fl.* first century CE) felt it necessary to explain that Jews did not fast on Sunday 'on account of the Christians' (*b. Ta'anit* 27b). The **liturgy** – through the creation of *birkat ha-minim* – was adapted to ensure that heretics, some of whom were identified as Christians (though scholars debate whether the term refers to Jewish Christians or included all Christians), could not easily participate in Jewish acts of worship. Although rabbinic knowledge of Jesus is extremely limited (and tells us nothing of the historical Jesus), it does shed light on early Jewish **polemic** against Christianity. For example, Christian teaching about the **Virgin Birth** resulted in the charge that Jesus was born out of wedlock; Christian rejection of the **Torah** led to the accusation that Jesus 'deceived and led Israel astray'; New Testament accounts of Jesus' miracles lay behind the criticism that Jesus was a magician who was put to death by 'Pinchas the Robber' (**Pilate**).

Once Christianity was established as the religion of the **Roman Empire** in the fourth century, the situation for Jews became more difficult, though this was a gradual process because the energy of Christian Europe was directed towards defeating pagans and Christian heretics. During this time the abundance of anti-Jewish writings (*Adversus Judaeos literature*) resulted in little violence against Jews; nor did it stir much of a Jewish response, possibly because until then Christianity, whilst seen as a contemporary oppressor of Judaism and ranking as the third or fourth of the four kingdoms predicted by Daniel, was viewed with little theological interest. The polemical text *Toledot Yeshu* seems to be an exception. On the other hand, there is some evidence to suggest that Jewish commentators were aware of Christian **exegesis**. The willingness of some Jewish exegetes to appropriate Christian interpretation, wrap it in Jewish garb and include it in Jewish biblical **commentary** suggests a closer relationship, at least as far as interpretation of scripture is concerned, than has previously been accepted. Rabbinic interpretation of the **binding of Isaac** is one example: the rabbis, like the **Church Fathers**, compare Isaac carrying the wood on his shoulder (Gen. 22.5) to 'a man who carries a cross' (*Genesis Rabbah* 56.3). This shows the influence of Christian interpretation adapted for a Jewish audience.

From approximately 1100 onwards, as Christendom became more homogeneous, Jews were seen as one of the last 'different' groups, and by the sixteenth century they had been expelled from most of Western Europe (*see* **expulsions**). Jews were liable to mass assaults, as witnessed in the **Crusades** from the eleventh century and in response to the **Black Death** in the fourteenth. Contemporary Jewish writings bear witness to violence, and increased political exploitation and legal discrimination, at the hands of Christians. This situation, in addition to widespread medieval Christian charges of **deicide**, **host desecration** and **blood libel**, resulted in the publication of anti-Christian writings such as the anonymous *Nizzahon Vetus*, which criticised Christianity as absurd and condemned Jewish converts as well as Christian attacks on the Talmud. During this period Christians were becoming increasingly aware of the existence of post-biblical Jewish writings such as the Talmud and denounced them accordingly. Similarly, the rabbis were familiar not only with the New Testament, but also with patristic writings and later Christian practices, which they used to condemn Christianity.

Since Judaism was a **minority** in both the Islamic world and Christendom, Jews were prompted to consider why God allowed these faiths to flourish. One view was that Christianity was a form of **idolatry**, perhaps not in the full biblical sense but through inherited patterns of idolatrous worship (*b. Hullin* 13b). Another approach categorised Christianity in terms of the **Noachide Laws**, which formulated moral standards without demand for **conversion** to Judaism. According to Rabbi Johanan ben Zakkai, whoever denied idolatry was deemed a Jew (a concept revived in the nineteenth century by Elia Benamozegh (1823–1900), who persuaded a would-be Catholic convert to adopt 'noahism'). Another view, propagated by **Judah ha-Levi** and

Maimonides, was that Christianity prepared the way for nations to worship the God of Israel and for redemption. Menahem ben Solomon **Meiri** put forward the most positive view during this period when he argued that Christianity should be understood as a form of monotheism and coined the phrase 'nations bound by the ways of religion' to relax certain rabbinic laws and facilitate a more fruitful interaction between Jews and Christians.

Jews viewed the **Reformation** as a positive development, partly because of its challenge to the unity of the Church, which seemed to divert Christian attention away from Judaism. The Protestant return to the **Hebrew Bible** and a number of reformers' awareness of Jewish commentaries probably contributed to a rise in messianic fervour among Jews, which was noticed by **Luther**. However, although Luther's early writings, such as *That Jesus Christ Was Born a Jew* (1523), suggested a dramatic change in Christian perceptions of Judaism, the bitter anti-Jewish treatises written towards the end of his life served to increase Jewish loyalty to the Catholic emperor. For example, the contemporary German Jewish leader **Josel of Rosheim** sided with the sovereign and called Luther 'impure' (*lo tohar* – a pun on Luther's name). Despite its early promise, therefore, as far as most contemporary Jews were concerned the Reformation saw the Christian 'teaching of contempt' continue unabated.

During the **Enlightenment** a small number of Jews, such as Moses **Mendelssohn**, reflected publicly and seriously on the future of Judaism and on the Jewish relationship with Christianity. In 1769 Mendelssohn was challenged by his friend Johann Lavater (1741–1801) to convert to Christianity. He rejected the call and, whilst extolling the teaching of Jesus and the virtues of Christianity, espoused the values of Judaism: 'Suppose there were living among my contemporaries a Confucius or a Solon, I could, according to the principles of my faith, love and admire the great man without falling into the ridiculous idea that I must convert a Solon or a Confucius.' Although Mendelssohn remained Jewish, the pace of change in society was matched by significant Jewish **assimilation** into either secularism or Christianity. Heinrich **Heine** famously called his conversion a 'ticket of admission to European culture'. The dramatic increase in assimilation in the nineteenth century was foreshadowed by the French Revolution, which offered Jews equality on condition of their abandoning their faith.

A shift in attitudes to Christianity among religious leaders can be noted in the years following the Enlightenment and Jewish **emancipation**. Reform figures such as Abraham **Geiger** and Stephen **Wise** embraced the Jewishness of Jesus, and even S. R. Hirsch (1808–88), one of the founders of **Orthodox Judaism**, argued that Jesus embodied the essence of Judaism. It was thus not a huge step for Martin **Buber** to call Jesus his 'elder brother'. Jewish philosophers such as Hermann **Cohen** and Franz **Rosenzweig** also made contributions to the Jewish understanding of Christianity, the former arguing that Jewish **ethics** were superior to Christian (heavily influencing Leo **Baeck**), and the latter that Christianity was a pathway to God for Gentiles. As liberal culture spread throughout Europe, East European thinkers also wrote on Christianity: for example, Abraham Isaac Kook (1865–1935), later Chief Rabbi of Palestine, praised Jesus but criticised Christianity for moving far from Judaism.

At the same time as exhibiting a more sympathetic understanding of Jesus, Jewish views of Christianity were affected by an increasing anti-Jewish prejudice and the rise of racial **antisemitism**. The Enlightenment doctrine that whilst society could be remade certain men were beyond redemption provided the basis for modern racism and reached a climax in the rise of **Nazism** and ultimately in the **Holocaust**. The failure of the Churches during 1933–45 resulted in anger towards and distrust of Christianity. An extreme example of this view is illustrated by Eliezer Berkovits (1908–92), who argued that the roots of Nazism can be traced back to the New Testament: 'Christianity's New Testament has been the most dangerous antisemitic tract in history. Its hatred-charged diatribes against the Pharisees and the Jews have poisoned the hearts and minds of millions and millions of Christians for almost two millennia. Without Christianity's New Testament, Hitler's *Mein Kampf* could never have been written.' The call at the first meeting of the **World Council of Churches** in 1948 for Christians to redouble their efforts to convert Jews reinforced the view that the Church had no respect for living Judaism.

However, the reassessment of Christian attitudes towards Judaism in the writings of Christian scholars such as James **Parkes**, which started in the first half of the twentieth century and accelerated after the Holocaust, began to have an impact on Jewish attitudes. In addition, Christian institutional statements such as *Nostra Aetate* in 1965 contributed to a reassessment of Christianity among Jews. The publication of *Dabru Emet* in 2000, exploring the place of Christianity in Jewish terms, represents the views of a significant proportion of Jews in English-speaking countries, although there are also many for whom Christianity is unimportant in their Jewish **identity** or who are critical of the document (particularly some Orthodox Jews). David Berger (b. 1943), for example, rejects what he considers to be 'theological reciprocity', while others are concerned about increasing antisemitism and a lack of Christian support for the **State of Israel**.

Some of the present-day concerns of Jews in their relationship with Christianity – fighting antisemitism and anti-**Zionism** – have remained the same for the last hundred years. However, new topics are also coming to the fore in **dialogue**, including theological conversations, such as joint projects on **biblical interpretation** and for social justice. *EDWARD KESSLER*

Christmas

The central event in the Advent–Christmas–Epiphany liturgical cycle, Christmas draws Christians into the mystery of the enfleshment of the Word of God in Jesus the Christ. Celebrating Jesus as **Immanuel** (God with us), the feast is an integral part of the Paschal mystery, focusing on an adult Christ rather than merely the biological birth of an infant. The central themes of this feast and cycle are among the most prominent in the Jewish–Christian **dialogue**. These include the Incarnation, **eschatology**, Messiah and the Messianic Era.

While the origin of the date of the feast (25 December) is unclear, its juxtaposition in the third and fourth centuries to the pagan observances of the winter solstice radically transformed their message and helped proclaim the presence of a new belief. The December feast was observed annually in Rome by the early fourth century and quickly spread in the West after the accession of **Constantine**. The fourth- and sixth-century controversies on the **Incarnation** and the Person of **Christ** doubtlessly contributed to the feast's growth in importance.

Given the proximity of Christmas to the Jewish celebration of **Hanukkah**, as well as their common emphases on the themes of light and God's presence in our midst, in the Western world the minor Jewish holiday with simple rituals has often expanded in importance in competition with this popular Christian feast. In many places this Christian liturgical feast and cycle has also become a secular season, a time when capitalist encouragement of frenetic Christmas gift-giving is also having a secularising and commercialising effect on Hanukkah. Regrettably, some of the beautiful liturgical and paraliturgical practices of the Advent and Christmas season have for centuries subtly and inadvertently promoted a **supersessionist** theology of fulfilment. Advent wreaths (on which a lit candle is added on each of the four Advent Sundays, culminating in the lighting of the Christ Candle) and **Jesse** Trees (on which images of Hebrew scripture personages prefiguring and preparing for God's ultimate manifestation in **Jesus** are progressively hung during the four Advent weeks) easily convey the message that the light (of Jesus) replaced the darkness (of the Jews), and that the Jews served merely as a preparation for the new People of God. Traditional Advent hymns with such lyrics as 'ransom captive Israel' and 'redeem the long lost fold' have significantly contributed to this. The season's **liturgies** show great continuity between the Hebrew and Christian scriptures, while at the same time raising questions about the nature of biblical **prophecy** and the relationship of the Church to the Jewish people. Such passages as **Isaiah**'s about the 'days to come', 'the people who walked in darkness', and the virgin giving 'birth to a son whom she will call Immanuel' – when immediately followed by the season's Gospel passages – convince the average Christian worshipper that Jesus is the fulfilment of the prophets' proclamation of hope and promise.

The Advent–Christmas reminder to the Christian community that it yet awaits the second and ultimate coming of Christ highlights the differences in the Christian and Jewish concepts of **Messiah**, as well as the similarity in the manner the two faith communities work and yearn for the Messianic Era.

See also **infancy narratives**   *AUDREY DOETZEL*

Christology *see* **Christ and Christology**

Chrysostom, John (c.350–407)

John Chrysostom ('the golden tongue') was born into a wealthy and powerful family in **Antioch**.

He studied under the well-known rhetor Libanius (314–c.394), and might have succeeded him had he not decided to be baptised in 368. Chrysostom retreated to the desert to study with monks and was ordained a deacon in 382 and presbyter in 386. In 398 he was summoned to Constantinople to become a patriarch, but at a synod in 403 was condemned as a result of the intrigue of Theophilus, Patriarch of **Alexandria** (r.385–412) and was deposed and exiled in 404.

Chrysostom delivered eight sermons, *Adversus Judaeos*, in 386–7 which demonstrate extreme antipathy to Jews and Judaism at an early stage of his career. They arose from his fear of the vitality of Judaism and the Jewish community in Antioch, which influenced his Christian congregants and threatened his authority. Chrysostom believed that Judaism and Christianity existed in a state of competition. Four elements in the close relationship between Jews and Christians particularly angered him: Christian participation in the festivals and fasts of the Jewish community, Christian belief that Jews and their synagogues were endowed with numinous aura, Christian admiration for Jewish observance, and Christian acceptance of Jews as the people of the **Hebrew Bible**. Chrysostom's comments indicate that Christians were attending both synagogue and church, and while his invective is directed at the Jew, his principal target is the **Judaising Christian**.

Chrysostom sought to protect Christian **identity** and **tradition** in a place and at a time when Christianity was a **minority** community struggling for survival against a Jewish and pagan majority in Antioch. In his first homily he accuses Jews of having 'degenerated to the level of dogs' who 'live only for their bellies' (*Adv. Jud.* 1.2; 845–46), and refers to the synagogue as a 'house of prostitution' (*Adv. Jud.* 1.3). Since the destruction of the Temple in 70 CE, he argued, Jews had lost their ministry and **covenant**; demons now live not only in the synagogue, but in the souls of Jews, who sacrifice their children to appease them (*Adv. Jud.* 1.6). Like **Melito**, Chrysostom accuses the Jews past and present of **deicide**, a claim that was to become central to the *Adversus Judaeos* tradition and official Christian teaching for centuries.

Chrysostom's first anti-Jewish sermon was delivered in September 386 before the festival of Rosh Hashanah. With the exception of the third homily, which was preached before **Passover**, all the homilies were delivered in September or October before the major autumn Jewish festivals, Christian participation in which he wished to discourage (*Adv. Jud.* 1.1; 844, and 4.3; 875). Similarly, Chrysostom's sixth homily must be understood against the background of the **Quartodeciman controversy** over the dating of **Easter**. The Judaisers in Chrysostom's Church were ignoring the ruling of the Council of Nicaea (325) that Easter should not be calculated according to the Jewish **calendar**, and by celebrating Easter and Passover together were, in Chrysostom's view, issuing a direct challenge to Christian truth and authority.

When evaluating these homilies we should bear in mind both the rhetorical conventions within which Chrysostom was working and the expectations of his audiences. He uses hyperbole, standard metaphors and similes; nor is his invective designed either as logical, truthful argument, or to be taken literally by listeners. No angry crowds stormed the synagogue as a result of Chrysostom's sermons; he aimed simply to win back Christians who had deserted the Churches. His attacks on Jews should also be seen in the context of his attacks on other groups. For example, his description of Judaism as a disease was used several days earlier with reference to the **Arians**; his description of Jewish **fasting** as a form of drunkenness was elsewhere applied to Christian moral laxity; and his characterisation of the synagogue as a gathering place for 'whores, thieves and the crowd of dancers' shares the language of his attack on **Julian the Apostate**.

However, the impact of Chrysostom's sermons can be seen in later generations, who enjoyed his **rhetoric** but either did not recognise or ignored its conventions. Passages were excerpted into Byzantine **liturgy** for **Holy Week**, and later writers drew freely from the homilies. They were translated into Russian in the eleventh century at the time of the first **pogrom** in Russian history under Prince Vladimir (956–1015), and were read in medieval Europe, in **Byzantium** and again in **Russia** when Christianity was the dominant religion and Jews were subject to repressive laws. Above all, Chrysostom's *Adversus Judaeos* sermons were used to support and encourage anti-Jewish attitudes in the Church and have had a significant impact on Christian theology for many centuries, particularly but not exclusively in the Eastern **Orthodox Churches**.

While his **anti-Judaism** was theological rather than racial, it is legitimate to consider his part, along with other **Church Fathers**, in the development of **anti-semitism**. His writings are thus acutely difficult for Jewish–Christian relations, in terms not only of the fourth century, but of their use and abuse over the following 1,600 years.   *EDWARD KESSLER*

Church and state

Christians vary in their understandings of the form relations between Church and state should take. Although Orthodoxy does not have the political principle of the state church at its basis, in Orthodox countries Church and state have usually been closely linked. In contrast, the **Historic Peace Churches** advocate separatism, in some instances shunning involvement in civic affairs. Catholics and Protestants generally hold intermediate positions, interpreting Mark 12.13–17 and Rom. 13.1–7 to require Christian involvement in the construction of **civil society** and obedience to the state.

Most historians agree that Jewish–Christian relations deteriorated after **Constantine**'s conversion and Christianity's establishment as the official religion of the **Roman Empire**. With Christendom's rise, Christians were able not merely to argue with, but to control Jewish activity: restrictions peaked in the medieval period, when legislation in numerous Western and Central European states responded to the papal desire (articulated in the Fourth **Lateran Council**) to see the socio-political realm embody **supersessionism**.

In the nineteenth century Jewish **emancipation** and increased contacts between Christians and Jews accompanied the weakening of legal Church–state ties. Critics of **dialogue** (e.g. **Berkovits**) have characterised ecumenical and interfaith activity as self-interested, strategic responses by the Western Churches to their loss of influence in state affairs. Conversely, the creation of **Israel** as a secular state inspired by Jewish tradition (predominantly a religious tradition) opens up new questions in Judaism that parallel those facing many Christian churches today. 'Church'–state relations may, therefore, prove a fruitful dialogue topic in the future.   *MELANIE J. WRIGHT*

Church and synagogue

In the study of Jewish–Christian relations it has sometimes been assumed that the term 'Church' (*ekklesia*) is equivalent to 'synagogue' (*beit ha-k'nesset*). In fact, their roles are significantly different, even though their origins are similar. In non-biblical Greek literature *ekklesia* refers to any gathering of people, Jewish, Christian or neither (Saldarini, *Matthew's Christian-Jewish Community* 116–20), and in the **New Testament** the Church is the gathering of people who follow **Jesus** of Nazareth. Similarly *beit ha-k'nesset* means a 'house of meeting', a place where Jews congregate, sometimes for prayer but on other occasions simply to participate in social events or to study scripture or other authoritative writings. Perhaps the nearest Jewish equivalent to Church is 'the Jewish people'.

Among the Gospel writers, only Matthew uses the term *ekklesia* ('on this rock I will build my church', 16.18), which **Roman Catholicism** interpreted institutionally, taking Peter as the first pope, through whom God transmits teaching authority (Lat. *magisterium*) via papal succession. As an episcopal polity developed which was unknown in Judaism, the meaning of 'Church' began to diverge from that of synagogue. For example, the Roman Catholic Church is led by bishops (Gk *episkopoi*), of whom the bishop of Rome is the first among equals. **Protestantism** also emphasises Matt. 16.18, but the focus is on faith, which is conveyed as a gift of grace to the whole **community**, leading to a more communal polity – clergy are ordained by the community to serve sacramental, teaching and leadership functions on their behalf, suggesting perhaps that the 'Church', as a non-hierarchical, communal polity of Protestantism, carries a meaning that is closer to synagogue. Consequently, Church teachings (*inter alia* about Judaism) under these distinctive ecclesiologies carry different degrees of authority.

After **Constantine**'s conversion, the Church became the religious institution of the **Roman Empire** and remained a powerful cultural force into modern times, symbolised in the Christian rites of medieval royal coronation. From this position of power, steeped in its *Adversus Judaeos* paradigm, the Church stressed the contrast of *ecclesia/synagoga*, assuring the marginal and oppressed position of Jews and also reinforcing a mistaken equivalence between Church and synagogue.

PETER A. PETTIT AND EDWARD KESSLER

Church Fathers

The Fathers (Latin *patres*) are the early Christian teachers who gave their name to the patristic age of Church history, lasting from the end of the first century to the early Middle Ages, and to the patristic literature, the main body of Christian texts from these years. Their localities include all the principal centres of Jewish population in antiquity, their languages were also used by contemporary Jews, and their writings form a rich and debated source for knowledge of Jewish history, Jewish–Christian relations and the history of the *aggadah*.

In the Church the name 'Fathers' has designated early teachers whose writings form an authoritative statement of **doctrine**; but patristic literature when viewed broadly is commonly taken to include authors, like **Origen**, whose authority has been doubted; writings from communities that have been judged heretical, notably **Gnostics**, **Arians** and Donatists; and acts of the martyrs, early lives of saints, and early texts of **liturgy** and church law. Prior and fundamental to this literature were the **Old Testament**, studied by the Fathers usually in the **Septuagint** and other translations, and the **New Testament**; both were read together with many related **apocrypha**, partly Jewish, partly amplified or composed by Christians. The Church also transmitted and translated the Greek biblical, historical and philosophical works of the first-century CE Jewish authors **Philo** and **Josephus**. There was some knowledge of pre-Philonic Greek Jewish biblical **exegesis**, preserved (mainly through the pagan Alexander Polyhistor (*c.*105–40 BCE)) in Clement of Alexandria (*c.*150–*c.*215) and **Eusebius**. Philonic biblical **allegory** as adapted in Latin sermons by Ambrose (339–97) aided **Augustine**'s return from Manichaeism to orthodoxy. Contributors to patristic literature range from Clement of Rome (*fl. c.*96) to **Isidore of Seville** in the west and to John of Damascus (*c.*675–*c.*749) in the east. Many Fathers were bishops, but important works come from teachers of lower clerical rank, notably Origen and **Jerome**, and there are a few lay authors, for example (probably) Julius Africanus in late second-century Judea and the Latin church poet Prudentius (348–*c.*410) in Gaul.

This literature is in the three main Christian languages of the **Roman Empire**: **Greek** in both east and west in the second and early third centuries,

Latin in the west from the second century onwards, and Greek with **Syriac** (a dialect of **Aramaic**) in the eastern Roman provinces and over the border. In the later patristic age the languages of the eastern Church also include Armenian, **Coptic** and Ethiopic. The forms of the literature need not have seemed alien to contemporary Jews, for the books follow literary models attested in earlier Jewish writing (**Hebrew**, Aramaic or Greek), including biblical **commentary**, homily, Church orders (comparable with the Qumran rule literature; *see* **Dead Sea Scrolls**), hymns and prayers. Apologetic, doctrinal and historical treatises develop Greek models already used by Philo and Josephus.

The light shed by this literature on the Jews in antiquity touches notable events, including the uprisings of the years 115–17 and 132–5 and the fifth-century **expulsion** of Alexandrian Jews, and aspects of communal life, as in Origen on the Jewish ethnarch in Judea or Synesius of Cyrene (*c*.370–*c*.414) on Jewish mariners. Impressions of Jews and Judaism also abound in apocrypha and martyr-acts. The value of patristic sources was shown by such historians of the Jews as J. Juster (*c*.1886–1916), L. Lucas (1872–1943) and Y. Kaufmann (1889–1963).

Patristic literature itself preserves some non-Hebrew writing by Jews, dating from the first century CE onwards. Among **Bible translations**, this includes the revised Greek versions in the names of Theodotion (*fl*. end of second century CE), **Aquila** and Symmachus (*fl*. probably late second century CE) (possibly a Christian Jew), the Syriac Pentateuch and perhaps some Jewish Latin renderings. Other probably Jewish texts in the patristic literature include, in Greek, an apologia for Judaism (*Clementine Homilies* 4–6), a second-century critique of Christian origins (quoted at length in Origen, *Contra Celsum*) and a number of prayers (*Apostolic Constitutions* 7–8), and in Latin, a comparison of Mosaic and Roman law (*Mosaicarum et Romanarum Legum Collatio*). Christian teachers of Jewish descent are cited, as by Clement of Alexandria in the second century. Works under the names of Jews who have accepted **baptism** include a (lost) second-century Greek *Dialogue* between Jason and the Alexandrian non-Christian Jew Papiscus, and tracts by Isaac in fourth-century Rome, in

Latin, and Joseph (on the newly baptised Jacob) in seventh-century Byzantine Carthage, in Greek.

The contact between Jews and Christians that these contemporary Jewish elements in patristic literature suggest is also suggested by writings 'against the Jews', *Adversus Judaeos*, sometimes in dialogue form. Like all **apologetic**, these books serve internal needs, but their presentation of the arguments put forward by Jews and proselytes is probably a reflection as well as an adaptation or invention. Continuing discussion of this point harks back especially to the Church historian Adolf von **Harnack**, who held that the Christian apologies, although ostensibly directed to Jews, were really concerned mainly with pagan arguments. Discussion with Jews is nonetheless mentioned by Origen (*Cels*. 1.55) and others, and a desire to dissuade Christians from being impressed by Jewish tradition is exemplified in **Chrysostom**'s homilies *Adversus Judaeos*, rebuking Antiochene churchgoers who frequent the synagogues. The ruling emphasis of the patristic apologies on biblical **proof-texts** continues in Jewish as well as Christian apologetic in the Middle Ages.

Patristic literature developed at the same time as the Hebrew and Aramaic literature of the **Talmud** and **midrash** grew up in Palestine and Babylonia. Some patristic awareness of rabbinic tradition emerges especially in third- and fourth-century Palestine in Origen, Epiphanius (*c*.315–403) and Jerome (whose exegesis and new Latin translation of the Hebrew biblical books sometimes reflect contemporary Jewish interpretation). Particularly striking, however, is the general overlap between patristic and rabbinic exegetical tradition; thus the Syriac biblical poetry of **Ephrem** Syrus has much in common with midrash and **Targum**, but specific indebtedness to contemporary rabbinic exegesis is less obvious. Jewish *aggadah* has been intensively studied in this connection by Samuel Krauss (1866–1948), Louis Ginzberg (1873–1953) and others. Contemporary Jewish–Christian contact can be seen, together with independent development from common sources. Jerome, one of a very few patristic authors who learned Hebrew, defends his own dependence on Jewish learning as a traditional Christian recourse (*Ruf*. 1.13).

Patristic literature exhibits side by side a differentiation between Christianity and Judaism and a Christian share in Jewish culture. Anti-Jewish argument has **antisemitic** aspects and contributes under the Christian emperors to restrictive measures and movements; but it is accompanied by recognition of the Jews as custodians of biblical tradition, and by many indications of contact between Jews and Christians, not least in biblical study. *WILLIAM HORBURY*

Church of England

The Church of England's attitudes to Judaism and the Jewish people have changed dramatically in recent years. The traditional attitude is illustrated in a collect for Good Friday, dating from the sixteenth century, to be found in the *Book of Common Prayer*. It prays that God will have mercy upon 'all Jews, Turks, Infidels and Hereticks, and take from them all ignorance, hardness of heart and contempt of thy Word and so fetch them home, blessed Lord, to thy flock, that they may be saved among the remnant of the true Israelites'. This reflects a **supersessionist** or replacement theology and assumes that salvation is only possible by membership of the church – the true Israel. Revised versions of the prayer in the *1928 Prayer Book* and the *1980 Alternative Service Book* reflect the same attitudes.

Even so, because both the morning and evening daily services of the Church of England required a reading from the '**Old Testament**' as well as of several **psalms**, clergy and devout laity were deeply versed in the Hebrew scriptures. Clergy were encouraged to learn **Hebrew**. In the nineteenth century some members of the Church of England actively supported missions to the Jews, especially through the Church's Mission to the Jews (subsequently the **Church's Mission among Jewish People**) (CMJ) and others protested against the persecution of the Jews in **Russia** and elsewhere. There was considerable sympathy for the **Balfour Declaration**, which promised the Jews a national home in Palestine. A pioneer of a new approach was James **Parkes**, a Church of England clergyman, who in the 1930s showed that Christian anti-Jewish teaching was the major cause of **antisemitism**. He and later Peter Schneider (1928–82) worked hard to counter unfair pictures of Judaism and to suggest that **Jesus** was a faithful Jew. Even in the 1930s Parkes opposed attempts to convert Jews and he and Archbishop William **Temple** and other members of the Church of England supported the formation of the **Council of Christians and Jews** in 1942, of which all

subsequent Archbishops of Canterbury have been Presidents.

The Church of England now repudiates antisemitism, and attempts have been made to purge the Church's teaching and liturgy of all anti-Jewish elements. The Good Friday collect is omitted from *Common Worship*, published in 2000. A good summary of current Church of England thinking is provided by *Sharing One Hope?*, published by the Inter Faith Consultative Group of the Archbishop's Council in 2001. This identifies seven areas of agreement: the repudiation of antisemitism; a recognition of the continuing vitality of Judaism; the unacceptability of '**replacement theology**'; the need for wider dissemination of recent findings of **New Testament** scholarship; the recognition of the Jewishness of Jesus; sensitivity in **liturgy**, especially in the public reading of passages that present 'the Jews' in a hostile light; and emphasis on the hope, shared by Jews and Christians, for the coming of God's kingdom. Four areas of continuing debate are noted: the relationship of the two **covenants**, the implications for **Christology** of a new appreciation of Judaism, the Land and **mission**. Reflection on the **Holocaust** has only had a limited influence on the thinking of the Church of England, although the recently introduced **Holocaust Memorial Day** may change this.

See also **Anglicanism**; **United Kingdom**

MARCUS BRAYBROOKE

Church's Ministry among Jewish People (CMJ)

CMJ is a society that seeks to share the gospel with Jewish people. Its missionary approach has often been controversial. The interdenominational London Society for Promoting Christianity amongst the Jews was established in 1809, with the support of leading evangelical churchmen, including William Wilberforce (1759–1833) and Charles Simeon (1759–1836). In 1815 Nonconformists withdrew. Adopting the name Church's Mission to the Jews, it became a **Church of England** voluntary society, although some members belong to other denominations. In 1995 the name was changed to Church's Ministry among Jewish People. The work has changed considerably over the years. For much of the nineteenth century CMJ was based in the East End of London, working with the many Jewish immigrants who had fled from persecution in **Russia**. After the Second World War, CMJ moved to north-west London, where many Jews lived.

The headquarters are now at St Albans. The society was for many years active in Eastern Europe, **Ethiopia** and Iran, and is beginning new work in the **Ukraine**. In England CMJ today seeks to combat **antisemitism**, to make Gentile Christians more aware of their faith's Jewish roots, especially through its 'Bible Come to Life' travelling exhibition, and runs Jewish evangelism training weekends. Its work in the Holy Land began early in the nineteenth century. Christ Church, in the old city of **Jerusalem**, was founded in 1842. CMJ has now handed its work over to an independent charity known as the Israel Trust of the Anglican Church (ITAC), which runs the Anglican International School in Jerusalem, where children from different communities learn together. ITAC runs Shoresh Study Tours to **Israel** and programmes in the Jewish roots of the Christian faith. **Messianic Jews** in Israel who accept Yeshua (Hebrew for Jesus) as the **Messiah** are supported, when they meet with hostility, by CMJ / ITAC. In the 1980s CMJ gave some support to evangelistic campaigns by **Jews for Jesus**, a group of Messianic Jews deriving from the **United States**. Church leaders distanced themselves from such evangelism, and George Carey (b. 1935), when he became Archbishop of Canterbury, unlike his predecessors declined to be a Patron of CMJ as, he said, this was incompatible with his position as Joint-President of the **Council of Christians and Jews**. At the time of the 1988 **Lambeth Conference**, leaders of CMJ argued against initial drafts of the section on **mission** because it did not recognise their position. CMJ seeks to communicate its belief that God's saving love to sinners was made known through the sending of his Son, the Messiah Yeshua, to be the only means of **atonement** and **righteousness**. CMJ holds that God's **covenant** with the Jewish people comes to fulfilment in Yeshua. It is supportive of Israel and is in fellowship with various sister societies, which carry on similar work – CMJ Ireland, Messiah's People in South Africa, Shoresh USA and Shoresh Australia. Other ministries in this area (not sister societies of CMJ) include Christian Witness to Israel, Messianic Testimony and the Lausanne Consultation on Jewish Evangelism.   *MARCUS BRAYBROOKE*

Cinema and film

The cinema – not just films themselves, but also the institutions that produce and distribute them, and the audiences who are their consumers – began almost simultaneously in the 1890s in France, Germany, the United Kingdom and the United States. Today it is a global phenomenon. Countries in Africa, Asia and Europe have noteworthy indigenous cinemas, although most of these define themselves in opposition to Hollywood, whose products have dominated screens since 1918.

Cinema has always been implicated in Jewish–Christian relations. Relationships between history, theology, the cinematic text, and its reception, are complex. Films do not simply reflect Jewish–Christian relations but actively constitute them. On occasion (most obviously, in Nazi propaganda pieces like *Jew Süss*; Harlan, 1940) film's affective qualities have been exploited with the aim of influencing attitudes. More commonly, intentions are less didactic, but a given film's subject-matter draws its makers and viewers into exploration of aspects of Jewish–Christian relations, present or past.

The first films to participate in Jewish–Christian relations were those with religious themes: keen to appease the middle classes, the nascent industry invested large resources in biblical films, especially screen lives of **Jesus** and **Moses**. (It has periodically revived these genres at other times when the threat of censure has seemed acute.) Pre-1960, biblical films typically propagated **anti-Judaism**. This is evident in Jesus films of the 1890s, which were series of tableaux, based on **Passion plays**. It is also apparent in silents like *King of Kings* (DeMille, 1927), which evokes Christian anti-Judaism in its depiction of Jesus' opponents, and the casting of Yiddish theatre actors as **Judas** and **Caiaphas**, and Orthodox Jews as extras. These moves implied continuity between Jesus' opponents and twentieth-century Jewry, and sparked protests from the B'nai B'rith. Such problems are not confined to Jesus films. In DeMille's *The Ten Commandments* (1956) **New Testament** themes and language are used in a manner that denies the specificity of Moses' life and promotes its interpretation as Christ-like (key scenes recall the Gospel accounts of Jesus' temptation and his mocking as 'King of the Jews'). It is only after **Vatican II** that non-Jewish filmmakers have to any serious extent tried to avoid anti-Judaism. Zeffirelli's *Jesus of Nazareth* (1977) reflects its director's reading of *Nostra Aetate* in its efforts to portray a Jewish Jesus and evoke the tragic consequences of the **deicide** charge. (Rabbi Albert Friedlander (1927–2004) a well-known participant in interfaith dialogue, was one consultant on the project.) However, the film is not without difficulties – those **Pharisees** whom it portrays positively are depicted as being such precisely *because* they are supporters of Jesus. The (from the standpoint of interfaith activists and film critics alike) only mixed success of *Jesus* raises pertinent questions about whether it is possible to make a Jesus film that is 'recognisable' to a Christian audience whilst avoiding **supersessionism** completely.

A significant proportion of commercial films are adapted from literary originals. These include Lean's *Oliver Twist* (1948) – celebrated as a cinematic masterpiece, but notable in this context for its reliance on Cruikshank's nineteenth-century sketches for the depiction of a demonic, animal-like Fagin. Amongst other prominent examples are Yiddish films *In Polish Woods* (Turkow, 1929) and *Hester Street* (Micklin Silver, 1972), which deal with Jewish participation alongside Christian Poles in the January Uprising of 1863 against **Russia**, and questions relating to Jewish **identity** and **assimilation** in the **United States** respectively. In addition to these adaptations, numerous fiction films have tackled interfaith relationships, either at the individual level (*Keeping the Faith* (Norton, 2000) flirts with the problem of **intermarriage**, but sidesteps the most difficult issues by downplaying Anna's Christianity and having her secretly embark on **conversion** classes before rabbi Jake proposes; *Valentín* (Agresti, 2002) offers an oblique treatment of similar issues in 1970s **Argentina**) or on the larger scale of inter-group relations, especially in relation to the **Holocaust**. Although most films downplay the religious dimension, some make specific reference to the Holocaust as a problem in Jewish–Christian relations. Based on Hochhuth's play 'The Representative', *Amen* (Costa-Gavras, 2002) is a polemical work about Vatican **silence** during the war, whilst Malle's *Goodbye, Children* (1987) deals more subtly with the issue of **bystanders**. Not all Holocaust films adopt a Jew/innocence–Christian/guilt schema, however. Depicting the Jew as a child or woman, protected by a strong Christian, is a strategy deployed in several examples (such as *Black Thursday*; Mitrani, 1974), suggesting that the relation between the two peoples is either symbiotic, or one of need and dependency.

Off-screen, debates about film **censorship** and regulation have been occasions for both **antisemitism** and more neutral-positive contacts between Jews, Christians and others. The early cinema was more accessible to immigrants than established industries, and Jews were among the founders of several American companies, including Paramount, MGM, Universal and Warner Brothers. In these contexts Jews and Christians have often worked successfully together, but relations were particularly strained during the 1920s, at the height of the Cold War, and more recently in the 1980s and 1990s. In the two earlier periods anti-semitism coloured the (successful) calls of Protestant and Catholic Christians for increased regulation of motion picture content. In the late twentieth century Christian opposition to the cinema issued from conservative fundamentalist circles. Generally **philosemitic** figures like Pat Robertson (b. 1930) have associated the permissiveness of the industry with the presence of 'Jewish intellectuals and media activists'. African-American nationalists (Muslim and Christian) have denounced Jewish filmmakers (especially Steven Spielberg (b. 1946)) as responsible for the suppression of Black liberation – criticism that overlooks the history of African-American and Jewish cooperation in lobbying *against* the pro-Ku Klux Klan *Birth of a Nation* (Griffith, 1915) and *for* modifications to the screenplay of *Gone with the Wind* (Fleming, 1939).

Some **Councils of Christians and Jews** have recognised the power of film, and have even produced videos in furtherance of their goals. However, interfaith professionals have typically struggled to come to terms with the nature and implications of the cinema as a locus of Jewish–Christian relations. Responses to *The Passion of the Christ* (Gibson, 2004), which was not motivated by antisemitism but reproduced elements of both Gospel anti-Judaism and modern antisemitic discourse, illustrate this trend. Viewed pessimistically, the film's contents and commercial successes revealed the extent to which Jewish–Christian relations is marginal to the concerns of many Christians (including traditionalist Catholics like Gibson) and a failure on the part of interfaith individuals and institutions to engage effectively with film (as art or industry). Conversely, *The Passion* phenomenon helped to secure temporarily a place for Jewish–Christian relations on the western religious agenda, and provided an opportunity for attempts to popularise modern scholarly constructions of Jesus' ministry and

death. Within cinema studies, aside from historical treatments of Jewish filmmaking, most scholarship focuses on individual films: whether Murnau's
cult horror film *Nosferatu* (1922) is an exercise
in antisemitism has, for example, been debated
at length. There is much scope for further work
in the field, particularly in the area of reception
studies.   *MELANIE J. WRIGHT*

Circumcision

In the Jewish–Christian encounter circumcision has
been both unifying and divisive. The practice itself
among Middle Eastern cultures predates **Abraham**
by several thousand years. But Judaism has invested
the ancient practice with its own unique meanings,
and ritual circumcision is now coterminous with
being an adult Jewish male.

Genesis 17 commands Abraham to remove the
foreskin (*orlah*) from the penis – not only his own,
but those of his sons and all other males who
are part of his extended household – as a sign of
the **covenant** between God and Abraham's descendants. Circumcision thus distinguished Israelites
from Philistines and other neighbours who did
not circumcise. In the late Second Temple period
(fourth century BCE to first century CE) it also distinguished them from **Hellenists** and Romans.

Not every male who joined the Hebrew people was circumcised: Naaman the Syrian (2 Kgs
5) seems not to be, and Second Temple synagogues frequently included sub-congregations of
'God-fearers', uncircumcised non-Jews who closely
identified with Judaism. Literature of the period
includes stories of conversion by **baptism** only
(e.g. Aseneth), and **Philo** interprets the circumcision of proselytes as metaphorical only. Perhaps
this explains why the earliest **Jewish Christians** so
readily accepted the uncircumcised in their midst.
Jesus and his disciples, and **Paul** and other members of the Jesus movement, would have all been circumcised, but as Christianity spread among Gentiles who were not, the Church reached one of its
earliest crises. Acts 15 records the decision of the
Jerusalem Council that Christians who were not of
Jewish origin would not be required to be circumcised. By the Rabbinic Period (second to sixth centuries CE) Judaism and Christianity had parted ways
on this issue, with Judaism requiring circumcision,
even of converts, and Christianity generally forbidding it as an unnecessarily literal reading of the
Bible. Christians were to 'circumcise their hearts'

(Rom. 2.28–29) and not their bodies. Even this
figurative interpretation could cite precursors in
Judaism (see Deut. 10.16 and 30.6).

For most of these two millennia circumcision
served the Jews as both a mark of **identity** and
a source of danger. Non-Christian emperors often
outlawed circumcision as government policy – the
first of these was Antiochus Epiphanes in the second
century BCE – but Christian emperors and theological councils outlawed it as well. What had once set
the Jews proudly apart became a dangerous mark
of difference. In medieval Europe Christians who
poured out of churches on Good Friday and **Easter**
in search of Jews to kill in revenge for Jesus' death
could easily identify potential victims by pulling
down their pants. The same mark made Jews easy
targets for the **pogroms** and Nazi persecution of the
nineteenth and twentieth centuries.

Modern practices of medical circumcision for
hygienic reasons in Western countries have no
relationship to ritual circumcision and are on
the decline. Neither Judaism nor Christianity has
a tradition of female circumcision (cliterodec-
tomy). Because there is no physical marking
of the female body as a sign of covenant
with God, **feminists** of both traditions consider
that circumcision confirms Judaism's patriarchal
character.   *PHILIP CULBERTSON*

Civil society

Jews and Christians have always had to work out
their relationship to larger society, but how they
have negotiated this has depended as much on
their relative status and power vis-à-vis the state
as on theological perspectives and principles. The
relation to civil authority at times complicated and
exacerbated tensions between the two traditions.
For example, the **Roman Empire** accorded Judaism
legal status and granted certain concessions (e.g.
the right to refuse military service, observe the **Sabbath** and substitute prayer for the emperor for participation in the imperial cult). In Rome's eyes, however, early Christianity appeared to be an illegal
association, an illicit cult (*see religio licita*). The
Christian need for legitimacy from Rome worsened
relationships with Jews, particularly after the Jewish War against Rome of 66–70 and the **Bar Kokhba**
revolt in 135. When Emperor Theodosius I (*r*.379–
95) made Christianity the official religion of the
Roman Empire in 379, a dramatic (and dangerous)
reversal took place. A debate that had been largely

theological in nature – the apologists' arguments with Judaism enshrined in the ***Adversus Judaeos*** literature – became institutionalised in legal strictures against Jews. The conflation of civil and religious power Christianity exercised in many places over the course of many centuries until the modern era relegated Jews to the status of a marginal, persecuted **minority** with few rights in society. Not until the **Enlightenment** and French Revolution, which led ultimately to the disestablishment of the church in most countries and offered the possibility of citizenship in most of Europe, did Jews enjoy legal equality. Yet **assimilation** into society was a temptation for newly emancipated Jews, as societal structures remained antisemitic. The advance of reactionary nationalism and the development of 'race science' made Jews pariahs to an unparalleled extent – vermin to be eliminated from society. History thus situates Judaism and Christianity differently in regard to civil society, at least in the West (in most Muslim countries Jews and Christians alike have a secondary status). Notwithstanding this history, contemporary Jews and Christians confront common issues in a globalised society. Jonathan Sacks (b. 1948) asks whether religions are prepared for the greatest challenge they have ever faced: 'a world in which even local conflict can have global repercussions' (*The Dignity of Difference*, 43).

Both have adherents who zealously defend traditional religion against the perceived encroachments of secularism. Living in enclave cultures, they regard the modern state as the enemy; only 'strong religion' will halt the erosion of religious identity and create alternatives to secular institutions and behaviours. Jews and Christians of less extremist mindsets explore ways in which religious commitment complements citizenship and fosters attitudes essential for pluralism. John Coleman argues that citizenship enhances religious **identity** (what he terms discipleship) by widening the reach of solidarity, inviting humbler service in the 'often intractable day-to-day reality of politics', and provides a taxing reality test for religious claims. Religious identity adds to citizenship by offering a utopian vision, countercultural practices and a sense of vocation ('The Two Pedagogies: Discipleship and Citizenship', 58–63).　　*MARY C. BOYS*

Coggan, Donald (1909–2000)

Archbishop of Canterbury (1974–80). As a schoolboy, Coggan attended a Hebrew class which, he said, 'created a lifelong interest in all things Jewish'. At Cambridge he read **Hebrew** and **Aramaic** and was a distinguished biblical scholar, subsequently becoming principal of London College of Divinity, Bishop of Bradford and Archbishop of York. In retirement, he became chairman of the **Council of Christians and Jews** (CCJ). He emphasised the importance of educating the clergy and engaging in discussion of theology and the situation in **Israel** – topics previously avoided as too controversial. Coggan was also an active supporter and honorary president of the International Council of Christians and Jews. In an address on the fiftieth anniversary of CCJ, Coggan said the time had come to move beyond **dialogue** to joint witness to the moral values shared by Judaism and Christianity.

See also **Anglicanism**; **Church of England**
　　　　　　　　　MARCUS BRAYBROOKE

Cohen, Hermann (1842–1918)

German philosopher. Cohen's philosophy is grounded in the ethical tradition of **Kant**. Only late in his life did Cohen turn to Jewish philosophy, applying Kantian principles to his evaluation of Judaism and in this making space for God in his previously atheistic philosophy. His description of Judaism as 'ethical monotheism' has gained influence in Jewish circles, notably for his student Franz **Rosenzweig**. Cohen's understanding of the Jewish task as working for the coming of the Messianic era by creating unity, justice and equality between human beings has gained importance in Christian theology since the **Holocaust**.　　*K. HANNAH HOLTSCHNEIDER*

Commandments

Arguments about the nature of 'commandments' go to the heart of the Jewish–Christian debate since they help define the nature of the relationship to God. Is it a collective, contractual arrangement requiring obligations on both sides, the Jewish view, or the result of an act of **grace** on the part of God, through the death and resurrection of **Jesus**, bestowed upon the individual Christian? Whereas the former inherits a systematised framework, based ultimately on the practice of tangible actions, the latter operates within a system of belief that is presumed to lead to appropriate action. Clearly there are positions between these extremes; nevertheless, both approaches imply obligations that need to be met by Jew and Christian alike.

The term 'commandment' translates the Hebrew word *mizvah* which occurs commonly in legal passages in the **Hebrew Bible**. The rabbis used it to preface **blessings** that are recited before performing ritual acts and religious duties. One of the early issues between emergent Judaism and Christianity lies in the question of the authority of biblical **law** and its application. Matt. 5.17–21 affirms the centrality of law, and elsewhere the Gospel focuses particularly on the **Ten Commandments** (Matt. 19.16–19). Indeed, it was Christian emphasis on the Ten Commandments, known biblically and in rabbinic tradition as the 'Ten Words', that led Jews to downplay their significance, removing them from a central place in the daily **liturgy**, and asserting that the **Torah** in its entirety was to be followed. Nevertheless, both traditions sought to express the essence of God's commandments. Matthew (22.37–40) emphasised the two commandments: to love God and your 'neighbour'; Rabbi Simlai offered a variety of biblical passages that summed up Jewish religious obligations, reducing them to one, choosing Amos 5.4, 'Seek me and live', or Hab. 2.4, 'the righteous shall live by his faith' (*b. Makkot* 23b–24a). Such a system of commandments, however, can operate only when the source of authority for the *mizvot* is unchallenged. Since the **Enlightenment** and **Emancipation** both the divine origin of the Torah and its commandments and the authority of the rabbinic tradition itself, and indeed of Christian institutions, have been seriously challenged by the inroads of secular **humanism** and, in the case of Jews, the growth of non-Orthodox religious movements.

Rabbinic Judaism assumes a total of 613 commandments (365 positive, 248 negative) which are to be found in the Hebrew Bible, though rabbinic authorities differ as to the exact enumeration. Within them are seven that are identified as the Seven Laws of the Sons of Noah (*see* **Noachide laws**). As the name suggests, these are universal laws given to humanity after the flood. In rabbinic thought whoever amongst the nations of the world adheres to these is certain of a place in the world to come, thus providing a basis in Judaism for the acknowledgement of the legitimacy of other faiths. From a Jewish perspective adherence to this minimalist programme provides a starting point for the acceptance of Christianity and legitimises the possibility of interfaith **dialogue**. *JONATHAN MAGONET*

Commentary

Interpretation of scripture, usually by a single author, organised according to the order of verses. **Midrash** is closely related to commentary, but, unlike midrash, the commentary treats the biblical verses in continuity. The commentator will therefore not intentionally interpret one verse in a manner inconsistent with his interpretation of a previous one. In this sense commentaries were written by some of the **Church Fathers**, but (except for **Philo of Alexandria**, whose Greek work was inaccessible to most Jews throughout the Middle Ages) Jewish commentaries do not appear before the tenth century.

The special dynamic of biblical commentary in the two traditions resulted from sharing a scripture that is read in dramatically different ways. Christian writers were often astonished at what they considered to be Jewish 'blindness': their failure to see and comprehend the truth proclaimed in their own sacred texts. Jewish writers were perturbed by Christian interpretations not rooted in the original Hebrew, or removed from their historical and textual context, or that abandoned completely the simple meaning of the words in favour of other significance. Jewish commentaries were written in many different languages, but (unlike Christian commentaries) were always based on the original Hebrew scriptural text. Church Fathers such as **Origen** and **Jerome**, whose **exegesis** is not free of **polemical** points, were helped in their biblical scholarship by Jewish teachers, who had greater mastery of Hebrew.

One of the most important modes in ancient Christian commentary was **typology**. **Augustine of Hippo**, for example, explained the figure of **Cain** to be a type for the Jewish people – guilty of murder, condemned to wander the earth in exile, yet given a sign of divine protection against violence.

Sometimes commentaries were explicitly driven by polemical or **apologetic** goals. Several medieval Jewish works treated only those biblical verses that Christians used to buttress their faith; in each case the Jewish commentator reports the Christian interpretation and then rebuts it. Some continue beyond the defensive by commenting on verses from the **New Testament** that raise problems for traditional Christian doctrine. Usually, however, the encounter with the other faith was more subtle.

Perhaps the most influential of all Jewish commentators was **Rashi** (Rabbi Solomon ben Isaac). Modern scholars have explicated his commentaries against their historical background – especially the deteriorating Jewish conditions and the intensifying pressure of the Christian environment – and have highlighted **anti-Christian** elements in his exegesis of the Bible. The same is true for his successors in northern **France** and for other medieval Jewish commentators in southern France and Christian **Spain**.

Not all the interaction was confrontational. The Christian teaching that scripture had four different senses – usually called 'historical' (the actual events), 'tropological' (moral instruction), 'allegorical' (doctrine linked with a non-literal reading) and 'anagogical' (teaching about the mystical spiritual realm) – was well established by the twelfth century. In Jewish thought an analogous conception of four senses – *peshat* (simple meaning), *remez* (philosophical **allegory**), *derash* (homiletical application) and *sod* (mystical symbol) – crystallised late in the thirteenth century, undoubtedly influenced by the Christian teaching.

Some medieval Christian scholars concluded that greater attention should be given to the 'historical' meaning of the text. For this the **Hebrew language** was needed, and that entailed study with Jews, who were themselves beginning to articulate more carefully the distinction between the homiletical interpretations of the midrash and the simple meaning of the biblical text. Contact between scholars of both communities can be documented most extensively in the School of St Victor, a Parisian Abbey (*see* **Victorines**). Biblical commentaries written there in the twelfth century are filled with references to Jewish interpretations, not for polemical but for more purely intellectual purposes, derived from both texts and conversations. Such Christian scholars as Herbert of Bosham (*c.*1115/20–*c.*1194) and Nicholas of **Lyra**, who had a major influence on **Luther**, cited Hebrew commentaries quite frequently.

Jewish typological interpretation, which is present in the midrash, received a new impetus with the commentary of **Nahmanides** (Moses ben Nahman), apparently influenced by Christian writers. The Spanish exegete Isaac Abravanel (1437–1508) had a broad knowledge of Christian exegetical literature, and seems to have been deeply influenced by the commentaries of the Spanish **Franciscan** Alfonso Tostado (*c.*1400–55). Jewish commentators were also influenced by Christian literary structures. Commentary organised by dividing the biblical text into small sections with conceptual unity and addressing underlying issues that transcend the individual verse first appears in late-medieval Jewish commentators. Levi Ben Gershom (1288–1344) concluded each section with a series of lessons for behaviour or belief (*to 'aliyyot*, apparently from the Latin *utilitates*). Isaac Abravanel raised a series of difficulties or 'doubts' (*sefekot*, from the Latin *dubitationes*) for each section, before resolving them in his ensuing discussion. Although the precise mechanism of influence remains unclear, both are certainly related to earlier Christian exegetical forms.

In the modern period the critical questioning of the Mosaic authorship of the entire **Pentateuch** through direct divine revelation, and the development of the 'documentary hypothesis', affected Jews and Christians in a similar manner. It was vehemently opposed by conservative thinkers in both traditions, while liberals in both camps made their peace with the new theories and began to incorporate some of the insights into their commentaries. Some Jews detected an anti-Jewish undercurrent in the **Wellhausen** School – dubbed by Solomon Schechter (1847–1915) the 'Higher **Antisemitism**' – because of its claim that the latest strata of the **Torah** (the Priestly document) reflected a degeneration of spirituality into a compulsively legalistic fixation on the details of a sacrificial cult.

For Jews, the most influential English-language commentary of the twentieth century was written by the British Chief Rabbi Joseph Hertz (1872–1946). Fiercely resistant to the documentary hypothesis, it is also extremely defensive. Hertz uses hundreds of quotations from Christian writers speaking about the exalted insight of the biblical text and the unique Jewish contribution to civilisation, while he strains to defend the Torah against any suggestion of ethical primitivism. During the past generation new commentaries on the Torah have been published by the movements of Reform Judaism and Conservative Judaism. Both of these commentaries show openness to the best of modern scholarship, while including considerable material from traditional Jewish commentators.   *MARC SAPERSTEIN*

Community

A generic term used by both Jews and Christians for larger and smaller assemblages of people sharing a faith **identity**. In contemporary usage the term usually denotes a wider group than the Jewish movements and Protestant denominations, though specific Roman Catholic religious orders still refer to themselves as communities. **Torah** usage (*kahal*) most often specifies '(all the) community of Israel'; where 'community of the LORD' occurs, Moses' leadership is under challenge. In the **Dead Sea Scrolls**, the term (*yahad*) identifies the group associated with the scrolls, as in the regulatory text 'The Rule of the Community' (1QS). **New Testament** usage (*koinōnia*) identifies specific groups or refers to their mutual sharing in religious realities such as sacrament, salvation etc. Medieval and early modern Jewish usage often identifies the local assemblage as the 'holy community' (*k"k = kehillah kedoshah*), which was organised to offer to Jews civic, religious and social services of all kinds in parallel to the Christian city. **Emancipation** and the emergence of the modern Jewish movements (Conservative, Orthodox, Progressive/Reform, Reconstructionist) pressed the term into service to mean all Jews, of whatever allegiance, in a particular place; the development of the Jewish Community Centre as a social and cultural institution reflects this. In Christian **liberation theology** the 'base community' (= local parish) is the proper *locus* of theological reflection, political engagement and social support.

In both Judaism and Christianity communal bonds are constitutive of religious identity; one is Jewish or Christian as part of a community of faith. Whether through the covenant of **circumcision** or the rite of **baptism**, initiation involves entry into a community that is local and global, contemporary and atemporal. With the late-twentieth-century Christian rejection of the 'teaching of contempt', the relationship of the Jewish and Christian communities has been re-examined. *Nostra Aetate* affirms that 'all humanity forms but one community'. Christian thinkers thus generally see more continuity between the two communities, while Jewish thinkers tend to emphasise the distinctiveness of the Jewish community from all who are outside the Sinaitic covenant (so even for Mordecai

Kaplan (1881–1983) and Reconstructionist thought, though the distinctiveness is not unique). Thus *Dabru Emet* refers consistently to 'two communities'. The question of communal identity and distinction is often reflected in discussions of **covenant** – whether Jews and Christians live within a single undifferentiated covenant, a single covenant mediated differently in history, two covenants, two of many covenants etc. In discussions of **canon** and **biblical interpretation**, advocates of canonical (or confessional) criticism have emphasised the role and **hermeneutics** of the community that receives and transmits scripture as critical in understanding the dynamics of normative scriptural authority and inspiration.

PETER A. PETTIT

Confessing Church

Protestant Christian movement in Nazi **Germany** opposing the movement of the self-styled German Christians who strove for full integration into the National Socialist state. The Confessing Church was founded at the General Synod of the Evangelical Church in Germany at Wuppertal-Barmen in 1934, resulting in the Barmen Confession. Karl Barth (1886–1968) and Dietrich **Bonhoeffer** were the leading theologians involved, together with activists such as Martin **Niemöller**. Barth's chief objective was the establishment of theological criteria for the independence of Christian conscience through the sole authority of Christ as taking precedence for Christian decision-making over any secular political authority. According to his reasoning the 'Jewish question' was subordinate to this principle, since if Christians were accountable first and foremost to the authority of Christ, protest and resistance against antisemitic policies and actions would be a logical consequence. Other members of the Confessing Church were more concerned with the Church's political independence and disagreed with Barth's theological reasoning, being opposed to Nazi rule only where secular authority proposed to determine questions of Church organisation and creed. Barth lost the struggle for the leadership of the movement and, with his return to his native **Switzerland**, became a supporter of and commentator on it rather than one of its leaders.

The 'Jewish question' was addressed by members of the Confessing Church through unwavering support of so-called 'Jewish-Christians', i.e. members of the Protestant Church who were defined as

Jewish under the Nuremberg Laws of 1935. Maintaining that sovereignty of the Church's internal affairs must rest with the Church itself, the Confessing Church condemned the German Christians, as well as regional churches which had split from the Confessing Church and individual parishes which followed the Nazi policy of expelling 'Jewish Christians' in an effort to create an 'Aryan Christianity'. While individual members of the Confessing Church such as Bonhoeffer and H. Grüber (1891–1975), Dean of Berlin, were involved in helping Jews to emigrate or find a place in hiding, such activities were not carried by an organisational policy. While criticism of **antisemitism** from within the Confessing Church was quite frequent, it was not necessarily supported by all its members or supporting organisations. Antisemitic statements and publications from representatives of the independent churches were common, as was the opinion that Jews deserved the discrimination and atrocities they were experiencing. As a whole the Confessing Church failed to speak out on the 'Jewish question' and did not seem to realise the implications of the state's antisemitic policies. Its struggle for confessional, organisational and legal independence from the Nazi state can be characterised more as an exercise in self-preservation than as a concerted effort to oppose the regime and its dehumanising policies.   *K. HANNAH HOLTSCHNEIDER*

Confession of faith

An open declaration and public avowal of the content of one's religious belief. For Judaism and Christianity, the *Shema* is the primal confession of faith. Proclaimed by God, **Israel** was enjoined to hear (Deut. 6.4) and then to profess (Deut. 6.7–9; 11.19–20) the *Shema*, which has remained the basic public avowal of faith in Judaism. Declared by **Jesus** in his response regarding the first and greatest **commandment** (Mark 12.29), the *Shema* formed the basis of Christian declarations of belief from nascent Christianity's spontaneous professions of new understandings, to the initial creeds formulated during the patristic era in response to perceived **heresy** and political opposition (Nicaea I, 325; Constantinople, 381; Nicaea II, 787). The effort to keep the monotheism of the *Shema* intact while articulating the new traditions of the revelation in Christ, especially the doctrine of the **Trinity**, continues to shape the profession of faith by Christians today.

Judaism's expressions of faith are primarily expressions of steadfast confidence and trust (*emunah, bittahon*) in the One God, rather than intellectual assents to theological propositions such as Christianity's more cognitive declarations, which convey the core elements of its **doctrine** and dogma. However, it is also true that Judaism's entire structure of beliefs and practices rests on cognitive presuppositions and that Christianity tacitly affirms the inseparable bond between creed, attitude and practice. On occasion, such as during its encounters with **atheism** during the Middle Ages, its interactions with Christianity, and its nineteenth-century Reform movement, Judaism's expressions of faith have verged more on the doctrinal, though never in a dogmatic manner (cf. **Maimonides**' 13 Principles, which were countered by the voluntarist school of **Judah ha-Levi** and **Crescas**). Christianity's numerous **particularistic** creedal formularies, which emerged in various historical periods and proliferated during and following the **Reformation**, gave its 'deposit of faith' a structured form and served as tests of orthodoxy.

Jesus' Great Commission in Matt. 28.19 underpins both Christianity's propensity for converting and its practice of preceding the **baptism** of catechumens (*see* **catechesis**) with a profession of faith. On numerous occasions during the past centuries Jews have been the objects of a selective interpretation of this Commission and have had to choose between a forced profession of Christian faith (*see* **conversion**) and **expulsion** or death.

Just as Christians make a collective profession of faith at the Sunday **Eucharist** and other key moments of the **liturgy** (e.g. at the **Easter** Vigil paschal celebration), so Jews begin and end their day with the *Shema* and recite it as a congregation at the conclusion of **Yom Kippur**. Pious Jews die with the *Shema* on their lips, as did many who were led to the gas chambers during the **Holocaust**. During the last century the impact of the Holocaust, along with existentialist philosophy, focused Jewish attention more on a mode of life and the nature of faith itself than on ultimate claims or public professions of faith. Christians who heed the lessons of the Holocaust express caution about the polarising potential of the absolutist claims in their professions of faith.   *AUDREY DOETZEL*

Confirmation *see* **barmitzvah; Progressive Judaism**

Consecration

The deeply human instinct to give special treatment to elements of the material world that are employed in the encounter with God is expressed in both Jewish and Christian religious ritual. In Christian theology and practice, consecration is the setting apart of persons, places and things for some holy use. Because that which is consecrated is understood to play a role in mediating the human encounter with God, rites of consecration generally take the form of praise of God for what is being consecrated, and include prayers that those who use the object of the consecratory action will experience an expansion of faith and insight. The closest Jewish counterpart to the Christian acts of consecration are the various forms of dedication (*hanukkah*), by which houses, synagogues and cemeteries are set apart by a '**blessing**' or 'benediction' (*berakhah*) accompanied by the reading of specified **Psalms**. Although we have little textual evidence, and no full texts, for either Christian or Jewish rites of consecration before about the eighth century CE, it is clear that even in the earliest stage they are theologically and ritually grounded in the biblical accounts of the dedications of the three great sanctuaries: the Sanctuary in the Wilderness (Num. 7), Solomon's Temple (2 Kgs 8; 2 Chr. 5–6), and the Second Temple (Ezra 3). In the Christian liturgical context the term 'consecration' has been used to refer to the prayers or sets of prayers said over church buildings and ritual objects that are to be used in services of **worship**, and also to the rite by which persons appointed for liturgical leadership roles are ordained. Within some Christian traditions consecration is most often used to describe the blessing of the **bread** and **wine** in the **eucharistic** rite, and more specifically to the particular words and actions that have been understood to effect the transformation of the elements into the body and blood of Jesus Christ, which at various times and among different Christian groups have been matters of great controversy. Some medieval and later halakhists used this close relationship between consecration and the presence of God to classify Christianity as an idolatrous religion. This same fear of **idolatry** led many Protestant Christians strenuously to resist the idea that inanimate objects could be consecrated through the actions and prayers of human beings, leading some Jewish scholars to consider Protestant Christians less idolatrous than Roman Catholics. For some Christians, the sacred character of places and objects that are consecrated for holy use can also be violated when the setting for worship or the objects used in worship are used for non-sacred purposes. This kind of desecration most commonly occurs when violence is done in a church building, when a suicide takes place in a church or cemetery, or when ritual objects are used as weapons. In these cases rites of reconsecration (which may often include forms of exorcism) are often performed to draw the consecrated place or object out of the realm of the profane. Some contemporary Jewish scholars have turned the understanding of consecration as 'setting apart' upside-down, claiming that since everything in the material world by its nature participates in the **holiness** of God, consecration should be seen as an act by which objects and persons are drawn from the realm of the sacred in order that they can be used with impunity by human beings in religious ritual. Although some Christian liturgists are intrigued by the implications of this idea for sacramental theology, it has yet to bear fruit in Christian theology more generally.

See also **liturgy; sacrament**   *SUSAN WHITE*

Conservative Judaism *see* **Progressive Judaism**

Constantine (*c*.285–337)

The first Roman emperor (306–37) to become a Christian. The significance of this choice, made on the eve of the Battle of Milvian Bridge (312) in which Constantine defeated Maxentius (r.306–12) and assumed undisputed control of the western Empire, is often exaggerated, though its influence on the history of Jewish–Christian relations is undisputed. The Christianisation of the **Roman Empire** was a long and complex process, not to be reduced to the religious policy of a single emperor: but the fact that the emperor was a Christian, and favoured the Church, was important, especially when in 324 Constantine assumed control of the eastern Empire as well. The motive for Constantine's choice, and the nature of his personal faith, remain elusive after much discussion. He had as emperor to work within idioms of public life that continued to be pagan, but he gave strong encouragement to the Church – by exempting clergy from civic burdens, by convening councils of bishops as instruments of public policy (especially at Nicaea in 325) and by sponsoring programmes of Christian building in Rome, Jerusalem and elsewhere. The decision to build a Christian capital for the reunited Empire at Constantinople was far reaching.

These developments came to change profoundly the setting in which Jews and Christians had dealings with one another. The Edict of Milan (313) grants 'both to Christians and to all others full authority to follow whatever worship each has desired', but this general extension of a **toleration** that was already customarily extended to Jews was principally intended to restore the position of the Christian Church after the Great Persecution. The corresponding edict of toleration for the eastern Empire is expressed in narrower terms: freedom of worship is extended to those 'who still persist in error', i.e. are not Christian. In his limited legislation concerning Jews in particular, Constantine reaffirmed earlier laws that tolerated Judaism but restricted proselytism. If a Jew buys and circumcises a non-Jewish slave the slave shall be freed, but no penalty is prescribed for the slave's owner. No extant law conforms to **Eusebius**'s statement (*Vit. Const.* 4.27) that Constantine prohibited Jews from owning Christian slaves at all. Constantine insisted that **Easter** must never coincide with **Passover**, although some Christians continued to celebrate Easter on the night of 14 Nisan.   *ANDERS BERGQUIST*

Conversion

The Latin *convertere*, 'to turn around, turn back', has the same fundamental meaning as its Hebrew equivalent, *teshuvah*: a profound transformation of mind, will and heart toward God. Christians are called to continuing conversion throughout their lives, most intensely during Advent, Lent and **Holy Week**, just as Jews, most particularly on **Yom Kippur**, are called to **repentance** and a renewed and deepened 'turning' to God. In a derivative, secondary sense, conversion came to mean joining the **people Israel**, and thus adhering to the God of Israel, as in the ancient conversion formula in the book of Ruth, 'Your people shall be my people and your God my God' (1.16). Esth. 8.17 relates a large-scale conversion of Persians out of fear of the Jews, which may refer obliquely to the forced conversion of the Idumeans and Itureans by the Hasmoneans. The latter part of the Second Temple period saw widespread conversion to Judaism, attested to in both **Josephus** (*Ag. Ap.* 2.39) and the **New Testament**, which speaks of **Pharisees** who 'traverse sea and land to make one convert [to Judaism]' (Matt. 23.15) and of 'Nicholas of Antioch, a convert to Judaism' (Acts 6.5). The term in this second sense is not, interestingly, used in the New Testament of Jews who become believers in the risen Christ, since this was not seen by the authors as a change from Judaism to a new religion.

Though many of the **Church Fathers**, including Augustine's great mentor Ambrose (339–97), argued that Jews, no less than pagan cults, should be converted by any means, **Augustine** argued that Jews should be allowed to worship freely, as had their ancestors. Though he did not challenge the charge of **deicide**, he argued that God maintained a special relationship with the Jews and that, like **Cain**, they were marked as reserved for God's will alone, since their witness to the validity of the '**Old Testament**' reinforced the essential validity of the Christian claim. Pope **Gregory the Great**, persuaded by Augustine's reasoning, established the basis of medieval **canon law** with *Sicut Judaeis non*, which rendered Judaism the only licit religion in the Empire apart from Christianity, banned forced conversion and urged Christians to bring Jews to conversion by the example of their love. At the same time, Gregory and subsequent popes developed numerous laws to inhibit and finally to prohibit Jews from proselytising Christians in order to convert them to Judaism. So the ancient Jewish missionary outreach ended not as an internal decision, but as an imposition from the majority community among whom they lived.

Aside from some relatively minor instances, especially in the Iberian peninsula, the first major breach of this tradition came with the First **Crusade**, when in 1096 a huge group of self-proclaimed 'Crusaders', overwhelming the small forces of the local bishops who tried in vain to oppose them, offered conversion or death to thousands of Jews in the Rhineland area of what is today **Germany**. Upwards of 10,000 Jews chose death rather than conversion, and most of those who did convert recanted. The episode established in European history a complex dynamic that worked itself out in succeeding centuries through **Passion plays**, **blood libel** charges, Jewish conspiracy myths and finally the **expulsion** of the Jews from virtually every region in Western Europe except the Italian peninsula. From this period, too, there dates a rich anti-conversion and polemical Jewish tradition seeking to discredit

Christian claims in the eyes of Jewish readers. It is no exaggeration to acknowledge that fear of Christian missionising and conversionism underlies much Jewish mistrust of Christians to this day.

Many Christian theologians today, however, are increasingly questioning the formerly presumed need for Jews to 'convert' to Christianity. This thinking is relatively advanced in official Catholic teaching, which proclaims that 'the Jewish faith, unlike other non-Christian religions, is already a response to God's revelation' (Catechism of the Catholic Church, no. 839). Thus, the one prayer for the Jews in the Catholic liturgy, which before **Vatican II** was a prayer for their conversion, the **Good Friday Prayer for the Perfidious Jews**, is now a prayer that Jews will be deepened in the faith given to them by God, and the Catholic Church has no sanctioned groups whose purpose is the conversion of the Jewish people to Christianity. While the implications of **_Nostra Aetate_** for this question have not yet been worked through sufficiently to become established doctrine in Catholic tradition, in 2002 two major statements, one (_Reflections on Covenant and Mission_) by Catholics involved in ongoing **dialogue** with the US National Council of Synagogues (which exists primarily as a vehicle for dialogue with Christians) and one by a joint group of Protestants and Catholics, the Christian Scholars Group on Christian–Jewish Relations, have questioned Christian efforts aimed at converting Jews not only from a pastoral, but also from a theological point of view. Protestant, Anglican and Orthodox Christian traditions have a variety of theological positions on this question and have not yet reached internal consensus in their official documents.

See also **mission**   _EUGENE J. FISHER_

Conversos

The term Conversos refers to those members of religious **minorities** in **Spain** and **Portugal** who adopted Christianity, voluntarily or under pressure, in the late Middle Ages, and to their descendants. Although there were many Muslim Conversos by the mid-sixteenth century (also known as Moriscos), the first wave of converts was predominantly Jewish; large numbers of Jews accepted **baptism** during and after the **pogroms** of 1391, including the senior rabbi of Burgos, and a new wave of converts was created by the decree of **expulsion** in 1492. The term **Marranos**, also used for the Jewish Conversos, was originally an opprobri-

ous one, but can be used helpfully to describe those Conversos who retained some knowledge of and interest in Jewish practices, although considerable numbers of Conversos became integrated into Iberian society and shook off any memory of their Jewish past, sometimes by adopting Spanish names at baptism. Two difficulties faced the Conversos, whether or not they remained secret Jews: the **Inquisition** had become a powerful arm of the government in Aragon and Castile after 1484, and relentlessly pursued false converts, who were seen as **Judaising** heretics; and popular opinion increasingly marginalised those with Jewish blood, leading officially to their exclusion from the universities and from high office on what can only be described as racial grounds. This could in fact stimulate a greater awareness among the excluded of their Jewish origins, as happened among the Xuetes ('little Jews') of Majorca in the seventeenth century; and many others, including noble families, successfully hid the fact of Jewish ancestry. For the Conversos were often seen as unwelcome competitors by those seeking a position at court and in society. Portugal remained a livelier centre of secret Judaism, which has survived to the present day at Belmonte. Some historians, such as Benzion Netanyahu and Henry Kamen, have denied that secret Judaism existed on a large scale, but most agree that the Conversos included many who knew or cared little about their new religion and maintained some Jewish practices.   _DAVID ABULAFIA_

Convivencia

The term Convivencia is used to describe the relatively easy coexistence, literally 'living together', of Jews, Christians and Muslims in medieval **Spain** and **Portugal**. It can be applied to the early Middle Ages, when, under Muslim rule, Umayyad Córdoba was the capital of a powerful state with a large Christian population (until about 900 probably a Christian majority) and an influential, though much smaller, Jewish community. Jews were present at court as royal physicians, and in the eleventh century, when the Córdoban state had fallen to pieces, Jews served as viziers to the Berber kings of Granada. It is important not to idealise this relationship: non-Muslims were _dhimmis_, subject to restrictions such as heavier taxation; on the other hand, there was no attempt to insist on the full rigour of these restrictions. With the coming in the late eleventh and twelfth centuries of the uncompromising Almoravid and Almohad rulers, Moroccan Berbers who had little experience of religious **minorities**, the outlook for Jews became darker, and many migrated to Christian Spain, where similar openness was visible at the courts of Aragon, Castile, Portugal and Navarre. By the fourteenth century, however, revived ecclesiastical legislation of the early Middle Ages excluded Jews from office, and rulers began to encourage their enclosure in **ghettos**. Jewish officials remained at court (Samuel Abulafia (c.1320–60) under Pedro the Cruel in the 1350s, Isaac Abravanel (1437–1508) under **Ferdinand** and Isabella in the 1480s), but they became the target of bitter critics. The age of Convivencia was dealt its death blow not by the **expulsion** of the Jews in 1492, but by the **pogroms** of 1391, which resulted in mass **conversions** and the increased marginalisation of those Jews who remained; **Islam**, too, was suppressed (Castile, 1502; Aragon, 1525), and Spain rejoiced in its special reputation as the most Catholic of monarchies.   DAVID ABULAFIA

Coptic Church

The words 'Copt' and 'Coptic', from the Greek (*Aigyptos*) and Arabic (*qibt*) words for 'Egypt', designate the Christian inhabitants of **Egypt** and the language used by them in their **liturgy**. The history of Jewish–Christian relations in Egypt is largely a story of the respectful coexistence of two *dhimmis* ('protected' **minorities**) that shared a common struggle for survival under **Islam**, as well as many linguistic, cultural, religious, liturgical and even national affinities. The Copts' Christian heritage includes the **biblical interpretation** and **Christological** debates of the **Church Fathers** of **Alexandria**, including the **anti-Judaism** in the writings of **Origen**, **Athanasius** and **Cyril of Alexandria**. But the Coptic Church's reverent deference to the **monastic** ethos of the desert fathers, foremost among them St Antony (c.251–356), and its sad experience of frequent **martyrdom** and persecutions – by Romans, Byzantines, Muslims and Crusaders alike – mitigated any triumphal posture or purpose regarding Jews and Judaism. Coptic piety emphasises the possibility of transformation through participation in the risen Christ present in the Divine Liturgy, rather than **atonement** and **salvation** through the propitiatory sacrifice of the **Son of God** on the cross, which dominated Western Christian thought and engendered the charge of **deicide** against Jews. The linguistic proximity of Coptic, Arabic and **Hebrew**, the mutual influence of Copts and Jews on each other's religious **architecture**, liturgical practices and communal structures, and the preservation by the Coptic Church of many elements of ancient Jewish rites and rituals, all nourished a cordial Coptic–Jewish nexus throughout most of the last 15 centuries. Like Jews, Copts have a sense of **nationhood** derived from their link with the legacy of pharaonic Egypt. Only in the wake of modern-day conflicts in the Middle East have tensions surfaced in the relations of the Coptic Church and the **State of Israel**, but they have not adversely affected Coptic–Jewish relations in Egypt.

See also **Orthodox Christianity**

DANIEL ROSSING

Cosmology

Cosmology (*kosmos*, world; *logos*, knowledge of) is the study of the original, constituent and final cause(s) of the world or material universe. It therefore studies the ultimate, metaphysical purpose(s) of the entire universe. Jews and Christians generally begin their cosmological study with the first chapter of Genesis. They see in this text that God is not only the ultimate cause or purpose of all that is, but is also intimately involved in creation (divine participation) and especially in human lives and history. **Creation** is a manifestation of God's love and concern for the universe. Everything in creation came to be because it was so willed by the Creator. The cosmos is God's gift to humanity. In the Christian vision of the world Jesus Christ plays a major role at the beginning of creation and also at the end of time, when all of creation will experience its final transformation and renewal. There is also in the Christian tradition the tendency to see creation as a sacramental manifestation of God, especially within the vision of Francis of Assisi (1182–1226) according to Saint Bonaventure (c.1217–74). Francis saw vestiges of God in all things that reflect God in their own way. Creation becomes a mirror that allows humanity a limited but dynamic vision of God. Francis saw everything in creation as interrelated and connected to the one source of all things. In the Jewish tradition cosmology more strongly emphasises the difference between creator and creation, and it is connected strongly with the prohibition against creating on the **Sabbath** and upholding God's involvement with the Jewish people in the **covenant** relationship. Jewish cosmology also contains a future-driven element in its doctrine of Messianic **redemption**.

Modern science has challenged the traditional view of cosmology and has raised the question of whether God is the primary cause of existence. This challenge has made it possible for Christians and Jews to re-evaluate the teleological outlook that has been passed down in their respective traditions. The effect of this re-evaluation has been a search for mutual understanding among Christians and Jews who continue to maintain a belief in God's involvement in the cosmos. For example, Greek Metropolitan Damaskinos Papandreou (b. 1936) has stated that cosmology (along with theology and anthropology) is a connecting point between Eastern **Orthodox Christianity** and Judaism.

Reflection on the *Shoah* has also raised the issue of God and cosmology. **Death of God theology** in both Jewish and Christian circles has created a challenge for theologians on both sides to come together in **dialogue** about the ultimate question of God's role and purpose in a world shattered by the suffering and death of millions of people. *STEVEN J. McMICHAEL*

Council of Centers on Jewish–Christian Relations *see* **Jewish–Christian relations, centres for the study of**

Council of Trent *see* **Trent, Council of**

Council(s) of Christians and Jews

Since the establishment of the National Conference of Christians and Jews in the **United States** in 1928, some 38 such Councils (by the year 2005) have been founded in various countries to foster **dialogue** between Jews and Christians and to counter **antisemitism** and other forms of prejudice. Each is an independent member of the International Council of Christians and Jews (ICCJ), which was founded in 1946 to serve as an umbrella organisation. The ICCJ holds annual conferences to bring representatives from each Council to meet and discuss issues, but it also has its own committees (also called 'councils') to address issues of international concern. Representatives from other bodies, in particular the Vatican and the **World Council of Churches**, send observers to its meetings to allow for liaising between the bodies, and the ICCJ in turn advises on issues related to Jewish–Christian relations. The ICCJ has now founded an Abrahamic Council to further dialogue with Muslims. *JAMES K. AITKEN*

Court Jews

Wealthy individual Jews who provided financial and commercial services to medieval princes, particularly in the sixteenth to eighteenth centuries. Court Jews were generally agents who arranged transfers of credit, rather than possessors of vast sums of capital in their own right. They were members of the prince's court, through which the state was governed, and were found in most principalities of the Holy Roman Empire. Protestant and Catholic princes alike opened their courts to Jews. Among the most well known was Christoph Bernhard von Galen (1606–78), elected Bishop-Prince of Münster in 1650, and Don Isaac Abravanel (1437–1508). Court Jews were exempted from both Gentile and Jewish courts but accountable to the Royal Court. Although exempt from paying protection money (*Schutzgeld*), they were dependent upon the protection and whim of the ruler and liable to exploitation. When a new ruler came to power he often dismissed a Court Jew or brought him to court to remove existing financial obligations. Many Court Jews converted to Christianity, although **conversion** was sometimes looked on askance by Christians, such as Friedrich Schleiermacher (1768–1834) who feared a 'judaisation of the Church'. Katz suggests that two-thirds of the Court Jews (or their descendants) converted to Christianity (*Out of the Ghetto*, 122). *EDWARD KESSLER*

Covenant

Covenant is a central concept in both Judaism and Christianity, and has been a key issue throughout the history of Jewish–Christian relations. The word itself derives from the Bible and has been reinterpreted many times in both traditions, mainly in opposition to each other. In both, two characteristics recur: God initiates a covenant with a **community** of people, and that community accepts certain obligations and responsibilities as covenant partners.

The word appears 287 times in the **Hebrew Bible** and is usually understood as a solemn and sacred agreement. Most exegetes, however, hold to the view that the Hebrew word *berit* should be translated not by 'covenant' but by 'obligation'. *Berit* expresses the sovereign power of God, who imposes his will on his vassal Israel: God promises in a solemn oath to fulfil his word to his people Israel, who have only to be faithful and obey.

In the writings that form the **New Testament** the concept of the covenant is reinterpreted through the experiences of the early Christian community. The Church accepted the story of **Jesus** as a new phase in the covenant-story of Israel. The change in emphasis marked by the translation of *berit* into the Greek *diatheke* ('decree') in the **Septuagint** was developed still further in the New Testament, where the concept acquired the meaning of a definitive 'last will and testament' on the part of God. The **Vulgate** used the word *testamentum*, which became the official designation of both parts of the Christian Bible – the **Old Testament** and the New Testament – with its inescapable implication of **supersessionism**.

In Jewish thinking the term 'covenant' has been constantly reinterpreted, in the first centuries in strong resistance to the Christian proclamation of the 'new covenant'. In *Tanhuma B.*, Ki Tissa 58b, for example, the reason is explained for God's gift of the **Mishnah** in writing: 'Moses said: "Lord, do you write it for them?" God said: "I did indeed desire to give it all to them in writing, but it was revealed that the Gentiles in the future will have dominion over them, and will claim the Torah as theirs; then would my children be like the Gentiles. Therefore give them the Scriptures in writing, and the Mishnah, Agada and Talmud orally, for it is they which separate Israel and the Gentiles".'

Early in its history the Church regarded the 'old covenant of Israel' as definitely abrogated; the text on the 'new covenant' in Jer. 31 was explained as pointing to fulfilment in **Christ**. Meanwhile, there was a growing emphasis in **Rabbinic Judaism** on the mutuality of the covenantal relationship between God and his People. This was summarised in a well-known **midrash**, in which God was depicted as travelling around the world asking various peoples to accept his **Torah**. None was willing to accept its yoke until God came to Israel and the Israelites answered in one voice: 'All that the Lord has spoken we will do, and we will be obedient' (in Exod. 24.7, after *Mekilta Bakodesh* 5.74a). In Christianity, by contrast, the one-sided initiative of God in the 'new covenant in Christ' was strongly emphasised. Much medieval Christian **polemic** against Jews was concerned with this issue.

The term covenant plays a less prominent role in **Roman Catholicism** and **Eastern Orthodox** tradition than in **Protestantism**, although there has in recent decades been a change discernible in the thinking of Catholic scholars like Erich Zenger (b. 1939) and John Pawlikowski (b. 1940). Among the Reformers, **Calvin**, together with Heinrich Bullinger (1504–75), was the leading exponent of the covenant concept, which is central to Calvinist theology. For Calvin the **salvation** revealed in the New Testament is the same salvation as in the Old, only in a new phase and a fuller light. He writes on dispensations of the one and eternal covenant, of which the basis is always the same, namely Jesus Christ. Calvin's high esteem for the Old Testament permeates the later **Calvinist** tradition, where it is often regarded as the 'proper Bible'. This may explain why soon after the Second World War Reformed Churches took the lead in new statements on Jewish–Christian understanding, in the **Netherlands** as early as 1949 and 1959.

It is much debated in the Jewish–Christian **dialogue** whether the concept of covenant, in its one-covenant version or in its two-covenants version, could function as a bridge between the two traditions. In the last decades of the twentieth century numerous official ecclesiastical statements declared that the covenant of God with his People was never abrogated. Covenant theology often assisted in the renewal of relations between Church and the Jewish People. The famous declaration *Nostra Aetate* (1965) of **Vatican II** follows the concept of the two covenants: 'The Church, therefore, cannot forget that she received the revelation of the Old Testament through the People with whom God in his inexpressible mercy deigned to establish the ancient covenant.' Pawlikowski elaborates on this line of thinking: for him the double covenant perspective helps to underline the distinctiveness of the revelation experienced in and through Christ. The German **Rhineland Synod**, in *Towards a Renewal of the Relationship between Christians and Jews* (1980), follows the one covenant perspective in its declaration: 'We believe the permanent election of the Jewish People as the People of God and realize that through Jesus Christ the Church is taken into the covenant of God with His People.'

The covenant concept is thus of great importance in Jewish–Christian dialogue. In the North American context Paul van Buren (1924–98) has most thoroughly integrated the theme into his theology. In what he terms 'the Jewish–Christian reality' Israel received the calling to be faithful in the covenant to the Torah because of the **creation**, and the Church received the calling to be faithful to Jesus Christ because of the same creation. Through the Jew Jesus the Christian community receives this calling to participate by faith in the covenant of **Abraham**. In **Germany** Friedrich-Wilhelm Marquardt (1928–2002) is Europe's most influential thinker on the theological consequences of the renewal of the relationship between the Church and the Jewish people. In his view the term 'covenant' is the most constructive biblical concept to describe both Christian **identity** and the Jewish–Christian relationship in our time. His conviction is that churches as representatives of the peoples of the earth can only hope to become partners in a covenantal relationship with the **people of Israel** if they are willing to accept the burden of Israel in sanctifying the name of God in the world, if they join in the calling of Israel to restore the world, and if they are ready to embark with Israel on its journey to the 'new covenant' with God that lies ahead.

The American-Jewish scholar Irving Greenberg (b. 1933) has defended the thesis that the covenant of God with Israel has undergone many renewals in the course of history. It was God's purpose from the very beginning to open up the covenant of Israel to a wider group of humanity. The shock of the ***Shoah*** and the empowerment of the Jewish People in the **State of Israel** have led to a new phase in the history of the covenant and of the Jewish–Christian relationship. The Israeli scholar David Hartman (b. 1931) also regards the covenant concept as central to his thinking. In his view Judaism is grounded in a covenant between people and God that is predicated on a belief in human adequacy and dignity. Also other religions, especially Christianity and **Islam**, have their own covenants with God and are called to celebrate their dignity and particularity.

See also **Romans 9–11**   *SIMON SCHOON*

Creation narratives

Jews and Christians have shared the same creation narratives since the Christian **canon** does not have any separate narrative. The story in Gen. 1.1–2.3 is a priestly document. It does not relate a *creatio ex nihilo* but describes the ordering of a chaotic cosmos. The narrative distinguishes between works of separation (days 1–3) and works of furnishment (days 4–6). At the climax of creation **Adam** appears

as a hermaphrodite. The second story in Gen. 2.4–26 is not strictly a creation narrative, but rather a narrative relating the origins of humanity and **sexuality**. The human person (Hebrew, *ha adam*) is derived from the earth (Hebrew, *ha adama*) in an obvious wordplay. Placed in a garden of **Eden**, God recognises that the single status of the human person is unhelpful. The subsequent parade and naming of the animals has a dual purpose: it expresses the God-given sovereignty of the human over the animals and it concludes that there is no helpmate among them. The woman is formed from the man's body. This etiology explains sexual attraction.

Christians and Jews have elaborated two differing anthropologies from the narratives. These have affected their respective theologies of the human person. Christianity during the patristic period was convinced that the humans in the two origin stories had been incorruptible and immortal. Therefore the conclusion was drawn that the subsequent sin-stories, beginning with the sinful action of Adam and **Eve**, explained that death was consequent on **sin** (see Wis. 2.23; Rom. 5.12). From this anthropology there developed the influential doctrine of **original sin**, which could only be remedied by Christian **baptism**. On the other hand, a Jewish anthropology identified in the human person the **evil** impulse (Hebrew, *ysr hara*) and the good impulse (Hebrew, *ysr hatov*). The *ysr hara* is not evil per se; it is undifferentiated between good and evil but, if undisciplined, will inevitably lead to sin and hence to death. It requires a counterforce, the *ysr hatov*, variously identified with **Torah**, the **Wisdom** of God and the Spirit of God. In fact, this anthropology underlies some of the thinking on human action in the Christian scriptures. Further, in pre-Christian times Jewish thought hypostatised Wisdom and the Word of God or **Logos**. Jewish thinkers were thus able to speak of the pre-existent and creative Wisdom and of creation by means of the Word. In the patristic period both Jews and Christians were confronted with **Hellenistic** culture and its concept of nature as eternal, autonomous and necessary. **Philo** had reconciled the conflict by introducing a mediating Logos as the agency to link God and the material world. Christians took up this line of thought and identified **Jesus** with the Logos and its creative force. Jewish thought also looked towards a renewal of the original creation: after the judgement of God on the present order there would be a new beginning (Ezek. 36.26–8) and this would include a new **covenant** relationship (Jer. 31.31–34). In a similar vein **Isaiah** spoke of a new heaven and a new earth (41.17–20; 66.22). These developments in Jewish thought prior to Christianity were adapted by Christians to their own thinking on creation, the belief that the cosmos, after the coming of the Christ, was already newly created (Rev. 21.1–4) and would undergo a cosmic transformation.

Jews and Christians thus shared a common worldview with variant interpretations relating to Jesus' role in it. It was the **Enlightenment** of the eighteenth century that broke the ties with this Judaeo-Christian worldview. Thereafter, in both traditions there were three possibilities. Creationism, reflecting an effort to relate a literal reading of the biblical text with developed ideas about God, humanity and the cosmos, defended the doctrine of a God who created the world and humans directly, appointing them to rule the world. At the opposite extreme the scientific theory of evolution was used to demonstrate the absurdity of the creation narratives. An intermediate position, maintained by many modern Christians and Jews, has been that science and faith are two separate modes of discourse and that scientific theory and creation narratives need to be read separately. On this issue of the interpretation of the creation narratives and the understanding of creation as a theological topic, Jews and Christians have generally followed a similar path.

See also **cosmology**   *ROBERT CROTTY*

Creed *see* **confession of faith; doctrine; early Church; Maimonides; religion; Shema**

Crescas, Hasdai (*c*.1340–1410)

From Barcelona, Hasdai Crescas represented the Jewish community at the court of the kings of Aragon in the 1380s and 1390s, and was considered one of the king's *familiares*, or close advisers, an increasingly rare achievement for a Jew at the end of the fourteenth century. Unfortunately, his family suffered badly in the **pogrom** of 1391, though Crescas himself was in Saragossa with the queen and escaped harm. The pogrom wrought terrible destruction on Catalan Jewry, and Crescas was entrusted with the task of trying to rebuild the Jewish communities of the Catalan lands, but his success was evidently limited. His sense of the need to defend and reconstruct Catalan Jewry was expressed in several of his books, such as an attack

on Christian beliefs written in Catalan (1397–8). He also distrusted Aristotelian philosophy, which he argued had distanced his fellow-Jews from Jewish beliefs. His *Or Adonai* was finished in 1410, shortly before he died, and attacked **Maimonides**' methods and views in the *Guide for the Perplexed*. Some have seen in this work an awareness of Christian theological writings of the fourteenth century, such as the works of Duns Scotus (1266–1308) and of William of Ockham (*c*.1280–*c*.1349), though this is hard to prove. He did, however, reveal considerable knowledge of leading Arabic scholars such as al-Ghazzali (1058–1111) and ibn Rushd (Averroes) (1126–98). Crescas's ideas of God, eternity and the **soul**, though derided by some, had a long afterlife, for example in the works of **Pico della Mirandola** and **Spinoza**.   *DAVID ABULAFIA*

Crimea

Peninsula on the Black Sea, since 1991 autonomous republic within **Ukraine**. According to a Karaite legend (concocted in the nineteenth century) the first Jews arrived there as early as the sixth century BCE. Effectively, the first Jewish communities appeared in the first centuries CE in Bosporus Kingdom and in the Roman (later Byzantine) colony of Cherson (where one of the most ancient synagogues was discovered, later replaced by a Christian basilica). In the eighth century part of the peninsula was conquered by the **Khazars**. At the end of the tenth century Cherson was devastated by the Russian Prince Vladimir (956–1015), who probably had been baptised there. In the thirteenth to eighteenth centuries the Crimea was ruled by the Tatars. The first **Karaites** (as well as Rabbanites – later called Krimchaks) settled in the thirteenth century in Solkhat (now Stary Krym), then in Qirqyer (later Chufut-Kale – Turkish: Jewish fortress) and Mangup (the centre of the Christian principality of Theodoro; the last two towns by the end of the Tatar rule became all-Jewish (mostly Karaite). In 1783 the Crimea became a part of **Russia**, and soon was included into the **Pale of Settlement**, so many Christians as well as Ashkenazi Jews from other parts of Russia settled there. During the nineteenth century the Crimean Karaites managed to achieve equal rights with the Christian population of the empire. Under Soviet rule in the 1920s several Jewish agricultural settlements were established in the Crimea. During the *Shoah* most Crimean Jews were killed (with the exception of Karaites). After the Second World War the project to establish a Jewish Soviet Socialist Republic in the Crimea was among the pretexts of the Jewish Antifascist Committee Trial, one of the key moments of Stalin's **antisemitic** campaign of 1948–53. *ARTEM FEDORTCHOUK*

Crispin, Gilbert (d. 1117)

Abbot of Westminster and pupil of **Anselm**, he published a popular Jewish–Christian disputation in 1092 entitled *Disputatio Iudei et Christiani*, based on his conversations with a Jew who lived in Westminster. The **disputation** uses many of the traditional arguments and **polemic** from the **Church Fathers**, but most of all reason and biblical **exegesis**. Although discussion between the Jew and Crispin is friendly, Crispin's concept of the Jew as unreasonable because he did not accept the rational Christian argument illustrated the deterioration of the position of Jews in Europe from the twelfth century onwards. *EDWARD KESSLER*

Cromwell, Oliver (1599–1658)

Soldier, leader of the Puritans, and ruler of England, Scotland and Ireland as Lord Protector, 1653–8. Cromwell was the person most responsible for the readmission of the Jews to England in 1656, following their **expulsion** in 1290. Jews would doubtless have returned to England at some point, but Cromwell ensured it was earlier than might otherwise have been the case and under very benign conditions at a time when Jews faced severe discrimination and hardship in many other parts of Europe. He had been petitioned by the Dutch rabbi **Menasseh ben Israel**, who saw England as a potential haven for Jews suffering widespread massacres in the **Ukraine**. Cromwell convened a conference in London in December 1655 to decide the issue. Those favouring readmission included **millenarianists** who argued that the Messianic age would dawn once the Jews were scattered to the four corners of the world, which necessitated entry to England. Cromwell himself was probably more influenced by the practical needs of the new Commonwealth and anticipated Jewish merchants playing an important economic role. Others, including especially clergy antagonistic on religious grounds, opposed readmission. When the conference failed to deliver a positive response, Cromwell dissolved it. Three months later a group of **Marranos** living in London and posing as Catholics openly professed their Jewish **identity** and petitioned Cromwell to allow them to establish a synagogue and cemetery. He gave his consent through a decision by the Council of State. The decision was one of very few acts of Cromwell not automatically repealed on the restoration of the monarchy. *JONATHAN ROMAIN*

Cross/crucifix

The principal symbols of Christianity. Appearing in a variety of configurations, the cross is most simply a vertical line transected by a perpendicular line at or near the top. The crucifix is a cross bearing the body of **Jesus** upon it, either suffering, dead or glorified. **Protestantism** has generally preferred the empty cross as a symbol of the **Resurrection**, **Roman Catholicism** the crucifix to signify Jesus' passion and death, while **Orthodox Christianity** uses a wide variety of elaborate and iconic crosses, often accompanied by textual graphics, that emphasise the Lordship of Jesus Christ.

This primary Christian symbol has antecedents in the late Second Temple and early rabbinic periods. Intersecting lines in a variety of arrangements formed geometric designs in many Jewish edifices, especially the *crux gammata* (swastika) formed by the convergence of four gamma Γ or L shapes. Cross-shaped symbols have also been found on Jewish sarcophagi at various sites dating from the first century BCE to the early third century CE (De Lange, *Origen and the Jews*, 116). This usage may relate to the text of Ezek. 9.4, in which the Lord commands, 'put a *mark* [Hebrew = *tav*, written in ancient Hebrew as X] on the foreheads of' the righteous. Recalling the blood on the doorposts in Exod. 12, those marked with the *tav* would be spared divine wrath. Thus, marking tombs with an X indicated the deceased's **righteousness**. The later rabbis also drew upon this Ezekiel verse when they commented that a *tav* on the foreheads of the righteous represented *tiḥyeh* ('you will live'), but the wicked had a *tav* in blood on their foreheads saying *tamut* ('you will die') (*b. Shabbat* 55a). The idea that the righteous were marked with this sign – in Greek the *tau* or T approximates the shape of crosses used in Roman **crucifixions** – would naturally resonate with early Christians. Thus in the apocalyptic **New Testament** book of Revelation, divine punishment hesitates until angels 'have sealed the servants of our God upon their foreheads' (Rev. 7.3; see also 9.4).

The centrality of the cross for Christian discipleship is seen in the earliest New Testament books, the letters written by **Paul of Tarsus**. For him, 'the word of the cross is folly to those who are perishing, but to us who are being saved it is the power of God' (1 Cor. 1.18). Church members should have the same attitude among themselves as did Christ, who had 'humbled himself and became obedient to the point of death – death on a cross! – [therefore] God also highly exalted him . . .' (Phil. 2.3–5, 8–9a). In the three Synoptic Gospels of Matthew, Mark and Luke each disciple is expected to 'take up his cross' and follow Jesus (Matt. 10.38; 16.24; Mark 8.34; Luke 9.23; 14.27).

A glimpse of the symbol being used in an early Christian–Jewish debate might be seen in the early second-century *Apocalypse of Peter*. In a vision to Peter, the glorified Jesus describes his return or **parousia**: 'So will I come upon the clouds of heaven . . . with my cross going before my face will I come in my majesty . . .' (Ethiopic text). If this text originated during the **Bar Kokhba** revolt (132–5), then **Jewish Christians** used the symbol of the cross while asserting the Messianic status of Jesus in opposition to other Jews who were hailing Bar Kokhba as **Messiah** (Bauckham, 'Jews and Jewish Christians').

By the mid-second century **Justin Martyr** understood the shape of a cross to mediate God's power, as his remarks on Exod. 17.11–12 show: 'Amalek was proportionally defeated, [because Moses] himself made the sign of the cross' (*Dial.* 90). **Tertullian of Carthage** in the early third century claims that 'at every forward step and movement, at every going in and out . . . in all the ordinary actions of daily life, we [Christians] trace upon the forehead the sign [of the cross]' (*Cor.* ch. 3). By the time Emperor **Constantine** adopted the cross as a military emblem in the early fourth century, it was already the characteristic symbol of Christianity. Thanks to his mother Helena's (*c.*255–330) 'discovery' of the 'true cross' in Jerusalem, pious veneration of **relics** of the cross spread, further intensifying the symbol's popularity and potency. Now made worthy of public reverence, it increasingly appeared on civic monuments and church shrines in the fourth and fifth centuries, and in medieval times was incorporated into heraldic designs and civic signage. From roughly the sixth century the figure of Jesus began to be added to crosses in Christian artwork.

Over the centuries the cross has held many meanings for Christians, including the triumph of Jesus over death, the victory of the Church over the **Roman Empire**, the establishment of God's will over the earth, the love of God as manifested in Jesus, God's hidden presence revealed in abject humility and suffering (**Luther**'s *theologia crucis*), the solidarity of God with the oppressed, or charitable service done in God's name. For late medieval and subsequent Jews who were persecuted by Christians, however, the cross symbolised oppression and domination, especially in the context of Good Friday observances or **Passion plays**. It was also associated with the **blood libel** that Jews tortured Christian children, sometimes by affixing them to crosses in mockery of Jesus, in order to use their blood to make **Passover** *maẓẓah* (Boys, *Has God Only One Blessing?*, 230–1). The **Shoah** intensified these negative connotations of the central Christian symbol not only because of its occurrence in 'Christian' Europe, but also because the Nazi emblem, the swastika, is a form of a cross (although with roots far back into pre-Christian antiquity). Deriving from these different historical experiences, the contrasting emotions that the cross generates among Jews and Christians often become evident during interfaith **dialogue** and played a major role in the controversy over the erection of a 14-foot cross at **Auschwitz** in 1988 and dozens of smaller crosses (removed a year later) in 1998. *PHILIP A. CUNNINGHAM*

Crucifix *see* **cross/crucifix**

Crucifixion

The term refers to the binding or nailing of an individual to a cross, which could be either a tree or a stake. Normally victims were alive at the time of crucifixion, but occasionally corpses were attached to crosses. As a military and political method of punishment, crucifixion was common in the ancient world. The Persians, the Greeks, the Carthaginians and the Celts practised it as a form of execution. Two key issues relating to the significance of the crucifixion of **Jesus** for Jewish–Christian relations are the identity of those responsible and the paradox of a crucified **Messiah**.

Though they differ in detail, the four evangelists provide a defensible historical account of the crucifixion. But who was responsible for sending Jesus to the cross? Christian tradition, following the view reflected in the Gospels, has blamed the Jews exclusively and exonerated the Romans. This has led to the charge of **deicide** being levelled against all Jews, past and present. **Augustine**, addressing Jews at the beginning of the fifth century, wrote, 'You, in your parents, killed Christ' (*Adv. Jud.* 7.10). But modern scholars, while recognising the part played by the Jewish leaders in the crucifixion, object to the total exoneration of the Romans. In their attempt to pacify Judea the Romans made extensive use of crucifixion, primarily because of its propaganda value. **Josephus** reports how Varus, governor of Syria, quelled a revolt in **Jerusalem** in 4 BCE by crucifying 2,000 of the inhabitants (*Ant.* 17.295). Ancient authors testify to its efficacy as a graphic warning to others of what will happen to them if they cause trouble (Quintilian, *Decl.* 274). If the Romans regarded Jesus as a disturber of the peace, nailing him to a cross would have seemed appropriate punishment.

Since crucifixion served as a public reminder to Jews that they were in bondage to a foreign power, it is hardly surprising that the most prominent feature of the crucifixion of Jesus, as far as they were concerned, was its shamefulness. The author of Heb. 12.2 refers to the 'shame' of the cross. **Paul** describes the crucified Christ as 'a stumbling block to Jews and folly to Gentiles' (1 Cor. 1.23). In Jewish thought the long-awaited Messiah would be a victorious king; there was nothing to indicate that he would endure a slave's death. The disgrace of crucifixion prompted **Celsus** to dismiss the redemptive work of Christ because he had been 'bound in the most ignominious fashion' and 'executed in a shameful way' (**Origen**, *Cels.* 6.10). Jesus did not fit Jewish Messianic expectations. Subjection to the greatest dishonour possible demonstrated that the victim was 'accursed by God'. According to Deut. 21.22–3, the body of a man convicted of a capital offence was to be 'hanged' on a tree. Evidence from Qumran (4QpNahum 3–4; 11QTemple 64.6–13) indicates that in Jewish tradition this text was applied to those who died on a cross. This form of the death penalty was brought into Judaism from the Gentile world. However, it would have been unacceptable to Jews as a means of execution as soon as direct rule from Rome began. Though thousands of Jews were crucified, the **cross** never became a symbol of Jewish suffering, primarily because of Deut. 21.23, but also because of its significance for Christians. The paradoxical claims about a crucified saviour are at the heart of Christian teaching and are expressed clearly in the early hymn found in Phil. 2.6–11.

See also **Passion narratives**; **trial of Jesus**

GARETH LLOYD JONES

Crusades

The Crusades (eleventh to sixteenth centuries) were holy wars preached by the papacy against those who were deemed to be the enemies of Christ and his Church and have been of profound significance in the history of Jewish–Christian relations. Holy wars were considered to be just because they were promulgated by authority against those who were seen to have caused injury to Christendom and because they were waged with the right intention, namely love for God. The Crusades appealed widely to Latin Christendom. The First Crusade was preached by Pope Urban II (*r.*1088–99) at Clermont in 1095 as an armed **pilgrimage** to the East to free **Jerusalem** from the Saracens. The Second and Third Crusades were expeditions aimed to re-establish the successes of the First in the Holy Land. Other crusades were aimed at conquering pagan lands, as for example from the middle of the twelfth century in the Baltic. The Albigensian Crusade, which was preached in 1208 by Pope **Innocent III**, was aimed at destroying Cathar **heresy**. In 1241 **Gregory IX** preached a crusade against the Mongols for the first time. Political crusades of the thirteenth and fourteenth centuries were wars promulgated by popes against their internal Christian enemies. Much of the Christian conquest of **Spain** from **Islam** was couched in crusading language. Crusading **preaching** concentrated on whipping up Christian emotions against unbelief or deviant forms of Christian belief. As crusading successes diminished in the Holy Land, sermons emphasised the need for Christian introspection and the purification of Christian society to regain God's favour. It is hardly surprising that this kind of language affected Christian attitudes towards Jews (and so-called unbelievers).

Urban's call to crusade in 1095 did not just result in the gathering of a number of princely armies. Unofficial bands of crusaders were recruited in north-eastern France, Flanders, Normandy and the Rhineland. Their departure for the Holy Land in spring and early summer 1096 preceded that of the official crusaders. On their land route through **Germany** they encountered prosperous Jewish communities in cities like Speyer, Worms, Mainz, Cologne and Trier. In all these cities the (arch)bishops concerned tried to prevent anti-Jewish violence. Not only were they anxious to uphold public order in their cities, they were committed to maintaining official Church policy, which did not permit Jews to be attacked or forcibly converted. In Speyer casualties stayed low, but many Jews died in Worms and Mainz and in the villages outside Cologne to which the archbishop had sent them for safety. Many of these Jews were killed or forcibly baptised by the crusaders and townsfolk who joined forces with them. Others died by their own hands as martyrs sanctifying God's holy name (*Kiddush ha-Shem*) rather than undergoing **baptism**. Three extant Hebrew narratives of the 1096 **pogroms**, which were written within about 50 years of the event, graphically depict the ritual slaughter of whole Jewish families. Although there is much scholarly debate about the historical reliability of these sources, corroboration from the Latin sources confirm that many Jews died in this way. At the same time it is probably true that the Hebrew narratives say as much about the feelings of those who survived the pogroms as about the feelings of those who did not. In Trier it seems that the majority of the Jewish community was forcibly converted. After the Crusade Emperor **Henry IV** permitted those who had been baptised against their will to return to Judaism. His ruling clashed with **canon law** which, notwithstanding its position against forced baptism, stipulated that anyone who had been baptised was a Christian. The princely armies did not persecute Jews in Europe. When Jerusalem fell to the crusaders in 1099 numerous Jews were killed alongside Muslims. Recent work has suggested, however, that wholesale slaughter of Jews did not occur.

Extensive loss of Jewish life was prevented by **Bernard of Clairvaux** during the Second Crusade in 1146. He put a stop to the anti-Jewish preaching of Ralph, one of his own Cistercian monks. Bernard firmly expected Christians to adhere to traditional Church policy protecting Jews. In the Third Crusade the Jews of York were massacred in 1190 in Clifford's Tower, while King Richard I (*r.*1189–99) was absent from England organising his own departure for the Holy Land. As far as later crusades are concerned, major violence against Jews was usually stemmed by those in authority. Some exceptions are the persecutions accompanying the preaching of the Crusade of 1309 in Brabant and the violence unleashed by the second Crusade of the Shepherds of 1320 in **France** to the south of the Loire.

What explains anti-Jewish violence by crusaders? Crusading preaching, calling upon Christians to wreak vengeance on the Muslims for dishonouring Christ, could easily spill over into the desire to avenge the death of **Jesus** on those who were judged to be guilty of the **crucifixion**. Growing identification of Christians with the figure of Jesus increased the likelihood of this happening. Our sources tell us how crusaders wondered why they should seek out Muslims in the Holy Land when there were Jews at home. In addition, the reality of crusading meant that large armies needed to get hold of provisions along the way. It is likely that crusaders felt it only right that Jews should in this way help finance the Crusades. The idea that Jews should suffer financially on behalf of crusading endeavours intensified as, by the end of the twelfth century, Jews had become important players in providing crusading loans (*see* **usury**). After the Jews died in Clifford Tower, the evidence held in York Minster of debts to Jews was destroyed.

The pogroms of 1096 mark the earliest serious well-documented medieval Christian attack on Jews (barring **Visigothic** persecution of Jews in seventh-century Spain). Although they do show how vulnerable their position was at times of heightened Christian fervour, it is important to note that they do not constitute a watershed in Jewish history. Jewish communities continued to develop during the twelfth and thirteenth centuries. Crusading hostility against Jews is only one factor among many that determined medieval Christian–Jewish relations.

Crusades have, nevertheless, had a continuing impact on Jewish–Christian relations. While 'crusade' is commonly used to denote a righteous endeavour, the word conjures up for Jews (and Muslims) the image of unjust religious persecution. Some Jews cite the Crusades as a reason not to engage in Jewish–Christian **dialogue**, others are convinced by the Crusades that the only purpose of dialogue is to prevent **antisemitism**. In 1999 some Christian pilgrims commemorated the 900th anniversary of the conquest of Jerusalem by asking **forgiveness** for the violence perpetrated by the crusaders.   *ANNA SAPIR ABULAFIA*

Crypto-Judaism *see* **Marranos**

Curses *see* **blessings and curses**

Cyprian (*c*.200–58)

Thascius Caecilianus Cyprianus, bishop of Carthage (248–58), was an admirer of **Tertullian**, and like him, and Hippolytus also, he systematised a collection of anti-Jewish **polemic** and rhetorically inspired **exegesis**. Cyprian had been a wealthy, cultivated adult convert from paganism. In the work *Testimonia ad Quirinum* he listed **proof-texts** and dealt with established topics of Christian **supersessionism**, including new **Law** versus old, Jews' loss of **Jerusalem**, the necessity of believing in **Christ** for understanding the scriptures, and culpable Jewish rejection of the Christ (cf. his *Dom. Or.* 10). Like Tertullian, and also **Pseudo-Cyprian** in the *Adversus Judaeos*, Cyprian envisaged **forgiveness** for the Jews, with baptismal washing cleansing them from blood guilt. He is best known for his teaching on episcopal authority, schism and **baptism** and regarding Christians who lapsed during persecution. Cyprian wrote treatises and letters that are important for understanding rigorist North African Christianity, where Carthaginian paganism ran deep and Christians of Carthage needed to respond to long-established and successful Jewish groups in the region. Writings such as the *Testimonia* educated Christians in 'proper' understanding of their relation to Jews and Judaism. At the same time Cyprian applied Jewish Levitical priestly and sacrificial categories to the understanding of Christian ministry and **sacraments** (*Epistle* 1). In arguing for the necessary *re*-baptism of schismatics, he pointed to analogies with Jewish ideas of **priesthood** and the danger of contaminating rites and people. He was persecuted in the reign of Decius (*r*.249–50) and martyred under Valerian (*r*.253–60).

CHRISTINE TREVETT

Cyril of Alexandria (*c*.375/380–444)

Patriarch of Alexandria in **Egypt** from 412 CE until his death. Cyril was a ruthless politician who used his patriarchal power to advance the agenda of the Christian **Roman Empire**, often at the expense of traditional Egyptian religion and **Rabbinic Judaism**. The Church historian Socrates (*c*.380–450) reports that Cyril was personally responsible for the **expulsion** of all Jews from the city of **Alexandria** following a riot that occurred there in 415. Despite this side of his legacy, Cyril is primarily known for his contribution to the development of classical **Christology** as it was articulated at the Council of Chalcedon in 451 CE.   *JOHN J. O'KEEFE*

Cyril of Jerusalem (*c*.315?–86)

Christian saint, probably a native of **Jerusalem** and from *c*.349/50 its bishop, who desired to elevate it as a Christian city and saw Emperor **Julian**'s short-lived attempt to facilitate the Jews' rebuilding of the **Temple** (see, e.g., *Catech.* 15.15). His 23 *Catechetical Lectures* (plus an opening address) are the oldest such writings to survive. Among these, the authorship of the five 'Mystagogic Catecheses' has occasionally been questioned, as also authorship of his letter to Emperor Constantius II (*r*.337–61). His episcopate suffered in a time of Christian theological disputes, but when Emperor Julian was discomforting some Christians by benefiting others Cyril could return to Jerusalem after banishment. His lack of opposition to the proposed Temple is attributed to God-given confidence that the venture would fail and Julian and the Jews would be confounded. The disputed letter, mentioning rebuilding, is extant in Syriac (Brock, 'A Letter Attributed to Cyril' original article 1977 (doubts authenticity) versus Wainwright, 'Recently Discovered Letter' (supports)). He made much of Jerusalem as an apostolic See, of its Holy Places and the relics of the True Cross available since **Constantine**'s reign. He may have instituted the **liturgy** for visiting the Christian **pilgrimage** sites, but for Gregory of Nyssa (330–*c*.395), who visited Jerusalem in the year 380, the city was faction-riven and morally corrupt (*Against Pilgrimages*). Cyril's *Catechetical Lectures* witness to the developing Christian **canon**. He quoted deutero-canonical writings and recorded the origins of the **Septuagint**, but thought that churches should use as **Old Testament** only those writings that were canonical for Jews (*Catech.* 4.33).   *CHRISTINE TREVETT*

Czechoslovakia *see* **Czechia; Slovakia**

Czechia

(Bohemia, Moravia and Czech Silesia.) Christianised after 863, with a Jewish presence from around the same time. Peaceful coexistence was interrupted by the **Crusades**, inciting a massacre in Prague in 1096 which was a precursor to further anti-Jewish measures in the following centuries. In 1254 Přemysl Otakar II (*c*.1233–78) granted Jews privileges based on the charter of **Frederick II**, but further anti-Jewish violence took place in the fourteenth century, evoking initial sympathy between Jews and the Hussite movement (1415–34), which was occasionally described by Catholics as a '**Judaising**' sect. However, eventual iconoclastic Hussite riots turned against both Jews and Catholics. The rule of Rudolph II (1576–1612), during which Prague attracted famous Jewish and Christian scholars, was a golden age in Jewish–Christian relations. Remarkably, after the defeat of the Czech estates in 1620, during which time Jews tended to support the Catholics, some Protestant families converted to Judaism rather than go into exile or convert to Catholicism. Edicts of **tolerance** were promulgated in 1781/2 and 1848 for Protestants and Jews. The Czech 'National Revival' movement (1790–1848) struggled with aristocratic and Jewish preference for German language and culture, while simultaneously commending Jewish culture and perceiving parallels between the Jewish and Czech national struggle. In 1939 120,000 Jews lived in Czechia; 40,000 survived the **Holocaust**, but only 14,000 remained. Many synagogues were transferred to use as Protestant Churches rather than being left for the use of the secular communist regime.

See also **Slovakia**   *PETR FRYŠ*

DDDD

Dabru Emet

'Speak truth', a Jewish statement on Christians and Christianity issued in 2000 by four American Jewish scholars, who met twice a year for eight years under the auspices of the Institute of Christian and Jewish Studies in Baltimore. Over 200 Jewish leaders, writers and rabbis, primarily from the **United States** but also from Europe and the Middle East, signed the document. *Dabru Emet* is addressed to the Jewish community, as is *Christianity in Jewish Terms*, a book edited by the same authors and published to coincide with the issue of the statement. A broad range of signatories, from both **Orthodox** and **Progressive Judaism**, indicates that it is the first detailed modern cross-denominational statement published in the name of Jews and Judaism, a significance highlighted by the previous lack of official Jewish statements about the Jewish understanding of Christianity: Jewish–Christian relations rarely feature in institutional statements and none has previously succeeded in crossing denominational boundaries.

A valuable reflection on the place of Christianity in contemporary Jewish thought, *Dabru Emet* stresses that it is time for Jews both to learn about the efforts of Christians to honour Judaism, and to reflect on what Judaism may now say about Christianity. The statement asserts eight points: Jews and Christians worship the same God; Jews and Christians seek authority from the same book (the **Bible**); Christians can respect the claim of the Jewish people upon the **land of Israel**; Jews and Christians accept the moral principles of **Torah**; **Nazism** was not a Christian phenomenon; the humanly irreconcilable differences between Jews and Christians will not be settled until God redeems the world; a new relationship between Jews and Christians will not weaken Jewish practice; and Jews and Christians must work together for justice and peace.

Dabru Emet is a positive affirmation of Christianity and has been well received by the Churches. Many Christian denominations have issued statements welcoming its publication, and an American Christian Scholars Group, which meets under the auspices of the Center for Christian–Jewish Learning in Boston, has responded explicitly by issuing its own statement entitled *A Sacred Obligation*. Some of the eight points have caused controversy within the Jewish community, however. For example, the statement that Christians worship the God of Israel and legitimately draw on the **Hebrew Bible** has been criticised by some Orthodox writers, such as David Berger (b. 1943), who argue that doctrines such as the **Trinity** and **Incarnation** compromise the integrity of Jewish monotheism. In response, some Christians have been surprised to discover that Christianity can still be criticised for a tendency towards **idolatry**. Another point that caused controversy was the assertion that Nazism was not an inevitable outcome of Christianity. Some Jews, concerned that Christians might feel completely exonerated, criticised *Dabru Emet* for going too far, while for some Christians it was troubling to learn that some Jews do view Nazism as the logical outcome of European Christian culture.

It is too early to evaluate the long-term impact of *Dabru Emet*. Certainly, those Jews who oppose theological **dialogue**, or for whom Christianity remains an object of fear and anger, will resist or ignore it. Nevertheless, in general Jews – and particularly those involved in interfaith dialogue – have welcomed the statement as an unprecedented Jewish response to the modern transformation in Christian understanding of Jews and Judaism.

See also **Christianity, Jewish perspectives on**

EDWARD KESSLER

Danby, Herbert (1889–1953)

Hebraist. Danby served as canon at St George's Cathedral, **Jerusalem**, before becoming professor of **Hebrew** at Oxford. He is representative of early twentieth-century British scholarship's growing interest in Judaism. His best-known work took the form of translations. Danby's *Mishnah* (1933) introduced rabbinic tradition to Christian readers, and is still widely used. He also translated **Klausner**'s work on **Jesus**. In 1927 Danby published a series of lectures, *The Jew and Christianity*, on **Jewish perspectives on Christianity**. In these he argued that Christian persecution of Jews was a major cause of the ongoing Jewish rejection of 'Jesus as Christ and Redeemer'. *MELANIE J. WRIGHT*

David

Son of **Jesse** and first dynastic king of Israel. The significance of David to the Jewish–Christian relationship stems from differing interpretations of two dimensions of his variegated biblical portrait. He is the king of **Israel** whose dynasty was expected to reign in perpetuity, and he was a prolific poet-musician who established **Temple** worship in **Jerusalem**. His image is shaped both by the historical narratives in Samuel–Kings and Chronicles, but also by the poetic accounts relating to the royal theology of Jerusalem found in the classical prophets, especially **Isaiah**, and in the book of **Psalms**. A unique divine **covenant** with David described in 2 Sam. 7 contains a twofold promise: that one of his descendants would always sit on the throne and that God would dwell in a temple in Jerusalem to be built by David's son. In some biblical passages the durability of the covenant is conditioned on faithful observance of the **Law** (Ps. 89, 132), but in any case, the covenant was expected to be eternal. Judaism and Christianity both hold Messianic hopes centred around the Davidic covenant. Needless to say, a major point of divergence between Jews and Christians is over whether the Messianic expectation focusing on a descendant of King David has been realised in the person of **Jesus** of Nazareth, whose line is traced from David in the **New Testament**, or whether the **Messiah** is yet to make an appearance. Petitions calling for the speedy return of God to Jerusalem and the request for a Davidic king to reign on its throne are the focus of the fourteenth and fifteenth blessings of the *Amidah*, the statutory daily prayer of Judaism.

The traditional view of David as the inspired author of the book of Psalms seems to have been rooted in narrative depictions of his activities, such as his soothing the melancholy of King Saul by playing his lyre. Musical gifts were closely associated with poetic and prophetic gifts in antiquity, and already in the **Hebrew Bible** David is said to have delivered an oracle as his life drew to a close. 2 Sam. 23 includes a poetic composition that purports to be the last words of David. His claim, in the second verse, that 'The spirit of the LORD speaks through me, his word is upon my tongue', seems to have contributed to the understanding of David as the prophetically inspired author of the psalms. A short composition found in one of the psalms scrolls from Qumran, 11QPs^a (*see* **Dead Sea Scrolls**) attributes 4,050 psalms and songs for temple worship to David, which he 'uttered through prophecy which was given him from before the Most High'. The authors of the New Testament cite psalm verses as prophetic oracles that are fulfilled in various aspects of Jesus' life. Although challenged by certain individuals throughout the centuries, both Judaism and Christianity held to the traditional notion of Davidic authorship or, minimally, editorship of the psalms until the influence of **biblical criticism** in the nineteenth century finally dislodged the notion among the majority of Jews and Christians who accept its results. *JUDITH H. NEWMAN*

Day of Atonement

Yom Kippur, the most solemn day (10 Tishri) in the Jewish calendar, biblically ordained as a day of **fasting** and abstinence and entitled 'the sabbath of sabbaths'. As long as the Jerusalem **Temple** stood, the central rituals of the day were conducted by the High Priest and were intended, through sacrifice, **incense**, confession and the killing of the scapegoat, to bring about **atonement** for all the people's sins and restore communal purity. Late in the Second Temple period educational and introspective content was added to the High Priest's activities that day. After the destruction of the Temple the rabbinic leadership encouraged a close knowledge of the rituals (*avodah*) but stressed the individual element in the acts of contrition and confession and the need for a genuine change of heart. Yom Kippur, together with Rosh Hashanah and **Sukkot**, was seen as the time for a fresh start and, unlike other fast-days, enjoyed the status of a major festival. During the talmudic period the role of priesthood was virtually replaced by that of the **rabbi**, and various religious alternatives, especially **Torah** study and daily precepts, were found for the Temple service and to strengthen the relationship with God.

In a chronologically parallel but theologically alternative trend, the Christian community was highly influenced by the notions of the priesthood, the holy place, the blood **sacrifice** and the scapegoat ritual and sought to apply them to the figure of **Jesus** and in the ceremony of the **eucharist** as a way of maintaining access to the divine presence. The respective Jewish and Christian interpretations of those parts of Leviticus that refer to Yom Kippur, as recorded in the patristic literature and the talmudic–midrashic sources, are at times parallel and also include examples of mutually antagonistic comments with **polemical** content. The close but tense relationship between the two communities is also demonstrated by the custom of the early Christians to observe the Yom Kippur fast, to the great consternation of such leading Church figures as John **Chrysostom**. The post-talmudic synagogal poets in the **land of Israel** restored the *avodah*'s centrality by relating it to the **creation** of the world, the election of Israel and the role of the diligent **priest** in achieving contact with God. They provided emotive descriptions of the whole ceremonial and of the High Priest's glorious appearance and ensured a virtual re-enactment of the original ritual. The more standard **liturgy** of the Middle Ages incorporated some of these elements and many other liturgical poems that took most of the day to recite, but generally returned to the theme of personal and communal **repentance** and atonement. An **Aramaic** formula for the annulment of foolish vows (*Kol Nidrey*) was added to the service for the eve of Yom Kippur and wrongly understood in some antagonistic Christian circles as an indication that the word of Jews could not be trusted. Jewish authorities responded by omitting it, altering its text or clarifying its authentic nature. Some modern Jewish communities were also averse to its inclusion and replaced the medieval poems with modern prayers of repentance.   *STEFAN C. REIF*

Day of Judgement

The Day of Judgement is an **eschatological** religious concept that permeates much of Jewish and Christian (and Islamic) thought, is especially prominent in apocalyptic literature and exhibits theological features and religious concerns that are common to both traditions. Its roots are found in pre-exilic Israelite prophecy where the 'Day of YHWH' is an important indicator of the expectation of a day of divine reckoning (Amos 5.18–20) and was expected to bring about the end of Israel (Isa. 2.12–17; Zeph. 1.14–18; Ezek. 7.10–27). In post-exilic prophecy the concept can acquire positive overtones (Joel 4.9–21; Zech. 14.1–21), and in **Hellenistic** Judaism the expectation of a day of reckoning becomes 'individualised' in the sense that the eternal fate of individuals and not just of the nation as such is decided upon. Similar views inform **New Testament** and early Christian writings. **Jesus** is presented as announcing the Day of Judgement (Matt. 12.36). The position of judge is assigned to Christ himself who, at his return, will judge human beings according to their deeds (Matt. 25.31–46; Acts 10.42; 17.30–31; 24.25; 2 Cor. 5.10; Heb. 6.2; Rev. 22.12).

In both Judaism and Christianity the Day of Judgement is linked with events of a cosmic scope: not just the social and political spheres are affected, but nature itself is drawn into the cataclysmic event of divine judgement. Judgement concentrates on the individual, but the whole of creation is its stage. The divine creator is expected to restitute his entire creation in the *eschaton*. Whereas the concept of a Day of Judgement was and remained central to Jewish **apocalypticism** since its inception in the Hellenistic period and was accepted into and transformed by **Rabbinic Judaism**, which made it a central tenet of the Jewish faith, Christianity modified it and linked it with the person of Christ, who is perceived as the eschatological judge of humankind. The image of Christ in judgement can be traced through the Christian **iconographical** tradition from late antiquity onwards. Through medieval **art** and **architecture** the concept of the Day of Judgement became part of the collective imagination of the West. Although the theologies and imageries derived from the concept of a Day of Judgement are very different, both Judaism and Christianity try to come to terms with the problem of theodicy: both expect eschatological **salvation** to be brought about by divine intervention, through retributive justice achieved in judgement, thus solving the theological problem posed by belief in the justice of God.

From the age of **Enlightenment** onwards, belief in a Day of Judgement has become less and less important to the religious imagination of both Jews and Christians, though recent decades have seen a 'renaissance' of the concept in both Jewish and Christian theologies.   *JOACHIM SCHAPER*

Dead Sea Scrolls

The Dead Sea Scrolls are a collection of manuscripts (primarily in **Hebrew** and **Aramaic**) dating from the third century BCE to the first century CE found in caves near Qumran on the Dead Sea, in and after 1947. They are one of a number of valuable sources for reconstructing Judaism in the period of the Second Temple (*c.* 538 BCE–70 CE). There have been some improbable attempts to identify the obscure figures named in the Scrolls as members of the early Christian community, but such reconstructions have been rejected by the majority of scholars. The dating of the manuscripts places them mostly in the pre-Christian era, and allusions to historical figures in them are for the most part imprecise. A suggestion that Greek fragments of the **New Testament** were found among the Scrolls has also been largely dismissed as unsubstantiated, since the fragments are too small to permit positive identification. There are some similarities that reflect a common tradition behind the community portrayed in the Scrolls and the early Christian community. These include the Scrolls' emphasis on a so-called 'Teacher of Righteousness' (comparable to **Jesus**' teaching ministry), their interest in communal **worship** (as presented too in Acts) and the combining of **wisdom** and **apocalyptic** traditions in a manner similar to Jesus' teachings. They also provide further evidence of early Jewish **biblical interpretation**, diversity of messianic belief, and parallels to Christian terminology (notably the expression '**son of God**'). For some period in its history the community in the Scrolls was celibate, which provides some evidence of Jewish **celibacy** that might account for such a strong tradition of celibacy in early **Syriac Christianity**.

JAMES K. AITKEN

Death

Judaism and Christianity both affirm the reality of death. Perhaps this should go without saying, but it bears asserting for the simple reason that, from ancient to **postmodern** times human beings have had difficulty accepting the fact that when we die, we are really dead. 'You are dust, and to dust you shall return' (Gen. 3.19) means that, unlike what ancient Egyptians believed, we have no need for worldly provisions to be buried with us; and, contrary to Canaanite custom, we must make no inquiries of the dead (Deut. 18.11), nor offer any sacrifices to them (Deut. 26.14). While Judaism and Christianity teach that death is real, not illusory, they also teach that death is not our final destination. As real as death is, there is life after death, understood both in terms of the **immortality** of the **soul** and **resurrection** of the dead. The former implies something about the God-given nature of human existence; the latter affirms that the Creator is also the Redeemer, whose **redemption** is not only in and of this world but also for the world to come.

The Jewish tradition contains paradoxical answers about why human beings die. Generally, death is accepted as a natural fact of creaturely existence, but some rabbinic authorities see it as resulting from sin. The latter view perhaps was developed in response to the Christian doctrine that all human beings inherit **original sin**, and consequently death, because of the sin of **Adam**. Those ancient rabbis who acknowledged the lethal yield of Adam's sin nonetheless stressed individual responsibility for sin, suggesting that people die because they sin. In their view human beings sin and die *as* Adam did, rather than *because* Adam did. In Christian teaching sin and death have come to all through Adam, and all are offered eternal life through Christ (Rom. 5.18–21) whose death conquered sin and death. All who are 'baptised into his death' are given 'newness of life' (Rom. 6.3–4). Because Christianity teaches that the death of **Jesus** was the great act of redemption, many Christians believe that 'dying was his reason for living'. And since Christians are to model their lives after Jesus, this view partly accounts for the longing for death or **martyrdom** that has been a part of the Christian tradition. According to Douglas John Hall (b. 1928), 'the hagiography of Christendom abounds in demonstrations of the principle that spiritual salvation implies physical destruction' (*Imaging God*, 29), a concept foreign to Judaism. Abraham Joshua **Heschel** points out that 'in spite of the excellence which the afterlife holds in store, there is no craving for death in the history of Jewish piety' ('Death as Homecoming', in *Jewish Reflections on Death*, 67–68). To be sure, some Jews have desired martyrdom as the ultimate expression of *Kiddush ha-Shem*, but rabbinic tradition mandates that only in order to avoid three cardinal sins – idolatry, murder and sexual crimes like incest and rape – should Jews be ready to sacrifice their lives. One of the fruits of contemporary Jewish–Christian relations is the recovery among many Christians of an emphasis on redemption in and of this world, while also trusting in eternal life. From this perspective, Christ's reason for living was to embrace the human condition, including death, in its entirety, and to extend thereby the redemption championed by Judaism to all who follow him.

See also **afterlife** *JOHN C. MERKLE*

Death of God theology

'Is God Dead?' asked *Time* magazine's cover story on 8 April 1966. That story's context included four Americans, among them the Jewish theologian Richard Rubenstein (b. 1924), whose influential book *After Auschwitz* (1966; revised 1992) was one of the first to probe the religious implications of the **Holocaust**. After the Holocaust, Rubenstein contended, belief in a redeeming **God** – one who is active in history – is no longer credible. The controversy caused by *After Auschwitz* linked Rubenstein to three Protestant thinkers: T. Altizer (b. 1927), W. Hamilton (b. 1924) and P. van Buren (1924–98). Neither the labelling nor the clustering was entirely accurate, but the four were dubbed 'death of God theologians'.

Contributing to a symposium on 'The Death of God and the Holocaust' at the 1996 meeting of the American Academy of Religion, Altizer contended that death of God theology, or radical theology as it was sometimes called, 'was the first Christian theology that was not only a response to the Holocaust but grounded itself in the ultimacy of a Holocaust that had ended every trace of a just or beneficent providence' ('The Holocaust and the Theology of the Death of God', 19). Despite Altizer's claim that the Holocaust was a generating cause of the death of God theologies, however, there was little in the early work of the principal Protestants in the movement to confirm his judgement. Their writings in the 1960s neither showed nor produced much Christian attention to the Holocaust or to the Jewish–Christian encounter. At least in postwar America, Christian attention to the Holocaust and to Jewish–Christian relations grew far more from the pioneering work done by F. H. Littell (b. 1917) and R. Eckardt (1918–98).

Altizer and Hamilton never became leaders in Jewish–Christian **dialogue**. On the other hand, after giving up many of the positions he held in the 1960s, van Buren made cutting-edge contributions to the Jewish–Christian encounter, especially with his three-volume *A Theology of the Jewish–Christian*

Reality (1980–9, reprinted 1995), which remains one of the most important revisions of Christian theology since the Second World War. Shortly before his death van Buren stated that it was not the Holocaust that led him to make the Jewish people and Judaism prominent in his theology, but instead 'being confronted with the living face of Israel, warts and all' ('From the Secular to the Scriptural Gospel', 35–6). By contrast with van Buren, Altizer and Hamilton, Rubenstein made the Holocaust pivotal for his radical theology in the 1960s and for his subsequent scholarship as well. Unlike the three American Protestants, who tended to see the death of God as a liberating experience, Rubenstein was saddened to conclude that the idea of a God of history lacked credibility after the Holocaust. For him the Holocaust shattered a system of religious meaning that had sustained Jews and Christians for millennia. To live in the time of the death of God, he cautioned, was no cause for celebration. Rubenstein's analysis of the Holocaust and its implications continues to provoke profound soul-searching, both among Jews and Christians and in their encounter.

See also **Holocaust theology** *JOHN K. ROTH*

Decalogue *see* Ten Commandments

Deicide, charge of

The term deicide means the killing of God and was used as an accusation against Jews by the Church for nearly 2,000 years. Coined as the phrase 'the charge of deicide', it formed the basis of what Jules **Isaac** called the Christian 'teaching of contempt' for Judaism and became 'the cornerstone of Christian antisemitism and laid the foundations upon which all subsequent antisemitism would in one way or another be built' (Flannery, *The Anguish of the Jews*). The charge of deicide refers to the belief that in killing Christ the Jews had killed God. Although the accusation that the Jews had killed Christ appears early in the **New Testament** (Matt. 27.25; Acts 2.36; 1 Thess. 2.15–16), the first recorded charge of deicide occurred in the second century CE with **Melito**, Bishop of Sardis. Melito was the first Church Father unambiguously to accuse the Jews of Jesus' generation and of all subsequent generations of deicide. The charge first appeared in his **Easter** sermon *Peri Pascha*, delivered around 180 CE, and was expounded by subsequent **Church Fathers** (including John **Chrysostom** and **Augustine**) and **Luther**, becoming official Church teaching until the twentieth century. It was used to justify the belief that God had rejected **Israel** as his **Chosen People** in favour of the Church. It was also attached to other myths about Jewish suffering and depravity (the Mark of **Cain, blood libel**, the **Wandering Jew**). The accusation was particularly evident annually around Eastertime when, especially in the medieval period, Jews had to hide on Good Friday for fear of the mobs who would attack them as 'Christ-killers'. The charge was repeated as late as 1942 by Archbishop Kmetko of Nietra (1875–1948) in response to the Jewish leaders who pleaded with him to intervene on the deportation of Slovakian Jews during the **Holocaust**.

Changes in official Roman Catholic teaching came in 1965 when **Vatican II** formally renounced the charge of deicide, as have other churches. The Church has now recognised that neither all Jews at the time of Jesus nor the Jews of subsequent generations can be blamed for the death of Christ, and this has led, with the aid of contemporary New Testament scholarship, to changes in the interpretation of the **Passion narratives** and the recognition that, whilst some Jewish leaders may have been involved in Jesus' death, **crucifixion** was a Roman punishment, and Jesus died under Roman judgement. This change in interpretation has also been reflected in the Oberammergau **Passion play** and in educational material for schools.

See also **anti-Judaism**; **antisemitism**; *hoi Ioudaioi*; **Sanhedrin**; **trial of Jesus**   *HELEN P. FRY*

Delitzsch, Franz (1813–90)

German Lutheran theologian and Hebraist. Delitzsch was the author of many **commentaries** on books of the Bible and a respected teacher. Combining adherence to conservative **Lutheran** orthodoxy with personal pietism, he connected impressive knowledge of Semitic languages and Judaism with dedication to Christian **mission** circles, founding the journal *Saat auf Hoffnung* ('Seeds for the Future') in 1863 and in 1886 an institution (later Institutum Judaicum Delitzchianum) to facilitate – lately increasingly rejected – Christian mission among Jews. On the other hand he became a passionate opponent of the increasing **antisemitism** of his time, confuting the superstitious hate-writings of August Rohling (1839–1931), such as his influential book *Der Talmudjude* (1871).

PETR FRYŠ

Demon/devil

The belief in demons and the devil was present in the ancient Near East in general, was shared by ancient Judaism and Christianity, and was later used in anti-Jewish **polemics**. The **Hebrew Bible** mentions spirits of the dead and refers to demons that are either theriomorphic or connected with the animal world (Lev. 16.8–10; Isa. 13.19–22; 34.9–15). The concept of the devil as the prime adversary of God is linked with that of demons, the former being depicted as the ruler of the latter (cf. 1QM XII13.1–6, 11–13). He is variously referred to as 'Satan' (Job 1), 'Belial' (Ps. 18.5; 2 Cor. 6.15) or 'Beelzebub' (2 Kgs 1.2–3, 6, 16; Mark 3.22). **Jesus** believed in the existence of demons and the devil and is depicted as exorcising demons. Medieval Judaism held demonological concepts received from biblical, talmudic and midrashic sources and from surrounding non-Jewish cultures. Kabbalistic thought especially was characterised by an extensive demonology. Belief in demons and the devil also played an important role in medieval Christian popular piety and contributed to a growing **antisemitism**. The Jewish people was often painted as the 'people of Satan', a concept that is the most prominent feature of antisemitism in the medieval and early modern periods, can be traced back to early **Gnosticism** and was employed in Nazi propaganda. The 'demonologies' which formed part of the medieval theological *summae* contributed to the persecution of 'witches' in the late medieval and early modern periods. In recent times the belief in demons and the devil has become far less important in both mainstream Judaism and mainstream Christianity.

See also **evil**   *JOACHIM SCHAPER*

Devil *see* demon/devil

Dialogue

The dialogue between Christians and Jews takes place in a wider context of interreligious encounter which itself is a phenomenon of the twentieth century. Much of the theory of dialogue was laid out by Martin **Buber**, who wrote as early as 1929: 'A time of genuine religious conversations is beginning – not those so-called but fictitious conversations in which none regarded and addressed his partner in reality, but genuine dialogues, speech from certainty to certainty, but also from one open-hearted person to another open-hearted person.' These words appear in his book *Zwiesprache*, or 'Dialogue', in which Buber intended to clarify the 'dialogical principle' set out in *I and Thou*. Even though *Zwiesprache* was not translated into English until 1947, it remains the pioneering theoretical work on interfaith dialogue, with its emphasis on experiencing 'the other side' of a relationship that has transformed itself from the I–It involved in everyday encounters to the I–Thou of genuinely human encounter. In it Buber not only pioneers the use of the word 'dialogue' itself for deliberate interreligious conversation (in this technical sense not in common usage until the early 1960s), but also points to a new moment in the history of the world's religious traditions. Jewish–Christian dialogue takes place against this background.

To be sure, there were moments of true dialogue before Buber – as, for example, in the London Society for the Study of Religion, founded in 1904, in which Jewish scholar Claude **Montefiore** played a prominent role. In **Germany** Franz **Rosenzweig**, a close friend of Buber, laid important foundations for Jewish–Christian dialogue (he once suggested that truth can exist in *two* forms, in Judaism and in Christianity) and remains perhaps more influential on Jewish partners in dialogue with Christians than Buber. Another key Jewish thinker was Emmanuel Levinas (1906–95), who extended the dialogical relationship beyond the 'I–Thou' to the 'We–Thou', entailing ethical commitment to and responsibility for the other person of faith. This 'We–Thou' relationship Levinas linked to the ethical relationship with God. As he once remarked, 'There can be no "knowledge" of God separated from the relationship with human beings'. On the Christian side stand, among others, James **Parkes**, the Anglican pathfinder of new Jewish–Christian understanding and witness against **antisemitism** in the 1930s and 1940s, and William W. Simpson (1907–87), a **Methodist** minister at work in wartime London building new relationships between Christians and Jews. Such movements and persons led to the founding in 1942 of the **Council of Christians and Jews** (CCJ), of which Simpson was the first General Secretary.

But this activity was but a prelude to large-scale commitment to dialogue, which can be dated to the 1960s with the promulgation of *Nostra Aetate* in 1965, a document that, without using the word dialogue, opened **Roman Catholic** doors to interfaith

dialogue. This was followed by the setting up in 1971 of the Dialogue with People of Living Faith and Ideologies (DFI) sub-unit of the **World Council of Churches**, into which the earlier work of the Consultation on the Church and the Jewish People was absorbed. The work of the DFI became a major force in **Protestant** and **Orthodox Churches**, and led in 1979 to the *Guidelines on Dialogue with People of Living Faiths and Ideologies*. This major statement, translated into scores of languages, sets out four principles of dialogue: (1) 'dialogue should proceed in terms of people of other faith, rather than of theoretical impersonal systems'; (2) 'dialogue can be welcomed as a welcome way of obedience to the commandment of the Decalogue: "You shall not bear false witness against your neighbour"'; (3) 'dialogue . . . is a fundamental part of Christian service within community'; (4) 'the relationship of dialogue gives opportunity for authentic witness . . . [W]e feel able with integrity to commend the way of dialogue as one in which Jesus Christ can be confessed in our world today' and 'to assure our partners in dialogue that we come not as manipulators but as genuine fellow-pilgrims'. This set of principles has formed the basis for commitment by member churches of the WCC to interfaith activity since 1979 and has stimulated much further reflection by scholars and theologians, as well as the 1982 document *Ecumenical Considerations on Jewish–Christian Dialogue* (*see* **ecumenism**).

The thinking behind these four principles of dialogue owes much to the Canadian scholar of religion Wilfred Cantwell Smith (1916–2000). Smith's insistence that 'religions' were not to be reified as 'impersonal theoretical systems' that could be juxtaposed and compared had been absorbed by the late 1970s. Smith's famous statement, 'Ask not what religion a person belongs to but ask rather what religion belongs to that person', lies behind the first principle. Like Buber before him, Smith affirmed that the distinctive quality of the human being was faith (Hebrew *emuna*) rather than his or her holding a set of beliefs ('the alleged ideal content of faith'), and that therefore dialogue was always from faith to faith, in Buber's words from 'one open-hearted person to another open-hearted person'. Similarly, Buber's assertion that genuine dialogue had to be 'from certainty to certainty' is affirmed by Christians in the fourth principle. Accordingly, authentic Jewish–Christian conversation must include the Christians' commitment to Jesus Christ, but equally Jews must testify to the truths of their own tradition. Consequently, Christians have welcomed *Dabru Emet: A Jewish Statement on Christians and Christianity* (2000) whose implications are that Jewish–Christian dialogue is best pursued if Jews cherish their own tradition. *Christianity in Jewish Terms* (2000), a follow-up book to *Dabru Emet*, admirably demonstrates the 'certainty' on the Jewish side, and has become a medium of authentic witness to Christians.   *KENNETH CRACKNELL*

Diaspora

Historically, Diaspora, Greek for 'dispersion', has described religious communities living outside their ancestral homelands. The Hebrew word for Diaspora, *golah*, shares the same root as *galut* or 'exile', but usually refers to the voluntary residence of Jews in lands other than Israel; *tfuzot* or 'circulation' is also used to describe the Jewish Diaspora. Members of Eastern **Orthodox Churches**, notably Greeks and Armenians, frequently speak of their Diaspora communities. In contemporary usage, the word is used to describe a religious community that perceives itself as living away from its population or spiritual centre. Some Christians define their traditional **pilgrimages** to the Holy Land as a spiritual return from a Diaspora.

While Jer. 44.1 mentions Jews living in **Egypt**, the first large Jewish Diaspora began with the Babylonian destruction of the Holy **Temple** in 586 BCE. Many exiles returned to **Jerusalem** 48 years later, following Persian King Cyrus's benevolent decree. During the Greco-Roman period perhaps five million Jews resided outside Israel. After the Roman destruction of the Second Temple in 70 CE, the Diaspora emerged as a central feature of Jewish life, even though Jerusalem and the **land of Israel** remained the religious focal point. Diaspora Jews continually prayed for its end and a physical 'return to **Zion**'.

The host communities, both Christian and Islamic, had significant impact upon Jews in the Diaspora, who often adopted the languages, dress, customs, names and even religious styles of the majority population. Examples include the many **Orthodox Jews** who today wear distinctive clothing similar to that of eighteenth-century Polish gentry. The **Reform Jewish** movement patterned its early worship services on German **Lutheranism**. Moses **Maimonides** and other Jewish philosophers wrote

in Arabic, and there is evidence that Jewish, Christian and Islamic **music** and religious thought were influenced by one another. The Yiddish language is an example of Ashkenazi Jews melding Hebrew with medieval German, Polish and other European languages. Sephardic Jews living in the Diaspora blended Hebrew and Spanish into Ladino. Despite living as a vulnerable **minority** within Christian Europe for centuries, there was extensive cross-fertilisation between Diaspora Jews and their host Christian communities. That interplay, both benign and negative, included the fervent **Messianic movements** that swept Europe in the sixteenth to eighteenth centuries. Some Jews believed the reforms of Martin **Luther** were a precursor to the Messianic era, and the Catholic **baptism** of Jewish Messianic pretender Jacob **Frank** was perceived by his adversaries as leading his followers to the Church.

In the nineteenth and twentieth centuries, even as the Zionist movement pressed for restored Jewish sovereignty in the ancient homeland, some Reform Jewish leaders theologically validated the Diaspora, asserting that God willed the dispersion as a means of spreading ethical monotheism. At the same time, Zionist/Israeli leaders urged an end to the Diaspora, calling Jewish life outside Israel spiritually and psychologically inferior and incomplete. **Zionism** attracted many Christians who strongly supported the creation, security and survival of the Jewish state. At the beginning of the twenty-first century the State of Israel and the Diaspora were both integral to Jewish continuity and to authentic Jewish–Christian **dialogue**.   *A. JAMES RUDIN*

Dickens, Charles (1812–70)

English novelist. Dickens was raised as an Anglican. Nostalgic attachment to Christianity is reflected in his fiction, which often satirises the hypocrisy of parish officials but idealises the piety of the poor. Several novels feature Jewish characters; Jewish–Christian relations are prominent in *Oliver Twist* (1837–9) and *Our Mutual Friend* (1864–5).

After **Shakespeare**'s Shylock, Fagin in *Oliver Twist* is the most famous Jew in **English literature**. Dickens drew on medieval and popular theatrical traditions, depicting him as a miser, both diabolic and subhuman. He was also influenced by newer ideas about heredity, conceiving Fagin's Jewishness in racial terms. Arguably, Dickens did not desire to fuel **antisemitism**, but participated in the prejudices of his day to construct a compelling image of archetypal evil to pit against Oliver, the novel's 'principle of good'.

Critics today disagree as to whether Dickens's achievement in creating Fagin should be assessed primarily in literary or moral terms. For Victorian Jewish readers the choice was unambiguous. Their objections (notably expressed by Dickens's correspondent, Eliza Davies), and the growing acceptance of Anglo-Jewry during the mid-nineteenth century, helped prompt the creation of the dignified and virtuous Mr Riah for *Our Mutual Friend*. Dickens used Riah to explore Jewish–Christian relations, but he remains a 'type', not a fully developed character; he is presented as an outcast, and as an oriental, 'feminine' Jew. In a sense, *both* Riah and Fagin are projections of Dickens's Christian allosemitism – the belief that Jews are in some sense radically and essentially different from all others. *MELANIE J. WRIGHT*

Didache

The *Teaching of the Twelve Apostles* (commonly referred to as the *Didache*) is a composite manual of church discipline, probably from the late first century CE (although only rediscovered in 1873). It provides us with some useful though indirect information about Jewish–Christian relations in this early period.

The first section, the 'Two Ways' tractate (chs 1–6), is a work of ethical instruction that has clear parallels with both canonical and non-canonical Christian sources but also resembles some Jewish literature from the **Dead Sea Scrolls** and elsewhere (e.g. 1 QS 3.18–4.26; the *Testament of Asher* 1.3–5). Indeed, apart from 1.3b–2.1 and 6.2–3 it is difficult to see any specific reference to Christian beliefs in this part of the *Didache* and so it is possible that the tractate is in fact Jewish in origin.

The second section consists of instructions about **worship** (chs 7–10) and ministry (chs 11–15). Although there are Jewish antecedents for the rituals described, notably **baptism** and the **eucharist**, it is possible that the command (8.1) to fast twice a week, but on Wednesdays and Fridays rather than Mondays and Thursdays, may be formulated in direct opposition to Jewish practice of the time (see Luke 18.12) (*see* **fasting**).

The final section (ch. 16) constitutes an **apocalyptic** appendix to the work. It is clearly inspired by such texts as Daniel, although evidently more influenced by Christian than Jewish apocalyptic.

It is striking that the *Didache* has none of the overt **anti-Judaism** found elsewhere in the **Apostolic Fathers**. There is nothing resembling the demonisation of Jewish practice found in the *Epistle of Barnabas* (e.g. 9.4), a text with which it has a direct literary relationship (see chs 18–20).

JUSTIN J. MEGGITT

Dietary laws/customs

The Jewish dietary laws/customs (*kashrut*) are a comprehensive set of rules governing the acceptability, preparation and consumption of foodstuffs. The **Torah** distinguishes between clean animals that can be eaten and unclean animals that are prohibited, and provides a comprehensive list of each category in Lev. 11.1–47 (cf. Deut. 14.3–20). Of those animals permitted to be eaten, no **blood** is to be consumed, since blood contains the life force (Lev. 3.17; 7.26–7; 17.10–14; 19.26; Deut. 12.16, 23–4; 15.23), and the tallow fat of the animal is likewise prohibited (Lev. 3.14–17; 7.22–5). The observance of these customs entailed that Jews and Gentiles could not readily eat together, and this led to the charge, often made in the *Adversus Judaeos* literature, that Jews were anti-social. Discussion of these dietary laws figured prominently in early Christianity. **Paul** declares that all foods are clean (Rom. 14.14, 20), while Mark 7.19 attributes this view to **Jesus**. In Acts Peter has a vision in which he is told that there is no longer any distinction between clean and unclean animals (10.9–16), while James proposes that Gentile Christians need to obey only the Jewish prohibition against the consumption of blood (Acts 15.20–1, 29). The author of the Gospel of Matthew seemingly represents a branch of Christianity that continued to follow the dietary laws in full. In accordance with his view that the Torah remains valid (Matt. 5.17–19), he omits the comment in Mark 7.19 that Jesus declared all foods to be clean. The **Jewish Christians** of later centuries also obeyed the dietary requirements in their entirety.

See also **food** *DAVID SIM*

Disputation

Disputation is a form of discourse where one party refutes the validity of the other in order to invalidate the foundation of the other's faith. Communication between Jews and Christians has been dominated by disputation from the earliest period until our era. The strength of disputation lies in its ability to maintain boundaries between religious **traditions,** while its weakness is that it can serve as the springboard for violence. As a form of argument, disputation originates in the **Hebrew Bible** with diatribes against polytheism and appears in the Gospels when **Jesus** refutes the interpretations of scripture proffered by **Scribes, Pharisees** and others. The book of Acts and the Pauline Epistles reveal evidence of disputations between members of the Christian community and Jews and pagans.

Early Christian authors compiled lists of **Testimonia** as warrants for their **Christological** interpretation of the Hebrew Bible. **Justin Martyr's** *Dialogue with the Jew Trypho* is the most sustained refutation of Judaism in this period. Both Latin and Greek literature of Early Christianity have a rich disputation literature. Rabbinic texts (**Mishnah, Talmud** and **midrashim**) of the first four centuries provide evidence of disputation with pagans and *minim* who are identified by some scholars as Christians. By the end of antiquity, the major themes of disputation had been established: (1) The Hebrew plural name for God: Was this an indication of the **Trinity**? (2) Did the righteous who lived before **Moses** observe the **commandments** of Sinai revelation? (3) Was the **Torah** given to the Jewish people as a benefit or punishment? (4) Who is the True Israel, the recipient of the biblical blessings? (5) What was the appropriate translation of *Shiloh* in Gen. 49.10 or *alma* (virgin or young woman) in Isa. 7.14?

With the rise of **Islam**, Jews, Christians and Muslims engaged in disputation and produced literary works in Syriac and Arabic. Saadiah Gaon's *Book of Beliefs and Opinions* (933) is a philosophical justification of **Rabbinic Judaism** with arguments against both Christianity and Islam. Internal sectarian arguments with the **Karaites** sharpened the ability of rabbinic Jews to defend their **biblical interpretations**.

The letters of **Agobard of Lyons** constitute the earliest evidence of Latin **polemic** against Jews in the Middle Ages. A series of Latin treatises, such as that of Gilbert **Crispin**, appear in the twelfth century in the circle of **Anselm of Canterbury**, introducing arguments from reason to augment the interpretation of scripture. Peter **Alfonsi** in Spain and **Peter the Venerable** in France wrote lengthy treatises utilising both reason and scripture – and extending the argument to Islam. Alan of Lille (1128–1203) rewrote

Gilbert Crispin's treatise to utilise new scholastic forms of argument. Jewish biblical **commentaries** from the circle around **Rashi** contain refutations of Christian interpretation. Joseph Kimhi's *Book of the Covenant* in Provence (*c*.1140), Jacob ben Reuben's *Wars of the Lord* in France (*c*.1140) and *Sefer Nizzahon HaYashan* in Germany (*c*.1350) represent a new genre of private disputation manual.

The rise of the mendicant orders in the thirteenth century, with their emphasis on maintaining Christian orthodoxy, marks the development of the public disputation. These gatherings in Paris (1240), Barcelona (1263) and Tortosa (1413–14) were part of a new direction in missionary efforts. Public disputations took the form of trials in front of an audience of nobility, clergy and laity. Christian participants were often baptised Jews and emphasised passages in the Talmud as blasphemous to Christianity and stumbling blocks to Jewish **conversion**. The Jews who participated in these disputations were highly regarded Jewish scholars such as Jehiel of Paris (d. *c*.1286), **Nahmanides** and Joseph Albo (1380–1430). They defended Rabbinic Judaism by historicising passages about Jesus in the Talmud or diminishing the authority of the *aggadah*.

Disputation literature continued to be written during the **Reformation** and **Renaissance** and through the modern period. The 1769 exchange between Moses **Mendelssohn** and Johann Kaspar Lavater (1741–1801) indicated that the extension of civil rights to Jews was insufficient to validate Jewish religious claims, and that their conversion was ultimately required. Mendelssohn's response to Lavater and his work *Jerusalem* (1783) did not impede a continuing literature of disputation aimed at the conversion of the Jews. This theme sadly echoes in the 1933 exchange between Martin **Buber** and Karl Ludwig Schmidt (1895–1956).

MICHAEL A. SIGNER

Disraeli, Benjamin (1804–81)

British statesman and novelist; Earl of Beaconsfield. Disraeli was born in London to Sephardi parents. In 1817, following a family dispute with the synagogue, Benjamin was baptised. Accordingly, his knowledge of Judaism was limited. Later in life he took pride in his roots, but his theological position was that of **supersessionism**. Disraeli was a journalist and writer before entering Parliament as a Conservative (1837). He rose to prominence in the 1840s, heading the 'Young England' movement.

Politically, he regarded the nation as a necessarily hierarchically structured organism; its well-being depended on crown, church and aristocracy. In 1868, and in 1874–89, he was Britain's prime minister, and is best remembered for his enhancement of the British Empire. Although some trace a link from his acquisition of a stake in the Suez Canal to the **Balfour Declaration**, Disraeli's Jewishness rarely informed his policies directly. His fiction more readily illustrates his ideas about Judaism and Jewish–Christian relations. In *Coningsby* (1844) Jewish banker Sidonia uses his wisdom and international connections to assist the hero, whilst in *Tancred* (1847) a young aristocrat's desire to restore English society leads him to Palestine, and an exploration of Jewish foundations of Christianity and (by extension) European civilisation. Disraeli's Jewish contemporaries saw him as one of their own, and his opponents also characterised his motives and actions pejoratively as 'Hebraic', but historians downplayed his Jewishness until recently. Current appraisals locate Disraeli in the contexts of nineteenth-century debates about English national **identity**, and the politics of Jewish **assimilation** and integration.   *MELANIE J. WRIGHT*

Dissenters

The term Dissenters refers to a number of Protestant denominations in England and Wales (particularly Baptists, Congregationalists, Presbyterians, **Unitarians** and **Quakers**) whose members were subjected to negative discrimination because they did not adhere to the tenets of the **Church of England** following its re-establishment in 1662. The legal restrictions on individual Church members (exclusion from membership of town corporations, civil and military offices, and the universities of Oxford and Cambridge; obligation to pay rates levied for the upkeep of Anglican churches) were chiefly removed in the nineteenth century, when the label Dissenter similarly gave way to 'Nonconformist'.

Despite diverse origins, Dissenters' common experiences of discrimination (which they shared with Anglo-Jewry) prompted them to make common cause with the Jewish community on numerous issues. In the eighteenth and nineteenth centuries the Dissenting Academies, intended primarily to train ministers, became centres of liberal education. A focus on **biblical interpretation** also made them sites of intellectual and personal con-

tact with Jews; noted Dissenter **Hebraists** include Unitarian R. Travers **Herford** and, more recently, Congregationalist W. D. Davies (1911–2001). Following their own **emancipation** Dissenters supported and actively campaigned for an end to Jewish disabilities, both as individual Churches and through the ecumenical board of Protestant Dissenting Deputies (formed in 1732, and a forerunner of the Board of Deputies of British Jews, which shares similar aims). Whilst some held a **supersessionist** view of Judaism, others espoused a form of **universalism**: all argued that religious opinion was no criterion of fitness for political or civic office.   *MELANIE J. WRIGHT*

Divorce *see* marriage

Doctrine

Disagreement between Jews and Christians about their respective doctrines ('teachings') cannot be removed, but what is common to both traditions is their view of the dynamic *from revelation to scripture to doctrine*. Doctrine then is a divinely enabled consequence of God's **revelation**: it is the cognitive component of divine revelation, which creates the conditions for its reception and interpretation by giving rise to teachings that communicate and preserve it. Both traditions see the need for this, viewing God's revelation as aimed at human minds and as leading to 'something understood'; the intellectual core of doctrine, both in the Bible and in subsequent teachings, is intended to preserve the core of what is grasped about God in relation to humans. Both traditions are internally subject to controversies about the relation of religious beliefs to reason, but aim to foster doctrine in ways that avoid the extremes that surface in each tradition: fideism (faith has no cognitive component), rationalism (faith is controlled by reason, narrowly conceived) and presumptive omniscience (everything can be clearly understood). Yet they differ with regard to the normative and symbolic status that doctrines play within each tradition.

Christianity develops a more comprehensive doctrinal system than does Judaism, because what is taught authoritatively is the index of the Church's appropriation of how Christ matters for God's dealings with human beings. By the end of the first century CE Christian doctrine rapidly develops in three related areas: **Christ** as divine, his death/**resurrection** as salvific, and God as Trinitarian (*see* **Trinity**). By contrast, the rabbis' insistence on the unity of God, the centrality of **Torah** as the expression of divine teaching and will and **Israel**'s vocation to witness to God's **holiness** required a less expansive doctrinal system. In the course of the centuries the Church forms statements about what it understands 'till what was an impression on the Imagination has become a system or creed in the Reason' (J. H. Newman, 1843). Hence orthodox Christianity recognises revealed truths, taught under divine guidance and not necessarily accessible to unaided reason, which through authoritative offices within the Church (councils, popes and bishops) come to be binding on believers.

Judaism too is concerned to express its interpretive beliefs and what is intellectually implied in them: **Philo**'s five principles (*Opif.* 61) and **Maimonides**' 13 principles are the classic ways of identifying the distinctive doctrines of Judaism. Maimonides, in a context of medieval scholastic intellectual systems which align revelation and reason, presents a taxonomy of Jewish beliefs centring on the one, eternal and incorporeal God, the divine origin of Torah and **eschatological** completion. By contrast, Moses **Mendelssohn** proposed that Judaism is free from binding doctrines; instead it is to be regarded as 'revealed law', whose central doctrinal tenets (the unity of God, providence and the immortality of the **soul**) come not from revelation, but from universal natural religion: 'faith accepts no commands; it accepts only what comes to it by way of reasoned conviction'. Although to a lesser extent than Christianity, Judaism thus also has its characteristic doctrines.　　*JOHN MCDADE*

Dominicans

Roman Catholic missionary order established (1216) by St Dominic (1170–1221) which formerly championed orthodox Christian **anti-Judaism**. Founded with the primary aim of extirpating **heresy** (initially that of the **Gnostic** Albigensians), the Dominican Order abandoned manual for intellectual labour and devoted itself to scholarship, **preaching** and education. Committed to corporate poverty, Dominican houses were established in larger cities and especially in universities. Renowned Dominican scholars included the leading philosophers Albertus Magnus (*c.*1200–80) and Thomas **Aquinas**.

In 1233 Pope **Gregory IX** appointed papal inquisitors, chiefly Dominicans and **Franciscans**, to root out Christian heresies. Inevitably, the eradication of

Judaising and the **conversion** of Jews soon became key foci of Dominican activity. Already in 1233 Dominicans burnt **Maimonides**' *Guide for the Perplexed* at Montpellier. Thibaut de Sezanne, one of many converts from Judaism, accused Jews of prioritising the **Talmud** over the Bible, thus adding myth to myth and fostering heresy. In 1240, on papal command, Jewish books were forcibly confiscated in France and the first public **disputation** between Christians and Jews was held in Paris. Following inquisitorial condemnation of the Talmud in 1242, 24 wagonloads of rabbinic commentaries were burned in Paris under Dominican auspices.

Ramon de Penyaforte (*c.*1185–1275) instigated anti-Jewish legislation in Aragon from 1228 and pioneered the study of Arabic and Hebrew for missionary purposes. Dominican **Hebrew** scholarship fostered biblical **exegesis**, underpinned **polemics** against Judaism and attracted apostates. Compendia of Latin translations of talmudic and rabbinic **commentary** were compiled, sometimes by converted Jews (Thibaut's *Quiver of the Faith, against the Jews*), sometimes by Christian polemicists (Raymond **Martini**'s *Pugio fidei*, 'Dagger of faith'), these testimonies providing an arsenal of anti-Jewish weapons to support Christianity and attack Judaism. Martini, with fellow Dominicans including Penyaforte and the convert **Paul the Christian**, had engaged in the momentous 1263 Barcelona disputation against **Nahmanides**, following which Dominicans enforced **censorship** of Jewish books.

While some Dominicans, including Berthold of Freiburg (thirteenth century), whose *Summa* in 1295 contested the validity of forced conversions, fostered relatively mild attitudes towards Jews, the Dominican Order was generally strongly hostile. It hunted out suspected Judaisers and their accomplices, and regularised conversionist sermons, which from 1278 were forcibly imposed on Jewish communities by papal decree. Raymond **Llull**, who probably knew **Judah ha-Levi**'s *Kuzari*, Maimonides' *Guide for the Perplexed*, and the **Kabbalah**, wrote model conversionist sermons and Christian doctrinal treatises for Muslims and Jews. St Vincent (Vicente) Ferrer (1350–1419), whose popular sermons often provoked anti-Jewish violence, inspired anti-Jewish legislation in Aragon and Castile following the 1391 persecutions and encouraged **expulsion** of Jews to prevent their influence on **Conversos**. The Dominican convert Johannes Pfefferkorn (1469–1522) led early sixteenth-century Dominican attacks on the Talmud, culminating in the Dominican Inquisitor-General, Cardinal Caraffa (1476–1559), instigating throughout **Italy** the seizure and burning of all copies of the Talmud in 1559. Dominican anti-Jewish activity was eclipsed by that of **Jesuits** following the Counter-Reformation. Its apogee had lain, perhaps, in the cruelty of the Spanish **Inquisition**, particularly under its first head, Tomas de Torquemada (?1420–98), Dominican confessor to **Ferdinand** and Isabella and instigator of the general decree of expulsion of Jews from **Spain** in 1492.

The Dominican Order still contains a significant number of converted Jews, but has relinquished missionary activities among Jews while yet maintaining fine Hebrew scholarship, exemplified by the Ecole Biblique in Jerusalem with its *Revue Biblique*. *MARGARET BREARLEY*

Domus Conversorum

'House of Conversion', home to Jews who converted to Christianity, established by **Henry III** in Chancery Lane, London, in 1232 as part of a wider process of reduction of civil liberties for Jews and abolished as an institution in 1891. It accommodated about 40 people and paid pensions to converts who lived outside, generally around 60 people. On conversion, Jews retained half their property with the remainder used for the upkeep of the *Domus*, which was also maintained through a poll tax levied on Jews. Although it declined after the expulsion of Anglo-Jewry in 1290, it was regularly used by converts visiting London. The office of Keeper of the *Domus Conversorum* was later combined with the judicial office of Master of the Rolls. Communal life in the *Domus* was based on **monastic** organisation with daily **worship** and offered support to Jewish converts who were regarded with scorn by Jews and with suspicion by Christians. The site later became the Public Record Office and is now a library of University College, London. *EDWARD KESSLER*

Donin, Nicholas (*fl.* first half of thirteenth century)

French **Franciscan**. He converted from Judaism after having been placed under the ban for deviant beliefs. In 1236 he presented to Pope **Gregory IX** a list of charges against the **Talmud**, most seriously

that it contains blasphemous statements about **Jesus** and is filled with expressions of hostility against Gentiles. The pope ordered that copies of the Talmud be seized and examined. King **Louis IX** of France complied; at Paris in 1240 leading rabbis tried to rebut the charges made by Donin in a public **disputation** and inquisitorial investigation, following which all the confiscated texts were burned. In the account written by R. Jehiel of Paris (d. *c.*1265), Donin is characterised with contempt as an 'ignorant heretic'. *MARC SAPERSTEIN*

Dress

Distinctive dress or uniforms set a group apart, but also tend to divest its members of their individuality, as, for example, in **monasticism**. In the history of Jewish–Christian relations, specific garments have sometimes served to distinguish between members of the two faiths, as well as to facilitate discrimination against Jews. Both Jewish and Christian leaders repeatedly attempted to segregate Jews and Christians by entreating or forcing the former to don special clothing, which suggests that in practice the two populations tended to dress similarly and that their common attire blurred the social borders between them.

The efforts of **Rabbinic Judaism** to preserve and protect Jewish **particularism** through communal dress regulations, no less than anti-Jewish discriminatory decrees of Church councils and Christian rulers, did produce specifically Jewish attire, which varied from one country or period to another. A well-known **midrash** argues that the children of Israel were redeemed from bondage because they did not abandon their traditional costume and customs during their forced sojourn in Egypt. In modern times ultra-orthodox Jews set themselves apart from both Gentile society and secular Jews by maintaining a distinctive dress that derives from a sixteenth-century adaptation of the characteristic apparel of Gentile nobility and upper classes. Christian rulers in many places reacted at the time to this Jewish adoption of Christian attire by compelling Jews to wear a distinctive mark, such as the **yellow badge**.

The practice of demarcating a religious **minority** by requiring its members to wear a distinctive vestment or emblem originated in **Islam**, which imposed dress restrictions on both Jews and Christians as early as the time of Caliph Omar II (717–20). Discriminatory dress regulations first entered canon law in 1215, when the Fourth **Lateran Council** adopted Canon 68, which required Jews to wear a special mark that would publicly identify them and discourage intercourse, particularly sexual relations, between Jews and Christians. In subsequent centuries the most common discriminatory marks imposed on Jews by ecclesiastical and civil authorities were some form of a badge and/or special *Judenhut*. At the time of the **Inquisition** and the **expulsion** of Jews from **Spain** and **Portugal**, some authorities argued that a special badge should be imposed even on **Conversos**.

Restrictions on Jewish dress had been removed throughout most of Europe by the eighteenth century. However, in the Papal States special dress requirements for Jews remained in effect until **Napoleon**'s armies abolished the **ghettos** and the humiliating Jewish badge. The widespread and increasing **assimilation** of Jews into Christian society in the course of the nineteenth and early twentieth centuries led to the disappearance of distinctive Jewish costume in the Western world, except amongst ultra-orthodox Jews. The Jewish badge was revived in the mid-twentieth century in the form of the infamous yellow star imposed on Jews by the Nazis as early as 1939.

The liturgical vestments used in both the Eastern and Western Churches appear to have derived originally from secular garments in use in the **Roman Empire** in the early Christian centuries, rather than from the dress of the priests in the **Temple**. However, certain prayers recited while vesting link the Christian presbyter with the priesthood of **Aaron**. There are no traditional rabbinical garments, although Ashkenazi rabbis often retained distinctive features of Jewish dress long after the laity had abandoned them. From the eighteenth century onward rabbis increasingly adopted the dress of their contemporary Christian counterparts, particularly in Germany, Holland, England and America.   *DANIEL ROSSING*

Dreyfus Affair

1894 trial and court-martial for treason of French Jewish captain Alfred Dreyfus (1859–1935), who was found guilty by antisemitic army officers on the basis of forged documents and sent to life imprisonment on Devil's Island off the coast of French Guyana. The Dreyfus Affair caused civil unrest in **France** and in 1898 was the subject of a front-page open letter in *L'Aurore* by Emile Zola (1840–1902) to the French President headlined *J'accuse . . . !*

At a time of paranoia in the French army, and against a background of increasing **antisemitism** in France following the 1886 publication of *La France Juive* by Edouard Drumont (1844–1917), Dreyfus, the only Jew on the General Staff, was accused of passing state secrets to **Germany**, which in its higher ranks was Catholic, anti-republican, monarchist and reactionary. Zola became convinced of his innocence and in *Le Figaro* in 1897 attacked Drumont's antisemites, concluding famously that 'truth is on the march and nothing can stop it'; further articles warned of the danger of a military dictatorship in alliance with the Catholic Church. French Protestants tended to support Dreyfus and Catholics to oppose him, and the affair split the country, with Dreyfus becoming a symbol either of the eternal Jewish traitor or of the denial of justice. The Catholic anti-Dreyfusards viewed the plot as an attempt to discredit the army, while the Dreyfusards argued that the Republic was no better than the *ancien régime*. (The French Jewish community kept very quiet.) Newspaper articles and cartoons supported both positions, and included on the one hand antisemitic images of Dreyfus as **Judas** and on the other Dreyfus being crucified, with the head of the army, General Auguste Mercier (1838–1921), dressed in ragged army clothes, offering him vinegar.

The publication of *J'accuse . . . !* was followed by antisemitic riots in France, notably in Catholic strongholds. Synagogues were attacked in 50 towns, and Zola was put on trial and fled to England to avoid imprisonment. Dreyfus was brought back from Devil's Island and underwent a second trial in 1899. The military judges again found him guilty but 'with extenuating circumstances', sentencing him to ten years' imprisonment; a few months later he was granted a pardon. When Zola died in 1902 – in suspicious circumstances – Dreyfus delivered the oration. Dreyfus became a *Légion d'honneur* in 1919.

The Dreyfus affair had a profound impact on Theodore **Herzl**, who was reporting the trial for a Viennese newspaper, and argued as a consequence that Jews could only be safe in their own land. It also led to a new left-wing government in France and to the foundation of the right-wing Catholic *Action*

Française, which was to play a part in the 1940 armistice and the Vichy government. In 1994 Monsignor Defois (b. 1931) apologised for the Catholic role in the affair, and in 1995 the French army officially declared Dreyfus innocent.

EDWARD KESSLER

Dura Europos

Discovered in 1932, the third-century synagogue of Dura Europos in Syria is the best preserved of all ancient synagogue buildings, and its significance for understanding contemporary Jewish–Christian relations has been a focus of inconclusive discussion. The *pièce de résistance* of this building is its breathtaking display of Jewish **art**: its walls were covered from floor to ceiling with 50 to 60 fresco panels displaying scenes from the **Hebrew Bible**, and above the Torah shrine on the synagogue's western wall are **Temple**-related depictions such as the menorah, the Temple façade and the scene of the **binding of Isaac** (which according to later tradition took place on the Temple Mount). Above these are scenes of **Jacob** blessing his sons and grandsons, **David** playing his lyre and an enthroned royal figure (David? the **Messiah**?) holding court. Flanking these upper panels are four large figures, one of which is clearly identified as **Moses**; numerous suggestions have been offered regarding the others. This display of Jewish figural art is the earliest and most comprehensive known to date. Moreover, some of the synagogue's **iconography** is similar to that appearing centuries later in the Byzantine churches of Italy. Thus, the Dura synagogue has been viewed as evidence of an early Jewish art that influenced later Christian depictions. Regrettably, however, it remains in splendid isolation, and no precedents and parallels have been uncovered elsewhere. As such, the question remains as to how widespread such Jewish art was at the time, or if the Dura synagogue art was indeed the product of this local community alone.

No less intriguing is the fact that the earliest church building discovered to date was found at Dura, not far from the synagogue. Built in 232, this church features a baptistery with frescoes depicting scenes drawn primarily from the **New Testament**. The church depictions are far fewer in number and considerably less sophisticated than those of the synagogue, and thus no real connection has been made between the art of these two buildings. No specific scenes are shared by synagogue and church, yet it has been posited that the very proximity of these two communities may have triggered some sort of **dialogue** or **polemic** that prompted the local Jewish community to respond to fundamental Christian theological claims (e.g. identifying references to **Jesus** in the Hebrew Bible, the notion of God's abandonment of the Jewish people, the claim that the Church was the true Israel etc.) in the choice of its biblical scenes and their presentation in their prayer hall. This view, however, has yet to be widely embraced.

See also **architecture**   *LEE I. LEVINE*

EEEE

Early Church

It is a matter of debate at precisely what point Christianity came into existence. The early Church has its roots in the activities of **Jesus** in Galilee and **Jerusalem** up to his **crucifixion** and **resurrection** in *c*.30 CE. Jesus, however, was no Christian but an observant Jew. Soon his adherents saw in him the **Messiah** announced in the **Old Testament** and confessed him as their Lord (John 20.28; Rom. 10.9; 1 Cor. 12.3), and the apostle **Paul** and others began to convert non-Jews (Gentiles) to Christ as the Lord. Thus a new religion consisting of Jewish and non-Jewish 'confessors of Christ' gradually emerged out of a Jewish sub-group and soon distanced itself from traditional Judaism. At a very early stage this new religious entity developed an independent organisational structure: by the end of the second century the governance of the individual congregations lay in the hands of a bishop who was assisted by presbyters (**priests**) and deacons. In the first three centuries the Church occasionally came under political pressure, since the rapid spread of Christianity threatened the traditional pagan cults, sometimes causing social unrest, but the last great persecution by the Roman authorities (303–11) ended with the rule of **Constantine**, who officially recognised Christianity and increasingly promoted it over the other cults. By 380 Christianity was the state religion of the **Roman Empire**, but pagan cults continued to exist.

As Christianity infiltrated the intellectual and social élite, there had been extensive theological debate within the Church over the essence of the Christian faith. Debate and controversy with representatives of Graeco-Roman culture and philosophy, but also with dissenting Christian views and with Judaism, led to the development of a coherent teaching of the central tenets of the Christian faith ('theology'). Sparked by the formation of a **canon** of specifically Christian Holy Scriptures (the '**New Testament**') towards the end of the second century, this debate increasingly focussed on the relationship between God the Father and Jesus Christ and between God the Father and the Holy Spirit, controversies settled by the formulation of the doctrine of the **Trinity** at the First and Second Ecumenical Councils in Nicaea in 325 and Constantinople in 381 (*see also* **Arianism**). The problem as to how Christ could have been both God and Man (which figured prominently in Jewish anti-Christian **polemics**) was debated at the Third and Fourth Ecumenical Councils in Ephesus in 431 and Chalcedon in 451. Not all Christian churches accepted the solution proposed by Chalcedon; some split from the Imperial Church. Among the leading theologians of this period, later called **Church Fathers**, were **Origen**, Basil of Caesarea (329/30–78), Gregory Nazianzen (*c*.329–*c*.390), Gregory of Nyssa (330–*c*.395) and John **Chrysostom** in the east, and Ambrose (339–97), **Jerome** and **Augustine** in the west. At the same time the gulf between the **Greek**-speaking Church in the eastern Roman Empire, with its centres ('patriarchates') at Constantinople, **Alexandria** and **Antioch**, and the **Latin**-speaking Church in the west and the south (Northern Africa), with its centre at Rome, continued to widen.

The relationship between Judaism and Christianity after the initial split remained a complicated one. On the one hand, the new religion had to assert its own right of existence in contradistinction to traditional Judaism and paganism. Christian apologists attempted to define the specificity of the Christian faith over against Jewish criticism. In the early Church these debates mostly centred on the messianic passages of the Greek Old Testament (**Septuagint**), which the Christians saw as fulfilled in the coming of Christ. At the same time, the influx of Gentiles meant that **Jewish-Christianity** soon became a small **minority** that was quickly marginalised.

On the other hand, the Church was always aware that it owed a large part of its theological and spiritual heritage to Judaism. Christian **liturgy** and **exegesis** had grown out of and continued to be deeply influenced by Jewish traditions. Christian festivals such as **Easter** and **Pentecost** had Jewish roots, and Christian **prayers**, such as the **Lord's Prayer**, were closely paralleled in Judaism. Many eminent Christian exegetes like Origen and Jerome drew heavily on Jewish interpreters of the Bible.

It is very controversial to what extent and in what respect the early Church was anti-Jewish (*see* **anti-Judaism**). In terms of theology there was, no doubt from a very early stage, a widespread view that the Jews were to be blamed for the crucifixion of Christ (*see* **deicide**) and that Judaism was an outdated religion that had been proved wrong once and for all in its messianic expectations by the coming of Christ. In this context the destruction of the **Temple** was seen as God's punishment for the unbelief of the Jews. As regards the legal and political situation in the first three centuries, the Christians were clearly in a worse position than the Jews, since, having no clearly defined legal status, they were under intermittent pressure from the Roman authorities, whereas the Jews, on the whole, were not. On a social level, however, there appear to have been no severe frictions between Christians and Jews.

Some recent research suggests that this situation of a by and large peaceful coexistence of Jews and Christians did not fundamentally change as a result of Christianity's becoming the privileged religion in the course of the fourth century. Although during the period 300–450 the legal position of the Jewish religion clearly worsened and ecclesiastical synods issued canons against the Jews, the effect of this on the ground appears to have been limited. In the fourth century Jewish persecutions by Christians were few and far between. There are reports, sometimes of dubious provenance, of synagogues having been converted into churches, and in c.387 a synagogue was burnt down in Rome; in 388 a similar incident occurred in Callinicum on the Euphrates. Reports of anti-Jewish incidents become more frequent in the early part of the fifth century: in c.413 Patriarch **Cyril of Alexandria** expelled the Jews from his city and confiscated their property and synagogues; in 418 there was an anti-Jewish **pogrom** on the island of Menorca, instigated by the local bishop Severus. There also appear to have been anti-Jewish riots of monks in Palestine. Yet these outbreaks seem to have been comparatively rare occurrences and to have shared their character with other forms of social unrest. Also, while some of the Church Fathers undoubtedly uttered vitriolic attacks against Jews and Judaism (*see* **Adversus Judaeos literature**), the most notorious perhaps being John Chrysostom in his *Discourses against the Jews* (386/7), the views of Judaism found in the writings of the Fathers are often less uniform than the secondary literature suggests. *WOLFRAM KINZIG*

Easter

Easter is the annual Christian festival which celebrates the resurrection of Jesus. It is one of the liturgical calendar's 'moveable feasts', with the date calculated by the same method used for determining the date of the Jewish festival of **Passover**. Easter is the pre-eminent of all Christian feasts, and becomes the ritual 'lens' through which all other celebrations, and indeed the Christian life as a whole, are viewed. Many Christians who do not attend worship services at any other time in the year are likely to be in church on Easter Sunday.

One of the earliest Christian controversies – the **Quartodeciman Controversy** – was over the question of the proper dating of Easter, and in particular whether it should be celebrated on the date of Passover, whatever date it happened to fall upon. Although the Quartodeciman debate lasted in some places for nearly five centuries, those arguing for a Sunday celebration of Easter ultimately prevailed, and the date of Easter continues to be calculated as the first Sunday after the first full moon after the vernal equinox.

The thematic links between the Christian Easter and the Jewish Passover are undeniable, such that the word for the Christian feast of the **Resurrection** in most Romance languages is identifiably related to the word for Passover (Fr. = *Pâques*, It. = *Pasqua*, Sp. = *Pascua*). In English, the festival borrowed its name from a pre-Christian Celtic goddess of the Spring, Eostre, whose feast-day occurred annually on the day of the vernal equinox (Easter celebrations remain heavily syncretistic, with elements from the pre-Christian Spring festivals playing a central role in the celebrations in both home and church). Although the earliest Christian writings are divided on the question of whether the **Last Supper** was a Passover meal (the Synoptic Gospels describe it as the Passover seder, while the Fourth Gospel claims that **Jesus** was crucified at the time of the slaughtering of the Passover lambs, making the Last

Supper a domestic meal on the night before the Passover), the relationship between the **crucifixion**/resurrection of Jesus and the Passover is undisputed, and the redemptive activity of God is Easter's overarching theme. For the earliest Christians, the blood of Jesus shed on the cross was likened to the blood on the doorposts of the Israelites in Egypt, a mark of God's persistent willingness to save. Because of this connection, Easter was in the early centuries of the Church the pre-eminent occasion for the **baptism** of new Christians, whose passage through the waters of baptism mirrored the passage of the Israelites through the Red Sea as a sign and guarantor of God's redemptive promises. During the next several centuries, however, these symbolic associations between Easter and Passover were gradually forgotten as Christianity lost touch with its Jewish roots, although some scholars would like to see a direct connection between a number of Easter and Passover ceremonies, such as the hiding of the *afikomen* during the Passover seder and the sequestering of the communion **bread** in a model sepulchre during the three days from Good Friday until the first **eucharist** at Easter. Indeed, during the Middle Ages the Easter Triduum (Good Friday, Holy Saturday and Easter Sunday) became the annual occasion for the intensification of Christian **anti-Judaism** and acts of violence, fuelled by the Easter readings (which tended to cast Jews in the role of the murderers of Jesus; *see* **deicide, charge of**), and the reading appointed to be said responsively between clergy and people called the 'Reproaches' which prayed for God's vengeance against Jews, infidels and heretics.

In the modern period, and particularly since the Second World War, the ancient Paschal roots of Easter have been researched and reclaimed by scholars of Christian **worship**. As a result, in many Christian denominations the Easter Vigil has been transformed into a service during which the whole sweep of God's dealings with the Jews, beginning with the Creation, and moving on through the Exodus, the Exile and the Prophets, is told in full as an indispensable part of the story of the **Resurrection** of Jesus. At the same time, as each Sunday Service has come to be understood as a 'little Easter', a weekly celebration of the Resurrection, the **Hebrew Bible** is more routinely read in ordinary services of Christian worship. New challenges are periodically raised to the dating of Easter,

which can be as early as 22 March and as late as 25 April, and calls have been made for the establishment of a fixed date for the sake of convenience. As the work of theologians, biblical scholars and liturgists on Jewish ritual and the theological context of the Christian Passover has begun to be appropriated by pastors of churches, many Christians have been encouraged to join with Jews in Passover seders, and to hold their own seders during the days before Easter. Although there has been some tendency to 'baptise' or 'Christianise' the seder for use in Christian congregations, adding **New Testament** readings and casting Jesus as the host of the meal, this has been strenuously resisted by those concerned with interfaith relations between Jews and Christians. Preachers have also been encouraged to treat with caution scripture readings appointed for the Easter period that suggest collective Jewish responsibility for Jesus' death (*see* **hoi Ioudaioi**). Cognisant of the place of Easter in the history of Christian anti-Judaism, many denominations and interfaith groups have issued guidelines for Christian worship during the Easter period. Many of these guidelines exhort Christians to a proper reverence for the Hebrew Bible and a respect for the Jewishness of Jesus during the celebration of Easter. More recently, the Easter season (the 50 days from Easter to **Pentecost**) has been commended as the most appropriate time for liturgical responses to the **Holocaust** in Christian churches.

See also **Good Friday Prayer for the Perfidious Jews**

SUSAN WHITE

Eastern Orthodox Christianity *see* Orthodox Christianity

Ebionite *see* Jewish Christianity

Ecclesia/Synagoga

Christian artists in the Middle Ages fashioned these female figures to represent Christianity's relationship to Judaism. The figures of triumphant 'Ecclesia' and defeated 'Synagoga' symbolised the Christian claim that Christ made Judaism obsolete. Well-known depictions represent the proud Ecclesia standing erect in contrast to the bowed, blindfolded figure of the defeated yet dignified Synagoga (e.g. the thirteenth-century stone figures in the cathedrals of Strasbourg, Freiburg, Bamberg, Magdeburg, Reims and Notre Dame, Paris). Like **Leah** of the weak eyes (Gen. 29.17), Synagoga was blind, failing to recognise the light of Christ. Her crown has fallen, her staff is broken, and the **Torah** has fallen to the ground. Hildegard of Bingen (1098–1179) images Synagoga as the dawn that recedes before the sun's brightness. One miniature from the *Bible moralisée* (*c.*1410) shows Synagoga lying helpless on the ground. Another represents her as a corpse in a sarcophagus, with Ecclesia at her head and Christ at her feet. In the Late Middle Ages Synagoga becomes a more contemptible figure. In a fifteenth-century portrayal of the crucifixion, Ecclesia holds a chalice to receive the blood from the pierced heart of Jesus; Synagoga turns away from him, in the clasp of a devil who rides on her neck and blinds her to the Christ by covering her eyes. The association with the **devil** evokes a malevolent Synagoga. Few Christians of the Middle Ages would have read the *Adversus Judaeos* **literature**, but the many who viewed these figures would have learned what those earlier writings taught: Christianity superseded Judaism, and thus Judaism no longer had reason to exist. In the present era, however, some artists are refashioning Synagoga and Ecclesia to represent the dramatically changed relation between Jews and Christians.

See also **Church and synagogue; supersessionism**

MARY C. BOYS

Ecology *see* environment/ecology

Ecumenical deal

A term coined by Marc Ellis (b. 1952), a North American Jewish liberation theologian, in his book *Unholy Alliance* (1997). Ellis condemns contemporary institutionalised Jewish–Christian **dialogue** for its readiness to operate according to strict, albeit unwritten, 'rules' which privilege particular voices (primarily those of white European and North American males) and limit the scope for discussion. He argues that institutional Jewish–Christian dialogue largely excludes significant perspectives (e.g. those of Palestinian Christians) and is unwilling to confront controversial or divisive issues (such as the challenges posed by **feminism**, postcolonialism and institutionalised racism). This 'ecumenical deal' reflects a new, disconcerting social and political reality in which Jews and Judaism emerge as part of the religious establishment in the West: 'it is strange for Jews to be grouped with dominant Christians over against struggling minorities . . . Jews are no longer an unempowered minority but rather an empowered one, which in America means identification with whiteness' (*Unholy Alliance*, 58).

A recurring theme in Ellis's work is his call for Jews and Christians to extend their discussion of power and institutionalised injustice beyond traditional historical and theological questions relating to Christian **anti-Judaism**, **antisemitism** and the **Holocaust**. Drawing upon feminist and postcolonial criticism, he draws attention to the failure of many participants in formal and informal Jewish–Christian dialogue fully to acknowledge their position of relative privilege and/or seriously to confront contentious issues such as **Black Christian–Jewish relations** (particularly in the **United States**), the role of Palestinian Christians, and the continuing perpetration of injustice both by and within institutional forms of Judaism and Christianity.

See also **liberation theology; Palestinian liberation theology** *ISABEL WOLLASTON*

Ecumenism

Ecumenism within the Christian Churches is a very recent movement. One convenient date for its inception is 1910 when a World Missionary Conference took place in Edinburgh. There for the first time Anglican representatives took their places alongside the churches of the Protestant Reformation. In 1948 these churches came together in Amsterdam for the founding of the **World Council of Churches** (WCC). Not until 1961 did the Orthodox Churches join the WCC and still today the Roman Catholic Church sends only observers to WCC Assemblies. Ecumenical Jewish–Christian relationships may be discussed from two aspects: (1) the ways in which the world ecumenical movement has attempted to relate to the Jewish community whether in **mission** or in **dialogue**, and (2) the larger question of how far the Jewish community should be seen to be intrinsically part of the ecumenical movement, as it seeks for the unity of humankind. Originally the ecumenical movement paid significant attention to Jews only as the objects of mission. The 1948 WCC Assembly condemned **antisemitism** but affirmed that the Jewish people were included in the Churches' evangelistic task, and this was reaffirmed at the Second Assembly in Eavaton, 1954: 'The Church cannot rest until the title of Christ to the kingdom is recognized by his own people according to the flesh.' But two factors caused a profound change of heart. First, the great Swiss theologian Karl Barth (1886–1968) insisted against the weight of all previous tradition that the Jews were *verus Israel*, the true Israel, and that it was appropriate to speak of 'the Church *and* Israel'.

Then in 1965 the **Second Vatican Council** affirmed 'the sacred spiritual bond linking the people of the new covenant with Abraham's stock' and repudiated the charge that Jews are rejected by God or are a 'deicide nation' (*Nostra Aetate*). Since the 1960s the WCC and its member churches have sought to build upon these insights. The Faith and Order Commission of the WCC expressed its conviction in the same year that the Jewish people still have theological significance of their own for the Church and began a study on the integral place of Jewish people within the whole People of God (*Aarhus Minutes*, 1965). This work bore fruit in the WCC 1982 document *Ecumenical Considerations on Jewish–Christian Dialogue*, where the Jewish people are seen as full partners in dialogue: 'The spirit of dialogue is to be fully present to one another in full openness and human vulnerability.' Yet mission to the Jewish people is not repudiated in this document, which was trying to reflect the many different views held by WCC member churches. But some clear statements have been made within the ecumenical movement. One member church, significantly in **Germany**, had been able by 1980 to affirm 'the permanent election of the Jewish people', that Jews and Christians are 'witnesses of God before the world and each other' and that therefore 'the church may not express its witness toward the Jewish people as it does its mission to the peoples of the world' (*see* **Rhineland Synod**). Similar forceful expressions of a new relationship are found in other Church statements, not always accessible or relevant beyond their own denominational boundaries, and are contributing towards the mutual understanding of Jews and Christians. There has been a widespread appreciation in ecumenical circles of *Dabru Emet*. The Office of Interreligious Relations in the WCC maintains cordial relations with the World Jewish Congress.

KENNETH CRACKNELL

Eden

Christian interpretations of the Garden of Eden story (Gen. 2–3), epitomised by its role in the **Christmas** liturgy, are coloured by the contrast between the 'Old **Adam**', symbol of **original sin**, and Christ as the sinless Second Adam. **Eve**, who 'was deceived and became a transgressor' (1 Tim. 2.14), is contrasted with the Virgin **Mary**. The 'tree of the knowledge of good and evil' has moral, frequently sexual associations, and the story is understood to be about a 'Fall' from grace into a state of original

sin. Jewish readings of the story, by contrast, are free of such theological dogma, and focus rather on the details of the narrative itself. The emphasis is thus rather on the discovery of **free will** and the ascent of humankind from a state of dependence to true humanity. The serpent's 'wisdom' is not wholly evil, 'good and evil' include all manner of knowledge and resourcefulness, and the newly discovered 'nakedness' of the humans refers more to their vulnerability than their sexuality. Eden, translated into Latin as *paradisus*, 'paradise', became a universal symbol of primeval bliss, applied to all kinds of situation from return to the **Promised Land** after exile (Isa. 51.3) to life after death (Luke 23.43). In rabbinic tradition and also in the **Kabbalah** there are two 'gardens of Eden', one terrestrial and one celestial. There is speculation about the location and dimensions of the terrestrial Eden, including the tradition that Alexander the Great discovered the entrance to it.

JOHN F. A. SAWYER

Edom

One of Israel's biblical enemies, Edom, the kingdom to the south, was also a name applied to Esau, likewise a figure that came to be seen as an opponent of **Israel**. The names Esau and Edom alternate in biblical texts arising from the naming of Esau as Edom (Gen. 25.30). *Genesis Rabbah* 63 interprets Esau's name as deriving from the colour 'red' (Hebrew *adom*; see Gen. 25.30) and demonstrating his bloodthirstiness. The tale in Genesis of the struggle between **Jacob** and Esau has become symbolic for both Jewish and Christian interpreters of the struggle with their enemies. The declaration in Mal. 1.2–3 that God loves Jacob but hates Esau has assisted in intensifying polarisation between the two traditions. In Judaism from as early as the Second Temple period Edom came to symbolise moral decay or more specifically **Rome**. In rabbinic literature Edom could still symbolise Rome but had also developed into an allusion to Christianity. Meanwhile Christian **typology** made use of the same Esau symbolism, **Paul**, for example, using it to portray siblings that follow two different paths (Rom. 9.10–13) and the Epistle to the Hebrews to speak of lawlessness (12.16–17).

JAMES K. AITKEN

Edward I (1239–1307)

King of England (1272–1307) responsible for the **expulsion** of the Jews. He initially used Jews as a source of funds, particularly for his **Crusades** and to support the *Domus Conversorum*. As prince,

Edward had personal contact with Anglo-Jewry when his father, **Henry III**, granted him all receipts from the Jewish community in 1262. Edward was influenced by popular hatred of Jews, **blood libel** charges and the Church's *Adversus Judaeos* teachings. Scholars also suggest that Christian piety lay behind his desire for Jewish **conversion**, compelling Jews to attend conversionary sermons by the **Dominicans** and to abandon **usury** upon conversion. When Jews did not convert *en masse*, and their financial contribution to the throne became limited through fiscal exploitation, he expelled, unusually for the time, the entire community from England in 1290.   *EDWARD KESSLER*

Egypt

From its initial conquest to its final loss, Aegyptus was one of the most important provinces in the **Roman Empire**. The fertile Nile delta, together with the North African provinces of Africa and Numidia further west, provided a substantial portion of the Empire's annual grain supply. Egypt was one of the 'bread baskets' of the Empire, and Alexandria, Egypt's great port, one of its most important cities. Because of the importance of Alexandria, and the proximity of the province to Roman Palestine, the province was home to a significant community of **Hellenised** Jews. Indeed, reliable evidence places Jews in Egypt as early as the third or fourth century BCE, and some estimate that the Jewish population of Egypt may have reached one million by the middle of the first century CE. The historian Hecateus (fourth century BCE), as reported by **Josephus** in *Against Apion*, is full of praise for the Jews and the role they played in Egypt at the time of Ptolemy I (*c.*300 BCE). Conversely, in the same text, Josephus reports on an account of the Jewish Exodus offered by the Egyptian priest Manetho. This Manetho claimed that the Exodus was the work of a rebel priest who changed his name to **Moses** and incited a rebellion of lepers against the Pharaoh. Both accounts, while of limited historical value, suggest centuries of Jewish presence in Egypt.

The vast majority of Egyptian Jews lived in the city of **Alexandria**, a key Jewish intellectual and cultural centre: **Philo** was a member of a prominent Alexandrian family, and Alexandrian Jewish scholars of an earlier generation were responsible for the creation of the **Septuagint** translation of the Bible. When Christianity came to Egypt and Alexandria in the first century, it profited greatly from this

Jewish legacy. Christian authors, such as Clement of Alexandria (*c.*150–*c.*215), studied the works of Philo to assist them in their own efforts to reconcile biblical faith and Greek philosophy. Indeed Philo's highly developed theology of the **Logos** had a profound effect on Christian use of the concept. **Origen** of Alexandria, perhaps the greatest of all ancient Christian commentators on the Bible, was clearly impacted by **dialogue** with Jewish interpreters in the city. Even the rise of Christian **monasticism** in the deserts of Egypt may have been inspired by the ascetical Jewish community that Philo called the *Therapeutae*, or 'healers'.

From the second century Jewish fortunes in Egypt changed for the worse. The Jewish revolts of 115–117 CE had a devastating effect on Alexandria's Jews. While the community recovered, it immediately had to face increasing conflict with developing imperial Christianity. This conflict reached a high point in 414–15 CE when the patriarch **Cyril of Alexandria** is reported to have expelled the entire Alexandrian Jewish community and permitted the looting of synagogues. From that point the influence of Alexandria's Jews declined rapidly. After the fifth century Egypt was no longer a centre of significant Jewish and Christian encounter.

JOHN J. O'KEEFE

Eisenmenger, Johann (1654–1704)

German orientalist. Eisenmenger studied rabbinic literature with Jewish scholars for 19 years, pretending he was a proselyte but in fact collecting material for his book *Entdecktes Judenthum* ('Judaism unmasked'; translated in 1732–4 as *The Traditions of the Jews*), finished in 1700. In this extensive work he selected rabbinic quotations critical of Christianity and also presented his hostile view of Judaism, reviving the **blood libel** claim. Due to the effort of Frankfurt's Jews and the intervention of Emperor Leopold I (1640–1705), publication of the book was delayed until 1711, but eventually gained formative influence on modern 'scientific' **antisemitism**, supplying antisemitic authors with their main arguments while paradoxically serving Christian scholars as an accessible source of quotations from **Talmud**.   *PETR FRYŠ*

Election *see* Chosen People; justification

Elijah

Ninth-century BCE Northern Kingdom (Israel) prophet. The Elijah cycle is to be found in the Tanakh/Old Testament, in 1 Kgs 17–2 Kgs 2. His name, 'Eliyahu' – 'my God is Yah' – symbolises his mission. Elijah, alongside **Moses**, is often seen as the prophetic figure *par excellence* by both Jews and Christians. He is also connected to Messianic expectation, a thematic born of the biblical texts and developed by both Jewish and Christian traditions.

Elijah, from Tishbe in Gilead, appears during the reign of Ahab, king of Israel, one of the many kings that 'did evil in the sight of God', introducing idol worship in **Israel**. Persecuted by his enemies, he was often forced to seek refuge outside the kingdom. However, God constantly manifested divine support for Elijah and Elijah's zeal for the Law of God characterised his life (1 Macc. 2.58). His miraculous ascent into heaven spurred the religious imagination for generations to come, giving rise to the expectation that he would return. This has roots already within the Tanakh/Old Testament. In Malachi, Elijah is to be sent as a herald of the **Day of Judgement** in order to reconcile fathers and children (Mal. 3.24, cf. Sir. 48.10).

In later Jewish tradition Elijah is to return to usher in the messianic age (*Leviticus Rabbah* 34.8). Jewish **mysticism** even ascribes to him the status of an **angel**, and he is often linked to Enoch, who also ascended alive into heaven (Gen. 5.24). In later Jewish writing Elijah is both an example of zeal (R. Samson R. Hirsch (1808–88)) and the model of final mystical union with God (R. Abraham I. Kook (1865–1935)). In Jewish practice Elijah is welcomed to the seder (**Passover** meal) as 'bearing good news, redemption and consolation' (prayer before *Hallel*) and it is customary to leave a chair empty for him at the table. He is also evoked to protect the child at the time of his **circumcision**.

In the **New Testament** Elijah is closely identified with the figure of **John the Baptist**, the forerunner of Jesus, who proclaims the need for **repentance**. In the Christian **canon** of scriptures the mention of Elijah at the end of the book of Malachi, the last book of the **Old Testament**, prepares for John's appearance at the beginning of Jesus' public life (Mark 1.2–4). John is described in the same terms as Elijah (Mark 1.6) and **Jesus** explicitly identifies the two (Mark 9.11–13). Elijah himself appears in the New Testament at Jesus' side, together with Moses, in the Transfiguration scene (Mark 9.4), Lawgiver and Prophet both legitimising Jesus as the **Messiah**. The Jews at the foot of the cross think that the crucified

Jesus is appealing to Elijah to save him as he utters his final cry before giving up the spirit (Mark 15.34–36). In later Christian tradition the **Church Fathers** presented Elijah as the greatest of the prophets. In the monastic tradition Elijah became an example of **asceticism** and **celibacy**, even being considered the founding figure for the Carmelite Order.

The expectation of Elijah is at the centre of both Jewish and Christian **eschatological** hope. His role as forerunner of the Messiah and reconciler could make him a focal figure for Jewish–Christian **dialogue**. *DAVID M. NEUHAUS*

Eliot, George (1819–80)

(Pseudonym of Mary Ann Evans.) Novelist and translator. George Eliot's novels reflected and participated in nineteenth-century debates about religion and society. A polymath, she translated German radical writers such as D. F. Strauss (1808–74) and L. Feuerbach (1804–72); her fiction may be read in part as literary exploration of their and others' ideas. Raised as an **evangelical**, Eliot rejected her upbringing but maintained a lifelong interest in Judaism, originally fuelled by her early reading of **Josephus**. The influence of **Spinoza**, whose *Ethics* she translated, can be detected in *Middlemarch* (1871–2). *Daniel Deronda* (1874–6) reflects most fully Eliot's Jewish studies and friendship with talmudist Emanuel Deutsch (1829–73). Its unprecedented (in non-Jewish fiction) advocacy of a territorial centre for Jewish national life inspired early Zionists, both Jewish and Christian.

See also **literature, English**; **Zionism**; **Zionism, Christian** *MELANIE J. WRIGHT*

Emancipation

In Jewish historiography emancipation refers to the legal processes by which Jews acquired civil and political rights in their countries of residence. In medieval Europe the possession of full rights was usually restricted to members of an established Church. Jews (and members of heterodox Christian denominations) lived as a generally tolerated **minority**, subject to legal and social restrictions. They maintained some autonomy, with many areas of life subject to the jurisdiction of their religious institutions (e.g. the *beth din*). Therefore, where emancipation replaced this arrangement with a new contract between state and (individual) Jew, this was regarded by some Jews as a welcome end to hardship and exclusion, and by others as a harbinger of **assimilation**.

Emancipation was not a single, uniform event, nor did it happen in a vacuum. For example, the Constitution of the **United States of America** was the first to grant Jews equality (1789). In **Italy** it happened in the context of national unification (1870); in Algeria it was imposed by the French colonial authorities, partly in response to pressure from the Alliance Israelite Universelle. In **Russia** emancipation came only in 1917, under the Bolsheviks.

What motivated those who framed the emancipatory legislation? In part, they were inspired by **Enlightenment** notions about the equality of peoples. But nationalism was another significant factor. Legislators wanted to create a unified state, populated by one people or *ethnos*: they hoped that removing legal restrictions would promote Jewish assimilation, so that Jews *qua* Jews would disappear.

Emancipation's impact on Judaism and Jewish–Christian relations was tremendous. For Jews, it brought the need to reconceive both communal organisation and the individual's relation to **tradition**. Most sought to balance in some way the demands of Judaism and non-Jewish mores (which in many countries were shaped by a Christian heritage). Modern forms of Judaism (Conservative, Orthodox, Reconstructionist, Reform and so on) are the result of this debate, first articulated eloquently by Moses **Mendelssohn**. For Jewish–Christian relations, emancipation's effects were generally positive. The opening up of previously restricted professions and institutions to Jews led to increased contacts between Jews and Christians in all walks of life. In the sphere of religious studies Judaism and Jewish religious texts became more accessible to Christian Bible scholars; this eventually led to a sea-change in **New Testament** scholarship. However, legal emancipation did not end negative discrimination or prevent the sporadic violence directed against Jews from time to time by the majority non-Jewish populations of continental Europe in particular. Moreover, some scholars trace the roots of modern **antisemitism** to non-Jewish disappointment at the Jewish 'failure' to respond as expected to the assimilationist 'bargain' offered to them at emancipation. As Jewish distinctiveness persisted, pseudo-scientific race theory was deployed by Wilhelm Marr (1819–1904) and his successors to suggest that by nature Jews could not be integrated into European culture. And the rights accorded to Jews at emancipation were suspended (in *de facto* or *de jure* terms) by the totalitarian regimes of mid-twentieth-century Europe. *MELANIE J. WRIGHT*

Emden, Jacob (1697–1776)

Talmudic scholar and fervent opponent of Shabbateanism (*see* **Shabbetai Zvi**). Despite his commitment to tradition, Emden believed that secular subjects could be studied (in the twilight hours) and was an admirer of Moses **Mendelssohn**. In *Seder Olam Rabbah Vezuta* he wrote positively about **Jesus** and **Paul**, utilising the **New Testament** in his argument that they had not sought to denigrate Judaism and that their teachings were primarily concerned to communicate the **Noachide laws** to Gentiles. Emden recognised 'true scholars' among contemporary Christians and appealed to them to protect the Jews against other Christians who wished 'to abolish the Law of Moses' and who ignored the fact that 'the Nazarene and his apostles . . . observed the Torah fully'. His view of Christianity as a legitimate religion for Gentiles was developed most famously in the twentieth century by Franz **Rosenzweig**. *DANIEL R. LANGTON*

English literature *see* literature, English

Enlightenment

The eighteenth-century European Age of Enlightenment, or Age of Reason, planted the seeds for modern liberal democracy, cultural **humanism**, science and technology and *laissez-faire* capitalism, and at the same time challenged not only the intellectual assumptions of traditional religion but also the political role of the Church and its leaders. The religious life of Jews was affected in similar ways to that of the Christians among whom they lived; the Enlightenment was conducive to increased contact between Jews and Christians and to a more balanced **dialogue**.

Jewish religious thinkers such as Moses **Mendelssohn**, the Reformers and even the reactionary S. R. Hirsch (1808–88) welcomed to a greater or lesser degree the political and intellectual achievements of the Enlightenment; others, including the Gaon of Vilna (1720–97) and Hasidic leaders such as Shneur Zalman of Liady (1745–1813), feared the potential of the new ideas to undermine religious tradition.

On the political front the Enlightenment led to the **emancipation** of the Jews, that is, to Jews gaining civil rights on a more or less equal footing with other citizens of the countries in which they lived. In the eighteenth century much of this 'civic improvement of the Jews' was inspired by men like John Toland (1670–1722) in England, Christian Wilhelm von Dohm (1751–1820) in **Germany**, and the Comte de Mirabeau (1741–91) in **France**, who argued that existing legislation disabling the Jews was motivated primarily by religious intolerance, hence contrary to the enlightened 'spirit of the times', and was also economically disadvantageous, since it excluded Jews from full participation in society. Attitudes were often ambivalent. **Voltaire**, the advocate of universal human rights, has also been seen by some scholars as the father of secular, racial **antisemitism**; Lord Byron (1788–1824) expressed sympathy for Jewish suffering in *Hebrew Melodies* but later opposed Jewish emancipation.

Legislation ameliorating Jewish civil rights in Europe fell short of the radical egalitarianism of the declarations and laws on freedom of conscience and religion accompanying the American Revolution, and was frequently linked to the hope that once Jews were 'civilised' they would readily adopt Christianity. Significant numbers did indeed convert, amongst them the German-Jewish poet **Heine**, who in his cynical remark that his baptismal certificate was an 'admission ticket to European culture' indicated something of the pressure under which Jews remained to conform, at least outwardly, to the dominant faith.

On the intellectual front, Enlightenment ideas were absorbed by the Jewish movement known as *Haskalah*, which, in addition, drew on earlier Jewish models from **Renaissance** Italy. The assumption was that there was one universal truth, attainable by reason, in which all might share, whether Christian or Jewish. Religious dogma was culture-based and uncertain; only the truths of reason, for instance in science, mathematics and **ethics**, were certain, and these were open to all. The philosophies of **Spinoza, Kant** and then **Hegel** were worked and reworked by both Christian and Jewish religious thinkers. On the Jewish side Moses Mendelssohn, awarded the Berlin Academy's prize in 1764 ahead of Kant, came close to Spinozan deism in his presentation of Judaism as the 'religion of reason'. In Germany the most distinctive product of *Haskalah* was the **Wissenschaft des Judentums** ('Science of Judaism') movement which, through men like

Abraham **Geiger** and Heinrich Graetz (1817–91), set the foundations for the modern academic study of Judaism. The distinctive product of 'Russian' (this term covers much of Eastern Europe) *Haskalah* was a popular scientific literature in Hebrew (Yiddish was also used, with some reluctance, since it was more widely understood), and the development in both **Hebrew** and **Yiddish** of secular literary genres. Though in both East and West the desire for **assimilation** was strong, and both German and Russian were cultivated, there was in the East also a growing Jewish national consciousness.

In sum, throughout the eighteenth and nineteenth centuries both Jews and Christians were struggling to come to terms with **modernity**, and in both camps there were both radicals and conservatives. If David Friedrich Strauss (1808–74) in *Das Leben Jesu* (1835) could reconstruct Lutheran theology while rejecting the historicity of the Gospels, Reform theologians could reconstruct Jewish theology while rejecting the historicity of much of the Hebrew scriptures. If Pope **Pius IX** could publish his reactionary *Syllabus of Errors* in 1864, denouncing 'modernism', that is, the Enlightenment, he was engaging in precisely the same battle as the rabbis who denounced *Haskalah*.

While post-Enlightenment thinkers reject the easy optimism of the Enlightenment and its confidence in human progress, they provide new ways to affirm the value of the 'other'. At the same time, while the extreme relativism that characterises **postmodernism** facilitates pluralism and dialogue, it also poses the dangers of indifference and syncretism. However, insofar as secularism is in part a legacy of the Enlightenment, it can be said to exercise a continuing influence on Jewish–Christian relations today. A common language of discourse, that of secular culture, is now available to Jews and Christians, just as in the Middle Ages the shared language of **Greek** philosophy was available to Jews, Christians and Muslims. One might even say that there are in reality three partners in the dialogue: Jews, Christians and the Enlightenment culture which provides both the universal language that makes dialogue possible and the separation of religion and power that enables its participants to communicate as equals.　　*NORMAN SOLOMON*

Environment/ecology

Judaism and Christianity are theocentric, not biocentric. To set anything other than God in the centre is to commit **idolatry**. Nature bears God's 'signature', mirrors his glory; yet to *equate* God with nature, as **Spinoza** did in speaking of *deus sive natura*, constitutes pantheism.

Human responsibility towards the natural environment can be summed up in six principles firmly rooted in the Hebrew scriptures and thus part of the common heritage of Jews and Christians: **creation** is good and reflects the glory of its creator (Gen. 1.31); biodiversity, the rich variety of nature, is to be cherished (Gen. 1 and 9); living things range from lower to higher, with humankind at the top (Gen. 1.27); human beings are responsible for the active maintenance of all life (Gen. 2.15); land and people depend on each other (the Bible is the story of a **chosen people** and a chosen land; prosperity of the land depends on the people's obedience to God's **covenant**); respect creation – do not waste or destroy (*Bal tashkhlt*, 'not to destroy' (Deut. 20.19), is the Hebrew phrase on which the rabbis base the call to respect and conserve all that has been created).

Whatever other arguments, for instance that of enlightened self-interest, lead us to conserve the natural world, the religious basis that demands respect for it is the concept of the world as God's creation, whether this be understood in naïve 'creationist' terms or in terms of organic evolution. Concern for the *bios* is an ideal enterprise to stimulate religions to work in harmony: either we all learn to share the planet, or we all perish. Amongst numerous examples of interfaith cooperation to this end are the Interfaith Ceremony at Assisi on the occasion of the twenty-fifth anniversary of the Worldwide Fund for Nature in 1986 and the Joint Declaration of Catholics and Jews on the Environment adopted at a meeting of the International Catholic–Jewish Liaison Committee at the Vatican in March 1998. The Joint Declaration notes how certain forms of human activity, including 'population increase in certain areas and heightened economic expectation among peoples', are leading to climate change, air and water pollution, desertification, resource depletion and loss of biodiversity. Though Jews and Catholics may differ in interpretation of some texts or in their methodological approaches, they have found, in turning to their scriptures, such broad agreement on certain fundamental values that they are able to affirm them together. Though the Declaration

was issued by Jews and Catholics, there is little doubt that its principles would be endorsed across the spectrum of Christian and Jewish denominations.   *NORMAN SOLOMON*

Ephrem (*c*.306–373)

Syriac theologian and poet. Ephrem spent the greater part of his life in Nisibis, moving to Edessa after the city's loss to Persia in 363. Ephrem served as a deacon in both cities, assuming a prominent role as a teacher, ascetic, spiritual guide and Church leader. His fame comes largely from his theological works, written in **Syriac** in both poetry and prose, the best known being his hymn cycles (*madrashe*) on themes such as faith, paradise, the Nativity, the Church, Lent, Pascha and virginity. In these hymns Ephrem puts forward a remarkable theological vision, pointing to the mystery of God not through definitions and categories but through metaphors and symbols: a truly poetic theology. In articulating this vision Ephrem displays many affinities with rabbinic **exegesis**, such as his treatment of the potent theme of the 'robe of glory' lost by **Adam** and **Eve** but regained through **baptism**, and his identification of **Melchizedek** with Shem, son of **Noah**. Ephrem was also very much involved in the debates of his day, fiercely attacking **Marcion** and the **Gnostics** and, notwithstanding the said affinities, engaging in fierce **polemic** with the Jews – with whom, especially in Nisibis, he would have been in close proximity. Like all Christian writers of his time, Ephrem is unambiguous about the redundancy of Judaism. He is, however, unusually bitter in lambasting the Jews for their collusion both in the **crucifixion** and in more recent persecutions. It is likely that the bitterness of his attack arises from the perceived Jewish involvement in the **antiChristian** persecution launched in the 340s by the Persian King Shapur II.   *MARCUS PLESTED*

Episcopus iudaeorum *see* leaders of the Jews, externally appointed

Epistle of Barnabas *see* Apostolic Fathers

Esau *see* Edom; Jacob

Eschatology

Derived from the Greek word *eschatos*, meaning 'final' or 'last', eschatology refers to teaching about 'the last things'. While many religions incorporate beliefs about the future, eschatology plays an especially central role in Judaism and Christianity, in part due to the prominent role played by eschatological hope in the scriptures that the two communities share. Since, however, Judaism and Christianity interpret their common scriptures differently, eschatology also differentiates the two traditions. Jews and Christians, one might say, are divided by a common eschatological hope.

The taproot of eschatology in the **Hebrew Bible** is the hope that God will act in the future to change the present course of events and to consummate God's purpose for God's people and for creation. This hope is fed by numerous strands of biblical tradition: God's promises to the patriarchs (Gen. 49.8–12; Deut. 33.13–17), traditions about **David**'s royal dynasty (2 Sam. 7), warnings of a coming 'Day of the Lord' and divine judgement (Amos 5.18; Isa. 8.8), cataclysmic conflict between good and **evil** (Dan. 7–12) and hopes of a perfected future (esp. Isa. 40–66). Drawing on these and other biblical and extra-biblical traditions, Judaism and Christianity have held a number of eschatological motifs in common down the centuries, including the coming of a promised heir of David (**Messiah**) who will inaugurate God's reign on earth, the bodily resurrection of the dead, God's final judgement condemning the wicked and rewarding the good (*see* **Day of Judgement**), and eternal life in a new and perfected creation. At the same time, Judaism and Christianity have configured these elements in characteristically different ways.

From the beginning, Christians have understood **Jesus** as the centre and turning point of God's eschatological plans for Israel and for creation, a fact reflected by Christianity's most central designation for Jesus: '**Christ**', or Messiah. This is not to say that early Christians understood Jesus as the fulfilment of any single pre-existing Messianic concept or eschatological schema. Rather, they adopted and transformed many such traditions in light of the unique features of Jesus' life and message, and, above all, his **crucifixion** and **resurrection**. The resulting eschatological vision is highly distinctive, emphasising both that God has already begun to implement God's reign on earth through the events surrounding Jesus and also that the fulfilment of God's reign remains a hoped-for future, to be consummated upon Jesus' own return as Lord and Judge of creation.

The eschatology of **Rabbinic Judaism** also manifests a certain twofold quality, although of a distinctive kind. After the Roman destruction of the **Temple** and brutal suppression of the **Bar Kokhba** revolt, the sages consolidated Rabbinic Judaism by affirming the indispensability of eschatological hope for Jewish life while adopting a cautious posture toward specific Messianic claims. Over the centuries Jewish tradition has balanced hopes for a suprahistorical 'world to come' with an insistence that the Messiah's role is to restore the dispersed exiles to the **land of Israel** and to bring peace to this world.

Jews and Christians have frequently appealed to eschatology in order to express what each regards as the crucial failing of the other tradition. Christians fault Jews for failing to recognise Jesus as the Messiah promised in scripture, while Jews fault Christians for embracing a false Messianic pretender. More subtly, Christians have charged Judaism with cultivating a vulgar, this-worldly conception of God's end-time **salvation** that distorts the scripture in a nationalist and materialist direction. In contrast, Jews have seen in Christianity a fundamentally unbiblical tendency to declare salvation 'already available' at the cost of making salvation an individualistic and spiritualised affair cut off from the world that needs redeeming. Yet both Judaism and Christianity possess eschatological frameworks that are rich and varied enough to permit more positive assessments of the other. **Maimonides**, for example, suggested that Christianity might be viewed as an instrument whereby God helps to prepare the Gentiles for the eventual coming of the Messiah-King. In the twentieth century numerous Christian theologians have argued that Judaism's insistence on the as yet unredeemed character of the world helpfully goads Christians to embrace a neglected dimension of their own faith, namely hope for the consummation of God's redeeming work on earth. Especially since the 1960s, participants in Jewish–Christian **dialogue** have often sought to qualify the abiding differences between Judaism and Christianity by emphasising the common biblical root of eschatological hope that the two traditions share.

Finally, it is important to note that secularised forms of Jewish and Christian eschatology such as Marxism and **Zionism** have proven enormously potent forces in the shaping of the modern world. While commonly regarded with deep reserve by more traditional forms of Judaism and Christianity, these movements have been embraced by more progressive religionists, especially in the case of Zionism among Jews and Marxism among, for example, Latin American **liberation theologians**. Among movements animated by biblical eschatology at the beginning of the twenty-first century, religiously inspired **Christian Zionism** is also likely to shape the context of Jewish–Christian relations in decades to come.   R. KENDALL SOULEN

Esther

Esther, and the book bearing her name, are inseparable from the festival of **Purim**, which has been contentious in Jewish–Christian relations. In recent decades, however, Esther has united Jewish and Christian scholars in new kinds of analysis of her deceptively simple biblical tale, a prose fiction *Diasporanovelle* set in Persia. Esther (Hebrew Hadassah, 2.7), consort of King Ahasuerus, was its heroine as it addressed problems of Jews' **minority** status. Purim commemorates the revelation of her **identity** as a Jew, her people's salvation from extermination and mastery of their foes (Esth. 9.20–28; 2 Macc. 15.36 and *b. Megillah*). The **Theodosian Code** (16.8.8) banned the public celebration of Purim, which through the *Purimspiel* has been rich in frivolity and theatricality, satire of Jew and Gentile and venting of emotion against opponents. Purim falls before the Christian **Easter**, when in some periods and places **Passion plays** were expressing anti-Jewish sentiments theatrically.

The Hebrew text of Esther lacks the divine Name (which is included in five of six *Additions* to Esther in Greek) and its canonicity was contested (*b. Megillah* 7a; *b. BabaBatra* 14b; *b. Sanhedrin* 100a; *t. Yadayim* 2.14). No copy of Esther was found at Qumran, nor was it in **Melito**'s second-century list of Jewish canonical writings (Eusebius, *Hist. eccl.* 4.26.14). Esther remained non-canonical for the Eastern church until the eighth century (*see* **canon**) and Martin **Luther** was hostile to it. Yet the story has featured much in the arts (including in the **Dura Europos** synagogue) and increasingly is studied by Jewish and Christian **feminist** scholars, as well as by students of the ancient novel, identity and ethnicity.   CHRISTINE TREVETT

Ethics

Any discussion of ethics in the context of Jewish–Christian relations needs to begin with a discussion of the law–gospel distinction that has been a centrepiece of classical Christian ethics. This distinction has argued for the basic inferiority of Jewish to Christian ethics on the grounds that the former is rooted entirely in **law** while **love** stands at the heart of the latter. This perspective dominated Christian thinking for many centuries, despite the fact that Catholic **canon law** often studied the Jewish legal tradition as an aid to making concrete moral decisions within the framework of Catholic case law. The supposed law–gospel distinction (also referred to as 'law–spirit') is patently simplistic. While Jewish ethics may not speak of love in the abstract as much as Christian ethics, an examination of its **halakhic** tradition clearly shows that a sense of love and compassion has permeated its process of reaching concrete ethical decisions. Ronald Green (b. 1942), a Jewish ethicist who has studied in depth the relationship between Jewish and Christian ethical thought, cites the following example as an illustration of the superficiality of such a distinction. When confronted with the question as to whether an adolescent who committed suicide could be buried in hallowed ground, the rabbis responded positively, arguing that parents should not endure the torment of exclusion from a deceased child. They so defined adolescent death that it could never be considered suicide. Green insists that we can find numerous examples of such humane and progressive reasoning tempering or even obliterating the letter of outdated laws. While Jewish ethics cannot be stereotyped along classical law–love lines, there is a somewhat greater stress on concrete legal decisions in Jewish ethics than in its Christian counterpart, though Catholicism has a casuistic moral tradition that draws somewhat on **talmudic** ethics. The moral life in Judaism has to be pursued through the development of legal reasoning. Generic neighbour-love, so central to much of Christian ethical thought, does not have the same importance in Judaism.

Green attributes the 'law' emphasis in the Jewish tradition to two principal factors. The first has to do with the fundamental goal of Jewish ethics, which can be defined as the creation of a 'holy community' in all aspects of life. The second is the emphasis on communal practice as the principal way of communicating and instilling ethical ideals. Some Jewish scholars have even questioned whether one can speak of Jewish ethics in the same way as ethics is defined as a theological discipline in Christianity. Clearly, Jewish and Christian ethics show considerable difference in terms of their basic modality. Yet, while Christianity has traditionally accorded overarching ethical principles a greater role in morality, Catholicism – particularly in what is known as the manualist tradition, which shaped ethical decisions in the context of the sacrament of **penance** – often relied on a type of ethical reasoning that closely parallels Jewish practice.

Another distinction between Jewish and Christian ethics concerns the particularity–universality polarity. Again stereotyping is not in order: the same tension has existed in both traditions over the centuries. But Green maintains that Christianity has generally emphasised the universalistic pole while Judaism has leaned far more towards the particularistic. He again illustrates his claim with a concrete example. The Good Samaritan story has been a quintessential aspect of the Christian ethical heritage. In Judaism, while the story has its parallels, it does not elicit the same profound response. Jewish ethics prescribes concern for the sojourner in one's midst, and the story of Ruth clearly shows openness towards the outsider. The highlight of the story of Ruth for Jews occurs, however, when she identifies her fate with that of the Jewish community and becomes a true 'daughter of Israel'.

A third point of general contrast between Jewish and Christian ethics comes in their respective approaches to the significance of suffering. Christianity, generally speaking, places a much higher value on the meaning of suffering than does Judaism. This is no doubt due in major part to the theological centrality of Christ's death in Christian faith. Suffering for Christianity is often seen as redemptive and morally purifying. With rare exceptions, such an attitude is absent from the Jewish tradition. Such statements as there are generally have more to do with the problem of how a God in **covenant** with the Jewish people can allow human suffering than with the significance of suffering as such. Jewish spiritual writers have certainly struggled with the issue of innocent suffering, but they assign no particular moral value to such suffering. And there is almost no emphasis in Judaism on self-imposed **asceticism**. Important talmudic scholars have in fact denounced any glorification of suffering and urged the forgoing of future reward if it meant enduring suffering in the process. Halakhic observance is normally willing to suspend any legal requirement if it jeopardises human life and health.

This third point surfaces in several recent discussions involving Christian and Jewish ethicists. In reflections on the moral implications of the **Holocaust**, where there has been considerable interchange involving scholars such as Irving Greenberg (b. 1933), Peter Haas (b. 1947), Didier Pollefeyt (b. 1965), John Pawlikowski (b. 1940), Jürgen Moltmann (b. 1926), John Roth (b. 1940), A. Roy Eckardt (1918–98), Michael Berenbaum (b. 1945) and Franklin Sherman (b. 1928), there has been a far greater willingness on the part of the Christians to find some source of meaning after the Holocaust through Christ's suffering death on the cross, though Eckardt and Pawlikowski have raised significant reservations about such an approach. We also see it operative in discussions about **abortion** and genetics, where there has been considerable willingness on the part of Jewish ethicists (especially geneticists) to embrace new technologies, in contrast to a pervasive moral reserve on the part of many Christian ethicists.

A final point of contrast between Jewish and Christian ethics has been the notion of natural law. Natural law, coming in significant part out of the Thomistic tradition, has been a core element in Christian ethics. Though this classical emphasis on natural law has been somewhat modified in Catholicism since **Vatican II** in favour of a more experiential and biblical basis (it was never central to the Protestant tradition), it remains an important feature of Christian ethics that has little parallel in Jewish tradition. David Novak (b. 1941) is one of the few Jewish scholars to have embraced natural law as a foundation for ethics.

While throughout history Christian ethicists have tended to focus attention on the contrast between Christian and Judaic morality, there are examples in more recent times of a recognition that Christianity can draw constructively from the Jewish tradition and work with Jews on issues of common moral concern. The Jewish–Christian **dialogue** in the **United States** owes much to the collaboration of Christians and Jews during the 1930s and 1940s in securing justice for the working class. Jews and Christians also worked together in the struggle for racial justice in America in the 1960s, with Jewish personalities such as Abraham **Heschel** joining Dr Martin Luther King (1929–68). And the ongoing Vatican–Jewish international dialogue has issued joint statements within the last decade on the ethics of family life and on **ecology**. Finally, Jews and Christians are beginning to recognise that both need to grapple with the meaning of God as a moral barometer within society in light of events such as the Holocaust and against the background of growing secularisation in Western society.

See also **medical ethics**   *JOHN T. PAWLIKOWSKI*

Ethiopia

Ethiopian Jews and Christians represent an issue within Jewish–Christian relations peculiar to Ethiopia, but also raise wider questions of **identity** and shared inheritance.

The Jews of Ethiopia, known as the Beta Israel or (originally pejoratively) as Falashas, share many affinities with the Orthodox 'monophysite' Church of Ethiopia. Until the late twentieth century they inhabited the same mountainous regions of north-western Ethiopia, speaking the same regional languages. The Ethiopian national saga *Kebra Nagast* ('Glory of the Kings'), compiled in the fourteenth century to legitimate the 'restored' Solomonic dynasty, ascribes the origin of the Ethiopian sacral kingship to the union between King Solomon and the Queen of Sheba. The tradition has had a mythopoeic influence, enshrined in the 1955 Ethiopian constitution, and accounts for the alleged presence of the Ark of the Covenant at Aksum (the ancient capital) and the use of the symbol of the Ark in Ethiopian churches.

Once seen as the lost tribe of Dan, Ethiopian Jews are non-talmudic and have some unique practices (e.g. **monasticism**). They seem to be either a people unconverted to Christianity and combining ancient Aksumite (including Judaic) elements or Christians who became increasingly emphatic on Pentateuchal teaching from the mid-fourteenth century. The first Christians in Ethiopia were probably traders like Frumentius (*c.*300–80), who was appointed the first bishop in the fourth century. Despite a major conflict between Jews and Christians in the sixth century, when trade routes were threatened, Jewish–Christian relations have been characterised by non-hostile interaction between the two communities, with a complex system of taboo that allowed close habitation and participation in each others' ceremonies and family events without any physical contact; to Jews Christians were impure, and both sides seem to have accepted the conventions for maintaining purity. Many Christians depicted the Jews as *Agaw*

('pagan') or *buda* ('hyena-man'), in African **folklore** a supernatural being able to work with fire; the Jews typically produced iron instruments and clay pots for the Christians, mostly as tenant farmers on Christian-owned land. Both communities share the liturgical language of Geez (Classical Ethiopic), while Christian traditions (in **biblical interpretation**, selection of scripture (e.g. *Ethiopic Enoch*) and practice) have many similarities with Jewish. Some practices (e.g. male and female **circumcision**) are undoubtedly derived from indigenous African culture; others may be remnants of ancient Christianity now lost elsewhere.

The movement of Ethiopian Jews to **Israel** began in 1977, and was completed with Operation Moses (1984) and Operation Solomon (1991).

JAMES K. AITKEN

Eucharist

Literally 'thanksgiving', derived from the Greek *eucharistia*, a term originally applied by Jews to a form of grace before and after meals. Central to most Christian communities, the eucharist is also called 'the Lord's Supper' (*kyriakon deipon*) and was a subset of *agape* (literally 'love' and applied to a religious meal shared as a sign of love), but later broke off from it to become a self-standing **bread** and **wine** rite. Prayers of thanksgiving during meals were a common feature of Jesus' ministry. The Gospels give particular attention to the **Last Supper**, which provides the basis for the eucharist, and Christian scholars believe that its origin is located in a Jewish meal presided over by **Jesus** in the context of the Jewish feast of **Passover** on the night before his **crucifixion**.

In the **New Testament** the earliest eucharists were complete meals shared by Jesus' Jewish followers in remembrance of him and in thanksgiving for what God had done in Christ. Early eucharistic texts indicate that the prayers were centred on thanksgiving, both for **creation** and for redemption in Christ. The ordering of the prayers remained close to the pattern of Jewish meal **blessings** for several centuries.

Liturgical scholar Gregory Dix (1901–52) remarked that 'the most important thing we have learned about the liturgy in the past 50 years is that Jesus was a Jew'. Dix realised that Christian **worship** was unintelligible without an understanding of the Jewish liturgical matrix out of which it came, yet it is also important to appreciate the distinctiveness and divergence of Christian worship from its Jewish parent.

The development of the eucharist during its first few centuries owes a great deal to the practice of Jewish worship. This is true not only of liturgical elements such as the Sanctus (the angelic hymn of Isa. 6.3) and the *kiddush* (the blessing spoken over the 'fruit of the vine'), but also of synagogue lections and expositions of scripture and perhaps even of the prolongation of the **Sabbath** to the dawn of the 'day of the Sun' (Justin, *1 Apol.* 67). In particular, it was through the pattern of promise and fulfilment that the eucharist was shaped as a meal that pointed to the consummation. This resembles features of Passover for Rabbi **Akiba** who, in answer to the question how the Passover Haggadah should conclude, insisted that it should conclude with the **redemption** that is to come. It is worth noting the increasing popularity of 'Passover seder re-enactments' in Christian churches during Holy Week, which aims not only at understanding the last days of Jesus' life, but also at giving people a sense of the roots of their communion practice. These have aroused mixed reactions among both Jews and Christians who are active in interfaith relations.

In Jewish practice every meal was a sacred occasion requiring a grace, but the Passover meal was especially **holy**, with a particular emphasis on **remembrance**. A meal reminds participants that eating, like praying, is a holy action. By retelling the story of redemption, the haggadah demonstrates the contemporary significance of an event that took place thousands of years before. Thus, Christians and Jews agree on the importance of retelling past events and acknowledging their significance and power in the present.

Nevertheless, the original Jewish context to the eucharist became lost over time; there was also a tendency towards standardisation, as well as an emphasis on the sacrificial aspects of the eucharist. As early as the second century the eucharistic action – the taking of bread and wine, the saying of the eucharistic prayer over them, the breaking of the bread and the distribution of both – became separated from the meal and located in a Christian service, perhaps in an attempt to avoid dependence on Judaism. At various stages in the history of Jewish–Christian relations Christians found themselves needing to distinguish themselves from Judaism, not least, paradoxically, in order to pre-

serve precisely the universality that they sought to affirm. This distinctiveness expressed itself particularly in aspects of the eucharist: the celebration of the risen and ascended presence of Christ in or at the **sacrament** and of the sacrament as a means of gracious, divine presence; the sacrificial nature ascribed to the eucharist as the 'full, perfect and sufficient sacrifice, oblation and satisfaction'; and ecclesiological interpretations of the 'body of Christ', stressing the church's catholicity, apostolicity, unity and **mission**.

During the Middle Ages in particular, when most Christians only made communion once or twice a year, the eucharist was viewed not as a meal but as an object of devotion, particularly among the laity. A sense of awe dominated popular piety, which believed that the physical presence of Christ existed within the bread and wine and that the entire **salvation** of the world was dependent upon it. Part of this was an exaggerated (and quite graphic) understanding of eucharistic presence, as expressed in popular tales of bleeding hosts and groaning hosts to underscore that this is the very selfsame crucified body of Christ that died on Calvary. This provides the background to Christian charges of **host desecration** against Jews in late medieval Europe. Violence against Jews, and even **expulsions**, often followed these charges.

The eucharist has not only divided Christians from Jews, but Christians from one another on matters of eucharistic **doctrine** (and in particular doctrines surrounding the presence of Christ in the eucharist). This came to the fore in the **Reformation**, but all Christians accepted that the eucharist was a memorial of all that God had accomplished in Christ and that it formed the core of the church's self-**identity**.

In the last century Christians have given renewed attention to the eucharist as part of a wider liturgical renewal. Since **Vatican II**, for example, **Roman Catholicism** has reaffirmed the centrality of the eucharist in making present the redeeming work of Christ. At the same time, ecumenical discussions have led to interdenominational agreement on the form and content of the eucharist. Joint Jewish and Christian scholarly studies of early Christian and Jewish worship have also taken place and resulted in an increasing knowledge of both the nature of early Jewish meal prayers and the earliest layers of Christian communion practice, several of which had previously been lost. As a result, the recitation of the acts of God in creation and **prophecy** – as in Jewish **liturgy** – which disappeared in the Western Church in the fifth century, has been reinstated. Another example of a recent Christian liturgical return to Jewish roots is found in the modern form of the Great Thanksgiving, which sums up the praises of the Father and concludes the eucharistic prayers. The prayer returns Christians to the themes of Jewish meal blessings – blessing God for creation and for redemption, asking God to act again here and now with the same creating and redeeming power, and looking forward to the coming of the **Messiah** in triumph.

IVOR H. JONES AND EDWARD KESSLER

Eusebius of Caesarea (*c*.260–339)

Bishop of Caesarea who held an ambivalent attitude to Judaism. In *Preparatio Evangelica* he advocates the superiority of Jewish religion above Greek religion and philosophy, but in *Demonstratio Evangelica* he establishes the superiority of Christianity over Judaism. Influenced heavily by **Origen**, Eusebius's value for Jewish–Christian relations lies in his history of the **early Church** (*Ecclesiastical History*). This became an indispensable source for all pre-critical records of this period because of its extensive collection of quotations. Stereotypically, he argues that Jews are responsible for their own fate, blaming them for the death of **Jesus**. However, he did not rejoice over that and consequently suggested that Christians deserved the persecution of Diocletian (*r*.284–305) as well. Nevertheless, the wide distribution and good reputation of *Ecclesiastical History* helped sustain Christian anti-Jewish stereotypes for many centuries. *PETR FRYŠ*

Euthanasia *see* medical ethics

Evangelical movements

'Evangelical' derives from the Greek *evangelion* meaning 'good news' or 'gospel'. By definition, Christianity is an evangelical religion and the 'Great Commission' commands Christians to 'convert the world to Christ'. However, contemporary usage of the term 'evangelical' usually refers to theologically conservative **Protestants**. Three features generally distinguish Evangelicals: belief in the 'inerrancy' of the Bible, both the Hebrew scriptures and the **New Testament**; a 'born again' religious experience culminating with acceptance of **Jesus** as a personal Saviour and **Messiah**; support of intensive missionary programmes aimed

not only at non-Evangelical communities (Jews, Muslims, Hindus, Buddhists, etc.) but also at other Christians, including **Roman Catholics**, 'mainline' Protestants and Eastern **Orthodox Christians** (*see* **mission**).

Evangelical–Jewish encounters in the **United States** greatly increased in the early 1970s and followed earlier Catholic–Jewish and mainline Protestant–Jewish initiatives. While many leaders and denominations representing mainline Protestant churches have been publicly critical of the **State of Israel**, Evangelicals are among Israel's strongest Christian supporters. Yet many Evangelicals actively seek the **conversion** of Jews to Christianity. As a result, the Jewish community, fully cognisant of the need to encourage and maintain Christian support for Israel, has in many localities carefully entered into a series of circumscribed programmes, encounters and relationships with Evangelicals. Besides a shared commitment to Israel's security and survival, Evangelicals and Jews were allies in the Soviet Jewry struggle of the late twentieth century. The two communities also work together on questions of human rights for religious believers in all parts of the world.

However, Evangelical–Jewish relations are frequently uneasy and ambivalent. One major area of contention between Jews and Evangelicals is the support given by some Evangelical leaders and Churches to **Jews for Jesus** and other missionary groups that specifically target the Jewish community. Another is the US public policy agenda: the majority of American Jews and Evangelicals differ on key issues including strict separation of **church and state**, gun control, women's rights and **abortion**. Other divisive issues are mandated prayer and Bible-reading in public schools, the teaching of evolution in public schools, and public financial aid to religiously sponsored private schools. The Jewish community is more surefooted in its relationships with Roman Catholics and mainline Protestants than it is with Evangelicals, who often have an inaccurate '**Old Testament**' image of Jews and Judaism, and are surprised to discover the significant religious differences within contemporary Jewry, as well as the existence of 'secular' Jews. Jews sometimes have difficulty differentiating among the wide variety of theological positions and groups extant among Evangelicals, including eschatology, faith healing, **antinomianism**, anti-modernism, speaking in tongues, charismatics and Pentecostals. Further complicating Evangelical–Jewish relationships was the revelation in 2002 that Billy Graham (b. 1918), the world's best-known evangelist and a long-time supporter of the State of Israel, uttered highly **antisemitic** remarks in a taped private 1972 White House conversation with US President Richard Nixon. Graham's remarks validated long-held suspicions among many Jews that Evangelicals, because of their conservative religious beliefs, remain antisemitic despite the growing number of positive encounters between the two groups. *A. JAMES RUDIN*

Evangelism

In the Christian community evangelism is telling the 'good news' (the gospel) of God's saving love and forgiveness of sin in Jesus Christ. This 'good news' is the content of the Church's **mission**, laid out at the end of the Gospel of Matthew and elaborated in the sermons found in the book of Acts. The Jewish community has not normally practised evangelism in the Christian sense of the term, although some post-exilic Jewish communities actively sought out converts. Throughout Christian history Jews have tended to be objects of evangelism along with non-Jews. **Evangelical** Christians (including members of the 'Free Churches', but also members found in all Church bodies today), particularly those who accept the Bible as literally true, understand this mandate as definitive of their very existence: evangelism aims at **conversion** and provides the passion for the Church's world mission. Conflicts still arise when Christian evangelists deny continuing meaning and validity to the Jewish witness and when Jewish converts to Christianity continue to affirm their religious adherence to Judaism (for example, **Jews for Jesus**).

A broader understanding of evangelism is widely held today. For many Church bodies evangelism does not necessarily aim at the conversion of non-Christians generally or Jews in particular; it is the sharing of the Christian message, a message intended for the entire human community. Such Christians share their faith in the tri-une God, confident that non-Christians also have much to share with them about the same God, believed never to be absent and never without witnesses in all times and places. Interfaith exchanges offer comparable forms of evangelism, in this sense, by Jews and members of other religious communities. *WALTER HARRELSON*

Eve

Eve – the name means 'life-giver', reflecting her procreative role – appears widely in Jewish and Christian biblical and extracanonical literature. As a prominent figure in Western **art**, literature and theology, she is often portrayed as a temptress, seducer and the embodiment of **sin**. According to the Bible (Gen. 2–3; 4.1–2) she was the first woman to be created by God from Adam's side (rib); later Jewish tradition suggests that she was created after **Lilith**. Outside the **Hebrew Bible** she appears in the **Pseudepigrapha**, the **New Testament**, the **Apocrypha**, rabbinic literature and early Christian writings. In Christian sources she is linked to the beginnings of sin, but in the Hebrew Bible the origin of sin is attributed to women who cohabited with evil **angels** (Gen. 6.1–4). The rabbis later attributed sin to **Adam** rather than Eve. Genesis 2–3 is called 'The Fall' in Christian theology; the linking of Eve to the fall of humankind is based on Christian interpretations heavily influenced by Platonic rather than Hebrew thought, although some scholars have suggested that the New Testament text of 1 Tim. 2.14 was influenced by Jewish **exegesis** of 'The Fall' (van der Horst).

In some texts Eve is mentioned by name (Tob. 8.6; 2 Cor. 11.3; 1 Tim. 2.13–14; Josephus, *Ant.* 1.34–51) whilst others only allude to her (Sir. 25.24; 40.1; 42.13; 4 Macc. 18.7). Scholars have suggested that Sir. 25.24 is the earliest of writings to link the origin of sin to Eve; others have argued that this was not typical in Jewish thought in the second century BCE (Kristen Kvam *et al.*). In rabbinic and early Christian sources, including **Gnostic** writings and the **Church Fathers**, there is no uniform picture of Eve. The rabbis differed on whether one or two Eves were created or whether the first being was androgynous and later given a gender. Genesis 2–3 was used by both Jewish and Christian commentators to justify the subordination and inferiority of women (**Philo**, Chrysostom, **Augustine**, Luther). Eve personified womanhood and was associated with sin, lust and sexual desire (Philo, **Tertullian**, Augustine). She was often rebuked as a temptress (Tertullian, *On the Apparel of Women*) and the sole reason for her creation was for procreation (Philo, Ambrose, **Chrysostom**). Many of the Church Fathers and Jewish commentators adopted an **allegorical** interpretation, understanding Adam and Eve as the archetypal husband and wife, where Adam represented the mind and rationality and Eve represented pleasure and desire (Philo, **Origen**, medieval commentaries). Augustine preferred the literal, plain meaning of the text, from which he developed the doctrine of **original sin**. The medieval Jewish commentator **Rashi** also preferred the philological and historical meaning of the biblical text. Egalitarian interpretations existed in *The Apocalypse of Moses* (15–30) and later in the writings of Hildegard of Bingen (1098–1179) and Christine de Pizan (b. 1364), where Eve (and women in general) personified **redemption** rather than sin. **Luther** argued that she was originally equal to Adam and shared dominion over the earth but forfeited that equality after 'The Fall'.

In contemporary exegesis Eve has been a prominent figure in feminist scholarship. Jewish and Christian feminists have redeemed the negative picture of Eve to focus on the egalitarian relationship between Eve and Adam. Any subordination that may exist in the text (Gen. 3.16) is explained as a distortion of the original story or used to explain the harsh realities of life for women in Palestine at the time the story was recorded (Carol Myers). Jewish and Christian interpretations of Eve have often been characterised by mutual influence, not only in **feminist writings**. The medieval period particularly, although not exclusively, was characterised by widespread scholarly interaction between Jewish, Christian and Muslim communities which affected the developing exegesis.   *HELEN P. FRY*

Evil

Evil, that which opposes or is the antithesis of what is good, is, along with questions about the nature of God, a concept receiving serious attention in Jewish and Christian philosophy and theology following the twentieth-century genocides, especially the *Shoah*. Frequently this study is pursued in the context of scholarly **dialogue**. Twenty-first century terrorism has intensified the nature of this work, given the absolutisation of evil, the establishing of dualism between good and evil, and the demonisation of others that frequently characterise responses to this phenomenon.

For both Judaism and Christianity the reality of evil has been a persistent problem, given their view of a benevolent, omnipotent God. While each accepts evil as an inevitable aspect of the world, and while the thinking of each is significantly informed by the references to evil in the Tanakh/Old Testament, a systematic understanding of it remains elusive for both. In the history of each, evil has been variously viewed as being permitted by God as a test of faith, or a divine warning, discipline or punishment. Considering suffering as evil, both have attributed to it redemptive value (e.g. as expressed in the **Isaiah** Servant Songs), though this is primarily a Christian understanding, reaching its depth of meaning in **Christ**'s suffering and death on behalf of all humanity – the act through which he triumphed over evil and death. Both also associate evil with sin and acknowledge humanity's capacity for sin due to the evil inclination or *yetzer* (in Judaism) and **original sin** (in Christianity). Both speak of evil in terms of Satan and the **devil**, the **New Testament** word *devil* (*ho diabolos*) coming from the Greek translation of Satan (*satan*), the designation in the Tanakh for a principle of evil warring against God and for a personal and superhuman evil force. Christianity, drawing on Old Testament **apocalyptic** passages regarding the final great struggle between the forces of good and evil, also speaks of the **Antichrist**, a hostile figure opposing the work of God, especially that accomplished through **Jesus** Christ. Within both Judaism and Christianity the distinction is commonly made between metaphysical, physical and moral evil. Though explicating and nuancing differently, Judaism and Christianity both acknowledge the limitation of finite creaturehood and its attendant tendency toward evil; both acknowledge the suffering and evil that lie in the wake of violent natural phenomena; and both attest to the essence of evil that resides in the perversity of will.

For centuries Christians theologically and popularly caricatured Jews as the personification of evil, a history that helped prepare the seedbed for the **Holocaust**. Given this centuries-long experience, a reciprocal Jewish perception of Christians has been that of *resha'im* (evil ones) – a sentiment expressed privately but rarely overtly due to church- and/or government-sponsored **censorship**.

The Holocaust and other twentieth-century genocides vividly illustrate the modern tendency to glorify the autonomy through which 'humans appoint themselves God and thereby become the devil' (cf. Greenberg 'Judaism, Christianity, and Partnership'). It is confronting this danger that post-Holocaust Jews and Christians committed to a life of faith see as a moral imperative in their responsibility to attend to the problem of evil at a time in history when humanity has the capacity to destroy creation and humanity itself. *AUDREY DOETZEL*

Excommunication

Expulsion from a **community**. In the Bible the Hebrew term *herem* meant setting someone or something apart from God, either devoting it to divine service or, in the context of war, destroying the person or thing so that no warrior would profit from it (see Exod. 17.14–16 and Deut. 25.17–19 on Amalek and 1 Sam. 13.1–35). John 9.22, 12.42 and 16.2 use the term *aposynagogos* ('put out of the synagogue') to describe expulsion of **Jewish Christians**, most likely by authority of the local leaders, not as a result of a decree of the Synod of Jabneh/**Jamnia**. Probably Jewish Christians were objects of a curse (*birkat ha-minim*) only after the Bar Kokhba revolt (132–5). During the early centuries after the Romans destroyed the **Temple** in 70 CE punishment of an offender was isolation from the community (*niddui*). Later the *herem* designated a harsher penalty, including curses. The **Talmud** listed 24 offences for which *niddui* was prescribed; seven more were added in the sixteenth-century *Shulhan Aruk* of Joseph Karo (1488–1575). The philosopher **Spinoza** was placed under *herem* by the Jewish community of Amsterdam in 1656.

Matthew 18.15–17, 1 Cor. 5.5, 13, Acts 5.1–11, 8.18–24 and 1 Tim. 1.18–20 describe expulsions from early Christian communities. Technically excommunication would affect Christians only, but in the Middle Ages 'a judgement of the Jew' might be applied indirectly to deal with a Jew who had offended by an act normally punishable by excommunication, e.g. striking a cleric. The bishop would forbid all Christians to contact him, under threat of excommunication. *LAWRENCE E. FRIZZELL*

Exegesis

Exegesis, or the interpretation of scripture, has always been at the centre of Jewish–Christian relations. Most if not all of the bitter **polemic** that divided Jews from Christians in the first centuries of the Common Era is rooted in scriptural exegesis, despite the fact that the principles and methods of rabbinic and patristic exegesis had much in common. The ancient Jewish exegetical literature, known as **midrash**, and the **commentaries** and homilies of the **Church Fathers** both acknowledged, for example, that texts have more than one meaning, a literal meaning and one or more other meanings. Almost all the early Jewish literature, including the **Dead Sea Scrolls** and the **New Testament**, was characterised by the conviction that sacred scripture must speak to the present, and encouraged the use of **Hellenistic** methods (e.g. **allegory**, etymology, *gematria*) to achieve this. Later the Church was divided between followers of the **Alexandrian** School in the West, where the allegorising tradition flourished, and the School of **Antioch**, which favoured a more literal interpretation of scripture. In the West references to **Christ**, the **Trinity** and the Virgin **Mary** were found in every book of the Bible from Genesis to Revelation. It is understandable that the Jews, who suffered more at the hands of the Greek and Latin Churches than in predominantly Syriac-speaking Christendom in the East, became increasingly wary of non-literal interpretations and sought to use the original Hebrew to counter Christian polemic. A notable exception is the mystical writers' exegetical method epitomised in the acronym PaRDeS ('paradise'): *Peshat* 'literal interpretation', *Remez* 'allusion', *Derash* 'non-literal interpretation', *Sod* 'mystical interpretation' (*see* **mysticism**).

Christian exegesis of scripture has been divided from Jewish in another way. While a relatively small number of specialist scholars like **Jerome**, **Andrew of St Victor** and **Pico della Mirandola** worked on the Hebrew text, Christian interpretation right down to the present has almost always been based on translations into Greek, Syriac, Latin, German, English and other languages, while Jewish exegesis has almost invariably been based on the Hebrew text. The sixteenth-century Reformers (*see* **Reformation**) and their Catholic counterparts encouraged the study of **Hebrew** but often more to expose and refute the errors of the Jews than to learn from them. Modern scholars' attempts since the eighteenth century to get back to one single 'original' meaning, by the use of archaeological data and comparative philology, continued to denigrate rabbinic interpretations as 'late' or 'fanciful'. Only towards the end of the twentieth century, in the shadow of the **Holocaust**, which called for new approaches to scripture, and in the light of new literary critical and linguistic insights, did an increasing awareness of the relevance of context, reception history, reader response and the plurality of meaning open up the way to mutually more positive evaluations of traditional Jewish and Christian interpretations of scripture.

See also **biblical criticism**; **biblical interpretation**; **linguistics** *JOHN F. A. SAWYER*

Exorcism *see* **consecration; demon/devil; magic**

Expatriate Christians in Israel *see* **Israel, expatriate Christians in**

Expulsions

Expulsions of Jews have occurred since antiquity, but the most significant for Jewish–Christian relations are the two great waves of expulsion that took place at the end of the thirteenth and the end of the fifteenth centuries. The former period reveals several types of expulsion. The expulsion of the Jews from Anjou, Gascony and England in 1289–90 involved the clearance of Jews from large areas by the decree of the ruling prince. In these cases the ruler cited Jewish **usury** as a central reason for expelling the Jews, but religious motives were also apparent: the expulsion decrees insist on the offence caused to Christians by the presence in their midst of those who denied Christ. The expulsions must be seen as the end of a process of marginalisation of the Jews, beginning with attempts at **conversion**, public **disputations** and the condemnation of the **Talmud**; the impetus came from the higher levels of society – rulers wished to curry favour with nobles and knights indebted to Jews, and also saw themselves as standard-bearers of Christianity, **crusaders** whose **mission** against unbelief should include Jews as well as Muslims. However, some rulers, such as the French kings, expelled Jews (1306) only to readmit them. The king of Naples expelled those Jews who refused to convert in 1290, apparently because of stories of ritual murder attributed to Jews which fanatical preachers had brought to his attention. England was unusual at this point in the completeness of the expulsion (*see* **Edward I**). In the late fifteenth century popular hostility to the Jews seems more noticeable. Tales of ritual murder of Christian children by Jews were revived (*see* **blood libel**), such as that of Simon of Trent (1475). Anti-Jewish riots in areas such as southern **Italy** were increasingly frequent, and the nobles and leading citizens often sought to protect the Jews from those calling for their expulsion (as in Sicily in 1492–3). The mass conversions in **Spain** were seen by the Crown as a model that could be imitated: the expulsion decrees of 1492 sought not so much to rid Spain of Jews as to encourage them to stay, but as Christians; its character was emphatically religious and not racial. Several rulers took advantage of expulsions to welcome Jewish craftsmen into their lands, as happened in Naples, Ferrara and even in Papal Rome. In the same few years several German and north Italian states decreed the expulsion of the Jews; the Polish king was the beneficiary of the flight eastwards of German Jews. Nor was blanket expulsion of all Jews the only method adopted by late medieval rulers for taking Jews out of society. Enclosure in Jewish quarters, surrounded by high walls, was practised in Majorca at the end of the thirteenth century as an alternative to expulsion (*see* **ghetto**). This way rulers could still draw benefit from the economic activities of the Jews. Indeed, the expulsion from Spain was criticised from the start for its deleterious effects on the economy. It is therefore not surprising that several expelled communities were allowed to trickle back, as in Milan at the end of the fifteenth century, or that expulsion could exclude the richest Jews, as in Naples in 1510. *DAVID ABULAFIA*

FFFF

Faith *see* **confession of faith; justification**

Falashas *see* **Ethiopia**

Fasting

Fasting, the complete or partial abstinence from food and/or drink, is common to both Judaism and Christianity. The two major Jewish fast-days are Yom Kippur (**Day of Atonement**) and the ninth day of the month of Av. There are also five minor Jewish fast-days. Prominent biblical citations for fasting include Isa. 58 and Exod. 34.

Despite his 40-day fast in the wilderness, the New Testament suggests that **Jesus** and his disciples rarely fasted. While **John the Baptist** (Mark 2.18) questioned this omission from traditional Jewish practice, Matthew (6.16–18) was critical of fasting. Despite Jesus' apparent lack of fasting, over the centuries Christians incorporated the ritual into their religious obligations as a means of freeing themselves from earthly desires and attachments. In the early period of the Church, Christians copied the Jewish twice-weekly fast-days (Monday and Thursday) but changed the days to Wednesday and Friday (cf. *Did.* 8.1). Ash Wednesday and Good Friday remain fast-days for many Eastern **Orthodox Christians**, but such practices have basically disappeared for most Protestants and Catholics (although fasting is now used by some Christians to protest social injustice). Unlike Christian fasting, Jews generally fast as a means of spiritual preparation for **atonement** and as a recognition of individual and collective sins.

Personal fasts are part of both Judaism and Christianity. Among Jews it is customary for the bride and groom to fast on their **wedding** day; fasting also takes place on the anniversary of a parent's death. Christians instituted fasts for important events like **baptism**, ordination to **priesthood** and receiving the **eucharist**. In recent times Christians and Jews have often called for joint public fasting to highlight specific causes including disarmament, world peace or the release of prisoners, e.g. Soviet Jews in the 1970s.   *A. JAMES RUDIN*

Feminism and feminist writings

Patriarchy – the social, legal, political and economic systems sanctioning and enforcing male dominion – shaped the origins and development of Judaism and Christianity, as well as the cultural contexts in which they were formed. Feminism, an ideology grounded in women's experience of gender-based subjugation, criticises patriarchy as destructive and dysfunctional. It is the belief that women have the same rights as do men, an alternative vision of how humans might relate to one another and to the earth, and a commitment to transform structures for the flourishing of all creation. Jewish and Christian feminists, therefore, share a common agenda in seeking to recover women's voices in their traditions and formulate new patterns and possibilities of relationships. Both work, as Judith Plaskow (b. 1947) has said, to 'render visible the presence, experience, and deeds of women erased in traditional sources'. Yet the **anti-Judaism** that has marred much of Christian feminist theology has divided Jewish and Christian feminists. Some contemporary scholars are attempting to heal this rift.

Feminism embraces a wide variety of approaches and perspectives; its diversity is apparent even in terminology. African-Americans, following the lead of novelist Alice Walker (b. 1944), may speak of themselves as 'womanists', and many Hispanics identify themselves as engaging in *mujerista* theology. There is increasing awareness that a term used with frequency and imprecision, 'women's experience', may obscure significant differences of social location, such as race, class and religion.

Nevertheless, common elements are evident within the varieties of feminist theology. Methodologically, feminists generally approach their religious tradition through complementary perspectives that biblical scholar Elisabeth Schüssler Fiorenza (b. 1938) terms a **hermeneutic** of 'suspicion' and a hermeneutic of '**remembrance**'. The first lens describes the process by which feminists scrutinise and question the **tradition**, searching for what has been overlooked, misinterpreted, oversimplified or misappropriated. The second denotes the process by which feminists seek to reconstruct the tradition, attempting to provide a more inclusive and complex reading of women's history and experience. These lenses challenge the way normative texts function in the community, and reveal tradition to be more variegated and multivalent than (male) authorities have defined it.

Thus, Jewish and Christian feminists have provided new insights on sacred texts, brought to light archaeological evidence pointing to women's leadership, challenged exclusively male images for God, and created **liturgies** and rituals expressive of women's lives. In so doing, they have challenged the mind–body dualism, which devalued the body (especially women's bodies), have questioned hierarchical arrangements of power, and have revealed the boundaries of religious tradition to be more porous than normative sources defined them to be.

Despite these deep commonalities, many Jewish and Christian feminists seem to operate in separate spheres. This division is due in large measure to the ways in which Christian feminists have characterised Judaism. Particularly in its early days, Christian feminist thought tended to be a treasure trove of anti-Jewish themes. It portrayed Judaism as hopelessly patriarchal in order to emphasise the liberating power of Christianity. Wrenching rabbinic sources from their context, Christian feminists portrayed Jewish women as subject to the whims of their husbands, forced into marriage at a vulnerable age, excluded because of menstruation, banned from giving witness or teaching, and barred from leadership. References abounded to the 'Jewish patriarchal system', while, as Amy-Jill Levine (b. 1956) has shown, similarly patriarchal cultures of antiquity were passed over in silence. Establishing a Jewish patriarchal system enabled Christians to portray **Jesus** as a liberator, the one 'who saves women from Judaism' in the critique of Mary Rose D'Angelo (b. 1946). By depicting Jesus as breaking the grip of patriarchy, Christian feminists argued for the return to the egalitarian, prophetic character of Jesus' movement as the norm for gender relations in the contemporary Church. Many Christian feminists used the laws of ritual purity, which the **Pharisees** are portrayed as championing, as the source of the clearest contrast between oppressive Judaism and the liberating Jesus. They portrayed Jewish women as 'enslaved' in a 'dehumanising situation'; menstruating women were 'discriminated against, degraded, and dehumanised'. Ignorant of the mores of antiquity, they faulted Judaism for patriarchy rather than probed the mindset of distant cultures.

Among some feminists, another critique developed over claims that matriarchal cultures, in which goddesses were worshipped, held sway over the ancient Near East until monotheism – that is, patriarchal Judaism – arose. In its more virulent form this argument attributed the rise of violence and war to monotheistic religions; devotion to the 'jealous' and one God of the **Old Testament** fostered intolerance.

Such views reveal inattentiveness to anti-Judaism in the Christian tradition and its tragic consequences. Three rules of formation have governed feminist distortions of Judaism, according to the analysis of Katharina von Kellenbach (b. 1960): Judaism is the antithesis of Christianity; Christian theology makes Judaism a scapegoat, whether for the death of Jesus or of the goddess; and Judaism is a relic of the ancient work, mere prelude to the fulfilment Christianity reveals.

A burgeoning literature, often fashioned collaboratively by Christians and Jews, offers correctives to these distortions. A host of studies, primarily at the scholarly level, opens new perspectives on the purity laws, reframes Jewish and Christian laws about women, documents the survival of goddess worship beyond antiquity, situates Second Temple Judaism in the context of Greco-Roman patriarchy, critiques **New Testament** depictions of Jews, and analyses the anti-Judaism that often blights postcolonial and liberationist biblical scholarship.

Many of these scholars participate as well in Jewish–Christian **dialogue**. While men dominate the public face of interreligious dialogue in general, and of Jewish–Christian exchange in particular, women have made substantial, if often unacknowledged, contributions from its earliest days. In more recent years feminist scholarship, to which men also contribute but to a lesser extent, has become requisite for well-informed discourse between Jews and Christians.   *MARY C. BOYS*

Ferdinand II (1578–1637)

Holy Roman Emperor (1619–37), king of Bohemia and Hungary. A dedicated Catholic and enthusiastic supporter of the Counter-Reformation, Ferdinand tried to extinguish **Protestantism** by force, allying himself with Jews to help finance his extensive military campaigns during the Thirty Years War (1618–48). Ferdinand introduced the institution of **Court Jews** and after 1622 raised one of the first Jews to the nobility in modern times in the person of his financier Jacob Bassevi (1570/80–1634) of Prague. In 1630, however, he ordered Jews of Prague and Vienna to attend Christian sermons every Sunday.   *PETR FRYŠ*

Ferdinand the Catholic (1452–1516)

King of Aragon who expelled the Jews from Spain. Ferdinand II (V of Castile) inherited the lands of the Crown of Aragon, becoming king of Sicily in 1468, on the eve of his marriage to his cousin Isabella of Castile, and king of Aragon, Valencia, Majorca and Sardinia, as well as count of Catalonia, following the death of his father John II in 1474. The recovery of royal authority there and in Castile became his first priority and was extensively supported by Jewish and Converso courtiers, but severe measures against Jews and **Conversos** in Andalusia heralded a more drastic policy: the Jews were expelled from the southern cities in 1483, and the **Inquisition** began serious work against the Conversos in 1484. Breaking with the policies of previous Iberian rulers, Ferdinand and Isabella decreed the **expulsion** of all confessing Jews from their lands following their conquest of the last Muslim kingdom in **Spain**, Granada, in 1492. Both acts were seen as part of the recovery of Spain's Christian **identity**, and the king and queen fervently hoped that many Jews would convert rather than depart, as many did. Ferdinand later took credit for the expulsion, and it is wrong to insist, as many do, that it was Isabella's idea. Thus, following his conquest of Naples (1503) Ferdinand sought to expel the Jews from southern **Italy**, though this proved a slow process. Ferdinand, mindful of the revenues they produced, did not expel the Muslims from Valencia and Aragon, however, even though Isabella suppressed **Islam** in Castile. Ferdinand saw himself as a redeemer king who would lead his armies to **Jerusalem** and usher in the Last Days.   *DAVID ABULAFIA*

Film *see* **cinema and film**

Finaly Case

Controversy over the upbringing of two Jewish children after the Holocaust. Fritz Finaly (d. 1944) and his wife, from Vienna, fled the Nazis after the *Anschluss* and moved to Grenoble, where they had two boys. Shortly before the parents were deported in 1944, they entrusted the children's care to the municipal school. Both parents perished in the **Holocaust**. After the war, Finaly's surviving sister claimed the boys, but the Director of Grenoble's Municipal Children's Home obtained formal custody and arranged for the children's **conversion** to Catholicism. The case lasted five years, while the children were moved from one Catholic institution to another. French Catholics were divided over the affair, and in 1953 France's highest court rejected the claim of the municipality and delivered the children to their aunt, who took them to live in **Israel**.   *EDWARD KESSLER*

Flood/Flood story

Narrative in Gen. 6–9 showing broad parallels to similar tales from 68 cultures and stimulating important, though largely independent, theological developments in Judaism and Christianity. Despairing of humanity's development, God resolves to blot out all animal life from creation; yet **Noah** 'found favour in God's sight'. God's unilateral **covenant** with all living things, never again to destroy all life by a flood, is the first covenant (*berit*) named in the Bible.

The tale has invited Jewish reflection especially on the morality of both humans and God. The character of antediluvian sin, the anthropopathism of God's regret at creating humans, the injustice of dooming innocent animals, the relative virtue of Noah, and the moral imperative on postdiluvian humanity all garner attention in Jewish sources. The alternation in divine names, later taken as a key to source-critical analysis of J and E strands (*see* **Wellhausen, Julius**), in early **commentary** signifies the competing divine attributes of mercy and judgement. The moral obligations of non-Jews in the rabbinic view are summarised in the '**Noachide Laws**', binding on all humanity descended from Noah and contrasted with the Sinaitic law that is given to Israel. **Philo** allegorises the flood as both passion and the cleansing of the soul, the ark as the body, and Noah's journey as an escape from mundane existence.

New Testament writers refer to the inattention of the antediluvian generation and the **righteousness** of Noah, whose rescue is exemplary of God's justice. Noah is one of the models of faith in Hebrews (11.7), and **baptism** is seen as the antitype of the flood (1 Pet. 3.20f.). Later Christian writers, like their Jewish counterparts, develop Noah's righteousness along moral lines, but also extend the **typological** connection with baptism and beyond it. Every detail of the story finds a Christian application, so the ark represents the Church, which contains a wide variety of people portrayed by the diversity of the animals, including those impious who, like the raven, leave and never return. Noah is understood as a **Christ**-figure, representing the turn of ages. It has been suggested that the parallel drawn between the wood of the ark and of the **cross** may reflect the practice of *gematria* known also in rabbinic literature: the number 300, which is the length of the ark in cubits, is represented in Greek by the letter *tau*, which is shaped like a cross.

In modern **dialogue** emphasis has been given to the role of the Noachide Laws in determining a framework for Jewish–Christian relations and to the character of the **covenant**, bearing on both Jews and Christians. *PETER A. PETTIT*

Folklore

Folklore is an umbrella term referring to various forms of vernacular culture, including beliefs, customs, legends, **music**, popular rites, songs and drama. Historically, folklore was regarded sceptically by elites, who viewed it as primitive, and likened it to **magic** and superstition. Since the early nineteenth century (prompted initially by Romanticism's nostalgic reaction against rationalism and interest in the distinctive 'characteristics' of peoples) the folkloric has been positively re-evaluated as a legitimate mode of cultural expression. Today folklore is recognised as a significant *locus* of Jewish–Christian relations.

Medieval European Christian folklore has long been identified as a vehicle for anti-Jewish prejudice. Phenomena such as the **Wandering Jew** legend and the cults surrounding **blood libel** 'martyrs' attest to a popular antagonism going beyond that officially sanctioned by Church authorities.

But a study of folklore can also challenge assumptions about the nature of Jewish–Christian relations during this period. For example, many Ashkenazi customs surrounding lifecycle events (e.g. glass-smashing at **weddings**, the holding of a vigil to protect a child from evil spirits on the night before **circumcision**) have their equivalents – perhaps their origins – in popular Christian practices, indicating that ordinary Jews and Christians did not live in total isolation from each other.

Nazism drew on anti-Jewish folklore, hence folklore has attracted the attention of **dialogue** and other activists. In 2001 the Dutch **Council of Christians and Jews** campaigned to end the public singing of anti-Jewish songs at **Easter** festivities in Ootmarsum; the Anti-Defamation League has focused on the presentation of Jews in Oberammergau's **Passion Play**. *MELANIE J. WRIGHT*

Food

Judaism's influence in the matter of food in Christianity is not as simple as might appear from Mark 7.19, which interprets **Jesus**' words as 'declaring all foods clean'. The **New Testament** itself indicates some continuing effect of *kashrut* (Jewish rules concerning what foods may be eaten and how food is prepared): first, at the apostolic council in Acts the eating of **blood** and things strangled was prohibited (15.20–29); secondly, epistle references indicate that Jewish dietary customs persisted in some circles (Col. 2.16–23; 1 Tim. 4.3); thirdly, the Jewish interdiction on idol food remained (Acts 15.29; Rev. 2.14, 20). A related problem in early Jewish–Christian relations was table fellowship, a factor at work in the **Antioch** incident at Gal. 2.11–14. Proto-orthodox Christianity viewed *kashrut* as one of many 'types' pointing to **Christ** and **allegorised** the Leviticus **dietary laws** (*Barn.* 10), something already done in **Alexandrian** Judaism (Ps-Aristeas, **Philo**), but in the latter case literal observance still applied; for Christians it generally did not. Yet apparently some early Christians were so affected by Jewish sectarian customs (Essene? Nazarite? Theraputae?) that they abstained from meat and/or **wine**, even to the point of celebrating the **eucharist** with water, though some see pagan influence here (McGowan, *Ascetic Eucharists*). The eucharist observance itself involves some **halakhic** elements, specifically the 'decorous liturgical order' common in Jewish *havura*-meals (Tomson, *Paul and the Jewish Law*, 140). In the **early Church**'s so-called paschal controversies one group evidently celebrated a memorial eucharist but once a year on Nisan 14 (Petersen, 'Eusebius'; cf. 1 Cor. 5.7). Thus labelled the **Quartodecimans**, they were castigated by their coreligionists for '**Judaising**'. **Jehovah's Witnesses** and **Seventh-Day Adventists** observe some of these customs. *FRANK SHAW*

Forgiveness

In considering the issue of forgiveness in the context of Jewish–Christian relations, it is appropriate to begin by noting the familiar caricature that the '**Old Testament**' God is a God of vengeance and retribution, while the '**New Testament**' God is a God of love and forgiveness. The reality is that even as the Hebrew scriptures depict God as just and zealous in exacting expectations of human obedience, at the same time God is understood to be merciful and forgiving of human shortcomings. Representative of numerous statements to that effect are the words of Exod. 34.6ff. which later Jewish tradition came to understand as 'the thirteen attributes of God', 'The Lord, the Lord a God compassionate and gracious, slow to anger, abounding in kindness and faithfulness. Extending kindness to the thousandth generation, forgiving iniquity, transgression and sin.' The theme of God's mercy and even eagerness to forgive underlies much of the prophets' chastisement of the people and their calls for the people to change their behaviour. The salience of God's forgiveness is the theme of the book of Jonah and is the reason that the rabbis included the reading of that book in the afternoon service of Yom Kippur/the **Day of Atonement**.

If forgiveness is understood as one of the essential attributes of God, it is no less felt to be a *desideratum* for human conduct. Perhaps one of the most powerful scenes of forgiveness and reconciliation in all literature is the depiction of **Joseph** disclosing himself to his brothers in Gen. 45. Forgiveness is enjoined explicitly in many places in the Hebrew scriptures (e.g. Lev. 19.17; Prov. 25.21).

The theme of forgiveness is carried on in both the Jewish and Christian traditions. The rabbis, rendering explicit what is implicit in the scriptures, teach that God (like human beings) has two natures. On the one hand, God is capable of judgement: rewarding and punishing human beings in exact recompense for their actions. On the other, God has the capacity and impulse to treat human beings with mercy, to forgive them their shortcomings and take

them back in love. In a powerful image one of the rabbis tells of discovering that God actually engages in prayer. When his colleagues inquired 'What can God pray for?', he replied, 'God says, "may My mercy suppress My anger, and that My mercy may prevail over My [other] attributes, so that I may deal with My children in the attribute of mercy, and on their behalf, stop short of the limit of strict judgment"' (*b. Berakhot* 7a).

In the **liturgy** of Yom Kippur the rabbis repeatedly depict God as 'eager to forgive', if only people performed *teshuvah* (*see* **atonement**), turned from their wicked ways and returned to God. In many tales told by the rabbis God is depicted as the parent of an errant child who sends messengers to beseech the child to return: 'come part way back to me and I will come the rest of the way to you'. That same theme is sounded in the New Testament. In the two versions of the **Lord's Prayer** God is called upon to 'forgive us our debts as we have forgiven our debtors' (Matt. 6.12) and, perhaps more germane to the issue at hand, 'forgive us our sins' (Luke 11.4). Indeed, the **parable** of the prodigal son (Luke 15.11–32) is very much in the rabbinic mould of parents eager to take back in love their children who have gone astray.

By the same token, people are required to forgive one another. If the ultimate human good is *imitatio dei*, then as we expect to be forgiven by God so must we forgive those who wrong us. This idea finds explicit articulation in the **Apocrypha**: 'forgive your neighbour his wrongdoing. Then when you pray, your sins will be forgiven' (Sir. 28.2). In delineating the process for *teshuvah*, the rabbis assert that, when someone comes to you and confesses the wrong they have done to you and makes atonement, you are required to forgive them. The rabbis call one who withholds such forgiveness 'cruel'. Indeed, they state that you must not only forgive the person who has wronged you, but you must also pray that God will forgive them too. The same injunction to forgive one another is expressed in the New Testament in more absolute and extreme terms. **Jesus** is repeatedly depicted as preaching the need to forgive one another. In Matt. 5.39 Jesus says, 'if any one strikes you on the right cheek, turn to him the other also', and a few verses later makes explicit the ideology that underlies this injunction, 'love your enemies and pray for those who persecute you' (Matt. 5.44). In the **Sermon on the Mount** Jesus makes clear the theological underpinning of this teaching: 'be merciful as your Father is merciful' (Luke 6.36). As he is being crucified Jesus is presented as embodying the quality of forgiveness when he says, 'Father forgive them, they know not what they do' (Luke 23.34). Such teaching may be regarded as representing an extreme version of the normative teaching about forgiveness of the Judaism of Jesus' time, but it does not constitute a break with it.

Where the Gospel traditions' depiction of Jesus does break with conventional Jewish teaching is in those instances where Jesus is represented as asserting that he himself had the authority to forgive sins – as in Matt. 9.2–6, Mark 2.5–11 and Luke 5.20–24: 'the Son of Man has the authority on earth to forgive sins'. In John 20.21–23, in his post-**Resurrection** appearance to the disciples in the upper room, Jesus is depicted as passing the authority to forgive sins to them, and implicitly to the Church which they represent: 'as the Father has sent me, even so I send you . . . If you forgive the sins of any, they are forgiven.' This is a perspective without antecedent in biblical or Jewish teaching, where no individual has the power to offer forgiveness to others.

One cannot conclude a discussion of the issue of forgiveness in the context of the Jewish–Christian encounter without noting that in recent years, as Jews and Christians have engaged in ever deeper conversations, the challenge has grown about what to make of 2,000 years of conflict and especially the tragic events of the **Holocaust**. The Catholic Church and various Protestant bodies, most prominently the **Lutheran** Church, have voiced **repentance** for the 'teaching of contempt' that has, over the centuries, resulted in violence against the Jews, but both Jewish and Christian writers have asked whether Christian bodies have sufficiently acknowledged the extent of their involvement. Conversely, Christian expressions of atonement present the Jewish community with a dilemma. Though instrumentalities exist to make atonement and to ask forgiveness, Jewish participants in the **dialogue** assert that no reciprocal mechanism exists in the Jewish community to grant forgiveness. Even more complicated is the ethical issue: is an assemblage of individuals in a position to grant forgiveness for wrongs not done directly to them? Put succinctly, who can forgive on behalf of the victims?

This issue will continue to play a significant role in the dialogue. DANIEL POLISH

Fourth Lateran Council *see* **Lateran Council (IV)**

France

From the **Roman** period until the present Jews have lived in France, which currently hosts Europe's largest Jewish community (600,000). The first documented community, in 465, was located in Brittany. At that time the Council of Vannes prohibited Christian clergy from taking their meals with Jews (thus suggesting good social relations between Jews and Christians). At other provincial councils bishops adopted measures to separate Jews and Christians and to mark the inferiority of the former, a tendency reinforced by **Agobard**, who condemned Christians for celebrating the **Sabbath** with Jews. During the eighth century Jews were active in commerce and medicine, and the Carolingian emperors allowed them to become accredited purveyors in the imperial court and involved in agriculture and especially viticulture, which they dominated, even providing wine for mass.

The **Crusades** had comparatively little effect on the Jews of France, but were followed by a long period of persecution. In some cities, such as Beziers, Jews were forced to pay a special tax every Palm Sunday. In Toulouse Jewish representatives had to go to the cathedral on a weekly basis to have their ears boxed, and France's first **blood libel** charge occurred in Blois in 1171 when 31 Jews, having rejected **baptism**, were burned at the stake. The cathedral of Notre Dame in Strasbourg, with its two statues, **Ecclesia and Synagoga** (*c*.1230), demonstrates the traditional *Adversus Judaeos* approach.

The situation worsened during the rule of King Philip Augustus (*r*.1180–1223), who imprisoned all Jews in his lands and demanded a ransom for their release. In 1215 the Fourth **Lateran Council** forced Jews to wear a badge in the provinces of Languedoc, Normandy and Provence (*see* **yellow badge**). In 1240 Jews were expelled from Brittany, and numerous **disputations** and anti-Jewish tracts were published. A notorious **Talmud trial** took place in Paris and 24 cartloads of the **Talmud** were burned in 1242, marking the decline in northern France of talmudic study, which had been built up by scholars such as **Rashi**. Violence against Jews culminated in their definitive **expulsion** from France in 1394, but the Jews of Avignon and Comtat Venaissin were spared a similar fate by papal intervention. Indeed the Jewish communities in that region were known as 'the Pope's Jews' and flourished.

From the 1500s **Marranos** settled in France, followed by Jews from **Poland** and **Ukraine** fleeing the Chmeilnicki massacres of 1648. Anti-Jewish laws began to be repealed in the 1780s, and the French Revolution granted Jews citizenship as individuals while depriving them of their group privileges. **Voltaire** called for religious tolerance but also described Jews in ways that suggested they had innate negative qualities. **Napoleon** considered the Jews 'a nation within a nation' and decided to create a Jewish communal structure sanctioned by the state, ordering the convening of a Grand **Sanhedrin** which paved the way for the formation of the consistorial system, making Judaism a recognised religion under government control.

While the situation improved for Jews thereafter, the 1840 Damascus Affair, which was one of the latest examples of the **blood libel** charge, led to outbreaks of anti-Jewish disorder in 1848. An upsurge of **antisemitism** began in the late 1800s, and Jews were blamed for the collapse of the Union Générale, a leading Catholic bank. The **Dreyfus affair** took place against this background, motivating Theodor **Herzl** to write his book *The Jewish State* in 1896 and Emile Zola (1840–1902) his article *J'accuse . . . !* and eventually led to the 1905 law separating **Church and state**.

When **Germany** invaded on 10 May 1940 an estimated 300,000 Jews lived in France. Twenty-five per cent perished in the **Holocaust**, a significantly lower proportion than in other European countries. France became a haven for postwar refugees, and within 25 years its Jewish population tripled. In 1948 the Amitié Judéo-Chrétienne was founded with the aim of improving relations between Christians and Jews, but the **Finaly Case** demonstrated ongoing obstacles, as did Jean-Paul Sartre's (1905–80) influential book *Anti-Semite and Jew*, in which he wrote that antisemitism 'derives not from thought but from fear of oneself and of truth . . . In a word, anti-Semitism is fear of being alive.' Nevertheless, individual figures such as Jules **Isaac** made a significant contribution to fostering better relations between Jews and Christians, and since 1965 and the publication of *Nostra Aetate* the Catholic Church in France has been at the forefront of con-

demning antisemitism. In 1997 the French bishops issued a 'declaration of repentance' for Catholic failings during the Holocaust. The Jewish community is currently facing growing antisemitism, notably among some French Muslims, stimulated in part by the increasing violence in the Middle East since 2002.   *EDWARD KESSLER*

Franciscans

Roman Catholic missionary order founded (1209) by St Francis of Assisi (1181/2–1226) which formerly promoted Christian **anti-Judaism**. From 1232 the Franciscan Order, based on poverty, **preaching** and mendicancy, was entrusted, together with the **Dominicans**, by Pope **Gregory IX** with the task of rooting out **heresy** (considered to be treason against God) by inquisitors. Like Dominicans, Franciscan friars were specifically trained for controversy with Jews and Muslims, studying **Hebrew**, Arabic and rabbinic **commentaries**, and having influence within universities. Mendicant friars, including apostate Jews such as Nicholas **Donin**, led Church denunciation of the **Talmud**. The papal bull *Turbato corde*, issued in 1267 by Clement IV and reissued by later popes, gave Franciscan and Dominican inquisitors permanent permission to use ecclesiastical punishment and the secular arm against Christian heretics, converted Jews who reverted to Judaism and their Jewish accomplices. The first Franciscan pope, Nicholas IV (1288–92), was stridently anti-Jewish, legislating that forcibly converted Jews who reverted were equivalent to heretics and that archbishops and bishops should aid the **Inquisition**. The Spanish Inquisition itself was founded by a Franciscan, **Alonso de Espina**, who wrote *Fortalitium fidei* ('Fortress of the Faith'), an influential treatise against the 'Jewish heresy' which urged **expulsion** of Jews.

A key Franciscan aim was to convert Jews. Nicholas of **Lyra** used his vast knowledge of rabbinic commentaries, including **Rashi**, to promote understanding of the literal biblical sense and to attempt methodically to convert Jews. Aggressively conversionist sermons were promoted, promulgated by the papal bull *Vineam sorec* in 1278 and forced compulsorily on many Jewish communities.

Virulently anti-Jewish sermons, like those of Berthold of Regensburg (before 1210–72), who claimed that Jews awaited **Antichrist** and were the **devil**'s allies, were matched by aggressive political policies, such as Duns Scotus's (*c*.1265–1308) urging the kidnap and forcible **conversion** of Jewish children. Such views hardened in the late fourteenth century due to internal pressures for reform and increasing opposition to Christian impoverishment attributed to Jewish moneylenders, especially in **Italy**.

The Order promoted implementation of all canonical anti-Jewish legislation, including segregation, wearing the Jewish badge (*see* **yellow badge**) and economic restrictions. Fiercely anti-Jewish sermons by Bernardino di Siena (1380–1444) typically conjured a vision of Christendom endangered, even destroyed, by poverty due to Jewish **usury** and the poison of Jewish influence. Such sermons to mass audiences, like those of St John of Capistrano (1386–1456), and St Bernardino da Feltre (second half of the fifteenth century), promoted and achieved expulsion of Jews from Italian and North European cities. In consequence of Franciscan anti-Jewish agitation, Jews were violently persecuted, as during allegations of the **blood libel** (Breslau, 1453 under Capistrano) and **host desecration** (Trent, 1475 under da Feltre), following which many Jews were tortured and executed, often by burning. While one or two Franciscans converted to Judaism, and **mysticism** within medieval Spanish Jewry was possibly influenced by the Spiritual Franciscans, several apostate Jews became Franciscans and expert anti-Jewish agitators.

In the modern period Franciscans, like Dominicans, abandoned any anti-Judaic agenda, and some Franciscan religious courageously saved Jews during the *Shoah*. In **Israel** the Franciscans, established in **Jerusalem** since 1229, are Custodians of the Christian Holy Places.

MARGARET BREARLEY

Frank, Anne (1929–45)

Teenage diarist. In 1942 the Frank family, including schoolgirl Anne, hid from Nazi persecution in an Amsterdam office building. Assisted by Christians, they survived until discovery in 1944. Anne went (via Westerbork and **Auschwitz**) to Belsen, where she died (March 1945). She is remembered for her diary, begun in 1942, and revised by her in anticipation of publication, following a radio appeal for people to record their wartime experiences for posterity. Its contents, reception and the development of Anne as a symbol of Jewish suffering in the **Holocaust** are relevant to Jewish–Christian relations.

The diary is a complex work, detailing the routine events and strains of life in hiding as much as more profound matters. It reflects Anne's upbringing in an assimilated Jewish family: she observes **Hanukkah** and **Christmas**, reads the **New Testament** and stresses the value of the individual's conscience. But Anne also rejects **conversion** to Christianity. She believes in God, and in a form of Jewish **chosenness** and **mission**. She locates her experiences within a broader history of Jewish persecution. *MELANIE J. WRIGHT*

Frank, Jacob (1726–91)

Polish Jewish religious leader and Messianic claimant. After travelling through Turkey, the heartland of Shabbetaianism (*see* **Shabbetai Zvi**), he returned (*c*.1755) home to Podolia (then in Poland, now in Ukraine) and gathered a following from local sectarian circles of the same origin. After 1763 he selected 12 apostles and assumed the role of the **Messiah**. Seeing Christianity as a transition stage on the way towards the future 'Messianic religion', he led his followers into **baptism**. Rejecting **Talmud** and claiming to find the doctrine of the **Trinity** in Kabbalah (*see* **mysticism**), the movement was originally accepted and supported by Christian political and religious leaders in Poland, Moravia and Germany as a disseminator of Christianity among Jews, but was eventually recognised as a sect. After 1816 Frankists were absorbed into the Roman Catholic Church. *PETR FRYŠ*

Frederick II of Babenberg (*c*.1210–46)

'The Quarrelsome'; last duke of the Babenberg dynasty in **Austria** (*r*.1230–46). In his struggle with Emperor Frederick II of Hohenstaufen (*r*.1215–50), he took both sympathetic and unsympathetic measures towards Jews: he secured himself the support of the citizens of Wiener-Neustadt by barring Jews from office, but in his famous charter from 1244 benevolently regulated the position of Jews, subjecting them directly to his own ducal, rather than imperial jurisdiction. The charter secured fair transit, trading and moneylending conditions, allowed some self-government, raised the value of Jewish oaths and protected Jewish children, synagogues and cemeteries. For almost two centuries similar charters in **Hungary, Poland,**

Bohemia and Silesia (*see* **Czechia**) were based on it.   *PETR FRYŠ*

Free will

When Aquinas wrote, 'Man has free choice, or otherwise counsels, exhortations, commands would be in vain' (*Summa* 1a, 83.a.1), he affirms the common view of both Jewish and Christian traditions that humanity has the capacity and obligation freely to do good and avoid evil, to love God and to exercise religious and moral responsibility. Neither religion is compatible with a strong deterministic denial of human freedom. But both are uncertain about how to reconcile freedom with divine foreknowledge – 'everything is foreseen, but freedom of choice is given' (*Avot* 3.15) identifies the tension rather than the solution – and about the impact of external and internal factors on our freedom. But the distinctive religious difference is that most Western Christian thinking on free will is shaped by **Augustine**'s analysis of the impact of **original sin** on our nature and his later pessimism that the human will is so impaired that only with the help of divine **grace** can the goal of achieved freedom be reached. For Augustine, if **evil** does not come from God, it must originate in and subsequently affect, the exercise of creaturely free will. Jewish thought sees no need to develop such explanatory, causal accounts, but is no less attentive to the problematics of human freedom.   *JOHN MCDADE*

French literature *see* literature, French

Freud, Sigmund (1856–1939)

Founder of psychoanalysis. A neurologist of Jewish origins, Freud is remembered for his studies of the unconscious mind and the motivations, desires and conflicts underpinning human behaviour. Judaism and Christianity were for him objects of critical enquiry. Freud likened religious rites to the obsessional behaviours of psychiatric patients, linking both to the repression of the sexual (or other self-seeking) instincts. He also deconstructed the founding narratives of both religions. Freud's career was overshadowed by **antisemitism**. The Nazis burned his books; he criticised Christian failure to intervene on behalf of Jews, which, he argued, contradicted any claim to practise love of enemies.   *MELANIE J. WRIGHT*

Fundamentalism

Although the term 'fundamentalism' is commonly associated with **Protestant** Christianity, there are similar religious movements within both **Roman** **Catholicism** and Judaism, some forms of which have increasing cross-religious links. Protestant, Catholic, and Jewish 'fundamentalism' is growing alongside similar movements in other world religions like **Islam** and Hinduism.

Protestant fundamentalism began in the **United States** during the 1830s and 1840s, and is rooted in Christian **millenarianism**. However, its greatest growth was in the early twentieth century. In 1902 the American Bible League issued 'The Fundamentals', 12 theological affirmations including the **Virgin Birth**, the Bible's inerrancy, the Second Coming of **Jesus**, and the **resurrection** and **atonement** of Jesus. Both Jewish and Christian fundamentalists reject modern scriptural criticism, particularly the documentary theory of biblical scholarship. Fundamentalists generally reject the Darwinian concept of human evolution, as well as **abortion** and euthanasia. In recent years American Christian and Jewish fundamentalist leaders, sometimes working together, have advocated a broad public policy agenda that opposes the strict separation of **Church and state** and 'secular **humanism**', a pejorative term used to describe opponents of fundamentalism. Once belittled by modernists, Protestant fundamentalism remains a major force within Christianity, especially among newly emerging Christian communities in Asia, South America and Africa.

There is also a form of Catholic fundamentalism, although it frequently bears the name 'traditional Catholicism', which affirms the centrality and authority of the **priest** and a diminution of the laity's recent involvement in Church governance, education and ritual. At its core traditional Catholicism seeks either the reversal or the elimination of many of the liturgical, educational and theological reforms adopted at **Vatican II**, including the *Nostra Aetate* Declaration that decried 'all forms of antiSemitism' and rejected the **deicide** charge against the Jewish people.

Jewish fundamentalists generally focus on issues related to the land and **State of Israel** and the City of **Jerusalem**. Such Jews are called *haredim*, or the 'trembling fearful ones'. In recent years they have emerged as a significant political and religious force within Israel as well as in the **Diaspora**. The *haredim* not only affirm the literal truth of the **Hebrew Bible**, but seek to impose many biblical and talmudic laws and ordinances, the *halakhah*, upon the modern State of Israel in key areas of life including education, medicine, food, transportation, law, the arts and government. Some *haredim* and other like-minded Jews, both within and outside Israel, have joined with Christian fundamentalists in calling for the erection of Judaism's Third Holy Temple in Jerusalem. Christian allies of the *haredim* believe the creation of the Jewish state in 1948 and the yet-to-be-built Third Temple are theological prerequisites for the Second Coming of Jesus. Some of these same fundamentalists also actively seek the **conversion** of Jews to Christianity.   *A. JAMES RUDIN*

GGGG

Gamaliel

Biblical character (Num. 1–10), also name of six rabbinic authorities, one of which is Rabban G. ha-Zaken ('the Elder') (first century CE), the (grand?) son of Hillel (end of first century BCE and beginning of first century CE), who is known for his *takkanot* (**halakhic** decrees), which were 'for the benefit of humanity' (*Gittin* 4.2f.). Acts 5.34 describes him as 'respected by all the people', and according to Acts 22.3 he was the teacher of **Paul**. In *Ps.-Clem.* 1.65 it is stated that he 'was secretly our brother in the faith [i.e. a Christian], but by our advice remained among them [i.e. the Jews]'. For a Jewish obituary, see *Sotah* 9.15.   *JESPER SVARTVIK*

Geiger, Abraham (1810–74)

Leading German Reform rabbi and scholar born into a distinguished family in Frankfurt. Throughout his career Geiger protested against and sought to correct Christian views of Judaism. He was a founder member of the Academy for the Scientific Study of Judaism (*see* **Wissenschaft des Judentums**), which was established in Berlin in 1872 and which he directed until his death. His collection of essays on Jewish history (*Das Judentum und seine Geschichte*, 1864) contains three that focus on **Jesus** and his disciples, reflecting a developing interest among some nineteenth-century Jews in Jesus in the context of Jewish **ethics**. For Geiger, Jesus was a Pharisaic Messianic claimant who generally affirmed the **Law** but whose lack of interest in material life and the joys of the world distinguished him from mainstream Pharisaism. He denied that Jesus taught anything original. A principle lying behind much of Geiger's work was a concern to challenge the contemporary Christian view of Christianity as the fulfilment of a flawed Judaism. Geiger argued that it should rather be seen as a tangential offshoot, and that the quest of Protestant scholars to uncover the **historical Jesus** would reveal that the beliefs of the founding figure of Christianity were essentially Jewish in nature. In this way he used

Jesus as a means by which to nullify **anti-Judaism** among Christian scholars. At the same time, the recognition of Jesus as a Pharisee would, he hoped, prevent Jewish **conversion** to Christianity, for the **Pharisees** had been a liberalising force and were, he argued, the spiritual ancestors of modern **Reform Judaism**.   *DANIEL R. LANGTON*

Gender *see* feminism and feminist writings

Germany

Until the late nineteenth century 'Germany' consisted of many states and principalities, and the nature of 'German' Jewish–Christian relations is thus difficult to define. While 'Germany' can loosely apply to all the German-speaking lands, following the **Enlightenment** it most commonly referred to the German-speaking territories caught up in the struggle between the Austro-Hungarian Empire and Prussia (thus not including **Switzerland**). Since 1945 the term is no longer used for the territories which the victorious Allies granted to other states, notably **Austria**.

The first Jewish presence in German lands is mentioned in records dating around 321 CE. Jews came in the wake of the Romans and settled in particular in Rhineland cities such as Cologne and Mainz. The Christianisation of the Empire put Jews in the precarious situation of a religious and economic **minority**. In the early Middle Ages Jews were not restricted in terms of their economic activity and could be found in all professions, even agriculture. Jews were under the protection of the emperors, a protection that was particularly valuable in the face of mob violence and **pogroms**. Valued economically by the ruling classes, Jews enjoyed privileges in cities, since their economic prosperity was seen as enhancing the value of the city as a whole. However, the local population did not always react favourably, and **expulsions** were not unheard of even before the **Crusades**, the first taking place in 1012 in Mainz.

The Crusades further altered the relationship between Christians and Jews in German lands. Now mob violence inspired by Christian **preaching** prevailed, and Jews in cities increasingly suffered. In terms of economic relations with the Christian population, Jews were increasingly expelled from the guilds and therefore found their professional opportunities diminished. With the Church prohibiting Christians from engaging in **usury**, this and pawnbroking became the main occupation of Jews, although they also continued to be involved in trade and even agriculture in a minor way. The Second Crusade, launched in 1146, saw the Jews seeking direct protection in castles and other property of the nobility until mob violence, inspired by local preachers, had passed. Yet, while Jews largely remained under the protection of the nobility, Church legislation of the Fourth **Lateran Council** in 1215 required them to wear a **yellow badge**, the so-called 'Jew badge', and 1235 saw Germany's first **blood libel** case, in the city of Fulda. From then onwards, the history of Jewish–Christian relations in Germany was primarily characterised by widespread expulsions, continuing until the fifteenth century. These signalled the social decline of the Jewish communities in Germany, moving the centre of Jewish life in Europe further to the east (see **Poland**, **Hungary**). However, while the history of expulsions had a negative impact on Jewish–Christian relations, the economic position of Jews in Germany improved. Increasing international trade offered Jewish traders the opportunity to break away from almost exclusive occupation with moneylending to engage in wholesale and act as welcome middlemen between Christian merchants.

Only with the **Reformation** did a more positive attitude among the majority Christian population come to bear on Jewish–Christian relations in Germany. The **humanist** tradition, in particular, emphasised the enduring qualities of Jewish religious teaching and took up **Hebrew** in the canon of scholarly languages along with **Greek** and **Latin**. The ensuing religious wars did also bring forth anti-Jewish violence, not least inspired by **Luther**'s tractate *On the Jews and their Lies* (1543), but smaller **philosemitic** Christian reform movements, such as the **Anabaptists**, fostered good relations with Jews. **Modernity** and the Enlightenment equalised the civil status of Jews with that of their Christian fellow citizens, but since this move was enforced by **Napoleon** it was reversed after his defeat. The German national revolution of 1848 reversed this development again, and with the founding of the German Reich in 1871 Jews gained equal rights of citizenship.

Jewish–Christian relations gained renewed religious importance to Christians with the Enlightenment and the Jewish **emancipation** in the eighteenth century. Poets such as **Lessing** were inspired by written exchanges between J. K. Lavater (1741–1801) and Moses **Mendelssohn**, the most significant play in this respect being Lessing's *Nathan the Wise* which propagates the equality of all religions. Many Jews sought equality in Christian society through **baptism**, the aim often being **assimilation**. Others, such as the poet **Heine**, saw their baptismal certificate as an 'entry ticket to European culture' and combined it with fervent social criticism of the 'enlightened' society which needed such validation of individuals. Jewish emancipation and the Jewish Enlightenment, Haskalah, also brought about a fragmentation of Jewish religious life, resulting in the establishment of an Orthodox and a Reform movement in Germany. With the emergence of the Christian scholarly movement **Wissenschaft des Judentums** at the end of the nineteenth and beginning of the twentieth century, Jews and Christians became embroiled in a struggle about the interpretation of Jewish history during biblical times and after. If for a while the emergence of chairs in Jewish studies at German universities appeared to offer Jews equal opportunities to Christians in teaching Judaism from a religious and historical perspective, the hopes placed on these developments were not fulfilled: since the chairs were mostly established in Christian theological faculties, Jews were often prevented from taking them up. Yet, inspired and led by people such as **Rosenzweig**, **Buber** and Hans Joachim Schoeps (1909–80), Jewish–Christian dialogues began to take place face to face in the Frankfurter Lehrhaus with Buber and in writing in the journal *Der Jude*, edited by Buber.

The advent of **Nazism** and the **Holocaust** destroyed many of the hopes of German Jews for a secure and equal future in Germany based on the insights of the Enlightenment and consistent with the burgeoning Jewish–Christian **dialogue**. Already during the Weimar Republic (1919–33) the dialogue movement had been disrupted by increasing popular and political **antisemitism**, in which the Christian participants in the dialogues were often implicated. However, in the Federal Republic of Germany, founded in 1949, a number of local Societies for Christian–Jewish Co-operation (Gesellschaften für christlich-jüdische Zusammenarbeit) were instituted by the American Allied Forces. While these endeavours proved controversial and gained little support from the German population, attitudes changed in the 1950s when Germans took over their leadership. Christians and Jews in Germany began to make contact with each other on their own terms, and the work of the societies continues in the present. In particular since the 1960s, Christian–Jewish conversations have taken on a much more public form. The institutional Churches, Catholic and Protestant alike, have made considerable efforts to initiate conversations with Jews, and these have prompted the establishment of institutions dedicated to Christian–Jewish conversations, such as the Martin Buber Haus in Heppenheim and the Hedwig Dransfeld Haus in Bendorf. With the Jewish community in Germany growing since the 1990s and thus establishing a more confident public presence, not least through the building of new synagogues and community centres, Christian–Jewish conversations after the Holocaust have entered a new phase, drawing on the resources of Christians and Jews who feel equally at home in Germany.

See also **Confessing Church**; **Hitler, Adolf**; **literature, German**; **Rhineland Synod**

K. HANNAH HOLTSCHNEIDER

Ghetto

Technically, the first ghetto was decreed in 1516 when Venice conditioned permanent Jewish residence on Jews living apart from the majority Christian population (the name *ghetto* comes from that of the island where Jews were ordered to live). Previously, **Spain** and German cities had fixed areas of Jewish residence, but none was as regulated as in Venice and, subsequently, elsewhere in **Italy**. The ghetto era truly began in 1555, when Pope Paul IV (1555–9) established a ghetto in Rome. In the succeeding 80 years ghettos appeared throughout Italy; the last, however, in Correggio (Reggio Emiglia), was decreed only in the 1760s.

Paul IV aimed at converting Jews through separation and restriction, viewing the ghetto as a social and cultural limbo which also guarded Christian purity. In 1873, three years after the Roman ghetto's

demise, **Pius IX** complained that Jews were 'barking' throughout the city, a limitless urban defilement reminiscent of the kind of noise pollution medievals said came from the 'barking' that substituted prayer in the synagogues; dogs were also a classic image applied to Jews accused of profaning the **eucharist** or 'sucking blood' by taking interest. Italian ghettos beyond the Papal State represented state acquiescence to a new, papally determined equilibrium. The old Jewish status of 'regulated, but free to roam' the medieval city did not suit the defensive post-Reformation papal strategy, let alone the Papal State itself.

Jews saw the ghetto as Jewish '**sacred space**', to be self-governed through institutions based on consensus, particularly a system of voluntary arbitration. In Rome Jewish notaries, at once rabbis and writing in Hebrew, created effective tools that made this system work. Some Jews preferred enclosure, and even celebrated a '**Purim**' in thanksgiving. In fact, ghettos were no salvation. Ghettoised Jews faced conversionary pressures and grave economic crises, especially in Rome. Crowding, bad sanitation but especially poverty grew geometrically. The historian of Rome, Ferdinand Gregorovius (1821–91), empathetically details this mid-nineteenth-century squalor.

The term 'ghetto' has been used in the twentieth century to apply to poor urban neighbourhoods, regardless of their residents' identity, but also to places like the Warsaw Ghetto established by the Nazis as holding areas prior to transporting Jews to extermination camps like **Auschwitz**.

See also **Pale of Settlement**   *KENNETH STOW*

Gnosticism

Gnosticism is a modern term coined from the ancient Greek word for knowledge, *gnosis*. Ancient 'Gnostics' would not have used this term as part of their religious self-description. The term 'Gnosticism' does not refer to a single ancient religious movement; rather it describes a set of theological ideas taught by a variety of ancient religious teachers, each of whom filtered them through their own personal religious vision.

Gnosticism was built upon a radicalised Platonism in which Plato's contrast between the superior intelligible world and the world of more or less neutral material reality is reread as a cosmic conflict between good and evil. Gnosticism is, thus, fundamentally dualist. The intelligible, or spiritual, world is the true home of all human beings. Through a massive deception, human spirits have become trapped in bodies. The physical world is the *locus* of **evil** and the enemy of spirit, and the only way to escape from this plight is to receive specialised revealed knowledge from a Gnostic teacher.

Modern understanding of the exact content of this knowledge is limited because it tends to have been passed verbally rather than in written form. However, scholarly understanding of Gnosticism was significantly enhanced during the twentieth century with the discovery of important textual records such as the dramatic find at Nag Hamadi in 1945. Because so much surviving Gnostic source material builds upon Christian themes, some scholars have suggested that Gnosticism actually originated within Christianity. Other scholars, citing the preoccupation of the Nag Hamadi literature with biblical figures like **Adam**, **Eve**, Enoch, **Melchizedek** and Sophia (**wisdom**), argue that the ultimate sources of Gnosticism lie in Alexandrian Judaism and that reference to the *minim* may at times indicate the presence of heretical Jewish Gnostics as opposed to Christians. Still others argue that Gnosticism was a religious movement broader than both traditions.

Whatever its origins, Gnosticism impacted emerging Christianity far more forcefully than it did emerging **Rabbinic Judaism**. Paul's tendency to distinguish sharply between the spirit of the **law** and the letter of the law lent itself readily to Gnostic interpretation. **Marcion**, seen by many as a Christian Gnostic, rejected all of the Bible and accepted only **Paul** as an authentic witness to the truth of Christ. Paul's desire to include the Gentiles in the Church, seemingly at the expense of ethnic **Israel**, was part of the engine powering the separation of Judaism and Christianity. Rabbinic commitment to **holiness** laws and to separation from Gentiles may have shielded Judaism from the Gnosticism that affected Christianity in the second and third centuries. Responding to the growing influence of Gnostic teachers (e.g. Valentinus (d. 160)), Christian theologians like **Irenaeus of Lyons** were forced to defend vigorously the integrity of the whole Bible and to argue that Gnostic celebration of spirit at the expense of body must be rejected. However, the frequent repetition of anti-Gnostic arguments in early Christian literature testifies to the magnitude of the challenge.   *JOHN J. O'KEEFE*

God

Contemporary Jewish–Christian **dialogue** began on modern terms. In the fashion of liberal religionists in eighteenth- and nineteenth-century Germany, the authors of post-Second World War dialogue assumed that theology is a private matter. With memories of modern Europe's religious wars and medieval Europe's religious **polemics**, they assumed that, when Jews and Christians talk about their intimate beliefs about God, the results are interminable debate and disagreement, which can even grow into hatred and violence. To avoid such results, contemporary dialogue was built on non-theological foundations: on talk about social ethics and about hopefully shared criticisms of religious **particularism** and shared visions of peace and understanding.

In the last two decades, however, Jewish–Christian dialogue has begun a new era of theological exchange. Recent discussants believe there is a third pathway to dialogue that reproduces neither the religious exclusivism of medieval debates nor the atheological **universalism** of modern times. For participants in this third way, knowledge of God is always contextual: God has spoken in particular ways to the particular communities of Israel and of the Church, and Jews and Christians lack the capacity to construct clearly universal propositions about the meaning of what God has spoken. For recent discussants, this is not, however, an impediment to dialogue but the condition of it. Dialogue presupposes real difference, and difference can lead to mutual exclusion only when *human beings* restate the difference as a clash of clearly stated universal beliefs. If, however, the difference is not only *about* God but also *authored by* God, then God alone knows what the difference means and how it can or should be mediated.

This third pathway to dialogue is promoted by a movement of what some label '**postliberal**' theologians, including Christian interpreters of both Karl Barth (1886–1968) and Thomas **Aquinas** and Jewish interpreters of Franz **Rosenzweig** and Emmanuel Levinas (1906–95). Emulating both the modern goal of interreligious understanding and the premodern goal of fidelity to the revealed Word, postliberal theologians believe that a certain discipline of scriptural study can provide a means of achieving both. These theologians read the text of Tanakh/Old Testament as a common source of narratives and namings that is received differently by differing communities of **Rabbinic Judaism** and early Christianity after the first century. Three characteristics of the one God become significant subjects for later theological interpretation: (1) one God creates all existence; (2) God creates humanity for the specific purpose of imitating God in the world and, thereby, serving as agent of what some will call 'God's self-knowledge' and others will call 'God's relation to another'; (3) God is displeased, however, with humanity's failures to live up to its purpose and, to correct these failures, God sends his Word directly to humanity, so that through it humanity will finally fulfil its purpose.

For the **New Testament** witness, the name of this redeeming Word is Jesus Christ, so that the redeeming word of God is incarnate in the earthly life of the Jew, **Jesus** of Nazareth. This Jew is rejected by most of his people, is handed over to Roman authorities who crucify him, and on the third day after his death he is resurrected and returns to earth to be seen by his apostles as the **Messiah** of the Jews and redeemer of humanity. As made more fully clear in the **early Church** Council of Nicaea, the Gospel narrative is a witness to the triune identity of the one God who is at once Father ('maker of all things both seen and unseen'), Son ('the only-begotten from the Father') and Spirit (*see* **Trinity**).

According to Jewish post-liberals, the Roman political authority that crucified Jesus also destroyed Israel's **Temple** in 70 CE and, at the end of the Jewish–Roman Wars in 135 CE, initiated Israel's exile by dispossessing Israel of its place in the Holy Land. How could the God who elected Israel abandon her to such a fate? The rabbinic sages' response to that question constitutes the elemental theology of Judaism. God remains *ohev yisrael*: one who 'loves Israel'. This does not mean that God's love is exclusive; God loves all the nations of the world. It simply means that Israel's destruction and exile were not signs that God's love abated. Israel was not divorced; her **covenant** with God remained intact; the words of **Torah** remained true and authoritative. Israel did now, however, recognise new meanings in those words. The rabbis taught, for example, that the God who instructed Israel to worship him through Temple **sacrifice** also invites Israel to serve him, outside any temple, through the worship of the heart: gathering in synagogues for verbal prayer and text study and in family units to offer **blessings** over

meals. According to this teaching, God is the god for whom no single description is adequate, but who, in answer to Israel's call, offers names to call him. Anticipating future disagreements between Christian and Jewish theologians, the rabbinic sages suggested that the two central names – *elohim* and *YHWH* – should be considered attributes of God, since God cannot be named in himself, but only in relation to his actions in the world. As attributes, *elohim* would signify divine justice and *YHWH* divine mercy.

From the beginning of the Exile through the time of **Constantine**, the communities of early Rabbinic Judaism and early Christianity nurtured mutually exclusive theological identities. In some ways the resultant schism helped each of these young religions define their **identity** boundaries, in other ways it led them to overemphasise their differences, transforming allusive scriptural accounts into two sets of sharply defined, irreconcilable **doctrines**. Jewish doctrines emerged out of readings of the written Torah, concerning God's unity (Deut. 6.4), God's otherness (Num. 23.19) and God's enduring love of Israel (Isa. 43.1, 2, 10). When addressing the issue of Christianity, the rabbinic sages tended to interpret such verses as proofs of the fallacies of the gospel. In the twelfth century, for example, **Maimonides** argued that Christians committed 'idol worship' by associating God with Jesus' creaturely body (*Commentary on the Mishnah, Avodah Zarah* 1.3; and *Mishneh Torah, Hilchot Avodat Kochavim* 9.4).

Christian doctrines emerged out of readings of the Gospel narratives and of **Paul**'s letters. These readings identified Jesus as God incarnate, redeemer of all creation, and Messiah of the Jews (Col. 1.15, 20; John 19.14–15). They identified the Jews as the elect of God (Rom. 11.11) who rejected the Messiah (Acts 7.51) and who suffer for their rejection until the end of days (Rom. 11.7–10). Patristic and medieval theologians tended to interpret these readings in **supersessionist** ways: claiming that the Church replaced Israel as God's covenant partner, that Israel's law is abrogated, and that Israel's suffering remains a public mark of her rejection. **Augustine**'s reading defined the centre of Christian theologies of Judaism from the patristic through the medieval periods: that Israel's impoverished station among the Christian nations would remain, until the end of days, a sign of both her enduring covenant and her calamitous sin (*Civ.* 18.46).

While there were also ameliorative voices – such as **Bernard of Clairvaux** among medieval Christians and Rabbi Menahem ben Solomon **Meiri** among medieval Jews – the modern vision of Jewish–Christian dialogue was shaped largely as a reaction against the memory of more violent interactions, Protestant–Catholic as well as Jewish–Christian. The vision moved, in fact, beyond dialogue itself to a vision of universal agreement that might smooth away religious difference altogether. For modern Jews this was a vision of **emancipation**: of being freed from socio-cultural isolation and being invited into equal citizenship in the European nation states. For everyday citizens the ticket to freedom was removing the most visible trappings of religious law. For scholars the ticket was making peace with European rationalism, which meant seeking ways to assimilate rabbinic understandings of God to the emergent, liberal vision of a God of universal reason and **ethics**. For modern Christians like Gotthold **Lessing** God is like a father who gave each of his three sons an identical ring, but each thought he possessed the true one. In his *Nathan the Wise* (1779) Lessing let Nathan (modelled on the Jewish philosopher Moses **Mendelssohn**) bear the enlightened Christian's vision of the brotherhood of humanity that united all three Abrahamic faiths.

After the Second World War the founders of contemporary Jewish–Christian dialogue drew on comparable **Enlightenment** resources for their rules of engagement. As illustrated in the work of Roy (1918–98) and Alice Eckardt (b. 1923), Christian participants were moved by compassion for the victims of centuries of Christian **anti-Judaism**. Anticipating the work of Rosemary Ruether (b. 1936), the Eckardts identified classical **Christology** itself as a source of this anti-Judaism. If God favoured the body of Christ instead of the body of Israel, then Christians would eventually forget that the Jews who suffered exile for their sins could also merit God's love. The only solution would be to reappropriate Enlightenment **humanism**, even if not its rationalism, identifying Christianity with a religion of the universal God whose attributes of love and compassion were displayed prototypically in the life of Jesus, but in a way that invited dialogue with humanists from all other faiths. The Jews who joined this dialogue tended to identify their religion with an even more humanistic variety of what the German Jewish philosopher Hermann **Cohen** called the 'religion of reason out of the sources of Judaism' (*Religion der Vernunft aus den Quellen des Judentums*). For two decades the resultant dialogue promoted a new degree of civic sharing among congregations of Jews and Christians and numerous projects of shared social justice.

The current epoch of Jewish–Christian dialogue emerges out of a critique of inadequacies in the previous one. The critique is informed, for one, by 'postmodern' criticisms of Enlightenment universalism as a human construct that had to represent, however subtly, the earthbound interests of the humans who constructed it. Thus, for example, Hermann Cohen discovered that his universalist colleagues in German academe could discriminate against him as a Jewish philosopher even though he had devoted his life's work to the project of universal, ethical theism. European universalism, it appeared, was inseparable from the nationalisms of the individual nations that promoted it. While inheriting such criticisms of the Enlightenment, the postliberal architects of current Jewish–Christian dialogue do not share **postmodernism**'s mistrust of religious belief and conviction. For the postliberals the only 'universal' that can stand up to postmodern criticism is the life of God and the revelation of God's living Word. This Word is revealed as an event that interrupts and reorders the intellectual and social constructions of those who receive it. The Word therefore interrupts both modern constructions of a universal religion of reason and premodern constructions of Judaism or of Christianity as sole embodiments of this universality. The body of this Word is scripture as received by its evolving communities and traditions of readers, whose own bodies belong to the social and natural orders of creation. Each community encounters God intimately in the way it receives the scriptural Word, but this encounter interrupts any effort to 'capture' this intimacy in concepts. God's presence is known, instead, by its fruit, and the fruit is displayed in action: in changed patterns of doing, speaking, caring, relating. Postliberal Jews and Christians believe that, in this epoch, the two communities have discovered that each is influenced by the ways the other receives the scriptural Word. This discovery leads them to try studying their scriptures together from time to time: not as academic scientists, but as believers; not united by one faith, but distinguished by different faiths and different ways of reading. They challenge and interrogate one another, but, abandoning both medieval and modern ways of constructing their differences, they find that the challenge uncovers something surprising. Without seeking or coming to any doctrinal agreements, they find they grow closer in friendship, in the way they see the presence of God in the other's different readings, and in the heightened intensity of their dedication to serving this God in the social and natural worlds. For the postliberals the goal of Jewish–Christian theological dialogue is not doctrinal agreement, but more profound relationship, with one another and with God.   *PETER OCHS*

Golden Calf

The name given to the story in Exod. 32.1–35 (cf. Deut. 9.7–29) which tells how, while **Moses** was on top of Mount Sinai receiving the **Torah**, the Israelites on the plain below made a Golden Calf and worshipped it. Israel's unfaithfulness at this pivotal moment in her history, when she was entering into a solemn **covenant** with God, perplexed and embarrassed Jewish commentators. The **Talmud** expresses the enormity of the sin by comparing Israel to 'a shameless bride who plays the harlot within her bridal canopy' (*b. Shabbat* 88b). The repercussions of this **apostasy** were felt throughout Jewish history: according to another talmudic dictum, 'there is not a misfortune that Israel has suffered, which is not partly retribution for the sin of the Calf' (*b. Sanhedrin* 102a). Uneasiness about the story surfaces early. **Josephus** (*Ant.* 3.89–101) entirely omits it (perhaps sensitive to accusations circulating in Rome in the late first century that Jews worshipped animals) and **Philo** (*Mos.* 2.161–73, 270–1) strikingly fails to mention Aaron's questionable role in the episode. In the second century CE the rabbis stipulated that, although the story could be read publicly in **Hebrew** in synagogue, only parts of it could be translated into **Aramaic** in the **Targum** (*m. Megillah* 4.10).

Christian writers tried to exploit the Golden Calf for polemical ends. In Stephen's speech in Acts 7.39–43 it is used to hint that the **covenant** between **Israel** and God was never fully consummated. The Israelites 'put aside' God's emissary Moses, and relapsed into the idolatrous practices that had marked their life in Egypt. As a result 'God turned away from them and handed them over to the worship of the host of heaven', finally exiling them to Babylon. The implication is that the redemption from Egypt never achieved its purpose of uniting Israel to the one true God. The Israelites proved to be irredeemable idolaters, so God finally banished them back into exile. This line of argument was developed more explicitly by *Barn.* 4.6–8, where it is argued that Moses' breaking of the Tablets of Stone when he saw the Calf represents the nullifying of God's offer of the covenant to Israel. That covenant was reoffered in **Jesus** the Beloved, the new Moses. Again rejected by Israel who spurned God's new emissary, it was accepted by the Church, the true heir of Sinai.

The parallelism between Moses and Christ, between Sinai and Golgotha, became a theme of Christian **preaching** (e.g. **Ephrem** Syrus, *Serm.* 3.421; and Cassiodorus, *Exp. Ps.* 105.19). The sin of the Golden Calf regularly appears in Christian catalogues of the sins of Israel, which prove the ingrained depravity of the Jews (e.g. Cyprian, *Test.* 1.1; **Ephrem** Syrus, *Comm. ev. conc.* 9.8; Raymond Martini, *Pugio Fidei*, II 1, ed. Carpzov, 261; III 3, 16, ed. Carpzov, 845).

Rabbinic texts, while acknowledging the enormity of the sin, attempt to mitigate its impact in various ways. They stress the efficacy of Moses' intercession on Israel's behalf, the cleansing of the camp of the idolaters, and the reoffering of the covenant in the second Tablets of the Law (*Exodus Rabbah* 41–45) – all points in the biblical story that Christian writers tend to ignore. They blame the apostasy on the 'mixed multitude' of Egyptians who came up with the Israelites from Egypt – possibly an implicit attack on proselytes or even on Christians as leading Israel astray from its allegiance to God (*Targum Canticles* 1.12). Some texts link the institution of the Tabernacle with the Golden Calf: the Tabernacle was given to Israel as a means of **atonement**, not only for the sin of the Calf but to ensure that other such sins should not irrevocably rupture Israel's relationship with God (*Targum Canticles* 1.5; 3.4). It was argued that even if the sin of the Calf had not been more or less immediately atoned for, it was already covered by the all-embracing merit of the Fathers, particularly by the **binding of Isaac** (*Targum Canticles* 1.13; 2.17). Above all, attempts were made to exonerate **Aaron** – attempts echoed in

Christian tradition as well (perhaps because Aaron was seen as a type of Christ).

Though the *aggadah* makes a concerted effort to play down the effects of the incident of the Golden Calf, it is not clear whether this was a response specifically to Christian **polemic**, or to more general theological unease. Probably both factors were at work. The unease began too early to be attributed solely to Christian influence, but later developments were almost certainly shaped by the growing Jewish–Christian debate.

See also **idolatry**   *PHILIP ALEXANDER*

Golden Rule

Since the eighteenth century the Golden Rule has been the name given to a maxim which Hillel the Elder (end of first century BCE and beginning of first century CE) formulated negatively as follows: 'What is hateful to you, do not do unto others: this is the entire Law; the rest is mere commentary. Go and learn!' (*b. Shabbat* 31a). Its positive formulation is found in the **New Testament**: 'Do to others as you would have them do to you' (Luke 6.31, cf. Matt. 7.12). The Golden Rule is a fundamental principle for balancing reciprocal interests. For a long time Christians saw a lesser ethic in Hillel's negative formulation, which was surpassed by the positive formulation of **Jesus** in the **Sermon on the Mount**. Today, however, Christian theology emphasises that both formulations have the same meaning. Both Jews and Christians accept the Golden Rule as a summary of and for ethical conduct.   *HANS HERMANN HENRIX*

Good Friday *see* Holy Week

Good Friday Prayer for the Perfidious Jews

Until the reform of the Roman Rite of the Catholic liturgy in 1970, following **Vatican II**, it had from ancient times been the practice on Good Friday to say a threefold prayer during the veneration of the cross. The Church first prayed for its own members, the *fideles* ('the faithful', full believers), then for the **conversion** of Jews, who were considered *perfideles* ('unfaithful' or perhaps 'half-believers', since they believed in the true God but not in Christ), and finally for the *infideles* ('non-believers, infidels'). Over the centuries, however, the theological **polemics** of Christian teaching against Judaism gradually drew out of the Latin word *perfidii* its modern connotations of treachery.

The prayer itself, as found in the 1962 Roman Missal, does not attribute the 'blindness' of Jews to **sin** or treachery, but asks God to 'withdraw the veil from their hearts' so they may 'acknowledge the light of your truth, which is Christ'. From patristic times, however, a gradual claim that moral failure was the cause of Jewish 'blindness' to Christ was advanced in both East and West. Pope Leo I (the Great) (*r*.440–61) repeatedly accuses the Jews of such (*Sermon* 52.5 and 70), while the corresponding 'guilt' of the Jews for their alleged crimes against **Jesus** is equated with *perfidia* in the catechetical homilies of the north African Quodvultdeus (*De Symbolo* 3.6; *Contra Iudaeos* 17.8). Prayer texts regarding *perfidia* in the seventh-century *Gelesian Sacramentary* (1.41, 45) would inevitably be read through this lens. By the medieval period the notion that the *perfidia* of the Jews was principally a kind of wickedness or sin was firmly in place in authors such as **Agobard** (*De insolentia Iudaeorum* 4) and routinely reinforced in the social and legal policies of popes such as **Innocent III** (*Licet perfidia Iudaeorum*, 1109) and Clement VI (*Quamvis perfidiam Iudaeorum*, 1348).

From the end of the Second World War discussions took place about removing or substituting the word *perfidiis* from the Good Friday prayer. On 10 June 1948 the Sacred Congregation for Rites, responding to a *dubium* or question, stated that 'it would not be inappropriate in vernacular translations . . . to render the sense of the prayer by *infidelity or unfaithful in believing*' (*Acta Apostolica Sedis* 40.342). In 1959, during his first Lent as pope, **John XXIII** ordered the term *perfidiis* be dropped altogether, leaving the prayer simply one for 'the conversion of Jews' in the 1962 Roman Missal. In 1965 the Sacred Congregation for Rites formally amended parts of the text to bring it into 'accord with the mind and decrees of the Second Vatican Council concerning ecumenism' (*Acta Apostolica Sedis* 57.412–13). In the 1970 revision of the Roman Missal the prayer was changed completely, asking God to strengthen 'the Jewish People' in the faith given to them by God, preserving the affirmation in *Nostra Aetate* of God's 'irrevocable covenant' with the Jews: 'Let us pray for the Jewish People, the first to hear the word of God, that they may continue to grow in the love of His Name and in faithfulness to His Covenant . . . Listen to your Church as we pray that the people you first made your own may arrive at the fullness of redemption.' 'Fullness of redemption' here is **eschatological**, mirroring the

Church's own prayers for herself. This is the only official prayer for Jews in Catholic **liturgy** today.

EUGENE J. FISHER AND DENNIS D. MCMANUS

Grace

The concept of grace is both problematic and fruitful in Jewish–Christian relations. The problems arise on both sides of the **dialogue**. The Christian tradition has a long history of opposing **Law** and grace on the basis of John 1.17 ('the law was given through Moses: grace and truth came through Jesus Christ') and the opposition of 'the law of sin and death' and the 'law of the Spirit of life in Jesus Christ' in Rom. 7–8. 'Law' in both cases translates the Greek word *nomos*, a term that takes us into the semantic field of codes and legalistic observances. In this context God became the Lawgiver, and the relationship with God was determined by the keeping of the Law. **Salvation** then came, so Christian theology has alleged, through works and not by grace, and Christian preachers have dwelt (and often still do) on this supposed contrast between Judaism and Christianity. One consequence of this profound Christian misunderstanding of law in relation to grace is that Jewish writers have avoided the use of the latter term. The Hebrew word for grace, *ḥen*, from the root *ḥanan*, has been translated in various ways but almost never as grace. As Larry Hoffman (b. 1942) has written, 'Jewish translators systematically avoid using theological language that they mistakenly think is purely Christian'. This has left Christian visitors to the synagogue to mistake the significance of a prayer like '*Avinu, Malkenu, ḥoneinu vaneinu ki ein banu ma'asim/Asei imanu zedakah va-ḥesed ve-hoshieinu*', which, Hoffman says, can mean nothing but 'Our Father, our King, respond to us with grace, for we have no good deed to our credit / Deal charitably and lovingly with us and save us' ('Jewish and Christian Liturgy', in *Christianity in Jewish Terms*, 2000). In the light of this we may revisit the affirmations in the Hebrew scriptures that indicate Israel's deep understanding that it exists through grace. The Land was the gift of grace; the **Torah** was given as an act of grace; the sacrificial system was a gift of grace; the **covenants** were always the acts of a gracious God; the deliverance from Egypt was a supreme sign of grace, for it belongs to the nature of God to pardon iniquity and delight in steadfast love (Mic. 7.18). Israel then becomes the manifestation in the world of God's presence and the permanence of his grace,

and Judaism a religion of grace (Gen. 12.3). It is in this area of Jewish–Christian dialogue that the concept of grace may bear real fruit, when Christians and Jews may discover that they are speaking of the same divine intentionality, indeed that they are speaking, as **Rosenzweig** once suggested, the same truth in Jewish and Christian forms. Further fruitful discussion will help resolve paradoxes that both Jewish and Christian theologies recognise, for example how God's graciousness to humankind is related to God's role as judge of all the earth. *KENNETH CRACKNELL*

Grace after meals *see* birkhat hamazon

Greek language and culture

The known history of the Greek language stretches back into the second millenium BCE, although the first major literary texts are the Homeric poems, which are now generally dated to the eighth century BCE. The greatness of fifth-century Athenian authors, in many genres, led to a pre-eminent position for the Attic dialect, which was maintained into modern times. Greek came to be the common language of the eastern Mediterranean area and of the Near East after the conquests of Alexander the Great (d. 323 BCE). The importance of Greek for Jewish–Christian relations derives from this phenomenon, for it was used by Jews from that time onwards, and subsequently by the first Christian communities. The Roman conquest did not lead to a Latinisation of the eastern lands, and Greek remained the language of the medieval **Byzantine Empire**.

According to a fairly reliable tradition, the **Torah**, or Pentateuch, was translated into Greek in **Alexandria** around the middle of the third century BCE. Among Jews of the **Diaspora** there developed a significant literary culture in Greek, and the language was widely used in Palestine as well, at least among the upper classes. The principal monuments of Judaeo-Hellenistic literature are the **Septuagint** and the voluminous writings of the philosopher **Philo** and the historian **Josephus**. Remains of Judaeo-Hellenistic literature from the post-**Bar Kokhba** era are sparse, although we know from various indications that throughout the eastern Mediterranean communities Jews continued to use Greek as their primary language. Christianity, for its part, as soon as it expanded beyond Palestine and the **Aramaic** environment, became a primarily Greek-speaking movement. Greek was the language of the synagogues of the **Diaspora**, where **Paul** often began his missionary activities, and also naturally became the medium through which the gospel was spread to the Gentiles. As Christians sought to define their community as an independent entity, they not only employed the Greek language, but also began to express themselves within a Greek cultural framework. This tendency becomes particularly manifest during the period of the Apologists (*c.*125–225 CE), and remains a characteristic of most of Christian literature throughout the patristic period, which corresponds approximately to the rabbinic period in Judaism.

In light of these circumstances, it is evident that most of the first Jewish–Christian discussions and **disputations** will have taken place in Greek. Moreover, since there is little reference to Christianity at all in surviving Judaeo-Hellenistic literature, and references to Christians and Christianity in the rabbinic corpus are often enigmatic or elliptical, one is forced to rely extensively on patristic literature in Greek (also in **Latin** and **Syriac**) for the reconstruction of early Jewish–Christian relations. Many works treat the subject only indirectly, but others are specifically concerned with Jewish–Christian debates. Of special interest are the **dialogues** between Jews and Christians, a famous early example of which is **Justin Martyr**'s *Dialogue with the Jew Trypho* (*c.*160 CE). This dialogue and numerous others like it were written in Greek and are set in a Greek cultural context. While these texts often represent literary constructions rather than verbatim accounts of what was actually said, no student of Jewish–Christian relations can afford to ignore them.

See also **Hellenism**   *ADAM KAMESAR*

Gregory I ('the Great') (540–604)

Pope (590–604) and a most significant figure in the intellectual and social history of Jewish–Christian relations. Gregory's writings reveal the influence of St **Augustine** with respect to the place of Jews and Judaism within the history of Christian **salvation**. However, his theological writings develop a more negative assessment of Judaism than Augustine by emphasising the role of Jews in the periods only prior to the coming of **Jesus** and at the very end of history when the Jews will convert to Christianity. The themes of blindness to the truth and the triumph of Christianity as the True Israel preclude any significant role for Jews prior to their **conversion**. By contrast, 28 of Gregory's 800 letters reveal a distinct tendency to protect the physical safety of the Jews. He intervened on several occasions to prevent violence against Jews, their synagogues and their cemeteries. When a synagogue was destroyed by a Christian mob he ordered the bishop to rebuild it. Gregory's most important contribution to Jewish–Christian relations was his letter to the Bishop of Palermo (598) that began with the words *Sicut Judaeis*. This document provided the formula for all subsequent letters of papal protection of Jewish rights in Christian Europe during the Middle Ages.   *MICHAEL A. SIGNER*

Gregory IX (d. 1241)

The pope (1227–41) who first ordered the **Talmud** burned (between 1239 and 1242). Gregory most likely was instigated by the secular Masters at the University of Paris, who were exploiting the accusation of (the probable convert) Nicholas **Donin**, who said that the Talmud was a *lex nova*, forbidden non-scriptural law, by which he was alluding – as popes from **Innocent IV** came to understand – to the formal legal compendium, the *Decretales*. This work, which Gregory IX himself had authorised in 1234, indeed does rest on non-scriptural law, principally edited papal dicta. The *Decretals* defined Jewish (canonically permitted) rights and made into permanently valid law the papal letter known as *Sicut Judaeis non*, first issued between about 1119 and 1191, which guarantees Jews peaceful existence and due legal process.   *KENNETH STOW*

HHHH

Hagar

Egyptian maid of **Sarah**, who gave her to **Abraham** so that God's promise of a son could be fulfilled (Gen. 16.1–16). Following **Philo of Alexandria** (*Leg.* 3.244), **Jerome** translated Hagar as *paroichia* ('alongside the house', i.e. alien) or pilgrim. Hagar and her son Ishmael were driven into the wilderness after Sarah became displeased because 'he played with her son Isaac' (Gen. 21.9). The rabbis and **Paul** interpret this to be mockery and persecution of the younger child (Gal. 4.29). In the effort to offset Galatian Christians' attraction to the **Law** of Moses, Paul contrasted the two wives of Abraham and their respective sons (Gal. 4.21–31). By use of '**allegory**' (or rather **typology**), Paul linked Hagar and Mount Sinai with contemporary **Jerusalem**, 'in slavery along with her children' (4.25). Implicitly the free-born Sarah is linked with 'the Jerusalem above', the mother of Christianity, children of the promise like **Isaac** (4.26, 28). This interpretation was the basis for **Church Fathers** to explore the relationship between Jews and Christians (Ambrose, *Abr.* 14.454; Augustine, *Civ.* 15.2; Jerome, *Comm. Gal.* 26.417). **Isidore of Seville** developed the identification of Hagar with the **Old Testament** and synagogue, and of Sarah with **New Testament** and Church. From Gen. 21.14 he linked Ishmael with 'the sinful and foolish people' clinging to the synagogue, 'expelled from her lands to wander the entire world and not to know well the way, which is Christ' (81.248). After the rise of **Islam**, John of Damascus linked the Saracens with the descendants of Ishmael; his derivation of the term Saracen (*Sarrakenoi*) is that 'Sarah sent [Hagar] away empty' (94.764).   *LAWRENCE E. FRIZZELL*

Halakhah

From a verb meaning 'to walk', *halakhah* refers to Jewish **law** developed over two millennia. However, there also exists a strand of Christian *halakhah*, in addition to the obvious fact that **Jesus**, as an observant Jew, followed Jewish law by, for example, attending synagogue on **Sabbath** and wearing fringed garments. Evidence for a Christian version is found in 1 John 2.6: 'Whoever claims to live in him [Jesus] must *walk* [italics added] as Jesus did' (cf. Rom. 6.4; 8.4; Eph. 4.1). For Jews, *halakhah* defines what they must do and not do, and is Judaism's answer to the question, 'What does the Lord your God require of you?' (Deut. 10.12). In the **New Testament** it is occasionally referred to as 'the tradition of the elders' (e.g. Mark 7.3, 5). From Matt. 23.3, referring to the **scribes** and **Pharisees** ('do whatever they teach you'), it would seem that Jesus' general attitude towards it was affirmative, although many of the arguments between Jesus and his fellow Jews were centred on conflicting interpretations of *halakhah*. The Pharisees and their successors, the rabbis, constructed a code of conduct of monumental comprehensiveness and specificity, going far beyond the scope of modern secular law. *Halakhah* covers every aspect of life – indeed, whatever can be expressed in the imperative 'you shall' or 'you shall not' – regardless of whether it is enforceable. Thus 'you shall love your neighbour as yourself' (Lev. 19.18) is as much part of the *halakhah* as the smallest details of civil and ritual law. Christianity from an early period sought to break the legal constraints of Judaism, building on the letters of **Paul** which indicate that, while he saw the law as excellent and divine, he also viewed it as a 'curse' because it revealed human sinfulness.

Halakhah effectively regulated Jewish individual and communal life and could be interpreted strictly or leniently. Relations with the non-Jewish world, including Christianity, influenced its development. For example, the ban on polygamy, generally attributed to Gershom ben Judah of Mainz (960–1028), was clearly influenced by Christianity, and it is no coincidence that polygamy was not banned for Jews living in Islamic countries. Louis Jacobs (b. 1920) suggests that the setting aside of the biblical law concerning converts from certain nations (such as the Ammonites or Moabites cf. Deut. 23.4) was also influenced by Christianity. According to the rabbinic interpretation, a member of one of these groups may not marry a Jewish woman, even after converting to Judaism, but the law does not apply to female converts – Ruth was a Moabite woman (*y. Yevamot* 8.3 (9c)). However, the **Mishnah** tells of a male Ammonite convert who was accepted (*m. Yadayim* 4.4, *b. Berakhot* 28a), concluding that 'Sennacherib confused the nations' (in other words, it was no longer possible to assume that anyone who claimed to belong to a nation really did belong), thus making **conversion** possible. Today **Orthodox Jews** maintain the undiminished authority of *halakhah*, while **Progressive Jews** either modify it conservatively or reconstruct it on the basis of a non-fundamentalist reading of scripture supplemented by modern consideration.

JOHN D. RAYNER AND EDWARD KESSLER

Ha-Levi, Judah *see* Judah ha-Levi

Halleluyah

A phrase in Hebrew **liturgy**, an imperative plural and a shortened form of Yahweh (the **tetragrammaton**), meaning 'praise Yah'. It occurs 23 times opening or closing (or both) the **Psalms** (intermittently 106–35; consistently 146–50). It appears to have lost its literal meaning early on and is found in various non-canonical works (Tobit, 3 Maccabees, **Dead Sea Scrolls**). It quickly moved into Christianity (Rev. 19.1–4, early ecclesiastical writings). Its vocalisation is one of only a few liturgical customs practised by Jews and Christians alike. *FRANK SHAW*

Ha-Meiri, Menaham ben Solomon *see* Meiri, Menahem ben Solomon

Hanukkah

A Jewish mid-winter festival of light, already associated in pre-Christian times with the victory of Judah the Maccabee over the Syrian general Lysias in 164 BCE and over the attempted Hellenisation of the Jewish homeland. The rededication (Hebrew *hanukkah*) of the **Temple** was celebrated for eight days and marked with **music**, praise, fire and palm branches, in a manner reminiscent both of Jewish (e.g. **Sukkot**) and non-Jewish feasts (e.g. Dionysia). In the first century **Josephus** refers to it as the festival of lights, and contemporary rabbinic sources refer to the kindling of lights, the recitation of *hallel*, and the prohibition of **mourning**. Like **Christmas**, Hanukkah takes place in mid-winter, starts on the twenty-fifth of the month (Kislev in the

case of Hanukkah) and involves the lighting of **candles**. During the talmudic and post-talmudic periods **Torah** readings were instituted and **liturgy** was adopted that stressed the miracle, summarised the physical deliverance and praised God for that and similar interventions. It also became customary to read an **Aramaic** version of the Hanukkah story, the Scroll of Antiochus, and to sing a domestic hymn chronicling the persecutions of the Jews. Medieval rabbinic law and tradition ensured an expansion of the festival's importance, with special roles for women and children. Some elements of these developments may conceivably reflect the influence of a Christian environment. Such current practices as the exchange of gifts, the sending of Hanukkah cards and more elaborate synagogal services, which emerged in the Jewish communities of the western and not the eastern world, have undoubtedly been adopted under the influence of Christmas festivities. *STEFAN C. REIF*

Haredi

Literally 'trembling'. 'Ultra-orthodox' Jewish community, its origins being the eighteenth-century development of the Ashkenazi movements of Hasidism and its opposition, Misnagdism, which found a mirror-image in the Sefardi world. Today the communities are largest in the **United States** and **Israel**. While largely secluded from mainstream society, following a tightly regulated lifestyle, haredi beliefs and moral understanding of the world are remarkably similar to those of some **evangelical** and – as demonstrated in research by Gershon Greenberg (1998) – **Orthodox Christian** communities. Concepts of human relationships with God and their distortion through **sin**, of spiritual purity and of gender roles find parallels in Christian thought which have recently become the focus of investigation and promise to open a new field of Jewish–Christian interaction hitherto largely unnoticed.

K. HANNAH HOLTSCHNEIDER

Harnack, Adolf von (1851–1930)

German Protestant theologian, professor in Leipzig, Giessen, Marburg and, from 1888, Berlin; ennobled in 1914. In 1899–1900 he held a series of lectures, the transcript of which was published in 1900 under the title of *Das Wesen des Christentums*. Criticising traditional Christian dogma, and stressing the personality and teachings of **Jesus** (i.e. God being a heavenly father, the infinite worth of personality and the commandment of love), he gave expression to the conviction that **Roman Catholic** and **Orthodox Christianity** are not compatible with the original teachings of Jesus. In emphasising the radicality and novelty of the teachings of Jesus he grossly misrepresented Second Temple Judaism to such an extent that leading Jewish authorities, Leo **Baeck** being the best known, set out a critique of Harnack's apologetic presentation. Baeck established that Harnack was incapable of separating *halakhah* from *aggadah*, which resulted in his comparing the **ethics** of Jesus, not with the ethics of the **Pharisees**, but with their ritual regulations. The portrait of Jesus in *Das Wesen des Christentums* has been highly influential and remains a stumbling-block in Jewish–Christian relations (see, e.g., **supersessionism**), since it tends to present a Jesus who is radically different from his contemporaries in every respect. In his book on **Marcion**, Harnack went so far as to advocate that the Hebrew scriptures be removed from the Christian **canon** altogether.   *JESPER SVARTVIK*

Hasidei Ashkenaz

A small but influential Jewish pietistic group in twelfth- and thirteenth-century **Germany**, which both reacted against and was influenced by contemporary Christian pietism. Their popular book *Sefer Hasidim* became a guide for pious Jewish living. It debates many questions of everyday life for Jews among Christians, strongly advising the pious Jew to abhor Christian customs, even to the extent of banning melodies used in church. In spite of this, the hasidim were willing to adopt what they considered to be praiseworthy Christian pietistic practices, such as exposure to excessive cold and flagellation as forms of **penance/penitence**. Earthly love became for them an **allegory** for the love of God, with the ideal being a monastic absence of passion.   *MICHAEL HILTON*

Hasidism *see* mysticism
Haskalah *see* Enlightenment
Hebraists, Christian

The term refers to Gentiles who became proficient Hebrew scholars, and usually applies to the period between 450 and 1800. Before Jewish studies became a recognised part of university curricula in the early modern period (*c.*1520), Christians studied Hebrew for various reasons. During the early centuries **Jerome** was motivated to trace the **Old Testament** back to its source in what he called the *hebraica veritas*. His expertise, gained

at the feet of Palestinian rabbis, was incorporated into the **Vulgate**, a version of the Bible much closer to the original than was once supposed. His commentaries also contain much exegetical material received from his Jewish teachers. The missionary orders of the thirteenth century regarded a knowledge of Hebrew as essential for purposes of **conversion**. If Jews were to be won for Christ, their religion had to be understood and their interpretation of certain biblical passages refuted. To this end Hebrew must be learned so that Christians could engage Jews in **disputations**. Nicholas of **Lyra**, whose knowledge of Hebrew and of the work of Jewish exegetes is indisputable, was anxious to discover the literal sense of scripture. Because his commentaries betray the influence of **Rashi**, he is credited with securing a place for traditional Jewish **exegesis** in Christian thought.

After Lyra's death what little interest had been shown by Christians in Hebrew studies waned. It was not until the **Renaissance** that we find a resurgence as Hebrew gained recognition as one of the historic languages of the West. By 1546 chairs of Hebrew had been established in the major European universities. **Pico della Mirandola** and his disciple Johannes **Reuchlin** stood at the forefront of this movement. Pico was the first Christian to take an interest in the **Kabbalah**. Both he and Reuchlin believed that fundamental Christian truths were to be found in the writings of Jewish mystics. This **humanist** desire to go *ad fontes* (back to the original sources) not only inspired Christians to study post-biblical Jewish literature, it also gave biblical translation a new impetus. New **Latin** versions of the Old Testament quickly assumed an important role in the field of biblical scholarship. Those of Pagninus (1470–1536), Müntzer (1489–1552) and Tremellius (1510–80) in particular played a crucial part in the transmission of rabbinic explanations of difficult texts. The **Reformation** emphasised the study of Hebrew even further. **Luther**, though antagonistic to rabbinic exegesis, had a high regard for the **Hebrew language** and recognised its importance for understanding scripture. In his *Rules for Translating the Bible* (1532) he states that he always consults experts to discover the exact meaning of a Hebrew word. In the following century John Lightfoot (d. 1675) demonstrated the significance of Jewish studies for the interpretation of the **New Testament**.

The Geneva Academy succeeded in drawing students from many different countries, with the result that **Calvinist** scholars became some of the leading Christian Hebraists of the seventeenth century. During this period Christian Hebraism became a weapon in the disputes between Protestants and Catholics. Sixteenth-century Protestant divines used the **Hebrew Bible** and rabbinic **commentaries** to support their case for scriptural over ecclesiastical authority in matters of faith, witness the extensive writings of Hugh Broughton (d. 1612). The role played by these Gentile scholars in the history of scholarship was considerable. They persuaded Christian theologians to attend not only to the original text of the Hebrew Bible, but also to the Jewish exegetical tradition. It was due to their influence that rabbinic explanations of difficult Hebrew words found their way into early vernacular **Bible translations**.   *GARETH LLOYD JONES*

Hebrew Bible

Heb. *Tanakh*; the 24 books comprising the scriptural **canon** of the Jewish community, which is also the Hebrew textual version of the Christian **Old Testament**. 'Tanakh' is an acronym of the names of its constituent parts, *Torah*, *Nevi'im*, *Ketuvim* (Torah, Prophets, Writings). The **Torah** is identified with the 'book of the Torah of Moses' that Ezra read to the Israelites who returned to Judea in the post-exilic period (Neh. 8) and is clearly recognised as scripture in the last centuries BCE, as evidenced by the **Dead Sea Scrolls** and **Philo**. Prophetic texts and the **Psalms** (part of the Writings) are interpreted by the *pesher* method in the Dead Sea Scrolls, indicating their acceptance at that time as divinely inspired texts. Traditionally, the final decisions regarding canonisation of the 24 books were made by the Council of **Jamnia/Yavneh** around 90 CE, but recent scholarship has found this difficult to substantiate. Canonisation was most likely a communal process, shaped around issues of Jewish **identity** and distinctiveness, both in the wake of the failed Judean rebellions of 66–73 and 132–5 CE and in response to continuing contact with Greco-Roman society and emerging Christianity. Talmudic discussions focus on the ritual status of individual books (whether or not they 'defile the hands' – *m. Yadayim* 3.2) and consistency with established authority (on Ezekiel and the Torah, see *b. Shabbat* 13b and *b. Hagigah* 13a) without enumerating a canonical list. Standardisation was achieved with the greater use of the codex and development of the Massoretic system, prior to the ninth century CE.

The use of the Hebrew Bible and its Greek version, the **Septuagint** (LXX), among early followers of **Jesus** to comprehend him as God's **Messiah** and **Son of God** has had lasting effects on the Jewish–Christian relationship. **Paul** summarised key elements of his witness as being 'in accordance with the scriptures' (1 Cor. 15.3–4). Subsequently, the writers of the four Gospels used the Hebrew Bible in manifold ways to establish the continuity of God's work in Jesus with God's work in biblical Israel. Matthew used explicit fulfilment citations throughout the birth narrative (see 1.23; 2.6, 15, 18, 23, etc., with variations on the formula, 'this took place in order to fulfil what had been spoken through the prophet'). The language and imagery of the Hebrew Bible is ubiquitous in the **New Testament**, with notable emphasis in the Gospel **passion narratives** and the books of Hebrews and Revelation. Both as an authority for the New Testament authors and as a **hermeneutical** key for New Testament readers, it is indispensable for understanding the earliest claims about Jesus.

Christian reliance on the Hebrew Bible spawned contradictory dynamics after the fall of the Jerusalem **Temple** in 70 CE, which triggered the eventual separation of Judaism and Christianity. Left to ask where God would be found if there were no Temple, Jews divided: some found the answer in the Torah as taught by rabbis, others found it in Jesus as fulfilment of the Torah, and others found it in the scriptures alone, whether Torah (**Samaritans**) or Tanakh (**Karaites**). As Christianity grew increasingly Gentile in its demographics, some with tendencies toward **Gnosticism** questioned the value of the Hebrew Bible for the Church; **Marcion** proposed to eliminate it from the Christian canon (along with much of the New Testament). Others saw it as vital testimony to the truth of Christian faith as God's fulfilment of the promises to biblical Israel. In the ***Adversus Judaeos*** writings of **early Church** theologians (**Church Fathers**), the distinction between Christian and Jewish understandings of key biblical texts becomes a defining characteristic of Christian self-understanding. Rosemary Ruether (b. 1936) has identified two patterns in these writings. The 'rejectionist' pattern bifurcates the message of Israel's prophets into condemnation, addressed to historical Israel, and promise, addressed to the New Israel, the Church. Thereby God reiterates the biblical pattern of promoting the younger sibling over the elder. The '**supersessionist**' pattern grants value to Israel's historical blessings, but asserts that Christianity moves forward with their spiritual fulfilments while carnal Judaism remains 'stagnant in useless antiquity' (Augustine, *Adv. Jud.* 6(8)). According to John **Chrysostom**, the law (Torah) that Israel repeatedly failed to observe has now been superseded by Christian faith, making Jewish efforts at Torah-observance especially perverse. Thus the theme of Jewish incompetence as readers of the Hebrew Bible became characteristic of Christian anti-Jewish **disputation**; **Augustine**'s enduring image of the Jews as a witness people included his assertion that the Christian doctrine of fulfilment was more credible for the fact that the fulfilled scriptures had been preserved by a people who did not believe them (the 'book-bearers').

The Hebrew Bible itself shows several cases of reinterpretation among the canonical books, as in the **Isaiah** book, which is expanded twice beyond the lifetime of the prophet, and the recasting of Samuel–Kings by the author of Chronicles. The writers of the Dead Sea Scrolls utilised interpretive techniques not unlike those known in early Christian circles, and the **Apocrypha** and **Pseudepigrapha** demonstrate the creativity of both Jews and Christians in carrying forward the biblical heritage. By the early centuries CE the Bible came to be understood as Written Torah, a closed canon, while a body of Oral Torah – traditionally understood to have come with the Written Torah to Moses at Mount Sinai – developed in **Rabbinic Judaism** as a complementary canon. Jacob Neusner (b. 1932) and others have explored the relationship of these two canons, which differ markedly in style, focus and authority. Rabbinic tradition in the post-Mishnaic period, in response to Christian reliance on biblical **prophecy** and psalms for **Christological** arguments, developed a principle of Torah priority over Prophets and Writings as theological authorities. Samaritans do not include the latter two collections in their canon, and Karaites reject the rabbinic use of Oral Torah and use the 'plain meaning' of the Hebrew Bible as their sole authority.

Medieval Jewish and Christian **biblical interpretation** ran parallel courses in their development of fourfold **exegesis**. The Jewish quartet of *peshat*, *remez*, *derash* and *sod* (abbreviated as '*PaRDeS*' and translated as 'plain, symbolic, homiletical and mystical') yielded similar interpretive possibilities to the Christian historical, allegorical, moral and anagogical senses, respectively. Common interests in biblical topics and the emergence of the university led to increasing interaction among Jewish and Christian scholars, and the twelfth to the seventeenth centuries saw a flourishing of **Christian Hebraists**, especially among the mendicant orders, the **Victorines** and the dissidents seeking reformation of the Roman Catholic Church. While the mendicants used their Hebrew learning to proselytise Jews, the latter groups followed the lead of the early church theologian **Jerome** in seeking clearer insight into biblical truth through the 'authentic Hebrew' (*hebraica veritas*) text. They also studied rabbinic and kabbalistic texts, believing that these preserved meanings that had come to be distorted by Church translations and interpretations.

Beginning with the rise of universities in the **Renaissance** and the sweeping intellectual changes of the **Enlightenment**, Jews and Christians found greater common ground in their approach to the Hebrew Bible through literary and historical criticism (*see* **biblical criticism**). Barukh **Spinoza**, in his *Tractatus Theologio-Politicus* (1670), severed the study of biblical history from doctrinal assertions by theologians much as Richard Simon (1638–1712) did in his *Histoire critique du Vieux Testament* (1678). Thereafter the 'liberal' approach to biblical interpretation would bear greater resemblances across the divide of faith than to 'traditional' methods within the same faith community. Such academic congruence afforded greater opportunity for interaction among Jewish and Christian scholars, but long centuries of **anti-Judaism** also continued to infect Christian biblical scholarship. Thus Julius **Wellhausen**'s late-nineteenth-century summation of the documentary hypothesis of Pentateuchal (Torah) composition, like his broader studies on the history of Israel, combined keen historical acumen with prejudiced caricatures of Judaism. The persistence of such bias in European and North American biblical studies prompted Solomon Schechter (1847–1915) to brand higher criticism a form of 'higher antisemitism' and contributed to the development of a twentieth-century Israeli school of thought. Yehezkel Kaufmann's (1889–1964) work on the history of biblical Israel; archaeological study by Benjamin Mazar (1906–95), Yohanan Aharoni (1919–76), and the father–son succession of Eliezer Sukenik (1889–1953) and Yigael Yadin (1917–84); the text-critical investigations of Shemaryahu Talmon (b. 1920), Moshe Goshen-Gottstein (1925–91) and Emanuel Tov (b. 1941) are all exemplary of distinctive Israeli approaches. In the last case, for instance, the Hebrew University Bible Project pursues its work toward a critical edition of the Hebrew Bible differently than the United Bible Societies, basing the work on a manuscript authenticated by **Maimonides**, entirely forswearing conjectural reconstruction of text forms that have no witness in the manuscript record, and including more evidence from traditional Jewish sources such as the **Talmud** and the masora. The distinctly Christian, even Protestant, development of **biblical theology** is one that has found little resonance in the Jewish academy. Albeit the biblical style was instrumental in Martin **Buber**'s articulation of the I–Thou character of divine–human relations, and Franz **Rosenzweig**'s theology took full cognisance of the biblical witness, their joint biblical project resulted in a translation of the Hebrew Bible rather than an explicit biblical theology. Isaac Kalimi (b. 1952) in 2002 called for greater attention to a Jewish biblical theology, notwithstanding its necessary differences from Christian biblical and '**Old Testament**' theology.

In the post-*Shoah* and **postmodern** era, the Hebrew Bible has become, in the words of the Christian 2002 statement *A Sacred Obligation*, something that 'both connects and separates Jews and Christians'. The optimistic rationalism of the modern era, already challenged by neo-Orthodox Christian theologians beginning with Karl Barth (1886–1968), exploded in the Final Solution, so that a neutral approach to the Hebrew Bible as a literary-historical product is no longer credible. Neither, however, can there be a return to the pre-modern, doctrinally determined mutual alienation of Jewish and Christian interpretation. A new understanding of canon and biblical authority is being fashioned among progressive thinkers in both communities.

One deceptively superficial symptom of the problem lies in disputes over the proper name of the canonical collection, with no satisfactory consensus emerging among the options of 'Hebrew Bible', 'Jewish Bible', 'Old Testament', 'First Testament', 'Shared Testament' etc. The Jewish Publica-

tion Society of America asserts 'Tanakh' convincingly as the title of its Bible for the Jewish community, while Paul van Buren (1924–97) makes a thoughtful, if not self-evident, case for retaining 'Old Testament' in Christian circles (1998). Yet, as an object of joint interest or of scholarly study, the heritage of biblical Israel seems too complex and multivalent to admit of a single adequate title.

Rather than exposing a failure of theological imagination, this inability to name the biblical writings univocally is a reflex of their radically communal character. James A. Sanders (b. 1927) set the new agenda for canonical studies, shifting the focus from their content or their inspired composition to the communities that revere them in different eras for varied reasons (*Canon and Community*, *Torah and Canon*). Thereby he has provided the historical and theoretical grounding for the spirit in which the Hebrew Bible has become a vehicle of common exploration and mutual self-disclosure among Jews and Christians, rather than a bone of contention over which to press exclusive claims. In his work lies the impetus for a new 'confessional criticism' that could elaborate a common Jewish and Christian exegetical method without surrendering distinctive theological claims to **modernity**'s rationalist norm, a project that is also being pursued by Peter Ochs (b. 1950) under the rubric of 'scriptural reasoning'.

Beginning with the recognition of modern biblical studies in the papal encyclical *Divino Afflante Spiritu* (1943), and the **Vatican II** repudiation of anti-Judaism in *Nostra Aetate* (1965), the Roman Catholic Church has undertaken its own rethinking of the place of the Hebrew Bible in Church and theology. Catholic revisions to the **lectionary** cycle in the 1970s led the way for all major liturgical denominations to re-examine their use of the Old Testament in **worship**. The Pontifical Biblical Commission, in its comprehensive 2001 publication *The Jewish People and their Sacred Scriptures in the Christian Bible*, affirmed the integrity of both the Jewish and Christian readings of the Hebrew Bible as 'irreducible' and affirmed that 'the Jewish reading of the Bible is a possible one, in continuity with the Jewish Sacred Scriptures . . . a reading analogous to the Christian reading' (II.A.7, §22).

The Hebrew Bible has been both battleground and weapon in the long conflict of Christianity and

Judaism that was largely forsworn in the latter half of the twentieth century. Both in shared study of these scriptures and in their respective recastings of theological language for a new era of mutual respect, Jews and Christians have begun to take up the challenge of discerning anew what role the Hebrew Bible will play in their relationship.

PETER A. PETTIT

Hebrew Christians

Hebrew Christians emerged as a group of Jewish converts to Christianity in the early nineteenth century, at the same time as the first translation of the **New Testament** into **Hebrew** (1838). The Hebrew Christian movement was established initially in England in 1865 but soon moved to the United States. The first **mission**, the 'Israelites of the New Covenant Movement', was established in Kishinev, Russia, in 1882 by Joseph Rabinowitz (1837–99), a member of a distinguished hasidic family, who developed a version of **Maimonides**' 13 principles of Jewish faith, as well as a version of the 39 Articles of the **Church of England**. Rabinowitz's attempt to combine a Jewish lifestyle with belief in **Jesus**' Messiahship caused great controversy but was supported by some Jewish-Christian leaders. An international body of **Jewish Christians** known as the Hebrew Christian Alliance was established in 1915 in New York. The Alliance grew significantly in the first half of the twentieth century and initiated missions to Jews in the US and in Europe. In the second half of the twentieth century there was increasing tension within the movement between a younger generation who wished to emphasise Jewish practice and maintain their own places of worship and the more traditionally minded who wanted to integrate into the Gentile Churches. Some left the movement to establish modern **Messianic Jewish** groups such as **Jews for Jesus**, and in 1975 the Hebrew Christian Alliance changed its name to Messianic Jewish Alliance, thus fulfilling Rabinowitz's vision.

EDWARD KESSLER

Hebrew language

Hebrew is the language of almost the entire corpus of the Hebrew scriptures, or **Old Testament**, except for Daniel and part of Ezra/Nehemiah. Hebrew *words* adopted into English and other languages include **Messiah**, Jubilee, Amen and **Halleluyah**; Hebrew *concepts* translated into those languages are far more numerous. This shared **vocabulary** forms a strong bond between Jews and Christians, but at the same time provides fertile ground for debate about interpretation.

In **Jesus**' time few Jews spoke Hebrew, and in the great community of **Alexandria** even the Bible was read in **Greek**. The rabbis and their followers, however, have continued to this day to use Hebrew for Bible, prayer and study, and in recent times it has revived as a spoken language in **Israel**.

Early Judaism and Christianity sought to justify themselves as fulfilment of the Hebrew scriptures. Gospels and **midrash** abound with **proof-texts** from the same scriptures. Jews had the advantage over Greek-speaking Gentile Christians, since they could always reject Christian interpretation on the grounds that it was based on a misunderstanding of the Hebrew text. The Church Father **Origen** of Alexandria composed his **Hexapla**, of which only fragments remain, not only to establish a correct biblical text, but to provide Christian scholars with material to rebut Jewish arguments. The Greek **Septuagint**, in varied recensions, became the definitive text for many **Orthodox Churches**. Following Origen, **Jerome**, who learned Hebrew and some midrash from Jews in Bethlehem, translated the scriptures from Hebrew into Latin. His **Vulgate** was accepted as the official version of the scriptures by the Catholic Church only at the Council of **Trent**; today the Church regards it as 'authentic from the judicial, but not from the critical point of view'.

The rabbis shared with Christians the notion that the text of scripture was literally the word of God. They held that the received text of the Five Books of **Moses** was free from error and redundancy, and comprehensive. In order to constrain the meaning of the Hebrew text so that it would accord with traditional teaching they devised rules of interpretation for both *halakhah* and *aggadah*, and these determine the limits of midrashic interpretation. These limits enabled them, by a close reading of the Hebrew text, to rebut both pagan critique of scripture and **Christological** readings. Though they looked on the Greek **Septuagint** with disfavour, the rabbis encouraged **Aramaic** translation; the **Talmud** several times adduces support for a particular understanding of a biblical word or phrase 'as Rav Yosef translated [into Aramaic]', and commended the regular reading, in public and private, of **Targum** (Aramaic translation), in particular that attributed to '**Onkelos** the Proselyte'.

Through the Middle Ages Jews enlarged the vocabulary of Hebrew and developed new styles, sometimes drawing on models from surrounding cultures. The formal study of Hebrew grammar and lexicography was well advanced by the late tenth century in Muslim **Spain**, when Judah ben David Hayyuj (*c*.940–*c*.1010) arrived from Fez and argued, against Menahem ibn Saruq (*c*.910–*c*.970), that all Hebrew roots were triliteral. It was, however, Menahem's *Mahberet*, or dictionary, that profoundly influenced the French commentator **Rashi** in his effort to recover the *peshat*, or plain meaning, of scripture. Rashi's **commentaries** were meant for the ordinary educated Jew, but they soon became known to Christians, both to those who hoped such knowledge would aid their conversionist aims, and to **Renaissance** scholars such as Hugh of St Victor (d. 1142) in Paris, who rather like Rashi set himself the task of rehabilitating the literal sense of scripture. Others, such as Robert Grosseteste (d. 1253), Bishop of Lincoln, and the *doctor mirabilis* Roger Bacon (1214–92) in Oxford, carried the work forward. In 1312 The Council of Vienne decreed that two teaching posts each for Greek, Hebrew, Syriac and Arabic should be established at Paris, Oxford, Bologna and Salamanca. Much of the new Hebrew scholarship is summed up in Nicholas of **Lyra**'s *Postillae*, strongly influenced by Rashi. The Lollard English Bible (1388), and successive translations into European vernaculars, were influenced in turn by Lyra's work.

It might be said that **Christian Hebraism**, and so indirectly Rashi and the Jewish grammarians, was responsible for the **Reformation**. Scholarly work on the original Hebrew text, as on the Greek of the **New Testament**, cast doubt on traditional Christian **exegesis**; it strengthened the hand of those, like **Luther**, who regarded only scripture (*sola scriptura*) as authoritative, and demanded freedom of interpretation. A similar questioning of traditional interpretation had occurred in the Jewish world, and it is ironic to see the Catholic Richard Simon (1638–1712), a pioneer of historico-critical biblical research, addressing a Protestant correspondent as 'mon cher Caraïte', and signing off 'Le Rabbaniste'.

Still today there are conservative Jews and Christians who do battle with 'proof-texts' and rehearse ancient debates as to whether *almah* in Isa. 7.14 means 'virgin' or 'young woman', or what is the precise meaning of *Shiloh* in Gen. 49.10, or other alleged **Christological** references. In the light of modern biblical scholarship such debates are futile. We must distinguish between the objective study of the biblical texts in their historical context and the use made of those texts within particular faith communities, Christian or Jewish – that is, Christian and Jewish **hermeneutic**. The objective study has its own disciplines, independent of later Christian and Jewish hermeneutic. The use of the Bible in the faith community is quite another matter; there is much for Jews and Christians to learn from each other's hermeneutic, but ultimately the question of what hermeneutic to adopt, and how this relates to the 'plain meaning', is a theological issue constrained but not completely determined by the study of the Hebrew language.   *NORMAN SOLOMON*

Hebrew literature *see* literature, Hebrew, modern

Hegel, Georg Wilhelm Friedrich (1770–1831)

Philosopher. A university lecturer and, from 1818, professor of philosophy in Berlin, Hegel dominated nineteenth-century philosophy and, particularly through his influence on Karl Marx (1818–83), significantly affected politics. Hegel believed his philosophy marked the high-water mark of human attempts to comprehend the 'absolute idea', or God. He considered Jewish religion limited in its apprehension of the absolute, but not wrong. Christianity he thought truer, but justified and fulfilled only in his philosophy. As a result, he lent philosophical credibility to the idea that Protestant Christianity is a more advanced form of religious belief than Judaism.   *STEPHEN PLANT*

Heine, Heinrich (1797–1856)

Born Harry Heine to Jewish parents, Heine converted to Christianity to make a civil service career possible, but is remembered as a poet and essayist. His work explored Judaism, Jewish–Christian encounter, and **antisemitism** in modern Europe. For example, his *Disputation* describes a **disputation** in medieval Toledo. Heine's biography is representative of a generation of Jewish intellectuals who abandoned Judaism only to return to it in later life. He famously regarded baptism as an 'entry ticket to European culture' and said of Judaism, 'I never left it'. Until recently his origins and politics made him a controversial figure in his native **Germany**. Under **Nazism**, his celebrated poem *Die Lorelei*, which has been set to **music** many times, was attributed to an 'author unknown'.   *MELANIE J. WRIGHT*

Hellenism

Three different if related uses of 'Hellenism' are to be distinguished: an ancient **Greek** term, a modern designation of a culture and its interaction in the ancient world, and a modern concept representing both cultural and intellectual movements. Confusion between the different denotations has caused misunderstanding, but has also in the modern era been used to promote anti-Jewish sentiments. A similar confusion has been the basis for an attempted resolution of difficulties in Jewish–Christian relations.

Hellenism first appears as an ethnic designation (as opposed to a cultural or linguistic one) in the apocryphal book 2 Maccabees (4.13). Used in parallelism with the term 'foreign', it denotes the charge levelled by the **Maccabees**, during their revolt against Seleucid rule (167–165 BCE), at the actions of those Jews they considered to be abandoning Jewish practice and succumbing to the ways of their overlords; it is thus presented as antithetical to Judaism. Hellenism in this context appears to be a term of propaganda against the Maccabean opponents, and it should not be considered that the Maccabees were against 'Greek' practices per se. Christian authors in antiquity expanded this ethnic usage to denote paganism in general.

In modern scholarship Hellenism denotes the spread of Greek cultural influence, whether in language, literature, thought or political institutions, throughout the Mediterranean and Near East in antiquity. Such cultural influence (which the Maccabees have erroneously been said to have opposed) was aided by the Empire of Alexander the Great and the kingdoms of his successors, but in most regions it seems that there was a symbiosis of Greek and native cultures rather than a dominance of one over the other. Both Jewish and Christian authors were influenced by Greek language (an influence found even in rabbinic **Hebrew**) and by Greek philosophical concepts and literary forms, and for many Jews in the **Roman Empire** Greek was the usual form of communication and expression. The synagogue, for example, could be said to have been a Greek institution only hebraised in late antiquity.

In the eighteenth century a revival of interest in the classical world, termed Neo-hellenism, produced a binary model of ethnic identity which distinguished between Hebraic and Hellenic, and which soon acquired broader cultural connotations. Drawing upon the work of the German classical scholar J. J. Winckelmann (1717–68), who championed the ideal of a Hellenic age, the historian J. G. Droysen (1808–84) applied the term 'Hellenism' to the cultural fusion of the period after Alexander the Great (d. 323 BCE) when Greek and Near Eastern traditions met. Rejecting the perception of this period as one of post-classical decline, he sought to rehabilitate it as an ideal epoch, a time of transition during which occurred the developments necessary for that fusion of the cultures of the pagan Greek world and the Semitic Eastern lands whose outcome was Christianity. The influence of **Hegel** detectable in the work of Winckelmann makes it possible to see this account of the meeting of Greek and Hebraic elements in Christianity as a Hegelian synthesis; while espousing a synthesis of the Hebraic and the Hellenic, Droysen held to the belief that they were opposed and required the brilliance of Christianity to unite them. The effect that such opinions had on the presentation of Judaism can be detected in a number of writers. Already in the works of Johann Gottfried von Herder (1744–1803) the superiority of the Greeks to the Hebrews had been claimed, with post-exilic Judaism being preferred to pre-exilic, and in the course of the nineteenth century many writers extolled the qualities of Hellenic Christianity in contrast to the more archaic Judaism. In France E. Renan (1823–92) argued that the Semitic (i.e. Israelite) contribution to the championing of paganism was not enough to prevent the charge of small-mindedness from being applied to the Semites, invoking once more the superiority of the Hellenic achievement over the Semitic and even claiming that **Jesus** should be considered a Galilean rather than a Jew. In England, meanwhile, Matthew Arnold (1822–88), under the influence of both Herder and **Heine**, claimed that England required a new Hellenic artistic spirit, seeing English tradition as a combination of Hellenism and the bondage of law and sin in Hebraism. Under Arnold's own influence as a literary critic, a Hebrew–Hellenic opposition has become a popular literary tool, without any prejudicial overtones, and is to be found in literary critics and philosophers, including Emmanuel Levinas (1906–95). This third use of the term Hellenism can often be confused with its designation of the ancient period in some modern studies of ancient Jewish history. Thus one sometimes finds the pre-Christian period portrayed as one of opposition between Judaism and Hellenism, as, for example, in the works of the historian Martin Hengel (b. 1926), who in similar Hegelian terms finds the resolution of such an opposition in a Christianity in which it is no longer possible to separate the two elements. The problem with all such reconstructions is that they do not conform to the historical evidence, which suggests a prevalence of symbiosis over opposition throughout the ancient period. The privileging as ideal of any one culture or age is also highly subjective.

Some Christian writers on Jewish–Christian relations, in an attempt to purge Christianity of its **anti-Judaism**, have resorted to a Hebrew–Hellenic opposition in their historical reconstruction of early Christianity. They have precedence in this from Martin **Buber**, who distinguished the faith of Jesus, as the biblical pattern of faith belonging to the **people of Israel** too, from the faith of **Paul**, a Greek propositional faith. Others have tried to return Christianity to its Jewish roots by downplaying Greco-Roman elements and emphasising a **wisdom** Christology rather than the Greek philosophical **Christology** of the early Councils. This overlooks the fact that early Judaism was itself Hellenistic and that to search for a pure Jewish or 'Hebraic' Christianity is thus a flawed enterprise.

See also **ancient authors**   *JAMES K. AITKEN*

Henry III (1207–72)

King of England (1216–72) whose reign saw the decline of medieval Jewry from a position of relative prosperity to one of complete ruin, buffeted by an increasingly hostile Church. Jews were seen as a source for royal income and, for example, Henry financed his son Edward's **crusade** from Jewish funds. Henry established the *Domus Conversorum* and ordered synagogue worship to be held quietly so that Christians passing by did not have to hear it. In 1217, shortly after **Lateran Council IV**, he ordered that Jews should wear the '**Jew badge**'; Jews were also forbidden to employ Christian nurses or maids or prevent other Jews from converting to Christianity.   *EDWARD KESSLER*

Henry IV (1050–1106)

Holy Roman Emperor and King of Germany (1056–1106) whose measures defined the status of Jews in **Germany**, often in opposition to the less liberal Pope Gregory VII (*r.*1073–85). He allowed baptised Jews to revert to Judaism, notably after the massacres and forced **conversions** of the First **Crusade** in 1096, and asked the Bishop of Speyer to shelter survivors of the massacre. He opposed forced **baptisms** and stated that Jews should come under his jurisdiction rather than the Church, partly because he viewed Jews as valuable property. In 1103, in Mainz, Jews were included for the first time in a *Landfrieden* (peace proclamation) – alongside clerics, women and merchants – in which the emperor pledged to protect certain classes.

EDWARD KESSLER

Herbert, George (1593–1633)

Anglican pastor and poet; his poems, often with biblical resonances, were collected under the title *The Temple*, published posthumously. His 12-line poem 'The Jews' is evocative, especially because he died well before Oliver **Cromwell** allowed Jews to return to England. The poem develops a theme of what might be called benign **supersessionism**. Jews lack vitality because their treasures have been usurped by Christianity. However, through the humble intercession of the Church, Jewish spiritual life will be revitalised. Probably this will take place before the final days. Influenced by Herbert, Henry Vaughan (1622–95) wrote a much longer poem with the same title.   *LAWRENCE E. FRIZZELL*

Heresy

From Greek *hairesis*, which originally meant a free choice, as in 'free-will offering' (Lev. 22.18 LXX), or a party of acceptable opinion, such as **Sadducees**, **Pharisees** and Christians (Acts 5.17; 15.5; 24.14). **Paul** perceived a pejorative in others' designating the Jewish-Christian community as a heresy ('everywhere it is spoken against') and preferred 'The Way'. By the end of the second century, influenced significantly by **Irenaeus** (see, e.g., his *Contra haeresis*), the term 'heresy' was used widely to describe and discredit Christian opponents but not Jews, who were viewed as unbelievers who had a special relationship with the Church. Irenaeus described his own position as orthodox (from *ortho*, 'straight', and *doxa*, thinking), condemning others as heretics. Although the term so understood does not exist in the **Hebrew Bible**, in post-Second Temple Judaism the rabbis used a number of terms to define a heretic, the most relevant to Jewish–Christian relations being *min*. The *minim* (pl.) referred to Jews of offensive theologies and practices and was likely at one time to have included Jewish Christians (*see birkat ha-minim*).

Christian persecution and elimination of Christian heresies tended to ignore Judaism, partly as a result of the influence of **Augustine**'s doctrine, reaffirmed consistently by medieval popes, that Jews were not to be killed or forced to accept **baptism** and that the continued existence of the Jewish people, observing its own faith, was God's will. Thus, after the conversion of **Constantine**, neither the widespread *Adversus Judaeos* **literature** nor Christian violence against Jews results in the elimination of Judaism. Although Jews were forced to live a life of dispersion, subjugation and inferiority, Christian **toleration** of Judaism was far more lenient than the Church's policy toward its own Christian heretics. For its part, Judaism was not beyond concern with heresy and persecution of Jewish heretics. This was sometimes supported by the Christian powers. For example, the Dutch Reformed Church encouraged the Amsterdam Jewish community in its measures against **Spinoza**, whose philosophy influenced Christianity. Since the **Enlightenment** the charge of heresy has carried less and less weight in Judaism and Christianity, although some **fundamentalist** groups still threaten **excommunication** for heretics. For example, ultra-Orthodox Jews accused Chief Rabbi Dr Jonathan Sacks (b. 1948) of heresy in 2002 on account of some statements in his book *Dignity of Difference*, such as his assertion that no one religion has a monopoly on truth. The ongoing power of the charge of heresy within these groups is illustrated by the fact that Sacks changed some of the offending language in the second edition. Controversies within the Jewish community affect Christian–Jewish **dialogue**: for example, significant pressure is brought to bear on Orthodox Jews to refrain from dialogue by the haredim.

EDWARD KESSLER

Herford, R(obert) Travers (1860–1950)

Christian scholar of **Rabbinic Judaism**. Following his education in London and Leiden, Herford served lengthy ministries at Manchester's Stand **Unitarian** Chapel and in London. Like other non-Jewish scholars in this field, Herford took up the study of Rabbinics as an inquiry into Christian origins. He is generally placed in the same class as Charles Taylor (1840–1908) and Herbert **Danby**, British Christians who were disturbed by the prejudices of earlier Christian scholars. Herford regularly translated *halakhah* as 'walking in the way' to deflect any sense of Judaism as legalistic, and

wrote of **Pharisaism**'s piety, loving concern and humaneness. His published works cite a particular indebtedness to the work of Jacob Lauterbach (1873–1942) and Leo **Baeck**. Of his nine books, three of the most significant remain *Christianity in Talmud and Midrash* (1903), *The Pharisees* (1924) and *The Ethics of the Talmud* (1945).

PHILIP CULBERTSON

Hermeneutics

Hermeneutics addresses the assumptions that underlie the process of interpretation. A history of the subject as it affects the interpretation of scripture would require an examination of the earliest theoretical discussions in Plato (427–347 BCE), through the practical rules to be found within both Jewish and Christian tradition, to the modern formal study of the subject following Friedrich Schleiermacher (1768–1834), Wilhelm Dilthey (1833–1911), Martin Heidegger (1889–1976), Hans-Georg Gadamer (1900–2002) and Paul Ricoeur (1913–2005). In the modern era the church would be represented by Rudolf Bultmann (1884–1976) and Karl Barth (1886–1968), the Jewish world by Hermann **Cohen**, Franz **Rosenzweig**, Martin **Buber** and Leo **Baeck**. The interaction between the two traditions in their engagement with the biblical text is a key element in Jewish–Christian relations.

Fishbane (b. 1943) distinguishes between *explicatio*, which addresses the philological or historical content of a text and *interpretatio*, which engages with the reception of the text by later generations. Regarding the former, the ongoing Jewish engagement with the Hebrew text led Christians to turn to the rabbis when seeking to uncover the 'plain' meaning of scripture. Thus **Origen** in the third century CE, the first Christian scholar to study **Hebrew**, consulted leading Jewish scholars during visits to the **land of Israel**. In the fourteenth century Nicholas of **Lyra**, in his commitment to a **commentary** on the literal meaning of the Bible, studied the commentaries of **Rashi**, in which regard he was following the similar step taken by **Andrew of St Victor**. Lyra in turn influenced the **Bible translations** of Wycliffe (*c*.1329–84) and of **Luther**. However, the 'traffic' was not simply in one direction, as Rashi's concern with creating a sentence-by-sentence commentary expounding the *peshat* (plain meaning) of **Torah** parallels the contemporary development in Christian circles of a movement that sought to emphasise the literal meaning of scripture.

On the level of *interpretatio* the rabbis derived hermeneutic rules (*middot*) for the interpretation of scripture: 7 *middot* are attributed to Hillel, 13 to Rabbi Ishmael and 32 to Rabbi Jose Galili. The former two addressed primarily issues of law, *halakhah*, while the latter addressed broader ethical and moral issues, *aggadah*. Similar methods can be found operating in the **New Testament**. Later Jewish commentary tends to reflect the need to counter Christian contentions regarding, for example, the divinity of **Jesus** and related Messianic expectations, sometimes fought out in the context of **disputations**. Hence a variety of Jewish interpretations of Isa. 52–53, the 'Suffering Servant' passage, identify this figure at various times with the Jewish people as a whole, with one of the prophets or kings, even with the 'yet-to-appear' **Messiah**, all of which served to combat Christian identification of the text with Jesus.

In **modernity**, with the radical change in the central authority of scripture, Christians and Jews face similar problems. The assault on the traditional view of scripture by historical criticism (*see* **biblical criticism**) affected both traditions equally. However, by the end of the twentieth century both had found ways of accommodating themselves to the challenge, either by an outward rejection of the approach, the 'neo-orthodox' or 'fundamentalist' position, or by emphasising the human contribution over time to the process of **revelation**. *JONATHAN MAGONET*

Herod/Herodian dynasty

Herod the Great, his son Antipas and his grandson Agrippa I are remembered differently by Jews and Christians. Rome appointed Herod (73–?4 BCE), grandson of an Idumean convert to Judaism, king of Judea, Galilee and Perea in 40 BCE. Matt. 2.1–18 depicts Herod as a new Pharaoh who slaughters Jewish children in the effort to kill the rival 'King of the Jews' mentioned by the Magi. Although some interpreters distinguish the evil Jewish Herod from the faithful Gentile Magi, Matthew's Gospel rejects such division: the holy family and slaughtered children are also Jews. Whereas today Jews remember Herod primarily for building the Western Wall (the Kotel), contemporary Jewish sources confirm Matthew's picture of a paranoid despot. **Josephus** suggests Herod died *c*.4 BCE, although Luke 2.2 sets the nativity when Quirinius governed Syria (*c*.6 CE). This possible discrepancy (the dates Josephus provides are not without problems) has served as an argument against the historicity of the Gospels. Herod's son Antipas (?13 BCE–?45), the tetrarch of Galilee, beheaded **John the Baptist** either because John condemned his incestuous marriage (so the Gospels) or as a pre-emptive strike against John's popularity (so Josephus). Christian writings describe Agrippa I (*c*.10 BCE–44 CE) unfavourably: he executed James, imprisoned Peter and, not having rebuffed the crowd's idolatry towards him, died ignominiously, devoured by worms (Acts 12.20–23). Jewish tradition emphasises his generous and compassionate nature and his observance of **halakhic** regulations (e.g. Josephus, *Ant.* 19.330f.). *AMY-JILL LEVINE*

Herzl, Theodor (1860–1904)

Budapest-born father of political **Zionism**. As a journalist he covered the **Dreyfus Affair** in 1895, which convinced him of the need for a radical solution to **antisemitism**. In *The Jewish State* (1896) he outlined a secular argument for the establishment of a Jewish state, not necessarily in Palestine. Despite a lack of interest in Jewish religious Zionism, Herzl was prepared to tolerate **Christian Zionism** insofar as it helped him to gain the support of European powers. One of Herzl's earliest supporters (present at the first World Zionist Conference, 1897) was the Anglican priest and Restorationist William Hechler (1845–1931) who pressed for a return to **Israel** and who introduced Herzl to a number of powerful contacts within the German ruling classes. *DANIEL R. LANGTON*

Heschel, Abraham Joshua (1907–72)

Philosopher, theologian, and social activist. Born in Warsaw, Poland, the descendant of long lines of renowned hasidic rabbis, Heschel eventually became the most prominent American Jewish religious thinker of the twentieth century. Raised to become a hasidic rebbe, he emerged as one of the most influential Jews with respect to Jewish–Christian relations. He earned his doctorate in philosophy at the University of Berlin (1933), succeeded Martin **Buber** as director of Jüdische Lehrhaus (founded by Franz **Rosenzweig**) in Frankfurt-am-Main (1937–8) and taught at Hebrew Union College in Cincinnatti (1940–5) and at the Jewish Theological Seminary in New York (1945–72).

A prolific writer, Heschel made scholarly contributions to the study of the **Bible**, rabbinic literature, medieval philosophy, Jewish **mysticism**, Hasidism and interfaith relations. His books – especially *The Sabbath* (1951), *Man Is not Alone* (1951), *Man's Quest for God* (1954) and *God in Search of Man* (1955) – have inspired countless Christians as well as Jews to perceive the spiritual grandeur of Judaism. Heschel's social activism also had great influence on Jewish–Christian relations. In 1963 he delivered the keynote address at the National Conference on Religion and Race, which led to widespread participation by rabbis and Christian clergy in the great 'march on Washington'. He often appeared with Martin Luther King (1929–68), who called Heschel 'a truly great prophet', and he walked by King's side in the front row of the march at Selma. Heschel and King forged a close friendship that became symbolic of fruitful Jewish–Christian encounter. A co-founder of the national interfaith group Clergy and Laity Concerned about Vietnam, Heschel inspired King to join him in publicly protesting against the war in Vietnam and in working to end it.

Active in formal interfaith relations, Heschel assumed a prominent role in negotiations between Jewish organisations and the hierarchy of the Roman Catholic Church before and during **Vatican II**. He was the most influential American Jewish delegate at the council, encouraging Church leaders to condemn **antisemitism**, to eliminate **anti-Judaism** from Church teachings and to acknowledge the integrity and permanent preciousness of Judaism. Although the final conciliar decree on interfaith relations, *Nostra Aetate*, did not fulfil Heschel's expectations, he considered it a landmark in the history of Jewish–Christian relations. Heschel also had far-reaching interfaith influence apart from formal interfaith **dialogue**. Through his writing, teaching and public lecturing, he taught Jews and Christians to recognise the sanctity of each other's religion and helped them realise the mutual spiritual benefits of interfaith encounter. Living his last decade of life in the midst of an interfaith revolution he helped create, Heschel had the opportunity to reach the Christian world in ways unknown to Jews of previous generations. And while he was one of many Jewish religious thinkers of the twentieth century to influence Christian thinking, he more than others fostered an enhanced appreciation of Judaism among Christians and a new Christian self-understanding vis-à-vis Judaism.   JOHN C. MERKLE

Hexapla

A compilation by **Origen** in parallel columns, the Hexapla contained the **Hebrew** text of the Tanakh/Old Testament, the Hebrew transliterated into **Greek** characters, the Jewish translation of **Aquila**, that of Symmachus (second century CE), the **Septuagint**, and the version of Theodotion (late second century CE?). It is preserved in quotations in the **Church Fathers**, marginal notes on manuscripts and a few manuscript leaves of the Hexapla itself. Its purpose is disputed, as its role may have been for textual criticism or education, but Origen (*Ep. Afr.* 9.5) claims he compiled it for debate with the Jews. **Eusebius** certainly made use of Aquila, Symmachus and Theodotion (sometimes known as 'the Three') for his *Proof of the Gospel*, which is an **apologetic**, and amongst *Adversus Judaeos* texts the *Anonymous Dialogue with the Jews* (sixth century?) employs them extensively.

See also **Bible translations, ancient**

JAMES K. AITKEN

Historic Peace Churches

The Historic Peace Churches (HPCs) – Brethren, **Quakers** and Mennonites (the largest of the **Anabaptist** family of churches) – are Christian communions that refuse to participate in war or to justify it theologically. They also share some common approaches to **Church and state** relations and to Jewish–Christian relations, and histories of persecution. Sociologist Max Weber (1864–1920) termed them 'believers' churches' because of their emphasis on voluntaryism. The groups have their origins in the Radical **Reformation** and English Revolution. The HPC umbrella label dates from 1935, when Church representatives met in Kansas to discuss how their pacifism could be ecumenically articulated. Since then the HPCs have come together periodically, most recently to influence the World Council of Churches' 'Decade to Overcome Violence' (2001–2010).

Debates about HPC identity were to the fore during and after the **Holocaust**. HPC members' responses during this period varied. Some European Mennonites abandoned pacifism and supported **Hitler**; their American counterparts, and the other HPCs, generally opposed **Nazism** but were slow to criticise **antisemitism**, at least before Kristallnacht. In keeping with the HPCs' general preference for implicit theology, they have issued no collective statements on issues in Jewish–Christian relations, although some individual HPC churches have done so. It is only very recently that HPCs have begun to examine how being a peace church informs relationships with other Christians and with those of other faiths, including Jews. Whilst many Quakers subscribe to some form of pluralism, the normative HPC position does not reject **mission** per se, but criticises much Christian witness, viewing it as abusive of power, reductionist in its emphasis on **doctrine** and ritual, and overly identified with Western culture.

MELANIE J. WRIGHT

Historical criticism *see* **biblical criticism**

Historical Jesus

Studies of the historical Jesus – an attempt to separate the pre-**Easter** historical figure of **Jesus** from the post-Easter **Christ** of faith – have been led by Christian theologians and scholars over several centuries, but were invigorated by Abraham **Geiger**'s multi-volume nineteenth-century work on the history of Judaism, treating Jesus as part of Jewish history, and Albert Schweitzer's (1875–1965) *The Quest of the Historical Jesus*. Several waves of intense research occurred in the twentieth century, with emerging focus on the Jewish roots of Jesus.

Many Christian and Jewish scholars today concur that Jesus was a hasidic Jew from the Galilee who developed a group of disciples and taught in the **Temple** and among the people. He was a miracle-worker who attracted the disinherited and outcasts, as well as some wealthy Jews. He had a relationship with the **Pharisees** and ties to renewal groups such as the Qumran sect. He proclaimed the rule of God as having arrived, and was crucified at the age of 33 after he refused to cooperate with either Temple or Roman authorities.

Jesus preached about the **Kingdom of God**, a central Jewish motif, and invited people to repent as a means of entering the Kingdom, also a Jewish mandate. Scholars contend that his **love** ethic, including love for the enemy, was based on the book of Leviticus (19.15–18), as were his urgings to turn away from revenge and retaliation. There is no evidence that Jesus sought to establish a new religion. Rather, as a prophet of renewal he sought to draw people back to covenantal faithfulness. He sought the unity of the Jewish people under the sovereignty of God. When he referred to himself as '**son of man**' (Mark 2.10 as

one of many examples) or used formulas such as 'In very truth I tell you . . .' (Mark 3.28, also one example) he drew from a well of unshakeable confidence in Judaism and a conviction that God loved him and all people.

Some of the finest portraits of the historical Jesus have been presented by Jewish scholars based in Jerusalem (Joseph **Klausner**, David Flusser (1917–2000), Scholem Ben Chorin (1913–99)). Other leading Jewish contributors include Samuel Sandmel (1911–79), Paula Fredriksen (b. 1951), Geza Vermes (b. 1924) and Martin **Buber**, who in 1919 (*Der Heilige Weg*; 'The Holy Way') referred to Jesus as 'brother' of the Jews and argued that Jesus was a representative Jew concerned about the unity of humankind who opened up the Jewish faith to the world.

Christian scholars and theologians now routinely teach that Jesus, his family and all his early followers were Jews, and that the **New Testament** was written within a Jewish context. Rediscovering the Jewish origins of Christianity has also led to a greater understanding of and appreciation for **Torah**, which Christians often pictured as a burden rather than as a joy (for delight in the Law, see Ps. 119.77, 174). In a Christian context this celebration of respect or awe for the Law appears in the *Epistle to Diognetus* (12.6) (*see* **Apostolic Fathers**).

WILLIAM KLASSEN

Hitler, Adolf (1889–1945)

German leader and antisemite. For Hitler, race, not religion, was the dominant motive for his objective of destroying Jews and Judaism. He believed that Jews were responsible for **Germany**'s defeat in the First World War, and in his autobiography *Mein Kampf* (1924) he wrote: 'The Jew has always been a people with definite racial characteristics and never a religion; only in order to get ahead he early sought for a means which could distract unpleasant attention from his person.' Yet if race provided the mythology and motivation for **antisemitism**, secularised religious language provided the justification. Hitler employed religious imagery and did not hesitate to use overtly Christian language to appeal to a pious audience. He wrote that the Jews' 'whole existence is an embodied protest against the aesthetics of the Lord's image' and affirmed that 'I am acting in accordance with the will of the Almighty Creator: by defending myself against the Jew, I am fighting for the word of the Lord'. Such statements show the legacy of the *Adversus Judaeos* literature and the Church's centuries of teaching of contempt. As Jules **Isaac** showed immediately after the war, it was this that sowed the seeds of hatred and made it so easy for Hitler to use antisemitism as a political weapon. Controversy still surrounds the actions of Cardinal Eugenio Pacelli (Pope **Pius XII**), who signed a concordat in 1935 guaranteeing the right of the Church 'to regulate her own affairs', the terms of which Hitler broke almost immediately. Hitler's actions against Jews started immediately after he gained power in January 1933, and when the war ended in 1945 so had a whole way of life for European Jews. *EDWARD KESSLER*

Hoi Ioudaioi

In biblical and non-biblical sources of the Greco-Roman period the expression *hoi Ioudaioi* ('the Jews') is mostly used in a neutral sense. In Jewish–Christian relations problems arise from the negative use of the term in the **New Testament**. Although a problematic use can also be found in 1 Thess. 2.14–16 and Matt. 28.15, scholarly discussion has focused mainly on the Fourth Gospel, where the expression 'the Jews' is used extensively, with frequently changing referents (the whole people, the authorities in **Jerusalem**, the **Pharisees**, the Judeans etc.) and in approximately half the cases with a pejorative meaning in the context of fierce conflict (with a climax in John 8.31–59). This evidence confronts Jewish–Christian relations with the question of whether **anti-Judaism** exists in the New Testament. The Fourth Gospel (John) is the most Judaeo-centric of the Gospels, and almost everyone we meet there is a Jew. Nevertheless, there are some among these Jews to whom the evangelist refers as 'the Jews'. The meaning associated with this expression has important implications for the question whether the Fourth Gospel has anti-Jewish dimensions: the broader the assumed meaning, the greater the potential for anti-Judaism; the narrower the meaning, the smaller the potential.

Many authors use historical, sociological, geographical or theological arguments to limit the referent of 'the Jews' (von Wahlde, 'The Johannine "Jews"', '"The Jews" in the Gospel of John', Motyer (*Your Father the Devil*), cf. the document of the Pontifical Biblical Commission *On the Jewish People and their Sacred Scriptures*, nr. 79 (2001)). In this way they can argue that John is not anti-Jewish, since he does not intend to refer to Jews of all times,

but to first-century Jews (historical); not to all Jewish social groups, but only to the Jewish authorities (sociological); not to all places, but to Judea (geographical); not to Jews of all faith convictions, but only to those who do not believe in the Johannine **Jesus** (theological). A limitation of the scope of 'the Jews' is in many cases the correct interpretation and avoids the danger of generalising the negative connotation to the entire **people of Israel**.

A number of authors have, however, raised critical questions about these attempts to limit the referent of 'the Jews' in John (e.g. Culpepper, *John the Son of Zebedee*, Reinhartz, *Befriending the Beloved Disciple*). While the expression frequently refers to the Jerusalem authorities, there are places, especially John 6.41, 52, where it clearly refers to the Jewish people as a whole. As to the geographical limitation, by the time of the New Testament the scope of the expression had taken on a religious meaning and included not only Judeans, but also Galileans (cf. John 4.9). Independently of its referent, however, the term tends to generalise and stereotype the people referred to. Even if a limited referent was originally intended, by using the general expression 'the Jews', with changing referents, it becomes possible for later readers to universalise its scope and in the extreme to include Jews of all times and places.

Here the question arises whether anti-Judaism can be limited to later interpreters, or whether the fourth evangelist himself is to be held responsible for the anti-Jewish potential of the text. This means that even the commonly accepted 'two-level drama technique' (Martyn, *The Gospel of John*), which sees in the Fourth Gospel a combination of the story of the earthly Jesus (level one) and the story of the Johannine community (level two), and which by the use of *hoi Ioudaioi* projects the conflict with opponents of the Johannine community onto the conflict with opponents of the earthly Jesus, cannot solve the problem. For the two-level drama technique is morally problematic, especially in the light of post-***Shoah*** Christian–Jewish relations, since it runs the risk of legitimating the 'transfer of hostility' from the time of Jesus to the time of the Johannine community and beyond. No matter how sophisticated the attempts to avoid an anti-Jewish understanding of the Fourth Gospel, the general expression 'the Jews' and its use in the (con)text confronts each reading of the Gospel of John with the risk of a new 'transfer of hostility' and raises the question how to deal with this problem in Christian life and in Christian–Jewish relations.

Several suggestions have been made to reduce the anti-Jewish potential of *hoi Ioudaioi*: leaving it untranslated, or even removing the most problematic text (John 8.43–50) completely from the Gospel; translating it as 'the Judeans' or 'the Jewish authorities'; putting 'the Jews' between quotation marks, or adding footnotes historically to contextualise the problem. However, none of these proposals addresses the underlying issue of the **Christology** of John. In John 'the Jews' are those Jews who remain 'disciples of Moses' and refuse to become 'disciples of Jesus': the negative use of the term is a barometer of the 'parting of the ways' between Christianity and Judaism. The fourth evangelist constructs his Christology in such a way that only those who believe in Jesus as the **Messiah** and the **Son of God** are authentic believers. But even though many of the statements of the evangelist tend towards exclusivism, the deepest message of the Gospel is inclusivistic insofar as it stresses that Jesus was sent for the **salvation** of the world (John 3.16, cf. 4.42), that is, of all. Some Johannine scholars (e.g. Schneiders, *The Revelatory Text, With Oil in their Lamps*) today stress God's universal salvific intention as the 'ultimate horizon' (Ricoeur (1913–2005)) of the Gospel of John. In a post-*Shoah* context, searching for a non-**supersessionist** theology, this theology implies that God's plan of salvation is so universal that the rejection of Christ as mediator of salvation is not necessarily a reason for excluding Jews from salvation. In this view the Fourth Gospel projects an all-inclusive 'alternative world' (Ricoeur, *The Conflict of Interpretation*) which transcends its anti-Jewish potential and therefore need not present a stumbling block for Jewish–Christian relations.

DIDIER POLLEFEYT AND REIMUND BIERINGER

Holdheim, Samuel (1806–60)

German Reform rabbi and scholar. A radical reformer, Holdheim personified the so-called nineteenth-century Christianisation of Judaism (*see* **Progressive Judaism**). Despite a traditional **talmudic** education, he shared a common Christian assumption that the destruction of the Second **Temple** and **Jerusalem** had been a sign from God that the civil and ritual laws were no longer necessary. If, he argued, only the moral teach-

ings remained, then **Rabbinic Judaism** should be regarded as an unhelpful development and of limited relevance to the modern Jew. Among the reforms he introduced at the Berlin congregation established in 1847 were such 'Christian customs' as Sunday services and bareheaded worship.   *DANIEL R. LANGTON*

Holiness

Though there are some differences of emphasis, holiness is a unifying concept in Jewish–Christian relations. For both Jews and Christians holiness derives from God himself. He is holy (*kaddosh*). The most common epithet for God in rabbinical literature is 'The Holy One, blessed be He', that is, set apart from his creation. (The title 'Holy One' is also frequent in Isa. 40–55.) Much of Jewish and Christian **liturgy** emphasises God's holiness as a cause for adoration. Jewish and Christian scripture contains numerous references not only to God's holiness but also to the consequent need for his people to be holy. This is worked out variously by Judaism and Christianity in both ceremonial and moral terms. Judaism tends to emphasise the idea of separation from and Christianity the idea of dedication to something, but the two processes are inextricably linked. By rejecting certain activities and thoughts, both Jew and Christian are believed to come closer to God. The so-called 'holiness code' of Lev. 17–26 spells out the requirements incumbent on a people who accept the invitation to be 'a priestly kingdom and a holy nation' (Exod. 19.6). The recurrent refrain of Leviticus is: 'You shall be holy, for I the LORD your God am holy' (e.g. 19.2). This is to be expressed in ways ranging from how they treat their neighbour to being distinctive by eating only permitted food (Lev. 19.17–18 and 11.44–47 respectively). 1 Peter presents Christians as inheriting this position as a **covenant** people (notably 1.15–16 and 2.9–10). Whether this implies the **supersession** of Judaism by Christianity remains a vexed question in Jewish–Christian relations. In both traditions writings, places, people, things and, supremely, times are set apart as holy. In his prose poem 'The Sabbath' **Heschel** writes: 'Judaism teaches us to be attached to holiness *in time* . . . The Sabbaths are our great cathedrals; and our Holy of Holies is the Day of Atonement.' So the *Kiddush* (meaning 'sanctifying') is recited at the beginning of Jewish festivals, setting the time apart. Other important Jewish prayers take their title from the opening word or phrase in

Hebrew or Aramaic, derived from the same Hebrew root for 'to be holy'. From the *Kedushah* comes the Christian *Sanctus*, both in turn deriving from the words of the seraphim in Isa. 6.3. **Nahmanides**, in his commentary on Lev. 19.2, argues that not only the holy man (*ha-kodesh*, a title reserved for the most saintly) but also the average Jew must go beyond the law in his cultivation of holiness. Jewish **mysticism** conceives of a particular unity with God achieved by the most holy. The hasidic practice of going to pray at the gravestone of famous rebbes may be taken to indicate belief in the great holiness of figures who are exceptionally close to God. Exceptional **sainthood** is also part of the Christian tradition, but so too is the notion that all God's people are called to be saints, combining the moral and spiritual connotations of Jewish holiness. As in Judaism, human beings attain holiness as they imitate God in all his attributes, such as mercy (*b. Shabbat* 133b), though, in Christianity, the model is seen as God in **Christ**, not only as a historical figure but as a present reality in the experience of his followers (for example, Francis of Assisi (1182–1226) and, most famously, Thomas à Kempis (1380–1471)). John **Wesley** drew on the Catholic tradition in his stress on the pursuit of holiness, combining it with the Protestant **justification** by faith in his ideas of 'perfection'. The Salvation Army's main act of worship is the 'holiness meeting' and there have been 'holiness movements' ranging from those in mid-nineteenth-century America to the Keswick Conventions in Britain. The largest holiness denomination in Britain today is the Church of the Nazarene with which three holiness groupings of British origin have joined. The defining characteristic of these Christian movements or denominations is a stress on God's action. Their members offer themselves to God trusting that he can work in them. In the late nineteenth century particularly they constituted a reaction against all the effort and endeavour of **Calvinism** as the road to **sanctification**. There are similarities here with the Jewish emphasis on holiness as something God uses in and for people. That what is vital is the power of the **Holy Spirit** is reflected in the scriptures of both traditions.   *CHRISTINE PILKINGTON*

Holocaust

The Holocaust is a central preoccupation of post-war Jewish–Christian relations. Yet it is frequently assumed that we know what the Holocaust was/is,

that all that is required is for the Churches to apologise for past actions or inaction and Jews and Christians can demonstrate their 'new' relationship through their shared commitment to commemorating the Holocaust, thus ensuring it never happens again. *Sharing One Hope? The Church of England and Christian–Jewish Relations* (2001) begs to differ and notes that 'many aspects of [the Holocaust's] history, its current commemoration, and its philosophical or theological interpretation arouse great controversy'.

'The Holocaust' is a complex metanarrative with multiple chronologies (histories of the Holocaust differed from country to country), incorporating numerous experiences and events (e.g. the *Kindertransports*, **ghettos**, hiding, resistance, the *Einsatzgruppen*, death camps) and perspectives (the 'classic' typology of victims, perpetrators and **bystanders**). How one experienced the Holocaust was influenced by factors such as gender, class, nationality, political and religious affiliation. The multifaceted, contested nature of the Holocaust provokes numerous controversies over appropriate commemoration of the Holocaust; recurrent disputes over the presence of Christian symbols at **Auschwitz** being the most obvious example (*see* **Carmelite controversy**).

Whilst there is agreement over the importance of remembering and studying these events, there is no consensus over how to interpret them. To take one example, there is deep-rooted disagreement over the uniqueness of the Holocaust and its relationship to Nazi persecution of 'other' victims, whether in the Euthanasia Programme or policies targeting Gypsies, Poles, Soviet POWs, homosexuals or **Jehovah's Witnesses**. Confronted with such disagreement, Christians making statements about the Holocaust can either follow the **Church of England**'s example and simply note alternative viewpoints, or risk articulating a more explicit position that, however well meant and carefully worded, will attract criticism from those with differing views. Thus, Pope **John Paul II** was heavily criticised for saying, as a Polish Catholic, to the Jewish community in Warsaw, 'the threat against you was also a threat against us; this latter was not realized to the same extent because it did not have the time to be fulfilled to the same degree' (14 June 1989 and 9 June 1991), and two of the more controversial elements of *We Remember: A Reflection on the Shoah*

(1998) were its robust defence of Pope **Pius XII** and the claim that **Nazism** was 'a thoroughly modern neo-pagan regime' which rejected Christianity and sought to destroy the Church or subject it 'to the interests of the Nazi state'.

Three areas continue to dominate discussion of the Holocaust in this context: **anti-Judaism/**antisemitism, the responses of Christians 1933–45 and post-Holocaust responses. *The Ten Points of* **Seelisberg** (1947) conceded that, whilst the church has 'always affirmed the un-Christian character of antisemitism, as of all forms of racial hatred', it failed 'to prevent the manifestation among Christians, in various forms, of an undiscriminating racial hatred of the Jews as a whole people'. Disagreement persists as to whether anti-Judaism/**antisemitism** should be seen as sinful and 'un-Christian' or as central to Christian self-understanding. Church statements adopt the first position; many Holocaust theologians the latter, for example, Rosemary Radford Ruether (b. 1936) insists that anti-Judaism is the 'left hand of Christology'.

Christian responses to the Holocaust varied enormously. Individuals and institutions failed to demonstrate solidarity with their Jewish neighbours by condemning and actively opposing Nazi policies. It is essential to differentiate between such failures and explicit endorsement of, and active participation in, Nazi policies, whether by groups (e.g. the *Deutsche Christen*) or individuals (e.g. Dr Jozef Tiso, a Catholic priest who, as leader of Slovakia, collaborated with **Hitler**). It is equally important to remember and reflect on Christian resistance, both individual and collective (e.g. The White Rose in **Germany**, Le Chambon in **France**). The bitter controversy over Pope Pius XII and access to the Vatican's archives for 1939–45 suggests that there has yet to be a full, unapologetic exploration of the complex and varied Christian motivations and responses during the Holocaust. In 1999 the International Catholic–Jewish Historical Commission was appointed (by the Vatican's Commission for Religious Relations with the Jews and the International Jewish Committee on Interreligious Consultations) with instructions to do precisely this. It suspended its activities in 2001 amidst considerable acrimony, demonstrating both the deeply rooted sensitivities and the practical difficulties involved in such a process.

Post-Holocaust responses take the form of statements on Christian–Jewish relations (the majority issued by Christian churches, with exceptions such as *Dabru Emet* (2000)) or post-Holocaust theologies outlining the impact that the Holocaust either has had, or should have, on Jewish and Christian self-understanding (by Jewish thinkers such as Marc Ellis (b. 1952), Emil Fackenheim (1916–2003), Melissa Raphael (b. 1960) and Richard Rubenstein (b. 1924); and Christian thinkers such as Alice (b. 1923) and Roy Eckardt (1918–98), Katharina von Kellenbach (b. 1960), Friedrich-Wilhelm Marquardt (1928–2002) and Ruether). Whilst these represent a start, *Sharing One Hope?* notes that 'much more needs to be done by Christians on [the Holocaust's] theological implications'. In recent years considerable changes have been made in the teaching of **Hebrew Bible** and **New Testament**, yet impact on the teaching of theology is less obvious. Post-**Holocaust theology**, when acknowledged at all (particularly in a European context), is generally studied on its own terms as a special subject, rather than as an integral part of courses on dogmatic or systematic theology.

Dabru Emet is typical in combining all three elements outlined above, performing a delicate balancing act. It begins by condemning Christian anti-Judaism (Nazi ideology would never have 'taken hold' or been 'carried out' but for the 'long history of Christian anti-Judaism'; many Christians 'participated, or were sympathetic to, Nazi atrocities against Jews', others failed to 'protest sufficiently'). Simultaneously, it insists that 'Nazism was not a Christian phenomenon', nor was it 'an inevitable outcome of Christianity', and the authors echo John Paul II in stating that if 'the Nazi extermination of the Jews had been fully successful, it would have turned its murderous rage more directly to Christians'. Finally, it applauds 'recent efforts in Christian theology to repudiate unequivocally contempt of Judaism and the Jewish people'. Unsurprisingly, this treatment of the Holocaust was the most controversial element of *Dabru Emet*. Responses ranged from outright condemnation to delight at the acknowledgement of fundamental change within the Christian churches. Commitment to remembering and reflecting on the Holocaust clearly continues to divide, as much as it unites, Christians and Jews.

See also **Holocaust education**; **Holocaust Memorial Days**; *Shoah*   ISABEL WOLLASTON

Holocaust education

Confronting the Holocaust (**Shoah**) is essential to the relation of Jews and Christians. Indeed, the principal impetus for scrutinising traditional Christian teaching about Jews and Judaism originates from facing ways such teaching prepared the ground on which the 'venomous plant of hatred for the Jews was able to flourish' ('Declaration of Repentance', Catholic Bishops of France, 1997). The 2001 *Leuenberg Document* from the Reformation Churches in Europe declares that the **Holocaust** demands 'permanent theological self-examination and renewal [that] compels us to investigate the causes of the hatred of Jews' that 'repeatedly breaks out anew' (*see* **Leuenberg Church Fellowship**). Moreover, Holocaust education is vital to counter claims of the 'myth' of the Holocaust spread by deniers who allege Jews have exaggerated, even invented, the charge of Nazi genocide. It is fundamental to fulfilling the hope expressed in the 1998 Vatican document *We Remember: Reflections on the Shoah*: 'The spoiled seeds of anti-Judaism and antisemitism must never again be allowed to take root in any human heart.'

Thus, many churches have a profound commitment to Holocaust education. Often collaborating with Jewish agencies and institutions, they have published resources, sponsored conferences and workshops for teachers, and designed curricula. They have encouraged rituals and prayers for Holocaust **remembrance**, particularly around *Yom HaShoah* (Day of Holocaust Remembrance, on 27 Nisan in the Jewish calendar, which is the fifth day following the eighth day of Passover; *see* **Holocaust Memorial Days**). The National Catholic Center for Holocaust Education, Seton Hill University in Greensburg, Pennsylania, working in cooperation with Israel's *Yad Vashem*, The Holocaust Martyrs' and Heroes' Remembrance Authority in Jerusalem, provides many resources for teachers.

Of course, study of the Holocaust, a serious interest of many committed to the elimination of intolerance, prejudice, discrimination and genocide, transcends the Jewish–Christian relationship. This widespread interest provides Christians and Jews with a burgeoning array of scholarly and popular resources. Universities offer courses that approach the Holocaust from diverse disciplines. The Facing History and Ourselves National Foundation, instituted in 1979 in Boston, Massachusetts, offers programmes, resources and speakers to help middle and secondary school teachers relate the teaching of the Holocaust and other instances of collective violence to contemporary issues. Private foundations underwrite collections of testimonies of survivors; the Shoah Foundation established by filmmaker Steven Spielberg (b. 1946) has videotaped some 51,000 testimonies in 32 languages from persons living in 57 countries. **Internet** sites offer a wealth of information, permitting computer users to study documentation, view maps and photographs, read interpretive essays, do virtual tours of concentration camp museums, and download resources for teaching. Some sites offer interactive materials for children.

Holocaust **museums** and educational centres offer a wealth of resources on which Jews and Christians may also draw. While the most notable is *Yad Vashem*, with its archives containing over 58 million pages of documentation, and its library more than 87,000 volumes, museums are widespread: Central and Eastern Europe, Australia (Sydney and Melbourne), Canada (Vancouver), Japan (Fukuyama City) and the United Kingdom (Nottinghamshire). In addition to the United States Holocaust Memorial Museum in Washington DC, at least 18 other cities in the United States house museums or centres.

MARY C. BOYS

Holocaust Memorial Days

Holocaust Memorial Days (HMDs) are government-initiated days of **remembrance** established as a relatively recent attempt to insert the **Holocaust** into formal narratives of national collective memory.

In 1951 the Israeli government established 27 Nisan as Holocaust and Ghetto Uprising Remembrance Day (*Yom HaShoah veHaGvurah*). Their hope was that *Yom HaShoah* would be a focal point for Israeli collective memory, and be observed by Jewish communities worldwide. Yet, over 50 years later, it is still not universally observed. It faced Orthodox opposition from the start with many **Orthodox Jews** preferring to remember the Holocaust on traditional fast days such as *Tisha Be'av* and *Asarah Betevet* (in 1948 the rabbinic authorities in Israel designated the latter as the appropriate date on which to say *Kaddish* and light *yahrzeit* candles for Jews who died in the Holocaust whose date of death is unknown).

Whereas *Yom HaShoah* falls within the Jewish **calendar**, most HMDs are designed by, and for, non-Jews as part of a national civic cycle of commemorative events. The Holocaust is remembered as part of a broader educational agenda promoting anti-racism, pluralism, multiculturalism and **civil society**. Local, regional and national events take place, with particular attention paid to participation of schools and representatives of each country's faith communities. This linkage of the Holocaust to broader educational, political and social issues, and to subsequent genocides, remains a source of controversy among both Jews and non-Jews.

Elie Wiesel (b. 1928), chair of the United States Holocaust Memorial Council (USHMC), played a key role in establishing the Holocaust in the American civic calendar. In 1980 Congress passed a law giving the USHMC responsibility for establishing and promoting annual (weeklong) Days of Remembrance. At Wiesel's insistence, the Days of Remembrance coincided with *Yom HaShoah*. Events are ecumenical and interfaith, reflecting the role the Holocaust now plays in American civil religion. There are an increasing number of interfaith **liturgies** (see, for example, those collected by Marcia Littell). In May 2000 the United **Methodist** Church's General Conference passed a resolution calling for the promotion of observance of *Yom HaShoah* in local congregations.

The Stockholm Forum on Holocaust Education, Remembrance and Research (2000), attended by delegates from 44 governments from around the world, played a crucial role in establishing and promoting HMDs: European government ministers committed themselves to establishing an annual day dedicated to Holocaust education and remembrance. Various dates were chosen, creating a national HMD alongside *Yom HaShoah*. Several countries, for example Estonia, Finland, Sweden and the UK, observe HMD on 27 January (the date **Auschwitz** was liberated). Others chose dates with particular national resonance, for example 3 May (the Czech Republic), 16 July (France), 4 July (Latvia) and 29 September (Lithuania).

HMDs are a vehicle for the civil religion of a particular country. Emphasis is placed upon education and ecumenical/interfaith cooperation. HMDs are an important vehicle for **Holocaust education**, particularly in schools. They provide Churches with an opportunity to disseminate new thinking on Jewish–Christian relations since 1945. Thus, when in 2003 HMD fell on a Sunday the Catholic Bishops' Conference of England and Wales published *Judaism and Christianity: Healing the Breach: Suggestions for Teachers and Preachers*. Despite such initiatives, observance of HMD in the UK is, as yet, nowhere near as firmly established in the national political and religious commemorative calendar as are the Days of Remembrance in the US or *Yom HaShoah* in Israel.

See also **memorialisation**   *ISABEL WOLLASTON*

Holocaust theology

The **Holocaust** is a term used to denote the systematic, state-sponsored campaign to persecute and eliminate the Jewish people during the Second World War. The implementation of Nazi policies that culminated in mass-murder required a fusion of expertise from virtually every profession. The complicity of a population baptised in Christian culture and educated at some of the most elite universities in the world continues to raise deeply disturbing questions about the moral and spiritual credibility of the Church and the academy. Holocaust theology has emerged as a response to an epoch-making disaster so catastrophic as to require a redefinition of the theological, ethical and spiritual contours of both Judaism and Christianity.

Both Jews and Christians are grounded in revelatory affirmations of God as the Creator, Sustainer and Redeemer of the world. The identity of God is disclosed not only in the natural order but also through the course of history, most especially in the election and covenantal formation of communities whose destinies are indissolubly bound to God's ongoing involvement in the world. Since God is understood as the Lord of all history, the evil as well as the good is classically attributed to the inscrutable will of the Almighty (see Isa. 45.7), and so disasters are traditionally interpreted as punishments that serve to reorient the wayward or as the necessary birth pangs of the Messianic era. The logic of this faith generates an untenable conclusion for Holocaust theologians: if God is not the author of the Holocaust, God at the very least shares responsibility for the tragedies and atrocities that have befallen the **people of Israel**. Holocaust theology is born out of the conviction that traditional theodicies buckle under the weight of the **Shoah** (Hebrew for 'total destruction'), and the magnitude of the theological collapse demands that Jews and Christians develop a radically different understanding of God and God's relationship to the world, which in turn requires our religious communities to redefine the horizons of their moral obligations.

The first generation of Christians and Jews to confront the enormity of the *Shoah* began with a probing examination of the pervasive and often elusive character of **anti-Judaism** within the Christian tradition. The pioneering work of Jewish scholars such as Jules **Isaac**, Eliezer Berkovits (1908–92), Emil Fackenheim (1916–2003) and Richard Rubenstein (b. 1924) was reinforced by Christian scholars such as James **Parkes**, Roy (1918–98) and Alice Eckardt (b. 1923), Franklin Littell (b. 1917), Edward Flannery (1912–98), Rosemary Ruether (b. 1936) and Paul van Buren (1924–98), all of whom underscored the ways in which Christian affirmations were advanced at the expense of Judaism and the Jewish people. Their scholarship demonstrated that Christian triumphalism has spilled into almost every corner of the Church. Indeed the vast majority of the most gifted preachers and teachers within the **Roman Catholic**, Protestant and **Orthodox Christian** traditions enshrined the teaching of contempt, and thereby provided biblical, historical and theological warrants for the marginalisation and persecution of the Jewish people.

With the acknowledgement that Christian anti-Judaism provided an ideological seedbed for the rise of modern **antisemitism**, the Roman Catholic Church and many **Protestant** denominations issued public documents that condemned racism and antisemitism as contrary to the Christian proclamation. The Third Assembly of the **World Council of Churches** in 1961 and the declaration known as *Nostra Aetate* of the Roman Catholic Church's **Second Vatican Council** in 1965 repudiated one of the most toxic teachings within the Christian tradition, namely the **deicide** charge. Subsequent documents have exposed some of the roots of Christian **supersessionism** and countered a theology of displacement by grounding their affirmations of God's enduring **covenant** with the Jewish people in the biblical axiom that God remains faithful to God's promises 'for the gifts and calling of God are irrevocable' (Rom. 11.29).

These official documents indicate that a revolutionary shift in the theological understanding of many Christians is in the making. The changes are clearing a path for a far deeper understanding of Judaism and opening up a far more constructive relationship with the Jewish people. While the changes signal an acknowledgement of Christian complicity, the Holocaust continues to raise significant theological issues for the Jewish–Christian encounter. Many Christians and Jews insist that Christian supersessionism will endure as long as the evangelical imperative to **conversion** of Jews to Christianity stands intact. A theological agenda that seeks to absorb the Jewish people into the Body of Christ registers in the hearts and minds of many as an ecclesiastical policy that sanctions the elimination of Judaism and legitimises spiritual genocide.

A second area for the Jewish–Christian encounter concerns the fact that the vast majority of Jews understand the **State of Israel** as a political and theological necessity in the aftermath of the Holocaust. Christians are profoundly divided in their appraisal of the State of Israel, and the pervasive conviction that God's presence is not determined by particular geographical attachments generates significant disjuncture with the Jewish people.

The most explicit Christian response to the Holocaust was the 1998 document issued by the Roman Catholic Church and entitled *We Remember: A Reflection on the Shoah*. While this statement demonstrates a profound act of **repentance**, the efforts to distinguish Christian anti-Judaism from modern antisemitism have evoked critical reactions. Most especially contested is the claim that the roots of antisemitism are found outside of Christianity.

The declaration entitled *Dabru Emet: A Jewish Response to Christians and Christianity* reflects the emerging possibility of ongoing theological engagement with respect to these and other concerns vital to both Christians and Jews. The assertion that 'Nazism was not a Christian phenomenon' has evoked searching debate and called both religious communities to a more nuanced reading of Western history. The statement that 'Christians can respect the Jewish people's claim upon the land of Israel' prompts both Jews and Christians to re-examine the particular terms of their own covenants with God and their relationship to one another. So Christians are challenged to struggle with a theological claim that is foreign to their own covenant in their assessment of God's promise of the Land to the Jews. Jews in turn encounter the problem of particularity when assessing the Christian affirmation that God was uniquely manifest in **Jesus** of Nazareth. How are Christians and Jews to make sense of the foundational claims of the other when these affirmations are unintelligible, if not offensive, precisely because of the particularity of the revelational claims within their inherited religious languages? The discovery that religious differences and disagreement can be a source of wisdom may prove the most critical achievement for Christians and Jews in the post-*Shoah* era.

Many of the most serious theological challenges evoked by the Holocaust revolve around questions of power, authority and obedience. Each community is struggling to come to terms with traditions that have often romanticised powerlessness and have failed to develop the disciplined practices of translating its ethical commitments into the political life of the larger society. For Christians the articulation of political theologies, which no longer isolate the **Kingdom of God** from the earthly kingdoms, is a fundamental challenge. For Jews the establishment and advancement of the State of Israel has a political significance inseparable from its religious import. While diverse religious and ethnic populations dispute the future of the land, Jews inside Israel are caught in a struggle to define a democratic order where political and religious concerns intersect. How will the State of Israel remain a Jewish country faithful to the core ethical values of its tradition in the midst of rival claimants to the land and to the state? Jews who live in other lands are exploring new ways of moving beyond the isolationism once imposed, bringing their distinct traditions to bear on civil life, and adjudicating the duelling claims of their religious and national loyalties.

Jewish and Christian scholars continue to debate the uniqueness of the Holocaust and to examine its relationship with respect to other genocidal catastrophes. At issue are the meanings that Jews and Christians find in the *Shoah*, and the theological understandings that they develop of one another.

Some Jewish scholars have maintained that the singularity of the Holocaust resides in the magnitude of the disaster, and yet they insist that these events need to be read and interpreted against the horizon of other catastrophes. Historians are concerned about descriptive language of uniqueness, for this discourse tends to mystify these events and undermines any analytic effort to explain the complex of historical factors. The emphasis placed on the Holocaust concerns other Jewish thinkers, who fear that this 'epoch-making event' may become the touchstone of Jewish **identity** and enculturate Jews to think of themselves as 'victims' and the rest of the world, most especially Christians, as 'perpetrators', '**bystanders**' and on very rare occasions 'rescuers'. If the Holocaust defines the terms of religious engagement, Christians and Jews often find themselves frozen in roles that stunt the growth of more creative and reciprocal partnerships. As the survivors of the Holocaust grow older and die, the legacy of the *Shoah* will suffer the loss of an exceptionally powerful voice. It remains to be seen if Christians will embrace the ethical demands of remembering this painful chapter in the history of Jewish–Christian relations. The southern hemisphere is becoming the demographic centre of the Christian population, and there are increasing numbers of people who do not see themselves reflected in the history of Europe. The prospect of sharing the burdens of this legacy will in large measure depend on the educational discovery that the spiritual and moral credibility of Churches everywhere is inseparable from an honest reckoning with this past. The kind of future that Holocaust theologians dare to envision depends upon a comprehensive memory.

See also **death of God theology; Jewish–Christian relations, modern scholarship in**

CHRISTOPHER M. LEIGHTON

Holy *see* **holiness**

Holy See's Commission for Religious Relations with the Jews *see* **Jewish–Christian relations, institutions**

Holy Spirit

Both Christianity and Judaism describe **God** as holy and as spirit, transcending matter of which God is creator. Distinctively, however, Christianity views the Holy Spirit as the Third Person of the Blessed **Trinity**, together with the Father and the

Son. In the **New Testament** the term 'spirit of God' indicates the influence of God on human actions, but there are also passages, notably in John and in **Paul**, that portray the Holy Spirit as divine, for example John 20.22–23 and 1 Cor. 6.11. Paul's comment, in Acts 28.25, that the Holy Spirit 'spoke to our fathers through Isaiah' mirrors the traditional Jewish understanding of Holy Spirit, based on the **Hebrew** term *ruaḥ ha-kodesh*, which indicates a force emanating from God that impels **prophecy** and other forms of divine **inspiration**. Thus, as the rabbinic scholar Marc Bregman (b. 1946) has pointed out, the rabbis understood the **Hebrew Bible** to have been composed by God or by means of the Holy Spirit. For example, Solomon is said to have composed the books attributed to him – Proverbs, Song of Songs and Ecclesiastes – in his old age 'when the Holy Spirit settled on him' just before death.

The Acts of the Apostles (2.2–4) describes the descent of the Holy Spirit on the **apostles**, indicating that the Holy Spirit will be the life of the church (cf. Jas 1.18) and an instrument in God's hands. The concept continues to be found in Christian **preaching**, with the Holy Spirit enabling a response of faith. Interestingly in Judaism, although direct divine inspiration came to an end after the **canon** was closed, the Holy Spirit continued to function, as indicated by the numerous stories of rabbis who are said to have 'seen by means of the Holy Spirit', indicating the prophetic aura of a seer. Abraham Joshua **Heschel** documents examples of rabbis in the Middle Ages who are said to have experienced prophetic inspiration by means of the Holy Spirit. Paralleling Christianity, the Holy Spirit is also personified in rabbinic literature. For example, the rabbis describe it leaving and returning to God or depict God as speaking with the Holy Spirit. It is particularly interesting that the rabbis conceive of the Holy Spirit in the form of a dove, as does the New Testament account of the baptism of **Jesus** (cf. Mark 1.10 and parallels). In the **Targum** on the Song of Songs 2.12, the phrase 'the voice of the turtle-dove' is paraphrased as 'the voice of the spirit of the Holy One'. *EDWARD KESSLER*

Holy Week

'Holy Week', or the seven days during which Christians commemorate the final week of Christ's life in **Jerusalem**, stretches from the Sunday before **Easter** (Palm or 'Passion' Sunday) through the following Saturday. The three-day period from the Thursday through the Saturday before Easter is known as the 'Paschal Triduum', in which the **Last Supper** of **Jesus**, together with his death and rising from the tomb, are marked with the most solemn liturgies. The observance of the triduum, done annually in Jerusalem by the third century, was undoubtedly the foundation of the entire week's celebrations. Historically, Holy Week has been tragically marked by four recurring issues which forged negative links with Judaism.

First, the ancient **Quartodeciman controversy** over the date of Easter – whether to observe the celebration of Easter on 14 Nisan, as per the Jewish **calendar**, or to keep it on the first Sunday that followed the Paschal moon – seems to have been an opportunity for anti-Jewish **rhetoric** by various **Church Fathers**, as hinted at by **Eusebius** (*Hist. eccl.* 5.23). No doubt the arguments of Appolinarius of Hieropolis (*Chronicon Paschale*) (*c*.186), Blastus (cf. *Hist. eccl.* 5.15 and 20) (*c*.175) and others spurred Pseudo-Tertullian's comment (*Adv. omn. haer.* 8.1) that Christian adherence to the Jewish calendar is nothing less than the continued '**Judaising**' of Christianity, long scorned by Christians in their attempt to establish an **identity** distinct from Judaism.

Second, the liturgies of Holy Week were progressively interpreted in an anti-Jewish way. An ancient petition for the Jews in the **Good Friday prayers** of the Roman rite, for example, was eventually offered *pro perfidiis Iudaeis*, or 'for the perfidious Jews'. The Gospel readings of the **trial** and death of Jesus, on both Palm Sunday and Good Friday, served as additional occasions on which anti-Jewish sentiment was fostered. Accompanied by anti-Jewish **preaching**, such observances were lethal for Jewish–Christian relations even late into the twentieth century. Not until the Roman liturgy's reform in 1970 (and subsequent revisions in most Protestant churches, such as can be found in the *Book of Common Prayer*), were texts such as the Good Friday prayers amended. Similarly, instructions by national bishops' conferences on the correct way to preach about Jews and Judaism (1988) in the **liturgy** have tried to correct for anti-Jewish homilies often given in earlier Holy Week liturgies.

Third, the medieval '**blood libel**' seems to have originated in Holy Week (*see* **William of Norwich**). The terrible association resulting in the Christian mind between the coincidental observance of **Passover** and Easter, along with alleged Jewish desire to use children's **blood** in the preparation of Passover *mazzot*, further vitiated the meaning of Holy Week for both communities.

Fourth, the production of **Passion plays** during Holy Week (most famously in Oberammergau, 1634), in which Jews were portrayed as 'Christ killers' in the drama of Jesus' last three days of life, only deepened the opprobrium of Christians towards Jews (*see* **deicide, charge of**). Remnant **anti-Judaism** can be seen today in surviving Passion dramas, such as the *Procession de los Borrachos* on Good Friday in Seville, Spain.

DENNIS D. MCMANUS

Homily *see* preaching

Homosexuality

While Judaism and Christianity individually have a great deal to say about homosexuality, the Jewish–Christian encounter maintains an ambiguous silence on the topic. Perhaps one of the mitigating factors is the problem of **vocabulary**. 'Homosexual' as an **identity** category was unknown until the early twentieth century. The traditional references are not to identities, but to activities. Thus homosexuals and homosexuality are not per se forbidden; rather, specific types of male-to-male sexual behaviour are prohibited, whether committed by homosexual or heterosexual men. There is little reference in either tradition to female-to-female sex.

Despite several biblical verses that are presumed by some scholars to refer to homosexuality (Gen. 38.4–10; Lev. 18.22; 20.13 in the **Hebrew Bible**; Rom. 1.27; 1 Cor. 6.9; 1 Tim. 1.10; Jude 7 in the **New Testament**), Jewish and Christian legal codes do not always explicitly prohibit male-to-male sex. In *m. Kiddushin* 4.14 Rabbi Judah prohibits two bachelors from sleeping together under one blanket, but at *b. Kiddushin* 82a the sages pronounce the safeguard irrelevant, as Jews are not tempted by male-to-male sex. Christian sources seem more pragmatic, perhaps because of the tradition of monastic **celibacy** that is absent from Judaism. Medieval codes of **penance** include specific restrictions on people sleeping together or even being found in suspicious circumstances. Such codes do not, of course, address how humans actually behave, but rather how they were expected to behave.

Once 'homosexuality' was recognised as an identity category by Kraft-Ebbing (1840–1902) and **Freud** early in the twentieth century, some parts of both traditions felt challenged to rethink their behavioural norms. Today both Judaism and Christianity are fractured in their attitudes toward homosexuals (and lesbians) and same-sex behaviour. **Orthodox Judaism** condemns all homosexuality, but Reform Judaism officially allows the ordination of homosexuals and the blessing of homosexual relationships. A Vatican encyclical of 1975 pronounced that homosexual identity has 'a strong tendency toward intrinsic moral evil'; yet a movement for the recognition of gays in the church has arisen within Catholicism. Protestants also have widely varying policies at both national and local level. For example, the Episcopal Church USA recognises that homosexuals 'deserve' God's love and the **sacraments** of the church, yet prohibits ordination of non-celibate homosexuals and the liturgical acknowledgement of gay relationships. These painful divisions could produce some interesting configurations within the Jewish–Christian encounter – such as the conservative wings of Christianity and Judaism in opposition to the liberal wings of both – but thus far no formal interfaith coalitions around **sexuality** seem to have emerged. *PHILIP CULBERTSON*

Hosanna

Greek transliteration of Hebrew *hoshana*: 'O deliver.' A cry of deep dependence and need in Jewish sources, 'hosanna' became one of affirmation and exultation in Christian **worship**. The word is used in Jewish worship as part of the prayer for rain during **Sukkot**, accompanied by the waving of palm branches. It also occurs as a cry to God for help ('We beg you, save us!') in Ps. 118.25, where it is associated with the exclusion of a pilgrim from the **Temple**; this passage was also used in Jewish **Passover** rites in **New Testament** times. Hosanna occurs six times in the New Testament: all are ascriptions of praise when **Jesus** enters **Jerusalem** (Matt. 21.9; Mark 11.9–10; John 12.13). A Messianic dimension may have been present in Judaic usage, but the anger of the chief priests and **scribes** at the public response to Jesus (Matt. 21.15) suggests that references to the **Messiah** were considered illegitimate in this context, as well as politically and religiously provocative (Pope, 'Hosanna'). *WILLIAM KLASSEN*

Host desecration

This accusation against the Jews of Europe developed in the thirteenth century in tandem with the rise in interest in the **eucharist** within Christian religious culture. From the twelfth century theologians and Church leaders emphasised the centrality of the eucharist among the seven **sacraments**. All sacraments offered Christians access to saving **grace**, but the eucharist was unique, as involving the physical presence of Christ in the bread and wine. As awareness of the doctrine of transubstantiation spread, greater anxiety was displayed about access to the eucharist, and greater care taken of the consecrated bread, which each church kept for ritual use. A vivid narrative developed, and was enacted in Paris in 1290, which attributed to a Jew – later to groups of Jews – the desire to desecrate a eucharistic wafer as re-enactment of the **crucifixion**. The narrative also claimed that the eucharist was not destroyed, but manifested its mystery by turning into flesh, or a child Christ, or a crucifix; once discovered, the accused Jew was invariably executed by judicial process or at the hands of a mob. The tale was recorded in Parisian chronicles and then spread further in sermons, exemplary tales inserted into sermons, and formed the basis for devotional images. For over a hundred communities in towns and villages of Franconia, Bavaria, Austria, Silesia and Catalonia, however, it was a painful lived reality: Jewish communities were destroyed, and chapels and cults were established on the sites of the alleged abuse. Grounded in the images of eucharistic worship, the host desecration charge was nonetheless criticised by some contemporary writers, and robustly rejected by several Protestant writers. **Luther** singled out for derision the cult that developed following a host desecration accusation at Sternberg in Mecklenburg in 1485.   *MIRI RUBIN*

Hugh of Lincoln

Two Saint Hughs of Lincoln were instrumental in Jewish–Christian relations: one was a Carthusian bishop of Lincoln (*c*.1140–1200) and the other was a child (usually designated 'Little Saint Hugh') whose death (1255) triggered one of the most notorious **blood libel** cases in medieval Europe.

Consecrated in 1181, Bishop Hugh was noted for holiness, his assertion of the liberty of the church vis-à-vis the monarchy, and a concern for marginalised groups including the poor, the sick and Jews. He intervened to suppress a blood libel cult in Stamford, Lincolnshire, and anti-Jewish violence in the diocese following Richard I's accession (1189) and departure on the Third **Crusade**.

According to the Latin sources, he was popular with Lincoln's Jews; they were amongst the mourners at his funeral.

'Little Hugh' was a boy allegedly imprisoned, tortured and killed by Lincoln's Jews (led by Koppin) in mocking re-enactment of the **crucifixion**. While Hugh did die, the story is false: it and Hugh's elevation as a martyr are (like that of **William of Norwich**) functions of medieval **anti-Judaism**. The libel led to the execution of 19 Jews. Others were imprisoned and released on payment of a fine. Little Hugh's tomb in Lincoln Cathedral became a place of **pilgrimage** (possibly instigated by **Edward I** in the 1290s) and his '**martyrdom**' a motif in English **folklore**. Chaucer alludes to it in the 'Prioresses Tale', as does Joyce in *Ulysses*. However, the cult was suppressed and the (Anglican) Cathedral now features an inscription asking **forgiveness** for the libel.   *MELANIE J. WRIGHT*

Huguenots

The Huguenots (the origin of the term is unclear) were a Protestant Church established in the sixteenth century by **Calvin**. Following persecution (most famously, the St Bartholomew's Day massacre of 1572), the majority fled their native **France** to other countries (especially the **United Kingdom** and the **United States**), preserving the French language and culture in these new locations for many generations. Others practised their religion secretly, rather like the '**Marranos**' in medieval **Spain**. Huguenot self-understanding likened the experience of persecution and dispersal to that of the biblical Hebrews. Consciousness of this heritage was a factor motivating the villagers of Le Chambon-sur-Lignon in southern France, who were descended from Huguenots, to shelter 5,000 refugees (mostly Jews) from the Nazis during the Second World War. Subsequently, they were collectively recognised as **Righteous Gentiles**. The Chambon Foundation was established after the **Holocaust** and is dedicated to protecting the memory of those who rescued Jews during the Holocaust.   *MELANIE J. WRIGHT*

Ḥukkat ha-Goy

Lit. 'practice of the nations', based on Lev. 20.23, refers to the biblical command not to follow immoral practices of the Gentile nations, extended by the rabbis to include idolatrous practices (*see* **idolatry**). On some occasions the rabbis applied *ḥukkat ha-Goy* strictly, particularly if Jewish

identity was seen as threatened – for example, the principle was applied against the use of an organ in synagogue or the wearing of canonicals by the rabbi and cantor (both clearly influenced by Christian custom). Many changes adopted by **Reform Judaism** were also condemned as ḥukkat ha-Goy, such as uncovering the head in prayer. In the context of contemporary Jewish–Christian relations, ḥukkat ha-Goy raises the question of how to respect the 'other' while remaining different and how to achieve integration without **assimilation**.

PETR FRYŠ

Humanism

Humanism has shaped the Jewish–Christian encounter in several ways. Many Jews and Christians have been inspired to collaborate in joint ethical projects by a shared commitment to humanism (defined as the 'affirmation of humanity'). Again, some Jews and Christians have created movements that aim to build a bridge with secularism and create a form of faith that denies any transcendent entity. And there is also some evidence that the emphasis on '**dialogue**' is itself a result of the modern emphasis on humanism.

Both Jews and Christians seem to have been involved in the initial development of classical humanism. It was in the fourteenth and fifteenth centuries, in the so-called northern European Renaissance, that the term 'humanism' came into widespread use. In that context most humanists were religious, and the goal was the purification and renewal of Christianity, in ways that some Jews found very congenial. In keeping with the spirit of the **Renaissance**, humanists shared a cultural and educational programme that derived inspiration from antiquity and stressed the importance of eloquence. Today many traditional Christians and Jews want to affirm the humanist emphasis on the significance and value of people, and some, such as the Christian theologian William Schweiker (b. 1953), talk about a 'theological humanism' as the potential solution to the human preoccupation with materialism.

The modern term 'humanism', which arose during the nineteenth and twentieth centuries, is today used as a label by many who wish to affirm humanity while denying any metaphysics, and in this respect too it has shaped the Jewish–Christian encounter. Henri de Lubac (1896–1991) identifies three forms of humanism that dominate the

nineteenth century: the Nietzschean, the Comtean and the Marxist. Although very different, they all assumed **atheism** and that the task of philosophy is to enable people to cope with and accept this reality. There are forms of both Christianity and Judaism that describe themselves as 'humanist', meaning that they are 'non-theist', and Jewish and Christian groups draw heavily on each other's writings. The Society for Humanistic Judaism, founded in 1969 by Rabbi Sherwin T. Wine (b. 1928), explains that 'Humanistic Judaism embraces a human-centred philosophy that combines the celebration of Jewish culture and identity with an adherence to humanistic values and ideas'. Many **Unitarian** Universalists share a similar commitment: William Murry argues that a majority identify with 'religious humanism', which involves a commitment to people and agnosticism about metaphysics. Unitarian Universalists are the fastest growing liberal church in New England, and significant numbers of Jews are joining the movement. Such forms of Christianity and Judaism are seen as an important bridge to modern Western secular culture and hope to attract those who find the metaphysics implausible.

Humanism has been significant in creating the culture in which 'dialogue' is viewed as supremely important. The spirit of the Renaissance stressed the importance of the Socratic discourse (conversation as a means to truth), which in turn influenced the creation of a climate favourable to conversation between Jews and Christians.   *IAN MARKHAM*

Hungary

Formerly part of the Habsburg Empire, Hungary was granted some degree of self-government in the Compromise of 1867 and established as an independent state in 1918. Aligned with Nazi **Germany** in the Second World War, it was transformed into a single-party Communist state after 1945. Since 1990 it has had a multi-party democratic government. From the eleventh century **Roman Catholicism** has been the dominant religion. Jews had been given full citizenship rights in 1867 and by the Second World War were highly integrated into Hungarian culture, numbering nearly 5 per cent of the population. However, from 1938 to 1941 antisemitic laws were promulgated, reflecting both Nazi pressure and indigenous nationalist sentiments, the latter promoted in the 'Szeged Idea' of right-wing government based on 'Christianity' and nationalism, which influenced the Hungarian ruler Admiral Horthy (1868–1957) and was prevalent in racial form among Church dignitaries. Such concern as there was for Jews in these circles tended to be reserved for those who had converted to Christianity. In 1941 725,007 Jews were recorded in Hungary; by the end of the war 564,500 had been killed (*see* **Holocaust**). The institutional presence of Judaism under Communism was minimal, and the Catholic Church was persecuted. Such common political cause as existed between Jews and Christians, however, resulted in little positive change in the encounter. The liberation of Hungary from single-party Communist rule in 1989 has led to some resurgence of right-wing nationalism and **antisemitism**, but also to such fruitful meetings between Christians and Jews as the Lutheran–Jewish conference on 'Antisemitism and Anti-Judaism Today' in September 2001 and statements such as the November 1994 *Joint Statement on the Fiftieth Anniversary of the Holocaust* by the bishops of the Hungarian Catholic Church and the Ecumenical Council of Churches in Hungary.

DAVID WEIGALL

Hutterites *see* **Anabaptists**

Hymnody *see* **Andrew of Crete; music; piyyut; Romanos Melodos**

Ibn Ezra, Abraham ben Me'ir (1089–1164)

Spanish philosopher, astronomer, mathematician, linguist, poet and biblical exegete. Ibn Ezra was widely travelled, and his numerous works contributed substantially to cultural learning between the three Abrahamic faiths. For example, his philosophical poetry *Hayy ben Meqits* was a source of inspiration for Dante's (1265–1321) *Divina Commedia*. Ibn Ezra's study of the Bible remains influential – his Bible **commentaries** are still printed in all editions of the *Mikraot Gedolot* (rabbinical Bibles) – and he is viewed by some as the father of **biblical criticism** as a result of his suggestion that Deut. 1.1 implies that **Moses** could not have written the whole **Torah**. His view was developed by **Spinoza**, whose writings undermined the traditional understanding of a perfect and divine scripture. *STEFAN SCHREINER*

Ibn Gabirol, Solomon ben Judah (*c*.1020–*c*.1057)

Known in Arabic as Sulayman ibn Yahya ibn Gabirul, and in Latin as Avicebron, Solomon ibn Gabirol was one of the most outstanding Jewish poets in Muslim **Spain** during the era of the taifa or 'party' kings, as well as a philosopher whose works were esteemed throughout Christian Europe. His poetry survived as part of the **liturgy** of the Sephardi Jews, including pieces such as 'Shahar Abashkeshcha' ('At Dawn I Seek You'), which became part of the daily morning prayers. His 'Fountain of Life', or 'Fons Vitae' as it was known in Latin Europe, was written in Arabic, but that version is lost, though parts survive in a later Hebrew translation; the fullest surviving text is that in Latin, attributed to Avicebron, whom medieval Christian readers generally assumed to be a Muslim. This is testimony to the way that ideas about the nature of God and the purpose of creation in medieval Judaism, Christianity and **Islam** concerned common intellectual problems and allowed for some sharing of concepts. *DAVID ABULAFIA*

Iconoclasm

The deliberate destruction of religious **art** has occurred at many points in history with communities of both Jews and Christians, as well as among Muslims. Although the often-stated justification for such destruction was the divine injunction against 'graven images' as conveyed by the so-called 'second commandment', as well as the fundamental concern that religious images either led to or constituted the sin of **idolatry**, most iconoclastic episodes emerged out of a complex web of religious, cultural and political circumstances, and were often justified by complex theological arguments. The first of the two most famous episodes of widespread and systematic icon-smashing began in the eighth century, when the Byzantine Emperor Leo III (*r*.717–41) ordered the destruction of all icons, arguing that they inhibited the **conversion** of Jews and Muslims to Christianity since these two groups would have found icons to be essentially idolatrous. By contrast, the second period of iconoclasm, associated with the sixteenth-century Protestant **Reformation**, had little relevance to Jewish–Christian relations. *ROBIN M. JENSEN*

Iconography

'Iconography' generally refers to pictorial images in visual **art**, and specifically to visual art that encompasses religious themes or motifs. Scholars who study iconography focus more on the meaning or subject matter conveyed by the imagery in a work of art than on the work's formal or stylistic aspects, and are especially interested in the interplay of visual imagery and religious belief and practice. The parallels as well as clear differences between the iconographic themes apparent in Jewish and Christian iconography serve as material evidence of the continuing interaction (or lack of interaction) between the two communities.

From the beginning of the third century both Jewish and Christian iconography employed symbolic images as a means of representing aspects of their faith or specific liturgical practices. For example, early Christians used the anchor, fish or dove as symbols of constancy, baptism or salvation. Jews included the menorah, lulav or shofar in the frescoes of their burial places in Rome, as references to their rituals as well as to their **identity**. Although far more common in Christian iconography in late antiquity (e.g. the Roman catacomb frescoes or sarcophagus reliefs), both groups also portrayed episodes from particular Bible stories, for instance the **binding of Isaac** and the crossing of the Red Sea. Some scholars have offered the appearance of certain common scenes in the art of both communities as indicating a shared iconographic model or prototype (perhaps an illuminated copy of the **Septuagint**), which in turn suggests a certain degree of continuing interaction between the two communities, or perhaps evidence that the communities employed the same artists' workshops. In addition, the appearance of certain details borrowed from Jewish **midrashic** writings indicate Christian familiarity with this literature.

Both communities adapted popular iconographic motifs from the secular and religious art of their surrounding environment. For this reason both Christian and Jewish visual art reveal striking similarities to the art of their polytheistic neighbours. For example, the Christian Good Shepherd looks much like Hermes carrying a ram over his shoulders, Jonah is portrayed in the posture of the classical hero Endymion, and representations of Daniel draw from the standard presentations of Hercules or other heroes from classical mythology. Both **Jesus** in Christian imagery and **David** in Jewish art (e.g. the mosaic pavement found in the sixth-century Gaza synagogue) were shown with the attributes of Orpheus, the mythological singer who tamed the wild beasts. Christians may have seen this as an **allegory** for the salvation of the soul from its baser passions, while Jews may have borrowed the representation of Orpheus in order to portray David as musician and poet. Similarly the figure of Sol or Helios occurs in both Jewish and Christian iconography. For Christians the figure was understood to represent Christ/**Logos** as the bringer of light out of darkness.

After the fourth century monumental Christian art focuses more on iconic and dogmatic imagery (especially portraits of Jesus, **Mary** and the saints),

while narrative imagery based on scripture stories is mostly found in the emerging art of manuscript illumination. The conversion of **Constantine**, and subsequently the establishment of Christianity, stimulated a tremendous output of monumental Christian art, along with new iconographic themes and styles. On the other hand, from the late sixth to the thirteenth century figurative art all but disappears from the Jewish archaeological record, and scholars may only offer hypothetical artistic links between the two communities.

When Jewish **illuminated manuscripts** begin to appear in the thirteenth century they seemed initially to be more influenced by Muslim than by Christian artworks. During the high Middle Ages, while Christian narrative imagery concentrates on Bible illumination, the richest Jewish iconography comes from medieval *haggadah* manuscripts. Nevertheless, most scholars believe that a large degree of mutual influence can be seen in both Jewish and Christian iconography from the period: that Jews borrowed Christian motifs while Christians often hired Jewish workshops or purchased illuminated Bibles from them.

In the modern era, despite important attempts to create a Jewish style or characteristic iconography (e.g. the efforts of Vladimir Stasov (1824–1906) in Russia), both Jewish and Christian artists are as much or more patronised by secular clients than by their own religious communities, leading to a great degree of assimilation to contemporary culture and taste on all sides.

See also **Dura Europos**   *ROBIN M. JENSEN*

Identity

Christians have defined themselves and their religious beliefs from the earliest times in contradistinction to Jews and Judaism, yet at the same time claimed continuity. Jews and Judaism, too, have been profoundly shaped by their reactions to, and the influence of, Christianity. Thus issues of identity lie at the heart of the study of Jewish–Christian relations. Depending upon the perspective and the criteria adopted, the so-called 'parting of the ways' – the emergence of two faith communities that saw themselves and each other as distinct religious groupings – can be said to have occurred at different times and places throughout the **Roman Empire**, sometime between the first and fifth centuries. From a Christian perspective the Jews became 'the other' as the result of the need to explain theologically the Jewish refusal to acknowledge Jesus as **Messiah** and as a result of the influence of **Paul**'s teachings that encouraged a Gentile Christian constituency. Socio-political factors encouraged divided loyalties, for example when many **Jewish Christians** would not unite under the self-proclaimed Messiah **Bar Kokhba** during the rebellion against Rome, 132–5. From a Jewish perspective the gradual growth of influence of rabbinic authority among synagogues throughout Palestine and **Diaspora** Jewish communities, and the sidelining of those who did not subscribe to the interpretation of the oral **law** according to **Rabbinic Judaism**, meant that legal (halakhic) definitions of Jewish identity and of **heresy** (*minut*) became theologically significant factors. Christian claims regarding the divine nature of their **Christ**, and increasing Gentile dominance of the movement with its attendant **antinomianism**, would have alienated them from the wider Jewish community. From the contemporary external viewpoint Roman legislation represents an alternative criterion for distinguishing between Jews and Christians. From the modern historical perspective the issue is further complicated by the question of whether one focuses upon popular or official behaviour among the two groups, and the issues of who and what define Jewish and Christian identities. A particularly complex area, today as in ancient times, involves those who regard themselves as both Jewish and Christian. Whether Ebionites during the first few centuries or **Hebrew Christians** in the nineteenth century or **Messianic Jews** in the twentieth century, such groups have provoked acute reactions from both Jewish and Christian communities. **Conversion** practices also reveal striking differences in terms of identity among Jews and Christians. Until relatively recently, Jewish identity has tended to be defined according to *halakhah* in terms of Jewish matrilineal descent or by a process of conversion that adheres to approved ritual. Complications have arisen as a result of the emergence of **Progressive Jewish** denominations, which are prepared to set the *halakhah* to one side, and also as a consequence of the creation of a secular, Zionist **State of Israel**, whose legal definition of a Jew corresponds more closely to historical perceptions of Jewishness than it does to the *halakhah*. In contrast, Christian identity does not incorporate the Jewish emphasis upon peoplehood. It tends rather to stress spiritual membership within a universal body of Christ, often reinforced by rituals such as **baptism**, and self-definition according to creed. The exploration of non-religious Jewish identities must also be taken into account in any discussion of Jewish–Christian relations in the post-**Enlightenment** era. *DANIEL R. LANGTON*

Idolatry

Idolatry, in the biblical sense of the worship of different gods, particularly through the use of tangible images, clearly plays little part in the contemporary encounter between Jews and Christians within Western culture. Indeed, both would take for granted their shared exclusive belief in the One God. Nevertheless, in earlier periods Jews, alongside Muslims, had considerable difficulty in differentiating the Christian use of images of the crucified **Jesus**, of **Mary** and of the **saints** from pagan forms of worship.

The **Hebrew Bible** presents itself as a record of the struggle to establish in the world the concept of the One God of the universe, which is the particular vocation of the children of **Israel**. At all stages in biblical Israel's history different concepts of **religion** formed the background to this task, each associated with the seductive temptation to 'worship other gods'. Nevertheless, as the Israelites emerged from each of these encounters they also incorporated elements from the host culture, transmuted and hence subsumed under the monotheistic quest.

Rabbinic Judaism pronounced the end of idolatry. Thus confronted with the statues of the gods of Rome they could argue: 'They do not say, "let us make a bath for Aphrodite" [i.e. worship the goddess], but "Let us make an Aphrodite as an adornment for the bath!"' (*m. Avodah Zarah* 3.4). An entirely different challenge was presented to the Jewish world by Christianity, particularly in the Middle Ages. The use of images within churches was puzzling, if not offensive, to Jewish sensitivities. The talmudic abbreviation *akum*, made up of the initials of the words *avodat kokhavim u mazalot*, 'the worship of stars and planets', could be reread as *avodat kristus u maria*, the worship of Christ and Mary. The difficulty of understanding the **Trinity** was and remains a theological puzzle for Jews, and indeed for many Christians. Nevertheless the kabbalistic concept of the *sferot*, ten emanations whereby the transcendent God becomes immanent in the world, may be recognised as an analogous system.

In the modern period the majority of Jews are less interested in the beliefs and practices of Christianity and more in the impact of Christian teachings on behaviour towards the Jewish people. Nevertheless, Jewish reactions against the affirmation of **Dabru Emet** that Jews and Christians worship the same God suggest that old doubts still persist. Christians have rarely viewed Jewish religious practices as idolatrous.

In the context of Jewish–Christian **dialogue** the approach to the issue of idolatry by Erich Fromm (1900–80) opens up an area for a shared task of exploration. He argues: 'An idol represents the object of man's central passion; the desire to return to the soil-mother, the craving for possession, power, fame, and so forth. The passion represented by the idol is, at the same time, the supreme value within man's system of values.' Thus the exploration of the nature of idolatry, which would include a rigorous self-examination of the history of values and practices of both religions, offers a common ground for a shared exploration of past and present lapses.

See also ***Avodah zarah***; **Golden Calf**

JONATHAN MAGONET

Ignatius of Antioch (*c*.30–107 CE)

Bishop of Antioch in Syria from *c*.69 CE, known especially for a series of epistles written while under escort from **Antioch** to his **martyrdom** in Rome – a prospect he looked forward to with great enthusiasm. The epistles lay down some of the basic principles of orthodox ecclesiology and **Christology** – seeing the bishop as the locus of Church unity and arguing for the full divinity and humanity of Jesus Christ. They also mark a key stage in the self-definition of Christianity, emphasising Christianity's **supersession** of Judaism and the need for Christians to dispense entirely with Jewish customs.

See also **Apostolic Fathers**; **early Church**

MARCUS PLESTED

Illuminated manuscripts

Illuminations of the **Bible** are a particular kind of narrative **art**, directly associated with an actual text, in contrast to visual representations of scriptural stories in other venues (church walls, pavements etc.). The proximity to a text itself inhibits non-canonical insertions into the artwork, while at the same time highlighting certain passages by giving them visual portrayal, sometimes in sequential images. Although narrative art was common in Christianity from the third century onwards, based on the surviving examples, Christian book illumination seems to date from the fifth century, the earliest example being the six surviving leaves from the book of Kings in the Quedlinburg Itala. By contrast, the earliest existing Jewish examples date to the ninth century and were, at first, entirely geometric or calligraphic in their design. Despite the monumentally important example of narrative painting in the **Dura Europos** Synagogue, no illustrated manuscript of a Jewish Bible can be dated prior to the thirteenth century.

Despite the lack of examples, a theoretical connection between early Christian art and Jewish manuscript illumination has been posited by many scholars, who pointed to the extensive **iconography** of the third-century Dura Europos synagogue as evidence of a Jewish source or model for Christian iconography, from third- and fourth-century Roman catacomb frescoes to the first Christian Bible illustrations. These scholars argue that Christian iconographic themes or motifs were derived from lost earlier copies of presumed Jewish prototypes that no longer exist. These theoretical Jewish prototypes include illustrated Bibles (in both Hebrew and Greek) as well as the pattern books used by artists' workshops to decorate synagogues like the one at Dura. According to scholarly premise, such Bibles or pattern books were then 'borrowed' by Christians who wished to decorate tombs, churches and eventually Bibles, especially for artistic representation of scenes from the Hebrew scriptures. Extra-canonical elements from rabbinic *aggadah* and **midrash** on these stories that appear in Christian paintings provide evidence for such Christian adaptation. The difficulty with this argument is the problem of proving the existence of a lost model, and the possibility that both iconographic and oral traditions were simultaneously transmitted and mutually influential between Christians and Jews.

The difficulties in establishing direct links between theoretical Jewish illuminated Bibles and Christian iconography in Late Antiquity notwithstanding, the mutual influence of Jewish and

Christian iconography is clearly apparent in the art of the Middle Ages. Christian workshops may even have produced Bibles for Jewish clients, although certain medieval Jewish illuminators and clients also are known by name. Additionally, Jewish manuscripts have certain distinguishing characteristics. For example, the lack of a capital letter in Hebrew script prevents the development of the initial letter as in Christian manuscripts, and certain liturgical implements or elements unique to Judaism may be seen in certain examples. Finally, although Christians began to portray God **anthropomorphically** as an old man, Jewish illuminations resisted portraying the divine and continued the long-established tradition of suggesting the presence of God with a hand or light beams coming from the heavens. Thus early Jewish influence on Christian illuminations can only be theoretically supposed, while later Christian influence on Jewish illuminations seems to have been limited by particular Jewish traditions and theological sensibilities.   *ROBIN M. JENSEN*

Imago Dei

'Image of God'. As the apex of **creation**, human beings (male and female) are in the image and likeness of God (Gen. 1.26–28; 5.1–3; 9.6; Ps. 8.5–8; Sir. 17.1–14). Both Jewish and Christian theologians have pondered at length the precise content of this doctrine. In the Middle Ages they focused on the intellect and will, residing in the immortal **soul**, as distinguishing humanity from other animate creatures. More recently scholars have looked for the meaning that the doctrine would have evoked for pre-philosophical communities. In the context of the creation hymn (Gen. 1.1–2.4) the human being is the viceroy, the representative of God in caring for the earth and its inhabitants. Secondly, human beings are created to be in a covenantal dialogue with God and to represent the rest of creation as the high priest mediating worship of the Creator. In the **Torah** only two earthly realities are created according to a heavenly model: the human being and the tabernacle in the wilderness (Exod. 25.40; 26.30 etc.). Just as the tent of meeting (and later the **Temple**) was the context within which sacrificial worship would be united with the celestial cult, so the human person should recognise the responsibility of reflecting God's presence and ordering the innate capacity of all creatures to serve God.

The concept 'image of God' (1 Cor. 11.7; Jas 3.9) is the foundation for the call to imitate God (Lev. 19.2; Matt. 5.48; Luke 6.36; 1 Pet. 1.16) by recognising the divine presence in one's neighbour (1 John 4.20, see Matt. 25.31–46). For Christian theologians Jesus is *the* image of the invisible God (Col. 1.15), and through him people conform to the divine exemplar (Rom. 8.29; 2 Cor. 3.18). Christ is the last **Adam**, whose obedience provides the foundation for human transformation (1 Cor. 15.45–50). Jewish teachers drew upon Gen. 1.26–28 as a foundation for doctrinal and moral insights into the meaning of life and respect for the inherent dignity of every human being. When discussing the responsibility of judges regarding the death penalty, for example, the sages noted: 'A king stamps many coins with one seal and they are all alike; but the King of Kings, the Holy One Blessed Be He, has stamped each human being with the seal of the first man, yet not one is like his fellow' (*m. Sanhedrin* 4.5).

Imago Dei is the doctrinal foundation for both Jews and Christians to grapple with virtually all issues of the moral order, from the challenge for each person to conform human life to the divine exemplar, to a self-respect that acknowledges the basic equality of all persons, to the human responsibility for the rest of creation.

LAWRENCE E. FRIZZELL

Immanuel

Although it occurs only three times in the **Old Testament** and **New Testament** (Isa. 7.14; 8.8; Matt. 1.23), the word *Immanuel* (literally, 'God with us') has left a significant impression in the Christian imagination, principally because it occurs frequently in Christian hymnody, especially around the music-rich Advent and **Christmas** liturgical seasons and epitomically in the hymn 'O Come, O Come Emmanuel' (a frequent alternative spelling). Its significance to Jewish–Christian relations lies in Matthew's interpretation of Isa. 7.14 as a Messianic prophecy fulfilled in Jesus: 'All this took place to fulfil what the Lord had said through the prophet: "The virgin will be with child and will give birth to a son, and they will call him Immanuel" – which means, "God with us"' (Matt. 1.22–23). Translations of this passage rendering the Hebrew *almah* as 'young woman' rather than as 'virgin' have removed some of the traditionally apologetical edge from the Christian prophecy-fulfilment rendering.

See also **Messiah**   *MICHAEL MCGARRY*

Immortality

Literally 'the state of not being subject to death'. The concept of an immortal **soul** does not appear in the Hebrew **canon** or the **New Testament**. Both *corpora* present the soul as dying (Judg. 16.30; Ezek. 18.4, 20; Acts 3.23; Rev. 16.3), the opposite of ancient Greek immortality; a 'dead soul' (Lev. 21.11; Num. 6.6) is contradictory in terms of Platonic philosophy. Late in the **Old Testament** period, when the resurrection is conceptualised, immortality is never mentioned with it. Certainly adoption of the immortal soul occurs in the more **Hellenised** circles of ancient Judaism (**Philo, Josephus,** *Wisdom*), but it is not generally found in Palestinian literature. Sir. 17.30 states that humankind is not immortal, implying only God is. Both at Qumran (Puech) and in the **Mishnah** (*Sanhedrin* 10.1) resurrection, not the immortal soul, is the basis for a share in the world to come. In the New Testament immortality is an inherent attribute of God alone (1 Tim. 6.16) but is attained by Christians through a spiritual resurrection (1 Cor. 15.44–6 *contrasts* this resurrection with the mortal, physical soul). As Judaism and Christianity continued, pervasive Greek thinking worked its way more fully into both. In rabbinic writings this is difficult to pinpoint (Grintz); for Christianity it appears quickly (*Diogn.* 6.8; Athenagorus, *Legatio* 27.2), though Christians and Jews had problems melding the Jewish and Greek concepts (**Justin Martyr,** *Dial.* 4–5; Tatian, *Oratio* 13; 2 Esd. 7.75–101). Early Jewish–Christian interaction likely hastened fusing the originally foreign notions, especially from Hellenised Judaism to nascent Christianity. Today the immortal soul notion is normative to many in both (and other) faiths.   *FRANK SHAW*

Incarnation

Incarnational **Christology** sees Jesus as 'the incarnate (enfleshed) Word of God'. It originates in the way early Christian teachers read Jewish poems about personified divine **Wisdom** (Prov. 8.22; Wis. 7–10; Sir. 24): they present the Word/Wisdom of God coming to dwell in human history, not in Torah as Sir. 24.23 suggests, but in Christ who radiates the divine *kabod* ('glory') (John 1.1–16). It develops central Jewish themes in relation to Christ and the character of God with consequences that come to exceed the limits of normative Judaism because it thinks of God's self-diffusive goodness towards the creation as culminating in the union of God's Word with **Jesus** of Nazareth. As a result, the concept of incarnation is generally viewed as one of the main dividing lines between Judaism and Christianity. Its 'maximalist' estimate of Christ's significance – nothing less than the actuality of divine love, wisdom, self-expression is mediated through him – develops in conjunction with a Trinitarian account of God as a generative mystery of self-expression (Word) and self-bestowal (Spirit), contact with which enables humanity to participate in the divine life (*see* **Trinity**).

Incarnational Christology envisages not a Zeus-like metamorphosis into creaturely form, but a union of the divine and the human in one person in ways that maintain the transcendent character of the divine and the dependent status of the created order. Judaism insists no less strongly than Christianity on the condescension of the transcendent God in being with his people, and the theme of the **Shekinah** is the closest Jewish analogue to Incarnation: 'when they [Israel] went into Egypt, the Shekinah went with them; in Babylon the Shekinah was with them' (*b. Megillah* 29a). Analogously, Jewish tradition thinks of the divine origin of **Torah** as the vehicle of God's self-bestowal to **Israel**, but it never treats Torah as the self-manifestation of God in the way Christian theology treats Christ as the Son/Word who 'bears the very stamp of God's nature' (Heb. 1.3).   *JOHN MCDADE*

Incense

While the **Temple** stood incense was offered twice daily by the officiating priests on a golden altar standing in the Holy Place before the entrance to the Holy of Holies (Exod. 30.1–10). It belonged to the category of most holy things, and its manufacture and use outside the Temple were strictly forbidden. Profound symbolism was often attached to it: Ben Sira (*c.*180 BCE) listed its ingredients as redolent of that Wisdom which is **Torah** (Sir. 24.15); **Philo** regarded it as thanksgiving for the rational spirit in humankind (*Spec.* 1.171) and accounted one grain of greater worth than blood **sacrifice** (*Spec.* 1.274–7). Some Christians of the first century CE viewed it as symbolic of **prayer**: it features in the Apocalypse of John in the heavenly liturgy there described (Rev. 5.8; 8.3–5), which probably owes a good deal to Jewish prototypes. Incense was not used in Christian **worship** at first, however, since its offering at altars dedicated to the Roman emperor was an essential element of cult paid to that personage, which Christians regarded as **idolatry**. Those who temporised and offered the incense were contemptuously dubbed *thurificati*; and it was only some time after **Constantine** that its use in Christian worship became general. Once adopted, it inevitably suggested that such worship was related in some way to the service of the Jewish Temple; and it ranks along with other solemn ceremonies described in the Bible and adopted by the Church, like the **anointing** of priests, the purification of women after childbirth, and the use of a breastplate with 12 precious stones by certain archbishops. Its place in Jewish–Christian relations is two-edged, since its prominent place in Christian worship inside church buildings and outside in processions could suggest to Jews a triumphalist appropriation of solemn Jewish rites: at the same time, however, its use by present-day Christians, particularly in the West, sometimes carries with it a high regard for the Hebrew scriptures and for Jewish ceremonies generally.   *C. T. R. HAYWARD*

India

India provides an intriguing example of a country where both Jews and Christians flourished under the benevolent rule of a third religious community, Hindus. Different groups of Jews and Christians have prospered in India. The earliest Jewish community to be located in the **Diaspora** is found in Cochin, Kerala, and claims to be descended from traders from the **land of Israel** during the reign of King Solomon. One group was given copper plates by a local Hindu ruler in 379 BCE, bestowing 'princely rights' for contributing to the prosperity of his territories. Most Indian Jews testify to the tolerance of Hindus, as do Christians. The latter have been in India since the middle of the second century CE and possibly since the days of the apostle Thomas. Ironically, their first persecutors seem to have been Portuguese Christians in the fifteenth and sixteenth centuries who attempted to correct Orthodox Indian Christians to Catholic faith; the Jewish community was left in peace.

MARTIN FORWARD

Infancy narratives

The common designation for the first two chapters of the Gospels of Matthew and Luke that narrate the circumstances surrounding the birth of **Jesus**. Although these two Gospels agree on certain details of the story, their differences are striking. Both Gospels name the parents of Jesus as

Mary and Joseph, a descendant of the Davidic line, note the announcement by a heavenly figure of the impending birth, and state that although legally engaged Mary and Joseph had not yet come to live together, hence the circumstances of conception were implicitly 'problematic'. Both narrate that the conception of the child by Mary happened not through normal intercourse but by the agency of the **Holy Spirit**, and agree that the birth of Jesus happened at Bethlehem. Beyond those shared details, other elements of the two accounts differ markedly, as Matthew's story comes from Joseph's perspective and is situated in Bethlehem, while Luke's story is told through Mary's eyes as the couple leave their home in Nazareth to travel to Bethlehem to register in the census. As the contradictions attest, midrashic and theological elements mark these stories more than accurate historical memory. Their attempts to emphasise Jesus' Davidic descent, his similarity with biblical ancestors (**Joseph**, **Moses**) and his filial relation to God through the power of the Holy Spirit are problematic claims and together contribute to a portrait of Jesus as the fulfilment of biblical prophecy and the replacement for Jewish mediations of God's presence in the world (*see* **supersessionism**).

BARBARA E. BOWE

Innocent III (1160/1–1216)

Pope (1198–1216). Born in Italy as Lotario dei Segni. During his pontificate, which marks a highpoint in the medieval papacy, Innocent dealt with problems of **heresy** and major issues of Church **doctrine** like transubstantiation. In 1207 Innocent preached the Albigensian **Crusade** against the Cathars. He was favourable to the new rules of the **Franciscans** and **Dominicans**, recognising the potential of both orders for his fight against religious deviance. As far as Jews were concerned, Innocent upheld the traditional papal policy of broad **toleration**. In a bull of 1205, however, he emphasised the superiority of Christianity over Jews by declaring that Jews had to live in a state of Perpetual Servitude. Although the term was new, the underlying concepts were not. **Augustine**'s witness theory subsumed the idea of Jewish subservience. The term did not imply slavery or serfdom in a strictly legal sense. The bull demanded that Jews no longer employ Christian wet-nurses: scandal had been caused by rumours that Jews did not want their children to receive breast milk from women just after they had been to Mass at **Easter**. In 1198 Innocent ruled that crusaders should not be charged interest on their loans from Jews whilst on crusade (*see* **usury**). On forced **baptism** Innocent ruled in 1201 that, notwithstanding the illegality of the procedure, the forced convert could not return to his original faith because that would constitute an insult to the **sacrament**. The apogee of Innocent's reign was the Fourth **Lateran Council** of 1215, which contained a number of important canons on the Jews.   *ANNA SAPIR ABULAFIA*

Innocent IV (*c*.1200–54)

Pope (1243–54). A renowned canonist, he asserted the Jews' right to justice, illustrated by his support for Jews who sought to recover debts owed to them in Champagne in 1247; he also set a precedent by condemning the **blood libel** on more than one occasion. On the other hand, he decreed the burning of the **Talmud** and other Jewish books and often reminded rulers of the need to implement the decisions of **Lateran Council (IV)** such as the wearing of the **yellow badge** and other distinctive clothing. Innocent was also eager to facilitate the **conversion** of Jews, often supporting Jewish converts to Christianity in arguments with local rulers.

EDWARD KESSLER

Inquisition

The Inquisition (the 'Holy Office of the Inquisition') began in the thirteenth century against heretical groups in southern **France** and lasted off and on until the nineteenth century. From its beginnings it was not primarily concerned with Jews and Judaism per se, but at various times Judaism was a major factor. For example, a type of Inquisition was held against Jews when Church leaders became concerned about the teachings of the **Talmud** concerning Christianity in Paris in the 1240s. After the 1391 riots that began in Seville and spread throughout the Iberian peninsula, a group called the **Conversos** (*see also* **Marranos**) came into existence when a number of the Jews converted to Christianity under the choice of **baptism** or death. These converted Jews were a cause of much suspicion, and therefore Church leaders felt the need to ensure that their conversions were valid and real, especially in the later half of the fifteenth century. **Alonso de Espina** and others argued for an institution that would eradicate **apostasy** and **heresy** in **Spain**. The National Spanish Inquisition was founded in 1478 by Pope Sixtus IV (1471–84) and officially began its

work in 1481 as an attempt to deal not only with Conversos but also the threat of Jews who were influencing the apostasy of these converts. This was not an attack on Judaism itself, but an attempt to stop Christian **Judaising** and the influence Jews and Judaism had in relation to the Conversos. **Apostasy** was held to be a greater sin than unbelief according to Thomas **Aquinas** and other medieval theologians. The main problem with the Inquisition in regard to Jews and Judaism was the line of demarcation between Conversos and the non-converted Jews: what right did the Church have to protect and defend its own (Conversos) and to pursue Jews as Jews? The line was crossed during the **Talmud trial** of Paris in the 1240s, and although for the most part the Inquisition went after relapsing Conversos, there was the tendency to think that the Inquisitors had a right to go after non-converted Jews because of the supposed threat they posed to the Conversos and their relapsing back into Judaism. The Inquisition caused much hardship on the part of the Jewish community and it certainly contributed to other behaviours detrimental to the Jewish community in Europe: **expulsions** (for example, from Spain in 1492 and **Portugal** a few years later), confiscation of property and expropriation of all rights as citizens within a host country. A major controversy is the role of the converts themselves in the persecution of their former religionists: in some cases the Conversos themselves became the major enemy of Jews living in their midst.   *STEVEN J. MCMICHAEL*

Inscriptions, ancient

Inscriptions and their study (epigraphy) shed light indirectly and sometimes directly on Jewish–Christian relations in antiquity. Subjects illuminated include Jewish names, marriages, occupations, organisation, languages and localities; proselytes and godfearers; synagogues; **conversion** to Christianity; and formulae and symbols of Jewish and Christian loyalty.

The ever-increasing body of inscriptions sponsored by or concerning Jews (over 2,000) illuminates Judea and Syria together with some places for which Christian literary documentation is richer than Jewish, notably the lands around the Mediterranean from Asia Minor to Spain, and from Arabia and Egypt to North Africa. The main languages are Aramaic, Hebrew, Greek and Latin. Most are funerary inscriptions, ranging from names on ossuaries and plaques to full epitaphs. Dedications relating to synagogues are also numerous. Epitaphs likewise predominate in the far larger body of contemporary Latin and Greek Christian inscriptions.

It has often been suggested (by scholars including E. L. Sukenik (1889–1953) of the Hebrew University and B. Bagatti (1905–90) of the Jerusalem Franciscans) that the names or symbols of Christian Jews occur in Judean inscriptions of the first and second centuries, but it remains hard to present a clear example. Some alleged epigraphic indications of communal loyalty are therefore doubtful, but in general such indications shed light on Jewish–Christian relations. Thus Jewish inscriptions often include explicit description as Hebrew, Jew or proselyte, occasionally with further reference to Judaism; so Polycharmus, benefactor of a synagogue at Stobi in Macedonia, had 'governed his life in every way according to Judaism' (c.150–250; *CIJ* 694). Comparably, many Christian inscriptions from the second century onwards include such descriptions as 'faithful', 'Christian' or 'catechumen'. Common epigraphic symbols of Jewish loyalty include shofar, menorah, ethrog and lulav (compare Christian use of **crosses** or monograms); signs of hope shared by Jewish and Christian epigraphy include the dove and the palm. Half-hidden expressions of faith are less prominent in Jewish than in Christian inscriptions, but famous allusions to **afterlife** occur in the Roman Jewish Latin verse epitaph of Regina (third–fourth century; *CIJ* 476). The importance of proselytes and godfearers is confirmed by inscribed listing of names from Aphrodisias in Caria (probably third century) published by J. M. Reynolds and R. Tannenbaum (*Jews and God-fearers at Aphrodisias*). Baptismal names taken by Jews who became Christians are inscribed for instance in Grado in north Italy (CIJ i^2 643a).   *WILLIAM HORBURY*

Inspiration

The notion that people compose scriptures under the influence of divine inspiration (Latin *inspiratio*) is found in many religions. The concept of inspiration is fundamental for understanding scripture and **tradition** in Judaism and Christianity. Both traditions start with biblical statements, but develop their understanding of inspiration differently.

The **Torah** takes a central place in the Jewish understanding of the divine origin of the sacred scriptures: 'You must diligently observe everything that I command you; do not add to it or take anything from it' (Deut. 13.1, Hebrew Bible). This uniqueness of the Torah corresponds to the incomparability of **Moses** who received it on Mount Sinai directly from God. 'The **Holy Spirit**' (*ruaḥ ha-kodesh*), however, inspired the writings of the other prophets. Understood as the spirit of **prophecy** in **Rabbinical Judaism**, the Holy Spirit comes from God and is given to the prophets to an unequal degree (*Leviticus Rabbah* 15.2). If a writing was inspired by the Holy Spirit it was counted among the books of the biblical **canon** in addition to the Torah (Pentateuch). After a long process of development the 'early prophets' (Joshua–2 Kings) and the 'major prophets', as well as the 'Hagiographa' (Psalms–2 Chronicles), achieved this canonical status.

The significance attached to 'the law and the prophets' in Judaism during the period of the Second Temple makes it understandable that 'the scriptures' played an important role in early Christianity (Matt. 5.17–19 and *passim*). For the early Christian community it was one and the same God who 'spoke to our ancestors . . . by the prophets, but in these last days . . . to us by his Son' (Heb. 1.1f.). It regarded sacred scripture as 'inspired by God' (2 Tim. 3.16). 2 Pet. 1.21 says of the scriptures of Israel that 'no prophecy ever came by human will, but men and women moved by the Holy Spirit spoke from God'; the fulfilment of this prophecy took place in the Christ event (Matt. 1.23f.; 2.17f., and *passim*). Thus the hermeneutic shifts: in the **New Testament** the Torah is no longer incomparable; the prophets are now ranked higher (cf. The Pontifical Biblical Commission, no. 11 and *passim*) and inspiration is attributed to the New Testament itself. The Holy Spirit – understood ever more clearly as the self-communicating and communicated gift of God himself and not, as in Judaism, as a gift that, while coming from God, is not itself divine – has 'inspired each one of the saints, whether prophets or apostles; and that there was not one Spirit in the men of the old dispensation and another in those who were inspired at the advent of Christ is most clearly taught' (**Origen**, *Princ.* 1, *Praefatio* 4). For the Catholic Church **Vatican II** states that everything 'the inspired authors . . . affirm should be regarded as affirmed by the Holy Spirit'; the biblical writings 'firmly, faithfully and without error, teach that truth which God, for the sake of our salvation, wished to see confided to the sacred Scriptures'

(*Dei verbum* 11). The question of how the 'Holy Spirit' or God's Spirit and human authors work together has continued to preoccupy Jewish and Christian scholars, including **Rosenzweig**, **Buber** and Karl Rahner (1904–84).

HANS HERMANN HENRIX

Institute of Christian and Jewish Studies (ICJS) *see* **Dabru Emet**; **Jewish–Christian relations, centres for the study of**

Institute of Judaeo–Christian Studies *see* **Jewish–Christian relations, centres for the study of**; **Oesterreicher, John**

Intercessions

Drawing on shared biblical models, prayers for the benefit of the community and its members are integral to public worship for Jews and Christians. Jewish intercessions appear in the petitions of the weekday *Amidah*, in private supplicatory prayers (*tahanun*), and in prayers accompanying the **Torah** reading. The first two categories are largely Messianic, asking God for redemptive amelioration of the current situation. In these, non-Jews, including Christians, appear primarily as persecutors and enemies whom God should overthrow. Modern liberal **liturgies** generally eliminate this negative portrayal. An early modern intercession that accompanies the Torah reading, documented first in Europe, prays for the monarch – usually Christian. Christian intercessions, also called the Prayer of the Faithful or bidding prayers, appear first in **Justin Martyr** (*1 Apol.* 65), where they also follow the scripture reading. Christian intercessions ask for God's blessing on members of the church and civil leaderships, the deceased, the living, humanity globally and the agricultural realm. There was great variation in the placement and content of these intercessions before they largely disappeared from medieval rites, to be replaced by various litanies and bidding prayers. Only the Good Friday intercessions continued in the Roman Catholic rite, until 1959 (*see* **Good Friday Prayer for the Perfidious Jews**). Twentieth-century liturgical reforms revived regular intercessory prayer, often encouraging free response to contemporary issues and events. Prayers for Jews' wellbeing are not uncommon.

See also ***birkat ha-minim*** *RUTH LANGER*

Intermarriage

Intermarriage – defined as **marriage** between members of different faiths, each of whom maintains their own religious **identity** – has long been a contentious issue for both Judaism and Christianity. It has become even more pronounced in recent decades with the decline of social and cultural barriers that previously reinforced the religious division between members of the two faiths.

The objections of Judaism are rooted in the concern of **Abraham** that his son should not marry any of the local pagan Canaanites lest they lead him astray religiously (Gen. 24.3–4). The biblical ban against intermarrying with the seven nations in the **land of Israel** (Deut. 4.1–4) was extended by rabbinic authorities to all Gentiles (*b. Avodah Zarah* 36b; *b. Yevamot* 45a). The **emancipation** of Jews and their integration into general society during the eighteenth century led to a rise in intermarriage, despite continued rabbinic opposition. Following the Second World War the **Holocaust** was often cited as providing additional reasons against intermarriage: first, as evidence that Jews could never fully trust the Gentile world; secondly, according to Emil Fackenheim (1916–2003), Jews had a duty not to give **Hitler** posthumous victory by disappearing, a danger posed by intermarriage; thirdly, Jews had a duty to replenish the 6 million lost Jewish lives by having Jewish children. Christian objections to intermarriage also stem from the very beginnings of the faith. **Paul** forbids Christians to marry non-believers (1 Cor. 7.12–16; 2 Cor. 6.14–16). His justification is theological: that Christians are living parts of the Church, which is the body of **Christ**; thus they are part of Christ's body, a spiritual oneness that would be sullied if they married out of the faith (Eph. 5.21–31). This ban later led to the introduction of the **yellow badge** and the **ghetto** as ways of preventing intimacy between Jews and Christians.

In recent times both Jewish and Christian authorities have had to confront the reality of the secularisation of society and an ever-increasing intermarriage rate even amongst those attached to their faith. By the 1990s the intermarriage rate for Jews in Britain was 44 per cent and in the **United States** 52 per cent. Amongst Catholics it was over 65 per cent in both countries, while it was a serious issue for Anglicans and other Protestant groups too. The reaction of some religious leaders was to oppose intermarriage even more vehemently, with, for example, the Chief Rabbi of **Orthodox Jewry** in Britain, Immanuel Jakobovits (1921–99), describing it as a 'cancer'. More liberally minded priests, rabbis and vicars regarded intermarried couples as an inevitable result of a pluralist society and sought to accommodate them by welcoming them into their communities and respecting their religious differences. Several Churches have published advice for their ministers on how to conduct such ceremonies (e.g. the Church of England's 1992 'Guidelines for the Celebration of Mixed-Faith Marriages in Church'). Despite these efforts at inclusion, Jewish and Christian ministers alike fear that intermarriage is a threat to religious continuity, in terms of both the observances of the couple themselves and the education of any children they may have. The Catholic Church will often insist that they will only officiate at an intermarriage if the Catholic partner agrees to bring up any children in the Catholic faith, while most rabbis decline to be present at either a marriage or blessing ceremony involving a non-Jewish partner. The **Church of England** is legally obliged to marry anyone resident in one of its parishes, but also has to keep to the Trinitarian formulation of its marriage service. The overall result is that although most Jewish–Christian couples wish to receive God's blessing on their union, they reluctantly decide that a registry office **wedding** is the only acceptable option. By contrast, marriages officiated jointly by Jewish and Christian ministers are common in North America, where many in the clergy feel it is more constructive to help the couple unite their two traditions than to refuse to assist them. Another concern of ministers of both faiths is the pastoral aspect: that unless couples are fully prepared for the possible difficulties they can face, they could find that differences in religious practice, cultural expectations and family pressures cause a serious strain on the marital relationship. Ministers themselves can face an acute dilemma: they wish to preserve their own faith tradition by discouraging intermarriage, yet want to respond positively to intermarried couples who approach them for help.

The issue has also affected Jewish–Christian **dialogue**, insofar as the fear of engaging in any action that might be seen to encourage blurring of religious boundaries has led many rabbis to shun interfaith activities. The ground-breaking Jewish statement on Christianity published in 2000, *Dabru Emet*, acknowledged the prevalence of such concerns and sought to allay them by declaring that

'An improved relationship will not accelerate the cultural and religious assimilation that Jews rightly fear . . . nor increase intermarriage between Jews and non-Jews'. For those engaged in dialogue, the issue has thrown into sharp relief the question to what extent the two faiths accept each other: if both are considered valid paths to God, then intermarriage should not pose any theological problems, even though it may still raise practical difficulties for those involved. The traditional teachings of both faiths regarding intermarriage have also been challenged by the pluralism within society at large. In an era in which many children are brought up to oppose intolerance of any kind and to value individuals in their own right, it has become increasingly hard for both ministers and parents to insist on the need to keep separate from those of a different religious identity. This has been exacerbated by the way in which, for many people, faith has become 'privatised': something to be practised by individuals in their own way and which need not have an impact on others in the same family. In this climate a person from a different religious background is regarded as no less suitable as a marriage partner.

See also **assimilation**   JONATHAN ROMAIN

International Catholic–Jewish Liaison Committee
see **Jewish–Christian relations, institutions**

International Christian Embassy

Established in 1980, the International Christian Embassy in Jerusalem (ICEJ) is one of the foremost organisations of advocates of **Christian Zionism**. ICEJ officially repudiates **replacement theology** and any **liberation theology** that scapegoats Jews and Judaism. Its supporters, drawn largely from among **fundamentalists** and **evangelicals**, affirm that Jews are still the **Chosen People** and that the **Promised Land** is theirs as 'an everlasting possession by an eternal **covenant**'. They believe that the modern-day restoration of the **State of Israel**, with **Jerusalem** as its capital, is in fulfilment of biblical prophecies, and thus scripture commands Christians to support this divine scheme. ICEJ's flagship activity is an annual nine-day Christian celebration of the Feast of Tabernacles in Jerusalem during **Sukkot**, which attracts some 5,000 persons from more than 100 countries. Other projects include financial assistance to bring Jews to Israel, social aid in Israel and 'bless Israel' events in local churches and communities worldwide. ICEJ monitors **antisemitism** and anti-Israel biases in the secular and religious **media** and strives to counter them through publications that present a 'biblical Zionist' understanding of current affairs affecting the Jewish people and the State of Israel. The embassy has organised several Christian Zionist congresses, first in Basel in 1985 and most recently in Jerusalem in 2001. ICEJ's Christian critics include both conservatives, who fault them for failing to evangelise Jews, and liberals, who censure their unconditional support for the State of Israel. Right-wing Israeli politicians publicly salute ICEJ's support, while left-wing parties and liberal Jewish circles are circumspect in their contacts with the embassy.   *DANIEL ROSSING*

International Council of Christians and Jews
see **Council(s) of Christians and Jews**
International Jewish Committee for Interreligious Consultations *see* **Jewish–Christian relations, institutions**

Internet

The Internet as a new medium of communication has taken many by surprise in its speed of development and universal application. It has raised concern over the accessibility of a wide range of positive and negative information, but has also presented new opportunities to be explored. Its manifestation in the World Wide Web (since 1991, with the creation of the Web consortium in 1994) will be most familiar, but the Internet as a method of communication between individuals is much older. It has allowed communication between scholars and individuals who are geographically dispersed, has improved cooperation and has allowed for discussion groups to operate virtually. One of the oldest and more successful discussion groups in the humanities has been the Ioudaios-list, specialising in Judaism in antiquity. The consequences of the new developments provided by the web for Jewish–Christian relations are significant.

The available resources for research into the field are many. Gateways providing organised links to other sites that are specifically focussed on Jewish–Christian relations are few, but gateways for the study of the ancient world are common, including the ABZU resources for the ancient Near East and 'Biblical Studies on the Web' (bsw.org), which provides access to a range of journals. For Jewish–Christian relations the JCRelations.net website has become the most visited site. It contains articles and discussions on key issues, the latest news, and a

useful collection of statements by Jewish and Christian groups. On a smaller scale but with a similar type of content is the website of the Baltimore Institute for Christian and Jewish Studies. The site of the Avraham Harman Institute of Contemporary Jewry in Jerusalem also provides articles and a searchable bibliography. As databases have become a standard backend to many websites, the scale of material that one may now access is greater than ever. Specialist bibliographic resources can be searched from databases, including the RAMBI catalogue of Jewish studies, but apart from the Harman Institute's resources, little can yet be found for Jewish–Christian relations specifically. It is likely, however, that in the future such resources will become increasingly available, allowing the searching of texts and discussions in depth.

As distance learning has become a common mode of course delivery, the Internet has been utilised in course teaching, including courses on Jewish–Christian relations. The Centre for the study of Jewish–Christian Relations (Cambridge, UK) has been particularly active in this regard. Small institutions are enabled to provide courses for people in many parts of the world without the additional costs of travel or accommodation. In particular teachers, and not just the students, may be in different locations, bringing an international flavour to the educational experience. One may therefore offer, for example, contemporary perspectives from Poland, Israel and Germany in a course based in the USA. Web pages can provide access to course materials, in the manner of a book, but with hyperlinks allowing for further exploration of topics on external sites. Discussion groups provide some of the experience of **dialogue**, again with the possibility of contact with people in disparate locations, but the future might see significant development in this area as technology allows the improved exchange of live images and sound.

The provision of publications on the Internet was an early goal. Ioudaios has published since the early 1990s book reviews and occasional articles on ancient Judaism and Christian origins, and many free publications still exist. The web journal *Crosscurrents*, for example, contains articles on contemporary religious issues, and JCRelations.net regularly includes discussions of issues relevant to Jewish–Christian relations. Some journals are available on the web by subscription, and a site such as 'Biblical studies on the web' provides a comprehensive list, indicating level of access to the information. Other types of publication available are reviews of books or films, statements by organisations, transcripts of parliamentary proceedings and press releases, all of which could be useful for research in the area.

The presence of racist and **antisemitic** websites, and **Holocaust** denial pages, and the propagation of such material by email, have been a particular concern. The situation is monitored by the Anti-defamation League (ADL) and the Avraham Harman Institute of Contemporary Jewry in Jerusalem. Although this is a new form of communication, the material is not new and the same issues apply as with more traditional **media**. Websites tend to be viewed by those already looking for them, and this material need not reach new audiences, although certain groups are clearly targeted. The difference with the Internet is that any person can establish a site for little cost and can promote opinions anonymously. The speed of exchange of information globally also allows for an issue to be spread extremely quickly and for immediate response, which has both positive and negative applications. The fact that sites can be viewed in any country allows the propagation of hate to those who might not have been able to reach it before. In particular, a site can be established in one country but viewed in another where such a site might be illegal. The use of 'spam' for the distribution of racist information is also common, although spam-blockers often reduce this threat. While Internet providers can block access to particular sites, and governments can legislate against certain types of material (albeit only within the confines of their jurisdiction), such measures have raised concerns over freedom of speech, especially on the Internet. Campaigns by pressure groups and the public can also be effective, such as that against certain discussion groups at Yahoo, which was led by the ADL, or the public-wide pressure on Amazon not to sell *Mein Kampf* and other hate literature. As always, education is the best solution, and the Internet provides an opportunity for websites promoting **tolerance** and understanding. *JAMES K. AITKEN*

Ireland

While Jewish settlement can be said to have begun around the time of the **expulsions** from England (1290), it was not until the early nineteenth century that more than a handful of Jews inhabited Ireland. This did not discourage active **mission** work, for example among Dublin Jewry in the eighteenth century. In 1846 legal discriminations against Jews desiring naturalisation were abolished and a statute prescribing a special **dress** for the Jews was repealed. Although conditions were not always favourable, its small size, its low profile and the Irish preoccupation with British oppressors meant that the Jewish community attracted little overt **antisemitism**, most Catholic antagonism being reserved for Protestants. Exceptions included the anti-Jewish riots in Limerick (1884) and Cork (1894), which followed the arrival of refugees from **pogroms** in Eastern Europe, and the boycott of the Jewish community in Cork from 1904, an explicitly antisemitic campaign led by Father John Creagh (1870–1947). However, the all-pervading culture of conservative Catholic triumphalism that followed the independence of Ireland from Protestant Britain in 1922 reinforced a sense of alienness felt by many Jews, often experienced as polite or silent antisemitism. Nor were relations with Irish Protestants, a fellow **minority** group, much warmer; the Church of Ireland Jews Society (for **Hebrew Christians**) represented one institutional effort to engage with Jews. During the 1930s and throughout the Second World War Ireland took very few Jewish refugees, its envoy in Berlin was a notorious antisemite, and despite his admiration for Chief Rabbi Herzog (1888–1959), who publicly supported Irish nationalist claims, Eamon De Valera (1882–1975) even paid his condolences to the Nazi delegation in Dublin at the death of **Hitler**. Reflecting Vatican reservations, Ireland only extended *de jure* recognition of the **State of Israel** in 1963. An abortive attempt at Jewish–Christian **dialogue** was made during the war; initiated in 1942 by lay Catholics, the Pillar of Fire society ceased its activities after the third meeting. An Irish **Council of Christians and Jews** was established in 1983.

DANIEL R. LANGTON

Irenaeus of Lyons (*c*.130–*c*.200)

Bishop of Lyons and **Church Father**. A native of **Asia Minor**, Irenaeus spent the greater part of his life in Gaul. He is best known for his theological works (*Against the Heresies* and *Demonstration of the Apostolic Preaching*), in which he clearly delineated Christian orthodoxy from **Gnostic** heresy (particularly through his conception of the apostolic tradition and the unity of the two Testaments), incidentally producing the first great synthesis of Christian **doctrine**. Irenaeus has little sympathy for the Jews. Notwithstanding their special election by God, they have not heeded the prophets and have connived in the **crucifixion** of Christ (and indeed in later **anti-Christian** persecutions). Judaism has therefore been comprehensively superseded by Christianity (*see* **supersessionism**). Irenaeus also takes issue with certain points of Jewish **exegesis** (e.g. regarding Isa. 7.14) and laments the survival of Jewish practices in certain Christian groupings.

MARCUS PLESTED

Isaac

Son of **Abraham** and father of **Jacob**, Isaac is the patriarch least commented upon in Jewish and Christian writings, although much attention has been given to the significance of the **binding of Isaac** (Gen. 22). The other two main events in his life, according to the biblical narrative, are his marriage to Rebecca and his blessing of Jacob over Esau. In early Christian thought Isaac's importance lies in his being the son of the exemplary figure of faith (Abraham), who received a son as God promised (e.g. Rom. 9.7, identified with **Christ** in Gal. 3.16). As the child of promise, Isaac is also contrasted with Ishmael (Rom. 9.7, 10; Gal. 4.28; Heb. 11.18) (*see* **Hagar**). The rabbis too compare Isaac favourably with Ishmael, but this may represent a response to Islamic tradition rather than to Christianity.

EDWARD KESSLER

Isaac, Jules (1877–1963)

French historian of **antisemitism**. His wife and daughter died in the **Holocaust**. In 1946, at an international conference of Jews and Christians, Isaac was largely responsible for the 'Ten Points of **Seelisberg**', influential guidelines for Christian preachers and teachers concerning Jewish–Christian relations. In *La genèse de l'antisémitisme* (1956) and *The Teaching of Contempt: Christian Roots of Anti-Semitism* (1964) Isaac revealed the Christian roots of antisemitism and coined the phrase 'teaching of contempt'. He was instrumental in persuading Pope **John XXIII** to attend to relations with Jews and Judaism at **Vatican II** as a result of their meeting in 1960, at which time he presented him with a document on the Church's involvement in promoting the teaching of contempt. Isaac urged the Pope to tackle the legacy of **anti-Judaism** and antisemitism; this resulted in the creation of a subcommission to study the Jewish question. Eventually incorporated into the deliberations of Vatican II, it thus helped shape the 1965 declaration *Nostra Aetate* repudiating the charge of **deicide** and calling for Jewish–Christian **dialogue**. Despite the loss of his family, Isaac did not hesitate to enter into dialogue with Christianity, envisaging an optimistic future and aspiring to positive relations between both religions.

STEPHEN PLANT

Isabella of Castile *see* Ferdinand the Catholic

Isaiah

Of the biblical prophets none has played a more crucial role in Jewish–Christian relations than Isaiah. He was one of the eighth-century prophets who, like Hosea, Amos and Micah, witnessed the Assyrian invasions of Israel and Judah, but unlike them also lived through the long and relatively prosperous reign of Hezekiah and saw the unexpected survival of **Jerusalem** in 701 BCE. Not all of the 66 chapters that bear his name, however, could have been written in the eighth century: large parts of the book, especially chs 40–66, as the medieval Spanish Jewish commentator **Ibn Ezra** recognised, appear to have been written much later, after Jerusalem had been destroyed by the Babylonians in the sixth century BCE. The division into three clear sections (1–39, 40–55 and 56–66) is now considered an oversimplification: some parts of 1–39 ('Proto-Isaiah'), notably the 'Isaiah Apocalypse' in 24–27, are almost certainly later than 'Deutero-Isaiah'. Still later are the works known as the *Martyrdom and Ascension of Isaiah*, which have come down to us in both Jewish and Christian versions.

Uniquely Isaianic is the focus on Jerusalem, the 'daughter of **Zion**', and the power of the 'Holy One of Israel' to intervene in history on her behalf. This gives the whole book an impressive unity and ensured its central role in the history of both Judaism and Christianity from the beginning. Isaiah is exceptionally prominent among the **Dead Sea Scrolls** and in the **New Testament** as well as in the Jewish **lectionary**. The special place that Isaiah held in the hearts of Jews can be illustrated by the Kedushah (6.3) and the 'consolation readings' from Isa. 41–61, as well as by the disproportionate frequency of Isaianic allusions in modern Jewish history and philosophy: Ariel, Rishon LeTzion, Nes Harim, Neveh Shalom, Yad Vashem, El mistater ('God who hides himself').

It was the Church, however, that made Isaiah peculiarly their own, in particular finding in the numerous 'Messianic' prophecies, such as those in chs 7, 9, 11, 35, 42, 49, 53 and 61, the language and imagery they needed to express their beliefs about **Christ**. For **Jerome** Isaiah was more evangelist than prophet because he described Christ's life and work in detail as though it had already happened (e.g. 9.6; 53), not as a prophecy of what was to come. References to the **Trinity** (6.3; 42.1), the Virgin **Mary** (7.14), the **eucharist** (55.1), even bishops (60.17b Greek *episkopoi*), were readily found in Isaiah, together with countless expressions that came to be integral parts of Christian vocabulary, like **Immanuel**, a voice crying in the wilderness, man of sorrows, good news to the poor. Indeed, modern Jewish Bible translators could not use the phrase 'Prince of Peace' because of its Christian associations. Sadly Isaiah's role in the history of Christian **anti-Judaism** and **antisemitism** was crucial. Not only were some of the best-known disputed texts in Jewish–Christian debate to be found in Isaiah (7.14; 53 – see **'Suffering Servant'**), but the venom that Isaiah so frequently directed at his own people provided the Church with scriptural authority to hurl at the Jews in all periods all manner of accusations, not least that of **deicide** (Isa. 1.15; cf. Matt. 27.25). The post-**Vatican II** emphasis on social justice (1.17; 11.3–5; 16.3–5; 32.16–20; 61.1–2) and widespread interest in the female images of God (42.14; 49.14–15; 66.13) in Isaiah (*see* **feminism**) promise more peaceable exchanges in future.   *JOHN F. A. SAWYER*

Ishmael *see* Hagar

Isidore of Seville (*c*.560–636)

Archbishop of Seville, last **Church Father** of the Western Church and one of the greatest scholars of the early Middle Ages. He and his influential family distinguished themselves in political and religious struggle against the **Arianism** of the **Visigothic** kings. Isidore's encyclopedia, the *Etymologiae*, a compilation that embodied the medieval knowledge of classical culture, was greatly admired for centuries, and his work became the main source for all later medieval history-writing in Spain. His *De fide catholica ex Veteri et Novo Testamento contra Iudaeos*, where, in comparatively moderate terms, he invokes Jews to accept Christianity, was much translated and widely read. Isidore opposed King Sisebut's (*r*.612–20) decree aimed at enforcing general **baptism** of all the Jews of Spain (613), the first of such scope, and he condemned forced conversions. Nonetheless, the fourth Toledan Council of 633, with Isidore at its head, prohibited converts from returning to their original beliefs and thus nullifying accepted sacraments.   *PETR FRYŠ*

Islam

In one sense Islam's influence upon Jewish–Christian relations can be dealt with under its general **supersessionist** attitude to other religions. Muslims believe that Islam was the final religion revealed by God through the Prophet Muhammad (*c*.570–632), and many thus have difficulty in responding positively to a religiously plural world. Islam condemns not only more recent religions, like Sikhism, but also polytheistic faiths.

Islam sees itself as perfecting other previous monotheistic religions. Muhammad's religious practice at first owed much to Arabian Christians and especially Jews: Muslims faced **Jerusalem** in prayer and fasted during the **Day of Atonement**. But after Muhammad failed to gain the support of both other groups, his became a separate religion, claiming to be the fulfilment and reformer of previous revelations, including Judaism and Christianity. He expelled two Jewish groups from Medina; finally, a third group was severely treated, the men being killed and women and children sold into slavery. Muhammad showed a similar though less violent ambivalence towards Christians: the Qur'an describes them as 'nearest in love' to the believers (5.82), yet condemns their **Christological** and Trinitarian beliefs.

Muhammad's ambivalent attitude towards Judaism and Christianity continued into later history. In medieval times Jews and Christians were often (not always) well-treated under Muslim rule, regarded (unlike polytheists and atheists) as *dhimmi*s, 'people of the book', who were, on payment of a tax, allowed to practise their faith and even to participate in political and social life. Even so, this attitude was one that regarded Jews and Christians as believers who had not understood the logic of their faith as pointing to the finality of Islam; it treated them as clients rather than as equals.

To the extent that Muslims have become involved in interfaith **dialogue**, they have much to discuss with Jews and Christians. Islam is more alike to Judaism than Christianity. Both have problems with

Christian Trinitarian theology, stress religious law, and have no **priesthood**. Like Christianity, however, Islam has a strong sense of **mission** to people of other religions. These similarities and dissimilarities could provide the substance of fruitful and respectful debate. There are problems to this scenario, however. For example, Islam's Wahabi sect, which has a following among many Muslims, including among Diaspora communities in the West, seeks to return to an idealised form of certain early Islamic values, and strongly condemns many other forms of Islam, as well as other religions. Many Wahabis as well as some other Muslims are vehemently opposed to Israel, whose control of Jerusalem is seen as a particular grievance, since it is Islam's third holiest city. Indeed, the great mosque on the Temple Mount and near to the Church of the Holy Sepulchre, the Dome of the Rock, finished in 691 or 692 CE, was intended as an early signal to both Jews and Christians that their corrupted faith had been replaced by a pure one. But Jerusalem has not always been seen by Muslims as centrally important to their faith. The fall of Jerusalem to Christians in 1099 did not initially cause overwhelming interest in the region, and even after it was recaptured by Muslims in 1187, in 1229 a Muslim ruler ceded it to the emperor Frederick II (*r*.1215–50). It was retaken in 1244 after crusaders tried to make it a wholly Christian city.

Since the creation of the **State of Israel** in 1948 many Muslims have emphasised Muhammad's harsher teachings towards Judaism and Christianity and regard Jewish–Christian relations with suspicion as an attempt to marginalise and disempower them. The recent creation of an Abrahamic Faiths forum within the International **Council of Christians and Jews**, which includes Muslims alongside Jews and Christians, may help to change this negative point of view, but more positive contemporary Muslim relations with Jews and Christians are greatly dependent upon intra-Islamic discussions that would admit more internal diversity, and articulate and apply more generous attitudes towards other religions than the noisiest ones that presently emanate from the worlds of Islam. Muslim **minorities** in significant numbers now live in the **United States**, the **United Kingdom** and elsewhere, but often play only a small role in the wider community. However, some Muslims are beginning to join in interfaith movements, particularly those that bring together Jews and Christians, though what results this will have it is, as yet, too early to predict.

See also **trialogue**   *MARTIN FORWARD*

Israel Council on Interreligious Relations *see* **Jewish–Christian relations, institutions**

Israel, expatriate Christians in

Only a very small proportion of the Israeli population are Christians. Of the 6 million inhabitants of the **State of Israel** about 18 per cent are non-Jewish. Most of them are 'Israeli Arabs' or 'Palestinian Arabs'. Of this group in Israel about 80 per cent is Muslim and 20 per cent is Christian, part of **Arab Christianity** in the Middle East. The specific numbers are not exactly known and are often the subject of socio-political debate. There is a small group of about 4,000 '**Jewish Christians**' or '**Messianic Jews**' in Israel. Beside these two groups, there are expatriate Christians in Israel, who came to the country for very different reasons. Any classification of these Christians must be somewhat arbitrary, but the following assessment is based upon their different motivations for coming to Israel.

'Guardians of the Holy Places' claim to have very ancient rights in the Land, which they usually call the 'Holy Land'. Most of these groups date their origins back to the time of the **Crusades**, some to even earlier. Their presence is devoted to defending the status quo of the Holy Places and to celebrating the **liturgy** on these sites. Most of the Holy Places are in the possession of Greek Orthodox, Roman Catholics and Armenians. Protestants, traditionally less impressed by holy sites, nonetheless maintain their own 'Garden Tomb', a supposed site of the **Resurrection** of Jesus, near the Damascus Gate in **Jerusalem**. The Guardians, especially the Order of the **Franciscans**, see it as their duty to preserve the Christian attachment to Jerusalem, the Holy Land and especially the Holy Places, the scenes of God's special revelation.

There are also scores of religious orders and thousands of devotees present in Israel. Most of them did not come especially to guard the Holy Sites. Some of them live a strictly contemplative life, others are very much integrated in the socio-cultural landscape and the State of Israel. They live both in the Jewish and in the Arab sectors in Israel, mostly strictly separated.

'Solidarity groups', another type of Christian presence, can be described as seeking 'solidarity with Israel', as for example in the Christian village **Nes Ammim** in West Galilee. This solidarity is based upon the conviction that there is a special relationship of the Christian Churches toward the Jewish people, and on the awareness that Christians bear historical responsibility for centuries of **anti-Judaic** teaching and **antisemitism**.

There are numerous institutes and organisations, especially in Jerusalem, that concentrate on biblical studies, archaeology or Jewish–Christian–Muslim relations. If the Guardians of the Holy Places could be designated 'Helena-types', looking after the original places of the revelation as did the Empress-Mother Helena in the fourth century, the students of this group could be called 'Hieronymus-types', attracted to the Land, like Helena's contemporary the monk Hieronymus, by its archaeological treasures and rich libraries.

Finally, some Christians, in particular **Evangelicals**, regard the Jews as a very particular missionary target, especially in the State of Israel. They see this state as a sign of the approaching end of times and hope to convert as many as possible of the Jews as a kind of 'setting of the stage' for the imminent events of the Second Coming and/or Apocalypse. Some groups, mainly **Millenarian** Christians, abstain from **mission** to Jews, because they believe God himself will do this in due time, but wait in the land of Israel, where, according to their conviction, the End of Time event will soon happen.

SIMON SCHOON

Israel, land and State of

Israel is often a cause of controversy in Jewish–Christian relations. For Jews the centrality of the land of the Bible as well as the survival of a third of world Jewry, is at stake. Christians, for their part, not only disagree as to the place of Israel in Christian theology, but also feel particular concern for **Arab Christians** who live in Israel and Palestine. Israel cannot be viewed simply as a geographical and political entity whose emergence is like the establishment of any new state. Political, social, cultural and religious concerns all affect its place in the Jewish–Christian relationship.

The land and State of Israel are intricately related to a number of subjects in that relationship. For example, it is impossible to examine the **covenant** of Israel with God if no account is taken of the place of land. In the Bible possession of the land of Israel was an indispensable condition of self-fulfilment both for the individual and for the community. When dispossession and powerlessness arose as a result of the destruction of the **Temple** in 70 CE, the Jewish response consisted both of the hope of divine restoration and of the mystical idea that God was also exiled with his people. Both Jews and Christians agreed that the exile occurred partly as a result of divine punishment. Traditional Christian interpretation emphasised punishment for failing to believe in **Christ**, whereas Jewish interpretations emphasised God's Presence (*shekinah*) joining the exile and the positive consequence of ensuring that Jewish teaching was spread far and wide. The traditional Christian emphasis on divine punishment provided the basis for **supersessionism** and **replacement theology** – in other words, the belief that Christians have replaced Jews as the people of God. This teaching became dominant through the centuries, contributing greatly to the development and maintenance of **antisemitism**. In the words of **Origen**, 'not only was Jerusalem destroyed and Israel sent into exile for crimes, but their divine election was revoked; they were destined to stand in perpetual opposition to God' (*Cels.* 4.22). The **Church Fathers** consistently used the historical tragedies of the Jewish people as 'proof' that God had rejected them definitively because of their rejection of **Jesus**. Thus, the possibility of a rebuilt Temple and the associated re-establishment of sacrifices in **Jerusalem** caused great concern, especially when the rebuilding programme began under Emperor **Julian** in the fourth century. As long as Jerusalem and the Temple lay in ruins, and Jews remained in exile, it appeared that Christians were correct in claiming that Judaism had lost its legitimacy.

The views expressed by the Church Fathers have obviously been undermined by the emergence of the State of Israel, in which Jews are a sovereign majority and Judaism the majority religion. In addition, Christianity is forced to acknowledge its **minority** status, which is emphasised by the diminishing number of Christians living in Israel. Genuine contact between Arab Christians and Jews is limited and often overshadowed by the Israeli–Palestinian conflict. As a result, **dialogue** between Jews and Christians (and Muslims) is often transformed into dialogue between Jews and Palestinians or Jews and Arabs, with national identities emphasised far more than religious differences. A further complication for interfaith relations is the fact that, while in other parts of the world where the Churches have conducted missionary activity the Church leadership is almost completely in the hands of local Christians, in Israel the Churches are controlled by foreigners (to the indigenous Arab Christians) such as Greeks, English or Germans – and this despite the fact that Arab Christians trace their Christianity back to the first-century Christians.

In recent times a Palestinian theology of liberation has developed out of replacement theology and the everyday experiences of Palestinian Christians living in Israel since 1948. It is not too extreme to state that the Palestinian Church has faced a major theological crisis since the establishment of Israel. A considerable part of this crisis has been due to a belief that the Bible has been used as a political Zionist text. Naim Ateek (b. 1937) argues that 'before the creation of the state, the Old Testament was considered an essential part of Christian scripture, pointing and witnessing to Jesus. Since the creation of the state, some Jewish and Christian interpreters have read the Old Testament largely as a Zionist text to such an extent that it has become almost repugnant to Palestinian Christians' (*Justice and Only Justice*, 77). The continuing problems faced by the Palestinian people have added to the crisis. Replacement theology has been revitalised by **Palestinian liberation theology** and there is also great frustration among many Arab Christians that they have had to pay the price of Western Christian antisemitism.

As far as Jewish hopes of liberation were concerned, the will to survive in the **Diaspora** generated Jewish Messianic hopes of **redemption**, which occasionally led to a high level of anticipation and the extraordinary claims of self-appointed **Messiahs** such as **Bar Kokhba** and **Shabbetai Zvi**. One of the common features of these times of Messianic fervour was that the **Promised Land** became a symbol of redress for all the wrongs that Jews had suffered. Thus, modern **Zionism** is in part the fusion of Messianic fervour and the longing for **Zion**. Jews took their destiny into their own hands and stopped waiting for a divine solution to their predicament. This was a dramatic break from the Diaspora strategy of survival, which advocated endurance of the status quo as part of the covenant with God. For many Jews the Jewish state offered the best hope

not only for survival in response to the breakdown in Europe in the late nineteenth and early twentieth centuries, but also for fulfilment. Yet not all Jews supported a Jewish state, particularly before the **Holocaust**. Indeed, Jewish attachment to the land of Israel caused great controversy, and vociferous arguments over the appropriateness of Zionism took place between all Jewish groups.

From the Christian perspective, perhaps because land is not central to Christian theology Christians have found it hard to grasp that the Jews feel tied to a particular territory. Walter Brueggemann argues that the subject of 'land' should move to the centre of Christian theology and suggests that Christians cannot engage in serious dialogue with Jews unless they acknowledge land to be the central agenda. In his view the State of Israel highlights the lack of a theology of place in contemporary Christianity. W. D. Davies (1911–2001), in contrast, argues that land is relatively unimportant and that Jesus paid little attention to the relationship between God, Israel and the land. He refers to the **New Testament** for support, pointing out, for example, that of the 47 references to Israel in the New Testament only three refer specifically to the land, while the overwhelming majority pertains to the Jewish people.

That it is highly unlikely the early Christians ignored the land of Israel, however, is suggested by the liturgical cycle. The early Christian **liturgy** traced the path of Jesus from birth in Bethlehem, through upbringing and early ministry in the Galilee and teaching and healing throughout Israel to suffering, death and resurrection in and around Jerusalem. **Pilgrimages** also illustrate the importance of the land of Israel to the early Christian community, and figures such as **Melito of Sardis** and **Eusebius of Caesarea** both visited the 'Holy Land'. In the fourth century CE **Constantine**'s conversion to Christianity led to an increasing number of Christian pilgrimages. He also initiated the building of many churches on the sites of the most significant events of Jesus' earthly ministry. The ruins found at Jewish sites (such as the Temple) symbolised the 'old' Jerusalem, in comparison to the basilicas rising in the 'new' Jerusalem. A further increase in the number of Christian pilgrims occurred when Constantine's mother Helena (*c.*255–330) made her own pilgrimage and discovered the 'True Cross' on which Jesus was crucified.

In 360 the Church of the Resurrection (*Anastasis*) was dedicated (on part of which today stands the Church of the Holy Sepulchre). From the very beginning, therefore, Christians were keenly aware of the fact that the land of Israel in general, and Jerusalem in particular, provided evidence for the most momentous acts of history. Christians soon identified the land of Israel as the Holy Land and Jerusalem as the Holy City.

In contrast to the numerous interpretations of the destruction of the Temple and the Dispersion of the Jews in the writings of the Church Fathers, there was a noticeable lack of Christian comment in response to the establishment of the State of Israel in 1948. Alice Eckardt (b. 1923) argues that Christian reluctance to tackle this topic is explained by Israel's challenge to the traditional stereotype of Jews as a suffering and persecuted minority, transforming the victim into a victor. The first modern Christian document to discuss the place of Israel in some detail was published in 1970 by the Synod of the Reformed Church of Holland. The Synod stressed that Christians must appreciate the significance of the land of Israel for Jews. Another significant document was produced by the Synod of the Evangelical Church of the Rhineland in 1980 (*see* **Rhineland Synod**). This stated that 'the continuing existence of the Jewish people, its return to the Land of Promise, and also the creation of the State of Israel, are signs of the faithfulness of God towards His people' (*Towards a Renewal of the Relationship between Christians and Jews*, 2.3). This view has been endorsed by other Protestant denominations such as the United **Methodist** Church (USA), which in 1996 accepted 'the theological significance of the holy land as central to the worship, historical traditions, hope, and identity of the Jewish people' (*Building New Bridges of Hope*, sec. 9).

Some evangelical Christians go further and believe that the State of Israel is the fulfilment of biblical **prophecy**. They refer to the uniqueness of the ingathering of people from over 100 countries, the revival of **Hebrew** as a spoken language after its removal from daily conversation for over 1,500 years and the survival of Jews after repeated massacres and dispersions throughout the world. American evangelists such as Jerry Falwell (b. 1933) and Pat Robertson (b. 1930) view biblical prophecy as predictive in nature and argue that biblical texts can be interpreted and applied to contemporary events.

For example, Isa. 11.10–14 is seen as predicting the capture of the Sinai and Gaza in the Six-Day War in 1967 and Luke 21.24 the return of Jerusalem to Jewish control. However, it is worth remembering that such rejoicing in the Jewish return to Zion is sometimes theologically self-interested because Jews are viewed as pawns on the chessboard of history, being used to fulfil the final predetermined game-plan. These views are representative of a **remnant theology**, which is based on the premise that God is still faithful to the Jewish people and that his covenant with Israel is eternal (**Romans 9–11**). As this was a covenant of both land and people, the land of Israel was viewed as the rightful home of the Jewish people, to which God assured their return. Many people have presumed that remnant theology is the result of the growth of the modern **evangelical movement**, but its origins can be traced back at least as far as the Puritans of the seventeenth century. Today there are many manifestations of this position, particularly among the evangelical and charismatic section of the Church, and adherents are often called **Christian Zionists**. While it may appear to be a fairly clear-cut and unified theology, there are many subdivisions, one of which concerns the **conversion** of the Jewish people. The influential group the **International Christian Embassy**, located in Jerusalem, speaks out publicly against all evangelistic activity among Jews, but others such as the **Church's Ministry among Jewish People** (CMJ) disagree.

From the **Roman Catholic** perspective, prior to **Vatican II** Jews were traditionally seen only as victims rather than as capable of power and sovereignty. However, the 1965 document *Nostra Aetate*, while not explicitly mentioning Israel, began the process that eventually led to the Vatican's recognition of the State of Israel in 1994. The statement assured those who were dubious of or opposed to *Nostra Aetate* that no value judgement was intended on the Jewish political reality of Israel at that time. Although Vatican II failed to address the subject, the debate began within the Catholic Church as to whether the State of Israel should be discussed at all.

Increasing awareness among Roman Catholics of the place of Israel became much more noticeable during the papacy of **John Paul II**. His acknowledgement of its significance to Jews can be seen as early as 1984 when in his Good Friday Apostolic Letter he wrote: 'For the Jewish people who live in the State of Israel, and who preserve in that land such precious testimonies to their history and their faith, we must ask for the desired security and the due tranquillity that is the prerogative of every nation and condition of life and of progress for every society.' Ten years later the State of Israel and the Holy See exchanged ambassadors, and the process begun in 1965 reached another significant landmark with the pontiff's pilgrimage to Israel in 2000.

See also **Israel, people of**   *EDWARD KESSLER*

Israel, people of

'Israel, the People of God' is a title claimed by both the Jewish people and the Christian Church. It is regarded by Jews as being at the very core of their self-understanding. For nearly two millennia the Church saw itself as the 'True Israel' and the heir of all the biblical promises towards Israel. This rivalry produced in the course of history a vast range of **polemical** and **apologetic** writings, by both Christians and Jews. The Christian *Adversus Judaeos* tradition claimed that the Church as the 'New Israel' had replaced the 'Israel of Old' and was now the heir of God's election and promises.

The phrase 'the People of God' is derived from the Tanakh/Old Testament. The so-called 'covenant formula' reads: 'I will be your God and you will be my people' (cf. Exod. 6.2–8; Lev. 26.12; Jer. 31.33b). According to the Song of Deborah, Israel is 'the People of JHWH' (Judg. 5.11, 13). The basis of the **covenant** is God's election of Israel as his people (cf. Deut. 7.6; 14.2). This choice implied that the people so elected acquired duties commensurate with that role, a responsibility to live in ways appropriate for the people of God, and is the reason the prophets criticised their people so fiercely, in passionate and moving appeals to return to the Way, the **Torah**. It was never meant that the covenant of God with his people could ever be irreparably broken.

According to Judaism the election of Israel as God's People is not a matter of an idea or an article of faith; it is a historical phenomenon that is connected to the concrete corporeal reality of the Jewish people, as the 'Body of Faith' (so Michael Wyschogrod (b. 1928)). The terms 'People of Israel' and 'People of God' cannot be deduced from a general, already accepted concept 'people' that is then applied to the special case of Israel. The Hebrew name for 'holy people' (*goy kadosh*, Exod. 19.5) is actually untranslatable, and its meaning can only be outlined and broadly explained in theological, sociological and political language. It indicates a community that is set apart by God's special election. It is experienced in the solidarity of a group of people in a community of destiny that has been called into being by God. The origin of this community is not natural, but a matter of election and **grace**. The faithful goodness of God's election is only realised in the 'natural' physicality and concrete history of the people Israel. The **circumcision** makes it clear that Israel is of the flesh as well as of the spirit. Giving up the names 'People of Israel' and 'People of God' would mean for Jews **assimilation** in the world of the nations and therefore the discontinuation of Jewish **identity**.

The use of the concept 'God's People' for the Church in the **New Testament** and in the varied traditions of Christianity make it impossible for most Christians to drop it. But there is a growing recognition that waiving the claim to self-definition as 'God's People' would not rob the Church of her identity. The use of the term 'God's People' for the Church is by no means clear of all traces of **anti-Judaism**. In classical Christian dogmatic theology the people of Israel have merely a role of 'foreshadowing', in the time of the **Old Testament**, the coming of the Church in the time of its fulfilment in Christ. It is noteworthy that in a totally different context, namely in the practice of many churches in the Third World, the concept 'People of God' is used as a liberating term for the poor and oppressed, without any anti-Judaic connotation.

The Church is not called by the name 'Israel' in the New Testament (see the writings of Krister Stendahl (b. 1921)), and only in a few texts is the Church called 'People of God'. But in a centuries-long anti-Judaic and **antisemitic** *Wirkungsgeschichte* of these few texts the use of the titles 'Israel' and 'People of God' for the Church was central in Christian **replacement theology** and practice. In the twentieth century many Christians and churches rediscovered the Jews as 'God's **Chosen People**'. This was expounded in numerous official statements and declarations. But this recognition opened up new theological problems and challenges in the context of Jewish–Christian relations. For example, there is the danger that the new Christian outlook on Israel as 'God's People' leads to unreasonably high moral and political expectations towards the present Jewish people and Jewish state. And for Christian theology there is the challenge to redefine the place of the Church as 'people' after the rediscovery of Israel.

In Jewish–Christian **dialogue** there will always remain an irreducible element of dispute and even rivalry between the 'People of Israel' and the 'Church of God', because of the fact that the 'joint heirs of the promises' interpret these promises of God differently. However, many Christians have learnt a new language – for example to speak of Israel as 'the first-chosen People of God' and of the Church as 'the also-chosen ecumenical People of God from all the nations'. Christians learn to accept in dialogue that the Church is not the first and not the only one that is chosen to be God's People.

See also **Israel, land and State of**; **supersessionism**
SIMON SCHOON

Italy

The continuous presence of significant Jewish communities in the Italian peninsula from the Roman period onwards makes Italy a prime location for the study of Jewish–Christian relations, but 'Italy' as a political unit is a creation of the mid-nineteenth century. The greater part of the history of Jewish–Christian encounter 'in Italy' has therefore to be written as a whole series of histories, of the relations of Jews and Christians in **Rome**, Naples, Venice, Florence, Padua, Sicily, Umbria and the other cities and regions that were included in the later Italian state. Each of these major centres has been the subject of extensive scholarly study. The richness of the evidence available for many of them, and the particular ways in which local political, economic and religious circumstances shaped the encounter of Jews and Christians in any of them, make generalisation hazardous. At the risk of oversimplification, however, some trends may be noticed. Even where (as in the Venetian **ghetto** from the early sixteenth century) Jews were physically segregated from other citizens, and enjoyed or were compelled to a degree of autonomy in the government of their own community, they remained an integral part of the economic fabric of their city. Certain categories of Jewish professional were highly esteemed (there were regularly Jewish physicians in the medieval papal court). Anti-Jewish **polemic**

was articulated most vigorously by the mendicant orders, as part of their programme of defending Christian orthodoxy, as in the **preaching** of the Franciscan Giacomo della Marca (1394–1476) in east-central Italy, but this polemic does not seem to have stimulated systematic anti-Jewish violence: there is nothing to match the **expulsions** of Jews from thirteenth-century England or from fifteenth-century Spain. In southern Italy Jews were an important element in the empire of Frederick II (*r*.1215–50). Exegetical and theological encounter between Jews and Christians tends to run on familiar lines, determined by the agenda of Christian apologists, but there are exceptions, such as the researches of the Florentine philosopher **Pico della Mirandola** into Kabbalah and other esoteric Jewish writings; Pico, however, is an unusual figure by any standard.

There was a strong element of anti-clericalism and post-Enlightenment **liberalism** in the movement for the unification of Italy. The Italian state was founded at the expense of papal government, and Jews were enfranchised in Italian parliaments from the beginning. The long tradition of accommodation with Jewish communities helps to explain why anti-Jewish measures were brought into force only slowly under fascism, and why their application varied from one place to another (Giorgio Bassani's (b. 1916) novel *The Garden of the Finzi-Continis* (1962) evokes the complex dynamics of the period). Only under direct Nazi occupation were there systematic deportations of Jews. The **silence** of the papacy during this episode continues to be intensely controversial (*see* **Pius XII**). Another Christian response is illustrated by the extraordinary example of Assisi, where the bishop and many religious houses were active in the rescue of Jews – possibly with a degree of connivance from the German authorities. These complexities form the background to the development of Jewish–Christian relations in the postwar period, when significant Jewish communities remained in all the major cities. The visit of Pope **John Paul II** to the principal synagogue (Tempio Maggiore) of Rome in 1986, following an earlier meeting with the Chief Rabbi of Rome, marked an important symbolic moment, but the history of Jews and Christians had been continuously intertwined in Italy to an unusual degree.
ANDERS BERGQUIST

JJJJ

Jacob

Also named Israel, last of the three biblical patri-archs, son of **Isaac** and grandson of **Abraham**. Jacob's story is recounted in Gen. 25.19–50.14, tak-ing up a major part of Genesis. Jacob is the father of 12 tribes who would constitute the people going out from Egypt to the **Promised Land**. Jacob-Israel came to represent the whole **people of Israel** in later biblical literature and in both Jewish and Christian traditions. Through centuries of **polemics**, both Jews and Christians have claimed to be the authen-tic descendants of Jacob, the true Israel.

Jacob was born into a situation of conflict with his twin, Esau. Before their birth, their mother Rebecca was told that 'Two nations are in your womb . . . and the one shall be stronger than the other, and the elder shall serve the younger' (Gen. 25.23). Esau, emerging first, was followed by Jacob, grasping Esau's heel. The name Jacob derives from *ya'aqov* ('he followed on the heel of'), evoking *aqev* ('heel'). Strife, trickery and competition characterise the brothers' relationship. Jacob eventually flees Esau's wrath after having tricked him out of his birthright as firstborn. After a long sojourn in Mesopotamia, Jacob decided to return home, accompanied by his wives, concubines and children. The description of the preparation for the meeting with Esau is among the finest examples of biblical narrative. On the eve of the meeting Jacob wrestled with an angel and received the new name 'Israel' – 'because you have striven with God' (Gen. 32.29). The next morning Esau embraced him in a surprising reconciliation (Gen. 33.1–11). After ch. 37 the focus moves to the story of **Joseph**, and Jacob is portrayed as the griev-ing father who has lost his favourite son only to receive him back in **Egypt**. After blessing his sons Jacob died and was embalmed in Egyptian style, but his body was buried in the tomb purchased by Abraham in Hebron (Gen. 50.13). In the rest of biblical literature, particularly in the Prophets and

the **Psalms**, the name Jacob is often a synonym for Israel, referring to the whole people, whilst Esau represents the people of **Edom** (see Isa. 14.1; 27.9; 41.8; 60.16; Jer. 49; and Obadiah). However, in Hosea there is an understanding of Jacob's trick-ery of Esau that is less complimentary to Jacob (Hos. 12.3–6).

In their reading of the Bible both Jews and Christians claimed the blessed son as their ances-tor and designated the other son as the ances-tor of the other. Jacob and Esau are evoked in both rabbinic and Christian literature as extreme opposites, representing virtue, fidelity, peaceful-ness versus dissipation, treachery and violence. For Jewish commentators the territorial basis for con-flict is replaced by the religious-cultural conflict: Jacob is identified with the Jewish people and Edom is first identified with **Rome**, after 70 CE, and then with Christianity after the fourth cen-tury (*b. Megillah* 6a). Many of these commen-tators described the reconciliation of the broth-ers as an act of deception on the part of Esau. For example, Rabbi Jannai is quoted as saying that Esau did not kiss Jacob but bit him (*Gene-sis Rabbah* 78.9). The commentators saw the con-tinued hostility between the brothers as a symbol of continuing hostility between Jews and Chris-tians (cf. *Pirke de Rabbi Eliezer* etc.). Laban the Aramean, who deceived Jacob in Mesopotamia, is also seen as a forerunner of Rome, as oppressor of Israel (the Hebrew word *arami* is tied to the words *romai* (Roman) and *rammai* (trickster), cf. *Gene-sis Rabbah* 70.19). However, it was the identifica-tion of Edom/Esau with Christianity that repeated itself often in Jewish literature in the Middle Ages (cf. **Nahmanides** on *Perashat Vayishlah*, Abarbanel on Isa. 35).

Of particular interest in the Jewish–Christian polemics engendered by the biblical figure of Jacob is the debate over the correct interpretation of the textually problematic blessing of Judah in Gen. 49.8–12: 'The sceptre shall not pass from Judah, nor the mace from between his feet.' Christian commentators have insisted on reading these verses as an important **Old Testament** prophecy regarding the coming of **Jesus** Christ. Another particularly important reference to Jacob for the development of Jewish–Christian polemics has been Mal. 1.2–3, 'Yet I loved Jacob, but Esau I hated', cited by **Paul** in Rom. 9.13. It is here that Paul insists that promise/election and not physical descent/flesh determine the status of the one called in faith. Those who believe in Jesus Christ are the sons of the promise, Jacob (and Isaac), while those who refuse Jesus are like Esau (and Ishmael). The **Church Fathers** further develop this identification (see **Justin Martyr**, *Dial.* 134; **Origen**, *Hom. Gen.* 12 Ambrose, *Jacob and the Happy Life* etc.). **Irenaeus of Lyons** writes typically, 'the latter people (the Gentiles) has snatched away the blessings of the former (the Jews) . . . just as Jacob took away the blessing from Esau' (*Haer.* 4.21). The Christian identification of the Jews with Esau was even used in medieval **canon law** to justify why Jews could not own Christian slaves, 'for the older shall serve the younger'.

It should not be forgotten, however, that the story of Jacob and Esau in the biblical text is free of the stark hostility introduced in later Jewish and Christian interpretations. The founder of neo-Orthodoxy, R. Samson R. Hirsch (1808–88), commenting on Esau's tears on meeting his brother after the long separation, discards the common traditional suspicion of Esau. He writes, 'It is only when the strong, as here Esau, fall round the necks of the weak and cast the sword of violence far away, only then does it show that right and humaneness have made a conquest' (on Gen. 33.4). Modern commentators, Jewish and Christian, have painted a more sympathetic portrait of Esau and a less flattering portrait of the deception worked by Rebecca in favour of Isaac. The brothers are truly reconciled on Jacob's return to the Land and together they bury their father Isaac (Gen. 35.29) and live side by side. This narrative can be liberated from the long tradition of polemics and reclaimed for **dialogue**.

DAVID M. NEUHAUS

James I (1204–76)

King of Aragon-Catalonia (1213–76). King James the Conqueror (in Catalan, Jaume or Jacme)

presided over a significant expansion in territory which brought under his rule large numbers of non-Christians to add to the Jews and Muslims who already inhabited parts of Aragon and Catalonia. He encouraged Jewish immigration into Majorca and issued ordinances in favour of Jewish butchers on the island. Yet James took a growing interest in missionary campaigns to convert the Jews and Muslims, in which Catalan friars, notably Ramon de Penyafort (*c*.1185–1275) and Raymond **Martini**, developed the strategy of learning the language and beliefs of the unbelievers in order to combat them on equal territory. He thus agreed to preside over the **disputation** of Barcelona in 1263, between **Nahmanides** and **Paul the Christian**, one consequence of which was an attempt to make Jews attend Christian sermons – a threat soon effectively commuted to taxation of Jews and other non-Christian subjects. Jewish life flourished in Barcelona and Girona, the extensive Jewish quarters of which cities were not forcibly enclosed. James saw the Jews as a financial asset and displayed similar ambivalence to many of his contemporaries, who devoutly aspired to their **conversion**, but perhaps not quite yet. *DAVID ABULAFIA*

James, brother of Jesus

Although the figure of James, the brother of **Jesus**, is of little consequence in understanding Jewish–Christian relations throughout most of the last two millennia, he is of vital, if disputed, significance in making sense of the initial phase of the relationship.

For some interpreters, James can be seen as the most prominent leader of the Jesus movement following his brother's death, and as advocating that it should remain firmly within the Judaism of its day. Indeed, if he had not been killed in 62 CE and the **Temple**, the focus of the piety of this early community, had not been destroyed a few years later, it is quite possible that 'Christianity' would have remained a Messianic sect of Judaism.

Such a picture of James's significance is plausible, although historical evidence that sheds light on him is sparse and difficult to interpret. It is undeniable that James was a key figure in the **Jerusalem** church (Gal. 1.19; 2.9; Acts 15.13; 21.18), having probably joined the movement following a resurrection appearance (1 Cor. 15.7 and **Jerome**, *Viv. ill.* 2). There are also good grounds for arguing that James remained, like his brother, a devout, law-observant Jew (Hegesippus, quoted by **Eusebius**, *Hist. eccl.* 2.23.4–18; see also Acts 21.18) who was convinced that Gentile converts to the new movement should likewise follow the full **Torah** if they were to be included in the community (Gal. 2.12ff.). This interpretation of James might be confirmed by the epistle of James, although its relationship to the historical figure is problematic. The epistle appears to have a high estimation of the **law** and takes direct issue with the gospel of **Paul** over its place (perhaps most obviously by contesting Pauline understanding of the implications of the **Abraham** narrative). The veneration of James the brother of Jesus by a range of Jewish-Christian groups, such as the Ebionites, may also support this picture. It is also, perhaps, telling that amongst those books that were later ascribed to him, the *Protoevangelium of James*, a second-century birth narrative, is striking in its positive portrayal of Jewish religious authorities and their religious practices.

However, the historical James may be a rather more complex figure and rather less positive in his understanding of the relationship between the formative Church and Judaism. **Josephus** records that the high priest Ananus had James put to death as a law-breaker (*Ant.* 20.200–1) and it is also notable that in Acts of the Apostles, as well as the ***Pseudo-Clementine*** *Recognitions* (a fourth-century work containing much earlier traditions) James is presented as a figure who does not advocate the **circumcision** of Gentile converts. Indeed, in Acts, he mediates between two wings of the **early Church** (Acts 15.1–20; 21.20), initiating the compromise of the so-called apostolic decree (Acts 15.20, 29; 21.25) – a set of regulations that would allow Gentiles full membership of the new community without the need for them to observe the whole Torah – something that would guarantee that the movement became distinct from Judaism (despite the resemblance of the regulations to the **Noachide laws** – Gen. 9.8ff., *b. Sanhedrin* 56a). As well as being venerated by **Jewish Christians**, James could also become the hero of the *Second Apocalypse of James*, a **Gnostic** work with many analogies to **Marcionism**, and the *Gospel of Thomas* (logion 12), a text that is incompatible with normative Jewish **identity** of the time.

James is a crucial but also frustratingly elusive figure for those wishing to understand the earliest period of Jewish–Christian relations. It is no surprise that estimation of his importance varies so markedly between interpreters.

JUSTIN J. MEGGITT

Jamnia/Yavneh, Council of

The existence in antiquity of a 'Council of **Pharisees**' had been mooted by **Spinoza** in the seventeenth century, and this in turn was located at Jamnia (Hebrew: Yavneh) by the nineteenth-century German-Jewish historian Heinrich Graetz (1817–91), whose aim was to highlight the communitarian nature of Judaism. The Council was thought to have met in *c*.90 CE in this largely Jewish city on the coastal plain south of Jaffa. Seeing it as modelled on early Church synods, nineteenth-century scholars attributed to it the fixing of the Hebrew **canon**, the exclusion of Christianity from Judaism and the codification of Jewish law, and therefore considered it decisive in the split between **Church and synagogue**. The hypothesis of such a Council has, however, been widely rejected. At the end of the first century R. Gamaliel II (*fl. c*.80–110) is credited with introducing the curse of the *minim* (see ***birkat ha-minim***) into the ***Amidah*** (*b. Berakhot* 28b–29a), and his successor Eleazar ben Azariah (late first century) with fixing the canon (*m. Yadayim* 3.5). The use of the term 'on that day' (*m. Yadayim* 3.5–4.4; *b. Berakhot* 28a) gave the impression that there was one meeting in the manner of a Council, but despite the tradition that Vespasian (*r*.69–79) granted Johanan ben Zakkai (first century) permission to establish an academy there, Jamnia between the Jewish revolts (68–72 and 132–135 CE) appears to have been a temporary centre of Jewish life that was only partially formative. **Rabbinic Judaism** developed over time, and the real need for codification would probably have been felt after **Bar Kokhba** (d. 135 CE) with the movement of rabbis to Galilee. The continuation of close contact between Jews and Christians for centuries (see, e.g., John **Chrysostom**), and of rabbinic diversity and discussion on canonic and related issues, supports the case that there was no Council with authority.

JAMES K. AITKEN

Jehovah's Witnesses

Jehovah's Witnesses (the label dates from 1931, but the movement began in nineteenth-century America) differ from mainline Christianity in several respects, including their insistence on 'Jehovah' as the divine name, an unwillingness to celebrate **Christmas** or birthdays (because of the pagan roots of these practices) and a refusal to accept blood transfusions. Moreover, although Jehovah's Witnesses view **Jesus**' death as a ransom for human sin, they reject the doctrine of the **Trinity**, in favour of a theology close to early **Arianism**. Significantly for Jewish–Christian relations, Jehovah's Witnesses are most widely known for their extensive and energetic **mission** (directed at all non-Witnesses including Jews and other Christians), which is a consequence of the belief that in 1914 Christ's 'unseen presence' on earth began, signalling the beginning of the last days and the imminence of Armageddon. Today there are approximately six million active, evangelising Witnesses (known as 'publishers') in over 200 countries.

During the Second World War many Jehovah's Witnesses died in Nazi concentration camps. Whilst the movement initially came under suspicion for what were perceived as 'Jewish' characteristics (extensive use of biblical-style language; practices derived from interpretations of **Hebrew Bible** texts), the ultimate basis of Witnesses' opposition to **Nazism** was a belief in the exclusive Lordship of Jehovah. Unlike some other millennial movements, Jehovah's Witnesses do not regard the foundation of the **State of Israel** as religiously significant. They spiritualise 'Israel' and 'Jerusalem' and see **Zionism** as a political and human movement that does not advance the **Kingdom of God**.

MELANIE J. WRIGHT

Jerome (c.342–420)

(Eusebius Hieronymus.) A Christian ascetic, presbyter and student of classical literature, Jerome acquired a knowledge of the **Hebrew language** which marked him out from other Christian scholars of his day and of later times. Born in Dalmatia of orthodox Christian parents, and educated at Rome by the distinguished scholars Donatus (*fl.* late fourth century CE) and Victorinus (fourth century), at Aquileia he befriended the scholar monk Rufinus (*c.*345–410). The later violent disruption of this friendship typifies Jerome's personality, a combination of generosity and spite which even his admirers have found perplexing and which is significant for all his relationships. After travels in Gaul, he journeyed east, fetching up in **Antioch**, where he renounced pagan literature, becoming a hermit in the desert of Chalcis (373–9). Here he learned

Hebrew and probably elements of the local **Aramaic** dialect, although his claim to know 'Chaldean' (see the Prologue to his **Vulgate** translation of Tobit) may be exaggerated. He now devoted himself to biblical study, being ordained presbyter (379) before visiting Constantinople, where he met Gregory Nazianzen (*c.*329–*c.*390). In 382 Pope Damasus I (366–84) summoned him to Rome and ordered him to prepare a new **Latin** version of the Bible. The **New Testament** and two versions of the Psalter were complete when Damasus died. Jerome's volatile personality and friendship with Roman women, whom he encouraged to learn Hebrew, made enemies at Rome, and on Damasus's death he retired to Antioch, joined by the rich widow Paula (347–404) and her daughter.

Eventually Jerome settled in Bethlehem, presiding over a monastery founded by Paula and working on his translation of the **Old Testament**, originally planned as a major correction of the **Septuagint** in the light of Hebrew witnesses. Growing familiarity with the Hebrew text and recognition of the chaotic state of the Septuagint soon persuaded him to abandon this as impractical and to translate directly from the Hebrew which, he became convinced, represented the authentic voice of scripture, *Hebraica veritas*. Books outside the **Hebrew Bible** but in the Septuagint he dubbed **Apocrypha**; and his apparent downgrading of these and other aspects of the Septuagint in favour of *Hebraica veritas* elicited the charge that he followed Jews, and earned him disapproval from authorities like **Augustine**. His earlier studies of Hebrew had involved close contact with Jews; he described to Damasus a visit from a Jew bearing scrolls from the local synagogue to help him in his researches. Scholarly converse with Jews continued in Bethlehem; he tells, among others, of his teacher 'Baraninas' and of a Jewish scholar who helped him translate Job. From his Jewish teachers Jerome acquired knowledge of exegetical traditions which he incorporated into his Latin versions of the biblical books, **commentaries** and many letters; most of these can be traced in extant Jewish sources, while others may represent otherwise lost Jewish interpretations of scripture.

Jerome often declares that Jewish traditions are true, and his *Hebrew Questions on Genesis* (completed 393?) testifies to a delight in Jewish learning. The Vulgate, although not entirely his, incorporates much of his translation work, with its

Jewish colouring, and remains his chief memorial. However, Jerome copied material from **Origen** (who knew some Hebrew) and other Christian scholars, frequently without acknowledgement; and his Latin translations are indebted to the earlier endeavours of **Aquila**, Symmachus (*fl.* probably late second century CE) and Theodotion (*fl.* end of second century CE) and to other Greek renderings collected by Origen in his **Hexapla**. While judging some Jewish traditions true, others he calls fables; he attacks Jewish rituals, sneers at Jewish prayer, is downright hostile to **Judaising Christians** and repeats stock Christian objections to Judaism. Respect for individual Jewish scholars he could offer; positive regard for Judaism and its practices seems to have been beyond him. His place in Jewish–Christian relations is difficult to assess. On the one hand he undoubtedly alerted contemporary Christians to their indebtedness to Jews and Judaism at almost every turn; yet his work could also be seen as exploitative of Jewish tradition for narrow, partisan, Christian purposes. In this regard he may have contributed to a Christian attitude which was willing to learn about Judaism only to use that learning to attack Jews and their beliefs.   *C. T. R. HAYWARD*

Jerusalem

For both Jews and Christians, Jerusalem is an icon of the divine–human encounter, which links **creation** and **redemption** and heaven and earth. Here the **Temple** stood and the *Shekinah* indwelt. Here the Word of God became flesh in **Jesus** and the **crucifixion** and **resurrection** took place. In Jerusalem the **people of Israel** became a nation and the Church was established through the descent of the **Holy Spirit** on **Pentecost**. Overlooking Jerusalem's man-made Temple Mount is the Mount of Olives, a kind of divinely designed eschatological temple where the living and the dead crowd together, awaiting resurrection and redemption in the end of days. Jerusalem's centrality for Jews and Christians made the metropolis, both as temporal urban centre and as symbol of an eternal celestial reality, a major point of contention between *Ecclesia* **and** *Synagoga*.

Some 3,000 years ago King **David** made Jerusalem the religious and national nucleus of the Jewish people. The cultic and political roles of Jerusalem under the monarchy were given a patriarchal prehistory by associating the city with both the **binding of Isaac** and **Abraham**'s meeting with the priest-king

Melchizedek. **Zion**, a synonym for Jerusalem, eventually came to mean not only a city, but also a land, and especially a people, whose historical existence is intimately linked with the metropolis, as a child is nurtured by its mother (cf. Isa. 66.10–13). Even when Titus destroyed the temple in 70 CE and Jews lost sovereignty over the sacred city, Jerusalem continued to serve as the pre-eminent symbol of the people's covenantal bond with the land of Israel. Fervent hope for a future ingathering of the exiles in a restored Jerusalem became the lifeblood of Jewish faith and piety; the longing for Zion found expression in every aspect of Jewish religious and communal life. **Zionism** took its name from the city.

The Christian approach to Jerusalem is characterised by ambiguity. On the one hand there is a strand in the tradition that seems to deny Jerusalem and the Temple any importance, as, for example, in the story of Jesus' encounter with the Samaritan woman (John 4.1–42), or in Stephen's speech (Acts 7.1–53) before he was stoned. On the other hand the notion of the **Incarnation** bestows sacramental significance on the tangible places connected with the life, death, resurrection and ascension of Jesus. **Paul** displays special regard for the Jerusalem Church as an important link between the Gentile Church and **Jewish Christianity**. But ultimately for Paul the true home of all Christians is not the 'present Jerusalem' but 'the Jerusalem on high' (Gal. 4.21–27). As the animosity between Jews and Christians deepened in the course of the first five centuries of the Christian era, the **Church Fathers** increasingly usurped Jerusalem by spiritualising the terrestrial entity and transforming it into a non-geographical **eschatological** 'heavenly' Jerusalem, which they identified with *mater ecclesia*, Mother Church, as the true earthly manifestation of 'the city of God'. In the Christian scheme of **sacred space** Christ is the temple and the 'new' Jerusalem is every place where the Christian community gathers as the body of **Christ**.

Christians nonetheless took a most active interest in the earthly Jerusalem. **Constantine** transformed the city into a major hub of the Christian *ecumene*, much as David united the Israelites around Jerusalem. Pilgrims subsequently streamed to the holy city and **relics** were carried back to churches everywhere, thus constantly nourishing the bond with Zion. The **Byzantines** banned Jews from their holy city and left the Temple Mount in ruins as a visible sign that God had rejected them and transferred the power and glory to Christianity, as confirmed by the grandeur of the nearby Constantinian Basilica of the Resurrection. Muslims allowed Jews to return to the city when they took control of it in 638. The **crusaders** reconquered Jerusalem for Christianity in 1099, butchered and burned the entire Jewish population, and established a Latin Kingdom of Jerusalem. Muslim control, and with it a Jewish presence, was re-established within a century.

Just as Christianity's stress on the primacy of the 'heavenly' Jerusalem did not impede a lively involvement with the terrestrial city, so also the intimate bond of the Jewish people with the historical Jerusalem did not prevent the development of an idea of a Jerusalem 'above'. Such a notion clearly is present in late-biblical and rabbinic literature. But when confronted with the Church's claim to be the sole heir to the 'heavenly' Jerusalem, the rabbis reiterated the primacy of the earthly Zion in the divine plan. In **apocalyptic** literature written in Muslim lands in the Geonic period (seventh to eleventh centuries) Jewish authors more freely develop the idea of a normative heavenly Jerusalem that is pre-existent and pre-eminent, and not simply a projection of an ideal earthly city.

Throughout much of the past 1,400 years the relations of Jews and Christians – until recent centuries, mainly Eastern **Orthodox Christians** – in Jerusalem were tempered by the circumstances of life as *dhimmis* ('protected' minorities) under the rule of a Muslim majority. As the **Ottoman Empire** declined in the nineteenth century two major developments greatly altered Jewish–Christian relations in the city. Factors as diverse as the quest for the **historical Jesus** and colonial interests led to an influx of representatives of Western Churches and Western secular powers. Parallel with, and related to, this Christian rediscovery of the Holy Land, the Zionist movement emerged in Europe and Jews began to return to Jerusalem. Some Christians welcomed and supported this restoration as a prelude to the **parousia**. Others, like Pope Pius X (1903–14), insisted that the Church could not condone the return of the Jewish people to Jerusalem and that if Jews insisted on going there Christian missionaries would be waiting to convert them. The establishment of the **State of Israel** in 1948, with

Jerusalem as its declared capital, and the extension of Israeli sovereignty over the entire city in 1967 further polarised opinions concerning the future of the city. The Vatican initially lobbied for internationalisation of the city, but since the late 1960s has called only for international guarantees to safeguard its sacred character and Christian interests in it. Whereas Pope **Paul VI** shunned all contact with Israeli leaders when – the first reigning pontiff to do so – he visited Jerusalem in 1964, the pilgrimage of Pope **John Paul II** to the holy city in March 2000 included all diplomatic formalities required by an official visit to the State of Israel. In 1980 **Christian Zionists** established an **International Christian Embassy** in the city to support the Jewish people in Zion. The local, largely **Arab Christian** communities now collectively comprise a tiny **minority** in the city, which is the reverse of the minority–majority roles in Jewish–Christian relations in the West. To date, formal Jewish–Christian **dialogue** in Jerusalem takes place mainly between Jews and **expatriate Christians in Israel** rather than indigenous Christians. *DANIEL ROSSING*

Jerusalem Talmud *see* **Talmud**

Jesse

Ancestral figure in the lineage of the **Messiah**; specifically, the father of King **David** (1 Sam. 16–17; Ps. 72.20). His relationship to the Messianic line makes him a symbolic figure in Christianity, which may in part account for the limited attention that Jewish tradition pays to him. 'Son of Jesse' was a pejorative circumlocution for David in the mouth of Saul (1 Sam. 20, 22), but otherwise is a standard patronymic. Jesse's identification as an 'Ephrathite of Bethlehem' (1 Sam. 17.12) is consistent with Messianic expectation (Mic. 5.2). His descent from Boaz by Ruth the Moabite (his grandmother – Ruth 4.17, 22) draws attention to the association of the Davidic line with those outside Israel. His name is twice the focus of Messianic promises in Isa. 11: 'a shoot shall come out from the stump of Jesse' (v. 1) and 'the root of Jesse shall stand as a signal to the peoples' (v. 11). The latter appears to be **Paul**'s reference in Rom. 15.12, as evidence of the Messiah's role with the Gentiles. In Acts 13.22f. Paul is quoted as referring to 'David, son of Jesse . . . of [whose] posterity God has brought to Israel a Saviour, Jesus, as he promised'. John Mason Neale's (1818–66) Advent hymn 'Oh Come, Oh Come, Immanuel' incorporates the epithet

Rod of Jesse (Isa. 11.1) in its third verse, drawing on antiphons used in Christian vespers as early as the ninth century. The Jesse tree is decorated throughout Advent by the daily addition of a symbol of **Jesus**' 'spiritual heritage'. When European Christians initiated an ecumenical Christian moshav in northern **Israel** in the 1970s, they named it **Nes Ammim** ('signal to the peoples' – Isa. 11.11). PETER A. PETTIT

Jesuits (Society of Jesus)

Catholic religious order. Attitudes towards and relationships with Jews have known sharp ups and downs in the history of the order. Founded in 1540 by St Ignatius of Loyola (1491–1556), the Jesuits engaged in the defence and reform of the Catholic Church in the face of the Protestant **Reformation**. The Jesuits founded schools and universities and quickly became a leading missionary order. Often regarded with suspicion, they were suppressed in 1773 due to political pressure on the pope. Re-established in 1814, Jesuits played a formative role in the Catholic reaction to **modernity**. However, in the twentieth century Jesuits were among the leading reformers at **Vatican II**.

Ignatius, though traditional insofar as **mission** to the Jews was concerned, was a Judeophile at a time when **anti-Judaism** raged. He refused to sanction the anti-Jewish 'purity of blood' ideology, welcoming those of Jewish origin into the order. However, in 1593 the Jesuits gave in to pressures and forbade converted Jews from entering the order (a decision abrogated in 1946). Within the context of the Catholic reaction against 'modernism', some Jesuits promoted nineteenth- and twentieth-century expressions of **antisemitism** in Europe. The influential Jesuit review *Civiltà Cattolica* published some virulent articles about supposed Jewish influence in Europe. Certain Jesuits were also among those who led the anti-**Dreyfus** camp in France. However, during the Second World War there were Jesuits who defended and saved Jews and opposed **Nazism**. During Vatican II the leading German Jesuit Augustin **Bea** was among the promoters of the changes in Church teaching that led to *Nostra Aetate*. Today an international forum of Jesuit scholars and activists meets regularly to study and promote Jewish–Christian **dialogue**. Established in Kraków and at **Auschwitz** in 1998, this forum convened in **Jerusalem** in 2000 to study the significance of the **State of Israel** for contemporary Judaism. DAVID M. NEUHAUS

Jesus (*c*.4 BCE–*c*.29 CE)

The Jewish founder of Christianity (the religion of the **Christ** or **Messiah**). The details of Jesus' life and career are a matter of much controversy, but the basic outlines seem clear. He was a wandering Galilean preacher and healer, whose vocation may have been between one (the implication of the first three Gospels) and three years (the impression of John's Gospel) long; it ended in execution by **crucifixion**. Jesus has mostly been the focus of disunity between Jews and Christians. The major reasons for this lie in the realms of religious discourse and of historical events.

Jesus lived his life not as a Christian but as a Jew, obedient (with very few exceptions) to the Jewish **Law**. Yet within a few years after his death, the faith his early followers placed in him led them to espouse a rather different kind of **religion** from that followed by most Jews. Judaism, like **Islam** after it, is strongly rooted in religious law; Christianity ceased to be so. Judaism, also like Islam, has a strong belief in the unity of God; Christianity came to place such great store in Jesus and subsequently in the doctrine of the **Trinity** that it has seemed to many other monotheists to be, in essence, a refined form of polytheism. Gradually, Christian religion came to look less like an authentic, even if eccentric, form of Judaism, and more like a completely different religion.

During the Second Temple period there were many internal arguments about what it meant to be Jewish. Did religious law permit one to acquiesce in Roman occupation, or to fight it? How did the law reconcile justice and mercy? These must have been common debates, which one can see mirrored in the Gospels' accounts of Jesus' disputes with contemporary religious leaders. Yet there were other disagreements between him and them which indicate that he espoused some very eccentric points of view. We cannot be certain of Jesus' views, for the Gospels are a highly interpretive genre of literature, coloured by their contributors' and editors' reflections on events that had happened 40 and more years before, in the light of the momentous events that had occurred in the intervening years. Even so, his attitude towards **dietary laws** recorded in Mark's Gospel shows little interest in the minutiae of what they require that Jews eat and drink. This unusual interpretation eventually became common for Christians: certainly the food laws gradually became a thing of the past, as accounts in Acts and the Pauline letters illustrate. Moreover, although Jesus' message of the **kingdom of God** was clearly within mainstream Jewish tradition, the Christological references about him and his meaning are less so. Numbers of people have claimed and been deemed to be Messiah; some have even stayed within mainstream Jewish religion. But the association of Messiah with terms like **Son of Man** and **Son of God**, which developed a profusion of meanings, soon led to exalted claims for Jesus that few Jews felt able to follow. Even within the **New Testament** this is so; by the time of the full-blown Trinitarianism of the fourth-century creeds this gap was unbridgeably wide.

Historical events created and accentuated these religious differences. Early Christianity differed from other Jewish interpretations in opening its insider membership to Gentiles, who soon became the majority of Christians. Although the apostle **Paul** struggled to hold together Jews and Gentiles within one faith in Jesus as Messiah and Lord, he did not succeed in this enterprise, and was greatly responsible for Christianity eventually becoming a separate, mostly non-Jewish religion. This 'parting of the ways', however, took place over many decades and even centuries. It began in part in Christianity's desire to prove itself to Roman authority as a peaceful religion. Christians did not feel able to worship the emperor, and many paid the price in the Neronian persecutions of 64–5 and in later maltreatment. But they distanced themselves from Jews who rebelled against Rome. This distancing can be seen in a number of Gospel passages, for example in the **Passion narratives**, which attempt to blame Jews alone for the death of Jesus; and in the Fourth Gospel's deprecatory references to 'the Jews' (*see hoi Ioudaioi*).

In time, Christianity became the state religion of the **Roman Empire** (381). The Christian incapacity to understand why Jews failed to see Jesus as Messiah thereafter linked them to real political power and made possible extensive reprisals against Jews. There were isolated outbreaks of **anti-Judaism** in the early medieval period, but these grew stronger during the period of the **Crusades**

from the end of the eleventh to the fifteenth century. A strong religious reason for this anti-Judaism was the belief that Jews had been guilty of **deicide** in killing Jesus, a charge that goes back at least as far as **Melito of Sardis**. Of course, economic and other factors were often of primary importance for actions taken against Jews, but these could be justified by an appeal to centuries-old claims about the Jewish failure to recognise the true importance of Jesus.

It is not surprising that many Jewish scholars have either ignored Jesus or believed him to have been a Jew gone astray, or even a sorcerer, or else insulted him, as in the *Toledot Yeshu*. As the Middle Ages proceeded, the wisest counsel for Jews was generally to keep quiet about him, though in the **disputations** Jewish scholars carefully and politely refuted Christian accusations that Jews slandered and libelled Jesus. In the *convivencia* in Muslim **Spain**, Jews and Christians lived and worked together, often in remarkable amity, though religious differences remained, as they did in the European **Reformation**. Then Christian views about Jews often mirrored intra-Christian disputes: Martin **Luther** may at first have hoped that Jews would convert to his purified form of Christianity that stressed **salvation** by faith in Jesus Christ; but in his disillusionment his 1543 tract *On the Jews and their Lies* retraces with bile much of the medieval **polemic** against them. The **emancipation** of Jews in the nineteenth century may have owed something to contemporary Christian views of Jesus that regarded him as more human than divine, but was more probably spurred on by the marginalisation of religion in a Western Europe that had become wearied by devastating wars of religion.

Even so, views that emphasised the humanity of Jesus over against his divinity and that credited Paul with creating a new religion, Christianity (based on works by, e.g., Joseph Ernest Renan (1823–92) and Adolf von **Harnack** and still found today in works of certain New Testament scholars, such as Gerd Lüdemann (b. 1946)), enabled certain positive Jewish voices about Jesus to be heard: Claude **Montefiore** proposed that Jesus walked in the footsteps of the eighth-century BCE prophets, and Joseph **Klausner** and others echoed this presentation of him as an ethical teacher of **righteousness**. Another strand of Jewish reflection has proposed Christianity and Judaism as complementary yet mutually exclusive: building on the work of Franz **Rosenzweig**, Pinchas Lapide (1922–97) has seen Christianity as the 'judaising of the pagans'.

Geza Vermes's (b. 1924) book *Jesus the Jew* (1973) drew wide attention among Christians to Jesus' Jewish origins, though Christians earlier in the twentieth century (R. T. **Herford**, George Foot Moore (1851–1931)) had also explored this trend, which has now become widespread and crucial within Jesus studies. At least until the 1970s it was common for German New Testament scholars to portray Jesus as a kind of prototype exponent of idealism. Many of them betrayed an instinctive **antisemitism**. They depicted Judaism at the time of Jesus as 'late Judaism' (*Spätjudentum*), as if Jewish religion had ended with the destruction of the Temple in 70 CE, or should have. This position was based on the conviction that post-exilic Judaism had ossified and betrayed the prophetic faith of **Israel**. It contends that Jesus stands outside such a hardened, legalistic religion, a stranger to it, condemning the **scribes** and the **Pharisees** who were the fathers of **Rabbinic Judaism** and who have thus misled modern Judaism into perpetuating this sterile, legalistic religion. One of the tools by which some Gospel scholars have assessed (as some still do) the genuineness of a saying or deed of Jesus is the criterion of dissimilarity, which focuses on those words and works of Jesus that cannot be derived from the Judaism of his day (or, indeed, from the **early Church**). For example, using this criterion, some scholars would claim an authentic word from Jesus when Matthew records his sweeping prohibition of all oaths (5.34, 37; but cf. Jas 5.12). Yet (among other objections to it) this tool divorces Jesus from the Judaism of his day. He was a Jew, deeply influenced by its unusual emphasis upon belief in one God and his gift of the **Torah** to his people. Jesus was not an alien intruder in first-century Palestine. Whatever else he was, he was a reformer of Jewish beliefs, not an indiscriminate faultfinder of them: so, at least, much up-to-date New Testament scholarship suggests (a notable example is E. P. Sanders (b. 1937)).

The fact that the Nazis took advantage of Christian antisemitism to justify and carry out the **Holocaust** led many individual Christians and even specific denominations to rethink teaching about God's relations with Jews. The reforms of the **Second Vatican Council** and official statements of the Protestant churches built upon the early stages of a new biblical and theological understanding of Jesus in relation to Judaism, and encouraged even greater exploration of this issue. Looking back, it is possible to argue that pioneers, in their understandable eagerness to mend fences, played down important Christian beliefs. For example, it was argued that anti-Judaism is the left-hand of **Christology** (Rosemary Ruether (b. 1936)), as also that modern research tends to deny that Jesus ever thought of himself as Messiah, so Jews and Christians can agree upon that (Marcus Braybrooke (b. 1938)). The latter point is highly controversial, and the former implies that it is impossible for Christians to drink the cup of **repentance** and reconciliation, since the well is poisoned at its source. It may be that Christians will discover that Jesus was in fact a wandering healer and teacher of righteousness, whose real meaning is located more in the Synoptic Gospels than in the more developed Christologies of John and Paul (Vermes); or this may come to be seen as an old (early nineteenth-century), stale and anachronistic interpretation. A second and third generation of Christian (and Jewish) interpreters of Jesus may find it easier to disagree respectfully, rather than seek a consensus where none is likely to exist.

Some modern Christologies that have not taken Jewish–Christian relations into account have fallen into a reflex and implicit antisemitism. For example, early stages of Christian **feminist** theology often condemned the **Old Testament** notion of God as patriarchal, which they saw Jesus, alone among his Jewish contemporaries, as challenging. More recent feminist studies of Jesus have been much more nuanced and have included significant and positive contributions by Jewish writers (e.g. Judith Plaskow (b. 1947)).

Recently Jews have begun to respond generously to Christian attempts to undo their centuries of anti-Judaic teaching. *Dabru Emet* is a recent (2000) statement by Jewish scholars. Jesus is mentioned only briefly in one of its eight subheadings. The relevant passage begins: 'The humanly irreconcilable difference between Jews and Christians will not be settled until God redeems the entire world as promised in Scripture. Christians know and serve God through Jesus Christ and the Christian tradition. Jews know and serve God through Torah and the Jewish tradition.' This apparently cautious statement (and the text as a whole) has not been welcomed by all Jews. In one sense such a statement merely represents a stream of thought dating back at least to Rosenzweig. Yet in another it represents a significant step forward among Jewish scholars and indicates that, in mutual respect yet not in perfect agreement, Christians and Jews have begun to discuss the vexed issue of Jesus as one of the real differences between them.

See also **historical Jesus**   *MARTIN FORWARD*

Jew badge *see* yellow badge

Jewish–Christian relations, centres for the study of

Organised centres for the study and promotion of Jewish–Christian relations began appearing in the aftermath of the *Shoah*, but in the last quarter of the twentieth century their number has increased rapidly, especially in academic settings.

John M. **Oesterreicher** founded the first such centre in 1953 at Seton Hall University in East Orange, New Jersey, USA. His Institute of Judaeo–Christian Studies published an influential series of yearbooks entitled *The Bridge* that explored theological concepts that would inform **Vatican II**'s 1965 declaration *Nostra Aetate*.

Beginning in 1967, the **Sisters of Sion** published in French and English a periodical called *SIDIC* (*Service International de Documentation Judéo–Chrétienne*). They established a SIDIC Centre in Rome (sidic.org) to support the periodical and went on to start similar centres and initiatives in several countries, including the SIDIC Centre in Paris, the Micael Center in Montreal, and other centres in London, Sao Paulo, Australia, Spain, Austria and Costa Rica. These centres promoted local interfaith **dialogue** and disseminated the teachings of *Nostra Aetate*.

In 1969 the Faith and Order Commission of the National Council of Churches (USA) gathered a 'Study Group on Christian–Jewish Relations' to encourage scholarly research in the field. These Catholic and Protestant academicians met semi-annually under the sponsorship of various agencies. Currently known as the Christian Scholars Group on Christian–Jewish Relations (CSG), its members over the past decades have included some of the most significant US authors and researchers in Jewish–Christian studies. In 2002 the CSG issued the important summative statement

A Sacred Obligation: Rethinking Christian Faith in Relation to Judaism and the Jewish People. The Center for Christian–Jewish Learning at Boston College currently hosts the CSG's activities and archives (bc.edu/csg).

Starting in 1973, Catholic, Jewish and Protestant leaders in the **United States** jointly sponsored periodic National Workshops in Jewish–Christian Relations. To date 16 have been held in various cities. Local leaders who had collaborated in preparing for the workshop held in Baltimore in 1986 decided that their combined efforts should continue. This led to the establishment of the Institute of Christian and Jewish Studies (ICJS), one of the larger such centres in the United States. Among the notable achievements of the ICJS was the sponsorship of a group of Jewish scholars who published in 2000 the groundbreaking *Dabru Emet: A Jewish Statement on Christians and Christianity*.

Since the 1980s more and more university-based research institutes have appeared, such as the Centre for the study of Jewish–Christian Relations (CJCR) at Cambridge in the **United Kingdom** (cjcr.cam.ac.uk). In 2002 the Council of Centers on Jewish–Christian Relations (ccjr.us) was established 'for the exchange of information, cooperation, and mutual enrichment among centers and institutes for Christian–Jewish studies and relations in the United States'. Its 25 regular members represent academic centres in 14 states, including in the cities of Baltimore, Boston, Chicago, Cincinnati, Minneapolis, New York and Philadelphia.

The increasing number of such academic centres or institutes suggests that post-Shoah encounters between Christians and Jews have begun to consider questions that require the scholarly resources of universities. This represents an unprecedented and positive development in the long-shared history of Christianity and Judaism.

See also **Jewish–Christian relations, institutions**; **Jewish–Christian relations, modern scholarship in**   *PHILIP A. CUNNINGHAM*

Jewish–Christian relations, institutions

The last three decades of the twentieth century witnessed efforts, on the part of both Jews and Christians, to establish and creatively advance formal institutional relationships and opportunities for official consultation and **dialogue**. To help transform mutual animosities and misunderstandings into reconciled and informed relationships, leaders in the Jewish, Protestant, Eastern Orthodox and Roman Catholic communities established formal bodies such as the International Jewish Committee for Interreligious Consultations (IJCIC), the Liaison and Planning Committee (LPC) and the International Catholic–Jewish Liaison Committee (ILC).

With the leadership of World Jewish Congress General Secretary Gerhart M. Riegner (1911–2001), IJCIC was founded in 1970 to facilitate Jewish–Christian consultation on concerns relating to Jewry's historic, religious and political claim to **Israel**, the effects of Christian **supersessionist** teaching, and the **silence** and passivity of the Christian churches during the **Holocaust**. The 12 religious and non-religious IJCIC member organisations now include: American Jewish Committee (AJC), Anti-Defamation League (ADL), B'nai B'rith International, the Israel Council on Interreligious Relations, World Jewish Congress (WJC) and bodies representing the three major Jewish denominations.

The rapport established during the Second World War between Riegner and **World Council of Churches** (WCC) General Secretary Wilhelm Visser't Hooft (1948–66) compelled them to seek a formal and sustainable relationship. The first IJCIC–WCC international meeting was in the early 1970s. These joint efforts helped facilitate the publication of such WCC documents as *Ecumenical Considerations on Jewish–Christian Dialogue* (1982). With the leadership of Bartholomaios I, Ecumenical Patriarch of Constantinople, and Mgr Damaskinos, Metropolitan of **Switzerland**, four Jewish–Orthodox Christian consultations took place in: Lucerne, Switzerland (1977) on the notion of law in Judaism and Christianity; Bucharest (1979) on the role of **tradition** in both religions; Athens (1993) on continuity and renewal; Ma'aleh HaChamisha, Israel (1998) on the encounter of Christian Orthodoxy and Judaism with **modernity**.

In December 1970, under the leadership of Cardinal Johannes **Willebrands** and Gerhart Riegner, ILC was founded to enable official relationships between the Holy See's Commission for Religious Relations with the Jews and the international Jewish community through IJCIC. The Holy See's Commission, established on 22 October 1974 by Pope **Paul VI**, was preceded by the Office for Catholic–Jewish Relations headed by Cardinal Augustin **Bea** and is closely linked with but distinct from the Pontifical Council for Promoting Christian Unity. With the chairmen of IJCIC, the Commission Presidents – Cardinals Willebrands (1974–89), Edward **Cassidy** (1989–2001) and Walter Kasper (2001–) – have co-chaired ILC. With the expressed aims of improving mutual understanding, exchanging information, and cooperating in areas of common responsibility and concern, ILC has had several formal meetings in various venues in Europe, North America and Jerusalem. Consultation through ILC helped inform the Holy See's Commission in its publication of *Guidelines and Suggestions for Implementing the Conciliar Declaration 'Nostra Aetate' n. 4* (1974), *Notes on the Correct Way to Present the Jews and Judaism in Preaching and Catechesis in the Roman Catholic Church* (1985), and *We Remember: A Reflection on the Shoah* (1998). ILC has also issued joint statements on **antisemitism** (1990), the family (1994), the **environment** (1998) and education in Catholic and Jewish seminaries (2001).

These joint efforts in consultation and dialogue have been fraught with real and potential conflict. The WCC–IJCIC relationship has struggled with: Protestant resistance to IJCIC's insistence on determining WCC's Jewish consultation and dialogue partners; critical voices from Christian churches in the Middle East highlighting Protestant concerns about the Palestinian cause and dialogue with Muslims; the need to extend Jewish–Christian efforts to countries in Africa and Asia; and the Protestant effort, in the pursuit of justice, to incorporate political advocacy into its efforts in dialogue. After the first 20 years of the Holy See–IJCIC relationship delicate issues such as the **Carmelite controversy** at Auschwitz, the beatification of Edith **Stein** and the visit of Kurt Waldheim (b. 1918) to the Vatican cast a heavy shadow over the work of ILC. The 1990 ILC meeting in Prague, calling for reconciliation and good will, attempted to address the prevailing spirit of suspicion, resentment and distrust. In the following years severe criticism of the Commission's statement *We Remember: A Reflection on the Shoah*, Jewish disapproval of the proposed **canonisations** of Popes **Pius IX** and **Pius XII**, and the demise of the International Catholic–Jewish Historical Commission led the Vatican co-chair to consider dissolving the ILC relationship. Internally, IJCIC leaders and members have been in disagreement over such issues as: Jewish over-aggressiveness in IJCIC's relationship with the Vatican; the degree of emphasis to be put on a political agenda; engaging in theological interfaith dialogue, an activity opposed by Joseph **Soloveitchik** who prohibited it for Orthodox Jews; and the question of whether IJCIC has outlived its usefulness.

The ability to sustain these official Jewish–Christian relationships, in spite of the problems encountered, attests to the quality of the work done and the good will and commitment of those involved. The new century is seeing IJCIC attempt to re-energise and redirect its efforts through the appointment of new leadership: IJCIC chairman Rabbi Israel Singer (2002) and IJCIC governing board chairman Rabbi Joel Meyers (2002). Renouncing a confrontational approach and espousing compromise, they favour a moderating social and diplomatic presence. The new President of the Holy See's Commission, Cardinal Walter Kasper (b. 1933), continues to relate to IJCIC and its constituencies. However, he is also attempting to open new doors with a greater variety of dialogue partners, including those of European Jewish leaders and Israeli officials. WCC leaders – General Secretary Konrad Raiser (1993–) and Programme Executive for Christian–Jewish Relations and Dialogue Hans Ucko (1989–) – continue to explore ways to work effectively with IJCIC by building mutual trust and creating a culture of dialogue.

In many countries institutional efforts at dialogue and partnership are multiplying at national and local levels. These are facilitated and supported by such bodies as national conferences of Protestant and Orthodox Churches, national conferences of Catholic Bishops, AJC and ADL. One example of a national partnership is that of the US Bishops' Ecumenical and Interreligious Affairs Committee and the National Council of Synagogues – a partnership that has resulted in five joint statements, including *Reflections on Covenant and Mission* (2002). AJC, since its inception, has been committed to strengthening understanding and communication across religious lines. Through the leadership of its National Directors of Interfaith Affairs, Rabbis Marc Tanenbaum (1961–1983) and James Rudin (1983–2000), AJC has made major contributions through organisational partnerships and coalitions, academic conferences, publications and personal interaction. Since the 1970s ADL's

Department of Interfaith Affairs, through the leadership of its Director Rabbi Leon Klenicki (1974–2000), has devoted itself to Jewish–Christian understanding on both theological and communal levels, and to reducing religious prejudice and defamatory stereotyping of the other. It has participated in numerous Jewish–Christian dialogues with the Vatican, WCC, and American Protestant and Catholic clergy.   *AUDREY DOETZEL*

Jewish–Christian relations, modern scholarship in

Since the publication of ***Nostra Aetate*** in 1965 there has been a transformation in Christian scholarly writings about Judaism, as well as a willingness among a small but growing body of Jewish scholars to create a Jewish theology of Christianity. Several major themes have emerged from these writings.

Beginning with biblical studies, modern scholarly works demonstrate a willingness to take the **Hebrew Bible** seriously on its own terms, rejecting the traditional approach of the ***Adversus Judaeos* literature**, which had rendered it virtually impossible for Christians to know how to write an **Old Testament** theology. It is increasingly accepted that Christian **biblical theology** can only be developed in **dialogue** with Judaism.

Associated with biblical theology are studies of the **New Testament**. Profoundly influenced by the Oxford scholar Geza Vermes (b. 1924), modern scholarship, which itself has influenced contemporary official Church statements on this topic, emphasises that the ministry of **Jesus** can only be understood in the historical context of first-century Palestinian Judaism, since Jesus was a Jew who taught his fellow Jews, some of whom followed his teaching while others did not. Scholars point out that Jesus' Jewish followers argued amongst themselves about the conditions under which Gentiles might be admitted to this new Jewish movement and with other Jews over issues such as **Torah**-observance and claims about Jesus. The New Testament bears witness to the disputes, which were vigorous and often bitter. Nevertheless, until recently scholars neglected almost completely the fact that the arguments were between Jews, about a Jew or about Jewish issues. Traditionally, polemical passages were read as if they were 'Christian' arguments against 'Jews'. Modern scholarship has shown that to read them this way is to misread them and that this misreading resulted in the Christian 'teaching of contempt'.

For example, Rosemary Ruether (b. 1936), building on the scholarship of James **Parkes** and Jules **Isaac**, argued that the root cause of **antisemitism** lay within Christian anti-Jewish teaching, specifically **Christology** and the *Adversus Judaeos* tradition. As she put it, 'Anti-Judaism developed theologically in Christianity as the left-hand of Christology. That is to say, anti-Judaism was the negative side of the Christian claim that Jesus was the Christ.' Ruether suggested that when Jews refused to accept the Christian teachings regarding Christ, Christians felt obliged to undermine their opponents' views. This was achieved by anti-Jewish Christian teaching and supersessionist **polemic**.

One of the most influential postwar New Testament scholars is Ed Parish Sanders (b. 1937) whose work is informed by a study of early Judaism in its own right, not just as 'background' to the story of Christian origins. In dialogue circles it is praised for having placed issues central to Christian–Jewish debate at the heart of academic biblical study. Another important biblical scholar is Krister Stendahl (b. 1921). In his studies of **Paul**, Stendahl maintains that the apostle's chief concern was not introspective and individualistic but historical and communal, that is, the question of how, while the Jews remain within the Abrahamic **covenant**, Gentiles also can be adopted into it; 'justification by faith' means that this can be done without strict Torah-observance. Stendahl argues that Paul's experience on the road to Damascus was less a 'conversion' than a 'call', a distinction that bears significance for Jewish–Christian relations. As a result of these and other New Testament studies, scholarship tends to describe the relationship between Judaism and Christianity in terms of siblings (the metaphor of elder and younger brothers being the most common) rather than in terms of a father (Judaism)–daughter (Christianity) relationship.

Stendahl's work on Paul has been influential on many Christian scholars, both Protestant and Catholic. For example, German Catholic theologian Franz Mussner (b. 1916) interprets **Romans 9–11** as an affirmation of Judaism as a positive way to God. While much of Mussner's work is concerned with the life of Jesus, an important contribution to Christian theology concerns the nature of the changes necessary in Christianity after the **Holocaust**. Another German theologian, Protestant scholar Jürgen Moltmann (b. 1926), explored the significance of the Jewish 'no' to Jesus as the **Messiah**, suggesting that Christians should postpone the question of who will be revealed as the Messiah to the end of time, and learn from Jews what it means to live in the present in an unredeemed world. His view is mirrored in the 2002 statement by the Pontifical Biblical Commission (*The Jewish People and their Sacred Sciptures in the Christian Bible*) that 'the Jewish messianic expectation is not in vain'.

The study of antisemitism and the Holocaust are of central concern to modern scholarship, as illustrated by continuing controversies over the role of **Pius XII** and the lack of access of the Vatican archives for Holocaust scholars. Franklin Littell (b. 1917), a Methodist theologian who was in Germany immediately after the Second World War, stresses the failures of the Churches, notably Protestant 'peddlers of cheap grace'. He promoted the study of the Holocaust in the development of Christian theology, suggesting that Christian–Jewish conversation would help free it from antisemitism. Karl Barth's (1886–1968) writings are also an important topic. Barth's opposition to **Nazism** and antisemitism was based on the view that the relationship between the Jewish people and the Church was unbreakable because of God's election of the Jew Jesus, which made opposition to antisemitism the duty of every Christian. However, Barth has been criticised for using supersessionist language and would not engage in Jewish–Christian dialogue. He was concerned that dialogue would contradict the togetherness of Jews and Christians as revealed in the word of God, thus either relativising the claims of faith of both or leading to **mission**. According to Barth, the Jewish–Christian relationship is comparable to the relationship between the various Christian churches. Catholic writers such as Edward Flannery (1912–98) have also examined the history of Christian antisemitism, and Charlotte Klein (1915–85) uncovered the surprisingly fixed ideas of some New Testament scholars, who contrasted **law** and **grace** in Pauline teaching and continually referred to first-century Judaism as 'late Judaism' (*Spätjudentum*). Among the scholars whose prejudices she revealed are Martin Noth (1902–68), Rudolf Bultmann

(1884–1976), Otto Dibelius (1880–1967) and Joachim Jeremias (1900–79). A similar contribution has been made by Katharina von Kellenbach (b. 1960) whose study of certain **feminist** theologians revealed a prejudicial portrait of Judaism as the antithesis of feminist values, associating it wholly with patriarchy. The writings of Ruether can be cited in this regard, since she maintained a view of the coming of Jesus as heralding the liberation of oppressed women from a patriarchal, oppressive Jewish culture.

As far as the Holocaust is concerned, a number of Jewish thinkers have been particularly influential on Jewish and Christian theological writings, especially Richard Rubenstein (b. 1924), Emil Fackenheim (1916–2003) and Irving Greenberg (b. 1933). Rubenstein sets the mechanical non-humanity of the perpetrators of the **Shoah** in a vast historical context, on the one hand of slavery (essentially making humans into consumables) and on the other the rise of the inhuman city, where functionaries survey the lives of the city-dwellers from behind closed doors. Rubenstein rejects any notion of God acting in history (*see* **death of God theology**). After **Auschwitz** only human beings can create value and meaning, and Judaism has a particular role in this renewal and reintegration.

In response, Fackenheim, himself a survivor, seeks to interpret the significance of the *Shoah*, where **evil** went beyond all explanation. God and Israel are still in relationship, and the Jewish people are precluded from despair or abdication of responsibility. Fackenheim's thesis of a 614th commandment for Jews to remain Jewish and thus not to grant **Hitler** a posthumous victory gained wide recognition among Jews and Christians, and he called on Christians to support Israel as a guarantor for the future survival of the Jewish people and for Jews and Christians to work together for *tikkun olam* (mending of the world). An example of Fackenheim's influence can be seen in the writings of Roy Eckardt (1918–98) who, following Fackenheim, called for a Christian return into the ongoing history of Israel.

Irving Greenberg developed an interest in Jewish–Christian relations, seeing the Holocaust as an event that needs to lead to the re-evaluation of Christian **identity** and relations with Jews. His concept of 'voluntary covenant', according to which Jews after the Holocaust are no longer commanded but choose to take on the continuity of Judaism,

has been discussed and incorporated into Christian **Holocaust theology**.

Roy and Alice (b. 1923) Eckardt were profoundly shocked that the Christian churches had for 20 years remained silent about the Holocaust and continued to remain silent about contemporary Jewish existence (Roy called it 'the new Christian **silence**'). Only, he suggests, by becoming the younger brother once again in the house of God the Father of Israel will the Church be able to live authentically. With his wife Alice he pleaded for a 180-degree reversal of inherited Christian theology, indeed a 'starting all over again' to eliminate all vestiges of **supersessionism**. Both saw historic Christian **anti-Judaism** as directly connected to modern antisemitism and as providing the soil in which the seeds of Nazism could flourish. Their influence can be seen in the writings of scholars such as Clark Williamson (b. 1935) whose book *A Guest in the House of Israel: Post-Holocaust Church Theology* (1993) seeks to reshape fundamental Church teachings on God, Jesus, Paul, covenant, scripture and the nature of the Church itself.

The Eckardts also devoted themselves to interpreting the significance of the **State of Israel** and vigorously defending it against its critics. As a source of Jewish–Christian controversy, Israel has been the subject of much discussion. The most critical scholars include Christian **liberation theologian** Naim Ateek (b. 1937) and radical Jewish theologian Marc Ellis (b. 1952) who take issue with other theologians by suggesting that Holocaust theology has failed by neglecting to analyse the contemporary use of power, which has now passed into Jewish hands in Israel. Ellis sees solidarity with the Palestinian people as Jewish theology's decisive test and suggests that Jews have to learn from the mistakes of Christians.

A number of Christian theologians have attempted to develop a systematic revision of Christian theology, the most detailed study being by Paul van Buren (1924–98). In his trilogy *A Theology of the Jewish–Christian Reality* (1980–7) he considers the implications that emerge within Christianity when the continuing validity of the covenant between God and the Jewish people is acknowledged. Van Buren argued that the foundational document of the Church is the Hebrew Bible; as a record of God's conversations with Jews, these scriptures belong to Israel, and Christians are committed overhearers. Because the covenant between God and Israel continues, Churches must reformulate all Christological statements that denigrate Judaism. He viewed Judaism and the Jewish people as partners with Christians on the same 'Way' to the kingdom of God. His work has been continued by Catholic scholar John Pawlikowski (b. 1940) who has reflected on issues associated with covenant, **mission** and especially Christology in the light of Jewish–Christian dialogue.

Other recent studies have also considered developments in educational and liturgical materials. Philip Cunningham (b. 1953) has studied **textbooks** used in Catholic schools and **religious education** programmes and has also written concise introductions to the Sunday readings (following the Roman Catholic **lectionary**). Mary Boys (b. 1947) has tackled specific implications of Jewish–Christian dialogue (traditionally dominated by male voices) for Christian education and biblical studies. Her most important work, *Has God Only One Blessing?*, addresses Christian supersessionism and suggests new ways for the Christian message to be proclaimed without anti-Judaism.

For their part a small but growing number of Jewish scholars have considered the theological implications of Jewish–Christian relations for Judaism. The Jewish community does not subject itself to the discipline of public statements like the numerous Christian statements of the Catholic and Protestant Churches. In part this is because of the asymmetrical nature of the history of persecution of Jews by Christians and the teaching of contempt, and in part because of the distinctive nature of Jewish religious polity. However, the publication of ***Dabru Emet*** in 2000 and of the book that followed, *Christianity in Jewish Terms*, symbolises a growing awareness among Jewish theologians of the theological implications of Jewish–Christian relations. An important Jewish study has been penned by David Novak (b. 1941) who analyses the **Noachide laws** and the significance of Martin **Buber** and Franz **Rosenzweig** towards developing a Jewish theology of Jewish–Christian dialogue.

A notable feature of modern scholarly writings is the increasing number of studies either co-edited by Jewish and Christian scholars or consisting of conversations between Jews and Christians. Among the more significant publications are the dialogue between Karl Rahner (1904–84) and Pinchas Lapide (1922–97) (*Encountering Jesus – Encountering Judaism: A Dialogue*); the jointly hosted seminar by Walter Harrelson (b. 1919) and Randall M. Falk (b. 1921) (*Jews and Christians: A Troubled Family*); the reflection on Israel by David Burrell (b. 1933) and Yehezkel Landau (b. 1949) (*Voices from Jerusalem*); and the study guide of the New Testament and rabbinic texts by Michael Hilton (b. 1951) and Gordian Marshall (b. 1938) (*The Gospels and Rabbinic Judaism*). Institutes specialising in Jewish–Christian relations, such as the Centre for the study of Jewish–Christian Relations (CJCR) in Cambridge, UK and the Catholic Theological Union's Cardinal Joseph Bernardin Center in Chicago have also produced important works, and the American publisher Paulist Press publishes a series dedicated to scholarly studies of Jewish–Christian relations.   *EDWARD KESSLER*

Jewish Christianity

There is no evidence in the ancient world for the use of the terms Jewish Christianity or Jewish Christian. They are in fact invented terms, probably introduced into the English language in the seventeenth century and subsequently used, in part, to describe a group in ancient Christianity that was seen to play a greater or lesser role in the evolution of that religion.

Precisely because it is not used in antiquity, settling upon a definition of the term is difficult. Some have sought to define it ethnically (a Jewish Christian is a Jew who has converted to Christianity – this brings out well the sense of the German word *Judenchrist*); others have defined it with reference to specific practices (a Jewish Christian is someone who observes certain laws associated with Judaism, e.g. **circumcision**, **sabbath** and **dietary laws**); and others with reference to certain beliefs (a Jewish Christian is a person who holds distinctively Jewish beliefs). Most scholars would probably agree that the second of the definitions, that related to praxis, is the best – the other two, it is argued, are too general in their orientation to define anything distinctive. But there remain problems with this definition, too. How might one, for instance, distinguish between a Judaiser and a Jewish Christian? By reference to the Jewish origins of the latter? But how might these be determined? And what practices or combination of practices made someone a Jewish Christian?

In the beginning all Christians were Jewish Christians – that is, they were a part of a Messianic sect within Judaism. It was only when a **mission** to the Gentiles began, and the need for converts to observe distinctive Jewish practices was questioned by some, that one can begin to talk about Jewish Christians as a group within Christianity distinct from Gentile Christians. Something of the controversy sparked off by the issue of Gentile Christian entry into the Church can be seen in Acts 15 and Gal. 2–5. The decision, recorded in Gal. 2.7f., to set up two separate missions (one to the Gentiles, the other to the Jews) probably served to reinforce a sense of division, and **Paul** appears to have been dogged by those who questioned his view that Gentiles could enter the Messianic community without being circumcised (see Galatians above and Phil. 3.5f.).

It was only gradually that the Jewish Christians began to lose their influence in the evolving Church. So, for instance, it seems clear that the community in **Jerusalem**, led by **James, the brother of Jesus** and subsequently by others associated with Jesus' family, wielded considerable influence well beyond the environs of Palestine. Such influence probably began to decline as a result of the death of James (see Josephus, *Ant.* 20.197–203; and Eusebius, *Hist. eccl.* 2.23.11–18) and the Jewish revolt of 66–70 CE when **Eusebius** records that the Jerusalem community was forced to flee to Pella in the Transjordanian district (Eusebius, *Hist. eccl.* 3.5.3), and of the growing influence of Gentile Christianity. Although the community probably returned to Jerusalem, the **Bar Kokhba** revolt, which led to the **expulsion** of the Jews from Palestine, significantly diminished their influence, a fact that may have become inevitable as non-Palestinian Christianity became a more Gentile-centred movement. A strong Jewish-Christian presence has also been posited for **Rome, Antioch** and Syria in general with the last of these places possibly boasting a strong Jewish-Christian presence well into the third century. By the time of **Justin Martyr** around the middle of the second century the presence in the Christian movement of Jews who continued to observe Jewish practices had become a hotly disputed point, with Justin's more liberal position an apparent exception (*Dial.* 47). By the time of **Irenaeus**, writing towards the end of the second century, such people were viewed as heretical by the majority Church and given

the name Ebionite (Elchasaites, Symmachians and Nazarenes were also names subsequently associated with Jewish Christians), although it is unclear whether such a name was a self-designation, possibly of some antiquity ('Ebion', meaning poor, is a word often applied in the Hebrew scriptures to the oppressed of God). But in spite of this hostility, it is possible that some **New Testament** texts such as Matthew, John, James, the epistles of Jude and 2 Peter, and Revelation, to name the most obvious, contain Jewish-Christian material.

Non-Christian Jewish reaction to Jewish Christians is not easy to determine. The Acts of the Apostles indicates some hostility on the part of certain sections of society, but interestingly **Josephus**, in his account of the death of James, implies a more complex reaction in which some Jews, implicitly including himself, questioned the legality of James's death. Strikingly, in this same passage, written in the 90s CE, Josephus appears to view James and his followers as Jews. Negative reaction appears to be more in evidence during the revolt of 66–70 CE and the later Bar Kokhba revolt (132–135 CE), perhaps resulting from the Messianic character of these events and the refusal of Jewish Christians to be a part of the nationalistic fervour dominant at these times. As relations between Jews and Christians became worse, attitudes amongst some Jews to Jewish Christians hardened. In this context some scholars have argued, controversially, that the reference to *minim* in the *birkat ha-minim*, or twelfth Benediction of the *Amidah*, was principally aimed at Jewish Christians, an observation partially supported by logic (it would only have affected those still in the Jewish community who attended synagogue) and by some patristic references, although called into question by others. The notion that Jewish Christians were an entity outside the Jewish community by the middle of the second century is further implied by the fact that any ongoing link to the Jewish community is not clear in references to, for instance, the Ebionites or Elchasaites, although certainty on this point cannot be arrived at. Just as we cannot speak of a uniform Christianity at this stage in history, so we cannot speak of a uniform Judaism, and we must, therefore, entertain the possibility that attitudes to Jewish Christians varied between different Jewish communities. Moreover, it seems clear that the Nazarenes, whose name may in fact go back to an early designation of the Christians (Matt. 2.23; Acts 24.5), saw themselves as operating from within the Jewish community, as their commentary on **Isaiah**, quoted by **Jerome**, appears to imply (*Comm. Isa.*. 8.11–15; 9.1; 19.17–21). Some rabbinic references may also support such an internal Jewish profile. Jerome appeared to give voice to this quest for a dual **identity** when he stated polemically that the 'Nazarenes' sought to be both Jews and Christians but were in fact neither (*Epist.* 112.13).

As stated above, it is difficult to make sweeping statements about the beliefs and practices of the Jewish Christians. In relation to the latter, a commitment to the observance of certain Jewish laws seems central, and we have some evidence of distinctive liturgical practices and places of worship called synagogues. Traditionally they have often been associated with what became heretical **Christological** beliefs in which the **Virgin Birth** was denied and Jesus' adoption as God's **Messiah** was emphasised, and with a hostility to the figure of Paul, whose association with the supposedly **antinomian** party made him repugnant to some of them. But again these are generalisations that do not include all groups normally thought to be Jewish Christian (the Nazarenes, for instance, held conventional Christological views and did not deride Paul). Jewish Christians wrote gospels (these are normally referred to as *The Gospel of the Hebrews*, *The Gospel of the Nazarenes* and *The Gospel of the Ebionites*) and histories of the Church (the section of the ***Pseudo-Clementine*** *Recognitions* 1.37–71 is usually taken to be from a Jewish-Christian 'Acts' source, possibly called the *Anabathmoi Jakobou*, or *Stepping Stones of James*), but these survive only in fragmentary form.

We hear very little about Jewish-Christian groups, at least in Christian sources, after the fifth century. Some evidence for their ongoing existence may be discerned within Arabic sources of a later date. Groups of a broadly Jewish-Christian profile, some of whom have their origin in the nineteenth century, can be found in Europe, **Israel** and the **United States** today (*see*, e.g., **Hebrew Christians**; **Jews for Jesus**; **Messianic Jews**).

See also **Christians, Judaising**

JAMES CARLETON PAGET

Jewish perspectives on Christianity *see* **Christianity, Jewish perspectives on**

Jewish pope *see* **Pope, Jewish**

Jews' bishop *see* **leaders of the Jews, externally appointed**

Jews for Jesus

Based in California, the Jews for Jesus movement emerged out of the **Hebrew Christian** Alliance in the 1970s under the leadership of Moishe Rosen (b. 1932), who was anxious to maintain Jewish practice and culture within the setting of a belief in Yeshua (**Jesus**) as the long-awaited **Messiah**. The movement is active in **missions** towards Jews and its charter states that 'we believe in the lost condition of every human being, whether Jew or Gentile, who does not accept salvation by faith in Jesus Christ, and therefore in the necessity of presenting the gospel to the Jews'. Despite this, Jews for Jesus are insistent that the Jewish component of the movement's ethnic identity should be a vital feature of the faith and that they should be seen as part of the **Messianic Jewish** movement. As part of its evangelical activity Jews for Jesus seek to generate publicity by, among other things, controversial advertising such as the full-page advert that appeared in the UK press on **Holocaust Memorial Day** in 2004 featuring a Holocaust survivor who came to Jesus. In addition to its missionary activity, which Jews generally receive with deep dislike, the movement also aims to challenge Gentile Christians about their relationship with Judaism and to increase their understanding of the Jewish roots of Christianity. Although mainstream Christianity is not as negative towards the movement as the Jewish community, Jews for Jesus remain on the periphery of the Church.

EDWARD KESSLER

Joachim of Fiore (da Flora) (*c*.1130/5–1201/2)

Italian Cistercian mystic, prophet and theologian. Joachim's highly influential **eschatology** envisaged tripartite division of history: **Old Testament** – Father, Law; **New Testament** – Son, Crucifixion, Sacraments; and finally an imminent third age of Spirit, liberty, love, to be inaugurated (1200–60) by two new spiritual Orders (hermits and preaching monks), who would convert the world and all Jews. The **Antichrist** was already alive (1190), though not Jewish. Joachim's **millenarianism** was posthumously radicalised: mid-thirteenth-century Spiritual **Franciscans** – frequently anti-Jewish – identified themselves as Joachim's predicted conversionist monks. His tripartite eschatology (partially condemned 1215, 1263) influenced millenarian sects and, indirectly, German Idealist philosophers: **Lessing**, Schelling (1775–1854), Fichte (1762–1814), **Hegel**; even, perhaps, the vision of the 'Third Reich'.

MARGARET BREARLEY

John Chrysostom *see* Chrysostom, John

John Paul II (1920–2005)

Pope (1978–2005). John Paul II's pontificate saw more progress in Catholic–Jewish relations – the area of the Church's ministry that embodies some of the most ancient and potentially divisive issues posed to the Church by its own history – and certainly more dramatic gestures toward the Jewish people by the Bishop of Rome than occurred during the reigns of all of his predecessors combined. Karol Wojtyła grew up in Wadowice, **Poland**, a town with a sizeable Jewish population. He entered the University of Kraków in 1939, just before the Nazis invaded Poland and shut down higher education. During the Second World War he worked in a stone quarry, clandestinely studying in an underground seminary and engaging in anti-Nazi resistance. Ordained in 1946, he was consecrated auxiliary bishop of Kraków in 1958, archbishop of Kraków in 1964, and cardinal in 1967. He participated in **Vatican II** as bishop from 1962 to 1965, being credited with the compromise that produced the Council's pastoral constitution on 'The Church in the Modern World' (*Gaudium et Spes*, 1965).

Elected pope in 1978, Wojtyła chose a name, John Paul II, that paid homage and made a commitment to his immediate predecessors: **John XXIII**, who called the Council, and **Paul VI**, who implemented that mandate and institutionalised it through the creation of the Holy See's Commission for Religious Relations with the Jews in 1970. Wherever he went throughout the world, John Paul reached out to and met with local Jewish communities, giving new life and energy to Jewish–Catholic relations in Europe, North and South America, the Middle East, Asia and Australia. He made addresses and remarks on Judaism on numerous occasions and in a remarkably wide range of locations throughout the world. Many of Wojtyła's classmates and friends from his youth were Jewish, and perished in the *Shoah*. This then was the first (and perhaps the last) pope to have

had an intimate knowledge of the great civilisation of Eastern European Jewry and to have mourned its passing as a deep, personal loss, which may explain his personal passion for Jewish–Christian relations.

One can discern in John Paul's addresses over the years a growth and development in understanding and appreciation of how 'the Jews define themselves in the light of their own religious experience' (12 March 1979). He was the first pope to visit a death camp, **Auschwitz**, and to pray there for its victims (1979); the first to visit a synagogue and to pray there with its congregation (1986); the first to have a speaking knowledge of Yiddish as well as Hebrew and to quote approvingly post-biblical Jewish thinkers; the first to exchange ambassadors with the **State of Israel** (1994); and the first to visit the central Jewish symbolic sites of **Jerusalem**, Yad Vashem and the Kotel (the Western Wall). He personally tackled, and led Catholic thinkers not only in the Curia but around the world in tackling, all of the major areas of the Catholic–Jewish agenda, from **liturgy**, biblical studies and **mission** in the realm of theology, to the *Shoah* and the State of Israel on the practical, historical level. Protestant scholars, no less than Catholics, have picked up the challenge of his far-reaching insights in Christian–Jewish relations.

While the pontificate of John Paul II was marked by the most solid and extensive advances in Catholic–Jewish relations in the history of the Church, it also saw some of the most vocal controversies between Catholics and Jews since Vatican II: the meeting with Kurt Waldheim (b. 1918), the **Carmelite controversy**, the canonisation of Edith **Stein**, the rise and demise of the International Catholic–Jewish Historical Commission (*see* **Jewish–Christian relations, institutions**). All these controversies and others revolve in the main around the **Holocaust**. In 1994 John Paul II arranged for a memorial concert within the Vatican to commemorate *Yom HaShoah* (**Holocaust Memorial Day**). In 1997 he personally charged the Pontifical Biblical Commission with studying the roots of Christian **anti-Judaism** in traditional polemical misunderstandings of the Bible. In 1998 he welcomed the Vatican document stating the Church's repentance for the Holocaust, *We Remember: A Reflection on the Shoah*, with a most unusual personal letter strengthening its text. In 2000, before his **pilgrimage** to Israel, he presided at St Peter's Basilica in Rome over a millennial liturgy of repentance which devoted one of its seven categories of major sins of the Church to repentance for Christian teaching against Jews and Judaism over the centuries and for the failures of the Church during the *Shoah*. This, in turn, was the basis for the prayer he placed in the Kotel: 'God of our fathers, we are deeply saddened by the behaviour of those who in the course of history have caused these children of yours to suffer and, asking your forgiveness, we wish to commit ourselves to genuine brotherhood with the people of the Covenant' (26 March 2000).

The Jewish response to John Paul's sponsorship of improved relations was, at first, hesitant, given his Polish background. Despite setbacks and controversies, however, he gradually won the trust of many Jews, not least in Israel with his pilgrimage there, that the Christian *teshuvah* (*see* **repentance**) he preached and modelled is genuine, albeit far from complete, in the Christian churches. In retrospect, he was a prophetic figure in leading his Church, and many in other Churches too, into a new, more hope-filled third millennium of the Jewish–Christian relationship.

EUGENE J. FISHER

John the Baptist

John, son of Zechariah and Elizabeth, a pious but childless old couple of priestly stock (only Luke 1.5–25, 57–80), was a teacher of renown in Judea who was executed by **Herod** Antipas (Matt. 14.1–2; Mark 6.14–29; Luke 9.7–9; Josephus, *Ant.* 18.5.2, 116–19). All these sources describe him as baptiser of people seeking **repentance** for sins; he challenged them to reform their lives in practical ways to prepare for impending judgement (Matt. 4.11–12; Luke 3.3–17). The fourfold gospel presents John as forerunner of the **Messiah**, fulfilling the role of **Elijah** the prophet according to Mal. 3.23–24 (Matt. 17.10–13; Luke 1.16–17). However, some pilgrims to the festivals in **Jerusalem** carried his message to **Alexandria** (Acts 18.25) and Ephesus (Acts 19.1–7), and in remote places adherents held on to his message for several generations.

Perspectives in the **Dead Sea Scrolls** concerning the proximity of the final days and the symbolic use of ablutions to depict turning from sin are found in John's message, but direct dependence on this group (Essenes?) need not be postulated.

The **baptism** of **Jesus** by John is interpreted by the evangelists as the Messiah declaring solidarity with sinners because he had come to serve them, to reconcile them with God (Matt. 3.13–17; Mark 1.9–11; John 1.24–34).

Tertullian declared that John constitutes the point at which Judaism ceases and Christianity begins (*Marc.* 4.33. 47–8). Until John there existed only the burdens of the **Law**, not its remedies; then Christ abolished the yoke of works, but not the precepts (*pud.* 6.3). **Origen** understood John's baptism as putting an end to the old order, but not as inaugurating the new (*Comm. Rom.* 5.8); however, the spirit and power of John must come upon the soul of those who believe in Christ to prepare for the Lord a perfect people (*Fr. Luc.* 4.6).

Typical of the **supersessionist** stance of early theologians is William Durand's (?1230–96) statement in *Rationale Divinorum Officiorum*, the great liturgical commentary of the thirteenth century, that 'John was like a cornerstone, joining the Old and New Testaments . . . he was a mediator between the Testaments because he was the end of the Old and the beginning of the New Testament, for "all the Prophets and the Law prophesied until John" (Matt. 11.13) . . .' (Book VII, ch. 14). Not until **Vatican II** did the Catholic Church officially recognise that 'from the Jewish people sprang the apostles' (*Nostra Aetate* no. 4) and by extension that John the Baptist lived and died a faithful witness to the God of Israel.

LAWRENCE E. FRIZZELL

John XXIII (1881–1963)

Pope (1958–63). By launching the Second Vatican Council (**Vatican II**) and insisting that it direct its attention to the age-old question of the Church's understanding of God's **people, Israel**, John XXIII brought about the greatest revolution in Church teaching on the question since the time of St **Paul**. Born Angelo Giuseppe Roncalli, he served as a parish priest and seminary professor from 1904 to 1925 when he was appointed nuncio to Bulgaria by Pope Pius XI (1922–39). As nuncio in Istanbul, Turkey, during the Second World War, Roncalli was instrumental in gaining papers for Jewish refugees seeking to enter Palestine, sending thousands of such documents also to the papal nuncio in Budapest, Angelo Rotta (1872–1975), who was working closely with Raoul Wallenberg (1912–?1947) and other neutral diplomats to save tens of thousands of Jewish lives. Roncalli and Rotta used the convents of the **Sisters of Sion** to communicate clandestinely through occupied Europe. Roncalli also intervened personally with the queen of Bulgaria to help protect the Jews of that country. He was given the important post of nuncio to **France** in 1944 and named primate of Venice in 1953. Already 72, and thus seen as a transitional figure who would do nothing too radical until a successor was ready, Roncalli was elected pontiff in 1958, surprising everyone with his boldness in announcing on 25 January 1959, less than 90 days after his election, that he was calling 'a general Council for the universal Church'. In March 1959 John suppressed the term 'perfidious' from the **Good Friday Prayer for the Jews**.

In October 1960 Pope John received a delegation of American Jewish leaders for the first time in Vatican history. They presented him with a Torah scroll in gratitude for the Jewish lives he had saved during the **Shoah**. He replied, 'We are all sons of the same heavenly Father. Among us there must ever be the brightness of love and its practice.' Then, stretching out his arms, he concluded, 'I am Joseph (Giuseppe), your brother' (Gen. 45.4). In using his baptismal name, the Pope made an unprecedented gesture of personal and filial warmth toward his guests, acknowledging their full dignity as descendants of the Patriarchs of the Bible. The statement was pregnant with theological implications that would come to fruit in the years to follow.

Already on 13 June 1960 John had received Jules **Isaac**, who argued for specific changes in Church teaching on Jews and Judaism. The first request from a Catholic source that the Council consider the sacred bond between the Church and the Jewish people had come on 24 April 1960 when the Pontifical Biblical Institute of Rome presented its formal *petitio*, arguing on the basis of the Pauline epistles and the Council of **Trent** that it was part of 'the deposit of faith' that the Jews could not be seen as 'rejected' by God or collectively guilty of the death of **Jesus**, despite the 'erroneous interpretation of certain **New Testament** citations' over the centuries. Likewise, recommendations for such changes came before the Council from European bishops, especially German, British and French, and the US bishops, for whom it was a major goal. The Pope assigned the task of developing a corrective statement on Judaism to Cardinal Augustin

Bea, his personal confessor and a biblical scholar. The declaration ***Nostra Aetate*** was overwhelmingly approved by the Council Fathers on 28 October 1965.   *EUGENE J. FISHER*

Josel of Rosheim (c.1476/1480–1554)

Successful Jewish advocate of German Jews during the turbulent years of the **Reformation**. From 1507 he represented the local Jewish community, quickly acquiring respect and eventually a mandate to represent German Jewry in both juristic and religious matters in the Reichstag and before the emperor. His personal skills and courage repeatedly secured letters of protection for all German Jews and prevented impending **expulsions**. Josel also blocked anti-Jewish legislation and frequently defended Jews, including himself, against **blood libel** charges, and was much in demand by other European Jewish communities. After a split with **Luther** and other initially sympathetic Reformers, Josel increasingly oriented his politics towards support of the Catholic emperor rather than the Protestant aristocracy.   *PETR FRYŠ*

Joseph

Eleventh son of **Jacob**, the biblical patriarch. As with many other biblical figures, **midrashic** interpretation of Joseph in Jewish tradition influenced his portrayal in Christian writings. According to Genesis, Joseph was born in the Mesopotamian town of Haran as the elder of **Rachel**'s two sons. Joseph's story is told in a tightly crafted narrative in Gen. 37–50. Scholars have long noted that the literary character of the Joseph novella is distinct from the rest of Genesis and Exodus because of its unified plot and cohesive narrative. A central dimension of the novella's theology is the absence of God, who remains in the background rather than as a theophanic presence as elsewhere in the book of Genesis.

Joseph has captured the imagination of many Jewish and Christian interpreters. In rabbinic tradition Joseph earned the sobriquet 'the righteous', in part because of exegetical elaboration on the episode with his master Potiphar's wife, known in extra-biblical literature as Zuleika. Already in the **Hellenistic** period his continence during the seduction attempt was a central feature of his reputation. 1 Macc. 2.53 reads: 'Joseph in the time of his distress kept the commandment, and became lord of Egypt.' One of the latest midrashic works, *Sefer ha-Yashar*, contains an elaborate reworking of the Joseph story. As James Kugel has demonstrated (*In Potiphar's House*, 1990), many of the midrashic elaborations of the story are rooted in a particular detail or peculiarity of the Hebrew text itself. In Gen. 39.14 Potiphar's wife says, 'See (plural imperative), my husband has brought a Hebrew among us to sport with us'. The anomalous first person plural is taken to suggest that she first made her false report to an assembly of women in her household. Such interpretive elements found their way into Christian depictions of the Joseph story. One example is the sequence of illustrations in the Eastern Christian illuminated Bible, the *Vienna Genesis*. Joseph is mentioned twice in the **New Testament**: Stephen's recapitulation of the story in Acts 7.9–15 mentions Joseph's God-given wisdom as the reason for his success in **Egypt**; Hebrews includes Joseph as an exemplar of faith along with other biblical heroes. The **Church Fathers**, such as Gregory of Nyssa (*c.*330–95) and Basil (*c.*330–79), shared the perspective of early Jewish interpretation by extolling Joseph's chastity and restraint. Others are more influenced by Hebrews' portrayal of Joseph as a man of constant faith. Christian interpreters take Joseph's exemplary status one step further and view Joseph as a type of **Christ**. Ambrose (*c.*339–97), for instance, finds **typological** parallels between events in the life of Joseph and **Jesus**, relating to their betrayal, suffering, endurance and ultimate triumph over life's circumstances.

JUDITH H. NEWMAN

Joseph II (1741–90)

Holy Roman Emperor (1765–90). Influenced by **Enlightenment** notions of 'benign despotism' (Sonnenfels) and Christian championing of Jewish civil **emancipation** (Dohm), Joseph influentially promoted partial emancipation of Jews, abolishing the Jewish poll tax and **yellow badge**. His Edict of Tolerance (January 1782), welcomed by *Haskalah* leaders, encouraged German-speaking schools, opening of universities to Jews and abolition of certain economic restrictions. Yet, because of prohibiting official use of Hebrew and Yiddish (1781), forcing Jews to adopt German names and decreeing military service (1787), abolishing rabbinical jurisdiction (1784), decreeing **expulsion** for offences against Christianity and limiting Jewish residence rights, Joseph's stringent reforms were perceived by traditionalists as *gezerah*, 'disaster'. They tended to become a dead letter under his successors, in part due to Jewish reluctance to assimilate.

MARGARET BREARLEY

Josephus (Flavius Josephus) (37/38–?100)

Jewish–Greek historian; Jerusalem priest, of Hasmonaean descent. A religious education under different authorities was followed by a prominent political role, first in an embassy to Rome and subsequently with the outbreak of revolt against Rome, when the Jerusalem leadership put him in military command of Galilee. Josephus accompanied the Roman forces during the suppression of the revolt, and records his own unsuccessful efforts to persuade the defenders of **Jerusalem** to surrender. After the war Josephus received Roman citizenship and economic support from the emperors Vespasian (*r.*69–79) and his son Titus (*r.*79–81). Of his subsequent activities we know only of his work as a writer of Jewish history. He is the author of four extant works, composed in Greek: (1) a seven-volume history of the Jewish War, from the Maccabaean Revolt to the Fall of Masada (composed before 79); (2) the *Jewish Antiquities*, in 20 books, comprising a history of the Jews from creation to the outbreak of the Jewish War in 66, designed to prove the antiquity of the Jews and to make Jewish history comprehensible in Greek terms (completed 93/94); (3) Josephus's *Life*, an apologetic defence of his activities in Galilee (appended to the *Antiquities*); (4) *Against Apion* (Book 2.52–113 in Latin) arguing for the greater antiquity and morality of Judaism vis-à-vis Greek culture, and refuting anti-Jewish detractors.

From an early period Josephus's writings were transmitted and translated in Christian circles, and played a fundamental role in arguments for the authenticity of Christian teaching and in the development of ideas about the relationship of Christianity to Judaism. The *Antiquities* provide rare testimony outside the **New Testament** to central figures in Christian history: **John the Baptist** (though Josephus does not connect him with Jesus); **James the brother of Jesus**; and, most crucially, **Jesus** himself. The description of Jesus as the **Messiah**, resurrected on the third day, is to be regarded as the work of an early Christian interpolator. Doubts about the authenticity of the 'Testimonium Flavianum' (as Josephus's testimony to Jesus became known) go back to the sixteenth century – partly reflecting the view among Christians and Jews that a Jew could not have written so positively about Jesus. Nevertheless, many Christians continued to revere Josephus as a Jew who proclaimed Christ. Josephus's interpretation (in the *Jewish War*) of the fall of Jerusalem as punishment for the sins of a few is developed in Christian **apologetics** to prove the depravity of the Jews, the fulfilment of Christ's prophecies of the destruction of the **Temple**, and the punishment of the Jewish people for the rejection of Christ.

In Christian scholarship and popular culture Josephus's writings functioned until the modern era as a trustworthy guide to the history, geography (for **pilgrims** and **crusaders**) and religious practices of the Jewish world. By contrast, his neglect in early Jewish tradition may be partly attributed to his positive evaluation among Christians. Medieval Hebrew versions of Josephus's works served Jewish scholars as a historical sourcebook for understanding **Rabbinic Judaism** and as the basis for arguments against Christian emendations of Josephus (in translation, they also proved influential among some Christians).

In modern scholarship, Jewish and Christian, Josephus is rightly viewed as the fundamental source for understanding the diverse Jewish world within which both Christianity and Rabbinic Judaism developed. His writings show no consciousness of Christianity as a movement separate from Judaism. *SARAH J. K. PEARCE*

Judah ha-Levi (*c*.1070/75–1141)

Poet, philosopher, apologist and physician. He was born in Tudela (**Spain**) and died in **Egypt** on his way to the **land of Israel**. Judah was one of the most important Hebrew poets and religious philosophers of the Middle Ages. His importance for Jewish–Christian relations lies in his treatise *Sefer ha-Kuzari*, which is one of the first comprehensive attempts at a systematic representation of Jewish teaching. Based on a fictitious dialogue between the king of the **Khazars** and a representative from Aristotelianism, Christianity, **Islam** and Judaism (the king realises that Christianity and Islam are both based on Judaism), the treatise allows ha-Levi to demonstrate the superiority of Judaism as a prophetically mediated religion over other religions, in particular Christianity and Islam, to which he nevertheless grants a place as *praeparatio messianica* because they contain authentic Jewish elements. His rejection of Christianity and Islam is based not on their faith claims but rather on the fact that, unlike Judaism, they cannot base their doctrines on an unequivocal historical **revelation** such as the one at Sinai witnessed by 600,000 people. He develops a theology of the *galut*, which sees in the exile not primarily a 'punishment', but rather a task ordained by God: as in the body no organ can exist without the heart, so also is Israel's existence among the nations vital to lead them to the way of revelation. *EDWARD KESSLER*

Judaisers *see* Judaising Christians

Judaising Christians

'Judaising Christians' is a term used in various periods of Church history that generally refers to Christians who have gone beyond an appreciation of Judaism to be actually observing some aspect of the Jewish cult or Jewish rituals. In various periods of history, especially in the **Reformation**, the term Judaiser was used polemically for those who were judged to be abandoning Christianity for Judaism.

Judaising among Christians has been seen as a problem for Christians since the very beginnings of the Church. The role of the Mosaic Law and other elements of Judaism served as an **identity** issue for the early Christians. In the **New Testament** there is evidence that the early Christian community was divided over the issue. For example, one possible reading of the **Sermon on the Mount** (Matt. 5.17–20) suggests that the early Christians continued to believe that some form of **Law** observance was necessary, while it appears that **Paul** of Tarsus was against any sort of Jewish observance for Gentile converts. Even the New Testament is not totally consistent in reporting what happened at the Jerusalem Council that was convoked to decide whether it was necessary for Gentile converts to be **circumcised** and practise certain Jewish **food** laws: Acts 15 indicates that Christians were not to eat blood or the meat of strangled animals, whereas Paul (Galatians) does not mention such prohibitions. In the early Christian period there is mention of Judaising when Christians continue to observe Jewish customs and rituals, such as **fasting** on Jewish days of fasting and going to the synagogue for various rituals. Charges of 'Judaising' among Christians are seen in the discussions of the establishment of the Lord's Day (Sunday) and the dating of **Easter** in relation to **Passover**. The sermons of John **Chrysostom** reveal that Christians were 'Judaising' well into the fourth century when, for example, he criticised his church members for attending Jewish **Sabbath** services. Certain groups (e.g. Ebionites) maintained their strong Jewish roots for which they were chastised as Judaisers by other Christians. Many of the anti-Jewish materials from the **early Church** stem from a desire to put a stop to Jewish influence and the allure that Jewish rituals and faith had for Christians.

From the early Church to the Middle Ages there appears much legislation to keep Christians separated from Jews. Underlying this legislation and other forms of **anti-Judaism** is the constant fear of the supposed Jewish threat. All these legal documents are evidence that there were actual positive social relationships between Jews and Christians throughout the Middle Ages. The papal bull *Cum nimis absurdum* of 1555 of Pope Paul IV (1555–9), which solidified the tendency toward total separation by demanding that all Jews in the Papal States be forced into a **ghetto**, was partly intended to eliminate Jewish influence within Christian society.

The sixteenth century also saw a limited return to a Judaising tendency within Christianity as small groups of Protestants, in the rediscovery of the Hebrew scriptures, felt compelled to return to Jewish Sabbath observance (for example, the **Sabbatarians**) and were thereby condemned by most Protestants. **Luther**'s study of scripture brought him a greater awareness of the Jewishness of **Jesus** (*That Jesus Christ was Born a Jew*, 1523) – by which he may have opened himself up to the charge of Judaising by his opponents – but this did not lead him to Judaise in any way; rather, it reinforced his condemnation of this Judaising tendency in Christianity (which he saw as promoting 'works righteousness') and raised his hopes for the **conversion** of Jews to a renewed and reformed Christian community. Luther's attack on Sabbatarians and Jews (*On the Jews and their Lies*, 1543) not only expressed Luther's rejection of this Judaising tendency, and his agony over the failure to convert Jews, but also his defence against what he thought was an attempt on the part of the Jewish community to seek the conversion of Christians to Judaism.

In the last hundred years, and especially since *Nostra Aetate* in 1965, there has been increasing understanding of and appreciation for the Hebrew scriptures and Judaism among Christians. Many Christians have rediscovered the roots of their faith in Judaism. The Roman Catholic Church and many Protestant denominations now teach the ongoing validity of the Jewish **covenant** with God as well as the significance of the Jewishness of Jesus for Christian self-understanding. These changes have taken place without lapsing into Christian Judaising. The serious study of Judaism as a living faith, and its relationship with Christianity, are viewed as an essential non-marginal part of Christian formation today, and Christians are now urged to learn about Jews and Judaism from the Jewish people themselves, to be in **dialogue** with Jews, and to be promoters of mutual respect and esteem. *STEVEN J. MCMICHAEL*

Judaism, Christian perspectives on

While the earliest Christian community originated within the Jewish world of Eretz Israel under Roman rule, its future lay in the external Gentile world of the **Roman Empire** and for a number of centuries in other parts of the East. **Paul**'s missionary work helped spread the Christian movement, while the Roman destruction of **Jerusalem** and its **Temple** (70 CE) and periodic persecution of Christian groups influenced the Gospels' downplaying of **Pilate**'s role in the execution of **Jesus**. Gradually the Church came to view Judaism as the preliminary and now outdated **covenant** people replaced by the newly covenanted people of the *ecclesia*, thus influencing the understanding of the finalised Gospels' **anti-Judaic** passages from the second century into the present. Yet many Christians in the early centuries were attracted to the synagogues and their services, especially at the High Holy Days and **Passover**. Consequently such Church leaders as **Chrysostom**, Gregory of Nyssa (*c.*332–398) and **Jerome** produced defamatory writings and sermons and insisted that Jews did not understand that the **Old Testament** was a prefiguring of Christ and the Church (cf. *Epistle of Barnabas*). In the second century Bishop **Melito of Sardis** embedded the first unambiguous accusation of **deicide** in **liturgy**. Later **Augustine**'s theology portrayed degraded Jews as children of **Cain** whose dispersion and woes were God's punishment; thus they served as witnesses to their own evil and to Christian truth. Even so, they were not to be harmed but preached to with love. This basic theology continued until the sixteenth century, though with many variations in the mercy or degradation shown to Jews.

Before the **New Testament** documents were assembled the Jewish scriptures remained the major sacred writings for both communities, even though they were understood differently by Christians as they sought to establish their own distinctive and legitimate relationship with Israel's God. As the Church spread outside Palestine it increasingly denied the significance of that land despite the presence of indigenous Christian communities. However, Emperor **Constantine** gave Christianity special status and supported the building of large churches on significant sites of Jesus' life and death. Monastic orders followed suit. From the end of the fourth century until the Muslim conquest in 638 Palestine was a Byzantine Christian country with Jerusalem as a patriarchal see. In the fifth and sixth centuries more than 500 churches built there attracted thousands of Christian **pilgrims**, and residents claimed that the grace of God was more abundant in Jerusalem than elsewhere. Increasingly the term 'holy land' was used, though rejected by such **Church Fathers** as **Origen** and **Eusebius** who insisted that the biblical passages regarding promise and restoration referred to the future Church. Jerome focused on combatting Jewish restoration expectations, and Emperor **Julian**'s late fourth-century plan to rebuild the Temple and restore Jerusalem to the Jews worried several generations of Christians even after his early death terminated the project.

In the Eastern **Byzantine Empire** the **Justinian Code** (535–53) removed many Jewish rights granted by the **Theodosian Code** (438). Severe restrictions on synagogue practices enabled local authorities to outlaw Judaism, close synagogues and enforce **baptisms**, despite some Church council opposition to such baptisms (e.g. Nicaea 787). In Western Europe Pope **Gregory the Great** insisted that the Jews' limited legal rights be respected and their internal affairs not be disturbed. Even so, he exhorted his bishops to work for Jewish conversions. While Gregory's policy of humanity and relative protection was the official Church position through the later Middle Ages, it was more often ignored than observed. In the early seventh century ranking churchmen of **Spain** and **France** attempted to counter the civil authorities' anti-Jewish measures which stripped Jews of their rights, put severe restrictions on their religious practices and finally ordered them to convert or leave. By contrast,

from 751 to 877 the Carolingian Christian emperors' reversal of this policy was fiercely opposed by vituperative Church leaders such as **Agobard of Lyons**. But after 879 Jews were once again viewed as Judases and left to the Church's harsh treatment without protection or legal redress. During the First Crusade (1096), despite some protection offered by local bishops, up to 10,000 Jews in eastern France and **Germany**'s Rhineland perished as they chose death over forced **conversion**. Popular hostility to Jews increased in the aftermath, and subsequent **Crusades** over several centuries led to more deaths, despite some countervailing Church efforts. From the twelfth century on a number of popes denounced accusations of Jewish ritual murder of Christian children, **host desecration** and causing the **Black Death**, all of which usually led to group executions. The religious orders of **Dominicans** (1216) and **Franciscans** (1209), founded during **Innocent III**'s papacy, became fiercely anti-Jewish in their activities. They initiated the **Inquisition**, burned thousands of **Talmuds** and other Jewish books (Paris, 1240), preached conversionist sermons at which Jewish attendance was compelled by order of Pope Nicholas III (1263), held enforced public **disputations** (Paris 1240, Barcelona 1263), accused Jews of **blood libel** (1246, 1475), instigated massacres in Navarre (1328), and agitated for the wearing of a distinctive badge which the Fourth **Lateran Council** (1215) authorised (*see* **yellow badge**). Converted Jews were separated from non-converts. By the fifteenth century Jews had been removed from most of Western Europe, with only small numbers remaining in some German principalities.

The early Protestant Reformers, particularly **Luther** and his colleagues, used vitriolic language in urging harsh repressions for Jews, though **Calvin** and **Calvinist** churches were less antagonistic and held a more positive view of Judaism's adherence to Old Testament teachings. This produced more **tolerance** for Jews in the **Netherlands** and later in the American colonies, where the proliferation of many denominations, the separation of **Church and state**, and emphasis on the rights of humankind helped create a more hospitable milieu for Jews. The reactionary Catholic Counter-Reformation became more radically anti-Jewish when Pope Paul IV (1555–9) overturned Augustine's theology by insisting that Jewish survival was tied to their converting.

He imposed on Rome's Jews a walled **ghetto** and many harsh restrictions. Further repressions continued within the Papal States until 1870. In the sixteenth century a small English Protestant **millenarian** movement emphasised Jewish restoration to the Land as an essential element in the Second Coming. This spread to Europe and in the eighteenth century to America. While the nineteenth century witnessed political **emancipation** of Jews, missionary activities to convert Jews multiplied in European **Protestantism** and some American Churches. During the years of the Third Reich, while most German Churches accepted the state's 'race, soil, and blood' stance, the Reformed Churches in the Netherlands began to question traditional theology about Judaism and the necessity of Jewish conversion. In 1947 Christians and Jews meeting at **Seelisberg**, Switzerland, called on the Churches to revise their thinking and **preaching** about Judaism and its people. Yet in 1948, while acknowledging and regretting the Churches' contribution to **antisemitism**, both the Evangelical Church in Germany and the **World Council of Churches** at Amsterdam still insisted Christians were obligated to include Jews in their evangelistic work since Israel's election had passed to the Church.

Deep-seated theological change came only two to three decades after the **Holocaust**. Consideration of the Church's 'teaching of contempt' for the Jewish people was put on the **Second Vatican Council**'s agenda by Pope **John XXIII** at the urging of Jules **Isaac** and resulted in *Nostra Aetate* (1965). Its insistence that 'Jews should not be presented as rejected . . . by God' was a significant turning point for the Catholic Church and has been followed by further documents. When Pope **John Paul II** led the Vatican to recognise the **State of Israel**, he overturned centuries of teaching that tied Jewish eviction from their land to their sinful rejection of Christ. Pope John Paul II repeatedly enhanced appreciation of Judaism and its people. Yet the Church as representative of God and Christ on earth is not seen as guilty of any error or wrong (*We Remember: A Reflection on the Shoah*, 1998). Since 1970 mainline Protestant Churches have adopted statements reflecting newly positive views of Judaism and rejecting **supersessionism**. The Evangelical Church of the Rhineland's 1980 document (*see* **Rhineland Synod**) was a major turning point in Europe with

its assertion that Jews were permanently elected as God's people, and that the Church was taken into this covenant with God through Jesus Christ the Jew. Hence the Church has no **mission** to the Jews. In 1982 the Texas Conference of Churches also stressed 'avoidance of any conversionary intent or proselytism' since Christ's coming did not dissolve the covenant between the Jewish people and God. The United Church of **Canada** also repudiates efforts to convert Jews since it insists God's covenant with Israel is irrevocable (2002). An ecumenical American scholars' group repeated these assertions, along with seeing contempt for Jews as dishonouring God, and affirming the redemptive power of God's enduring covenant with the Jewish people (*A Sacred Obligation*, 2002). The **Orthodox Church**, many of the Churches in the land of Israel, along with fundamentalist and biblically conservative Churches generally, have not participated in these theological revisions and many Churches still insist on the missionary obligation.

See also **Christianity, Jewish perspectives on**

ALICE L. ECKARDT

Judas Iscariot

Of the 12 **apostles** mentioned in the **New Testament**, none is more widely discussed or maligned than Judas, viewed by many Christians as the 'betrayer' of **Jesus**. Over the centuries Judas came to be seen as the archetypal Jew. As a result no other disciple of Jesus has figured so prominently in Jewish–Christian relations.

In New Testament sources Judas is always listed at the end of Jesus' 12 apostles. He carried the purse for the disciples (John 12.6) and handed Jesus over to the Temple authorities during **Passover**. When he became aware that Jesus had been transferred to **Pilate**, the Roman governor, he rushed back to the authorities to proclaim Jesus' innocence (Matt. 27.4). He then either committed suicide (Matt. 27.5) or died from a fall in the Valley of Gehinnom (Acts 1.18).

The Gospels' portrait of Judas has been complicated by centuries of mistranslation. In the original Greek only once is Judas referred to as a traitor (*prodotes*; see Luke 6.16). All other Gospel references are to 'informer' and 'handing over'. Recent scholarship has finally noted these errors, most significantly by changing *Bauer's Greek–English Lexicon* (2000 edn) reference for *paradidomi* from 'betray' to 'hand over'.

The earliest Gospel, Mark, speaks of handing Jesus over to the Chief Priests (Mark 14.1; 10.43), but Mark sees this as an act of God and foreseen by Jesus (Mark 14.17–21). By contrast, John says it occurred after Satan entered into Judas (John 13.21–7). Yet Matthew has Jesus and Judas warmly embracing at the time of Jesus' arrest, with Jesus saying, 'Friend, this is what you are here for' (Matt. 26.50). The earliest mention of the death of Jesus in **Paul** refers to 'the Jews' killing Jesus (1 Thess. 2.14–16); a later reference cites Jesus' arrest (1 Cor. 11.23) but makes no mention of Judas or his deed.

The **early Church** exempted Judas and Jews collectively from the salvific effect of Jesus' prayer from the cross, 'Father, forgive them for they do not know what they are doing' (Luke 23.34), on the ground that they knew what they were doing in condemning him (Flusser, '"Sie wissen nicht was sie tun"'). Early Jewish sources neither maligned nor praised Judas; they could not understand, however, why Christians condemned him (Bammel, 'Judas in der jüdischen überlieferung'). Despite the contention of some prominent Christians that Judas had a place in the divine plan (the second-century 'Gospel of Judas' and the writings of **Origen**), the later response of the Church contributed to centuries of persecution and violence by Christians against Jews. In visual **art**, especially paintings of the **Last Supper**, Judas was often depicted as the evil Jew with hook nose and money bag. The name of Judas, *yehudah* in Hebrew, signified infamy for Christians; in **Germany** parents were forbidden by law to name a child Judas. However, in recent years Judas has been viewed with more sympathy, as witness his depiction in the rock musical *Jesus Christ Superstar* and the Negro spiritual, 'When you get to heaven, rub poor lil' Judas' head'.

WILLIAM KLASSEN

Judgement *see* **Day of Judgement; immortality; salvation; soul**

Julian ('the Apostate') (331–63 CE)

(Flavius Claudius Julianus.) Emperor (361–3). **Constantine**'s nephew and a key figure in the evolution of both Christianity and Judaism and of relations between them, he might have stemmed the tide of Christian history and altered the direction of Jewish history, but in trying to use Judaism to thwart Christianity he did neither. Julian had studied Neoplatonism and later publicly and vituperatively abandoned Christianity as both inferior to **Hellenism** and Judaistic, while lacking the antiquity of Judaism's **Law**. As emperor he introduced fiscal changes to benefit pagans and Jews, reversed anti-Jewish laws, removed clergy privileges and disadvantaged Christian teachers of **rhetoric**. Capitalising on Christianity's internal rifts and its antipathy towards the Jews, Julian planned to revive both pagan worship (a Caesarea Philippi **inscription** bears witness to the fact that pagan temples were restored) and a traditional Temple-centred Judaism. Hillel II was Jewish **Patriarch** in Tiberias and **Cyril** bishop in **Jerusalem** when Julian met Jewish representatives in **Antioch**. In his address *To the Community of the Jews* (cf. also *Epistle* 204) he announced that Jerusalem would formally be accessible to the Jews again, the city and Temple rebuilt and **sacrifice** reinstituted (lacking sacrificial rites, Christianity would become anomalous). Thus the increasingly Christian architecture of Jerusalem would be challenged and **Jesus**' much-cited prophecy ('no stone left on another', Matt. 24.2) invalidated. Jewish sources of the fourth century are unforthcoming about relations with paganism and Christianity, but Christian sources tell of Jews' enthusiasm for Temple-building, and a Temple Mount inscription quoting Isa. 66.14 suggests Jewish hopefulness. However, establishing a Jerusalem High Priest would have demoted the Patriarch, and the sparseness of talmudic evidence may suggest Palestinian rabbis' hesitation.

Work began on the **Temple** in 353 CE. Reports are overlaid with legend – 'balls of fire' and an earthquake figure in them – but it is clear that building work ceased. Relations between Christians and Jews became fraught and accounts (of varying reliability) report mutual recriminations and violence in Julian's reign: Christian deaths and ransacked churches in Palestine, Syria and Egypt, and Jews massacred in Edessa; pagans suffered too. Within a few weeks of the events Julian, emperor for just 19 months, died of wounds in battle against the Persians. His war against them – in particular a desire to gain the support of Persian Jewry – may have been another factor motivating his plan for the Temple. 'Vicisti Galilaee' ('O Galilean thou hast conquered') were allegedly his deathbed words. After a lull Christian **anti-Judaism** flourished, ensuring that Jews' civil status was affected adversely, and while in the fourth century Judaism was to assert its own understanding of **covenant**, **Messiah**, land and scripture in material gathered for **midrash** and Palestinian **Talmud**, Christianity dominated the period culturally and politically.

Ephrem, John **Chrysostom**, Rufinus (*c.*345–410), Socrates Scholasticus (*c.*380–450), Sozomen (fifth century) and others wrote negatively about Julian and in some cases about Jews; the **Theodosian Code** preserved the relevant edicts. Julian's own writings (especially *Against the Galileans*) and Ammianus Marcellinus (*c.*330–395) are important sources for the history of events and of Jewish–Christian relations during this formative period. The funeral oration by Libanius of Antioch (314–*c.*393) (sophist and Julian's friend) contrasts well with *Against Julian* by bishop Gregory Nazianzen (*c.*329–*c.*390), formerly Julian's Athens classmate. *CHRISTINE TREVETT*

Justice

From its biblical roots, justice (*zedakah*) evokes **righteousness**, right order, harmony, vindication of the innocent, fairness and so on. The notion generates multiple connotations (juridical, ethical, religious) in both traditions, both of which rely on the Jewish scriptures for the insight that justice is an attribute of God who is supremely 'just' in his actions towards all and whose justice is compatible with the exercise of his mercy. Consequently, because God is just in his relations with humans, justice and right behaviour towards God and others are what are required of his people if they are to witness to the character of God. The Jewish tradition teaches Christians that **worship** of God requires moral and social expression in attending to the needs of the poor and the defenceless. A commitment to social and economic justice is required by the dynamic of both traditions (Deut. 18ff.; Jas 2.14).

Judaism and Christianity differ, of course, in how they understand the self-disclosure of the just God. Religiously, the key statement in the Christian tradition is made by **Paul**'s words to the Romans that God's justice is revealed in the gospel of Christ: it is 'the power of God for salvation to everyone who has faith' (Rom. 1.16–17). God's action in Christ is thus the decisive expression of God's will to bring all into union with Christ – in Paul's eyes this justice has been disclosed 'apart from Torah' (3.21), and contact with it is through faith. The reordering of human life in its fulfilled form ('justice') is through living out the consequences of being 'in

Christ'; ethical living flows from this (1 Cor. 6.15ff.). The Jewish interpretation of justice focuses on the divine imperatives communicated in **Torah** and intensified by the prophets: from its experience of God, Israel becomes a covenantal people in the land given by God, and serves God through Torah and *mizvot*. Because the truth of God cannot be thought conceptually, but can only be lived out in obedient witness, Jewish fidelity to Torah, as enacted in the ideal of the righteous man (*zaddik*), is declarative of the truth of God by inseparably linking the religious and the ethical **commandments**: 'Act with justice and do no wrong or violence to the alien, the orphan and the widow, or shed innocent blood in this place' (Jer. 22.3). From the perspective of this powerful association of religious and social imperatives – the moral life is true justice and the foundation of the common, social good under God – justice could be regarded as the source and the goal of what is intended by the religious practice of both traditions. *JOHN MCDADE*

Justification

A Christian doctrine articulating the grounds and process whereby sinful human beings are restored to righteousness before God. **Paul** focuses on it in his letters to the Romans and the Galatians, although elsewhere in the **New Testament** it garners little attention. **Augustine** developed the doctrine in opposition to Pelagianism, and Martin **Luther** set it at the centre of his **Reformation**, making it definitive of **Protestant** theology and central to modern Protestant–Catholic disputes. 'Jewish legalism', '**Judaising**' and 'works righteousness' are often projected as the counterpoint to a proper understanding of justification, so the **doctrine** has become a focus for both Christian **anti-Judaism** and Jewish–Christian **dialogue**.

Paul speaks of 'justification by faith apart from works of the law' (Rom. 3.28; Gal. 2.16), giving to subsequent theology an adversarial theme on which pervasive Christian anti-Judaism capitalised. If faith is opposed to works/**law** and Paul is arguing for Christian faith against legalistic Jewish alternatives, then Christianity at its core is found to be the corrective to Judaism. Indeed Luther indicts as a Judaiser everyone – papist, Muslim, iconoclast and more – who fails to acknowledge this central doctrine by which 'the church stands or falls'. Whether understood forensically as 'declaring' the sinner righteous or effectively as 'making' the sinner righteous, justification is centred in God's act on behalf of the sinner and contrasted to every form of **righteousness** centred in human effort, epitomised for centuries in the Christian caricature of self-righteous, Torah-observant Judaism.

Krister Stendahl (b. 1921) shifted the discussion of Paul's meaning from abstract theological theory about individual **sin** and **redemption** to the specific problem Paul addressed in Romans and Galatians: how Gentiles can be included in the people of God without requiring Torah-observance. This shift undercuts the long-standing, dominant presupposition that Paul presents Christianity and Judaism in opposition. Rather, Paul affirms that Jews are justified (Rom. 1.16f.; 3.29f.; Gal. 2.15f.) and asks how Gentiles also can be. He asserts that both Jews and Gentiles are justified by God's **grace**, through faith (Rom. 3.24), for which his biblical model is Gen. 15.6: '[Abraham] believed the Lord, and the Lord reckoned it to him as righteousness.' This reckoning and God's accompanying **covenant** are the ground of Jewish justification; the **Torah**, dated by Paul as 430 years later, does not annul it (Gal. 3.17). Whatever else the Torah avails – and Paul affirms it as 'holy and just and good' – Jews do not need it for justification; neither, then, do Gentiles. Thus it is finally God who is justified in choosing to include the Gentiles within the people of God (Rom. 3.4, 25f.), apart from the requirements of Torah.

The Pauline understanding of justification presupposes an essential human sinfulness (Rom. 2.12; 3.9–26) that lays the groundwork for the doctrine of **original sin** but that is unfamiliar in Judaism. Justification thus finds its closest parallel in Jewish thought not in the cognate semantic arena of righteousness (*zedek/zedakah*), but in the realm of election, or of that constitutive redemption that freed Israel from bondage in Egypt (*see* **Chosen People**).   *PETER A. PETTIT*

Justin Martyr (? *c.*110–167 CE)

Christian apologist and writer. Justin Martyr was born a 'pagan' in Samaria, converted to Christianity after exploring a variety of philosophies, and later moved to Rome as a Christian teacher, where he died a martyr. He is best known for his two Apologies (the second an appendix) addressed to Antoninus Pius (*c.*156) and for the *Dialogue with the Jew Trypho*, conventionally situated in Ephesus close to **Bar Kokhba**'s revolt but written later at Rome (155–60 CE). His *Apology* develops the idea of the

pre-existent **Logos**, and of those who lived according to the Logos as Christians before Christ, including Socrates, Heraclitus, **Abraham** and the three in the fiery furnace. He claims the scriptures for the Christians, citing the story of the translation of the **Septuagint** in defence of their authenticity. Purporting to describe a real encounter, the *Dialogue* develops many of the arguments that continued to be used in later *Adversus Judaeos* **literature**: that **Jesus** is already present as Lord in the theophanies of the scriptures; that his death and **resurrection**, and the coming to faith of the Gentiles, were prophesied therein; that the **Law** was given because of Israel's hardness of heart but is now replaced by faith in Jesus as the only means of **salvation**; that Christians are the heirs to all God's promises and thus are the True **Israel**. Justin also asserts Jewish hostility against and cursing of Christians. Much more detailed than similar subsequent literature, and betraying some knowledge of Jewish interpretation, the *Dialogue* probably does testify to genuine Jewish–Christian encounters, but remains the literary creation of its author.   *JUDITH LIEU*

Justinian I (483–565)

Eastern Roman emperor (527–565). Born at Tauresium in Illyricum, probably of Slavic parents, Justinian, named originally Uprauda, was adopted by the Emperor Justin I (518–527), taking a variant form of his name: he was educated at Constantinople, but spoke Greek with a foreign accent all his life. Becoming expert in ecclesiastical matters, he advised Justin on Church policy before becoming co-emperor with him for the last months of his reign. In 523 he married Theodora, she and Justinian effectively co-ruling the Empire from 527. Justinian was a staunch upholder of orthodox Christianity, expressing attitudes to the Jews principally in his legal activity. He systematically consolidated earlier Roman Law in five stages, simplifying and bringing order to unwieldy and sometimes contradictory legal texts. This process resulted in two digests of laws, the second of which (*Codex repetitae praelectionis* of 534) is known simply as the Digest or Code of Justinian. This huge enterprise of legal reform was undertaken by skilled jurists led by Tribonium (late fifth century to 546/7), who presided over the various commissions and was highly influential in determining the final forms of the texts. While his initial endeavours preserved earlier laws against the Jews (*see* **Theodosian**

Code), Justinian's law of 531 preventing heretics or Jews testifying in court against orthodox Christians pointed to a new severity. His Digest omitted all reference to Judaism as *religio licita*. Subsequent imperial ordinances (*Novellae*) introduced anti-Jewish rulings in *Novellae* 37, 45, 131 and 146, issued in 535, 537, 545 and 553 respectively. In all but the last of these Jews are listed with heretics (*Novellae* 37, 45, 131), **Samaritans** (*Novellae* 45 and 131) and pagans (*Novella* 131). *Novella* 37 legislated for Justinian's newly acquired North African province: Jews and heretics were forbidden to worship, and their buildings were to be taken over by the Church; an ancient synagogue at Borion was a victim of this law. *Novella* 45 refused exemption from minor public office to religious officials, Jews being permitted only the 'pains and penalties' of such duties and none of their rewards; Jews holding offices higher than orthodox Christians were to be fined. *Novella* 131 prohibited sale of Church property to Jews, and synagogues built on land shown to belong to the Church were to be confiscated. *Novella* 146 dealt exclusively with the Jews, forbidding the reading of the **Torah** in Hebrew, but permitting use of the **Septuagint** or **Aquila**'s version, while forbidding the *deuterōsis*, a term which certainly included in its meaning the **Mishnah** and probably the teachings of the rabbis in general, who were already described as *deuterōtai* in **Jerome**'s writings (e.g. *Comm. Isa.* 10.1; *Comm. Habac.* 2.9). This final *Novella* supports the opinion of some students that Justinian regarded Judaism as a **heresy** and himself as final judge in all matters religious in his realm. The effect of his laws during his reign was limited, for they were poorly enforced; but provision was made for bishops as well as provincial governors to enact them, opening the way for direct ecclesiastical interference in Jewish affairs.

C. T. R. HAYWARD

Justinian Code *see* **Justinian I**

KKKK

Kabbalah *see* **mysticism**

Kaddish *see* **Lord's Prayer**

Kant, Immanuel (1724–1804)

The paradigmatic philosopher of the modern era, Kant viewed Christianity, Judaism and their relation in terms broadly characteristic of the European **Enlightenment**. Kant held that true religion was moral religion, which could be wholly derived from human reason alone. He esteemed positive religions such as Christianity and Judaism only insofar as they could be made to serve the interests of moral religion. Measured by this standard, Kant regarded Christianity as moderately useful and Judaism as utterly without value. **Jesus**' moral teaching contains the essence of moral religion, while Judaism scarcely qualifies as a religion at all, since it elevates statutory law and national interest above the claims of morality. Early Christians appealed to Jewish scriptures out of temporary pedagogical need, but their subsequent decision permanently to retain Jewish elements was the original source of the Church's moral corruption. Christianity would better serve moral religion, Kant believed, if it were purified of its residual Jewishness. In sum, Kant espoused a typically modern form of Christian **anti-Judaism**, viewing Judaism not as a superseded instrument of God (the traditional view), but rather as a foreign religion essentially unconnected to Christianity and the universal moral values it represents.

Despite his negative view of Judaism, Kant has proven influential among both Christian and Jewish thinkers for over two centuries. Jews in particular have sought to appropriate Kant by detaching his moral philosophy from his judgements about the relative value of Judaism and Christianity. The German Jewish philosopher Hermann **Cohen**, for example, championed Kant's ethical interpretation of religion, but argued that Kant badly misunderstood the true nature of Judaism. Cohen's neo-Kantian ethical idealism in turn influenced a generation of liberal Protestant pastors and theologians. Whether in fact Kant's moral philosophy can be detached from his assessments of the revealed religions is an open question. What is certain is that his thought has been a fruitful medium of intellectual cross-fertilisation between Christians and Jews for generations, leaving its mark on figures such as Karl Barth (1886–1968), Martin **Buber**, Emmanuel Levinas (1906–95) and others.

R. KENDALL SOULEN

Karaites

Jewish sect (*Kara'im*; Hebrew: 'scripturalists' or 'propagandists') that originated as a current within Judaism opposed to Rabbanite Judaism. The Karaite doctrine is characterised by its denial of the Oral **Law** and recognition of the scriptures as the sole and direct source of religious **revelation**. According to the Karaites, their confession was founded by Anan ben David, a Jewish religious leader who was active in Iraq in the mid-eighth century CE. Karaism spread from Iraq to Iran, Egypt, the **land of Israel** and other countries, and for several centuries presented a serious challenge to Rabbanite Judaism, compelling it to redefine itself against Karaism.

In the thirteenth century the Karaites settled in the **Crimea**, and by the end of the fourteenth century in the Grand Duchy of Lithuania. The most important Karaite author in Lithuania was Isaak b. Abraham Troki (1533–94) who wrote an important **anti-Christian** treatise *Hizzuk Emuna*. In the late eighteenth century, after the partitions of **Poland** and Russian conquest of the Crimea, East European Karaites found themselves within the bounds of **Russia**. The restrictions imposed upon the Jews (including the **Pale of Settlement**) prompted East European Karaites to distance themselves from the Jews. The collector and archaeologist Abraham Firkowicz (1786–1874) invented the **myth** that the Karaites came to the Crimea in the sixth century BCE with Persian troops. In the second half of the nineteenth century Russian legislation separated the Karaites from the Jews and they were given full civil rights, equal with the Christian population. In the early twentieth century the idea became dominant that East European Karaites were descendants of the **Khazars**, which eventually saved them during the *Shoah*.

ARTEM FEDORTCHOUK

Khazars

A national group of Turkic type, the core of the Khazar Khaganate, a powerful state in Eastern Europe between the seventh and tenth centuries CE, the rulers of which were converted to Judaism in the eighth or ninth century. The semi-legendary circumstances of the Khazars' **conversion** are described in several Hebrew as well as Arabic sources. A common feature of all these versions is the so-called Choice of Faith, which included a religious debate between representatives of Judaism, Christianity and **Islam**. This legend most probably reflects the realpolitik of the region – throughout its history the Khazar Khaganate was sandwiched between the Christian **Byzantine Empire** and the Muslim Caliphate, so the Khazar rulers choose the third option to escape subordination to one of them. After the debate the king of the Khazars (Bulan, according to one version) accepted the religion of Israel. This story is reflected in **Judah ha-Levi**'s famous apologetic dialogue *Sefer ha-Kuzari*, and also possibly in the Russian Primary Chronicle's account of the conversion of the Russian Prince Vladimir (965–1015) to Christianity (where the prince chooses among several religious missions, including that of the Khazar Jews). The problem of Khazar influence (and the influence of Khazar Judaism) on the formation and early history of the Russian state, as well as of the Russian **Orthodox Church**, is much discussed. The question of the Khazar legacy was at the origin of several nineteenth- and twentieth-century **myths** which played an important part in Jewish–Christian relations (e.g. the theory of the Khazar origin of Ashkenazi Jewry, popularised by Arthur Koestler (1905–83); the theory of the Khazar origin of East European **Karaites**). In Soviet and post-Soviet **Russia** the history of the Khazars became a subject of many (generally **antisemitic**) speculations by 'patriotic' authors. *ARTEM FEDORTCHOUK*

Kibbutz

Voluntary, collective settlement in Israel. An offshoot of **Zionism**, the first kibbutzim were founded in the early twentieth century, by pioneers anticipating the establishment of a Jewish homeland. Momentum gathered during and after the **Holocaust**. Today, there are 267 kibbutzim, some of which are significant sites of Jewish–Christian encounter.

The kibbutz has socialist roots. Members have little private wealth or family life. Work is valued and mandatory for all who are able; elected committees and officers are responsible for community welfare. Most kibbutzim have agricultural roots, although many have diversified into industry. In recent years the movement has been shaken by the individualist desires of some members, the need to employ outside labour, and a tendency towards the re-emergence of traditional gender roles. Whereas many earlier kibbutzim were secular, and observed only those festivals that resonated with their experience of working the land, later ones are shaped by varied political and religious beliefs. Many kibbutzim rely on seasonal volunteer labour, often young Europeans, who inevitably become involved in what the **World Council of Churches** terms 'dialogue of life'. Some kibbutzim run guesthouses popular with Christian **pilgrims**. Religious kibbutz Lavi has responded to this by opening an education centre, aimed at developing Christian understanding of Judaism. Shared experience of living in **community** has also formed the basis of contacts between Jewish kibbutz members and those **Anabaptist** churches that eschew private property, such as the Hutterian Brethren. Inspired by the kibbutz model, **Nes Ammim** was established in **Israel** by Christians seeking to create an environment of interfaith cooperation.

MELANIE J. WRIGHT

Kiddush *see* **wine**
Kiddush ha-Shem

The literal meaning of *Kiddush ha-Shem* is the **sanctification** of God's name. It became associated more specifically with **martyrdom** during the period of Roman persecutions in Palestine in the early second century CE. Rabbi **Akiba** formulated an understanding of martyrdom as an act and public declaration of **love**, as yet another means of expressing love of God. Jewish ideas developed within a world that offered examples of Christian martyrdom, especially under Emperor Diocletian (*r*.284–305). Another formative stage was the period of massacres of Jews perpetrated by French and north German contingents which gathered to march westwards and form part of what came to be known as the First **Crusade**, inspired by the preaching of Pope Urban II in 1095. As they marched through the rich Rhineland cities, home to old and prosperous Jewish communities, these armed pilgrims began the work of **holy war** by attacking local Jews. Within their quarters, and even when protected by local prelates, many Jews chose to take their own lives and those of their children rather than endure forced **conversion** or be killed by the attackers. The Hebrew chronicle accounts that followed elaborated a powerful **myth** of self-immolation, attributing to the martyrs ritualised gestures (like the blessing of the knife, prayer) and extraordinary courage. These events marked Jews as well as Christians powerfully in following centuries. They offered Jews examples for emulation, which were commemorated in **liturgy**; and in Christians they aroused puzzlement, which sometimes led to further demonisation of Jews as unnatural child-killers. Although it affected only a small minority of Jews in any generation, *Kiddush ha-Shem* remained a powerful moral example, invigorated by ever new examples of people choosing to commit public, ritualised self-killing in the face of violence and the threat of forced **baptism**.　　*MIRI RUBIN*

Kimhi, David (1160–1235)

Jewish exegete, grammarian and controversialist of southern France (known as Radak from the acronym Rabbi David Kimhi). His father, Joseph (1105–1170), wrote *The Book of the Covenant*, a response to Christian polemical arguments. Most of David's references to Christianity are in his biblical **commentaries**, especially on **Psalms** (first printed in 1477). After reporting **Christological** interpretations of Pss 2, 21, 45, 72, 87 and 110, he provides answers to be used by Jews in rebuttal, most of which are based on the plain meaning of the correct biblical text. These passages were **censored** from printed editions beginning in the sixteenth century. Kimhi's writings reveal knowledge of the **Vulgate** and the **New Testament**.　　*MARC SAPERSTEIN*

Kingdom of God

A term describing God's sovereignty and rule over **Israel** and, by extension, over the nations. Without using the specific phrase, the **Old Testament** reg-ularly affirms God as King (Deut. 33.5; Judg. 8.23; Isa. 43.15). 1 Chron. 17.14 locates the reign of God specifically in the house of **David**, and the **Psalms** hail God as king over the nations (Pss 22.28; 47.2, 7–8). God's reign was both a present (Pss 93; 95) and a future reality related to judgement (Pss 96.13; 98.9). Prophetic hope looked to a future time when God's rule of **justice** and **peace** would be established forever (Jer. 30.9; Ezek. 37.24–26). During the post-exilic period Jews longed for the coming of God's rule to break the political power of their Hellenistic and Roman overlords. The phrase appears in the Qumran texts (1QM 6.6) (*see* **Dead Sea Scrolls**), and was known to **Philo** (*Spec.* 4.164) and used in the *Amidah* and *Kaddish* prayers. **Jesus** proclaimed that the kingdom of God had come near (Mark 1.15; Matt. 4.17). Matthew's Gospel prefers the circumlocution 'kingdom of heaven' and so avoids using the name of God. In the prayer that Jesus taught his disciples, the '**Lord's Prayer**', Christians pray for the coming of the kingdom of God (Matt. 6.10; Luke 11.2). Jesus' **parables** claim that the kingdom has already come, while for Luke the exorcism of **demons** points to God's powerful reign present in Jesus (Luke 11.20). Surprisingly, the Gospel of John makes little mention of the kingdom of God, but Christian apostolic **preaching** (e.g. Acts 8.12; 19.8) took up the proclamation of the kingdom where the apostles preached in the **Diaspora** synagogues. Christians and Jews today both continue to pray for God's kingdom of justice and peace in hope (*see* ***Dabru Emet***).　　*BARBARA E. BOWE*

Kingdom of priests

In the chapter preceding the list of the **Ten Commandments**, Israel is called a kingdom of priests (Exod. 19.6). This is usually understood as a cultic metaphor in a collective sense comprising every member of the entire people, since a specific **priesthood**, the Levites, was appointed without geographical inheritance in the Land (Josh. 13.33). After the fall of the second Temple, **Rabbinic Judaism** came to emphasise scholarship, not heredity, thereby relativising the role of the priests (who are actually lacking in the chain of religious authorities in *m. Avot* 1.1).

Two polemical understandings of this concept have hampered its interpretation: (1) Christians have at times referred to 1 Pet. 2.9 (which quotes Exod. 19.6; see also Rev. 1.6; 5.10) as a justification for the **replacement theology** paradigm (see also Heb. 7–9 where Christ is portrayed as a heavenly high priest who makes the old **covenant** void). (2) Refuting what he understood as a Roman Catholic abuse, **Luther** repeatedly referred to 1 Pet. 2.9 when arguing in favour of a universal priesthood of all Christian believers, stating that every Christian through **baptism** is consecrated as a priest. Since then, the heat of the debate has abated, and **Vatican II** (e.g. *Lumen Gentium* 10) and the *Catechism of the Catholic Church* (§§1546f.) seem to affirm Luther's proposals.

Present-day biblical scholarship tends to argue that Exod. 19.6 and 1 Pet. 2.9 are best understood as a collective vocation to **holiness**, rather than as an agenda of rights and privileges granted to an individual, or, even worse, as an instrument to depreciate the ordination of the priesthood of another religious community. *JESPER SVARTVIK*

Kittel, Gerhard (1888–1948)

Kittel is remembered by Bible scholars as editor of *The Theological Dictionary of the New Testament*. He was also a Nazi, joining the party (1933) and its Reich Institute for the History of the New Germany (1936). He openly supported Nazi policies against Jews (whom he believed to be morally and racially degenerate) with the possible exception of genocide. After the war Kittel was imprisoned. He defended his views, arguing that he was no more **antisemitic** than **Paul**, that his motivations were Christian and his methods scientific. Released in 1946, he briefly resumed his researches, but not his university career at Tübingen.

MELANIE J. WRIGHT

Klausner, Joseph (1874–1958)

Born near Vilna, his PhD at Heidelberg formed the basis for *The Messianic Idea in Israel* (1903–4), which emphasised the centrality of Messianism to Judaism (*see* **Messianic movements**). After moving to Palestine in 1917, as the first Professor of Hebrew Literature at the Hebrew University he reflected on the origins of Christianity in books on **Jesus** (1922) and **Paul** (1939). An ardent **Zionist**, he saw Christianity as partaking of Jewish Messianism, and Jesus and Paul as figures in the history of his country. *JAMES K. AITKEN*

Kolbe, Maximilian (1894–1941)

Polish **Franciscan** who perished in **Auschwitz**. During the 1920s Kolbe built a friary near Warsaw, called the City of Mary Immaculate (Niepokalanów), which became Poland's main Catholic publishing house. Kolbe knew little about Jews and Judaism, although he appears to have believed in the veracity of the ***Protocols of the Elders of Zion*** and as a missionary expressed hope for the **conversion** of the Jewish people. He was involved in hiding 2,000 Jews in Niepokalanów, arrested in January 1941 and transported to Auschwitz. When a prisoner escaped, 10 inmates were ordered into the starvation bunker, and Kolbe took the place of Franciszek Gajowniczek, because he had a wife and children. Two weeks later, only Kolbe and three others were still alive; they were killed by an injection of carbolic acid. He was beatified by Pope **Paul VI** and canonised by Pope **John Paul II**.

STEPHEN NICHOLLS

Kristallnacht *see* **pogroms**

LLLL

Lamb of God *see* **Paschal lamb**

Lambeth Conference 1988

Once each decade the Archbishop of Canterbury invites the bishops of the Anglican communion to conference at Lambeth in London. The 1988 assembly was the first to consider Jewish–Christian relations in depth.

The Bishop of Oxford (Richard Harries (b. 1936)) and Orthodox Jewish scholar Norman Solomon (b. 1933) led a working group which drafted a text for debate at the meeting. After much discussion it was rewritten, largely in response to the insistence of Jerusalem Bishop Samir Kafity (b. 1933) that the **dialogue** must include **Islam**. The final text, *Jews, Christians and Muslims: The Way of Dialogue*, was commended by the bishops and appeared as an appendix to the conference report. It is a landmark document in Anglican–Jewish relations.

Three sections in the document explore 'The Way of Understanding', 'The Way of Affirmation' and 'The Way of Sharing'. Judaism is affirmed as a living religion and as 'a people and a civilisation'. Scholarly re-evaluation of difficult **New Testament** texts is commended and the history of Christian **anti-Judaism** acknowledged. The document rejects **supersessionism** and advocates common action on matters of social justice; it was one of the first such statements to proclaim 'common mission'. The most contested sections discuss Christian **mission** to Jews. Whilst proselytism is rejected, a range of positions is recognised. Anglicans still disagree about what constitutes appropriate and inappropriate sharing of their faith with Jews.

Other sessions at Lambeth also touched on interfaith matters, especially in relation to the **land of Israel** (resolution 24), and since 1988 Anglicans have continued to debate related areas of faith and practice, including recently the **Church of England**'s attitude towards Jewish believers in **Jesus**.

See also **Anglicanism**   *MELANIE J. WRIGHT*

Land of Israel *see* **Israel, land and State of**

Langton, Stephen (*c*.1150–1228)

Archbishop of Canterbury (1207–28). Langton was one of the leading figures of the **Lateran Council (IV)** of 1215 and promoted its regulations in England, including those about Jews – especially the compulsory wearing of the badge (*see* **yellow badge**) introduced in 1218 and 1222, restrictions on intercourse of Jews and Christians, and a ban on new synagogues. However, he also opposed anti-Jewish riots by English **crusaders**. As a longstanding professor at the University of Paris, he stood in the tradition of the **Christian Hebraists**. He is also believed to be responsible for the division of the **Bible** into today's chapters, a custom the eventual adoption of which into Jewish Bibles attests to the mutual influence of Jewish and Christian biblical scholarship.   *PETR FRYŠ*

Last Supper

The common designation for the last meal **Jesus** shared with his disciples before his death in **Jerusalem** during the festival time of **Passover**. Almost every aspect of this meal has been matter for scholarly debate: whether it was indeed a Passover meal, who attended, what if any **eschatological** overtones were present, what words and actions did Jesus use, and what are the salvific and theological implications of this event for Christians? This final meal should be seen in light of the patterns of Jewish festive meals in general and the meal traditions at Qumran, and in light of the many table fellowship meals Jesus shared with others, including outcasts and sinners, during his lifetime. In these meals the participants would share common food as a sign of friendship. The Gospels differ in their description of who gathered with Jesus. Mark and Matthew note that two 'disciples' made the preparations for the supper and then Jesus came with the Twelve, implying that the group consisted of more than just the Twelve. Luke refers to both 'disciples' and 'apostles' at different points, and

John speaks only of disciples. Those gathered at the supper, then, were not designated by name nor limited only to the Twelve. The Gospels differ also in the exact chronology of the meal. The Synoptics identify the meal as a Passover meal (Mark 14.12–16 and parallels) whereas John locates the meal on the Preparation Day for Passover (John 19.14, 31, 36). Attempts to explain these differences by appealing to two different **calendars** in use at the time have not proved convincing. But despite this difference, all three Gospels interpret the meal within a Passover context, a fact supported also by **Paul** (1 Cor. 5.7). In addition, Paul's first letter to Corinth (1 Cor. 11.26) points to the eschatological dimension of the supper which 'proclaim[ed] the death of the Lord until he comes'. Two different traditions convey the actual words and actions of Jesus at the meal, one followed by Mark and Matthew, the other in Paul and Luke. Mark's account of Jesus' words over the **bread**, 'took, *blessed*, broke, gave', are closer to the familiar Hebrew *barak* than to Paul and Luke's reference to Jesus 'giving thanks'. But the Pauline/Lukan words over the cup 'this cup is the new covenant in my blood' preserve the oldest tradition of the cup **blessing**. In both, however, sacrificial language and the emphasis on the bread and cup 'given for you' signal the meal's atoning and salvific significance for Christians and explain why they continue to celebrate Jesus' action in eucharistic ritual meals. The Passover context for Jesus' words and actions at the supper before he died has generated in recent years a resurgence of interest among Christians in the meaning and significance of the Passover meal. It has prompted many synagogue communities to invite Christian guests to their Passover seder meals and to provide explanation and greater understanding of this shared meal tradition.

See also **eucharist**   BARBARA E. BOWE

Lateran Council (IV)

General Council of the Church, summoned by **Innocent III**, opened November 1215, attended by some 400 bishops, 800 abbots and priors, and lay representatives of various European nations. In addition to addressing significant political and doctrinal issues (including transubstantiation and confession), several decrees attempt to regulate the position of the Jews in Christendom. Some reaffirmed ancient rules. It was prohibited to appoint a Jew to a position of authority over Christians. Converts from Judaism must be constrained from observing any of the former Jewish practices. Jews were ordered to refrain from public appearance during the days before **Easter**, especially on Good Friday (a ruling said to prevent mockery of Christian sensibilities, but also perhaps partly for the Jews' own protection). A more current issue was **usury**: Christians must boycott Jews who extort 'heavy and unrestrained interest'; kings should act to restrain Jews in this area, and force them to remit interest to Christians who set out on a **Crusade**. Most influential was the decree compelling Jews (and Muslims living under Christian rule) to wear distinctive, recognisable **dress**, in order to avoid 'prohibited intercourse' (sexual relations, perhaps excessive socialising) based on mistaken **identity**. The context was a society in which it was assumed that the legally defined category to which every individual belonged (e.g. nobles, serfs, clergy and members of various religious orders) should be identifiable by dress. Furthermore, the decree appeals to the biblical precept that Jews should wear distinctive fringes on their garments (Num. 15.38). Nevertheless, it was generally perceived by Jews as mandating a 'badge of shame', and in this sense a similar ordinance requiring a **yellow badge** was imposed by the Nazis in occupied Poland, Germany itself and elsewhere.   MARC SAPERSTEIN

Latin

Study of the use of Latin, both by Christians and to a lesser extent by Jews, provides evidence of the influence of Jewish **biblical interpretation** on early Christian **exegesis**. Familiarity with Latin in the **land of Israel** is attested by papyri from Muraba'at, Latin **inscriptions** in the **Temple** warning Gentiles not to trespass beyond their court, and the number of Latin loan words in the **Mishnah**. At **Rome**, however, only about a quarter of Jewish funerary inscriptions in the catacombs (ranging from first century BCE to early fourth century CE) are in Latin, **Greek** being preferred. Likewise, Roman Christians used Greek until the time of Pope Victor I (189–198 CE), when the use of the Old Latin (*Vetus Latina*) versions of the Bible seem established in Roman North Africa and Southern Gaul. These probably represent a number of different Christian translations of the **Septuagint**, some of which indicate knowledge of **Hebrew** and Jewish exegetical tradition. The rabbis of Jerome's day regarded Latin as a language fit for war (*y. Megillah* 1.11); and it was evidently little esteemed (*b. Gittin* 80a). Remarkable among

Jewish medieval scholars for his knowledge of Latin was the poet Immanuel ben Solomon ben Jekuthiel of Rome (c.1261–1328): he was evidently familiar with and admired the work of Dante (1265–1321), and some of his own Hebrew poetry was translated into Latin. But the **Renaissance** saw Jewish scholars generally renew interest in Latin, among them Azariah dei Rossi (c.1511–c.1578), whose *Me'or Einayim* makes extensive use of the Latin Fathers.

See also **Bible translations, ancient**; **disputation**

C. T. R. HAYWARD

Latter-Day Saints

There are several hundred Churches (popularly (mis)named Mormon) which trace their origins to Joseph Smith, Jr's (1806–44) Christian revivalist ministry. The largest of these is the Church of Jesus Christ of the Latter-Day Saints (LDS). LDS thought radicalises traditional Christian claims to be the **people Israel**; adherents see themselves as Jews descended from Ephraim, and Jews as descendants of Judah. Accordingly, whilst the LDS is not immune from **antisemitism**, members feel themselves to be specially related to the Jewish people and the **State of Israel**. Some smaller Saints' churches have adopted **Judaising** practices, including **dietary laws** and **Sabbath** observance. The LDS also holds that Native Americans are descendants of the lost tribes of Israel, and that the true **Eden** and **Zion** are located in the **United States**. These ideas are found in the *Book of Mormon*, which Smith is believed to have recovered and translated (1827–30), and *The Pearl of Great Price* (a later collection of visions). The LDS believes that these texts contain a true account of the ancient history of God's people. (Some liberal Saints view *The Book of Mormon* as **myth**.) For this reason, most Christians do not share the LDS definition of itself as a Christian Church. This has limited LDS participation in organised ecumenical and interfaith activities. A further source of tension in recent years has been the extension of the LDS ritual of **baptism** of the dead (derived from 1 Cor. 15.29) to **Holocaust** victims. In 1995, following extensive **dialogue** with Jews offended by this practice, the LDS formally ended the posthumous baptism of Jews who were not direct ancestors of Mormons. However, the controversy resurfaced in 2002 and 2004. For practical and doctrinal reasons, it is unlikely that the Church will guarantee that no future baptisms of deceased Jews will occur, or the names of Holocaust victims will be removed from its registers.

MELANIE J. WRIGHT

Law

The place of law in religion has been the focus of considerable attention in Jewish–Christian relations, much of it generated by failure among Christians to appreciate the true meaning of the Hebrew term 'Torah'. Though 'law' is used in most English Bibles to translate **Torah**, the word reflects the ancient Greek (**Septuagint**) and Latin (**Vulgate**) versions of scripture, which have *nomos* and *lex* respectively. This translation has given rise to the misapprehension that Judaism is based entirely on legalism, but modern scholarship has helped to clarify the true significance of the original **Hebrew**. While the Torah does contain **commandments** and precepts that are binding on Jews, it has another, equally important characteristic, namely 'instruction' or 'revelation'. It has within it elements of both *halakhah* (ordinance) and *aggadah* (story).

Though many Christians find it hard to believe that Jews are able to embrace willingly the scrupulous observance of a host of commandments or *mizvot*, the rabbis regard the *halakhah* not as restriction but as liberation, not as a demand but as a gift. God has decreed the commandments and expects them to be kept, but humans have been given the intellectual freedom to interpret and apply them. In rabbinic thought there is much emphasis on human initiative. The ordinances, as interpreted by rabbinic authorities, enable the faithful to live as God's people.

Another issue that has polarised Jewish and Christian exegetes is the continuing validity of the legal parts of the Torah. Is the *halakhah* still valid as a source of divine **revelation**, or has it been abolished through the coming of Christ? Traditionally, the Christian Church has taken a **supersessionist** standpoint, claiming that God rejected his **covenant** with the old **Israel**, which was based on law, in favour of that made with the new Israel (the Church) based on **grace** through faith. Judaism became a fossilised religion. Such thinking is characteristic of the early **Church Fathers** and the Protestant Reformers. But in recent years revisionist theologians have radically reassessed this view, claiming that it stems from a misunderstanding of the teachings of Jesus and Paul. Properly understood, the writings of the **New Testament** do not nullify the Torah. Two brief examples must suffice.

According to Matt. 5.17, **Jesus** claims that he has not come to abolish the Torah but to complete it. He said nothing that led his disciples to disregard it. E. P. Sanders (b. 1937) finds only one example of Jesus transgressing the biblical ordinances: the demand made on the man whose father had died (Matt. 8.22). However, 'there is clear evidence that he did not consider the Mosaic dispensation to be final or absolutely binding' (*Jesus and Judaism*, 268). **Paul** had only one Greek word (*nomos* = law) at his disposal when he discussed the Torah. He therefore could not differentiate between its aggadic and its halakhic content. When he calls for freedom from the Law he is not condemning the Torah as a whole, as Christian commentators once thought. For in the sense of 'instruction' the Torah teaches **justification** by faith, witness the case of **Abraham** in Gen. 15.6. What Paul objects to are ritual observances, namely **circumcision**, **Sabbath** observance, **dietary laws** and purity regulations. Such precepts are not binding on the Christian (see, e.g., Galatians), but the Torah, in the sense of divine revelation, has lost none of its significance.

See also **antinomianism**   *GARETH LLOYD JONES*

Leaders of the Jews, externally appointed

Jews in the Middle Ages sought to govern themselves internally. However, from the earliest period, they had to balance an internally selected leadership against that imposed from outside. Through the eleventh century, especially in the Rhineland, the two were the same, easing the inherent tensions. Afterward, and in other locations, this was not so. In the Rhineland the externally chosen, or at least confirmed, Jews' Bishop (*episcopus iudaeorum*), who was also a person of the Jews' own choosing, first appeared after the demise of the Carolingian Empire, where a Christian *magister* had once been loosely responsible for Jewish affairs. The title was interchangeable with *archisynagogus*, the ancient Jewish communal head. Its possessor was invariably the same person called the *parnas* (the provider) in Hebrew sources, who usually belonged to one of the leading rabbinical families like the Kalonymides. Charters, like that of Bishop Rudiger of Speyer in 1084, prescribed that 'Their (Jewish) *archisynagogus* shall judge in any dispute which occurs among them and against them, just like the city tribune among the towns-people', and Jews may have had to litigate before him. Renewing Rudiger's text six years later, Emperor **Henry IV** said, 'If it should happen that one of them, a perfidious person, should wish to hide the truth of something done among them, the man who governs the synagogue for the bishop shall make this person confess the truth according to their law.' This power was new. By contrast, ninth-century charters of Louis the Pious (*r*.814–840) say, 'If any of them, Christian or Jews, should wish to hide the truth, the (Christian) count of that place shall make each of them reveal it, through appropriate investigation and according to his law'.

Nevertheless, the *episcopus* was a tribune, a regent who governed the synagogue *for* the bishop and at his behest; appeals were heard by the bishop himself, so that dissatisfied Jews could circumvent the *episcopus*'s decisions, and Jewish leaders were constantly forced to seek new means to prevent Jews from looking for redress to outside sources. Put otherwise, the *episcopus* was in danger of becoming more and more an intermediary and administrator: he served first the emperor, count or bishop who conferred power upon him; halakhic primacy, although ascribed to him internally, was secondary. The initiatives of the office might also be circumscribed. Internally, *episcopi* like Rabbi Solomon b. Samson, mentioned in Henry IV's charter of 1090 to the Jews of Worms, had to share headship with representatives of the five leading local rabbinic families. Externally, the *episcopus-archisynagogus* evolved (over the centuries) into either a governmentally appointed 'state rabbi' or a secular head chosen by wealthy non-rabbinic Jewish factions. And just as the unity of internal and externally appointed leadership was normally beneficial in the earlier Middle Ages, by contrast, the dichotomous leadership of the later period frequently created tensions. Moreover, the *episcopus-archisynagogus*, or his equal, eventually became an agent of Jewish constitutional isolation, enhancing the Jews' juridical uniqueness, a situation that had grown ever clearer since the late eleventh century, when the Jews' legal and 'constitutional' status began to break loose from its moorings and Jews became ever more exposed to the whim of lay rulers who also were committed, of their own volition, to applying restrictive Church canons.

Parallel to the Rhenish *episcopus* was the English Presbyter of the Jews, the Jews' Priest. Five such Presbyters were royally appointed for 'life' between 1199 and 1290. The Presbyter functioned as head of all English Jews. Thirteenth-century kings used the Presbyters as their chief collectors of abusive taxes. Presbyters were directly answerable to a non-Jewish royal official, the *Dominicus Iudaei*, and eventually to a 'Justiciar of the Jews'. One may liken the Presbyter to the later fourteenth-century French 'chief rabbis' (appointed only between 1360–94, the final **expulsion**). The Presbyter had lesser powers than did his peers, the autocratic, and often lay, *Rab de la Corte* in Castile (1255–1492) or the *Dayyan Kelali* in Aragonese Sicily (1386–1447, suppressed by internal Jewish demand). The *Imperial Hochmeister*, or *Landesrabbiner*, began to function in 1407. A true rabbi, he was consistently opposed by yeshiva-heads, and forced to operate against the background of the weak power structures of the empire itself. *KENNETH STOW*

Leah

Biblical figure, elder sister of **Rachel**, first wife of patriarch **Jacob**. The reconsideration of Leah and other female biblical characters has been a fruitful source of collaboration among Jewish and Christian **feminist** biblical scholars and serves to counterbalance some of the anti-Jewish depictions of Leah in patristic writings and Christian **iconography**.

Jacob was tricked into marrying Leah after promising to work for Laban for seven years for the hand of Rachel, the woman he preferred. Together, Rachel, Leah and their two servants, Bilhah and Zilpah, produced 12 sons, the eponymous ancestors of the 12 tribes of Israel. Although the older sister Leah is portrayed as the less attractive and less beloved of her husband, her descendants nonetheless included the dynastic house of priests through her son Levi and the dynastic Davidic royal house through Judah. Jewish and Christian commentators focus on various dimensions of Leah's story. Jewish commentators often focused on the physical description of Leah in Gen. 29.17. Leah is not mentioned in the **New Testament**, but in patristic and medieval writings she is considered a type of the active life as against Rachel's contemplative life (e.g. **Augustine**, *Contra Faustum*), analogous to the depiction of **Mary** and Martha in the New Testament. Other Christian interpretations reflect **supersessionism**: with her weak eyes, Leah

is negatively portrayed as a type of the synagogue (e.g. Commodian, *Instructiones* 39), and the contrasting depiction of Leah and Rachel is echoed in the ***Ecclesia/Synagoga*** figures.

JUDITH H. NEWMAN

Lectionary

A lectionary is a collection of biblical readings for proclamation at **liturgy**. Christians borrowed both the concept of the lectionary and its cyclic arrangement of readings from Jewish synagogue practice. **Sabbath** readings were ordinarily taken from the **Pentateuch** and the Prophets, as can be seen in Jesus' visit to the synagogue at Capernaum (Luke 4.16–21), followed by **preaching**, such as Paul's in the synagogue at Pisidia (Acts 13.14–16).

By the time of **Justin Martyr**'s *Apologia 1* 67 (*c*.155), Christians had begun to combine the letters of **Paul** and the Apostles with the traditional Jewish sources, often extending the length of the liturgy. By the second half of the fourth century, the *Apostolic Constitutions* 8, 5, 11 required a reading of the **Law**, the Prophets and the letters, Acts and Gospels. Psalmody was eventually placed between readings as a way of meditating upon and responding to the reading just proclaimed; this practice was in place at least by the time of **Tertullian** (*c*.225).

However, in an important development away from Jewish practice, Christian lectionaries eventually paired readings of the **Old Testament** with those of the New, thereby interpreting the Hebrew scriptures typologically (*see* **typology**). This trend would mark another definitive liturgical break between the two communities. While many Jewish scholars consider the **New Testament** as a kind of **midrash** or meditative reading of the Hebrew scriptures which produces meanings beyond the literal one, Christian lectionary schemes have always implied that the full meaning of the law and the prophets is found in the reading given to them by **Jesus**. The most recent reform of Catholic and Protestant lectionaries maintains this lectionary scheme. *DENNIS D. MCMANUS*

Leon of Modena (1571–1648)

Venetian Jewish scholar. As orator, rabbi and poet, Leon was a profound interpreter of Judaism to the Christian world, where he was in demand as a consultant on Jewish learning. Analogically to the anti-papal struggle of the Republic of Venice, Leon challenged rabbinic authority, attacking the

Talmud and the whole legal canon; he remained, however, a respected member of the rabbinate. Usually attributed to him, *Kol Sakhal* (first published in 1852) argues against traditionalism. Other decisive **polemics** include *Ari Nohem* (1840), an attack upon the reliability of the Kabbalah (*see* **mysticism**), which he blames for its alleged compatibility with Christian Trinitarianism. He also argues in *Magen ve-Herev* against what he sees as the scriptural and dogmatic inconsistencies of Christian teaching.   *PETR FRYŠ*

Leontius of Neapolis (mid-seventh century)

Churchman, hagiographer and controversialist. Perhaps the most important witness to the spirit of open religious competition between Jews, Christians of all stripes and others (e.g. **Samaritans** and Manichees) that occurred after the early Islamic conquests in the Middle East, he was bishop of Neapolis (near modern Limassol) in Cyprus, and possibly attended the Lateran Synod of 649 that condemned the doctrine that Christ had only one (divine) will (monothelitism); he is mainly known as a hagiographer. Fragments (preserved in collections of citations by defenders of icon-veneration in the next century) survive of an *Address to the Jews*, in which Leontius responds to Jewish accusations that Christian veneration of icons, **relics** and the **cross** amount to **idolatry**, and also to criticisms of Christian Trinitarianism (*see* **Trinity**). His response takes such accusations seriously and responds on the basis of passages from the **Torah**. It is not clear from the fragments whether Leontius was responding to written texts or to Jews he had himself encountered, though there is other evidence of actual **disputations** between Christians and Jews in this period.   *ANDREW LOUTH*

Lessing, Gotthold Ephraim (1729–81)

Dramatist, critic, philosopher and a leading figure of the **Enlightenment** who advocated tolerance, spiritual freedom and a cosmopolitan attitude of mind towards all social, religious and ethnic groups, including Jews. This revolutionary viewpoint is expressed in his early play *The Jews* (1749), which focuses on Jews' marginal position in society. The theme of universal **tolerance** comes to fruition in his late play *Nathan the Wise* (1779), the title character being based on his close friend and fellow philosopher Moses **Mendelssohn**, which deals with Christianity, Judaism and **Islam**. All are given equal

status, and the conduct of the individual is seen as superseding religious dogma.

STEPHEN NICHOLLS

Leuenberg Church Fellowship

The Leuenberg Church Fellowship consists of the Reformation Churches in Europe. In 2001 it published a document entitled *Church and Israel*, which marks the first joint theological contribution on Judaism of the Reformation Churches in Europe since the Reformation and demonstrates that, while its effects remain unclear, a fundamental shift has occurred in recent Christian theological thinking about Judaism. The document discusses the relationship between the Churches and the Jewish people and stresses the importance of education and **dialogue**. It was approved by the Leuenberg Church Fellowship General Assembly, which requested the Churches to 'receive the results of the doctrinal conversations and to take them into account in Christian/Jewish dialogue and in their own work on the issue'.

Church and Israel illustrates that the historical change in attitudes towards Judaism within **Roman Catholicism** has also taken place in many of the **Protestant** Churches. The document demonstrates a radical transformation, including acknowledgement of the Christian contribution to **antisemitism** and 'the failures of the churches' which were a result of 'wrong interpretations of texts from the Bible and the terrible theological errors to which they led'. It stresses the 'indissoluble bond' between God and the Jewish people and states that Christian dialogue with Judaism is 'an indispensable necessity'. *Church and Israel* calls for Christian support of both **Israel** and the Palestinian people and states that the Churches should counteract any Christian tendencies to denigrate the **Zionist** movement. The document concludes with a series of recommendations on pursuing Jewish–Christian dialogue in the parishes and educating parishioners about the right relationship with Judaism. Educational programmes should include studies of Jewish interpretation of scripture and exchange programmes with Jewish educational institutes.   *EDWARD KESSLER*

Liberal Judaism *see* Progressive Judaism
Liberalism

The emergence of liberalism as a social and political ideology through the English Revolution of the

1640s and the American and French Revolutions in the eighteenth century had a considerable impact on Jewish–Christian relations. Christianity, **Roman Catholicism** in particular, came to view liberal ideology as representing a fundamental threat to its dominance over public life and morals in Europe, especially in countries with substantial Catholic populations such as Germany, France, Poland and Austria. In Italy liberalism was perceived by the Vatican as undermining the very existence of the Papal States as a political entity. As a result popes took a strong stand against its 'pernicious' influence, labelling liberalism's fundamental notions of freedom of conscience and human rights as totally unacceptable. In an 1832 encyclical Pope Gregory XVI denounced supporters of liberalism, and in the 1864 'Syllabus of Errors' Pope **Pius IX** condemned liberalism as an 'absurd principle', especially its notion that the state should treat all religions in equal fashion. In North America liberalism advocated the separation of **Church and state**, but did not generally assume the anti-religious stance it took on in Europe. Jews often took a more positive view of liberalism as a gateway to enhanced equality in terms of basic citizenship in those areas such as the Papal States where they had been denied such equality. The significant embrace of liberalism within the European Jewish community led many in the Christian Churches to identify Jews with this despised liberal tradition. As a result, in the latter part of the nineteenth and the first half of the twentieth century Jewish involvement with liberalism and, as it became known, freemasonry, constituted a potent new source of **antisemitism**. Freemasonry, which originated in eighteenth-century English Deism, became associated with liberalism in the writings of such anti-liberal figures as Edouard Drumont (1844–1917) and Gougenot de Mousseaux (1805–76), who spoke of a supposed 'Judaeo-Masonic plot' whereby Jews and their secularist companions sought to destroy Christian hegemony in Europe. This new form of antisemitism became especially prominent in France and Poland, and played a significant role in shaping Christian attitudes towards Jews and Judaism during the **Holocaust**, coming to rival the older Christian expression of antisemitism rooted in interpretations of the Gospels and the teachings of the **Church Fathers**, with which it

retained some connections. It also found considerable support in Latin America. It had a presence in North America but less political influence than in Europe. **Vatican II**'s Declaration on Religious Liberty severely undercut the basis for an antisemitism based on opposition to liberalism, even though it still surfaces from time to time within the Churches.

JOHN T. PAWLIKOWSKI

Liberation theology

Liberation theology combines the insights of Marxist social criticism with (primarily) Christian belief and practice and argues that Christians are required to take an active role in eradicating exploitation, discrimination and oppression. Leading liberation theologians, many of whom live in the Third World, notably **South America**, emphasise the importance of the **Old Testament**, and particularly the biblical account of the Israelites as an oppressed people. The exodus story, an account of freedom after slavery, is often mentioned as an inspiration for their writing – see, for example, *A Theology of Liberation* (1973), one of the first writings of this type, by the Peruvian priest Gustavo Gutierrez (b. 1928). Although Christian liberation theologians stress the significance of the **Hebrew Bible**, some Jewish and Christian scholars involved in the study and teaching of Jewish–Christian relations, such as John Pawlikowski (b. 1940) and Norman Solomon (b. 1933), have expressed concern about some stereotypical assumptions (such as **Law** versus **Grace**), which lie behind their writings. Leading liberation theologians such as Jon Sobrino (b. 1938) from El Salvador and Leonardo Boff (b. 1938) from Brazil have been criticised for their ignorance of Judaism, for reinforcing the traditional 'teaching of contempt' found in the *Adversus Judaeos* literature and for espousing a form of **replacement theology**. According to Christian liberation theology, **Jesus** is pre-eminently a liberator, calling the people back to true worship of God. On the other hand some Jewish writers see liberation theology as a means for Jews and Christians to set aside previous **Christological** barriers to interfaith **dialogue** and concentrate on a shared prophetic vision. Instead of rejecting Jesus as a blasphemous heretic, the emphasis of liberation theology has enabled Jewish liberation theologians such as Dan Cohn-Sherbok (b. 1945) to see in their lives a reflection of the prophetic ideals of Israel. Liberation theology is notable for its support of Palestinian Christians and its criticism of the **State of Israel**. Well-known **Palestinian liberation theologians** include Anglican scholar Naim Ateek (b. 1937). A handful of radical Jewish thinkers, such as Marc Ellis (b. 1952), have offered their own understanding of a Jewish liberation theology, but Ellis's vehement condemnation of **Zionism** has ensured that his views are rejected by the vast majority of the Jewish community. *EDWARD KESSLER*

Life

Judaism and Christianity both are life-affirming religions, based on the belief that life is a sacred gift from God and that it is our supreme duty and privilege to cherish and cultivate this gift. God has created us with the ability to choose between life and **death**, and we are commanded to 'choose life' (Deut. 30.19). All life is created by God and therefore worthy of reverence, especially human life, which embodies 'the image of God' (Gen. 1.27). Therefore, according to the **Talmud**, all the laws of the **Torah** except three – the prohibitions against idolatry, murder and sexual crimes like incest and rape – must be set aside if keeping them would prove life-threatening. Christian theologians often claim that earthly human life must be preserved except at the cost of turning away from eternal life. For both Judaism and Christianity, then, human life is of infinite value, but is not an absolute value demanding the sacrifice of all other values.

According to both Jewish and Christian teachings human life is both physical and spiritual. But Jews more than Christians have emphasised the unity of the physical and spiritual dimensions of life. The celebration of the sacred significance of the physical is deeply ingrained in Jewish religious practice, while Christian spirituality (despite the doctrine of the **Incarnation**) often manifests an ambivalence towards earthly life. Indeed, there are holistic forms of Christian spirituality, but the bifurcation of the spiritual and the physical has been more characteristic of Christianity than of Judaism. One of the outcomes of contemporary Jewish–Christian encounter, as acknowledged by numerous Christians, is a newfound Christian appreciation of the sanctity of physical life.

Both Judaism and Christianity also teach that human life is both temporal and eternal, but each tradition has its own emphasis. While traditional Judaism affirms belief in an **afterlife**, it stresses life in this world, the sanctity of **time**, and the eternal in the temporal (particularly in the form of the **Sabbath**) rather than the eternal beyond time. Many modern Jews even emphasise the temporal at the expense of the eternal. Christianity affirms the goodness of life in this world, but it emphasises eternal life, which, though beginning in time, is fulfilled only beyond time. Many Christian spiritual writers have even revealed a heaven-bent eagerness to be done with the temporal life. As a result of contemporary Jewish–Christian relations, many Christians have grown in their appreciation of the **holiness** of temporal life, while many Jews have recovered interest in eternal life beyond time. *JOHN C. MERKLE*

Lilith

Meaning 'wind' or 'demon of the night', Lilith is the feminine **demon** of Babylonian origin, mentioned only once in the Bible in an oracle against **Edom** (Isa. 34.14). Contemporary interpretations of the Lilith **myth** have been most prominent within the field of **feminist** studies. Jewish and Christian feminists have rehabilitated the negative image that was portrayed of her within their religions.

Lilith's origins lie in a Sumerian storm demon (*c.*3000 BCE) which by biblical times had taken on the characteristics of the Babylonian demon Lamashtu. In Jewish and Islamic traditions she is Adam's first wife, created before **Eve**. Jewish tradition also says that she is a danger to pregnant women and tries to kill all newborn babies; in kabbalistic literature she symbolises lust, sexual desire and temptation. The most eloquent expression of the myth appears in *The Alphabet of Ben Sira* (*c.* ninth century CE), where God creates her on the same day as **Adam** and of the same material. Here she is equal to him and rejects his patriarchal dominance. She quarrels with him and escapes by flying over the Red Sea into the desert. Jewish feminists have redeemed and reclaimed Lilith by creating a new **midrash** where she is cast as a strong woman who prefers to be banished from the garden rather than submit to Adam's dominance (Judith Plaskow). Adam's efforts to keep his second wife Eve from Lilith's influence by building high walls around the garden are futile when eventually Eve climbs the wall and meets Lilith. The impact of this myth beyond the Jewish feminist circle is evident in its use by Christian feminists to create their own midrash and write their own rituals (Carol Christ). Jewish and Christian feminists have used it as an empowering image of egalitarianism and sisterhood. As with the reclamation of other marginalised women in the Bible, their work on Lilith has often resulted in **dialogue** and mutual influence between Jewish and Christian feminists on biblical **exegesis**.   *HELEN P. FRY*

Linguistics

The interpretation of a sacred text, written many centuries ago and in a language foreign to the vast majority of its readers, calls for a variety of linguistic strategies beginning with translation in the ancient world and culminating in modern scientific linguistics. The origin of the scientific study of the **Hebrew language** can be traced back to the work of the medieval Hebrew grammarians who, adapting Arab methods, produced the first Hebrew grammars and dictionaries. Christian scholars, never as committed to the study of the Hebrew original as their Jewish counterparts, did not seriously engage with Hebrew linguistics until the sixteenth century (*see* **Hebraists, Christian**). Thereafter the dominance of comparative philology for 300 years led to widespread and erroneous 'etymologising' descriptions of Hebrew meaning (e.g. *hoshia* 'to save' from Arabic *awsa'a* 'to give room to'). Another consequence of the over-reliance on comparative Semitic philology was that Christian scholars neglected the Jewish sources, despite the fact that rabbinic, medieval and modern Hebrew is closer in various obvious respects to biblical Hebrew than Arabic, Akkadian and Ugaritic. The modern application of more sophisticated linguistic theory, which incidentally owes not a little to the work of missionaries working on **Bible translation**, shifts the emphasis away from historical linguistics towards subtler synchronic descriptions of the meaning of words and phrases in the social and political contexts in which they are actually used, and for this Eliezer Ben-Yehudah's *Complete Dictionary of Ancient and Modern Hebrew* (1908–59) often comes into its own. Finally, the application of socio-linguistics and pragmatics has thrown light on the way people use language and the effect it has had on others down the centuries, not least on women and Jews.   *JOHN F. A. SAWYER*

Literature, American

American literature was from early days influenced by the encounter between Judaism and Christianity. The Puritan founding fathers of the **United States** saw Jews as the precursors of Christianity, and as millennialists they believed them to hold the key to the Second Coming. Writing in 1850 in *White-jacket*, Herman Melville (1819–91) observed: 'We Americans are the peculiar, chosen people – the Israel of our time: we bear the Ark of the liberties of the world.' Biblical language allowed Melville to voice a sense of American uniqueness, just as the American Revolution gave Jews a language of citizenship. At the same time as American Jewish immigrant writers were keen to become more fully American – Harvard's first Jewish Faculty member, Judah Monis (1683–1764) was founder of Jewish American literature but converted to Christianity – the Christian Pilgrims dreamed of being Jews, or at least ancient Hebrews arriving in the Promised Land. This provides the context for Benjamin Franklin (1706–90) to propose an image of the Israelites crossing the Red Sea for the original seal of the United States.

A key poet of the nineteenth century was Emma Lazarus (1849–87), an admirer of both Heinrich **Heine**, whose work she translated, and of George **Eliot**. Alerted by the **pogroms** to the repeated plight of immigrant Jews, she argues that Jews are the most evident manifestation of such truth as American Christianity contains. However, for other contemporary Jewish authors a sense of loss, emptiness and alienation dominates (not least linguistically). For example, in Lithuanian immigrant Abraham Cahan's (1860–1951) *Yekl: A Tale of the New York Ghetto* (1896) and *The Rise of David Levinsky* (1917) the leading characters' attempts to become fully Americanised prove intolerably frustrating. But assimilationist narratives can also indicate the advantages of Jewish experience. Drawing on the tradition of Jewish socialism, Theresa Malkiel's (arr. USA, 1890) *Diary of a Shirtwaist Striker* (1910) finds Christian narrator Mary identifying with her Jewish co-workers as their courage during the 1912 labour strike alerts her to the realities of class and gender prejudice.

Reacting to the linguistic environment, Henry James (1843–1916) denounced East Side cafés as 'torture chambers of the living idiom' (*The American Scene*, 1904). His reactions can be compared fruitfully with those of Ezra Pound (1885–1972), Mark Twain (1835–1910), F. Scott Fitzgerald (1896–1940), Edith Wharton (1862–1937), Willa Cather (1873–1947) and **philosemitic** poet John Berryman (1914–72), whose essay 'The Imaginary Jew' (1945) is a key work. Accused violently of being a Jew by a drunken Irishman in Central Park, the author eventually decides that, bearing those characteristics that apparently define Jewishness, he is one after all. He succeeds in accommodating an imaginary Jewish self in a way that T. S. Eliot (1888–1965) and Pound, locked in phobias, notably fail to do.

Jewish writers whose first language was Yiddish include Henry Roth (1906–95), Bernard Malamud (1914–86), Saul Bellow (1915–2005), Delmore Schwartz (1913–66), Nobel prizewinner Isaac Bashevis Singer (1893–1944), Isaac Rosenfeld (1918–56), Grace Paley (b. 1922) and Cynthia Ozick (b. 1928). Their multilingual 'literary' idiom problematises the encounter with the Christian world. Henry Roth described the Statue of Liberty wearing 'spikes of darkness' and holding her lamp like a 'black cross against flawless light'. His 1934 novel *Call it Sleep*, in which he defines a relation between Easter and Passover, explores the evolving identity of the hero who is torn between the Yiddish-speaking immigrant world and the broader secular one and ends up physically paralysed.

Many Jewish writers expressed solidarity with African Americans to emphasise the failure of European Christians to save them from the Nazis. In 1942 Karl Shapiro (b. 1913) wrote, 'to hurt the Negro and avoid the Jew / is the curriculum'. Those questioning American WASP culture from this perspective include Muriel Rukeyser (1913–80), Nathanael West (1903–40), Norman Mailer (b. 1923), Arthur Miller (1915–2005), Tillie Olsen (b. 1913), E. L. Doctorow (b. 1931), Philip Levine (b. 1928) and Allen Ginsberg (1926–97). Equally committed to the political, Adrienne Rich (b. 1929) describes herself (1960) as 'Split at the root, neither Gentile nor Jew./Yankee nor Rebel'. Marxist, lesbian, patrilineal Jew, she succeeds in finding a unique voice clearly distinguished from the WASP. So too does Irena Klepfisz (b. 1941). In her poem 'Bashert' (1982) she consid-

ers Elza, a survivor whose sense of fragmentation drives her to suicide. As a child, in order to survive the **Holocaust**, she has had to impersonate a Roman Catholic. Subsequently she absorbs and is absorbed by the Roman Catholic reading that attributes blame to the Jews. She finds that her adoptive American identity leaves her feeling empty. Only inhabiting a Jewish identity could have saved her. Art Spiegelman's (b. 1948) *Maus* (1986) explores a similar predicament, but having pretended to be Roman Catholic, once in America Artie's father becomes anti-Black. This chimes with James Baldwin's (1924–87) idea that the Negro condemns the Jew if he becomes a white man. Lore Segal's (b. 1928) *Her First American* (1985) also challenges the advantages of assimilation, where Vienna-born Ilka Weissnix ('I know nothing/I know whiteness') perceives African American Carter Bayoux as a 'real American'. Christian prejudices are satirised, while differing experiences of victimisation are juxtaposed.

By 1953 Nobel prizewinner Saul Bellow had given the Jewish voice the authority to speak for an integrated America. Early in his career he and Isaac Rosenfeld had written a Yiddish parody of T. S. Eliot. In *Henderson the Rain King* (1959) a stereotypical Protestant visits mythic Africa. The text resonates with the 'laughter and trembling' that Bellow finds typifies Jewish literature. Replacing Kierkegaard's 'fear' with Jewish 'laughter', Bellow defines both a distance from and a closeness to Christian culture. Grace Paley's story 'The Loudest Voice' (*Little Disturbances of Man* (1959)) does the same. A school's attempt to integrate the children of immigrants through acting in a Nativity play that incorporates the crucifixion is thwarted as actor Albie Stock escapes his captors and introduces a humane, vaudeville ending. At home the narrator kneels to recite the ***Shema***, confident that she will be heard.

Bernard Malamud's *The Jewbird* further complicates the Christian–Jewish encounter when he Judaises Poe's (1809–49) *The Raven* in an exploration of Jewish self-hatred and the legacy of the Holocaust. *The Assistant* (1957) draws on his own intermarriage in portraying the relationship between an Italian crook and the daughter of a Brooklyn Jewish grocer. Human love reveals similarities between the religions. For Isaac Bashevis Singer human love is as beguiling as both the lost world of Warsaw and the new American world. *Enemies, A Love Story* (1960) sees him exploiting the Christian notions of Hell and Purgatory and introducing a **Righteous Gentile** who embraces both Judaism and the hero dazzlingly to relate past to present and future. Philip Roth (b. 1933) complicates the social scene when in *The Human Stain* (2000) he shows that the attempt at tolerance can provoke violence. In *The Counterlife* the rite of circumcision permits a discussion of Christian fantasies and the resulting dangers to Jews.

Facing a crisis of identity in Allegra Goodman's (b. 1967) *Paradise Park* (2001), Sharon Spiegelman looks for a diverse spiritual community. Quoting Augustine as an epigraph, her quest interrogates both the Christian idea of pilgrimage and 'the chosen people stuff'. Richly layered rather than painfully fragmented identity is the subject of Victor Perera's (1934–2003) autobiographical *The Cross and the Pear Tree: A Sephardic Journey* (1995). Suspecting a Roman Catholic priest of being a relative, Perera pretends to be a Christian. The **Converso** past of his Sephardi ancestors becomes a crucial part of his Jewish present. Equally concerned with what he calls 'core-core culture confrontation', Chaim Potok's (b. 1929) *My Name Is Asher Lev* (1972) addresses the problem of the Second Commandment. Asher Lev paints his Brooklyn Crucifixions not to be transgressive, but because the image mediates most fully his own and his mother's suffering.

Aryeh Lev Stollman (b. 1954) takes enormous risks in choosing to universalise a Holocaust narrative in *The Far Euphrates* (1997). Signifying those marginalised by Western society, a homosexual and a transsexual occupy the centre of this novel. 'Elchanan, son of David, has chosen to live what is left of his life after the devastation of the camps as a woman and, even more significantly, as a Christian.' Stollman allows this character to survive death as a **Shekinah** (God's presence) who becomes analogous to the 'Holy Ghost'. Unable to procreate, this ghostly character can still generate figuratively – and Jewishly – by endlessly raising questions. Stollman's work demonstrates that the Jewish–Christian encounter continues to play a role in American literature.   *JANE LIDDELL-KING*

Literature, English

Medieval English texts largely depend on popular piety and **folklore** for their image of 'the Jew' as the Christ-killer or demonic abuser of innocents who is ultimately trumped by Christian virtue (or guile): Geoffrey Chaucer's (*c.*1342/3–1400) *The Prioress's Tale* (written in the aftermath of the **Black Death**) recounts the story of a boy murdered by 'cursed Jews' who are punished cruelly following **Mary**'s miraculous intervention. References to **ghettos** and **Hugh of Lincoln** notwithstanding, the tale is opaque as a 'window' onto contemporary realities: the Jews, like the Prioress, are ciphers within a narrative of broader didactic intent. But given fourteenth-century England's ideologically Jew-free status, such literature was significant in the construction of Jews and Judaism in national culture and consciousness.

The constructive influence of one text upon others can be clearly traced in relation to **Renaissance** drama. **Shakespeare**'s *Merchant of Venice* (1596/7), part of a larger body of contemporary 'flesh-bond' dramas (including Christopher Marlowe's (1564–93) *The Jew of Malta* (1589?)) provides a point of departure for many subsequent fictional treatments of Jews in England and still appears regularly on school examination syllabuses. On the one hand the avaricious Shylock appears as a diabolic figure, eventually defeated by an alliance of **Church and state**. His literary heirs include the grotesque and avaricious Jew in Daniel Defoe's (1660–1731) *Roxana; the Fortunate Mistress* (1724; interestingly, the novel's eponymous heroine is a **Huguenot**) and more significantly Fagin, the villain who fails to corrupt the eponymous hero of **Dickens**'s *Oliver Twist* (1837). Conversely, Shylock's daughter Jessica, who undergoes voluntary **conversion** to Christianity, is locatable within a tradition of more positive (albeit **supersessionist**) treatments of Jewish women. As their titles evidence, many such conversion narratives are revealing generally of English (usually Protestant) perceptions of Jews and Judaism. Examples include Amelia Bristow's (1783–1850) *Emma de Lissau: A Narrative of Striking Vicissitudes and Peculiar Trials; With Notes, Illustrative of the Manners and Customs of the Jews* (1828).

For critic Harold Fisch (1923–2001) the ambivalent treatment of Jews was not distinctively Shakespearean, but a general trend in English literature, rooted theologically in Christian notions of Jews as at once a **deicide** nation and a people privileged as the historic bearers of divine promises (*The Dual*

Image, 1959). Recent critics have attributed a less determinative role to theology, emphasising such factors as the rise of scientific discourse (Goldie Morgentaler, *Dickens and Heredity*, 2000), the **myth** of English national **identity** (Michael Ragussis, *Figures of Conversion*, 1995; Bryan Cheyette, *Constructions of 'the Jew' in English Literature and Society*, 1993) and a psychologically motivated need for male authors to inscribe their gender anxiety and conflicted feelings for women (Andrea Freud Loewenstein, *Loathsome Jews and Engulfing Women*, 1993). These latter factors are a reminder that the categories 'Jew' and 'Christian' do not signify religious 'difference' alone; nor are all texts with Jewish (or Christian) authors, characters or readers of equal significance for Jewish–Christian relations.

The nineteenth century saw the development of a mass reading public and ever more complex engagements with Jewish–Christian relations. In response to criticism of Fagin, Dickens created the kindly Riah in *Our Mutual Friend* (1864) as a vehicle for discussion of the ways in which 'it is not, in Christian countries, with the Jews as with other peoples'. However, from a literary perspective Riah is an unsatisfactory creation, more symbolic than human. Anthony Trollope's (1815–82) *Nina Balatka* (1867) is set in a fictionalised Prague, but anticipates the difficulties its author perceived in the integration of Jewish immigrants to England ('Nina Balatka was . . . a Christian – but she loved a Jew'). Although best remembered for its proto-**Zionism**, George **Eliot's** *Daniel Deronda* (1874–7) satirised the London Society for Promoting Christianity amongst the Jews (now the **Church's Ministry among Jewish People** (CMJ)) and, developing a trend seen earlier in Walter Scott's (1771–1832) *Ivanhoe* (1819), reversed the ideology of conversion in its account of Christian Gwendolen Harleth's moral education by Jewish Deronda. However, this novel, too, is shot through with tensions, at once both distinguishing 'Jews' and 'Englishmen' and arguing for their affinity.

It was in the mid-nineteenth century that literature by Jewish authors first achieved popularity in England. Benjamin **Disraeli**'s fiction, written after his conversion to Christianity, offered portraits of Jews (most obviously Sidonia in *Coningsby* (1844)) whose character traits the author believed could help to revivify England's mission as an empire-building nation. Other writers aimed primarily at the Anglo-Jewish reader. Grace Aguilar's (1816–47) *The Vale of Cedars; or, The Martyr* (1850) addressed the **evangelical** belief that Jewish women (following *The Merchant*'s Jessica) were more readily converted than men, by attributing the survival of Jewish culture in **Spain** to their 'martyr strength'. Amy Levy (1861–89) tackled conversion to different ends: *Reuben Sachs* (1888) ridicules Christian conversion to Judaism and associates it with idealised images of Jewish life in *Daniel Deronda*. At the same time the novel's New Testament allusions and imagery hint at Levy's participation in the surrounding Christian culture. Whilst the acerbicism of *Reuben Sachs* was not widely popular, the gentler wit of Levy's contemporary, Israel Zangwill (1864–1926), was favourably received. A plea for Jewish–Christian amity is an important theme in several of Zangwill's stories. 'The Model of Sorrows' (*Ghetto Comedies*, 1907) describes how a Christian artist's portrait of **Christ** is changed by his experience of working with a Jewish life-model, whilst in 'A Tragi-Comedy of Creeds' (*The King of Schnorrers*, 1894) a rabbi finds himself administering 'last rites' to a Protestant. A more problematising account of **Orthodox Judaism**'s fate is offered in *Children of the Ghetto* (1892). However, even here, it is suggested that the estrangement of those Jews who opt for **atheism** or Christianity is not permanent.

In the earlier part of the twentieth century racial representations of Jews are to the fore, with the result that many literary texts may be more accurately described as depicting Jewish/non-Jewish, rather than Jewish–Christian, relations. Thus several recently revived works by Jewish authors (examples include Leonard Woolf's (1880–1969) *The Wise Virgins* (1914) and Betty Miller's (1910–65) *Farewell Leicester Square* (1941)) juxtapose the experience of **antisemitism** with the English sense of class, rather than any theologically driven prejudices. Jewish characters appear as negative foils to the Christian orthodoxy championed by **Roman Catholic** author G. K. Chesterton (1874–1936) (see, for example, *The Ball and the Cross* (1910)), but he, too, drew extensively on the vocabulary of 'race' that was commonplace in English society at the time. Against the deterministic impulses of its times, James Joyce's (1882–1941) *Ulysses* (1922) – sometimes described as *the* novel of the century – offers a fluid picture of Jewish identity in the figure of Leopold Bloom. Bloom, who is partly symbolic of his creator's ambivalence towards Christianity, is a kind of alienated Everyman. The wandering son of an Irish Catholic and a Hungarian Jew who converted to Christianity, he is haunted by half-remembered Hebrew phrases, and carries Zionist literature in his journey around Dublin.

Jewish identity persists as a not insignificant theme in postwar English literature, especially in relation to the **Holocaust** and antisemitism. However, authors have tended to present events not in terms of Jewish–Christian relations, but as questions of Jewish–German relations, or as examples of wider questions relating to memory and identity. Thus Stevie Davies's (b. 1946) *The Element of Water* (2001) confronts fascism and antisemitism with the intention of drawing comparisons between the largely secularised imperialisms of England and **Germany**; in Norman Lebrecht's (b. 1948) *The Song of Names* (2002) Christian **anti-Judaism** is a device used to create unflattering images of the inadequate amongst the northern English middle classes, but the novel is primarily an exploration of the shifting relationship between two Jewish men. Similarly, the prejudice encountered in London and Palestine by the protagonist of Linda Grant's (b. 1951) *When I Lived in Modern Times* (2001) has discernibly Christian roots, but the book's attentions are focussed instead on the determination of Evelyn and other postwar immigrants to be 'modern'. Throughout David Peace's (b. 1967) *GB84* (2004) manipulative millionaire Stephen Sweet is referred to as 'the Jew'. This intentionally disturbing allusion to older literary stereotypes brings us full circle to the language of Chaucer, but is not explicitly linked by Peace to Christian–Jewish relations. *MELANIE J. WRIGHT*

Literature, German

Since the early medieval period the recurrent negative figure of the marginalised Jew, often the focal point of controversy on the political landscape of greater **Germany**, has attracted much attention in German fiction and political literature. Seen as a religious deviant accused of **deicide**, who for centuries dressed and spoke differently and was always engaged in seemingly dubious practices, few writers regarded the Jew in a positive light. At best they were ambivalent, if not critical, at worst hateful.

During the medieval and pre-**Enlightenment** period literary accounts of Jews took the form either of tirades against their religion and way of life, as with Martin **Luther**'s two venomous anti-Jewish leaflets in 1542 and 1543, or of personal records, as with the detailed autobiography in German-Jewish of Glückel of Hameln (1646–1724) who travelled extensively in Germany. During the Enlightenment **Lessing** was the first to plead for tolerance and understanding in his plays *The Jews* (1749) and *Nathan the Wise* (1779). Nathan is based on Lessing's Jewish friend Moses **Mendelssohn**, who encouraged Christian Wilhelm von Dohm (1751–1820), a Prussian civil servant, to write his treatise *On the Civil Amelioration of the Jews* (1781–3), in which he advocated the state lifting the restrictions on its Jewish residents, while urging them to follow more respectable professions and assimilate. Wilhelm von Humboldt (1767–1835), the minister of education in the new Prussia, advocated immediate **emancipation** in his *On the Framework for a New Constitution for the Jews* (1809). A selection of letters (published 1834) by the Jewish-born Berlin salon hostess Rahel Varnhagen (1771–1833) reflects the intellectual atmosphere between Jews and Gentiles during the period of reform in Prussia.

In his essay *The Spirit of Hebrew Poetry* (1782) Johann Gottfried von Herder (1744–1803) defended the poetic language of the **Old Testament** but was more critical of modern Jews; if he abhorred what he saw as their parasitic practices in the economy, he hoped emancipation would improve their morality. Friedrich Schiller's (1759–1805) essay *The Mission of Moses* (1790) compared Jews to pariahs, and G. W. F. **Hegel** is also highly critical of Judaism in his early theological writings (published 1907). The philosophers Ludwig Feuerbach (1804–72) and Immanuel **Kant**, who disliked Lessing's Jewish hero, also expressed their distaste and distrust of Jews in their works and letters. Johann Wolfgang von Goethe (1749–1832), whose poetry was considerably influenced by the Old Testament, praised the qualities of leading Jewish figures of his time, yet opposed Jewish emancipation, a view he expresses in his Bildungsroman *Wilhelm Meister's Years of Travel* (1821–9). In 1815, three years after the Toleration Edict for Prussian Jews, the brothers Jacob and Wilhelm Grimm (1785–1863; 1786–1859) published the second volume of their *Children's and*

Household Tales, which included 'The Jew in the Thorns' (originally written as a rhymed theatre piece in 1599). As the cruel title suggests, the Jew is seen as the scourge of Christendom, whose laceration and hanging is justification for his apparent exploitative treatment of humankind. The Jew in Georg Büchner's (1813–37) revolutionary social drama *Woyzeck* (1836) fulfils a lethal role – it is he who sells with relish the murder weapon. The Jewish-born feature journalist Ludwig Börne (1786–1837), who converted to Christianity, was an early protagonist of **liberalism** who advocated emancipation, while the poet and essayist **Heine**, who also converted, and the revolutionary political scientist Karl Marx (1818–83) were bitter critics of both Jew and Gentile.

In the mid-nineteenth-century novels of Wilhelm Raabe (1831–1910) and Gustav Freytag (1816–95) the honest Christian was pitted against the cunning male Jew, while Jewish women, who were not regarded as economic rivals, were exotic attractions. Theodor Fontane's (1819–98) portraits of Jewish personalities in his late nineteenth-century novels about the declining Prussian nobility are far less acerbic than those in Freytag's *Debit and Credit* and Raabe's *The Hungry Pastor*, but dominant Jewish influence on the cultural and political life of Germany greatly vexed him (in 1881 he stated in a letter that 'the German spirit is infinitely superior to the Jewish one'). Although the central character in the play *Social Aristocrats* (1896) by Arno Holz (1863–1929) is a Christian journalist, his language is akin to the Jewish idiom.

If nineteenth-century Christian writers viewed the Jew as the perpetual and untrustworthy outsider, twentieth-century Jewish writers like Arthur Schnitzler (1862–1931) and Stefan Zweig (1881–1942), both Viennese-born, Jakob Wassermann (1873–1934) from Fürth in Franconia and Arnold Zweig (1887–1968) from Gross-Glogau in Silesia attempted to analyse in detail the pain and torment of their social exclusion while praising the enormous Jewish contribution to European culture; both Wassermann and Stefan Zweig wrote poignant autobiographies. On the other hand, the Viennese-born Karl Kraus (1874–1936) heaped merciless criticism on Jews and liberalism in his newspaper *The Torch*. The Christian–Jewish world of Joseph Roth (1894–1939) from Schwabendorf in Eastern Galicia is destroyed by the Great War, after which his char-

acters suffer a sense of dislocation. Others, such as Theodor Lessing (1872–1933) from Hanover, a fierce exponent of Jewish self-hatred, travelled to **Poland** to observe and write about the *Ostjuden*. Yet none of these authors displays the nightmarish quality of the world of Franz Kafka (1883–1924), in which man doggedly struggles to gain a foothold in a society that is always just beyond his reach and which may be viewed as an outworking of Kafka's double alienation – from both (as a Jew) the predominantly Christian German community in Prague, and (as an intellectual) from the traditions of Judaism. In most of his works Thomas Mann (1875–1955) reveals an ambivalent, if not negative, attitude towards his wide range of fictional Jewish characters, even in his post-**Holocaust** novel *Dr Faustus*; whether as philosophers, musicians, writers or entrepreneurs, their activities are seen as counterproductive. Only in his Joseph tetralogy does Mann extol the virtues of Jewish creativity flourishing in exile under the Pharaohs – his idea of Jewishness is no longer perceived as something alien.

Since 1945 some German authors continue to view Jews in a negative light. In Günter Grass's (b. 1927) *The Tin Drum* (1954) Sigismund Markus, the toyshop owner, is an unattractive single male hankering after a German woman and leading a worthless existence. In Hans Scholz's (1911–88) *On the Green Beach of the Spree* (1955) Jews are cruel and repulsive, in Alfred Andersch's (1914–80) *The Red Woman* (1960) the Italian jeweller is an unsympathetic Jew who buys Franziska's ring at a knockdown price, while in *Efraim* (1967) Andersch's eponymous Jewish hero is the author's unconvincing spokesman, an atheist who claims there is no clear explanation for the Holocaust. The most odious postwar image of the Jew is undoubtedly in Rainer Werner Fassbinder's (1945–82) play *Trash, the City and Death* (1975), whose intended stage production in Frankfurt-am-Main was blocked ten years later. Other postwar German authors see fit to trivialise the German-Jewish tragedy, or fail to mention Jews when writing about the history of their regions, including the former eastern territories, but there are writers who are very conscious of the German destruction of European Jewry. Johannes Bobrowski (1917–65), a devout Christian from Tilsit, grew up in the multicultural and multiethnic atmosphere of this north-eastern corner of the Reich on the Lithuanian border; his novels, short stories and evocative poems depict a lost multinational world. Horst Bienek (1930–90) hailed from Gleiwitz in Upper Silesia, and his tetralogy is set in this southeastern corner of the Reich near the Polish border; he views this thriving Jewish community positively. Arno Surminski (b. 1930) is the youngest of these authors with a duty to remember the past. His birthplace is Jaglack near Rastenburg in East Prussia; if his rural Jews are traders or artisans, their urban counterparts are doctors, and all are respected members of their communities until their ostracism in 1933.   *STEPHEN NICHOLLS*

Literature, modern, Hebrew

Modern literature in the **Hebrew language** was created in **Germany** at the turn of the nineteenth century by 'enlightened' Jews (*maskilim*) who, not willing to become Christian, strove for a respected Jewish-European existence. At first, under the influence of Romanticism, historical novels and long poems on Jewish biblical themes were the most common literary genres, where no Christian characters appeared. Romanticism was highly problematic, however, because of its clash with traditional Judaism. Under German and later Russian influence modern Hebrew literature absorbed and transformed Christian ideas and motifs, as part of its European **modernity**.

Christian literary characters appear in prose writing together with descriptions of social Jewish–Christian relations. Persecution of Jews by antisemitic Christians and the dangerous seduction of proselytism become dominant themes. At the turn of the twentieth century Christians appear in realistic characters as part of Jewish–Christian social and economical tensions. In his stories M. Y. Berdychevsky (1865–1921) described personal Jewish–Christian relations, motivated by unconscious, especially sexual, drives. Love between a Jew and a Christian became a frequent theme in Hebrew literature at the beginning of the twentieth century (Berdychevsky, H. N. **Bialik**, Sh. Tchernikhovsky (1875–1943), U. N. Gnessin (1879–1913), Y. Steinberg (1887–1947), S. Y. Agnon (1888–1970), D. Vogel (1891–1944) and others). Here love is tragically frustrated not because of different socio-cultural backgrounds or religious beliefs, but because of deterministic genetic differences. In Bialik's *Behind the Fence* (1910), Berdychevsky's 'Without Her' (1899) and *The Two* (1912) and in

Vogel's *Marriage Life* (1929–30, English: 1988, 1998) male Jews are yielding to the power of sexual seduction and are seen by the writer as responsible for the suffering they bring on themselves and on their Christian partners.

In his story 'Circles of Justice' (1923) Agnon depicts the Orthodox Jew's complete ignorance of the theological and ritual world of Christianity. In contrast, early Christian theology, and especially the image of **Jesus**, was a centre of interest for Hebrew writers during the twentieth century, together with their criticism of modern **antisemitism**. Even the influential Bialik, the 'Poet of Jewish Revival', included in his poetry **mystical** elements that are common to Christianity and to Kabbalah, such as the divine, Madonna-like Woman or the Jesus-like poet ('The Scroll of Fire', 1905). Circa 1913–14 J. C. **Brenner** wrote, 'We sometimes see in the story of Jesus a world tragedy and our heart goes to him, the tortured prophet . . . and sometimes we see in the whole business of prophecy a ridiculous and comic matter, and in his disciples fools who deviated from the way of the world'. Uri Zvi Greenberg (1894–1981) wrote in 1935 in a foreword to *Sadan* 1–2, which he edited, 'the pain of the pure Christianity – this is the pain of the stabbed Judaism. The wound is in our flesh under the skin, not theirs.' While fiercely attacking contemporary Christianity, Greenberg identifies himself with Jesus in his early Hebrew and Yiddish poetry. Attraction to early Christianity and especially the proposal to 'broaden the borders' of modern Judaism by seeing Jesus as 'our brother' and by including the **New Testament** in the Jewish **canon** gave rise to stormy **polemics**.

Interest in Jesus and in early Christianity continued in Hebrew literature in pre-state **Israel**. In the 1910s–20s Greenberg, Avraham Shlonsky (1900–73), Yitshak Lamdan (1899–1954) and Brenner mythologised the sufferings of the **Zionist** pioneers using Christian symbols. Hayyim Hazaz (1898–1973), in his 'Revolution Stories' cycle (1924–25), portrayed young Jews taking part in the Bolshevik revolution in the image of Jesus or of **John the Baptist**. In Avigdor Me'iri's (Foiershtein) (1890–1970) autobiographical story 'On Behalf of Jesus the Nazarene' (1928) a Jewish soldier who was taken captive by Russian soldiers during the First World War was forced to drink human blood, crucified and buried alive by a Russian commander.

Natan Bistritski's (1896–1980) drama *Judas Iscariot* (1930), Aharon Kabak's (1883–1944) novel *Narrow Path: The Man of Nazareth* (1936, English 1968) and Hayyim Hazaz's unfinished novel on Jesus (1947–48) portray the **historical Jesus** with deep sympathy, seeing him as the founder of one of the many sects into which Judaism was split at his time. The purity of Jesus is distinguished from the heathen Christianity of his **apostles**. The speech of Jesus and the other characters is stylised according to post-biblical Hebrew mixed with **Aramaic** elements, thus making Jesus' sermons an organic part of contemporary Judaism.

The life and sexual drive of nuns is the focus of interest in K. Y. Silman's (1880–1937) short story 'Pilgrims' (1929), A. Lifshitz's (1901–86) story 'The Sister and the Nun' (written in the 1930s, published in 1982) and Shoshana Shababo's (1910–92) novel *Maria: A Story of a Nun* (1932).

After the ***Shoah*** a new wave of writing on Jewish–Christian relations appears in the work of Greenberg, Agnon and Aharon Appelfeld (b. 1932). These writers present antisemitism as a deterministic law, demonising the seduction of Christian culture and its cruel disappointment. In his novels *Katarina* (1989, English 1990) and *Railroad* (1991) Appelfeld warns against sexual attraction of Jews to Christian women and against the seduction of proselytism for the sake of social success. Appelfeld's deterministic worldview denies the chances of conciliation between Jews and non-Jews.

Yigal Mossenzon's (b. 1917) historical short novel *Judas* (1962, English 1963) depicts Christianity as an anti-Roman underground organisation. The writer sympathises with Jesus as well as with the banished **Judas Iscariot**. Amos Oz's (b. 1939) short historical novel *Unto Death* (1971, English 1992) is a diagnosis of the Christian pathological attitude to Jews, depicted on the historical background of the **Crusades**. 'My historical account with Christian Europe is bitter and more frightening than the quarrel with the Arabs and Islam, which is just an episode', said the writer in 1991. Common to Mossenzon and Oz is the image of the Jew as a warrior who, in terms of bravery and moral values, is superior to the Christian soldier. Oz has been interested in Christianity since his early story 'The Trappist Monastery' (1962), where an Israeli soldier, having just experienced death and sacrifice, learns about the vow of silence taken by the monks of

this monastery, situated near Jerusalem. He reacts towards Christian **asceticism** with ambivalent feelings of reverence and horror. This ambivalence is part of Oz's general attitude to Christianity. In the 1950s–70s neo-romantic attraction to early and medieval Christianity appears in the prose writings and poetry of Pinchas Sadeh (1929–94), Yonah Wollach (1944–85) and Avot Yeshurun (Perlmutter) (1904–92). For the young Sadeh the search for Christianity, mixed with admiration of Nietzsche (1844–1900), was a revolt against Israeli mediocrity and an expression of an extreme, almost perverse yearning for spiritual purity and mystical experiences. In the 1980s–90s Christianity together with Buddhism and Zen attracts Yoel Hoffman (b. 1943). Binyamin Shvili's (b. 1956) two novels *Kastoria* (1998) and *Down from the Cross* (2000) are autobiographical poetic accounts of the writer's spiritual search for his own religious **identity**. He cites the New Testament, together with hasidic stories, excerpts from Plato and Sufi poetry. Although charmed by Christianity, the narrator never questions his Jewish identity.

The growing interest in Christianity in Israeli literature at the turn of the twenty-first century can be explained by intellectual curiosity and emotional attraction, almost free from the trauma of Christian antisemitism and from victim psychology.

See also **literature, Yiddish**

HAMUTAL BAR-YOSEF

Literature, Russian

Russia acquired Eastern Christianity through the mediation of Balkan Christians who were touched by Bogumil **heresy**, believing the **Old Testament** was a devilish book and the Jews agents of Satan. Such attitudes penetrated early Russian literature in spite of the Church, for whom the Old Testament was a sacred book forbidden to laymen. Biblical motifs and plots found their way into early Russian literature through **liturgy**, but on the whole the early Russian reader knew little of the Bible and viewed it with suspicion; the book at his disposal was a selection of popular biblical episodes. However, impact from the Jewish ***aggadah*** and **Talmud** was felt, mainly in the **apocrypha** and **folklore**. An eleventh-century sample of Russian literature, *The Word on Law and Grace* by a Kiev Bishop, Ilarion (first half of eleventh century), argued that the **New Testament** was preferable to the Old. In a popular story, *The Descent of the Virgin to Hell*, the Virgin

Mary obtains **salvation** for all sinners in Hell except the Jews.

By the late fifteenth century Jewish–Christian relations in Russia worsened: the heresy of the Judaisers spreading in Moscow and Novgorod was stamped out and was followed by an anti-Jewish campaign. Thereafter the Jews as a whole were seen as unwanted strangers in Russia. Their massive presence in modern Russia was the result of Russian occupation of eastern **Poland** during the reign of Catherine II (1729–96). Late eighteenth- to early nineteenth-century Russian culture distinguished between the respected biblical Jews and the detested modern ones. As a poet Gavrila Romanovich Derzhavin (1743–1816) translated the **Psalms**, but as a public servant he accused the Jewish population of the **Pale of Settlement** of all possible vices. After the 1812 war official Russia developed **mystical** inclinations: the Bible Society was allowed into Russia and the Bible was for the first time translated into Russian. The idea of the return of the Jews to **Zion** prophesied by the Protestant Judeophile mystic Johann Heinrich Jung-Stilling (1740–1817) was appropriated by the Decembrist revolutionaries, who planned a Jewish state in Asia Minor. But society remained anti-Jewish: in the classic Russian literature that originated in 1820–30 Jews were mostly treated as enemy spies in spite of their proven loyalty in the 1812 war. Among steadfast Jewish stereotypes were a smuggler, a traitor, a poisoner, a moneylender and a bar owner who is ruining the local population (Aleksandr Pushkin (1799–1837), Nikolay Gogol (1809–52)). Under Western influences the cruel old Jew symbolising the Old Testament was counterbalanced by the young beautiful Jewess in love with a Christian and longing for Christianity (Mikhail Lermontov (1814–41)).

Mid-nineteenth-century depictions sometimes merged humane notes with the obligatory negative feelings (Ivan Turgenev (1818–83)), but the liberal reforms of 1861 were followed by a conservative reaction, with Jews seen as breeders of dissent and agents of world anti-Russian conspiracy (Nikolay Semyonovich Leskov (1831–95), Aleksey Feofilaktovich Pisemsky (1821–81)); soon this idea transformed into a conspiracy of world Jewry. Jews began to be seen as capitalists, servants of the **Golden Calf**, in both conservative and leftist social-oriented literature (Nikolay Alekseyevich Nekrasov (1821–77)).

In the 1880s, following the first wave of **pogroms** after Alexander II's assassination in 1881, Russian **philosemitism** arose and was given a Christian ecumenical meaning by philosopher **Soloviev**. Leskov published a treatise and some stories defending the Jews. German racial theories influenced Fyodor Mikhaylovich Dostoevsky (1821–81), while Anton Chekhov (1860–1904), who in his youth depicted Jews with cold unfriendliness, tried to be fair to them in his drama *Ivanov* and especially the story 'Rothschild's Fiddle' written during the **Dreyfus Affair**. Leo Tolstoy (1928–1910) abstained from the argument: such distancing from the problem, common in the coming twentieth century, was dubbed 'asemitism'.

By 1900 Jewish presence in Russian letters (and press), art and theatre was noticeable: Russian-Jewish literature appeared. The Jewish question polarised society: the newspaper *Novoe Vremja* attacked the Jewish role in Russian culture, while philosemitic tendencies strengthened at the turn of the century in the work of Maxim Gorky (1868–1936), Leonid Nikolayevich Andreev (1871–1919), Aleksandr Ivanovich Kuprin (1870–1938), Evgenij Nikolaevich Chirikov (1864–1932) and others. Jewish themes became popular in the Russian literature and theatre of the 1900s. But some writers, like Andrey Belyj (pseudonym of Boris Nikolaevich Bugaev (1880–1934)) were irritated at the massive penetration of the Jews into literature. The Beilis case in 1913 marked a new stage of Judeophile activity, with the Religious-Philosophic society excluding **Rozanov** who had supported the accusation of **blood libel** against Beilis. During the First World War dozens of writers took part in the effort to help Jewish refugees exiled from the Pale.

After the October Revolution of 1917, in view of what many people saw as over-representation of the Jews in the new regime, the shocks and stresses of the period were blamed on the Jews, particularly by less important literary figures. Major writers, however, such as Ivan Alekseyevich Bunin (1870–1953), Marina Ivanovna Tsvetaeva (1892–1941) and Vladimir Nabokov (1899–1977) tended to take a philosemitic stand. In Soviet Russia **atheism** was imposed and all religion persecuted, including Judaism. The Jews who in the 1910s began to play a role in Russian culture – **Pasternak**, Osip Mandelstam (1891–1938), Isaak Emmanuilovich

Babel (1894–1941), Eduard Georgiyevich Bagritsky (1895–1934) and hundreds, if not thousands, of others – assumed in the 1920s a place of unprecedented importance in Soviet literature. A creeping and cryptical nationalist reaction followed in the 1930s, when Jews began to be ousted to the periphery of the literary process, but many of them kept their positions in children's literature, or in literary translation, like Samuil Marshak (1887–1964) who excelled in both; others were irreplaceable as writers for the theatre or **film** industry. During the Second World War the **Holocaust** caused shock and sympathy for the Jews among leading Russian writers: Ilya Grigor'evich Erenburg (1901–67), together with Vasili Semenovich (Iosif Solomonovich) Grossman (1905–64), compiled *The Black Book* – a collection of documentary evidence of the mass extermination of the Jews by the Nazis, which was suppressed and destroyed by Soviet **censorship** in 1948 (the manuscript survived and was smuggled out of Russia, appearing only in 1980 in Jerusalem); Grossman also spoke of the Catastrophe in his novels. Ethnic Russians Andrey Platonovich Platonov (Klimentov, 1899–1951) and Viktor Platonovich Nekrasov (1911–87) wrote philosemitic stories. Open **antisemitism** reappeared only after the war, but without any overt religious overtones (e.g. the 1946 campaign against 'cosmopolitans'). In the spirit of the Khrushchev 'thaw' there was a surge of new philosemitism. In 1961 poet Evgenii Evtushenko (b. 1933) wrote about the Holocaust, identifying Jews with the crucified Christ. The religious revival which followed the thaw brought with it awareness of the traditional interfaith conflict. Pasternak in his novel *Doctor Zhivago* took a Russian Orthodox stand that Jewish existence loses all sense after the coming of Christianity. The nationalist camp, which was in the 1960s restricted to a group of so-called 'village writers' (Viktor Petrovich Astafiev (1924–2001), Vasili Ivanovich Belov (b. 1932), Valentin Grigor'evich Rasputin (b. 1937)), blamed the Jews for the fall of old Russia and especially for the spiritual ruin of the Russian people. Following the collapse of the Soviet regime and the ensuing economic and social crisis the nationalists have become strong as never before. They publish their own newspaper *Zavtra*, enjoy the support of a large segment of the ruling elite and are acquiring legitimacy; their leader Aleksandr Andreevich Prokhanov (b. 1938) has received a 2001 National Bestseller prize. Liberal dissident literary intelligentsia tended toward philosemitism (Andrey Donatovich Sinyavsky, who wrote under the pseudonym 'Abram Terz' (1925–77), Andrey Georgievich Bitov (b. 1937), Vladimir Nikolaevich Voinovich (b. 1932), Sergey Donatovich Dovlatov (1941–90) and numerous writers of Jewish origin). The most outstanding writer of the 1970s exiled as a leading opponent of the Soviet regime, Aleksandr Solzhenitsyn (b. 1918), sounded several antisemitic notes in his novels and in the documentary *Gulag Archipelago*; his antisemitism has lately come to the fore in his two-volume attempt at a history of Russian–Jewish relations *Two Hundred Years Together (1795–1995)*.

Since the exodus of Jewry from Russia from the 1970s, and the legalisation of Jewish religious, cultural and community life which took place there in the 1990s, there remains interest in Jewish themes among Jewish (Asar Isaevich Eppel (b. 1935)), half-Jewish (like Aleksandr Motel'evich Melikhov (b. 1947), who described a conflict between the Russian and the Jewish halves of his personality) and even several non-Jewish writers.   *MICHAEL WEISSKOPF*

Literature, Yiddish

In late nineteenth-century Yiddish literature the Jewish experience of **antisemitism** is a central theme, often depicted from a humorous or satirical point of view. The seduction of deserting Judaism for the sake of convenience or even for love is viewed as a tragedy, even by the prominent humorist Sholem Aleichem (1859–1916) in his serial *Tevie the Milkman* (published from 1895 on, later filmed as *Fiddler on the Roof*).

During the first third of the twentieth century the image of **Jesus** and other Christian symbols and narratives attracted Yiddish writers. Der Nister (Pinkhas Kahanovitch (1884–1950)) ended his poetry collection *Thoughts and Motifs* (1907) with the prayer of **Mary** for the birth of a son despite Satan's warnings of the tragic fate that would await him. The 'problem of the Crucifixion' became central in Yiddish literature from 1909, following the sensational publication of Lamed Shapiro's (1878–1948) 'The Cross' and Scholem **Asch**'s 'In a Carnival Night' in the monthly *Dos Neie Leben* in New York.

Messianism and **apocalypticism**, the roots of which are common to Judaism and Christianity, became central in Yiddish literature throughout the first half of the century. Examples are H. Leivik's (pseudonym of Leivik Halperin (1888–1962)) trilogy of dramas, written between 1907 and 1932. Itsik Manger (1901–69) gave his collection of poetry *Stars on the Roof* (1929) the subtitle 'Ballads, Poems of Christ and Poems of the Baal Shem'. In this Jesus appears as a symbol of human tragedy, and the cross indicates the poet's inner suffering

Uri Zvi Greenberg (1894–1981) in his 1910s and early 1920s expressionist poetry often compared himself to Jesus and referred to him as 'my brother'. Jesus was for the young Greenberg a symbol of universal human suffering, emptied of his humanity by 2,000 years of distance from his native land, still being crucified by the Christians. In 1922 Greenberg published in his Yiddish journal *Albatros* a 'concrete' poem in the form of a cross, which was entitled 'Uri Zvi before the Cross/INRI'. In this poem he says that the **cross** has become a meaningless symbol, while Jesus is the representative of the Jewish fate. In his 'A World on a Slope' (1922) the poet expressed his nihilistic loss of his former faith in Christian ideals. Using expressionistic style, Greenberg attacked and caricatured the image of Christ.

Isaac Bashevis-Singer (1904–91) described Jewish–Christian sexual relations, basing their common ground on demonology, which represents the writer's psychoanalytic attitude to human behaviour. Interest in Jewish–Christian relations faded in scanty Yiddish literature written in **Israel** during the second half of the twentieth century.

See also **literature, Hebrew, modern**

HAMUTAL BAR-YOSEF

Liturgy

A consideration of liturgy in Jewish–Christian relations must begin with the Jewish roots of Christian liturgy. As late as 1968 Louis Bouyer (b. 1913) bemoaned 'the continued persistence of the state of mind . . . that the Christian liturgy sprang up from a sort of spontaneous generation, motherless and fatherless like Melchizedek' and that scholars looked to every source except Judaism for Christian liturgical antecedents. However, today it no longer appears startling for Christians to acknowledge the Jewish roots of virtually all aspects of Christian **worship**.

Jesus prayed as a Jew, teaching his followers the **Lord's Prayer**, with its many biblical and synagogue resonances (Matt. 6.9–13; Luke 4.2–4) such as the description of God as Father to Israel (e.g. Exod. 4.22f.; Deut. 30.9; Hos. 2.1; Jer. 3.19; Isa. 1.4; Mal. 1.6). Likewise, the most ancient doxologies in the **New Testament** (e.g. Rom. 11.33–36) and the liturgy (e.g. at the end of the Roman Canon) are not directed to Jesus but to the 'Father'. Acts 2.42–46 clearly depicts Jesus' disciples after the Resurrection continuing their Jewish way of worship in a way that did not distinguish them from other Jews, and Christians only gradually adapted their Jewish prayer life to the new condition of faith in Christ as **Son of God**, on the one hand, and an increasingly Gentile community on the other, even as **Rabbinic Judaism** was adapting to worship without **Temple** sacrifice after 70 CE. The term for 'church', *ecclesia*, like the word *synagoga*, is an equivalent of the Hebrew *kahal*, 'assembly'.

The Christian order of the **eucharist** takes its form and structure from combining elements of the traditional synagogue service with elements of the Jewish **Passover** meal and the *birkat hamazon*. The use of liturgical translations reflects the development of the Aramaic **Targumim** as the homily on the cyclic scripture reading reflects the **midrash**. It is also easy to discern the Jewish background of the Christian liturgy cycle. **Easter** and **Pentecost** are adaptations, with dates modified according to the solar **calendar** of the Gregorian reform, of Passover and **Shavuot**, as the Christian liturgy itself acknowledges. The Jewish autumn cycle of Rosh Hashanah and **Yom Kippur** have parallels in theme and content with Christian Advent, the beginning of the Christian liturgical year, a six-week period of preparation and spiritual renewal roughly corresponding to the six 'Sabbaths of Preparation' of the Jewish calendar. The two periods share penitential themes and the use of prophetic writings, particularly from **Isaiah** (e.g. Isa. 40.1–26 and 60.1–22 on Messianic hope). In the same cycle the festivals of Epiphany and **Sukkot** include celebrations of water and light (see *m. Sukkah* 5.3), features that are better preserved in Eastern Christianity than in the West, as is true also of elements shared by Jewish and Eastern Christian **wedding** ceremonies. The theological and liturgical aspects of Yom Kippur, however, migrated in Christian practice to Lent and the celebration of the Easter Triduum, where they are linked to Christ's death and resurrection. The Christian reading of 'The Divine Office' at certain times of the day reflects the *tehillim* (hymns and psalms). Beyond the annual cycle specific Christian **sacraments** derive essential themes and elements from Jewish ritual, for example **baptism** owes its origin to the purifying and initiating ritual of the *mikveh* (ritual bath).

The central, ongoing feasts of the two traditions are the **Sabbath** and Sunday. Just as every Sabbath is an extension of the Passover, so is every Sunday an Easter. The Eastern Churches in the early centuries, with the exception of **Alexandria**, kept the Sabbath as a day of liturgical assembly, banning **fasting** on it just as did rabbinic tradition. It may be that Sunday worship in Christianity developed as a sequel and conclusion to the Sabbath, with the faithful gathering for the breaking of bread after sunset to avoid travelling during the Sabbath itself (see Acts 20). Both Sabbath and Sunday contain a dynamic tension between the celebration of **creation** and an **eschatological** foretaste of the **kingdom of God**. Though it was not until the fourth century in the West, when **Constantine** ordered Sunday to be observed as a day of rest, that Sunday took on this sabbatical aspect, the practice has raised the issue of Sunday as a day of rest ever since. The notion of Sunday as both the first day of creation and at the same time the eighth day, the day of the *parousia*, reflects the Jewish understanding of Sabbath.

In terms of Jewish–Christian interaction it seems that Jewish liturgy and its Christian equivalent were not, respectively, progenitor and offspring but exercised mutual influences during the formative periods of both religious practices. When the Jewish communities of the post-talmudic period in the Islamic environment adopted for their rabbinic texts the codex that had long been known in the classical and Christian worlds, the first prayerbook (*siddur* in Hebrew, signifying 'order [of prayers]') emerged in a small and simple format consisting of a few stitched gatherings and some basic texts. Through the Middle Ages this medium, perhaps under the influence of its equivalents in the Church, grew in size, elegance, content and authority and came to cover much of rabbinic ritual, even including prayers for non-Jewish rulers.

Polemic has also been commonplace in the liturgy. In the early period it is likely that some rab-

binic **prayers** had a few phrases that were intended or regarded as critical of Christianity such as *birkat ha-minim*. The cursing of heretics, which probably also included **Jewish Christians**, was mentioned by some of the early **Church Fathers** and manuscript evidence has also been found in the **Cairo Genizah**. However, scholars still dispute to what extent the curse was aimed at heretics in general or Christians in particular. An additional complication is that different rites evolved among Jews and phraseology was subjected to external Christian **censorship** as well as internal theological and linguistic adjustment. Also, Jewish liturgy was based on an oral tradition for many hundreds of years, the first prayerbook being written as late as the ninth century CE. Interestingly, the prayerbook's format was affected by the invention of printing and by Christian liturgical prototypes, and over time its content has been seriously altered by progressive groups in modern central and western Europe to take account of views of the Temple, **Zion**, spirituality, **nationhood** and gender that were more acceptable in the dominant Christian environment.

In Christian liturgy anti-Jewish elements are much more obvious. The early Christians saw themselves primarily as Jews, and the destruction of **Jerusalem** (70 CE) confronted both with the same problem: how was **sacrifice** to be offered without a Temple? For Jewish Christians the Letter to the Hebrews resolved this crisis, asserting that earthly liturgy shared in the sacrifice of **Christ**, who was now 'high priest' within the heavenly temple (Heb. 8). The *Didascalia Apostolorum* 5 (*c.*220 CE) marked an important shift in Christian liturgical self-awareness: Christians should not think of themselves as Jews, nor observe Jewish ceremonial law. This was developed by the Church Fathers, who understood the liturgy as non-Jewish, since by the third century most converts were no longer from Judaism, and strong anti-Jewish **preaching** in the form of the *Adversus Judaeos* **literature** invaded liturgical preaching as a biblical **hermeneutic** and sought to establish differences between the rites of the 'old' and 'new' **covenants**. From 500 CE forward liturgy was used for virulent **anti-Judaism**, as in the prayers for the consecration of a church that had formerly been a synagogue (*Liber Sacramentorum Romanae Ecclesiae, Assemani Codex* 4.2.91). Even more bitterly anti-Jewish were local feasts celebrating the martyrdoms of so-called child victims of the '**blood libel**', in the boy-saints Simon of Trent (*c*.1472) and Andreas of Rinn (*c*.1462). Most of these were not observed throughout the Roman rite, and both have now been suppressed.

The Churches of the **Reformation** shared many of the attitudes of the medieval Catholic Church. Although the reformers continued the polemics of their Catholic predecessors, their liturgical texts were not as overtly anti-Jewish because many of the most problematic texts such as the **Holy Week** liturgies were replaced with preaching services. Nevertheless, anti-Judaism prevailed in the preaching of the minister, who was free to preach on biblical texts of his own choice and at length.

After the **Holocaust** Christians have become very sensitive to the experience of the Jewish people and to the contribution of worship to **antisemitism**. As rites and texts have been revised and created anew, care has been taken to remove texts that may be perceived as antisemitic. In the Holy Week liturgies, when the Roman Good Friday liturgy was adopted, either the *Reproaches* and the solemn intercessions have been edited to remove offensive texts or alternatives have been substituted. The Second Vatican Council's *Nostra Aetate* 4 (1965) condemned antisemitism and anti-Judaism, although three years earlier **John XXIII** had begun to change the disparaging **Good Friday Prayer for the Jews** (*pro perfidiis Iudaeis* or 'for the wicked Jews'), ending in **Paul VI**'s corrections to the Roman Missal of 1970 (for 'the Jews first to hear the word of God'). **John Paul II**'s Apostolic Letter, *Dies Domini* 8–18 (1998), pointed appreciatively to the Jewish background of the principal weekly (Sunday) and yearly (Easter) feasts of Christianity, while the Vatican's Congregation for Divine Worship and the Discipline of the Sacraments (2001) warned against exegeting rites and texts in a discriminatory way against Jews (*Liturgiam authenticam* 29).

In North America the main Churches have all provided Good Friday liturgies from which antisemitic material has been carefully excluded. Similar revisions have taken place in the British Isles. As well as liturgical developments, the *Revised Common Lectionary* has been adopted by the major denominations. The listing of scripture readings for Sundays and major feasts have been chosen to allow the texts taken from the Jewish scriptures to speak for themselves and to let them be seen in a positive light. In addition, many of the Churches have adopted new or revised translations of the scriptures for use in worship. The most commonly accepted version of the scriptures in English is the *New Revised Standard Version*, which takes care in the translation of the New Testament phrases and words that might foster antisemitism, while at the same time attempting to be faithful to the meaning of the original Greek text (*see* **Bible translations, modern English**).

It is increasingly becoming common practice for Christians and Jews to gather for prayer on special occasions throughout the year. Guidelines and suggestions for such interfaith services are beginning to appear in order to address questions of how Christians and Jews can pray together. In North America the major professional organisation of persons engaged in teaching about worship and in the preparation of liturgical materials, the North American Academy of Liturgy, has Jewish members who actively contribute to its work. It is to be hoped that such organisations will eventually appear in other parts of the world.

EUGENE J. FISHER, DENNIS D. MCMANUS AND ALAN DETSCHER

Lloyd George, David (1863–1945)

British Prime Minister (1916–22) at the time of the **Balfour Declaration** (1917). Lloyd George himself explained British policy as a reward for the scientific contributions to the war effort of Chaim **Weizmann**. Alternative explanations for his support for **Zionism** relate to his Welsh Baptist background, with its deeply rooted, literalist **biblical interpretation** and interest in Messianic expectation. Lloyd George wrote that 'I was taught far more about the history of the Jews than about the history of my own people', and a romantic interest in the survival of the people of the Old Testament certainly reinforced his political determination that Protestant Britain should control the Holy Places.   *DANIEL R. LANGTON*

Llull, Ramon (1232–1315/16)

Born in Majorca, Ramon Llull or Lull was an exceptionally prolific author of conversionist tracts in Catalan and Latin, aimed at Jews, Muslims and schismatic Eastern Christians and at Catholics who needed guidance on how to live a better life. He underwent a personal conversion and in the 1270s began to elaborate ideas about how to demonstrate Christian truth to unbelievers, developing what has been called a 'holy algebra', a system for classifying and describing the material world and the world of concepts, in an attempt to prove the Trinitarian structure of all things. Popular presentations of his ideas included the novel *Blaquerna* and his *Book of the Gentile and the Three Wise Men*, which offered a characteristically unaggressive account of Judaism and **Islam**, which he regarded as partial truths. He insisted, unusually at a time when **preaching** campaigns had become increasingly strident, on the need to show respect to his interlocutors; he had personal contact with several Catalan rabbis. *DAVID ABULAFIA*

Logos

As Gentile Christianity began to spread and to distinguish itself from its Jewish past, its apologists had perforce to account for the worship accorded to **Jesus** by developing a **Christology** comprehensible to the intellectual currents of the day. A central aspect of this process was their employment of the concept of Logos. A Greek term of wide semantic range, signifying principally 'word', 'speech', 'reason', it had been used as a theological designation of Jesus by the author(s) of the Fourth Gospel and the first Johannine epistle. The Gospel, in imitation of the opening of Genesis, states that the Logos was in the beginning, was with God and was God; that he became flesh and tabernacled among us so that we saw his glory (John 1.1, 14). The epistle describes Jesus as the word of life (1 John 1.1), life being also a trait of the Logos according to the Gospel (1.4), along with light (1.1–4, 9). Greek philosophers had used Logos in different senses. Thus for Heraclitus (*fl.*500 BCE) Logos was a general order in the universe analagous to reason in human beings; for the Stoics it represented the ordering principle of reason active in the world, consisting of fire (so Zeno (335–263 BCE)) or fire and air (so Chrysippus (*c.* 280–207 BCE)), and might be called *pneuma*, 'spirit'; and Middle Platonists, differentiating God's transcendent inner being from his actions towards the world (e.g. in **creation**), sometimes spoke of the latter in terms of Logos. Among Jews the **Septuagint** translators used Logos most often to represent Hebrew *dabar*, 'word' or 'thing', especially in the prophetical books and the Psalter: according to this Bible version, it was the Logos of the Lord that constituted the medium of prophetic **revelation**, and through the creative Logos of the Lord that the heavens were made firm (LXX Ps. 32.6). Thus Logos took on some of the colouring

of its **Hebrew** original: Jewish thinkers like Aristobulos (second century BCE) could associate it with **wisdom** in God's ordering of the cosmos; while the author of Wisdom of Solomon (late first century BCE to early first century CE) could speak of God's formation of the world by his Logos, and concomitantly of human beings by his wisdom (9.1–2).

But it was principally **Philo** who drew together scripture and Greek philosophy, speaking of the Logos both as 'boundary figure' between God and the universe and, like the Stoics, as an active principle of order in the cosmos (*Fug.* 110). The highest of intelligible beings, the Logos in Philo's scheme 'holds together', as it were, the two principal divine powers, the kingly and the creative, themselves represented in scripture by the two cherubim on the ark of the covenant from between which the divine Word addressed **Moses** (Num. 7.89). Legislative authority and creative power are here united by Logos; and Philo urges his readers to train the **soul**, under instruction from the Logos as coach, to practice detachment from the passions, to rise above ephemera, to communicate with the Logos, and to become 'one who sees God', the expression he uses as an explanation of the name **Israel**, and also as a description of the Logos itself.

The background to the Johannine use of Logos is complex. It may be related to some or all of these ideas, so as to appeal to both Jewish and Greek readers. It may also be coloured by Jewish tradition preserved in the **Aramaic** Targumim of Gen. 1 and Exod. 12.42, where the *Memra* ('word, utterance') of the Lord is associated with creation, light and glory. Once established in Christian **vocabulary**, it is used regularly to speak of the second person of the **Trinity**; and its antecedents in Greek philosophy proved helpful in defence of Christianity to pagans (*see* **Justin Martyr**) and crucial for later theological development. In particular, **Athanasius** refined and developed the notion that the Logos assumed and was united to human nature when the Christ became incarnate, and integrated the term into his systematic account of the Christian doctrine of the **atonement** and the **redemption** of humanity. Among Jews, however, use of the term Logos as found in Philo's writings and as a philosophical term seems largely to have disappeared, presumably partly in response to its centrality in Christian theology. *C. T. R. HAYWARD*

Lord's Prayer, The

The Lord's Prayer is found in the Gospels and not in the Hebrew scriptures. Likewise, it has been incorporated into Christian liturgies but not into Jewish worship. As a result one could assume that it represents a point at which the two traditions find no confluence. But the reality is that the Lord's Prayer offers a window into the origins of Christianity within Judaism and provides a fertile area for Jews and Christians to engage in mutual exploration. At the very least, there is nothing in the Lord's Prayer (other than the connotations of the name ascribed to it) that is offensive to Jewish sensibilities, and nothing that is unfamiliar to Jewish ears.

Often called the Paternoster after its first words, the Lord's Prayer is found in longer form in Matt. 6.9–13 and shorter form in Luke 11.2–4. It is often regarded as the Christian prayer *par excellence* and perhaps one of the most familiar sections of the **New Testament**. Nonetheless, its precise meaning continues to be the subject of scholarly disagreement, with New Testament exegetes offering varying interpretations. The existing text also presents the challenge of identifying the original formulation. Widespread agreement exists, however, that the original was in **Aramaic**, though some have posited that it was first articulated in **Hebrew**.

Unlike many other statements attributed to **Jesus**, the Lord's Prayer contains no direct quotation from, and some of its phraseology has no antecedents in, the Hebrew scriptures. However, the prayer in its entirety contains nothing that is antithetical to those scriptures or to the post-biblical Jewish context in which the New Testament represents it as being first enunciated. More significantly, the general spirit of the prayer, and many of its particular formulations, have clear antecedents both in the Hebrew scriptures and in the liturgical structure of the early synagogue, and may well be understood as derivative from those sources.

Various scholars find the inspiration of all or parts of the Lord's Prayer in elements of Jewish **liturgy**. David de Sola Pool (1885–1970) writes that Matt. 6.9c–10a 'have their exact equivalent on the Kaddish, except for differences in person' (*The Kaddish*, 112, cited in Petuchowski and Brocke (eds), *The Lord's Prayer* 81); Baruch Graubard has characterised the whole as 'like an abbreviation of the Prayer of the Eighteen Benedictions' (Petuchowski and Brocke (eds), 61); Joseph Heinemann (1915–78) finds the inspiration in the rabbinic practice of private prayer or charismatic prayer (Petuchowski and Brocke (eds), 88). There appears to be general consensus that the prayer, as it appears in Matthew, begins with the main concerns of the *Kaddish* and then moves to the petition elements of the Eighteen Benedictions. Many scholars note that it follows the tripartite outline of the Eighteen Benedictions: praise, petition and thanksgiving. The **Didache** included the instruction that the Paternoster be recited three times each day (8.2), just as the Eighteen Benedictions are in the Jewish tradition.

Closer examination of particular phrases and formulae in the Lord's Prayer reveals antecedents in Hebrew scriptures and Jewish practice. For example, God is addressed as Father, the term Jesus is depicted as using most regularly in prayer. Some might assume this is indicative of Jesus' sense of having a unique intimacy with God, or even of Jesus' own self-understanding as the **Son of God**. But closer examination reveals that Jesus is represented as prescribing this phrase not as a self-description, but for the use of his disciples and those who come after them. The practice of addressing God as Father had earlier currency in Hebrew scriptures (e.g. Deut. 32.6; Isa. 63.16; 64.7; Jer. 31.20), and in Jewish liturgy it figures prominently in the *Avinu Malkeinu* ('Our Father, our King') prayer of the High Holy Day liturgy. It is employed in the Eighteen Benedictions and the Sim Shalom prayer of the daily morning service. Furthermore, God is depicted as a Father in heaven. This image is expressed in composite form in Isa. 63.15–16, and in Jewish liturgy can be found in the *Kaddish*. As **Oesterreicher** notes, it appears in rabbinic literature in *m. Avot* 5.23, *Sifre Deuteronomy* par. 306; *Sifra Kedoshim* 11 and *Deuteronomy Rabbah* 1.6 (Petuchowski and Brocke (eds), 130f.). Again the hallowing of God's name is an essential part of the Lord's Prayer, but it is not unique or original to it, being integral to the *Kaddish*. Similarly, reference to the coming of God's Kingdom is part of the second sentence of the *Kaddish*.

The appeal for **forgiveness** included in the Lord's Prayer has its parallels in Jewish liturgy – most prominently in the Eighteen Benedictions. The theme of forgiveness is, of course, central to the Days of Awe and is addressed throughout the liturgy of those days. The plea to 'deliver us from evil' has two possible interpretations, each with its own set of Jewish associations. If the phrase is a plea to rescue us from those who do evil, it echoes many of the **Psalms** (e.g. 79.9; 31.16; 7.2–3). If the sense is to save us from the effects of our own evil deeds, antecedents can also be found in the Psalms (e.g. 39.9 or perhaps 79.9). In either case, its inclusion in the Lord's Prayer represents a reiteration of a familiar theme, not the introduction of a new perspective. Some versions of the Paternoster add a concluding Doxology that sounds very like **David**'s prayer in 1 Chr. 29.11ff. and, in Jewish liturgy, in the *Kaddish*. Alternative versions include the phrase 'blessed be Your name forever', which appears in Ps. 113.2 and in Dan. 2.20; in Jewish liturgy it constitutes the second line of the Barchu prayer, which is part of the liturgy of every service.

The most salient fact about the relationship of the Lord's Prayer with Judaism is its consonance with Jewish religious teaching. De Sola Pool has written, 'there is complete conformity of the Paternoster with Jewish norms of Prayer' (*The Kaddish*, 112, cited in Petuchowski and Brocke (eds), 81; Samuel Sandmel (1911–79) states, 'the words themselves are quite congruent phrases of prayer in habitual use in the Talmud' (*A Jewish Understanding of the New Testament*, 150); **Wellhausen** writes, 'True prayer is a creation of the Jews, and the Paternoster follows Jewish models although it is not simply put together *ex formulis Hebraeorum*' (cited in Petuchowski and Brocke (eds), 134). The Lord's Prayer fits comfortably within Jewish religious sensibilities and yet, for all that, is very much a *novum*. For this reason it is often pointed to as a bridge linking Jewish and Christian spiritualities, and offering a meeting place for the two communities and traditions. The Jewish scholar Jakob Petuchowski (1925–91) created a 'Hebrew version' of the Lord's Prayer, which sought to approximate what the original may have sounded like. In more recent times the Lord's Prayer has become a familiar subject of discussion in workshops on Jewish–Christian relations and has served as a focal point of scholarly conferences. *DANIEL POLISH*

Louis I ('the Pious') (778–840)

Frankish Emperor (814–40). Continuing his father Charlemagne's (742/7–814) Jewish-friendly policy, Louis granted Jews protection from both clergy and barons, appointed a special protector of Jewish rights, enabled free movement throughout the Empire, tolerated Jews having Christian servants, and even endorsed Jewish observance of the **Sabbath** by shifting markets to Sunday. These special Jewish privileges irritated Archbishop **Agobard of Lyons**, who eventually supported Louis' three sons against him, his second wife Judith and their child Charles the Bald (823–77), the future guardian of his father's Jewish policy. Both the sympathetic and hostile attitudes towards Jews at and around the court are illustrated by the example of Bodo, Louis' deacon, who, distracted by the immorality of the Church, provoked controversy and reaction by his sensational conversion to Judaism.

PETR FRYŠ

Louis VII (1120–80)

King of France (1137–80). In 1144 he prohibited converted Jews from returning to Judaism under penalty of death, since this would nullify received **sacraments**. However, professing Jews were not affected and even enjoyed his moderate protection. Together with the emperor Conrad III (1093–1152), Louis was major proponent of the Second **Crusade**. He responded to the preaching of **Bernard of Clairvaux** and the papal bull *Quantum praedecessores* (1145) by cancelling interest payments on the debts crusaders owed to Jewish moneylenders, but did not allow confiscation of the whole principal as suggested by **Peter the Venerable**. *PETR FRYŠ*

Louis IX (1214–70)

King of France (1226–1270), **crusader;** his **canonisation** in 1297 was highly unusual for a political ruler. Known for his ascetic Christian piety, he was the most anti-Jewish monarch of his age, fostering a comprehensive programme to convert Jews. He intensified the campaign against Jewish moneylending, defining **usury** as any payment beyond the principal and ending governmental enforcement of contractual debts to Jews. When, in 1239, Pope **Gregory IX** ordered the seizure of all Jewish books, to be investigated for **blasphemy** by **Dominican** and **Franciscan** friars, Louis IX was the only king to enforce the decree. The resulting public burning in Paris of the **Talmud** and other rabbinic manuscripts had a devastating impact on Jewish morale. *MARC SAPERSTEIN*

Love

Love as the keynote of religion is usually associated with Christianity. It is important in Jewish–Christian relations, however, to recognise that Judaism is no less a religion of love. Love of God and love of neighbour are the primary principles of both Judaism and Christianity. The key texts come in Deut. 6.5 and Lev. 19.18. The first is part of the three passages that make up the *Shema*, the most important Jewish prayer and sometimes described as the creed of Judaism because it encapsulates Jewish belief in terms of one God who demands the loving response of the whole person. The second is part of the **holiness** code which spells out the forms of behaviour that love of God entails, specifically, in vv. 17–18, not to nurse a grudge but to love your neighbour simply because he is a human being like yourself. Both these texts are taken straight into Christianity by **Jesus** quoting them jointly in response to a question about which is the most important **commandment** (Mark 12.28–34) and saying that they together sum up 'the law and the prophets' (Matt. 22.40). The latter comment may be compared with that recorded in Matt. 7.12: 'In everything do to others as you would have them do to you: for this is the law and the prophets.' This has come to be known as the '**Golden Rule**'. Rabbi Hillel (end of first century BCE and beginning of first century CE) is reported to have met the request to teach a prospective convert to Judaism the whole of the **Torah** whilst the listener stood on one leg: 'That which is hateful unto thee do not do unto thy neighbour. This is the whole of the Torah. The rest is commentary. Go and study.' (*b. Shabbat* 31a). Christians sometimes describe Jesus' version as positive and Hillel's as negative, but this is a false contrast, commonly stemming from a failure among Christians to recognise the source of Jesus' summary of God's commands as his own Jewish scriptures. In reality it is often easier to work out how one would not like to be treated than it is to define love in terms of how one would like to be treated. Jesus' emphasis on love is not new and those who contrast it with a supposed '**Old Testament** religion' of **law**, fear and justice misrepresent the Bible of both Jews and Christians. The **Hebrew Bible** emphasises that God loves his people and this is the sole reason why he chooses them and makes demands on them (Deut. 7.7–8). His love is everlasting; therefore, he is faithful even when his people are not (e.g. Jer. 31.3). That God is the source and inspiration of love is reiterated in the **New Testament**, notably in John 3.16 and 1 John 4.7–12.

Also in common between both Judaism and Christianity are other vital contentions about love. Firstly, it can be commanded. **Hebrew** and **Greek** both have a range of words for 'love'. Those used for the human response to God and to neighbour denote not so much a feeling as an attitude, even an act of will. Most commonly the Hebrew *ahavah* (e.g. Lev. 19.34) and the Greek *agape* (1 Cor. 13) are used of this human loving. *Ahavah* is also used of God's love for human beings (e.g. Isa. 43.4), though more common is the Hebrew *ḥesed*, which carries the connotation of steadfastness (e.g. Hos. 2.19). *Ḥesed* can also be used for human love of God (e.g. Hos. 6.6). Secondly, Judaism and Christianity insist that love entails action. The rabbis go so far as to say that this is how people can cultivate love: by studying and doing the Torah (so their commentary on Deut. 6.5). 1 John 1.3–6, 9 similarly describes obedience to God's commands as the only proof of love, particularly as regards loving others. Thirdly, both religions have a more **mystical** strand which envisages love of God coming about through contemplation. The intense desire for God, with disciplined devotion, can create union with God. In Hebrew, *kavanah* (intention/concentration) can produce *devekut* (cleaving).

CHRISTINE PILKINGTON

Luther, Martin (1483–1546)

Theologian and biblical scholar. Martin Luther is considered the initiator of the **Reformation** and its most powerful voice. He perpetuated with medieval crudity of language the **Church Fathers**' view of the Jews as God's enemy. His writings about Jews should not be seen as totally separate from his denunciations of the pope, false Christians and the Turks (Muslims), all of whom he saw as the devil's legions. Yet he saw Jews as unique deniers of Christ and, though his hostility was not racial, they remained the negative element in the bedrock of his theology. He asserted the true Church had existed since **Adam** whenever patriarchs and prophets trusted God in faith alone, and the 'hypocritical church' of heretics and works-righteous advocates since **Cain**'s rebellion (*Lectures on Genesis*, 1537). The older Luther's views cannot legitimately be divorced from the younger Luther's, though his later words were much more brutal. His earliest words on the Jewish issue (1514–15) in lectures on the **Psalms** affirmed God's wholesale rejection of this people and insisted that by their obduracy they continued to show themselves as active foes of Christianity. His 1523 critique of Judaism (*That Jesus Christ Was Born* a Jew) chastised the Church for its treatment of Jews and then expressed hope for some Jews' **conversion** under a new approach. Since Jews were not back in their own land but remained scattered and despised with no sign of an end to their exile, God's promises to **Abraham** regarding his descendants could not apply to them but must apply to Abraham's spiritual heirs, Christians. For Luther, as for virtually all others at the time, truth allowed no room for **tolerance**. He saw the evangelical proclamation of faith as the last chance for misguided Jews and Christians alike, since God was working in the Reformation to extricate all from the **Antichrist**. The anticipated future did not contemplate the coexistence of peoples of various faiths, for 'the holy Christian Church' separated true Christians 'from all other peoples on earth' (*Large Catechism*, 1529). The Reformation was a grace period, a postponement of the end of time; yet Luther believed that the greatest threats would arise within its own circles. Hence he reacted savagely against all who differed with his theology, especially the **Anabaptists**, **Sabbatarians** and **Christian Hebraists**, whose efforts he saw being strengthened by the very successes of the Reformation. In 1536 he urged Christian authorities to expel Jews if they would not convert. By 1543 his vehement publication, *On the Jews and their Lies*, counselled rulers to confiscate rabbinical texts, forbid the rabbis to teach, and burn down synagogues along with Jews' homes, so that Judaism's falsehood could no longer be taught. If these actions caused Christians to fear Jewish retribution, all Jews should be driven out of the country 'for all time'. Despite these admonitions, Luther claimed he had held to his advice to treat Jews 'in a friendly manner', though he admitted to advocating 'severe mercy'. In a letter to his wife, 2 January 1546, Luther said the Jews were responsible for perverting his own health on top of attempting to convert all Christians and make them their servants. Despite the realities of the Jewish people's eviction from virtually all of Western Europe, he saw Jews as evil 'lords of the world' and thus as the most dangerous foes (*On the Jews . . .*).

See also **Lutheranism**   *ALICE L. ECKARDT*

Lutheranism

Form of Protestant Christianity growing out of the work of the sixteenth-century Reformer Martin **Luther**. Numbering some 65 million adherents worldwide, Lutheranism is the largest **Protestant** denomination. It is the predominant faith in certain regions of **Germany** and the whole of **Scandinavia**, and is strongly represented in several African countries and elsewhere. In the **United States** it is the fourth largest denomination after Roman Catholics, Baptists and Methodists. Lutherans do not regard Luther's voluminous writings as having creedal authority, but his anti-Jewish treatises have been a fateful legacy. Objections were made to them at the time by some of Luther's closest colleagues, and few if any of his infamous 'recommendations' with regard to the treatment of the Jews were acted on. The desk editions of Luther's works typically used by the Lutheran clergy did not include these writings, and for long periods they were in effect unknown. However, excerpts from them, especially the 'recommendations', have been circulated by **antisemitic** movements, and in the twentieth century the Nazis eagerly cited Luther as providing historical and theological sanction for their anti-Jewish measures. Certain elements in Lutheran theology, in addition to the **supersessionism** common to most Christian theology, made German Lutherans especially vulnerable to this appeal. These included a view of the relation of **Law** and 'Gospel' which tended to see the former as rigid and punitive, ignoring the positive meanings of **Torah** for Jews, and a doctrine of the Two Kingdoms (the realm of faith and the realm of politics) that too often inculcated an uncritical obedience to government authority.

Theologians and Church leaders during the Nazi period such as Dietrich **Bonhoeffer** and Hans Lilje (1899–1977), however, laboured mightily to overcome these tendencies. In Norway Luther's struggle against the papacy was cited by Bishop Eivind Berggrav (1884–1959) and other anti-Nazi leaders as a model of resistance to tyranny, while Denmark, an almost wholly Lutheran country, was the scene of the heroic rescue of 95 per cent of the Danish Jews, who were ferried across the straits to neutral Sweden. In 1984 the Lutheran World Federation formally renounced Luther's anti-Jewish views, stating that 'all occasions for similar sin in the present or the future must be removed from our churches'. The Evangelical Lutheran Church in America, in its 1994 'Declaration to the Jewish Community', repudiated Luther's anti-Jewish writings, acknowledged their tragic effects on subsequent generations and affirmed its 'urgent desire to live out our faith in Jesus Christ with love and respect for the Jewish people'. Lutheran Church bodies in Europe, **South America** and **Australia** have issued similar statements. Numerous Lutheran–Jewish **dialogues** and scholarly symposia have been held at the local, national and international levels, leading Lutherans to a renewed awareness of their indebtedness to the Jewish heritage and a deeper appreciation of the vitality of Jewish life and thought today.

With regard to the Israeli–Palestinian conflict, many Lutherans, influenced by a close sense of identification with Palestinian Lutherans and the Lutheran educational and medical institutions in the area, have been strong advocates for Palestinian self-determination.   *FRANKLIN SHERMAN*

Lyra, Nicholas of (c.1270–1349)

Medieval exegete. Born in Normandy, Lyra entered the Order of Friars Minor, taught at the University of Paris and later served as a **Franciscan** provincial. His *Postillae perpetuae*, a running **commentary** on the entire Bible, was widely used in subsequent centuries. Lyra emphasised the literal meaning of the text, grounded in the study of philology, grammar and history, though not to the exclusion of mystical and **Christological** interpretations. He mastered **Hebrew** and made extensive use of the **Talmud**, **midrashic** literature and rabbinic commentaries, especially those of **Rashi**. Despite this reliance on Jewish sources, his work is filled with anti-Jewish **polemic**, both in the *Postillae* and in two anti-Jewish treatises.   *FRANKLIN SHERMAN*

Maccabees

The story of the revolt in the 160s BCE of the high priestly family of the Maccabees against their Seleucid ruler Antiochus IV (*r*.175–164 BCE) in Palestine is recorded in books 1 and 2 of the Maccabees and in **Josephus**. It is unclear whether it was internal conflict in **Jerusalem** or the imposition of religious laws on the Jews by Antiochus that instigated the revolt. 2 Maccabees presents it as a group of traditional Jews fighting against a 'Hellenised' minority who were abandoning Judaism, and this has given rise to theories of opposition between Judaism and **Hellenism**. Antiochus's restrictions, whether they instigated the revolt or were a response to it, have often been taken as the first recorded instance of **antisemitism**, although others have argued it should be traced back to fourth-century BCE **Egypt**, or instead should not be properly so called until the Middle Ages or after the **Enlightenment**. The **martyrdom** of a mother and her seven sons in 2 Macc. 7 influenced both Jewish and Christian views of martyrdom. The Maccabean martyrs remain the only pre-Christian Jews commemorated in the Western Church **calendar** (1 August), although they are often obscured by their commemoration falling on Lammas day (also known as St Peter's chains), a feast of St Peter.

JAMES K. AITKEN

Magic

Magic has played a contrary but important role in the history of Jewish–Christian relations throughout the last two millennia. Despite the myriad of problems of definition and interpretation that beset its analysis, magic could be said to be a cause of both unity and conflict between Jews and Christians.

Both religions share an antipathy towards practices perceived as magical that is a consequence of their common biblical heritage. A number of strong injunctions against engaging in magic can be found in the **Hebrew Bible** (most notably Exod. 22.18; Lev. 19.26, 31; 20.27; Deut. 18.10–11, 1 Sam. 28; Mal. 3.5)

and there is plenty of evidence that in both early Judaism and early Christianity such prohibitions remained influential (see, for example, *m. Avot* 2.7; Acts 19.18–20; 2 Tim. 3.13; Rev. 21.8; 22.15). However, it should be noted that there is little substantive difference between some of the practices outlawed as magical and others deemed acceptable in the normative traditions of both communities. In both Judaism and Christianity magical practices are most usefully understood as unsanctioned religious activities, and the term 'magic' is often employed as a pejorative, polemical label, rather than an empirically verifiable description.

It is no surprise, therefore, that, given the strained nature of Jewish–Christian relations over the centuries, accusations of magic, designed to stigmatise those accused, have been common. For example, it is probably seen in the early tradition, found in the Synoptic Gospels, in which **Jesus** is accused by some of his Jewish contemporaries of using demonic powers to effect his exorcisms (Matt. 12.24; Mark 3.22; Luke 11.15; see also **Justin**, *Dial.* 69; **Origen**, *Cels.* 1.38, 68; *b. Sanhedrin* 43a; and the sixth-century ***Toledot Yeshu***). Christians likewise accused Jews of such practices from the earliest period of the Church's existence. Although the association of Jews with magic was something known in the Greco-Roman world (e.g. Pliny the Elder, *Nat.* 30.11), Christian writers appear to have been particularly keen to make this claim. Acts of the Apostles, for example, shows a clear interest in presenting Jews as magicians (see 13.6; 19.11–20). Over time the nature of this accusation seems to have changed: not only individual Jews but also Jewish religious practices per se became associated in Christian **polemic** with magic and were held responsible for innumerable outrages and calamities, real and imagined, that befell Christian communities. The accusations of witchcraft made against Jews and **Conversos** in the case of Santo Nino of La Guardia in 1490 provides a chilling example of the enduring consequences of such thinking. Stereotypes set in earliest periods of Jewish–Christian relations have a long history and impact beyond their respective traditions – the last remaining Jew of Kabul was accused of witchcraft in 1999.

It is clear that, for all the polemical use of the accusation of 'magic', it is not just something in the eye of the beholder. Some individuals and groups within Judaism and Christianity self-consciously practised what they understood to be magic or closely related activities such as alchemy. Their activities present a little studied but fascinating insight into informal Jewish–Christian contact and cooperation. Indeed, some drew clients from across the religious divide – as we can see, for example, in the bitter words of John **Chrysostom** against the use of Jewish magical healers by his congregation in fourth-century **Antioch** (*Adv. Iud.* 8.6).

The reinvention and reclamation of 'magic' in neo-pagan movements that have grown up in Western countries since the nineteenth century in response to a perceived failure of organised religion represents a common challenge to both Judaism and Christianity and is yet another example of how magic can unite as well as divide the traditions.

JUSTIN J. MEGGITT

Magnificat

First word of the Latin designation (*Magnificat anima mea Dominum* – 'My soul magnifies the Lord') of the song of **Mary** of Nazareth in the **infancy narrative** of Luke 1.46–55 and probably modelled on Hannah's song in 1 Sam. 2.1–10. This is one of four hymnic songs in Luke 1–2, the others being Zechariah's canticle (Luke 1.67–79), the hymn of the angels (Luke 2.13–14) and the hymn of Simeon (Luke 2.18–32). Numerous **Old Testament** allusions mark the Magnificat hymn as a product of Jewish–Christian reflection on the birth of **Jesus** in the early stages of the Christian movement. Mary, portrayed by Luke as a woman of Old Testament faith, sings this **psalm** of praise upon meeting with her cousin Elizabeth in the hill country of Judah. Both women, pregnant with sons **John the Baptist** and Jesus, felt the babes leap in their wombs, a sign that they interpret as God's intervention in the births of their two children. The song reflects classic Hebrew parallelism and meter common in the Hebrew psalter and expresses Mary's belief in God's powerful salvific acts on her behalf. She praises

God for exercising divine justice and compassion on behalf of the lowly, both for herself and for Israel as 'God's servant'. With language echoing the prophets or the **eschatological** hopes of Israel reflected in **Maccabees**, she expresses trust that God's justice is shown in 'bringing down the mighty from their thrones'. With the **covenant** reference to **Abraham**, she claims this moment as an act in continuity with God's promises and blessings in the past. This hymn preserves the depth of both Jewish and Christian **prayer** marked by humility and trust in God's power to save. It has been the inspiration for countless musicians, including **Bach**, Telemann (1681–1767), Palestrina (*c.*1525–94) and Liszt (1811–86).

BARBARA E. BOWE

Maimonides (Moses ben Maimon) (1135–1204)

Jewish physician, philosopher, legal authority. Maimonides lived his entire life in Muslim countries (Spain, Morocco, Egypt), but statements about Christianity in his legal works had a major influence on later Jews. One was his insistence that Christianity, unlike **Islam**, was **idolatry**; consequently the **talmudic** laws severely regulating Jewish interaction with Gentiles applied to contemporary Christians. Later Jewish thinkers in Christian Europe tried to modify this view, although many continued to refer to Christians, especially Catholics, as idolaters. Second, at the conclusion of his comprehensive *Code of Jewish Law* (*Mishneh Torah*), discussing Jewish Messianic doctrine, Maimonides insists that **Jesus** only imagined he was the **Messiah**, but instead of improving the lot of the Jewish people, made it incomparably worse. Yet Christianity, along with Islam, providentially spread knowledge of God and scripture throughout the world, thereby preparing the way for the true Messiah. This passage was eliminated from printed versions of the text by Christian **censors**. (Another negative reference to Jesus is in his celebrated 'Epistle to Yemen'.) Finally, Maimonides' statement that 'The pious of the Gentile nations have a share in the world to come' (*Code, Laws of Kings* 8.11) has been frequently cited by modern Jews as evidence of Jewish inclusiveness, sometimes contrasted with Christian doctrine (although it is unclear whether Maimonides, who excluded idolaters from eligibility, meant to include pious Christians in his statement). Maimonides' philosophical masterpiece, the *Guide for the Perplexed*, was quickly translated into Latin and used by Scholastic philosophers including Thomas **Aquinas**, who refers to 'Rabbi Moses the Egyptian' with respect. The 13 Principles of Jewish Faith in his *Commentary on the Mishnah* attempt to define Jewish **identity** in doctrinal terms (*see* **doctrine**). These include the absolute unity of God, the uniqueness of Mosaic prophecy, the immutability of the divinely revealed **Law**, and the future advent of the Messiah, which clearly differentiate Jewish from Christian belief. Made into a popular liturgical hymn *c*.1400 ('*Yigdal Elohim Hai*'), the Principles' 1914 English 'translation' for use in the liturgy of American Reform Judaism was so universalised that it has been incorporated into Protestant hymnals as 'Praise to the Living God'. *MARC SAPERSTEIN*

Mandate

The system of British administration of Palestine, a territory previously controlled by the Turkish empire, established following the First World War. The Mandate represented the first Christian administration there since the **Crusades**. It was granted at San Remo in April 1920, was ratified by the League of Nations, and came into effect on 1 July 1922. British responsibilities were to make good the promise of the **Balfour Declaration** (1917) to reconstitute the Jewish national homeland. This was to include the facilitation of Jewish immigration, Jewish settlement and self-governing institutions. The Mandate was entrusted to preserve the civil and religious rights of all the inhabitants of Palestine, irrespective of race and religion. Despite its formal internationalist credentials, the Mandatory power was Christian, and this provoked among contemporaries excited expectations and a wave of triumphalism throughout Europe. Even before the ratification of British control (the allies captured Jerusalem in December 1917), Pope Benedict XV (1854–1922) had spoken of 'the rejoicing of all good men' that the Holy Places had been freed from 'the domination of infidels' and had 'finally returned into the hands of Christians'. During the Mandate period contending claims relating to the Holy Places proved a constant headache, so much so that among the various post-Mandate solutions contemplated was the creation of a separate State of **Jerusalem**. Successive Arab and Jewish revolts (which rarely involved **Arab Christians**, who tended to express their opposition to **Zionism** diplomatically) eventually persuaded the Mandatory power that they could not solve the diplomatic challenges.

The matter was handed over to the United Nations with the result that the Mandate was terminated on 14 May 1948 upon the establishment of the **State of Israel**. *DANIEL R. LANGTON*

Marcion (? *c*.90–155 CE)

Christian 'heretic'. Marcion came from Sinope on the Black Sea and moved to Rome where he was excommunicated for his radical theology, which is known to us only from refutations by his opponents, particularly **Tertullian** and **Ephrem**. He drew a sharp distinction between the Creator God of the Jews, characterised by a spurious justice, deceitfulness and inconsistency, and the eternal, distant 'stranger' God, revealed as the Father of Jesus Christ. Apparently seeking to excise any taint of what he labelled 'Judaism' from Christianity, he rejected the **Old Testament** and appealed only to **Paul**'s letters and to an edited version of the Gospel of Luke. The source of his ideas, which included a strong **asceticism**, is debated – radical Paulinism, **Gnosticism** or a philosophical dualism. Tertullian labelled him 'ally of the Jews' because, adopting a more literal reading, he denied that the Old Testament spoke of the Christian God or prophesied **Jesus** as **Messiah**; however, rabbinic assertions of the unity of God, and of God's justice and love, and defences of God's actions in Egypt, may also oppose him. Forced by Marcion to justify retention of the Old Testament without its literal observance, Christian writers reaffirmed Israel's hard-heartedness which necessitated the **Law**, and blindness to the true meaning of the scriptures; in this way anti-Marcionite and anti-Jewish **polemic** reinforced each other. Little is known about how long Marcionite communities survived; however, the term has often been used of subsequent tendencies in Christian thought to devalue the Old Testament and the 'God of retributive justice' detected therein. *JUDITH LIEU*

Marranos

Marranos (literally 'swine' or one who 'mars' or damages the Christian faith) is a derogatory term, originating in the fifteenth century, that constitutes a sub-category of **Conversos** or 'New Christians'. Conversos is used to distinguish recently converted Jews from Old Christians – Christians by birth/blood with no Jewish affiliation or lineage whose **conversion** to Christianity was sincere. The title Marranos refers to those Jews who converted to Christianity and either continued to observe certain Jewish rituals (e.g. lighting of **candles** on **Sabbath**) and practices (e.g. keeping a modified kosher diet) or were accused of doing so, especially in areas in which these converts and their descendants settled after their **expulsion** from **Spain** and **Portugal** at the end of the fifteenth century. Another term used for this phenomenon is 'Crypto-Judaism', because of the underground or covert nature of the practice of Judaism of Marranos living among Christians and, in some cases, Jews. One of the major problems of research is to determine whether individuals or groups are in fact Conversos or Marranos, which is hard because of the secrecy surrounding Marrano Jewish practice. Since they could not practice Judaism openly, Marranos are known to have developed elaborate ways of maintaining Sabbath and the Jewish holidays. Certain Jews helped the Marranos to maintain their Jewish rituals and practices as best they could in situations of fear and suspicion. Conflicts were inevitable as Jews, Conversos and Marranos tried to live among Old Christians in a predominantly Christian society. Practising Jews were looked upon with suspicion as instigators of the return of a convert to the Jewish faith. Did they help these converts to maintain certain Jewish practices and beliefs? Certainly some members of the **Inquisition** thought this influence was real, and therefore Jews were always suspect because of their **Judaising**. Marranos themselves were a primary target of the inquisitors' investigation because of their Judaising and **apostasy** from the Christian faith. The crime they were committing, apostasy, was considered by the Church to be worse than the sin of unbelief. There were tensions between Conversos and Marranos in that the Marranos themselves became enemies of their former religionists (practising Jews and Conversos) because of the desire by the latter to fully integrate into Christian society. A definite problem arose in regard to the attitude of the local populace toward Marranos, as they tended to see Conversos and Marranos as a single entity: Judaisers in their midst. Because of fear and persecution, many of the Marranos found shelter in other parts of Europe, the New World or in Muslim lands where they could continue to observe certain Jewish practices. Problems also arose among the Marranos in regard to their Jewish beliefs and practices in that 'their notions of what constituted Jewish practice would, of necessity, become blurred

with the passage of time' (Jane S. Gerber, *The Jews of Spain*, 121).   *STEVEN J. MCMICHAEL*

Marriage

The story of **Adam** and **Eve** has been seen in both traditions as proclaiming the value of marriage, ordained by God for **sex**, for procreation and for companionship. The high value placed on fidelity within marriage in both traditions has been an important factor in encouraging social harmony between Jewish and Christian communities. In the **Roman Catholic** tradition marriage is considered a **sacrament**, whereas Jewish marriage is based on a written contract, a *ketubah*, which includes provisions for maintenance. **Celibacy** has never been considered an ideal within Judaism, and divorce has always been permitted (Deut. 24.1–4, cf. 1 Cor. 7). In biblical times men often took more than one wife. Polygamy was outlawed for Ashkenazi Jews (those living in Christendom) by the decree attributed to Gershom ben Judah of Mainz (960–1028) about the year 1000. This was undoubtedly due to the influence of the surrounding Christian culture. Adultery has been defined by Judaism as a sexual union between a man and a married or betrothed woman, by Christianity as a sexual union between a married person and one unmarried, or between a married person and the spouse of another. Modern societal trends have affected the stability of both Jewish and Christian marriage, as well as encouraging **intermarriage**, debates about **homosexuality**, and the recognition of gay relationships.

See also **weddings**   *MICHAEL HILTON*

Martin, Raymund *see* **Martini, Raymond**

Martini, Raymond (c.1220–85)

(= Martin, Raymund.) Spanish **Dominican** friar and prominent anti-Jewish polemicist. His work *Pugeo Fidei* ('The Dagger of Faith', *c*.1280) purported to demonstrate the truth of Christianity and the falsity of Judaism by citations from the Hebrew scriptures, the **Talmud** and other rabbinic literature, finding in them **proof-texts** for Jesus as the **Messiah**, the doctrine of the **Trinity** and so on. Martini assisted the Christian apologist **Paul the Christian** in the famous **disputation** with the Jewish scholar **Nahmanides** at Barcelona in 1263. His anti-Jewish writings were utilised by **Lyra** and other medieval polemicists and were also cited by **Luther**. Long resident in Barcelona, Martini also spent some years in Tunis pursuing missionary work among Jews and Muslims. He was well versed in **Hebrew** and served King **James I** of Aragon as a **censor** to examine Jewish books for allegedly **anti-Christian** passages. His numerous quotations from rabbinic sources provide the only evidence of some rabbinic texts that were not otherwise preserved.   *FRANKLIN SHERMAN*

Martyrdom

Derived from the Latin *martus*, literally a witness, the concept first appears in the Bible in Daniel (3.8ff. and 6) and later in the **apocrypha** during the **Maccabean** revolt. In the **early Church** 'martyr' referred to a Christian who suffered persecution and death for the sake of faith in Christ. The **New Testament** records Jewish persecution of the first followers of Jesus, such as Stephen, a Greek-speaking Jew who is remembered as the first Christian martyr (Acts 7.51ff.). The **Church Fathers** also charged Jews with involvement in the persecution of the early Church, alongside pagans. The Jewish understanding of martyrdom is best explained by the Hebrew term *Kiddush ha-Shem* (lit. 'the sanctification of God's name') which refers to acts that glorify God's name, the highest form of which is to give up one's life for God. Over many centuries, particularly after the reign of **Constantine**, Jews have suffered martyrdom at the hands of Christians.

In the New Testament Christ is viewed as the first martyr (Rev. 1.5) and his actions are viewed as a witness to love (cf. John 15.12ff.). Martyrdom's association with death was reinforced by persecution of Christians for their faith in the first few centuries. A cult of martyrs soon emerged, in which Christians recounted the faith and death of martyrs. This was used as a source of encouragement to Christians, particularly in times of trial. For Jews acts of *Kiddush ha-Shem* were also recounted – as they are today – and likewise provided encouragement as well as solace. For Jews two paradigms of mass suicide developed. First, suicide after armed resistance had failed, as took place at Masada when the Romans were about to overrun the Jewish defences; second, suicide without resistance, as took place along the Rhine during the **Crusades** when Jewish communities decided that they would not fall into the hands of the crusaders and prepared themselves for death by ritual bathing, prayer and fasting. The stories of these communities, often called the Akedahs, after the **binding of Isaac** (which was viewed as the exemplary act of a martyr),

are central to Ashkenazi **liturgy** and recited every year.

The subject of martyrdom has become particularly sensitive to the Jewish–Christian encounter since the **Holocaust**, because the events of 1933–45 have called these paradigms into question. While there were those who were martyrs affirming their belief in God, there were many others who died denying a faith in God. There were also, of course, millions who had no choice of martyrdom, but were summarily executed or murdered. For them there was no **sanctification**, but it is common for Jews and Christians to view these people as martyrs and, from a Jewish perspective, as involuntarily sanctifying God's name. David Blumental (b. 1938) has argued that the martyrdom of the Holocaust is the deepest motif in the contemporary Jewish pysche, and its impact clearly extends to Jewish–Christian relations.   *EDWARD KESSLER*

Mary

Mary's primary role in the **New Testament** is as mother of **Jesus**. Her body is the *locus* of divine activity. To be sure, Mary's body is the body of a Jewish woman; Jesus is brought up in Judaism by his mother (Luke 2.22–4). Jesus is Mary's child (Mark 3.31; Matt. 12.47; Luke 8.19): Matthew's birth narratives displace Joseph as father and situate Mary within the patrilineal genealogy of Jesus (Matt. 1.16). Her name is actually Mariam, a Hebrew Semitic form appropriate for Nazarenes (so Luke 1–2 and the Greek and Sahidic Coptic texts at Matt. 13.55). This is the Semitic form of the name found in, for example, the Greek translation of **Miriam** at Exod. 16.20. Thus it is as a Jewish woman, Mariam, that Mary receives the angel (Luke 1.34, *see* **Magnificat**). The annunciation scene has analogies with angelic visits paid to **Hagar** (Gen. 16.7–14) and the mother of Samson (Judg. 13.2–5). However Pseudo-Philo's *Biblical Antiquities* 9.10 also reports Miriam's dream in which an angel tells her of the birth and career of her brother **Moses**. Mariam's acceptance of her role as slave/servant of the Lord in Luke 1.38 puts her alongside the great leaders of Israel: **Abraham** (Ps. 105.42), Moses (Mal. 3.22), Joshua (Josh. 24.29) and **David** (Ps. 89.3) and compares her favourably to apostolic leaders such as Peter and **Paul** portrayed in Acts.

As *mater dolorosa*, 'mother of sorrows', Mary's anguish and grief at the cross joins that of **Rachel** lamenting dead children (Matt. 2.17–18) and other mourning parents. The second-century *Protevangelium of James* relates further information about Mary's childhood elaborated from Hebrew scriptures. Only once as Mariam does Mary prophesy on the journey to Egypt: 'Joseph, I see . . . two peoples, one weeping and lamenting, one rejoicing and exulting' (17.2–3 cf. Luke 2.34).

Apocryphal texts describe the purity of Mary's body and her words. In the third-century *Questions of Bartholomew* Mary teaches cosmic mysteries to the apostles. Dormition and Assumption **apocrypha** from the fifth century onwards include an Ethiopic *Liber Requiei* describing Mary's departure from this world, *De transitu Mariae apocrypha aethiopice*. Anglo-Saxon death and assumption traditions of Mary developed from Latin translations of earlier texts and contained anti-Jewish elements (some Jews attempt to sabotage the funeral).

Current interest in Mary seems primarily historical. It traces modes of worship centred on Mary and the theological discussions that led to the formulations of the early Ecumenical Councils. Forms of devotion to Mary developed in the medieval centuries with an emphasis on Mary's role as intercessor for sinful humans. The **Reformation** and Counter-Reformation rethought and further elaborated Mary's place, during the period that saw her figure reach all over the globe through conquest and **mission**. These centuries also saw a growing sense, expressed in the miracle tales and religious works, of the fundamental chasm that separated Jews from an appreciation of Mary. Jews were accused of desecrating Marian images, deriding her cult and blaspheming.

Future interfaith **dialogue** might ponder theologically on Mary's role as mediator, on women's (and men's) parenting experiences, including anguish (Luke 2.48) and attentive reflection (Luke 2.19).

See also **Virgin Birth**   *DEIRDRE J. GOOD*

Masorti Judaism *see* **Progressive Judaism**

Media

Reporting to the general public raises a number of issues of specific concern to Jewish–Christian relations. These include sensitivity over the choice of language, such as the use of the term '**antisemitism**' (particularly with reference to reporting on Israel) or adoption of the phrase 'the Jews'. Some journalists no longer use the latter owing to the pejorative meaning the phrase carries in popular Christian culture. The religion correspondent of *The Times* of London, for example, has argued that ***hoi Ioudaioi*** still echoes today and prefers where possible to use 'Jewish people' instead of 'the Jews'. The selection by journalists and reporters of appropriate words and phrases has become even more important since the public have immediate access to news reports from around the world through the **Internet**. Sometimes religious difference can be highlighted by adoption of a phrase in the non-English speaking world. For example, Jewish–Christian relations in **Poland** are reported in the Polish media as Polish–Jewish relations. The term 'Pole' is used as a synonym for Catholic: it is not claimed by or applied to Jews. For an English-speaking observer, it would have been thought self-evident that the Polish national community consists of both Catholics (as well as Protestants) and Jews and that 'Polish–Jewish relations' implies that Polish Jews are not Poles. One eminent English journalist, Clifford Longley (b. 1940), commented that he was 'someone who regards himself as fully Catholic and fully English, who would not dream of suggesting, and would be deeply shocked to hear it suggested by others, that Jews cannot be just as English as I am. Indeed, I would regard someone who suggested such a thing as coming very close to committing the crime of incitement to racial hatred' (Kessler *et al., Jews and Christians in Conversation*, 2002, 172).

The stresses and demands of modern journalism, including a straightforward lack of space in newspapers or exposure on television, means it is not always possible to provide stories with the detail they deserve. For example, journalists are told to take into account that the Jewish and the Christian **community** consist of a number of different groupings. Thus, it can cause annoyance in the Free Churches when the Archbishop of Canterbury is used as the main Christian spokesman in Britain and they are left unquoted. Likewise, some in the Progressive Jewish community can become exercised when the Chief Rabbi is taken as a spokesman for the whole Jewish community.

Another example of the role of the media in reporting Jewish–Christian relations can be seen in the portrayal of the **State of Israel**. There is a widespread expectation within the Jewish community and the Jewish media that Christians have a particular responsibility to show understanding for and sympathy towards Israel. On the other hand some Christian media exhibit huge sympathy for the Palestinians, which influences their coverage of the issues. Consequently, the media are often accused of bias, in favour either of Israel or of the Palestinians. At the same time journalists are aware that antisemitism sometimes hides beneath a veneer of anti-Israeli sentiment. The situation is complicated further by the existence of strong anti-**Zionist** sentiments among some sections of the ultra-Orthodox Jewish community. The coverage of a 16-year-old suicide bomber who surrendered to Israeli troops on the Gaza strip in 2003 caused particular concern, as did the Bethlehem siege the preceding year. The Israeli government accused one BBC correspondent of 'total identification with the goals and methods of the Palestinian terror groups' and the Israeli media also criticised reporters from *The Times*, Sky television and several French papers.

However, wide coverage of issues related to Jewish–Christian relations illustrates the extent to which the topic has become central to media interest. For example, the huge coverage of Mel Gibson's **film** *The Passion of the Christ* (2004) demonstrated a surprising level of interest in Jewish–Christian relations among the general public. Generally, Christian media welcomed the film as much as the Jewish media condemned it, but commentators in both communities raised concerns about its potential for stirring up antisemitism.

RUTH GLEDHILL

Medical ethics

Medical ethics, or bioethics, refers to the **ethics** of all aspects of human experimentation, health care, reproductive technology and genetics. Its recent history dates from the Nuremberg Code, itself a response to the atrocious experiments conducted during the **Holocaust**. Conflict between the individual's perceived needs and those of society at large is central to much bioethics. From the 1970s to the mid-1990s the research and discussion was largely led by Jewish and Christian ethicists. The *Journal of Medical Ethics* and the Institute of Medical Ethics in Britain, the Hastings Center in New York (*Hastings Center Report*) and the Kennedy Institute at Georgetown (*Kennedy Institute of Ethics Journal*) though arising out of religious backgrounds fuelled wider interest in the issues. More recently the emergence of the journal *Bioethics* and of the International Bioethics Society marked the broadening of that base well beyond any religious domain. The principle of fairness as enunciated by John Rawls (1921–

2002) in *A Theory of Justice* and Amartya Sen's (b. 1933) social capital and capabilities are important examples of secular confluence with Jewish and Christian values. Jewish and Christian ethicists have generally shared a concern to see the principles of their tradition applied in bioethics. They differ in some key understandings: in matters of reproductive technology and **abortion** Jewish thought emphasises, distinctively, the obligation to work with the Creator to propagate the race. Hans Jonas (1903–93) is one whose eminent work has been universally valued and through whom such Jewish emphases have become accepted in secular and Christian thought. Similarly, Jonas has extended the notion of therapeutic research by the principle of identification to include experimentation that, although it could not benefit this patient, has the potential to produce a cure for this patient's disease. Non-therapeutic research is then ruled out in all other clinical situations on the grounds both of human dignity and of the nature of the doctor–patient relationship. Genetic engineering and possible human cloning on the one hand and the allocation of money, resources and treatment on the other are perhaps the biggest bioethical issues for the immediate future: the demography of the AIDS epidemic adds to the magnitude and urgency of the task. Larger in impact will be the continuing debate about abortion, euthanasia and assisted suicide as individuals face the effects of medical advances. Governments have come to rely upon expert committees, usually including prominent religious ethicists, to advise on major bioethical issues, and it is here that shared religious insights have had an impact upon public policy.   *COLIN HONEY*

Meiri, Menahem ben Solomon (1249–1316)

Talmudist, Bible exegete and philosopher of Perpignan (Provence), author of a talmudic **commentary** (*Beit ha-Behirah*) and halakhic novels (*Hiddushei ha-Rav ha-Me'iri*). As a philosopher follower and defender of **Maimonides**, he distinguished between religious teachings that can be established rationally (as, for example, the existence, unity and incorporeality of God) and religious teachings that are a matter of faith (as, for example, creation, retribution, providence and miracles). His philosophical opinions made it possible for him to be one of the few Jewish scholars of the Middle Ages who maintained a certain openness and **tolerance** towards other religions.

Meiri amends the talmudic conception of the *ger toshav*, the non-Jew who keeps the **Noachide laws**, and declares that Christians and Muslims, 'though they are, measured by our own faith, in some points mistaken', are nevertheless not idolaters but *ummot ha-gedurot be-darkhei ha-datot*, 'nations restricted by the ways of religion', and therefore stand between Jews and idolaters (*see* **idolatry**). This positive view of Christianity and **Islam** allows Meiri also to see the *meshummad*, the apostate, in a different light: while the rabbinic ***halakhah*** classifies them as heretics towards whom the Jew has no obligations, Meiri recognises the possibility of a religious **conversion** when he legally puts apostates and members of religions to which the conversion occurred into the same category.   *STEFAN SCHREINER*

Melchizedek

The obscure figure of Gen. 14.18 and Ps. 110.4 is presented as God's assistant in the **Dead Sea Scrolls** (11QMelch), perhaps as part of a tradition reflected in later rabbinic identification with the archangel Michael. Melchizedek's appearance in **Gnostic** writings may be connected with the Melchizedekian sect, which insisted on the humanity of Christ, as recorded by Epiphanius (fourth century) and Mark the Monk (fifth century). A Christian **supersessionist** tendency appears in Heb. 5–7, where the levitical **priesthood** is portrayed as insufficient and the priesthood of Christ 'after the order of Melchizedek' is preferred (Ps. 110.4). This becomes an issue in Jewish–Christian controversy in the first few centuries and is debated in the ***Adversus Judaeos* literature**. In one rabbinic passage Melchizedek is still said to reappear in the Messianic era (*b. Sukkah* 52b). Melchizedek came to be identified with the patriarch Shem by both Christians and Jews, and although it has been argued that the Shem–Melchizedek identification was a Jewish reappropriation of Melchizedek, the origins of Shem's priestly status are pre-Christian. The omission by some **Targumim** of reference to his priesthood may have been a response to the Christian use of Melchizedek.   *JAMES K. AITKEN*

Melito of Sardis (? *c.*140–185 CE)

Early Christian writer sometimes seen as influential in the development of the charge of deicide. **Eusebius of Caesarea** says he was bishop of **Sardis** and gives a survey of his writings, most now lost. Among these are: an Apology to the Emperor Marcus Aurelius (121–80 CE), describing the Chris-

tian philosophy, although originating among 'the barbarians' (i.e. Jews), as having blossomed with the Empire; the *Extracts*, giving a list of the writings of the **Old Testament** (the first use of this term), which he learnt as one of the earliest pilgrims to 'the place where it was preached and happened' (*Church History* 4.26). The 'two books *On the Passover*' are generally identified with the *Concerning the Pascha*, surviving in two Greek papyri first published in 1940 and 1960, and in later versions in Latin, **Coptic**, Syriac and Georgian. This highly rhetorical homily, apparently addressed to Christians who followed the **Quartodeciman** observance, presents the Exodus and **Passover** as prefiguring the death of **Jesus** and the **redemption** brought by him; supporting the **typology**, a spurious etymology links *Pascha* (Greek transliteration of **Aramaic** *pesach*) with the verb 'to suffer', *paschein*, used both of Christ's death and of the human situation he entered. Melito's language and imagery sometimes echo Passover aggadic and related traditions, suggesting contacts between the two faiths. Melito attributes Jesus' murder to 'Israel', indicts **Israel** directly, and has Israel admitting to killing him 'because he had to die' (*Concerning the Pascha* ll. 528–9). The charge of **deicide** – 'God is murdered, the King of Israel is killed by an Israelite right hand' (ll. 715–16) – arises out of his **Christological** identification of Jesus with God and his heated **rhetoric**, but was to be a significant theme in the history of Christian **anti-Judaism**.   *JUDITH LIEU*

Memorialisation

While Jews and Christians as members of historical communities have always engaged in acts of **remembrance**, the discussion of concepts of memorialisation as part of communal and individual practice are more recent occurrences. Regarding the **Holocaust**, calls for a liturgical remembrance of the murder of European Jews have resulted in specially composed **liturgies** which are enacted by part of the Jewish community. At the same time the establishment of a **civil society** in the **State of Israel** has resulted in the development of civil religion, which includes the establishment of **Holocaust Memorial Day** and the memorialisation of other events significant to the State of Israel. Holocaust Memorial Day has also been recently established in Britain (Holocaust remembrance in **Germany** and **Poland** has taken place on 27 January for some years) and is marked by civic activities as well as educational programmes in churches and synagogues. Recently studies of collective memory have gained influence also in the study of religion and Jewish–Christian relations. This is particularly the case in relation to the Holocaust, where the communities of victimisers and victims have developed different patterns of relating to the legacy of their families and communities. The study of these patterns one, and now already two or three, generations removed offers a new area of Jewish–Christian encounter in the present that is brought to bear on the study of the history of Jewish–Christian relations.

K. HANNAH HOLTSCHNEIDER

Men', Aleksandr Vladimirovich (1935–90)

Russian Orthodox priest (Moscow region). Men' was baptised as an infant at the same time as his Jewish mother. In later years he was to speak with satisfaction of his Jewish roots, which allowed a particular 'participation in the sacred past'. Soviet circumstances inhibited involvement in overt or extensive **dialogue** with Judaism, but his reading and commitment provided firm foundations for such work. In a Church heavily burdened with **anti-Judaism** and **antisemitism** he was accused of fostering a Judeo-Christian movement, though there was nothing to suggest that such was his concern: rather, he rejected the use of **Hebrew language** or ritual in support of Jewish converts. His Jewish ancestry was held to define him as an interloper by fellow-members of his Church; there were also Jews who saw him as a traitor to their cause. He welcomed individuals' acceptance of the Christian faith, but never sought converts, and was convinced that the **covenant** on Sinai could not but endure throughout the ages; hence his delight at St **Paul**'s insistence that 'the gifts and the calling of God are irrevocable' (Rom. 11.29) and his reluctance to accept the **supersessionist** stance of his Church. It took courage to argue, as he did (in conformity with **Vatican II**), that anti-Judaism should have no place in the life and worship of the Church, yet he shared such thoughts with a *samizdat* journal, and a Jewish one at that (1975). Here also he protested against the **blood libels** of the Russian past. His writings circulated widely in *samizdat* and abroad, but with the end of Soviet rule, during which his ministry had constantly attracted the attentions of the KGB, he became a public figure. Conservatives of various kinds still saw his generous spirit as a

threat, and on 9 September 1990 he was axed to death by unidentified assailants. A minority of his fellow-Orthodox acclaim him as a martyr; others regret his **liberalism** and his **tolerance** of other faiths. Patron and promoter of Jewish–Christian **dialogue** in **Russia** though he might become, his reputation in his homeland is not yet sufficiently secure for this to carry weight. *SERGEI HACKEL*

Menahem ben Shelomo Ha-Me'iri *see* Meiri, Menahem ben Solomon

Menasseh ben Israel (1604–57)

Rabbi in the Portuguese Jewish community of Amsterdam. His writings in Latin, Spanish and English on biblical **exegesis**, Jewish character, Messianic hope and the fate of the **soul** produced a substantial reputation among European Christian intellectuals, many of whom corresponded with him. One of his books was illustrated with four plates by Rembrandt (1606–69), who also etched his portrait. His 1655 mission to England, attempting to convince Oliver **Cromwell**'s government to reverse the 1290 **expulsion** of the Jews, generated vigorous debate about the Jews. He died believing he had failed, as his proposal for a formal recall of the Jews was not accepted, but his efforts led to a *de facto* **toleration** of Jews living openly on British soil. *MARC SAPERSTEIN*

Mendelssohn, Moses (1729–86)

German philosopher and man of letters. Often regarded as the father of the Jewish Enlightenment or *Haskalah*, Mendelssohn was an observant Jew who embraced the wider **Enlightenment** culture. He upheld the traditional rejection of Christianity in his open correspondence (1769–70) with the Zurich theologian Johann Kaspar Lavater (1741–1801), arguing that rationality was the criterion by which to assess religious claims, and regarded Christianity as lacking in comparison with Judaism. In *Jerusalem* (1783) he urged **tolerance** for other religious groups based upon a common humanity, and regarded the practice of religion as a private affair for the individual and for the community concerned. *DANIEL R. LANGTON*

Mennonites *see* Anabaptists

Merchant of Venice, The

Comedy by William **Shakespeare**. Written in 1596/7, *The Merchant of Venice* endures as one of Shakespeare's most staged and studied plays. It is also controversial in its portrayal of Jews and Jewish–Christian relations.

Shakespeare's play depicts Jews and Christians ambivalently. Shylock, the principal Jewish character, is both villain and victim. He is an avaricious moneylender (*see* **usury**), a Christian-hater who tries to take a pound of flesh from merchant Antonio in payment for a debt (I.iii; II.v). But the play also depicts greedy, prejudiced Christians (I.i; I.iii; II.ii) and Jewish suffering is highlighted (IV.i) when Shylock falls foul of the Venice authorities, loses half his property, and is subject to forced **conversion**. *Merchant* can be read as making a plea for **tolerance**, although it is often forgotten that the famous 'hath not a Jew eyes' speech (III.i) functions as a justification for revenge.

Shakespeare's sources (medieval flesh-bond stories, Marlowe's *Jew of Malta* (1589?), and the execution of **Converso** Roderigo Lopez (1594) are likely influences) and intentions are hard to determine. What is clearer is the significance of *Merchant* in reflecting and shaping subsequent Jewish–Christian relations. For example, influenced by Romanticism's interpretation of 'the Jew' as symbol of tragic endurance, many nineteenth-century productions depicted Shylock sympathetically. Conversely, 'Shylock' passed into English as a term of abuse. With some justification it may be argued that Jewish characters in much later **English literature** (for example in the novels of **Dickens** and **Eliot**) are developments of or reactions against those portrayed in *The Merchant of Venice*.

MELANIE J. WRIGHT

Messiah

From the Hebrew *mashiaḥ*, meaning 'anointed', translated into the **Septuagint** (third century BCE) by the Greek word *christos*, which in the **New Testament** is the title of **Jesus**, rendered into English by **Christ**. The difference of Messianic beliefs can be regarded as the classic distinction between the two faiths. The **Lambeth Conference 1988** said, 'There are those Christians whose prayer is that Jews, without giving up their Jewishness, will find their fulfilment in Jesus the Messiah'. However, the recent official **Roman Catholic** document *The Jewish People and their Sacred Scriptures in the Christian Bible* (2002) states that 'the Jewish messianic expectation is not in vain'. This represents a huge shift in traditional Christian thinking about the Jewish Messianic hope.

Both Jews and Christians often make debatable assumptions about Messianism: Christians may envisage a unified doctrine of the Messiah in Judaism at the time of Christ; and Jews may assume that a Christian is one who claims Jesus was the Messiah. In fact, 'Messiah' was only one of a wide range of terms and titles used for Jesus, others being 'Master', 'Lord', 'Prophet' and '**Son of Man**'. It has often been argued, for example by Jacob Neusner (b. 1932) in his controversial book *Messiah in Context* (1984), that the concept of the Messiah was not a well-known one in the Jewish world at the time of Jesus. The Lord's anointed in the **Hebrew Bible** is normally the present king, but the prophetic time of 1 Sam. 2.10 makes it easy to apply the phrase to the coming Davidic king envisaged in such prophecies as Isa. 11.1–9 (*see* **Isaiah**). Yet although the prophetic texts that give a vision of a peaceful future quoted by the Gospel writers, especially Matthew, may refer to a king, they do not use *mashiaḥ* as a title. On the other hand, a central scene in the Gospels is the acknowledgement of Jesus as Messiah (Mark 8.29 and parallels). Its historical value for the reconstruction of the life of Jesus is debated, but on any interpretation it shows the importance of Messianism for early Christians who were still in touch with Jewish opinion.

How are we to understand the charismatic figure of Jesus? We can make a distinction between Messianic doctrine and a **Messianic movement**: a popular movement around a Messianic figure need not imply a unified **doctrine**. Judaism hoped for a coming Davidic king, as attested in the *Psalms of Solomon* (first century BCE). Movements that can be called Messianic in a broad sense are mentioned by Judas the Galilean (6 CE) and Theudas (46–8 CE); in Acts 5.36–37 the respected **Gamaliel** is presented as comparing them with the activity of Jesus. In the Hasmonean period the **Dead Sea Scrolls** seem to have envisaged two Messiahs as the King and Priest of the end time, including the Davidic Messiah fulfilling the prophecy of the lion of Judah (Gen. 49.10). To go back further, the oracles of **Balaam** in Num. 24.7, 17 are rendered in the Septuagint so as to understand the expectation of a coming Jewish conqueror. These hopes appear to have been the basis for Shimon **Bar Kokhba**, who led a rebellion against the Romans from 132 to 135 CE and whom, according to the Jerusalem **Talmud** (*Ta'anit* 68d), Rabbi **Akiba** himself believed to be the Messiah as the star prophesied in Num. 24.17. After his death Messianic expectation probably lessened, but it did not disappear and provides part of the background of the debate with Christianity.

The Babylonian and Jerusalem Talmuds are works edited and completed after the **Roman Empire** became Christian – the idea that the Messiah had not yet come is now given an elaborate doctrinal form which can also be viewed as a rabbinic response to a dominant Christianity. The Church says the saviour of humanity has arrived: the Synagogue will now elaborate this doctrine, but place his arrival firmly in the future. The Babylonian Talmud (edited 500–600) has an extended passage on Messianism in *Sanhedrin* 97a–99a: the coming of the Messiah will be preceded by a time of trouble; it is not advisable to calculate the time of his coming; the history of the world can be divided into three parts, the third of which is the time of the Messiah; God will send the Messiah to a generation that is worthy of it and repents; the Messiah will be from the House of **David**; his coming will be announced by the return of **Elijah**; others suggest he is here already, but we fail to recognise him sitting among the poor. The Talmuds specifically link the coming of the Messiah with the keeping of the **Sabbath**. This too may reflect a debate with **Jewish Christians** who were discarding the celebration of the day in favour of Sunday, the 'Lord's Day'. Those who proclaimed the Messiah had come were in fact, by their heresies, postponing his arrival yet further. Christian teaching both before and after **Constantine** had insisted on the idea of two advents of the Messiah, one still to come; and this second advent was expected, especially by second- and third-century **Church Fathers** such as **Irenaeus** and **Tertullian**, to initiate a reign of Christ in **Jerusalem** (millennium).

In the Bible **commentaries**, **disputations** and **polemics** of the Middle Ages the topic of the Messiah was again a central topic of dispute between Jews and Christians. The same arguments were repeated, with Christians arguing that texts from the Hebrew prophets foretold the two advents of Jesus as Messiah, and Jews replying that the promised Messiah has not yet arrived. At Barcelona in 1263 the Messiah was the first and principal topic of discussion. The Christian disputants found it difficult to cope with **Nahmanides**' arguments that a biblical passage can carry a wealth of alternative explanations: 'As for the *Midrash*, if anyone wants to believe in it, well and good, but if someone does not believe in it there is no harm.' They were also puzzled by his statement that the Messiah was not as important to Jews as Christians seemed to think: 'My lord King, hear me. The Messiah is not fundamental to our religion. Why, you are worth more to me than the Messiah! You are a king, and he is a king.' Nahmanides criticised **Maimonides**' making the Messiah a Principle of the Faith.

The debate continues today in the Jewish world since the death in June 1994 of Rabbi Menachem Mendel Schneerson (1902–94), leader of the Lubavitch movement, many of whose followers proclaimed him as the Messiah. The Messianic hope rooted in scripture was a powerful factor in the origins of Christianity. Yet one could well argue that had it not been for Jewish–Christian debate *neither* faith would have since been so preoccupied with Messianism. Official religious leaders would not otherwise have accepted a doctrine so threatening, so potentially subversive and revolutionary, and so rooted in popular culture.

MICHAEL HILTON

Messianic Jews

Messianic Judaism consists of Jews (individuals with Jewish ancestry) and Gentiles who believe that by accepting Yeshua (**Jesus**) into their lives they can live a fulfilled Jewish life. The movement emerged out of **Hebrew Christianity** in the latter decades of the twentieth century and emphasises its attachment with Judaism rather than with the Church. Messianic Jews, such as **Jews for Jesus**, observe many of the same customs as Jews, including biblical festivals and post-biblical lifecycle events such as **barmitzvah**. Messianic Judaism is proactive in seeking Jewish converts and is condemned by the vast majority of the Jewish community. Although a Jewish convert to Christianity may still be categorised a Jew according to a strict interpretation of the *halakhah* (Jewish law), most Jews are adamantly opposed to the idea that one can convert to Christianity and still remain a Jew or be considered part of Jewish life. From a mainstream Christian perspective Messianic Judaism can also invoke hostility for misrepresenting Christianity. Although there is sympathy for the difficulties faced by Messianic Jews, many involved in Jewish–Christian **dialogue** view Messianic Judaism as undermining the mutual respect that has been built up in recent years. Its syncretism confuses Christians and Jews, and it is not surprising that Messianic Jews feel rejected and misunderstood by both Judaism and Christianity. *EDWARD KESSLER*

Messianic movements

The term is generally employed to label those people who have acclaimed a given individual to be **Messiah** and in the process have become followers of that figure. Messianic movements in Judaism and Christianity share many of the same features, such as the belief that their leader is the awaited Messiah who will help bring about God's rule and restore the autonomy of **Israel**. In the **New Testament** Gospel accounts of the teachings of **Jesus** the concept was directly related to the **kingdom of God**. A further key element of a Messianic group is that the adherents view their leader as actively ushering in the new era, by promoting particular patterns of behaviour and/or by advocating the taking up of arms. The latter is best illustrated by the tradition that **Akiba** acclaimed **Bar Kokhba**, the leader of the second Jewish revolt (132–5CE), as Messiah (*y. Ta'anit* 4.8 68a). There is no further evidence, however, to suggest that Bar Kokhba tried to present his cause as a Messianic movement, although he was condemned in Christian writings.

Jewish history incorporates several examples of Messianic movements, but the majority of attention centres on the period in which Christianity emerged. The New Testament provides the most detailed exposition of the activity and identity of a Messiah figure in its depiction of Jesus of Nazareth. In turn this has fostered the notion that Messianic expectation was a dominant concern of Jews in the late Second Temple period. It has also resulted in a tendency within Christian scholarship to view the various groups and movements during the period as a broad single expression of zealot ideology (e.g. M. Hengel (b. 1926)). However, the recent work of R. A. Horsley and D. M. Rhoads has established that each group described in the extant sources needs to be understood in its own right.

The brutal suppression of the Bar Kokhba revolt helped to ensure that **Rabbinic Judaism** did not actively promote aspirations for helping to usher in the Messianic era. This quietist approach has remained in place in Jewish thinking, with two notable exceptions. One was the seventeenth-century movement connected with **Shabbetai Zvi**, who was acclaimed by his followers as the Messiah and generated much Christian interest. The other recent claim by members of the Lubavitch hasidim

regarding Menachem Schneerson (1902–94) has caused great controversy within Judaism, both towards the end of Schneerson's life and after his death, because, in remarkable parallel with Christian teaching about the *parousia*, some of Schneerson's followers expect him to return and inaugurate the Messianic age.

See also **eschatology**; **millenarianism**

JAMES S. MCLAREN

Messianism *see* **Messianic movements; Messiah**

Methodism

A movement of the eighteenth-century British evangelical revival, and an offshoot of **Anglicanism**. Its founder, John **Wesley**, recorded a small number of meetings with Jews in his journals, but in his sermon 'On Faith' (1788) he wrote that 'with heathens, Mahometans, and Jews, we have at present nothing to do'. More important for Methodism than his chance encounters with people of other faiths was his inclusive Arminian theology, rather than an exclusive **Calvinism**, which he explicitly repudiated. Methodism is now found as a number of different denominations in many countries of the world; it is also a participant in a number of united Churches (notably in Australia, Canada and India). Methodism's strong sense of God's universal **grace** and the need for social **holiness** or **sanctification** has led a number of Methodists into positive interfaith, including Jewish–Christian, relations. One notable pioneer was William W. Simpson (1907–87), the first secretary of the International **Council of Christians and Jews**. Like many Churches in recent years, various Methodist Churches have made positive statements about relations with Jews: notably the British Methodist Church in 1993 in the course of a wider ranging document on interreligious relationships; and especially the American United Methodist Church in its important 1996 document *Building New Bridges in Hope*. The latter, offering nine guiding principles for Jewish–Christian relations, goes further than many Church documents in a positive appraisal of post-Christian Judaism as an authentic and ongoing revelation of God. It espouses **dialogue** rather than **mission** and respects 'the legitimacy of the **State of Israel**'.

MARTIN FORWARD

Midrash

(Pl. = midrashim.) Hebrew term for asking, searching, inquiring and interpreting. It generally refers to a genre of rabbinic literature, although it has been argued by some Christian scholars, such as Raymond Brown (1928–88), that there also exists a specifically Christian form of midrash, notably in the **New Testament**. In **Rabbinic Judaism** midrash consists of an anthology and compilation of homilies, including *halakhah* (Jewish law) and *aggadah* (general ethical, anecdotal or homiletical material). Consequently, midrash is considered a religious activity as well as a **commentary** on a particular book of the Bible. In Jewish services midrash is often part of the exposition of the **Torah** reading, as found, for example, in the **Targums**, which are supposed to be merely translation but nevertheless allow for development. Thus, midrash is not merely an attempt to understand the biblical text but to make sense of it, i.e. to create meaning, not simply to offer biblical **exegesis**.

Midrash sometimes sheds light on the Jewish–Christian encounter in Late Antiquity and can demonstrate rabbinic awareness of Christianity. For example, a midrash on the phrase 'let us make man' (Gen. 1.27) may represent an early Jewish response to Christian teaching about the relationship between the Father and the Son. Christians interpreted this phrase **Christologically**, interpreting it to mean that the Father (God) discussed the creation of humankind with the Son (Jesus Christ). In one midrash, however, God is portrayed as 'taking counsel with the works of heaven and earth' or in an alternative suggestion 'taking counsel with His own heart'. **Justin Martyr** quotes this midrash in *Dialogue with Trypho* (62) when he accuses the rabbis of misrepresenting scripture.

Rabbinic literature also includes midrashim on biblical legends such as the tradition that the Torah was given to Moses by angels, rather than by God. This midrash is known by Barnabas (*see* **Apostolic Fathers**), who warns Christians against being influenced by Jewish **biblical interpretation** and suggests that the Torah was given by an evil angel as a punishment to the Jewish people for their sins. A very small number of midrashim mention Christianity explicitly, such as the eighth-century Palestinian midrash, *Aggadat Bereshit* (31), which in a polemical comment on the *Akedah* condemns the view that God had a son.

An example of Christian midrash can be found in the differing birth stories in Matthew and Luke. The two stories may be described as Christian midrash because they look at the historical facts – the birth of

Jesus – and add related stories which interpret and amplify the original historical event. Brown argues that Christian midrash builds a bridge between the stories of the **Old Testament** and the life of Jesus.   *EDWARD KESSLER*

Millenarianism

Also known as millennialism or chiliasm. This term is often applied loosely to any religious outlook that envisages a transformation of earthly life and the ushering in of a golden age, in which, commonly, a faithful group are rewarded. The core doctrines of millenarianism are found in prophetic Judaism and early Christianity. In the latter the reference in the book of Revelation (20.1–5) – clearly itself rooted in contemporary Jewish interpretation – to a period of a thousand years in which Christ will reign in person on earth has encouraged the expectation of a collective, imminent, terrestrial **salvation** according to a divine plan and has exercised a pervasive influence in the history of Christianity. The millennium is an interval in the war of good and evil which the Christian **revelation**, following Hebrew **apocalyptic**, sees as the pattern of all history. It is obsessive preoccupation with, rather than belief in, this idea that separates cultic extremists from the rest of Christendom. Christian and Jewish millenarianism share the revolutionary concept of **redemption** in which the old order is destroyed. As a form of **eschatology** concerned with the chronology of future events, three positions have emerged which try to interpret the return and millennial rule of Christ. Pre-millenarianism asserts that Christ will return to earth before his millennial reign begins; post-millennialism, which is more allegorical, teaches that Christ's return will follow a millennial period on earth; while amillennialism rejects the notion of a literal thousand-year period and emphasises the coexistence of the **kingdom of God** with the kingdom of **evil** until the end of history. Pre-millennialists have frequently given the Jewish people a prominent role in the future age. Over the centuries there have been various attempts by Christians to restore Jewish sovereignty in the Holy Land rooted in the belief that the return of the Jews is a biblically designated precondition to the Second Coming of Jesus (*see* **Christian Zionism**). The primary concern here has been the **conversion** of Jews to Christianity. In modern times, particularly since the Six Day War of 1967, this interest has been reflected in very strong Christian **fundamentalist** support for the **State of Israel**, notably in the **United States** and among **Evangelical** Protestants, such as Pentecostal and Adventist churches.

In rabbinic teaching the eschatological Messianic hopes for the re-establishment of the **Temple** and of a Jewish kingdom were often treated with caution and moderation; but they continued to play an important part throughout the medieval and later periods, as can be seen in writers like Saadiah Gaon (882–942) and Don Isaac Abravanel (1437–1508) and even, in a sophisticated form, **Maimonides**. The widespread movement of Messianic hope focussed on **Shabettai Zvi** aroused the keenest interest among contemporary Christians. The most recent example of Jewish millennial fervour is demonstrated by the Lubavitch hasidim, some of whom suggested that their rebbe, Menachem Mendel Schneerson (1902–94), was the **Messiah**. After his death he was expected to return and bring in God's Messianic kingdom.

See also **Messianic movements**   *DAVID WEIGALL*

Minorities

In its origins Christianity, like Judaism but with less legal protection (*see* **religio licita**), was a minority religion in the **Roman Empire**. However, this changed after the conversion of **Constantine** in 312 CE, and since the end of the fourth century Christianity has been the dominant partner in the relationship with Judaism, and Jews the minority. The *Adversus Judaeos* **literature** thus illustrates, among other things, the frustration experienced by a majority power in its relationship with a minority group. The respective populations today indicate that Christianity remains the majority power, but an increasing number of Christians in the West are aware that they live in a multicultural and multifaith world and that, consequently, both religions are now minorities. This has led a number of contemporary Christian scholars, such as Krister Stendahl (b. 1921), to develop a theology of the interfaith encounter that takes into account its minority status.

In Western Europe and North America, where Roman Catholic and Protestant theology has changed dramatically in recent years, most notably since *Nostra Aetate* in 1965, Christian–Jewish **dialogue** takes place with Christians being a majority and Jews a minority. However, the situation is different in other historical and cultural contexts. In Israel, for example, dialogue takes place where Christians are a minority among a Jewish majority. Here the context is further affected by a complex asymmetry in the dialogue of Christians and Jews with Muslims: in Western Europe Muslims are a minority, but in the Middle East they are a large majority; yet in Israel Muslims are a minority, but larger than the Christian minority.

For Christians, accepting a minority position, alongside Judaism, requires a rethinking of the place of the Christian Church, the specific mission of Christ and the way in which the mission of the Church fits into God's total plan. **New Testament** texts, such as Matt. 28.19 ('Go therefore and make disciples of all the nations baptising them in the name of the Father and of the Son and of the Holy Spirit') are being re-read alongside passages such as Matt. 10.5 and 23 ('Do not go to any Gentiles... You will not lack cities in Israel before the Son of Man appears'), with Stendahl, for example, arguing that Matthew's understanding of the **mission** of the Church is based on a minority model which sits comfortably alongside the Jewish understanding of mission (cf. Isa. 42.6 and the calling of Israel 'to be a light to the nations'). He suggests that the Jewish emphasis on a revelatory non-universalism – in other words, on being a particular people – may help Christians respond to the self-evident fact, particularly in the West, that they are no longer a majority. Being faithful and obedient to God but not claiming a monopoly on God's revelation may provide the basis for Jews and Christian to explore together what it means to have minority status.

See also **particularism**; **universalism**

EDWARD KESSLER

Miriam

Jews and Christians associate Miriam's name with prophecy, music and ritual dance, salvation and prophetic dissent. Miriam, sister to **Moses** and **Aaron**, is the first woman in scripture to be called prophet (Exod. 15.20, cf. Philo, *Contempl.* 86–7), though there is no example of her prophesying (cf. *b. Sotah* 12a–13a; *b. Baba Batra* 120a; *L.A.B.* 9.9–10 and 9.15; *Mekilta Shirata* 10). Modern biblical scholars concur that Miriam was once of greater significance in Israel's history than the biblical texts allow, and women in particular have found Miriam an inspiring, subversive figure. Jewish and Christian feminist scholars say much about the way she has been portrayed in tradition.

Jewish **midrashim** explored and explained anomalies and the unclear sibling-relationships in the Hebrew texts about her, sometimes enhancing Miriam's role (see Cohen, *The Origins and Evolution of the Moses Nativity Story*). Mic. 6.4 points to what some suspect, namely that she, no less than her siblings, had led the exodus from Egypt. **Wisdom** and **salvation** combined in the traditions about Miriam's well, which appeared because of her merits (so Pseudo-Philo and rabbinic interpretation, see Ginzberg, *Legends* III), but originally Miriam may have been a priestly figure. After she and Aaron criticised Moses, Miriam alone was punished with a polluting skin disease and seven days of separation (Num. 12.1–15). Christian and Jewish commentators struggled to explain this seeming injustice, but for some that separation has suggested a parallel with the seven days of priestly consecration (Exod. 29.35), and a condensed and legendary reference to women's demotion from **priesthood**.

Just as modern Jewish women and feminists try to recover the spiritual legacy of Miriam, so Christian women past and present have appealed to her example, sometimes to claim a right to public ministry or priesthood, or in exploring spirituality and **liturgy**. Clement of Rome (*c*.95 CE) likened Miriam's challenge to a threat to properly constituted Church leaders (*Cor.* 4.11). In second- to fifth-century Montanism Miriam was proof that females might validly be publicly active prophet-teachers (Origen, *Fr. 1 Cor.* 14.36), while later Quintillian Montanists cited her in support of female clergy (Epiphanius, *Medicine Box* 49.2). Among Catholics, in the fourth-century *Apostolic Constitutions* she was named in the ordination prayer for deaconesses, who were likened to the **Holy Spirit**.

Miriam was probably the unnamed sister of the infant Moses in the narrative of his rescue (Exod. 2.1–10) and thus a means to her people's deliverance. In turn Moses' infancy story influenced that of **Jesus** in Matthew's Gospel. Since the *Song of Moses* and of the men (Exod. 15.1–18) probably belonged originally to Miriam and the women (cf. 15.20–21), it was she who figured at the beginning (Moses' birth) and end of the exodus salvation story, as did **Mary** (in name another Miriam) in Jesus' story, beginning with Luke's **Magnificat** and ending at the cross. Miriam and Mary seemingly converge again in the Qur'an, where Mary/Maryam is also 'sister of Aaron' (cf. Exod. 15.20; 1 Chr. 6.3; Num. 26.59; *Sura* 3.31 *House of 'Imran*; *Sura* 19.29 and cf. 66.11–12). Muslim authorities offer differing explanations for this.   *CHRISTINE TREVETT*

Mishnah

A comprehensive compendium of rabbinic law from the early third century CE, perhaps the earliest of all rabbinic works, which formed the base-text of the **Talmud**. The fact that it makes no reference to Christians or Christianity may be due partially to the marginality of Christianity in third-century Palestine, in spite of individuals such as **Origen** (who seems unaware of this work); it is also a reflection of general early rabbinic indifference towards non-Jewish or non-rabbinic religions. The **eschatological** prediction that 'the Kingdom will convert to heresy (*minut*)' (*m. Sotah* 9.15), presumably referring to **Constantine**'s conversion to Christianity, is a later interpolation which may be dated to the fourth century. The term 'Mishnah' means 'teaching (by oral repetition)', but it was also interpreted as meaning 'second' (in relation to scriptures), hence the Greek term *deuterosis* used by fourth-century and later **Church Fathers** (e.g. Eusebius, Jerome), and by **Justinian** in his decree against it in 553 CE (a decree that is unlikely to have been effectively implemented). In this decree the *deuterosis* is described as 'unwritten', which may confirm the widely held opinion that the Mishnah, in this period, was still an oral composition. However, 'unwritten' may simply mean 'not in the scriptures'. The term *deuterosis*, moreover, is likely in early Christian sources to refer to Jewish non-scriptural teachings in general, rather than to the specific work of the Mishnah. In an early medieval **anti-Christian** polemic, exclusive possession of the Mishnah is presented as evidence that the Jews are the true **Israel** (*Pesikta Rabbati* 5.1, etc.).   *SACHA STERN*

Mission

Mission is one of the most contentious and sensitive areas in Jewish–Christian relations, partly because, for Jews, it conjures up images of centuries of persecution by the Church and partly because Jews are frustrated with Christian missionary activity that fails to understand their 'no' to **Jesus**. Any attempts to convert the 'other' destroys the trust that is building between the two faiths. Terms sometimes used synonymously with the word 'mission' include 'evangelism', 'conversion', 'witness' and 'proselytism'.

Mission is the sending out of someone to fulfil a particular task. Both Judaism and Christianity have a missionary vocation in the sense that their adherents are commissioned by God to carry out a specific witness in the world. Christian missionary activity has traditionally been understood as converting non-Christians to belief in Christ, and that has included Jews. Generally, Jews have not understood their mission as converting others to Judaism but as faithfulness to **Torah** and the covenantal obligations; therefore non-Jews are not targets for **conversion** because the righteous of all nations will have a share in the world to come if they keep the **Noachide Laws**. Jews understand their mission as being a witness to the One God, as a 'light to the nations'; however, between the second and third century CE the **Pharisees** may have actively sought converts, although scholars disagree as to when within this period they did so (Feldman, Goodman). A number of diverse texts are relevant when considering Pharisaic missionary activity during this period, for example: Matt. 23.15; *Letter of Aristeas* 226; **Josephus**, *Ant.* 13.9.1; 13.11.3; 20.2.3; also *J.W.* 7.3.3; **Philo**, *Virt.* 102; 219; Esth. 8.17. The missionary approach of the Pharisaic movement may have influenced early Christian mission (Georgi, Nock, Segal).

Jesus' mission was focused on the imminent coming of the **kingdom of God** (Mark 1.15; 6.7f.). He commissioned 12 disciples to represent **Israel** and accompany him during his ministry, specifically asking them not to go to any Gentile town but only to 'the lost sheep of the house of Israel' (Matt. 10.5). He later sent out 70 disciples in pairs to extend this mission. It is generally accepted in **New Testament** scholarship that the Gentile mission occurred not during Jesus' lifetime but after the **resurrection** when the Christ-event was understood to have universal relevance (Matt. 28.19; Luke 24.47). Immediately after Jesus' death the disciples directed their **preaching** at Jews and some godfearers (Gentiles attracted to Jewish monotheism, but who did not convert to Judaism) in the synagogues, proclaiming that God had raised him from the dead. The catalyst for the mission to the **Samaritans** and Gentiles can be located in the dispute between the Jerusalem Church (the Hebrews) and Stephen and the Hellenists in Acts 6–7. The

Hellenists had developed a negative view of the **Temple**, based on that part of the Jesus-tradition which prophesied the destruction of the Temple (e.g. Mark 14.58 and par.). Prior to Paul's conversion to Christianity it was these Christians whom he had persecuted; and consequently they were driven out of **Jerusalem** and began preaching their message to Samaritans and Gentiles (Hahn, S. Brown, Gager). Acts 10 records the conversion and **baptism** of the centurion Cornelius by the apostle Peter and is interpreted by some scholars as an attempt to root the Gentile mission in a key disciple-figure (S. Brown). The incorporation of the Gentiles into the Church gathered momentum with **Paul**, known as 'an apostle to the Gentiles'. He based his mission on two convictions: first, that he had been specially commissioned by the risen Christ to go to the Gentiles (Gal. 1.15–17) and second, the belief that God was the God of Gentiles as well as Jews (Rom. 3.29; 15.8f.). When the gospel was preached in the synagogues with little success, the Church had to come to terms with the Jewish 'no' to Jesus, a situation that Paul wrestles with in **Romans 9–11**. The gradual parting of the ways between the communities led to a severely hostile relationship that was to intensify with competition between the two faiths for converts on the mission-field until the fourth century. The continued attraction of Judaism provoked harsh anti-Jewish sermons from the **Church Fathers** (e.g. **Melito**, John **Chrysostom**).

During the first three centuries CE the Church's mission to Jews was coupled with anti-Jewish **polemic** because the Jews had failed to convert to Christianity. The Church developed an exclusive understanding of **salvation** – *extra ecclesiam nulla salus* – outside the Church no salvation. This teaching became the central support for its mission to Jews as well as pagans. The conversion of **Constantine** to Christianity in 312 CE was a turning point for Jewish–Christian relations, where missionary policy became bound up with anti-Jewish legislation, severely restricting Jewish influence on society and prohibiting Jews from converting Christians to Judaism. Christianity became the official religion of the **Roman Empire**, which meant that the Church's mission to Jews was officially endorsed by the state and that those who did not convert were to experience brutal activity. In 438 the **Theodosian Code** made missionary activity legal for Christians but illegal for Jews. The **Justinian Code** of the sixth century severely restricted the public status of Jews and led to a wave of aggressive missionary activities and forced baptisms. Historically, the 'failure' of large numbers of Jews to embrace Jesus continued to baffle the Church and precipitated the development of various **myths** of Jewish depravity and blindness. The anti-Jewish policies were challenged by some Church leaders: for example, Pope **Gregory the Great**, who wrote to the Bishops of Arles and Marseilles explaining that these measures against Jews were counterproductive. Some measure of **tolerance** was suggested by the Second Council of Nicaea in 787, which decreed that Jews who had converted to Christianity but continued to practise their Judaism were not Christians and could practise their faith openly. There was always some ambiguity in the Church's understanding of mission and Jews: on the one hand it sought to bring as many Jews as possible into the fold, at times by force if necessary; on the other hand it had a deep respect for the tradition that was at the root of Christian faith. The Church sought to preserve the **identity** of the Jewish people because of the belief that the Jews were the recipients of God's providential care as the **Chosen People** and that eschatologically they had a role in the final act of **redemption**. This raised a tension on the mission-field between belief that the conversion of the Jews was an essential part of Christian mission and not wanting to thwart God's final salvific plan. This tension has still not been adequately addressed by the Church.

The Middle Ages brought some measure of tolerance and peaceful coexistence, but also periods of brutal persecution and aggressive mission when Jews were forced to accept immediate baptism and compulsory attendance at Church, and Jewish children whose families had not converted to Christianity were taken from their homes and raised with Christian families. During the fifteenth and sixteenth centuries Jews were given the choice of converting to Catholicism or **expulsion** from their land (for example, from **Spain** in 1492). The early **Reformation** period saw the positive beginnings of **dialogue** rather than missionary activity. However, this changed with Martin **Luther**. The young Luther was tolerant of Jews because he hoped that when the gospel was stripped of its Catholic inter-

pretation the Jews would convert to Christianity. In his missionary tract of 1523, *That Jesus Christ Was Born a Jew*, he sought to make the gospel more acceptable to Jews. The tract was seen as a success by many Christians at the time, but it sowed the seeds for his later disappointment because the Jews did not convert as expected, and this was to provoke him to write some of the most anti-Jewish tractates in Christian history. For him the conversion of the Jews was an essential part of heralding the Second Coming of Christ. By 1543 he had categorised Jews as beyond redemption and dismissed any mission to them as useless, and wrote three anti-Jewish tracts that suggested measures against those who had not converted which were to have later parallels in Hitler's anti-Jewish laws of the 1930s. John **Calvin** did not consider mission to Jews an urgent priority in his early ministry, partly because he worked in an area with few Jews. Another position emerged during the Reformation which minimised conversionary activity because of the belief that in the end times all Jews would convert; consequently Christians should have a positive attitude towards Jews rather than seeing them as the objects of mission or polemics. This attitude was carried into many discussions by Protestant theologians in the sixteenth and seventeenth centuries. Jews were rarely baptised, and there were few organised attempts to proselytise them; for example, the Pietist movement did not expect the widespread conversion of Jews until the end days and their missionary policy thus encouraged a positive relationship, with conversion by gentle persuasion. During this period missionary activity was less aggressive and began to take a new direction with missionaries learning the languages of Jews (**Hebrew** and Yiddish) as well as studying Jewish religious practices and customs. This led to the inculturation of the gospel with Jewish ideas and language to attract Jews to Christianity, marking a new approach towards Jews in Protestant missionary work. The nineteenth century saw a surge in missionary activity with the founding of new societies for promoting the gospel to Jews (e.g. the London Society for Promoting Christianity amongst the Jews; *see* **Church's Ministry among Jewish People**). The missionaries combined their evangelistic approach with support for a Jewish homeland, a position now termed **Christian Zionism**. In this period the first **Hebrew Christian** groups and Messianic Jewish congregations were founded, which combined the traditional missionary message with the possibility for Jews to keep Jewish customs and identity whilst believing in Christ. This new face to Christian mission was primarily rooted in nineteenth-century Protestant theology. During the twentieth century individual figures like James **Parkes** suggested a non-missionary approach towards Jews. Some organisations took a new position regarding mission: the Roman Catholic order the **Sisters of Sion**, originally founded to convert Jews, renounced its missionary stance in favour of a dialogical relationship with Jews. The various **Councils of Christians and Jews** around the world are non-missionary organisations which believe that mission is incompatible with dialogue. The **International Christian Embassy** in Israel, a Christian Zionist organisation, has a particular **eschatology** which affects its understanding of mission, believing that Christians have forfeited their right to evangelise Jews because of the **Holocaust** and because only after the Second Coming of Christ will all Israel be saved. Other evangelistic groups, like **Jews for Jesus** and **Messianic Jews**, continue to defend a missionary approach, working for the conversion of all Jews to belief in Christ as a necessary requirement for their salvation.

The Holocaust was a further, and perhaps the most significant, catalyst for changes in Christian understandings of mission. The Church began to acknowledge that centuries of anti-Jewish teaching and brutal missionising had laid the foundations for secular **antisemitism** in Europe. The Jewish response often argued that the Christian conversionary attitude towards Jews was in reality no different from Hitler's policies because for centuries the Church had tried to do spiritually what **Hitler** had sought to do physically: to wipe out Jews and Judaism. Contemporary Christian understandings of mission and Jews remain ambiguous but can be placed in three main categories: first, those who seek the conversion of all Jews because there is no exemption from the need for salvation in Christ; second, those who witness to faith in Christ, without targeting Jews specifically, and believe in sharing the Christian faith with all people; and third, those who have no conversionary outlook towards Jews, where mission is understood as mutual influence and a joint ethical witness in an unredeemed world. This latter model has been termed 'critical solidar-

ity' or 'mutual witness' by the American theologian Clark Williamson (*A Mutual Witness*, 1992). The change in Christian mission is clear from a number of statements that clearly reject any coercive proselytising directed at Jews. The **Roman Catholic** Church in **Nostra Aetate** condemns any attempts to set up organisations with the sole aim of converting Jews. The **World Council of Churches** has moved away from a missionary approach to a dialogical relationship (the *Sigtuna Report* of 1988, 4 and 5) and the *Leuenberg Document on the Church and Israel* (*see* **Leuenberg Church Fellowship**) calls for a sensitivity in its methods of witness because of the experience Jews have had of Christian missionary activity and for engagement in appropriate witness within the context of dialogue (3.2; 3.2.2). Nothing has been forthcoming from the **Orthodox Churches**. The first Jewish statement on Jewish–Christian relations, **Dabru Emet**, does not mention Jewish or Christian mission, but does speak about the joint ethical witness of Jews and Christians.

Since the publication of two study documents, *Reflections on Covenant and Mission* (August 2002) and *A Sacred Obligation* (September 2002), mission has been the subject of fierce debate in the **United States**, not only amongst Roman Catholic scholars and leaders, but also in the conservative and **evangelical** wings of the Protestant churches. The Roman Catholic theologian John Pawlikowski (b. 1940) strongly argues that new understandings of mission and covenant in relation to Jews have their roots in *Nostra Aetate*, and necessitate a rethinking of **Christology** and Christian identity. It is this reassessment that remains highly contested between institutional leaders such as Cardinal Dulles (b. 1918) and scholars and activists in Jewish–Christian relations. The issue of mission remains problematic in Jewish–Christian relations. The Churches have no clear consensus of belief in this area and therefore a number of differing positions remain. When groups like the Church's Ministry amongst the Jewish People (CMJ) and Jews for Jesus seek to participate in the dialogue, the problem of mission is inevitably raised. Many Jews expect that if they dialogue with Christians there should be no hidden missionary agenda or secret desire for their conversion. Much missionary theology rests on Christian claims that salvation is only possible through Christ, and therefore any solution to 'mission and Jews' will need to address the issue of salvation. Many Jews, and an increasing number of Christians, see efforts to convert Jews as incompatible with dialogue, and a joint ethical mission is deemed appropriate. *HELEN P. FRY*

Modern Hebrew literature *see* **literature, Hebrew, modern**

Modernity

Modernity is an umbrella term referring to both the cultural and intellectual consequences of the **Enlightenment** and the historical epoch with which they are associated. Its origins may be located philosophically in the work of figures like John Locke (1632–1704) and **Voltaire**, and the commitment to autonomous human rationality and progress through science. However, the rise of modernity is also inextricably linked to particular institutions, namely industrial capitalism (based on technology and rational forms of organisation) and the modern nation state (characterised by representative democracy and the increasing bureaucratisation of life).

Modernity's implications for Jewish–Christian relations are complex. On the one hand the associated processes of social and political **emancipation** of Jews and **minority** Christian groups have created conditions of pluralism in which adherents of different worldviews are brought into close proximity with one another. The separation in the modern state of the public sphere of wage-earning from the increasingly privatised realm of kinship and religious life has created opportunities for interaction and **dialogue**. Within academe the rise of modern biblical scholarship (predicated, like **Wissenschaft des Judentums**, on rational procedures of investigation) has been crucial to the reappraisal of **New Testament** texts and, consequently, Christian **catechesis** and **doctrine** on Judaism.

Interestingly, whilst these shifts are commonly associated with improved Jewish–Christian relations, resistance to aspects of modernity has emerged recently as a platform for interfaith cooperation. The offering of a shared response to secularism (inherent in modernity's privileging of rationalism over belief in the transcendent and supernatural) is a goal of several **Councils of Christians and Jews**, whilst the Society for Textual Reasoning (primarily a body of postmodern Jewish philosophers with diverse influences, including Martin **Buber** and Franz **Rosenzweig**) has increasingly attended to relations between Judaism, Christianity and **Islam**.

This ambivalence stems generally from modernity's challenge to traditional religious authority and belief. In the context of Jewish–Christian relations it may also draw support from the arguments of those, like Zygmunt Bauman (b. 1925), who have suggested that the **Holocaust** is best understood not as an aberration, but as the logical outworking of modernity. From this perspective the attempted genocide of Jews not only depended on modern technologies and bureaucratic processes for its implementation, it was also fuelled by the ordering, classifying nature of modernity, which constructed the unassimilable 'conceptual Jew' as a threatening, challenging presence within the nation state. As such, modernity signalled not the demise of anti-Jewish prejudice, but rather its mutation into a more deadly form, underpinned by the pseudo-science of race theory and eugenics.

If (*contra* Anthony Giddens (b. 1938)) theorists such as Bauman and Fredric Jameson (b. 1934) are correct in suggesting the demise of modernity (witnessed in the increasing problematisation of **identity**, a decline of confidence in science to deliver progress etc.), this has significant implications for the future conduct of Jewish–Christian relations. Since many of the subject's current physical and conceptual structures are the products of modernity, they must alter or lose relevancy with the passing of the epoch. However, the implications of **postmodernism** – with its interest in identity formation and difference – for Jewish–Christian relations are as yet largely unclear. *MELANIE J. WRIGHT*

Molcho, Solomon (*c*.1500–32)

Portuguese **Marrano** Diego Pires, who returned to Judaism and was burned at the stake during the **Inquisition**. After his return to Judaism following a meeting in 1525 with David Reuveni (1490–1538) who claimed to be representative of the ten lost tribes of Israel, Molcho studied **Kabbalah** and settled in Salonica where he wrote *Sefer ha-Mefo'ar* and gained a reputation for prophecy. Returning to Italy by 1529, he preached the coming of the **Messiah** among Jews and Christians. Pope Clement VII (*r*.1265–8) befriended him on account of his successful prophecies and he travelled with Reuveni to Emperor Charles V (*r*.1519–58) to convince him to let the Jews fight against the Turks. The emperor delivered him and Reuveni to the Inquisition. Many attributed Messianic qualities to Molcho, even refusing to believe in his death, and he was an influence on **Shabbetai Zvi**.   *PETR FRYŠ*

Monasticism

Monasticism is a phenomenon of Christian life that has no exact Jewish equivalent. It originates in the decision of some Christians, from about the third century CE, to withdraw from ordinary society into a life of intense **asceticism** in the deserts of Syria, Egypt and the Holy Land. A distinction was soon made between solitary (eremetical) and communal (coenobitic) modes of monastic life, and the principles governing this life were codified into Rules. The Rule of St Benedict (*c*.540 CE) has been most influential in the West, and the Rule of St Basil (from 360s CE) in the East; there are many others, and they regulate the life of a great variety of religious orders. Monasteries, which developed into a dominant economic and cultural force in the medieval West and continue to play an important role in contemporary Christianity, especially in the Roman Catholic Church, have sometimes been centres of hostility to Jews, as well as to those who were (in the monks' eyes) unorthodox Christians, but monastic history also includes episodes of courageous hospitality to Jews (as in Assisi, 1942–4). The nearest Jewish analogy to monasticism is probably to be found in the remote and ascetical community at Qumran (*see also* **Dead Sea Scrolls**), but one must be alive to the danger of drawing too much on Christian monastic categories (e.g. refectory, scriptorium) in interpreting the archaeology of the site. Some of the ascetic customs of the hasidim are also analogous to Christian monastic practice.

ANDERS BERGQUIST

Montefiore, Claude (1858–1938)

Anglo-Jewish leader and scholar. Claude Montefiore was a pioneer in Jewish–Christian relations in the **United Kingdom**. Born into what has been called the 'Cousinhood' – the Anglo-Jewish aristocracy – Montefiore studied at Oxford and came under the wing of Benjamin Jowett (1817–93), who was to be a lasting influence upon him. He also studied under Solomon Schechter (1847–1915), whose influence can be seen in the Hibbert Lectures (Montefiore was the first Jew to be invited to deliver the

Lectures, in 1892). As well as publishing numerous works on fields relating to Judaism and Christianity, he co-founded the *Jewish Quarterly Review*. He was the leader of the Liberal Jewish Movement and crucial to its development in England; his Liberal Jewish views form the basis of all his writings. Montefiore's studies focused on four subjects: the **Hebrew Bible**, the **New Testament** and Christianity, **Rabbinic Judaism**, and **Liberal Judaism**. His was one of the earliest attempts by an English Jew to interpret the history of the Bible in accordance with the conclusions of **biblical criticism**. He wrote *The Synoptic Gospels* (1909), a two-volume introduction, translation and commentary on the first three Gospels, and co-authored *A Rabbinic Anthology* (1938), an important work on Rabbinic Judaism.

Montefiore argued for a change in negative Jewish attitudes towards Christianity. His approach was based on the Liberal Jewish understanding of progressive **revelation**, which located revelation not only in the **Pentateuch**, but also in the Prophets, Writings and rabbinic literature, as well as in other religions. He believed the time had come for a Jewish reappraisal of Christianity and *vice versa*, and his writings reached their climax in a call for a Jewish theology of Christianity, though he made no attempt to forge one himself. In presenting the New Testament to a Jewish audience, he argued that it was an entirely Jewish book with no Christian elements. He saw the teaching of **Jesus**, whom he regarded as a great teacher but in no sense God, as 'a revival of prophetic Judaism', pointing forward to Liberal Judaism. Jesus 'started the movement which broke down the old barriers and brought about the translation of Judaism into the Gentile world . . . with many modifications, curtailments, additions both for the better and worse, good and evil' (*Hibbert Journal*, 3 (1904), 779).

Study of the New Testament led Montefiore to respond to the anti-rabbinism which went hand in hand with **antisemitism**, particularly in **Germany**. Scholars such as Rudolf Bultmann (1884–1976) and Wilhelm Bousset (1865–1923) stressed the antithesis between the teachings of Jesus and Rabbinic Judaism, and argued that by the end of the biblical period the Jewish God had become so transcendent and remote as to have been almost purified away. Montefiore countered that the close relationship between the rabbis and God occurred as a result of the **Torah**. He showed the extent to which the Torah had been venerated, and stressed that it deepened the life of the rabbinic Jew. Montefiore compared the position of Torah to the position of Jesus: both supplied the motive for love and passion; both became mediators between God and the people and the means of bringing God close to the people.   *EDWARD KESSLER*

Montefiore, Moses (1784–1885)

Philanthropist and public office holder, Montefiore occupied a unique place in the nineteenth century for his ability to combine being a strictly **Orthodox Jew** with participating fully in British social and political life. He served as a captain in the Surrey militia and was elected sheriff of London in 1837, while he was President of the Board of Deputies, the representative body of British Jewry, almost continuously from 1835 to 1874. His many diplomatic missions abroad on behalf of oppressed Jews included two cases that echoed longstanding conflicts in Jewish–Christian relations but which were becoming increasingly unacceptable to Western society. The **blood libel** that erupted in Damascus in 1840 led Montefiore to journey there to intervene on behalf of Jews falsely accused of the ritual murder of a local priest, Father Thomas; he achieved their release. He was less successful in the case of Edgar **Mortara**, a six-year-old Jewish boy kidnapped from his parents in 1858 by the Catholic Church; Montefiore travelled to Rome, but was refused a papal interview. Montefiore was highly regarded within British society at large both for his defence of Jewish rights and his wider philanthropy, and was knighted and later awarded a baronetcy by Queen Victoria (*r.*1837–1901). At a time when others were pressing for Jews to enjoy full political rights, he personified the ideal Jew who was loyal to both his country and his faith.   *JONATHAN ROMAIN*

Mormons *see* **Latter-Day Saints**

Mortara Affair

Controversy surrounding the Catholic abduction of an Italian Jewish child. In 1858 Edgardo Mortara (1851–1940), aged six, was abducted by the papal police from his home in Bologna and taken to Rome. The boy had been secretly baptised six years earlier by a Christian domestic servant who thought he was about to die. The parents vainly attempted to get their child back, and the case caused an international uproar. Napoleon III (*r.*1852–70) protested and Moses **Montefiore** attempted to secure the child's release. The founding of the Alliance Israelite Universelle in 1860 was due partly to this case. Pope **Pius IX** rejected all petitions, believing the Church had a legal obligation to raise the boy in the Catholic faith. Edgardo thus became a ward of the Church and, under its tutelage, grew up to become a Catholic priest. In 1870, with the end of papal secular rule in **Italy**, Mortara was free to return to his family, but he refused and became a missionary.   *EDWARD KESSLER*

Moses

The biblical story of Moses, who led the Hebrews out of slavery in Egypt and at Sinai gave them their identity as 'a **kingdom of priests** and a holy nation' (Exod. 19.6), is as familiar to Jews as it is to Christians. But for Christians down the ages Moses was primarily a Lawgiver, while for Jews he is *Moshe rabbenu*, 'our teacher Moses'. References to him in the Bible outside Exodus–Deuteronomy are predominantly to the 'Torah of Moses' or the 'Book of the Law of Moses', and it is clear that from a very early date the laws in the Torah/**Pentateuch** were believed to have been revealed to Moses at Sinai. In the Gospels Mosaic authority is frequently cited in legal discussions, and in rabbinic tradition the 'Law' revealed at Sinai included not just the written **Torah** but also the Oral Torah, that is to say, the **wisdom** handed down orally from generation to generation until finally collected as the sayings of the rabbis in the **Mishnah** and **Talmud**. It is said that Moses actually appealed to God to write down the Oral Torah at Sinai as well. There is also a famous tale that Moses once overheard Rabbi **Akiba** discussing the Law with his disciples and could not understand them, although they claimed Mosaic authority for what they were saying. Rather surprisingly, he is not mentioned in the Passover *haggadah*. Mystery surrounds the death of Israel's greatest leader. An early Jewish tradition describes a dispute between the archangel Michael and the Devil over his body (Jude 9) and another that, like **Elijah**, he ascended miraculously to heaven. He is said to have met the **Messiah** in heaven before his death, and his resurrection from the dead is prophesied, according to a well-known, if rather contrived, interpretation of Deut. 31.16. Moses was the yardstick against which prophets (Deut. 18.15) and kings (2 Kgs 23.25) were judged. Already in biblical tradition he was 'unparalleled in all the signs and wonders he performed' (Deut. 34.10) and for **Philo** he was 'in all respects the greatest and most perfect of men'.

Comparisons with **Jesus** were made from the very beginning. Matthew's Gospel follows the pattern of the life of Moses (e.g. massacre of the innocents, flight into Egypt, 40 days' temptation in the wilderness, **Sermon on the Mount**), while John, in his version of the Gospel narrative, specifically alludes to Moses' brazen serpent, manna in the wilderness and the **Passover**. In the **Golden Calf** story Moses offers to die for his people (Exod. 32.32), while in Deuteronomic and perhaps also Deutero-Isaianic tradition, like Jesus, he plays the role of **suffering servant** bearing the sins of his people (Deut. 1.12; Isa. 53.4, 12; Matt. 8.17). His exceptional humility is referred to in Num. 12.3. Elsewhere in the **New Testament** a contrast is made between Moses, the servant to whom God entrusted his house, and Jesus who was more like a son (Heb. 3.5–6). **Paul** draws a contrast between the old **covenant** of Moses written on tablets of stone and Christ's new covenant in the hearts of believers. If the face of Moses shone when he appeared to Israel with the tablets of the old law, how much more splendid will be the light of Christ, the new Moses. From Paul there grew up the belief that Moses actually placed a veil over the faces of the Israelites (2 Cor. 3.12–15) so that when the Messiah came they could not recognise him: hence the image of the synagogue as a woman blind-folded, graphically depicted in numerous works of art from the early Middle Ages onwards (*see **Ecclesia/Synagoga***). In Muslim tradition too he is sometimes accused of misleading the Jews. He is not infrequently depicted with a saint's halo, however, a feature of Christian **iconography** perhaps less well known than the horns he is given by Michelangelo (1475–1564) and others as a consequence of the erroneous Latin translation of Exod. 34.30 (Hebrew 'rays').

No extrabiblical evidence has so far come to light to confirm or deny the existence of Moses, and modern scholars have questioned the historicity of most of the biblical story, though his Egyptian name and his marriage to the daughter of a pagan priest seem very unlikely to have been invented. Belief in the Mosaic authorship of the Torah, the 'Five Books of Moses', against all the evidence of modern critical scholarship (e.g. anachronisms like Gen. 12.6b and abrupt changes of style), remains a distinguishing feature of both **Orthodox** **Judaism** and conservative **evangelical** Christianity. Cecil B. de Mille's epic **film** *The Ten Commandments* (1956) successfully appealed to both Jewish and Christian audiences by adhering as closely as possible to the biblical text while at the same time skilfully incorporating elements of Jewish liturgical tradition and explicit visual references to Christian iconography. More recently the animated cartoon *Prince of Egypt* (1998) adds some interesting aggadic details to the story, such as the stormy waters of the Nile on which Moses' basket is tossed about and barely survives, and Moses' poignant compassion for his defeated 'brother' Rameses at the end. For Christians he remains one of several legendary biblical champions of justice, while in Judaism he is unique, both as a source of legal and ethical authority and as an inspiration to the people he created.   *JOHN F. A. SAWYER*

Mourning

The distinctive mourning rites of Judaism appear at first sight to have no parallel in Christianity, but many detailed customs were borrowed from the Catholic Church in a rich period of innovation in the twelfth and thirteenth centuries. Ever since **Abraham** purchased a place of interment for **Sarah** (Gen. 32), **burial** rather than cremation has remained the norm in both faiths. The most ancient surviving Jewish mourning rituals are tearing the clothes, *keriah* (Gen. 37.34), and a seven-day mourning period, *shiva* (Gen. 50.10). In the Middle Ages rituals in both faiths were thought of as elevating the **soul** of the dead. In Jewish practice the ancient *Kaddish* prayer took on this function and was recited by mourners (*Machzor Vitry*, from 1208); Catholic Masses for the Dead had a similar function. After the first **Crusade** Jews in Christian lands adopted from Catholics the custom of lighting **candles** for deceased parents on the anniversary (*yahrzeit*) of the death. In 1296 in Mainz Rabbi Isaac ben Samuel began his *Memorbuch* recording the names of dead **martyrs**, thus mirroring the cult of **saints** in the Catholic Church. Many Jewish mourning customs come from twelfth- or thirteenth-century **France** and **Germany**. These include pouring out all the water from the house where a death occurred and putting earth from the **land of Israel** into the grave, which seems to be derived from the crusader practice of carrying earth from the Holy Land. Other practices adopted from contemporary Christians include the use of a coffin for burial and the recital of Ps. 23 in memorial prayers. The wearing of black by mourners was common among Jews in the days of the **Talmud**, but later prohibited as a non-Jewish custom. The placing of flowers on the coffin or grave is discouraged for the same reason. A recent innovation in Jewish mourning rituals is the ceremony for the setting up of a tombstone. A stone-setting ceremony is known from the **Ukraine** and Belarus in both the **Roman Catholic** and Ukrainian **Orthodox Churches**. *MICHAEL HILTON*

Muhammad *see* **Islam**

Museums

Museums in the West record the self-understanding of the dominant group which is, generally speaking, at least nominally Christian. For example, the subject matter of medieval and Renaissance **art** is predominantly Christian, although artists' preoccupations began to change with the coming of **modernity**. Since the nineteenth century **minorities** have become increasingly assertive in publicly **memorialising** their past, presenting it as a significant part of national history (e.g. the National Museum of American Jewish History (1976)). Many Jewish museums, for example Prague (founded 1906) and Berlin (founded 1933), were looted or destroyed during the **Holocaust**. Today's Jewish museums, often located in former Jewish quarters, restored synagogues or communal buildings, present themselves as 'living memorials' celebrating the life and mourning the death of local and national communities. Whilst they include positive references to coexistence and cultural symbiosis, the primary emphasis is on what was lost, and the host community's responsibility for, or indifference to, this destruction. Part cultural centre, part educational tool, these museums educate Jews and non-Jews (particularly Christians) about Jewish history and culture. 'Jewishness' is represented in largely ethnic or cultural terms with an emphasis on the value of pluralism and multiculturalism.

There is a contemporary resurgence of interest in Jewish culture, reflected in the number of museums, festivals (e.g. Kraków's Festival of Jewish Culture, established by two non-Jews in 1988) and organisations (e.g. the Council of American Jewish Museums (1977)). As Ruth Gruber notes, Jewish culture is increasingly produced and consumed by non-Jews: 'in scores of cities, villages, and towns where few or no Jews live today, local Jewish history is being reclaimed, recognised, exhibited, and exploited as part of local Jewish heritage' (*Virtually Jewish: Reinventing Jewish Culture in Europe*, 75). In part, such interest stems from the growing popularity of roots/heritage tourism. In part, particularly in central and eastern Europe, it is a genuine attempt to rethink local and national **identities** by integrating a country's relations with its Jewish community into its own self-understanding and history.

A different approach is evident in the **State of Israel**, where a Jewish majority commemorates its own past, presenting the non-Jew (primarily Christians and Muslims) as a largely hostile 'other'. Beth Hatefutsoh, the Museum of the Jewish Diaspora, records the Jewish experience in non-Jewish lands, celebrating the diversity and creativity of Jewish culture. The permanent exhibition begins with a replica of a relief from the Arch of Titus, and, at a central point, the Memorial Column and 'Scrolls of Fire' commemorate Jewish **martyrdom** through the ages. Thus, despite a section, 'Among the Nations', stressing the reciprocal relationship with Christianity and **Islam**, diaspora experience is framed within a story of **antisemitism**, martyrdom and the struggle to survive.

The representation of Jewish–non-Jewish relations in Jewish and Holocaust museums is significant given the role they play in educating non-Jews (particularly schoolchildren) about Jews and Judaism. Holocaust museums present Jewish–Christian relations as a history of antisemitism, with **Righteous Gentiles** exceptions that prove the rule (even in museums established by Christians, such as Beth Shalom in Nottinghamshire, England). More recent Jewish museums, such as New York's Museum of Jewish Heritage – A Living Memorial to the Holocaust, adopt a more nuanced approach, striving to avoid stereotypes and reflecting on a multicultural history, combining coexistence (peaceful or otherwise) and cultural symbiosis (reflected in the existence of a variety of different Jewish cultures). *ISABEL WOLLASTON*

Music

The question of Jewish–Christian relations in music has as yet been little addressed by scholars. Encompassing issues including aesthetic choices, theological representation, professional and personal contact and reception history, the Jewish–Christian encounter has nevertheless had – and continues to have – a profound effect on many areas of musical life.

There is no one tradition either of 'Jewish' or of 'Christian' music; rather, within both religions many traditions, both sacred and secular, have existed and developed side by side. Their relationship is complex: most borrow material from surrounding music cultures – and not only between Jewish and Christian groups – as well as retaining their own distinctiveness. Additionally, examples of musicians crossing between the Jewish and Christian communities when performing or composing music arise frequently. Discussion of Jewish–Christian relations in music is further complicated by terminology. The terms 'Jewish' and 'Christian' have generally been used in an asymmetric manner when describing music. Seen as an outsider to the predominantly Christian art, folk and popular traditions of the West, Jewishness in music has largely been defined by ethnic group (whether of composers, performers or origins of musical material). By contrast, there has rarely been call to define 'Christian' music, since the normative Western musical canon is historically based upon Christian roots, felt even in 'secular' music.

Music is central to both Jewish and Christian **worship**; biblical texts, especially the **Psalms**, frequently mention the use of instruments and song in praise of God. Nevertheless, these descriptions largely relate to practices that ceased with the destruction of the **Temple**. Several scholars have posited musical links between early Christian singing and that of Jewish contemporaries. While a shared history and evidence of shared liturgical material suggest that commonalties were likely, in the absence of notated musical examples there is no substantial proof of this; further, Hebrew musical terms appear to have taken on new meanings in Greek translation. As the two religions developed, approaches to the liturgical use of music have differed widely – not only between Judaism and Christianity, but also within their denominations. While chant and song are used in all Jewish traditions, **Rabbinic Judaism** has traditionally been opposed to the use of musical instruments in the synagogue. By contrast, the Church has fostered the Western art music tradition, cantatas, masses and oratorios becoming core genres in the canon.

Jewish musical material frequently draws upon aspects of the musical traditions of the wider culture within which it has developed, a pattern common to both sacred and secular repertories. Indeed, the earliest surviving manuscripts of Jewish music owe their existence to contact with Christian monks, who developed systems for the accurate notation of melodies. The **Cairo Genizah** collections include the two earliest manuscripts of Hebrew texts with music, whose notation is attributed to Obadiah the Norman Proselyte (second half of eleventh to first half of twelfth century). Further, the first accurate record of the melodies used for chanting the **Torah** was made by Christian scholars during the fifteenth century.

In more recent centuries the hasidim adapted melodies including military and popular songs into *nigunim*, wordless spiritual songs. This process was seen as elevating material to a higher use; however, songs directly connected with Christian worship were not considered suitable. By contrast, the Reform movement (*see* **Progressive Judaism**) modelled its musical practices on those of the Church, seeking to increase the respectability of Jewish worship. Organs and choirs were introduced to synagogues in the early nineteenth century, causing much controversy. Viennese cantor Salomon Sulzer (1804–1900) sought to 'cleanse' traditional melodies from embellishments, harmonising them instead in a classical style. This move to integrate synagogue music into the non-Jewish aesthetic world was accompanied by an interest in synagogue music among Christian composers. Several visited the synagogue, and Christian Viennese composers, including Schubert (1797–1828), contributed to Sulzer's anthology *Shir Zion* (1840, 1866). Reform hymnody was likewise heavily based on Christian models; however, more recent hymnals reflect a move towards greater diversity and a more identifiably 'Jewish'-sounding music.

Jewish musical sources have, by contrast, impacted far less upon Christian worship. Historically, Jewish **liturgy** has inspired Christian hymnody; more recently, Jewish music has been sought by Christians seeking to explore a connection with the Jewish roots of Christianity, or through a post-**Holocaust** desire to connect with European Jewish culture. Nevertheless, interest in Jewish music by Christians has frequently been connected with missionary activity (*see* **mission**): groups such as **Jews for Jesus** use Jewish-sounding music to convey a Christian message; some Jewish-style songs of missionary origin have now become part of the mainstream modern Christian canon. Conversely, others have attempted to introduce Christianity to Jews via Church melodies: a Yiddish translation of an American Christian hymnal was published in America in many editions during the first part of the twentieth century.

Outside regular worship, music has frequently played a major role in events seeking to promote Jewish–Christian relations, including the presentation of Jewish and Christian repertories side by side in numerous concerts, and the use of song and dance as tools to introduce Jewish culture to Christian groups. Among scholars, recent research touching upon the subject of Jewish–Christian relations reflects issues current in the wider field: critics have turned to historical works, questioning the portrayal of the Jews in frequently performed compositions such as J. S. **Bach**'s Passions. Further, music scholarship can itself have wider repercussions in the field of Jewish–Christian relations. In researching the music and liturgy of the Jews of **Ethiopia**, Kay Kaufman Shelemay writes that 'what began as a study of music and ritual ends with implications for our view of Falasha liturgical history' (*Music, Ritual and Falasha History*, 2), challenging conventional explanations of the history of this group.

The issue of Jewish–Christian relations in music is by no means confined to the liturgical spectrum; rather, this interaction is equally visible in classical, popular and folk music, in which Jews have played a prominent role as performers, composers and scholars. Evidence of Jewish–Christian contact within courtly music dates at least back to the early sixteenth century. A number of instrumentalists at the court of Henry VIII (*r*.1509–47) have been identified as Jewish immigrants from **Portugal** and **Italy**; they were, nevertheless, required to pass as Christians. Conversely, several sixteenth-century composers parody 'Jewish' music in their works, mimicking Jewish ritual song and dances.

An exception to the usually limited scope for Jewish involvement in **Renaissance** musical life was Salamone Rossi (*c*.1570–*c*.1630). Living in Mantua and working for Christian patrons, Rossi was the first Jewish musician to make an impact on European music history as a composer. Unlike his Christian contemporaries, Rossi wrote no liturgi-

cal music for the Church. Instead, he composed and performed secular madrigals and instrumental works for his patrons, alongside music for the Jewish community; his 'Songs of Solomon' are the first known collection of polyphonic works set to Hebrew texts.

After Rossi it is not until the nineteenth century that Jewish composers of similar importance appeared within Western classical music. While freer to participate in musical life, the careers and reception of these composers have similarly been constrained by the attitudes of their contemporaries and critics. Some, like Felix Mendelssohn (1809–47) (grandson of Moses **Mendelssohn**) and Gustav Mahler (1860–1911), furthered their careers through **conversion** to Christianity. Nevertheless, both clearly continued to feel affiliation to the Jewish community, and continued to be seen as Jews by Jews and non-Jews alike, who identified Jewishness with race as well as with faith. Other composers of Jewish birth achieved popular success while remaining professing Jews. Giacomo Meyerbeer (1791–1864) and Fromental Halévy (1799–1862) dominated the nineteenth-century French grand opera scene; Jacques Offenbach (1819–80) was one of the most outstanding composers of popular music and operetta of his time. Many have sought to identify 'Jewish' characteristics in the works of these and other composers of Jewish ancestry. Nevertheless, all were working in a predominantly Christian environment, and very little overt expression of Jewishness is evident. Indeed, like their Christian contemporaries, all these composers wrote music exploring explicitly Christian themes, including Mendelssohn's *St Paul* oratorio, Mahler's 'Resurrection' symphony (no. 2, in fact written before his conversion) and Meyerbeer's opera *Les Huguenots*; Mendelssohn, Meyerbeer, Halévy and Offenbach all wrote choral settings of Christian liturgy. While they enjoyed enormous success and made an outstanding contribution to nineteenth-century music, however, the reputations of these and other composers of Jewish origin were tarnished by **antisemitism**, both that of critics, particularly **Wagner**, and later by the Nazis; the impact of this negative reception upon their place in the canon continues today.

Nazism had a heavy impact upon the careers of Jewish musicians. Jews had been particularly influential within Austro-German musical life, historically the centre of the Western classical scene. The Nazis sought to remove the historical 'Jewish influence' from the German musical canon; anti-Jewish policies included the blacklisting of musical works by Jews and foreigners and the removal of Jews from musical posts. These policies operated on racial grounds, encompassing Jewish musicians who converted to Christianity and music written by Jewish composers on Christian themes. Much of the music preferred by the Nazis dealt with secular nationalist and folk subject material; however, the Reich Chamber of Music encompassed a Reich Union of Church Musicians, headed by prominent organist Karl Straube (1873–1950). Jewish musicians were forced to perform in camps, sometimes ordered to perform 'Jewish' music as a sport for the SS, at other times made to sing Christian music, including a performance before Eichmann of Verdi's Requiem in Terezin.

During the twentieth century Jewish composers have increasingly presented explicitly Jewish themes in their work. Leonard Bernstein (1918–90), Ernest Bloch (1880–1959) and Arnold Schoenberg (1874–1951) are among those to have written substantial choral works incorporating elements of Jewish liturgy. Nevertheless, this material is framed within classical forms derived from specifically Christian musical genres: the oratorio and the cantata. Since the late nineteenth century non-Jewish composers, such as Maurice Ravel (1875–1937) ('Kaddish', 1914) and Max Bruch (1938–1920) ('Kol Nidrei', 1881), have also drawn upon Jewish material as part of a wider enthusiasm for folk music and exotica.

Different patterns of Jewish–Christian relations emerge in the field of popular music, an industry to which American Jews have made a prominent contribution since its beginnings in the mid-nineteenth century, and dominated during the 1910s–40s. While a relative lack of antisemitism made the music industry an attractive choice for Jews to find employment, until much later in the twentieth century Jews tended to play background roles as publishers, promoters and songwriters, leaving the limelight to non-Jewish, and often avowedly Christian, stars. While few completely abandoned their Jewish origins, Jewish musicians tried to be highly assimilated Americans, ironically contributing to the negative, caricatured images of immigrant Jews often expressed in songs, yet also writing some of the songs most symbolic of America and its Christian holidays, including Irving Berlin's (1888–1989) 'White Christmas', 'Easter Parade' and 'God Bless America'.

Conversely, however, popular music has also served as a vehicle for Jewish material to enter the American mainstream: Jacob Jacobs and Sholom Secunda's 'Bei mir bistu schön', originally written for the Yiddish theatre, became a hit in English translation for the Andrews Sisters in 1938. During the 1960s Jewish songs such as 'Tzena Tzena' formed part of the popular folk repertory; groups including the Weavers recorded Jewish and Christian numbers side by side. From the 1960s onwards several Jewish singers have achieved great prominence in the pop scene; nevertheless, mainstream pop music has seen little overt expression of Jewish **identity** by singer-songwriters. Conversely, the conversion of Bob Dylan (b. 1941) to evangelical Christianity in 1978, expressed both in his music and in the press, was much publicised, as has been speculation about his relationship to Judaism and Christianity since this time.

In the folk music of central and eastern Europe Jewish–Christian contact is evident since the Middle Ages. Many folk songs are found in both Jewish and non-Jewish versions; specific Christian references in ballads tend to be neutralised or Judaised in Jewish versions. While few songs directly address the Jewish–Christian relationship, many variants, both Christian and Jewish and spanning several centuries, exist of a song known as 'Die Jüdin' (The Jewish woman), which describes the relationship of a Jewish girl and her non-Jewish lover. Instrumental music, too, illustrates reciprocal and extensive contact between Jewish and non-Jewish musicians; parts of the repertory of pre-Second World War east European Jewish klezmer musicians were shared with co-territorial non-Jewish musicians. The relationship of Jewish musicians with the Christian establishment varied, however: examples of Jews performing at Christian weddings and in church ceremonies are balanced by periods of restrictions placed upon Jewish musicians by Christian authorities. The Holocaust put an end to the klezmer tradition in Europe; while the repertoire thrived for a few decades among Jewish immigrants in America, by the late 1940s a desire for **assimilation** had all but eradicated the tradition.

Since the mid-1970s klezmer music has undergone a massive revival in America and, later, in Europe. In America the music continues largely to be played by Jews as an expression of Jewish identity; nevertheless, a handful of non-Jewish artists play prominent roles, and the music has gained a wide audience as a popular genre on the world music scene. In Europe the majority of musicians are non-Jewish, forming part of a wider enthusiam for Jewish culture among a younger generation, particularly in **Germany**. While not all non-Jewish musicians involved in klezmer music are professing Christians, this enthusiasm has been catalysed in part by changing attitudes of the Catholic Church towards Jews and the Holocaust, and churches have frequently hosted performances of Jewish music.

In the Sephardi world Jewish, Christian and Muslim music thrived in the Iberian peninsula before the 1492 **expulsion**. During the twentieth century there was considerable romanticisation and revival of Sephardic history and culture in **Spain**. Today many 'Jewish' festivals are held; local songs are often held to be 'Jewish' or 'Sephardic' regardless of their roots; conversely some Judeo-Spanish songs have also been adopted into local folk repertories.

Not only has the Jewish–Christian encounter shaped many areas of secular music over the past centuries, but individuals across many musical genres have also sought to represent the encounter itself through music. Everyday issues predominate, from the complex Christian–Jewish love affair portrayed in Halévy's opera *La Juive* (*The Jewess*, 1835), to the pressures of assimilation portrayed in Alan Crosland's 1927 film *The Jazz Singer*.

Today the widespread availability of recorded music from diverse Jewish and Christian traditions, coupled with information accessible via the **Internet**, gives the curious an unprecedented degree of access to the music of Jewish and Christian others. Nevertheless, while the 'world music' genre has supported Jewish music and **Orthodox Christian** music alike, this label has also paradoxically re-inscribed the alterity of these traditions, which continue to be cast as 'outside' the Western mainstream. *ABIGAIL WOOD*

Mysticism

Mysticism is here used to describe the attitudes and practices employed to attain immediate and trans-formative contact with God. Mysticism is one of the elements shared by Judaism and Christianity, along with such other aspects of religious life as institutions, laws, doctrine and ritual. Jewish and Christian mystical traditions display many comparable features due to their dependence on a partly shared Bible. Here, however, we will not study the comparative dynamics of the two mystical traditions, but will rather explore the more direct historical links between Jewish and Christian mysticism. While these contacts are admittedly of secondary importance to the internal development of mysticism within the two faiths, the mutual interactions between the two traditions were at times significant and also possibly more extensive than we know given the **polemical** context of much of the history of Jewish–Christian relations.

The most important link between Jewish and Christian mysticism is in their common background in Second Temple Judaism, especially its apocalyptic strands. The heavenly ascents recounted in Jewish apocalypses (e.g. *1 En.* 14; *2 En.* 22), though rooted in the theophanies of the **Hebrew Bible**, express a new way of conceiving the relation between the human and divine worlds, not only in the portrayal of the seer as actually going up to heaven, but also in the preparation for the experience of God by prayer, ascetical effort and theurgical activity. Equally important in the Second Temple period was the emergence of a **hermeneutical** mentality which made the interpretation of the sacred text, and often the search for its hidden meaning (the original meaning of 'mystical'), a central aspect of religious life. The apocalyptic ascents paved the way for the earliest forms of Jewish mysticism, the Hekhalot texts (perhaps second to sixth centuries CE), where the seer ascends to heaven to see the divine majesty enthroned on the Merkavah (i.e. chariot), to participate in the celestial liturgy, and even to undergo deification.

The mystical and apocalyptic elements of Second Temple Judaism were united in at least some strands of the early Jesus movement. This is evident in the teaching of the converted Pharisee, **Paul**, whose preaching about life 'in Christ' has a strong mystical element and whose description of his own ascent into the third heaven, and even into paradise, where he heard 'unutterable things'

(2 Cor. 12.1–12), is the only first-person apocalyptic ascent account. The way in which Jesus was seen as the 'Glory of the Lord' in the Pauline and Johannine literature may reflect a Christian version of Jewish speculation about how ascending seers, such as Enoch, came to be identified with the divine *kavod*.

During the course of the second century CE nascent Orthodox Christianity and **Rabbinic Judaism** emerged as related, if estranged, rivals to the heritage of Second Temple Judaism. Nevertheless, there was still significant interchange between the two religions, though admissions of direct borrowing from the rival were naturally rare. The most prominent example of Jewish influence on emerging Christian mysticism is the impact of **Philo of Alexandria**'s melding of Greek philosophical mysticism and biblical **revelation**. Philo's thought was a major resource for **Origen**, the first Christian mystical theologian. Philo was also known to fourth-century Christian mystics, not only in the East, but also in the West (e.g. Ambrose (339–97)). Christian enthusiasm for Philo helps explain why he played little role in Judaism before the modern period.

Far more difficult to assess are the possible contacts between Hekhalot mysticism and developing Christian mysticism, especially in the light of the **Gnostic** texts. One shared concern, and possible source of connection, was the interpretation of the Song of Songs, a book that was to remain central to both mystical traditions. Origen was aware of Jewish **exegesis** of the Song, but his interpretation emphasised the necessity of reading the physical descriptions of the Song as a message about the **soul**'s inner activation of the spiritual senses to reach loving union with the incarnate **Logos**. In Jewish mysticism the Song was given a major role by the early rabbis because it was seen as an account of the love between God and the community of **Israel**. This exoteric reading, however, suggested an esoteric one in which the depictions of the male lover's body (e.g. Song 5.11–16) were seen as divine self-descriptions. This reading contributed to the accounts of the dimensions of the divine body such as those found in the *Shi'ur komah* (possibly sixth century), a work that had an impact on the mystical eroticism of the Kabbalah. Early **Jewish Christianity** and some patristic traditions seem to have featured similar ascensions to the heavenly

world, the glorification of the seer, and speculations on the form and dimensions of the divine body, as we can see in the case of the Elchasaites, the **Pseudo-Clementine** homilies (fourth century), the **anthropomorphite** monks of Egypt, and especially in some **Syriac** authors (e.g. **Aphrahat**, **Ephrem**, and the Pseudo-Macarian *Homilies*).

After the era of formation (first to sixth centuries CE) the evidence for direct contact between Jewish and Christian mysticism is sporadic, not only due to the hostile relations between the two communities, but also because of the ignorance of **Hebrew** among Christians. The flowering of Jewish mysticism, first among the German Pietists and then with the emergence of Kabbalah in **France** and **Spain** (twelfth to thirteenth centuries), presents us with some possible connections with Christianity, although these remain problematic, and hence it is not easy to know if we are dealing with actual contacts, parallel developments or forms of mutual interaction whose parameters are easier to suggest than to demonstrate. From the Christian perspective the interest in esoteric Jewish lore as proof of Christianity's **supersession** of Rabbinic Judaism that eventually led to the Christian Kabbalah of the **Renaissance** is evident as early as the twelfth century in figures such as **Joachim of Fiore**, and around 1300 in Ramon **Llull**. Possible Christian influence on Kabbalah has been controversial, though in recent years a number of investigators have argued for Christian impact on some features of theosophical Kabbalah (e.g., Y. Liebes, *Studies in the Zohar*, A. Green, 'The Shekinah', E. Wolfson, 'The Tree that Is All', P. Schäfer, *Mirror of his Beauty*), noting, for example, the parallels between the Christian Marian cult and the emergence of the **Shekhinah**. The four modes of exegesis advanced by some Kabbalists (expressed in the acronym PaRDeS) may show the influence of the Christian four senses of scripture. There were also contacts between the ecstatic Kabbalist Abraham **Abulafia** and the **Franciscan** Spirituals and their Joachite mystical **apocalypticism**. These contacts, intriguing as they are, do not appear to have been central to the new forms of Jewish mysticism.

The late fifteenth and sixteenth centuries saw the flowering of Christian Kabbalah in figures such as Giovanni **Pico della Mirandola**, Johannes **Reuchlin** and Guillaume Postel (d. 1581). Each had first-hand acquaintance with Jewish mystical sources. Postel's knowledge was particularly extensive; he even translated a number of Hebrew texts into **Latin**, including the *Sefir ha-Bahir* and the *Zohar* (could this have helped stimulate the first Hebrew editions of this esoteric text?). The polemical intent of Christian Kabbalah is evident in the insistence of these authors that the true inner Judaism of the *Zohar* and other mystical texts was identical with Christianity, especially in belief in the **Trinity** and acceptance of Christ as **Messiah**. Some Christian Kabbalists, however, went further in claiming that Kabbalah revealed that Christian belief and practice also needed amendment and reformation. Postel, the most mystical of the three major Christian Kabbalists, believed in an imminent age of Christian Judaism, claiming, 'We are Christian Jews much more truly than those literal Jews of long ago, and we are Israelites as it were, because we accept and adore the King of the Jews and King of Israel, Jesus . . .' The trajectory of thought found in Christian Kabbalah continued to have an influence on a few early modern mystics, such as the esoteric Lutheran Jacob Boehme (d. 1624), but the role of Kabbalah on Christian mysticism decreased in the seventeenth century. Later Jewish mysticism also seems to display few direct contacts with Christianity. The hasidic movement that arose in the eighteenth century, however much it may be compared to some forms of Quietism, seems to have been largely untouched by Christianity, including the mysticism of contemporary Russian Orthodoxy.   *BERNARD MCGINN*

Myth

Myths are stories providing metaphorical and symbolic accounts of how things came to be, and why they are 'this way' rather than some other. Featuring human characters, or other beings, they are typically set in a time beyond that known to their consumers, are often rehearsed in ritual contexts, and may be incorporated into other cultural forms, including scripture and **art**. Unlike **parables**, myths are generally assumed by their consumers to have historical bases. However, increasingly since the **Renaissance**, critics have argued about whether it is possible to find value in myth regardless of historicity, or whether the only valid approach is a literalist one. These understandings of myth are significant for the study of Jewish–Christian relations.

The theological problem of **supersessionism**, a cause of Christian **anti-Judaism**, may be interpreted partly as one of competing mythologies. Both Jews and Christians identify themselves as **Israel** – God's **Chosen People**. Each community locates this status in a narrative-blend of myth and history (Exodus-Sinai; the life of Jesus), which has become the basis for ritual practices. During these (the seder and the **eucharist**) time 'collapses', as events of the past are integrated into the participants' own experiences of God in the present (Jews 'become' part of the exodus generation; Jesus' 'real presence' is in the **bread** and **wine**). These competing claims to chosenness are exacerbated by the presentation of Jews as characters in Christianity's foundation-myth. Building on a process that begins in the **New Testament** (the Johannine conflation of Jews as historical agents with 'the Jew' as metaphor/symbol; *see **hoi Ioudaioi***) the Church adopted a dehistoricised, *presentist* approach to Jews, seeing them less as human beings and more as mythological creatures – sub- and superhuman, and perpetually guilty of inciting Jesus' death.

Biblical scholarship has questioned scripture's historicity, drawing on ethnology, archaeology and the study of ancient civilisations. However, (perhaps in itself an illustration of the elasticity of the Christian myth of Jewish perfidy) nineteenth-century critics such as D. F. Strauss (1808–74) tended to see 'primitive' Jewish influences behind the mythological in Christianity. It is only more recently that insights on myth have been exploited by those seeking to improve Jewish–Christian relations.

Demythologising the New Testament (e.g. reassessing the **Virgin Birth** as a metaphorical expression of the doctrine of the **Incarnation**) provides one route into a re-evaluation of **Jesus** the Jew; it also contributes to readings of difficult texts as retrospectively generated accounts (designed in part to explain later Church–Synagogue tensions) rather than as records of actual disputes between Jesus and the **Pharisees**.

Postmodernism, and growing awareness of the ways in which events may be variously interpreted by different people, also leads some (following Claude Lévi-Strauss (b. 1908)) to talk of the ways in which history may acquire mythological functions. This has implications for the historiography of events in Jewish–Christian relations (e.g. the **Holocaust**). It also raises questions about the new construction of Jewish and Christian origins by contemporary scholars. For example, Arthur A. Cohen (1928–86), Martin E. Marty (b. 1928) and Jacob Neusner (b. 1932) have critiqued 'the myth of a common tradition'. Current claims to identify a 'Judaeo-Christian' heritage and **mission** are, they suggest, misfounded attempts to elide two distinctive world-views into one another, and to construct a shared history and **vocabulary** that does not, strictly speaking, exist. From the viewpoint of religious studies, given the human tendency to mythopoesis, it would be surprising if Jewish–Christian relations were *not* generative of its own mythologies. However, the contours of today's myths will only be clearly visible after they have ceased to function as accepted accounts of reality.   *MELANIE J. WRIGHT*

NNNN

Nahmanides (1194–1270)

Moses ben Nahman, referred to in Hebrew sources by the acronym Ramban or as Moses Gerondi, was the dominant philosophical voice among Spanish Jewry in his day, and an important leader who withstood attempts to spread Christianity among the Catalan Jews, building on his apparently warm relationship with King **James I**. As a young man he became involved in the bitter controversy over **Maimonides'** writings that wracked the academies of southern France. Alongside many shorter talmudic and halakhic tracts, his major work was a Bible **commentary** that has a strongly prophetic streak; the theme of **redemption** was also the subject of his *Sefer ha-Geullah* of *c*.1263. His works were among the first to be printed by the Hebrew printers of late fifteenth-century Naples and Rome.

Late in life Nahmanides was summoned by James I to defend Judaism against the argument that the **Messiah** had already come. The **disputation** of Barcelona of 1263, held in the king's presence, is recorded both in Nahmanides' version and in a Christian **polemic** which, not surprisingly, awards victory to the rabbis' opponent, **Paul the Christian**. The disputation marked a new intensification of attempts at **conversion** of the Jews in which the friars were notably active and in which attacks on the **Talmud** became increasingly intense, following the mass burning of the Talmud by **Louis IX** in France. Nahmanides was treated courteously by James I, who gave him money but, following attempts to have Nahmanides tried for insulting Christianity, the king made it plain that he would do well to leave Spain. In 1267 Nahmanides travelled to the Holy Land. He established a small community in Muslim-ruled Jerusalem, but became rabbi of Acre, the seat of government of the Latin kingdom, where he died soon after. *DAVID ABULAFIA*

Napoleon Bonaparte (1769–1821)

French emperor (1804–1814/15) whose ambiguous attitude towards the Jews was profoundly shaped by Christian assumptions. Napoleon was inclined to link contemporary Jews with institutions from their distant past; in 1798 he proclaimed the leaders of the Cairo Jewish community High Priests of the Jewish Nation and in 1807 he attempted to resurrect the **Sanhedrin**. Prepared to believe traditional **anti-semitic** complaints about the moneylending activities of the Jews of Alsace from 1801 (*see* **usury**), Napoleon called for an Assembly of Jewish Notables in Paris in 1806 to agree publicly a kind of declaration as to the limits of Jewish tradition upon loyal Jewish European nationals. These principles were to be confirmed as a set of religiously binding decisions by the creation of the French Sanhedrin the following year, it having supposedly the authority to establish a second body of legislation after **Moses**. During his unsuccessful campaign in Palestine (1799), the first sustained contact between the Christian West and the land's inhabitants since the **Crusades**, rumours had spread that Napoleon had issued a public proclamation that the Jews were free to return to their biblical homeland. This was almost certainly campaign propaganda, but the image of Napoleon as a new Cyrus was to prove enduring. The Sanhedrin itself was a failure, its rulings ignored by most European Jews. But there would be a lasting legacy. In his determination to fix the limits between religion and the state, Napoleon had attempted to regularise Jewish life under the authority of a Central Consistory (a term borrowed from their fellow **minority** group, the Protestants). In doing so he had assumed that Judaism could be redefined as a Christian-like religion and organised hierarchically. These ideas would later resonate with **Reform Judaism** and the **State of Israel** respectively. *DANIEL R. LANGTON*

Nationhood/nationality

The Hebrew scriptures tell the story of a nation strongly aware of its **identity**. The focus of that identity is a covenantal relationship with its God, analogous to the relationships the surrounding nations claimed with their gods. Since Christians read the Bible and Muslims absorbed much of its content, they both continued, throughout the age of religious domination, to regard Jews as a separate nation. The significance of this became apparent with the rise of European nation states, but became acute only with the rise of romantic nationalism in **Germany**, **Italy** and the **Balkans** in the eighteenth and nineteenth centuries. As Elie Kedourie wrote (*Nationalism*): 'Nationalism is a doctrine invented in Europe at the beginning of the nineteenth century . . . [T]he doctrine holds that humanity is naturally divided into nations, that nations are known by certain characteristics which can be ascertained, and that the only legitimate type of government is national self-government.' Nationalism depends on transforming ethnic characteristics such as language and social custom into ultimate values for which the individual citizen is prepared to kill and die.

To what extent is religion constitutive of national consciousness? For instance, must a 'good' Pole be Roman Catholic, or a 'true' Englishman be an Anglican? If this is answered in the affirmative, Jews cannot be Poles or Englishmen, Catholics cannot be English, and Anglicans cannot be Polish. Such a philosophy supports prejudice and discrimination, and aggravates relationships between Catholics, Protestants and Jews. The problem has been solved in large part by the emergence of the secular state, in which government is impartial as between religions, and citizens are equal before the law irrespective of religious affiliation. This development has had a profound impact on Jewish–Christian relations, since it enables Jews and Christians to meet as equals; on the other hand, the rise of secularism is in itself a challenge to both faiths.

The tension between nationalism and universalism that rent nineteenth-century Europe was manifested in the Jewish national movement, and with one further complication: Jews had to choose whether to abandon part or all of their Jewishness by adopting the local European nationalism or whether to opt out of Europe into a nationalism of their own. On the whole, **assimilation** was chosen where practicable, provided that a Jewish religious identity could be maintained. But where Jews were not accepted, or only very grudgingly accepted, as nationals in the countries in which they lived, a drive to a separate Jewish nationhood made itself felt, eventually flowering in **Zionism**, a political transformation of the religious 'yearning for Zion'. Zionism has posed questions for Jewish–Christian **dialogue** not only at the political level but because it raises the theological issue of how to interpret biblical **prophecy** about the Land.

Early Christianity proclaimed itself a universal religion ('for the Gentiles'), **Rabbinic Judaism** chose to emphasise its particularity. In recent times, by contrast, **Reform Judaism** has re-emphasised the universal dimension of Judaism, while Christians, reacting from their earlier imperialism, have discovered the significance and value of 'local theologies', whereby particular cultures or nationalities express Christian practice and belief in their own terms. In both cases an internal tension remains; Christians and Jews might profit from each other in learning how to accomplish a balance between the universal and the particular, between faith and nation, between the secular and the religious.

See also **Israel, land and State of**

NORMAN SOLOMON

Nazism

A contraction of the term *Nationalsozialismus* (National Socialism), Nazism identifies a type of fascism, essentially linked to Adolf **Hitler**, that emphasised **antisemitism**, single-party dictatorship, a state-controlled economy, opposition to communism, and territorial expansion through war. The involvement of Christians in advocating a racist form of nationalism that led to the **Holocaust** is a significant issue of debate within Jewish–Christian relations.

When Hitler came to power on 30 January 1933 German culture had its secular strands but it remained deeply Christian. Conventional interpretations have often claimed that Nazism and Christianity were enemies. They stress examples of Nazi **rhetoric** that were anti-Christian, as well as Christian protest against the Third Reich and Nazi persecution of Christian dissenters. Nevertheless, Nazism enjoyed strong Christian support, particularly because of its emphasis on restoring the national power and prestige that had been lost through defeat in the First World War and the Versailles Treaty, its resistance to Marxism, and its yearnings for a superior German *Volk* that would not be corrupted by alien influences. Thus, an overwhelming majority of **Germany's**

Christians and members of the Nazi Party endorsed, in one way or another, Hitler's proclamation that he was doing 'the work of the Lord' (*Mein Kampf*, 65).

When Hitler wrote those words he referred specifically to actions against the Jews. That fact is crucial, because Nazism was driven by what Saul Friedländer (b. 1932) has called 'redemptive antisemitism' (*Nazi Germany and the Jews: The Years of Persecution, 1933–1939*, 73–112, 1997), which alleged that Jews were the most potent force in history for radical evil. Building on the anti-Jewish stereotypes, such as the medieval **blood libel** accusations, it regarded Jews as conspiring to destroy European civilisation and dominate the world. It held them responsible for Germany's defeat in the First World War and for the Bolshevik Revolution, as well as for all of the moral, financial, political and social problems that beset Germany and the world thereafter. With Hitler and the Nazi movement as the Messianic forces that would save Germany from disaster and guarantee its hegemony, Nazism's 'logic' entailed that the Jews must be eliminated, one way or another, once and for all. Not all Christians in Nazi Germany embraced that logic, but they supported or at least complied with Nazism more than they resisted it.

We Remember, the Roman Catholic Church's 1998 statement on the Holocaust, contends that Nazi antisemitism 'had its roots outside of Christianity', but controversy swirls around that proposition because Nazism's targeting of the Jews cannot be explained apart from anti-Jewish images – Christ-killers, wilful blasphemers, unrepentant sons and daughters of the Devil, to name only a few – that have been long and deeply rooted in Christian practices. Other Christian statements, such as the **Leuenberg Church Fellowship**, accept that Christian **anti-Judaism** provided essential background, preparation and motivation for Nazism. Those factors help to explain why, from 1933 to 1945, Germany's overtly Christian resistance to Nazism and the Holocaust was as scarce and sporadic as it turned out to be (*see* **bystanders**).

See also **Dabru Emet**   *JOHN K. ROTH*

Neo-hellenism *see* **Hellenism**

Nes Ammim

Nes Ammim, located in the North of Israel, between the cities of Acco and Nahariya, is an ecumenical Christian village. It was founded by Christians from the Netherlands, Switzerland and Germany at the beginning of the 1960s, in recognition of the almost 2,000-years-old alienation between Christians and Jews, and in hope for a new era of understanding after the atrocities of the **Shoah**. Since its foundation hundreds of (mainly young) people have lived there. Based on the support of an international movement, Nes Ammim aims to give a 'sign of the nations' (name derived from Isa. 11.10), a sign of reconciliation and solidarity towards **Israel**. In addition, the village is a model of a Christian living, working and learning community. In recent years many Israeli groups, both Jews and Arabs, have met in Nes Ammim for a period of peace education.   *SIMON SCHOON*

Netherlands, the

The earliest Jews arrived in the Low Countries – present-day Belgium and the Netherlands – during **Roman** times, but reliable documentary evidence dates only from the 1100s. Jews were expelled on a regular basis and experienced violence at the hands of Christians, notably in 1349 when they were accused of spreading the **Black Death**. Beginning in the sixteenth century, the Netherlands became home to numerous Portuguese merchants as the region, and particularly Amsterdam, became a centre of world trade. Among these merchants were **Marranos** who had been forced out of **Spain** by the **Inquisition** in 1492.

By the seventeenth century the Netherlands' Jewish community was more integrated economically and socially than anywhere else in Europe. Jews played a role in the economic expansion of the Netherlands into a world power and lived in a Jewish quarter which they were free to leave and which was frequented by non-Jews – Rembrandt (1606–69), for example, lived and worked there. Violence against Jews, prevalent in **Germany** and eastern Europe, was non-existent in the Netherlands. Christian conversions to Judaism, while not common, were not unheard of, and the Synod of Dordt (1618–19) demonstrated a close relationship between Jews and Christians: at a time of **blood libel** charges elsewhere in Europe, scholars in Amsterdam were studying the **Mishnah** and the **Talmud**, and even composing poetry in **Hebrew**. The controversy surrounding **Spinoza**, who was excommunicated by the leaders of both Jewish and Christian communities in Amsterdam, also demonstrates the closeness of relations between them.

The Netherlands granted Jews full equality and citizenship in 1796. Their full integration into Dutch society contributed to the fact that **Zionism** did not achieve there the same popularity as elsewhere in Europe. In 1940, when the Netherlands was occupied by Germany, 170,000 Jews lived in the country. Most were sent to **Auschwitz** and Sobibor, but some survived the **Holocaust** either by hiding with non-Jews or by forging documents with the help of non-Jews. The Frank family is a famous example and survived for several years hidden in an Amsterdam building (*see* **Frank, Anne**). In 1946 there were 30,000 Jews in the Netherlands, and this number has remained steady since.

The Holocaust remains an important factor in modern Jewish–Christian **dialogue** in the Netherlands, and a feeling of co-responsibility for the fate of Dutch Jews has led Dutch Christians, especially **Calvinists**, to rethink their relations with the Jewish people. In its constitution of 1951, the Netherlands Reformed Church was the first Church body to include a special section on dialogue with the Jews. The establishment of the **State of Israel** met with considerable sympathy in the Netherlands, and many Dutch Christians saw in it a fulfilment of **Old Testament** prophecies. The 1970 General Synod of the Netherlands Reformed Church stated that the return of Jews to **Zion** was a 'special sign of God's will'. There has also been great sympathy for the problems of the Palestinians, and in 1979 the Council of Churches in the Netherlands called for a two-states solution to the Middle East crisis. At the same time, an increase in the number of Muslim immigrants has led to social tensions in the Netherlands, creating a need for both Christians and Jews to reflect on relations between all three Abrahamic faiths. *EDWARD KESSLER*

Neve Shalom/Wahat al-Salam

'Oasis of peace'. A community of Israeli Jews and Palestinians founded in 1972 on a barren hilltop between Jerusalem and Tel Aviv by Bruno Hussar (1911–96), a **Dominican** friar, with the aim of peaceful reconciliation between Jews, Muslims and Christians. Husar, an Egyptian Jew who converted to Catholicism, dedicated his life to encouraging peaceful coexistence between Jews and Arabs. The community's name is drawn from Isa. 32.18, 'my people shall dwell in an oasis of peace'. Husar explained that he had in mind 'a small village composed of inhabitants from different communities

in the country. Jews, Christians, and Muslims would live there in peace, each one faithful to his own faith and traditions, while respecting those of the others.' The community has grown to 50 families, has hosted over 35,000 youth and adults at its internationally recognised School for Peace, and educates almost 300 students in its bilingual bicultural primary school. *WILLIAM KLASSEN*

New Christians *see* Conversos

New Testament

The New Testament, the second part of the Christian Church's **canon**, both marks the separation between Christianity and Judaism and contains substantial historical and exegetical information on the connections between these two movements. On the one hand the 27 books in this canon, in varying degrees, are the principal sources for discussions about **supersessionism** and the origins of the 'teaching of contempt'; on the other they provide information about varieties of first-century Jewish practice and belief, as well as interpretations of the books both Church and synagogue regard as holy (*see* **Old Testament**). Both for its historical information and for its legacy in Jewish–Christian relations, the New Testament today serves as a major site of interfaith discussion.

Questions of supersessionism begin with the canon's designation. 'New Testament' (Greek: *Kaine Diatheke*; Latin: *Novum Testamentum*), can also be translated 'new covenant'. Although *Diatheke* usually meant the disposition of an estate, the title derives in part from Jer. 31.31–4. Jeremiah anticipated a 'new covenant' (*Berit Hadashah*) distinct from the Sinaitic **covenant** that **Israel** often failed to follow, to be inscribed on the heart and to include the forgiveness of sin. Rabbinic texts rarely cite Jer. 31.31–4. The few discussions interpret it to mean that God reminds people what they have forgotten concerning **Torah** (*Midrash* Song 8.14) and that forgetting Torah is a sign of this world but not the world to come (*Midrash* Eccl. 2.1; *Midrash* Song 1.2). The Qumran scrolls anticipate a new covenant, but the term is primarily associated with the Church. 1 Cor. 11.25 quotes Jesus: 'This cup is the new covenant in my blood'; 2 Cor. 3.6 speaks of 'ministers of a new covenant, not of letter but of spirit'; Heb. 8.8–12, setting the new covenant in contradistinction to the faulty 'first covenant', quotes Jer. 31.31–4; and Heb. 9.15 (see 12.24) identifies **Jesus** as the new covenant mediator who redeems humanity from 'transgressions under the first covenant'. The longer version of Luke's Gospel (22.20), as well as a few manuscripts of Mark and Matthew that record Jesus stating, 'This cup . . . is the new covenant in my blood', may be scribal adaptations to 1 Cor. 11.25. Thus 'new covenant' or 'new testament', when first used by Christian writers, indicates the Christ's mediatory role in forgiving sins and, perhaps, in abrogating the Old Covenant. This soteriological focus remains a point of division within Christianity. Some Christians teach that the New Testament/New Covenant replaces the old one, and so view Judaism as having been replaced by the Church. Appeals to such passages as the Parable of the Vineyard (see Mark 12.1–9) and the epistle to the Hebrews are cited in support. Others, citing **Romans 9–11**, see the 'Old Covenant' as having eternal value and so view the Church as a co-heir with Judaism.

The shift from a soteriological to a canonical meaning was prompted in part by the reference in 2 Cor. 3.14 to the Mosaic 'old covenant' or 'old testament' (*Palaia Diatheke*) read in synagogues. **Melito of Sardis** first used 'Old Testament' to designate scripture. **Tertullian, Eusebius** and others then used 'New Testament' for Christian texts viewed as inspired. By the fourth century 'New Testament' and 'Old Testament' became the common Christian terms for canonical materials. The New Testament thus became both the fulfilment of the Old (Jesus is a new **Adam** (Rom. 5.12–21) and because of **Eve**'s sin women gain their salvation by bearing children (1 Tim. 2.13–15); those who persevere will gain the Garden of Eden (Rev. 2.7)) and the template through which the Old Testament is to be interpreted. The ending of the Christian Old Testament (minus the **apocrypha**) with Malachi's prediction of the coming of **Elijah** facilitated this promise-fulfilment design.

The New Testament shares with Judaism the synagogue's scriptures (i.e. the Old Testament/the Tanakh), although it usually cites the **Greek** translation rather than the **Hebrew** original (e.g. Matt. 1.23 cites the **Septuagint**'s reference to a 'virgin' in Isa. 7.14; Luke 4.18–19 depicts Jesus reading from the Septuagintal Isaiah). In addition to direct citation, the New Testament is replete with scriptural allusions. Stephen summarises Israel's history (Acts 7.2–47); Hebrews catalogues examples of

faith from Abel (11.4) to 'David and Samuel and the prophets' (11.32). Jesus is a new **Moses** in Matthew's Gospel and the replacement for Moses in Hebrews; he appears with Moses (representing Torah or the Law) and Elijah (representing the Prophets) at his Transfiguration. Rom. 4.1–12 speaks of **Abraham** as 'justified by faith' while Jas 2.21–4 claims faith and works justified Abraham. Matthew's Joseph the son of Jacob resembles **Joseph** the son of **Jacob** of Genesis. New Testament allusions to scriptural scenes include the meeting of a man and a woman at a well (John 4, cf. Gen. 24.10–27; 29.1–12; Exod. 2.15–21); raising a widow's son (Luke 7.11–17 cf. 1 Kgs 17.17–24); creating food miraculously (Mark 6.30–44 cf. Exod. 16.13–35; Num. 11.1–35; 1 Kgs 17.8–16); a child born to an aged couple (Luke 1.5–80 cf. Gen. 21 *et al.*); and women's songs of liberation (Luke 1.46–55 cf. 1 Sam. 2.1–10). The book of Revelation, although offering no direct quote, is steeped in scriptural reference.

Church and synagogue came to emphasise different aspects of shared scripture. The New Testament tends to relegate Torah to a secondary or even negative role, whereas it is paramount for the synagogue; the New Testament reads the Prophets selectively in attesting to the role of Jesus and the Church, whereas the rabbinic tradition sees the Prophets as speaking to the situation of (non-Christian) Jews. The Jewish tradition highlights the book of **Esther**; it is ignored in the New Testament (as it is in the **Dead Sea Scrolls**). In 2001 the Pontifical Biblical Commission highlighted both the connections and the divergences between the two parts of the Christian canon as well as between the Church and the synagogue in *The Jewish People and their Sacred Scriptures*.

Although the Church decided that the Old Testament and New Testament formed its canon, the connection between the two collections was a matter of debate. In the second century **Marcion** concluded that the God of the Jews was inept and distinct from the Deity revealed by Jesus. He then compiled a Christian canon (perhaps the first canon) consisting only of select Pauline epistles as well as a version of the Gospel of Luke stripped of Old Testament allusions. Responding to Marcion as well as to certain Gnostic ideas (*see* **Gnosticism**), **early Church** teachers insisted that the Old Testament was inspired, but that Jewish readings (e.g. readings that insisted on the practice of Mosaic Torah; readings that did not find anticipations of Jesus) were incorrect. Although Marcion's teaching became regarded as **heresy**, residual Marcionism survives in the false claim that the Old Testament presents a wrathful God of **law** whereas the New Testament offers a loving God of **grace**.

Because 'Old Testament' can bear negative connotations (old as outdated, surpassed or replaced), and because 'New Testament' can sound supersessionist, alternative designations arise. Substitutions include Christian Testament (problematic because the Old Testament is also in the Church's canon), Second Testament (problematic both because 'second' can imply secondary and because Heb. 8.7–8 views the 'first covenant' as superseded), and Greek Testament (problematic both because some Churches hold the Greek Old Testament canonical and because the Old Testament apocrypha/deutero-canonical texts have Greek originals). Nor is it likely all denominations will change the title of their scripture from *The New Covenant Commonly Called The New Testament of Our Lord and Saviour Jesus Christ* (New Revised Standard Version, following the King James Version).

Written in *Koine* Greek (with occasional **Latin** and **Aramaic** expressions) and dating from the mid-first to the early second century CE, the New Testament addresses congregations of both Jews and Gentiles (in various proportions). Although often speculative, determinations of authorial identity and intent, as well as the composition of the community to whom each text is addressed, serve as bases for judging whether the New Testament is anti-Jewish (the definition of which is itself subject to endless debate). The primary argument for exculpating the New Testament of charges of **anti-Judaism** relies on the identification of author and audience: if the author of a New Testament book were Jewish and/or if the text were addressed primarily to Jews, the text cannot be anti-Jewish. This argument has several inherent flaws. First is the problem of determining who was a 'Jew'. For example, while scholars often regard the Gospel of Matthew as written by a Jew to a Jewish (or mixed Jewish and Gentile) Church, Matthew's own language (28.15) distances author and reader from 'Jews' (*Ioudaioi*).

John's Gospel, often regarded as a response to the separation of believers in Jesus from their synagogue, uses 'Jews' primarily to refer to those who oppose Jesus. Second is the lack of consensus on authors and audiences. The canonical Gospels were all originally anonymous; 'Matthew, Mark, Luke and John' are names assigned by the Church. The composition of the Gospels' original audiences is also unknown, although within two generations these audiences were primarily Gentile. **Paul**, although a self-identified Jew (Phil. 3), writes primarily to Gentile congregations, and some documents promulgate the erasing of distinctions between Jews and Gentiles (e.g. Ephesians).

Several other approaches seek to acquit the New Testament of anti-Judaism. One strategy classifies problematic texts (e.g. Mark 12.1–12; Matt. 23; the **passion narratives**; John 8; Hebrews; Rev. 2.3–9) as excoriations of the Jewish leaders rather than of the Jewish people or practice. While having merit, the thesis fails in that the majority of Jews chose not to follow Jesus. A second argument labels the **polemic** conventional (cf. the Dead Sea Scrolls), but the comparison is inexact because the scrolls were not taught to Gentiles. Another approach, common among many Christians today, recognises the potency of invectives such as the anti-Pharisaic screed of Matt. 23, but labels them warnings to the faithful against hypocrisy, greed and so on. Negative references to 'the Jews' (***hoi Ioudaioi***) are sometimes seen to refer to 'Judeans'. 1 Thess. 2.14–16, describing the *Ioudaioi* as having 'killed the Lord Jesus', is often mitigated by being labelled an interpolation inconsistent with Paul's positive view of Judaism found in Romans. Some interpreters argue that Jews prompted the invective: John 8, wherein Jesus labels 'Jews' as 'from your father the Devil' (8.44), is seen as a response to the synagogue's expulsion of Jesus' followers (see John 9, 12, 16). Rarely do these interpreters inquire into why John might have been expelled (preaching exclusivist soteriology? encouraging Gentiles to stop eating food offered to idols?). Finally, some Christian theologians insist that the New Testament cannot be anti-Jewish because anti-Judaism is incompatible with divine **inspiration**.

Whether the New Testament is anti-Jewish will remain a matter of debate. Nevertheless, because the text has been used to support the teaching of contempt, its anti-Jewish potential must be addressed. Proposed solutions to anti-Jewish readings include educating Christians about the New Testament's historical context and anti-Jewish legacy, recognising that Jesus and his earliest followers were all Jewish, expunging offensive verses, offering alternative translations (such as 'officials' for 'the Jews'), revising **lectionaries** so that the New Testament material is not seen as a positive antithesis to the Old, and having New Testament passages studied together by Jews and Christians. Joint study facilitates acknowledging potentially problematic passages even as it aids both Jews and Christians in recovering shared history. Jewish scholars such as Claude **Montefiore** and Martin **Buber** found in the New Testament (especially the words of Jesus in the Synoptic Gospels) sentiments consistent with the rabbinic tradition; their studies also helped to combat the tendency of Christian theologians and historians to divorce Jesus from his Jewish context. Since the ***Shoah***, and especially with the opening of Departments of Religion as distinct from theological schools and seminaries, the number of Jewish scholars who study the New Testament (e.g. Samuel Sandmel (1911–79), David Flusser (1917–2000), Geza Vermes (b. 1924), Alan Segal (b. 1945), Paula Fredriksen (b. 1951), Daniel Boyarin (b. 1946), Adele Reinhartz (b. 1953), A.-J. Levine (b. 1956)) continues to increase. The Reform movement requires rabbinical candidates to take a course in the New Testament (*see* **Progressive Judaism**).   *AMY-JILL LEVINE*

New Year

Human New Year festivals began as a remembrance of the **creation** of the world on its supposed anniversary. Jewish tradition assigns this significance to the autumn festival of Rosh Hashanah ('head of the year'). **Rabbinic Judaism** (*M. Rosh Hashanah* 1.1) records other new years, of which only Tu Bishvat, the late winter new year for trees, survives. The Jewish celebration is unusual among new years in marking the start of a penitential season, which was developed by Rabbinic Judaism in the shadow of the loss of **Jerusalem** and the Temple in the early days of Christianity. The story of the **binding of Isaac** (from Gen. 22) is the main feature of the **Torah** reading. This narrative was popular in the Church as a prototype of the sacrifice of Christ, and its inclusion in the Jewish **lectionary** allowed the preacher to counter

with his own view of the text. The prayer *avinu malkenu* 'our father our king' (attributed to Rabbi **Akiba**) uses the designation of God as 'father' popularised by **Jesus** in the **Lord's Prayer**. The *aleinu* prayer, attributed to the third-century teacher Rav, was censored as **anti-Christian** in many Jewish prayer books (*see* **censorship**). In the Middle Ages most of Christian Europe celebrated 25 March as the beginning of the year. 1 January was the New Year's Day of the Gregorian Calendar (1582), restoring an ancient Roman practice. In the Church **calendar** both dates have links to the birth of Christ, 25 March marking the Annunciation and 1 January the Circumcision.   *MICHAEL HILTON*

New Zealand

Christians and Jews were already living in harmony in New Zealand before the nation's foundational document, the Treaty of Waitangi, was signed in 1840. About 45 years after Captain Cook (1728–79) first sighted New Zealand (1769) Anglican missionaries arrived, and 15 years after that Solomon Levy established a law firm in Lyttelton (Christchurch) as a branch of his Sydney office. Other early Jewish names included the families Montefiore, Hort, Keesing, Joseph and Nathan. Jewish traders and settlers worked cooperatively with the local Christian residents, teaching **Hebrew** to Christian seminarians, and contributing financially to the building of churches. Some early Jewish settlers intermarried with the indigenous Maori population, others with Christian settlers, primarily from England. The Jewish population of New Zealand has never been large, but has been influential in business and politics. In the 1996 census out of 3.7 million residents, just under 5,000 were Jews (about 1.5 per cent). The most influential forms of Judaism today are Liberal/Reform or Orthodox. Because the Jewish community is so small, many of its younger members emigrate to Australia, Canada or England.

The **Council of Christians and Jews** (CCJ) began as a core group in Auckland in 1987, headed by Selwyn Dawson (Methodist) and Ann Gluckman (Jewish), in cooperation with CCJ Australia. In 1990 they became members of the International Council of Christians and Jews. Relations between Christians and Jews in New Zealand remain relatively amicable, though periods of **antisemitism** have occurred as world tensions rise, most recently around issues of peace in the Middle East. *PHILIP CULBERTSON*

Nicaea, Council of *see* **Easter; Quartodeciman controversy**

Nicholas of Lyra *see* **Lyra, Nicholas of**

Niemöller, Martin (1892–1984)

Protestant minister. Best known as a representative of organised Christian opposition to aspects of **Nazi** politics, the **Confessing Church**, Niemöller's attitudes towards Jews and his contribution to Christian–Jewish relations found direct expression in his solidarity with baptised Christians, including converted Jews, under the Nazi regime and his favouring of the Stuttgart Confession of guilt for the Churches' involvement in National Socialism and the **Holocaust**. From a patriotic German family, Niemöller fought in the First World War, opposed democracy in the Weimar Republic and voted National Socialist from 1924. He began to oppose the German Christians who were closely linked to Nazi organisations when they interfered in what Niemöller regarded as Church affairs, that is, Christian **confessions of faith** and Church membership. Imprisoned in Sachsenhausen and Dachau for his anti-Nazi activities, Niemöller rethought his Christian faith and changed in postwar years to advocate the ecumenical movement and radical pacifism. *K. HANNAH HOLTSCHNEIDER*

Nizzahon Vetus

An anthology of northern European Jewish **polemical** arguments against Christianity probably compiled in the thirteenth century, *Nizzahon Vetus* reveals literary links to the polemical work *Sefer Yosef HaMeqqaneh* by Joseph ben Nathan Official (*fl.* thirteenth century). The author is unknown, and this work is often confused with *Sefer HaNizzahon* written by Yom Tov Lippman Muelhausen of Prague (fourteenth–fifteenth century). The work is marked by an aggressive **rhetorical** approach to Christian **exegesis** of the **Hebrew Bible**, Christian dogma, **liturgy** and ritual. There are passages that describe Christianity in scatological terms and others that mock Christian beliefs. By contrast, the beliefs and practices of Judaism are exalted, especially Jewish **martyrdom**. *Nizzahon Vetus* is organised according to the books of the Hebrew Bible, offering appropriate responses to Christian interpretations. It then offers an anthology of refutations of the **New Testament** and Christian practices such as **baptism**, priestly **celibacy**, **relics** and confession. It is an important source of Jewish assessments of Christianity during the medieval period.

See also **anti-Christian Jewish teaching**

MICHAEL A. SIGNER

Noachide laws

The Genesis account portrays **Noah** as a pious believer in God who worshipped him through obedience and sacrifice and was given divine commands, including those prohibiting murder and the consumption of blood. He is therefore seen by Judaism, Christianity and **Islam** as one of antiquity's righteous personalities and a prototype of simple religiosity vis-à-vis God, humanity and animals. According to the pre-Christian book of *Jubilees*, he was given a specific set of principles by which to live, and this concept appears in its early rabbinic form as 'the seven laws of the children of Noah'. Non-Jewish men and women are to be defined and treated as monotheists if they adhere to these basic social and religious values and their subsets. They should establish law-courts; refrain from **blasphemy**, **idolatry**, murder, theft and forbidden sexual relationships such as incest; and not perform vivisection. They are then regarded by rabbinic codifiers (e.g. **Maimonides**) as 'the pious of the gentile peoples' and worthy of the same eternal bliss guaranteed to Jews who observe the **Torah**'s 613 commands. In the Middle Ages the concept was widely applied to Muslims and, after some early doubts about the **Trinity**, was also used in the Jewish theological definition of Christians. In the modern period Jewish thinkers such as Moses **Mendelssohn** used the idea to justify the equal treatment of monotheistic non-Jews in the social application of religious legislation, but the response was sometimes to regard this as religious condescension. There are, especially in the **United States** and **Israel**, contemporary movements among Jews and non-Jews (Noachides, Bnai Noach) that seek to encourage non-Jews to adopt the Noachide laws and to spread their basic teaching, and the United States Congress officially recognised them in 1991. *STEFAN C. REIF*

Noah

Antediluvian biblical ancestor. As a non-Israelite living prior to the law-giving at Sinai, who was nonetheless considered righteous in the biblical account, Noah has been important to Jews in providing expectations for Gentile behaviour. The universal dimension of the story was also important to early Christians in arguing for their freedom from Sinaitic **commandments**.

Noah is first mentioned in Gen. 5.29 as the son of Lamech, the ninth generation after **Adam**. The story of Noah and the **flood** is narrated in Gen. 6–9 from two distinct sources that differ in various details. As the patriarchal head of the only household to survive the flood, Noah is portrayed as the ancestor of all people on earth through his sons Shem, Ham and Japheth. Outside the book of Genesis the **Hebrew Bible** mentions Noah explicitly only in Isa. 54.9, Ezek. 14.14, 20 and the genealogy of 1 Chr. 1.4. The figure of Noah held a special appeal for the Jewish community at Qumran (see **Dead Sea Scrolls**) and those responsible for writing such **Pseudepigraphic** works as *1 Enoch* and *Jubilees*, perhaps because of their **apocalyptic** eschatology, which envisioned an imminent battle between the wicked and the righteous. Parallels were seen with the tale of Noah, who was deemed righteous by God in the midst of a wicked generation and viewed as a prototype of the marginalised and alienated community itself, at odds with the rest of the Jewish people, particularly in regard to the **Temple** in **Jerusalem**.

Although Noah is mentioned only rarely outside of the book of Genesis, Christian and Jewish exegetes found the story rich with meaning. In Christian **exegesis** the story of Noah's family surviving the great deluge was read typologically to represent Christian **baptism**. First evidenced in 1 Pet. 3.20, which mentions that eight people were saved with Noah in the ark, Clement of Rome (*fl.* 96 CE) and other **Church Fathers** would reaffirm this typological interpretation. The **typology** was extended so that the ark represented the Church, without which no one could be saved, a view that represents a problematic issue for Jewish–Christian relations. In traditional Christian liturgical practice the waters contained in the baptismal font symbolise not only the waters of the ancient flood, but also the primordial waters of chaos over which God ruminated, and the waters of the Red Sea, which God divided in order to save the Israelites. **Justin** found Noah particularly useful in his *Dialogue with the Jew Trypho*. Unlike the rabbis, who insisted that the patriarchs observed the **Law** before it was given at Sinai, the

Church Fathers used Noah to demonstrate that law observance was unnecessary – indeed, it was given as punishment. For example, Noah and his children were all uncircumcised (*Dial.* 19.4). There are a number of similarities between early Jewish and Christian scriptural interpretation of Noah to which J. P. Lewis has drawn attention (*A Study of the Interpretation of Noah and the Flood*, 1968). The lifespan of 120 years decreed by God in Gen. 6.3 is thought to have related to the years a generation was permitted for **repentance**. In Genesis Noah is referred to as 'righteous in his generations', but the rabbis debated whether this was **righteousness** relative to the comparative wickedness of those around him or whether he was righteous in an absolute sense. In Jewish tradition the so-called seven **Noachide laws** came to be understood as minimum normative laws to be observed by non-Jews and be considered righteous from a Jewish perspective. *JUDITH H. NEWMAN*

Nonconformists *see* Dissenters
Non-violence *see* peace
Nostra Aetate

Promulgated on 28 October 1965, the fourth section of the **Vatican II** declaration on non-Christian religions, *Nostra Aetate*, achieved nothing less than a radical reversal of what Jules **Isaac** called the Church's ancient 'teaching of contempt' against Jews and Judaism. It is easily the most significant document concerning Jewish–Christian relations in Church history since **Paul** in **Romans 9–11**. In 15 sentences it rejected **anti-Judaic** theological **polemics** and condemned **antisemitism**, and replaced them with the foundations for a renewed vision of the continuing role of the Jewish people in God's plan of **salvation** for all humanity. Uniquely among the conciliar statements, it referred only to scripture, not to the **Church Fathers** or previous Councils, as these had no doctrinal relevance to the issue. Noting the **New Testament** records that some 'authorities of the Jews ... pressed for the death of Christ', it stated that what happened 'cannot be blamed upon all the Jews then living, nor upon the Jews of today'. With this simple statement an entire theological edifice, built over centuries, collapsed. If the Jews were not and are not collectively responsible for the death of **Jesus**, then it is impossible to view the destruction of the Jerusalem **Temple** in 70 CE and the **Diaspora** of the Jews as 'divine punishment'. Rather, as the Holy

See's 1985 *Notes on the Correct Way to Present Jews and Judaism in Catholic Preaching and Catechesis* were to conclude, the Diaspora 'allowed Israel to carry to the whole world a witness – often heroic – of its fidelity to the one God' (no. 25). Positively, the Council emphasised the Jewish origins of Christianity and that the Church draws (present tense) spiritual 'sustenance' from the people of God of the 'Ancient Covenant'. The Jews 'still remain most dear to God' and 'have [present tense] the glory and the covenant and the Law and the worship and the promise . . . for the gifts and the call of God are irrevocable'. Subsequent statements of the pope and the Holy See have developed and underscored this acknowledgement of Judaism as a salvific, living tradition.

The statement on the Jews was one of the earliest on the Council's agenda and among the last to be promulgated. It found opposition from conservatives on the one hand and from bishops representing **minority** Christian communities in the Muslim world and Asia on the other. The biblical and theological scholarship of Augustin **Bea** and the drafters of the text, such as John **Oesterreicher** and Gregory Baum (b. 1923), countered the former theologically. The so-called 'Wardi Affair', in which an antisemitic tract was surreptitiously given to all the Council Fathers, served only to galvanise support for the document. The objections of Eastern bishops resulted in the text being taken out of its original context in the conciliar statement on **ecumenism** (*Christian Unity*) and set up on its own, complemented by positive statements concerning **Islam**, Hinduism, Buddhism and traditional religions. This did not weaken but, in the eyes of many, strengthened the document's reception throughout the Catholic world.

Most Protestant scholars engaged in Jewish–Christian relations attest to the positive impact of *Nostra Aetate* on discussions within their own communions. While statements of the **World Council of Churches** pre-date the Second Vatican Council in addressing 'the Christian approach to the Jews' (Holland, 1948) and condemning antisemitism (New Delhi, India, 1961), the sheer weight of the Catholic Church within Christianity seemed to endorse and energise progressive movements within the Protestant Churches that sought to reform their own traditions' received theological presumptions about Jews and Judaism. In turn, it must be noted that the great pioneers of modern biblical scholarship whose work made possible the radical change in Christian attitudes toward Jews and Judaism represented by *Nostra Aetate* were, until Pope **Pius XII**'s groundbreaking encyclical *Divino Afflante Spiritu* (1943) empowered Catholics to engage in critical biblical scholarship, virtually all Protestant.

EUGENE J. FISHER

OOOO

Oberammergau *see* **Passion narratives**

Odo of Sully (*c*.1160–1208)

Bishop of Paris from 1196. Under the influence of Pope **Innocent III**, he attempted to restrict social relations between Jews and Christians. For example, he prohibited priests from standing security for a Jew and forbade Christians from using grapeskins that had been pressed by Jews (except as food for pigs or as fertiliser). He also threatened Christian laymen with **excommunication** if they engaged in debating articles of faith with Jews.

EDWARD KESSLER

Oesterreicher, John (1904–93)

One of the architects of *Nostra Aetate*, who pleaded for the reconciliation of Christians and Jews in word and writing. Born in Moravia of Jewish parents, Oesterreicher became a Catholic during his studies in Vienna (1922–4) where he was ordained to the priesthood in 1927. As priest, editor and broadcaster, in **Austria** and later in Paris, he worked against **Nazism**, narrowly escaping the Gestapo. Arriving in the **United States** in 1940, he was founding Director of the Institute of Judaeo-Christian Studies at Seton Hall University in New Jersey from 1953–93 where, between 1955 and 1970, he edited five volumes of *The Bridge: A Yearbook of Judaeo-Christian Studies*. Called to Rome in 1961 to work on the 'subcommission for the Jewish questions', he attended the last three sessions of **Vatican II** and remained consulter to the Secretariat for Christian Unity until 1968. *AUDREY DOETZEL*

Old Testament

The Christian term Old Testament, referring to the first part of the **canon**, has been taken by some as a support for **supersessionism**, the belief that the **New Testament** has superseded the 'Old'. The inference is that the Old (i.e. Jewish) **Covenant** is no longer valid and has been replaced by a New (superior) one. The term 'old covenant' first appears in 2 Cor. 3.14, perhaps as a counterpoint to the new covenant of Jer. 31.31, but it is **Melito of Sardis** who

first uses it collectively of the biblical books (*c*.180). The supersessionist tendency has induced many in Jewish–Christian relations to find alternative terms, such as 'Prior Testament', 'Former Covenant', 'Prime Testament', 'Common Testament', '**Hebrew Bible**' or 'First Testament', to prevent it from being seen as a redundant text. Of the more common preferences 'Hebrew Bible' draws attention to its origins within Judaism and the fact that it has an integrity of its own, even if it is not the term used by Jews, who prefer 'Tanakh'. However, others have argued that Old Testament is a technically correct designation for Christians, since until the time of **Luther** the Church primarily relied on the Greek **Septuagint** text, and since the ordering of the books within the Christian canon to this day differs from the Hebrew order. The Christian Old Testament concludes with the prophecy of Malachi, an ending appropriate to Christian theology in its prediction of the returning **Elijah**. 'First Testament' is a term preferred by some, provided it does not imply primacy, a danger apparent in the alternative suggestions for the Old and New Testament of 'Prime Testament' and 'Appendix Sayings' respectively, or 'The Scriptures' and 'Apostolic Writings'.

See also **Pentateuch**; **Torah** *JAMES K. AITKEN*

Onkelos (2nd century CE)

Traditionally, the author of the anonymous official **Targum** to the **Pentateuch** (*b. Megillah* 3a); often identified as 'the proselyte'. One tradition, of uncertain date and suppressed by the censors, reflects **anti-Christian** propaganda: the spirit of **Jesus**, in Gehenna for offences against 'the wise', confirms to the prospective convert that the Jews have the highest status in the world to come (*b. Gittin* 56b, 57a). Such a view may reflect the influence of Palestinian sources which identify Onkelos with **Aquila** the proselyte, whose activities were interpreted by some in antiquity as hostile to Christianity. Thus, Epiphanius (*c*. 315–403) presents Aquila's hebraising Greek version of the **Hebrew Bible**, favoured by the rabbis, as intended to displace the **Septuagint** used by Christians. By contrast, **Jerome** and **Origen**, reflecting their reverence for the Hebrew Bible, are much more favourable to Aquila.   SARAH J. K. PEARCE

Ordination *see* **priest; rabbi**

Origen (*c*.185–*c*.254)

Priest, biblical scholar and catechist. Origen was the son of a Christian martyr (Leonides Adamantius) in **Alexandria**. Amongst all the **Church Fathers**, Origen is considered the most erudite in his knowledge of Hebrew letters, rabbinic **commentaries** and scriptural texts, but with only a fair reading knowledge of **Hebrew** itself. His most influential work is the **Hexapla** (completed *c*.245) or Greek–Hebrew comparative-critical text of the **Old Testament**, which assembled usually four, but as many as seven, different **Greek** versions (at least three of which were done by **Aquila**, Symmachus and Theodotion – Jewish scholars of the first two centuries CE) of a given passage in parallel columns. Origen's corrected transcription of the **Septuagint** (LXX) was noted for its accuracy by its diligent comparison with the Masorah. Unlike any other Christian of his day, he displayed a commanding knowledge of **halakhic** debate (cf. *Princ*. 4.3.2; *In Sermone Matthei*, 11). The balance of his writings comment on every aspect of scripture and the Christian mysteries, but the *De Principiis* stands out as his most comprehensive and speculative work. The weight given to rabbinic ideas in his commentaries and close textual work would decisively influence Christian biblical **hermeneutics**. His corpus of writings which, according to **Eusebius** (*Hist. eccl.* 4) and **Jerome** (*Epist.* 33), was composed of nearly 2,000 books, is considered as influential for Christian theology in the East as **Augustine**'s has been for the Latin West.

Origen's acquaintance with the Jews of Alexandria and later, of Palestine, was extensive and presented him with a dilemma: on the one hand, their knowledge of the scriptures and of rabbinic **exegesis** was greatly desirable (*Ep. Afr.* 6), as was their friendship (cf. *In Mattheo* 11.9); on the other hand Origen's theological understanding of Jews and Judaism could be extremely negative (cf. *Cels*. 3.1; 1.49), obliging him to a kind of religious disdain for Jews as killers of Christ (*Cels*. 2.18; 8.42) (*see* **deicide, charge of**). Though often debating with Jews in public and frequently criticising what he

regarded as their literalistic interpretations of biblical texts (*Princ*. 2.3.1), he also defended them against the vicious attacks of the pagan authorities (cf. Celsus' *Alethes Logos* 5.41ff.). Indeed, Origen found the Jews an admirable people, but one whose teachings could appeal to all men only if broadened out (*Cels*. 5.42). Origen would refer to Jews and Christians together as 'all of Israel' (*Cels*. 6.80), which awaited the **salvation** of God.

Origen's theology of Judaism is therefore more complex than at first seems. On the one hand his derogatory **rhetoric** and **supersessionist** remarks place him among the emerging *Adversus Judaeos* thinkers of the **early Church**. For example, in Origen (cf. *Cels*. 4.3) charge over the **kingdom of God** has been given to Christians and taken from the Jews, who remain a **Chosen People** but somehow in exile until brought back to Christ through the mysterious *apokatastasis*, or return of all mankind to God. For Origen and many of his Christian contemporaries the Old Testament was replete with **prophecy** fulfilled only through Christ. Origen taught that Jews who demurred in accepting **Jesus** as the true **Messiah** did so principally because they read the Bible in an exclusively literal way and hence could not understand it through Christ (cf. *Princ*. 4.2.1), the **Logos** or 'living word' of truth. In these and other ways Origen helped to promote an overtly anti-Jewish theology which later fathers and medievals would exploit at will. On the other hand Origen's appreciation for Jewish insight and thought is immense. The truth of God's **revelation** was validly found in the way in which Jews read the scriptures, though the following of Jesus would demand further elaboration. In an age where Christian life was still socially blended in close proximity to Jewish practice and belief, Origen's teachings can be seen as both appreciative and condemnatory of Judaism and anxious for the establishment of a separate Christian **identity**.   DENNIS D. MCMANUS

Original sin

A Christian belief (based on Gen. 3 and Rom. 5.12–21) that the sin of **Adam** has been passed on to all humanity and can only be expiated through **baptism** in Jesus **Christ**. It is often said that belief in original sin is one of the main differences between Judaism and Christianity. Mainstream Judaism, both in antiquity and today, certainly does teach that each person is responsible for his or her guilt, but the existence of an innate sinfulness in each human being was discussed in biblical (cf. Gen. 8.21; Ps. 51.5) and post-biblical texts, which may provide an insight into the development of the Christian theology of **sin**. Passages in the **apocrypha** and **Pseudepigraphic** literature are pessimistic indeed: *4 Ezra* 4.30–31, for example, states that a 'grain of evil seed was sown in Adam's heart from the beginning', a concept that appears remarkably Christian. There is also an oft-quoted and unique teaching in the **Talmud** (*b. Avodah Zarah* 22b) which states that the serpent seduced **Eve** in paradise and impregnated her with spiritual-physical 'dirt' which was inherited through the generations. The revelation at Sinai, when **Moses** received the **Torah**, cleansed **Israel** (like baptism) of this sin. Although it is clear that belief in some form of original sin did exist in Judaism, it did not become mainstream teaching, nor dogmatically fixed. Rather, it remained at the margins of Judaism while becoming a central tenet of Christian faith.   *EDWARD KESSLER*

Orthodox Christianity

Early toleration of the Jewish world by Christians did not outlive the fourth-century promotion of Christianity as the principal religion of the **Roman Empire**. The establishment of Constantinople as an eastern capital for that Empire (330) was to initiate and eventually to encourage the separate development of a distinctive (**Byzantine**) culture, in which the Orthodox Church was to play an all-important role. It was a role that various independent Orthodox Churches were to inherit in centuries to come. In those first decades of Byzantine history the propriety of social and devotional participation of Jews and Christians in each other's worlds was to be severely questioned. New calculations for the date of **Easter**, designed to prevent coincidence with **Passover**, were introduced in the early fourth century to separate the two communities. More important was the antagonism preached by such prominent figures in the Eastern Church establishment as John **Chrysostom**, which was not countered by other Christian apologists at the time. Rather, it established a norm which long outlasted the rhetorical conventions of the time: Chrysostom's writings, the authority of which is seldom if ever disputed, remain the fount for much **anti-Judaic** thought in the Orthodox milieu to this day.

Equally long-lasting, since never yet rescinded, are the **canon laws** which encouraged separation of the Jewish and Christian communities. Thus the Quinisextum council (691–2) prohibited Christians from having recourse to doctors of the Jewish faith; nor were Christians to share the public baths with Jews. However, the separate existence of the Jews was reluctantly tolerated. The Byzantine emperor Theodosius II (*r.*408–50) went out of his way to declare that a Jewish believer should not suffer contumely for his religion (438). **Conversion** to the Christian faith was welcomed, but rarely enforced. Even so, the **Theodosian code** prohibited the building of new synagogues in the Eastern Empire (438); nor were existing synagogues necessarily safeguarded – in the fifth century some were burned. While formal dialogue was of course rare, there was nonetheless some Christian adaptation and assimilation of Judaic modes of **worship**: much of the Bible was regularly read in public (though the **Septuagint** was deemed to be the standard text); **Psalms** were the principal ingredient of the daily office; biblical patriarchs and prophets were commemorated with the saints.

In a conservative Church, with its veneration of **tradition**, none of these practices were to be abandoned in the centuries to come. Also safeguarded, however, were subsequent (medieval) additions to the services of **Holy Week**. Lengthy texts included in the matins of **Good Friday** remain as anti-Judaic as anything proposed for Christian worship at the present time, yet there is no Orthodox liturgical commission that works for their amendment or excision, nor has biblical scholarship prompted revision of attitudes and texts in modern times. Much of the textological work that is taken for granted in non-Orthodox Churches has been ignored or deemed improper. In the twentieth century communist restrictions prevented the Orthodox of the USSR and Eastern Europe from engaging in such work; in the aftermath, a tendency to isolationism has inhibited fresh work in this sphere. Rather is there anti-Judaic zeal in some Church circles, where early medieval **rhetoric** is still employed to denigrate perfidious Jews. Furthermore, such rhetoric is often not condemned by the leaders of the given Church. In **Russia** the chief proponent of anti-Judaic if not **antisemitic** attitudes, Metropolitan Ioann Snychev (1927–95), was himself a member of the Moscow patriarchate's ruling synod. By contrast, the patriarchate of Constantinople has sponsored a research centre at Chambésy (Switzerland) where Orthodox isolationism has been steadfastly counteracted. Its director for many years was Metropolitan Damaskinos Papandreou (b. 1936). One of the centre's prime concerns has been to foster Orthodox relations with Judaism. To this end four international academic meetings have been held (1977, 1979, 1993 and 1995), with wide representation from the Christian Orthodox and Jewish worlds. It should be noted that members of the Christian Orthodox diaspora tend to be less hampered in their dealings with the Jewish world than their co-religionists at home, whether in Eastern Europe or the Middle East.

In the preceding period the inherited attitudes of many Europeans were necessarily tested in the crucible of the *Shoah*. But the experience of the Jews prompted no public reconsideration of Christian Orthodox attitudes to Judaism or the Jews. It is not as if the Churches lacked the opportunity to ponder questions of this kind. In 1961 a series of pan-Orthodox deliberations began on a variety of subjects, yet fear of controversy prevented any treatment of Jewish–Christian themes. Even so, a general council of the Orthodox Church (the first since 787) is at least in prospect, and might permit the formulation of post-**Holocaust** concerns. For the present there is no parallel to *Nostra Aetate* or anything else that emerged from **Vatican II**. Yet there is some promise in the fact that individual Churches (each with its peculiar culture and its independent managerial structures) were able to demonstrate commitment to fellowship with Jews in their plight under Nazi domination, some more consistently than others. In Greece it was not only the primate of the established Church, Archbishop Damaskinos Papandreou (1891–1949), who encouraged the hiding and the succour of the victims; most of the population was ready to support them. At one stage as many as 600 priests refused to preach anti-Judaic sermons and were imprisoned by the occupation forces for their stand (1943). Most notable of all was the commitment of the Bulgarian Orthodox Church. Clergy and laity alike ensured that the Jews of Bulgaria were never rounded up and so survived the Nazi-sponsored onslaught on their lives. Such fellowship offers

promise of **dialogue**. It also suggests that inherited anti-Judaic attitudes could yet be overcome in other Churches of the Orthodox communion.

See also **early Church**; **Syriac Christianity**; **Ukraine**

SERGEI HACKEL

Orthodox Churches *see* **Orthodox Christianity**

Orthodox Judaism

This term was adopted in the nineteenth century when new varieties of Judaism emerged in central and western Europe and it was necessary to offer a characterisation of the group(s) least likely to alter earlier ideas and practice. It has come to be applied to a range of religiously committed Jews who have a traditional notion of divine **revelation** and place *halakhah* at the centre of the decision-making process. They range from those who interpret its application to modern life as broadly as possible to those who consistently prefer pre-modern precedents. The former pursue daily professional activities while devoting spare time to **Torah** study, while the latter view non-Torah involvement as a waste of effort and resources. They also differ about **Zionism**; at one extreme there are crocheted *kippa* (skull-cap) wearers who are enthusiastic about the modern Jewish state and its institutions, while at the other there are black-hatted side-locked Jews who opt for a closed communal existence in, say, Jerusalem, London or New York and have, at best, little concern as to who runs the government at large.

Before the **Holocaust** and the establishment of the modern **State of Israel**, attitudes to Christianity on the part of such Orthodox Jews developed differently in the liberal democracies of Europe and America than in Eastern Europe and the Islamic world. In the latter geographical spheres the less one had to do with non-Jews the better, since they were seen as intent on exploitation, persecution, **conversion** or **expulsion**. Where Jews began to benefit from social **emancipation** and intellectual enlightenment, Orthodox Jews, such as Moses **Mendelssohn** in late eighteenth-century Berlin and David Sinzheim (1745–1812) at the Paris **Sanhedrin** in 1807, debated the nature of the relationship with non-Jews in general and Christians in particular, especially on the basis of the talmudic and rabbinic sources. Prayerbooks compiled by Wolf Heidenheim (1757–1832) and Seligmann Baer (1825–97) were careful to distinguish non-Jews from heathens. There were also highly practical aspects to the problem. For example, the talmudic corpus records prohibitions against non-Jewish wine, cheese, bread and oil, however technically 'kosher' their ingredients may be, with the intention of discouraging fraternisation and, ultimately, **intermarriage**. Did this refer exclusively to heathens or to all non-Jews? The issue in the modern period was, as it had been in the less antagonistic periods of the Middle Ages, whether monotheistic non-Jews could be regarded in some meaningful way as religious partners and therefore accorded at least some of the privileges available to fellow Jews. Alternatively, did their beliefs and practices still have elements of **idolatry** in them that disqualified them from such treatment? Even if that were theoretically the case, another argument for a more tolerant approach might be on grounds of *darkey shalom* (literally, 'ways of peace'), that is, the promotion of good neighbourly relations.

Orthodox rabbis such as S. R. Hirsch (1808–88) and D. Hoffmann (1843–1921) in **Germany** argued strongly in the late nineteenth century for treating Christians as monotheistic brethren. Although the Jewish communities of Eastern Europe and the Islamic countries have virtually ceased to be major factors in the past half-century, the remnants of their views and lifestyle have had a major impact on the situation in Israel, particularly since many Israelis have the impression that the non-Jewish world is broadly hostile to Jewish statehood, religion and culture. Attempts at forging a **dialogue** or a **trialogue** in Israel, though partly underway, have not therefore been blessed with conspicuous success. In the Jewish **Diaspora**, Orthodox authorities continue to argue different positions. The total rejection of an exchange of any sort is still to be found in voluntarily ghettoised ultra-Orthodox circles, while those who opt for some kind of relationship have reached no overwhelming consensus. It has been suggested, and even ruled by no less a prominent a figure than the late Rabbi J. B. **Soloveitchik**, that interfaith relations devoted to social and political issues of mutual concern are permitted while those of a theological nature are to be eschewed. Against such a standpoint, it has been argued that such a distinction between various parts of life is foreign to traditional Jewish notions and values and less honest than a total

ban. There have been numerous Orthodox rabbis, among them the British Chief Rabbi Jonathan Sacks (b. 1948), who have questioned the idea that Jews possess the whole truth and pointed, with some degree of respect and even admiration, to the contributions made by other faiths to humanity's spiritual development. That has at times been met with angry ripostes from other rabbis, including members of the London Bet Din of Rabbi Sacks, who see it as an admission that Judaism is defective.

The point has been made that the divide today is not so much between different varieties of monotheism as between religion and secularism; Orthodox Jews should therefore find allies wherever they can in order to promote spiritual values in a world that distinctly lacks them. Another issue is reciprocity. If dialogue means asking the other faith to amend some of its beliefs and practices to give less offence to its neighbours, does this not surely rule it out for Orthodox Jews? In that case it is better for them to make no suggestions about alleged inadequacies on the part of the religious other for fear that parallel suggestions will be made to them. What some Orthodox Jews fear is the coming together of Jews and Christians in a kind of ethical monotheism which blurs the distinctive features of each faith and may, as they see it, lead to the gradual extinction of both. For them there will be elements in the faith of the other that they find unacceptable and it is best to leave these issues unresolved and undebated. On the other hand there will inevitably be other aspects of alternative religious lifestyles that are worth discussing together and that may be adjusted without damage to the authentic message but to the advantage of mutual respect and a thawing of theological ice. Many Orthodox Zionists are troubled by the fact that non-Jews with liberal attitudes to other religions are often those least sympathetic to the politics of the Jewish state.

Regarding the **Hebrew Bible**, Orthodoxy has little sympathy with the continuation of aspects of nineteenth-century Protestant scholarship in the theologically biased style of such literary historians as Julius **Wellhausen**. There are, however, Orthodox university teachers, particularly in North America and Israel, who are beginning to consider the less tendentious historical and critical study now being more widely followed. STEFAN C. REIF

Ottoman Empire

For nearly five centuries the Ottoman dynasty founded by Osman I (*r.*1280–1324) governed a vast Islamic empire that, at its height, spread across the **Balkans**, **Asia Minor**, the Middle East and North Africa and embraced a medley of ethnic and religious **minorities**, including Jews and a variety of Christian communities. Ottoman rule generally improved the situation of Jews living in those areas previously controlled by the **Byzantine Empire**, under which Jews suffered humiliation and servitude for centuries. In the sixteenth and seventeenth centuries Jews fleeing the **Inquisition** and persecutions in **Spain**, **Portugal** and other parts of Europe found refuge in the Ottoman realm, where many **Conversos** returned to Judaism. The Ottoman Turks, like earlier Islamic regimes, imposed discriminatory laws and special taxes on both Christians and Jews, but they granted their communities considerable autonomy in the conduct of their cultural and religious life. In the early centuries of Ottoman hegemony Jews enjoyed some advantage over Christians, for they were not suspected of having political sympathies with Christian Europe, the Ottomans' principal adversary. However, as the Western powers and European Christian **missions** increasingly penetrated the Middle East in the eighteenth and nineteenth centuries, the situation of Jews deteriorated relative to that of the Greeks and Armenians, who now benefited from Western patronage. In the nineteenth century there were instances of Christian-instigated **blood libel** against Jews, of which the Damascus Affair in 1840 is one of the most infamous. In part under the influence of European concepts of ethnic and territorial **nationhood**, numerous national movements arose throughout the Balkans and the Middle East during the century prior to the demise of the Ottoman Empire in the First World War. The Jewish national movement, **Zionism**, was opposed both by the Ottomans and by the emerging Arab national movements, in which **Arab Christians** played a prominent role.

DANIEL ROSSING

PPPP

Pablo Christiani *see* Paul the Christian

Pacifism *see* peace

Pale of Settlement, the

The Russian state had been reluctant to countenance the presence of Jews on its soil since medieval times. At the end of the eighteenth century the expansion of the Russian empire westwards abruptly posed the question of how the resulting incorporation of many hundreds of thousands of Jews could be managed. New laws were promulgated in 1791 and refined with each succeeding partition of **Poland** in 1792, 1793 and 1795. With further redefinitions in 1835, a pale of residence for Jews was established that was to last until 1917. It involved vast areas of the Russian empire, 15 provinces at least. Not only were Jews required to reside within the stated limits, they were simultaneously required to gather in the larger villages and towns, regardless of their capacity to do so. Only a limited elite was allowed to penetrate beyond these borders for residence or trade. Those who chose to be baptised certainly gained a key to professional or economic advancement. At one stage (1817–33) the government promoted the cause of would-be converts, who were described as 'Israelite Christians'. Large tracts of unencumbered land were set aside within the pale to benefit such people, but the scheme was roundly scorned. The requirement for Jews to provide their quota of recruits for the army (1827) could bring young soldiers to the outside world, but their access to it was rendered more legitimate if they agreed to be baptised. Nicholas I (*r.*1825–55) saw such 'conversions' as 'the chief benefit' of the brutal recruitment system. But some recruits turned to suicide instead. Resettlement beyond the boundaries of the pale was possible for Jews whose education, income or profession suited them for public life on Russian soil. The comparatively liberal legislation of Alexander II (*r.*1855–81) allowed some classes of Jews to live outside the pale.

See also **Russia**   *SERGEI HACKEL*

Palestinian liberation theology

Contemporary trend in Christian Palestinian Arab theology, also known as 'local', 'incarnational' or 'contextual' theology. Often hotly contested by promoters of Jewish–Christian **dialogue**, this theological trend also claims to present an alternative agenda for such dialogue, founded on peace and justice in Israel/Palestine.

Palestinian liberation theology refers to the writings of Christian Palestinians from diverse denominations, in both **Israel** and the Palestinian territories. A pioneering publication, *Theology and the Local Church* (1987) from the ecumenical Liqa Center, formulated the driving question of this theological reflection: 'We are Christian Palestinian Arabs: How do these elements come together to form our identity?' The first to call his writing '**liberation theology**' was the Anglican theologian Naim Ateek (b. 1937), whose book *Justice and Only Justice* was published in 1989, at the beginning of the first Palestinian uprising against Israeli military occupation. Other writers close to this current include Roman Catholics Patriarch Michel Sabbah (b. 1933) and Rev. Rafiq Khoury (b. 1943), Lutherans Bishop Munib Younan (b. 1950) and Rev. Mitri Raheb (b. 1962), Greek Catholics Rev. Elias Chacour (b. 1939) and Dr Geries Khoury (b. 1953) and Anglican Bishop Riah Abu Al-Assal (b. 1937).

Although primarily concerned with formulating a Christian ecumenical theology and a theology of dialogue with the majority Muslim population, underlining the shared Arab heritage of Muslims and Christians, some have also sought dialogue with Jews, particularly those critical of aspects of **Zionism** and Israeli policy. Some Jews, like Marc Ellis (b. 1952) and Jeremy Milgrom (b. 1954), have taken up the challenge and established a Jewish–Christian dialogue where the Israeli–Palestinian conflict and the search for **peace** and **justice** are indeed the central issues. This is a dialogue that recognises the Jews as an empowered majority and the Christians as an embattled **minority** within the context of Israel/Palestine.

These theologians have been critical of existing Jewish–Christian dialogue. They point out that, after the *Shoah*, some Western theologians saw the biblical election of Israel and the promise of the land as a ratification of modern Zionism, seemingly ignoring the existence of the Palestinian people. Palestinian theology insists that Christians cannot ignore the Palestinian people, their loss of homeland and struggle for liberation. The Palestinian theologians search for a biblical **hermeneutic** (particularly of the **Old Testament**), focussing on justice and peace, that universalises the themes of election and promise of land. This dimension is often in reaction to Zionist and Evangelical **Christian Zionist** readings of the Bible. In much of this theological reflection Jewish–Christian relations are reduced to the specifically political dimensions of the Israeli–Palestinian conflict, focussing on a criticism of Zionist ideology and Israeli policies. In turn, some participants in Jewish–Christian dialogue have been suspicious of Palestinian liberation theology, accusing its writers of being politically partisan, hostile to Jews and Judaism and naive about the possibilities of dialogue with increasingly militant Arab **Islam**. It remains to be seen, however, whether the dialogue that has been established between this theological trend and Jewish peace activists might indeed bear fruit for Jewish–Christian dialogue in the context of the Middle East.

See also **Arab Christianity**   DAVID M. NEUHAUS

Palestinian Talmud *see* **Talmud**

Parables

Parables are conventionally understood to be extended fictional narratives that serve to convey a particular message, usually of a theological nature. Although they are popularly associated with the teaching of **Jesus**, his use of them, as presented in the Gospels of Matthew, Mark and Luke, in fact helps to locate him within the cultural world of **Rabbinic Judaism**. In the Hebrew scriptures, while the literary prophets and the **Psalms** make extensive use of images and metaphors, there are only two real parables to be found: the challenge of the prophet Nathan to King **David**, in which he told the story of the poor man's ewe lamb (2 Sam. 12); and **Isaiah**'s tale of the vineyard that yielded wild grapes (Isa. 5). By contrast, post-biblical Judaism, to the present day, is rich in its use of parables as

a vehicle for religious teaching. Most significantly, the rabbis told many parables: *mashals*, **allegories** and extended tales – often **midrashim** (elaborations on biblical stories) – intended to convey a teaching to simple people in graphic, tangible and easily comprehended terms. Jesus' use of parables has the same purpose. Indeed, the parable of the prodigal son (Luke 15.11ff.) sounds very like the familiar rabbinic trope about the son of a king who wandered away from his father's palace and the efforts to which the father went to be reunited with him. Similarly, the parable of the talents (Matt. 25.14ff.) has numerous analogues in rabbinic literature about a master testing his servants and their various responses.   *DANIEL POLISH*

Parkes, James (1896–1981)

Anglican minister and pioneer in the study of the roots of antisemitism. Parkes graduated in theology in 1923, becoming a priest in 1926. He was devoted to fighting **antisemitism** and seeking out its origins, which he found in the writings of the **early Church**, including the **New Testament**. During the Nazi period he helped mobilise British opinion on behalf of Jewish victims, playing a leading role in helping refugees escape, and in the formation of the UK **Council of Christians and Jews** in 1942. Courageously outspoken, he was the target of a Nazi assassination plot. In his doctoral thesis, published in 1934 as *The Conflict of the Church and Synagogue: A Study in the Origins of Anti-Semitism*, Parkes argued that the Church bore much responsibility for the development of antisemitism, a view that caused great controversy. He later wrote that he was 'completely unprepared for the discovery that it was the Christian Church, and the Christian Church alone, which turned normal xenophobia and normal good and bad communal relations between two human societies into the unique evil of antisemitism' (*Voyage of Discoveries*, 1969, 123). He called for the Church to abandon proselytism to Jews.

Generations ahead of their time, Parkes's writings continue to have a significant influence on the Christian understanding of Judaism. He left his library to the University of Southampton, UK, where it is held in the Parkes Centre.

EDWARD KESSLER

Parousia

Parousia is a New Testament term (e.g. 1 Thess. 2.19; 3.13; 4.15; 5.23; Jas 5.7–8; 2 Pet. 1.16; 1 John 2.28) for the return of Jesus as final judge of all. According to **Paul** and the other **apostle**-authors, **Jesus**' return in glory would occur on 'the day of the Lord' – a term adapted by Christians from Amos 5.18, in which God threatens his coming in judgement against wrongdoers (*see* **Day of Judgement**).

Much of the **New Testament**'s description of the *parousia* is borrowed from Jewish **apocalyptic** sources. Though Paul develops this doctrine in particular, especially in his letters to the Thessalonians, John also uses similar images throughout the Book of Revelation, while Matthean texts (24.15–31) build on the apocalyptic appearance of the '**Son of Man**' in Dan. 9–12.

There are two other points of connection with Judaism. First, Jesus' *parousia* would have capped the Messianic expectations of his disciples. In the multiple Messianic concepts of first-century Judaism Christianity was typically Messianic in its being opposed by established authority which attempted to destroy it (cf. Matt. 26.1–6; Acts 4.1–22), but unique in its commitment to a non-violent, communal life of prayer and mutual support (Acts 4.32–17; 5.1–11), not intent on overtly overthrowing the religious or political order. And secondly, both ancient and medieval **millenarianists** who looked for an imminent *parousia* would be quick to insist on the **conversion** of the Jews as its necessary precondition, in line with their reading of the New Testament (e.g. of **Romans 9–11**) and the Christian belief in the ultimate Jewish acceptance of **Christ**. Such was the case, for example, with **Joachim of Fiore**, whose preaching on the conversion of the Jews and the *parousia* would become a model for the millenarianist thinkers who followed him.   DENNIS D. MCMANUS

Particularism

Jewish–Christian relations take place amid increased awareness of an extraordinary global religious diversity. An example of that diversity is the fact that every religious group in the world is represented within the **United States**, with each community asserting its particularisms of faith and belief. While there has been significant progress in developing positive Christian–Jewish **dialogue** in many parts of the world, deeply held particularities of faith will always remain. They are, in fact, irreducible and irrevocable, and should be viewed as such by participants in interreligious dialogue. Religious particularism among Jews and Christians is central to their identities as 'peoples of God'.

Jewish particularism emphasises the love, study and life of **Torah**, a term that has historically been broadly defined. Torah is a religious imperative and commitment that defines the Jews' **covenant** with God. The inextricable corporeal link of the Jewish people with the **land of Israel** is another example of religious particularism. For most Jews the link with the Land transcends contemporary politics and is, instead, a firmly held form of religious particularism. Christian particularism focuses on the core belief that the life, death and **resurrection** of **Jesus** of Nazareth were historical events of universal meaning for all humanity and for all time. Many Christians hold the particularist belief that there can be no human **salvation** without personal acceptance of Jesus as the **Christ**/God. In addition, both communities present particular, profoundly different views about which one constitutes the true 'Israel'.

Attempts to minimise particular religious beliefs increase the likelihood of failure in any authentic Jewish–Christian encounter. Particularisms of faith, like the meaning of Torah for Jews or the centrality of the Jesus event for Christians, cannot be glossed over for the purpose of achieving either a superficial accommodation between the two communities or a watered-down syncretism. Genuine Christian–Jewish dialogue goes far beyond merely acknowledging that there are diverse religions in the world. Instead, a mature dialogue recognises, even celebrates, the particularisms that will always be present in both Judaism and Christianity. However, Jewish and Christian particularism is no barrier to successful dialogue. Indeed, such an affirmation is a necessity.

Facing the challenge of affirming one's faith in a world of religious particularisms has frequently elicited two opposing responses from Christians and Jews. Some leaders assert that, despite unique faith commitments, all religions, including Christianity and Judaism, have equal validity and share the same value system despite their distinctive outer trappings. Other spiritual leaders turn inward and urge increased exclusivism. They assert that their particular faith commitment is the sole path for all people to follow. Neither approach is helpful in the Christian–Jewish encounter. The former results in a bland relativism, where all religious faiths are viewed as the same with no significant differences or particularities; the latter often results in bigotry or fanaticism. Accepting the reality of religious particularism affords Jews and Christians the right to self-definition on their own terms as well as affirming the same right for their dialogue partners.   *A. JAMES RUDIN*

Pascal, Blaise (1623–62)

French religious philosopher, scientist and mathematician who, despite his conventional anti-Jewish theology, expressed profound admiration for Jews. Pascal exerted influence on letters, theology and science (inventing in the 1640s the first digital calculator, the syringe and the hydraulic press). After 1646 Pascal's strict **Roman Catholicism** was tempered by encounter with Port-Royal's austerely Augustinian Jansenism. Pascal entered Port-Royal convent in 1655 following his 'night of fire' mystical encounter with the 'God of Abraham, God of Isaac, God of Jacob, not of the philosophers and men of science' (*Memorial*).

Pascal subsequently wrote *Les Provinciales* attacking **Jesuit** morality and theology in scintillating prose. Although placed on the *Index* (1657), *Les Provinciales* influenced later papal activity against the Jesuits. Pascal's unfinished *Apologie de la religion chrétienne*, published as *Pensées* (1670), a work of **apologetics** and biblical **exegesis**, stressed interiority and the primacy of emotion. It influenced Rousseau (1671–1741), Bergson (1859–1941) and the existentialists. In *Pensées* traditional **anti-Judaic** motifs abound: the wretchedness and blindness of Jews; a rebellious and accursed people; their oral law absurd. Pascal interpreted the Hebrew scriptures figuratively and argued that God had rejected the entire Mosaic **covenant** (*Pensées*, 444). Yet he praised Mosaic **Law** as the most perfect law and Jews for their long survival, sincerity, zeal and unexampled willingness to observe, and die for, the Law. Outlining their unique singularity, Pascal expressed himself astounded by his encounter with, in his view, a people consisting entirely of brothers, worthy of study and entitled to special veneration.   *MARGARET BREARLEY*

Paschal lamb

Throughout the ritual history of ancient Israel the lamb or ram is a central figure of **sacrifice**. Even from **Abraham**'s time the offering of a ram (Gen. 22.13) was a prized holocaust. While still in Egypt the Israelites were commanded by God to slay a male lamb on the evening of Nisan 14 (Exod 12) as a **Passover** offering. *Pesachim* 5–9 of the **Mishnah**, and the tracts *Tamid* and *Zevahim* 5 of the **Talmud**, give the ancient regulations for the annual commemorative offering of the paschal (Passover) lamb through the Second Temple period.

It is in connection with this important Jewish setting that Christians apply the term 'paschal lamb' to the person of **Jesus** at his death during a Passover celebration. **Paul** (1 Cor. 5.7) and John (1.31–34; 6; 19.36) are the principal agents of this identification between the ancient Hebrew symbol of the Passover lamb as the guilt offering of the people and the person of Jesus. John further elaborates by placing the title 'Lamb of God' in the mouth of **John the Baptist** at Jesus' baptism (John.1.31–34). The evangelist may well have relied on the double meaning of the **Aramaic** term *talya* as both 'servant' and 'lamb', as found in the **Targum** of Ps. 117 and elsewhere, as the basis for this title. John's conflation of the two distinct but allied meanings of the term applied to Jesus within a sacrificial context is unique.

Almost immediately within a developing Christian theology the term 'Passover lamb' is taken to mean the person of Jesus as offered in **atonement** for the sins of the world. The patristic **exegesis** of the term is extensive (cf. Clement of Alexandria (*c*.150–*c*. 215) *Paed.* 1.5.24.4; **Origen**, *Comm. Jo.* 6.52; Gaudentius (d. early fifth century), *Tractatus* 2.14.17) and dominated by a typological **hermeneutic** such as that of **Melito of Sardis** (*Peri Pascha*), who extends the imagery to include **Mary**: 'he was the silent lamb, the lamb who was slain, born of Mary, the fair ewe'. Gradually, a discounting of the Passover lamb of ancient **Israel** as no more than a forerunner of **Christ** 'the true Lamb' (*Exsultet*, fourth century) begins to take hold in the Christian **liturgy**, so that by the time of Thomas **Aquinas** the Passover lamb of Exodus is referred to as *agnum typicum*, or 'the lamb which was a type', in his well-known hymn *Sacris solemnis juncta* (1264). Israel's Passover lamb then becomes only a foreshadowing of the Christian reality in the mind of Western believers. When Thomas à Kempis (1380–1471) composes his influential devotional work *De Imitatione Christi* (*c*.1418), and adopts

Aquinas's phrase, contrasting the Jewish paschal lamb as a mere 'type' to Christ, the 'true Lamb', the notion becomes a part of **eucharistic** vocabulary for the ordinary Christian. This same term, with its **typological** interpretation, is found in the revised Roman rites of **Holy Week** (1970) for the liturgies of Holy Thursday and the **Easter** Vigil. *The Book of Common Prayer* (USA, 1979) retains identical language in its Proper Preface for Easter. Present-day communion rites of many Christian Churches herald Christ under the title 'Lamb of God'. *DENNIS D. MCMANUS*

Passion narratives

These are the narrative accounts of the suffering, death and burial of **Jesus** found in the four canonical Gospels and in other non-biblical literature, especially the apocryphal *Gospel of Peter*. In general, these accounts tend to exaggerate Jewish responsibility for the death of Jesus and to downplay Roman responsibility and have been, therefore, both problematic and harmful through the centuries in Jewish–Christian relations. In telling the story of Jesus' death, Christians sought to explain the meaning of this ignominious end, marked as it was by shameful public ridicule and execution by **crucifixion**. The passion narratives, therefore, narrate not only events surrounding the circumstances of Jesus' death but the Christian interpretation of those events. References to Jesus' death in **Paul**'s letters (Gal. 3.1; 1 Cor. 2.2; Rom. 6.4), as well as the many varied elements included in the passion narratives of the four Gospels, point to a lively oral tradition of the passion story that continued to circulate among Christians even after the four Gospels were written. Christian texts from the second to the fifth centuries CE confirm the continued telling and elaboration of the passion story (e.g., Papias, Barnabas, **Ignatius** of Antioch (*Trall.* 9.1), *Odes of Solomon* 28, **Justin Martyr** (*1 Apol.* 35; *Dial.* 98–106), **Melito of Sardis** (*Homily on the Passion*)). In form and genre the story of Jesus' suffering and death resembles those of many Jewish accounts of the death of righteous people, beginning with the **Suffering Servant** of Second Isaiah and such texts as Dan. 3 and 6, 2 Macc. 7, and Wis. 2, 4 and 5 (*see* **wisdom**). Most scholars argue that an already continuous narrative (perhaps in written form, though the exact content of this is much debated) with fixed narrative form existed prior to the writing of the canonical Gospels and that each

of the four evangelists expanded in different ways on this basic story. The common elements include: betrayal by **Judas Iscariot**, the arrest at night, interrogations by both Jewish and Roman authorities, mockery and abusive treatment, condemnation by **Pilate**, the sentence of death by crucifixion, and burial.

Each of the canonical Gospels exhibits a number of unique features in the shared story of Jesus' passion and death. Matthew's account, for example, adds a number of elaborate details not found elsewhere, some of which serve to exaggerate even more the accusation of Jewish responsibility for Jesus' death. Only Matthew includes a tortured Judas who commits suicide (Matt. 27.3–10) and the story of Pilate's wife warning her husband to have nothing to do with 'that righteous man' (Matt. 27.19). Matthew alone adds the people's damning cry of 'His blood be upon us and our children' (Matt. 27.24–25), the cosmic signs after the death of Jesus (Matt. 27.51–54) and the clearly apologetic detail that narrates the posting of a guard at the tomb of Jesus (Matt. 27.65–66). Among the unique features of Luke are the collusion of Jewish authorities in Jesus' arrest (Luke 22.52), a morning (not night-time) interrogation by the **Sanhedrin** (Luke 22.66) and a trial before **Herod** (Luke 23.7–12). Many of the actual historical details surrounding the suffering and death of Jesus remain clouded behind these very different, and explicitly theologically motivated, Gospel accounts. A number of specific, thorny problems surround the passion stories: for example, the question of the Jewish interrogations in the **trial of Jesus**, the degree of influence and instigation wielded by the Jews in the final Roman sentencing and execution, the chronology of the events and their relation to the **Passover** feast, the Gospel reference to a custom of Passover amnesty – to name the most debated issues. Obvious **Old Testament** allusions mark the passion narratives as already reflecting the interpretive process of the early Christians who turned to the biblical tradition in search of an explanation for the meaning of Jesus' ignominious death. The texts of Isa. 53, 2 Macc. 6–7, the lament **psalms**, especially Ps. 22, provided structures of meaning enabling Christians to see in the death of Jesus the pattern of the death of a righteous person who was then vindicated by God. But all the Gospel accounts reflect the deepening early Christian **polemic** against the Jews as responsible for the death of Jesus.

This polemical tendency found powerful dramatic expression in the Christian tradition of the medieval passion plays, the most famous of which since 1634 has been the passion play performed once every ten years at Oberammergau in the Bavarian alps. But in modern times, especially in the wake of the **Vatican II** document *Nostra Aetate*, Christians as well as Jews have called for and achieved far-reaching changes in this very influential dramatic production. A jointly authored Jewish–Christian statement, published by B'nai B'rith in 1984, outlined 24 recommended changes in the text and the dramatic embellishments at Oberammergau. These changes aimed to remedy the excessive stereotyping of Jewish characters in the drama that has contributed to anti-Jewish sentiment among Christians. It called for a more historically accurate portrait of a Jewish Jesus and a recognition in the text of the passion play that the struggle leading to Jesus' death was a struggle internal to Judaism, not a struggle between Jews and Christians. Even more than the Gospel passion narratives themselves, the text of the passion play depicts **Pilate** as a noble and righteous, though weak, character when history tells us that he was a tyrannical ruler who spared nothing to protect his own power. Changes were called for not only in the text of the passion play itself, but also in the costuming and staging that had exaggerated anti-Jewish features, as in the example of the Jewish priests wearing outlandish robes and hats with horns symbolising their connection with the '**devil**'. Many of these suggested changes were put in place for the Oberammergau performance in 2000 but only after repeated appeals from Jews and Christians alike. The example of the Oberammergau passion play is indicative of the lasting, powerful effect, and often harmful potential, of the Gospel passion narratives. *BARBARA E. BOWE*

Passion plays *see* **passion narratives**

Passover

A major Jewish festival, Passover features in Jewish–Christian relations only insofar as Christians associate the timing and the imagery of the festival with the death of **Jesus**. Both aspects are, however, of great significance for Christians, especially in relation to the **Last Supper** which Jesus shared with his disciples before his **crucifixion**, and the emerging **sacrament** of the **eucharist**. The eucharistic **liturgy** during the **Easter** season includes the words: 'Christ our Passover is sacrificed for us. Therefore let us

keep the feast.' These words derive from **Paul**'s theology as found in his first letter to the Corinthians (5.7–8), where he compares clearing out the bad elements of their lives with getting rid of the old yeast or leaven.

Some maintain that the Jewish festival of unleavened **bread** was at first separate from the following Passover festival, the former being an agricultural festival and the latter pastoral. What is important for Judaism, however, is that the festivals either were or became at some point combined. Agricultural and pastoral elements were connected to the historical commemoration of the exodus from Egypt. Exod. 12.34 indicates that there was no time for the bread to rise before the urgent escape, and vv. 3–6 narrate how on the eventful night every Israelite family was commanded to offer and eat a lamb. The **Torah** later commands the Israelites to sacrifice a lamb every year to recall this (Deut. 16.2, 6–7). Deut. 16.3 refers to unleavened bread as 'the bread of affliction', remembering the Egyptian oppression. As sacrifice could be offered only in the **Temple** in **Jerusalem**, Israelites endeavoured to go there for Passover. It thus became one of the foot or **pilgrimage** festivals, alongside **Shavuot** and **Sukkot**. Since the destruction of the Second Temple in 70 CE sacrifice is no longer offered. Nonetheless, alongside the two other pilgrimage festivals, together with **Yom Kippur**, Passover is a major festival and widely observed by Jews worldwide. Beginning on 14 Nisan, it is a seven-day festival (eight in the **Diaspora**) with work restrictions on the first (two) and last (two) days. The lamb is still represented (in the form of a lamb bone) in the seder, the meal held on the first night of Passover in **Israel** (the first two nights in the Diaspora). Whilst sometimes Christians have paralleled the bread and **wine** of the eucharist with the unleavened bread and the wine of the seder, in reality they carry quite different meanings. The notion of bread symbolising someone's body, of wine symbolising someone's blood, and of both being consumed is totally alien to Judaism. The most that could be said for a common understanding is that both the unleavened bread of the Passover and the bread or wafer of the eucharist have come to be symbols of **salvation** and deliverance. (Some scholars, e.g. John Pawlikowski (1991), draw attention rather to possible links between the weekly **Shabbat** meal in Judaism and the so-called 'table-fellowship' in Christianity.)

There is considerable debate over the timing of the Last Supper, stemming from the differences in chronology between John's Gospel (John 19.14) and the other three Gospels. If it is accepted that, as John says, the meal was held on the night before Passover, then all the emphasis falls on Jesus as the **paschal lamb**. This may also be linked with John's references to Jesus as the lamb of God, though in Judaism it is not the sacrificial lamb but the scapegoat that is seen as taking away the people's **sin**. From the accounts in the Synoptic Gospels we may conclude an identification of the Last Supper with the Jewish seder. The feast of unleavened bread is identified as Passover (Luke 22.1) and the 'institution' of the eucharist is seen as centering on Jesus presenting the bread as his body and the wine as his blood (Luke 22.19–20). It may be observed that both **Josephus** and **Philo** state that 14 Nisan was both the Feast of Passover and the day of the Passover **sacrifice** and that there have long been attempts to bring John's chronology in line with that of the Synoptics, for instance by Annie Jaubert (*La date de la Cène*). For Christian liturgists the answer to the question of timing is not crucial. There are no exclusively paschal practices in the Church's eucharistic celebrations and it is the general atmosphere of the Jewish Passover that Christians associate with the Easter period. There are dangers in the celebration of 'Christianised' seders, a practice begun in the 1960s whereby Christianising formulae were introduced into the Jewish celebration. Whilst their intention may be to help Christians understand their Jewish roots, the result can be unhelpful as representing conflation rather than genuine **dialogue** between the two religions. They seem to confuse two different types of **remembrance**, which might be called affective and effective respectively. In Judaism remembrance is not so much a matter of trying to replicate an event in order to draw out a human response but of dramatising the event as part of a living tradition. God's word, *davar*, is declared and something happens. Thus **Luther**, in insisting that a sermon accompany the ritual memorial of the Last Supper, was perhaps nearer to drawing on Judaism than Christian attempts to recreate this supper 'as it was'. The central significance of Passover as a celebration of freedom is captured for Christians in the Easter vigil (*pasch*), begun on Easter eve and going through into the early hours of Easter Sunday morning. The first part of the vigil involves the lighting of a paschal **candle**, the reciting of psalms and other passages from the **Hebrew Bible** depicting the deliverance of the children of Israel from slavery to freedom and thus from darkness to light. The imagery of physical **redemption** lies at the heart of the Christian celebration of redemption from sin as believed to be brought about by Jesus through his crucifixion and confirmed by his **resurrection**. Thus it is the Easter Vigil and not the seder which expresses Christian continuity with the Jewish Passover.

Passover has come to be associated with manifestations of **anti-Judaism** through the Christian accusation against Jews known as the **blood libel**. Modern Christian statements emphasise the need for care in liturgy and particularly in dramatisations when association is made between Easter and Passover. For instance, the Canadian Catholic Bishops Conference in 1988 issued *Revised Directives for the Liturgical Reading of the Passion Narratives in Holy Week.*   *CHRISTINE PILKINGTON*

Pasternak, Boris Leonidovich (1890–1960)

Writer and Nobel laureate. Born to a Jewish family in Moscow, Pasternak was baptised by his nurse and became a Russian **Orthodox Christian** in the 1930s. He worked as a librarian, poet and translator (of **Shakespeare**, Byron and Goethe) but is chiefly remembered for the epic novel *Dr Zhivago* (1956). Although influenced by Jewish tradition, Pasternak sought spiritual fulfilment and identification with the Russian eth(n)os through Christianity. Indeed, David Ben Gurion (1886–1973) called *Zhivago* 'despicable', because it advocated Jewish **assimilation**, both politically and spiritually. Pasternak opposed **Zionism** and believed that Judaism had been superseded by Christianity (*see* **supersessionism**).   *MELANIE J. WRIGHT*

Paul

Apostle and Christian theologian. As the first Christian missionary to the Gentile world, Paul has played a unique role in Jewish–Christian relations. Convinced that God had called Gentiles to be members of his people, Paul insisted that what had happened through the death and resurrection of **Christ** was the fulfilment of God's promises to **Israel**. Tragically, later generations read his letters out of context, and so lost sight of his emphasis on continuity, misinterpreting his words as an attack on Judaism.

Our knowledge of Paul is derived from his letters and from the Acts of the Apostles. Acts records Paul's travels in some detail, but scholars differ in their assessment of its accuracy. The letters tell us little about Paul's life and background, and what information they provide occurs incidentally. He speaks of his Jewish upbringing (Phil. 2.5–6), and refers briefly to an experience that he himself clearly regarded as a call (Gal. 1.15–16). Luke describes this event three times (Acts 9.1–19; 22.3–16; 26.4–18), and he, like Paul, says that Paul was called to preach the gospel to Gentiles (Acts 9.15; 22.15, 21; 26. 17–18). Luke's dramatic accounts of the 'Damascus Road experience' have, however, led to it being seen as Paul's 'conversion'. Yet Paul was certainly not converted from one **religion** to another. Rather he became convinced that the God whom he had worshipped all his life had now revealed himself in a new way through the death and **resurrection** of his Son **Jesus**. The interpretation of the event as a conversion reflects the subsequent split between Judaism and Christianity.

Of the 13 letters attributed to Paul, we may be confident that he wrote Romans, 1–2 Corinthians, Galatians, Philippians, 1 Thessalonians and Philemon; there is less certainty about 2 Thessalonians and Colossians, and considerable doubt concerning Ephesians, while the 'Pastoral Epistles' (1–2 Timothy and Titus) appear to have been written later. All his letters are in fact 'pastoral' – written to deal with issues that were causing concern, either to the Churches or to Paul himself.

It is clear from his letters that Paul had been trained both in Greek **rhetoric** and in Jewish methods of **exegesis**. There is no evidence to support suggestions that he was influenced by contemporary mystery religions: the basis of his theology was Jewish. As a Jew, Paul judged everything by the **Torah**. He had originally thought of the crucified Jesus as having come under the curse of God (Deut. 21.23); now, convinced that Jesus had been raised by God, he was forced to look at the scriptures in a new light. His message, he insisted, was in no way contrary to the Torah (Rom. 3.31), which was holy and good (Rom. 7.12): God was faithful to the promises that he had made to his people Israel (Rom. 3.3–4; 9.6). The gospel (or 'good news') that Paul proclaimed was the fulfilment of promises made by God in the holy scriptures concerning Jesus, who was God's **Messiah** (Rom. 1.1–3; cf. 9.5). In this he was in agreement with other Christians.

Paul's conviction that he had been sent to evangelise Gentiles, however, led to a dispute with some of his fellow-Christians, who assumed that Gentiles who accepted a gospel about Jesus as God's Messiah should become Jews, accepting all the obligations of obedience to the Torah. But the Christian gospel centred on Jesus' resurrection, and Paul was convinced that this had in some sense inaugurated the Age to Come. Hope for the future age had included the expectation that Gentiles would acknowledge Israel's God and come to worship in **Jerusalem** (Isa. 2.2–4; Zech. 2.11; 8.2–23): they would not need to become Jews. Paul went further, applying to the Gentiles texts that had once referred to repentant Israel: those who had not been God's people were now called 'my people' (Hos. 1.10; 2.23; Rom. 9.25–6); the barren woman now has children (Isa. 54.1: Gal. 4.27).

Paul's justification for doing so was twofold. The first was that Gentiles who had responded to the gospel had received the gift of the **Holy Spirit** (the promise of the Last Days, Joel 2.28–9; Acts 2.14–21), and had already been received by God as his children (Gal. 3); obedience to the Torah was thus unnecessary. A similar argument is used in Acts 10.9–11.18. Paul concluded that the grace of God had been poured out on Jew and Greek alike: 'everyone who calls on the name of the Lord will be saved' (Joel 2.32; Rom. 10.13).

The second was based on the exegesis of scripture. Gen. 15.6 had referred to Abraham's *faith* or *trust* in God, and nothing more had been required of him: the true children of **Abraham**, therefore, to whom the promises had been made, were those who – like Abraham – trusted in God, not those who were his physical descendants (Gal. 3.6–29; Rom. 4.1–25). The **covenant** with Abraham did not require obedience to the Mosaic **Law**, which had been given subsequently as an interim measure until the coming of the Messiah. For Gentiles to put themselves under its requirements was thus a denial of the privileges that they had already received by being 'in Christ'.

The Mosaic Law had been given to Israel (Rom. 9.4), and obedience to it was seen as Israel's response to what God had done at the exodus. Now he had saved his people again – not Israel alone, but the Gentiles also – and the response expected of them was obedience to 'the law of Christ' (Gal. 6.2), which was the command to **love**; this was the fulfilment of the whole Law (Rom. 13.8–10; Gal. 5.14). Paradoxically, however, it was fulfilled, not by striving to keep the Law, but by God's Spirit at work in the human heart (Rom. 8.3–4). Although God revealed himself to **Moses**, and his glory was seen on Sinai, he had revealed himself more fully in Christ, who is the very image of God (2 Cor. 3.2–4.6). It is, then, in Christ, not in the Torah, that we see the supreme revelation of God's purpose. To many of Paul's Jewish contemporaries, this seemed like an *attack* on the Torah.

The Christian community owed its existence to the belief that Jesus had been raised from the dead. This left Christians with a problem, however. Why had God allowed his Messiah to be crucified? What had happened to him must have been part of God's plan, and so had taken place 'according to the scriptures'. But why had Christ's death been necessary? Like other early Christians, Paul saw it as a redemptive act – a second Exodus – and as 'for sins'. He drew on a wealth of **Old Testament** imagery: Christ had 'redeemed' believers (Gal. 3.13; 4.5), had been sacrificed as a Passover lamb (*see* **paschal lamb**) (1 Cor. 5.7) and as a sin-offering (Rom. 8.3); he is even described as a *hilasterion* (Rom. 3.25), the mercy-seat of Lev. 16.13–16, where **atonement** was made for Israel, and now, in Christ, for the whole world.

Central to Paul's understanding of the gospel was his belief that Christians *share* Christ's death and resurrection, which had inaugurated the Age to Come. **Baptism** into Christ therefore meant sharing his death to **sin**, which dominates the present age, and sharing his resurrection life. As God's Messiah, Christ was a representative figure, like **Adam**, whose actions affected others. Just as Adam's disobedience had brought sin and death into the world, so Christ's obedience had brought an end to the era of sin and death (Rom. 5.12–21) and inaugurated the new **creation** promised by the prophets (2 Cor. 5.17). Final salvation and restoration lie in the future (Rom. 8.18–25; 1 Cor. 15.20–58). Paul emphasises Jesus' humanity (Rom. 8.3; Gal. 4.4; Phil. 2.7). At the same time he insists that God was at work through him (Rom. 5.15–17; 8.3; 2 Cor. 5.18–21). Like Israel's kings, and like Israel herself, Christ can be described as '**Son of God**', but with far more reason, since he

is obedient to God and totally committed to God's purpose.

In **Romans 9–11** Paul agonises over Israel's failure to respond to the gospel. Since God is faithful to his promises to his people (Rom. 9.1–5), Paul is confident of Israel's final **salvation** (Rom. 11.26–9): he dismisses indignantly any suggestion that God has rejected his people (11.1–2). Jewish rejection of the gospel meant that it was being preached to the Gentiles, but they have not replaced the Jews (Rom. 11.13–24). Rather, the **conversion** of the Gentiles would, eventually, lead Israel to respond (Rom. 11.11–32).

The inclusion of the Pauline letters in the **New Testament** made them authoritative for the whole Church. Letters addressed to particular situations were now regarded as providing instructions for all Christians. The break between Judaism and Christianity meant that they were read in very different contexts: Paul's arguments concerning Gentile Christians were seen as an attack on Judaism. In the second century **Marcion** totally misinterpreted Paul's teaching. Paul's Jewish roots were ignored, and his writings were twisted to justify anti-Jewish prejudice.

For Paul, the pressing problem discussed in Romans was the salvation of Israel. Later generations were more interested in the salvation of the individual. **Luther** interpreted Rom. 1–8 as the answer to this problem, laying great emphasis on Paul's insistence that '**justification**' (or being brought into a right relationship with God) came through faith, not works. The Protestant emphasis on 'faith' was a direct attack on Catholic reliance on 'works' (or 'merit', such as indulgences); the parallel with Paul's insistence that God saved those who trusted in him, not those who trusted in 'the works of the Law', meant that Paul's teaching was seen as an attack on Judaism. 'The gospel' was now regarded as opposed to 'the Law', Judaism as a legalistic religion over against Christianity, the religion of **grace**.

In the early twentieth century Paul was often understood to have been influenced by Greek ideas. More recently, following the work of W. D. Davies (1911–2001), scholars have emphasised his debt to Judaism. Others sought to correct the common caricature of Judaism. E. P. Sanders (b. 1937), whose name is the one most often associated with what has been termed 'the new perspective on Paul', built on the work of G. F. Moore (1851–1931) in emphasising that the doctrine of God's grace in saving Israel lay at the heart of Judaism.

Paul has often been described as the real founder of Christianity. This is a gross exaggeration. The gospel he preached seems to have been essentially the same as that proclaimed by other early Christians. There are similarities, too, between his teaching and that of Jesus. In contrast to the latter, however, Paul's teaching was Christocentric. This shift was due to the conviction of Paul and his fellow-Christians that Jesus was the Messiah, through whom God's righteousness and salvation were at work. It was God who sent his Son, gave him up to death and raised him to life, God whose grace was seen in Christ, God to whom men and women are now reconciled.

In his letters Paul explored the significance of these beliefs for the Christian community. His conviction that he had been sent to evangelise the Gentiles was largely responsible for changing belief in Jesus as the Messiah from a Jewish sect into a worldwide religion. *MORNA D. HOOKER*

Paul the Christian (thirteenth century)

Often wrongly called Pablo Christiani (Pablo being a Castilian name alien to Catalonia and Languedoc), Paul was born a Jew in Montpellier but converted to Christianity after some exposure to Jewish learning. He then entered the **Dominican** Order where, in the entourage of Ramon de Penyafort (*c.*1185–1275), he became engaged in anti-Jewish **polemics**. Penyafort had become interested in using friars with a deep knowledge of Judaism or **Islam** on **missions** to unbelievers, hoping that their ability to argue with the leaders of other faiths using knowledge of **Hebrew** or Arabic texts would show the superiority of Christianity. Paul was assigned the task of debating in public before King **James I** of Aragon concerning whether the **Messiah** had come; his opponent was the elderly leader of Catalan Jewry, **Nahmanides**. Both a Latin and a Hebrew account of this **disputation**, held in Barcelona in 1263, survive, offering different viewpoints. What was distinctive was Paul's attempt to use the **Talmud** to demonstrate that the Messiah had come. Nahmanides argued that he was not obliged to believe as literal truth the **aggadic** material – that is, the stories and **parables** – in the Talmud. Paul

mocked this position. Neither side 'won', in the sense that the king could not possibly declare that a Jew had been victorious, and the aim of the disputation had been to discredit Jewish belief; Paul thereafter maintained pressure on Nahmanides, who was threatened with a trial. Paul interceded with Pope Clement IV (*r.*1265–8), who demanded that the leading ecclesiastic of Catalonia, the archbishop of Tarragona, must arrange for the Talmud to be checked for **blasphemies**. Paul also appears to have encouraged the king to force Jews to attend the missionary sermons he and other friars would give in synagogues. However, the Jewish communities regularly paid their way out of this obligation, which became, in effect, a way of taxing them. Paul's aggression also extended to **France**, where he encouraged King **Louis IX** to impose the wearing of a badge on Jews (*see* **yellow badge**). His fanatical hatred of Judaism helped initiate more hostile approaches to the Jewish refusal to convert in the thirteenth century. *DAVID ABULAFIA*

Paul VI (1897–1978)

Pope (1963–78) and reformer. Born Giovanni Battista Montini in Concesio, Italy, he grew up in an upper-middle-class family active in political life and social issues. Ordained a priest in 1920, he entered the Vatican's diplomatic service and worked for more than 30 years in the Secretariat of State. In 1937 he was appointed Substitute for Ordinary Affairs, and was thus intimately involved in the Vatican's wartime policies under **Pius XII**, with whom he had nearly daily contact for 15 years and whose character he later vigorously defended. Upon the election of **John XXIII** in 1958, Montini was the new pope's first nomination as cardinal. Five years later he was elected to the papacy himself.

Paul's papacy began in the midst of the **Second Vatican Council** (1962–5), over whose deliberations he presided, and whose direction he would implement for the rest of his life. He combined a concern for Church **tradition** with a desire to be open to modern culture and other religions, and his personal influence was crucial in the passage of several controversial sections of ***Nostra Aetate***, the Council's document on Judaism and other non-Christian religions, which he promulgated in 1965. In January 1964 Paul became the first pope in 150 years to leave Italy, travelling to the Middle East and making a short visit to Christian holy sites in **Israel**. This historic **pilgrimage** was also noteworthy for the fact that the Pope did not use the word 'Israel' during any of his public addresses, did not visit any Israeli monuments, and declined to meet with Israel's chief rabbi – largely because of differences over Israel's political statehood and a desire that the visit be seen as a purely religious act, avoiding any kind of political considerations. The contrast with **John Paul II**'s visit 36 years later is striking.

Paul's pontificate was marked by a spirit of openness, **dialogue** and outreach, and in October 1974 he established a Commission for Religious Relations with the Jews. He presided over a period of great turbulence and flux in Catholic life, and was widely criticised for upholding traditional Catholic teachings on birth control and priestly **celibacy**. His precedent-setting international journeys made him the most widely travelled pope up to that time, a legacy that Pope John Paul II continued and developed considerably. In 1969 Paul received Abba Eban (1915–2002), the foreign minister of Israel, and Prime Minister Golda Meir (1898–1978) met with him in 1973, although the significance of this meeting was downplayed because of pressure from several Arab states, and Paul remained ambivalent towards Israel's character as a Jewish state. His most important contribution to Jewish–Christian relations can be seen in the ongoing work of the Commission that he established four years before his death.

LUCY THORSON AND MURRAY WATSON

Peace

Peace (*shalom* in Hebrew) is both a state (the absence of war) and a process of living in wholesome relationship with others, ideally where partners and participants trust each other, act with integrity and are dedicated to the common good rather than threatening each other. It has been called the 'ultimate purpose' of the **Torah** (Zvi Werblowsky, 'Peace'). In this respect Christianity is a true child of Judaism, laying particular emphasis on the admonition in the Hebrew **psalm** 'Seek peace and pursue it!' (Ps. 33.15), which occurs only once in the **Hebrew Bible** but four times in the **New Testament** (Heb. 12.14; 1 Pet. 3.11; Rom. 14.19; 2 Tim. 2.22).

The Sayings of the Fathers (the *Pirke Avot*) affirm that the world rests on three things: justice, truth

and peace (m. Avot. 1.12). Drawing from this heritage, **Paul** also affirms that the **kingdom of God** consists not of food or drink but of justice, joy and peace (Rom 14.17). **Jesus** pronounced a special blessing upon peacemakers (Matt. 5.9) and used the term 'person of peace' as a normative self-designation (Luke 10.6) for his disciples, leading his followers to be reconciled with their enemies instead of annihilating them. His contemporaries invited people to be sons of **Aaron**, who was known as a great reconciler. Jesus invited people to be peacemakers and thus become children of God, a 'God of Peace', a phrase Paul uses seven times and Hebrews once.

Despite this, there is in Judaism and Christianity both a time for peace and a time for war: God is both a warrior, as expressed in the Song of Miriam (Exod. 15.3) and a God who is peace, as celebrated by Gideon in Judg. 6.24. Thus neither religion can be said to be fundamentally pacifist. However, the fifteenth and sixteenth centuries saw the development within Protestantism of **Historic Peace Churches**, who continue to affirm a commitment to pacifism and non-violence built on the life of Jesus, and in recent years Jews and Christians have together protested against wars: Martin Luther King (1929–68) and Abraham **Heschel** brought study and action together in the organisation Clergy and Laity Concerned about Vietnam. In Israel and the Palestinian territories non-violence is vigorously supported by groups such as Oz ve Shalom (Peace through Strength) and Sabeel, the **Palestinian liberation theology** movement.

WILLIAM KLASSEN

Penance/penitence

First-century Judaism held that a sinner's return to God (*teshuvah*) required remorse for sins (*haratah*), the avoidance of evil (Isa. 33.15; Ps. 24.4) and the doing of good (Jer. 26.13). In a Jewish context penance was restitution to others for the repair or restoration of what was damaged through wrongdoing. The Jewish **liturgy** prizes **repentance** and penitence throughout the penitential season (*Asere Yemei Teshuvah*) and the observance of **Yom Kippur** in particular.

Rabbinic teaching on repentance would eventually centre on the question of how to put right the wrong done against one's neighbour, since wrong done against God could not be restituted for in any material sense. However, wrong done to another could be atoned for through cultic offerings, alms-giving, the payment of fines, **fasting** and works of charity. Penance is meant to be a constant prac-tice for Jews, with the reminder of *m. Avot* 2.10 to do penance one day before death – it being under-stood that since one's day of death is unknown, then every day must be lived in penance.

Much of **Jesus**' teaching was consistent with this same doctrine, as can be seen in the prodigal son story of Luke. 15.11–32, wherein a change of heart or will (Ezek. 18.31; Jer. 4.4) was needed for repentance. However, by the second century Christian notions of penance had developed radically. Christians focused on penance as restitution to God through **Christ** for all humankind's offences, with a belief in Christ's own death as their principal reparation. However, the individual's debt for **sin** was satisfied through a penance given by the **priest**, who for-gave sins in the name of Jesus. Such penances were also intended as medicinal remedies for the effects of sin in the **soul**, as seen in the great medieval compilations of virtue–vice lists such as Hildegard of Bingen's (1098–1179) *Liber Vitae Meritorum* (completed 1163). Much of traditional Jewish belief in the efficacy of restitution through what the **Church Fathers** would call the 'sacred tri-pod' – prayer, fasting and almsgiving – survived in the penances assigned in the medieval penitential books, such as *Capitula iudiciorum* or the *Burgun-dian penitentials*.

However, a tragic use of the Christian doctrine of repentance was made against Jews in the period of the **Crusades** from 1095 until *c*.1464, during which Jews were forced to accept every kind of depriva-tion, beatings and even death as 'penance' for their supposed collective guilt in the death of Jesus (*see* **deicide, charge of**). Despite attempts by **Bernard of Clairvaux** and others to defend the Jews against such attacks, they were nonetheless caught up in the turmoil. Godfrey of Bouillon (*c*. 1058–1100), for example, in 1094 vowed retribution against the Jews for their role in the killing of Jesus, demanding that they pay *poenitentiam justitiae divinae*, or punish-ment of divine justice. Such tactics were also used in the **Inquisition** against Jews who were regarded as heretics for returning to Judaism, even after forced **conversions** to Christianity. The full renun-ciation of this practice came definitively in the **Vatican II** document entitled ***Nostra Aetate*** (no. 4) in 1965. *DENNIS D. MCMANUS*

Pentateuch

Formed from two Greek words, *pente* (five) and *teu-chos* (scroll), and meaning five scrolls, the term is used in Greek and Latin writings from the second century CE to designate the first five books of the Bible. In Jewish tradition this section of the Bible is known as the **Torah**. For Jews and Christians it occupies a supreme place as a source of **revelation** about the created universe and the moral impera-tives enjoined by the creator. While Orthodox Jews and conservative Christians believe that **Moses** was the author of the Pentateuch, critical scholarship assigns its composition to the redaction of many sources and supplements over a long period of time.

See also **Wellhausen, Julius** *JOHN ROGERSON*

Pentecost

Pentecost Sunday, also known as Whitsunday, marks the end of the **Easter** season and occurs 50 days after Easter Sunday just as **Shavuot** occurs 50 days after **Passover**. Pentecost also refers to the 50-day season itself, though this sense was lost over time and Pentecost came to be seen as an isolated feast celebrating the birth of the Church. Since **Vatican II** reforms of the liturgical **calendar**, there have been attempts to restore this sense of Pentecost as a celebration of 50 days. Pentecost as mentioned in the Acts of the Apostles (2.2–4) is a description of the descent of the **Holy Spirit** on the **apostles**. Pentecost is what Greek-speaking Jews called the feast of Shavuot, the Feast of Weeks, which occurred 50 days after the feast of Passover and was in its origins the final celebration of the harvest. Later Jewish tradition has Shavuot com-memorating the events of the giving of the **Torah** at Sinai and the season acquires a penitential tone. However, as a Christian feast, it does not appear until the end of the second century, when it marks a 50-day period of rejoicing. In the fourth century the fiftieth day emerges as a special day which com-memorates both the ascension of the Lord and the coming of the Holy Spirit; it is the first element in this understanding that seems to emerge from a Jewish background, where the feast of the renewal of the **covenant** with its focus on the ascent of **Moses** on Mount Sinai is likened to the ascension of **Jesus**. *LIAM M. TRACEY*

People of Israel *see* **Israel, people of**

Peshitta

The Peshitta is one translation of the **Old Testament** and **New Testament** into Syriac, used in the **liturgy** of the Syrian Churches to this day. Other Syriac versions are revisions of it or, in the case of the Old Testament, translations based on the **Septuagint**, but they do not have the same authoritative status. The Peshitta may date as early as the second century CE, being cited by **Aphrahat** and **Ephrem**, and some of the Old Testament translation reflects Jewish interpretation, inducing some scholars to posit a Jewish origin for the translators, perhaps Jewish converts to Christianity.

See also **Syriac Christianity**   *JAMES K. AITKEN*

Peter the Venerable (*c*.1090–1156)

Abbot of Cluny, one of the most respected figures in twelfth-century Christendom. His longest work, the *Book against the Inveterate Obstinacy of the Jews*, is a fierce sustained attack against 'the absurd and utterly foolish fables' of the **Talmud**, which he learned about through a Jewish apostate. In a letter to King **Louis VII** of France supporting the Second Crusade, Peter insisted that the Jews, 'vile blasphemers and far worse than the Saracens', should not be allowed to prosper at home while the Crusaders went off to battle the Muslims; he urged the king to confiscate Jewish property in order to defray expenses of the **Crusade**.   *MARC SAPERSTEIN*

Pharisaism *see* **Pharisees**

Pharisees

The negative connotation associated with the term in everyday modern language reflects the pivotal role a comprehensive understanding of the group plays in Jewish–Christian relations. The caricature of the Pharisees as equating with hypocritical and legalistic behaviour has resulted in much misunderstanding about the period to which Christianity and **Rabbinic Judaism** trace their origins.

The Pharisees were one of several Jewish groups known to have been in existence during the late **Hellenistic** and the early Roman periods. The earliest reference to their activities relates to the rule of John Hyrcanus (135–104 BCE). The group and/or individuals identified as Pharisees are then mentioned in relation to the reign of Alexander Janneus (103–80 BCE), Alexandra Jannaea (80–67 BCE), **Herod** (40–4 BCE), the governorship of Pontius **Pilate** (26–36 CE) and the Jewish revolt (66–70 CE). There has, however, been an unfortunate tendency to presume the presence of Pharisees in many of the events from the period even though there is no clear evidence for doing so.

Direct reference to the Pharisees is made in two major sources: the writings of **Josephus** and the **New Testament**, especially the Gospels. There is general agreement that pre-70 CE sages whose teachings are preserved in rabbinic literature should be identified as Pharisees. It is also possible that the Pharisees are the 'seekers of smooth things' alluded to in the **Dead Sea Scrolls**. Not one of these sources, however, is a first-hand witness of Pharisaic thought. Josephus claims to have chosen to join the Pharisees (*Life* 12), but his writings always refer to the group in the third person. The second-hand nature of the sources means that caution is required in reconstructing the history of the Pharisees. The comments of Josephus are presented as part of comparative summaries of the Jewish philosophies, written and shaped for a Greco–Roman audience, in which a key purpose is to compare the Pharisees with the **Sadducees**. According to Josephus the Pharisees believed in a life after death and that although fate plays a part in human affairs individuals control their own destiny. They developed an oral tradition regarding *halakhah* and claimed to be accurate in the interpretation of the law. Josephus also claims that public worship was structured according to Pharisaic teachings because of their standing within the community (*Ant.* 18.15). However, very few people named in his narrative are identified as Pharisees, and the group is mentioned only spasmodically in the description of events. In the New Testament the Pharisees are prominent as the main rivals of **Jesus** in the Gospel accounts of his ministry. The conflict between Jesus and the Pharisees generally centres on interpretation of the **law**, especially in terms of observing the **Sabbath, dietary laws** and issues of purity. In contrast, however, the Pharisees are notable by their absence from the **passion narratives**. Although **Paul** of Tarsus describes himself as a Pharisee, it is difficult to establish what, if any, of his writings reflect specific Pharisaic teachings. In the Acts of the Apostles **Gamaliel** is presented as a Pharisee who defended the followers of Jesus before the **Sanhedrin** by opposing the Sadducees. In the rabbinic literature the Pharisees are depicted as being scrupulous in their observance of the law, especially with regard to matters of purity, the Sabbath and tithing. They consciously separate themselves from other Jews who are deemed to be less strict in their observance of such requirements. Of particular note is the figure of Hillel (end of first century BCE and beginning of first century CE).

Coupled with the absence of any direct testimony from the Pharisees and the particular interests and concerns of the surviving second-hand accounts, the Pharisees have been the subject of much caricaturing by subsequent generations of Christians and Jews. Drawing heavily on the Gospel accounts, Christianity has consistently depicted the Pharisees as the leaders of the Jewish people at the time of Jesus, who oversaw a legalistic, exclusive religion lacking any sense of charity and compassion. In particular, the harsh **polemic** against the Pharisees contained in the Gospel of Matthew (e.g. Matt. 23) was read at face value as accurately describing the historical situation. The negative picture of the Pharisees in the Gospels became a crucial component in the effort to assert the supposed superiority of Christianity over and against Judaism. Inadvertently, the prominence afforded to the Pharisees in Jewish circles as the predecessors of the rabbinic movement compounded the degree to which the Pharisees were seen as the antithesis of what Jesus taught and did. Modern scholarship has provided important correctives to the traditional picture of the Pharisees. The pioneering work of Jacob Neusner (b. 1932) established the need for caution regarding the attributing of all pre-70 CE sayings in the rabbinic corpus to the Pharisees. Another key figure in developing a clearer understanding of the role of the Pharisees in the late Second Temple period is E. P. Sanders (b. 1937). He shows that the Pharisees were active in the community throughout the entire period, but that they were not the governing party and that they did not control public worship. There is also recognition that there were several schools of thought within the Pharisaic group (e.g. House of Hillel, House of Shammai). At the same time scholars, especially with regard to the polemical interests of the New Testament, now readily acknowledge the importance of a critical reading of the source material pertaining to the Pharisees. The harsh criticism of the Pharisees in the Gospels is recognised as having as much to do with rivalry between the communities in which the texts were written (especially the Matthean community) as with anything that

happened during the lifetime of Jesus. Indeed, the level of overlap and coherence between the teachings of Jesus and the Pharisees probably outweighs the areas of difference of opinion. It is in this context that the Roman Catholic Church has released documents designed specifically to provide a corrective to the traditional negative picture of the Pharisees (e.g. *Notes on the Correct Way to Present Jews and Judaism in Catechesis and Preaching of the Roman Catholic Church*, 1985).

See also **scribes**   JAMES S. MCLAREN

Philo of Alexandria (*c*.25 BCE–*c*.50 CE)

Jewish-Greek scholar and political representative of the Jews of **Alexandria**. In the political sphere Philo is known as the leader of an embassy (39–40) to Gaius Caligula (*r*.37–41) to speak for the rights of the Jews of Alexandria, and is an important witness to the crisis in Jewish–non-Jewish relations that stands behind this. His accounts of events (*Against Flaccus* and *Embassy to Gaius*) portray the persecution of the Jews at the hands of an Alexandrian faction, and their ultimate vindication through divine providence. Several Philonic treatises bring a Mosaic perspective to important questions in Greek philosophy, including the nature of God, providence and the eternity of the world. But the great majority of Philo's writings are philosophical commentaries on the Greek **Pentateuch** (which he regarded as an inspired 'sister' version of the 'Chaldaean', *Mos.* 2.40): the *Allegorical Commentary*, devoted to the allegorical reading of Genesis; the *Exposition of the Law*, presenting the lives of the ancestors and the laws of Moses to readers educated in Greek philosophy but not necessarily within the allegorical discourse, and perhaps including non-Jews; and the *Questions and Answers* on Genesis and Exodus. Philo is primarily an interpreter of scripture, not a systematic philosopher, but the language and ideas of Greek philosophy, with marked affinities to Middle Platonism (characterised by Stoic and Pythagorean traditions), are put to the service of explaining scripture. Philo's appeal is universal, calling all who seek wisdom to become disciples of **Moses**, attentive to the deeper meaning of his words as revealed by **allegory**, which alone leads to true knowledge of the eternal God.

In early Jewish circles Philo is mentioned with admiration by **Josephus**, but otherwise largely neglected until the revival of interest in sixteenth-century Italy, marked especially by Azariah dei Rossi (c.1511–c.1578) and his *Me'or Enayim* (*Light of the Eyes*, 1573). An important factor in the neglect of Philo in **Rabbinic Judaism** is the Christian appropriation of his legacy from early on. Responding partly to a long tradition of Christianising readings of Philo, dei Rossi's work represents the first critical study of Philo's place within Judaism, setting the standard for future work, and effectively challenging the authority of Philo as used by Christian theologians.

The early belief that Philo's treatise *On the Contemplative Life* described a proto-Christian community (**Eusebius**, *Hist. eccl.* 2.17.1), a view unchallenged until the Protestant **Reformation**, was very influential in the preservation of his writings among Christians. Indeed, early Christian traditions report the conversion of Philo to Christianity, and he is included among the **Church Fathers** by **Jerome** (in *Vir. ill.* 11), though a later tradition reports his subsequent **apostasy** (Photius, *Bibliotheca* cod. 105). From the fourth century, however, Philo was viewed more cautiously in Christian orthodox circles, which tended to associate him with heretical Christianity.

Modern scholarship affirms that, though an exact contemporary of **Jesus**, Philo shows no knowledge of the existence of the Christian movement. Moreover, Philo's thinking is substantially different from that of the earliest Christians on questions of central importance to Christian faith, such as **eschatology** and Messianic hope. At the same time, 'Philo's pages contain exegetical ideas that constantly seem like anticipations of St Paul, St John and the author of the Epistle to the Hebrews' (H. Chadwick, 'Philo' 1967, 157), reflecting their place in the wider world of **Hellenistic** Judaism.

Later Christian theologians looked to Philo above all as a model for relating the traditions of Jewish scripture and philosophy, his interpretations adapted in the service of Christian **doctrine** by Alexandrian theologians like Clement (*c.*150–*c.*215) and **Origen**, and transmitted in time to the Latin Church which made Philo, as mediated through Christians, known to the Western world.

SARAH J. K. PEARCE

Philosemitism

Probably coined in analogy to terms such as 'philhellenism', the term 'philosemitism' first emerged in the 1880s in **Germany** in the context of the scandal surrounding an antisemitic article by the historian Heinrich von Treitschke (1834–96), with whom it may even have originated, and was initially invariably used in opposition to '**antisemitism**'. It is thus originally an antisemitic term denouncing an 'exaggerated' friendliness towards Jews.

The first known occurrence of the adjective 'philo-Semitic' in English is found in Cecil Roth's (1899–1970) *Life of Menasseh Ben Israel* (1934, p. 146), indicating that its use was by no means restricted to antisemites. This is particularly true for the English-speaking world, where philosemitism is often used by historians to describe a particular historical phenomenon, though the appropriateness and referents of the term remain a matter of debate. An alternative sometimes advanced, 'Judaising', is likewise not free from antisemitic overtones (*see* **Judaising Christians**).

Independent of the question of usage, however, careful historical research has, over the past 50 years or so, shown that time and again in history a friendly attitude of Christians towards Jews can be observed that is not just identical with an absence of antisemitism but reveals a positive interest in Jews and Judaism, sometimes leading to actions supporting and helping Jews. Often, however, philosemitic attitudes among Christians have been subordinate to other concerns not in themselves philosemitic, as for example the **conversion** of Jews to Christianity, or a **humanism** extending to all humankind. It is thus necessary to distinguish 'primary' philosemitism (where Christians take an interest in Jews *as Jews*) from 'secondary' philosemitism (where this interest is steered by other motives).

Paradoxically, primary philosemitism shares its fascination with Judaism with (some types of) antisemitism. Both philosemites and antisemites attribute to Judaism a significance above that of other peoples and religions, but they assess this significance in diametrically opposing terms. Thus understood, primary philosemitism can be observed throughout the history of Jewish–Christian relations. It occurs most often in the context of **eschatological** speculations attributing to the Jews a special role at the end of times, often culminating in the idea of the **salvation** of all Israel (Rom. 11.25–32) and sometimes of a (political) restoration of Israel and the **Temple**. Representatives of this type of philosemitism are found, for example, in the **early Church** (Cerinthus (first century), Apollinarius of Laodicea (*c*.315–*c*.390)), but also, much later, in Dutch and English **Calvinism**, especially between 1640 and 1700, where various philosemitic eschatologies were propagated by theologians such as Thomas Brightman (1562–1607), Joseph Mede (1586–1638) and Petrus Serrarius (1600–69), as well as by sectarian groups such as the Ranters or Arise Evans (1607–after 1660) and his followers. A singular kind of eschatological philosemitism was championed by Isaac la Peyrère (1596–1676), who envisaged a reductionist Church of Jews and Christians, stripped of all the doctrines offensive to Jews. La Peyrère strongly influenced the Amsterdam rabbi **Menasseh ben Israel**, who maintained close relations with leading Christian millenarians (*see* **millenarianism**). This millenarian philosemitism was also influential among radical German pietists (e.g. Ernst Christoph Hochmann von Hochenau (1669/70–1721) and others). Other types of philosemitism await further investigation.

Philosemitism has never been nearly as strong as antisemitism, and both terms, as representing extremes on a wide scale of possible interactions between Jews and Christians, fail fully to describe the complex history of Jewish–Christian relations.   *WOLFRAM KINZIG*

Pico della Mirandola, Giovanni (1463–94)

A member of a minor princely family in northern Italy, Pico was the key figure in the transmission of Jewish **Kabbalah** to Christian readers, even offering a number of theses derived from Kabbalah for public discussion in Rome in 1486. His views have been described by the leading modern authority on Pico's Kabbalah, Chaim Wirszubski, as no less a kabbalistic interpretation of Christianity than a Christian interpretation of Kabbalah. His interest in **Hebrew** and **Aramaic** reflected the **humanistic** culture of Renaissance **Italy**, which sought to return to the ancient sources of knowledge, generally the classical but also in some instances Jewish and Arabic ones. Thus Pico took an interest in Averroistic writings and studied both mainstream kabbalistic sources built around the *Zohar* (then assumed to date from the time of the destruction of the Temple), as well as the ecstatic Kabbalah of Abraham **Abulafia**, whose works could be found in the Biblioteca Laurenziana in Florence. Pico also repre-

sents the mystical strand within **Renaissance** culture, linked to the Platonism of Marsilio Ficino (1433–99).   *DAVID ABULAFIA*

Pilate, Pontius (governed 26–36 CE)

The prime textual and archaeological sources when reconstructing the life of the fifth Roman procurator of Judaea, under whose rule **Jesus** was executed, are Josephus, Philo, the New Testament and apocryphal Gospels, Ignatius, Eusebius and an **inscription** found in 1961 in Caesarea Maritima. The various portraits of Pilate in the Jewish and Christian traditions illuminate their importance to Jewish–Christian relations. Whereas Jewish sources (**Philo**, *Legat.* 299–305; **Josephus**, *J.W.* 2.8; *Ant.* 18.3f.) portray him in fairly homogeneous terms, that is, as a despotic and ruthless dictator, who was finally forced by the **Samaritans** to resign from office, modern scholarship points out that the ancient Christian sources contain a great deal of diversity in their characterisation of Pilate. They tend to refer to him in three different ways: (1) In the letters of **Ignatius** (*Magn.* 11; *Trall.* 9; *Smyrn.* 1) and in the Creeds he is referred to in order to emphasise the trustworthiness and historicity of the passion of Jesus. (2) **Eusebius** (*Hist. eccl.* 2.7) argues that Pilate committed suicide and that this was a fitting fate for him: 'Divine justice, it seems, did not long protract his punishment.' Other traditions understand him as a wanderer, finally meeting death in the Alps, where his grave is still shown. (3) An understanding of particular importance to Jewish–Christian relations, however, is the third interpretation, according to which Christian sources seek to exculpate him from the death of Jesus, a tendency that certainly can be detected as early as in the **New Testament** Gospels (see, e.g., the crowd's rejection of his offer in Matt. 25.27) but, to a much larger extent, in later passion accounts, for example the *Gospel of Peter*, where 'the Jews' (*hoi Ioudaioi*) not only wish to see Jesus dead, but also are responsible for the actual execution. Thus, whereas the Jewish people has had to suffer for being accused of **deicide**, Pilate, being the political potentate in Judea at the time, without whose consent no one would be put to death, has gradually been understood as being opposed to the execution of Jesus. Most scholars understand this as an attempt to present the Christian message as in no way threatening to the Roman authorities. The corollary, however, has been to interpret Pilate as not only interested in the truth (John 18.38) but, indeed, convinced of the veracity of Christianity (**Tertullian** *Apol.* 21.24). In the **Coptic** and **Ethiopian** Churches he is highly revered.

See also **Easter**; **Holy Week**; **passion narratives**; **trial of Jesus**   *JESPER SVARTVIK*

Pilgrimage

Pilgrimage is generally connected with a particular, usually distant, **sacred space** or shrine to which the pilgrim journeys as a religious duty or a penitential, spiritual or devotional exercise. In the history of Jewish–Christian relations pilgrimage preserved Christianity's living links with the historical geography of the **Hebrew Bible**. But it also served Christianity's **supersessionist** claim to be the sole heir to the '**Old Testament**' and to the **Promised Land** itself. Only in the modern era has pilgrimage become 'an occasion for better understanding between the pilgrims and the peoples and religions in Israel', as recommended in the Fundamental Agreement between the Holy See and the **State of Israel** of December 1993, and as exemplified by the historic pilgrimage to the Holy Land of Pope **John Paul II** in March 2000.

In **Rabbinic Judaism** the three annual pilgrim festivals prescribed by the Torah – **Passover**, **Shavuot** (Pentecost) and **Sukkot** – recall the formation of the **people of Israel** through the Exodus and their desert trek, and highlight the centrality of the land of Israel, **Jerusalem** and the **Temple** in their **covenant** with God. From the outset Christianity exhibited a marked ambivalence regarding the significance of specific sacred space and the merits of pilgrimage. There is a strand in the **New Testament** (cf. John 4.19–24 and Acts 7) and in the writings of some **Church Fathers** that rejects the notion that **holiness** can be spatially localised and thus contests the value of pilgrimage to any particular sacred precinct. **Jerome**, for example, questioned the efficacy of pilgrimage to Jerusalem but journeyed to the Holy Land and settled in Bethlehem. Protestant reformers of the sixteenth century emphasised the need to de-territorialise holiness, but nineteenth-century Protestant pilgrims were enthralled by the power of the Promised Land and biblical archaeology to verify and vivify scripture.

Christian pilgrimage to the Holy Land began in earnest in the fourth century when Christianity became the legal religion of the **Byzantine Empire**. The impressive shrines established in Jerusalem and Bethlehem by **Constantine** and his mother Helena (*c.*255–330) and the endearing accounts of the pilgrimages of Egeria (*fl.* 380s?) and others inspired an influx of pilgrims and a corresponding outflow of **relics** that linked the Christian ecumene with the Holy Land. The proliferation of holy places and pilgrim services throughout the land gradually Christianised the country and crowded out Jews. Centuries later the **Crusades**, which combined the spiritual paradigm of pilgrimage to the Holy Land with the notion of holy war, massacred Jews *en route* to Jerusalem and in the holy city itself.

Despite its anti-Jewish bias, Christian pilgrim literature includes valuable information on Jewish life in the land of Israel from medieval times to the modern era. In modern times, and particularly since the founding of the **State of Israel** in 1948, pilgrimage to the Holy Land has afforded many Christians an opportunity not only to rediscover the Jewish roots of Christianity and the Jewishness of the **historical Jesus**, but also to discern the intimate link between the Jewish people and the land of Israel and **Zion**. Although most Jews and Christians visit Israel without meeting one another, there are an increasing number of groups who make the Jewish–Christian encounter the heart of their pilgrimage. Another recent phenomenon concerns encounter with the **Holocaust** through pilgrimage to **Auschwitz** and other sites of the extermination process of the Nazi era.   *DANIEL ROSSING*

Pius IX (1792–1878)

Pope (1846–78). Born Giovanni Maria Mastai-Ferretti. His attitude towards Jews is defined by the **Mortara Affair**, the forced removal in 1858 of six-year-old Edgardo Mortara (1851–1940) from the home of his Jewish parents because he had allegedly been baptised by a Christian servant as a sick infant. Pius, who took a personal interest in Edgardo, knew of international outrage but was convinced he had acted in the boy's interests and believed that in the Papal States the laws of man and God coincided.

As bishop of Imola, Mastai-Ferretti gained a reputation for pastoral zeal and as an advocate of reform. His election in 1846 chimed with popular hopes for a reforming papacy. Jews in the Papal States petitioned him for an end to injustices to which the Jewish community was subject. Pius ended the requirement for Jews regularly to hear Christian sermons and instituted an enquiry into conditions in the **ghetto**, but had no intention of granting wider civil liberties. Until the break-up of the Papal States in 1870 he upheld restrictions on Jews living in the ghetto, which was the last of its kind in Europe until the Nazis reintroduced the idea more than half a century later.

In 1848, a year of revolution throughout Europe, Pius fled Rome. Restored in 1850 by French troops, he was convinced thereafter that **liberal** values were at odds with Catholic religion. His 1864 Syllabus of Errors condemned freedom of religion and used the phrase 'synagogue of Satan' to describe the enemies of the Church (cf. Rev. 2.9 and 3.9). In 1870 his temporal authority over the Papal States ended; in the same year the first Vatican Council asserted the doctrinal infallibility of the Church and the pope.

STEPHEN PLANT

Pius XII (1876–1958)

Pope (1939–58). Pius XII's response to the **Holocaust** is the subject of a vigorous historical debate of profound significance for contemporary Jewish–Christian relations. Born Eugenio Pacelli in Rome, the son of a Vatican lawyer, he entered the Vatican diplomatic service in 1901. On his appointment as papal nuncio to Bavaria in 1917 he was consecrated Archbishop. He became fluent in German. He was in Bavaria when it was declared a Soviet Republic in 1919, an experience that possibly informed his deep antipathy towards Communism. Following appointment as Vatican Secretary of State, Pacelli was responsible for the Reich Concordat of 1933 that effectively neutered Catholic political opposition to the Nazis. He protested against violations of the Concordat and, when elected pope in 1939, was widely regarded as anti-Nazi.

As Pius XII he condemned the effects of the war on its innocent victims but did not single out the persecution of the Jews or publicly protest the transportation of Rome's Jews to the concentration camps in 1943. He refused pleas for help on the grounds of neutrality, while making statements condemning injustices in general. For example, during his Christmas Eve radio broadcast in 1942 he referred to the 'hundreds of thousands who, through no fault of their own, and solely because of their nation or race, have been condemned to death or progressive extinction' but never mentioned Jews by name. Privately, he may have sheltered a small number of Jews and spoken to a few select officials, encouraging them to help Jews.

Rolf Hochhuth's (b. 1931) controversial 1963 play *The Representative* dramatically portrayed Pius as more concerned with safeguarding Vatican interests than with the fate of the Jews, igniting historical and moral debate. Critics suggest Pius was bound by centuries of anti-Jewish attitudes and practices in the Papal States. Some suggest he was **antisemitic**. Defenders, in the context of current moves to beatify Pius, point to his great personal piety, the unprecedented complexity of issues faced during his papacy and the naivety of assumptions that the pope could have made any difference to the progress of Nazi genocide, and presume his tacit blessing of acts of sanctuary afforded by Catholics to Jews.

Pius's lack of public advocacy for Jews was a result of a number of factors, including a fear of Nazi reprisals, a feeling that public speech would have no effect and might harm Jews, the idea that private intervention could accomplish more, the anxiety that acting against the German government could provoke a schism among German Catholics, the Church's traditional role of political neutrality, and concern about the growth of Communism were the Nazis to be defeated.   *STEPHEN PLANT*

Piyyut

The Hebrew word *piyyut* (plural *piyyutim*) from the Greek *poietes* 'poet' was first recorded in a Jewish homiletical text (fifth–sixth century CE) where the second-century sage El'azar bar Rabbi Shim'on is called a *paytan*. The *piyyut* is a hymnic composition that embellishes the statutory prayers. As to origins, testimony from the eighth century points to the **Justinian** suppression of Jewish worship in the sixth century as a possible catalyst, impelling the Jews to develop additional modes of religious expression, while a text from the **Dura Europos** synagogue (destroyed *c.*256 CE) contains *piyyut*-like elements.

Some characteristics indicate possible influences from early Eastern Christian hymnology. As with the early *piyyutim*, the fourth-century Syriac poet **Ephrem** employed regular syllable stresses and acrostics and the Syriac *enyana* were interwoven into a biblical text. The Hebrew use of rhyme perhaps suggests that the *piyyut* was the mature form. There are also parallels with the Greek Christian poetry of **Byzantium**. The *kontakion* hymns composed by **Romanos Melodos** are similar in form to the Hebrew *kerovah* championed by his Jewish contemporary Yannai (sixth century): both forms rely on rhyme assonance, biblical allusion, word-play and emblematic words, and turn to homily for thematic inspiration.

There are five distinct periods of *piyyut*, from an anonymous period of unclear origin sometime before the sixth century to the 'golden' age of poetry in Islamic **Spain**. The *piyyut* was later used by Ashkenazi Jews as a vehicle for martyrological laments recording the persecution of Jewish communities in Northern Christian Europe.

REBECCA J. W. JEFFERSON

Pogrom

A Russian word meaning 'devastation', this term originally denoted attacks on Jews in late nineteenth- and early twentieth-century **Russia**. In the history of **antisemitism** and Jewish–Christian relations, however, pogrom refers to violent attacks on Jewish persons, communities and properties in any part of the world. Provoked by antisemitic charges that Jews, in one way or another, have acted treacherously against the majority population's national, economic or religious interests, pogroms often appear to be spontaneous, but closer scrutiny shows that they are usually condoned, if not organised, by political leaders and governments. Although massacres against Jews had already been taking place in Christendom for many hundreds of years, pogroms directly foreshadowed the **Holocaust**, the worst being in Russia in 1881, 1903 and 1905, in **Ukraine** during the Russian Civil War (1918–20) and with regularity in **Poland** between 1918 and 1939. The Nazis themselves also initiated pogroms such as Kristallnacht ('the night of broken glass') which swept through **Germany** and **Austria** on 9–10 November 1938. Pogroms continued after the end of the Second World War, one of the most notorious being at Kielce, Poland, in July 1946 when **blood libel** allegations falsely claimed that a temporarily missing Polish child had been murdered by Jews for ritual purposes.

JOHN K. ROTH

Poland

In 990 AD Mieszko I (*c*.930–92), who had been baptised in 966, placed Poland under the protection of the pope. Since then the Catholic Church and Poland and its inhabitants have been inextricably related in history. Though Protestant beliefs spread widely in the sixteenth century in Poland and for a while the country enjoyed a **toleration** not experienced elsewhere on the Continent, the energetic efforts of the supporters of the Counter-Reformation, notably the **Jesuits**, established **Roman Catholicism** as the official state religion, an identification dramatically underlined in 1666 when Jan II Kazimierz declared the **Virgin Mary** to be Queen of Poland. The rights of other religious groups were diminished. Jews had lived in Poland since the ninth century, but in 1764 the autonomy previously granted to Jewish communities was abrogated 'in perpetuity'. This Roman Catholic identification was, paradoxically, further encouraged by the partitions of Poland in 1792, 1793 and 1795 between **Russia**, Prussia and **Austria**. While the partitioning powers advanced **Orthodox Christianity** and **Protestantism** as a means of Russification and Germanisation, Polish Catholicism became a means of asserting Polish national **identity** against oppression, and has remained so through the traumas of its history. Nineteenth-century nationalism even advanced a quasi-mystical belief in the relationship between the **resurrection** of Christ and the restoration of Poland. Historically, Polish conservative nationalism has also been strongly antisemitic.

The end of the First World War saw the emergence of an enlarged and free Poland and a strong advance of Catholicism. Ten per cent of the population at this time, over 3 million, were Jewish. The Jewish communities themselves were divided between assimilationists and **Zionists**. The interwar years also saw significant antisemitic discrimination, in particular economic boycotts. The Catholic–Pole equation continued under the Nazis and Soviet Communism, the clergy strongly asserting the relationship between Catholicism and Poland in response to Communist attempts to minimise the role and significance of religion in Polish history. In October 1978 the cardinals elected a Polish pope in Karol Wojtyła, **John Paul II**, who, though theologically conservative, consistently denounced **antisemitism**. Since 1989 the Church has participated in the democratisation of Poland. The immediate post-Communist conservative resurgence of Catholic nationalism, though, has re-emphasised old tensions and Judeophobia. The **Holocaust** reduced the Jewish population to 300,000 and continuing antisemitism, including a **pogrom** in Kielce in 1946 and an officially inspired campaign for Jews to leave, has reduced the population to approximately 25,000 today. Jews have found themselves being accused variously of aiding the tsar, undermining Christianity, supporting Communism and Stalin (the myth of Stalinism as 'Jewish colonisation'), encouraging counter-revolution against Stalinism, corrupting traditional society with capitalism and supporting **Israel** in the Cold War.

In recent years there have been a number of positive developments, such as the activities of the Polish **Council of Christians and Jews**, episcopal initiatives and interreligious events. In 1997, for example, the Roman Catholic Church in Poland instituted an annual 'Day of Judaism' (17 March). At the same time there have been conflicts such as the **Carmelite controversy** and intense debates such as that provoked by the story of the massacre at Jedwabne.   *DAVID WEIGALL*

Polemics

Polemics are the rhetorical arguments and declamatory strategies by which one group defines itself over and against its competitors and/or opponents. In the wake of the ***Shoah***, scholars have directed considerable attention to the significance of the polemical language used within and between religious communities, most especially those long-standing rhetorical practices employed by Christians to justify their affirmations at the expense of Judaism and the Jewish people. While some scholars claim that this ancient antipathy arises from within the **New Testament**, others maintain that an anti-Jewish bias was superimposed onto it by an evolving Church predominantly composed of Gentiles and increasingly estranged from its Jewish roots. Either way, Christians now find themselves under a moral and theological imperative to re-examine the ways that they have historically read and interpreted their scriptures and take bold measures to blunt the anti-Jewish polemical edges.

Recent scholarship has placed polemical discourse within a broader literary context and directed particular attention to the social setting out of which the argumentation arose. In their assessment of the polemics within the New Testament, biblical scholars have noted that the art of verbal assault pervaded the varied philosophical schools and religious communities in the Greco-Roman era. Adversarial discourse followed rhetorical conventions that in large measure determined the form and content of verbal combat. Luke Timothy Johnson (b. 1943) has described the deployment of slanderous **rhetoric** in the **Hellenistic** period, luridly illustrating how the disputatious rivalries among competing philosophical schools became intensely personal. **Josephus** recorded the verbal attacks of Gentiles such as Apion who assailed the **Diaspora** Jews by charging them with sedition, human sacrifice and the idolatrous worship of the head of an ass (*Ag. Ap.* 2.6.68; 2.8 .92–6; 2.7.80). Josephus reciprocates by portraying hostile Gentiles as 'blasphemers', 'liars' and 'crazy fools' who are themselves guilty of the very slanders that they project onto the Jewish people (1.11.59; 2.7.86; 2.6.71). The polemics within the **Dead Sea Scrolls** reflect the profound hostility the Essenes directed to outsiders. Johnson therefore maintains that the vitriolic diatribes in Matt. 23 mirror the rhetorical conventions of the surrounding literary culture; even the identification of 'the Jews' with 'the devil' in John 8.44 echoes a familiar literary trope (*see **hoi Ioudaioi***).

In the study of polemical discourse literary critics urge readers to examine the social context in which the struggle for **identity** is unfolding and to distinguish those verbal arguments that are directed at competitors within the community from those attacks that assail opponents outside the community's ranks. When the Hebrew prophets subject their own community to polemical exhortations, the governing motivation is to reform the life of the **people Israel**; when the **Church Fathers** invoke the same prophetic critique in order to condemn the Jewish people and Judaism, the original text is conscripted to serve a theological agenda that undermines the theological and moral integrity of those who also lay claim to these writings. Literary critics also insist that the power dynamics governing relations between opponents require careful scrutiny. When an oppressed **minority** deploys polemical arguments to differentiate its own group from the dominant culture, these rhetorical strategies enable the group to resist their opponents' encroachments, to defend the group's legitimacy, to reinforce its identity boundaries, and to marshal a commitment to remain faithful. Not only does the New Testament contain polemical arguments against Jewish opponents, for example; there are also potent, albeit carefully coded, polemical attacks against the **Roman Empire**. One of the most potent rhetorical devices emerges when a besieged minority adopts the sacred texts used against it, inverts the oppressive meanings of the dominant culture, and finds support and solace for their own struggle. In assessing the uses and misuses of polemical discourse, readers need to survey the political landscape and identify the nature of the conflicts, and then decipher the text to determine both the intended audience and the purposes that the arguments are designed to advance. The art of rhetorical criticism is not only indispensable in the appraisal of ancient arguments, but also in enabling contemporary readers to assess more carefully the fever-pitched debates that accompany, for example, Vatican declarations about the *Shoah*, Christian **evangelism**, the Israeli–Palestinian conflict, and the separation of **Church and state**. The polemical strategies within Jewish communities will also require critical analysis so that readers can discern to what extent 'Christianity' is framed as an immutable opponent and foil over and against which the distinctive genius of Judaism shines brightly. To prevent the hardening of polemical discourse and the paralysis of Jewish–Christian relations, readers will need to recognise when there are changes in the circumstances out of which the original polemics grew. The impassioned **disputations** of our own day demonstrate that the legacy of adversarial group-definition continues to haunt both the Jewish and Christian communities.

CHRISTOPHER M. LEIGHTON

Poliakov, Léon (1910–97)

Historian. Poliakov became a founder-member of the Centre de Documentation Juive Contemporaine in Paris as soon as the German occupation came to an end (1944). Some of his earliest work, such as his assembly of materials for the Nuremberg trials and his pioneer study *L'Etoile jaune* (1949), was directly involved with its concerns. His doctoral thesis (Eng. trans. *Jewish Bankers and the Holy See* (1971)) addressed the history of a peculiar Jewish–Christian cooperation in the thirteenth to the seventeenth centuries. Much of Poliakov's teaching career was spent at the Ecole Pratique des Hautes Etudes. His volumes *The History of Anti-Semitism* (1955–77, Eng. trans. 1965–85) and his study *The Aryan Myth* (1971, Eng. trans. 1974) provide a social and intellectual context for Jewish–Christian, as well as Jewish–post-Christian, encounters in the European world.

SERGEI HACKEL

Polycarp *see* Apostolic Fathers
Pontius Pilate *see* Pilate, Pontius
Pope, Jewish

Legendary Yiddish account of a medieval pope who had been born and raised as a Jew but was kidnapped as a child, which sheds light on Jewish cultural **identity** in the context of mainstream Christianity. The legend originated in the late fifteenth century when **ghettos** were first introduced and went through numerous retellings, most recently in 1943. The story describes how Rabbi Shimon of Mainz's son, Elkhanan, was kidnapped by his Christian nurse, baptised and brought up in the Church. After he became pope, he arranged to meet his estranged father and shortly afterwards reversed anti-Jewish edicts in Mainz and secretly returned to Judaism.

EDWARD KESSLER

Portugal

Portugal came into existence in the twelfth century as Christian armies conquered the western flank of Muslim **Spain**. Jews are documented as part of the royal entourage in 1190, when the Jews of Lisbon were described as 'servants of the king'. Although in later centuries the Portuguese Jews did not achieve the importance culturally, economically and politically of those in Castile and Catalonia, families such as the ibn Yahya enjoyed royal protection and looked after the king's finances. Regulations concerning the Jews, for example under King Afonso V in the fifteenth century, were a mixture of restriction and protection. There is no evidence for serious popular anti-Jewish sentiment, and the decision of Manuel I to expel the Jews in 1497 is generally attributed to pressure from Spain, many of whose Jews had taken refuge in Portugal after their **expulsion** in 1492. However, the treatment of these Castilian Jews was severe; their children were deported to Portugal's colonies on the equator. The expulsion was in any event replaced by a mass **conversion**, accompanied by a promise not to unleash the **Inquisition** for a generation. The Portuguese **Conversos** could thus maintain Jewish practices more easily than in Spain, and Portugal long remained a reservoir of (secret) Judaism, which still survives at Belmonte in the north. However, open Judaism was only possible in the Portuguese Jewish **Diaspora** that developed in Amsterdam, London, Hamburg and the Caribbean.

DAVID ABULAFIA

Postliberalism

Postliberalism has taken two opposite directions. One is the postmodern response (*see* **postmodernism**). The other is much more conservative in orientation. Contrary to its postmodernist counterpart, it is unwilling to declare the end of ideology. It too recognises the challenge to a comprehensive framework of meaning that modernism raises, and the profound dismemberment of meaning brought about by the **Holocaust** and other modern genocides. But, contrary to Irving Greenberg (b. 1933), who argues that it is possible to recover only 'fragments of meaning' in the post-Holocaust world, representatives of this form of postliberalism such as George Lindbeck (b. 1923) and Hans Frei (1922–88) maintain that we need to recover a biblical rootage for our self-understanding. Part of that recovery involves making the prophetic call to justice integral to human meaning today. But for this to become a reality there is also need to recapture an ecclesial framework for human meaning within the Christian community. The otherwise noble attempt by the Social Gospel movement in Christianity failed in the end because of the absence of an ecclesial framework. (The Social Gospel movement grew up within American Liberal **Protestantism** in the first part of the twentieth century and attempted to give Christianity a decidedly social justice orientation. Its detractors regarded it as low on theological content despite its admired social commitment, and it was perceived as attempting to 'Christianise' the general liberal agenda for society. It tended to be transdenominational in its approach and hence did not establish strong roots in any sector of the Christian community.) The Church cannot be viewed as a 'voluntary' institution. Restoring the Church as **Israel** (without expropriating the image of Israel from Jews) is key to such a revival of human meaning that has social commitment at its heart. This commitment to the corporate character of Christian faith stands at the heart of postliberalism. For Frei and Lindbeck, and close associates such as Stanley Hauerwas, David Ford and Michael Baxter, Christian faith and its prophetic vision of a just society cannot be realised without a strong sense of Church among its adherents. That is why they remain strongly interested in what Jewish ethicist Ronald Green (b. 1942) has called the ideal of the 'holy community' in Judaism,

and why some postliberal Christian scholars such as David Ford (b. 1948) are very interested in rabbinic interpretations of the scriptures because, as Green has insisted, such concrete interpretations are critical for the sustainability of that 'holy community'. Postliberal Christian scholars join ranks with certain Jewish religious scholars such as David Hartman (b. 1931) and Peter Ochs (b. 1950) who argue that the reinterpretation and revitalisation of the Jewish covenantal tradition, both biblical and post-biblical, remain central for the maintenance of a communal religious **identity** in Judaism. These Christian scholars regard a communal religious identity as vital for the generation of a countervailing set of societal values over against the dominant secular values in contemporary Euro-centred societies.

See also **liberalism**   *JOHN T. PAWLIKOWSKI*

Postmodernism

Postmodernism is an umbrella term, referring to a range of cultural and intellectual positions, which question the **Enlightenment** belief in reason and objective knowledge, natural (as opposed to divine) law and progress. Friedrich Nietzsche (1844–1900), Karl Marx (1818–83) and Martin Heidegger (1889–1976) are influential in postmodernism's 'development', but popular reference to postmodernism and postmodernity (contemporary forms of social organisation, characterised by new modes of communication, globalisation and consumerism) dates from the work of Jean François Lyotard (1924–98), Jacques Derrida (1930–2004), Michel Foucault (1926–84) and others in the mid-1980s. In 'everyday' usage postmodernism is associated with parody and relativism. It entails a denial of hierarchical boundaries between 'high' and 'low' culture and an interest in the local and the specific, rather than the universal or generalisable.

The implications of postmodernism for Jewish–Christian relations are varied. On the one hand postmodern relativism could be seen to argue against Christian **mission** to Jews, and to advocate positions of pluralism. Post-**Holocaust**, many Jews and Christians share postmodernism's lack of confidence in Enlightenment ideas about human progress. Moreover, current dialogue's emphasis on listening to the 'other' draws on the work of postmodern Jewish philosopher Emmanuel Levinas (1906–95). Conversely, postmodernism's scepticism about truth claims may be regarded as threatening all positions of (religious) commitment. Although many noted postmodernists are Jews, Nazi use of Nietzsche, and Heidegger's support for **Hitler**, lead some to view postmodernism as a dangerous phenomenon; historians like Deborah Lipstadt (b. 1947) trace links between postmodernism's emphases on relativism and deconstruction, and Holocaust denial.

Postmodernism has prompted some thinkers to question essentialist definitions of **religions**, stressing instead their malleability and dynamism. For those who accept this idea, interfaith relations and **dialogue** are transformed. Instead of the modernist approach, which sees 'Jew' and 'Christian' as two separate, readily definable, coherent identities which relate to, but remain discrete from, one another, postmodernist dialogue sees the boundaries between 'Jew' and 'Christian' as fluid and permeable, and emphasises the fact that encounters inevitably lead to changes in self-image, **identity** and practice.

See also **modernity**   *MELANIE J. WRIGHT*

Post-supersessionism

Post-supersessionism designates not a single viewpoint but a loose and partly conflicting family of theological perspectives that seeks to interpret the central affirmations of Christian faith in ways that do not state or imply the abrogation or obsolescence of God's **covenant** with the Jewish people, that is, in ways that are not supersessionist. Positively expressed, a theology is post-supersessionist if it affirms the present validity of God's covenant with **Israel** as a coherent and indispensable part of the larger body of Christian teaching. Strictly speaking, the term applies to theological viewpoints that emerge out of ecclesialogical contexts that once espoused **supersessionism**. Therefore, post-supersessionism should be distinguished from the views of dispensationalist Christian movements that originated in the nineteenth century and continue to enjoy widespread popularity today, even though these latter also affirm in some fashion the present validity of God's covenant with the Jewish people.

The emergence of post-supersessionism was first occasioned by the **Holocaust** and the return of the Jewish people to their ancient homeland, and has been sustained since then by a growing consensus among Christians that traditional Christian teaching on the Church's relation to the Jewish people was inherently flawed (*see* **replacement theology**). Significantly, post-supersessionism has been embraced not only by individual Christians, but by many Christian denominations in North America and Europe, which have incorporated post-supersessionist perspectives in a variety of official teaching documents (e.g. **Vatican II**'s statement *Nostra Aetate*). Arguably, therefore, the emergence of post-supersessionism represents the most significant development in Christian teaching on the Jewish people since the second and third centuries, when supersessionism originally solidified as the Church's dominant outlook.

The development of post-supersessionist theology since the 1950s can be divided into three broad stages. A first stage (until 1970) was characterised by historical scholarship (e.g. that of Marcel Simon (1907–86) and James **Parkes**), establishing the fact and extent of **anti-Judaism** in Christian history and by the first steps to affirm the unrevoked character of God's covenant with the Jewish people (e.g. *Nostra Aetate*). The systematic connection between supersessionism and other Christian doctrines remained relatively unexplored. During a second stage (roughly 1970–85) theologians sought to explore the systematic connections between supersessionism and other Christian beliefs, concluding that supersessionism could not be corrected without radically rethinking virtually the whole body of Christian divinity, especially the Church's **Christology** (Rosemary Ruether (b. 1936), Franklin Littell (b. 1917), Alice (b. 1923) and Roy Eckardt (1918–98)). This period was dominated by a broadly liberal theological ethos that tended to assume that post-supersessionist gains could be achieved only by a corresponding willingness to jettison or minimise traditional Christian affirmations, for example that **Jesus** is the Christ, was raised from the dead and so on. A third period (1985 to date) has been characterised by the increasing prominence of what some have called a **postliberal** approach to the problem of supersessionism, as represented by theologians such as George Lindbeck (b. 1923), Berthold Klappert (b. 1939) and Robert Jenson (b. 1930). (Arguably, the important figure of Paul van Buren (1924–98) straddles the second and third stages.) Typically, a 'postliberal' post-supersessionism affirms the systematically entrenched character of traditional supersessionism, but holds that a post-supersessionist theology can be successfully developed by reinterpreting rather than rejecting or minimising such traditional Christian affirmations as, for example, Jesus' Messiahship, the **incarnation**, the **Trinity** and so on.

See also **biblical theology; recognition theology**

R. KENDALL SOULEN

Prayer

Human means of seeking communication with God by way of petition, confession or praise. In **Hebrew** to pray is *hitpalel*, a reflexive meaning 'to work on oneself'. It well describes the inner psychological need to pray. In Deut. 11.13 we read 'serve him with all your heart'. Says Midrash *Sifre*: 'What service is with the heart? It is prayer.' The Jewish emphasis on prayer as a duty can be contrasted with prayer for one's own needs, as emphasised by **Jesus**. 'I tell you, then, whatever you ask for in prayer, believe that you have received it and it will be yours' (Mark 11.24). The structure of Jewish prayer services develops the imagery of the worshipper approaching God directly; Roman Catholic tradition encourages prayer to God alone, but also mediation through the action of Christ, and intercession through the action of **Mary**, the **angels** and the **saints**. The basic unit of prayer as developed by the rabbis is the *berakhah* or **blessing**, an utterance that has power to transform any everyday act into one that acknowledges God's role in the world. Both faiths have developed regular forms of prayer that have grown and changed in parallel to and in contradistinction from each other. In some Christian rites the communicant gives thanks after partaking for the gift of eternal life; a blessing thanking God for eternal life is said in synagogue by each person called to the reading of the **Torah**, after hearing or reading the text. Thus the Jewish worshipper gains life through the reading and quoting of scripture, the Christian worshipper through the body of the living Christ. *MICHAEL HILTON*

Prayer of the Faithful *see* **intercessions**
Prayerbooks *see* **liturgy**

Preaching

Pulpit discourse, usually in the context of a **worship** service, in which classical religious texts are expounded to address the intellectual or spiritual needs of the listeners. In the pre-modern period, preaching was one of the most important means of mass communication, through which ordinary people received the ideas they lived by. Many listeners believed that the preacher was actually divinely inspired, speaking the word of God. The representation of Jews and Christians in the sermons of the other could therefore have an enormous effect on the way people thought and behaved.

Among the other roles that he played, **Jesus** of Nazareth was apparently a gifted preacher. No first-century records of Jewish sermons are preserved in internal Jewish sources, so the accounts in the Gospels are an important source for what Jewish preaching was like. The **parables** – a specialty of Jesus – and the novel exposition of a familiar biblical verse, seem to be distinctively homiletical forms of communication.

After the death of Jesus arguably the most important medium of propagating the message that would become Christianity was the spoken word, delivered by believers who travelled throughout the Mediterranean world, addressing assemblies of Jews and others open to hearing about the new faith. The precise forms of their discourse during the first generations are not clear, but they certainly included an exposition of scripture (what Christians began later to call the **Old Testament**) in light of the new reality, instruction in the teachings of Jesus, admonition and rebuke, exhortation and consolation, often framed in familiar Greek rhetorical patterns. This message was often communicated in open competition with Jewish preachers who had no use for the new tidings.

As the hierarchy of the Church crystallised, it became one of the recognised responsibilities of the bishops to instruct their flocks on worship occasions, and stenographers were commissioned to record their words. One of the earliest recorded Christian homilies, *Concerning the Pascha*, attributed to **Melito**, second-century bishop of Sardis, includes a strong condemnation of the Jews for the crime of **deicide**. A far more sustained attack was launched in the late fourth century by one of the most gifted preachers of antiquity, John **Chrysostom**, whose series of sermons attacking Christians in his own church who went to the synagogue to watch Jewish observances not only denied any efficacy or legitimacy to contemporary Jewish worship, but also demonised it. In the sermons of **Augustine of Hippo**, the element of attack is far more subdued. When preaching on Hebrew scripture, his central purpose seems to be not so much to tear down the Jews but to expound the biblical narratives in such a way as to validate their application to the Church, through appeal to a deeper, spiritual meaning. He frequently resorts to **typology** in his sermons, as in his works of biblical **commentary**.

There is no doubt that sermons were delivered in synagogues on a regular basis throughout the first centuries of the Christian era. But we have no record of sermons by individual rabbis that can compare to those of the **Church Fathers**. The **Talmud** and **midrash** are collective works, recording individual teachings only as juxtaposed by later editors with the teachings of other rabbis who may have lived hundreds of miles away or generations later. Jewish preachers may indeed have referred to the new faith and its spectacular success in the pulpit discourse of the first five centuries. But what precisely they said, and how important the subject was for them, cannot be reconstructed.

In the Middle Ages Christian preaching about Jews and Judaism became more hostile, shifting from stereotypical references to Jews of antiquity to pointed attacks against contemporary Jews. Scholars have associated this development with the emergence of the mendicant orders of **Franciscans** and **Dominicans** in the early thirteenth century. Especially during the Christian **Holy Week**, sermons could lead to physical attacks. In **Spain** Ferrant Martínez (*fl.* last quarter of the fifteenth century), archdeacon of Ecija, undertook a campaign of anti-Jewish preaching in the vicinity of Seville that was instrumental in fomenting the deadly violence that began in that city in June 1391 and quickly spread through much of the Iberian peninsula, with devastating results for Jewish life. A generation later one of the most acclaimed medieval popular penitential preachers, Vicente Ferrer (1350–1419), travelled through Castile, Aragon and even into **France**, addressing mass audiences wherever he went. Part of his message of Christian **repentance** called for isolation of the Jews; while the violence of 1391 was not repeated, Jewish communities felt extremely vulnerable wherever he went. In fifteenth-century **Italy** popular mendicant preachers fomented widespread antagonism against Jews, to the point where popes and local officials felt compelled to try to restrain their anti-Jewish **rhetoric**. Preachers such as Antonio Bettini, bishop of Foligno, went far beyond the theological,

invoking vivid metaphors of the Jew as a malicious source of danger to Christian society.

Especially in **Portugal**, the sermon became an integral component of the *auto-da-fé*. Before execution 'heretics' convicted by the **Inquisition** were given the opportunity to listen to a sermon intended to inspire them to confess and repent. The texts of these sermons are a major source for attitudes toward Judaism and the Jew held by the leadership of the Inquisition.

Frequently Jews figured as characters in dramatic *exempla* used by Christian preachers. In many of the stories the Jewish character is carnal, lustful, gluttonous, greedy, a source of danger to Christian children, an assailant against the Virgin **Mary**, a would-be torturer of the body of Christ. Sometimes the Jewish characters are won over to Christian faith by a miraculous event. Occasionally, Jews figure in a more positive role, as representing alternatives to the behaviour being criticised by the Christian preacher. Thus Jews are praised for their devotion to the observance of their holy days, their refusal to utter **blasphemy**, their commitment to education, their willingness to die as martyrs. Jewish preachers also sometimes invoked Christians in this manner within the context of self-criticism, as a model worthy of emulation.

Christians and Christianity do not play a central role in medieval and early modern Jewish preaching, at least insofar as can be documented from the extant records. Nevertheless, some Jewish preachers did address aspects of the rival religion from the pulpit. Jacob Anatoli, a thirteenth-century philosopher, rarely engages in **polemics** against the central doctrines of Christian theology; his references to Christianity generally come in the context of an internal Jewish argument, asserting that certain contemporary Jewish beliefs (e.g. in demons) and practices (e.g. of an ascetic nature) should be rejected because they are too similar to those of the Christians. A preacher who devoted significant energy to attacks against Christianity was Saul Levi Morteira (1596–1660), rabbi in Amsterdam. Addressing a congregation composed almost entirely of former Portuguese **Conversos**, his sermons, mostly directed against Catholicism, contain strong polemics against Christian doctrines of God, **Torah** and **redemption**, and claim that Catholics consciously falsify the Bible in their translations.

In the early Middle Ages a Christian writer (**Agobard of Lyons**) reported with shock that simple Christians said the Jews preached better than their own elders. By the late Middle Ages the pattern was reversed: Spanish Jews were said to listen to Christian sermons and come away impressed by the high calibre of the discourse, complaining that Jewish preachers fell short by comparison. And indeed, Spanish Jewish preachers adapted the model of the scholastic thematic sermon for their own use, incorporating such Christian forms as the 'disputed question' into their preaching.

As sermons were delivered in the vernacular, members of each community sometimes listened to the preachers of the other, with motivations ranging from curiosity to suspicion. Jews sometimes attended the sermons of renowned Christian preachers; Christian intellectuals listened to the sermons of acclaimed Spanish and Italian Jews; the Venetian rabbi **Leon of Modena** was especially proud that friars and priests, nobles and dignitaries would come to hear him.

Quite different was the conversionary sermon, in which Jews were compelled to listen to a Christian preacher (sometimes a convert) try to convince them of the truth. Forced attendance (mandated by the king) was initiated in the mid-thirteenth century; one of the greatest medieval Spanish scholars, Raymon **Llull**, spent many years preaching to Jews in this manner, and Vicente Ferrer insisted that Jews attend his sermons. Reinvigorated in the Papal States during the Counter-Reformation, the practice, with sporadic interruptions, continued until the middle of the nineteenth century.

Even before **emancipation**, the modern period brought a greater affinity between Jewish and Christian preaching. In cities of Europe and the **United States**, Jews and Christians gathered in their synagogues and churches on occasions of national mourning or celebration, and the sentiments expressed from the pulpits were often quite similar. The same fashions of oratory influenced both communities. The new style of nineteenth-century German Jewish preaching was clearly modelled on the German Protestant edificatory sermon. The sermons of the Rev. John Haynes Holmes (1879–1964) and Rabbi Stephen **Wise** were similar both in content and in style.

Polemical and **apologetic** sermons continued. In late nineteenth-century Britain both the Orthodox Rabbi Hermann Adler (1829–1911) and the Reform leader David Woolf Marks (1811–1909) published books containing a series of sermons defending Jewish belief against the arguments of the 'London Society for Promoting Christianity amongst the Jews' (*see* **Church's Ministry among Jewish People**).

In the twentieth century certain themes – such as the pressures upon Jews of the **Christmas** season and issues of **Church and state** – have remained constant topics of pulpit discourse. Others come into fashion. Stephen Wise aroused heated controversy by a 1925 sermon in which he maintained that 'Jesus the Jew' was 'of the very fibre of our Jewish heritage'. In the 1960s the new openness of the Catholic Church accompanying **Vatican II** was discussed with enthusiasm in many Jewish pulpits, but so was the issue of papal policy towards **Nazism** and the **Holocaust**. '**Jews for Jesus**' and other similar groups became a hot topic in the 1970s and 1980s.

One component of the new attitude towards Judaism following from Vatican II was an effort to remove **anti-Judaism** from the Christian pulpit. There is a widespread recognition, especially in Western Churches, that scriptural passages that may convey negative stereotypes of Jews when read in public worship must be contextualised and defused by preaching. The sermon is therefore seen to be crucial for translating the enlightened outlook of official Church statements into the actual message heard in the pews.   *MARC SAPERSTEIN*

Presbyter of the Jews *see* **leaders of the Jews, externally appointed**

Priest/priesthood

It is in Christianity, not Judaism, that the biblical concept of priesthood has been preserved. In the Hebrew scriptures priests offered **sacrifices** in the **Temple**, blessed the people in God's name, sounded the *shofar* (ram's horn) and cast lots to determine God's will. After the destruction of the Temple in 70 CE the sacrificial system came to an end and with it the priesthood, although Jews who claim priestly descent have some privileges in Orthodox synagogues (*see* **Orthodox Judaism**). **Rabbis**, who are experts in the **Torah**, have no priestly functions nor, at first, did Christian leaders. **Jesus** drove the sheep and cattle out of the Temple, emphasised virtuous behaviour rather than ritual and was accused of prophesying the Temple's destruction. Yet even in the **New Testament** he is spoken of as a great High Priest and his death was compared to the **Passover** sacrifice. The earliest Christian leaders were presbyters or elders, not priests. The word 'priest' is itself an Old English contraction of the Latin *presbyter*. Gradually the ordained became a class apart, and the Fourth **Lateran Council** decreed that only they could pronounce **absolution**, give a blessing and celebrate the mass. At the **Reformation** this sacerdotalism was rejected and the 'priesthood of all believers' affirmed. The ordained became known as pastors or ministers. In the **Church of England**, although the term 'priest' is retained, the word 'clergy' is more common. Many Protestant and Anglican churches now ordain women to the priesthood. The work and lifestyle of clergy and rabbis are similar, but it is important to remember the differences in their functions.

MARCUS BRAYBROOKE

Progressive Judaism

Modern movements in Judaism, known as Progressive, have taken their inspiration from earlier pietistic movements within the Church, and have played a major role in modern Jewish–Christian **dialogue**. The term 'Progressive' is normally used to describe all modern interpretations that differ from **Orthodox Judaism** in various ways. These include Conservative, Liberal, Masorti, Reconstructionist and Reform Judaism. The term as sometimes used excludes Masorti or Conservative Judaism. Early histories of Progressive Judaism used the term 'The Jewish Reformation' to describe the origins of the movement in the nineteenth century. There were many unconscious parallels with the **Reformation** in Christianity, including the desire to break away from established tradition, to pray in the vernacular, to return to older and simpler forms of **worship**, and to retrieve the biblical text from the weight of **talmudic** interpretation. **Protestantism** in Christianity also exerted a direct and obvious influence on forms of Progressive Jewish worship, most notably the use of an organ, and a synagogue **architecture** that placed the leader at the front of the building facing the congregation, instead of at the centre facing the Ark. The very terms Orthodox and Reform were borrowed from the Church, and community **rabbis** in modern times have taken on pastoral roles like Christian ministers.

Religious reform of Judaism was only conceived after profound changes had taken place in the civil status of Jews in **France, Germany** and the **Netherlands**, and Jews began to attend non-Jewish places of education and mix socially with Christians. From the opening of the first Reform Temple in Seesen, Germany, in 1810 until today the building of good relations with local Christians has formed an important part of Progressive practice. Progressive scholars have played a vital role in elucidating the Jewish background to the life of **Jesus** and early Christianity, most notably Claude **Montefiore**, Jacob Neusner (b. 1932) and Samuel Sandmel (1911–79). The modern biblical scholarship begun by Christian and secular scholars led to what became known as the 'Scientific Study of Judaism', **Wissenschaft des Judentums**. The new scholarship was also applied to liturgical innovations in Reform Judaism. Many of these, such as the discarding of prayers for the restoration of animal sacrifices, have the effect of bringing the **liturgy** closer to the Church. One motivation of the first Reformers was to prevent Jews joining the Church. This 'radical **assimilation**', as it has been called, was new to Germany, but had been found in England since the early eighteenth century, because wealthier Jews had moved with ease in Gentile society. A style of **prayer** closer to the Church was thought to be more appealing to such people, and would facilitate **conversion** to Judaism of non-Jewish partners of mixed marriages (*see* **intermarriage**). The new rite of confirmation, of which the name, idea and many specific features were borrowed from the Church, was an early and popular innovation, first recorded in 1803. At first the ceremony took place at home or at school, with the teacher asking the 13-year-old boy to give well-rehearsed answers to questions about his beliefs and the Bible. Confirmation became popular in nearly all Progressive synagogues, and gradually evolved into a group ceremony sometimes completely replacing the traditional **barmitzvah**. The first confirmation ceremony for girls was held at Berlin in 1817. Permitting men and women to sit together in synagogue was an innovation of Isaac Mayer Wise (1819–1900) in Albany, New York in 1851, following the practice of most American Churches. The practice spread widely among American Reform Congregations. Only some 50 years later did the 'family pew', as it was called, begin to spread eastwards from the USA to Europe. Yet the history of Progressive Judaism shows a constant struggle between the more traditional and the radical wings. The traditionalists wished to retain rituals when a meaning relevant to their time and society could be found. The disagreement was such that in the **United States** it proved impossible to sustain a single non-orthodox Judaism: Zecharias Fraenkel (1801–75) left the 1845 conference of Reform Rabbis when they declared that **Hebrew** was not absolutely necessary for Jewish prayer. The more traditional Conservative Judaism which he helped to found proved very popular in the USA. At the other end of the spectrum radicals such as Abraham **Geiger** wished to conduct a total reappraisal of all rituals. At the radical New Year Services led in Berlin by Rabbi Samuel **Holdheim** from 1847 most of the men prayed bareheaded, which Jewish tradition considered a Christian custom. Most of the traditional liturgy was discarded in favour of new prayers in German, and the prayerbook opened from left to right. The Association for Reform in Judaism, as the group was known, became the only European Congregation to conduct its weekly service exclusively on Sunday. The Sunday **Sabbath** did not take root in Germany, but was vigorously promoted in the USA. Isaac Mayer Wise promoted late Friday night services as an alternative for those working on Saturday to attend. The Sunday service movement passed its peak, but the popularity of Friday night services remains a feature of Progressive Jewish life. A new concentration on the ethical values of Judaism accompanied the changes in ritual: Protestant Christian claims to ethical primacy were countered with accounts of a moral and universal Judaism. But rabbis now became sensitive to the criticism that their 'reforms' were merely imitations of Christian practice. They felt a need to justify the changes in terms of Jewish **tradition**: an organ had been used in the Temple; choral singing was not new; all the traditional codes stressed that prayers could be said in any language; the sermon was a well-known part of Jewish tradition.

During the second half of the twentieth century Progressive Jewish and Protestant and Free Church Christian groups have explored many innovations together, most notably the appointment of women rabbis and clergy, and the use of inclusive language for prayers. But in other respects the more recent history of Progressive Judaism is marked by a gradual return to tradition. **Zionism** and links with the State of Israel renewed interest in Hebrew prayers, and renewal movements with increased emphasis on traditional forms of observance and study run parallel to similar movements in many Churches, as both faiths seek to come to terms with an increasingly secular world.   *MICHAEL HILTON*

Promised Land

Historically, the 'Promised Land' was a leitmotif in Christian–Jewish **polemics**, though only after the late 1960s did the purpose and conditions of the biblical promises feature in Christian–Jewish **dialogue**, following decades of deliberate evasion of the subject.

Referred to in the **Torah** as 'the land', 'the land of Canaan', or 'the land which I will show you' (e.g. Gen. 12; 13; Deut. 11), God's promise to **Abraham** and his descendants of an agricultural land suited to the godly life is 'forever', though temporary exile will follow periods of national **sin**. The implications of the promise received greater attention in rabbinic writing than in the earliest Christian texts, reflecting, *inter alia*, divergent attitudes to the Torah. With the beginning of the Christianisation of **Byzantium** in the fourth century, however, 'the Holy Land' also featured in triumphalist Christian thought, recalling the 'dispossession' of the Jews – in addition to the destruction of the **Jerusalem** Temple – as evidence that the promise was transferred to the Church. Centuries of Muslim rule (see **Islam**; **Ottoman Empire**) did little to shake Christian confidence that the Jews' weakness in the Holy Land signalled the permanent transfer of the biblical promises to the Church, and would not end once the punishment of exile had redeemed Israel's sins, as rabbinic texts averred. Equally, this ideology meant that the Holy Land of **Christ** and of the Christians has long been viewed in relationship to the 'Jewish' associations of the land of the '**Old Testament**'. This has been particularly so in Protestant traditions according to which some biblical promises still apply to contemporary Jews, a belief that has recently spread in the Catholic Church.   *GEORGE R. WILKES*

Proof-text

The term 'proof-text' describes an exegetical practice that uses the content of the **Bible** to draw conclusions without regard to historical context. Specifically, a proof-text would be an individual passage from the Bible that has been lifted from its location both in time and in the narrative and pressed into the service of solving an unrelated theological or exegetical problem. This entire process is often called proof-texting. Since this style of interpretation ignores fundamental principles of historical-critical interpretation (*see* **biblical criticism**), generally the term 'proof-text' carries a pejorative meaning, and interpretations based upon such a method are usually rejected as unhistorical, misleading and self-serving. (**Fundamentalist** Christian readings of the Bible are often criticised as the result of proof-texting.)

A classic example of this practice appears in **Justin Martyr**'s *Dialogue with the Jew Trypho*. The text faithfully captures a conversation between a Christian and a Diaspora Jew in the middle of the second century CE. (It is likely that an actual Jewish source lies behind the dialogue in its current form.) Justin, a Christian, attempts to persuade his opponent Trypho, a Jew, that the Bible predicts Christianity and that Christianity is the fulfilment of God's promises. Trypho argues contrary positions, also citing biblical example. Both engage in 'proof-texting'. Consider the exchange between Justin and Trypho over the question of Gentile observance of the **Law**. Justin, of course, claims Gentiles do not need to keep the Law to be included in the **covenant**, while Trypho argues for the centrality of the Law. Justin cites Isa. 42.6–7, 63.15–19 and 64.1–12 – all of which deal with the extension of the covenant to the Gentiles – as 'proof' that his position is biblical, but this 'proof' ignores the actual historical context of Isaiah's composition. The application of Pauline visions of Gentile inclusion to Isaiah is anachronistic. Trypho, for his part, retorts that Justin only picks passages he likes and ignores those that make it clear that the law must be faithfully observed, such as Isa. 58.13–14, but his objection is equally uninterested in Isaiah's meaning in context. Similarly, in a classic reflection on the meaning of Isa. 7.14, which in the **Septuagint** says that a 'virgin shall conceive and bear a son', Justin claims the text as proof that the circumstances of Jesus' birth were predicted by the prophet. Later, using a similar technique, Trypho cites Isa. 11.1–3 as proof that **Jesus** could not be what Christians claim him to be because the prophet implies that the 'shoot from the stump of Jesse' will receive the gifts of the spirit and not be born with them as Justin seemed to claim. To the extent that Justin and Trypho are representative of ancient Jewish and Christian approaches to the Bible, we can see how

common it was to employ what many today call 'proof-texts'.

In assessing ancient interpretive techniques one should take care to avoid blanket condemnations. Dismissing these practices as 'proof-texting' ultimately leads to the dismissal of all ancient **biblical interpretation**: Christian readings of the Bible that use **allegory** and **typology**, as well as rabbinic **midrashic** exegesis, would all be disqualified if one were to apply the standards of contemporary historical critical **exegesis**. All pre-modern exegesis was, in some way, unhistorical. With this in mind, many scholars of ancient Judaism and Christianity believe the pejorative term 'proof-text' should be abandoned and replaced with the more neutral term 'intertextual reading'.   *JOHN J. O'KEEFE*

Prophecy

In traditional Jewish and Christian theology there is broad agreement as to the nature of prophecy: prophecy is linked with 'the **Holy Spirit**', seen basically as a divine power entering the prophet, in virtue of which he or she is enabled to speak the word of the Lord. 2 Pet. 1.21 offers a classic statement of this doctrine: 'no prophecy ever came by human will, but men and women moved by the Holy Spirit spoke from God'. Similar ideas are found in rabbinic literature, which claims that the Holy scriptures were 'spoken in the holy spirit' or 'the spirit of prophecy' (*t. Yadayim* 2.14; b. *Megillah* 7a), the expressions being synonymous. Christianity developed the Second Temple period doctrine of the Holy Spirit much more fully than **Rabbinic Judaism**, in orthodoxy transforming the spirit into the third person of the **Trinity**. In rabbinic thought, however, the Holy Spirit remained an impersonal force or influence.

Both traditions agree in classifying the whole of the Old Testament/Tanakh as 'prophecy': **Moses** and **David** are as much prophets who were inspired by the Holy Spirit as **Isaiah**, Jeremiah and Ezekiel. **Inspiration** in this sense was the most important theological criterion for determining whether or not a writing should be included in the **canon** of scripture. However, they differed sharply as to the relative authority of the ancient prophets, and hence of the parts of the canon. Rabbinic Judaism consistently stressed the supremacy, indeed the incomparability, of Moses – a claim grounded in the fact that scripture speaks of God communicating with Moses 'face to face' (Exod. 33.11) or 'mouth to mouth' (Num. 12.8) and directly dictating to him the **Torah**. Such language is used of no other prophet. For Rabbinic Judaism, therefore, the Torah of Moses is the heart of the canon. The rest of the scriptures, though inspired, are of lesser authority, and are sometimes dubbed, somewhat dismissively, 'words of tradition' (*divrei kabbalah*). For Christianity, however, the heart of the Old Testament/Tanakh has tended to be located in the writings of the Prophets, narrowly defined (Isaiah, Jeremiah, Ezekiel, the Twelve and Daniel), because they were seen as foretelling the coming of **Christ**. The Torah of Moses was traditionally regarded as a passing phase in God's dealings with humanity, a view that was anathema to Rabbinic Judaism.

Both Rabbinic Judaism and Christianity agree that the phenomenon of prophecy is time-bound. There had been a great period of prophecy in the past that had produced the canonic writings of scripture. When this period came to an end was not clearly defined. The rabbis suggested the time of Ezra (mid-fifth century BCE) or Alexander the Great (d. 323 BCE). The Christians regarded Malachi as the last of the classic prophets, though they are vague as to when he lived. However, both sides agree that classic, biblical prophecy did come to an end and was followed by a period of prophetic silence. Both also agree that prophecy will be restored at the end of history, in the Messianic age. Since Christians believed that **Jesus** was the **Messiah**, they logically claimed that prophecy returned when he came. His ministry was inaugurated by a **baptism** in the Holy Spirit (Mark 1.9–11), and he was seen as 'a prophet mighty in deed and word' (Luke 24.19). He held the status of the supreme prophet, and the revelation which he brought was believed to supersede the Torah of Moses. His followers also, it was believed, had received the Spirit after his ascension to heaven, and so spoke authoritatively God's truth (Acts 2). Later Christian orthodoxy came to regard this second outpouring of prophecy also as time-bound, though again there was uncertainty as to when precisely it ceased. Later Church authorities dealt harshly with claims to continuing prophetic inspiration, and regarded the closed canon of early Christian prophetic writings (the **New Testament**) as offering sufficient guidance to the Church and as rendering obsolete the need for living prophets.

Rabbinic Judaism, since it rejected Jesus as Messiah, logically held that Christian prophecy was false, and Jesus an imposter. It postponed the return of prophecy to the future, to the coming of the true Messiah. It held, however, somewhat contradictory views as to whether the Messianic age would witness a new **revelation**. The standard view, forged in the fires of Jewish–Christian controversy, was that the Torah of Moses would not be superseded even when the Messiah came. However, under the impact of prophetic inspiration new and hidden meanings would be discovered in it. Some, however, hinted that there would be a new Torah in the Messianic age. The most radical form of this thinking is found the medieval **mystical** tradition, the Kabbalah, where it is argued that since the Torah of Moses clearly addresses a fallen, broken world, it cannot be adequate for the perfections of the world to come. There will be need for a new Torah that will fit the conditions which then prevail.

For Christianity predictive prophecy was central to the **Old Testament**. From the very beginning of its history Christians claimed that the life and death of Jesus, and the events that befell the **early Church**, were clearly foretold in scripture. Jesus himself may have believed that he was personally fulfilling prophecy. After his death his followers engaged in an intensive searching of the scriptures and found there, as they thought, all manner of foretellings of what had happened. They were following a known way of interpreting the prophetic writings, attested also in the **Dead Sea Scrolls** Pesharim, which discovered in Habakkuk and other biblical prophecies cryptic references to events in the Pesharists' own day. One of the key passages for the Christian exegetes came to be Isa. 53: it seemed almost self-evident to them that the **Suffering Servant** mentioned there could only be Jesus. This approach was eventually to culminate in the claim that all the prophetic promises to Israel in the Old Testament were spiritually fulfilled in the Church. Jewish exegetes strongly disputed these claims, arguing, for example, that the Suffering Servant of Isaiah is the nation of Israel personified.

In the nineteenth and twentieth centuries, under the influence of rationalism and historicism, liberal Christian biblical scholarship discounted the possibility of predictive prophecy. Instead the Hebrew prophets were celebrated for the universal ethical principles, such as **justice** and **righteousness**, that they advocated. They were seen as the champions of an austere, ethical monotheism. Some of these ideas found a sympathetic hearing among Jews, particularly in the Reform movement, that abandoned many of the Mosaic laws as incompatible with the modern spiritual condition of humankind. **Orthodox Judaism**, however, continued to look and pray for a more or less literal fulfilment of the promises that Israel would be restored to her ancient land (*see* **Zionism**). In contemporary Jewish discourse, particularly since the Six Day War of 1967, there is a widespread tendency to speak of the **State of Israel** in language that echoes the biblical prophecies. The emergence of the State of Israel has sharpened the debate with the Church over the fulfilment of the ancient prophecies. So long as the Jews were oppressed it was easy for the Church to claim to be the spiritual heir of the promises, but with the emergence of an independent Jewish state that has become much more difficult: it looks as if the prophecies have been literally fulfilled.

An influential strand of Christian thought would agree. Since the early nineteenth century some **fundamentalist** Christian Bible exegetes have argued that the prophecies are too precise and concrete to be other than literally fulfilled. To see them as only spiritually fulfilled in the Church is to trifle with the plain sense of scripture. This Christian restorationism resulted in **Christian Zionism** that has been widely espoused among Southern Baptists in the **United States** and has had considerable influence on US policy towards the State of Israel. Though these Christian Zionists regard the present State of Israel as fulfilling, at least in part, the biblical prophecies of restoration, they see the founding of the state as the first step in a chain of events that will culminate in the second coming of Christ, and in the Jews acknowledging him as their Messiah.   *PHILIP ALEXANDER*

Proselytism *see* **conversion; evangelism; mission**

Protestantism

The term designates the beliefs and practices of non-Roman Catholic and non-Orthodox Christian Churches. The movement arose in sixteenth-century Europe under the leadership of Martin **Luther** and others, protesting certain beliefs and practices of Catholic Christianity.

In its early days the Protestant **Reformation** had certain affinities with Judaism that could have

brought the two communities into a close working relationship. Both were **minority** movements in a religious setting that viewed them with suspicion. The **Hebrew Bible** was central to Protestantism in a way in which it had not been for **Roman Catholicism** and **Orthodox Christianity**, since Protestantism claimed the authority of 'scripture alone' (*sola scriptura*) for faith, the ordering of the community, and its moral life. And both upheld the prophetic principle of holding all human institutions and achievements under the critical eye of a God of uncompromising **justice** who had a special concern for the poor and the oppressed of earth. Yet these affinities failed to lead Protestant Christianity to build a positive relationship with Jews and Judaism. On the contrary, some of the most virulent Christian assaults on Jews came from Luther. Moreover, at the nadir of Christian–Jewish relations in Germany – the **Hitler** years – many Protestant clergy and laypersons supported **Nazism**, while several Protestant theologians voiced anti-Jewish views throughout the Second World War and beyond. By the end of the twentieth century, however, most Protestant Church bodies had adopted new and positive attitudes towards Jews and Judaism.

The Protestant Reformation's emphasis upon the sole authority of the Bible produced close working relations between Jewish and Christian scholars, at least intermittently, throughout the years up to the present. While the **Old Testament** was read and understood primarily in the light of the **New Testament**, in their study of it Reformers such as John **Calvin** made extensive use of Jewish textual and interpretive aids. Protestant concentration upon the Old Testament meant that the Reformers necessarily worked with Jewish scholars, using Jewish grammars, dictionaries, concordances, and turning to Jewish teachers of biblical **Hebrew**. The Reformers also claimed the same books of the 'Old Testament' as Jews, eliminating the deutero-canonical books (the **apocrypha**). However, until recent times several lines of **biblical interpretation** ensured that Protestantism maintained the traditional *Adversus Judaeos* approach. For example, more than other Christians, it seems, Protestants interpreted the Old Testament with the aid of polarities such as promise/fulfilment, law/grace, old/new, judgement/love and so on. They affirmed the history of God's saving deeds on behalf of humankind, with a major place for both Jews and Christians, but the history of the Jewish people easily became the history of a great failure: God provided the **Torah**, but Israel failed to keep the Torah; God's 'old' **covenant** with Israel was broken and the 'new' covenant was made with the Christian community. Some prominent Protestant theologians such as Emil Schürer (1844–1910), in fact, insisted that Judaism was doomed to fail because of its **particularistic** commitments: a single ethnic group, a particular land, an exclusive covenant. While the Reformers and their successors did not always draw the harsh conclusion that there was no religious/theological reason for the continuing existence of the Jewish people – a view all too often expressed in the history of the Church – they generally agreed that the Church had succeeded Israel as the people of God. **Supersessionism** was firmly in place.

In Europe **Enlightenment** and post-Enlightenment Protestantism, which made common cause with Reform and other liberal Jewish groups, did little to alter this understanding. Evolutionary readings of the history of Israel and of Christianity always favoured the Christian 'religion of Jesus' – **grace** over **law** – ignoring the fact that most of Jesus' moral teaching was shared by his contemporaries and earlier Jewish interpreters and that grace provided the setting of Torah for Jews as well (*see* **Ten Commandments**). Even those Protestant interpreters who became experts in the interpretation of post-biblical Judaism, such as Gerhard Kittel (1888–1948) and Rudolf Bultmann (1884–1976) in some early writings, rarely departed from the above-mentioned polarities. Nevertheless, by the late nineteenth century Jewish and Protestant scholars worked closely together in Europe, Great Britain and North America, particularly in relation to biblical studies. In Great Britain the influence of Claude **Montefiore** and David Ginsburg (1831–1914) (a convert to Christianity) helped to moderate the successionist outlook. In North America relations between Protestants and Jews developed along different lines. When European settlements began to multiply in the seventeenth century, some colonies of Jews also made their way to North America. English Baptists and others from Great Britain made common cause with some of these Jewish settlers, particularly in Rhode Island. The US Constitution and its First Amendment in par-

ticular assured that the **United States** would have no Christian establishment and that religious freedom would be a hallmark of the new land. Partly as a consequence, Jews have flourished in North America.

The Protestant Churches in the last 60 years have slowly come to the recognition that the **Holocaust** in Europe made forever unacceptable the view of Christianity as the successor religion to Judaism, as though Judaism had no legitimate place or vocation in the world once Christianity had come. Most of the Protestant Church bodies have now produced statements, such as the 2001 *Church and Israel* published by the **Leuenberg Church Fellowship**, that seek to lay out a proper relationship of their communities to the Jewish people and to Judaism, and speak of God's eternal covenant with both Israel and the Church – either one covenant in two modes or two inseparable but distinct covenants. One of the constant themes in these statements is taken from Rom. 11.29: 'The gifts and the calling of God are irrevocable.' Protestant colleges, universities and theological seminaries, such as Brite Divinity School at Texas Christian University, have joined with public universities in appointing professors of Judaism or Jewish literature and thought to their faculties. Throughout the world scholarly societies for biblical and theological research have Jewish members working along with Protestant, as well as Orthodox and Catholic, members. These interfaith associations and societies are often brought into existence and heavily supported by Protestants.

Many Protestant bodies work on social and humanitarian projects with the Jewish community, and some vociferously support the **State of Israel**, although it is not altogether clear whether they have laid aside their theology of supersession. The vigorous support of Israel by **Christian Zionists** and other Protestant groups is balanced by other more ambivalent Protestant attitudes. Some Protestant groups have close ties with **Arab Christians** in the Middle East (Baptists, Lutherans, Mennonites, Methodists, Presbyterians, United Church of Christ), as do Orthodox, Roman Catholic and Anglican churches. These connections, together with Protestant efforts to lend support to Palestinian refugees and others in need, have made it difficult for many Protestant bodies to offer the kind of support for the State of Israel that some of their fellow Protestant and Jewish colleagues have sometimes anticipated.

This situation illustrates the variety of opinion among Protestants. Some groups adopt an interim theology, firmly convinced that it is God's purpose to bring the Jewish community into the Christian fold at the end, and among some of these Christian groups a '**mission** to the Jews' is still firmly in place. The more radical of such Christian groups can even assert that 'God does not hear the prayers of the Jews'. Protestant **fundamentalists** differ markedly in their relations with the Jewish people and their understanding of God's covenant with Israel, and many Southern Baptists, for example, not only maintain a 'mission to the Jews', but believe that the only positive future for the Jewish people lies in their **conversion** to Christianity. Many still lack the language, the rhetoric and the style that would enable them to affirm the truth and enduring adequacy of the revelation of God in Jesus Christ without insisting that this truth, this adequacy, leaves all other religions, all other truths inconsequential.

For many Protestant Church leaders and theologians, too, along with a large number of clergy and laypersons, the New Testament itself stands in the way of improved relations between Jews and Christians. Just as they read the denunciations of Israel by Israel's prophets in the 'Old' Testament as factual reports rather than theological judgements, so also they read the **polemics** in the New Testament against **Pharisees**, scribes and lawyers as applicable to all Pharisees, all **scribes**, all teachers of the law. Despite a century of efforts to interpret such New Testament texts in their contexts, the influence of the late nineteenth-century German liberal Protestant scholars such as Julius **Wellhausen** and Adolf von **Harnack** still holds fast. For many Protestants the critical assessments of Israel's leaders in Jesus' day is evidence of the moral decline in Jewish life since the return from Babylonian exile and they have continuing difficulty distinguishing between 'some Jewish leaders' in Jesus' day and 'the Jews' (*see **hoi Ioudaioi***).

Protestant Christianity – especially its **evangelical** and Free Church forms – is growing rapidly in several parts of the non-Western world, particularly in sub-Saharan Africa and Latin America. Many Churches in these areas, however, appear to be relatively untouched by the transformation in Christian attitudes towards Jews and Judaism in the West. The New Testament texts that have fomented suspicion or outright hatred of the Jews through the centuries stand in Bibles without comment that might reduce the harm they do to Jewish–Christian relations. And the very confidence in the exclusive truth of Christianity among many of the new adherents would seem to obviate the need to learn from Jews or any others. Protestant Christianity worldwide bears a heavy responsibility to address these two aspects of Christian understanding of Judaism that have prevented earlier development of positive relations between the two communities. All too rarely have Protestants and other Christians engaged in serious study of Judaism: its history, its thought, its sacred writings (beyond the Old Testament itself), its ways of **worship**, its moral commitments. Thus far, Protestant Christianity has worked more diligently to clarify and correct its past relations with Judaism than it has on seeking to understand the world of Judaism, past and present.

WALTER HARRELSON

Protocols of the Elders of Zion

Also known as *Protocols of the Learned Elders of Zion*. Late nineteenth-century antisemitic forgery, which appeared in **Russia** in the early 1900s and aimed at showing the existence of an international Jewish conspiracy for world domination. The idea of a Jewish conspiracy is based on medieval Christian anti-Jewish legend, such as charges of ritual murder (*see* **blood libel**), **host desecration** and well poisonings. From the **Enlightenment** such accusations took on a political dimension. The *Protocols* were written to influence the policies of Tsar Nicholas II (*r.*1894–1917) and were based on a French document (1864) accusing Napoleon III (*r.*1852–70) of ambitions towards world domination. The *Protocols* became widely known from 1919 onwards, notably in Russia and **Germany**. Today it remains freely available in Russia, but also in Arab countries where it continues to be used to generate **antisemitism** and anti-**Zionism**.   *EDWARD KESSLER*

Psalms

The biblical book of Psalms plays a large – and similar – role in the lives of Jews and Christians. For both traditions the book of Psalms, the authorship of which is traditionally ascribed to King **David**, provided the model upon which the worship service was patterned. The themes, specific subject matter, style and language of Psalms is echoed in both

Jewish and Christian **liturgy**; indeed, entire psalms are included verbatim in both liturgies. Phrases or verses from still other psalms are woven into the prayers of both communities, while yet other prayers paraphrase one or more psalms.

Both Jews and Christians are in the habit of making Psalms the focus of private devotion. It has been a custom in both the Jewish and Christian communities to create separate volumes containing the Psalms (known by Christians as the *Psalter* and by Jews as the *Tillimbuch*, a term derived from the Hebrew word for Psalms: *tehillim*), which were often treasured as a source of solace or encouragement.

Notwithstanding these profound commonalities in their approach to, and use of, the book of Psalms, significant differences exist between the Jewish and Christian traditions. In the first place, there is the matter of numbering the psalms themselves and their verses. There is often a difference of one number between the Hebrew text and the Greek version used by many Churches in identifying Pss 10 to 147. Also, in some modern translations there can be a difference of usually one number, sometimes more, in assigning numbers to the verses of many psalms. This is because some translations do not count the superscription at the beginning of many psalms as a separate verse. In addition, the Orthodox Churches include one more psalm in their **canon** than is found in the Hebrew scriptures. Emblematic of these differences is the intersection of Jews, Christians and psalms which occurred in 589. In that year, the Council of Narbonne issued an edict forbidding Jews to sing psalms during funerals. The purpose of this prohibition can only be surmised.

Of greater consequence is the history of interpretation. For millennia, Psalms was read typologically by the Church (*see* **typology**). Thus, many of the psalms were understood as prefiguring the life and career of **Jesus** – as, for instance, Ps. 110 which was interpreted as meaning that God, the Father, called Jesus to ascend a throne next to him in heaven. The medieval Jewish **polemic** *Teshuvot La-Noẓrim* by David **Kimhi** is devoted to a refutation of such typological reading and an insistence on the plain meaning of the text.

Another difference is the Christian discomfort with some of the psalms' treatment of the theme of 'enemies' and the psalmist's rage against them.

Christian writers regularly comment that Christians have difficulty with vengeance and violence in the Psalms directed particularly against enemies, clearly as a result of the Gospel tradition in which Jesus teaches love for one's enemies (Matt. 5.44; Luke 6. 27–29). Entire psalms or sections of psalms are excluded from Christian liturgy or from the calendar of readings because of this discomfort. The excluded sections, or complete psalms, consistently involve curses directed against enemies. Even though there exists a strand of thought in the Jewish tradition that is in consonance with the ideas ascribed to Jesus in the Gospels, there is perhaps less Jewish discomfort about reading psalms containing the sentiments that are problematic to many Christians. *DANIEL POLISH*

Pseudepigrapha

Writings with false superscriptions, titles or authors; a modern designation of a collection of **Hellenistic**-early Roman period Jewish writings not included in the **Hebrew Bible** or Greek **canon** of the Christian **Old Testament**. First brought to prominence by the Lutheran scholar J. A. Fabricius (1668–1736), responsible for the first collection of the 'Pseudepigrapha of the Old Testament' in 1731, most of the 'Pseudepigrapha', as the term suggests, are pseudonymous, appealing for their interpretation of the present to the authority of antiquity, as they claim to communicate the words of the patriarchs and prophets of ancient Israel. Modern scholarship, Jewish and Christian, is divided on the usefulness of the term as a collective category.

While the majority of the so-called Pseudepigrapha are usually reckoned originally Jewish compositions, a few are Christian, rooted in the literary models and religious language and ideas of early Judaism. Of the Jewish Pseudepigrapha, most were transmitted in Christian circles, some in their Jewish form, others rewritten to reflect distinctively Christian beliefs. They show that, like non-Christian Jews of the period, early Christians put great emphasis on the power of appeal to the authority of ancient Jewish tradition to confirm their interpretation of information about the divine. Citations of the Pseudepigrapha in sources including **Josephus**, the **New Testament** and, most extensively, early patristic writings indicate their status as authoritative religious writings in some Jewish and Christian circles. Within rabbinic tradition, however, the Pseudepigrapha are hardly reflected, perhaps in part because they came to be viewed as Christian writings.

Most early study of the Pseudepigrapha was undertaken by Christian scholars for the primary purpose of explaining Christian origins, leading sometimes to influential but inaccurate representations of first-century Judaism as dominated by rabbinic legalism. By contrast, Charlesworth's edition of the Pseudepigrapha (1983, 1985) represents a call to cooperation between Jews and Christians, and celebrates these writings as the heritage of both Jews and Christians. Modern scholarship increasingly emphasises the significance of studying the Pseudepigrapha in their own right, as testimony to the diversity and richness of religious thought that characterised early Judaism and Christianity. The Pseudepigrapha are also rightly viewed as fundamental for illustrating the Jewish context of earliest Christianity: particular attention is given to shared theological language and symbolism including 'the **kingdom of God**' and 'the **Son of Man**'; and to rare, but significant, evidence in the Pseudepigrapha for early Jewish Messianic beliefs.

SARAH J. K. PEARCE

Pseudo-Clementine Writings

Clement of Rome (*fl. c.*95 CE) did not write the so-called Pseudo-Clementine writings which purport to deal with his eventful life. They derive partly from ascetic **Jewish Christianity** and in anthropology and dualism show the influence of **Gnosticism**. The Pseudo-Clementine literature has been much developed (probably in the third and fourth centuries) but an underlying source was hostile to the 'enemy', **Paul**, a view many Jews would have shared. Here is an important witness to the anti-Pauline strain of Christian thought. Paul appears as an **antinomian** pseudo-apostle, thinly disguised in the character of Simon Magus (cf. Acts 8.9–24). The writings honoured Peter, **James brother of Jesus** and the earliest **Jerusalem** Church, respecting the traditions of the Jews and the 'word of truth' of **Moses** as important precedents for Peter's 'lawful' proclamation. **Jesus** was the true Prophet, who had reappeared in different guises through history. Subsequent redactions and interpolations made these writings home to more than one heterodox **Christological** teaching, however. Two letters, from Peter to James and

from Clement to James, appear with the Pseudo-Clementine *Homilies*, plus a response (the *Contestatio*). The Pseudo-Clementine *Recognitions* shares characteristics with the genre of the ancient secular romance. It is generally granted that the (possibly *c.*200 CE) *Kerygmata Petrou* was an early source for the corpus, and some scholars have taken this reconstructed *Kerygmata Petrou* as a template of Jewish Christianity. Jewish Christian groups such as Ebionites and Elkesaites have been cited in relation to the Pseudo-Clementine literature, but the dates, recensions, interpolations and theological affinities of its surviving forms are contested.

CHRISTINE TREVETT

Pseudo-Cyprian

A North African or Italian homily ***Adversus Judaeos*** is one of several third-century writings formerly and wrongly associated with **Cyprian**. It probably represents Christian reaction to a confident and influential local Jewish community, though some critics think the work was for discussion and **catechesis** *internal* to Christianity, and concerned Christian Jews. Formerly attributed to **Melito** among others, it uses both Jewish traditions (e.g **martyrdoms** of the prophets) and common anti-Jewish themes (**deicide**, Jews' loss of their temporal and spiritual inheritance), but envisages **repentance** and **baptism** for Jews. **Supersessionist** and anti-Jewish elements are also found in the pseudo-Cyprianic *De Pascha Computus* (on **Easter**), *Ad Vigilium* and *De Montibus Sina et Sion*, which makes extensive use of Jewish and Christian texts and traditions.

CHRISTINE TREVETT

Purim

An early spring festival (14–15 Adar, usually in March) that marks the deliverance of the Jews in Persia from the attempt by Haman, a favourite nobleman of King Ahasuerus, to massacre them. It celebrates their vengeance and victory over their non-Jewish enemies, as related in the biblical book of **Esther**. It has been traditionally popular at the Jewish communal level but has often raised problems in the minds of Jewish and Christian religious thinkers. The festivities, like the biblical book itself, which makes no mention of God and gives little specific attention to religious ideas, are generally of a mundane character, with the exception of the synagogue ritual surrounding the formal reading of the Esther scroll (*megillah*). This ritual was important enough in the early Christian centuries to be permitted in **Greek** as well as **Hebrew** and to be obligatory on women as well as men. It is conducted on the second day in walled cities and is marked by attempts to drown out the name of Haman each time it is read out. Given the lack of alternative historical verification of the story, the Persian names of the heroes Queen Esther and Mordechai, her cousin and mentor, and the timing of the festival, the origins may well be in some sort of pagan **new year** festival known in the **Diaspora** of the late biblical period. The feasting, revelry, gifts, fancy dress, parodies and even licit drunkenness traditionally associated with Purim would support such a theory. Though formally a minor festival, Purim became popular among Jews by the early Christian era and received major attention from the talmudic teachers. There were always Jewish authorities who were uneasy about the alleged lack of decorum and spirituality, and Christian theologians, already in Byzantine times, who resented the use of the biblical book and the Purim festivities for an indulgence in what they regarded as Jewish chauvinism and **anti-Christian** behaviour. The text of one of the post-*megillah* hymns contrasted Jews and non-Jews and was altered because of Christian **censorship**. In the Middle Ages aspects of Purim celebrations were reminiscent of Carnival and Twelfth Night, perhaps indicating elements of direct mutual influence. **Luther** and the later proponents of **biblical criticism** expressed their opposition, and some early Reform Jews abandoned the celebration of the festival. At that stage it was therefore more likely to be a cause of friction than a factor that bound the monotheistic communities together. As the worlds of Judaism and Christianity became more secular in the twentieth century, and the Purim festivities came to be centred on carnival and dietary delicacies (especially in **Israel**), so the objections lessened. The concept of an occasion on which to rejoice about the rescue of Jews from a potential disaster was widely applied in the Middle Ages and the modern period to other similarly miraculous events. A host of 'Purims' marking incidents in which Jews unexpectedly overcame Christian and Muslim attempts at persecution were added to the Jewish calendar in the relevant communities. Many of these marked what were seen as miraculous rescues from **blood libels** and threats of massacre and they were especially common in Italy and North Africa in the early modern period. *STEFAN C. REIF*

QQQQ

Quakers (Religious Society of Friends)

One of the **Historic Peace Churches**, Quakerism began during the English Revolution. 'Quaker' was originally a nickname, evoking George Fox's (1624–91) call for people to tremble before God. Based on early Friends' beliefs in realised **eschatology** and a universal human capacity to receive the Light (Spirit) of Christ, distinctive Quaker practices emerged. These include **worship** meetings based on waiting for God in **silence**, and the equality of the genders, who share responsibility for church affairs.

Quaker relations with Jews are shaped by their own shifting positions vis-à-vis mainstream Christian theology. Seventeenth- and early eighteenth-century Friends were Christian **universalists**, as articulated in Robert Barclay's (1648–90) description of the Church as consisting of all those 'obedient of the holy light and testimony of God in their hearts . . . There may be members therefore of this . . . church both among heathens, Turks, Jews, and all the several sorts of Christians . . .' They also described **Jesus** as a moral prophet, as well as a priestly figure. This position, and a rejection of compulsion in religion, enabled Quakers to make theological space for Judaism. Although intense **millenarianism** led Margaret Fell (1614–1702) to address her evangelical message 'A Loving Salutation, to the Jews of the world' to Amsterdam Jewry (**Spinoza** was possibly its Hebrew translator) Quakers did not develop any organised **mission** to Jews.

Following early trends, most nineteenth-, twentieth- and twenty-first-century Friends have adopted a Christian universalist approach to other faiths, including Judaism. However, there are some Quakers who reject this position, shun Christian language and interpret the Quaker concept of 'that of God in everyone' in **humanistic** terms, as suggestive of the worth and dignity of all people. Such perspectives have often made it hard for Quakers to locate themselves within ecumenical and interfaith activity. The question of Quaker **identity** is particularly acute in Jewish–Christian relations. Jewish members constitute a significant **minority** of Quakers in Britain and North America today. (One notable example is Harvey Gillman, Outreach Secretary for Quaker Home Service in Britain, 1983–2001.) Many became attracted to Quakers for pragmatic reasons (some at a time when most synagogues did not respond constructively to **intermarriage**; others were child refugees from **Nazism**, raised by Quakers) and do not regard themselves as Jewish converts to Christianity, although many **dialogue** participants (and many Jews) might do so.

This complexity makes it hard to speak of Quaker–Jewish relations, in the sense of two discrete entities encountering one another. The presence of openly non-Christian members, and the Quaker rejection of creeds, ordained ministry and outward **sacraments**, are perennial issues in Friends' relationship with ecumenical and interfaith organisations like the **World Council of Churches**. Other tensions surrounding Quaker involvement in Jewish–Christian relations concern Friends' support for Palestinians and **Palestinian liberation theology**, which conflicts with the pro-**Israel** stance of most dialogue participants. Finally, although Quakers protested against Kristallnacht and nearly all members in **Germany** hid Jews during the **Holocaust**, Friends are not immune from (chiefly ethical) **supersessionism** and **anti-Judaism**. And whilst the absence of a hierarchy of Quaker authorities challenges all members to take responsibility for this, this same organisational structure makes it hard to effect revolutionary advances in relations with the Jewish people.

See also **Dissenters**   *MELANIE J. WRIGHT*

Quartodeciman controversy

'Quartodeciman' designates an early Christian practice, later to become heretical, of observing

Easter on the 14th day of the lunar month, at the same time as the Jews observed **Passover**. It is likely that the first Christians commemorated the passion on the date when **Jesus** had been crucified, that is, the Jewish Passover, of which Easter was only a Christian reinterpretation. Evidence regarding the early Christian Easter is, unfortunately, almost non-existent. The earliest information about the date of Easter pertains to the 190s CE, when a controversy erupted between the Churches of **Asia Minor** (led by Polycrates, bishop of Ephesus; Christians in Palestine and **Egypt** may also have been involved), which observed Easter at the same time as the Jews on the 14th of the lunar month, and the Church of Rome, which celebrated Easter on the following Sunday, as has become universal practice today (Eusebius, *Hist. eccl.* 5.23.1). The issue does not appear to have been the separation of Christianity from Judaism (which did dominate the debate on the date of Easter at the Council of Nicaea in 325 CE, where the question was the determination of the lunar month in which Easter was to be celebrated), but rather an 'internal', theological question regarding the most appropriate day for observing Easter. Quartodecimans may have appeared again in Asia Minor in the later fourth and fifth centuries (so Socrates, *Ecclesiastical History* 6.11 and 7.29, and Sozomen, *Ecclesiastical History* 7.18), but at this stage they were regarded as heretical and probably of marginal importance both to Christianity and to Jewish–Christian relations.

See also **calendar**   SACHA STERN

Qumran *see* **Dead Sea Scrolls**
Qu'ran *see* **Islam**

RRRR

Rabbi

Rabbis are often regarded as 'Jewish clergy', but historically their role is different. A rabbi is a teacher of **Torah** and qualified to interpret Jewish law. The term derives from *rav*, which means 'great man', 'master' or 'teacher'. The suffix 'i' means 'my'. Rabbinic ordination, like Christian ordination, involves the laying on of hands. **Jesus**, according to Matthew, criticised the rabbis' desire for respect and told his disciples not to be called rabbi (23.7–8), but in John's Gospel he is addressed as rabbi on five occasions. In **talmudic** times rabbis were expounders of scripture and interpreters of the oral **law**, but in the Middle Ages they became spiritual leaders of a particular Jewish community with teaching, **preaching** and administrative functions. After **emancipation**, rabbis were expected, like clergy, to be cultured and at home in Western as well as rabbinic learning. Jews' College, which provided both, was founded in London in 1855. Today rabbis in the West are expected to perform functions similar to Christian ministers and often represent the community to the outside world and explain Judaism to Gentile audiences. In the twentieth century, Conservative, Liberal and Reform traditions, like Protestant churches, started ordaining women. In the Middle Ages kings sometimes appointed a 'chief rabbi' to represent the Jewish community. In Britain the office was modelled in part on that of the Archbishop of Canterbury. **Israel** has both an Ashkenazi and a Sephardi chief rabbi.

See also **priest/priesthood**

MARCUS BRAYBROOKE

Rabbinic Judaism

Rabbinic Judaism is the form of Judaism followed by the majority of Jews from Late Antiquity down to the present day. It emerged out of Second Temple period **Pharisaism** and rebuilt Judaism in Palestine after the destruction of the **Temple** in 70 CE. Gradually gaining in strength, the rabbinic party by the third century CE was probably the dominant force in Palestinian Judaism. A turning point in its fortunes is marked by Judah ha-Nasi (late second–early third centuries CE), both a rabbi and a man of substantial wealth in good standing with the Roman authorities, with whose approval he acted as Patriarch of the Jewish community in Palestine. Rabbinic Judaism was carried to Babylonia in the third century CE by Palestinian scholars who soon eclipsed in prestige their counterparts in Palestine. The rabbis also largely succeeded in bringing the Jews of the western **Greek**-speaking **Diaspora** under their aegis. The process by which they achieved this remains obscure, but it must have involved, at least during the first few centuries of the common era (*see* **CE/BCE**), a running battle with the expanding Christian **mission**. Marcel Simon (b. 1907) argues strongly that competition for converts between Christianity and Judaism continued until the conversion of **Constantine** in 312 CE.

All the major varieties of Judaism today, across the religious spectrum from the most orthodox to the most liberal, can be classified as rabbinic, though they observe the rabbinic norms in varying degrees. Rabbinic Judaism is thus by no means monolithic, embracing Haredi, Modern **Orthodox**, Conservative, Masorti, Reform and Liberal (*see* **Progressive Judaism**). Even non-religious or secular Jews recognise the importance of the rabbinic movement in Jewish history, and regard the classic rabbinic literature as an inalienable part of the Jewish cultural heritage.

Rabbinic Judaism can also be defined by texts, institutions and beliefs, each of which sheds light on the Jewish–Christian encounter. For example, aware that Christians regarded the Written **Torah** as part of their own scriptures, the rabbis viewed the **Mishnah** and ongoing oral tradition as setting Judaism apart from Christianity. Other key texts include the **Talmud**, law codes and Bible **commentaries** known as the **midrashim**. Rabbinic Judaism is further defined by a set of institutions that have determined its social structure. The most fundamental of these is the rabbinate. Historically speaking, a **rabbi** is a legal scholar, whose role is to expound and apply the Torah in everyday life. He or (in some modern varieties of Judaism) she is normally ordained to the role by competent authority after intensive study at a rabbinical academy, a yeshivah. Yet even here it is clear that Christianity has to some extent influenced the role of the rabbi. For example, in the **United Kingdom** the office of the Chief Rabbi is modelled on that of the Archbishop of Canterbury, and most rabbis, like ministers, now lead their community in **worship**, although historically this was not expected of them. The fundamental rabbinic principle that 'the law of the state is the law' (*dina de-malkuta dina*) demonstrates that a characteristic feature of Rabbinic Judaism is its ability to digest the mores and customs of the surrounding culture, as Louis Jacobs (b. 1920) has convincingly shown in works such as *A Tree of Life* (1984). Finally, Rabbinic Judaism is defined by a set of beliefs, which constitute its distinctive worldview. Underpinning this worldview is Torah, which comprises not only the Written Torah (*Torah she-bikhtav*) found in the first five books of Tanakh, but also the Oral Torah (*Torah she-be'al peh*), a body of teaching equally deriving, it is claimed, from **Moses** on Sinai, which gives the true interpretation of the Written Torah. The doctrine of the Oral Torah, which is seen as embodied in the Mishnah, Talmud and other authoritative rabbinic texts, and can be accessed only by studying with the right teachers in a chain of tradition going back to Moses, is an emphatic way of asserting the legitimacy of the rabbinic tradition against alternative interpretations of scripture, such as those advanced by Christians.

The relationship between Rabbinic Judaism and Christianity, both of which have their roots in the religious diversity of late Second Temple Judaism, has until recently been dominated by mutual antagonism. In the opening centuries of the common era both fought for the hearts and minds of Jews. The rabbis largely succeeded in neutralising the Christian mission to Israel, successfully categorising the Christians as 'heretics' (*minim* – see **birkat ha-minim**) to be excluded from the synagogue and Jewish social life. The Christians, in turn, when they found themselves in a position of political power

from the time of Constantine onwards, persecuted the rabbis in various ways, closing their schools, dispersing their leaders, censoring or even, in the Middle Ages, destroying the Talmud and other rabbinic texts (*see* **censorship**) and forcibly converting their followers. Christian theology persistently vilified Rabbinic Judaism. It was depicted, particularly within **Protestantism**, as a dry-as-dust legalism, which, by its obsessive attention to the minutiae of the **Law**, squeezed all joy out of religious life. The burdened condition of the Jew groaning under bondage to the Law was contrasted with the freedom of the Christian saved by **grace** and filled with the Spirit. Better acquaintance with the classic sources of Rabbinic Judaism, notably from the end of the nineteenth century, and with the realities of Jewish life, led many Christian scholars such as R. Travers **Herford** and James **Parkes** to question this view of Judaism. Rabbinic Judaism, for its part, has not been above vilifying Christianity. For example, the *Toledot Yeshu*, elements of which are found in the Talmud, offers a scurrilous alternative life of **Jesus**, which denigrates both him and **Mary**. More recently, however, some Jewish scholars, such as Geza Vermes (b. 1924) and Amy-Jill Levine (b. 1956) have made a concerted effort to understand Jesus as a genuinely Jewish teacher and to reclaim him for Judaism.

There have also been down the ages many instances of more positive interaction between the two traditions. For example, Christians relied for many centuries on rabbinic knowledge of **Hebrew** to gain access to the **Old Testament** in its original language, and the great medieval rabbinic Bible exegetes **Rashi**, **Kimhi** and Abraham **ibn Ezra** had a profound influence on Christian **Bible translations**, such the Authorised Version of 1611. And in recent times forms of Christian ministry and Christian religious community have had a considerable impact on the rabbinate and the synagogue in the western world, particularly in Progressive Judaism. The fact that Rabbinic Judaism has survived for 2,000 years, despite dispersion, persecution and its lack of a strong, centralised organisation, testifies to its resilience and an adaptability that includes reacting to and to a certain extent being influenced by Christianity.   *PHILIP ALEXANDER*

Rachel

Biblical figure, sister of **Leah**, second wife of **Jacob**. Rachel's status as Jacob's preferred wife according to the biblical narrative has factored into her role in the Jewish–Christian relationship.

Like all the biblical ancestors in the book of Genesis, the narratives about Rachel and her relationship with her family members reflect later socio-political relationships in ancient **Israel**. She is Jacob's favourite, and as the mother of two sons, **Joseph** and Benjamin, she represents an exalted strain of later Israelite polity. Rachel is one of the four biblical matriarchs who is mentioned with some frequency in Jewish **liturgy**. Although in biblical genealogies her name appears in birth order after her sister's, in Jewish liturgy her name appears first before her elder sister Leah's name. In contrast to her role in Judaism, Rachel does not figure prominently in Christian liturgical tradition or theological thought, although she has been, along with other figures from Genesis, a favourite subject of artists. Among others, the **Church Father** Commodian (third century CE) viewed Rachel as a type of the Church; her older sister Leah with her weak eyes is negatively depicted as a type of the Synagogue (*Instructiones* 39). This contrasting depiction between two women, one positive and one negative, is also seen in medieval **iconography** in Christian **art** and **architecture** in the *Ecclesia/Synagoga* figures. Not all Christian interpretations of Leah and Rachel reflect such **supersessionism,** however. In *Contra Faustum* **Augustine** looked upon Leah as a type of the active life, and Rachel, the contemplative. This interpretation influenced subsequent patristic and medieval commentators. The supposed site of Rachel's tomb between Jerusalem and Bethlehem has been a **pilgrimage** site for both Jews and Christians through the ages.

JUDITH H. NEWMAN

Rashi (1040–1105)

Rabbi Solomon ben Isaac of Troyes. Rashi is the founder of the Northern French School of exegesis. His **commentaries** on almost the entire **Hebrew Bible** and most tractates of the **Talmud** continue to serve as normative understanding of these fundamental works of **Rabbinic Judaism**. At the core of Rashi's **hermeneutics** is an attempt to balance the *peshat*, the plain meaning of the text, with the *derash*, the multiple levels of rabbinic interpretation. Comments about Christian interpretations of scripture appear both explicitly and by implication in Rashi's biblical **exegesis**. The commentary on **Psalms** has several 'answers to the Christians'

(*teshuvah leminim*), and his introductory comments to each book of the **Pentateuch** stress God's continuing love for **Israel**. In the introduction to the Song of Songs Rashi emphasises that Israel will endure 'exile after exile' and how much God still loves them. Rashi and his disciples were a source for the twelfth-century canons of St Victor (*see* **Victorines**), who renewed emphasis on the literal sense of scripture as the basis for Christian theology. Nicholas of **Lyra** quotes the commentaries of Rashi throughout his comprehensive *Postillae perpetuae* on the Hebrew Bible. Through Lyra's writings, Rashi became an important source for **Luther's** exegesis.

MICHAEL A. SIGNER

Ratisbonne, Theodore (1802–84) and **Alphonse** (1814–84)

The Ratisbonne brothers were born into a wealthy, assimilated Jewish family in Strasbourg, Alsace. Theodore was baptised a Catholic in 1827 and ordained a priest in 1830. Alphonse was baptised in 1842, after having a vision of the Virgin Mary in Rome, and soon after entered the **Jesuits**. At this same time Theodore was founding the **Sisters of Sion**. In 1852 Alphonse left the Jesuits in order to join his brother. The two, although believing that Jews should accept Jesus Christ and formally enter the Church, insisted on a particular love of the Jewish people, the Jewish origins of Christianity and the Jewish identity of **Jesus**, long before this became widely accepted in the Church. They also dissuaded the Sisters from active proselytism. While Theodore directed the growth of the Congregation in France, Alphonse established the Congregation in **Jerusalem**, where three centres were built between 1856 and 1878.

See also **Ratisbonne, Pontifical Institute**

DAVID M. NEUHAUS

Ratisbonne, Pontifical Institute

Institute for Jewish studies. Its unique status as (since 1998) a pontifically established institution and its location in **Jerusalem** made it a significant point of encounter for the Catholic Church with the Jewish people. Alphonse **Ratisbonne** erected the building in 1873 as a school. With the changes in orientation of the Roman Catholic Church towards the Jewish people in the 1960s, Ratisbonne Institute became an international ecumenical centre for the study of Judaism under the direction of the Fathers of Sion. Its location and links with the Hebrew University facilitated the setting up of a programme of Jewish studies for Christian students, ensuring an authentic meeting with the Jewish living and textual traditions. Former students have promoted Jewish–Christian **dialogue** and positive teaching on the Jews within their local churches. In 2002 the Vatican closed Ratisbonne and transferred its activities to the Cardinal Bea Center at the Gregorian University in Rome, which aims to continue the Institute's aims.

DAVID M. NEUHAUS

Recognition theology

In the last several decades a growing group of Christian theologians have advocated a transformation of Christian understanding of the relationship between Judaism and Christianity and have sought to overturn the traditional Christian views of **supersessionism** and **replacement**. Recognition theology, as the name suggests, is based on the recognition by Christians that Judaism has a continuing role in God's plan of **revelation** and **salvation**, and that Judaism is a valid and valuable path to God and a partner with Christianity in God's plan. These theologians recognise that the Jewish roots of Christianity are essential to Christianity and that Christianity is unintelligible without them. They recognise that **Jesus** lived and died as a Jew, that God's **covenant** with the Jewish people endures forever, and that Judaism is a living and vibrant faith today. They acknowledge and abhor the evil Christians have done in the name of supersessionism. Recognition theologians insist that accepting these positions is essential to a coherent and credible theology. The greatest challenge these theologians face is integrating these positions into the rest of their theology.

'Recognition theology' is not the only name for this movement; it is also called 'theology of continuity', '(Christian) theology of Israel', 'theology of the Jewish–Christian reality' and so on. The most prolific and influential recognition theologians include A. Roy Eckardt (1918–98), Eugene Fisher (b. 1943), F.-W. Marquardt (1928–2002), John Pawlikowski (b. 1940), Paul van Buren (1924–98) and Clark Williamson (b. 1935). *JOANN SPILLMAN*

Reconstructionist Judaism *see* Progressive Judaism

Redemption

The concept of redemption (*redemptio* in Latin or *ge'ulah* in Hebrew) plays a central role in both Christianity and Judaism. Its original meaning refers to paying a ransom price to a temporal ruler to obtain physical security. However, in religious usage the term describes personal and collective efforts to gain divine deliverance from **sin**, oppression or slavery.

While both faiths affirm God as the Ultimate Redeemer, and employ the same term, 'redemption', there are clear differences between Jews and Christians that have implications for interreligious relations. Traditional Christianity asserts that because humans are born 'in sin', they can achieve redemption only through belief in the vicarious saving power of **Jesus**. Jews, however, believe redemption requires the faithful performance of God's **commandments** (*miẓvot* in Hebrew) and the lifelong study of **Torah**. There are significant differences among Christians as to whether Jesus brought a redemption that is 'complete, integral in all points, perfect and truly admirable' (Council of **Trent** (1545–63)), or whether there is redemptive predestination: 'that salvation is freely offered [by God] to some, and others are prevented from attaining it' (**Calvin**, *Institutes of the Christian Religion*, 1559). Unlike Christianity's emphasis on individual redemption, Judaism stresses *ge'ulah* for the entire Jewish people, a development that began with the biblical exodus from Egyptian servitude, but is yet to be fulfilled.

Despite the differences between Christians and Jews, the two communities theologically intersect on some aspects of redemption. In recent years Jews have stressed the concept of *tikkun olam* or 'the mending/repair of the world' as an active tangible means of achieving redemption. The concept of perfecting human society has resonated among those Christians who emphasise spiritual redemption in this life. Although Judaism does not accept the Christian concept of **original sin**, it does recognise that sin is ubiquitous in human existence. Redemption from sin involves confession to God, followed by sincere regret, and finally *teshuvah* or **repentance**, a strong resolve not to repeat the sin. This is the redemptive theme of Yom Kippur, the **Day of Atonement**. Many Christians have been influenced by Martin **Buber**, who reflects basic Jewish thinking in his *The Two Foci of the Jewish Soul* (1930) by recognising 'that God's redeeming power is at work and at all times, but that a state of redemption exists nowhere and never . . . in a world which still remains unredeemed'. Similarly, the Christian theologian Reinhold Niebuhr (1892–1971) has influenced Jewish religious thinkers with his emphasis on the omnipresence of sin in this life and his insistence on pursuing a vigorous course of human action to confront that condition as a means of achieving redemption. Niebuhr taught that religion must redeem society from the sins of the economic, social and political spheres, calling his redemptive actions 'Christian Realism'.

A. JAMES RUDIN

Reform Judaism *see* Progressive Judaism

Reformation

The Reformation has been called one of the greatest revolutions in the history of Western thought. It broke the religious monopoly of the **Roman Catholic** Church for all foreseeable time and introduced many alternative theologies and Churches. While generally considered to have been initiated by the compelling ideas and actions of Martin **Luther** in German areas, another movement of reform was taking place in Switzerland under Huldreich Zwingli (1484–1531) followed by John **Calvin**. Still others would emerge in the early to mid-sixteenth century. Most reformers retained the antithetical and conversionist attitudes toward Jews and Judaism of previous centuries. Certainly this was true for Luther and for his early colleague Martin Bucer (1491–1551). Bucer advised Landgrave Philipp of Hesse in 1538–9 that he should deprive Jews of everything but the bare means of existence so that they would see their errors and convert to Christianity, since **New Testament** admonitions for **tolerance** applied only to **Jewish Christians**. Justus Jonas (1493–1555) held that Jews had been led astray by Talmudic hair-splitting, just as Christians had by scholastic subtleties. Each could be won to Reform, Christians by recovery of their holy scriptures, Jews by the unadulterated Tanakh. He lauded the 'doctors of theology' who existed among biblical Israelites, and held that Christians are guests in the house of **Abraham** as latecomers to the promise of God. In somewhat similar fashion Wolfgang Capito (1478–1541) believed that the ancient tradition was sound but that contemporary Jews had lost sight of those early truths by following human reason rather than the word of God. He denied that Jews were **demon**-possessed or were plotting to overthrow nations, and urged they be treated with kindness and compassion. Andreas Osiander (1498–1552) was also outspoken in his condemnation of **blood libel** accusations against the Jews, as well as in his criticism of Luther's late *Vom Shem Hamphoras* ('Concerning the Ineffable Name'). Reformers in Switzerland, especially Calvin, took somewhat more positive views of Judaism. In Zurich Zwingli launched a reform movement through a series of sermons attacking **fasting**, **celibacy** and other abuses of the Church. Zwingli saw the Lord's Supper not as a repetition of Christ's sacrifice, as Luther did, but as a remembrance of that sacrifice made for all. Zwingli taught that God's **covenant** with **Adam** was fundamental and of benefit for all humankind. It was renewed for the **people of Israel** through Abraham, and Abraham anticipated God's saving act in Jesus Christ for their faith was essentially the same. When the **early Church** abandoned Judaic ceremonies and undertook the **mission** to the Gentiles it was reaffirming the universal character of the covenant with Adam. Heinrich Bullinger (1504–75) carried Zwingli's idea about the covenant with Adam and the unity of **salvation** further when he held that the covenant made with Abraham was directed to all people, not just Israel. Since God's saving act in Christ can only be understood in that framework, the Old Covenant is the interpreter of the New. Calvin insisted on the value of the **Torah** in its teaching about God's will and human duties. Further, he insisted that God had not abrogated his covenant with Israel. Calvin's theology was preeminent in shaping the Reformed Church in its theology and structure as it spread into France, Holland, Germany, Hungary, Poland, England and Scotland. Adding to the ferment of the Reformation were **Anabaptists**, **Sabbatarians** and **Christian Hebraists**.

See also **Protestantism**   ALICE L. ECKARDT

Reformation Churches *see* Leuenberg Church Fellowship

Reformation, Jewish *see* Progressive Judaism

Reformed Churches *see* Leuenberg Church Fellowship; Protestantism; Reformation

Relics

Relics refer to both the material remains of a holy person after their death and to objects that come into contact with those remains. The Greek word *leipsana* and the classical Latin word *reliquiae* mean any mortal remains; only later does the word assume religious connotations. The origin of the practice of relics is to be found in the veneration of the dead, a common practice in many religions and cultures. This veneration often focused on the place of **burial**, where monuments were erected and religious gatherings were held. In Judaism special honour was paid to the tombs of the patriarchs. Early Christians also honoured the burial places of their holy ones, especially the **martyrs**; in Christianity, by the fourth century in the East and the eighth century in the West, as the bodies of the martyrs were moved to shrines and churches for a variety of reasons, the focus of veneration shifted from the place of burial to the remains themselves. The moving of bodies was often seen as a barbaric practice by Jewish writers and other non-Christian commentators. While for Judaism many tombs were and are still venerated, they were not promoted by Jewish leaders in the same way Christian leaders promoted the tombs of their **saints**, though the **pilgrimages** of some hasidic groups to the tombs of their rabbis mirror the Christian practice of pilgrimage to particularly important shrines on the feast-day of the saint or even throughout the year.

LIAM M. TRACEY

Religio licita

The phrase *religio licita* was coined by **Tertullian** (*Apol.* 21.1) to refer to Roman **tolerance** of Judaism as a 'permitted religion'. The phrase was not used by the Romans themselves. Judaism, as Tertullian correctly observes, enjoyed a special status in imperial legislation. Generally, the Romans did not interfere with the religious practices of conquered people; they were content to add new deities to the existing pantheon and continually to expand the pluralistic religious environment of the Empire. The Jews offered a particular challenge because their strict monotheism prevented them from accommodating themselves to Roman pluralistic attitudes. However, because the Romans respected the antiquity of the Jews as a people, they were willing to concede special status to them when it came to religious matters. This accommodation was not without friction, and the Jews had to work hard to maintain it.

When Christianity appeared on the scene the Romans tended to lump Christians together with Jews. Suetonius (*c.*70–140 CE) reports that Claudius expelled the Jews from Rome because of disturbances caused by 'Chrestus' (*Claud.* 25.4). Eventually, in part through the protests of the Jewish community, Roman authorities recognised Christianity as a new sect that was not subject to legal protection because it was not an ethnos and because it lacked the ancestral pedigree of the Jews. Pliny's (*c.*61–*c.*113 CE) letter to the emperor Trajan (*r.* 98–117) (*Ep. Tra.* 10) famously captures this change in Roman perception. The surviving writings of early Christian apologists suggest that Christians made significant efforts to secure for themselves the same kind of religious protection that had traditionally been extended to the Jews. This effort was not successful until the conversion of **Constantine** in the fourth century.

JOHN J. O'KEEFE

Religion

Historically, the category 'religion' is almost entirely alien to the Jewish–Christian encounter. There is, for example, no straightforward translation of the word 'religion' in Hebrew. The two words that sometimes are translated as 'religion' are *dati*, which means observance, and *emunah*, which means faith. There are significant differences between Christianity and Judaism that the term 'religion' can obscure. For example, beliefs in the terms of a creed are extremely important in Christianity, while practice is much more important in Judaism. Indeed, the case can be made that it was only the rise of **Islam** that forced Judaism to start articulating a distinctive creed, perhaps with the 13 principles of faith formulated by **Maimonides** in the twelfth century. Before this it was story and practice that mattered: the stories of '**covenant**' and the obligation to be '**Torah**-observant' were the defining features of the Jewish faith.

Yet of course the very fact that Jewish–Christian dialogue can be described as 'interreligious dialogue' reveals that the word has become important. The word 'religion' has a Latin root *religio*, which captures a sense of fear or awe invoked by a god or spirit. However, it has come to describe a generic commitment to any faith tradition. Thus in popular usage the term implies that both Judaism and Christianity are 'religions' (i.e. systems of belief and practice that require the worship of a transcendent deity), and it is in this sense that the term 'interreligious **dialogue**' is used. *IAN MARKHAM*

Religious education

The education of most Christians and Jews over the ages has generally contributed to the development of an oppositional **identity**; both traditions have fostered in their adherents a self-understanding that contrasted with an oversimplified notion of the other. Christians have typically been taught that the divine promises made to the Jews were fulfilled in Christ, whom the Jews rejected and crucified. Judaism was thus a religion of the past, a preparation for Christianity, which superseded it. Jews have characteristically learned that Christianity, with its doctrine of the **Trinity** and claims about the divine status of **Jesus**, is **idolatry**. The bitter legacy of **anti-Judaism** and **antisemitism**, moreover, made Jews sceptical of Christianity's moral integrity and wary of Christians.

A number of factors make possible a different religious education today. The *Shoah* (**Holocaust**) challenged theology in a radical way. **Vatican II** set in motion a serious re-examination by many Churches of their teaching about Jews and Judaism. A burgeoning field of biblical scholarship opened new avenues for understanding the complexities of Christian origins in relation to Second Temple Judaism. Important studies challenged the anti-Jewish theologies that had shaped Christian self-understanding. Jewish agencies worked in tandem with ecumenical and interreligious offices sponsored by the Churches. Synagogues and Churches initiated programmes and publications as resources for teachers and preachers. Friendships formed: Jews and Christians studied with each other, worked on collaborative projects and engaged in **dialogue** in both formal and informal settings.

Scholars in the field of religious education itself initiated studies of the way **textbooks** presented the other tradition. These studies, first appearing in the early 1960s in the United States, in Europe in the mid-1970s, and with further analyses in the US in the late 1970s and mid-1990s, gave impetus to more accurate texts for many Roman Catholic and mainline Protestants. Other scholars focused on developments in biblical studies and theology that necessitated replacing the **supersessionist** paradigm of salvation history so influential in Christian education with a more nuanced framework for interpreting scripture. Continuing education opportunities for teachers have deepened their grasp of changes in texts, as well as involved them in the dramatic, if painstaking, work of rethinking previous understandings. In some cases Jewish and Christian educators study together, confronting some of the difficult and delicate questions history and theology raise. Such interreligious learning has enabled participants to gain understandings of the other tradi-

tion in ways not possible in homogeneous settings. Moreover, the recent educational thrust toward multiculturalism and religious pluralism tends to overlook the specificity of relations between Jews and Christians.

The **Internet** offers rich resources for deepening understanding of the Jewish–Christian relationship, often in collaboration with the various **centres for Jewish–Christian relations** that have been established in recent years (see, e.g., www.jcrelations.net and www.bc.edu/research/cjl). In a world in which too many peoples learn their religious tradition in ways that inadequately define (and even demonise) the religious other, the progress in relations between Jews and Christians is powerfully instructive.
MARY C. BOYS

Religious Society of Friends *see* Quakers

Remembrance

The cycle of the religious year as well as lifecycle events in Judaism and Christianity all contain elements of remembrance by which Jews and Christians are called to place themselves in the history of their respective communities. History, in this context, can mean different things. While it may mean the history of **communities**, recalling events that are thought especially important to shape the mindset of subsequent generations, other elements include the history of ideas, such as concepts important for the development of faith and expectations of **salvation**. Since most Christian festivals are modelled on aspects of Jewish festivals (Easter–Pesach, followed after 50 days by Pentecost–Shavuot), the different ways in which the seasons of the year are invested with meaning by Jews and Christians offer insights into interfaith relations. How Jews were and are now portrayed, for example, in the **liturgies** of Lent and **Easter**, has been an important point in interfaith **dialogue** in recent decades, where the impact of **Vatican II** and subsequent documents has been particularly significant. (Jewish portrayals of Christians in liturgical events are not common.) The remembrance of historical events occurring in the lifetime of present-day communities is a matter of religious controversy, as demonstrated by the difficulties of finding ways of commemorating the **Holocaust** in Jewish and Christian communities. While for parts of the Jewish community the inclusion of a separate Holocaust remembrance in the liturgical **calendar** is halakhically difficult, Christians struggle with the difficulty of remembering members of their own communities as perpetrators, **bystanders** and victims.

See also **Carmelite controversy**; **Holocaust Memorial Days**; **memorialisation**; **museums**

K. HANNAH HOLTSCHNEIDER

Remnant theology

Remnant theology proposes the continuity between the Hebrew scriptures and the **New Testament** in terms of the ongoing election of the Jewish people. Although it claims biblical roots, notably **Romans 9–11**, remnant theology is a much later development, and its origins can be traced back to the desire of seventeenth-century English Puritans to study the scriptures in their original languages. Whilst there were sufficient **Latin** and **Greek** scholars, few had an understanding of **Hebrew**, and Puritans sought guidance not from **Calvinists**, but from rabbis, notably from Amsterdam. This resulted not only in a greater knowledge of Hebrew, but in a new understanding of **covenant**, and perhaps also contributed to Jews being encouraged to return to live in **England**. Remnant theology rejected classical **replacement theology** by arguing that God's covenant with the **people of Israel** was eternal, a view that parallels contemporary Christian teaching that the covenant between God and the Jewish people is 'irrevocable' (cf. Rom. 11.25).

In the eighteenth and nineteenth centuries the Brethren movement, influenced by dispensationalist **eschatology**, argued that the rejection of **Jesus** by the majority of Judaism only postponed God's promises for Israel until Christ's second coming. This *parousia* would bring in the millennial reign of Christ, during which time all God's plans for Israel would be restored and come to full fruition. The book *Israel my Glory* (1889) by John Wilkinson (1824–1907) was highly influential at the beginning of the twentieth century, not least on many politicians, including Arthur Balfour (1848–1930), and in shaping the British government's support for the establishment of a homeland for the Jewish people in Palestine (*see* **Balfour Declaration**).

The political consequences of remnant theology have been considerable. As the biblical covenant referred to both land and people, there was a reassessment of attitudes towards Palestine, viewing it as the rightful homeland of the Jewish people to which God would eventually ensure Jews would return. This view provided the theological basis for modern **Christian Zionism**. Today there are many manifestations of remnant theology, embodying differences over issues such as the **conversion** of the Jewish people. While influential groups such as the **International Christian Embassy** in Jerusalem publicly speak out against evangelical activity among Jews, others, such as the **Church's Ministry among Jewish People**, actively encourage Jewish conversion to Christianity. Nevertheless, all groups holding remnant theology agree that the modern **State of Israel** is intrinsically related to the Israel of biblical **prophecy** and a direct fulfilment of it.

See also **millenarianism**   EDWARD KESSLER

Renaissance

In general terms, the Renaissance of the fourteenth and fifteenth centuries denotes a revival of culture which marked the end of the Middle Ages. It was an era in which the ancient world was rediscovered. Part of the drive to restore the vanished splendours of the past was a renewed interest in classical literature. This enthusiasm for antiquity was expressed in the **humanist** battle cry *ad fontes* (back to the original sources), which was reflected in the Christian theologians' rejection of scholasticism.

The revival of learning profoundly affected Jewish–Christian relations, primarily through the development of Hebrew scholarship among Christians (*see* **Hebraists, Christian**). Acknowledgement of **Hebrew** as one of the three historical languages of the West, alongside **Latin** and **Greek**, had several significant results. First, the teaching of Hebrew was placed on an official footing. Between 500 CE and 1450 CE very few Gentiles had undertaken detailed study of the language. However, by the beginning of the sixteenth century it was rapidly becoming a recognised part of every biblical scholar's training. Initially, Christian humanists received instruction privately from Jews: Manetti (d. 1459), **Pico della Mirandola**, Egidio of Viterbo (1469–1532) and **Reuchlin** all had Jewish teachers. Such cooperation became one of the chief characteristics of humanistic scholarship in **Italy**. But if Hebrew was to be taken seriously it had to be included in the academic curriculum at universities. It had to be taught by competent teachers and supported by enthusiastic patrons. Such official recognition is a mark of the Renaissance. Reuchlin spent most of his life as professor of Hebrew at Tübingen, Jerome Busleiden (d. 1517) endowed the Collegium Trilingue at Louvain, and Robert Wakefield (d. 1537) was the first salaried Hebrew lecturer at Cambridge. Second, the study of Hebrew undermined the traditional reverence for the **Vulgate** as a translation of the scriptures. **Jerome**'s version was less readily accepted as the final authority in textual matters because knowledge of Hebrew gave scholars direct access to the **Old Testament** in its original form. This eventually led to a drive by Catholics and Protestants for fresh and independent Latin translations based on the *hebraica veritas*. Among them are those of Pagninus (1470–1536), Müntzer (1489–1552), Jud (1482–1542) and Tremellius (1510–80), all of which feature prominently as channels of Hebrew scholarship in the lineage of the English Bible. Third, Christians began to take a serious interest in post-biblical Jewish literature. Pico and Reuchlin pioneered the Christian study of the Kabbalah, primarily because they were convinced that Jewish **mystical** teaching could be employed to reinforce Christian convictions, but also because they believed in the practical value of the Kabbalah as a means of making contact with the celestial world and enlisting the help of angelic powers. A knowledge of Hebrew gave Christians access also to the writings of **Rashi**, **Kimhi**, **Ibn Ezra** and other medieval rabbinic exegetes. Sixteenth-century scholars who produced Latin and vernacular translations of the scriptures were greatly assisted by the explanations of textual difficulties provided in Jewish biblical **commentaries**. In sum, the humanists of Renaissance Europe laid durable foundations for the development of Hebrew scholarship and enabled Christians to appreciate the mystical and exegetical traditions of the Jews.   *GARETH LLOYD JONES*

Repentance

Jews and Christians share certain biblical notions regarding repentance, but also diverge sharply on this concept in their respective traditions. For Jews, biblical teaching comprises two acts that must be realised in the repentant sinner: true sorrowing for **sin** (2 Sam. 13.13), and putting an end to evildoing, while at least beginning to do good (Ps. 24.4). This is captured in the Hebrew verb *shwb* ('to return'), whereby repentance is understood as a 'change of direction' of the heart (Ezek. 18.31; Jer. 4.4) or will. Eventually, the rabbinic concept of *teshuvah* would come to summarise this doctrine.

Christians derive their notion of repentance partly from these concepts, but also from the example of **Jesus** in the Gospels. There, Jesus depicts God as a father who welcomes home his prodigal son (Luke 15.11–32) returning in sorrow for his misdeeds. While this image is consistent with the Judaism of his day, Jesus' later placing of himself uniquely in the role of the forgiver of sins (Matt. 9.5–6) was considered **blasphemy** by onlookers (Luke 5.21). His teaching on repentance emphasises first the mercy of God over the judgement of others and suggests that the social condition of the sinner neither guarantees nor inhibits true repentance, for example with prostitutes and adulteresses who turn from sin (Luke 7.44–50; John 8.11), or tax collectors and brigands (Luke 19.1–10; 23.39–42; 7.50; 23.43). In some cases sin remains due to the self-deceit of the sinner (John 9.41). True repentance is known as *metanoia*, or 'a change of heart' and is not equivalent to mere 'remorse', which must precede it (cf. Matt. 27.3 and Luke 12.10); failure to repent risks God's judgement (Luke 13.5). Early Christians, such as **Paul** of Tarsus, taught identically on the mercy of God (cf. Rom. 2.4 and 2 Cor. 7.9–11) and sorrow over sin for true repentance.

Following the separation of Jews and Christians, repentance becomes more distinctive in each community. The loss of the **Temple** and the rise of rabbinic teaching brought the concept of *teshuvah* to the fore, concentrating on the question, How can wrongdoing be made right? Talmudic discussion affirmed the mercy of God as the only one who can forgive sins, especially when repentance is made from love and not from fear alone (*b. Yoma* 86b). Christian notions, however, developed in conjunction with a belief that **baptism** marked true repentance, after which only one repentance from sin was allowed (cf. Herm. *Mand.* 4.1.8; **Tertullian**, *Paen.* 7.9.10). Emphasising the role of the **priest** in forgiving sins in the name of Jesus, Christian ideas on repentance centred on reconciliation with the Church and **atonement** for punishment (owed both in this life and the next) through **ascetic** practices.

Tragically, many Christians saw the collective guilt of Jews for the death of Jesus (*see* **deicide, charge of**) to be the same as an 'unrepentant Judaism'. Consequently, Jews were made to 'repent' through forced baptism, especially during the **Crusades**, despite official Church bans on this practice. Inevitably, these false **conversions** were marked by remorse and the need to 'reconvert', occasioning Jewish and Christian literature that deplored forced baptism unto repentance and reinstated affected Jews (cf. **Maimonides**' *Mishneh Torah*). In 1965 **Vatican II** formally repudiated the notion that Jews are cursed or forsaken by God in retribution for their supposed killing of Jesus (*Nostra Aetate* no. 4). In his Lenten liturgy of repentance for 2000, and subsequently in his visit to **Israel**, Pope **John Paul II** repented of Christian injuries against Jews, asking for **forgiveness** and the acceptance of true repentance.

See also **penance/penitence**

DENNIS D. MCMANUS

Replacement theology

Replacement theology has entered the parlance of contemporary theology in recent decades to refer to the traditional Christian teaching that with the coming of Jesus Christ the Church has taken the place of the Jewish people as God's elect community. The term is substantially equivalent to **supersessionism**, and the two terms are sometimes used interchangeably. Both designate a theological perspective that interprets Christian faith generally and the status of the Church in particular so as to claim or imply the abrogation or obsolescence of God's **covenant** with the Jewish people.

Replacement theology took shape during the second century CE, based upon a selective and embellished reading of the **New Testament**, and was a generally accepted staple of Christian theology from the third century onward. Christian theologians found various ways to express the central idea that the Church had supplanted the Jewish people and henceforth was the true **Israel** (*verus Israel*) of God. Some (e.g. **Justin Martyr**, **Tertullian**) emphasised the persistent failure and disobedience of the Jewish people, culminating in their **crucifixion** of **Jesus** and rejection of the Easter gospel. According to this view God finally cast off unbelieving Jews because of their sins and gave their inheritance to another people, the Gentile Church. Others (e.g. **Melito of Sardis**, **Augustine**) emphasised the idea that God had always intended the Jewish covenant to be temporary in character, an earthly foreshadowing of heavenly goods to be made available in the Church. On this perspective the distinguishing features of Israel's covenant (temple, sacrifices, participation through carnal descent etc.) naturally lost their validity with the birth of the Church which offered the old benefits in a new and superior form. While the two perspectives are compatible, and indeed are often found side by side in the same authors, their emphases differ. The first portrays the Jewish people as disobedient in fact, while the second portrays the Jewish covenant as obsolete in principle. In modern times the second view has been especially prominent among apologetically minded theologians who have advocated a developmental or progressivist interpretation of Christian faith (e.g. Schleiermacher (1768–1834), **Hegel**, **Harnack**).

Although a re-evaluation began in the first half of the twentieth century, it was the **Holocaust** that prompted many Christians and Christian denominations in Europe and North America to embark upon an unprecedented critical examination of Christianity's traditional teachings regarding the Jewish people. A major outcome of this reassessment has been the formation of a broad (though not universal) consensus regarding the inadequacy of replacement theology, which is now perceived to have formed the linchpin of Christianity's historic 'teaching of contempt' toward Jews. Accordingly, the identification, analysis and repudiation of replacement theology have occupied a prominent place among Christians seeking to put the Church's relationship to the Jewish people on a new theological footing. However, there is less agreement among Christians about what replaces replacement theology. Clearly, the rejection of replacement theology entails some affirmation of the continuing validity of God's covenant with the Jewish people. But Christians differ about the implications of the rejection of replacement theology for other central Christian doctrines such as the **Trinity**, the person and work of Jesus Christ and the universality of the Church's **mission**. Pioneering among Europeans has been the work of the Roman Catholic Franz Mussner (b. 1916) and the Protestant Friedrich-Wilhelm Marquardt (1928–2002), who have appealed in different ways for a renewed appreciation of the Jewish roots and dimensions of all aspects of Christian faith. In North America the dominant voices of the 1970s and 80s (e.g. Rosemary Ruether (b. 1936), A. Roy Eckhart (1918–98), Paul van Buren (1924–98)) argued that a thoroughgoing rejection of replacement theology requires a corresponding rejection of certain doctrines traditionally regarded as constitutive of Christian **identity** by the ecumenical church (e.g. that Jesus is the **Christ**). Since then theologians on both sides of the Atlantic have increasingly embraced the view that the most promising avenue for future exploration lies in reinterpreting rather than rejecting traditional affirmations in light of the Church's new understanding of God's continued fidelity to God's covenant with Israel (*see* **postsuspersessionism**; **recognition theology**).

R. KENDALL SOULEN

Resurrection narratives

Influenced by the Jewish pharisaic belief in a future resurrection, the **New Testament** 'resurrection narratives' are stories in the Gospels of Matthew (Matt. 28.1–20), Luke (Luke 24.1–51), John (John 20–1), and the later ending of Mark (Mark 16.9–20) that describe Jesus' followers coming to the tomb and finding it empty, narrate appearances of **Jesus** after his death and burial, and as a consequence of these experiences proclaim the belief that Jesus was vindicated and raised by God from the dead. Earlier New Testament traditions about the resurrection of Jesus appear already in the Pauline and post-Pauline letters in the form of creedal statements and hymns (e.g. 1 Cor. 15.3–4; Phil. 2.6–11; Rom. 4.24; 8.11; Gal. 1.1; Eph. 1.20; Col. 2.12; 1 Pet. 1.21; cf. Rom. 10.9) that celebrate Jesus' life, death, resurrection and ascension to God.

For Jew as well as Christian belief in an **afterlife** is fundamentally a consequence of firm confidence in God's judgement on evildoers and in the divine providential care for righteous humankind. In Jewish tradition Enoch (Gen. 5.24) and the prophet **Elijah** (2 Kgs 2.1–15) were rewarded for their piety and were 'taken to God' in mysterious ways that prefigure later resurrection beliefs. Ezekiel's prophetic vision of the 'dry bones' (Ezek. 37.1–14) similarly attests to the conviction that God's power can revivify even the dry, lifeless bones of the dead. The earliest biblical attestation for a belief in resurrection, however, usually turns to the texts of Daniel (Dan. 12.1–3) and the 'Isaian apocalypse' (Isa. 26.19). Daniel comes from the turbulent time of the Maccabean revolt (167–161 BCE) and reflects the Jewish apocalyptic mood of the day with its belief that God would soon intervene in the world, bringing it to its final consummation. At the end time God would raise the dead bodies, pronounce judgement on the evil and the just, and sentence them to either eternal punishment or eternal reward. This faith in bodily resurrection at the end time became one of the hallmarks of **Pharisaic** piety and the subject of their fierce debates with the **Sadducees**, who rejected such notions of afterlife.

The New Testament resurrection narratives can be understood only against this Jewish **apocalyptic** background: the Jews who became disciples of Jesus were convinced that God had vindicated his righteous life and raised him from the dead, ushering in the final New Age. Two different types of resurrection stories circulated among Christians: appearance stories and empty tomb stories. The earliest New Testament tradition is attested in **Paul's** creedal statement in 1 Cor. 15.5–8, but because Paul did not mention the empty tomb, only a list of appearances, some scholars claim that the empty tomb narratives developed later and had a distinct **apologetic** function to counter Jewish claims that the body of Jesus had been stolen. In keeping with this apologetic function, Matthew's Gospel alone narrates the posting of a guard at the tomb (Matt. 27.62–6). Others see in the stories of the empty tomb the earliest Christian attestation of bodily resurrection and Jesus' victory over death. Despite differences in the New Testament accounts, the constant Christian affirmation stands firm: 'the tomb was empty and he is alive!'

Although belief in God's power to bring to life those who have died is a conviction shared by Jews (for example, the *Amidah* states, 'Blessed are You, O Lord, reviver of the dead') as well as Christians, the belief in the resurrection of Jesus is a key dividing line between the two religions.

BARBARA E. BOWE

Reuchlin, Johannes (1455–1522)

German lawyer and Hebraist. Reuchlin's interest in the language, **mysticism** and literature of the Jews lies behind his lasting contribution to scholarship. Taught by a Jew, he became a proficient Hebraist. As professor of Hebrew at Tübingen he published a grammar-cum-dictionary, *De rudimentis hebraicis* (1506) and a treatise on accents, pronunciation and synagogue **music**. Influenced by **Pico della Mirandola**, he made a detailed study of the Kabbalah, which, he believed, confirmed Christian truth. He published his views in *De verbo mirifico* (1494) and *De arte cabbalistica* (1517). His appreciation of post-biblical Jewish literature emerged in a bitter controversy with the **Dominicans** which raged for almost a decade. The Emperor Maximilian (1459–1519), at the instigation of the Dominicans, had ordered that all **Hebrew** books considered inimical to the Christian faith should be burned. Reuchlin came to the defence of Jewish literature. His success in this 'battle of the books' was a victory for Jews and Christian **humanists** alike.

See also **Hebraists, Christian**; **Renaissance**

GARETH LLOYD JONES

Revelation

Christians in their encounter with Judaism have wanted to stress the recognition that Christianity has built on the 'revealing' of God to Judaism. Both traditions stress that knowledge of God depends on God 'revealing' Godself to humanity. The Hebrew word for revelation is *nirah*, which literally means 'see'. While Christians want to see the **New Testament** (literally 'New Covenant') build effortlessly on the **Old Testament**, Jews do not see the **Hebrew Bible** as one uniform document. In Judaism all of scripture is a testimony to the disclosure of God in history in a variety of ways (prophets, priests, kings and the written word). The Tanakh is the preferred term for the Jewish scriptures; the term is made up from the initial letters of Torah (the Pentateuch), Neviim (Prophets) and Ketuvim (Hagiographa). The ultimate revelation of God is the **Torah**, which primarily refers to the **Pentateuch** (the first five books of the Bible), although the word can apply to the teaching of a rabbi. In the **Talmud** the Torah is God's blueprint for **creation** – a text that predates the creation. Although written by **Moses**, it was received from God and is therefore infallible.

In the encounter between Christianity and Judaism, the way that Christianity builds on the Hebrew Bible has been very contentious. Christianity talks of the 'revelation' of God in the person and work of **Jesus** of Nazareth. The Gospel of John starts by proclaiming Christ as the **Logos** (the word) of God. The author is deliberately creating a link between Jesus and God's revelation in nature (in Gen. 1, at the start of the Hebrew Bible), which was brought about by the words of God. In addition, reformed Christians, in particular, talk about the Bible as the Word of God. The crucial text here is 1 Tim. 2.16: 'all scripture is inspired by God'.

Christian and Jewish attitudes to the text have shaped each other. In both traditions we find the distinction between 'propositional revelation' (that in some sense the text or doctrinal formula is the very Word of God) and 'non-propositional revelation' (that the revelation lies behind the text, located within the experience of those who wrote it – see J. Hick, *Philosophy of Religion*, 61–4). The propositional view is held by such people as James Packer (b. 1926) (Christian) and Norman Lamm (b. 1927) (Jewish), while on the non-propositional side C. H. Dodd (1884–1973) (Christian) and A. J. **Heschel** (Jewish) line up together. The former position tends to be much more suspicious of the historical-critical approach to scripture (*see* **biblical criticism**), while the latter position is much more sympathetic to it.

IAN MARKHAM

Reverend

An honorific, ordinarily associated with Christian clergy. First used in the Church in the fourteenth century, and since the seventeenth century prefixed to the names of clergy as a formal title. It can be applied equally to men and women, as well as to those in religious orders. It has also been used in Judaism in England and some Commonwealth countries where, before rabbinical diplomas were required for rabbis in the twentieth century, it was adopted to honour the spiritual leadership of those who served Jewish congregations. A student of the London School of Jewish Studies (formerly London Jews College) still graduates, and is qualified to accept a position, with a minister's diploma, which is less than the rabbinical diploma and carries with it the title 'reverend'. In all other countries, and among Reform and Conservative as well as Orthodox Jews, the only title borne by the spiritual leader is **rabbi**, except for the Sephardi congregations, which use the title *hakham*.

PHILIP CULBERTSON

Rhetoric

Rhetoric refers to the art of communication that enables the speaker/writer to define a concern and to frame a presentation that will effectively move an audience towards a consensual goal. The importance of rhetoric was grounded in the conviction that the meaning of the spoken and written word depended not only on *what* was stated, but also on *how* it was declared. The teaching and **preaching** of Christians and Jews that grew out of the **Hellenistic** world was profoundly indebted to the prevailing practices of rhetoric. The arguments Christians and Jews advanced within their own ranks, as well as the conflicts that emerged between these divergent religious communities, cannot be deciphered without careful regard for the rhetorical norms that shaped their discourse.

The value of rhetoric depreciated in the wake of the **Enlightenment** as knowledge was increasingly identified with observable fact. Rhetoric was reduced to nothing more substantial than an outcropping of subjectivity and disregarded as an ornamental expression of the imagination. In recent decades literary critics have revived cultural interest in the dynamics of rhetoric by exploring the relationship between language, persuasion, personal knowledge, political/religious contexts and social control. Rhetorical criticism has generated some fresh insights that have great bearing on Jewish–Christian relations.

Stanley Stowers (b. 1948), for example, demonstrates that a failure to understand the literary context and the rhetorical purposes of Paul's letter to the Romans has generated some serious misunderstandings of Judaism. The traditional reading of Romans sees **Paul** as a critic of 'Jewish legalism' and 'Jewish ethnocentrism'. This rendering yields a radical doctrine of **sin** that is said to overturn the 'external' character of Jewish observance and its empty promise of **salvation**. Stowers echoes Krister Stendahl's (b. 1921) critique and argues that this interpretation of Romans reflects the concerns of **Augustine** and **Luther**, but has little to do with Paul or the community he addressed. Instead, Stowers advocates a reading of Romans that identifies classical rhetorical conventions and reveals a Pauline argument that enabled Gentile believers to stand within the mystery of God's purposes as an authentic extension of the People of God, namely the **people Israel**.

Scholars are also applying the study of rhetoric to patristic literature. Robert Wilken (b. 1936) demonstrates the importance of rhetorical conventions in his analysis of John **Chrysostom**'s sermons *Against the Jews*. Not only do contemporary readers need to understand that indictments of Judaism and the Jewish people are modelled on an established rhetorical framework of invective, they also need to identify Chrysostom's audience, most especially his opponents. Chrysostom developed an argument that condemns 'Judaisers' who are luring his congregants into the observance of Jewish rituals, and he assails this dynamic within his congregation by attacking the vibrant religiosity to which these **Judaisers** are pointing. While Paul and

Chrysostom may have directed their arguments against enemies within their ranks, these rhetorical texts can live many lives. What Nazis found within Chrysostom's sermons is certainly different from what Chrysostom's congregation heard. In contemporary controversies in Jewish–Christian relations there are rhetorical expressions that carry potent emotional payloads, and the deployment of these terms can evoke explosive reactions, as evidenced in references to contested real estate as either 'Palestine' or 'Israel', or in applying the name '**Holocaust**' as a description of injustices and atrocities other than those perpetrated during the Nazi era. Readers will need to examine the ways in which different audiences receive rhetorical arguments in different circumstances, and then scrutinise the various purposes that these arguments serve.

See also **polemics** *CHRISTOPHER M. LEIGHTON*

Rhineland Synod (1980)

The statement of the Synod of the Evangelical Church in the Rhineland (EKiR) *Towards a Renewal of the Relationship between Christians and Jews* is often praised as one of the most important documents for Christian interpretation of Jewish–Christian relations. It was the first statement of a German Protestant Church to recognise the theological importance of the subject. In the wake of the study *Christians and Jews* (1975), in which the Evangelical Church in **Germany** focused on the history of Jewish–Christian relations, the EKiR formed a commission to draft a further document, which was presented to the Synod in 1980, accepted and recommended for study by Church congregations. The commission had a number of Jewish advisors, notably Rabbi Yehuda Aschkenasy (b. 1924). The statement outlines five areas that are of concern for Jewish–Christian relations (the **Holocaust**, the **Bible**, **Jesus**, the people of God, and **mission**) and recommends conversations between Jews and Christians. Reactions to the statement were varied. Based on **covenant** theology, the statement assumes that Christians are dependent on Jews for the development of their own faith and **identity**, and hence need Jewish partners in conversation in order to understand themselves. While many theologians and activists in Jewish–Christian conversations welcomed this, a few prominent professors of theology wrote a letter of objection, suggesting that the statement gave up fundamental Christian beliefs and asserting that **salvation** could be attained only through **Christ**. The few Jewish reactions to the statement were positive, recognising the enormity of the theological step taken by the Synod and expressing hope for the future of Jewish–Christian relations. In 1996 an addition to the constitution of the Rhenish Church was ratified which was suggested as a consequence of the 1980 statement and which embeds Jewish–Christian relations in this Church's self-definition. The constitution carries the following unique addition: 'She [the Evangelical Church in the Rhineland] confesses God's faithfulness, who holds fast to the election of His people Israel. Together with Israel, she hopes for a new heaven and a new earth.'   K. HANNAH HOLTSCHNEIDER

Righteous Gentiles

Righteous Gentiles, or Righteous among the Nations, is a term originating in rabbinic literature, where it is applied to non-Jews who are good god-fearing people. However, it is used today for those non-Jews who risked their lives to save Jews during the **Holocaust** and is often linked to a statement from the **Talmud** that 'a person who saves a life is as if he saved an entire world' (*b. Sanhedrin* 37a). Since 1963 an Israeli commission has been charged with the duty of awarding the honorary title Righteous among the Nations, and at Yad Vashem over 11,000 'Righteous Gentiles' are honoured, 5,000 of whom are Polish.

Examples of Christians who acted to rescue Jews include the Metropolitan Andrii Sheptytsk'kyi (1865–1944) in Lvov, who hid about 150 Jews in monasteries in eastern Galicia, and the French **Huguenot** pastor André Trocmé (1901–71), who converted the Huguenot village of Le Chambon into a mountain hideout. Lay Catholics, such as the German Dr Gertrude Luckner (1900–95), who headed the Caritas Catholics, also extended help to Jews and non-Aryan Christians in **Germany**. In addition to active help, some clergymen protested the mistreatment and deportations of Jews as violations of divine and human laws. The Catholic pastor of St Hedwig's Cathedral in Berlin, Bernard Lichtenberg (1875–1943), prayed publicly for the Jews until his arrest; he died on the way to Dachau. The rescue work of Righteous Gentiles has become increasingly well documented and plays an important role in contemporary Holocaust **remembrance**.

                EDWARD KESSLER

Righteousness

The English word 'righteousness' is often used to translate the Hebrew nouns *zedek* and *zedekah*, and the Greek word *dikaiosune*. Its range of meanings encompasses the ethical, the state of acting in the correct or right manner, as well as the forensic, where it indicates the acquittal or the vindication of the person(s) involved. In both the Jewish and the Christian traditions righteousness is closely related to other concepts, such as justice, justification and salvation.

In the **Hebrew Bible** righteousness has its basis in the **covenant** between God and his people. Righteousness characterises the **people of Israel** when they are obedient to the **commandments** (Ps. 18.20–24; Jer. 22.3; Ezek. 18.5–9, 25–29). The prophets hoped for a future Davidic king whose reign would be marked by **justice** and righteousness (Isa. 9.7; 11.1–5; Jer. 23.5; 33.15). The righteousness of God (Ps. 119.142) is displayed in his loyalty to the covenant agreement (Neh. 9.8; Dan. 9.13–16), in his judgements (Pss. 9.8; 119.137) and in his acts of vindication and **salvation** (Ps. 71.2; Isa. 46.13; 51.5; 54.14; 62.1–2; Jer. 23.6). These senses of righteousness are found in later Jewish literature. The **Torah** itself can be described in terms of righteousness (*T. Dan* 6.10), while those who follow its precepts are characterised by righteousness (*Pss. Sol.* 9.3; 1 Macc. 2.29; *Jub.* 20.2–3). In the sectarian writings from Qumran (*see* **Dead Sea Scrolls**), there is mention of the Teacher of Righteousness who taught a particular understanding of the Law (CD 20.28–33; 1QpHab 8.1–3).

In the Christian tradition the Gospel of Matthew stands firmly within contemporary Judaism by coupling obedience to the Torah with righteousness. **Jesus** stipulates that the **Law** is to be obeyed in its entirety (Matt. 5.17–19), and he demands that the righteousness of his followers in fulfilling the Torah must be superior to that of the **scribes** and **Pharisees** (5.20). By contrast, **Paul** of Tarsus is adamant that righteousness (or **justification**) comes not through observance of the Law but through faith in Christ alone (Phil. 3.9; cf. Rom. 9.30–1; 10.3–13). For Paul the righteousness of God is manifested in his acts of salvation. It is revealed through faith in Christ and in his **forgiveness** of sin (Rom. 3.21–6; cf. 1.16–17).

At the time of the **Reformation** the Pauline view of justification (or righteousness) by faith alone and not by works of the Law became the catch-cry of the Protestant reformers. Martin **Luther** saw his attack upon the medieval Catholic Church as replicating Paul's attack on contemporary Judaism. Luther maintained that just as the Catholic Church emphasised salvation through works and achievements, so too did first-century Judaism with its emphasis on Law-observance and human effort. Despite objections from Jewish scholars, this caricature of Judaism as a religion of legalism and merit that had forgotten the **grace** of God dominated Protestant scholarship for centuries, and severely compromised Jewish–Christian relations during that time. This view, however, was strongly and convincingly criticised in the works of E. P. Sanders (b. 1937).

DAVID SIM

Ritual murder, accusation of *see* blood libel

Roman Catholicism

Roman Catholicism is a historical, religious, political and sociological reality. It denotes those Christians who claim to be in possession of a historical and continuous **tradition** of faith and practice and who are in communion with the Pope in Rome. The term is used particularly of Catholicism as it has existed since the sixteenth-century Protestant **Reformation**. However, following the East–West schism (traditionally dated 1054 CE) after which the Eastern Church described itself as 'orthodox', it also frequently denotes Western Christianity, which referred to itself as Catholic and in union with Rome. Organisationally, it is a centralised, hierarchical structure of bishops, priests and laity with the pope at its head. In dialectical relationship with this official Church is popular Roman Catholicism which incarnates the basic beliefs and practices within the concrete conditions of human life.

Following the schism of 1054 Roman Catholicism's relationship with Jews and Judaism retained many of the understandings and attitudes that marked Christianity of antiquity and the early Middle Ages. This included the strains of political and spiritual triumphalism which, in contradistinction to the status of the Jewish people, viewed the Church's historical victory and success as clear evidence of divine approval (*see* **supersessionism**). The association of synagogue and Jews with the demonic, rooted in the **New Testament** and graphically asserted by such early **Church Fathers** as **Chrysostom**, undergirded late medieval

and early modern **anti-Judaism**. **Augustine**'s theory that Jews should be permitted to live in a Christian realm because they were valuable as the 'guardians of Scripture' and living proof of the truth of Christian faith was incorporated into papal legislation. Though not allowing Jews to flourish, Augustine insisted upon physical safety for the Jews to enable them to fulfil their function of attesting to their status of being accursed. The **Crusades** of 1095 and 1147 and the **William of Norwich** ritual murder charge in 1144 were omens of profound changes in the popular Church. Though local bishops and persons such as **Bernard of Clairvaux** attempted to protect the Jews, and popes condemned charges of ritual murder and Jewish international conspiracy as baseless, the local masses were not restrained from violence and bloodshed by official edict or **doctrine**. Their twelfth-century attack on the **Talmud** was endorsed for a time in the thirteenth century by popes who perceived talmudic interpretations of biblical laws as perverting divine revelation. Though the papacy soon reversed itself, it was not before there had been a papal **inquisition** and a public book-burning in Paris. This increasing popular hostility was fed by fear of Muslim expansion, an emerging economic order in which Jews were perceived as calculating for profit, and the emerging bureaucratic institutions in a society whose proclivity for persecution required the identification of an enemy. This also effected a change of attitude in Roman Catholic leadership which particularly affected those Jews suffering from the **expulsions** from Western Europe. For example, 1084 saw the Bishop of Speyer offering a charter of protection to expelled Jews, while in 1519 the Bishop of Speyer quarantined his diocese against them. Though Jews were deeply opposed to the Church, they refrained from expressing this publicly, especially in face of the thirteenth-century increase in prohibitions and condemnations. Defensive apologetic texts such as those of Abraham **Ibn Ezra** and Joseph Kimhi (1105–70) were the exception. The Fourth **Lateran Council** (1215) convoked by Pope **Innocent III**, looking back to the Roman Law of the Christian emperors, specified new restrictions placed on Jews. The founding of the **Franciscan** and **Dominican** mendicant orders in the early thirteenth century, in reaction to threats against the institutional Church, affected all non-Christians within the Christian frontiers. The attitudes and actions of the popes generally combined both positive and negative elements – sincere attempts to restrain anti-Jewish zealots, and active repression of whatever appeared to border on **anti-Christian** influence. Paradoxically, in many places during this period Roman Catholic relationships with Jews were also positive, and Jewish cultural, biblical, legal, philosophical and scientific contributions were often received with appreciation. The work of the school of St Victor (*see* **Victorines**) attests to significant Jewish contributions to the spiritual life of the Church, particularly through their command of **Hebrew**. Just as Judaism stimulated the Church's creative reflection and reformulation of old understandings, so the Church was a factor in helping Jews hone and develop their thought and vision. In spite of prohibitions and persecution, there was at no time a Jewish majority relocation to the Islamic world.

During the fourteenth- to eighteenth-centuries Western and Central European transition from the medieval to the modern world, the new spirit of **humanism**, initiated by the **Renaissance**, was followed by the **Protestant** Reformation. The parallel hierarchies of Church and nobility lost power as old secular and religious authority was questioned. The shattering of the monolith of Western Christendom by the Reformation evoked a militant response within Roman Catholicism, including an increase of anti-Jewish **rhetoric** and actual confrontation. Caught in the crossfire of verbal warfare, the familiar scapegoat was linked with these upheavals in Christendom and charged with seditious conspiracy at a time when European Jewry was in a severe crisis situation, having just been forced to choose between **baptism** and expulsion amidst **pogroms** and massacres in **Spain**. After-effects of the Spanish 'purity of blood' preoccupation and of the 1480 Inquisition had spread to northern Europe, intensifying anti-Jewish sentiment there. In 1553 the Jews of **Italy** felt Roman Catholicism's militant resurgence of intolerance in the form of public book-burnings in Venice and Rome, and in 1555 in the form of a **ghetto** established in Rome and 24 Jews being burned at the stake. With its confidence gravely shaken by the Reformation, the Church sought assuagement through efforts at mass **conversions** of Jews. This was central to the Counter-Reformation efforts of Pope Paul IV (1555–9), and to the 1577 papal bull *Vices eius nos* which required Jews in the Papal States to attend conversionist sermons.

Ultimately the Reformation, along with the **Enlightenment**, was the harbinger of such positive developments as religious liberty, pluralism and religious **toleration**. However, accusations of unbelief and treason, in the context of a nationalism significantly intensified by national Churches and close alliances between **Church and state**, continued to mark a virulent anti-Judaism. The profound reordering of society effected by the French and American revolutions at the end of the eighteenth century formally moved religion from the centre to the margins of political social structures. With the various faiths now equal before the law, religions were forced to establish new relationships. While they presented the greatest challenge to these liberal ideals, Jews – due to depletion in numbers, and their social and political status – did not play a dominant role in this process, though their influence in the religious field and the purely philosophical realm increasingly affected the universities of the West and newly developing areas of cultural creativity. The modernist movement within Roman Catholicism which sought to bring the tradition of Catholic belief into closer relationship with these changes was encouraged by Pope Leo XIII (1878–1903) but condemned by Pius X (1903–14) in 1907.

In the midst of this preoccupation with modernism, Roman Catholicism entered the 'century of genocide' which included the experience with **Nazism** and the watershed event of the **Holocaust (*Shoah*)**. Nazi racial hatred and dehumanisation of the Jews from 1933 to 1945 took to the extreme the Enlightenment declaration that the genetic nature of some people rendered them inherently inferior. The debate over the '**silence** of the Vatican' during this period may remain forever unresolved. However, the fact remains that while the popes in previous centuries had consistently condemned excessive violence against the Jews, and while Pius XI's (1922–39) 1937 anti-Nazi encyclical and 1938 words declared total opposition between Christianity and Nazism (5 September; Christmas Allocution), the words and actions of **Pius XII** in the face of this Nazi aggression appear woefully inadequate. There was clearly a radical reversal of the Middle Ages, when popular and lower-clergy anti-Jewish agitation was confronted by popes. During the Holocaust laity and lower clergy were far more willing directly to resist the 'final solution' than official leaders.

More than at any other time in its history, Roman Catholicism was caught in the dilemma of being both a political entity and a religious moral force. The Vatican's hesitation to violate its neutrality in the war or the 1933 Concordat with the Nazi regime stands in sharp contrast to the actions of some local German bishops and the papal representatives in such countries as Turkey, Slovakia and **Hungary**.

Pope **John XXIII**, who as Apostolic Delegate in Turkey and Bulgaria witnessed Jewish suffering and rescued thousands from deportation, began his brief pontificate (1958–63) with a clear moral imperative. His 1959 directive that the phrase *perfidia Judaica* be deleted from the intercessory prayers for the Jewish people (*see* **Good Friday Prayer for the Perfidious Jews**) was but a foreshadowing of the effect this experience was to have on **Vatican II**. He warmly received the French Jewish scholar and Holocaust survivor Jules **Isaac** and heard Catholic voices from Rome's Biblical Institute and elsewhere expressing the hope that the Council review the Church's relationship with Jews and Judaism. Under the leadership of Cardinal Augustin **Bea** the Council deliberations on this matter were promulgated in 1965 as Article 4 in *Nostra Aetate*. However, the efforts to arrive at this brief statement, the result of considerable compromise, had given rise to the Council's most controversial sessions, in which Pope John himself at times directly intervened. At issue were diplomatic sensitivities and pastoral/theological considerations which coalesced mainly around concern for Catholic **minorities** in Arab states and the explicit rejection of the charge of **deicide**.

Nevertheless, under the leadership of Pope **Paul VI** and Pope **John Paul II** this statement provided the foundation of Roman Catholicism's most radical rearticulation of Christian self-understanding. Taking seriously the document's call to **dialogue**, its rejection of the charge of deicide and its reaffirmation of God's **covenant** with the Jewish people, Church leaders, clergy and scholars – in dialogue with their Jewish counterparts – contributed to the carefully delineated theological, pastoral and ethical directives in the following documents issued through the Holy See's Commission for Religious Relations with the Jews: *Guidelines and Suggestions for Implementing Nostra Aetate*, §4 (1975); *Notes on the Correct Way to Present the Jews and Judaism* (1985); *We Remember: A Reflection on the Shoah* (1998). Along with statements from national and local episcopates, these directives now guide the Church in its teaching about Jews and Judaism. They reject proselytism, repudiate **antisemitism** and call Christians to **repentance**. Roman Catholic dioceses and parishes throughout the world are gradually implementing these directives into their teaching and ministries. Meanwhile, in-depth dialogue continues on historical, theological and pastoral themes which include concerns regarding scripture, **Christology**, soteriology, evangelisation and **liturgy**. These efforts in dialogue are strengthened by the Commission's partnership with the International Jewish Committee for Interreligious Consultation (IJCIC), and by national and international Roman Catholic participation in the International **Council of Christians and Jews** (ICCJ).

Trust of the other, fostered by several decades of honest and open dialogue, has enabled Roman Catholics and the international Jewish community to engage constructively on such conflictual issues as: the beatifications and **canonisations** of Pope Pius XII, Pope **Pius IX** and Edith **Stein**; the **Carmelite controversy** at Auschwitz; the papal receptions of such controversial figures as Kurt Waldheim (b. 1918) and Yasser Arafat (1929–2004); and the opening of the Vatican archives on the Second World War. It also helped sustain the Roman Catholic–Jewish relationship in the years leading up to the Fundamental Agreement (30 December 1993) and Diplomatic Exchange (15 June 1994) between the Holy See and the **State of Israel**. The delay raised in Jewish memories Pope Pius X's response to Theodor **Herzl** in 1904 and Pope Pius XII's refusal to support the emigration of Jews to Palestine during the Holocaust.

The September 2000 *Dabru Emet* response by an interdenominational group of rabbis and Jewish scholars to these late twentieth-century changes in Christianity bears witness that a mutual enterprise of renewal and reconciliation is in process. Speaking more powerfully of this changed and changing relationship than political negotiations and theological reformulations are the profound symbolic moments when a deeply moved Pope John XXIII, upon meeting a group of grateful Jewish leaders, extended his arms and greeted them with 'I am Joseph your brother' (1960), when Pope John Paul II visited the Great Synagogue of Rome (1986), and when this same pope, during his visit to **Jerusalem** (2000), wept at Yad Vashem and stood in silent prayer at the Western Wall. These moments impress upon the pages of history the reality of a new sibling relationship, Roman Catholic respect for the Jewish religion, a repudiation of triumphalism, and a humble admission of the Church's weakness, error and sin. *AUDREY DOETZEL*

Roman Empire see Rome, Roman Empire

Romanos Melodos (*fl.* sixth century)

Byzantine hymnographer. Renowned as Byzantium's greatest liturgical poet, Romanos was born in Emesa in the late fifth century, quite possibly to Jewish parents. He eventually settled in Constantinople in the early sixth century and died sometime after 555. Romanos is credited with the composition of a prodigious number of hymns, including the famous Akathist Hymn to the Mother of God, of which only about 60 survive that are generally accounted genuine. The hymns are known as *kontakia* and consist of a short prelude followed by a number of longer strophes in identical metre, separated by a repeated refrain, and united by an acrostic. In terms of poetic form there are affinities with the poetry of **Ephrem** and, arguably, with Hebrew liturgical poetry (*piyyut*). Romanos's hymns deal mainly with biblical events and reveal him as a loyal supporter of the policy of enforced Christian orthodoxy vigorously pursued by the Emperor **Justinian**. For all his zeal against Christian heretics, Romanos displays a remarkably temperate attitude to the Jews at a time when official **toleration** was appearing increasingly reluctant. Romanos has no doubts that the Jews are in error, but accepts that at the Last Day they will be judged according to the **Law** (cf. Rom. 2.12). They will certainly bewail their error in not recognising **Christ** and confessing the **Trinity**, but they will not be punished for it. Equally, in his treatment of the passion of Christ he singularly fails to lambast 'the Jews', preferring the less inflammatory 'the lawless'. In advocating a position that upholds the integrity of the Christian revelation without denying the ongoing special dispensation accorded to the Jews, Romanos represents a significant and constructive voice of continuing relevance. *MARCUS PLESTED*

Romans 9–11

Paul of Tarsus wrote to the Christian community of **Rome** about 57–8, in anticipation of his first visit. This letter presents Paul's mature thought on a number of issues pertinent to Christian–Jewish relations. It has made a tremendous impact on Western Christianity.

Paul's thesis is that both Jews and Gentiles **sin** and fail to achieve the purpose of human existence and are under divine judgement. But the descent of God's wrath in judgement is offset by the work of Jesus, **Messiah** and **Son of God**. Through his self-giving in obedient love, **Jesus** merits divine blessings for all humanity. God's love (*agape*) is revealed through the presence of the **Holy Spirit**, enabling Christians to attain the destiny of sharing the risen life of Jesus. This new gift of **justification** moving toward the fullness of **salvation** does not contradict God's promises to Israel. Themes from the Jewish scriptures have been the basis for Paul's argument that **Abraham** is the model of believers and the father of those adopted into God's family through **baptism**. Romans 9–11 constitutes the longest **New Testament** reflection on the situation of the Jewish people and the relation of Gentile Christians to them. In contrast to 1 Thess. 2.14–16, the occasion is not so polemical and the issues are discussed at length. Using techniques from Jewish **preaching** and scriptural **exegesis**, Paul builds a case from **Torah**, Prophets and Writings for his analysis of the non-response of many Jews to the gospel.

Major themes that have been integrated by many generations of Christians into both **polemics** and genuine **dialogue** include the seven enduring characteristics of the Jewish people (9.4–5; absence of a verb implies present tense), the mystery of election favouring the unlikely younger sons (**Isaac** and **Jacob**) in relation to divine mercy (9.6–29, see 11.30–2) and **righteousness** grounded on faith (9.30–3; see 3.21–4.25). Christ is the *telos* (end, goal) of the Law (10.4) in relation to **Moses** and Jonah (10.6–8 in light of *Targum Neofiti* on Deut. 30.12–13). Isa. 65.1–2 is interpreted as contrasting the favorable lot of Gentile Christians with 'a disobedient and contentious people' (Septuagint) in Rom. 10.19–21. God has not rejected his people (11.1) but a remnant has always remained faithful (10.2–10). The positive response of Gentiles to the gospel should make Jews jealous (11.11, 14) for all are sanctified by the first fruits and the root of the cultivated olive tree to which Gentiles are grafted (11.16–24). When 'the full number of the Gentiles comes in all Israel will be saved'; they are beloved because of the patriarchs, 'for the gifts and the calling of God are irrevocable' (11.25–9). Ultimately, this is a mystery whose solution is reserved to God (11.33–6).

Origen offered the first extant **commentary** on Romans, during his time in Caesarea, after 230; it survives in extensive **Greek** fragments and in Rufinus's (?345–410) translation into **Latin**. Origen believed that Paul addressed Gentile Christians 'to demonstrate that salvation is from the Jews, the Law being the foundation on which the truth of Christ is built' (Peter Gorday, *Principles of Patristic Exegesis*, 50). He considered that Paul intended to pray in Rom. 9.3–4 for the true Israel, composed of those 'who see God', Abraham's spiritual progeny. Rom. 9:24 shows that divine mercy has reached an outcast people, the Gentiles and ultimately to every human heart that is ready to respond (Gorday, 78). Origen uses Rom. 11.25 in reference to the purification of every soul (*Hom. Jos.* 8.4–5) and to speak of the eventual reconciliation of the Church and the synagogue (*Hom. Num.* 6.4).

As a priest in **Antioch** in 386–97, John **Chrysostom** preached 32 homilies on Romans. Against Jews who complain that God is unfaithful to them, he showed that Paul argued that God is faithful. The anti-Jewish tone of these homilies is an echo of his eight virulent sermons against the Jews of the city.

Augustine of Hippo did not complete a commentary on Romans but reflected on Israel's destiny in the *City of God*, letters and sermons. Just as Esau was supplanted by Jacob, so Israel's blindness regarding the Messiah serves Christians. A day will come at the end of time when there will be one people (*Sermon* 122). In arguing against Pelagius (late fourth–early fifth century), who emphasised the importance of good works, Augustine castigated the Jews for their supposed adherence to works in contrast to Paul's theology of **grace** as the foundation for salvation. The Israel that will be saved (Rom. 11.25–26) are the predestined elect, Jews and Gentiles, called into unity.

Augustine's influence on the issue of 'grace versus works', with its negative view of the Jewish position, came to the fore in the writings of Martin **Luther** and John **Calvin**. In his commentary of 1515–16 Luther is very negative about the fate of the Jews. In an irenic appeal to the Jews in 1523 (*That Jesus Christ Was Born a Jew*) he commented on Rom. 11.25 as a call for the **conversion** of the Jews at the end of time, which he hoped would come soon. Later he returned to his previous stance, referring to the obscurity of Rom. 11. Commenting on Isa. 59:20 (quoted in Rom. 11.26), Calvin spoke of the indomitable obstinacy of the Jews and opined that only a remnant would come finally to Christ. The Reformers were heirs of a general anti-Jewish prejudice that interfered with an effort to grapple with Paul's message.

In his epochal commentary on Romans (1919) Karl Barth (1886–1968) did not dwell on 'the Jewish question', but reacting to Kristallnacht of 9–10 November 1938 he wrote in 1939 that the Church cannot be separated from Israel (referring to Rom. 11.17–24). In 1944 the Swiss Catholic theologian Charles Journet (1891–1975) published a work that lamented the tragedy of the ***Shoah*** and presented a response to Léon Bloy's (1846–1917) *Salut par les juifs* (1892). He reviewed the positions of earlier interpreters on Rom. 9–11 and presented his own synthesis: 'The full number of the Gentiles' in Rom. 11.25 refers to nations, not individuals; so 'all Israel' in 11.26 designates not all individually but the mass of the people, in contrast to those already converted. Will this return bring history to its consummation? Rather, this reintegration may fall within history and influence its development for centuries to come; then in Rom. 11.15 'resurrection from the dead' would not be the resurrection for final judgement but an outpouring of divine love comparable to a return of the dead to life. Journet's and other European studies of Rom. 9–11 since the Nazi period have begun to elucidate how Christians may place Paul's theology of Jews and Judaism in a modern context.

Declarations of many Churches on Christian–Jewish relations draw upon themes of Romans as a foundation for sensitivity to the place of the Jewish people in the divine plan of salvation. Thus **Vatican II**'s 'Declaration on the Church's Relationship to Non-Christian Religions' (***Nostra Aetate*** 4) recognises that Christians are Abraham's children according to faith. They have been grafted onto the good olive tree, drawing sustenance from its root. The privileges of Israel (9.4–5) perdure because 'the Jews still remain most dear to God because of their Fathers', for the divine gifts and calling are irrevocable. References regarding Jews and Judaism in the New Testament must be studied in context and integrated into a theological synthesis that takes into account the vicissitudes of subsequent history. *LAWRENCE E. FRIZZELL*

Rome, Roman Empire

The history of ancient Rome is traditionally divided into three periods: regal (753–509 BCE), republican (509–31 BCE) and imperial (31 BCE–476 CE). The **Byzantine Empire**, the name for the Roman Empire that survived in the East, lasted until 1453. Although Jewish contacts with the Romans date back to the second century BCE, Christian history begins only in the imperial age, and it is therefore this period that is most relevant for the history of Jewish–Christian relations. The significance of the Roman Empire lies in the fact that it constituted the political and legal framework within which the two communities lived and interacted with each other during the formative period. Before the time of **Constantine** this interaction took place primarily outside Palestine, so it is the setting of the **Diaspora** (to employ Jewish terms) that is of major concern here.

Under the **Hellenistic** kings Jewish communities in the Diaspora seem to have enjoyed a recognised legal status as independent ethnic units, often alongside a Greek *polis*. Under the Roman Empire this situation may have gradually changed, especially as more and more Jews, at first within the city of Rome but also outside it as time went on, became Roman citizens. Accordingly, Jews came to be recognised not so much as members of a national community, but as members of legal *collegia* or associations, which in many cases no doubt took the form of synagogues. When **Tertullian** speaks of Judaism, he speaks of a *religio licita*, or a legal religion (*Apol.* 21.1). Christians, on the other hand, as they came to be distinguished from Jews by the Roman authorities, did not enjoy a similar legal status. Indeed, they were often persecuted, although the actual legal grounds for this, at least before the time of Decius (*r.*249–51), may be buried deep within Roman bureaucratic operations. It is remarkable that Pliny, who served as the Roman governor of Bithynia (*c.*110–12), seems to have persecuted Christians on the basis of precedent without knowing the precise reason for doing so (Pliny, *Ep.* 10.96). The difference in legal status of the two communi-

ties was significant for the development of Jewish–Christian relations for many reasons, but perhaps chief among them is the fact that it gave a concrete political expression to the broader cultural principle of *presbyteron kreitton* or 'older is better'. For the formal recognition of the Jewish religion was connected with its venerable antiquity, whereas Christianity seems to have been unable to obtain a similar recognition (whatever the reason for the original persecutions) largely because of its 'novelty' and lack of an ancestral foundation or **tradition**. This circumstance goes a long way in explaining why the **Church Fathers**, even as they defined Christians as a *tertium genus* or 'third race', needed to maintain a claim on Jewish tradition and acknowledge their historical links to it.

With the Edict of Milan (313 CE) and the conversion of Constantine to Christianity this situation changed. Christianity came to be tolerated and later favoured by the Roman government. The status of Judaism, on the other hand, suffered certain setbacks, a fact observable in the legislation preserved in the **Theodosian Code** and in the codification of **Justinian**. Indeed, the late Roman laws sanction the verity of Christian orthodoxy, as opposed to the 'error' of Judaism, heralding medieval conceptions. Nevertheless, the exercise of the Jewish religion, in contrast to that of pagan cults, was not banned, and some legal measures may have even strengthened or at least consolidated the position of Judaism in the Empire and consequently vis-à-vis Christianity. *ADAM KAMESAR*

Rosenstock-Huessy, Eugen (1888–1973)

Law historian and critic. Born to Jewish parents, Rosenstock was baptised at the age of 16. He worked as an academic and subsequently in business in Leipzig, Frankfurt and Breslau, emigrating to the United States in 1934. His influence on Franz **Rosenzweig** was important for Jewish–Christian relations: in 1913 Rosenstock, a strong advocate of **revelation**, urged Rosenzweig as a representative of philosophy to abandon his faith in reason and be baptised; Rosenzweig, accepting his Jewishness as a cultural reality, found his way to the Judaism of faith instead. This exchange became the topic of an uncompromising correspondence in 1916: Rosenstock was convinced that Christianity had a civilisational **mission**, even vis-à-vis Judaism, while Rosenzweig insisted that Judaism and Christianity have equal status in their relationship to the truth.   *HANS HERMANN HENRIX*

Rosenzweig, Franz (1886–1929)

Jewish philosopher. Emmanuel Levinas (1906–95) praised him for being the first to say that truth can exist in two forms, in Judaism and in Christianity. Rosenzweig asserted the equality of both forms and justified this understanding in his magnum opus *The Star of Redemption* (1921).

Born in Kassel (Hesse), Rosenzweig's early years were not spent with practising Jews. 1913 was a fateful year for him: in debates with his close cousins Hans (1883–1958) and Rudolf Ehrenberg (1884–1969) and his friend Eugen **Rosenstock-Huessy**, all of whom had converted to Christianity, he likewise faced the decision of whether to be baptised. However, he did not want to take this step as a 'pagan', a representative of reason and philosophy, but as a Jew. He thus began to study the origins of Judaism and consciously participated in the High Holy Days services. He wrote to his cousin Rudolf: 'So I will remain a Jew . . . We agree upon the meaning of Christ and His Church in the world: No one comes to the Father except through him. No one *comes* to the Father – but it is different if one does not have to come to the Father because he or she *is* with Him already. And that is the case with the people of Israel (not the individual Jew)' (*Gesammelte Schriften I*, 132ff.).

Rosenzweig's 1913 decision, for Judaism as **revelation** and against **baptism**, determined his entire life and way of thinking. The *Star*, which he drafted on army postcards on the Balkan front between 1916 and 1918 and completed in book form in 1919, represents the sum and substance of his thought. He decided not to pursue an academic career, contacted Hermann **Cohen** and devoted himself to adult education. Despite degenerative illness, he kept up an extensive correspondence, translated poems by **Judah ha-Levi** and worked on a translation of the Bible with Martin **Buber**, a friend since 1921, until his death.

Rosenzweig's thought has had a deeper impact on Jewish self-awareness than, for instance, that of Buber. He made significant contributions to the rediscovery of Jewish authenticity and to the clarification of the relationship between Judaism and Christianity. His *Star* deals with God, World and Humankind: creation or 'the past' takes place in the relationship between God and World; revelation or 'the present' in the relationship between God and Humankind; and **redemption** or 'the future' in the relationship between Humankind and World. Redemption is the 'situation in which the "I" learns to say "you" to a "him or her"' and anticipates eternity. Judaism anticipates redemption as an eternal *people* who (as the inner fire of the star of redemption) live eternity now in the yearly course of liturgical feasts and prayers. Christianity creates community across all nations as an eternal *way* (the rays of the star) and lives the anticipation of the **kingdom of God** in that way. The entire truth is neither in the Jewish people nor in the Christian way: only 'God is truth' (*The Star of Redemption, II*, 423). Jews and Christians have separate missions, but only together do they form the star of redemption.

Contemporary attempts in Christian theology and the Jewish philosophy of religion to conceptualise the relationship between Judaism and Christianity refer in a fundamental way to Rosenzweig. He made **prayer** and the **liturgy** the centre of his magnum opus ('prayer establishes the human world order': *ibid.*, 268). Both Jewish and Christian thinkers (Levinas, Bernhard Casper (b. 1931) and others) have followed his lead, seeing in prayer the expectation of the kingdom of God.

HANS HERMANN HENRIX

Rozanov, Vasily Vasilyevich (1856–1919)

Russian conservative writer and journalist who wrote on the Jewish question, combining Judeophilia with Judeophobia. In his books Rozanov admired Judaism as a religion of flesh and sex, preferring it to 'fruitless' Christianity which 'rejected life' (*Solitaria*, 1912 and 1916; *The Dark Face: A Metaphysics of Christianity*, 1911, *People of Moonlight*, 1913). However, modern Jewry was in his opinion a threat to the organic basis of Russian life embodied in grass-roots Orthodoxy and monarchy. The resulting dualism towards the Jews was reflected in *The Fallen Leaves* (1912 and 1915). During the Beilis trial of 1913 Rozanov published a series of strongly **antisemitic** articles later gathered in *The Olfactory and Tactile Relation of Jews to Blood* (1914). He supported the **blood libel** precisely because he saw in Judaism a 'natural religion' connected intimately with blood. Publication of his next book of essays on the alleged seizure of Russian economy and culture by the Jews, *Sakharna*, was made impossible by the 1917 revolution.

MICHAEL WEISSKOPF

Russia

By the beginning of the twentieth century no less than half the world's Jewish population was located within the bounds of the Russian Empire. Most Russian Christians then belonged to the established Orthodox Church of the realm. Encounters between the two kinds of population were at best neutral.

For many centuries Jews and Christians were kept apart. In the early Middle Ages a small Jewish **minority** played little part in public life. From the sixteenth to the eighteenth centuries Russian rulers were unwilling to admit Jews to their realm at all. Only with the assimilation of **Poland** to the Russian crown under Catherine II (*r.*1762–96) did Jews become a major demographic factor in the western regions. In order to contain them, an extensive **Pale of Settlement** was established (1791), intended as a home from which the Jews might move to other (nominally Christian) areas only with permission. Such permission would be granted readily for those who chose to be baptised, and Alexander I (*r.*1801–25) published an edict to this effect in 1817. But this was hardly a procedure that predisposed anyone to **dialogue** between the faiths. In any case, there was often no common language to facilitate discussions of this or any other kind. Hebrew was needed for the studies and the worship of the Jews, Yiddish for diurnal life. Only a promoter of the *Haskalah* might urge that acquisition of other languages was proper for the Jewish population. Such was Itzhak Ber-Levinson (1786–1860), who was prepared to engage in Russian-language correspondence with representatives of Church and state. This involved his acceptance that there were Gentiles who should be considered 'pious men'. At the same time he was anxious to combat Jewish 'blood guilt' libels (*see* **blood libel**) and published a book on this theme (1837). In its Russian translation it was to remain in print until the trial of Mendel Beilis (1913). By that time it had demonstrated its relevance many times over, for the neutral encounters between the Christian and the Jewish populations of the realm were all too often punctuated by aggression vented by the Russians on the Jews. Not for nothing is the word **pogrom** derived from Russian roots. While the pogroms might be prompted by social and economic factors, they were also coloured by religious ignorance disguised as zeal. Accusations against individual Jews, like Beilis, of killing Christian children at Passover to use their blood for *mazzot* were repeatedly made, and believed, from the beginning of the eighteenth century. Further, it was generally believed that each and every Jew could be considered guilty of Christ's crucifixion (*see* **deicide, charge of**). Matt. 27.25 was used to justify this view, and the Orthodox Good Friday services confirmed it year by year. There were Church leaders who condemned the pogroms and made every effort to prevent recurrence of them. Among them was the most senior of Russian bishops, Antonii Vadkovskii (1846–1912), metropolitan of St Petersburg. Another bishop, Platon Rozhdestvenskii (1866–1934), faced a Kievan mob on his knees while endeavouring to still the pogrom of 1905. But there were other churchmen (like the monks of Pochaev) who fostered the venom of the day. In such a milieu there was a ready welcome for the ***Protocols of the Elders of Zion***, which first appeared under Russian auspices and on Russian soil (1903). Here, as elsewhere, **antisemitism** and **anti-Judaism** were equally involved. It was rare for an Orthodox Christian not only to counteract the former, but to rise above the other and welcome Judaism as it stands. This was the achievement of Nikolai Ziorov (1850–1915), Russian Orthodox archbishop of Warsaw, in 1912; Vladimir **Soloviev** had already pointed in the same direction. However, the succeeding age was to encourage little in the way of interreligious dialogue, since all religions were to be victims of the Soviet state. A new obstacle to any convergence between Judaism and Christianity was the myth that the Soviet government in its first years was predominantly Jewish, hence its persecution of the Russian Orthodox Church, a myth that ignored the Soviet persecution of Judaism in the period.

But the worst persecutions were yet to come. The Nazi invasion of the Soviet Union (1941) involved initiation of the ***Shoah*** in those parts of a newly expanded Soviet Union that were then inhabited by several million Jews. Belarus and Western **Ukraine** had been incorporated into the USSR (1939), as had Lithuania (1940). The fact that many Gentiles played their part in the extermination of their Jewish neighbours added yet another impediment to Christian–Jewish convergence which even the witness of the **Righteous Gentiles** was not strong enough to countermand. Nor did appraisal of the *Shoah*, which was delayed and muted in the FSU, affect Christian–Jewish relations there as it did in other parts of the world. There was never an equivalent climactic moment to **Vatican II**. Even Jews whose families had passed through the **Holocaust** were provided with little education on the experience. Rather, the Soviet authorities continued Stalin's black-out on specifically Jewish implications of the Nazi onslaught. The writings and monuments devoted to the subject dwelt on the victims exclusively as Soviet citizens.

All the more, therefore, were Christians left unchallenged in their attitudes to Judaism and to Jews. Furthermore, Soviet restrictions had long inhibited biblical research, and Russian Orthodox scholars were in no position to offer fresh assessments of such **New Testament** material as might fertilise Christian encounters with the Jewish world. In any case, there was a conservative and nationalistic streak in Russian Orthodox churchmanship that included the kind of antisemitism and anti-Judaism that fed on the *Protocols of the Elders of Zion* and other pamphlets of a bygone age. A range of semi-official groups promoted their ideology, among them a 'union of Orthodox brotherhoods' (1990) and a 'union of Orthodox banner-bearers'

(1993). Its most prominent spokesman was a recent metropolitan of St Petersburg, Ioann Snychev (1927–95), whose extremist views were never seriously disputed by his peers.

One incident which seemed to promise something different took place abroad when the patriarch of Moscow, Aleksii Ridiger (b. 1929) brought an address of reconciliation to a gathering of rabbis in New York (1991). It involved a generous acceptance of Judaism and its eternal values, and quoted the words of Archbishop Nikolai Ziorov, which the speaker accepted as his own. But the speech caused outrage in conservative Church circles in the home milieu. The patriarch feared a backlash and denied that his speech should be seen as 'programmatic'. He has not revisited the subject since. Only the occasional Jewish–Christian consultation at the grassroots level takes the matter further, sponsored on two occasions (St Petersburg, 1997 and 1998) by the International **Council for Christians and Jews**. Even so, each of the partners is burdened by the stubborn constraints of the past.

See also **literature, Russian; Orthodox Christianity**

SERGEI HACKEL

SSSS

Sabbatarianism

Doctrine that Christians should refrain from work on Sunday (the Christian **Sabbath**) in strict accordance with the fourth **commandment**; its radical implementation was occasionally associated with **Judaising** tendencies.

Scottish and English Reformers, including John Knox (*c*.1513–72), developed a uniquely rigorous Sabbatarianism unparalleled among Continental Reformers. Nicholas Bownde's (d. 1613) *The Doctrine of the Sabbath* (1595) urged Sunday Sabbath-keeping according to **Old Testament** strictures; banned and burned, its teachings gained many adherents, including clergy. Sabbatarianism, a political issue in the struggle of Parliament against crown and Church, was attacked by Anglicans, including Peter Heylin (1599–1662) in *The History of the Sabbath* (1636) and Archbishop Laud (1573–1645), and by James I (*r*.1603–25), whose controversial *Book of Sport*, imposed in 1618 and republished in 1633 under Charles I (*r*.1625–49), urged Sunday recreational sports. Parliament burned James's *Book* in 1645 and legislated to impose the Puritan Sabbath. Puritan **iconoclasm** replaced the traditional Church **calendar** with scrupulous Sunday observance, the strict Sabbath becoming the defining Puritan hallmark in England, the Netherlands and North America.

More extreme reformers, notably the clergyman John Traske (*c*.1585–1636), argued for Saturday-Sabbatarianism as biblically commanded moral law dating from creation, and therefore permanently valid. Though without known direct influence from Jews, Saturday Sabbath-keepers were accused of Judaising. (Despite Church prohibitions, some Christians, from Spain to Syria, had retained the Jewish Sabbath until the fifth and sixth centuries – in Lyons even until the ninth century.) Traske and his followers were harshly persecuted, imprisoned and heavily fined. Theologically, most retained orthodox Christian beliefs; some recanted, others became Baptists, a few fled and converted to Judaism in Amsterdam. Traske's example had far-reaching consequences; Henry Jessey (1603–63), a Saturday-Sabbatarian Baptist, championed Jewish readmission, corresponded with Rabbi **Menasseh ben Israel** and collected alms for Jerusalem Jews. Internationally, **Seventh-Day Adventists** (Protestants: membership three million worldwide) still rigorously observe Saturday as Sabbath. *MARGARET BREARLEY*

Sabbath

The key questions about the Sabbath in Jewish–Christian relations concern the purpose of the day. Is the Sabbath mainly a day of rest or a day of **worship**? Is there some connection between rest and celebration and, if so, what is it? The answers given to these questions raise vital issues of continuity and discontinuity between the two religions.

The word 'Sabbath' translates the Hebrew *Shabbat* from the Hebrew root *shavat*, 'to cease'. Resting from creative work in order to remember God as creator is the purpose of this festival. The day is observed from Friday sunset until Saturday nightfall, day following night in the Jewish calendar (deriving from the account of **creation** in Gen. 1.1–2.4a). The Sabbath is the only festival to be mentioned in the **decalogue**, in both versions of the fourth commandment (Exod. 20.8–11; Deut. 5.14–15). In Exodus the reason given is that God ceased from his work of creation on the seventh day (Gen. 2.2–3), thus creating a **holy** day. In Deuteronomy the benefits of rest are linked to **redemption**. The freedom to rest was given to the Israelites by God's redeeming them from slavery in Egypt. Recognising the need for rest from work, they must therefore ensure that all have this day of rest. Thus the Sabbath is seen as God's gift to his people, and the Sabbath **liturgy** speaks of God's hallowing this day as a remembrance of both the work of creation and the exodus from Egypt. The opening *Kiddush* and closing *Havdalah* ceremonies set it aside as a holy, that is, separate day. Not Saturday but Sunday is the weekly festival of Christians, in celebration of the **resurrection**. Nonetheless, elements of the Jewish Sabbath have been incorporated into the Christian Sunday at various periods in the history of Christianity, sometimes leading to confusion in the popular understanding of both Sabbath and Sunday.

The **New Testament** references to the Sabbath are of particular importance in Jewish–Christian relations. In many Gospel passages Jesus is depicted as coming into conflict with Pharisaic Judaism for breaking the rules of Sabbath observance. From these accounts have come perpetual misrepresentations by Christians of Jews being legalistic in the sense of being more concerned with detailed rules than with their purpose. Jesus is presented as needing to draw the attention of his fellow-Jews to the fact that 'the sabbath was made for humankind, and not humankind for the sabbath' (Mark 2.27). Christians often miss the thoroughly Jewish sentiment of this dictum. 'The Sabbath is given to you, not you to the Sabbath' appears in **midrash** (*Mekhilta* 31.14) and **Talmud** (*b. Yoma* 85b). Further possibilities for misunderstandings between Jews and Christians arise from the fact that in some of these so-called 'conflict stories' in the Gospels what Jesus is purportedly accused of would not in reality have been judged by his critics as breaking the Sabbath at all (e.g. healing, as in Matt. 12.9–14; John 7.19–24). This is best explained by remembering that by the time the Gospels were being written their authors wanted polemically to distance the emergent new religion of Christianity from Judaism. Matthew's predominantly **Jewish-Christian** community, it may be surmised, observed the Sabbath and came into conflict with other Jews as to what was allowed on that day. This has a bearing on the whole vexed issue of the Jewishness of Jesus' teaching and the degree to which he intended to supersede Jewish **Law**. On the one hand Jews dislike the caricature of the **Pharisees** in the past and themselves in the present as people missing the point of God's commands. On the other hand many Christians are not convinced by the suggestion that Jesus was at one with the Pharisees in his attitude to the law, particularly as it pertained to the Sabbath. (The debate has implications for the whole position of law in the theology of **Paul**.)

The following assertions are often made about the Sabbath: Sabbath was a cornerstone of religious practice in ancient **Israel**; Sabbath was a day of worship for Jews in Old Testament times; Jews worshipped in synagogues on the Sabbath in New Testament times; Jesus of Nazareth attended regular worship in synagogues on the Sabbath. Heather McKay has significantly challenged all of these (*Sabbath and Synagogue*) and concludes that any degree of certainty should rather be reserved for the following claims: the Sabbath became the most important holy day in Israel during the last two centuries BCE; the Sabbath was not a day of worship for the ordinary Jewish believer in Old Testament times; Jews studied in the synagogue on the Sabbath in first-century Palestine, but worship is not described; Jesus did not attend Sabbath services of worship, for there were none at that time. This may make too sharp a distinction between study and **prayer**, and thus underestimate the part played by study in Jewish worship. Whether all McKay's conclusions are accepted largely depends on how prayer and worship are defined. However, she issues a valuable warning against assumptions, some of which may cloud Jewish–Christian relations.

There is debate about when the Jewish Christians of New Testament times stopped observing the Sabbath, when they began observing Sunday, and what they transferred from Sabbath to Sunday observance. It is unlikely that Gentile Christians had an interest in adhering to the work restrictions of Judaism, but just what elements constituted Christian worship and exactly when they took place is difficult to establish. From the biblical texts that mention Sunday (Acts 20.7–12; 1 Cor. 16.2; Rev. 1.10) scholars come to varied conclusions. The **Seventh-Day Adventist** Samuele Bacchiocchi (b. 1938), for instance, maintains that Sunday observance began only in the second century CE (*From Sabbath to Sunday*), whilst most scholars believe that in the first century Christians chose to differentiate themselves from Jews by beginning the first day of the week on Saturday evening with a **eucharist**. Once **Easter** began to be celebrated on a Sunday, there also appears to be variation in Christian observance of **fasting** and vigils associated with Jewish **Passover** activities. (In Syria and Egypt, for example, third-century Christians extended a Saturday fast back by two days.) This has a bearing on what later Christian groups have taken from the Jewish Sabbath. **Sabbatarianism** judged the fourth commandment to be binding on Christians, claiming that 'the Christian observance of Sunday has its basis not in ecclesiastical tradition but in the decalogue' (P. Collinson, *Godly People*, 429). In mid-seventeenth-century England Puritan rulers introduced short-lived laws banning any form of recreation on Sunday, taken to be the Sabbath. This point of view is today represented by the Lord's Day Observance Society. Besides representing a **supersessionist** view in taking upon itself a uniquely Jewish **commandment**, it seems also to miss the key purpose of the Jewish Sabbath which is precisely to 'recreate' the human spirit by freeing time to concentrate on God. Whether in home or synagogue, Jewish observance is characterised by joy rather than avoidance of anything pleasurable. The Jewish idea of resting in order to focus on God as creator has made it possible for Christians to apply the Sabbath commandment to the observance of Sunday. Establishing the common ground between their respective holy days as a weekly opportunity to celebrate key theological themes of both faiths, notably reassurance and hope, and the need for recreation in relation to each other and the created world, may also be seen as an opportunity for greater closeness in Jewish–Christian relations.

CHRISTINE PILKINGTON

Sacrament

In contemporary Christian practice a sacrament refers to a specific liturgical rite. The majority of Christian communities accept **baptism** and **eucharist** as sacraments, while Roman Catholics along with some other Christians add confirmation, **marriage**, orders, **penance** and the **anointing** of the sick to the number of sacraments. However, early Christian writers often described the whole ensemble of their liturgical practices as mysteries (Greek, *mysterion*; Latin, *mysterium* or *sacramentum*). The word *mysterion* and some of its synonyms does appear in some post-exilic books of the **Hebrew Bible**, where it refers to the plan of God for the **salvation** of humanity and the **revelation** of that plan by an angel, a prophet or even God. **Paul** takes up this meaning and mainly uses the word to indicate that **Jesus** is the revelation of the saving plan of God.

Systematic theology, aided by contemporary philosophy (especially phenomenology) and patristic scholars, has pushed beyond Aristotelian and neo-scholastic presentations of sacrament to an understanding of sacrament as founded in the person of Jesus and embodied in the Church. This has led to an abandonment of an earlier theology which saw sacraments as present in the Hebrew scriptures within a **typological** framework of promise and fulfilment. Contemporary theologians have again expanded their use of the word 'sacrament' to indicate any encounter or thing that mediates an experience of God. In this regard, in 2002 Cardinal Walter Kasper (b. 1933) described Judaism as 'a sacrament of every otherness that as such the Church must learn to discern, recognize and celebrate'. Since Judaism is not sacramental – and some would argue that it has no understanding of sacraments – such a comment is particularly striking.

LIAM M. TRACEY

Sacred space

Because Judaism and Christianity are revelatory religions operating within human history, the physical sites where defining events – births, deaths, miracles, visions, revelations, victories and defeats – are believed to have taken place are important. Such sites become sacred space: places for **pilgrimages**, the focus of devotion. For Christians and Jews questions of sacred space remain an integral part of interreligious relations, since sacred space is the place where divinity and humanity encountered one another and where God's power was revealed. But there are major differences between the two religions, especially in the dichotomy between the Christian view of **Jerusalem** as a 'heavenly' city and the importance given to the 'earthly' Jerusalem by Jews. Historically, these differences vis-à-vis Jerusalem have impacted directly upon Jewish–Christian relations. The entire city of Jerusalem is sacred space for Jews, not merely the holy places associated with Judaism; and since it is also the political capital of the **State of Israel**, Jewish sovereignty over the entire city is a religious as well as a political imperative. While Christians revere the city where **Jesus** died and was resurrected, their attachment is frequently to a spiritualised Jerusalem that transcends earthly existence; as a result, the issue of political sovereignty over Jerusalem is often less important to Christians than the existence of an internationally guaranteed statute that permits them to visit holy places in peace and security.

Since Christians believe Jesus is the fulfilment of the **Hebrew Bible**, he represents definitive sacred space. As a result, Christianity emphasises a strong spiritual perspective on holy places. Protestant scholar W. D. Davies (1911–2001) has called this Christian de-emphasis on geographical or terrestrial specificity 'disenlandisement', but on the other hand Walter Brueggemann feels that Christianity needs to develop a theology of land precisely because land is traditionally not central to Christian theology. The Christian approach to sacred space contrasts with the Jewish concept. Sacred space is a central motif of the Hebrew Bible, and in **Rabbinic Judaism** *makom*, the Hebrew for 'place', is another name for God. The hope expressed in many Jewish prayers is for the physical return of Jews to the divine presence in **Zion**, notably the remaining outer stone rampart of the Holy **Temple** – the Western Wall, a destination of Jewish pilgrims for centuries. Christians emphasise pilgrimages to sacred sites linked to the life and ministry of Jesus, particularly in Jerusalem, Bethlehem and the Galilee. But despite these differences, visits to sacred space, even if highly 'spiritualised', can be a profound religious experience for pilgrims of both faiths.

A. JAMES RUDIN

Sacrifice

While sacrifice (an offering) is something that is conceived as alien to contemporary Western society, it was a fundamental way to express human interaction, homage and relationship with the divine in the ancient world, Judaism and Christianity being no exception. In Judaism one can see various attitudes to sacrifice, from the idealised priestly theology of the books of Leviticus and Numbers to the sharp critical **rhetoric** of some of the prophetic writers. In post-biblical Judaism the study of sacrificial texts in the **Pentateuch** has ensured that the significance of sacrifice retains an important place, particularly in **Orthodox Judaism**, although clearly not as central as when the **Temple** stood.

For some of the writers of the **New Testament**, offering a material sacrifice was seen not as a Christian activity, but as associated with pagan cults or with the Jerusalem Temple. Yet the writings of **Paul** and deutero-Pauline are filled with spiritualised or bloodless sacrificial language and images. These texts can refer to the sacrifice of **Christ**, or envision Christians as a new **priesthood** or temple, or speak directly or indirectly of the sacrifice of Christians. For early Christians the whole of their lives were seen as a sacrifice of praise offered to God. Prayer and their central prayer of thanksgiving, the **eucharist**, was inevitably seen as part of the Christian sacrifice. This sacrifice or offering of praise was seen to be in direct contradiction to the blood sacrifices of Judaism and the contemporary Greco-Roman world, yet drew on some of the ideas of **Philo** and the Qumran community. The ***Didache*** sees the eucharist as fulfilling the 'pure sacrifice' of Mal. 1.11, a theme also taken up in **Justin Martyr** and often used in anti-Jewish **polemic**. Already in the writings of Justin Martyr we find the notion that the **bread** and **wine** of the eucharist fulfil the oblations of the Hebrew scriptures, and the Christian offering came to be seen as the offering of the bread and cup. Over the next centuries, especially in the post-Constantinian liturgical transformation, ever more use was made of the language of sacrifice found in the Hebrew scriptures, and even language from pagan cultic practices finds its way into Christian descriptions of the eucharist. Some recent scholarship has argued that a plurality of views – sacrificial and anti-sacrificial – are to be found in the early Christian movement and that even the use of sacrificial language may be an attempt to subvert the religious meaning of sacrifice away from its cultic connotations and to assert its ethical implications for the Christian believer. This view has similarities with the Progressive Jewish understanding of the biblical sacrifices that took place in **Jerusalem**: they were a step towards the rejection of a cultic religion and a move towards an ethical monotheism and a sacrifice of the heart.

LIAM M. TRACEY

Sacrifice of Isaac *see* binding of Isaac
Sadducees

Adherents of a first-century CE Jewish sect, listed by **Josephus** as one of the 'three philosophies' (alongside **Pharisees** and Essenes: *J. W.* 2.108–66). Sadducees are mentioned in the **New Testament** in **polemics** with **Jesus** (Mark 12.18–27 and parallels) and as members of the **Sanhedrin** that tried **Paul** (Acts 23.7–8). They first appear in **Jerusalem** in the second century BCE, when according to Josephus (*Ant.* 13.288–98) the Hasmonean kings converted to their sect. The Sadducees subsequently became a powerful faction in Judean politics, but seem not to have survived the destruction of Jerusalem in 70 CE (however, this may just reflect our lack of sources for the post-70 CE period). Sadducees were mainly wealthy aristocrats, but the assumption that they were all priests (or that all priests were Sadducees: a traditional extrapolation from Acts 5.17) has now been largely discarded (note that Josephus, a priest, was a Pharisee). The passage in Acts 23.7–8 certainly suggests that they were only partially in control of the Sanhedrin, and the same is likely to have applied to the Jerusalem **Temple**. Sadducees rejected the authority of ancestral traditions upheld by the Pharisees (their main opponents), relying exclusively on their own interpretation of scriptures; they also rejected (if our sources, largely anti-Sadducean, are to be trusted) divine providence, the existence of angels, the afterlife, resurrection and other related beliefs. Some passages of the **Dead Sea Scrolls** may reflect Sadducean origins. According to Josephus (*Ant.* 20.197–203), it was a Sadducee high priest, Ananus, that brought about the execution of **James, brother of Jesus**, leader of the Jerusalem Church, in 62 CE. It has been suggested that the Sadducees, as aristocrats, may have disliked James because of his preference for the poor (evident at least in the *Epistle of James*).

SACHA STERN

Saint James, Association of

Association of Hebrew-speaking Catholics in Israel (Mif'al Ya'aqov HaTsadik) named for St **James, brother of Jesus**. Founded in 1955 by the **Roman Catholic** Patriarch of Jerusalem for Catholics of Jewish origin and Catholics living in Jewish society in Israel, there are communities in the four major cities of **Jerusalem**, Tel Aviv-Jaffa, Haifa and Beer Sheba. Members give expression to their faith in **Hebrew**, with a profound appreciation of the Jewish roots of their faith and practice, and seek to understand the relationship between Christianity and contemporary Judaism, as well as the reality of the **State of Israel**. Members tend to see the Association as the revival of a Judeo-Christian community within a Jewish environment, recalling the earliest Church. Some of its leaders have been central figures in the Jewish–Christian **dialogue** in Israel, including the **Dominican** priests Bruno Hussar (1911–96) and Marcel Dubois (b. 1920). In August 2003 Pope John Paul II appointed the head of the Association, Benedictine Abbot Jean-Baptiste Gourion (b. 1934), himself of Jewish origin, auxiliary bishop to the Patriarch of Jerusalem, a move designed to strengthen the Hebrew-speaking Catholics in Israel. *DAVID M. NEUHAUS*

Sainthood

Historians and phenomenologists of religion consider sainthood to apply generally to persons of all religions who are leading or have led lives of heroic virtue. However, sainthood is primarily a Christian category, the term 'saints' (*hagioi*) having been used in Acts (e.g. 9.13, 32, 41) and by **Paul** (e.g. Rom. 12.13; 15.25) to refer to the entire Christian community, and during the patristic era to refer to exceptionally holy persons worthy of veneration. The cult of saints became increasingly elaborate during the Middle Ages, during which time the episcopacy and eventually the papacy controlled the declaration of sainthood through the formal process of **canonisation**. Sainthood plays a minor role in Judaism, which, given its lack of institutional hierarchy, has no official notion of sainthood. The Christian emphasis on holy individuals worthy of imitation and veneration is generally incompatible with Jewish focus on the people collectively. However, Judaism has always held up, in the Bible and in rabbinic literature, and continues to acknowledge, saintly persons held in high esteem for their extraordinary piety, goodness and **covenant** faithfulness through such categories as *hasid*, *kadosh* (set apart, separate, holy) and *tzaddik* (righteous one). There is a sense, particularly in communities influenced by traditions of Lurianic **Kabbalah** or by cults of saints in **Islam**, that there are saints who can act as heavenly intercessors – leading to such practices as worship at their graves. These similarities in Judaism and Christianity's expressions and appreciation of saintliness (lived **holiness**) are rooted in the call to the children of **Israel** in Lev. 19.2: 'Ye shall be holy; for I the Lord your God am holy.' Christianity's self-understanding is also shaped by this call to holiness which is extended to them through **New Testament** writers (e.g. 1 Pet. 1.15, 16; 1 Cor. 1.2; Eph. 1.4; 1 Thess. 4.3). To be near to God is to be holy; therefore saintliness, if not sainthood, is possible for all.

See also **righteousness**; **sanctification**; **Stein, Edith**
AUDREY DOETZEL

Saints *see* canonisation; sainthood
Salvation

Salvation is a key area for the Jewish–Christian encounter. The early Christian understanding of salvation was dependent upon Judaism, as demonstrated by the Hebrew word for salvation *yeshuah*, meaning 'divine deliverance'. It runs parallel to a range of related concepts such as 'redemption', and perhaps 'life after death'. The theme of deliverance is a significant one in the **Hebrew Bible**. It is associated with the need for deliverance from sickness (Ps. 6.4), danger (Ps. 10), captivity (Exod. 14.30) and, in particular, exile (Isa. 49.25). Ps. 33.16–19 explains that God alone brings about salvation. The theme is also significant in terms of ritual. On the seventh day of the festival of **Sukkot** is Hoshana Rabba, which includes prayers that ask God for salvation. In addition, Alan Unterman (b. 1942) argues that the concept of *mizvah* includes certain notions of punishment and reward that implies 'a doctrine of salvation by works rather than faith, [although] this does not necessarily imply a mechanistic view of salvation' (Unterman, *Jews*, 32).

Christians inherited much of this description of salvation. However, it was significantly modified by using the term to describe primarily the work of God in Christ, made possible by the life, death and resurrection of **Jesus**. Humanity is saved from five different problems and situations: these are (1) **sin** (Matt. 1.21), (2) judgement or condemnation (1 Pet. 4.17–18), (3) losing one's life (Mark 8.35), (4) death (Jas 5.20) and (5) the 'wrath of God' (Rom. 5.9). From these different images the doctrine of **atonement** and **redemption** emerged. For Christians in the Reformed tradition, the emphasis is upon 'salvation from hell', which is made possible by accepting the work of atonement that God performed in Christ on the cross or to use **Paul**'s instruction to the gaoler in Acts 16: 'Believe in the Lord Jesus, and you will be saved, you and your household.'

The Christian doctrine of salvation can be a major problem for constructive relations between Christians and Jews. Part of the reason for the animosity towards '**Messianic Jews**' (those Jews who have accepted Jesus as the Jewish **Messiah** and Saviour) is the sense that these groups are requiring Judaism to convert to Christianity otherwise they will not be saved. Hermann **Cohen** has argued that, on the topic of salvation, Judaism has the advantage over Christianity: the Jewish emphasis on the priority of **ethics** over belief means that ultimately people are judged by their behaviour, not by their beliefs, which are often determined by culture and can be muddled, confused and partial.

In recent years there has been a major debate in Christianity over 'soteriology' (the study of salvation). Alan Race (b. 1951) in 1982 organised the debate around three positions: '**exclusivism**' – salvation is only through conscious knowledge of the saving activity of Jesus; 'inclusivism' – salvation is only possible through Jesus, but Jesus can save faithful adherents of other faith traditions without their conscious recognition; and 'pluralism' – all the major faith traditions are different and independently authentic contexts of salvation. The debate has since generated a vast literature. Whereas Messianic Jews and Evangelicals tend to be exclusivists, inclusivism and pluralism are strategies that seek to redefine the language of salvation so it can respect the integrity of Judaism.

Some Jewish scholars have started to use the same taxonomy, for example, Dan Cohn-Sherbok (b. 1945) has described himself as a Jewish pluralist. There has been some interesting work exploring the concept of '**covenant**' between the two traditions, with some contemporary theologians talking of a 'two-covenant' approach, according to which Christ does not displace or supersede the covenant with Judaism. Other theologians have stressed how the '**Noachide laws**' are an inclusivist strategy within Judaism; they assume the truth of the 'symbol-system' of Judaism, but make provision for a moral Gentile.   *IAN MARKHAM*

Samaritans

An ethnic and religious group, whose members are few in numbers today (*c.*500 persons today live mainly in Nablus (ancient Shechem at the foot of Mt Gerizim) and outside Tel Aviv). They identify themselves as descendants of the tribes of Ephraim and Manasse, that is, those Jews who were not deported by the Assyrians in 722 BCE. They regard themselves as faithful to the ancient traditions; calling themselves *ha-Shamerim*, 'those keeping [the Law]'. Cultural and religious clashes between the Samaritans and those Jews who returned from the exile led Jews to accept neither their offer to help rebuild the **Temple**, nor their wish to convert to Judaism (2 Kgs 17.24; Ezra 4). They were regarded as idolatrous immigrants from Kuth and were not allowed to convert to Judaism.

In New Testament times the animosity was already proverbial (John 4.9; 8.48), which may well be the reason for the positive characterisation in the **parable** of the good Samaritan (Luke 10.33) and in the story about the ten lepers (Luke 17.16) – although the characterisation is not consistent (cf. Matt. 10.5; Luke 9.52f.). In early Christian missionary reflection the Samaritans played an influential role; they were understood as the first group outside the Jewish people that was proffered and accepted the Christian gospel. This is seen in both the programmatic verse in Acts 1.8 and the entire eighth chapter where Luke depicts the transition from Jews to Gentiles. Important also is the conversation between an anonymous Samaritan woman and the Johannine **Jesus** who encourages her to preach the gospel (John 4.39). *JESPER SVARTVIK*

Sanctification

As with the closely related concept of **holiness**, sanctification is important in both traditions, Christianity inheriting many central connotations from Judaism. In Jewish–Christian **dialogue**, however, it may be necessary to recognise that each religion has its distinctive emphases in interpreting the term. At the root of the concept is the notion that God alone is holy and that through him times, places, objects and people can become sanctified. The Hebrew *Kiddush* and the Greek *hagiasmos* denote a state or the outcome of an action or process. So the reciting of *Kiddush* declares the holy days as set aside by God, and the sanctification of **marriage** is expressed in the term *kiddushin*. Jews can be sanctified by God's **commandments** (e.g. in the blessing recited on kindling the **Sabbath** lights). A **priest**, in ancient Israel, was sanctified and needed to retain his sanctity (Lev. 21.6–8). God's name can be sanctified or hallowed as, in Christianity, in the **Lord's Prayer** and in Judaism in the so-called 'Mourner's Prayer', the *Kaddish*, whose opening words are: 'Magnified and sanctified be his great Name' and which is, in effect, a hymn of praise to God's kingship. In Judaism, *kedushat ha-Shem* ('the sanctification of the Name') becomes the third blessing of the daily **Amidah** ('the sanctification of the day', *kedushat ha-Yom* is the blessing used in the Sabbath or festival *Amidah*). **Kiddush ha-Shem** is also a term used in Judaism for **martyrdom**, and implies that the mysteriously holy God reveals himself in the reality of the martyr's faith, the martyr thus helping God by manifesting his presence in the world. In both Judaism and Christianity martyrs may be witnesses to their faith, standing firm against opposition from members of another faith; Jews have, for example,

often preferred martyrdom to forced **conversion** to Christianity.

On its own, the Hebrew word for 'sanctification', *Kedushah*, denotes a prayer celebrating God's majesty and glory. To join in this heavenly *sanctus* (the opening words of which are in Isa. 6.3) is regarded as the climax of the mystic's ecstasy, as seen in *Merkavah* **mysticism**. In the Old and New Testaments 'sanctification' carries a range of meanings. In the first instance the sense of God's separateness dominates (compare Rudolf Otto's (1869–1937) sense of the 'numinous' in *The Idea of the Holy*, 1923), but the connotation of morality soon comes through in injunctions accepted by both faith communities to 'be holy for I am holy' (a recurrent refrain, notably in Leviticus). **Jesus**' command in Matt. 5.48 ('Be perfect, therefore, as your heavenly Father is perfect') has been interpreted variously by Christian movements, notably Arminian groupings where the effort of the 'believer' over a lifetime is usually emphasised. In both Jewish and Christian traditions people can grow in holiness, whether suddenly or gradually. **Aquinas**, drawing on the Jewish concept of the sanctification of a whole people, conceived of the Israelites receiving 'sanctifying grace' through the gift of faith in God and his **revelation**. Quoting Isa. 26.12 and Hos. 13.9 to emphasise that sanctification comes from God rather than through human effort, Aquinas states that Christians are sanctified in **baptism** or at conversion from sin. Again the stress is on joining a community that is sanctified by God. Supremely in Christianity, sanctification is the work of the **Holy Spirit**. The **Lambeth Conference** of Anglican Bishops in 1988 emphasised the shared mission of Jews and Christians in sanctifying the world in the sense of promoting God's intended purposes of justice, peace and harmony. This manifestation of sanctification draws on the powerful Jewish concept of *tikkun olam*, variously rendered as 'mending', 'healing' or 'repairing' the world.

CHRISTINE PILKINGTON

Sanhedrin

Sanhedrin, a Hebraicised form of the Greek *sunedrion* (literally, 'sitting together'), Second Temple Judaism's legislative and judicial council in **Jerusalem**, appears differently in Christian and Jewish sources. The Church vilified the Sanhedrin as complicit in the death of **Jesus** and the persecution of his followers; the rabbinic system praised it;

Josephus mentions it in connection with the death of **James, the brother of Jesus**.

Discrepancies among the various early sources concerning the Sanhedrin's composition and responsibilities complicate any analysis. Mark 14.64 and Matt. 26.66 depict the Sanhedrin, led by the high priest and composed of chief priests, elders, **scribes** and, according to Acts and John, **Pharisees**, as seeking to kill Jesus (Mark 14.53–5) and suppress his followers; thus it epitomises Judaism's corruption. Rabbinic sources call the Sanhedrin the *Bet Din* ('house of judgement'), attest it had 71 members (see Num. 11.16) and mention two leaders, the *Nasi* (prince) and the *Av bet Din* (father of the house of judgement). Whereas these texts ascribe the office of *Nasi* to such figures – usually identified as Pharisees – as Hillel, his son Simon and his grandson **Gamaliel** I, Josephus (*Ant.* 20) and the **New Testament** (Matt. 26.5–6; John 11.49) assign the presidency of the Sanhedrin to the high priest. Whether the Sanhedrin had the power of capital punishment in the late Second Temple period remains debated. John 18.31 (cf. *Ant.* 20.9.1 and *b. Sanhedrin* 18a, 24b) claims that death sentences required Roman confirmation, but *m. Sanhedrin* 6.1–4 and *y. Sanhedrin* 24, 25 describe procedures for capital punishment. Some interpreters suggest that John sought to vilify the Jewish council by suggesting that the Sanhedrin would have executed Jesus themselves if they had the power. Josephus (*Ant.* 20.197–203) records that the high priest Ananus convened the Sanhedrin during an interregnum between Roman governors to condemn James the brother of Jesus and others for 'having transgressed the law', although it is not clear that the charge was the proclamation of Jesus. He also notes that 'those of the inhabitants of the city who were considered the most fair minded and were strict in the observance of the Law [Pharisees?] were offended by this'.

Jewish sources (*Sota* 9; *Echa Rabbati* on Lam. 5.15) lament the Sanhedrin's demise during the First Revolt, and Jewish leaders reconstituted the Sanhedrin in **Jamnia**, Tiberias, Usha and especially Beit She'arim where the institution lasted until the cessation of the Patriarchate in 425. Although Church assemblies (e.g. Acts 15, the Councils) bear some similarity to the Jerusalem Sanhedrin, there is no direct connection. Most Roman cities had councils or senates as well as law courts, and voluntary societies held administrative and disciplinary meetings. The **Samaritans** also had a 'supreme council' (*Ant.* 18.4.8).

In 1807 **Napoleon Bonaparte** convened a 'Grand Sanhedrin' modelled after rabbinic descriptions, to provide religious credibility to the assimilationist resolutions of the 'Assembly of Jewish Notables'. Six of the 12 issues it debated related directly to the interaction between Jews and their Christian neighbours and addressed traditional concerns regarding Jewish clannishness, divided loyalties, **intermarriage** and **usury**. At the time, the Sanhedrin generated considerable excitement, including condemnations from the **Lutheran** Church in Prussia and from the tsar who, encouraged by the Russian **Orthodox Church**, described Napoleon as the '**Anti-Christ** and the enemy of God' for liberating the Jews.
AMY-JILL LEVINE

Sarah

Wife of **Abraham**, mother of **Isaac**, and claimed by both Jews and Christians as their matriarch. Consequently, Sarah is both a point of contact for Jews and Christians and a point of separation. Sarah plays a role in five narratives recounted in Genesis. The focal point in her complex story is the fourth episode in which, by God's miraculous intervention, the infertile Sarah gives birth and so becomes the mother of the Jewish people. Thus she plays an essential role in the fulfilment of God's **covenantal** promise. The other incidents provide a context for this fourth episode. The **New Testament** adds additional layers to the Christian interpretation of Sarah, and parts of **Paul**'s treatment of Sarah in Romans and Galatians seem to separate her from the Jewish people and thus undermine her potential as a bond between Jews and Christians.

The biblical account of Sarah raises many troubling issues for contemporary readers, in part because it reflects the worldview of patriarchal society at the time of Abraham and of the composition and compilation of Genesis. While Sarah has the prestige of being the first matriarch, she is certainly not an equal to or partner of Abraham and she is described primarily in terms of her relationships with and attractiveness to men. She is a victim of the limitations imposed on women in her society and she in turn victimises her slave **Hagar**. The story of Sarah raises other disturbing questions because it takes for granted the institution of slavery. As a slave, Hagar is treated as property – given to Abraham as a concubine, mistreated and then discarded.

The New Testament contains several references to Sarah. In Rom. 4.19 Paul praises Abraham for his faith in the divine promise of progeny, even though both he and Sarah are too old to have children, and treats Sarah's barrenness as a challenge to Abraham's faith. 1 Pet. 3.6 cites Sarah as a model of wifely submission to her husband. In the New Testament too, therefore, Sarah is described in terms of her relationship to men. Heb. 11.11 offers some redress of the balance by focusing on Sarah rather than on Abraham and by praising her faith in the divine promise.

Paul's treatment of Sarah presents great challenges to those concerned to promote positive relations between Christians and Jews. He cites the story of Abraham and Sarah to illustrate and explain his understanding of God's covenantal promises, of election as God's free act, and of **justification** by faith. In Galatians Paul allegorises the story of Sarah and Hagar in order to illustrate his understanding of faith and election. He not only appears to separate her from the Jewish people – or at least from some of the Jewish people – but also to appropriate her as the mother of Christians only. This may not have been his intention – this **allegory**, employing as it does forms of argument common among Jews of Paul's day, drawing on **midrash** and at times using exaggeration and irony, is one of the most difficult passages in the entire body of Paul's writings, and its interpretation remains a subject of scholarly debate – but whatever Paul's intention, some later Christian writers did in fact claim that Christians have replaced Jews as the children of Abraham and Sarah, thus making Sarah a symbol of supersession.

In recent decades there has been a growing interest in the study of the women of the Bible, especially among **feminists**. As both Jewish and Christian scholars try to recover and understand the role of women in their traditions, Sarah has become a point of convergence for Jewish and Christian feminist scholars who are rediscovering her voice and offering new and sometimes radical interpretations. For instance, developing the midrash in *Genesis Rabbah* that Sarah died immediately after the episode of the **binding of Isaac**, Christian theologian Phylis Trible wrote an influential essay entitled 'The Sacrifice of Sarah' (1999), while Jewish scholar Ellen Umansky

in *Weaving the Visions* (1989) 'revisions' Sarah, also via midrash. Finally, a growing number of Christians have come to reject theologies of **supersessionism** and **replacement**, and feminist scholars in particular may find a shared heritage as children of Sarah.

JOANN SPILLMAN

Sardis

The synagogue in Sardis, a major urban centre in south-western **Asia Minor** (modern-day Turkey) has played a major pioneering role in the re-evaluation of Jewish–Christian relations in Late Antiquity. Discovered in 1961, this very impressive structure was located on the city's main thoroughfare, occupying a wing of the municipal bath-gymnasium complex. The building was c.80 m long; in its final stage it was subdivided into a 60 m-long sanctuary and a 20 m-long atrium. The remains of its extraordinarily rich interior include an elaborate courtyard with a fountain, two *aediculae* (one of which undoubtedly housed Torah scrolls), a massive stone table with Roman-style eagles engraved in relief on each of its two supporting stones, a lavish mosaic floor and a three-tiered semicircular bench at the western end of the hall. Remains of 19 *menorot* were found along with 86 **inscriptions** (79 of which are in **Greek**).

The synagogue was initially dated to the late second and early third centuries, but recent studies have suggested a late third- and fourth-century context. The building as we see it today is largely a product of extensive renovations conducted in the latter half of the fourth century, that is, a clearly **Byzantine** setting, and it remained as such until the fall of the city to the Persians in 616 CE. The Sardis synagogue is the first and most dramatic archaeological testimony for the continued presence and acceptance of a Jewish community even after Christianity had become the dominant force in society. The degree of **tolerance** and acceptance reflected in this and several subsequent archaeological remains goes a long way in balancing the rather negative picture of Jewish–Christian relations portrayed in contemporary literary sources, such as the **Church Fathers** and some imperial edicts. There is no more striking example of the contrast in attitudes toward the Jews than the comparison of the impressive Sardis synagogue remains with the harsh anti-Jewish **polemic** preached by **Melito**, bishop of Sardis in the second century. His condemnation of the Jews and Judaism was not reflective of the city's population generally (to wit, the synagogue enjoyed a prominent position on the urban landscape throughout Late Antiquity), of the Christian laity, at least in the Byzantine period, or of the involvement of members of the Jewish community in political affairs. The inscriptions found at the site reveal that 16 synagogue donors identified themselves as citizens of Sardis and 9 as members of the city council; 3 others held imperial posts, and 6 were referred to as *theosebeis* (godfearers, or Gentiles (Christians?) who associated with the synagogue). Finally, it has even been suggested that the community itself might not have been Jewish, but was rather a non-Jewish association closely related to Judaism.

See also **architecture**   *LEE I. LEVINE*

Satan *see* **demon/devil**

Scandinavia

There are indications of Jewish–Scandinavian encounters during the Viking period, but it was not until the seventeenth century that Jews were allowed to settle in Scandinavia (Denmark 1619; Sweden 1774). Although the ways to estimate the size of the Jewish population differ (according to the *American Jewish Year Book* 2000: Denmark 6,400; Finland 1,100; Norway 1,200; Sweden 15,000), Scandinavian Jewry is comparatively small and well integrated. This may also explain the wave of sympathy with the fate of Scandinavian Jewry during the Second World War, which made possible the rescue of some 7,500 Danish Jews who, in spite of German occupation, in October 1943 were smuggled to Sweden in small boats, thereby escaping the fate of the Norwegian Jews.

In the autumn of 1942 the Norwegian Nazi party leader Vidkun Quisling (1887–1945) ordered the deportation of the Norwegian Jews. Thus, almost all of those who had not escaped the country perished. Finnish soldiers – among them Jews – fought the Soviet Union, that is, on the same side as German soldiers. Paradoxically, a number of Jewish soldiers were awarded the German Iron Cross (although refusing to accept it), and a tent served as a Finnish field synagogue with a Torah Scroll for the Nyland brigade ('Scholka's shul').

In the postwar era Jewish–Christian relations have improved, perhaps more in Sweden than in the other countries. There are local **Councils of Christian and Jews** in Sweden, the *Swedish Theological Institute* in **Jerusalem** was founded in 1951

and has become an important meeting place for scholars and interfaith groups alike, and the exegetical and theological contribution of Krister Stendahl (b. 1921) is groundbreaking. One of the most tangible examples of this improvement is that the Evangelical-Lutheran Church of Sweden passed its first declaration on Jewish–Christian relations in 2001, *The Ways of God*, in which **antisemitism** is declared to be a sin, the **deicide** charge is condemned and **replacement theology** is abandoned.

JESPER SVARTVIK

School of St Victor *see* **Andrew of St Victor; Victorines**

Scribes

Both Judaism and Christianity are indebted to scribal activity; without the dedicated work of scribes over many centuries the documents essential for tracing the history and self-understanding of religious movements would never have survived. The availability and quality of those documents, written by Jewish and Christian scribes, control the reliability of texts within the **canon** and within non-canonical texts. The technical description of 'scribe' varies in reference and significance throughout Jewish literature: the **Septuagint** favours the function of scribes as administrators, officials, instructors and judges, and bearers of **wisdom** and ethical traditions (Sir. 6.34; 7.14; 8.33; 39.1–4); sociological study of the Second Temple period recognises their political relationship to priestly parties (*1 En.* 92.1–5); as an honorific term 'scribe' is used of **Moses**, Enoch, **David** and Ezra (1 Esd. 8.7); within the early relationships of Jews and Christians, as the Synoptic Gospels indicate, it could be used as a term of general criticism – of scribal commitment to the written **Torah**, of an implied failure to match understanding of the Torah with appropriate behaviour, or of involvement in opposition to **Jesus** and his followers (Mark 8.31; 9.16). That usage of the term should not, however, inhibit the scholar today from a deep appreciation of aspects of the spirituality of the scribe as portrayed in Sirach, where meditation, worship, theology and learning are fused, nor from appraising the positive attitude to scribal activity which is also found in each of the Synoptic Gospels (Matt. 13.52; 23.2; Mark 12.28–34; Luke 10.25–28). The early interdependence of Jewish and Christian scribal activity, in terms of translation, **exegesis**, form, composition and content, is well illustrated by comparisons between the Gospel of Matthew, the Qumran material (*see* **Dead Sea Scrolls**) and the scribal methods as evidenced in **Mishnah** *Avot*.

IVOR H. JONES

Second Vatican Council *see* **Vatican II**
Seder *see* **Last Supper**; **paschal lamb**; **Passover**
Seelisberg Conference

The newly formed International **Council of Christians and Jews** (founded 1946), under the general secretaryship of the Revd W. W. Simpson (1907–87), met in the Swiss town of Seelisberg in 1947. Delegates attended from European countries in East and West and from Australia, as did representatives from many organisations, including UNESCO, the **World Council of Churches** and the 'Historic Peace Churches'. At this second conference of the Council the main issues on the agenda were the establishment of human rights and the combating of **antisemitism**. A declaration by the Christian participants was issued, known as the 'Ten Points of Seelisberg: An Address to the Churches', in which the Christians, in consultation with Jews, tackled the problem of Christian antisemitism. The 'Ten Points' drew attention to the Jewishness of **Jesus** and of the early Christian community, and reminded that Jews and Christians are bound by a common **commandment** to love God and one's neighbour. It proceeded to indicate what should be avoided in the presentation of Jews by Christians, including the misrepresentation of Jews as enemies of Jesus, portraying the passion as if all Jews were responsible for Christ's death, or choosing critical passages from the **New Testament** without noting their universal application to humanity and not just to Jews. The 'Ten Points' anticipated many later Church statements in its understanding of Jesus and the **early Church**, and in its concern for care in **preaching** and **catechesis**. *JAMES K. AITKEN*

Septuagint (LXX)

The Septuagint originally denoted the (Old Greek) translation of the **Pentateuch**, but from the second century CE onwards the term came to be used for the whole of the **Old Testament** in **Greek**, including the **apocryphal** books, not all of which were translations. Within the Church it has held a special position as the version of the Bible quoted in the **New Testament** and as the version used by many **Church Fathers**. The Eastern Fathers too relied for their Old Testament on ancient translations from the LXX. It was also important within Judaism, despite a lack of other Jewish literature

in Greek from after the first century CE (although Jewish Greek **inscriptions** have survived), its value being indicated by **Philo**, who recorded an annual festival in **Alexandria** celebrating the translation. In rabbinic literature criticism of it is found only rarely, and it is often spoken of approvingly. Such approval might be indicated by the continued use of the Greek text, at least in the version of **Aquila**, in the synagogue as late as **Justinian** (sixth century). The use of Greek by both Jews and Christians in the Mediterranean region, and respect for the LXX, account for the preference of the LXX over the **Hebrew Bible** in Jewish–Christian **disputations** in the first couple of centuries, and suggest that such disputations might reflect genuine contact. The inclusion of apocryphal books in the Christian **canon** was not a matter of dispute, but the accuracy of the text and its interpretation were. **Justin** (*Dial.* 71.1) implies some Jews wished for a more accurate translation than the current LXX, and in the second century the apparently Jewish versions of Aquila, Symmachus and Theodotion were produced. Aquila's version rendered the Hebrew much more closely than any other, and its Jewish origin might be implied by a similar version still in use among Jews in the medieval period (attested in the **Cairo Genizah**). All three Jewish versions render, for example, Isa. 7.14 with the word 'young woman' rather than 'virgin' to counter Christian claims of the virginal birth of Christ (cf. Justin, *Dial.* 43.8; 67.1). The *Dialogue of Timothy and Aquila* (late second to fourth century) specifically attacks Aquila's version for mutilating the text, and the ongoing dispute concerning the text of the LXX might be reflected in the rabbinic response that the day of the translation was as the day when the **Golden Calf** was fashioned (*Megillat Ta'anit* 13). Some Christian commentators, notably **Melito of Sardis**, **Origen** and **Jerome**, were aware of deficiencies in the LXX, and referred to the Hebrew for clarification. Origen's **Hexapla** (*c.*250 CE), which aligned various LXX translations with the Hebrew text, may have been produced, among other reasons, to counter Jewish arguments on the text. In Justin's *Dialogue with the Jew Trypho* Jews are accused of omitting passages from the LXX, although in reality these are usually Christian additions. The *Epistle of Barnabas*, for example, discusses the Christian reading of the LXX of Isa. 45.1, where the addition of one letter has changed 'my anointed one, Cyrus [*kyro*]' to 'my anointed one, Lord [*kyrio*]', a reading that Jerome actually denounces. The LXX continued to be the text discussed in disputations as late as the **Byzantine** period, appearing in the **anti-Christian** text *Nestor the Priest*, although the version there is different from extant LXX versions. The authority of the LXX remains a matter of discussion in Christianity, it being advocated, for example, by Bishop John Fisher (sixteenth century), E. Grinfield (nineteenth century) and M. Müller (twentieth century). **Orthodox Churches** continue to use the Septuagint (in the case of the Greek Orthodox) or its daughter translations (e.g. **Coptic**, Ethiopic, **Armenian**, Old Slavonic), which, given their incorporation of theological alterations influential on early Christian writers, can reinforce the position of the Old Testament simply as a typological precursor of the New. *See also* **Bible translations, ancient**; **biblical interpretation**   *JAMES K. AITKEN*

Sermon on the Mount

The Sermon on the Mount (Matt. 5–7) is the first of five major discourses in the Gospel of Matthew (perhaps the most Jewish of the four Gospels of the **New Testament**). A number of biblical scholars have suggested that the five discourses are intended to parallel the five books of the **Torah**. The Sermon on the Mount can be further divided into five major sections beginning with the **beatitudes** and concluding with exhortations to live a radical type of discipleship. In addition, it has a section consisting of six statements – 'You have heard it said . . . but I say to you' – in which Torah law is expanded or reinterpreted, and another section on purity of intention in **prayer**, **fasting** and almsgiving – important elements of Jewish piety.

The most controversial element of the sermon is Matt. 5.17–20, which begins 'Do not think I have come to abolish the law or the prophets: I have come not to abolish but to fulfil.' While many Christians do think that **Jesus** came to abolish Mosaic **Law**, it is clear from the sermon that the Matthean Jesus is not speaking of eliminating the law but of calling people to live their **covenant** relationship in a radical, more intensive way. In this, Jesus is following in a long tradition of reformers and prophets of Jewish history. Recall, for example, Jeremiah's call to a new covenant written on the heart (Jer. 31.31–4).

The literary context of the Sermon on the Mount confirms this interpretation. In the stories that precede the sermon Matthew describes the infant Jesus being sought out by Gentile astrologers and dream interpreters, who call him 'the king of the Jews' (Matt. 2.1–12). Immediately afterwards Jesus' parents take him to Egypt to protect him from **Herod**, who kills all the baby boys of Bethlehem. Later, they return to fulfil the prophecy, 'Out of Egypt I have called my son' (Matt. 2.13–15). An observant reader quickly recognises allusions to Jewish Messianic hopes, Moses' childhood escape from death, and the exodus.   *STEVEN J. MCMICHAEL*

Service International de Documentation Judéo-Chrétienne (SIDIC) *see* Jewish–Christian relations, centres for the study of

Seventh-Day Adventists

The Seventh-Day Adventist church is distinguished from mainline **Protestantism** by its belief in the imminent pre-millennial Second Advent (return) of **Christ**, and observance of the biblical seventh-day (Saturday) **Sabbath** and **dietary laws**. With roots in the teachings of Baptist William Miller (1781–1849) and Ellen G. White (1827–1915), the Church was formally organised in 1863 and now has over 11 million members. Energetic **mission** is a consequence of the belief that universal proclamation of the gospel is a precondition of the Second Advent.

As **Judaising Christians**, Adventists constitute a **minority** in all countries, and are prominent campaigners for religious liberty, lobbying for implementation of the United Nations' Declaration on Human Rights, and **Church and state** separation. However, whilst several individual Adventists helped Jews to escape the **Holocaust** (John Weidner (1912–94) is recognised as a **Righteous Gentile** for his organisation of an 'underground railroad' that rescued 800 people), the German Adventist Church supported **Hitler** and attempted to distinguish itself from Judaism in the minds of the authorities by publishing articles in support of anti-Jewish measures, permitting Sabbath work and military service.

Adventist practice was re-established in postwar Europe, but the Holocaust has had limited impact on Adventist–Jewish relations. Individuals like John Graz (b. 1945) have called for recognition of Christian complicity in the Holocaust and a re-evaluation of Adventist theology of the Jewish people, but Adventist–Jewish relations remain largely those between propagators and targets of conversionary mission. In several countries Adventists are primarily African, African-American or African-Caribbean in origin; Adventist–Jewish relations may therefore be located partly in a context of wider **Black Christian–Jewish relations**. *MELANIE J. WRIGHT*

Sex/sexuality

In today's world the subject of sexuality is increasingly complicated. Sex is a physical and emotional activity; sexuality is an **identity** category, generally privileging heterosexual concepts of power, ownership, social role and status in the eyes of God. In the face of modern insights into gender, sexual identity and sexual orientation – all non-biblical categories – both Judaism and Christianity are struggling to find enough common ground to formulate definitive joint declarations concerning many sexual issues.

Historically both religions sanction only one option: a carefully delimited heterosexuality, regulated by religious authority. Both assume that a 'normal' man–woman relationship should culminate in **marriage**. All other sexual activity is traditionally understood to be contrary to nature as intended by God.

The Gospels say little about sexual behaviour (**Paul** spoke only slightly more) and nothing at all about sexuality. **Early Church** writers often understood marriage as a distraction from full devotion to God; hence **celibacy** is much more common in the history of Christianity than in Judaism. The **creation narrative** models monogamy, though the Bible also contains examples of 'sanctioned' polygamy. Christianity has from the beginning insisted on monogamy, a proscription also adopted by Judaism from the eleventh century.

Though adultery is often used in the Bible as a metaphor for intentionally turning away from right relationship with God, neither religion tolerates human adultery. In the prophetic literature adultery could be forgiven by God, though there is little biblical evidence that humans should forgive. In both traditions marriage is also a common metaphor – God to Israel, the Lamb to the Church, God to the human soul. Both Kabbalah and early medieval **mysticism** drew erotic parallels between the sexual act and the mystical union with God. In Judaism God's sexuality is also **anthropomorphised** as female and heterosexual. **Wisdom** and the *Shekinah* are feminine aspects of God; **Torah** and **Sabbath** are also described as female.

Body–soul dualism, valuing the **soul** and devaluing the body, entered Christianity from outside Judaism, probably from Greek philosophies. Chris-

tianity's approach–avoidance relationship with sex and sexuality is further complicated by the fact that in the Bible, while God is usually referred to by male pronouns or male titles, God has no clear genital configuration in contrast to all other divine figures of the ancient Near East and of Hellenistic cultures. Each religion dealt with this discrepancy differently. Sexual love is celebrated in the **Hebrew Bible**, and sex is spoken of frankly in rabbinic literature. Sexual love in the **New Testament** is often equated with lust, and thus condemned. **Original sin** (**Augustine**, early fifth century) was virtually equated with sexual passion, so every act of conception was intrinsically evil. The difference between the two traditions can be summarised as follows: in Judaism sexual activity is characterised by temperance and self-control; in Christianity by **asceticism** and self-denial.

In 1993 the Synagogue Council of America and the US National Conference of Catholic Bishops issued a joint statement decrying the proliferation of pornography, for it 'reduces the Creator's gift of sexuality to a level . . . devoid of personal dignity, commitment and spirituality'. In 2003 a joint statement by the Pontifical Commission for Religious Relations with the Jews and the Chief Rabbinate of Israel Commission for Jewish–Catholic Dialogue affirmed 'the family unit as the basis for a wholesome society', arguing that God has sanctified marriage between a man and a woman (Gen. 1.27). The statement ends: 'We cannot agree to alternative models of couples' union and the family.'

But other voices within both Judaism and Christianity do seek to explore and endorse alternative models. With the rise of **biblical criticism** and the influence of **Freud**'s psychology, and in a world of **postmodern** contextuality, attitudes toward sex and sexuality have begun to change in Judaism and Christianity. Both religions agree that sexual abuse, paedophilia, bestiality and non-consensual sex are offensive to a loving God who desires healthy human relationships. However, both religions are at present characterised by intra- and inter-community disputes on issues of sexual identity and orientation, and divine sanction, so that a rocky road lies ahead in this area of Jewish–Christian relations. We are more likely to find agreement among Jewish and Christian liberals, or Jewish and Christian traditionalists, than we are across the traditionalist/postmodern divide.

See also **homosexuality**   *PHILIP CULBERTSON*

Shabbat *see* **Sabbath**

Shabbetai Zvi (1626–76)

Self-proclaimed **Messiah** and founder of Shabbeteanism, a Jewish **Messianic movement** which gained an enormous following among Jews, particularly in the **Ottoman empire** through which he travelled widely from his home city of Smyrna, and was seen by some Christians as a precursor to the return of **Jesus** Christ. The rise in violence against Jews, particularly in **Russia** and **Poland** (for example, the Chmeilnicki massacres of 1648), contributed to his success, as did the increase in popularity of Kabbalah, especially in its Laurianic form which combined Messianism with **mysticism**. In 1665 Nathan of Gaza (1644–80) acknowledged Shabbetai Zvi as the long-awaited Messiah. Shabbetai Zvi's actions, such as appointing apostles to represent the 12 tribes of Israel, attracted the interest of Christian **millenarians** in England, the Netherlands and Germany who expected Christ to return in 1666; for example, in Amsterdam Peter Serrarius (1600–69) spread news of Shabbetai Zvi to his many Christian correspondents. Fasts, ritual baths and mortifications of an extreme character were the order of the day among the Shabbeteans. Many communities in Europe made preparations or even left for the **land of Israel** in Messianic expectation. In 1666 Shabbetai Zvi was imprisoned by the sultan and given the choice of converting to **Islam** or being put to death. He chose the former, as did thousands of his followers. Nathan of Gaza explained that the scandal of his **apostasy** was necessary in order to redeem the entire world: although outwardly he submitted to domination by an earthly power and took on the shame of being a traitor, this was a last stage before he revealed himself as Messianic redeemer. Gershom Scholem (1897–1982) compares the Shabbetean movement to Christianity, suggesting that what **Paul** had called the scandal of the cross was as shocking as the scandal of an apostate Messiah. In both cases the disciples proclaimed the birth of a new form of Judaism, which had replaced the old. Both groups believed that the **Torah** had been replaced by the new law of the Spirit and developed an incarnational conception of God (*see* **incarnation**). After his conversion Shabbetai Zvi sent Nathan to Rome to perform a secret ritual to hasten the fall of the pope and Christendom. Shabbeteanism continued to flourish after their deaths, but the movement disintegrated in the following century when most followers converted to Christianity or **Islam**. The best known Shabbetean was Jacob **Frank**, whose followers later converted to Catholicism. Catholic Frankists survived until the mid-twentieth century, although their influence diminished significantly from the mid-nineteenth century.   *EDWARD KESSLER*

Shaftesbury, Anthony Ashley Cooper, 7th Earl of (1801–85)

Early Christian Zionist. Shaftesbury urged Jews to immigrate to **Israel**, partly because, like other early Christian Zionists, he saw Jews playing a key role in Christ's Second Coming, which would occur only when Jews lived in a restored Israel – he argued the Jewish people were vital to a Christian's hope of **salvation** – and partly from a desire to see Europe free of Jews. The contradictory co-existence in his writings of **antisemitism** (e.g. 'The State and Prospect of the Jews' (1841)) and exaltation of Jews as God's **Chosen People** is not unusual in early **Christian Zionism**. Shaftesbury was among a small number of early Christian Zionists who influenced leaders such as **Lloyd George**, Arthur Balfour (1848–1930) and Woodrow Wilson (1856–1924).

EDWARD KESSLER

Shakespeare, William (1564–1616)

English playwright, poet and actor. Parish records from his birthplace Stratford-upon-Avon indicate that (as the law required) William Shakespeare belonged to the **Church of England**; the **Bible** and the Book of Common Prayer influenced his work. Several of his 38 plays treat Jews and Jewish–Christian relations in ways that contemporary readers find problematic, including *The Two Gentlemen of Verona* and *Macbeth* which contain passing antisemitic references (II.iii and v, and IV.iv respectively) and *The **Merchant of Venice***. Opinion is divided as to whether the latter is an antisemitic play or a play about **antisemitism** (or both).

Little is known of Shakespeare's biography, including his religious beliefs. The family had recusant connections and there is a tradition that Shakespeare was a Catholic. This theory has more credibility than the (rare) suggestion that he was Jewish, but remains unproven. There have been many attempts to deny or explain Shakespeare's negative attitude towards Jews. For some interpreters as a 'great writer' Shakespeare must necessarily have been (by contemporary standards) a 'great person', and so cannot have shared in the prejudice of his age. Alternatively it is sometimes argued that Shakespeare's attitude stems from ignorance; Jews were expelled from England in 1290. However, there were Jews in sixteenth-century London, where Shakespeare worked. Moreover, scholars like James Shapiro (b. 1955) have recently argued for a reappraisal of the impact of Jewish questions in early modern England, implying that Shakespeare certainly participated in Jewish–Christian relations on an ideological level, if not in terms of everyday life encounters. What is undeniable is that Shakespeare's pre-eminence in the literary canon has ensured the continuing influence of his work on popular perceptions of Jews and Judaism.   *MELANIE J. WRIGHT*

Shalom *see* **peace**

Shavuot

Jewish festival precisely parallel to the Christian festival of **Pentecost** (which was also the name given to the Jewish festival by Greek-speaking Jews). Shavuot is linked to **Passover** in the same way that Pentecost is linked to **Easter** by a period of seven weeks (Lev. 23.15). Acts 2 describes how at the festival the **Holy Spirit** descended on the whole assembly with the disciples speaking in tongues, to take the Christian message out to the peoples of the world. The narrative precisely parallels the revelation at Sinai, with its thunder and fire and God's **revelation** to the whole of the **people of Israel**. Rabbis countered Christian claims to have a more universal message with the retort that **Torah** had been offered to other nations but refused. In the **Hebrew Bible** Shavuot is simply a harvest festival, and the precise date of the revelation at Sinai is not mentioned. Shavuot as celebrating God's revelation finds its written testimony firstly in Acts, secondly in rabbinic writings. The third-century Rabbi Elazar ben Pedat declared that the Torah was given on Shavuot (*b. Pesahim* 68b), thus making the festival similar in theme to the parallel Christian festival. The more recent development of the two festivals shows further links. As early as the fifth century **baptisms** into the Church were common at Pentecost. It became the custom at Shavuot to read the book of Ruth (*Machzor Vitry*, from 1208), which

deals with the theme of **conversion** to Judaism. Shavuot in medieval times marked the beginning of children's formal study and in modern times has been favoured for Jewish confirmation and religion school graduation ceremonies. The Anglo-Saxons called the feast White Sunday (Whitsunday), from the white clothes worn by those baptised. In modern Israel public processions are held for which white is worn.   *MICHAEL HILTON*

Shekinah

The idea of the *Shekinah* seems to originate with God's glory 'dwelling' over the tabernacle (Exod. 40.35) and comes to be associated with divine presence and continuity. In the **Aramaic** translations of the Bible the term *Memra* serves the same purpose. An important image of the *Shekinah* is the continuity of the divine presence even when in exile, seen in the cloud and fire leading the people in the Exodus account, and later taken to be present after the fall of the **Temple** in 70 CE. In the Wisdom of Solomon (first century BCE) the figure of **Wisdom** was associated with the *Shekinah* and this contributed to the Christian view of **Jesus**. The prologue to John's Gospel might have been developing similar concepts, especially with the allusion there to the 'tabernacling' of the Word. Drawing upon a pun in Greek where the word for 'tent' is similar to the Hebrew for 'to dwell' (1.14), Jesus, the Word of God, is depicted as encamping with the people of the world. The similarity of Jewish and Christian concepts of divine presence could serve as a theological issue of **dialogue** and understanding between the faiths.   *JAMES K. AITKEN*

Shema

Shema is the singular imperative of the Hebrew verb 'to hear' and the first word of Deut. 6.4, 'Hear, O Israel'. The *Shema* is the name of the most important declaration of faith for Jews, and consists of Deut. 6.4–9, 11.13–21 and Num. 15.37–41. It begins by asserting the unity of God ('the Lord our God, the Lord is one') and it enjoins the love of God with one's whole being and possessions. The second part of the *Shema* links obedience to God's commandments to material blessing, while the third part commands the wearing of fringes or tassels as a reminder of the exodus from Egypt and the obligation to obey God's commandments. The recitation of the *Shema* is at the heart of the daily morning and evening service, but it is also used on other occasions, such as at the culmination of the **Day** of Atonement. In the **New Testament** the opening words (Deut. 6.4–5) are described by Jesus as 'the first and great commandment' (Matt. 22.37–8), and Anglican **liturgies** from the eighteenth century have included this passage in the opening section of the **eucharist**, thereby putting it at the heart of their worship.

See also **confession of faith**   *JOHN ROGERSON*

Shittuf

A halakhic term which means 'partnership' or 'association' of an additional power with God and is used in **Orthodox Judaism** to describe non-Jewish religions, especially Christianity and **Islam**. It is applied to religions that are not considered idolatrous but are viewed as combining elements of Judaism and paganism, resulting in a contamination of the absolute monotheism revealed at Sinai. However, because a *shittuf* religion has not degenerated into polytheism and **idolatry**, it was not condemned, and (commercial) contacts with its representatives were deemed acceptable. According to the medieval view, it was understandable that such religions contain truth and error, because their representatives were not at Sinai and did not take on the obligatory commitment to uncorrupted worship of God and fulfilment of God's **commandments** that covers all generations. The view that God might have had a partner in **creation** was first refuted in **Rabbinic Judaism**'s interpretation of the **Golden Calf**, which was described as a false 'mixing' (*shetaf*) of the Name of God with an alien cult. A pragmatic position eventually emerged that while *shittuf* compromised monotheism and was thus prohibited to Jews, it was not incompatible with the **Noachide laws** and thus Christians were not actual idolaters (*t. Sanhedrin* 63b and *t. Bekhorot* 2b).

EDWARD KESSLER

Shiloh

An obscure word in Gen. 49.10, and part of a **blessing** by **Jacob**, which was interpreted in **Rabbinic Judaism** and in the **early Church** as a Messianic prophecy: 'The sceptre shall not depart from Judah, nor a lawgiver from between his feet, until *Shiloh* comes; and to him shall be the obedience of the people.' 'Sceptre' was understood by both the rabbis and by the **Church Fathers** as the 12 tribes of **Israel** or as Judah, and *Shiloh* as the **Messiah**. In Christian tradition *Shiloh* is identified with **Jesus**, but for the rabbis *Shiloh* has not yet arrived (cf. *b. Sanhedrin* 98b)   *EDWARD KESSLER*

Shoah

Hebrew term used to describe the murder of Jews during the Second World War. It is biblical in origin, meaning 'total destruction' (e.g. Ps. 35.8; 63.10; Prov. 1.27; Job 30.14; Isa. 6.2; 19.3; 47.11). In English it is used by some as an alternative to the term **Holocaust** which, also biblical in origin, is the Greek translation of the Hebrew *olah*, meaning 'whole burnt offering'. Describing the victims with a word that originally denoted sacrifices to God, as well as the use of the term 'holocaust' in other contexts, is offensive to some Jews and Christians. Yet just as the term 'holocaust' has been used in a variety of contexts to describe scenes of violence and destruction, *shoah* is used similarly in modern Hebrew, for example in association with nuclear disasters and air accidents.   *K. HANNAH HOLTSCHNEIDER*

Sicut Judeis

Sicut Judeis is the name of a Papal Bull, first promulgated during the pontificate of **Callixtus II** (1119–24). Its purpose was to protect Jews against Christian violence. Even while protecting Jews, however, the document reflects the depth of Christian ambivalence about the continued vitality of Jewish communities. This can be clearly discerned in the document's opening line: 'Even as the Jews ought not have the freedom to dare do in their synagogues more than the law permits them, so ought they not suffer curtailment of those [privileges] which have been conceded them.' The most likely context for the original promulgation of Callixtus's Bull is the increasing Christian–Jewish violence that characterised the First **Crusade**.

Specifically, the Bull forbids the forced **baptism** of Jews, and it condemns such crimes as the wounding, killing or robbing of Jews. It also forbids Christians from interfering with Jewish **worship** and festival celebrations. Although first promulgated during the medieval period, similar legal pronouncements date back to the pontificate of Pope **Gregory the Great**, one of whose letters begins with the words *Sicut Judeis*. For Gregory the context was local Roman policy toward the Jews. As the power of the Pope grew, local Roman policy began to have more universal influence on issues affecting the whole Church. The Bull was frequently reissued by a succession of popes during the Middle Ages, testifying to its limited success in controlling violence against the Jews. *Sicut Judeis* became part of the foundational texts for the developing tradition of **canon law**, and for centuries it represented official Church policy towards the Jewish community. Reflecting the Church's generally defensive posture following the **Reformation**, the Bull fell into disuse; Church policy became more restrictive and remained so until the twentieth century, when official policy went far beyond the bare **tolerance** that characterised *Sicut Judeis* and condemned **antisemitism**. *JOHN J. O'KEEFE*

SIDIC *see* **Jewish–Christian relations, centres for the study of**

Silence

Silence may describe a number of different states, including the condition of being silent or still, or a failure to speak out on an issue. Silence in each of these senses has a role in Judaism, Christianity and Jewish–Christian relations.

Both Jews and Christians use silence in **worship**. It is customary for Jewish congregations to recite the *Amidah* silently before its repetition by the leader (following *m. Berakhot* 5.1), and the **Kabbalah** (drawing on texts like Ps. 62.2; 5.2; *Zohar* 2b) views silence as the authentic medium of **prayer**, a discipline to be practised by those seeking to draw near to the Eternal. Christianity roots silent, private prayer in the examples of **Mary** (Luke 2.19, 51) and **Jesus** (Luke 5.15; Matt. 6.5–8). Members of religious orders regularly observe silence (especially during the night hours, or 'Great Silence'); **Quakers** are noted for their tradition of silent 'waiting upon the Lord'.

In Jewish–Christian relations silence as failure to resist **evil** is associated primarily with the failure of Christians to protest the **Holocaust** or address their complicity afterwards. Much contemporary **dialogue** and **remembrance** activity is predicated on the fear that the absence of conversation within and between faiths on these issues is only partly a stunned or respectful silence, and may in fact attest to indifference or forgetfulness.

Some meetings of **Councils of Christians and Jews** (and similar bodies) and other interfaith events use silence as an opportunity for spiritual reflection and sharing. In the absence of commonly accepted **liturgies** reflecting new appreciations of the bonds uniting Jews and Christians, this avoids problems associated with verbal ministry, but can become characterless and lack genuine spirituality. *MELANIE J. WRIGHT*

Sin

Sin is an important issue in the Jewish–Christian encounter. A shared concept, the word sin in Hebrew, *het*, means 'that which goes astray' and carries connotations of an arrow that misses the target, while for Christianity the Greek word *hamartia* means 'missing the mark'. In both cases the word implies failure to meet expectations of **holiness** or goodness. As **Paul** puts it in Rom. 3.23, 'all have sinned and fall short of the glory of God' (New Revised Standard Version). One key difference between Christianity and Judaism is over the issue of '**original sin**'. There is, however, a major similarity in that both Judaism and Christianity stress the importance of the mercy of God. God is willing and able to forgive those who turn to God for **repentance**. The idea shapes much of the drama of the **Hebrew Bible**, and Christians inherited the idea and made it central to their understanding of how God relates to the world.

The twentieth century, especially in the light of the **Holocaust**, generated a significant literature of Christian acknowledgement of the many sins committed against Judaism. Many of the major Christian denominations (e.g. Anglican, Lutheran, Presbyterian) organised working parties to look at the propensity to demonise the Jew both in scripture and tradition. Pope **John Paul II** made the acknowledgement of sin against Judaism a major theme of his pontifical teaching, culminating in his papal confession of sin at the Western Wall in Jerusalem during his pilgrimage to **Israel** in March 2000.

IAN MARKHAM

Sisters of Sion

The Congregation of Our Lady of Sion is an international Order of Roman Catholic religious women founded in Paris in the mid-nineteenth century by Theodore **Ratisbonne**. In accordance with the thought of the Church at the time, the order's aim was the **conversion** of the Jews – 'to cooperate in the fulfilment of the promises concerning the destiny of the Jewish people'. Following the Second World War, the impact of the **Holocaust**, the ecumenical and biblical movements, and new theological understandings led to a dramatic change in the aim of the Order. **Vatican II** and *Nostra Aetate* confirmed and encouraged this new thrust. The sisters are now called, through a variety of ministries, professions, schools and centres, to witness 'to God's faithful love for the Jewish people' and 'to promote understanding and justice for the Jewish community, and to keep alive in the Church the consciousness that, in some mysterious way, Christianity is linked to Judaism from its origin to its final destiny' (1984, Constitution §§ 13, 14). *AUDREY DOETZEL*

Slovakia

For almost ten centuries (tenth century–1918) Slovakia preserved its Slavonic language and character as a part of **Hungary**, a fact that also significantly influenced the relationship of Christians and Jews there. Thanks to the initially benevolent policy towards Jews of the Árpád dynasty (896–1301), Hungary and Slovakia witnessed relatively peaceful coexistence and even attracted Jewish fugitives from the West. A gradual change of mood was signalled by two **blood libel** charges from 1494 and 1529, which ended at the stake. After the defeat of Hungarian forces by the **Ottoman** army at the battle of Mohács (1526) Jews were banned from several towns, settling in suburbs where peaceful cooperation developed with rural Christian communities, especially in the districts of Liptovský Mikuláš and Trenčín. In the seventeenth century Slovakia again became a destination for Jewish refugees, who were sometimes even supported by Hungarian landlords in erecting places for worship and study. At the beginning of the nineteenth century Hatam Sofer (1762–1839) founded an officially recognised rabbinical orthodox seminary in Pressburg (Bratislava). New political conditions in the Austro-Hungarian Empire gradually led to greater cultural and political bonds between Slovak Jews and Hungary, which contradicted national Slovak feelings and created new tensions. Modern edicts of tolerance such as that in 1867 were therefore sometimes opposed by clergy and public. There was strong support for **Zionism** among Slovak Jews, and Pressburg hosted important Zionist congresses. The creation of Czechoslovakia in 1918 brought relative political and religious freedom, but this was interrupted between 1939 and 1945 by the controversial creation of an independent Slovak state which collaborated with the Nazi regime: some 100,000 people perished in the **Holocaust**, and of about 25,000 survivors only half resettled. Today about 6,000 Jews live in the modern state of Slovakia.

See also **Czechia** *PETR FRYŠ*

Society of Friends *see* **Quakers**
Society of Jesus *see* **Jesuits**
Soloveitchik, Joseph (1903–92)

Scion of the rabbinic family that led the prestigious Volozhin yeshivah, Soloveitchik studied philosophy in Berlin before becoming one of the most influential 'Modern Orthodox' rabbinic leaders and philosophers of twentieth-century America. Soloveitchik reacted to Western **liberalism** and to **Vatican II** with the same mixture of interest and mistrust. While Jews had a duty to resist religious acculturation, Soloveitchik ruled that American Jews could celebrate Thanksgiving as a religious festival, and he actively followed discussions of the role of religion in society. His public response to Vatican II ('Confrontation', *Tradition*, 1964) has often been read as a ban on theological or even all interfaith **dialogue**, restricting intergroup encounter to secular and social subjects. He subsequently made clear that this was not a **halakhic** ban but an exposition of the philosophical basis for an encounter in which Judaism would be respected as equal and independent, not subjected to triumphalist condescension, dogmatic **disputation** and missionary intent. In relating his suspicion that the Catholic Church was unlikely to abandon its **mission** to Jews, Soloveitchik also recalled the unscrupulous measures previously adopted by the Russian **Orthodox Church** in pursuit of Jewish converts. Nevertheless, his publications betray a profound engagement with prewar German Protestant thought, from **Kant** and Kierkegaard (1813–55) to Scheler (1874–1928) and Otto (1869–1937). From 1962 Soloveitchik was privately involved in discussions between Jewish organisations and the Vatican, insisting that limits on dialogue be set to avoid doctrinal divisions. His classic *Lonely Man of Faith* was first delivered at a Catholic seminary in 1965.

GEORGE R. WILKES
Solovyov, Vladimir (1853–1900)

Orthodox Christian Russian religious philosopher, poet and political thinker; the spiritual father of Russian religious renaissance during the early twentieth century. Solovyov's innovative pro-Jewish theses and arguments were part of his Christian **universalism** and ecumenist utopia. In his youth he studied **Kabbalah** and later read in Hebrew the **Old Testament** and parts of the **Mishnah** with his friend and teacher Feivl Getz (1853–1931). He used ideas, terms and citations from the Old Testament, sometimes in Hebrew, to illustrate his theosophical views. In his lectures at the St Petersburg University (1882) he praised the Jews as the **Chosen People** and defended their civil rights in **Russia**. He attributed to Jews deep religious belief and dedication to God; a developed personal and national self; and a materialist worship of God. He wished Jews were participants in a future ecumenist 'free theocracy', but in his 'The New Testament Israel' (1885) and later essays he realised that mass proselytism cannot be expected from Jews after the **pogroms**. In his 'The Jewish People and the Christian Question' (1884) he declared that the 'Jewish problem' in Russia derived from the non-Christian behaviour of the Christians. In an essay published in 1896 Solovyov enthusiastically rehabilitated the moral values of the **Talmud**. He defined Jewish theological innovation on the basis not of monotheism, but of belief in historical progress, thus giving hope to its believers. In his apocalyptic 'Three Discussions' and 'A Short Story on the Anti-Christ' (both 1899), Jews join Christians in a battle against the **Antichrist** and return to their Holy Land. Solovyov was politically active against **antisemitism** in Russia. On his deathbed he asked his attendants not to let him sleep so he could pray for the Jewish people. His lectures, writings and personality were highly valued by Jewish **Zionist** and non-Zionist writers, intellectuals and theologians, including S. Dubnov (1860–1941) and A. I. Kook (1865–1935), the Chief Rabbi of pre-state **Israel**.   *HAMUTAL BAR-YOSEF*

Son of God

Since the beginning of Christianity the question whether the expression 'Son of God' can be applied to **Jesus** has been a central issue of debate between Jews and Christians. In Jewish tradition 'son of God' has been used to refer to the **people of Israel** (Exod. 2.24; Isa. 1.2; Jer. 3.22; Hos. 11.1), the king (2 Sam. 7.14; Ps. 2.7; 89.27–8) and the heavenly court at God's throne (Job 1.6; Ps. 29.1; Dan. 3.25). In all these cases the expression 'son of God' is not referring to physical conception, but is associated with election and obedience, often with a commission to accomplish a task. In Christian tradition 'Son of God' as a title for Jesus has been used to express Jesus' divinity and his special relationship with God. In the Gospel tradition, in Acts and in the letters of **Paul** 'Son of God' is variously connected with

the pre-existence (John 3.16–17), **baptism** (Matt. 3.17; Mark 1.11; Luke 3.22), **trial** (Matt. 26.63; Mark 14.61; Luke 22.70; John 19.7), death (Matt. 27.54; Mark 15.39), **resurrection** (Acts 13.33; Rom. 1.3–4) and ascension of Jesus (John 20.17) and the *parousia* (1 Cor. 15.28). In the letters of Paul the believers become 'sons' or 'children' of God by adoption (Gal. 4.5–7; Rom. 8.14–15), but this 'sonship' has its origin in Jesus' unique 'filial' relationship with God. In present exegetical scholarship it is still an open question whether the **Messiah** was seen as 'son of God' prior to Christianity, but on the basis of 2 Sam. 7.14 and Ps. 2.7 (and their seeming interpretation in **Qumran**), many deem it possible. If this is so, then one needs to assume that **Rabbinic Judaism** deliberately avoided 'son of God' due to the fact that Christians made extensive use of this concept in their **Christological** reflection.

The confession of Jesus as 'Son of God' can be called a summary of the problem of Jewish–Christian relations. In the Gospels, and in the Gospel of John in particular, calling Jesus the 'Son of God' is at the heart of the disputes concerning Jesus' identity and ultimately leading to his accusation. It was not unusual in Jewish circles to consider human beings as 'sons of God'. Pious Jews, all Israelites or even all of humanity were at certain moments in history considered to be 'sons of God'. In the rabbinical period the expression 'son of God' disappeared into the background, according to some for the reason that the title 'Son of God' had taken a prevalent place in the parting of the ways. The specificity of the Christian understanding of 'Son of God' as applied to Jesus is that Christians believe that Jesus is the ultimate **incarnation** of God, which is and continues to be unacceptable from a Jewish perspective.

REIMUND BIERINGER AND DIDIER POLLEFEYT

Son of Man

The Hebrew *ben adam* and the Aramaic *bar (e)nash(a)* form the linguistic background of the Greek *ho huios tou anthropou* which is commonly translated as 'Son of Man'. In the Hebrew scriptures statistically the majority of the occurrences of the expression is found in Ezekiel, where God addresses the prophet as *ben adam*. Some scholars understand this expression to refer to the unique position of the prophet as the exceptional person chosen by God to fulfil a special task, while others see it as stressing Ezekiel's *mere* human status. Elsewhere in the Bible the term appears mainly in synonymous poetic parallelism, always in the second half, as a counterpart to nouns designating 'human being', predominantly in passages that point to human weakness and mortality as contrasted to God and **angels** (e.g. Ps. 8.5). There is a strong tendency in scholarship that assumes that the titular use of 'Son of Man' in the **New Testament** has its origin in a **Christological** explanation of Dan. 7.13 where it refers to a vision of the figure 'like a son of man' coming with the clouds to the Ancient of Days. The vision has been interpreted as symbolising a collective unity (the suffering **people of Israel**), an angel or divine figure (as a theophany), or the **Messiah** (prevalent in rabbinic literature, where he is mostly seen as an individual). In the New Testament the expression occurs in about 50 different sayings (mainly in the Gospels) almost always on the lips of **Jesus** in third-person sayings. It is likely that the expression 'Son of Man' in the New Testament has its origin in the **historical Jesus** himself. Scholars continue to discuss whether he might have used 'Son of Man' in a generic sense ('human being') or in a self-referential sense ('I'). It is now generally accepted that the Synoptic and Johannine Jesus refers to himself as the 'Son of Man'. The New Testament 'Son of Man' sayings can be divided into three categories, referring to his earthly ministry, his suffering and resurrection, or his future coming. Many authors understood the Gospels to use the expression 'Son of Man' to designate Jesus' humanity, stressing his truly human nature, some emphasise his lowliness ('weak man'), others his superiority ('ideal man'), still others his mere humanity ('simply human'). Based on Dan. 7.13 many scholars have interpreted 'Son of Man' as an **apocalyptic** title referring to one who comes on the clouds to judge and reign (e.g. Mark 13.26; 14.62). In the New Testament 'Son of Man' is only used in the context of **Jewish Christianity**, which seems to indicate that this terminology is only understood in continuity with Jewish tradition. Obviously the concept did not survive the move of early Christianity to a **Hellenistic** context. Christians who use 'Son of Man' today have to be aware that originally this concept was developed by Jewish Christians who tried to understand the meaning of Jesus Christ starting from the framework of their Jewish faith. They moved beyond the original meaning of 'Son of Man'

by using it not only in apocalyptic contexts, but also applying it to the suffering and resurrection of Jesus. In contemporary Jewish–Christian relations 'Son of Man' reminds Christians of their Jewish roots and Jews of the Christological line of interpretation Christians have developed starting from the First Testament.

REIMUND BIERINGER AND DIDIER POLLEFEYT

Soul

Although there was an earlier belief in some form of separate existence for the essential character of the human being (*nefesh*, *ruaḥ* and *neshamah*), the concept of the soul came into early Judaism through Greek thought. In early Christianity there is much discussion about the body/soul and flesh/spirit division of the human being, especially in the writings of the apostle **Paul**. Around the first century CE there seems to be a prevalent belief in both the **resurrection** of the body and the **immortality** of the soul that caused much reflection and argumentation in Judaism and Christianity. The resurrection of the body was a major item of debate between **Sadducees** and **Pharisees**. Neoplatonism strongly influenced early Christianity and Judaism in the development of the idea of a rational soul distinct from the physical body. Christians and many Jews believe that the soul is the innermost part of the human being because it reflects the 'image of God' (**Imago Dei**) (Gen. 1.27). Human beings are spiritual creatures and the soul is the spiritual principle within them that makes them images of God. The soul is united with the body to form one single nature. Christians believe that God creates the soul and unites it with the body at conception and that it will rejoin the body at the time of the final resurrection after being separated at death. Even though not many Jews believe in bodily resurrection, many Jews believe in the existence of a soul that will live on after death.

The main issue that concerns the soul in Jewish–Christian relations is the **salvation** of the soul after death. Certain Christians in history have held that the lack of belief in the divinity of Christ has resulted in Jews not being able to reach salvation and therefore they will suffer the loss of their souls at death. Contemporary Roman Catholic understanding of salvation holds that there is a possibility of salvation for the souls of non-believers (which would include Jews) who do not come to believe in Jesus Christ, though '*objectively speaking* [they] are in a grave deficient situation in comparison with those who, in the Church, have the fullness of the means of salvation' (2000 Vatican document *Dominus Iesus*, 22), but Jews are in a different situation from other non-Christians with regard to the salvation question in that they belong to 'the covenant that has never been revoked' (Pope **John Paul II**) (Vatican document *Notes on the Correct Way to Present the Jews and Judaism in Preaching and Catechesis in the Roman Catholic Church*, 24 June 1985).

STEVEN J. MCMICHAEL

South America

The Jewish–Christian encounter in South America started soon after the arrival of the first Christians around 1500. For example, Pedro Alvares Cabral (1467–1520), who discovered Brazil, brought with him Gaspar da Gama (*c*.1444–*c*.1510), a Polish Jew converted during the **Inquisition**. From then onwards the continent received many **Conversos** and **Marranos**. Even today it is common to come across Christian families who do not eat pork or who light **candles** on Friday night. The bulk of the Jewish community arrived in the nineteenth and early twentieth centuries as refugees, the majority fleeing **antisemitism** in Eastern Europe. Outside of **Argentina** the largest Jewish community is found in Brazil, where the population is estimated at 150,000 out of 170 million. The Jewish population in South America (excluding Argentina) is estimated to be approximately 250,000 out of a total population of 315 million (2002).

At least 80 per cent of Christians in South America are **Roman Catholic** and much of the Jewish–Christian **dialogue** is organised through the Latin American Council of Bishops (CELAM), which has organised regular meetings with leaders of the Jewish communities since *Nostra Aetate* in 1965. For example, in 1968, when Pope **Paul VI** visited Columbia, CELAM and the Anti-Defamation League organised the first official meeting of Catholics and Jews in Bogotá. In 1985 a document was issued entitled *To Dialogue in Order to Serve* which tackled some of the problems facing the interfaith dialogue, notably Christian prejudice and Jewish distrust of Jewish–Christian dialogue. In 1990, during a time of increasing antisemitism in Argentina, the Anti-Defamation League, the Latin American Jewish Congress and CELAM met to discuss historical and theological understandings of racism (*The Church and Racism: Towards a More*

Fraternal Society). As well as continental gatherings, some countries have organised national meetings. In 1981 the National Bishops Conference in Brazil created a National Commission of Dialogue for Catholic–Jewish relations, consisting of five priests and five Jewish representatives. This body has regularly produced documents and educational guides for local dioceses and has organised joint Bible study programmes. The **Sisters of Sion** and Brothers of Sion are particularly strong in Brazil. Similarly in Chile, according to Chief Rabbi Angel Brill (b. 1945) one of the most advanced Latin American countries in interfaith work, a joint Jewish–Catholic group has been established to help prisoners and families of prisoners who suffered under the Pinochet dictatorship.

In spite of these efforts, the relationship between Jews and Christians is markedly less developed in South America than in North America and Europe. Given the small size of Jewish communities in a continent where democracy is far from consolidated and economic and social turmoil are the rule, Jewish–Christian relations are perhaps unsurprisingly often relegated to secondary importance. Nevertheless, there is increasing awareness of the significance of South America in Jewish–Christian relations, as can be seen in the decision by the International **Council of Christians and Jews** to hold its annual meeting in Montevideo in 2002.

EDWARD KESSLER

Spain

Jewish settlement in Spain is very ancient. The **Hebrew Bible** reveals knowledge of Tarshish (Tartessos), probably a port near Cádiz. A large Jewish community existed in the sixth and seventh centuries under the **Visigothic** kings, who, however, decided to suppress Judaism, perhaps as part of their programme of conversion of the Goths from **Arian** to Catholic Christians, which led them to seek religious uniformity. It is uncertain how far the vicious legislation outlawing Jewish observances such as **circumcision**, **Passover** and the **Sabbath** was applied. However, the Jews appear to have welcomed as saviours the Arab and Berber invaders who came in 711, especially since the armies probably included Berbers of Jewish origin. As Muslim rule stabilised, the Jews became an accepted part of the religious landscape, subject to some restrictions like all non-Muslims, but widely tolerated. Jewish culture responded to contact with **Islam** by adopting similar styles of poetry and by engaging in the close study of Hebrew grammar, following Arabic methods of study. Some Jews even studied the Qur'an. In addition Jews were able to make contact with the communities of Babylonia across the vast open spaces of the Islamic world, acquiring a version of the Babylonian **liturgy** and **Talmud** texts. The Caliphs employed Jewish officials at court, and Lucena in the Berber kingdom of Granada became a formidable centre of Jewish scholarship and population. The advancing Christian kingdoms of the north in turn became welcoming when new Berber empires conquered the south and turned against religious **minorities**, so that Toledo took over the baton from Lucena. Jewish scholars were actively engaged, alongside arabised Christians, in the translation of Arabic scientific and philosophical books for the royal court. Toledo also became a very important centre of **Torah** study and kabbalistic study. For a while a similar openness to that found in early Muslim Spain existed in Christian Spain, and Jews and Muslims were accepted as part of the fabric of society (*see* **Convivencia**). The atmosphere turned sour as the Christian kingdoms began to assert more strongly their Christian **identity**: Aragon, Catalonia, Castile, León, Navarre and **Portugal** saw themselves as the front line of a **crusade** against the Moors, and inevitably other non-Christians were also seen as outsiders. Jews remained prominent at court, but attempts to force Jews to attend conversionist sermons were tentatively made under King **James I** of Aragon, and the **Dominican** friars began to develop a vigorous strategy of learning Hebrew and Arabic to a high level in order to challenge rabbis and imams using their own texts. The Disputation of Barcelona (1263) between **Paul the Christian**, a converted Jew, and **Nahmanides** was an important moment in this process. Thereafter conditions became gradually more difficult. Before 1300 the large Jewish community of Majorca City (the modern Palma) was enclosed in a Call, or **ghetto**, and walled Jewish quarters, partly for protection, partly for segregation, became widespread in the fourteenth and fifteenth centuries. The **conversion** campaigns were only moderately successful until force came into play, in 1391, when **pogroms** spread across Spain and led to mass conversions; in large areas of Catalonia the Jewish communities shrank almost to nothing. Thereafter the Jewish communities were divided between professing Jews and **Conversos**, and at first not much was done to keep them apart (after all, many converts were members of families some of whose members remained Jewish). But concern at the 'contamination' of converts by Jews led to the establishment of a Spain-wide **Inquisition** (1484) and culminated in the decree of **expulsion** of the Jews in 1492. This did not mark the end of Judaism in Spain, because secret Jews continued to practise their ancestral religion behind (literally) closed doors, but their numbers rapidly declined in all but a few outlying areas such as Majorca. Some Portuguese merchants managed to practise Judaism in Spain in the seventeenth century, but to all intents Judaism had ceased to exist there by then.

See also **Ferdinand the Catholic**; **Marranos**

DAVID ABULAFIA

Spinoza, Barukh (1632–77)

Philosopher. Spinoza was born into a Dutch **Marrano** family and received a Jewish education, but later study of Greek philosophy, Descartes and **Calvinism** led him away from orthodoxy. He rejected **free will** and a personal deity, understanding God as the Universe's immanent cause. He also argued that the Bible was human in origin. This precipitated his **excommunication** and estrangement from Amsterdam's Jewish community, although some critics have emphasised the continued influence of **talmudic** style and medieval Jewish philosophy on his reasoning. Spinoza subsequently spent time with **Anabaptists** near Leiden; they may have encouraged his advocacy of religious **tolerance**. His ideas were not generally popular with Christians. The **Enlightenment** led to reappraisal of Spinoza, and his thinking influenced **Eliot**, **Hegel**, **Heine** and Schleiermacher (1768–1834), amongst others.

MELANIE J. WRIGHT

Star of David

According to Jewish tradition the six-pointed star appeared on the shield of King **David** (magen David) and on King Solomon's ring (seal of Solomon). As a symbol it does not feature in the biblical or rabbinic literatures. In the Second Temple period both Jews and non-Jews used the hexagram for decoration. From the early Middle Ages it appears in Jewish magical works and at times was associated with the **Messiah**, for example by the followers of **Shabbetai Zvi**. From early in the nineteenth century a self-conscious concern to imitate Christianity (for example, among Reform or

Progressive Jews) meant that many Jews increasingly adopted the star as a symbol for Judaism, corresponding to the **crucifix** as the symbolic representation of Christianity. It also became a common feature of popular **antisemitic** imagery. Jewish political Zionists in the late nineteenth century took it as their own emblem, and by the time the philosopher Franz **Rosenzweig** published *The Star of Redemption* in 1921, it had become a universally recognised Jewish icon. Rosenzweig used the star as a means by which to illustrate the triangular interrelationships between God, humankind and the world, and also as a metaphor for the relationship between Judaism and Christianity, with Judaism as the centre of a fiery core and Christianity as the rays that radiate from the core to illuminate the pagan world. During the **Holocaust** the Nazis combined the hexagram with the **yellow badge** of shame as a means by which to distinguish and humiliate the Jews. Today the national flag of the **State of Israel** is a blue star on a white and blue background.

DANIEL R. LANGTON

State of Israel *see* Israel, land and State of

Stein, Edith (1891–1942)

Philosopher, Carmelite nun, saint. The youngest child of a Jewish family in Breslau (then **Germany**), Edith Stein converted to Catholicism in 1922, having explored Christian thought and practice following the shock of the First World War and having read the spiritual autobiography of Teresa of Avila (1515–82), reformer of the Carmelite order of nuns. In 1933 she was expelled from her teaching post in Münster because of her Jewish origin. Stein entered the Carmelite convent in Cologne in October 1933 and took her eternal vows in 1938, shortly before fleeing to the Carmel in Echt, Holland, following the **pogroms** of Kristallnacht. Stein and her sister Rosa, who also found refuge in Echt, were arrested by the Gestapo on 2 August and sent to **Auschwitz**-Birkenau, where they were murdered on arrival, presumably on 9 August, the date chosen as Stein's saint's day.

Controversy about Stein's significance for Jewish–Christian relations erupted with her beatification in 1987 and subsequent **canonisation** (1998). While the Catholic Church suggested that Stein's beatification recognised her Jewishness and that her '**martyrdom**' at Auschwitz was thus remembered in Catholic celebration of her life, Jews saw these events largely as damaging to Jewish–Christian relations, suggesting that placing such emphasis on a Jewish convert to Christianity would promote the idea of a renewed Christian **mission** to convert Jews. Three themes can be identified in the controversy. First, did Stein die as a Christian or a Jew – hence, whose 'martyr' was she? Secondly, is she a symbol of Jewish–Christian reconciliation or conflict? And thirdly, does her self-understanding and interpretation of her situation matter, and to whom? While Stein was a Christian, she was murdered not because of her Christian faith but because of her Jewish origin, as were many of her family; hence, it is controversial to claim her as a Christian martyr. At the same time, Jews are reluctant to claim Stein as Jewish, other than in the sense of a **Holocaust** victim, since a confessing member of another religion ceases to be able to claim their rights in the Jewish community. Stein herself interpreted her impending death as part of her 'Jewish fate', a joining of the 'sacrifice' of the Jewish people, seeing God's judgement enacted in the Holocaust and the persecution and murder of the Jewish people as the 'cross' of Christ. This further complicates understanding of her **sainthood** as a symbol of reconciliation between Christians and Jews. While the Catholic Church, making Stein's interpretation of her own fate normative for her sainthood, suggests she can be seen as a symbol of a new Jewish–Christian relationship of mutual understanding, Jews have criticised this vision: whether she saw Jews in the Holocaust as witnessing to the persecuted Christ or as a sacrifice for their own sins, clearly neither view voiced by a convert to Christianity coincides with Jewish self-understanding. A charge levelled against Stein during her lifetime was that she did not explore Jewish tradition before **conversion** (as, for example, did her fellow philosopher **Rosenzweig**) and that her understanding of Judaism therefore remained caught in Christian terms and stereotypes. Some commentators saw the Catholic Church's beatification of Stein as a confirmation of her interpretation of Jews in negative **supersessionist** terms and consequently as a step backwards in Jewish–Christian relations. Some Catholics, commenting on the same passages in Stein's work, interpreted them in the opposite sense, suggesting that her understanding of her own imminent death and her (disputed) willingness to embrace it demonstrated not only her solidarity with Jews, but also her saintliness in imitating Christ.   *K. HANNAH HOLTSCHNEIDER*

Strack, Hermann *see* Strack–Billerbeck rabbinic commentary

Strack–Billerbeck rabbinic commentary

German Protestant scholars, Paul Billerbeck (1853–1932) and Hermann Strack (1848–1922) jointly wrote the *Kommentar zum Neuen Testament aus Talmud und Midrasch*, which drew parallels between rabbinic texts and the **New Testament**. This became a standard text for Christian study of **Rabbinic Judaism**, but has been recently criticised because of alleged theological bias in its selection of texts, notably towards the theory that God was inaccessible in Rabbinic Judaism. E. P. Sanders (b. 1937), for example, has suggested that the **commentary** misled a generation of New Testament scholarship with a loaded interpretation of Rabbinic Judaism.

STEPHEN PLANT

'Suffering Servant'

The 'Suffering Servant' refers to a figure appearing in **Isaiah** 52.13–53.12. This is the final of a series of at least four texts describing the Servant (see 42.1–4; 49.1–6; 50.4–9) found in Deutero-Isaiah (chs 40–55), attributed to a disciple of Isaiah and written towards the end of the Babylonian exile, 539. These texts are at the centre of an often bitter debate between Jews and Christians regarding interpretation of the scriptures of Israel after the coming of Jesus Christ. Who is the Servant described in these texts? Exegetes have proposed four basic possibilities: the prophet himself; a contemporary of the prophet; the **people of Israel**; or the **Messiah**. The texts themselves focus more on the Servant's role than on his identity.

Deutero-Isaiah consoles the people, assuring them that God had not abandoned them and that they would experience a second Exodus and return to the Land. Within this context the songs of the Servant appear as cryptic and enigmatic evocations of a salvific figure: 'Behold My servant whom I uphold, My elect in whom My soul delights' (Isa. 42.1). In the fourth song the divine elevation and humiliation of the Servant at the hands of the people is described. The song contains the reflection of the people after the Servant has been rejected, has died and is buried. The people recognise that 'ours were the sufferings he bore' (53.1–11a) and God affirms that the Servant, though rejected by the people, has found favour with God, bearing the sins of many and making intercession for the transgressors

(53.11b–12). This figure of a Suffering Servant is taken up again in later texts, for example Zech. 12.10, Dan. 12.3, Sir. 11.12–13 and Wis. 5.1–7.

The writers of the **New Testament** were influenced by Isaiah in general, and the figure of the Suffering Servant seems to have coloured their understanding of the passion and death of **Jesus**. The New Testament narratives are marked by the mission and suffering described in the Servant songs (cf. citations in Matt. 8.17 and 12.18–21 and Acts 8.30–35 as well as in Mark 15.28, Luke 22.37, 24.26, 46). **Paul** in Rom. 4.25 and Phil. 2.6–11 and the author of Peter in 1 Pet. 2.21–4 paraphrase from the Suffering Servant text in order to describe Christ's sufferings. Even though the explicitness of the equation between Christ and the Suffering Servant is the subject of some debate with regard to the New Testament itself, later Christian literature used the Isaiah texts as **proof-texts** with regard to the identity of Jesus as Messiah. The **Church Fathers** insisted on a Christological reading, and the texts became the centre of a biblical **apologetic** for the understanding of Jesus as the **Christ** (see **Justin Martyr**, *Dial.* 89, **Tertullian**, *Marc.* 3.7.1–7, **Origen**, *Cels.* 1.55).

Much of traditional Jewish **exegesis** rejected the understanding of the Suffering Servant as an individual Messianic figure. Most Jewish commentators insist that the servant is in fact the people of Israel as a collective (**Rashi**, Radak (David **Kimhi**)). Saadiah Gaon (882–942) argues that the Servant was Jeremiah while **Ibn Ezra** summarises the various possibilities and then concludes that the figure is any servant in exile and most likely Isaiah himself. Some Jewish commentators, however, do maintain that the figure described is a Messianic one (*Targum Jonathan, b. Sanhedrin* 98b, **Maimonides**, *Letter to Yemen* 4).

In large part because of the Servant texts, Isaiah has been understood in Christian tradition as being 'the Fifth Evangelist'. The Servant texts are central in the liturgical readings during Holy Week, and the Suffering Servant text is read in Catholic and Anglican Churches on Good Friday. Christian belief that the Servant texts are a **prophecy** of Jesus Christ is probably what led to their exclusion from the **canon** of prophetic readings publicly recited in the synagogue on Shabbat (*haftorot*), many of which are derived from Deutero-Isaiah.

Modern exegesis of Isaiah has contributed much to the possibility for Jews and Christians to study these texts together. Christians are more apt today to understand the elements of collective **identity** that suppose that the Servant is the people of Israel (cf. Grelot). Modern Jewish commentators, on the other hand, are confronted with the significance in these texts of an innocent figure who carries the sins of the multitude, suggesting a redemptive theology of **atonement** through vicarious suffering. Joint Jewish–Christian study of the texts holds out much promise for the overcoming of centuries of biblical **polemics**.   *DAVID M. NEUHAUS*

Sukkot

As one of three annual pilgrim festivals (with **Passover** and **Shavuot**) in ancient Judaism, Sukkot or the Feast of Tabernacles celebrated in autumn the harvest of grapes and olives at the end of the season. It became associated with prayers for rain, and in the post-exilic period involved a water-drawing ceremony at the pool of Siloam and water libations at the **Jerusalem** altar, while the people processed carrying fruit and palm branches. To this day booths are built in remembrance of the Israelites dwelling in the wilderness and are decorated with branches (*lulav*) and fruits. It is possible that Sukkot came to signify Jewish national hope, it being the festival when Judas Maccabaeus rededicated the **Temple** on the first celebration of **Hanukkah** (1 Macc. 4), and it seems to have developed an **eschatological** dimension, as reflected in Zech. 14, which may then have been utilised by Rev. 7. For that reason there may be a resonance of the feast in Jesus' entry into Jerusalem (Mark 11), even though it is at the wrong time of year. John's Gospel, which mentions a celebration of the feast (John 7.2), draws on the water imagery of Sukkot in its designation of **Jesus** as the living water. In Jewish tradition, especially in the **Targumim**, the Tabernacles came to denote the indwelling presence of God, and it is perhaps a combination of that and the eschatological connotations that explains Peter's desire to build tabernacles at the Transfiguration of Christ (Mark 9.2–8 and parallels). As an annual **pilgrimage** festival the evangelical organisation the **International Christian Embassy** in Jerusalem has chosen Tabernacles for a gathering of Christians in **Israel** to witness and pray for the welfare of the country.

JAMES K. AITKEN

Supersessionism

From Latin *supersedere*: to sit above or be superior to. In general parlance to supersede means to take the place of someone or something, while to be superseded means to be set aside as useless or obsolete in favour of someone or something that is regarded as superior. In recent decades the term 'supersessionism' has gained currency among theologians and biblical scholars to refer to the traditional Christian belief that since Christ's coming the Church has taken the place of the Jewish people as God's chosen community, and that God's **covenant** with the Jews is now over and done. By extension, the term can be used to refer to any interpretation of Christian faith generally or the status of the Church in particular that claims or implies the abrogation or obsolescence of God's covenant with the Jewish people. Supersessionism is thus substantially equivalent to **replacement theology**, and the two terms are often used interchangeably.

Although never formally defined as a **doctrine** by the **early Church**, supersessionism has stood at the centre of Christianity's understanding of its relationship to the Jewish people from antiquity until recent times. During the second and third centuries Christian theologians (e.g. **Irenaeus, Tertullian**) often articulated its main elements in opposition to Marcionism (*see* **Marcion**) on the one hand and Judaism on the other. They condemned Marcionites for denying that the one God and Father of Jesus Christ had spoken in the **Old Testament**, and that he had indeed entered in some fashion into a special relationship with **Abraham**'s descendants according to the flesh. But they equally condemned Jews for failing to recognise that after Christ's **incarnation** God had irrevocably transferred all the benefits of this relationship from Abraham's carnal descendents to his spiritual ones, that is, to the Church, where the benefits were moreover available in superior form. After Christianity became the official religion of the **Roman Empire**, supersessionism provided a theological rationale for imperial policy towards Jews, with similarly two-sided implications. In contrast to paganism, which was driven underground and eventually extinguished, Judaism continued to enjoy some measure of official **toleration** and self-government, but on terms increasingly subordinate to Christianity and disadvantageous to Jewish institutions. Supersessionism also figures prominently in modern Christian thought, which has often portrayed the origin of the Church as a victory of universal, humanising values over ancient Judaism's narrow, self-interested, particularistic ones (**Kant**, Schleiermacher (1768–1834), **Harnack**).

After the Second World War, and particularly in the light of the **Holocaust**, Christians in Europe and North America gradually began to question the soundness of supersessionism on the grounds of its consistency with scripture (especially **Romans 9–11**), its coherence with other Christian beliefs (e.g. the fidelity of God) and its practical consequences (e.g. the inculcation of contempt toward Jews). By the 1990s many Church bodies had issued public teaching documents (e.g. the Evangelical Church of the Rhineland's *Toward Renovation of the Relationship of Christians and Jews* (1980) and the Presbyterian Church (USA)'s *A Theological Understanding of the Relationship Between Christians and Jews* (1987)) repudiating the belief that Christ's coming entails the abrogation or obsolescence of God's covenant with **Israel**. Alternatives to supersessionism concur in affirming the ongoing validity of God's covenant with the Jewish people, but beyond that vary widely among themselves. Some emphasise the relative independence of Christianity and Judaism as different but equally valid appropriations of a common religious inheritance rooted in biblical Israel (often called 'two covenant' approaches). Others interpret the Church and the Jewish people as interdependent players in a common history of **salvation** (so-called 'one covenant' approaches). To date North Atlantic Christians have taken the initiative in seeking **post-supersessionist** ways to express Christian faith; the long-term viability of their efforts will depend in part on whether and to what degree Christians in South America, Asia and Africa also begin to consider and address the fundamental theological issues at stake.

See also **recognition theology**

R. KENDALL SOULEN

Switzerland

Switzerland has had a Jewish community since the thirteenth century, made up of Jews from **Germany** and **France**. The medieval community flourished until the mid-fourteenth century when, during the **Black Death**, Jews were accused of poisoning wells and of murdering a Christian boy named Rudolf (*see* **blood libel**). Many Jews were killed and Jewish children forcibly baptised. Regular **expulsions** followed, and although Jews often returned

to their homes within a few years, in some cities such as Basel (edict in 1434) they were required to attend proselytising sermons. Jews began to return in greater numbers in the sixteenth century when Christian printers began printing **Hebrew** texts. **Emancipation** was granted in 1874. Prior to and during the Second World War Switzerland gave refuge to about 23,000 Jewish refugees, and its role in the **Holocaust** has become the object of fierce debate, notably in the 1990s. For example, the Catholic Bishops' Conference in Switzerland issued a statement on the subject in 1997, acknowledging the failure of the Churches. In 1947 Switzerland hosted a group of Jews, Protestants and Catholics in **Seelisberg** to consider the implications of the Holocaust; this marked the establishment of the International **Council of Christians and Jews**. The **World Council of Churches** and the Orthodox Center of the Ecumenical Patriarchate are based in Switzerland, increasing its importance in modern Jewish–Christian **dialogue**. In 1977, for example, an Orthodox Christian–Jewish conference took place in Lucerne, a city that houses an institute for Jewish–Christian dialogue founded by Swiss Catholic theologian Clemens Thoma (b. 1932) who has written a number of important works on Christian–Jewish relations.

EDWARD KESSLER

Synagogue *see* **Church and synagogue**

Syriac Christianity

The Syriac language is a form of **Aramaic** spoken in the region of Edessa from shortly before the beginning of the Christian era. It is therefore closely related to the form of Aramaic spoken by **Jesus** himself. Syriac Christianity refers to the form Christianity took in the lands where Syriac was spoken, where there were active Christian communities from the beginning. It was a region where there had long been important Jewish communities, especially in Edessa. From the beginning relations between Jews and Syriac Christians were close, displaying both shared traditions and sharp antagonisms. This is illustrated by the fifth-century *Doctrine of Addai*, which on the one hand accuses Jews of killing Christ but on the other indicates that Christians had friendly relations with Jews and may have attended the synagogue. Because Syriac Christianity retained its original Semitic expression, it was thus less affected than Christianity in the rest of the **Roman Empire** by the need to negotiate the thought-world of **Hellenism**, and remained open to Jewish traditions, both targumic and rabbinic. The principal version of the scriptures (and still the authorised version of the Syriac-speaking Churches) is the **Peshitta**, the **Old Testament** of which was probably made from the Hebrew original in the early part of the second century for the Jewish community in Edessa; it betrays the influence of **targumic** interpretations. In the **New Testament** the Gospels exist in two forms: a Syriac translation of the *Diatessaron*, a harmony of the Gospels composed in **Greek** by the Syrian Tatian (the original Greek is lost), and a later 'Gospel of the Separated', that is, the four separate Gospels, known as the 'Old Syriac'. The Peshitta included Acts and the major Catholic epistles and the Pauline epistles (in that order), but not the Apocalypse, or the lesser Catholic epistles (2 Peter, 2 and 3 John, and Jude). The earliest forms of Syriac Christianity – *Odes of Solomon*, Bar-Daisan, *Acts of Judas Thomas* (containing the beautiful 'Hymn of the Pearl') – were from the point of view of Greco-Roman Christianity tainted with '**Gnosticism**', though more recent scholarship has tended to see them as indebted to **ascetic** Jewish traditions, such as those of the **Qumran** community or the Essenes (if they are not one and the same). Syriac Christianity, in this deeply ascetic form, was embraced by those who called themselves the 'sons of the covenants', or the 'single ones' (*ihidhayeh*), celibate followers of the 'Only-begotten' (same word in Syriac). The separation of Syriac Christianity from mainstream Mediterranean Christianity should not, however, be exaggerated. The greatest Syriac writers of the fourth century, **Aphrahat** and **Ephrem**, supported the great Greek fathers of the fourth century in their rejection of **Arianism**, and in the following centuries the Syriac fathers were as deeply involved in the continuing **Christological** controversy and the controversy over Origenism as the Greek fathers. In their writings Aphrahat and especially Ephrem betray extensive knowledge of Jewish exegetical traditions, both targumic and rabbinic, in their interpretation of scripture, some of which no longer survive in the rabbinic literature. This Jewish influence is manifest as late as the seventh century. The influence of Semitic literary genres partly explains Ephrem's fondness for metrical forms, which probably influenced the development of liturgical poetry in the Greek Church. From the fifth century onwards Christian antagonism to Jews led to attacks on synagogues. With the rise of **Islam**, Syriac first acted as a bridge between Greek and Arabic (especially for philosophical works), but increasingly became an artificial language, used largely liturgically.

ANDREW LOUTH

TTTT

Talmud

A generic name (literally 'Teaching') for the most important works of **Rabbinic Judaism**. The Palestinian Talmud (*y.*) (also known as 'Jerusalem Talmud') dates from the second half of the fourth century CE, while the Babylonian Talmud (*b.*) (far more important in medieval and later Jewish tradition) was redacted from the fifth to the seventh centuries CE. Both are structured as commentaries on the **Mishnah**, but include much more than **commentary**: they present and discuss a wide range of legal and non-legal sources (*halakhah* and *aggadah*), often digressing into **ethics**, biblical **exegesis**, anecdotes and stories. Talmud and contemporary Christian literature were written, it seems, without knowledge of each other; mutual influence is generally unlikely.

As the main source-text of Judaism, the Talmud has long been at the centre of Jewish–Christian controversies. However, references to Christianity and Christians are sparse in the Talmud and related literature. This is surprising, considering the high level of Christian presence in Palestine from the fourth century, and that a large proportion of the Babylonian Talmud is based on traditions of Palestinian origins. It may also appear surprising that the few talmudic passages that mention **Jesus** or Christians (see below) are almost entirely confined to the Babylonian Talmud. This may reflect self-censorship by the authors or early transmitters of the Palestinian Talmud who lived (until the seventh century) under increasingly oppressive Christian rule, unlike the Babylonians who lived under non-Christian rule; but this remains entirely speculative. The scarcity of references to Christianity in both Talmuds more probably reflects a general lack of interest, in early Rabbinic Judaism, towards other religions: specific pagan cults are rarely mentioned in the Talmuds, but simply bundled into the catch-all category of *avodah zarah*. One passage (*b. Avodah Zarah* 6a and 7b) suggests, indeed, that Christianity belongs to the category of *avodah zarah*, although it is not explained in what respect it should be regarded as idolatrous, polytheistic or 'pagan'. The assimilation of Christianity with other religions into the single, halakhic category of *avodah zarah* may thus explain its apparent rarity in the Talmud. Another category frequently associated with the Christians is *min* (pl. *minim*), literally 'type(s)', a term generally applied to (Jewish) heretics, including Christians, and by extension applicable (in some cases) to non-Jewish Christians; although the extent to which the term *min* in the Talmud should be identified as 'Christian' has been grossly overestimated. One *min*, Jacob of Sikhnin, is said to have healed 'in the name of Jesus' and conveyed an exegetical teaching of Jesus to Rabbi Eliezer (early second century; the latter subsequently regretted his action: *b. Avodah Zarah* 16b–17a, 27b); he is certainly to be identified as Christian. The same probably applies to the *minim* of Caesarea who are said to have challenged Rabbi Abbahu (late third century) about the meaning of Amos 3.2 and its implications regarding the election of **Israel** and its current sufferings (*b. Avodah Zarah* 4a; see also the dialogue of Rabban Gamaliel and a *min* in *b. Yevamot* 102b). This story, if historical, would suggest that some Palestinian rabbis had polemical encounters with Christians.

Explicit references in the Talmud to the figure of Jesus are more detailed, and in some ways more interesting. 'Jesus the Christian' (*Yeshu ha-noẓri*) is depicted as a pupil of Rabbi Joshua ben Perahyah who was expelled by his master because of his lewdness, and subsequently apostasied to **idolatry** (*b. Sotah* 47a; *b. Sanhedrin* 107a). He was tried, executed and hung on the eve of **Passover** by the Jewish high court, for practising **magic** and luring the Jews into idolatry (*b. Sanhedrin* 43a). These sources are defiant rather than apologetic: there is no attempt, for example, to deny that the Jews killed Jesus. However, it must be remembered that the Talmud is addressed exclusively to a Jewish rabbinic readership. It is difficult to relate these stories to anything contained in the Gospels, the detailed contents of which are ostensibly unknown to the talmudic authors (save for one paraphrase of the **Sermon on the Mount**, and a pun on the word *evangelion*, in *b. Shabbat* 116a–b). Talmudic stories about Jesus are certainly polemical (e.g. the gibe, in coded language, on the virginity of Miriam/**Mary**: *b. Sanhedrin* 67a), but their source remains unclear; they are more likely to represent later literary creations than the legacy of some early historical tradition. These stories later formed the basis of the medieval compilation *Toledot Yeshu*.

Besides the passages so far discussed, the Talmud appears in some places to polemicise against Christianity, but without any explicit mention of Christianity or Jesus. The identification of these passages as **anti-Christian** polemics is naturally contentious; but we may point, for example, to a saying attributed to R. Abbahu that if someone claims to be God or the **'son of man'**, he is a liar (*y. Ta'anit* 2.1, 65b) – this saying is more likely aimed at Jesus than at pagan, deified men. In *b. Sanhedrin* 46b a **parable** is cited of a robber who was hanged, but whom onlookers mistook to be the king. This source (already attested in the third century Tosefta) may well be a parody of the **Crucifixion**, not least because it is part of an exegesis of Deut. 21.22–3, and may thus be a covert response to Gal. 3.13. Implicit **polemics** of this kind, however, are far more frequent in the contemporary and later works of **midrash**; even if correctly identified, their historical significance and *Sitz im Leben* is yet to be established.

From the thirteenth century the Talmud became the object of Jewish–Christian controversies and **disputations**. In 1240 the disputation in Paris of Nicholas **Donin** led, two years later, to the public burning of 24 cartloads of Talmud (and presumably other books). The Talmud suffered further repression from Christian authorities (e.g. **Innocent IV**) in this and subsequent centuries, and was included in the first Index of forbidden books in 1559, although **Christian Hebraists** such as Johannes **Reuchlin** attempted to defend it. The text of the Talmud also suffered from **censorship**, either at the hand of Christians, or by Jews anticipating Christian censors. The Basel edition of 1578–80 was particularly mutilated by Christian censorship. This led to the expurgation from standard editions (including the now standard Vilna edition of 1880–6) of all explicit references to Jesus and Christians (i.e. the passages referred to above), as well as of words considered offensive such as *min*, 'non-Jew', or even 'Talmud'.

See also **Talmud trials**   SACHA STERN

Talmud trials

Allegations against the **Talmud** had already been made in the twelfth century by, for example, Peter **Alfonsi** and **Peter the Venerable**, Abbot of Cluny. What is new in the thirteenth century is much greater first-hand knowledge of Jewish post-biblical writings amongst Christians. In 1236 the Jewish convert Nicholas **Donin** wrote to Pope **Gregory IX** accusing the Talmud of blaspheming **Jesus** and the Virgin, maligning non-Jews and altering scriptural precepts. The charge that Jews followed precepts of the Talmud rather than those found in the Bible was an especially serious threat to the Jews whose presence in Christian society was safeguarded by the principle, formulated by **Augustine of Hippo**, that they bore witness to the truth of Christianity by upholding the books of the **Old Testament**. Pope Gregory instructed the **Dominicans** and **Franciscans** to confiscate the Talmud. In **France** the Talmud was put on trial in Paris in 1240. After Rabbi Jehiel ben Joseph of Paris (d. before 1267) was unsuccessful in combating the allegations brought against it, and an ecclesiastical court headed by Eudes (Odo) of Chateauroux (d. 1273), chancellor of the University of Paris, condemned it, cartloads of volumes of the Talmud were publicly burnt in 1242. Some years later Pope **Innocent IV** commissioned Eudes, by then cardinal-bishop of Tusculum, to reinvestigate the Talmud. This led to further condemnation of the text. The remainder of the thirteenth and the fourteenth centuries witnessed various instances of confiscation, burning or **censorship** of the Talmud. In general, however, it seems as if popes were hesitant to deprive Jews permanently of their sacred texts altogether, however much they were concerned about their contents. Traditional papal policy towards the Jews did ensure that Jews were allowed the wherewithal to practice their religion.

In 1263 the Talmud was subjected to another public investigation in the **disputation** of Barcelona between **Paul the Christian**, a convert from Judaism, and **Nahmanides** in the presence of

James I of Aragon. By this time Christian scholars did not just reject the whole Talmud as an affront to Christianity, they incorporated the Talmud in their efforts to convert Jews by interpreting various passages as attesting to Christian belief. Thus in Barcelona Paul attempted to demonstrate that the Talmud proved that the **Messiah** had come and that Christian teaching was therefore correct. Nahmanides' long Hebrew report reflects the earnest attempts made by the Jewish community to deflect this new and dangerous conversionary tactic. Subsequent work by the Dominicans greatly perfected Paul's jejune efforts. In his *Pugio Fidei* ('Dagger of Faith', *c.*1278) the Dominican Raymond **Martini** quotes countless passages of post-biblical Jewish writings in **Hebrew** and **Aramaic** in order to prove the veracity of Christianity to Jews. Condemning the Talmud whilst at the same time identifying **prooftexts** from it for Christianity was once again on the agenda at the public disputation staged in Tortosa in 1413–14 by anti-pope Benedict XIII (*r.*1394–1417). Over a period of almost two years of relentless conversionary effort many Jews were converted. Later Joseph Albo (*c.*1380–*c.*1435), who took part in the disputation, wrote his *Sefer ha-Ikkarim* (Book of Principles) in an effort to bolster Jewish confidence.

ANNA SAPIR ABULAFIA

Tanakh *see* Hebrew Bible; Old Testament

Tantur Ecumenical Institute

On the border between south **Jerusalem** and the Palestinian West Bank, the Tantur (literally 'hilltop') Ecumenical Institute embodies the shared dream of **Paul VI** and the official observers at **Vatican II**: an international, intercultural, ecumenical community of prayer, study and **dialogue** in the Holy City. The institute, under the guidance of both Protestant and Roman Catholic rectors, focusses ecumenical and interfaith relations through study, research and international or local meetings with Christians, Jews and Muslims. Since Tantur's opening in 1973 over 4,500 scholars, teachers, parish clergy and other Church workers have participated in its programmes, conducted principally by local Christian, Jewish and Muslim teachers, on topics such as biblical studies, field trips, Abrahamic spiritualities, the bases and practices of ecumenical and interreligious relations, human rights and non-violent conflict resolutions in the Holy Land.

MICHAEL MCGARRY

Targum

A Jewish translation of the **Hebrew Bible** into **Aramaic**, dating from Late Antiquity (first to eighth centuries CE). There are Targums for all the biblical books, with the exception of Ezra–Nehemiah and Daniel, which already contain substantial portions in Aramaic. In many cases several Targums, either in whole or in part, are extant for the same books. For example, besides the official Babylonian Targum to the **Pentateuch** known as **Onkelos**, a complete Palestinian Targum to the Pentateuch, known as Codex Neofiti 1, survives, as well as several incomplete Palestinian versions (the Fragmentary Targum and the **Cairo Genizah** fragments), and a curious late text, Targum Pseudo-Jonathan, which combines elements of both Onkelos and the Palestinian tradition. The institution of the Targum originated in the early synagogue's practice of orally rendering the Hebrew biblical lections into the vernacular. Many Targums contain paraphrases and expansions of the biblical text which make them valuable repositories of early Jewish **exegesis**, on which **Rashi** and other medieval Jewish Bible commentators draw from time to time.

The Targums have long attracted the interest of Christian scholars. It is possible that **Jerome**'s knowledge of Jewish Bible exegesis was derived, at least in part, from a Targum, known either to himself, or to one of his Jewish informants. Medieval **Christian Hebraists** such as Nicholas of **Lyra** also studied the Targums, but it was not until the **Reformation**, with its return to the Bible in its original languages, that Christian scholars truly mastered this literature. Texts of the Targums were included in the great Christian polyglot Bibles, starting with the Complutensian Polyglot (Alcalá de Henares, 1514–17), and culminating in the London Polyglot, edited by Brian Walton (1665). They can also be found, without Latin translations, in the Rabbinic Bibles printed by Daniel Bomberg and others (1525 etc.). Though printed under Christian auspices, the texts of the Targums were prepared by Jewish scholars, who in some cases were converts to Christianity (e.g. the Spaniard Alfonso de Zamora (d. 1531), whose editions of the Targums, still preserved in manuscripts in Madrid and Salamanca, were used in the Complutensian Polyglot and the Biblia Regia, Antwerp). Christian scholars pioneered the study of the Targums, and as a result they were rather neglected and marginalised among Jews. A notable exception was the Jewish biblical scholar Samuel David Luzzatto (1800–65), who wrote an important study of Targum Onkelos.

Christian interest in the Targums focussed on: (1) Their language. The Targums were used by Christian scholars to reconstruct the Aramaic spoken by **Jesus** and the first Christians. Debate has raged as to which targumic Aramaic dialect is closest to the language of Jesus. Gustav Dalman (1855–1941) argued that it is Onkelos; Alejandro Díez Macho (1916–84) that it is the Palestinian Targumim. (2) Their exegesis. Though the 'official' Targums (Onkelos to the Pentateuch and Jonathan to the Prophets) have been heavily influenced by **Rabbinic Judaism**, the Targums are not in origin rabbinic, and they contain interpretations that are sometimes at variance with the official rabbinic view and closer to Christian exegesis. Thus, they interpret Isa. 53 (*see* **'Suffering Servant'**) as referring to the sufferings of the **Messiah**, and not of the Jewish people as a whole – the standard rabbinic opinion. Christian apologists have seized on this to argue that the Targums reflect earlier Jewish exegesis which the rabbis suppressed because it supported Christianity. Less controversially, Christian scholars have used the Targums to illuminate **New Testament** exegesis of the **Old Testament**. By assuming that the Targum's interpretation was current in the first century, a flood of light can sometimes be thrown on the early Christian use of the Old Testament/Tanakh. The Targums have played an important role in demonstrating how rooted early Christianity was in Jewish tradition. More recently, however, Jewish scholars have attempted to reclaim the Targums, along with the **apocrypha**, other deutero-canonical texts, and the **Dead Sea Scrolls**, as a part of the Jewish heritage.   *PHILIP ALEXANDER*

Temple

The Jerusalem Temple, first built by Solomon after the example of other Syro-Phoenician temples as a state sanctuary around 960 BCE (1 Kgs 5.16ff.), destroyed by troops of the Neo-Babylonian Empire in 587, rebuilt by the returnees from the Babylonian exile and rededicated in 515, desecrated by Antiochus IV Epiphanes (*r.*175–164 BCE) in 167 and again rededicated by Judas Maccabaeus in 164, suffered final destruction at the hands of the Roman military leader Titus (39–81) in 70 CE. Until the

Josianic Reform in 622 BCE the **Jerusalem** Temple had been one of many in the **land of Israel**. The reform centralised the cult and made the Jerusalem sanctuary the only remaining legal one. It contained, until 587, the Ark of the Covenant, which was never replaced. From its beginnings the Temple served as the focus of ancient Israelite and Jewish religious and cultural self-understanding and as an economic centre; after its final destruction it became a focal point for nostalgia and for fervent **eschatological** expectation. In Christianity the Temple was used as the negative background for the **salvation** brought about by Christ: although **Jesus** is described as a devout practitioner of the **Law** (Matt. 21.12, 23), he prophesies the destruction of the Temple (Mark 13.2), and at the moment of his death the veil protecting the holy of holies is rent asunder (Mark 15.38). However, for the earliest Christians in Jerusalem, who considered themselves no less Jewish than their fellow Jews, the Jerusalem Temple continued to be the centre of their religious lives (Luke 24.53; Acts 2.46) until 70 CE. The rebuilding of the Temple remains one of the hopes of **Orthodox Judaism** (e.g. the *Shemoneh Esre*). From the Christian perspective the sacrifice of Christ rendered the Temple obsolete: there will be no Temple in the New Jerusalem (Rev. 21.22).   *JOACHIM SCHAPER*

Temple, William (1881–1944)

As Archbishop of York (1929–42) and Canterbury (1942–4), Temple played an important role in the formation of the **Council of Christians and Jews** (CCJ). A creative theologian, Temple, who keenly supported **ecumenism**, became increasingly interested in the application of the gospel to social problems. In 1941, in discussion with Chief Rabbi J. H. Hertz (1872–1946) and others about the formation of CCJ, Temple insisted that, rather than just combating **antisemitism**, CCJ should emphasise the fundamental ethical values shared by Judaism and Christianity, which provided the basis for European civilisation and which were under attack by **Nazism**.   *MARCUS BRAYBROOKE*

Ten Commandments

The Ten Commandments, also known as the Decalogue ('Ten Words' in Exod. 34.28 and Deut. 10.4), are highly honoured in the Christian community, despite the contrast long drawn by Christians between Judaism as a religion of divine **law** and Christianity as a religion of divine **grace**. This contrast between law and grace, supported especially by reference to **Paul**'s epistles to the Galatians and Romans, is called into question precisely by the Ten Commandments, thus making the Decalogue a potentially fruitful subject in Jewish–Christian relations.

The Ten Commandments of Exod. 20.1–17 and Deut. 5.6–21 summarise the demands of God placed upon **Israel**. They do so, however, in a way that makes them applicable to all peoples and all times. While the opening commandments are tied to Israelite faith (YHWH delivered Israel from bondage in Egypt, is the only deity who counts, forbids **idolatry** and the misuse of the divine name), even these carry a meaning applicable to all peoples (the mercy and uniqueness of the deity). The commandments are not so much law as the foundation for particular laws. They were probably committed to memory in the home and recited periodically in public gatherings for the reaffirmation of the **covenant** between Israel and the deity.

The commandments as read and observed in Judaism begin with Exod. 20.2 (Deut. 5.6): 'I am the LORD your God (better: 'I the LORD am your God') who brought you out of the land of Egypt, out of the house of slavery', a declaration rather than a commandment, but one that firmly establishes God's love and grace as the motivation and ground for the demands that follow. Since the twentieth century this grounding of Israelite law in divine grace has been widely affirmed by Christian as well as Jewish interpreters. Three commandments stand out as highly distinctive from those of neighbouring communities, all with consequences for relations between Judaism and Christianity. The prohibition of the making of carved images resulted over time in a rejection of all images of the deity, even though the Israelites surely knew that such images were *representations* of the deity, not objects of worship as such. Strict fidelity to this prohibition by some Christian groups brought division within the Christian community, while laxity by both Jews and Christians through the centuries often resulted in bitter conflict within and between the communities. The command to observe the **Sabbath** or seventh day came to divide Christians over how to relate Sabbath and Lord's Day (Sunday). And the prohibition of the taking of human life has offered a challenge of interpretation for both Jews and Christians. How is the Hebrew term *raẓaḥ* to be understood? Does it refer to murder or to any taking of human life? Does the command rule out **capital punishment**, warfare, euthanasia, **abortion**? Joint debates between Jews and Christians over these commandments have proved highly productive, especially as each community has come better to understand the long traditions of interpretation by the other. In Christian history the negative form of most of the commandments has caused Christian interpreters to contrast Jewish prohibitions with Christian positive commands that sum up the entire law (Matt. 22.36–40; Mark 12.28–34; Luke 10.25–8; Rom. 13.9), but the positive import of short, pithy prohibitions, easily remembered, in providing orientation and guidance for the community is unmistakable. Christian communities have made regular use of the Ten Commandments in both instruction and **worship**. More critical for Jewish–Christian relations is the whole question of how law itself is best understood. Studies of texts in praise of God's teaching or **Torah** (e.g. Pss 19 and 119), plus the relation of Torah to **wisdom** (Sir. 24; Bar. 3.9–4.4), have radically altered much Christian understanding of law in the Bible, bringing about a renewed appreciation of the form, contents and function of the Ten Commandments and of the very meaning of Torah within the Jewish community.

Controversy has arisen in the **United States** over the posting of the Ten Commandments in public places, an issue still not resolved. The controversy is primarily among Christians and does not greatly affect Jewish–Christian relations thus far.

WALTER HARRELSON

Tertullian of Carthage (second century CE)

Church Father. The author of ***Adversus Judaeos***, a prominent example of the literary genre to which it gave its name, Tertullian was principally concerned with being a Christian in a pagan society and his knowledge of Judaism seems to have been limited. Scholars are divided as to his view of, and the extent of his contact with, Jews and Judaism, some arguing that he saw Jews and Christians as rivals jointly fighting the evil of **idolatry**, others that *Adversus Judaeos* was written to convert not Jews but pagans. All agree, however, that Tertullian believed Christianity, not Judaism, was the spiritual heir of Israel (*see* **supersessionism**).

See also **Church Fathers**; **early Church**

EDWARD KESSLER

Testaments

Belonging to the category of the **Pseudepigrapha**, testaments can be classified as a genre of **Hellenistic** Jewish literature, with forerunners in **Aramaic** Jewish literature. They played a significant role in their Jewish context, and some were taken over and modified by the **early Church**. There are several distinctive elements characterising testaments: after introductory remarks and an opening formula, a dying father addresses his offspring, or a teacher or leader directs a farewell discourse at his successor, his followers, his disciples or his people. The discourse tends to comprise references to events in the speaker's past, moral exhortations directed at the listeners, and forebodings of the future, ending with a concluding formula. The testament as a whole ends with the death and burial of the central character. They are modelled on biblical farewell discourses, such as Gen. 27.1–40, 49, Deut. 1.1–4.40, Josh. 23–24 and 1 Sam. 12. The most characteristic examples of the genre are the *Testaments of the Twelve Patriarchs*, the *Testament of Job*, and the *Assumptio Mosis*. Some of the writings commonly called testaments are in fact not representatives of the genre, like the *Testament of Abraham* and the *Testament of Solomon*. The testaments were intended to exhort, sustain and educate their readers by referring to exemplary characters in Israel's past and were used, in modified form, for similar purposes by early Christians, to whom they appealed because of their paraenetic character. The most famous testaments, the *Testaments of the Twelve Patriarchs*, are Christian in their present form and contain components that range from the second century BCE to the second century CE, witnessing to the interest of Christian communities in Hellenistic Jewish theology and incorporating elements from both traditions.

JOACHIM SCHAPER

Testimonia

Testimonia are collections of uncommented quotations, especially from the Bible, which are organised around common themes. They were produced and used in ancient Judaism and in the **early Church**. Collected as **proof-texts** in order to support certain theological viewpoints, testimonia were made to serve didactic, paraenetic, polemical and liturgical purposes respectively. Amongst such testimonia were: the oldest Christian collection extant, **Cyprian**'s *Testimonia ad Quirinum*; the collection

presumably put together by Gregory of Nyssa (330–*c*.395); a compilation of Old Testament quotations attributed to **Melito of Sardis** (cf. Eusebius, *Hist. eccl.* 4.26.12ff.) and the compilation produced by Bar Salibi, of which a Syriac text is extant. However, testimonia had already been compiled in **Hellenistic** Judaism: amongst the **Qumran** writings was found what is probably the earliest example of a collection still in existence, viz. 4Q175 (4QTest), a collection of Messianic/eschatological texts. The thesis proposed by J. R. Harris (*Testimonies, passim*), according to which all Christian testimonia collections can be traced back to one original testimony book of **Old Testament** prophecies intended to demonstrate that **Jesus** was the **Messiah**, was subjected to fierce criticism by, amongst others, C. H. Dodd (1884–1973) and Krister Stendahl (b. 1921). The existence of 4Q175 indicates that the genre of testimonia collections predates the beginnings of Christianity and was 'inherited' from Hellenistic Judaism. Rabbinic testimonia are not known. The basic concept informing the collectors of testimonia, both in Judaism and in Christianity, was their view of scripture as containing texts that could be used to show the truth of **eschatological** and Messianic predictions. *JOACHIM SCHAPER*

Tetragrammaton

Greek term meaning '[comprising] four letters' signifying the name of **God** in Hebrew, YHWH, often shortened to tetragram. First found in **Philo** (*Mos.* 2.115), the designation was taken up by early Christian writers. The tetragram's original vocalisation is uncertain, but there is evidence (**Samaritan** usage, **Church Fathers**, the shortened form Yah) that it was probably pronounced 'Yah-weh'. In the late biblical period the name's pronunciation began to fall into disuse for several reasons (Martin Rose, 'Names of God in the OT'). It was once believed that the name's usage ceased completely by the time of the **Septuagint** (LXX), whose translators employed *kyrios* ('Lord') for YHWH, reflecting the Palestinian practice of substituting *adonai* ('Lord'). However, with the twentieth-century discovery of pre-Christian LXX manuscripts containing Hebrew tetragrams (or the Greek trigram *Iao*) written within the Greek text, scholars revised this assumption, some postulating that it was Christians who replaced the tetragram with *kyrios*. Evidence for the history of the name's gradual disuse, both oral and written, is contradictory, and various scenarios postulated by certain academics are inadequate for explaining this complex issue. A number of scholars find various evidence for the name in the **New Testament**; some pagans and early Christians knew the name especially in its pronounced Greek form (McDonough, *YHWH at Patmos*; Shaw, 'The Earliest Use of Ιαω'). 'Jehovah' came about when late medieval Roman Catholics and early Reformers began studying **Hebrew** and, unaware of the Masoretic practice of pointing YHWH with the vowels for *adonai*, misread the tetragram and produced this designation, used in Church hymns and some **Bible translations** until the mid-twentieth century. Most Bibles today utilise the device LORD to indicate the name. *FRANK SHAW*

Textbooks

United States and European studies of how Christian and Jewish religion textbooks present the other tradition have proven to be useful measures of reform. Textbooks are defined herein as grade-level-specific books used for classroom religious instruction.

In the late 1950s in the **United States** the American Jewish Committee sponsored studies of the treatment of different ethnic, racial and religious groups in Jewish, Catholic and Protestant secondary textbooks. In the Catholic study Rose Thering OP discovered that positive comments about Judaism were restricted to praising Judaism as the forerunner of Christianity. The widespread negative assertions about Jews mostly referred to the **New Testament** themes of the supposed Jewish rejection of Christ and their consequent divine punishment, the role of Jews in Jesus' **crucifixion**, or **Pharisaism** (Pawlikowski, *Catechetics and Prejudice*). In the Protestant study, Bernhard Olson (*Faith and Prejudice*) examined textbooks from fundamentalist, conservative, liberal and neo-orthodox Christian publishers. He was concerned that the frequent mention of Jews in 64 per cent of all lessons could make them a 'vulnerable target'. Thering's list of negative topics was replicated by Olson, with the additional biblical subjects of early conflicts between **Church and synagogue** and Gentile admission to the Church. Olson believed that the authors' pre-existing attitudes towards other religious communities shaped their interpretations of pertinent New Testament passages. The Jewish study of Bernard D. Weinryb ('Intergroup Content in Jewish Textbooks') found that only 14 per

cent of lessons referred to Gentile religious groups. Over 90 per cent of those references were either neutral or intended to combat prejudice. Negative comments were more numerous concerning other segments of the Jewish community. These United States studies were made known to Pope **John XXIII** and contributed to his wish that **Vatican II** prepare a document on Jews and Judaism; *Nostra Aetate* was thus partially the consequence of textbook research.

Beginning in 1967, the Sperry Center for Intergroup Learning sponsored analyses of Italian and Spanish Catholic textbooks published between 1940 and 1964 and of French Catholic textbooks used from 1949 to 1964. Jews were mentioned twice as often as Protestants in Italian textbooks and six times more often in Spanish materials. The ratio of negative to positive references to Jews in Italian texts was found to be roughly 5 to 1 and about 3 to 2 in the Spanish books, although the Spanish negative comments were more vituperative. The French texts were generally more balanced, but the positive comments mostly referred to Jews before the time of Jesus. These studies concluded that young European Catholics were being taught that 'the Jews' killed Jesus and were punished by God, that Jews had rejected Jesus because they were materialistic, that the unfaithful Jews cannot be saved, and that Judaism has been superseded by Christianity and now has no meaning (Bishop, *How Catholics Look at Jews*).

In 1972 the American Jewish Committee sponsored research by Gerald S. Strober to determine if the 1963 Olson study had affected US Protestant materials (*Portrait of the Elder Brother*). Strober concluded that the same topics remained problematic.

In the early 1970s Eugene J. Fisher studied primary and secondary US Catholic textbooks and found that 'American Catholic religion materials are significantly more positive toward Judaism than they were before the Vatican Council' (*Faith without Prejudice*). The idea of a divine punishment of Jews, for instance, had vanished or was condemned. However, there were still topics that produced negative scores according to the statistical instrument Fisher employed. It should be noted that 'negativity' in this statistical sense means 'inaccuracy'. These topics were: (1) Jesus and Jewish contemporaries, (2) Pharisaism, (3) the crucifixion, and (4) the relationship of the **Old Testament** to the New Testament. A study by Philip A. Cunningham of late-1980s Catholic primary and secondary textbooks (*Education for Shalom*) found that the negative topics in Fisher's study remained negative, although noticeably less so. The exception was the more negative treatment of the crucifixion in secondary textbooks because of careless remarks that sweepingly implicated Jews or Jewish leaders. Cunningham also concluded that 'the most important single deficiency in present textbooks is the minimal application or complete lack of critical biblical insights'. Stuart Polly studied US Protestant junior and senior high school textbooks and Sunday school materials within a year of the Cunningham study. He found that 65–80 per cent of Protestant lessons referred to Jews as compared with about 50 per cent in the Cunningham Catholic study. Polly also discovered that materials for younger students tended to be more negative to Jews because they lacked the extended and nuanced presentations of high school materials. Collectively, the nine Protestant curricula that Polly evaluated had about an equal number of positive and negative references to Jews. However, this ratio ranged from almost entirely positive for one publisher to largely negative for another. Polly's list of negative topics mirrored those of the other studies.

Ronald Kronish conducted an informal assessment of Israeli textbooks in 1998. He noted that the few lessons on Christianity were mostly historical rather than religious in nature. This led to a danger of Christians being mentioned only as oppressors of Jews. Kronish also observed little interest in recent changes in the teachings of some Christian churches.

The following overall conclusions can be drawn:

1. Christian textbooks had been predominantly negative in their portrayal of Judaism until the mid-1960s. Then some Christian Churches began to revise their textbook lessons, most notably the Roman Catholic Church in the wake of Vatican II. Protestant curricula vary more widely in terms of how Jews are portrayed.
2. Certain recurrent biblical topics are consistently problematic in Christian education depending on whether a textbook employs various forms of **biblical criticism**.
3. Jewish educational materials are less concerned with teaching about the religious other. There is some tendency to portray Christians only as historical oppressors and to overlook recent changes in Christian theology.

Future research should examine **lectionary**-based curricula and the curricula in continents and Churches not previously examined. Previous studies should be updated regularly.

See also **religious education**

PHILIP A. CUNNINGHAM

Theodoret of Cyrrhus (393–466)

Christian bishop, theologian, exegete and historian of the Antiochene tradition. Theodoret's literary work is extraordinarily wide in scope, encompassing biblical **exegesis**, Church history, **Christology** and a comprehensive refutation of paganism. He displays a conventional but comparatively moderate hostility to the Jews, regularly lamenting their misunderstanding of scripture and their infidelity to God's purposes. He reports the enthusiasm of Jews across the Empire for **Julian the Apostate**'s proposal to rebuild the **Temple** and also notes that the various woes of the Jews under the **Roman Empire** were the direct result of their rejection of Jesus Christ. Theodoret notes instances of forced **conversion** of Jews with apparent approval but also hints at a more tolerant approach, remarking that Jews are commanded to follow the pious ways of their fathers and aiming his criticism not so much at Jews in general but rather at particular instances of perceived impiety.   *MARCUS PLESTED*

Theodosian Code

Collection of imperial legislation dating from 312 onwards promulgated in 438 by the Emperor Theodosius II (*r.*408–50). The Theodosian Code witnesses the passage of Christianity from the favoured religion of the emperor to the official religion of the **Roman Empire**. A number of prescriptions against the Jews are laid down (without necessarily being rigidly or universally applied): they are forbidden to proselytise, own Christian slaves, marry Christians or to hold public office. Judaism, however, remains very clearly a licit religion (*see **religio licita***): freedom of worship is upheld, as are the fiscal privileges of the Jewish clergy. The stance is one of reluctant **toleration**, in marked contrast to the Code's decidedly harsh treatment of Christian heretics.

The Theodosian Code became one of the principal building-blocks of the more famous Justinian Code (see **Justinian I**), its prescriptions against the Jews being (again) reconfirmed and extended by the later collection. The regularity with which disabilities are laid upon the Jews by the Christian emperors may be taken as an indication that enforcement was often far from comprehensive.

MARCUS PLESTED

Time

Time has played an acute role in Christian **anti-Judaism**. This is superficially surprising, since Jewish and Christian perceptions of time have much in common, especially an optimistic, linear vision of time, markedly distinct from the orientation of pagan mythology towards a past Golden Age or the cyclical vision of time prevalent within Buddhism and Hinduism. Just as Genesis embodied 'the rejection of space, the espousal of time' (André Neher, *Moses and the Vocation of the Jewish People*), so biblical and rabbinic writers rejected the emphasis on **sacred space** inherent within pantheistic paganism. They invested time, not space, with spiritual significance, its passage replete with meaning due to God's perceived active role in history. Thus Jews became 'builders in time', their Sabbaths and festivals approximating to 'cathedrals in time' (Heschel), reliving – and anticipating – God's interventions in Jewish history.

Within Christianity the profoundest significance attached to time was **Christological**; Jewish biblical history was interpreted as culminating in Christ, while Christian festivals, like the sacraments of **eucharist** and **baptism**, ritually perpetuated the past of Christ's birth, life, death and resurrection. Although for several centuries, despite the force of **canon law** and anti-Jewish preaching such as that of John **Chrysostom**, some Christians continued to observe their festivals at Jewish times and with Jews, to pray and light **candles** in synagogues, keep the Jewish **Sabbath** – until the ninth century around Lyons (see **Sabbatarianism**) – and even Jewish festivals, the early Christian divorce from Jewish time – to discourage **Judaising**, to distinguish Christianity as uniquely salvific – was inevitable. Commemoration of the **resurrection** on Sunday, stressed by **Ignatius**, led to its substitution for the Jewish Sabbath, urged by the second-century anti-Jewish *Epistle of Barnabas* and formalised during the fourth century. Similarly, Tuesdays and Fridays were substituted for the Jewish fast-days of Monday and Thursday (see **fasting**).

Momentously, Christian interpretations of biblical time demonised the Jews, polarising **Old Testament** figures into bad Jews and good Hebrews (Gavin Langmuir, *Toward a Definition of Anti-Semitism*). Typically, Hilary of Poitiers (*c.*315–67) argued that before the **Law** the Jews were demon-possessed; the Mosaic Law temporarily drove out their unclean **devil**, which returned immediately after they rejected Christ. The association of **Rabbinic Judaism** with devil worship, articulated by Chrysostom and other **Church Fathers**, resulted in both Jewish space (the synagogue) and Jewish time (festivals, especially **Passover**) being maligned as demonic; from the thirteenth century Christian propagandists linked allegations of Jewish ritual murder to Passover. Medieval Christian persecution of Jews was often specifically timed to coincide with the holiest Jewish times, Sabbaths and festivals: the mass-suicide in York to pre-empt mass murder occurred on the Sabbath before Passover, 1190.

Moreover, persecution and massacres of Jews often coincided with the holiest Christian times, notably Lent (Jewish books were confiscated in France on the first Sabbath in Lent, 1240), Palm Sunday (in Beziers and elsewhere Christians stoned Jewish houses), **Holy Week** (anti-Jewish sermons, **passion plays**), **Easter** (ritual murder allegations – see **blood libel**) and Corpus Christi (accusations of **host desecration**). **Expulsions** were sometimes symbolically timed; all Jews had to leave England by All Saints' Day, 1290. Because Christian **eschatology** envisaged the **conversion** of all Jews prior to the **Messiah**'s return, mass forcible conversions could occur, especially at times of millenarian fervour.

Today **millenarian** eschatology more benignly underpins **Christian Zionist** observance of **Sukkot** in Jerusalem, while Christian–Jewish relations are widely fostered by interfaith ceremonies on **Holocaust Memorial Day** and events like the Polish Catholic 'Day of Judaism'.

MARGARET BREARLEY

Toledot Yeshu

The first extant **anti-Christian** tract, the *Toledot Yeshu* ('family history of Jesus') has survived in a number of varying versions in **Hebrew**. A complete form of the text exists from the tenth century, but the variety of versions indicates that it has had a long history. It derives its core from the Gospels, presenting the life of **Jesus**, whose **Virgin Birth** is explained as the result of a rape or an abandonment by the father. The precocious youth Jesus shows great wisdom but is disrespectful of the sages, and when he grows up performs magical tricks, including his **resurrection**, which is explained as a trick intended to deceive. The tract's **polemic** is drawn from a number of similar traditions, found, for example, in the ninth-century *Alphabet of Ben Sira*, where the Virgin Birth is seen to be the result of a masturbator's semen floating in a pool and where the young child has wisdom beyond his age. The **Talmud** too presents Jesus as a magician, and many of the other themes in the *Toledot*, including misuse of the divine name and a shameful death, can be traced in Jewish–Christian **disputations** and literature. In its final form the *Toledot* reads like a folktale, but was probably written for the education of Jews about Christianity and to respond to Christian arguments and prevent **conversion**.

JAMES K. AITKEN

Tolerance/toleration

Marcus Vipsanius Agrippa in 27 BCE designed the Roman Pantheon as a home for all gods. When it was dedicated in 609 CE as the Church of the Santa Maria Rotonda, or *ad Martyres*, the gods were driven out to be replaced by the One God. Pagan tolerance was swept away by Judeo-Christian intolerance of 'other gods'. Worse than that, Jews and Christians were no longer prepared to tolerate each other, or even dissidents within their own ranks; as Christians gained the upper hand, Jews became a barely tolerated **minority** under Christian rule, and Christian–Jewish relations deteriorated to a low ebb.

Despite this, dormant seeds remained to support the rediscovery and re-growth of tolerance in the modern age. Those seeds were germinated by the blood of the Wars of Religion and nurtured through the **humanism** of a secular **Enlightenment**. The Peace of Augsburg (1555) allowed for both Catholic and Lutheran states to coexist within the Habsburg Empire, but made no allowance for the autonomy of individual conscience, a concept clearly formulated by Pierre Bayle (1647–1706) more than a century later in his plea for religious toleration even for **atheists**. John Locke (1632–1704) in his *Epistola de Tolerantia*, influenced by the latitudinarians and published anonymously at Gouda in 1689, was ready to allow Jews freedom to worship in England, but drew the line at atheists and Catholics, believing that they would undermine the stability of the state.

Jews did not exercise political power over people of other religions, but as a minority they had an interest in demonstrating their own tolerance. Moses **Mendelssohn**, in his 1782 preface to **Menasseh ben Israel**'s *Vindiciae Judaeorum*, denounced the practice of **excommunication** by which the rabbis had until then enforced religious conformity. A year later, in *Jerusalem*, he argued for the complete separation of **Church and state**. He also sought, like many Jewish apologists before and after, to demonstrate that Judaism was inherently more tolerant than Christianity; he claimed that it was a 'rational' religion, free of dogma, non-conversionist, and through its concept of the 'Seven Laws of Noah' (*see* **Noachide Laws**) acknowledged that other people might approach God in different ways while upholding the moral and ethical values that were the essence of **Torah**. His Judaism has much in common with the less dogmatic Christianity advocated by Locke in *The Reasonableness of Christianity* (1695). Political implementation of the new ideas was piecemeal. The *Toleranz-Patent* (1781–2) of **Joseph II** of Austria, one of a series of patents granted to the major, non-Catholic denominations of **Austria**, aimed at encouraging the integration of the Jews into Christian society. It retained some traditional restrictions and, though welcomed by many Jews, was opposed by Mendelssohn, who feared that the proposed method of education would lead Jews to **apostasy**, as well as by conservatives who saw that it would lead to the break-up of traditional communal discipline.

The 'Declaration of the Rights of Man and of the Citizen' adopted in 1789 by the National Assembly during the French Revolution asserts unequivocally (article 10) that 'No one may be disturbed on account of his opinions, even religious ones, as long as the manifestation of such opinions does not interfere with the established Law and Order.' This principle has become the norm in Western societies, even though its implementation has been imperfect. It was adopted by **Israel** in its Declaration of Independence, which states: 'The State of Israel . . . will ensure complete equality of social and political rights to all its inhabitants, irrespective of religion, race, or sex; it will guarantee freedom of religion, conscience, language, education and culture; it will safeguard the Holy Places of all religions.'

While **dialogue** is possible within a regime of 'toleration', successful dialogue needs to be based on full affirmation of the other as an equal. This is possible under secular government, but where the representatives of a specific religious denomination control the government it is *ipso facto* impossible. From the theological point of view dialogue is easier when participants are able to make 'theological space' for one another. This is relatively easy in Judaism, where the concept of the 'Seven Laws of Noah', and the classic statement of Rabbi Joshua ben Hananiah (second century) that 'the righteous of all nations have a portion in the World to Come', provide 'space' for people other than those of the Jewish faith. Statements such as *extra ecclesiam nulla salus* ('there is no salvation outside the Church') make such a position more difficult for Christians, though many modern Christian theologians have adopted a less exclusive, pluralist view.   *NORMAN SOLOMON*

Toleration *see* **tolerance/toleration**

Torah

Literally teaching, instruction, often translated as **law**, Torah carries a wide variety of meanings. Traditionally misunderstood by Christian scholars as solely a collection of laws, more recently it is being seen as a common link between Judaism and Christianity.

Torah can be used to describe the Five Books of **Moses** (Written Torah) or the Word of God (cf. Ps. 119). The latter is of particular interest to **New Testament** scholars because it was translated in the **Targums** as *memra*, indicating the means by which God's will is made known to the **people of Israel** and by which that will is fulfilled. Most striking is the Targum on Exod. 19.17, which states that the people went out to meet the Word of God (*memra*) rather than to meet God as stated by the biblical text. Although *memra* became a periphrasis for God, it is most unlikely to have been understood as a separate person, as in Christian Trinitarianism (*see* **Trinity**).

Torah in its broadest sense can also be equated with the whole body of Jewish teaching and law (Oral Torah). The latter explains what the **Pentateuch** means and how it should be interpreted, which is a process that has continued from bib-

lical times to the present day and has resulted in the completion of works such as the **Mishnah** and **Talmud**, as well as the **midrashim**. Rabbinic Judaism taught that Moses received the Torah from Sinai (*m. Avot* 1.1) but there was also a **tradition** that the Torah was in existence before the **creation** of the world (e.g. Sir. 1.1–5), or even before the creation of the Throne of Glory (*Genesis Rabbah* 1.4). Torah was equated with **Wisdom** (Prov. 8.22) and **Philo** wrote about the pre-existence and role in creation of the word of God (**Logos**), which he identified with the Torah (*Migr.* 130). Although Philo did not have the same understanding of the incarnate Logos that is found in the prologue to John's Gospel, it is striking that a Jew who lived at the same time as the authors of the New Testament, and who probably never even heard of **Jesus**, spoke of the fatherhood of God and of the Logos as his image: 'Even if we are not yet suitable to be called the sons and daughters of God, still we may be called the children of his eternal image, of his most sacred word (*logos*)' (*Conf.* 147). Later, Christian theology understood Logos as the 'Word of God', which referred to Jesus as God Incarnate.

Rabbinic Judaism also personified Torah, describing how God discussed the creation of the world with the Torah (Gen. 1.27). On another occasion the Torah is described as Israel's bride. Another feature of the Torah according to the rabbis is that it was eternal. Jesus' statement in Matt. 5.17 that he has come not to destroy but to fulfil the Torah is reminiscent of the rabbinic teaching of its non-abrogability. The rabbis taught that the Torah would exist in the world to come, but interestingly it was also argued that changes to the Torah would take place in the Messianic age (*Genesis Rabbah* 98.9), although this was later rejected by **Maimonides**, who held there would be no change after the coming of the **Messiah**.

Torah was translated in the **Septuagint** as *nomos* (in order to emphasise the traditions and customs of Israel), by **Jerome** in the **Vulgate** as *lex*, and finally into English as 'law'. Each translation narrowed the meaning of the term until Judaism came to be seen by many Christians simply as a form of legalism. In the late nineteenth and early twentieth centuries in particular Christian biblical scholars such as Schürer (1844–1910) and **Wellhausen** described Judaism as a cold, unfeeling, legal religion, in contrast to Christianity, the religion of love and brotherhood. Judaism, especially **Pharisaic** and Rabbinic Judaism, which were generally described as 'late Judaism' (*Spätjudentum*), was compared negatively with the teaching of Jesus. The Jewish context was almost entirely ignored or rejected.

Although Jewish law lies at the heart of Torah, particularly in the teaching of **Orthodox Judaism**, a large part of Jewish law is about social action. Thus, acts of kindness are deemed part of Jewish law; the word *mizvah* (**commandment**) is commonly used to mean any good deed. This is illustrated by the Talmud's account of a pagan who visited Hillel (end of first century BCE and beginning of first century CE) and told him that he would convert to Judaism if Hillel could teach him the whole of the Torah while he was standing on one foot. Hillel replied: 'What is hateful to yourself, do not do to your fellow man. That is the whole Torah; the rest is just commentary. Go and study it' (*b. Shabbat* 31a). This **Golden Rule**, which was negatively expressed by Hillel, was declared as a positive pronouncement by Jesus (Luke 6.31, cf. Matt. 7.12), indicating that both Judaism and Christianity place correct ethical conduct at their core.

Most recently Jewish scholars of and activists in Jewish–Christian relations have argued that the Torah illustrates a number of shared values between the religions. For example, *Dabru Emet* states that 'Jews and Christians accept the moral principles of Torah' and that 'this shared moral emphasis can be the basis of an improved relationship between our two communities'.   *EDWARD KESSLER*

Tradition

The notion of tradition is fundamental to both Judaism and Christianity. Both depend on the idea that the disclosure of the divine self, and of the divine purposes for the **Chosen People** or for all humankind, need to be handed on securely from one generation to another. The nature and content of what is handed on varies within and between both religions, and debates over the limits and character of tradition have played an important part in both their histories. 'Tradition' has often been used to refer in particular to insights and instructions that are handed on in parallel with the teaching to be found in the written law or the Christian scriptures, and the authority of this 'tradition' has been a subject of lively debate. Early Christian writers use the terms *paradosis* (in Greek) and *traditio* (in Latin); they can refer to both the process and the content

of handing on. Jewish **vocabulary** is able to distinguish between the point of view of the tradent and of the recipient: *kabbalah* is 'that which is received' and *masoret* is 'that which is passed on'.

In **Rabbinic Judaism** a special importance attaches to the *halakhot*, or directions for right conduct, given to **Moses** on Mount Sinai, and transmitted orally from one generation of teachers to another. This constitutes a body of law held to be of equal authority to the laws of the written **Torah**. This kind of 'tradition' is presupposed in Mark 7.1–23, where **Jesus** is questioned about his disciples' refusal to follow its precepts. It is interesting that some of Jesus' contemporaries apparently expected him to keep traditions that were not universally observed. His reply need not be read as a negation of the value of the traditions as such, but as emphasising the primacy of an ethic of **love** within which alone they become acceptable; it can thus be construed as a perfectly Jewish answer to a Jewish question. Around the traditions of both the oral and the written law grew traditions of commentary and interpretation, especially in the **Mishnah** and the **Talmud**. The characteristic rabbinic way of approaching the task of **commentary** by balancing different possible interpretations against one another gives a dynamic quality to the transmission of tradition.

Paul uses the concept of tradition positively: it is important to him to hand on what he has received (1 Cor. 11.23–24; 15.3; Gal. 1.9; 1 Thess. 2.12). It became important to Christians to define the boundaries of this *paradosis*. Against esoteric teachers who initiated their disciples privately into **Gnostic** traditions, **Church Fathers** like **Irenaeus of Lyons** sought to define a public body of tradition. During the **Reformation** the relation between the greatly expanded body of Church 'tradition' (embracing both teaching and practice) and scripture became highly controversial, and those controversies are still being worked out in different Christian attitudes to tradition today. The Council of **Trent**, in response to the Reformers' critique of tradition, insisted that scripture and tradition were to be esteemed equally (1546). This insistence could easily be taken to mean that tradition was a source of revelation alongside scripture. **Vatican II's** *Dogmatic Constitution on Divine Revelation* (1963) was careful to deny the inference, but continued to allow an important place to tradition in determining how

Christians should believe and live. Between Trent and Vatican II comes the spread of theories of evolution and change, and especially the work of John Henry Newman (1801–90) on the development of **doctrine**, which understood tradition to mean development as well as transmission. This understanding of the development and transmission of tradition is noticeably similar to Judaism's emphasis on the ever-developing oral Torah, which is handed down from generation to generation.

ANDERS BERGQUIST

Trent, Council of

A council of Roman Catholic bishops, held intermittently between 1545 and 1563 and regarded as the nineteenth ecumenical council. Although Trent gave little attention to Jews and Judaism, its importance to Jewish–Christian relations lies in the new catechism that resulted from it and that served for centuries as a basic resource for Catholic **catechesis**. The Council declared that Christian sinners were more to blame for the death of Christ than Jews, thus rejecting accusations of **deicide** against Jews. According to the 1985 *Notes on the Correct Way to Present the Jews and Judaism in Preaching and Catechesis*, the Council taught that whilst Jews 'knew not what they did (cf. Luke 23.34)' 'we [Christians] know it only too well' (Pars I, caput V, Quaest. XI). The Council is also mentioned in the American Catholic *Criteria for the Evaluation of Dramatizations of the Passion* (1988), warning Christians not to allow **passion plays** to stir up anti-Jewish prejudice. *JOANN SPILLMAN*

Trial of Jesus

The events that led to Jesus' death have been debated over the centuries, and assessment of these events has fuelled hostility against Jews as 'Christ-killers'. In general, the Gospels tend to exaggerate the responsibility of the Jewish leaders in Jesus' death and to exculpate **Pilate** and the Romans. The **New Testament** Gospels record multiple and contradictory traditions associated with different 'trials' convened to accuse and to judge **Jesus**, one Jewish and another Roman. The earliest Gospel, Mark (14.53, 55–65, see parallel Matt. 26.57, 59–68), records a first arraignment and interrogation during the night before the Jewish religious leaders (Mark 14.53 'high priest, chief priests, elders and scribes'), whereas John records two Jewish trials, one before Annas and another at the house of the high priest **Caiaphas** (John 18.13, 19–24). Schol-

ars regard these Jewish trials as informal interrogations, not as a formal meeting of the **Sanhedrin**, since later practice suggests that the Sanhedrin would not have met at night, nor did they convene during the festival days. Whether these procedural rules were fixed already in the first century, however, cannot be determined with certainty. The charge brought against Jesus by the Jewish authorities was one of '**blasphemy**' (Mark 14.64), although Mark also implies that Jesus was seen as a threat to the **Temple** (Mark 14.58). Mark records the abusive treatment and mockery of Jesus by the religious leaders (Mark 14.65), and Matthew and Luke embellish this tradition in order to depict Jewish hostility to Jesus even more emphatically. Once charged with blasphemy, Jesus was then led to the Roman governor Pilate because, as John records, the Jews had no right to try capital offences at this time in Palestine (John 18.31). Whether this detail is historically sound is another matter of inconclusive debate. The Roman trial before Pilate corresponds to procedural customs of the time for the trial of a non-citizen. The charge brought against Jesus in the Roman trial is that he claimed to be 'King of the Jews' (Mark 15.2), a title that may suggest his perceived role as 'leader of the resistance'. It was, therefore, a political charge of sedition against **Rome**. The Gospel portrait of Pilate as an indecisive and compassionate ruler who three times declares Jesus' innocence is in sharp contrast to the historical Pilate, whom history records as a cruel and brutal ruler. Except for John's Gospel, the others depict a silent Jesus who gave no response to Pilate's questions, but this detail seems expressly designed for **apologetic** purposes to cast Jesus in the role of the Isaianic **Suffering Servant** who was silent, 'like a sheep before the shearers' (Isa. 52.13–53.12). Another questionable detail in the Gospel accounts is their reference to a custom of 'Passover amnesty' whereby the governor would release a criminal at the time of **Passover**. We have no extra-biblical corroborating evidence for this so-called custom, although we cannot rule out the possibility of an occasional incidence of amnesty granted. The intended irony indicated by the confusion of names, 'Jesus Barabbas or Jesus who is called Messiah' (Matt. 27.17), suggests redactional intent. Finally, Pilate's sentence of death by **crucifixion** for Jesus' political crime, despite attempts to shift blame onto the Jewish crowd, was the decisive judgement leading to Jesus' death. The enduring effect of the Gospel trial scenes has been to dismiss Roman responsibility and to focus instead on the trials before Caiaphas (Matt. 26.57; Mark 14.53; Luke 22.54; John 18.24), Annas (John 18.13–23) and even **Herod** (Luke 23.6–12) as a way to demonstrate Jewish responsibility and guilt for Jesus' death.

See also **deicide, charge of**; **passion narratives**

BARBARA E. BOWE

Trialogue

The term 'trialogue' designates a 'trilateral dialogue' between Judaism, Christianity and **Islam** that goes beyond both bilateral dialogues – Jewish–Christian, Muslim–Christian and Jewish–Muslim – and a general dedication to multi-religious encounter. The foundation of this trialogue is monotheism: Judaism, Christianity and Islam share belief in one God, and all three regard **Abraham** as the ancestor of their faith.

Despite the challenge to search for a common language and potential symbiosis, there are huge doctrinal and psychological barriers to trialogue within all three monotheistic religions. Collective memories prevent uninhibited **dialogue**: for example, most Jews think of Christianity in terms of suffering and persecution; while Muslims have not forgotten the **Crusades**, and see in Western aspirations for world hegemony the old crusader mentality in a new guise. All three religions have wide experience in **polemics** and **apologetics**, but not in real dialogue, for which addressing one's own theological agenda is an essential preparation.

For Jews the traditional assumption that Judaism constituted the only fully authentic expression of divine **revelation** had been modified by the third century CE to accord the status of *ger toshav* ('resident alien') to individuals who abandoned **idolatry**, a recognition formalised in the **Noachide laws**. In Jewish philosophy there were several attempts – for example by Saadiah Gaon (882–942), developed by **Judah ha-Levi** and **Maimonides** – to find 'theological space' for the other: Islam and Christianity were 'in error', but could be accommodated as part of the divine design to bring the nations gradually to God. A further step was made by the Yemenite philosopher Netanel ibn Fayyumi (d. *c.*1164), who asserts the authenticity of the prophecy of Muhammad, as revealed in the Qur'an, and at least the possibility that there are additional authentic revelations: 'He sends a prophet to every people according to their language.'

In Christian circles **anti-Judaism** has not yet been banished entirely from Church and theology, and Islamophobia is a widespread phenomenon. Of the three monotheistic religions it is Christianity that has most consistently excluded others from ultimate **salvation**. Jews may regard Muslims and Christians as 'sons of **Noah**'; Muslims may regard Jews and Christians as 'people of the book'. For many centuries, however, Christians have adhered to the tenet *extra ecclesiam nulla salus* ('no salvation outside the Church'). To find space for the other, attempts have been made in recent years to develop a more dynamic **covenant** theology, and to emphasise a theology of the **Holy Spirit** – a conviction that Abraham's promise has been directed to all peoples by the outpouring of the Holy Spirit at **Pentecost** – which might accommodate the theological question whether Muhammad can be seen as a special envoy of God. Some theologians, for example, regard it as a special work of the Holy Spirit that the Name of the God of the Bible has been brought to the lips of the Arab and many other peoples by means of the prophet Muhammad.

Trialogue does not mean looking for a harmonising common denominator: the core beliefs of Judaism, Christianity and Islam cannot be harmonised. The place that **Torah** holds for Jews is for Christians held by **Jesus** Christ and for Muslims by the Qur'an as the infallible and literal revelation of Allah through Muhammad, the seal of all the prophets before him. Although there are some promising new approaches, where dialogue partners are looking at the fruitfulness of theological differences between religions, the emphasis within the trialogue has thus tended to be on **ethics** rather than on theology. Indeed, Jewish–Christian–Muslim trialogue remains limited. An example is the long-established annual study conference, held in Bendorf in **Germany**, in which Jews, Christians and Muslims participate. In **Israel** the Interreligious Coordinating Council in Israel and the Israel Interfaith Committee are active in the field of trialogue.

see also **vocabulary**   *SIMON SCHOON*

Trinity

The Christian **doctrine** of Trinity achieved its classic expression in the Nicene creed, according to which Christians believe in 'One God the Father . . . and in one Lord Jesus Christ, the Son of God . . . that is from the substance of the Father . . . and the Holy Spirit . . . who proceeds from the Father and the Son'. From earliest times Christians have argued there is no inconsistency between a belief in the Trinity and a belief in the one **God**. Although the doctrine of the Trinity has undergone numerous developments, it remains the central Christian teaching about the Godhead and also marks not only difference between Judaism and Christianity, but also profound mistrust. For its part, from its biblical roots to the present day, Judaism affirms monotheism (cf the *Shema* and Deut. 6.4–10), and rabbinic writings demonstrate concern about dualism and tri-theism. The **Talmud**, for example, contains numerous condemnations against **idolatry** (*see* ***avodah zarah***) and the rabbis were keen to refute Trinitarian claims such as the Christian interpretation that the three references to God in the *Shema* applied to the Trinity. For patristic Christianity the Trinity measured what Judaism was missing: above all, recognition that the Second Person of God is incarnate in **Jesus**. For **Rabbinic Judaism** it marked what Christianity lost: the ability to remove divinity from all levels of creaturehood. Medieval Jewish philosophers identified belief in the Trinity with the heresy of ***shittuf***, or limiting God's infinity by associating his divinity with creaturely being. In the modern epoch liberal Christians as well as Jews tended to denounce the doctrine as introducing a metaphysical system alien to Christianity's biblical roots.

In the present epoch, however, **postliberal** Christian and Jewish theologians have opened possibilities of constructive **dialogue** between Trinitarian Christians and rabbinic Jews. According to the Lutheran theologian Robert Jenson (b. 1930), the doctrine has been misrepresented by theologians who identify the triune God with the Greek philosophic concept of 'timeless being'. 'Being is not a biblical concept', but a philosophical concept designed to answer the question 'what do we mean when we say "x is?"' (*Systematic Theology I*, 207ff.). The doctrine of Trinity names the discovery that God lives in endless relation to the three persons, which Jenson retranslates, following **Tertullian**, as God's three *dramatis personae*, or 'identities'. Israel remains alive in these identities, since God's relations are narrated in scripture and his faithfulness to Israel is central to this narrative.

For the Methodist theologian Kendall Soulen Jenson's scriptural account enables Christians to remember how God named himself in relation to Israel: the **Tetragrammaton** of Exod. 3. Because YHWH remains the name of God the Father to whom Jesus prays 'hallowed be thy name', YHWH must also name the one with whom Jesus identifies himself (Matt. 28.18) and the Spirit (Rom. 1.4, Acts 5.9). If so, Soulen concludes, YHWH must name the one whom Christians name 'The Father and the Son and the Holy Spirit'.

The current epoch brings Jewish theologians into fruitful dialogue with Christian theologians who portray the Trinity as a doctrine about God's relationality. Elliot Wolfson (b. 1956), for example, argues that, like the Christian doctrine, the Jewish **Kabbalah** narrates the relations God establishes with himself and his creation, each relation constituting one of God's identities. Students of the Jewish philosopher Franz **Rosenzweig** write of the triadic relations among God, God's word (**Torah**) and God's addressee (**Israel**). Charles Peirce (1839–1914) based his triadic logic of science on a model of three-part relations in the Trinity. And the patristic scholar Robert Markus (b. 1924) suggests that Peirce's logic fulfils what **Augustine** sought: a thoroughly triadic logic of triune relations. As suggested by these hints, Jewish and Christian theologians have much more to discuss about God's relationality.   *PETER OCHS*

Tyndale, William (c.1494–1536)

Bible translator. B. F. Westcott (1825–1901) notes: 'the history of the English Bible begins with the work of Tyndale and not Wycliffe' (*A History of The English Bible*, 316). William Tyndale produced in 1525 or 1526 his hugely influential translation of the **New Testament**; in 1530 he produced the **Pentateuch**, and in 1537 Joshua to 2 Chronicles and Jonah. His New Testament translation was influenced by the German translation of Martin **Luther** and replicates Luther's anti-Jewish features. However, Tyndale translates Luke 19.46 as 'den of thieves' rather than *Moerdergrube* (gang of murderers) and his 'Exposition of the Fifth, Sixth and Seventh Chapters of Matthew's Gospel' makes clear that he understood Jesus in Matthew to criticise the **Pharisees** for their exclusionary practices but that scripture itself is 'the well of Abraham'. By 1530, in contrast to Luther, Tyndale began to display a positive attitude to the laws of the Hebrew scriptures. He praised Deuteronomy as 'a boke worthye to be rede in daye and nyghte and neuer to be oute of handes . . . a very pure gospel'. Tyndale's translation reflects his assessment that the Hebrew scriptures nurture the beginning of an education in love of God and love of neighbour.   *DEIRDRE J. GOOD*

Typology

The term 'typology' refers to a particular variety of interpretation and is generally discussed in tandem with the similar practice of **allegory**. More generally, typology, like its cousin allegory, is a form of non-literal or figurative reading of the Bible. The ancient Christian and Jewish communities extensively cultivated both of these practices as they attempted to reinterpret the **Hebrew Bible** in the light of faith in **Jesus** and the new reality facing Judaism after the destruction of the Temple (70 CE). Discerning the exact way in which typological **exegesis** differs from allegorical exegesis can be a challenge to the modern student of antiquity. In general a typology is a figural reading that discerns in an event or person in the past a model that illuminates an event or person in the present. For example, when Christians claim that the exodus anticipates the liberation from sin and death in baptism or when **Zionists** liken the establishment of **Israel** to post-exilic restoration, they are using typology. Allegory, on the other hand, is a figural reading that sees the literal text as standing for something else: both Christians and Jews read the Song of Songs as something other than erotic love poetry. For the former it was about the soul's relationship to Christ, and for the latter it described God's relationship with Israel. **Philo of Alexandria** pioneered figural reading of the Bible and influenced the exegetical work of Clement (*c*.150–*c*.215) and **Origen**. When Philo, Clement and Origen laboured to reconcile respectively Judaism and Christianity to Platonism, the person of **Moses** frequently appears as a 'type' of the true philosopher.

Typological interpretation also functioned in the struggle between Christians and Jews over who was and was not the 'true' Israel, a title to which both religious groups laid claim. Christian exegetes, for example, frequently maintained that the story of **Jacob** and Esau typologically depicted the relationship of the Church to Israel: the elder (Judaism) shall serve the younger (Christianity). Surprisingly, some Jewish scholars report that the rabbis also used this same text to claim that Esau was the Christian church and Jacob was faithful Israel. Christianity, they argued, was the elder Rome in new form, while Jacob was the younger, and seemingly weaker, Israel. More negatively, typology has made frequent appearances in Christian **supersessionism**. Christianity, the new Jacob, claimed to replace Esau, the elder Israel. The old levitical priesthood and Temple sacrifice were seen as types of the new single atoning sacrifice of Christ who renders the old obsolete. The circumcision of the heart replaces the literal **circumcision** of the Jews. The Pauline contrast between the justified faith of **Abraham** and the **law** given to Moses has often been used in Christian history typologically to cast Jews in the role of closed-minded legalists whom God has rejected and Christians in the role of heirs to God's promise.

This mixed legacy of typology, however, should not detract from its usefulness. Any community attempting to engage an ancient text and make it relevant in the lives of contemporary believers will likely make use of this powerful interpretive technique. As a final example, one might recall that the American civil rights leader Martin Luther King (1929–68) once exclaimed that he had 'been to the mountain top and seen the promised land'. In doing so, he likened the struggle of African-Americans against discrimination to Israel's liberation from Egypt and filled that struggle with divine purpose.   *JOHN J. O'KEEFE*

431

UUUU

Ukraine

Poland, Russia and the Austrian-Hungarian Empire have each dominated portions of Ukraine until its present independence. With the exception of the Soviet period, when **atheism** was officially imposed, the ruling classes since the Middle Ages have been Christian, whether Roman Catholic, Orthodox or (since 1596) 'Uniate' (Greek-Catholic). But there was also a sizeable proportion of the population that was Jewish. The Russian **Pale of Settlement** included Ukraine. By the beginning of the Second World War Jews amounted to no less than 8 per cent of the population in Soviet Ukraine, recently expanded westwards as it was (1939).

The earlier history of Jewish–Christian relations had been deeply troubled. Almost all the **pogroms** of the late nineteenth and early twentieth centuries had taken place in Ukraine. Ingrained **antisemitism** meant that the Nazi onslaught on the Jews (1941) found considerable support among the local people. All the more notable was the public stance taken by the Greek-Catholic metropolitan of L'viv, Andrii Sheptytsk'kyi (1865–1944). He personally sheltered Jews and encouraged fellow-Christians to do the same. The actions of a Christian burglar, Leopold Socha, in sheltering a company of Jews in the sewers of L'viv for 14 months (1943–4) also deserves to be remembered. Among the Orthodox who risked their lives to save Jews under Nazi occupation should be mentioned Aleksii Glagolev (1902–72), who was a priest in Kiev. But in general the history of the **Righteous Gentiles** in Ukraine remains to be explored. Theirs was a dialogue in dramatic terms, which anticipated any dialogue of words. Neither was furthered by the Soviet **antisemitic** campaign of the postwar period, much of it masked as anti-**Zionism**. The independence of Ukraine (1990) provided the would-be protagonists of Jewish–Christian **dialogue** with some new perspectives, which were judged to be positive enough for the International **Council of Christians and Jews** to convene its annual conference in Ukraine in 1999.

See also **Poland**; **Russia**   *SERGEI HACKEL*

Unitarians

Unitarianism is a diverse movement originating within Christianity during the **Reformation**, although some major groups claiming the label are now only tenuously associated with it. As its name suggests, Unitarianism was distinguished by the anti-Trinitarian convictions of its founders, such as the sixteenth-century reformers Michael Servetus (1509–53) and Francis David (1520–79), but for many contemporary adherents Unitarianism is a non-creedal religion that encompasses a wide range of beliefs, and does not presuppose or proscribe any particular faith commitment.

Around 10 per cent of the current membership of the Unitarian Universalist Association (1,000 congregations in North America) identify themselves as Jewish, a figure only slightly less than those who define themselves as 'liberal Christians'. This complexity makes it hard now to speak of Unitarian–Jewish relations, in the sense of two discrete entities encountering one another. The predominance of non-Christian (often non-theist) members, and the rejection of creeds, are perennial issues in Unitarians' participation in ecumenical and interfaith organisations. Although there is superficial affinity between Judaism and traditional Unitarianism in their respective assertions of the unity of God, there have been few formal relations between the two. There are some notable exceptions: the Socinian Unitarian Szymon Budny (1550–93) of Lithuania was praised by Hezekiah David Abulafia (eighteenth century) for his knowledge of **Talmud**; nineteenth-century Unitarian scholar R. Travers **Herford** had a particular interest in the ethical traditions of early Judaism. Also in the nineteenth century, Unitarians joined other **Dissenters** in campaigning actively for religious **toleration** and Jewish **emancipation**. Perhaps the most striking, albeit untypical, episode in Unitarian–Jewish relations is that of the Transylvanian Sabbatarians (**Sabbatarianism** spread among some Hungarian Unitarians in the late sixteenth century) who, in a move echoing that of the **Khazars**, converted *en masse* to Judaism.   *MELANIE J. WRIGHT*

United Kingdom

Christianity has been the dominant religion in the United Kingdom, but some Jews have lived in Britain for much of the last 2,000 years, except between 1290, when they were expelled by **Edward I**, and 1656 when they were readmitted by Oliver **Cromwell**.

Christianity reached Britain by the second century CE, and there is evidence of an organised Church from the fourth century. Archaeological evidence also suggests a few Jews lived in Roman Britain between 43 and 400 CE. After Roman rule collapsed Christianity in Britain was influenced by the Celtic Church, which survived for some centuries in **Ireland**. Elsewhere, following the **mission** led by St Augustine of Canterbury (d. between 604 and 609), who landed in Kent in 597, and the Synod of Whitby (664), papal authority was established and Roman usages were accepted. Some Jews may have visited Britain during the Anglo-Saxon period, but there is no firm evidence of Jewish settlements until after the Norman Conquest of 1066, which also brought the English Church into the mainstream of European religious life. The Jews who accompanied William I to England from Rouen received royal protection. Communities were established in London – on a site still known as Old Jewry – in Lincoln, Oxford and some other centres. There were a number of debates between clergy and **rabbis**, and Brother Gilbert **Crispin** of Westminster Abbey in a letter to St **Anselm**, Archbishop of Canterbury, refers to one with an unnamed Jewish 'friend', although the report has not survived.

Relations, however, deteriorated by the middle of the twelfth century. Royal power became weaker and less able to protect Jews, who, in any case, were unable to provide the excessive sums of money demanded by the kings. The barons, to whom the Jews lent money, encouraged popular disturbances in which Jewish homes were ransacked and records of debts destroyed. The clergy became more hostile, and popular prejudice was fed by the '**blood libel**' which originated in England with the case of **William of Norwich** in 1144. In 1190 massacres of Jews occurred in several cities, most notably in York at Clifford's Tower. A century later Edward I ordered the **expulsion** of all Jews from the realm. Despite the expulsion, some **Marranos** – Jews from **Spain** who had converted to Christianity – may have come to Britain during late medieval and Tudor times; **Shakespeare**'s Shylock (*see* **Merchant of Venice**) was perhaps modelled on one of them.

The Tudor and Stuart periods were dominated by the struggles of the **Reformation**. Henry VIII (*r.*1509–47) repudiated papal control and established the **Church of England**, and in Scotland, under the leadership of John Knox (*c.*1513–72), a more thoroughgoing Reformation led to the establishment in 1560 of the Church of Scotland. In the seventeenth century there was new interest in the Jews, especially from Puritans, who attached great importance to the study of the scriptures, including the **Old Testament**, and some of whom, as a **minority** themselves, advocated religious **tolerance**. Oliver Cromwell, himself a Puritan, aware of the economic benefits of Jewish tradesmen and financiers, allowed Jews to return in 1656. This policy was continued by Charles II (*r.*1660–85). Bevis Marks, the oldest synagogue in Britain, was opened in 1701, and in 1760 Sephardi and Ashkenazi communities together formed the Board of Deputies of British Jews, as it is now known.

In the nineteenth century the disabilities of Roman Catholics, Nonconformists and Jews were gradually removed, although the Church of England, as the established Church (*see* **Church and state**), retained certain privileges, such as the presence of some bishops in the House of Lords. Jews gradually gained political **emancipation**, although, partly because of opposition by the bishops, it was not until 1858 that Lionel de Rothschild (1808–79) was formally admitted as the first Jewish Member of Parliament. The nineteenth century was a period of Jewish organisational consolidation. The office of Chief Rabbi was established and the Board of Deputies strengthened, thanks especially to Sir Moses **Montefiore**. The nineteenth century also saw the beginning of divisions in the Jewish community with the opening of the West London Synagogue – the first Reform synagogue in Britain – in 1840; the United Synagogue was founded in 1870 and the Union of Liberal and Progressive Synagogues in 1902. There were also divisions in the Churches – notably between **Methodists** and the

Church of England and between members of the **Evangelical** revival and the higher Church Oxford Movement – while **biblical criticism** and the evolutionary views of Charles Darwin (1809–82) caused great theological debate. During the nineteenth century some Jews took their place in high society and others, including Claude **Montefiore**, were from its beginning in 1904 members of the Society for the Study of Religions. The late nineteenth century also saw an influx of Jewish refugees fleeing from persecution in **Russia**. In the period 1881 to 1914 the Jewish population rose from about 25,000 to nearly 350,000. Some Christians joined protest meetings against Russian persecution, and Christian missionary centres in East London and other cities provided practical help.

Even before the rise of **Nazism**, some British Christians, such as James **Parkes**, recognised Christian responsibility for **antisemitism**, and the founding of the (London) Society of Jews and Christians in 1927 saw the beginning of organised **dialogue**. Many British Jewish leaders and some Christians were strong supporters of **Zionism**. Nazi persecution led to another influx of refugees, and again Christians and Jews came together to provide practical help and oppose Nazi ideology. The **Council of Christians and Jews** was founded in 1942. The number of Jews in Britain today is about 300,000, including those of Jewish birth who have no affiliation with a synagogue. Since the readmission Jews in Britain have been spared serious outbreaks of violence, but antisemitism, which has never had official approval, remains latent, and attacks on Jewish buildings and cemeteries still occur.

There are three mainstreams of Christianity in Britain today: Anglican, Roman Catholic and Free Church or Protestant – consisting of the Methodist, United Reformed and Baptist Churches. There are also some Greek, Russian and Oriental Orthodox Churches, as well as Pentecostal Churches, often with many members of Afro–Caribbean ethnic origin, and a growing number of 'charismatic' house Churches. The Society of Friends, known as **Quakers**, has a distinctive peace witness. **Unitarian** Churches do not believe in the Trinity or the divinity of Jesus. Many Churches work together through the Council of Churches for Britain and Ireland (CCBI), which in 1994 produced guidelines on Christian–Jewish relations called *Christians and Jews – A New*

Way of Thinking. Although most Churches have made significant efforts to eliminate anti-Jewish teaching and are committed to maintaining good relations with the Jewish community, there is a danger that the conflict in the Middle East may spill over into Britain, and bodies such as the Three Faiths Forum try to ensure good relations between Jews, Christians and Muslims. Attitudes to **Israel** often cause division between Jews and Christians in Britain, and the conversionist efforts of some Christian groups also cause tension. *Sheḥita* – the ritual slaughter of animals – may provoke the opposition of Christians committed to animal rights. There is public debate about the place of faith-based schools in contemporary Britain. Yet, despite tensions, there are friendly relations between many leaders of Jewish and Christian communities and between local churches and synagogues. Most religious communities, however, are experiencing a loss of membership in an increasingly secular society.

See also **Anglicanism**; **literature, English**

MARCUS BRAYBROOKE

United States of America

Since the Second World War, in which two-thirds of European Jewry, along with its rich array of centres of learning, were destroyed, the United States has been in the vanguard of Jewish–Christian relations internationally. While Israel has the world's second largest Jewish community after the US, and a wealth of academic institutions to foster serious study, its Christian community is too small to hold its own in a **dialogue**. Until recently only in the US have both communities enjoyed the institutional and academic strength for serious and sustained dialogue.

The first group of Jewish families arrived in 1654 in New Amsterdam (renamed New York in 1664) following the fall of Recife, Brazil, to the Portuguese. By the time of the founding of the Republic, small groups of Jews, often merchants and dominantly Sephardic, existed in cities along the coast. In the early nineteenth century Ashkenazi synagogues were established. In the years between 1820 and 1870 some 7,500 Jews emigrated to America, and more than 70,000 in the 1870s. **Pogroms** launched in **Russia** after the assassination of Alexander II in 1881 led to a great wave of immigration: a third of the 4 million-plus Jews of Eastern Europe had fled their homelands by the outbreak of the First World War, many to the US.

For these Jews the American experience was marked both by lack of a feudal heritage determining the 'caste' of its citizens and by an individualist ethic, derived from the **Enlightenment**, set within a legal framework of civil equality and separation of government from any particular religious tradition – the result of accommodation with earlier and contemporary waves of immigrants, many Catholic, from **Ireland**, **Germany**, and southern and eastern Europe. Given the antipathy with which these Catholic 'ethnics' were greeted, Jews were seen as simply one more group of 'huddled masses', no more alien to the 'Protestant Establishment' than were Italians or Slavs. These groups all faced similar levels of cultural, economic and political discrimination, and reacted, often, in parallel fashion, if not in coalition.

In the US no Church had an exclusive historic association with an inherited aristocracy; Church affiliation often cut through social classes, as individuals of different denominations achieved success. There was thus no distinctive drama of 'Jewish **emancipation**', since there were neither legally prescribed **ghettos** nor a distinct place in society for Jews as a group to be emancipated from. After the Civil War, while 'genteel' discrimination kept Jews, Catholics and Protestants of the non-'mainline' Churches out of many of the better universities and neighbourhoods, as well as the more prestigious law and medical practices, banking firms and so on, a generally booming economy and mobile social structure opened opportunities.

The history of the American labour movement is at the same time a history of Catholic–Jewish relations in the US for the last half of the nineteenth and the first half of the twentieth centuries. The needs of both communities, comprising as they did so much of American 'ethnics', were shared, giving rise to an unprecedented economic and social coalition, which also had political implications, for example in the influence of labour (i.e. Catholics and Jews) on the domestic and foreign policy stances of the Democratic Party with regard to support for the **State of Israel**. However, such coalitions, replicated in many ways in different communities, seldom gave rise to religious dialogue as we know it today; accommodating each other's food requirements was about the limit of religious discussion.

One can find traditional, European-derived stereotypes and negative religious images of Jews in both Protestant and Catholic literature in the nineteenth century, but in neither the nineteenth nor the twentieth centuries were religious-based prejudices politically potent as they were throughout Europe. Because of their numbers, Catholics rather than Jews were seen as the greatest threat to American civilisation, spawning remarkable anti-Catholic political parties such as the Know-Nothings. The nineteenth century was marked by strong attempts of the Protestant majority to missionise America's immigrants – Jews and Catholics alike – through the 'public' schools, where numbers gave them control of the curriculum. (While Catholic belief led to a desire to 'save' Jewish as well as Protestant souls, efforts to convert Jews never took on the same priority or aggressiveness as in the Protestant **Evangelical** community.) The Jewish community responded with increasingly sophisticated works of **apologetics** and, by the 1920s, with the establishment of two major 'defence' organisations, the American Jewish Committee and the Anti-Defamation League.

In 1928, as **antisemitism** began to rise to political prominence in Europe, anti-Catholicism determined the outcome of a presidential race when the first Catholic ever to be nominated by a political party, Alfred E. Smith (1873–1944) of New York, lost amid a flurry of stereotypes and Vatican conspiracy theories. Shocked, key figures of the Protestant Establishment sought to counteract what they perceived as a threat to American religious pluralism with the foundation of the National Conference of Christians and Jews. This became the first forum of religious exchange in the US, though its platforms of 'minister, priest, rabbi' most often stuck to generally acceptable social values and affirmations rather than delving into the dangerous waters of theology. During the 1930s and 1940s major Catholic and Protestant publications expressed concern for the plight of the Jews of Europe and condemned antisemitism at home; the 'radio priest', Charles Coughlin (1891–1979), whose antisemitic fulminations in the late 1930s were heard by millions, was among the clergy a notorious exception to the norm. Both Catholic and Protestant publications, however, were split among themselves on the issues of **Zionism** and a Jewish state in Palestine. While the American labour movement, heavily Catholic, supported the cause from the beginning, fears were expressed in Catholic magazines, at times reflecting similar concerns coming from Rome, that a Jewish state would dispossess the Catholic minority in the Holy Land and close access to the Holy Places.

Just as the US varies from region to region, so does the quality and character of Jewish–Christian relations. The concentration of Catholics and Jews, as well as Protestants, in the large cities of the North-east resulted in various patterns of economic and political alliance and sometimes conflict. In the predominantly Baptist South both Jewish and Catholic communities were from the beginnings of the Republic tiny **minorities** that often got along quite well. It was not unusual after the Civil War, for example, for Catholic schools in the South to have numerous Jewish students, whose parents felt they were less likely to be proselytised than in the public schools. A relative openness to innovation and difference characterised much of the 'pioneering' culture of the Midwest and West, enabling an ease of mingling between ethnic groups not always present in the more socially stratified East and South. In Detroit in 1942, for example, three major social groups, Knights of Columbus (Catholic), B'nai B'rith (Jewish) and the Masonic Lodge (Protestant), jointly launched a series of annual banquets that lasted well into the 1970s, raising hundreds of thousands of dollars to help the war effort and, later, a variety of social causes.

The Second World War was a unifying struggle for many ethnic Americans, while the GI Bill (1944) gave hundreds of thousands the opportunity of higher education and entry to the middle and upper-middle classes, ultimately bringing to an end the era of the dominant Protestant Establishment – an ending symbolically marked by the election in 1960 of the first Catholic President, John F. Kennedy (1917–63), which was cheered as much by Jews as by Catholics. As it was a Protestant initiative that first picked up the challenge of religious bigotry among its own after the First World War, so immediately after the Second World War the early American pioneers of Jewish–Christian dialogue – notably Reinhold Niebuhr (1892–1971) and H. Richard Niebuhr (1894–1962), Roy (1918–98) and

Alice Eckardt (b. 1923) and Franklin Littell (b. 1917) – were Protestants, most of them deeply concerned with the logical result of Jew-hatred that was the **Holocaust** and the role of traditional religious doctrine and images in the development of modern, racial antisemitism.

In American Catholicism the work of the great French theologian Jacques Maritain (1882–1973) first raised the issue as a serious theological concern. In 1955 John **Oesterreicher** established at Seton Hall University the first Institute of Judeo-Christian Studies at any institution of higher learning in the history of Christianity, bringing to the fore a generation of Catholic pioneers such as Edward Flannery (1912–98) and George G. Higgins (1916–2002) and providing a constructive focus for the postwar sympathy of many Catholics toward Jews. This positive attitude resulted in a key role for American bishops at the Second Vatican Council (1962–5) in securing a strong statement on the Jews (*Nostra Aetate*), along with statements on **ecumenism** and religious freedom.

Even before **Vatican II**, Catholics, Jews and Protestants had in the early 1960s become involved in specifically religious dialogues, locally as well as nationally, leading not only to several significant statements by the Churches but also to joint Jewish–Christian statements on a variety of social and religious topics, the series issued by the US Conference of Catholic Bishops (USCCB) and the National Council of Synagogues being perhaps the most consistent example. Co-founded by Rabbi Mordecai Waxman (1917–2002) and Cardinal William Keeler (b. 1931) in 1987, the consultation has produced joint statements on topics such as *Moral Values in Public Education* and *Reflections on Covenant and Mission*, as well as condemnations of pornography and Holocaust revisionism.

The National Workshops on Christian–Jewish relations, jointly sponsored by all three religious communities, began as a Catholic–Jewish dialogue in 1973 in Dayton, Ohio. Held in varying cities across the country, the workshops have provided the opportunity for scholars and local laity and clergy to meet and enrich each other's perspectives. There are now over two dozen institutes and centres across the country promoting Jewish–Christian studies, many affiliated with Catholic universities. A source of solid scholarship and programmes to support the ongoing efforts of Church and synagogue bodies, they have joined to form the association the Center of Centers of Jewish–Christian Relations.

See also **literature, American**

EUGENE J. FISHER

Universalism

Universalism – belief in a collection of universal truths applicable to everyone and at all times – is often defined in contradistinction to **particularism**. It is sometimes assumed that one of the major differences between Judaism and Christianity is that the latter is a universal and the former a particularistic religion. Thus Judaism has been accused by Christians of lacking an emphasis on universalism while Christianity has been accused by Jews of religious imperialism. These generalisations derive from an oversimplification of the teachings of both religions. While Judaism clearly possesses particularistic features, such as attachment to the **land of Israel**, there is also a strong emphasis on universal values, as witnessed from the writings of the biblical prophets in the eighth century BCE through to the development of Reform Judaism (*see* **Progressive Judaism**) in the nineteenth and twentieth centuries CE. Yet it is doubtless true that in its emphasis on land and culture as well as religion Judaism combines particularism with universalism, and there are also clearly examples in the history of Christianity of the fusing of religious and national or ethnic elements, as in the nineteenth-century Anglican missions to Africa, which sought to propagate both religious and national, in this case British, **identity**.

For Christianity, universalism is generally understood as God loving or saving all people (cf. 1 Tim. 2.4): God wills all to **salvation**, but there remains disagreement as to whether salvation is limited to believers only (*extra ecclesiam nulla salus* – outside the Church there is no salvation) or is open to all. Some Christian theologians have explored the universal salvific will of God; Karl Rahner (1904–84), for example, proposed the concept of 'anonymous Christianity' and was concerned with how God can save all people while Christ remains the mediator of salvation. Unsurprisingly, Jews (and other non-Christians) do not welcome the title of 'anonymous Christian'. For Christians, universalism requires a reconsideration of the meaning of **mission** and thus of whether **conversion** remains at the heart of their faith. For Jews, by contrast, conversion to Judaism is not necessary for salvation: adherence to the **Noachide laws** is sufficient. *EDWARD KESSLER*

Usury

From the earliest days of the Church Christian thinkers were faced with the challenge of interpreting the biblical prohibition of the taking of interest from co-religionists. The **proof-texts** most often cited are Exod. 22.25, 'If you lend money to my people, to the poor among you, you shall not deal with them as a creditor; you shall not exact interest from them', as well as Lev. 25.36. The highly commercialised Roman economy was supported by laws that defined and allowed the enforcement of contracts regulating interest on loans. Jewish law had a complex set of definitions, which allowed for investment and shared compensation for risk. In their desire to differentiate themselves from both Jewish and Roman practices the taking of interest beyond the principal of the loan came to be prohibited by the **Church Fathers**. In the first instance, in the Council of Nicaea (325) clerics were forbidden to take interest, a prohibition extended in the next century to the laity. Pope Leo I's letter of 444 against the taking of interest formed the basis of a legal tradition enshrined in canonistic collections, a position reiterated and invigorated by the canons of the Second Lateran Council of 1139. The Third Lateran Council of 1179 ordered **excommunication** of usurers and the annulment of wills that dispensed usurious gains. This position clashed dramatically with the realities of urban growth and commercialisation of the European economy from around 950. It also existed in acute tension with the interests and initiatives of secular rulers who habitually licensed interest-taking by setting regional rates of interest and licensing specific groups to undertake moneylending and pawnbroking. It is in the late medieval centuries that Jews were simultaneously excluded from many occupations and encouraged to engage in financial services. But they were never the sole providers of loans, although they were increasingly providers of small subsistence loans. In England the crown developed an ingenious system of protection and licensing of Jewish moneylending and the enforcement of contracts between Christians and Jews. Copies of contracts were deposited in carefully guarded urban chests (*archae*) the incomes of which were scrutinised by a department of state, the Exchequer of the Jews. The Holy Roman Emperors protected Jews in the imperial cities as 'servants of the imperial fisc', parts of an imperial fiscal policy. Large-scale loans could be disguised as forms of investment and so the restriction on moneylending at interest usually applied only to smaller loans, and lending against pawns. In these transactions Jews came into contact with the poorer sections of urban societies, contacts that often created malaise and resentment. Such feelings converged with the competitive animosities of guild-members in German cities and ultimately led to the **expulsion** of Jews from several urban centres in the fifteenth century during anti-usury campaigns by preachers. Although moneylending at interest was a widespread and necessary economic reality, it became a byword for Jewish evil, and for the harm that Jews intended to inflict on Christians. In late medieval Italy preachers and urban elites attempted to rid themselves of the need for Jewish subsistence lending by setting up charitable low-interest banks (*monti di pietà*) with the encouragement of **Dominican** and **Franciscan** preachers, banks that usually failed after a short while. The visual image of the Jew as usurer was transformed in more modern times into the figure of the Jewish banker, or even into conspiracies of bankers. In the twentieth century the traditional imagery was revived most powerfully in **antisemitic** publications of Nazi, Soviet anti-capitalist and anti-Israeli Arab propaganda.   *MIRI RUBIN*

VVVV

Vatican II

The Second Vatican Council was, in the counting of the **Roman Catholic** Church, the twenty-first ecumenical (literally, 'the whole world') council of the Church. The defining event for Catholicism in the twentieth century, it marked a turning point in the history of Jewish–Christian relations, particularly with the promulgation of *Nostra Aetate* (October 1965), the council's declaration on interfaith relations. While ecumenical councils, which are gatherings of bishops from throughout the Catholic world, have been held in order to respond to doctrinal disputes, to determine official ecclesiastical teaching, and to take disciplinary measures, Pope **John XXIII** convened Vatican II for the purpose of *aggiornamento*, 'updating'. It was in this spirit that the council issued 16 documents initiating Church reform in a variety of areas, including interfaith relations with Jews.

Nearly a year before *Nostra Aetate*, the council declared, in *Lumen Gentium* (November 1964), that the Jewish people 'remain most dear to God'. Thus, 'in a single phrase, the Roman Church reversed at least 16 centuries of popular Christian teaching' (Cunningham, *Education for Shalom*, 35) and signalled a reversal of the traditional **replacement theology** or **supersessionism** that, for most of Christian history, had marked the Church's self-understanding vis-à-vis Jews and Judaism. Not only has this reversal positively affected Jewish–Christian relations, it also has fostered renewal of Catholic life and theology based on a new-found appreciation of the **Hebrew Bible**, of the Jewishness of **Jesus** and his ministry, and of Jewish approaches to God and to **covenant** with God, to **community**, to the relationship of the physical and spiritual dimensions of life, and to **redemption** in and of this world.   *JOHN C. MERKLE*

Verus Israel *see* **Chosen People; people of Israel; supersessionism**

Victorines

Augustinian canons of Saint-Victor Abbey in Paris, founded in 1113 by William of Champeaux (*c.*1070–1121). Victorine scholars exerted a major influence on twelfth-century biblical **exegesis**, **mysticism** and liturgical poetry. Breaking with **Augustine**'s allegorical tradition, they returned to **Jerome**'s literal and historical approach to biblical study and took rabbinic **commentary** tradition seriously. Hugh of St Victor (d. 1142), whose vast erudition in the liberal arts and theoretical and practical sciences resulted in an early encyclopaedia, *Didascalicon* (*c.*1127: 'Teaching'), was the first medieval theologian to urge the importance of the natural world for understanding God. Hugh's prolific Bible commentaries established the Victorine tradition of literal interpretation and historical study of scripture, inspired in part by his considerable indebtedness to **Rashi**. Hugh knew some **Hebrew** and frequently cited Jewish sources, including Rashbam (Samuel ben Meir) (*c.*1080/85–1174) and oral traditions. He warned against overly **Christological** interpretation of the **Pentateuch**.

Andrew of St Victor wrote important commentaries on the Octateuch, Prophets, Proverbs and Ecclesiastes, based on Hugh's exegesis and close attention to the literal text; like Hugh, Andrew juxtaposed Christian with Jewish interpretations, frequently and sympathetically. Richard of St Victor (d. 1173), an early and scintillating teacher of mystical theology, opposed some of Andrew's 'Jewish' interpretations, yet innovatively used portions of Hebrew scripture to explore 'the steep stairway of love', the **soul**'s union with the Bridegroom-Word through betrothal, marriage, wedlock and fruitfulness.   *MARGARET BREARLEY*

Virgin Birth

The Christian belief that Christ was born of a virgin who was intact at the time of his conception and remained so after his birth became central to Christian theology by the early Middle Ages. It formed part of the emergent theology and homiletics that underpinned the belief that **Jesus** was both God and man. Yet this was also one of the claims that met the most visceral rejection from Jews.

The Gospel accounts of Jesus' birth provide relatively little detail about his mother. Luke 1.26–35 recounts the encounter between **Mary** and the angel, who announces that although she is a virgin she will conceive by the work of the **Holy Spirit**. What the Gospels left out was clearly a subject of some speculation and discussion among the many groups engaged in **polemic** and persuasion: **Jewish Christians**, Gentile Christians, Jews, pagans. By the early second century a version of Mary's early life was provided by the Greek *Protogospel of James*. This work emphasised the chastity of her elderly parents and rendered her own birth miraculous; each tale demonstrated Mary's purity, in her life in the Temple, during her chaste youth, and in her marriage to the widower Joseph.

While Mary's virginity was upheld in these early Christian accounts, important thinkers – **Origen**, **Tertullian** – rejected the growing belief that Mary remained intact after the birth of her son. The Virgin Birth continued to grow in importance as it was blended into the claims that resulted from the formative **Christological** debates. In the Nicene creed (325) Virgin Birth and **incarnation** were intertwined. In opposition to those sects that emphasised one nature in Jesus, the dual formulation – man and God – depended on his birth in the flesh of a woman, yet a birth pure and unique, of a virgin. The efforts of exegetes were poured into interpretation of the Bible, rendering the phrase *alma* ('maiden' in Hebrew) in the prophecy of Isa. 7.14 as *virgo* ('virgin') in Jerome's translation of the **Vulgate**. By the council of Ephesos of 431 the formulation *theotokos* – 'bearer of God' – was authorised to describe Mary.

Jewish opinion expressed in polemical texts rejected the idea of Virgin Birth as unreasonable because unnatural, and even suggested that it masked Mary's adulterous pregnancy. *Toledot Yeshu*, a parodic and polemical version of Christ's life, inverted Christian belief and called Mary impure (*nidda*). Jewish rejection of Virgin Birth formed part of the denial of the incarnation. The *Book of Nestor the Priest*, a Jewish polemical text

of the ninth century, rejected the thought that God would have dwelt in a 'womb, in the filth of menstrual blood, in the confinement and imprisonment and darkness for nine months'. Conversely, in medieval Christian polemical writings, such rejection of Virgin Birth was imputed to Jewish interlocutors; Odo of Tournai (*c*.1100) had the Jew in his *Disputation with the Jew Leo* claim that Mary's womb was 'uncleanliness of woman, the obscene prison, the fetid womb'. Jewish rejection of Virgin Birth also resulted in a view of the Jews as particular enemies of Mary, an understanding that was explored in medieval polemic, **art** and miracle tales. The polemical thrust became newly apparent during the **Reformation**, when, although it was without scriptural basis, Mary's perpetual virginity was not rejected by **Luther**.　　　　*MIRI RUBIN*

Visigoths

The Visigoths ruled the Iberian Peninsula from the later part of the fifth century until 711 when Islamic forces took it over. In the early period there is evidence that there were friendly social relations between Christians and Jews, such as sharing in festivals and dining together. With the conversion of King Recared (*r*.586–601) in 589 from **Arianism** to Catholic orthodoxy, a different attitude to the Jews arose. Social and economic forces, along with a desire to unify the kingdom, seem to have moved Christian leaders to enact legislation harmful to the Jews. At the Third Council of Toledo in 589, the decision was reached that Jews were no longer able to marry Christians, hold public office or possess slaves. After a period of relaxing of these laws, King Sisebut (*r*.612–21) ordered that all Jews be baptised. Although many did not convert, many of those who did wanted to return to their Jewish faith, which created the first **Conversos** controversy in **Spain**. During the reign of the subsequent kings Reccesuinth (*r*.649–72) and Ervig (*r*. 680–7), further legislation was enacted to curtail the influence of Judaism in the kingdom: **Passover**, **dietary laws**, Jewish **marriages**, **Sabbath** and other Jewish rituals were forbidden, and ownership of property was taken away from Jews. There is much debate about the extent to which this anti-Jewish legislation was enforced, and about the respective roles in it of the Church leadership and the government. Also at issue is whether these leaders were trying to suppress Jews and Judaism per se or Jewish influence over Christians in a country that was attempting to unite under the banner of Christianity. *STEVEN J. McMICHAEL*

Vocabulary

Vocabulary is a key issue in Jewish–Christian relations in several respects. As modern **linguistics** have shown, words gain their meanings from the contexts in which they are used and the social conventions that lie behind them, and since they can of course have more than one meaning, or different referents in different situations, if not used wisely they can cause misunderstanding or misrepresentation.

When comparing Judaism and Christianity, for example, it is common to speak of each as a '**religion**', but such a term has been questioned. When used of ancient religion (Latin: *religio*) the term refers to the ancient practices of sacrifice and worship, and is not to be associated with the dogma or institutionalisation of the modern term. The concept of 'religion' as developed by Christianity was such that by the fourth century it represented a practice that committed the believer to a set of rules and beliefs separate from lifestyle. One could argue, therefore, that by this definition Judaism is not a religion. At the same time, to draw such a rigid distinction is to emphasise differences rather than commonalities.

When the same word is applied to different phenomena or events, it both identifies their relationship and implies a connection that might not exist. For example, '**antisemitism**' always applied to any verbal or physical attack on Jews implies the continual presence of hatred and the essentialist nature of Jewish suffering, whether in antiquity or more recently. However, in contrast, to define the term too precisely by social and historical conditions can obscure the real connections that do exist. Likewise, one may speak generally of an '*Adversus Judaeos*' tradition, in the light of *Adversus Judaeos* texts. But as an actual tradition it might not exist beyond the texts themselves, and to generalise such a term can lead to statement without a supporting argument. The presence of texts by that name, if those texts might be for internal Christian education only, cannot necessarily be used to support a tradition of continual attack on, or Christian critique of, Judaism.

Other words have caused confusion from a misunderstanding of their origins. '**Holocaust**' has been objected to as a religious term, and *Shoah* and other terms have been preferred. But whilst 'holocaust' is used of sacrifices in English translations of the Bible (from Greek 'wholly burnt'), it has been used in the English language since the eighteenth century of any major destruction. For this reason it came to be used of the destruction of Jews and others in the Third Reich, and for the same reason is initially capitalised in that specific context. Again, '**dialogue**' when it includes a third party is sometimes referred to as a '**trialogue**', but this presupposes, incorrectly, that 'di-' in 'dialogue' means 'two': in fact, the whole word dialogue denotes 'discussion' without indication of number. (At the same time, it is of course in the nature of language that new words may be coined for specific needs, and often through false etymology.) It should also be borne in mind that dialogue is different from relations, the former a subset of the latter. 'Relations' refers to the study of contact in all its forms between Jews and Christians, and need not be theological or reconciliatory, as is implied in 'dialogue'.

The handling of vocabulary in religious texts is an issue of particular sensitivity. As words derive force from their context of use, apparently innocent words can be applied in communities with negative effects: for example 'the crowd' in John's Gospel, which could be taken disparagingly to refer to a Jewish mob. But by the same token such misapplications can be reinterpreted within communities and need not call for excision of the offending word. Similarly, in translations no one word will convey the full range or connotation of the source language, and education is needed for a proper understanding of the meaning. To explain a religious term through recourse to its 'root' sense or the presumed mind of the speaker, without any reference to actual usage in texts, is thus a futile enterprise. *JAMES K. AITKEN*

Voltaire (1694–1778)

(Pseudonym of François-Marie Arouet.) Voltaire was a prolific **Enlightenment** author. His writings called for religious **tolerance.** Although built on rationalist foundations, they assumed a detailed familiarity with the Bible, suggesting (for example) that the first Christians did not distinguish themselves from Jews, and that Christian **anti-Judaism** was a later aberration. However, Voltaire's work was not free of traces of the same anti-Jewish prejudices that he sometimes ridiculed, and, more distinctively, he discussed Jews in ways that suggested they had innate negative qualities. In the *Philosophical Dictionary* (1764) Voltaire described avarice, superstition and hatred of others as Jewish traits, which meant that they 'deserve[d] to be punished'. For this reason, scholars like Arthur Hertzberg (b. 1921) have traced a line from Voltaire's views to modern racial **antisemitism** and **Nazism**. This assessment neglects the inconsistent and satirical character of much of Voltaire's *oeuvre*. His main target was the *ancien régime*, established privilege in French society.

See also **literature, French**   *MELANIE J. WRIGHT*

Vulgate

Jerome was commissioned to produce a new translation of the Bible into **Latin** by Pope Damasus I (366–84). Known as the Vulgate, owing to its 'common' (i.e. widespread) use in the Latin Church, it was intended as a revision of an earlier Latin translation, the *Vetus Latina*. Jerome sought to return to the *hebraica veritas* ('the Hebrew truth') by translating the **Old Testament** from the **Hebrew** rather than from the **Septuagint**. Using a Jewish informant, he justifies in his **commentaries** a reading on the basis of **exegesis** that often seems to be Jewish in origin. Nevertheless, he remains in part dependent on the Septuagint for his translation, sometimes contradicting his own commentaries. The influence of the Vulgate continues today, through **Luther**'s translation that was based upon it and Luther's influence in turn upon the Authorised Version.

See also **Bible translations, ancient**

JAMES K. AITKEN

Wagner, Richard (1813–83)

German composer and essayist. Wagner associated Judaism with corruption and degeneracy. His essay *Das Judentum in der Musik* (1850) drew on deterministic race theories, arguing that Jews were innately avaricious and sought world domination. Unassimilable, they must be removed from European cultural life. Wagner's politics are reflected in his operas: *Parsifal* (1882) blends pagan and Christian stories and motifs to glorify the German *Volk*; Beckmesser's character in *Die Meistersinger von Nürnburg* (1868) is influenced by **antisemitic** stereotypes. Wagner influenced later antisemites, including **Hitler**. For these reasons, public performance of his **music** in **Israel** is rare and controversial.   *MELANIE J. WRIGHT*

Wandering Jew

The Wandering Jew is a recurring and much studied motif in Christian **folklore**, finding expression in stories, songs, poems, the visual arts and the popular name for the trailing plant *tradescantia zebrina*. In common with other legends, there are many versions of the tale, but its core is relatively constant. A Jerusalem cobbler (often named Ahasuerus) refuses **Jesus** rest near his house on the road to the **crucifixion**. For this he is cursed, forced to wander eternally until Jesus' second coming. The story is recorded by thirteenth-century chroniclers Roger of Wendover and Matthew Paris, with a 1602 German publication (the *Kurtzse Beschreibung*) being the earliest to identify the wanderer as Jewish. However, the tale is probably ancient. It may originate in popular **exegesis** of Matt. 16.28 and John 21.20–2; there are also significant resonances with the story of **Cain** (Gen. 4.1–15), where longevity and wandering are divinely imposed punishments for wrongdoing. Many versions of the legend are shaped by negative prejudice towards Jews and Judaism: arrival of the wanderer invites disaster. But in some variants he is a positive figure, whose presence brings blessing. Post- **Enlightenment**, each of

these impulses found new expression. Nazi propaganda recast the wanderer as an international criminal, both sub- and superhuman. This contrasts with the approach of the Romantic poets, such as Shelley (1792–1822), Wordsworth (1770–1850) and Coleridge (1772–1834), for whom he was a universal symbol of dignified endurance. A recently rediscovered Yiddish **film**, *Der Vanderner Yid* (George Roland, 1933), is believed to have been the first American feature film to deal with the subject of Nazi oppression of Jews.

MELANIE J. WRIGHT

Weddings

Christian and Jewish **marriage** ceremonies have a common origin, but have developed many opposing customs. Wedding ceremonies derive from the Romans, including the giving of a ring and the cutting of the bride's hair. Roman custom drew a clear distinction between the *sponsalia*, or preliminaries, and the marriage itself, culminating in the procession of the bride to her husband's house. In most Christian rituals these two parts have become intertwined, but at a Jewish wedding the two original parts can still be made out, the giving of the ring forming the *erusin* or betrothal ceremony, and the *sheva berakhot* (seven benedictions) forming the *nissuin* or wedding ceremony. These two parts were combined into one ceremony from the twelfth century. By this time the Roman origin of wedding ceremonies was forgotten, and Church and synagogue developed opposite customs. For example, it is the Jewish custom that the bride stands on the bridegroom's right: in the Church the bridegroom stands on the bride's right. It has always been the custom at a Jewish wedding for the bridegroom to place the ring on the forefinger of the bride's right hand: the Church also preferred the right hand until the sixteenth century, but used the third finger. Many wedding customs, including the veiling of the bride and the Jewish custom of breaking a glass by the bridegroom, were originally intended to protect against evil spirits. In **talmudic** times it was customary to strew food, such as nuts and parched corn, before the bridal pair: during the Middle Ages wheat was thrown by both Jews and Christians. The celebration of marriage at the church door was the norm in Western Christendom from the tenth to the sixteenth century. Jewish weddings were held in private homes at that time: from the fifteenth century they were held in synagogues and then out of doors in the courtyard, especially in Eastern Europe. Early Reform Jews were considered to be adopting a 'Christian' custom in seeking to hold the ceremony in the communal place of worship.

MICHAEL HILTON

Weizmann, Chaim (1874–1952)

First president of the **State of Israel** (1948–52) and president of the World Zionist Organization (1920–31 and 1935–46). Through a combination of charismatic personality and scientific contributions, Weizmann became known to leading British politicians including **Lloyd George**. In his intensive lobbying which led to the **Balfour Declaration** (1917) he consciously appealed to **Christian Zionist** sympathies among the British statesmen, later commenting, 'They understood as a reality the concept of Return. It appealed to their tradition and their faith.' Likewise, in his dealings with US President Harry S. Truman (1884–1972), he based his presentation of the Zionist cause on the biblical history and geography with which Truman was intimately familiar. *DANIEL R. LANGTON*

Wellhausen, Julius (1844–1918)

German orientalist best known for *Prolegomena to the History of Israel* (1883), which proposed a three-stage development of Israelite religion, each stage corresponding to a literary source of the **Pentateuch**: a period of spontaneous religion with worship at many shrines (ninth to eighth centuries, the sources using the divine names *J*ehovah and *E*lohim); centralisation of worship in **Jerusalem** under the influence of prophetic teaching (seventh century, *D*euteronomy); the post-exilic period with increasing emphasis on sacrificial **atonement** (the *P*riestly source). Orthodox Jewish and conservative Christian scholars have been united in their rejection of this view, in which some Jews, such as Solomon Schechter (1847–1915), have detected an undercurrent of **antisemitism**, but which, however, remains a milestone in the critical study of the Bible. *See also* **biblical criticism**   *JOHN ROGERSON*

Wesley, John (1703–91)

Anglican clergyman and founder of **Methodism**; his view of non-Christian religions was unusually open in an eighteenth-century cleric. As a fellow of Lincoln College, Oxford, Wesley led a group dedicated to study, prayer and good works nicknamed 'methodists'. Following a religious experience in 1738, Wesley travelled extensively in Britain and Ireland, establishing Methodist societies. By 1784 Methodism had effectively separated from the **Church of England**.

In 1737 Wesley learned Spanish to converse with Sephardic Jews in his parish. In 1757 he baptised a Portuguese Jew. His journal for 23 February 1770 records his visit to the Aldgate Synagogue where he was impressed by the solemn doxology which 'might strike an awe upon those who have any thought of God'. Wesley believed that Jews are at a stage of faith beyond materialists, 'Mahometans' and 'heathens'. He argues that though Jews are God's elect, 'the veil is still upon their hearts', yet concludes that 'it is not our part to pass sentence upon them' (Sermon 106). But Wesley's chief interest in Judaism was as a rhetorical device to encourage **evangelical** faith: he goaded Christians by pointing to good Jews.

Charles Wesley (1707–88), Anglican clergyman and poet, co-founded Methodism with his brother John. He wrote nearly 10,000 hymns, many employing a **Christological** reading of Hebrew scriptures: for example, 'Come, O thou Traveller unknown' identifies the stranger at the Jabbok ford (Gen. 32) with Christ. Charles emphasised the doctrine that Christ died for all people, a **universalism** that may explain why he rarely singled Jews out for comment. *STEPHEN PLANT*

Willebrands, Johannes (b. 1909)

Dutch Catholic churchman and ecumenist. Monsignor Willebrands was Secretary of the Secretariat for Promoting Christian Unity (SPCU) when the Office for Catholic–Jewish Relations (OCJR) was created under Augustin Cardinal **Bea** in 1966 and attached to the SPCU. In 1974 the OCJR became the Holy See's Commission for Religious Relations with the Jews (CRRJ) under the presidency of now Cardinal Willebrands. Although successive secretaries of the Commission were responsible for its ongoing activity, Willebrands continued to follow its development closely until his retirement in 1989. He clarified the Commission's mandate by inserting in its name the qualification 'religious' relations.

LUCY THORSON AND MURRAY WATSON

William of Norwich

The traditions associated with the life-story of William of Norwich told that his 12-year-old body was found in Thorpe Wood outside Norwich, England, on 24 March 1144. His mother claimed that he had been taken away by a man who offered the boy employment; his uncle, Godwin Sturt, blamed the Jews of Norwich, but this accusation did not result in any action. It was with the arrival at Norwich Cathedral priory in 1150 of the monk Thomas of Monmouth (*fl.*1150–60) that the local tale became a notorious one. For Thomas wrote an account of the life of William of Norwich, a history of his passion (*Passio*). This was a hagiographical treatment, which claimed to be based on careful research conducted by Thomas, and to be based on the testimony of a Jewish convert, Theobald. Thomas attributed sanctity to the body, which had not been touched by the birds of the forest and was left intact and incorruptible. Thomas's account, in a manuscript of around 1170, also recorded tens of miracles that were believed to have taken place around William's tomb, and later around the shrine that was built for it once the body was moved to Norwich cathedral. William of Norwich attracted **pilgrims** who sought in particular cure for children's diseases and the ailments of women.

This early tale established a narrative that imputed to Jews the desire to 're-crucify' Christ in the figure of an innocent Christian boy. Although it did not gain official recognition, the following decades saw similar cases enacted in English towns – Harold of Gloucester in 1168, Robert of Bury in 1181, Adam of Bristol in 1183 – and later in France. The narrative was also elaborated further as the **blood libel**. The cult of William of Norwich ebbed and flowed, particularly in East Anglia, where a number of fifteenth-century roodscreens included him among martyrs and saints (as in Litcham and Lodden). *MIRI RUBIN*

Wine

By the first century CE, when **Jesus** shared wine with his disciples at the **Last Supper**, most known Jews marked certain elements of domestic life as sacred by performing rituals in conjunction with a cup of wine. As documented in early rabbinic texts, such rituals included the inauguration and conclusion of Sabbaths and festivals, most lifecycle rituals, the Grace after Meals (**birkat hamazon**), particularly in a festive setting, and parts of the **Passover** seder. Their thick wine always required dilution, so cups were always 'mixed'. The origins of this ritual practice are unknown, but among the factors that doubtless led to its emergence were that wine, a local and high-quality product in **Israel**, was widely considered a choice drink both for human consumption and for ritual use in temple contexts. Pagan and Jewish sacrificial rites involved wine libations. All of these rabbinic rituals required a **blessing** (*berakhah*) over the wine in conjunction with the blessing(s) appropriate to the specific ritual that addresses the actual content of the event. The prayer of **sanctification** (*Kiddush*) before a **Sabbath** or festival meal and the grace after that meal bracket it with wine-related rituals, marking the whole as particularly sacred time.

Jesus and his disciples were clearly familiar with this structure, particularly with the integration of a ritual cup of wine into a meal setting. The Synoptic Gospels all record that at the Last Supper Jesus 'took a cup, gave thanks, and gave it to them . . .' (Mark 14,23; cf. Matt. 26,27; Luke 22,17). He continues with an explanation of the meaning of the cup. However, it is with this explanation that Jesus and his followers broke with the Jewish model; at this meal and in subsequent Christian **eucharistic** rites it is the cup's contents, the fruit of the vine, that holds symbolic value rather than wine's creating the context for another ritual. This wine combines the Jewish domestic and sacrificial rituals. While derived from a home table setting, as the blood of Christ it echoes distantly the libations of the **Temple**, but even more so the blood of the sacrificial animals that was ritually sprinkled on the **altar** as part of the offerings. However, humans consumed neither the libations nor the sprinkled blood; the shared eucharistic wine therefore maintains elements of its original social function. Requirements in most Churches that the wine be mixed with water, although explained **Christologically**, also derive from the ritual's cultural origins.

Rabbinic concern that Jews might consume wine intended for pagan libations led to **halakhic** requirements that Jews only drink wine prepared by other Jews. This, along with other **dietary laws**, severely limited socialisation between Jews and non-Jews. Even medieval acceptance of Christians as monotheists did not alter this restriction. Many contemporary kosher wine-makers, especially in the **Diaspora** where Jews and Christians often socialise together, now pasteurise their wines. This removes the product from the halakhic category of 'wine', thus circumventing the prohibition. Few non-orthodox Jews observe this prohibition today. *RUTH LANGER*

Wisdom/Wisdom Literature

The term 'Wisdom Literature' is used to identify a distinct category of biblical books whose purpose is to provide moral and religious instruction. Within the **Hebrew Bible** it refers to the books of Proverbs, Job and Ecclesiastes; in the **apocrypha** it includes Tobit, the Wisdom of Solomon and the Wisdom of Ben Sira (Ecclesiasticus). Israelite wisdom is to be understood in two ways. First, as a characteristic. It has been defined as 'the ability to cope', inasmuch as it has a practical rather than theoretical meaning. Skilled workmen, capable administrators and successful statesmen are described as 'wise'. The sages, or teachers of wisdom, provided sound advice on matters of daily living. Second, as a person. In Prov. 8 wisdom is personified as a woman and honoured as the first of God's creations. She was present as an active participant when the world was formed. As wisdom theology developed in Judaism, she was equated with the **Torah** (Sir. 24.23).

A greater appreciation of the Israelite wisdom tradition has led Christian theologians to recognise the marked affinity between it and the **New Testament** teaching about Jesus Christ. As a result of the current drive to explore Christianity in Jewish terms, and the recognition of the common ground shared by Jews and Christians, **Jesus** is recognised as wisdom's voice. The Synoptic Gospels place much emphasis on Jesus' sayings; they record many **parables** and over 100 aphorisms – for example 'You cannot serve two masters'; 'you cannot get grapes from a bramble bush'; 'no one pours new wine into an old wineskin' – which are the bedrock of the Jesus tradition. Wisdom from the Hebrew Bible lies behind this collection of sayings. Like the Israelite sages, Jesus is portrayed as one who disturbs his listeners and provokes them to think for themselves.

But in the New Testament Jesus is not only a teacher of wisdom, he *is* wisdom. In the letters of **Paul** and in John's Gospel we see the move from teacher to wisdom personified. The motif of wisdom as a person invested with divine attributes was rooted in Jewish thought. In Wis. 7.22–7 she is given qualities usually attributed to God. **Philo** refers to her as 'the daughter of God, the mother of the creative word' (*De Profugis* 9.20). In both Judaism and Christianity this concept developed under the influence of Greek philosophy and was adapted by the first Christians to suit the needs of their **mission** to the Gentiles. It is to be found in the hymn extolling the cosmic Christ in Col. 1.15–20 and in the prologue to John's Gospel where Christ is described as the **Logos** or Word which has been with God from the beginning of time, assisting in the creation of the world. Jesus is the **incarnation** of divine wisdom. It has been claimed that this Wisdom **Christology** is the earliest attempt to understand and express the relationship between Jesus and God, predating **Son of God** Christology. *GARETH LLOYD JONES*

Wise, Stephen (1874–1949)

Budapest-born American Reform rabbi and **Zionist** leader. Wise studied independently in New York and was ordained privately. As a rabbi he was a radical and charismatic leader who disregarded ritual and pioneered interfaith activities, conducting services for both Jews and Christians. In 1922 he established the Jewish Institute of Religion, a cross-denominational rabbinical seminary and educational centre. His contribution to the Jewish reclamation of **Jesus** took the form of a public sermon in 1925 in which he controversially endorsed Joseph **Klausner**'s positive biography of Jesus. An outspoken, liberal preacher, he was active in social rights work, protesting alongside Christian leaders such as the Baptist minister Walter Rauschenbusch (1861–1918) of the Social Gospel movement in America, and was among the first in the US to warn against the dangers of **Nazism**. He co-founded the representative body, the World Jewish Congress, in 1936. *DANIEL R. LANGTON*

Wissenschaft des Judentums

German term for the 'Science of Judaism' (Hebrew *ḥokhmat yisrael*) that flourished primarily in **Germany** and **Austria** from the early nineteenth century until the Second World War and promoted the critical, historical and literary study of Judaism and Jewish sources. Born out of the *Aufklärung* or enlightenment that accompanied Jewish **emancipation**, its methodological ancestry was in the European intellectual developments that had been primarily inspired by the Christian **Reformation**. It set out to record Jewish history in a scholastically sound and modern way, to present Jewish learning in a manner acceptable to the dominant Christian environment and to emancipated Jewry, and to fuse the best academic traditions of both Jews and Christians. Its proponents were prolific scholars, especially in the areas of manuscript (and then Genizah) research, who edited a number of important new periodicals, but their degree of commitment to Jewish belief and practice ranged from the intensely traditional to the minimal. The early leading figures were Leopold Zunz (1794–1886), S. J. Rapoport (1790–1867), Samuel David Luzzatto (1800–65) and Nachman Krochmal (1785–1840), and the methodology was championed in the rabbinical seminaries and subsequently at some (essentially Christian) universities of central and western Europe. It provided much of the intellectual stimulus for the evolution of Reform (A. **Geiger**), Conservative (Z. Fraenkel (1801–75)) and Modern Orthodox (D. Hoffmann (1843–1921)) forms of Judaism, encouraged a closer engagement with Christian sources and perhaps led to early forms of modern **dialogue**. Members of the traditional rabbinate of Eastern Europe were generally antagonistic to its principles and influences. Its impact on cultural **Zionism** and interplay with Jewish nationalism are represented by the Hebrew University and other Israeli educational institutions, and its effect, in moderated form, is still being felt in the Jewish studies departments of universities around the world, most of them of Christian foundation. *STEFAN C. REIF*

Word of God *see* Logos

World Council of Churches (WCC)

Established in Amsterdam in 1948, the WCC is a fellowship of approximately 350 mainline Protestant and Orthodox Churches. Its make-up is so heterogeneous that its approach to Judaism has to steer a difficult course through the great variety of attitudes represented by the constituent Churches.

At its first Assembly in 1948 the WCC addressed issues associated with the destruction of European Jewry during the **Holocaust**, stating: 'We call upon all the churches we represent to denounce anti-Semitism, no matter what its origin, as absolutely irreconcilable with the profession and practice of the Christian faith. Anti-Semitism is sin against God and man.' Tackling **antisemitism** has continued to be a concern, as has the question of **mission** to Jews. The selfsame 1948 report called for a

redoubling of efforts to convert Jews, recommending that the Churches should 'seek to recover the universality of our Lord's commission by including the Jewish people in their evangelistic work . . . and because of the unique inheritance of the Jewish people, the churches should make provisions for the education of ministers specially fitted to this task.' This position is no longer held by the WCC, although mission to Jews remains a controversial topic, as does the significance of the **State of Israel** and especially the Israel–Palestinian conflict. The WCC has been deeply involved in **liberation theology**, and the strongly pro-Palestinian Middle East Council of Churches (consisting in the main of Arab Churches – *see* **Arab Christianity**) is a constituent body and has influenced its attitudes beyond the specific political issues of the Middle East. The WCC Assembly has regularly endorsed anti-Israel statements, including an approval of the 1975 UN resolution equating **Zionism** with racism. The hostile attitude to Israel underwent a certain thaw with the peace process of the 1980s and 1990s and the 1993 Israel–PLO agreement but has reverted to the critical following the collapse of both in 2002.

In 1971 the WCC established a Sub-unit for Dialogue with People of Living Faiths and Ideologies, which also provided a desk for Jewish–Christian **dialogue**. New partners, particularly from member Churches in the South, have become involved in the dialogue through consultations in Nairobi (1986), Hong Kong (1992), Cochin (1993), Johannesburg (1995) and Yaoundé (2001). Important statements were issued in 1982 and 1988, but the diversity of opinion within the WCC resulted in their being toned down versions of the original drafts. Nevertheless, the 1982 document called on Christians to understand the Jews 'on their own terms', acknowledged the continuing creativity of Judaism as a living religion, and encouraged dialogue. The 1988 document affirmed that the Jewish people have not been rejected by God but remain the continuation of the biblical Israel, enjoying God's love and faithfulness. Yet for all their positive statements, neither of these documents was promulgated at the top level of the WCC because it was felt that they would not be passed by the Central Committee. In 2004 the WCC began a process of considering the implications of Jewish–Christian dialogue for Christian self-understanding. *EDWARD KESSLER*

Worship

Worship is understood in a religious sense as giving due honour and reverence to the divine. As such it is a communal and public activity that is seen as central in defining the **identity** of a religious group, a fact central to the Jewish and Christian understanding of worship. For Jews, worship takes place at home and in the synagogue at set times and in a set way, its central motif being praise. For Christians, worship is understood to be a public activity of the Christian **community**, the offering of praise and glory to God for the gift of Jesus Christ in the power of the Spirit by a gathered community. Both Jewish and Christian worship gathers together different strands of **time** in its celebration. The past is remembered as a manifestation of God's saving love for humanity, especially the **covenant** with the people of Israel. Christians recall the life, ministry, suffering, death, resurrection and ongoing saving presence of **Jesus** as the central point of this remembrance. Sometimes problematic for Jewish–Christian relations in this regard is appropriation by Christians for themselves of the **vocabulary** and identity of the **people of Israel**.

The study of worship as an academic discipline continues to grow. From its roots in the disciplines of history and archaeology, it now embraces theology and has more recently drawn extensively on the human and social sciences. More specifically, the study of the relationship between Jewish and Christian worship is of increasing interest to scholars in the field, in respect not only of the earliest interactions between the emerging Jesus movement and Second Temple and **Rabbinic Judaism**, but of the ongoing influences between the two communities in the **Roman Empire** and into the medieval and modern world. Liturgical scholars have noted that modernising nineteenth-century reforms of Jewish worship adopted many forms of Protestant worship, including the introduction of a sermon or having it in the vernacular, the shortening of the service, and the use of choirs. As in Christian worship, these reforms provoked strong reactions and **polemics**. Students of worship engaged in the contemporary Jewish–Christian encounter are particularly attentive to how the 'other' is portrayed in worship; the 'other' may have been portrayed as 'faithless' or 'heretical', or not been mentioned at all. Christian liturgists have shown how worship patterns and claims have led to **antisemitism** and **supersessionism** in Christian worship, especially in some Christian liturgical use of the **Hebrew Bible**. The possibilities and problems of interfaith worship have also drawn the attention of scholars. Nowadays Jewish and Christian worship traditions are faced with many challenges in common; for example, the role of women in worship as participants and as leaders of the worshipping assembly; what language should be used for worship; how should it be inclusive of all those present; how 'sacral' should it be; how much communal participation should there be; and who or what defines that participation. Despite these questions, worship remains the central public self-identification of both Jewish and Christian communities.

See also **liturgy**

LIAM M. TRACEY

Yavneh, Council of *see* **Jamnia, Council of**

Yellow badge

From medieval times Jews were often required to wear badges to distinguish them from their Christian neighbours. **Augustine** had taught that the Jews were set apart, the cursed bearers of 'the mark of **Cain**'. A tradition had developed of a fear of inter-relations, which was clearly articulated at **Lateran Council IV** in 1215 and which led to the sporadic introduction throughout Europe of 'the badge of shame'. In England the yellow badge showed the tablets of the **Law**, representing the **Old Testament**, while elsewhere other designs were used. The conquests of **Napoleon** freed many Jews from this discriminating practice. During the **Holocaust** the Nazis enforced the wearing of a yellow **star of David** or variations of it (for example, white armbands with blue stars) for Jews from as young as six years old.   *DANIEL R. LANGTON*

Yiddish literature *see* **literature, Yiddish**

Yom Kippur *see* **Day of Atonement**

Yugoslavia *see* **Balkans**

ZZZZ

Zealotry

The phenomenon of zeal is an important aspect of the ancient Hebrew religion, with the fervour of God affirmed in countless texts, indicating divine passion against sinners and in support of **justice** and **peace** (Exod. 20.5; 34.14; Deut. 4.24; 5.9; 6.15; Nah. 1.1–2; Isa. 9.7, where 'zeal' is also translated as 'jealous love'; 37.32; 2 Kgs 19.31). All occurrences of 'zealot' in the Greek Bible, the **Septuagint**, are in reference to God and the Lord's self-disclosure.

During the Second Temple period the figure of Phineas (Num. 25. 6–13), much discussed by such leading figures as Josephus, **Philo** and Pseudo-Philo, became for Jews a model of zeal, enacting justice on behalf of God without waiting for official action if something abhorrent to **Torah** was encountered. Jews referred to as zealots were active from the time of the **Maccabees** until they were destroyed during the last Jewish revolt against Rome in 135 CE. During the first century CE they kidnapped Jews as hostages for ransom, stole from caravans and killed their own people whom they regarded as traitors. **Josephus** accuses the zealots of destroying the **Temple** and eventually **Jerusalem** in the war against Rome in 66–70 CE.

There are indications that Jews who made up the **early Church** accepted zeal as a virtue, but chose not to encourage believers to imitate God's zeal. At least one of Jesus' disciples was a zealot (Simon the Zealot, Luke 6.15). Only once is an act of **Jesus** attributed to zeal: when he rages in the Temple, John 2.17 echoes a passage from Ps. 69.9: 'the zeal for your house consumes me'. Of the 16 references to zeal in the **New Testament**, by far the majority are laudatory. **Paul** boasts that, prior to his conversion, he was zealous for the law and in his persecution of Christians (Gal. 1.13–16). One of his greatest contributions, however, was his effort to remove from passionate devotion to God any need to kill the transgressor or the 'other'. Instead, he urges his people to be zealous (Greek, *zelos*) for love and for the good of the neighbour (1 Cor. 12.31; 14.1).

WILLIAM KLASSEN

Zion

Zion is a place name that Jews and Christians use to express realities that are beyond geography but nonetheless rooted in history. Both traditions proclaim and claim Zion as the city of God and of 'the great king', and especially as the setting and symbol of **salvation** in an idealised 'end of days'. For both Jews and Christians Zion is a spiritually and politically loaded symbol that carries within it life-giving truths that sustain the communal **identity** of each group.

Zion, or Sion, is synonymous with **Jerusalem** in the Tanakh, but became more evocative of **eschatology** than the later name. Zion's meaning was constantly expanded and extended: from a designation for a specific site and a name for a city to an allusion to the entire **land of Israel** and a symbol of the historic fate of the **people of Israel**, and finally to a vision of universal **redemption** and a concept of cosmic concord. Zion's multiple layers of meaning and its power to evoke a radically new era or reality are reflected in the use of the term by groups as diverse as **Anabaptists** (who founded their Kingdom of New Zion in Münster in 1534), **Mormons** (for whom America is the land of Zion where the new Jerusalem will be established) and the founders of **Zionism**. Many African and Protestant Churches and sects incorporate the word Zion in their name. Today in Jerusalem Mount Zion denotes the hilltop at the south-west corner of the Old City, which is elevated by its association with the site of the institution of the **eucharist** at the **Last Supper** and of the founding of the Church at **Pentecost**, as well as with the traditional tomb of King **David**.

Ever since the Babylonian exile, Jewish faith and life have been animated by the hope of religious and political renewal in Zion, which ultimately will include the restoration of the **Temple** and an idealised kingdom of David. Redemption is inconceivable without *shivat zion*, 'return to Zion', as the material and spiritual centre of Jewish existence. Jewish **liturgy**, festivals, rites of passage and everyday life are permeated with longing for Zion. Zionism – the modern-day, largely secular, Jewish movement for national renaissance – takes its name from Zion as the most evocative symbol of the Jewish people's eschatological aspirations.

For Christians, 'the great king' is **Christ** and Zion is *mater ecclesia*, the Church or body of Christ, the city of God on earth. The sequence, or liturgical hymn, composed by Thomas **Aquinas** for the Mass of Corpus Christi is entitled *Lauda Sion* ('Praise Sion'). As the place where the first church – the Church of Jerusalem or of the Apostles – was founded, Holy Zion is also the earthly mother of all Churches. Zion is sometimes equated with **Mary**, the virgin daughter of Zion who became the holy mother and the ark that bore the **incarnation**. Beginning with the **Church Fathers**, classical Christian **biblical interpretation** generally applied the praises and promises for the 'daughters of Zion' to Christians, while directing criticisms and condemnations at Jews. Modern **biblical criticism** isolated a 'Zion tradition' with a royal trajectory, which, particularly in **liberation theology**, is negatively contrasted with the Christian gospel of freedom deriving from the 'exodus' or 'Mosaic tradition'.

The centrality of Zion symbolism and consciousness in both Jewish and Christian tradition points to the common patrimony of the two faiths. But the very interrelatedness of these traditions betrays the causes of their interreligious rivalry and historical conflicts. Ultimately, their dispute over the meaning of Zion as the city of God reflects rival claims to be the true Israel, or people of God, and the chosen forebears of the future.   *DANIEL ROSSING*

Zionism

No other single topic in the modern history of Jewish–Christian relations has generated such intense and often divisive debate among Jews and Christians as has Zionism, which raises important questions about core components of traditional Christian and Jewish self-understanding. From its beginnings in the second half of the nineteenth century the main goals of Zionism have been the return of the Jewish people to **Zion** and the establishment of a secure national home for Jews in the

land of Israel, both through political action and by practical settlement of the land. This restoration and national renaissance severely undermined the age-old Christian claim that the '**Wandering Jew**' is divinely doomed to eternal exile and suffering and the corollary charge of **deicide**, which have buttressed **replacement theology** and the **supersessionism** inherent in the notion of the Church as the New Israel. For Jews, the path of modern secular nationhood required reconsideration of the classical notions of **Chosen People**, reward and punishment and **redemption**. Zionism, like Christianity, is both an ideal and a reality, and thus it evokes for Jews and Christians alike the issue of the relationship between **universalism** and **particularism**. The ongoing debate about Zionism mainly revolves around the question of whether Zionism is an integral part of being Jewish, as the vast majority of Jews and many Christians now maintain, or is intrinsically incompatible with Judaism, as some Christian critics and most ultra-**Orthodox Jews** adamantly insist. At best, Christian opponents argue that a particular nationalism cannot coexist with a universal religion of ethical monotheism; at worst, they insist that Jews have no right to terminate the exile imposed on them as punishment for failing to recognise **Jesus** as their **Messiah**. Orthodox Jewish opposition to Zionism derives from a firm belief that return and restoration can come about only under divine auspices and that any human attempt to 'hasten the end' through political means is heretical.

Religious, philosophical, social and political factors converged and interacted to produce Zionism. The movement drew heavily – not least through its chosen name – on the religious faith that in the end of days God would return the Jewish people to **Jerusalem**, but it largely secularised traditional **Messianism** by translating it into political means and goals appropriate to the modern Western discourse. Zionism was a natural outgrowth of **emancipation** and **enlightenment**, but it was also a reaction to the failure of enlightened **liberalism** and rationalism to eradicate the popular **antisemitism** – epitomised by the **Dreyfus Affair** – that thwarted full **assimilation** of Jews into Western European society and fuelled **pogroms** in Eastern Europe and **Russia**. The rise of modern nationalism in the middle of the nineteenth century, with its romantic concept of the unique soul of a particular 'folk' rooted in a specific land and language, also hampered integration of Jews. However, the new notions of **nationhood** and national renaissance offered Jews an alternative path to a secure place in the modern world, not as assimilated universalised individuals or as a reformed religion like all other religions, but as a particular nation like all other nations.

Ideological debates among the early Zionists produced a variety of visions of the desired character of a renewed national Jewish existence, which were influenced as much by current trends in Western Christian society as by ancient Jewish traditions. Zionism's founding father, Theodor **Herzl**, envisioned an elitist, aristocratic liberal European polity, and at one point even considered establishing it in Uganda. Ber Borochov (1881–1917), a champion of Marxism, argued for a nation that would be the vanguard of the international class struggle, with the **kibbutz** as its hallmark. Ahad Ha'am (Asher Zvi Ginsberg (1856–1927)) advocated a 'cultural Zionism' and a small nation of the spirit that would be a vital corrective to the dominant nationalisms of power. In sharp contrast, Jewish revisionists, led by Vladimir Jabotinsky (1880–1940), insisted that Jews were doomed in the **Diaspora** by an impending 'onrush of lava' and only an ironclad state with considerable military power could guarantee Jewish survival. The common aim of these and other plans was to secure and 'normalise' Jewish existence, which required the cooperation of Gentile nations.

Zionism benefited from the Christian West's rediscovery of the Holy Land in the nineteenth century, as well as from the climate created by numerous influential Christians like George **Eliot**, who advocated the restoration of the Jewish people to the **Promised Land**. The collapse of the **Ottoman Empire** in the First World War, the capture of Palestine by General Allenby (1861–1936) and the publication of the **Balfour Declaration** in 1917, and the decision of the League of Nations to award Great Britain the **Mandate** over Palestine all facilitated the political and practical progress of the Zionist movement.

In the aftermath of the **Holocaust** Zionism became a pre-eminent part of Jewish **identity**, even though Jews continue to argue passionately over its place in Jewish history and its desired future course. Christian attitudes towards Zionism are often confused, and sometimes extreme. Many major Christian statements on the new relationship of the Church and the Jewish people stammer or even fall silent on the subject of Zionism and the State of Israel. In 1969 Edward Flannery (1912–98) argued cogently that the Christian psyche is subliminally predisposed to anti-Zionism, which provides an outlet for suppressed or unconscious antisemitism. The complexity of the issue is illustrated by the case of the American Catholic scholar Rosemary Ruether (b. 1936), who published a penetrating study of the theological roots of antisemitism as well as a later work whose **polemic** against Zionism is more virulent even than the harsh critique of the movement featured in **Palestinian liberation theology**, where Zionism is presented as 'a retrogression of the Jewish people' and 'a step backward in the development of Judaism'. **Roman Catholicism's** official attitude towards Zionism changed greatly in the course of the twentieth century. In 1904 Pope Pius X (r.1903–14) rejected Herzl's plea for support unequivocally: 'The Jews have not recognised our Lord, therefore we cannot recognise the Jewish people.' Nine decades later the Holy See established official diplomatic relations with the State of Israel, and Pope **John Paul II**, during his historic visit to the Holy Land in March 2000, displayed deep respect for the nation of the Jewish people. **Orthodox Christianity** has been guarded in its response to Zionism, particularly in Arab lands and countries of the former Soviet bloc, where the political climate dictated a negative attitude to the Jewish national movement. **Protestantism** is deeply divided by polar positions on Zionism. Christian Zionists, including **fundamentalists** and **evangelical movements** associated with the **International Christian Embassy**, believe that God is working through Zionism to fulfil biblical **prophecy** and usher in the Messianic age. Most mainline Protestants firmly oppose such prophetic dispensationalism and reject **millenarianism**, but nonetheless endorse Zionism, as did Paul Tillich (1886–1965) and Reinhold Niebuhr (1892–1971), as a necessary and morally justified response to antisemitism. Some Protestants make absolute moral demands on Israel and conclude that Zionism represents a profane corruption of Judaism's true prophetic mission. Opposing views on Zionism also find expression in the politics of **pilgrimage**: Christian Zionist tours to Israel emphasise the amazing accomplishments of God's Chosen People in the land given to them by God. Churches and Christian organisations that are hostile to Zionism tend either to ignore modern Israel in their Holy Land itineraries or to sponsor tours that feature the worst sides of Israel and thus reinforce and enhance participants' negative attitudes to Zionism and the State of Israel. The intense debate about Zionism among Christians is mirrored in the international political arena. Zionism has been extolled as the national liberation movement *par excellence*, and condemned as a form of racism by the United Nations General Assembly in a 1975 resolution which most major Churches condemned at the time and which the General Assembly rescinded two decades later.

See also **Zionism, Christian**   *DANIEL ROSSING*

Zionism, Christian

Commonly used to refer to Christian support for the **State of Israel**, 'Christian Zionism' also denotes the doctrine that the return of Jews to the '**Promised Land**' will fulfil biblical **prophecy** and inaugurate the end times.

From the eighteenth century a steadily growing minority of Protestants in Europe and America argued that a Jewish 'Restoration' in the Holy Land would accompany the creation of Christian nation states elsewhere, fulfilling one of the 'dispensations' leading to the millenial **redemption** prophesied in the Old and New Testaments. Christian Zionists have thus also been known as Restorationists, Dispensationalists or pre-**millenarians**, believing (in contrast to post-millenarians) that the redemption will begin before the Second Coming.

A handful of nineteenth-century Christian Zionists, like W. Blackstone (1841–1935) and W. Hechler (1845–1931), were instrumental in the advance of modern **Zionism**. Historically, however, Christian Zionists had little contact with Jewish Zionists. The 1970s saw a new level of contact between the Israeli government and its American Christian supporters, claiming to represent 65 million Southern Baptists and other **Evangelicals**. Most Christian Zionists believe Jews must convert to Christianity by the completion of the Restoration, though the **International Christian Embassy** in Jerusalem also includes Christians who believe it is they who must fit into a Jewish religious framework.

Christian movements have generally identified '**Zion**' with their own religious and national fulfilment, and Jewish appropriations of the biblically promised Land have been viewed variously with sympathy or scorn. Until 1945 some Church support for Zionism was tinged with the aspiration to rid Christian lands of Jews. A range of nativist 'Zionisms' continue to respond to the **Old Testament** 'Zion' traditions without reference to post-biblical Judaism – notably in Africa and the African Diaspora (Swazi Zionists, Rastafarians; *see also* **African theology**).   *GEORGE R. WILKES*

Zohar *see* mysticism

Zola, Émile *see* Dreyfus Affair

Bibliography

Bible

Abrahams, Israel, *Studies in Pharisaism and the Gospels* (first series, Cambridge, Cambridge University Press, 1917, second series, Cambridge, Cambridge University Press, 1924).

Adamo, David T., *Reading and Interpreting the Bible in African Indigenous Churches* (Eugene, OR, Wipf & Stock, 2001).

Adams, William Seth, 'Christian Liturgy, Scripture and the Jews: A Problematic in Jewish–Christian Relations', *Journal of Ecumenical Studies* 25/1 (1988), 39–55.

Aletti, Jean-Noël, *Israel et la Loi dans la lettre aux Romaines* (Paris, Cerf, 1998).

Anderson, G. A., *The Genesis of Perfection: Adam and Eve in Jewish and Christian Imagination* (Louisville, Westminster John Knox Press, 2001).

Bach, Alice (ed.), *Women in the Hebrew Bible: A Reader* (London, Routledge, 1999).

Bammel, E. (ed.), *The Trial of Jesus; Cambridge Studies in Honour of C. F. D. Moule* (London, SCM Press, 1970).

Bammel, E., *Judaica et Paulina: Kleine Schriften II* (Wissenschaftliche Untersuchung zum Neuen Testament 9) (Tübingen, J. C. B. Mohr, 1997).

Barr, James, *Holy Scripture: Canon, Authority, Criticism* (Philadelphia, Westminster Press, 1983).

Barrett, C. K., 'The Allegory of Abraham, Sarah and Hagar in the Argument of Galatians', in *Rechtfertigung: Festschrift Ernst Käsemann* (Tübingen, Mohr-Siebeck, 1976), 1–16; reprint *Essays on Paul* (Philadelphia, Westminster Press, 1982), 154–70.

'The Lamb of God', *New Testament Studies* 1 (1954), 210–18.

Barth, Markus *The People of God* (Sheffield, JSOT Press, 1983).

Barton, J. (ed.), *Cambridge Companion to Biblical Interpretation* (Cambridge, Cambridge University Press, 1998).

Barton, John (ed.), *The Biblical World*, Vol. II (London, Routledge, 2002).

Baskin, J. R., *Pharaoh's Counsellors: Job, Jethro, and Balaam in Rabbinic and Patristic Tradition* (Brown Judaic Studies 47) (Chico, CA, Scholars Press, 1983).

Beal, T. K., *The Book of Hiding: Gender, Ethnicity, Annihilation and Esther* (London, Routledge, 1997).

Beaton, Richard, *Isaiah's Christ in Matthew's Gospel* (Cambridge, Cambridge University Press, 2002).

Beck, Norman, *Anti-Roman Cryptograms in the New Testament* (New York, Peter Lang, 1997).

Beckwith, R. T., *The Old Testament Canon of the New Testament Church* (London, SPCK, 1985).

Bell, Richard H. *Provoked to Jealousy: The Origin and Purpose of the Jealousy Motif in Romans 9–11* (WUNT 2/63) (Tübingen, J. C. B. Mohr (Paul Siebeck), 1994).

Bellis, Alice Ogden and Joel S. Kaminsky (eds), *Jews, Christians, and the Theology of the Hebrew Scriptures* (Atlanta, Society of Biblical Literature, 2000).

Blenkinsopp, Joseph, *A History of Prophecy in Israel* (Philadelphia, Westminster Press, 1983).

'Tanakh and New Testament: A Christian Perspective', in Boadt, Lawrence, *et al.* (eds.), *Biblical Studies: Meeting Ground of Jews and Christians* (New York, Paulist Press, 1980), 96–119.

Blowers, P. M. (ed.), *The Bible in Greek Christian Antiquity* (Notre Dame, University of Notre Dame Press, 1997).

Blintzler, J., *The Trial of Jesus* (Cork, Mercier, 1961).

Boadt, Lawrence, *et al.* (eds), *Biblical Studies: Meeting Ground of Jews and Christians* (New York, Paulist Press, 1980).

Borg, M., *Meeting Jesus Again for the First Time* (San Francisco, Harper 1994).

Borgen, P. (ed.), *The New Testament and Hellenistic Judaism* (Aarhus, Aarhus University Press, 1995).

Bori, Pier Cesare, *The Golden Calf and the Origins of the Anti-Jewish Controversy* (South Florida Studies in the History of Judaism 16) (Atlanta, Scholars Press, 1990).

Boyarin, Daniel, *Intertextuality and the Reading of Midrash* (Bloomington, Indiana University Press, 1990).

A Radical Jew: Paul and the Politics of Identity (Berkeley, University of California Press, 1997).

Boys, Mary C., *Biblical Interpretation in Religious Education* (Birmingham, AL, Religious Education Press, 1980).

Brenner, A. (ed.), *Ruth and Esther: A Feminist Companion to the Bible* 2nd series (Sheffield, Sheffield Academic Press, 1999).

Bronner, L. L., *From Eve to Esther: Rabbinic Reconstruction of Biblical Women* (Louisville, Westminster John Knox Press, 1994).

Brooks, Roger and Collins, John J. (eds), *Hebrew Bible or Old Testament?: Studying the Bible in Judaism and Christianity* (Notre Dame, IN, University of Notre Dame Press, 1990).

Brooks, Roger (ed.), *Unanswered Questions: Theological Views of Jewish–Catholic Relations* (Notre Dame, IN, University of Notre Dame Press, 1990).

Brown, Raymond E., *The Birth of the Messiah* (New York, Doubleday, 1993).

A Coming Christ in Advent: Essays on the Gospel Narratives – Preparing for the Birth of Jesus (Matthew 1 and Luke 1) (Collegeville, MN, The Liturgical Press, 1998).

The Death of the Messiah (New York, Doubleday, 1994).

Brown, Schuyler, 'The Matthean Community and the Gentile Mission', *Novum Testament* 22 (1980), 193–221.

Brueggemann, W., *An Introduction to the Old Testament: The Canon and Christian Imagination* (Louisville, Westminster John Knox Press, 2003).

Bruteau, Beatrice (ed.), *Jesus through Jewish Eyes: Rabbis and Scholars Engage an Ancient Brother in a New Conversation* (Maryknoll, NY, Orbis Press, 2001).

Büchmann, Christina and Spiegel, Celina (eds), *Out of the Garden: Women Writers on the Bible* (San Francisco, Harper Collins, 1994).

Burns, R. J., *Has the Lord Indeed Spoken Only through Moses? A Study of the Biblical Portrait of Miriam* (SBL Dissertation Series 84) (Atlanta, Scholars Press, 1987).

Caird, G. B. *The Language and Imagery of the Bible* (Philadelphia, Westminister Press, 1980).

Campbell, W. S., 'Israel', in Hawthorne, Gerald F. and Martin, Ralph P. (eds), *Dictionary of Paul and his Letters* (Downers Grove, IL, InterVarsity Press, 1993), 441–6.

'Judaizers', in Hawthorne, Gerald F. and Martin, Ralph P. (eds), *Dictionary of Paul and his Letters* (Downers Grove, IL, InterVarsity Press, 1993), 512–16.

Carr, D. M., 'Canonization in the Context of Community', in Weis, R. D. and Carr, D. M. (eds), *A Gift of God in Due Season* (Sheffield, Sheffield Academic Press, 1996).

Carroll, J. T. and Green, J. B., *The Death of Jesus in Early Christianity* (Peabody, Hendrickson, 1995).

Catchpole, D. R., *The Trial of Jesus* (Leiden, E. J. Brill, 1971).

Charlesworth, James H. (ed.), *Jesus and the Dead Sea Scrolls* (New York, Doubleday, 1992).

Jesus' Jewishness: Exploring the Place of Jesus in Early Judaism (Philadelphia, American Interfaith Institute; New York, Crossroad, 1991).

The Messiah: Developments in Earliest Judaism and Christianity (Minneapolis, Fortress Press, 1992).

Chester, Stephen J. *Conversion at Corinth: An Exploration of the Understandings of Conversion Held by the Apostle Paul and the Corinthian Christians* (Edinburgh, T&T Clark, 2003).

Childs, Brevard S., *Biblical Theology of the Old and New Testaments* (Minneapolis, Fortress Press, 1992).

The New Testament as Canon: An Introduction (Philadelphia, Westminster Press, 1984).

Chilton, Bruce, *Judaic Approaches to the Gospels* (University of South Florida international studies in formative Christianity and Judaism 2) (Atlanta, Scholars Press, 1994).

Targumic Approaches to the Gospels: Essays in the Mutual Definition of Judaism and Christianity

(Lanham, MD, University Press of America, 1986).

Chilton, Bruce and Evans, Craig (eds), *James the Just and Christian Origins* (Leiden, Brill, 1999).

Chilton, Bruce and Neusner, Jacob, *Comparing Spiritualities: Formative Christianity and Judaism on Finding Life and Meeting Death* (Harrisburg, PA, Trinity Press International, 2000).

Judaism in the New Testament: Practices and Beliefs (London, Routledge, 1995).

Chilton, Bruce and Neusner, Jacob (eds), *James, Brother of Jesus* (Louisville, Westminster John Knox Press, 2001).

Clines, D. J. A., *The Esther Scroll: The Story of the Story* (JSOT Supplement Series 30) (Sheffield, JSOT Press, 1984).

Coats, G. W., *Moses: Heroic Man, Man of God* (Sheffield, JSOT Press, 1988).

Cody, Aelred, 'Aaron: A Figure with Many Facets', *Bible Today* 88 (1977).

A History of Old Testament Priesthood (Rome, Pontifical Biblical Institute, 1969).

Cohen, J., *The Origins and Evolution of the Moses Nativity Story* (Suppl. to Numen 58) (Leiden, Brill, 1993).

Cohn, Haim, *The Trial and Death of Jesus* (New York, Ktav Publishing House, 1971).

Collins, Adela Yarbro, 'The Function of "Excommunication" in Paul', *Harvard Theological Review* 73 (1980), 251–63.

Conrad, E., *Reading Isaiah* (Minneapolis, Fortress Press, 1991).

Coote, R. B. and Ord, D. R., *In the Beginning: Creation and the Priestly History* (Minneapolis, Fortress Press, 1991).

Cosgrove, Charles H., *Elusive Israel: The Puzzle of Election in Romans* (Louisville, Westminster John Knox Press, 1997).

'The Law Has Given Sarah No Children (Gal 4:21–30)', *Novum Testamentum* 28 (1987), 219–35.

Cothenet, E. 'A l'arrière-plan de l'allégorie d'Agar et de Sara (Ga 4:21–31)', in *De la Torah au Messie: Festschrift Henri Cazelles* (Paris, 1981), 457–65.

Cowley, R. W., *Ethiopian Biblical Interpretation: A Study in Exegetical Tradition and Hermeneutics* (Cambridge, Cambridge University Press, 1988).

Crossan, J. D., *Who Killed Jesus? Exposing the Roots of Anti-Semitism in the Gospel Story of the Death of Jesus* (New York, Harper Collins, 1996).

Culpepper, Alan, *John the Son of Zebedee: The Life of a Legend* (Edinburgh, T&T Clark, 2000).

Cunningham, Philip A., *Sharing the Scriptures* (New York, Paulist Press, Stimulus Books, 2003).

Daniélou, J., *The Bible and the Liturgy* (Notre Dame, University of Notre Dame Press, 1956).

Davies, Philip R., *Scribes and Schools: The Canonization of the Hebrew Scriptures* (Louisville, Westminister John Knox Press, 1998).

Davies, W. D., *Paul and Rabbinic Judaism* (London, SPCK, 1948).

DeLorenzi, L. (ed.), *Die Israel Frage nach Römer 9–11* (Rome, St Paul's Abbey, 1977).

Dodd, C. H., *According to the Scriptures: The Sub-Structure of New Testament Theology* (London, Nisbet, 1952).

Driver, S. R. and Neubauer, A. D., *The Fifty Third Chapter of Isaiah According to Jewish Interpreters* (New York, Ktav, 1969).

Efroymson, David P., Fisher, Eugene J. and Klenicki, Leon (eds), *Within Context: Essays on Jews and Judaism in the New Testament* (Collegeville, MN, Liturgical Press, 1993).

Evans, Craig, and Hagner, Donald A. (eds), *Anti-Semitism and Early Christianity* (Minneapolis, Fortress Press, 1993).

Farmer, William (ed.), *Anti-Judaism and the Gospels* (Harrisburg, PA, Trinity Press, 1999).

Farris, Stephen, *The Hymns of Luke's Infancy Narratives: Their Origin, Meaning and Significance* (Sheffield, JSOT Press, 1985).

Feiler, Bruce, *Abraham: A Journey to the Heart of Three Faiths* (New York, W. Morrow, 2002).

Feliks, Yehuda, *Nature and Man in the Bible: Chapters in Biblical Ecology* (London, Soncino Press, 1981).

Fernández Marcos, N., *The Septuagint in Context: Introduction to the Greek Versions of the Bible* (Leiden, Brill, 2000).

Flusser, David, *Jesus* (Jerusalem, Magnes Press, 2001).

Judaism and the Origins of Christianity (Jerusalem, Magnes, 1988).

'"Sie wissen nicht was sie tun", Geschichte eines Herrenwortes', in Müller, Paul Gerhardt and Stenger, Wenger (eds), *Kommunität und*

Einheit, Studien für Franz Mussner (Freiburg, Herder, 1981), 391–410.

Fox, M. V., *Character and Ideology in the Book of Esther*, 2nd edn (Grand Rapids, Eerdmans, 2001).

Fredriksen, Paula, *Jesus the Christ* (New Haven, Yale University Press, 1988).

Frymer-Kensky, Tikva, *Reading the Women of the Bible: A New Interpretation of their Stories* (New York, Schocken Books, 2002).

Fuchs, E., *Sexual Politics in Biblical Narrative: Reading the Hebrew Bible as a Woman* (Sheffield, Sheffield Academic Press, 2000).

Gamble, H. Y., *The New Testament Canon: Its Making and Meaning* (Philadelphia, Fortress Press, 1985).

García Martínez, Florentino and Luttikhuizen, Gerard P., *Interpretations of the Flood* (TBN 1) (Leiden, Brill, 1998).

Gartner, Bertil, *John 6 and the Jewish Passover* (Lund, C. W. K. Gleerup, 1959).

Georgi, Dieter, *The Opponents of Paul in Second Corinthians* (Edinburgh, T&T Clark, 1987).

Gignac, Alain, *Juifs et chrétiens à l'école de Paul de Tarse . . . Romains 9–11* (Montreal, Médias Paul, 1997).

Good, Deirdre J., 'What Does it Mean to Call Mary Miriam?', in Levine, Amy-Jill (ed.), *Mary* (Feminist Companion to the New Testament Series) (forthcoming)

  Mariam, the Magdalen, and the Mother (Bloomington, Indiana University Press, 2005).

Gorak, J., *The Making of the Modern Canon* (London, Athlone Press, 1981).

Goulder, Michael D., *Luke: A New Paradigm* (Sheffield, JSOT Press, 1989).

Greene, John T., *Balaam and his Interpreters: A Hermeneutical History of the Balaam Traditions* (Atlanta, Scholars Press, 1992).

Greenspahn, Frederick, E. (ed.), *Scripture in the Jewish and Christian Traditions* (Nashville, Abingdon Press, 1982).

Grelot, Pierre, *Les poèmes du serviteur: De la lecture critique à la herméneutique* (Paris, Cerf, 1981).

Grenholm, Cristina and Patte, Daniel (eds), *Reading Israel in Romans* (Harrisburg, Trinity Press, 2000).

Gunneweg, A. H. J., *Leviten und Priester* (Göttingen, Vandenhoeck & Ruprecht, 1965).

Hahn, Ferdinand, *Mission in the New Testament* (London, SCM Press, 1965).

Hall, S. G., *Christian Anti-Semitism and Paul's Theology* (Minneapolis, Fortress, 1993).

Hansen, Walter, *Abraham in Galatians: Epistolary and Rhetorical Contexts* (Sheffield, JSOT Press, 1989).

Haran, M., *Temples and Temple Service in Ancient Israel* (Oxford, Oxford University Press, 1978).

Hayes, Richard B., *Echoes of Scripture in the Letters of Paul* (New Haven, Yale University Press, 1989).

Hayward, Robert, 'Shem, Melchizedek, and Concern with Christianity in the Pentateuchal Targumim', in Cathcart, K. J. and Maher, M. (eds), *Targumic and Cognate Studies: Essays in Honour of Martin McNamara* (JSOTSS 230) (Sheffield, Sheffield Academic Press, 1996), 67–80.

Hazleton, Lesley, *Mary: A Flesh and Blood Biography of the Virgin Mother* (New York, Bloomsbury, 2004).

Heaton, E. W., *The School Tradition of the Old Testament* (Oxford, Oxford University Press, 1994).

Hengel, M., *Crucifixion* (Philadelphia, Fortress Press, 1977).

  The Zealots (Edinburgh, T&T Clark, 1989).

Herberg, W. and Anderson, B. W. (eds), *Faith Enacted into History: Essays in Biblical Theology* (Philadelphia, Westminster Press, 1976).

Hill, David, *New Testament Prophecy* (Atlanta, John Knox Press, 1979).

Hodgson, R., 'Holiness Tradition and Social Description: Intertestamental Judaism and Early Christianity', in Burgess, S. M. (ed.), *Reaching Beyond: Chapters in the History of Perfectionism* (Peabody, Hendrickson, 1986).

Hoheisel, Karl, 'Hagar', *Reallexikon für Antike und Christentum* (Stuttgart, 1986), XIII, 305–13.

Hollenbach, Paul W., 'Social Aspects of John the Baptizer's Preaching Mission in the Context of Palestinian Judaism', *Aufstieg und Niedergang der römischen Welt* II, 19 (1979), 856–75.

Holmgren, F. C., *The Old Testament and the Significance of Jesus: Embracing Change – Maintaining Christian Identity: The Emerging Center in Biblical Scholarship* (Grand Rapids, Eerdmans, 1999).

Holtz, Barry W. (ed.), *Back to the Sources: Reading the Classic Jewish Texts* (New York, Summit, 1984).

Hooker, Morna D., *The Gospel According to St Mark* (London, A. & C. Black, 1991).

The Signs of a Prophet: The Prophetic Actions of Jesus (London, SCM Press, 1997).

Horbury, W., 'The Aaronic Priesthood in the Epistle to the Hebrews', *Journal for the Study of the New Testament* 19 (1983), 43–71.

'Extirpation and excommunication', *Vetus Testamentum* 35 (1985), 13–38.

Horsley, R. A. and Hanson, J. S., *Bandits, Prophets, and Messiahs: Popular Movements in the Time of Jesus* (Minneapolis, Winston, 1985).

Horton, J., *The Melchizedek Tradition* (Cambridge, Cambridge University Press, 1976).

Howard, George, 'Tetragrammaton in the New Testament', *Anchor Bible Dictionary* (New York, Doubleday, 1992), VI, 392–3.

Jantzen, G. J., 'Song of Moses, Song of Miriam: Who Is Seconding Whom?', *Catholic Biblical Quarterly* 54 (1992), 211–21.

Jaubert, Annie, *La date de la Cène: calendrier biblique et liturgie chrétienne* (Paris, J. Gabalda, 1957).

Jeansonne, Sharon Pace, *The Women of Genesis* (Minneapolis, Fortress Press, 1990).

Jeremias, Joachim, *The Eucharistic Words of Jesus* (trans. Norman Perrin; Philadelphia, Fortress Press, 1977).

Johnson, Luke Timothy, 'The New Testament's Anti-Jewish Slander and the Conventions of Ancient Polemic', *Journal of Biblical Literature* 108/3 (1989), 419–41.

Journet, Charles, *Destinées d'Israël* (Paris, Egloff, 1944).

Juel, D., *Messiah and Temple* (Missoula, Scholars Press, 1977).

Kabak, Aharon Avraham, *Narrow Path: The Man of Nazareth* (trans. Julian Louis Meltzer; Tel-Aviv, The Institute of Translation of Hebrew Literature, 1968) (Hebrew 1936).

Kaufmann, Y., *Christianity and Judaism: Two Covenants* (Jerusalem, Magnes Press, 1988).

Kee, H. C., *Who Are the People of God? Early Christian Models of Community* (New Haven, Yale University Press, 1995).

Kessler, E., *Bound by the Bible: Jews, Christians and the Sacrifice of Isaac* (Cambridge, Cambridge University Press, 2004).

Kim, Johann D., *God, Israel, and the Gentiles: Rhetoric and Situation in Romans 9–11* (Atlanta, Scholars Press, 2000).

Kinzig, Wolfram, 'Closeness and Distance: Towards a New Description of Jewish–Christian Relations', *Jewish Studies Quarterly*, vol. 10 (Nov. 2003).

'Philosemitismus', *Zeitschrift für Kirchengeschichte* 105 (1994), 202–28, 361–83.

Klassen, William, *Judas, Betrayer or Friend of Jesus?* (Minneapolis, Fortress Press/SCM Press, 1996).

Klassen, William, 'Jesus and the Zealot Option', in Huebner, Chris, Hauerwas, Stanley, Huebner, Harry, Tiessen Nation, Mark (eds), *The Wisdom of the Cross: Essays in Memory of John Howard Yoder* (Grand Rapids, Eerdmans, 1999), 131–49.

Klutz, Todd (ed.), *Magic in the Biblical World: From the Rod of Aaron to the Ring of Solomon* (London, Continuum, 2003).

Koenig, John, *Jews and Christians in Dialogue: New Testament Foundations* (Philadelphia, Westminster Press, 1979).

Kraemer, D., 'The Formation of the Rabbinic Canon: Authority and Boundaries', *Journal of Biblical Literature* 110 (1991), 613–30.

Kraemer, Ross (ed.), *Women in Scripture* (Grand Rapids, Eerdmans, 2000).

Krauss, S., *Das Leben Jesu nach jüdischen Quellen* (Berlin, S. Calvary, 1902).

Kugel, James L., *The Bible as It Was* (Cambridge, MA, Harvard University Press; London, Belknap, 1997).

In Potiphar's House: The Interpretive Life of Biblical Texts (New York, HarperCollins, 1990).

The Traditions of the Bible (Cambridge, MA, Harvard University Press, 1998).

Küng, H. and Lapide, P., *Jesus im Widerstreit: Ein jüdisch-christlicher Dialog*, 2nd edn (Stuttgart, Calwer Verlag; Munich, Kösel Verlag, 1981).

Kuschel, Karl-Joseph, *Abraham: Sign of Hope for Jews, Christians, and Muslims* (New York, Continuum, 1995).

Kvam, Kristen, Schearing, Linda and Ziegler, Valarie (eds), *Eve and Adam: Jewish, Christian, and Muslim Readings on Genesis and Gender* (Indianapolis, Indiana University Press, 1999).

Lachs, Samuel, *A Rabbinic Commentary on the New Testament: The Gospels of Matthew, Mark and Luke* (New York, Ktav, 1987).

LaCoque, A., *The Feminine Unconventional: Four Subversive Figures in Israel's Tradition* (Minneapolis, Fortress Press, 1990).

Lapide, P., *Am Scheitern hoffen lernen: Erfahrungen jüdischen Glaubens für heutige Christen* (Gütersloh, Gütersloher Verlagshaus Gerd Mohn, 1985).

Lapide, P. and Gollwitzer, H., *Hebrew in the Church: The Foundations of Jewish–Christian Dialogue* (Grand Rapids, Eerdmans, 1984).

Larsson, Goran, *Bound for Freedom: The Book of Exodus in Jewish and Christian Traditions* (Peabody, MA, Hendrickson, 1998).

Le Deaut, R., 'Miriam, soeur de Moïse, et Marie mère du Messie', *Biblica* 45 (1964), 198–219.

Levenson, J. D., *The Death and Resurrection of the Beloved Son: The Transformation of Child Sacrifice in Judaism and Christianity* (New Haven, Yale University Press, 1993).

The Hebrew Bible, the Old Testament, and Historical Criticism: Jews and Christians in Biblical Studies (Louisville, Westminster/John Knox Press, 1993).

Sinai and Zion: An Entry into the Jewish Bible (New York, Harper & Row, 1985).

Lewis, J. R., *A Study of the Interpretation of Noah and the Flood in Jewish and Christian Literature* (Leiden, Brill, 1968).

Lichtenberger, H., 'Täufergemeinde und frühchristliche Täuferpolemik in letzten Drittel des 1. Jahrhunderts', *Zeitschrift für Theologie und Kirche* 84 (1987), 36–57.

Lim, Timothy H., *Holy Scripture in the Qumran Commentaries and Pauline Letters* (Oxford, Clarendon Press, 1997).

Linafelt, T. (ed.), *Strange Fire: Reading the Bible after the Holocaust* (Sheffield, Sheffield Academic Press, 2000).

Linton, O., 'The Trial of Jesus and the Interpretation of Psalm CX', *New Testament Studies* 7 (1960–61), 258–62.

Lodge, John G., *Romans 9–11: A Reader-Response Analysis* (Atlanta, Scholars Press, 1996).

Lübking, Hans-Martin, *Paulus und Israel im Römerbrief* (Frankfurt, Peter Lang, 1986).

Luttikhuizen, Gerard P. (ed.), *The Creation of Man and Woman: Interpretations of the Biblical Narratives in Jewish and Christian Traditions* (Leiden, Brill, 2000).

Marshall, I. H., *Last Supper and Lord's Supper* (Grand Rapids, Eerdmanns, 1981).

Martyn, J. L., 'The Covenants of Hagar and Sarah', in Carroll, T. T. (ed.), *Faith and History: Essays in Honor of Paul W. Meyer* (Atlanta, Scholars Press, 1990), 160–92.

The Gospel of John in Christian History: Essays for Interpreters (New York, Paulist Press, 1979).

McAuliffe, J. D., Walfish, B. D. and Goering, J. W. (eds), *With Reverence for the Word: Medieval Scriptural Exegesis in Judaism, Christianity, and Islam* (Oxford, Oxford University Press, 2002).

Meier, John P., *A Marginal Jew: Rethinking the Historical Jesus: Mentor, Message and Miracles* (New York, Doubleday, 1994), Vol. II.

Mellinkoff, B., *The Mark of Cain* (Berkeley, University of California Press, 1981).

Metzger, Bruce, *The Canon of the New Testament* (Oxford, Oxford University Press, 1987).

Morgan, R. with Barton, J., *Biblical Interpretation* (Oxford, Oxford University Press, 1988).

Morray-Jones, C. R. A., 'Paradise Revisited (2 Cor 12:1–12): The Jewish Mystical Background of Paul's Apostolate. Part 1: The Jewish Sources; Part 2: Paul's Heavenly Ascent and its Significance', *Harvard Theological Review* 86 (1993), 177–217.

Morris, P. and Sawyer, D. F. (eds), *A Walk in the Garden: Biblical, Iconographical and Literary Images of Eden* (Sheffield, Sheffield Academic Press, 1992).

Motyer Stephen, *Your Father the Devil: A New Approach to John and 'the Jews'* (Carlisle, Paternoster Press, 1997).

Müller, M., *The First Bible of the Church: A Plea for the Septuagint* (Sheffield, Sheffield Academic Press, 1996).

Munck, Johannes, *Christ and Israel: An Interpretation of Romans 9–11* (Philadelphia, Fortress Press, 1967).

Murphy, Catherine M., *John the Baptist: Prophet of Purity for a New Age* (Collegeville, MN, Liturgical Press, 2003).

Murphy-O'Connor, Jerome and Charlesworth, James H., *Paul and the Dead Sea Scrolls* (New York, Crossroad, 1990).

Mveng, E. and Werblowsky, R. J. Z. (eds), *Black Africa and the Bible: The Jerusalem Congress on Black Africa and the Bible* (Jerusalem, Anti-Defamation League of B'nai B'rith, 1972).

Nanos, Mark D., *The Irony of Galatians: Paul's Letter in its First Century Context* (Minneapolis, Fortress Press, 2002).

Nehrer, André, *Moses and the Vocation of the Jewish People* (trans. Irene Marinoff; London, 1959).

Nickelsburg, George W. E., *Resurrection, Immortality, and Eternal Life in Intertestamental Judaism* (Cambridge, MA, Harvard University Press, 1972).

Niditch, S. (ed.), *Text and Tradition: The Hebrew Bible and Folklore* (SBL Semeia Series) (Atlanta, Scholars Press, 1990).

Nodet, Etienne, 'Jésus et Jean-Baptiste selon Josèphe', *Revue Biblique* 92 (1985), 497–524.

Ochs, C., 'Miriam's Way', *Cross Currents* 45/4 (1995), 493–510.

Ochs, Peter, *The Return to Scripture in Judaism and Christianity* (New York, Paulist Press, 1993).

Packer, James, *God Has Spoken: Revelation and the Bible* (London, Hodder and Stoughton, 1993).

Paffenroth, Kim, *Judas the Last Disciple* (Richmond, VA, Westminster/John Knox Press, 2001).

Painter, John, *Just James: The Brother of Jesus in History and Tradition* (Edinburgh, T&T Clark, 1999).

Peters, F. E., *Judaism, Christianity, Islam: The Classical Texts and their Interpretation* (Princeton, NJ, Princeton University Press, 1990).

Petuchowski, J. J., 'Hoshi 'ana in Psalm CXVIII, 25, a Prayer for Rain', *VT* 5 (1955), 266–71.

Petuchowski, Jacob and Brocke, Michael (eds), *The Lord's Prayer and Jewish Liturgy* (New York, Seabury Press, 1978).

Polzin, R., *Moses and the Deuteronomist: A Literary Study of the Deuteronomic History* (New York, Seabury Press, 1980).

Pomykala, Kenneth, *The Davidic Dynasty Tradition in Early Judaism: Its History and Significance for Messianism* (Atlanta, Scholars Press, 1995).

Pope, Marvin, 'Hosanna', *Anchor Bible Dictionary* (New York, Doubleday, 1992), III, 290–1.

Powery, Emerson B., *Jesus Reads Scripture* (Leiden, Brill, 2003).

Puech, Emile, 'Messianism, Resurrection, and Eschatology at Qumran and in the New Testament', in Ulrich, E. and Vanderkam, J. (eds), *The Community of the Renewed Covenant* (Notre Dame, University of Notre Dame Press, 1994), 235–56.

Redford, Donald B., *A Study of the Biblical Story of Joseph, Genesis 37–50* (Leiden, Brill, 1970).

Reinhartz, Adele, *Befriending the Beloved Disciple: A Jewish Reading of the Gospel of John* (New York, Continuum, 2001).

Reumann, John, *The Supper of the Lord* (Philadelphia, Fortress Press, 1985).

Richardson, Peter (ed.), with Granskou, David, *Anti-Judaism in Early Christianity, Vol. 1, Paul and the Gospels* (Ontario, Wilfrid Laurier University Press, 1986).

Rivkin, Ellis, *What Crucified Jesus?* (London, SCM Press, 1984).

Rodríguez Carmona, A., 'La figura de Melquisedec en la literatura targúmica', *Estudios Biblicos* 37 (1978), 79–102.

Rosenberg, D. (ed.), *Congregation: Contemporary Writers Read the Jewish Bible* (San Diego, Harcourt Brace Jovanovich, 1987).

Roshwald, M. and M., *Moses: Leader, Prophet, Man: The Story of Moses and his Image through the Ages* (New York, Thomas Yoseloff, 1969).

Rubenstein, Richard, *My Brother Paul* (New York, Harper, 1972).

Russell, Letty M. (ed.), *Feminist Interpretation of the Bible* (Philadelphia, Westminster Press, 1985).

Ruether, Rosemary, *Faith and Fratricide: The Theological Roots of Anti-Semitism* (Minneapolis, Seabury Press, 1974; New York, Search Press, 1975).

Sabourin, L., *Priesthood: A Comparative Study* (Leiden, E. J. Brill, 1973).

Saebo, Magne (ed.), *Hebrew Bible/Old Testament* (Göttingen, Vandenhoeck & Ruprecht, 2000).

Saldarini, Anthony J., *Matthew's Christian-Jewish Community* (Chicago, University of Chicago Press, 1994).

Sanders, E. P., *The Historical Figure of Jesus* (London, Allen Lane, 1993).

Jesus and Judaism (London, SCM Press, 1985).

Judaism: Practice and Belief 63BCE – 66CE (London, SCM Press, 1992).

Paul and Palestinian Judaism (London, SCM Press, 1977).

Sanders, James A., *Canon and Community* (Philadelphia, Fortress Press, 1984).

Torah and Canon (Philadelphia, Fortress Press, 1972).

Sawyer, J. F. A., *The Fifth Gospel: Isaiah in the History of Christianity* (Cambridge, Cambridge University Press, 1996).

Schneiders, Sandra M., *The Revelatory Text: Interpreting the New Testament as Sacred Scripture* (San Francisco, Harper, 1991).

With Oil in their Lamps: Faith, Feminism, and the Future (New York, Paulist Press, 1999).

Schneidewind, William, *Society and the Promise to David: The Reception History of 2 Samuel 7:1–17* (New York, Oxford University Press, 1999).

Schüssler-Fiorenza, Elisabeth (ed.), *Searching the Scriptures: An Introduction* (New York, Crossroad, 1993).

Segal, Alan, *Paul the Convert* (New Haven, Yale University Press, 1990).

Seitz, C., 'Old Testament or Hebrew Bible? Some Theological Considerations', *Pro Ecclesia* 5 (1996), 292–303.

Senior, Donald, *The Passion of Jesus in the Gospel of John* (Collegeville, MN, Liturgical Press, 1991).

The Passion of Jesus in the Gospel of Luke (Collegeville, MN, Liturgical Press, 1989).

The Passion of Jesus in the Gospel of Mark (Collegeville, MN, Liturgical Press, 1984).

The Passion of Jesus in the Gospel of Matthew (Collegeville, MN, Liturgical Press, 1985).

Sievers, Joseph, 'God's Gifts and Call are Irrevocable: The Reception of Romans 11:29 through the Centuries and in Christian–Jewish Relations', in Greenholm, C. and Palte, D. (eds), *Reading Israel in Romans: Legitimacy and Plausibility of Divergent Interpretations* (Harrisburg, PA, Trinity Press International, 2000), 127–73.

Sim, David, *The Gospel of Matthew and Christian Judaism: The History and Social Setting of the Matthean Community* (Edinburgh, T&T Clark, 1998).

Simon, Uriel, *Four Approaches to the Book of Psalms* (Albany, NY, SUNY Press, 1991).

'Joseph and his Brothers, A Story of Change', trans. Louvish, David in, *Seek Peace and Pursue It* (Tel Aviv, Bar Ilan University, 2002).

Smalley, Beryl, *The Study of the Bible in the Middle Ages* (New York, Philosophical Library, 1952; Notre Dame, University of Notre Dame Press, 1964).

Smiles, Vincent M., 'The Concept of "Zeal" in Second-Temple Judaism and Paul's Critique of it in Romans 10:2', *Catholic Biblical Quarterly* 64 (2002), 282–99.

Spiegel, S., *The Last Trial: On the Legends and Lore of the Command to Abraham to Offer Isaac as a Sacrifice: The Akedah* (New York, Schocken Books, 1967).

Stegemann, Hartmut, *The Library of Qumran: On the Essenes, John the Baptist and Jesus* (Grand Rapids, Eerdmans, 1993).

Stegner, W. R., 'Paul the Jew', in Hawthorne, Gerald F. and Martin, Ralph P., *Dictionary of Paul and his Letters* (Downers Grove, IL, InterVarsity Press, 1993), 503–11.

Stemberger, Günter, *Jewish Contemporaries of Jesus: Pharisees, Sadducees, Essenes* (Minneapolis, Fortress Press, 1995).

Stendahl, Krister, *A Final Account* (Philadelphia, Fortress Press, 1996).

Paul among Jews and Christians (Philadelphia, Fortress Press, 1976).

Swartley, Willard, 'War and Peace in the New Testament', *Aufstieg und Niedergang der Römischen Welt* II 26.3 (1996), 299–410.

Swetnam, J., *Jesus and Isaac: A Study of the Epistle to the Hebrews in the Light of the Aqedah* (Rome, Biblical Institute Press, 1981).

Talmon, Shemarayhu, 'The Signification of Shalom in the Hebrew Bible', in Evans, Craig and Talmon, S. (eds), *The Quest for Context and Meaning, Studies in Biblical Intertextuality in Honour of James Sanders* (Leiden, Brill, 1997), 75–115.

Taylor, Jean E., *The Immerser: John the Baptist within the Second Temple Judaism* (Grand Rapids, Eerdmans, 1997).

Thoma, Clemens and Wyschogrod, Michael (eds), *Understanding Scripture: Explorations of Jewish and Christian Traditions of Interpretation* (New York, Paulist Press, 1987).

Tomson, Peter J., *Paul and the Jewish Law: Halakha in the Letters of the Apostle to the Gentiles* (Compendia rerum iudaicarum ad Novum Testamentum 3.1) (Assen, Van Gorcum; Minneapolis, Fortress Press, 1990).

Trible, P., 'Bringing Miriam Out of the Shadows', *Bible Review* 5/1 (1989), 14–25 and 34.

Tyson, Joseph, *Images of Judaism in Luke–Acts* (Columbia, University of South Carolina Press, 1992).

Ulfgard, Håkan, *Feast and Future: Revelation 7:9–17 and the Feast of Tabernacles* (Lund, Almqvist & Wiksell, 1989).

Ulrich, E, 'The Canonical Process, Textual Criticism and Later Stages in the Composition of the

Bible', in Fishbane, M., Tov, E. and Fields, W. W. (eds), *Sha'arei Talmon* (Winona Lake, IN, Eisenbrauns, 1992).

van Buren, Paul M., *According to the Scriptures: The Origins of the Gospel and of the Church's Old Testament* (Grand Rapids, Eerdmans, 1998).

van der Horst, Pieter W., 'Eve in the New Testament', in Meyers, Carol and Craven, Toni (eds), *Women in Scripture* (Boston, Houghton Mifflin, 2000), 144–5.

van Kooten, G. (ed.), *The Creation of Heaven and Earth: Re-interpretations of Genesis 1 in the Context of Judaism, Ancient Philosophy, Christianity and Modern Physics* (Leiden, Brill, 2005).

Vermes, G., *The Changing Faces of Jesus* (New York, Viking, 2000).

Jesus the Jew (London, SCM Press, 1973).

The Religion of Jesus the Jew (London, SCM Press, 1993).

Scripture and Tradition in Judaism: Haggadic Studies (Studia Post-Biblica 4) (Leiden, E. J. Brill, 1961).

Visotzky, Burton L., *Reading the Book: Making the Bible a Timeless Text* (New York, Doubleday, 1991).

von Rad, Gerhard, 'The Joseph Narrative and Ancient Wisdom', in *The Problem of the Hexateuch and Other Essays* (New York, McGraw Hill, 1966).

von Wahlde, Urban C., 'The Johannine "Jews": A Critical Survey', *New Testament Studies* 28 (1982), 33–60.

'"The Jews" in the Gospel of John: Fifteen Years of Research (1983–1998)', *Ephemerides theologicae lovanienses* 76 (2000), 30–55.

Wagner, J. Ross, *Heralds of the Good News: Isaiah and Paul 'in Concert' in Letter to the Romans* (Leiden, Brill, 2003).

Weitzman, M. P., *The Syriac Version of the Old Testament: An Introduction* (Cambridge, Cambridge University Press, 1999).

Werner, E., 'Hosanna in the Gospels', *Journal of Biblical Literature* 65 (1946), 97–122.

Westermann, C., *Creation* (London, SPCK, 1974).

Whybray, R. N., *The Intellectual Tradition in the Old Testament* (New York, de Gruyter, 1974).

Wiener, Aharon, *The Prophet Elijah in the Development of Judaism* (London, Routledge and Kegan Paul, 1978).

Williamson, Clark M. and Allen, Ronald J., *Interpreting Difficult Texts: Anti-Judaism and Christian Preaching* (London, SCM Press, 1989).

Williamson, H., *The Book called Isaiah: Deutero-Isaiah's Role in Composition and Redaction* (Oxford, Clarendon Press, 1994).

Willis, W., *The Kingdom of God in 20th-Century Interpretation* (Peabody, MA, Hendrickson, 1987).

Wink, Walter, *John the Baptist in the Gospel Tradition* (Cambridge, Cambridge University Press, 1968).

Winter, P., *On the Trial of Jesus* (Berlin, de Gruyter, 2nd edn rev. 1974).

Yoder, John Howard, *The Politics of Jesus* (Grand Rapids, Eerdmans, 1972, 1994).

Young, Norman, *Creator, Creation and Faith* (Philadelphia, Fortress Press, 1976).

Younger, K. L., Hallo, W. W. and Batto, B. F. (eds), *The Biblical Canon in Comparative Perspective: Scripture in Context IV* (Lewiston, NY, Edwin Mellen Press, 1991).

Zeitlin, S, *Who Crucified Jesus?* (New York, Bloch, 4th edn, 1964).

Theology

Adam, Adolf, *The Liturgical Year* (New York, Pueblo Publishing, 1981).

Adler, Rachel, *Engendering Judaism* (Philadelphia, Jewish Publication Society, 1998).

Aitken, J. K. and Kessler, E. (eds), *Challenges in Jewish–Christian Relations* (New York, Paulist Press, 2006).

Altizer, Thomas J. J., 'The Holocaust and the Theology of the Death of God', in Haynes, S. R. and Roth, J. K. (eds), *The Death of God Movement and the Holocaust: Radical Theology Encounters the Shoah* (Westport, CT, Greenwood Press, 1999).

Aquino, Maria Pilar, Machado, Daisy, and Rodriguez, Jeannette (eds), *A Reader in Latina Feminist Theology* (Austin, University of Texas Press, 2002).

Ateek, Naim, *Justice and Only Justice, a Palestinian Theology of Liberation* (Maryknoll, NY, Orbis Books, 1989).

Bacchiocchi, Samuele, *From Sabbath to Sunday: A Historical Investigation of the Rise of Sunday Observance in Early Christianity* (Rome, Pontifical Gregorian University, 1977).

Baeck, L., *The Essence of Judaism* (London, Macmillan, 1936).

Judaism and Christianity: Essays (Philadelphia, Jewish Publication Society, 1964).

Banki, Judith H. and Pawlikowski, John T. (eds), *Ethics in the Shadow of the Holocaust: Christian and Jewish Perspectives* (Chicago, Sheed & Ward, 2002).

Barth, Karl, *Church Dogmatics II* (Edinburgh, T&T Clark, 1957).

Barton, Stephen C. (ed.), *Holiness: Past and Present* (London, T&T Clark, 2003).

Baum, Gregory, *Christian Theology after Auschwitz* (London, Council of Christians and Jews, 1976).

Bayfield, T., Brichto, S. and Fisher, E. (eds), *He Kissed Him and they Wept* (London, SCM Press, 2001).

Beauchamp, Tom and Childress, James, *Principles of Biomedical Ethics* (Oxford, Oxford University Press, 4th edn, 1994).

Bemporad, Jack, Pawlikowski, John T. and Sievérs, Joseph (eds), *Good and Evil after Auschwitz: Ethical Implications for Today* (Hoboken, NJ, Ktav, 2001).

Bemporad, J. and Shevack, M., *Our Age: The Historic New Era of Christian–Jewish Understanding* (New York, New City Press, 1996).

Berger, David, *The Rebbe, the Messiah and the Scandal of Orthodox Indifference* (London, Littman Library, 2001).

Berger, David and Wyschogrod, Michael, *Jews and 'Jewish Christianity'* (New York, Ktav, 1978).

Berkovits, Eliezer, *Faith after the Holocaust* (New York, Ktav, 1973).

Major Themes in Modern Philosophies of Judaism (New York, Ktav, 1974).

Bieringer, Reimund et al., *Anti-Judaism and the Fourth Gospel* (Louisville, Westminster John Knox Press, 2001).

Bishop, Claire Hutchet, *How Catholics Look at Jews: Inquiries into Italian, Spanish, and French Teaching Materials* (New York, Paulist Press, 1974).

Bokser, B. M., *The Origins of the Seder* (California, The University of California Press, 1984).

Borowitz, E. B., *Contemporary Christologies: A Jewish Perspective* (New York, Paulist Press, 1980).

Borresen, K. (ed.), *Image of God and Gender Models in Judeo-Christian Tradition* (Oslo, Solum Verlag, 1991).

Bouyer, Louis, *The Eucharist* (Notre Dame, University of Notre Dame Press, 1968).

Boyarin, Daniel, *Dying for God: Martyrdom and the Making of Christianity and Judaism* (Stanford, CA, Stanford University Press, 1999).

Boys, Mary C., *Has God Only One Blessing? Judaism as a Source of Christian Self-Understanding* (New York, Paulist Press, 2000).

Jewish–Christian Dialogue: One Woman's Experience (New York, Paulist Press, 1997).

Boys, Mary C. (ed.), *Education for Citizenship and Discipleship* (New York, The Pilgrim Press, 1989).

Seeing Judaism Anew: Christianity's Saved Obligation (Lanham, MD, Sheed & Ward, 2005).

Braaten, Carl E., *Justification: The Article by Which the Church Stands or Falls* (Minneapolis, Fortress Press, 1990).

Braaten, C. and Wilken, R. (eds), *Jews and Christians, People of God* (Grand Rapids, Eerdmans, 2003).

Bradshaw, Paul, 'Did the Early Eucharist Ever Have a Sevenfold Shape?', *The Heythrop Journal* 43 (2002), 73–6.

The Search for the Origins of Christian Worship (London, SPCK, 1992).

Bradshaw, P. and Hoffman, L. A. (eds), *Passover and Easter: Origin and History to Modern Times* (Notre Dame, Notre Dame Press, 1999).

Passover and Easter: The Symbolic Structuring of Sacred Seasons (Notre Dame, University of Notre Dame Press, 1999).

Brandon, S. G. F., *The Judgment of the Dead* (London, Weidenfeld & Nicolson, 1967).

Braybrooke, Marcus, *Christian–Jewish Relations: The Next Steps* (London, SCM Press, 2000).

'Praying Together: Possibilities and Difficulties of Interfaith Worship', *Dialogue and Alliance* 3/1 (Spring, 1989), 89–93.

Brueggemann, Walter, *The Land* (Philadelphia, Fortress Press, 1977).

Buber, Martin, *Between Man and Man* (Macmillan, New York, 1965 (1947)).

I and Thou (New York, Charles Scribner's Sons, 2nd edn, 1958).

Moses, the Revelation and the Covenant (Oxford, Phaidon, 1946; New York, Harper Torchbooks, 1958).

Burrell, David B., *Knowing the Unknowable God: Ibn Sina, Maimonides, Aquinas* (Notre Dame, University of Notre Dame Press, 1986).

Cairns, D., *The Image of God in Man* (Fontana Library of Theology and Philosophy) (London, Collins, 1973).

Cantwell Smith, Wilfred, *The Meaning and End of Religion: A New Approach to the Religious Traditions of Mankind* (New York, Macmillan, 1963).

Charlesworth, James (ed.), *Jews and Christians: Exploring the Past, Present and Future* (New York, Crossroad, 1990).

Overcoming Fear between Jews and Christians (New York, Crossroad, 1992).

Chauvet, Louis-Marie, *The Sacraments: The Word of God at the Mercy of the Body* (Collegeville, MN, The Liturgical Press, 2001).

Chilton, Bruce, *Redeeming Time: The Wisdom of Ancient Jewish and Christian Festal Calendars* (Peabody, MA, Hendrickson, 2002).

Chireau, Yvonne and Deutsch, Nathaniel (eds), *Black Zion: African American Religious Encounters with Judaism* (New York, Oxford University Press, 2000).

Christ, Carol and Plaskow, Judith (eds), *Womenspirit Rising: A Feminist Reader in Religion* (San Francisco, Harper Collins, 1979).

Chupungco, Anscar, *Liturgical Time and Space: Handbook for Liturgical Studies 5* (Collegeville, MN, The Liturgical Press, 2000).

Clifford, Anne M., *Introducing Feminist Theology* (New York, Orbis, 2001).

Cohen, Arthur A., *The Myth of the Judeo-Christian Tradition* (New York, Schocken, 1971).

Cohen, Arthur A. and Mendes-Flohr, Paul (eds), *Contemporary Jewish Religious Thought: Original Essays on Critical Concepts, Movements and Beliefs* (New York, Charles Scribner's Sons, 1988).

Cohen, H., *Reason and Hope: Selections from the Jewish Writings of Hermann Cohen*, trans. Jospe, E. (Cincinnati, Hebrew Union College Press, 1993).

Religion of Reason out of the Sources of Judaism, trans. with an introduction by Kaplan, S. (Atlanta, Scholars Press, 1995).

Cohen, Martin and Croner, Helga (eds), *Christian Mission – Jewish Mission* (New York, Paulist Press, 1982).

Collins, J. J. (ed.), *Apocalypse: The Morphology of a Genre* (Semeia 14) (Chico, CA, Scholars Press, 1979).

The Encyclopedia of Apocalypticism, vol. 1: The Origins of Apocalypticism in Judaism and Christianity (New York, Continuum, 1998, 2nd edn, 2000).

Collinson, P., *Godly People* (London, The Hambledon Press, 1883).

Cohn-Sherbok, Dan, *Judaism and Other Faiths* (London, Macmillan, 1994).

Messianic Judaism (London, Cassell, 2000).

Cracknell, Kenneth, *Wilfred Cantwell Smith: A Reader* (Oxford, One World, 2001).

Cunningham, Lawrence, *The Meaning of Saints* (San Francisco, Harper & Row, 1980).

Cunningham, Philip, *Proclaiming Shalom: Lectionary Introductions to Foster the Catholic and Jewish Relationship* (Collegeville, MN, The Liturgical Press, 1995).

A Story of Shalom: Religion Textbooks and the Enhancement of the Catholic and Jewish Relationship (Collegeville, MN, The Liturgical Press, 1995).

Danby, Herbert, *The Jew and Christianity: Some Phases, Ancient and Modern, of the Jewish Attitude towards Christianity* (London, The Sheldon Press, 1927).

Daum, Annette and Fisher, Eugene, *The Challenge of Shalom for Catholics and Jews: A Dialogical Discussion Guide* (New York, Union of American Hebrew Congregations and the US Conference of Catholic Bishops, 1985).

Davies, W. D., *The Gospel and the Land* (Berkeley, University of California Press, 1974).

Davies, W. D. (ed.), *Torah and Dogma* (Cambridge, MA, Harvard University Press, 1968).

Davies, W. D. and Allison, D. C. (eds), *Christian Engagements with Judaism* (Harrisburg, Trinity Press International, 1999).

Davis, J. D., *Finding the God of Noah: The Spiritual Journey of a Baptist Minister from Christianity to the Laws of Noah* (Hoboken, NJ, Ktav Publishing House, 1996).

Dawe, Donald, G., and Fule, Aurelia T. (eds), *Christians and Jews Together: Voices from the Conversation* (Louisville, Theology and Worship Ministry Unit, Presbyterian Church USA, 1991).

Delooz, Pierre, 'The Social Function of the Canonization of Saints', in Duquoc, Christian and Floristán, Casiano (eds), *Models of Holiness* (New York, The Seabury Press, 1979).

Di Sante, Carmine, *Jewish Prayer: The Origins of the Christian Liturgy* (New York, Paulist Press, 1991).

Dohmen, Christoph and Zenger, Erich, *Der neue Bund im alten: Studien zur Bundestheologie der beiden Testamente* (Herder Verlag, Freiburg, 1993).

Dorff, Elliot N. and Newman, Louis E. (eds), *Contemporary Jewish Ethics and Morality* (New York, Oxford University Press, 1995).

Duhaime, J. and Gignac, A. (eds.), *Juifs et chrétiens, L'avenir du dialogue théologique*, vol. 11 (Montréal, Université de Montréal, 2003).

Eckardt, A. Roy, *Christianity and the Children of Israel* (New York, King's Crown Press, 1948).

Collecting Myself: A Writer's Retrospective (Atlanta, Scholars Press, 1993).

Elder and Younger Brothers: The Encounter of Jews and Christians (New York, Scribner's, 1967; reprinted Schocken, 1973).

Reclaiming the Jesus of History: Christology Today (Minneapolis, Fortress Press, 1992).

Your People, My People: The Meeting of Jews and Christians (New York, Quadrangle, 1974).

Eckardt, A. Roy and Alice L., *Encounter with Israel: A Challenge to Conscience* (New York, Association Press, 1970).

Long Night's Journey into Day: A Revised Retrospective on the Holocaust (Detroit, Wayne State University Press; London, Pergamon Press, 1988).

Elbogen, Ismar, *Jewish Liturgy: A Comprehensive History*, trans. Scheindlin, Raymond P. (Philadelphia, Jewish Publication Society, Jewish Theological Seminary of America, 1993).

Erickson, Millard J., *Christian Theology* (Basingstoke, Marshall Pickering, 1983).

Eskenazi, J. C. et al., *The Sabbath in Jewish and Christian Tradition* (New York, Crossroad, 1991).

Evers, G., 'Die "anonymen Christen" und der Dialog mit den Juden', in Vorgrimler, H. (ed.), *Wagnis Theologie: Erfahrungen mit der Theologie Karl Rahners* (Freiburg, Herder Verlag, 1979), 524–36.

Fackenheim, E. L., *The Jewish Bible after the Holocaust* (Manchester, Manchester University Press, 1988).

The Jewish Return into History: Reflections in the Age of Auschwitz and a New Jerusalem (New York, Schocken Books, 1978).

To Mend the World: Foundations of Future Jewish Thought (Bloomington, Indiana University Press, 1994).

Feiler, Bruce, *Abraham: A Journey to the Heart of Three Faiths* (New York, W. Morrow, 2002).

Fiensy, David, *Prayers Alleged to be Jewish: An Examination of the Constitutiones Apostolorum* (Chico, CA, Scholars Press, 1985).

Fink, Peter, *Anointing of the Sick. Vol. 7: Alternative Futures for Worship* (Collegeville, MN, Liturgical Press, 1987).

Finkel, Asher and Frizzell, Lawrence, *Standing before God* (New York, Ktav, 1981).

Fisher, Eugene J., *Faith without Prejudice: Rebuilding Christian Attitudes Toward Judaism* (New York, Paulist Press, 1977; revised and expanded edn, New York, Crossroad; Philadelphia, The American Interfaith Institute, 1993).

Interwoven Destinies: Jews and Christians through the Ages (New York, Paulist Press, 1993).

The Jewish Roots of Christian Liturgy (New York, Paulist Press, 1990).

Fisher, Eugene J. (ed.), *Visions of the Other: Jewish and Christian Theologians Assess the Dialogue* (New York, Paulist Press, 1994).

Fisher, Eugene and Klenicki, Leon, *John Paul II on Jews and Judaism 1979–1986* (New York, US Catholic Conference and Anti-Defamation League of B'nai B'rith, 1987).

Fleischner, E., *Judaism in German Christian Theology since 1945: Christianity and Israel Considered in Terms of Mission* (Metuchen, NJ, Scarecrow Press, 1975).

Flannery, Edward H., *The Anguish of the Jews: Twenty-Three Centuries of Anti-Semitism* (New York, Macmillan, 1965; Mahwah, NJ, Paulist Press, 1985).

Flusser, David, Pelikan, Jaroslav, Lang, Justin (eds), *Mary: Images of the Mother of Jesus in Jewish and Christian Perspective* (Philadelphia, Fortress Press, 1986).

Friedman, F. G. and Rahner, K., 'Unbefangenheit und Anspruch: Ein Briefwechsel zum jüdisch-christlichen Gespräch', *Stimmen der Zeit* 177 (1966), 81–97.

Fry, H. P. (ed.), *Christian–Jewish Dialogue: A Reader* (Exeter, University of Exeter, 1996).

Fry, Helen, Montagu, Rachel and Scholefield, Lynne (eds), *Women's Voices: New Perspectives for the*

Christian–Jewish Dialogue (London, SCM Press, 2005).

Frymer-Kensky, Tikva, Novak, David, Ochs, Peter, Sandmel, David Fox and Signer, Michael A. (eds), *Christianity in Jewish Terms* (Boulder, CO, Westview Press, 2000).

Gale, R., *On the Nature and Existence of God* (Cambridge, Cambridge University Press, 1991).

Galvin, John (ed.), *Faith and the Future: Studies in Christian Eschatology* (New York, Paulist Press, 1994).

Garber, Z. (ed.), *Mel Gibson's Passion: The Film, the Controversy and its Implications* (Purdue University Press, 2005).

Gillet, Lev, *Communion in the Messiah: Studies in the Relationship between Judaism and Christianity* (London, Lutterworth Press, 1942).

Gillman, Neil, *The Death of Death: Resurrection and Immortality in Jewish Thought* (Woodstock, VT, Jewish Lights Publishing, 1997).

Green, Ronald, 'Jewish and Christian Ethics: What Can we Learn from One Another?', *Annual Society of Christian Ethics* (1999), 1–16.

Greenberg, I., *For the Sake of Heaven and Earth: The New Encounter between Judaism and Christianity* (Philadelphia, The Jewish Publication Society, 2004).

Living in the Image of God: Jewish Teachings to Perfect the World (Northvale, NJ, Jason Aronson, 1998).

Greenspahn, Frederick E. (ed.), *The Human Condition in the Jewish and Christian Traditions* (Hoboken, NJ, Ktav, 1986).

Griffin, D. R., *God, Power and Evil: A Process Theodicy* (Philadelphia, Westminster Press, 1976).

Griffiths, J. G., *The Divine Verdict: A Study of Divine Judgement in the Ancient Religions* (Leiden, Brill, 1991).

Hall, D. D. (ed.), *The Antinomian Controversy, 1636–1638* (Middletown, CT, Wesleyan University Press, 1968).

Hall, Douglas John, *Imaging God: Dominion as Stewardship* (Grand Rapids, Eerdmans, 1986).

The Stewardship of Life in the Kingdom of Death (Grand Rapids, Eerdmans, 1988).

Hanson, Paul D., *The Dawn of Apocalyptic* (Philadelphia, Fortress Press, 1975).

Happel, Stephen, *Conversion and Discipleship: A Christian Foundation for Ethics and Doctrine* (Philadelphia, Fortress Press, 1986).

Harrelson, Walter and Falk, Randall M., *Jews and Christians: A Troubled Family* (Nashville, Abingdon Press, 1990).

Harries, Richard, *After the Evil – Christianity and Judaism in the Shadow of the Holocaust* (Oxford, Oxford University Press, 2003).

Hartman, D., *A Living Covenant: The Innovative Spirit in Traditional Judaism* (New York, Free Press, 1985).

Hauerwas, S., *Sanctify Them in the Truth: Holiness Exemplified* (Edinburgh, T&T Clark, 1998).

Haynes, S. R., *Prospects for Post-Holocaust Theology* (American Academy of Religion Academy Series 77) (Atlanta, Scholars Press, 1991).

Haynes, Stephen R., and Roth, John K. (eds), *The Death of God Movement and the Holocaust: Radical Theology Encounters the Shoah* (Westport, CT, Greenwood Press, 1999).

Hays, Richard B., *The Faith of Jesus Christ* (Chico, CA, Society of Biblical Literature, 1983).

Hecht, N. S., Jackson, B. S., Passamaneck, S. M., Piattelli, D. and Rabello, A. M. (eds), *An Introduction to the History and Sources of Jewish Law* (Oxford, Clarendon Press, 1996).

Hellholm, D. (ed.), *Apocalypticism in the Mediterranean World and the Near East: Proceedings of the International Colloquium on Apocalypticism Uppsala, August 12–17, 1979* (Tübingen, J. C. B. Mohr (Paul Siebeck), 1983).

Heschel, Abraham Joshua, *God in Search of Man: A Philosophy of Judaism* (New York, Noonday Press, 1976).

Man Is Not Alone: A Philosophy of Religion (New York, Farrar, Straus and Young, 1951).

Man's Quest for God: Studies in Prayer and Symbolism (New York, Charles Scribner's Sons, 1954).

The Sabbath: Its Meaning for Modern Man (New York, Farrar, Straus, and Young, 1951).

Hick, J., *Evil and the God of Love* (New York, Harper & Row, rev. edn, 1978).

Philosophy of Religion (Englewood Cliffs, NJ, Prentice–Hall, 1963).

Hilton, Michael, *The Christian Effect on Jewish Life* (London, SCM Press, 1994).

Hoeckman, R., 'The Teaching on Jews and Judaism in Catholic Education', *Seminarium* 2 (1992), 346–59.

Holm, Jean and Bowker, John (eds), *Attitudes to Nature* (London, Pinter Publishers, 1994).

Myth and History (London, Pinter Publishers, 1994).

Holwerda, David E., *Jesus and Israel: One Covenant or Two?* (Grand Rapids, Eerdmans, 1995).

Isaac, Jules, *Jesus and Israel* (New York, Holt, Rinehart & Winston, 1971).

The Teaching of Contempt: Christian Roots of Anti-Semitism (New York, Holt, Rinehart & Winston, 1964).

Jackson, G., 'Jesus as a First-Century Feminist: Christian Anti-Judaism?', *Feminist Theology* 19 (1998), 85–98.

Jacobs, Louis, *Faith* (London, Valentine Mitchell, 1968).

Holy Living: Saints and Saintliness in Judaism (London, Jason Aronson, 1990).

Jewish Law (New York, Behrman House, 1968).

Principles of the Jewish Faith (London, Kuperard, 1995).

A Tree of Life: Diversity, Flexibility, and Creativity in Jewish Law (London, The Littman Library of Jewish Civilization, 2nd edn, 2000).

Jasper, R. C. D. and Cuming, G. J. (eds), *Prayers of the Eucharist Early and Reformed* (New York, Pueblo Publishing, 1987).

Jenson, Robert, *Systematic Theology I, The Truine God* (Oxford, Oxford University Press, 1997).

Johnson, Elizabeth A., *Friends of God and Prophets: A Feminist Theological Reading of the Communion of Saints* (London, SCM Press, 1998).

She Who Is: The Mystery of God in Feminist Theological Discourse (New York, Crossroad, 1992).

Truly Our Sister: A Theology of Mary in the Communion of the Saints (New York, Continuum, 2003).

Jones, Cheslyn, Wainwright, Geoffrey and Yarnold, Edward (eds), *The Study of Liturgy* (London, SPCK; New York, Oxford University Press, 1978).

Jones, David H., *Moral Responsibility in the Holocaust: A Study in the Ethics of Character* (Lanham, MD, Rowman & Littlefield, 1999).

Käppeli, Silvia (ed.), *Lesarten des jüdisch-christlichen Dialoges* (Bern, Peter Lang, 2002).

Katz, S. T., *Post-Holocaust Dialogues: Critical Studies in Modern Jewish Thought* (New York, New York University Press, 1985).

Kee, H. C. and Borowsky, I. J. (eds), *Removing Anti-Judaism from the Pulpit* (New York, Continuum, 1996).

Kellner, Menahem M., *Dogma in Medieval Jewish Thought: from Maimonides to Abravanel* (Oxford, Oxford University Press, 1986).

'Heresy and the Nature of Faith in Medieval Jewish Philosophy', *Jewish Quarterly Review*, 77 (1987).

Kessler, E., Pawlikowski, J. T. and Banki, J. (eds), *Jews and Christians in Conversation: Crossing Cultures and Generations* (Cambridge, Orchard Academic Press, 2002).

Kessler, E., and Wright, M. (eds), *Themes in Jewish–Christian Relations* (Cambridge, Orchard Academic Press, 2004).

Kieckhefer, Richard and Bond, George D. (eds), *Sainthood: Its Manifestations in World Religions* (Berkeley, University of California Press, 1988).

Kimelman, Reuven, 'The Literary Structure of the Amidah and the Rhetoric of Redemption', in Dever, William G. and Wright, J. Edward (eds), *The Echoes of Many Texts: Reflection on Jewish and Christian Traditions, Essays in Honor of Lou H. Silberman* (Brown Judaic Studies 313) (Atlanta, Scholars Press, 1997).

Kinzig, Wolfram and Kück, Cornelia (eds), *Judentum und Christentum zwischen Konfrontation und Faszination: Ansätze zu einer neuen Beschreibung jüdisch-christlicher Beziehungen* (Judentum und Christentum 11) (Stuttgart, Kohlhammer, 2002).

Klein, Charlotte, *Anti-Judaism in Christian Theology*, trans. Quinn, Edward (London, SPCK, 1978).

Klenicki, L. (ed.), *Toward a Theological Encounter: Jewish Understandings of Christianity* (Mahwah, NJ, Paulist Press, 1991).

Klenicki, Leon and Huck, Gabe, *Spirituality and Prayer* (New York, Paulist Stimulus, 1983).

Korn, E. B. and Pawlikowski, J. T. (eds), *Two Faiths, One Covenant? Jewish and Christian Identity in the Presence of the Other* (Lanham, MD, Rowman & Littlefield, 2004).

Kraemer, Ross Shepard, and D'Angelo, Mary Rose (eds), *Women and Christian Origins* (New York, Oxford University Press, 1999).

Krieg, Robert A., *Catholic Theologians in Nazi Germany* (New York, Continuum, 2004).

Kung, Hans and Kasper, Walter, *Christians and Jews* (New York, Seabury Press, 1975).

Kuschel, Karl-Joseph, *Abraham: Sign of Hope for Jews, Christians, and Muslims* (New York, Continuum, 1995).

Lamm, Norman, *The Condition of Jewish Belief* (London, Macmillan, 1988).

The Shema: Spirituality and Law in Judaism as Exemplified in the Shema, the Most Important Passage in the Torah (Philadelphia, Jewish Publication Society, 1998).

Lane, Dermot, *Keeping Hope Alive: Stirrings in Christian Theology* (New York, Paulist Press, 1996).

Langer, Ruth, 'Early Rabbinic Liturgy in its Palestinian Milieu: Did Non-Rabbis Know the "Amidah?"', in Harrington, Daniel, Avery-Peck, Alan J. and Neusner, Jacob (eds), *When Judaism and Christianity Began: Essays in Memory of Anthony J. Saldarini* (Leiden, E. J. Brill, 2004).

Lapide, P. and Moltmann, J., *Jewish Monotheism and Christian Trinitarian Doctrine*, trans. Leonard Swidler (Philadelphia, Fortress Press, 1981).

Lapide, P., *Auferstehung: Ein jüdisches Glaubenserlebnis* (Stuttgart, Calwer Verlag; Munich, Kösel Verlag, 3rd edn, 1980).

Lapide, P. and Rahner, K., *Encountering Jesus – Encountering Judaism* (New York, Crossroad, 1987).

Leaman, Oliver, *Evil and Suffering in Jewish Philosophy* (Cambridge, Cambridge University Press, 1995).

Leibniz, Gottfried W., *Theodicy: Essays on the Goodness of God, the Freedom of Man and the Origin of Evil* (Open Court, 1988).

Levack, B. (ed.), *New Perspectives on Witchcraft, Magic and Demonology*, 6 vols. (London, Routledge, 2002).

Levinas, Emmanuel, *Entre nous: On Thinking-of-the-Other*, trans. Smith, Michael B. and Harshav, Barbara (New York, Columbia University Press, 1998).

Otherwise than Being or Beyond Essence, trans. Lingis, A. (The Hague, Kluwer Academic Publishers, 1981).

Levine, L. (ed.), *Jerusalem: Its Sanctity and Centrality to Judaism, Christianity and Islam* (New York, Continuum, 1999).

Lévi-Strauss, Claude, *Myth and Meaning* (London, Routledge and Kegan Paul, 1978).

Lichtenstein, A., *The Seven Laws of Noah* (New York, The Rabbi Jacob Joseph School Press, 1981).

Lindsay, M. R., *Covenanted Solidarity: The Theological Basis of Karl Barth's Opposition to Nazi Antisemitism and the Holocaust* (New York, Peter Lang, 2001).

Littell, F. H., *The Crucifixion of the Jews: The Failure of Christians to Understand the Jewish Experience* (Macon, Mercer University Press, 1986).

Locke, Hubert G., *The Black Anti-Semitism Controversy: Protestant Views and Perspectives* (Selingsgrove, PA, Susquehanna University Press, 1994).

Learning from History: A Black Christian's Perspective on the Holocaust (London, Greenwood Press, 2000).

Searching for God in Godforsaken Times and Places: Reflections on the Holocaust, Racism, and Death (Grand Rapids, Eerdmans, 2003).

Lodahl, Michael E., *Shekhinah / Spirit: Divine Presence in Jewish and Christian Religion* (New York, Paulist Press, 1992).

Loewe, R., '"Salvation" is not of the Jews', *Journal of Theological Studies* 32 (1981), 341–68.

Maduro, Otto (ed.), *Judaism, Christianity and Liberation* (Maryknoll, NY, Orbis, 1991).

Magonet, Jonathan, *Talking to the Other: A Jewish Interfaith Dialogue with Christains and Muslims* (London, I.B. Taurus, 2003).

Maguire, Daniel C., *The Moral Core of Judaism and Christianity* (Minneapolis, Fortress Press, 1993).

Mamorstein, Arthur, *The Doctrine of Merits in Old Rabbinical Literature* (New York, Ktav, 1968).

Markschies, Christoph, *Alta Trinita Beata: Gesammelte Studien zur altkirchlichen Trinitätstheologie* (Tübingen, Mohr, 2000).

Marquardt, F.-W., *Von Elend und Heimsuchung der Theologie: Prologomena zur Dogmatik* (Munich, Chr. Kaiser, 1988).

Mascall, Eric, *Existence and Analogy* (London, Darton, Longman & Todd, 1966).

Maybaum, Ignaz, *Trialogue between Jew, Christian and Muslim* (London, Routledge & Kegan Paul, 1973).

McGarry, Michael, *Christology after Auschwitz* (New York, Paulist Press, 1977).

McGrath, Alister, *Iustitia Dei: A History of the Christian Doctrine of Justification* (Cambridge, Cambridge University Press, 1986).

McKay, H., *Sabbath and Synagogue* (Leiden, Brill, 1994).

Merkle, John C. (ed.), *Faith Transformed: Christian Encounters with Jews and Judaism* (Collegeville, MN, The Liturgical Press, 2003).

Metz, J.-B., *The Emergent Church* (London, SCM Press, 1981).

'Facing the Jews: Christian Theology after Auschwitz', in Schüssler Fiorenza, E. and Tracy, D. (eds), *The Holocaust as Interruption* (Concilium 175) (Edinbugh, T&T Clark, 1984), 26–33.

Metz, J.-B. and Moltmann, J., *Faith in the Future: Essays on Theology, Solidarity, and Modernity* (Concilium Series) (Maryknoll, NY, Orbis Books, 1995).

Mitchem, Stephanie Y., *Introducing Womanist Theology* (New York, Orbis Books, 2002).

Moltmann, J., *The Crucified God: The Cross of Christ as the Foundation and Criticism of Christian Theology* (London, SCM Press, 1974).

Theology of Hope: On the Ground and Implications of a Christian Eschatology (New York, Harper & Row, 1967).

The Way of Jesus Christ: Christology in Messianic Dimensions (London, SCM Press, 1990).

Moran, Gabriel, *Religious Education Development* (Minneapolis, Winston, 1983).

Morgan, M. L. (ed.), *The Jewish Thought of Emil Fackenheim: A Reader* (Detroit, Wayne State University Press, 1987).

Murphy, Madonna (ed.), *Faith, Moral Reasoning and Contemporary American Life* (Brighton, MA, Cambridge Center for the Study of Faith and Culture, 1995), 14–27.

Murray, R., *The Cosmic Covenant* (London, Sheed & Ward, 1992).

Mussner, Franz, *Tractate on the Jews: The Significance of Judaism for Christian Faith* (Philadephia, Fortress Press, 1984).

Neiman, Susan, *Evil in Modern Thought: An Alternative History of Philosophy* (Princeton, NJ, Princeton University Press, 2003).

Neufeld, Vernon H., *The Earliest Christian Confessions* (Grand Rapids, Eerdmans, 1963).

Neuhaus, David, 'Kehilla, Church and the Jewish People', *Mishkan* 36 (2002), 78–86.

Neusner, Jacob, *Messiah in Context: Israel's History and Destiny in Formative Judaism* (The Foundations of Judaism: Method, Teleology, Doctrine Part Two: Teleology) (Philadelphia, Fortress Press, 1984).

Nicholls, William, *Christian Antisemitism: A History of Hate* (Northvale, NJ, Jason Aronson, 1993).

Nickelsburg, George W. E., *Resurrection, Immortality, and Eternal Life in Intertestamental Judaism* (Cambridge, MA, Harvard University Press, 1972).

Novak, D. *The Image of the Non-Jew in Judaism: A Constructive Study of the Noahide Laws* (New York, Edwin Mellen Press, 1983).

Novak, David, *Jewish–Christian Dialogue: A Jewish Justification* (Oxford, Oxford University Press, 1989).

O'Hare, Padraic, *The Enduring Covenant: The Education of Christians and the End of Antisemitism* (Valley Forge, PA, Trinity Press International, 1997).

Ochs, Carol, *An Ascent to Joy: Transforming Deadness of Spirit* (Notre Dame, University of Notre Dame Press, 1986).

Oesterreicher, John M. (ed.), *The Bridge: A Yearbook of Judaeo-Christian Studies*, Vol. I–IV (New York, Pantheon Books, 1955, 1956, 1958, 1962) Vol. V (New York, Herder and Herder, 1970).

God at Auschwitz (South Orange, NJ, Seton Hall University, 1993).

The Israel of God (Englewood Cliffs, NJ, Prentice–Hall, 1963).

Racisme, antisémitisme, antichristianisme (Paris, Editions du Cerf, 1939).

Olson, Bernhard E., *Faith and Prejudice: Intergroup Problems in Protestant Curricula* (New Haven, Yale University Press, 1963).

Papademetriou, George C., *Essays on Orthodox Christian–Jewish Relations* (Bristol, IN, Wyndham Hall Press, 1990).

Parker, K., *The English Sabbath* (Cambridge, Cambridge University Press, 1988).

Parkes, J., *Voyage of Discoveries* (London, Gollancz, 1969).

Pawlikowski, John T., *Catechetics and Prejudice: How Catholic Teaching Materials View Jews, Protestants, and Racial Minorities* (New York, Paulist Press, 1973).

The Challenge of the Holocaust for Christian Theology (New York, Anti-Defamation League, 1978).

Christ in Light of the Christian–Jewish Dialogue (New York, Wipf & Stock Publishers, 1982).

'Christology after the Holocaust', in Merrigan, T. and Haers, J. (eds), *The Myriad Christ: Plurality and the Quest for Unity in Contemporary*

Christology (Leuven, Leuven University Press, 2000).

Jesus and the Theology of Israel (Collegeville, MN, Liturgical Press, 1989).

Sinai and Calvary: A Meeting of Two Peoples (Beverly Hills, Benziger, 1976).

Pawlikowski, John T. and Perelmutter, Hayim Goren (eds), *Reinterpreting Revelation and Tradition: Jews and Christians in Conversation* (Franklin, WI, Sheed & Ward, 2000).

Pawlikowski, John and Wilde, James, 'Advent: Rethinking the Fulfillment Theme', in *When Catholics Speak about Jews* (Chicago, Liturgy Training Publications, 1975).

Pecherskaya, Natalia (ed.), *Theology after Auschwitz and its Correlation with Theology after the Gulag* (Saint Petersburg, School of Religion and Philosophy).

Peck, Abraham, J. (ed.), *Jews and Christians after the Holocaust* (Philadelphia, Fortress Press, 1982).

Pelikan, Jaroslav and Hotchkins, Valerie (eds), *Creeds and Professions of Faith in the Christian Tradition* (New Haven, Yale University Press, 2003).

Pelikan, Jaroslav, *Credo: Historical and Theological Guide to Creeds and Confessions of Faith in the Christian Tradition* (New Haven, Yale University Press, 2003).

Perham, Michael, *The Communion of Saints* (London, SPCK, 1980).

Peterson, Michael, *God and Evil: An Introduction to the Issues* (Boulder, CO, Westview Press, 1998).

Pirani, A. (ed.), *The Absent Mother: Restoring the Goddess to Judaism and Christianity* (London, Mandala, 1991).

Plaskow, Judith, 'Feminist Anti-Judaism and the Christian God,' *Journal of Feminist Studies in Religion* 7/2 (Fall 1991), 99–108.

Standing Again at Sinai: Judaism from a Feminist Perspective (New York, HarperCollins, 1991).

Plaskow, Judith and Christ, Carol, *Weaving the Visions: New Patterns in Feminist Spirituality* (San Francisco, Harper Collins, 1989).

Poorthuis, Marcel and Schwartz, Joshua (eds), *Saints and Role Models in Judaism and Christianity* (Leiden, Brill, 2004).

Porter, Stanley E. and Pearson, Brook W. R. (eds), *Christian–Jewish Relations through the Centuries* (Sheffield, Sheffield Academic Press, 2000).

Procter-Smith, Marjorie, *In her Own Rite: Constructing Feminist Liturgical Tradition* (Nashville, Abingdon Press, 1990).

Rahner, K., 'Bekenntnis zu Jesus Christus', in Schulz, H.-J. (ed), *Juden Christen Deutsche* (Stuttgart, Kreuz Verlag, 1961), 151–8.

Race, Alan, *Christians and Religious Pluralism: Patterns in the Christian Theology of Religions* (New York, Orbis, 1982).

Rahner, Karl, *On the Theology of Death* (New York, Seabury Press, 1973).

Rahner, K. and Lapide, P., *Heil von den Juden? Ein Gespräch* (Mainz, Matthias-Grünewald-Verlag, 1983).

Rankin, O. S., *The Origins of the Festival of Hanukkah* (Edinburgh, T&T Clark, 1930).

Ratzinger, Joseph, *Eschatology: Death and Eternal Life* (Washington, DC, Catholic University Press, 1988).

Reif, Stefan C., *Judaism and Hebrew Prayer: New Perspectives on Jewish Liturgical History* (Cambridge, Cambridge University Press, 1993).

Reimer, Jack (ed.), *Jewish Reflections on Death* (New York, Schocken Books, 1974).

Rengstorf, K. H. and Kortzfleisch, S. von (eds), *Kirche und Synagoge: Handbuch zur Geschichte von Christen und Juden I* (Stuttgart, Ernst Klett, 1968).

Reumann, John H. P., *Righteousness in the New Testament: Justification in the Lutheran–Catholic Dialogue* (Philadelphia, Fortress Press, 1982).

Ricoeur, Paul, *The Conflict of Interpretation: Essays in Hermeneutics* (Evanston, IL, Northwestern University Press, 1976).

Romain, Jonathan A., *Till Faith us Do Part* (London, HarperCollins, 1996).

Rose, Martin, 'Names of God in the OT', *Anchor Bible Dictionary* (New York, Doubleday, 1992), IV, 1001–11.

Rosenbloom, Joseph R., *Conversion to Judaism: From the Biblical Period to the Present* (Cincinnati, Hebrew Union College Press, 1978).

Rosenzweig, Franz, *Die 'Gritli'-Briefe: Briefe an Margrit Rosenstock-Huessy*, Ruehle, Inken and Mayer, Reinhold (eds) (Tübingen, Bilam Verlag, 2002).

The Star of Redemption, trans. William Hallo (Notre Dame, University of Notre Dame Press, 1985).

Roth, John K. (ed.), *Ethics after the Holocaust: Perspectives, Critique, and Responses* (St Paul, MN, Paragon House, 1999).

Rousmaniere, John, *A Bridge to Dialogue: The Story of Jewish–Christian Relations* (Mahwah, NJ, Paulist Press, 1991).

Rubenstein, Richard L., *After Auschwitz: History, Theology, and Contemporary Judaism* (Baltimore, Johns Hopkins University Press, 2nd edn, 1992).

Ruether, Rosemary Radford, *Women and Redemption: A Theological History* (Minneapolis, Fortress Press, 1998).

   Women-Church: Theology and Practice (New York, Harper & Row, 1985).

Sacks, J., *The Dignity of Difference: How to Avoid the Clash of Civilisations* (London, Continuum, 2002).

Salkin, Jeffrey K., *Putting God on the Guest List* (Woodstock, VT, Jewish Lights, 1993).

Sandmel, David, Catalano, Rosann M. and Leighton, Christopher M., *Irreconciliable Differences?* (Boulder, CO, Westview Press, 2001).

Saperstein, Marc (ed.), *Essential Papers on Messianic Movements and Personalities in Jewish History* (New York, New York University Press, 1992).

Scholem, G., *Major Trends in Jewish Mysticism* (New York, Schocken, 1961).

   The Messianic Idea in Judaism and Other Essays on Jewish Spirituality (New York, Schocken, 1971).

Schwartz, H., *Evil: A Historical and Theological Perspective*, trans. Worthing, M. (Minneapolis, Fortress Press, 1995).

Schwartz, Richard, *Judaism and Vegetarianism* (Marblehead, MA, Micah Publications, 1982).

Senn, Frank C., *Christian Liturgy: Catholic and Evangelical* (Minneapolis, Fortress Press, 1997).

Shermis, Michael and Zannoni, Arthur E. (eds), *Introduction to Jewish–Christian Relations* (New York, Paulist Press, 1991).

Shokek, Shimon, *Repentance in Jewish Ethics, Philosophy and Mysticism* (Lewiston, NJ, Edwin Mellen Press, 1995).

Signer, Michael, A. (ed.), *Memory and History in Christianity and Judaism* (Notre Dame, University of Notre Dame Press, 2001).

Smith, Wilfred Cantwell, *The Faith of Other Men* (republished as *Patterns of Faith around the World*) (Oxford, Oneworld, 1998).

   The Meaning and End of Religion: A New Approach to the Religious Traditions of Mankind (New York, Macmillan, 1963).

   Towards a World Theology (Basingstoke, Macmillan; Philadelphia, Westminster Press, 1981).

Sölle, D., *Suffering* (London, Darton, Longman & Todd, 1975).

Solomon, Norman, *Judaism and World Religion* (Basingstoke, Macmillan; New York, St Martin's Press, 1991).

Soulen, R. Kendall, *The God of Israel and Christian Theology* (Minneapolis, Fortress Press, 1996).

   'Hallowed be Thy name! The Tetragrammaton and the Name of the Trinity', in Braaten, C. and Wilken, R. (eds), *Jews and Christians, People of God* (Grand Rapids, Eerdmans, 2003).

Stendahl, Krister, *Holy Week Preaching* (Minneapolis, Fortress Press, 1985).

Stravinska, Peter and Klenicki, Leon, *A Catholic Jewish Encounter* (Huntingdon, Indiana, Our Sunday Visitor, 1994).

Strober, Gerald S., *Portrait of the Elder Brother: Jews and Judaism in Protestant Teaching Materials* (New York, American Jewish Committee, 1972).

Stylianopoulos, Theodore, 'Faithfulness to the Roots and Commitment toward the Future: An Orthodox View', in Lowe, Malcolm (ed.), *Orthodox Christians and Jews on Continuity and Renewal: The Third Academic Meeting between Orthodoxy and Judaism, Emmanuel* 26/27 (1994), 142–59.

Swidler, L. (ed.), *Muslims in Dialogue: The Evolution of a Dialogue* (Lewiston, NY, Edwin Mellen Press, 1992).

Thoma, C., *A Christian Theology of Judaism* (New York, Paulist Press, 1980).

   Die theologischen Beziehungen zwischen Christentum und Judentum (Darmstadt, Wissenschaftliche Buchgesellschaft, 1982).

Talley, Thomas, *The Origins of the Liturgical Year* (Collegeville, MN, The Liturgical Press, 1991).

Tanenbaum, Marc, Marvin, Wilson and Rudin, James, *Evangelicals and Jews in Conversation* (Grand Rapids, Eerdmans, 1978).

Thornton, T. G. C., 'The Crucifixion of Haman and the Scandal of the Cross', *Journal of Theological Studies* 37 (1986), 419–26.

Thrower, J., *A Short History of Western Atheism* (London, Pemberton Publishing, 1971).

Trevett, C., *Montanism: Gender, Authority and the New Prophecy* (Cambridge, Cambridge University Press, 1996).

Unterman, Alan, *Jews: Their Religious Beliefs and Practice* (London, Routledge, 1981).

van Buren, P., *A Theology of the Jewish–Christian Reality, Part I: Discerning the Way* (New York, Harper & Row, 1980).

    A Theology of the Jewish–Christian Reality, Part II: A Christian Theology of the People of Israel (San Francisco, Harper & Row, 1983).

    A Theology of the Jewish-Christian Reality, Part III: Christ in Context (San Francisco, Harper & Row, 1987).

von der Osten-Sacken, Peter, *Christian–Jewish Dialogue: Theological Foundations*, trans. Kohl, M. (Philadelphia, Fortress Press, 1986).

Von Kellenbach, Katharina, *Anti-Judaism in Feminist Christian Writings* (Atlanta, Scholars Press, 1994).

Wainwright, Geoffrey, *Eucharist and Eschatology* (Peterborough, Epworth Press, 2003).

Weinryb, Bernard D., 'Intergroup Content in Jewish Textbooks', *Religious Education* 55/2 (March–April, 1960), 109–16.

Werblowsky, R. J. Z., *The Meaning of Jerusalem to Jews, Christians and Muslims* (Jerusalem, Israel Universities' Study Group for Middle Eastern Affairs, rev. edn, 1978).

Werblowsky, R. J. Z., 'Africa and Judaism: Retrospect, Problems and Prospects', in Olupona, Jacob K. and Nyang, Sulayman S. (eds), *Religious Plurality in Africa* (Berlin, Mouton de Gruyter, 1993).

Willebrands, Johannes, *Church and Jewish People: New Considerations* (Mahwah, NJ, Paulist Press, 1992).

Williams, A. Lukyn, *Adversus Judaeos: A Bird's-Eye View of Christian Apology until the Renaissance* (Cambridge, Cambridge University Press, 1935).

Williamson, Clark, *A Guest in the House of Israel* (Louisville, Westminister John Knox Press, 1993).

    Has God Rejected his People? (Nashville, Abingdon Press, 1982).

Williamson, Clark, *A Mutual Witness: Towards Critical Solidarity between Jews and Christians* (St Louis, Chalice Press, 1992).

Wischermann, C. (ed.), *Die Legitimität der Erinnerung* (Studien zur Geschichte des Alltags 15) (Stuttgart, Franz Steiner Verlag, 1996).

Wohlmuth, Josef, *Im Geheimnis einander nahe: Theologische Aufsätze zum Verhältnis von Judentum und Christentum* (Paderborn, Ferdinand Schöningh Verlag, 1996).

Wybrew, Hugh, *The Orthodox Liturgy: The Development of the Eucharistic Liturgy in the Byzantine Rite* (Crestwood, NY, St Vladimir's Seminary Press, 1990).

Wyschogrod, E., *Saints and Postmodernism: Revisioning Moral Philosophy* (Chicago, Chicago University Press, 1990).

Wyschogrod, Michael, *Abraham's Promise: Judaism and Jewish–Christian Relations* (ed. with an introduction by Kendall Soulen) (Grand Rapids, Eerdmans, 2004).

    The Body of Faith: God in the People of Israel (San Francisco, Harper & Row, 1989).

    'A Jewish Perspective on Karl Barth', in *How Karl Barth Changed my Mind*, ed. McKim, Donald (Grand Rapids, Eerdmans, 1986).

Yoder, John Howard, *The Jewish–Christian Schism Revisited* (London, SCM Press, 2002).

Zannoni, Arthur (ed.), *Jews and Christians Speak of Jesus* (Minneapolis, Fortress Press, 1994).

Zvi Werblowsky, R. J., 'Peace', *Oxford Dictionary of the Jewish Religion* (Oxford, Oxford University Press, 1997), 522–3.

History

The formative period of Judaism and Christianity – the first 500 years

Aitken, J. K., 'The Language of the Septuagint: Recent Theories, Future Prospects', *Bulletin of Judaeo-Greek Studies* 24 (1999), 24–33.

Alexander, P. S., 'The Parting of the Ways from the Perspective of Rabbinic Judaism', in Dunn, J. D. G. (ed.), *Jews and Christians: The Parting of the Ways: AD 70–135* (Grand Rapids, Eerdmans, 1989), 1–25.

    '"A Sixtieth Part of Prophecy": The Problem of Continuing Revelation in Judaism', in Davies, J., Harvey, G. and Watson, W. G. E. (eds), *Words Remembered, Texts Renewed: Essays in Honour of John F. A. Sawyer* (Sheffield, JSOT Press, 1995), 414–33.

Aptowitzer, V., *Kain und Abel in der Agada, den Apokryphen, der hellenistischen, christlichen und muhammedanischen Literatur* (Vienna, R. Löwit, 1922).

Attridge, Harold W., *Eusebius, Christianity, and Judaism* (Leiden, E. J. Brill, 1992).

Aune, D. E., 'On the Origins of the "Council of Yavneh" Myth', *Journal of Biblical Literature* 110 (1991), 491–3.

Prophecy in Early Christianity and the Ancient Mediterranean World (Grand Rapids, Eerdmans, 1991).

Avi-Yonah, M., *The Jews of Palestine: A Political History from the Bar Kokhba War to the Arab Conquest* (Oxford, Basil Blackwell, 1976).

Bamberger, B. J., *Proselytism in the Talmudic Period* (Cincinnati, Hebrew Union College Press, 1939).

Barclay, John and Sweet, John (eds), *Early Christian Thought in its Jewish Context* (Cambridge, Cambridge University Press, 1996).

Bardy, G., 'Le souvenir de Josèphe chez les Pères', *Revue de l'Histoire Ecclésiastique* 43 (1948), 179–91.

Barnes, T. D., *Athanasius and Constantius: Theology and Politics in the Constantinian Empire* (Cambridge, MA, Harvard University Press, 1993).

Barnes, Michael R. and Williams, Daniel H. (eds), *Arianism after Arius: Essays on the Development of the Fourth Century Trinitarian Conflict* (Edinburgh, T&T Clark, 1993).

Barnes, Timothy David, *Constantine and Eusebius* (Cambridge, MA, Harvard University Press, 1981).

Barthélemy, Dominique, *Les devanciers d'Aquila* (Supplements to *VT* 10) (Leiden, Brill, 1963).

Bartlett, John R., *1 Maccabees* (Sheffield, Sheffield Academic Press, 1998).

Barton, J., *Oracles of God: Perceptions of Ancient Prophecy in Israel after the Exile* (London, Darton, Longman and Todd, 1986).

Baskin, J. R. 'Rabbinic–Patristic Exegetical Contacts in Late Antiquity: A Bibliographical Reappraisal', in Green, W. S. (ed.), *Approaches to Ancient Judaism*, V (Atlanta, SBL, 1985), 53–80.

Bauckman, Richard, 'Jews and Jewish Christians in the Land of Israel at the Time of the Bar Kochba War, with Special Reference to the *Apocalypse of Peter*', in Stanton, Graham N. and Stroumsa, Gug G. (eds), *Tolerance and Intolerance in Early Judaism and Christianity* (Cambridge, Cambridge University Press, 1998), 228–38.

Beckwith, R. T., *Calendar and Chronology, Jewish and Christian* (Leiden, Brill, 1996).

Benoit A., Philonenko, M. and Vogel, C. (eds.), *Paganisme, Judaïsme, Christianisme* (Paris, E. de Boccard, 1978).

Bilde, P., *Flavius Josephus between Jerusalem and Rome* (Sheffield, JSOT Press, 1988).

Blanchetière, F., 'Julien, Philhellène, philosémite, antichrétien. L'affaire du Temple de Jérusalem (363)', *Journal of Jewish Studies* 31 (1980), 61–81.

Blumenkranz, B., 'Kirche und Synagoge: Die Entwicklung im Westen zwischen 200 und 1200', in Bori, P. C., 'The Church's Attitude Towards the Jews: An Analysis of Augustine's "Adversos Judaeos"', in *Miscellanea Historiae Ecclesiasticae* VI, 1 (*Bibliotheque de la Revue d'Histoire Ecclesiastique* 67) (Brussels, 1983), 301–11.

Bockmuehl, Markus, *Jewish Law in Gentile Churches: Halakhah and the Beginning of Christian Public Ethics* (Edinburgh, T&T Clark, 2000).

Revelation and Mystery in Ancient Judaism and Pauline Christianity (Wissenschaftlich Untersuchungen zum Neuen Testament 36) (Grand Rapids, Eerdmans, 1990).

Bowersock, G. W., *Hellenism in Late Antiquity: Thomas Spencer Jerome Lectures* (Cambridge, Cambridge University Press, 1990).

Julian the Apostate (London, Duckworth, 1978).

Boyarin, Daniel, *Dying for God: Martyrdom and the Making of Christianity and Judaism* (Stanford, CA, Stanford University Press, 1999).

Brennecke, Hanns Christof, *Hilarius von Poitiers und die Bischofsopposition gegen Konstantius II: Untersuchungen zur dritten Phase des arianischen Streites (337–361)* (Patristische Texte und Studien 26) (Berlin, de Gruyter, 1984).

Brock, S. P., 'A Letter Attributed to Cyril of Jerusalem on the Rebuilding of the Temple', in *Syriac Perspectives on Late Antiquity* (London, Variorum Reprints, 1984).

The Luminous Eye: The Spiritual World Vision of Saint Ephrem (Rome, Center for Indian and Inter-Religious Studies, 1985; Kalamazoo, Cistercian Publications, 1992).

Bronner, L. L., *From Eve to Esther: Rabbinic Reconstructions of Biblical Women* (London, Faber & Faber 1967).

Brown, Peter, *The Rise of Western Christendom: Triumph and Diversity 200–1000 AD* (The Making of Europe) (Cambridge, MA, Blackwell, 1996).

Bruns, J., 'Philo Christianus, the Debris of a Legend', *Harvard Theological Review* 66 (1973), 141–5.

Carleton Paget, James, 'Jewish Christianity', in Horbury, W., Davies, W. D., Sturdy, John (eds), *The Cambridge History of Judaism*, III (Cambridge, Cambridge University Press, 1999), 731–75.

Carroll, James, *Constantine's Sword: The Church and the Jews* (Boston, Houghton Mifflin, 2001).

Chadwick, H., *The Church in Ancient Society: From Galilee to Gregory the Great* (Oxford History of the Christian Church) (Oxford, Oxford University Press, 2001).

'Florilegia', *Reallexikon für Antike und Christentum* 7, 1131–60.

'Philo', in Armstrong, A. H. (ed.), *The Cambridge History of Later Greek and Early Medieval Philosophy* (Cambridge, Cambridge University Press, 1967), 137–57.

Charlesworth, James H., *The Messiah: Developments in Earliest Judaism and Christianity* (Minneapolis, Fortress Press, 1992).

Charlesworth, James H. (ed.), *Jesus and the Dead Sea Scrolls* (New York, Doubleday, 1992).

Chilton, Bruce and Neusner, Jacob, *Types of Authority in Formative Christianity and Judaism* (London, Routledge, 1999).

Cohen, S. J. D, 'The Significance of Yavneh: Pharisees, Rabbis, and the End of Jewish Sectarianism', *Hebrew Union College Annual* 55 (1984), 27–53.

Collins, J. J., *Between Athens and Jerusalem: Jewish Identity in the Hellenistic Diaspora* (New York, Crossroad, 1983).

The Scepter and the Star: The Messiahs of the Dead Sea Scrolls and Other Ancient Literature (New York, Doubleday, 1995).

Corwin, Virginia, *St Ignatius and Christianity in Antioch* (New Haven, CT, Yale University Press, 1960).

Daly, Robert J., *Christian Sacrifice: The Judaeo-Christian Background before Origen* (The Catholic University of America Studies in Christian Antiquity 18) (Washington, DC, The Catholic University of America Press, 1978).

The Origins of the Christian Doctrine of Sacrifice (London, Darton, Longman & Todd, 1978).

Danby, H., *The Mishnah* (Oxford, Clarendon Press, 1933).

Daniélou, J., *Origen* (New York, Sheed & Ward, 1955).

The Origins of Latin Christianity: A History of Early Christian Doctrine before the Council of Nicaea III (London, Darton, Longman & Todd, 1977).

de Jonge, M., *Outside the Old Testament* (Cambridge, Cambridge University Press, 1985).

Davies, Alan (ed), *Antisemitism and the Foundations of Christianity* (New York, Paulist Press, 1979).

De Lange, N. R. M., *Origen and the Jews – Studies in Jewish-Christian Relations in Third-Century Palestine* (Cambridge, Cambridge University Press, 1976).

Dimant, Devorah, 'Noah in Early Jewish Literature', in *Biblical Figures outside the Bible* (Valley Forge, PA, Trinity Press International, 1998), 123–50.

Doniach, N. S., *Purim, or The Feast of Esther: An Historical Study* (Philadelphia, Jewish Publication Society of America, 1933).

Doskocil, Walter, *Der Bann in der Urkirche* (Munich, Zink, 1958).

Drijvers, J. W. and Watt, J. W. (eds), *Portraits of Spiritual Authority: Religious Power in Early Christianity, Byzantium and the Christian Orient* (Leiden, Brill, 1999).

Dugmore, C. W., *The Influence of the Synagogue upon the Divine Office* (Oxford, Clarendon Press, 1944).

Dunn, J. D. G., *Jews and Christians. The Partings of the Ways: between Christianity and Judaism, and their significance for the character of Christianity* (London, SCM Press, 1992).

Dunn, J. D. G. (ed.), *Jews and Christians: A Parting of the Ways: A.D. 70 to 135* (The Second Durham-Tübingen Research Symposium on Earliest Christianity and Judaism) (Grand Rapids, Eerdmans, 1989).

Ehrman, Bart D., *The Apostolic Fathers* (London, Loeb Classical Library, 2003).

Eisenmann, R., *James the Brother of Jesus* (Penguin, Harmondsworth, 1998).

Emmel, S., 'The Recently Published Gospel of the Saviour: Righting the Order of Page and Events', *Harvard Theological Review* 95.1 (2002), 45–72.

Fahey, M. A., *Cyprian and the Bible: A Study in Third Century Exegesis* (Tübingen, Mohr, 1971).

Feldman, Louis, *Jew and Gentile in the Ancient World* (Princeton, NJ, Princeton University Press, 1993).

Feldman, L. and Hata, G. (eds), *Josephus, Judaism and Christianity* (Detroit, Wayne State University Press, 1987).

Feldman, L. and Levenson, J. (eds), *Josephus' Contra Apionem* (Leiden, Brill, 1996).

Fiensy, David, *Prayers Alleged to be Jewish: An Examination of the Constitutiones Apostolorum* (Chico, CA, Scholars Press, 1985).

Fine, Steven (ed.), *Jews, Christians, and Polytheists in the Ancient Synagogue* (London, Routledge, 1999).

Finkel, Asher, 'Yavneh Liturgy and Early Christianity', *Journal of Ecumenical Studies* 18 (1981), 231–50.

Flusser, David, *Judaism and the Origins of Christianity* (Jerusalem, Magnes, 1988).

Forkman, G., *The Limits of the Religious Community: Expulsion from the Religious Community within the Qumran Sect, within Rabbinic Judaism and within Primitive Christianity* (Lund, Gleerup, 1972).

Frankfurter, David, *Religion in Roman Egypt: Assimilation and Resistance* (Princeton, NJ, Princeton University Press, 1998).

Fredrikson, P., 'Excaecati Occulta Justitia Dei: Augustine on Jews and Judaism', *Journal of Early Christian Studies* 3.3 (1995), 299–334.

Frend, W. H. C., *The Early Church from the Beginnings to 461* (London, SCM Press, 3rd edn, 1991).

'Jews and Christians in Third Century North Africa', in Benoit, A., Philonenko, M. and Vogel, C. (eds), *Paganisme, Judaïsme, Christianisme* (Paris, E. de Boccard, 1978), 185–94.

The Rise of Christianity (Philadelphia, Fortress Press, 1991).

Gager, John G., *The Origins of Anti-Semitism: Attitudes toward Judaism in Pagan and Christian Antiquity* (Oxford, Oxford University Press, 1983).

'Proselytism and Exclusivity in Early Christianity', in Marty, Martin and Greenspahn, Frederick (eds), *Pushing the Faith: Proselytism and Civility in a Pluralistic World* (New York, Crossroad, 1988).

Glenthøj, J. B., *Cain and Abel in Syriac and Greek Writers (4th–6th Centuries)* (Corpus Scriptorum Christianorum orientalium 567/Subs 95) (Leuven, Leuven University Press, 1997).

Goldberg, Arnold, 'Der Heilige und die Heiligen: Vorüberlegungen zur Theologie des Heiligen Menschen im rabbinischen Judentum', *Frankfurter Judaistische Beiträge* 4 (1976), 1–25.

Goodman, Martin, *Mission and Conversion* (Oxford, Clarendon Press, 1994).

'Palestinian Rabbis and the Conversion of Constantine to Christianity', in Schäfer, P. and Hezser, C. (eds), *The Talmud Yerushalmi and Graeco-Roman Culture*, vol. 2 (Tübingen, Mohr-Siebeck, 2000), 1–9.

'Sadducees and Essenes after 70 CE', in Porter, S. E., Joyce, P., and Orton, D. E. (eds), *Crossing the Boundaries: Essays in Biblical Interpretation in Honour of Michael D. Goulder* (Leiden, Brill, 1994), 347–56.

Gorday, P., *Principles of Patristic Exegesis: Romans 9–11 in Origen, John Chrysostom, and Augustine* (New York, Edwin Mellen Press, 1983).

Grabbe, L. L., 'Aquila's Translation and Rabbinic Exegesis', in *Journal of Jewish Studies* 33 (1982), 527–36.

Grant, Robert M., *Irenaeus of Lyons* (London, Routledge, 1997).

Green, William Scott, 'Palestinian Holy Men: Charismatic Leadership and Rabbinic Tradition', *Aufstieg und Niedergang der Römischen Welt* (Berlin, de Gruyter, 1972–3).

Gutmann, Joseph, 'The Dura Europos Synagogue Paintings: The State of Research', in Levine, Lee I. (ed.), *The Synagogue in Late Antiquity* (Philadelphia, American School of Oriental Research, 1987).

'Early Synagogue Art and Jewish Catacomb Art and its Relation to Christian Art', *Aufstieg und Niedergang der Römischen Welt* 11/21.2, 1313–42.

Haas, Christopher, *Alexandria in Late Antiquity: Topography and Social Conflict* (Baltimore Johns Hopkins University Press, 1997).

Hall, Stuart G., *Melito of Sardis On Pascha and Fragments* (Oxford, Clarendon Press, 1979).

Halpern-Amaru, B., 'Portraits of Biblical Women in Josephus' Antiquities', *Journal of Jewish Studies* 39 (1988), 143–70.

Hanson, Richard P. C., *The Search for the Christian Doctrine of God: The Arian Controversy* (Edinburgh, T&T Clark, 1988).

Harland, Philip A., *Associations, Synagogues, and Congregations: Claiming a Place in Ancient Mediterranean Society* (Minneapolis, Fortress Press, 2003).

Harrington, Daniel, Avery-Peck, Alan J. and Neusner, Jacob (eds), *When Judaism and Christianity Began: Essays in Memory of Anthony J. Saldarini* (Leiden, E. J. Brill, 2003).

Harris, J. R., *Testimonies* (Cambridge, Cambridge University Press, vol. I, 1916, vol. II, 1920).

Hauschild, Wolf-Dieter, *Lehrbuch der Kirchen- und Dogmengeschichte, vol. I: Alte Kirche und Mittelalter* (Gütersloh, Chr. Kaiser, 2nd edn, 2000).

Hayward, C. T. R., *The Jewish Temple: A Non-Biblical Sourcebook* (London, Routledge, 1996).

Saint Jerome's Hebrew Questions on Genesis (Oxford Early Christian Studies) (Oxford, Clarendon Press, 1995).

Hazlett, Ian, (ed.), *Early Christianity: Origins and Evolution to AD 600. In Honour of W. H. C. Frend* (London, SPCK, 1991).

Heither, T., *Translatio Religionis: Die Paulusdeutung des Origenes in seinem Kommentar zum Römerbrief* (Cologne, Böhlau, 1990).

Hengel, Martin, *Judaism and Hellenism: Studies in their Encounter in Palestine during the Early Hellenistic Period*, 2 vols. (ET, London, SCM Press, 1974 (1969)).

Herford, Travers, *Christianity in Talmud and Midrash* (London, Williams and Norgate, 1903).

Hirshman, M., *A Rivalry of Genius* (New York, SUNY Press, 1996).

Hodgson, R., 'The Testimony Hypothesis', *Journal of Biblical Literature* 98 (1979), 361–78.

Horbury, William, *Jews and Christians in Contact and Controversy* (Edinburgh, T&T Clark, 1998).

Horbury, William, Davies, W. D. and Sturdy, John, *Judaism. Vol 3 The Early Roman Period* (Cambridge, Cambridge University Press, 1999).

Horner, Timothy J., *Listening to Trypho: Justin Martyr's Dialogue Reconsidered* (Leuven, Peeters, 2001).

Horsley, Richard and Tiller, Patrick, 'Ben Sira and the Sociology of the Second Temple', in Davies, Philip and Halligan, John (eds), *Second Temple Studies* III (Sheffield, Sheffield Academic Press, 2002).

Hurtado, Larry, W., *One God, One Lord: Early Christian Devotion and Ancient Jewish Monotheism* (Edinburgh, T&T Clark, 1988).

Instone-Brewer, David, 'The Eighteen Benedictions and the Minim before 70 CE', *Journal of Theological Studies* 54 (2003), 25–44.

Janowitz, Naomi, *Magic in the Roman World: Pagans, Jews and Christians* (London, Routledge, 2001).

Jones, F. S., *An Ancient Jewish Christian Source on the History of Christianity: Pseudo Clementine Recognitions 1.27–71* (SBL Texts and Translations 37) (Atlanta, Scholars Press, 1995).

'The Pseudo Clementines: A History of Research', *The Second Century* 2 (1982), 1–33, 63–96.

Juster, J., *Les juifs dans l'empire romain* (2 vols., Paris, Geuthner, 1914).

Kalimi, Isaac, *Early Jewish Exegesis and Theological Controversy: Studies in Scriptures in the Shadow of Internal and External Controversies* (Assen, Royal Van Gorcum, 2002).

Kamesar, A., *Jerome, Greek Scholarship, and the Hebrew Bible: A Study of the Quaestiones Hebraicae in Genesim* (Oxford Classical Monographs) (New York, Clarendon Press, 1993).

Kimelman, R., 'Birkat Ha-Minim and the Lack of Evidence for an Anti-Christian Jewish Prayer', in Sanders, E. P., Baumgarten, A. I. and Mendelson, A. (eds), *Jewish and Christian Self-Definition*, vol. 2 (Aspects of Judaism in the Graeco-Roman Period) (Philadelphia, Fortress Press; London, SCM Press, 1981), 226–44.

'The Literary Structure of the Amidah and the Rhetoric of Redemption', in Dever, William G. and Wright, J. Edward (eds), *The Echoes of Many Texts: Reflection on Jewish and Christian Traditions, Essays in Honor of Lou H. Silberman* (Brown Judaic Studies 313) (Atlanta, Scholars Press, 1997).

Klappert, Bertold, 'Die Trinitätslehre als Auslegung des NAMENs des Gottes Israels. Die Bedeutung des Alten Testaments und des Judentums für die Trinitätslehre', *Evangelische Theologie* 62 (2002), 54–72.

Klauck, Hans-Joachim, *Apocryphe Evangelien* (Stuttgart, Katholisches Bibelwek, 2002).

Klijn, A. F. J. and Reinink, G. J., *Patristic Evidence for Jewish–Christian Relations* (Leiden, Brill, 1973).

Kofsky, Aryeh, *Eusebius of Caesarea against Paganism* (Jewish and Christian Perspectives Series 3) (Leiden, Brill, 2000).

Krauss, S. and Horbury, W., *The Jewish–Christian Controversy from the Earliest Times to 1789. Volume 1 History* (Tübingen, J. C. B. Mohr (Paul Siebeck), 1996).

Kugel, James and Greer, Rowen, *Early Biblical Interpretation* (Philadelphia, Westminster Press, 1986).

Lander, Gerhart B., *The Idea of Reform: Its Impact on Christian Thought and Action in the Age of the Fathers* (New York, Harper and Row, 1967).

Langer, Ruth, 'Early Rabbinic Liturgy in its Palestinian Milieu: Did Non-Rabbis Know the 'Amidah?' in Harrington, Daniel, Avery-Peck, Alan J. and Neusner, Jacob (eds), *When Judaism and Christianity Began: Essays in Memory of Anthony J. Saldarini* (Leiden, E. J. Brill, 2003).

Lash, Archimandrite, *Ephrem, St Romanos the Melodist: Kontakia on the Life of Christ* (London, Harper Collins, 1995).

Levine, Lee I. and Weiss, Zeev (eds), *From Dura to Sepphoris: Studies in Jewish Art and Society in Late Antiquity* (Portsmouth, RI, Journal of Roman Archaeology, 2000).

Lewis, J. P., 'What Do we Mean by Jabneh?', *Journal of Bible and Religion* 32 (1964), 125–32.

Lichtenberger, H., Lange, A. and Römheld, K. F. D. (eds), *Die Dämonen/Demons: Die Dämonologie der israelitisch-jüdischen und frühchristlichen Literatur im Kontext ihrer Umwelt/The Demonology of Israelite-Jewish and Early Christian Literature in Context of their Environment* (Tübingen, Mohr Siebeck 2003).

Lieu, J., *Image and Reality: The Jews and the World of Christianity in the Second Century* (Edinburgh, T&T Clark, 1996).

Lieu, J., North, J. and Rajak, T. (eds.), *The Jews among Pagans and Christians in the Roman Empire* (London, Routledge, 1992).

Lim, Timothy H., *Holy Scripture in the Qumran Commentaries and Pauline Letters* (Oxford, Clarendon Press, 1997).

Limor, Ora and Stroumsa, Guy G., *Contra Iudaeos: Ancient and Medieval Polemics between Christians and Jews* (Texts and Studies in Medieval and Early Modern Judaism 10) (Tübingen, Mohr, 1996).

Linder, A., *The Jews in Roman Imperial Legislation* (Detroit, Wayne State University Press; Jerusalem, Israel Academy of Sciences and Humanities, 1987).

Lorenz, Rudolf, *Arius Judaizans? Untersuchungen zur dogmengeschichtlichen Einordnung des Arius* (Forschungen zur Kirchen- und Dogmengeschichte 31) (Göttingen, Vandenhoeck & Ruprecht, 1980).

Lucas, L., *Zur Geschichte der Juden im vierten Jahrhundert* (Berlin, Mayer & Muller, 1910; repr. Hildesheim, Olms, 1985). English trans. *The Conflict between Judaism and Christianity: A Contribution to the History of the Jews in the Fourth Century* (Warminster, Aris & Phillips, 1993).

Lüdemann, G., *Opposition to Paul in Jewish Christianity* (Minneapolis, Fortress Press 1989).

MacLennan, Robert S., *Early Christian Texts on Jews and Judaism* (Atlanta, Scholars Press, 1990).

Maier, J., *Jesus von Nazareth in der talmudischen Überlieferung* (Darmstadt, Wissenschaftliche Buchgesellschaft, 1978).

Martin, Vincent, *A House Divided: The Parting of the Ways between Synagogue and Church* (New York, Paulist Press, 1995).

Mason, S., *Josephus and the New Testament* (Peabody, MA, Hendrickson, 1992).

McDonough, Sean M., *YHWH at Patmos: Rev. 1:4 in its Hellenistic and Early Jewish Setting* (Wissenschaftliche Untersuchungen zum Neuen Testament 107) (Tübingen, Mohr Siebeck, 1999).

McGowan, Andrew, *Ascetic Eucharists: Food and Drink in Early Christian Ritual Meals* (Oxford, Oxford University Press, 1999).

McGuckin, John A., *St Cyril of Alexandria: The Christological Controversy, its History, Theology, and Texts* (Leiden, Brill, 1994).

McKinnon, J., *Music in Early Christian Literature* (Cambridge, Cambridge University Press, 1987).

McVey, Kathleen, *Ephrem the Syrian: Hymns* (New York, Paulist Press, 1989).

Meeks, R. A. and Wilken, R. L., *Jews and Christians in Antioch in the First Four Centuries of the Common Era* (Missoula, MT, Scholars Press, 1978).

Mendels, Doron, 'The Relationship of Christians and Jews during the Years 300–450: A Preliminary Report of the Christian Point of View', in Kinzig, Wolfram and Kück, Cornelia (eds), *Judentum und Christentum zwischen Konfrontation und Faszination: Ansätze zu einer neuen*

Beschreibung jüdisch-christlicher Beziehungen (Judentum und Christentum 11) (Stuttgart, Kohlhammer, 2002), 45–54.

Mimouni, Claude, *Le judéo-christianisme ancien: Essais historiques* (Paris, Cerf, 1998).

Minns, Denis, *Irenaeus* (London, Geoffrey Chapman, 1994).

Momigliano, A. (ed.), *The Conflict between Paganism and Christianity in the Fourth Century* (Oxford, Oxford University Press, 1963).

Murphy-O'Connor, Jerome and Charlesworth, James H., *Paul and the Dead Sea Scrolls* (New York, Crossroad, 1990).

Negev, A., 'The Inscription of the Emperor Julian at Ma'ayan Barukh', *Israel Exploration Journal* 19 (1969), 170–3.

Neufeld, Vernon H., *The Earliest Christian Confessions* (Grand Rapids, Eerdmans, 1963).

Neuhaus, Dietrich, 'Ist das trinitarische und christologische Dogma in der alten Kirche antijudaistisch?', in Mertin, Jörg (ed.), *'Mit unserer Macht ist nichts getan . . .': Festschrift für Dieter Schellong zum 65. Geburtstag* (Arnoldshainer Texte 80) (Frankfurt am Main, Haag und Herchen, 1993), 257–72.

Neusner, J., *Aphrahat and Judaism: The Christian–Jewish Argument in Fourth-Century Iran* (Studia Post-Biblica 19) (Leiden, Brill, 1971).

Jews and Christians: The Myth of a Common Tradition (London, SCM Press, 1991).

Judaism and Christianity in the Age of Constantine (Chicago, University of Chicago Press, 1987).

The Rabbinic Traditions about the Pharisees before 70, vol I: The Masters (Leiden, E. J. Brill, 1971).

Niederwimmer, Kurt, *The Didache* (Minneapolis, Fortress Press, 1998).

Nock, A. D., *Conversion* (Oxford, Oxford University Press, 1961).

Noethlichs, Karl Leo, *Die Juden im christlichen Imperium Romanum (4.–6. Jahrhundert)* (Studienbücher Geschichte und Kultur der Alten Welt) (Berlin, Akademie-Verlag, 2001).

Nordström, Carl-Otto, 'Rabbinic Features in Byzantine and Catalan Art', *Cahiers archéologiques* 15 (1965), 179–205.

Oegema, Gerben S., *The Anointed and his People: Messianic Expectations from the Maccabees to Bar Kochba* (Sheffield, JSOT Press, 1998).

Orlov, Andrei, and Golitzin, Alexander, '"Many Lamps are Lightened from the One": Paradigms of the Transformational Vision of the Macarian Homilies', *Vigiliae Christianae* 55 (2001), 281–98.

Orton, David, *The Understanding Scribe* (Sheffield, JSOT Press, 1989).

Parkes, James W., *Conflict of the Church and Synagogue* (New York, Hermon Press, reprint 1974 (1934)).

Parmentier, Martin, 'Greek Church Fathers on Romans 9', *Bijdragen* 50 (1989), 139–54; 51 (1990), 2–30.

Patout Burns Jr, J., *Cyprian the Bishop* (London, Routledge, 2001).

Pearson, Birger, *Gnosticism, Judaism, and Egyptian Christianity* (Minneapolis, Fortress Press, 1990).

Petersen, William L., 'Eusebius and the Paschal Controversy', in Attridge, H. and Hata, G. (eds), *Eusebius, Christianity, and Judaism* (Detroit, Wayne State university Press, 1992), 311–25.

Petrement, Simone, *A Separate God: The Christian Origins of Gnosticism*, trans. Harrison, Carol (San Francisco, HarperSanFrancisco, 1984).

Piétri, Charles and Piétri, Luce (eds), *Histoire du christianisme: Des origines à nos jours, vol. II: Naissance d'une chrétienté (250–430)* (Paris, Desclée-Fayard, 1995); revised German trans., *Das Entstehen der einen Christenheit (250–430)* (Die Geschichte des Christentums I) (Freiburg, Herder, 1996).

Piétri, Luce (ed.), *Des origines à nos jours, vol. I: Le nouveau peuple (des origines à 250)* (Histoire du christianisme) (Paris, Desclée-Fayard, 2000).

Pilhofer, P., *Presbyteron kreitton* (Tübingen, Mohr, 1990).

Plotkin, Albert, *Sacred Roots: Commonalities Expressed by the Early Church and Synagogue* (Phoenix, Fogfree, 2002).

Pouderon, B. and Doré, J. (eds), *Les apologistes chrétiens et la culture grecque* (Paris, Beauchesne Editeur, 1998).

Prigent, Pierre, *Les testimonia dans le christianisme primitif* (Paris, Gabalda, 1961).

Pritz, Ray A., *Nazarene Jewish Christianity* (Leiden, Brill, 1988).

Rajak, T., 'Jews and Greeks: The Invention and Exploitation of Polarities in the Nineteenth Century', in Biddiss, M. and Wyke, M. (eds), *The Uses and Abuses of Antiquity* (Bern, P. Lang, 1999).

Josephus: The Historian and his Society (London, Duckworth, 2nd edn, 2002).

Reif, Stefan C., *Judaism and Hebrew Prayer: New Perspectives on Jewish Liturgical History* (Cambridge, Cambridge University Press, 1993).

Reitemeyer, Michael, *Weisheitslehre als Gotteslob: Psalmentheologie im Buch Jesus Sirach* (Berlin, Philo, 2000).

Reynolds, Joyce and Tannenbaum, Robert, *Jews and God-Fearers at Aphrodisias: Greek Inscriptions with Commentary: Texts from the Excavations at Aphrodisias* (Cambridge, Cambridge Philological Society, 1987).

Ritter, Adolf Martin, 'Trinität, I. Alte Kirche', in *Theologische Realenzyklopädie* 34 (2002), 91–99.

Rives J. B., *Religion and Authority in Roman Carthage* (Oxford, Clarendon Press, 1995).

Rokeah, D., *Jews, Pagans and Christians in Conflict* (Leiden, Brill, 1982).

Rubenstein, Jeffrey L., *The History of Sukkot in the Second Temple and Rabbinic Periods* (Atlanta, Scholars Press, 1995).

Rubenstein, Richard E., *When Jesus Became God: The Epic Fight over Christ's Divinity in the Last Days of Rome* (New York, Harcourt Brace & Company, 1999).

Rudolph, Kurt, *Gnosis: The Nature and History of Gnosticsim*, trans. Wilson, R. (Edinburgh, T&T Clark, 1983).

Ruether, Rosemary, *Faith and Fratricide: The Theological Roots of Anti-Semitism* (Minneapolis, Seabury, 1974; New York, Search Press, 1975).

'Judaism and Christianity: Two Fourth Century Religions', *Sciences Religieuses/Studies in Religion* 2 (1972), 1–10.

Runia, D. T., *Philo in Early Christian Literature: A Survey* (Assen, Van Gorcum; Minneapolis, Fortress Press, 1993).

Russell, Norman, *Cyril of Alexandria* (London, Routledge, 2000).

Sacchi, Paolo, 'From Righteousness to Justification in the period of Hellenistic Judaism', *Henoch* 23 (2002), 77–85.

Sanders, E. P., *Jewish Law from Jesus to the Mishnah* (London, SCM Press, 1990).

Judaism: Practice and Belief, 63 BCE–66 CE (London, SCM Press, 1992).

Sanders, E. P., Baumgarten, A. I., and Mendelson, A. (eds), *Jewish and Christian Self-Definition*, 3 vols. (Philadelphia, Fortress Press; London, SCM Press, 1980–2).

Sandmel, S., *Philo of Alexandria: An Introduction* (Oxford, Oxford University Press, 1979).

Sandt, Huub van de and Flusser, David, *The Didache: Its Jewish Sources and its Place in Early Judaism and Christianity* (Assen, Royal Van Gorcum, 2002).

Schäfer, Peter, *Judeophobia: Attitudes toward the Jews in the Ancient World* (Cambridge, MA, Harvard University Press, 1997).

Mirror of his Beauty: Feminine Images of God from the Bible to the Early Kabbalah (Princeton, NJ, Princeton University Press, 2002).

Schiffman, L. H., *Reclaiming the Dead Sea Scrolls* (Philadelphia, JPS, 1994).

Schreckenberg, Heinz, *Die christlichen Adversus-Judaeos-Texte und ihr literarisches und historisches Umfeld (1.–11. Jh.)* (Europäische Hochschulschriften 23/172) (Frankfurt am Main, Peter Lang, 4th edn, 1999).

Die Flavius-Josephus-Tradition in Antike und Mittelalter (Leiden, Brill, 1972).

'Josephus und die christliche Wirkungsgeschichte seines Bellum Judaicum', *Aufstieg und Niedergang der Römischen Welt* 2.21.2 (1984), 1106–217.

Schreckenberg, Heinz and Schubert, Kurt, *Jewish Historiography and Iconography in Early and Medieval Christianity* (Minneapolis, Fortress Press, 1992).

Schürer, E., *The History of the Jewish People in the Age of Jesus Christ (175 B.C.–A. D. 135)*, revised and edited by Vermes, G., Millar, F. G. B. (with Black, M. (vols. I–II) and Goodman, M. (vols. III.1–2)), 4 vols. (Edinburgh, T&T Clark, 1973–87).

Schwartz, Seth, *Imperialism and Jewish Society, 200 B.C.E. to 640 C.E. (Jews, Christians, and Muslims from the Ancient to the Modern World)* (Princeton, NJ, Princeton University Press, 2001).

Segal, Alan, *Rebecca's Children: Judaism and Christianity in the Roman World* (Cambridge, MA, Harvard University Press, 1986).

Setzer, Claudia, *Jewish Responses to Early Christians* (Minneapolis, Fortress Press, 1994).

Sevenster, J. N., *Do you Know Greek? How Much Greek Could the First Jewish Christians Have Known?* (Leiden, E. J. Brill, 1968).

Sharf, Andrew, *Byzantine Jewry: From Justinian to the Fourteenth Century* (London, Routledge and Kegan Paul, 1971).

Shanks, H. (ed.), *Christianity and Rabbinic Judaism: A Parallel History of their Origins and Early Development* (London, SPCK, 1993).

Shavit, Yaacov, *Athens in Jerusalem: Classical Antiquity and Hellenism in the Making of the Modern Secular Jew* (London, Littman Library of Jewish Civilization, 1997).

Shaw, Frank, 'The Earliest Non-mystical Jewish Use of Ιαω' (Dissertation, University of Cincinnati, 2002).

Simmons, M. B., 'Julian the Apostate', in Esler, P. F. (ed.), *The Early Christian World*, II (London, Routledge, 2000), 1251–72.

Simon, M., *Verus Israel: A Study of the Relations between Christians and Jews in the Roman Empire (AD 135–425)* (The Littman Library of Jewish Civilization) (Oxford, Oxford University Press, 1986).

Sivan, H., 'Building Marital Boundaries in the Law: Rabbis, Bishops and Emperor on Jewish–Christian Marriage in Late Antiquity', in Mathisen, R. W. and Sivan, H. (eds), *Shifting Frontiers in Late Antiquity* (Aldershot, Variorum, 1996), vol. 2.

Skarasaune, Oskar, *In the Shadow of the Temple* (Downers Grove, IL, Intervarsity Press, 2003).

Smith, J. A., 'First-Century Christian Singing and its Relationship to Contemporary Jewish Song', *Music and Letters* 75/1 (1994).

Smith, R., *Julian's Gods: Religion and Philosophy in the Thought and Action of Julian the Apostate* (London, Routledge, 1995).

Smolar, L. and Aberbach, M., 'The Golden Calf Episode in Postbiblical Literature', *Hebrew Union College Annual* 39 (1968), 91–116.

Snaith, J., 'Aphrahat and the Jews', in Emerton, J. A. and Reif, S. C. (eds), *Interpreting the Hebrew Bible: Essays in Honour of E. I. J. Rosenthal* (Cambridge, Cambridge University Press, 1982).

Sparks, H. F. D., 'Jerome as Biblical Scholar', in Ackroyd, P. R. and Evans, C. F., *The Cambridge History of the Bible, volume 1: From the Beginnings to Jerome* (Cambridge, Cambridge University Press, 1970).

Sparks, H. F. D. (ed.), *The Apocryphal Old Testament* (Oxford, Clarendon Press, 1984).

Staats, Reinhart, *Das Glaubensbekenntnis von Nizäa-Konstantinopel: Historische und theologische Grundlagen* (Darmstadt, Wissenschaftliche Buchgesellschaft, 2nd edn, 1999).

Stanton, Graham N. and Stroumsa, Guy G. (eds), *Tolerance and Intolerance in Early Judaism and Christianity* (Cambridge, Cambridge University Press, 1998).

Stemberger, Günter, *Juden und Christen im Heiligen Land: Palästina unter Konstantin und Theodosius* (Munich, Beck, 1987); English trans., *Jews and Christians in the Holy Land: Palestine in the Fourth Century* (Edinburgh, T&T Clark, 2000).

'Judenchristen', in *Reallexikon für Antike und Christentam* 19 (1999), 228–45.

Stern, S., *Calendar and Community: A History of the Jewish Calendar, 2nd cent. BCE – 10th cent. CE* (Oxford, Oxford University Press, 2001).

Stökl Ben Ezra, D., *The Impact of Yom Kippur on Early Christianity* (Tübingen, Mohr Siebeck, 2003).

Stone, Michael E. (ed.), *Jewish Writings of the Second Temple Period* (Assen, Van Gorcum, Minneapolis, Fortress Press, 1996).

Strecker, G., *Das Judenchristentum in den Pseudoklementinen* (Texte und Untersuchungen 70) (Berlin, Akademie Verla, 2nd rev. edn, 1981).

Strecker, G., and Irmscher, J., 'The Pseudo-Clementines', in Schneemelcher, W. (ed., trans. Wilson, R. McL.), *New Testament Apocrypha*, II (Cambridge, James Clark & Co.; Louisville, KY, Westminster John Knox Press, 1992), 483–541.

Stylianopoulos, Theodore, G., *Justin Martyr and the Mosaic Law* (Missoula, MT, Society of Biblical Litertaure and Scholars Press 1975).

Sullivan, J. E., *The Image of God: The Doctrine of St Augustine and its Influence* (Dubuque, The Priory, 1963).

Taylor, Joan E., *Christians and the Holy Places: The Myth of Jewish Christian Origins* (Oxford, Clarendon Press, 1993).

Taylor, Miriam, *Anti-Judaism and Early Christian Identity: A Critique of the Scholarly Consensus* (Leiden, Brill, 1995).

Thornton, T. C. G., 'Problematic Passovers – Difficulties for Diaspora Jews and Early Christians in Determining Passover Dates during the First Three Centuries AD', in Livingstone, E. A. (ed), *Studia Patristica*, 20 (Leuven, Leuven University Press, 1989), 402–8.

Treu, K., 'Die Bedeutung des Griechischen für die Juden im römischen Reich', *Kairos* 15 (1973), 123–44.

Ullendorff, E., 'Hebraic-Jewish elements in Abyssinian (Monophysite) Christianity', *Journal of Semitic Studies* 1 (1956), 216–56.

Ethiopia and the Bible (London, Oxford University Press, 1968).

Ulrich, Jörg, *Euseb von Caesarea und die Juden: Studien zur Rolle der Juden in der Theologie des Eusebius von Caesarea* (Patristische Texte und Studien 49) (Berlin, de Gruyter, 1999).

Urbach, Ephraim E., *The Sages: Their Concepts and Beliefs* (Jerusalem, Magnes Press, 1975; reprint, Cambridge, MA, Harvard University Press, 2001).

Urbainczyk, Theresa, *Theodoret of Cyrrhus: The Bishop and the Holy Man* (Ann Arbor, University of Michigan Press, 1997).

Vaggione, Richard Paul, *Eunomius of Cyzicus and the Nicene Revolution* (Oxford Early Christian Studies) (Oxford, Oxford University Press, 2000).

van Damme, D., *Pseudo Cyprian Adversus Iudaeos, gegen die Judenchristen: Die älteste lateinische Predigt, Paradosis 22* (Freiburg, Universitätsverlag, 1969).

Van der Horst, P. W. (ed.), *Hellenism – Judaism – Christianity: Essays on their Interaction* (Kampen, Kok Pharos, 1994).

van Henten, Jan Willem, *The Maccabean Martyrs as Saviours of the Jewish People: A Study of 2 and 4 Maccabees* (Leiden, Brill, 1997).

VanderKam, James C. and Adler, William (eds), *The Jewish Apocalyptic Heritage in Early Christianity* (Assen, Van Gorcum; Minneapolis, Fortress Press, 1996).

VanderKam, James and Flint, Peter, *The Meaning of the Dead Sea Scrolls* (San Francisco, HarperCollins, 2002).

Veltri, G., *Eine Tora für den König Talmai: Untersuchungen zum Übersetzungsverständnis in der jüdisch-hellenistischen und rabbinischen Literatur* (Texte und Studien zum antiken Judentum 41, (Tübingen, Mohr, 1994).

Vermes, G., *An Introduction to the Complete Dead Sea Scrolls* (London, SCM Press, 1999).

Vernet, F., 'Juifs (Controverses avec les)', in *Dictionnaire de Théologie Catholique* (Paris, 1925), vol. 82, col. 1870–914.

Visotzky, B. L., 'Prolegomenon to the Study of Jewish Christianities in Rabbinic Literature', in *Association for Jewish Studies Review* 14 (1989), 47–70.

Wainwright, P., 'The Authenticity of the Recently Discovered Letter Attributed to Cyril of Jerusalem', *Vigiliae Christianae* 40 (1986), 286–93.

Walker, P. W. L., *Holy City, Holy Places? Christian Attitudes to Jerusalem and the Holy Land in the Fourth Century* (Oxford Early Christian Studies) (Oxford, Oxford University Press, 1990).

Wegner, J. R., 'Philo's Portrayal of Women – Hebraic or Hellenic?', in Levine, A.-J. (ed.), *'Women Like This': New Perspectives on Jewish Women in the Greco-Roman World* (Atlanta, Scholars Press, 1991), 41–66.

Weitzmann, Kurt, *Studies in Classical and Byzantine Manuscript Illumination*, ed. Kessler, H. (Chicago, University of Chicago Press, 1971).

Weitzmann, Kurt and Kessler, Herbert, *The Frescoes of the Dura Synagogue and Christian Art* (Washington, DC, Dumbarton Oaks, 1990).

Werner, Eric, 'Melito of Sardis: The First Poet of Deicide', *Hebrew Union College Annual* 37 (1966), 191–210.

The Sacred Bridge: The Interdependence of Liturgy and Music in Synagogue and Church during the First Millennium (London, Dennis Dobson; New York, Columbia University Press, 1959).

Westra, Liuwe H., *The Apostles' Creed: Origin, History, and Some Early Commentaries* (Instrumenta patristica et mediaevalia 43) (Turnhout, Brepols, 2002).

Whealey, A., *Josephus on Jesus: The Testimonium Flavianum Controversy from Late Antiquity to Modern Times* (Frankfurt, Peter Lang, 2003).

White, L. Michael, *Building God's House in the Roman World: Architectural Adaptation among Pagans, Jews, and Christians* (Baltimore, The Johns Hopkins University Press, 1990).

White, S. A., 'Esther: A Feminine Model for Jewish Diaspora', in Day, P. L. (ed.), *Gender and Difference in Ancient Israel* (Minneapolis, Fortress Press, 1989), 161–77.

Wilde, R., *The Treatment of the Jews in the Greek Christian Writers of the First Three Centuries*

(Washington, DC, Catholic University of America Press, 1949).

Wiles, Maurice, *The Archetypal Heresy: Arianism through the Centuries* (Oxford, Clarendon Press, 1996).

Wilken, R. L., *The Christians as the Romans Saw Them* (New Haven, Yale University Press, 1984).

John Chrysostom and the Jews: Rhetoric and Reality in the Late Fourth Century (Berkeley, CA, University of California Press, 1983).

Judaism and the Early Christian Mind (New Haven, Yale University Press, 1971).

Wilken, Robert L. and Wayne Meeks (eds), *Jews and Christians in Antioch* (Missoula, MT, Scholars Press, 1978).

Williams, Rowan, *Arius: Heresy and Tradition* (London, SCM Press, 2nd edn, 2001).

Wills, Lawrence, 'Scribal Methods in Matthew and Mishnah Abot', *Catholic Biblical Quarterly* 63 (2001), 241–57.

Wilson, Robert R., *Genealogy and History in the Ancient World* (New Haven, Yale University Press, 1977).

Wilson, Stephen G., *Related Strangers: Jews and Christians 70–170 CE* (Minneapolis, Fortress Press, 1995).

Wilson, Stephen G. (ed.), *Anti-Judaism in Early Christianity, vol. II: Separation and Polemic* (Studies in Christianity and Judaism 2) (Waterloo, Ontario, Wilfrid Laurier University Press, 1986).

Winkelmann, Friedhelm, *Euseb von Kaisareia: Der Vater der Kirchengeschichte* (Biographien zur Kirchengeschichte) (Berlin, Verlags-Anstalt Union, 1991).

Winston, D., *Philo of Alexandria: The Contemplative Life, the Giants and Selections* (Ramsey, NJ, Paulist Press, 1981).

Wood, Diana (ed.), *Christianity and Judaism* (Studies in Church History 29) (Oxford, Blackwell, 1992).

Yadin, Y., *Bar-Kokhba: The Rediscovery of the Legendary Hero of the Second Jewish Revolt against Rome* (New York, Random House 1971).

Yarnold, E. (ed.), *Cyril of Jerusalem* (Early Church Fathers Series) (London, Routledge, 2000).

Young, Frances, *Biblical Exegesis and the Formation of Christian Culture* (Cambridge, Cambridge University Press, 1997).

The Making of the Creeds (London, SCM Press, repr. 2002 (1991)).

Zeller, Dieter (ed.), *Christentum I: Von den Anfängen bis zur Konstantinischen Wende* (Die Religionen der Menschheit 28) (Stuttgart, Kohlhammer, 2002).

Medieval, early modern and Enlightenment

Abrahams, Israel, *Jewish Life in the Middle Ages* (London, Macmillan, 1896).

Abulafia, Anna Sapir, *Jews and Christians in Twelfth-Century Renaissance* (London, Routledge, 1995).

Abulafia, Anna Sapir (ed.), *Religious Violence between Christians and Jews: Medieval Roots, Modern Perspectives* (Basingstoke, Palgrave, 2002).

Adler, I., 'Les chants synagogaux notés au XIIe siècle (ca 1103–1150) par Abdias, le prosélyte normand', *Revue de musicologie* 51/1 (1965), 19–51.

Altmann, Alexander, *Moses Mendelssohn: A Biographical Study* (University, The University of Alabama Press, 1973).

Anderson, George W., *The Legend of the Wandering Jew* (Providence, RI, Brown University Press, 1965).

Bacharach, Bernard, *Early Medieval Jewish Policy in Western Europe* (Minneapolis, University of Minnesota Press, 1977).

Baron, Salo W., 'John Calvin and the Jews', in Lieberman, Saul, Spiegel, Shalum et al. (eds), *Harry A. Wolfson Jubilee Volume* (Jerusalem; American Academy for Jewish Research, 1965); repr. in Cohen, Jeremy (ed.), *Essential Papers on Judaism and Christianity in Conflict* (New York, New York University Press, 1991).

Beck, James, 'The Anabaptists and the Jews: The Case of Hätzer, Denck and the Worms Prophets', *The Mennonite Quarterly Review* 75 (2001), 407–28.

Becker, Adam H. and Reed, Annette Y. (eds), *The Ways that Never Parted: Jews and Christians in Late Antiquity and the Early Middle Ages* (Text and Studies in Ancient Judaism 95) (Tübingen Mohr Siebeck, 2003).

Ben-Sasson, Haim Hillel, 'Jewish–Christian Disputation in the Setting of Humanism and Reformation in the German Empire', *Harvard Theological Review* 59 (1966), 369–90.

'The Reformation in Contemporary Jewish Eyes', *Proceedings of the Israel Academy of Sciences and Humanities* 4 (Jerusalem, 1971), 241–326.

Berger, David, 'The Attitude of St Bernard of Clairvaux towards the Jews', *Proceedings of the American Academy of Jewish Research* 40 (1972), 89–108.

The Jewish–Christian Debate in the High Middle Ages: A Critical Edition of the Nizzahon Vetus (Philadelphia, Jewish Publication Society, 1979).

Blumenkranz, B., *Le juif médiéval au miroir de l'art chrétien* (Paris, Etudes Augustiennes, 1966).

Juifs et chrétiens dans le monde occidental, 430–1096 (Paris, Mouton, 1960).

Bolton, Brenda, *Innocent III: Studies on Papal Authority and Pastoral Care* (Aldershot, Ashgate Variorum, 1995).

Bonfil, Robert, *Rabbis and Jewish Communities in Rennaisance Italy* (The Littman Library of Jewish Civilization) (Oxford, Oxford University Press, 1990).

Brod, M., *Johannes Reuchlin und sein Kampf: Eine historische Monographie* (Stuttgart, Kohlhammer, 1965).

Brown, Peter, *The Cult of the Saints: Its Rise and Function in Latin Christianity* (London, SCM Press, 1983).

Burnett, S. G., *From Christian Hebraism to Jewish Studies* (Leiden, Brill, 1996).

Burrell, David B., *Knowing the Unknowable God: Ibn Sina, Maimonides, Aquinas* (Notre Dame, University of Notre Dame Press, 1986).

Chazan, Robert, *Barcelona and beyond: The Disputation of 1263 and its Aftermath* (Berkeley, University of California Press, 1992).

European Jewry and the First Crusade (Berkeley, University of California Press, 1996).

In the Year 1096: The First Crusade and the Jews (Philadelphia, Jewish Publication Society, 1997).

Medieval Jewry in Northern France (Baltimore, MD, Johns Hopkins University Press, 1973).

Chazan, Robert and Neal Kozodoy (eds), *Church, State and Jew in the Middle Ages* (New York, Behrman House, 1996).

Cohen, Jeremy, *The Friars and the Jews: The Evolution of Medieval Anti-Judaism* (Ithaca, NY, Cornell University Press, 1982).

Living Letters of the Law. Ideas of the Jew in Medieval Christianity (Berkeley, University of California Press, 1999).

Cohen, Jeremy (ed.), *Essential Papers on Judaism and Christianity in Conflict: From Late Antiquity to the Reformation* (New York, New York University Press, 1991).

Cohn, Samuel K., *The Black Death Transformed: Disease and Culture in Early Renaissance Europe* (London, Arnold, 2002).

Cooper, Wilmer A., *A Living Faith: An Historical Study of Quaker Beliefs* (Richmond, IN, Friends United Press, 1990).

Cooperman, Bernard Dov (ed.), *Jewish Thought in the Sixteenth Century* (Cambridge, MA, Harvard University Press, 1983).

Dahan, Gilbert, *The Christian Polemic against the Jews in the Middle Ages* (Notre Dame, University of Notre Dame Press, 1998).

Dan, Joseph (ed.), *The Christian Kabbalah: Jewish Mystical Books and their Christian Interpreters* (Cambridge MA, Harvard College Library, 1997).

de Lange, Nicholas R. M. (ed.), *Hebrew Scholarship and the Medieval World* (Cambridge, Cambridge University Press, 2001).

Dick, John A. R. and Richardson, Anne (eds), *William Tyndale and the Law* (Sixteenth Century Essays and Studies 25) (Missouri, Sixteenth Century Journal Publishers, 1994).

Douie, Decima L., and Farmer, David H., (eds), *Magna Vita Sancti Huganis: The Life of St Hugh of Lincoln*, 2 vols. (Oxford, Clarendon Press, 1985).

Dundes, Alan (ed.), *The Blood Libel Legend: A Casebook in Anti-Semitic Folklore* (Madison, University of Wisconsin Press, 1991).

Echevarria, Ana, *The Fortress of Faith: The Attitude toward Muslims in Fifteenth Century Spain* (Leiden, E. J. Brill, 1999).

Eckardt, Alice L., 'The Reformation and the Jews', in Fisher, Eugene J. (ed.), *Interwoven Destinies: Jews and Christians through the Ages* (Mahwah, NJ, Paulist Press, 1993).

Edwards, Mark U., Jr, 'Martin Luther and the Jews: Is There a Holocaust Connection?', *Shofar* 1 (1983); and *Face to Face* 10 (1983).

Feldman, Egal, *Dual Destinies* (Urbana, University of Illinois Press, 1990).

Friedman, J., *The Most Ancient Testimony: Christian Hebraica in the Age of Renaissance Nostalgia* (Athens, Ohio University Press 1983).

Friedman, Jerome, 'Alienated Cousins: Jews and Unitarians in Sixteenth-Century Europe', *Transactions of the Unitarian Historical Society* 22/1 (1990–1), 63–76.

Friedman, Yvonne, 'An Anatomy of Antisemitism: Peter the Venerable's Letter to Louis VII, King of France (1146)', in Artzi, P. (ed.), *Bar-Ilan Studies in History* (Ramat-Gan, Bar-Ilan University Press, 1978), 87–102.

Funkenstein, Amos, 'Basic Types of Anti-Jewish Polemics in the Later Middle Ages', *Viator* 2 (1971), 373–82.

Gaon, Solomon, *The Influence of the Catholic Theologian Alfonso on the Pentateuch Commentary of Isaac Abravanel* (Hoboken, NJ, Ktav, 1993).

Garrett, Don (ed.), *The Cambridge Companion to Spinoza* (Cambridge, Cambridge University Press, 1996).

Gemeinhardt, Peter, *Die Filioque-Kontroverse zwischen Ost- und Westkirche im Frühmittelalter* (Arbeiten zur Kirchengeschichte 82) (Berlin, de Gruyter, 2002).

Gerber, Jane S., *The Jews of Spain: A History of the Sephardic Experience* (New York, Macmillan, 1992).

Gilchrist, John, 'The Perception of the Jews in Canon Law in the Period of the First Two Crusades', *Jewish History* 3 (1988), 9–24.

Ginio, Alisa Meyuhan, *De bello iudaeorum: Fray Alonso de Espina y su Fortalitium fidei* (Fontes Iudaeorum Regni Castellae 8) (Salamanca, Universidad Pontificia, 1998).

La forteresse de la foi: La vision du monde d'Alonso de Espina, moine espagnol (?–1466) (Collection Histoires-Judaisme) (Paris, Cerf, 1998).

Glaser, Edward, 'Invitation to Intolerance: A Study of the Portuguese Sermons Preached at Autos-da-fé', *Hebrew Union College Annual* 27 (1956).

Goitein, S. D., *A Mediterranean Society: An Abridgement* (Berkeley, University of California, 1999).

Goodman, M. and S., *Johann Reuchlin: On the Art of the Kabbalah* (ET, New York, Abaris, 1983).

Goshen-Gottstein, M. and Jardine, L., *From Humanism to the Humanities: Education and the Liberal Arts in Fifteenth- and Sixteenth-Century Europe* (Cambridge, MA, Harvard University Press, 1986).

Grayzel, S., *The Church and the Jews in the XIIIth Century* (New York, Hermon, 1966).

'The Papal Bull "Sicut Judeis"', in Cohen, Jeremy (ed.), *Essential Papers on Judaism and Christianity in Conflict: From Late Antiquity to the Reformation* (New York, New York University Press, 1991).

Green, Arthur, 'The Shekinah, the Virgin Mary, and the Song of Songs', *Association for Jewish Studies Review* 26 (2002), 1–52.

Gregg, J. Y., *Devils, Women, and Jews: Reflections of the Other in Medieval Sermons Stories* (Albany, SUNY Press, 1997).

Gruenwald, Ithamar, *Apocalyptic and Merkavah Mysticism* (Leiden, Brill, 1980).

Güde, Wilhelm, *Die rechtliche Stellung der Juden in den Schriften deutscher Juristen des 16. und 17. Jahrhunderts* (Sigmaringen, Jan Thorbecke Verlag, 1981).

Gutmann, Joseph, *Hebrew Manuscript Illumination* (New York, George Braziller, 1978).

Gutteridge, Richard, 'Luther and the Jews', Appendix I, *Open Thy Mouth for the Dumb!* (Oxford, Basil Blackwell, 1976).

Hall, D. D. (ed.), *The Antinomian Controversy, 1636–1638* (Middletown, CT, Wesleyan University Press, 1968).

Harrán, D., *Salamone Rossi: Jewish Musician in Late Renaissance Mantua* (Oxford, Oxford University Press, 1999).

Hasan-Rokem, Galit and Dundes, Alan (eds), *The Wandering Jew: Essays in the Interpretation of a Christian Legend* (Bloomington, Indiana University Press, 1986).

Haverkamp, Alfred (ed.), *Juden und Christen zur Zeit der Kreuzzüge* (Sigmaringen, Jan Thorbecke Verlag, 1999).

Heffernan, T. J., *Sacred Biography: Saints and their Biographies in the Middle Ages* (New York, Oxford University Press, 1988).

Heilperin, Herman, *Rashi and the Christian Scholars* (Pittsburgh, University of Pittsburgh Press, 1963).

Hertzberg, Arthur, *The French Enlightenment and the Jews* (New York, Columbia University Press, 1990).

Hood, John Y. B., *Aquinas and the Jews* (Philadelphia, University of Philadelphia Press, 1995).

Horowitz, Elliot, 'Jewish Life in the Middle Ages and the Jewish Life of Israel Abrahams', in Myers, D. and Ruderman, D. (eds), *The Jewish Past Revisited: Reflections on Modern Jewish*

Historians (New Haven, Yale University Press, 1998).

Hsia, R. Po-Chia, *The Myth of Ritual Murder: Jews and Magic in Reformation Germany* (New Haven, Yale University Press, 1988).

Idel, Moshe, 'Reflections on Kabbalah in Spain and Christian Kabbalah', *Hispanica Judaica* 2 (1999).

Iogna-Prat, Dominique, *Order and Exclusion: Cluny and Christendom Face Heresy, Judaism, and Islam 1000–1150* (Ithaca, NY, Cornell University Press, 2002), 275–322.

Jedin, Herbert, *A History of the Council of Trent* (New York, Herder, 1957–61).

Kaplan, Yosef, *From Christianity to Judaism: The Story of Isaac Orobio der Castro* (London, Littman Library of Jewish Civilization, 1989).

Kaplan, Yosef, Méchoulan, Henry and Popkin, Richard (eds), *Menasseh ben Israel and his World* (Leiden, Brill, 1989).

Katz, J., *Exclusiveness and Tolerance: Studies in Jewish–Gentile Relations in Medieval and Modern Times* (London, Oxford University Press, 1961).

Out of the Ghetto (Cambridge, MA, Harvard University Press, 1973).

Kedar, B. Z., 'Canon Law and the Burning of the Talmud', *Bulletin of Medieval Canon Law* 9 (1979), 79–82.

Kellner, Menaham M., *Dogma in Medieval Jewish Thought: From Maimonides to Abravanel* (Oxford, Oxford University Press, 1986).

Kisch, Guido, *Forschungen zur Rechts und Sozialgeschichte der Juden in Deutschland während des Mittelalter* (Stuttgart, Kohlhammer, 1955).

Jewry-Law in Medieval Germany: Laws and Court Decisions Concerning the Jews (New York, American Academy for Jewish Research, 1949).

'The Yellow Badge in History', *Historia Judaica* 4 (1942), 95–144.

Kleiner, John W., *The Attitudes of the Strasbourg Reformers toward Jews and Judaism* (Ann Arbor, University Microfilms International, 1978).

Klenicki, Leon, *Passion Plays and Judaism* (New York, ADL, 1996).

Krauss, S. and Horbury, W., *The Jewish–Christian Controversy from the Earliest Times to 1789: Volume 1 History* (Tübingen, J. C. B. Mohr (Paul Siebeck), 1996).

Kristeller, P. O., *Renaissance Thought and its Sources* (New York, Columbia University Press 1979).

Lambert, Phyllis (ed.), *Fortifications and the Synagogue* (London, Weidenfeld & Nicolson, 1994).

Laver, Mary Sweetland, *Calvin, Jews and Intra-Christian Polemic* (Ann Arbor, University Microfilms International, 1987).

Leigh, John, *The Search for Enlightenment: An Introduction to Eighteenth-Century French Writing* (London, Duckworth, 1999).

Liebes, Yehuda, *Studies in the Zohar* (Albany, SUNY Press, 1993).

Lloyd Jones, G., *The Discovery of Hebrew in Tudor England: A Third Language* (Manchester, Manchester University Press, 1983).

Lloyd Jones, G. (ed.), *Robert Wakefield: On the Three Languages [1524]* (Mediaeval and Renaissance Texts and Studies 68, Renaissance Texts Series 13), (Binghamton, NY State University 1989).

Lubac, Henri de, *The Drama of Atheist Humanism* (London, Sheed and Ward, 1949).

Maccoby, Hyam (ed.), *Judaism on Trial: Jewish–Christian Disputations in the Middle Ages* (London, Littman Library of Jewish Civilization, 1993).

Manuel, F., *The Broken Staff: Judaism through Christian Eyes* (Cambridge, MA, Harvard University Press, 1992).

Marcus, Ivan G., *Rituals of Childhood Jewish Acculturation in Medieval Europe* (New Haven, Yale University Press, 1996).

Marcus, Jacob, R., *The Jew in the Medieval World: A Source Book 315–1791* (New York, Atheneum, 1981).

Marissen, Michael, 'The Character and Sources of the Anti-Judaism in Bach's Cantata 46', *Harvard Theological Review* 96/1 (2003), 63–99.

Lutheranism, Anti-Judaism, and Bach's St John Passion (New York, Oxford University Press, 1998).

Mason, Haydn, *Voltaire: A Biography* (London, Granada Publishing, 1981).

McAuliffe, J. D., Walfish, B. D. and Goering, J. W. (eds), *With Reverence for the Word: Medieval Scriptural Exegesis in Judaism, Christianity, and Islam* (Oxford, Oxford University Press, 2002).

McCulloh, John M., 'Jewish Ritual Murder: William of Norwich, Thomas of Monmouth, and the Early

Dissemination of the Myth', *Speculum* 72 (1997), 698–740.

McGinn, Bernard, 'Cabalists and Christians: Reflections on Cabala in Medieval and Renaissance Thought', in Popkin, R. H. and Weiner, G. M. (eds), *Jewish Christians and Christian Jews* (Dordrecht, Kluwer, 1994).

McKane, William (ed.), *Selected Christian Hebraists* (Cambridge, Cambridge University Press, 1989).

McMichael, Steven J., *Was Jesus of Nazareth the Messiah? Alphonso de Espina's Argument against the Jews in the 'Fortalitium Fidei' (c.1464)* (Atlanta, Scholars Press, 1994).

McNeill, John T., *The History and Character of Calvinism* (New York, Oxford University Press, 1954).

Mellinkoff, B., 'Cain and the Jews', *Journal of Jewish Art* 6 (1979), 16–38.

Mellinkoff, Ruth, *Antisemetic Hate Signs in Hebrew Illuminated Manuscripts from Medieval Germany* (Jerusalem, Hebrew University, 1999).

The Horned Moses in Medieval Art and Thought (Berkeley, CA, University of California Press, 1970).

Outcasts: Signs of Otherness in Northern European Art of the Late Middle Ages (Berkeley, University of California Press, 1970).

Milfull, Inge, *The Hymns of the Anglo-Saxon Church* (Cambridge, Cambridge University Press, 1996).

Momigliano, Arnaldo, 'A Medieval Jewish Autobiography', in Lloyd-Jones, Hugh, Pearl, Valerie and Worden, Blair (eds), *History and Imagination: Essays in Honour of H. R. Trevor-Roper* (London, Duckworth, 1981), 30–36.

Mormando, Franco, *The Preacher's Demons: Bernardino of Siena and the Social Underworld of Early Renaissance Italy* (Chicago, University of Chicago Press, 1999).

Morray-Jones, C. R. A., 'Transformational Mysticism in the Apocalyptic-Merkabah Tradition', *Journal of Jewish Studies* 43 (1992), 1–31.

Murry, William. R., 'Religious Humanism', in *The Journal of Liberal Religion: An Online Theological Journal Devoted to the Study of Liberal Religion*, 1/2 (Spring 2000).

Nadler, Steven, *M. Spinoza: A Life* (Cambridge, Cambridge University Press, 1999).

Noonan, John T., Jr, *The Scholastic Analysis of Usury* (Cambridge, MA, Harvard University Press, 1957).

Oberdorfer, Bernd, *Filioque: Geschichte und Theologie eines ökumenischen Problems* (Forschungen zur systematischen und ökumenischen Theologie 96) (Göttingen, Vandenhoeck & Ruprecht, 2001).

Oberman, Heiko A., *The Roots of Antisemitism: In the Age of Renaissance and Reformation,* trans. Porter, James I. (Philadelphia, Fortress Press, 1984).

'Three Sixteenth Century Attitudes to Judaism: Reuchlin, Erasmus, and Luther', in Cooperman, Bernard Dov (ed.), *Jewish Thought in the Sixteenth Century* (Cambridge, MA, Harvard University Press, 1983).

Overfield, T. M., *Humanism and Scholasticism in Late Mediaeval Germany* (Princeton, NJ, Princeton University Press, 1984).

Pakter, Walter, *Medieval Canon Law and the Jews* (Ebelsbach, Verlag Rolf Gremer, 1988).

Pauck, Wilhelm, *The Heritage of the Reformation* (Glencoe, The Free Press, 1961).

Pelikan, Jaroslav, *Bach among the Theologians* (Philadelphia, Fortress Press, 1986).

Popkin, Richard H. and Singer, Michael A. (eds), *Spinoza's Earliest Publication?: The Hebrew Translation of Margaret Fell's 'A Loving Salutation to the Seed of Abraham among the Jews, Wherever they are Scattered up and down upon the Face of the Earth'* (Assen, Van Gorcum, 1987).

Popper, W., *The Censorship of Hebrew Books* (New York, Knickerbocker Press, 1899).

Rack, Henry D., *Reasonable Enthusiast: John Wesley and the Rise of Methodism* (London, Epworth Press, 1992).

Reichardt, Klaus Dieter, 'Die Judengesetzgebung im Codex Theodosianus', *Kairos* 20 (1978), 16–39.

Reif, Stefan C., *A Jewish Archive from Old Cairo* (Richmond, Surrey, Curzon, 2000).

Reites, James, 'St Ignatius of Loyola and the Jews', *Studies in the Spirituality of Jesuits* 13/4 (1981).

Rice, E. F., Jr, *Saint Jerome in the Renaissance* (Baltimore, MD, Johns Hopkins University Press, 1985).

Riley-Smith, Jonathan, *The First Crusade and the Idea of Crusading* (London, Athlone Press, 1986).

Robinson, Jack Hughes, *John Calvin and the Jews* (Ann Arbor, University Microfilms International, 1991).

Roth, Cecil, *A Life of Menasseh ben Israel* (Philadelphia, Jewish Publication Society, 1934).

Roth, Norman, *Conversos, Inquisition and the Expulsion of the Jews from Spain* (Madison, The University of Wisconsin Press, 2002).

Rubin, Miri, *Gentile Tales: The Narrative Assault on Late Medieval Jews* (New Haven, CT, Yale University Press, 1999).

Rupp, Gordon, 'Martin Luther and the Jews' (London, Council of Christians and Jews (pamphlet), 1972).

Saperstein, Marc, 'Christianity, Christians, and "New Christians" in the Sermons of Saul Levi Morteira', *Hebrew Union College Annual* 70–71 (1999–2000), 329–84.

Moments of Crisis in Jewish–Christian Relations (London, SCM Press; Philadelphia, Trinity Press, 1989).

Decoding the Rabbis: A Thirteenth Century Commentary on the Aggadah (Cambridge, MA, Harvard University Press, 1980).

Jewish Preaching 1200–1800 (New Haven, Yale University Press, 1989).

Scholem, Gershom, *Major Trends in Jewish Mysticism* (London, Thames & Hudson, 1955).

On the Mystical Shape of the Godhead: Basic Concepts in Kabbalah (New York, Shocken, 1991).

Schoot, Henk J. M. (ed.), *Tibi soli peccavi: Thomas Aquinas on Guilt and Forgiveness* (Leuven, Peeters, 1996).

Schreckenberg, H., *Die christlichen Adversus-Judaeos-Texte und ihr literarisches und historisches Umfeld (1.–11.Jh.)* (Frankfurt am Main, Peter Lang, reprinted with Addenda and Corrigenda, 1990 (1982)).

The Jews in Christian Art: An Illustrated History (New York, Continuum, 1996).

Secret, F., *Les kabbalistes chrétiens de la renaissance* (Paris, Dunod, 1964).

Seiferth, Wolfgang, *Synagogue and Church in the Middle Ages: Two Symbols in Art and Literature* (New York, Frederick Ungar, 1970).

Shapiro, James, *Oberammergau: The Troubling Story of the World's Most Famous Passion Play* (New York, Pantheon Books, 2000).

Shapiro, James, *Shakespeare and the Jews* (Columbia, Columbia University Press, 1996).

Shatzmiller, Joseph, *Shylock Re-considered: Jews, Moneylending and Medieval Society* (Berkeley, University of California Press, 1990).

Sherman, Franklin, *Luther and the Jews: A Fateful Legacy* (Allentown, PA, IJCU; Baltimore, ICJS, 1995).

Sherman, J., *The Jewish Pope: Myth, Diaspora and Yiddish Literature* (Oxford, European Humanities Research Centre, 2003).

Signer, Michael and Van Engen, John, *Jews and Christians in 12th Century Europe* (Notre Dame, University of Notre Dame Press).

Simonsohn, S., *The Apostolic See and the Jews*, 8 vols (Toronto, Pontifical Institute of Medieval Studies, 1988–91).

Smalley, Beryl, *The Study of the Bible in the Middle Ages* (New York, Philosophical Library, 1952; Notre Dame, University of Notre Dame Press, 1964).

Sonne, I., *Expurgation of Hebrew Books – the Work of Jewish Scholars: A Contribution to the History of Hebrew Books in Italy in the Sixteenth Century* (New York, New York Public Library, 1943).

Southern, R. W., *Saint Anselm: A Portrait in a Landscape* (Cambridge, Cambridge University Press, 1991).

Steinmetz, David C., *Reformers in the Wings* (Philadelphia, Fortress Press, 1971).

Stow, Kenneth R., *Alienated Minority: The Jews of Medieval Latin Europe* (Cambridge, MA, Harvard University Press, 1992).

Catholic Thought and Papal Jewry Policy, 1555–1593 (New York, Jewish Theological Seminary of America, 1977).

Synan, Edward A., *The Popes and the Jews in the Middle Ages* (New York, Macmillan, 1965).

Tabraham, B., *The Making of Methodism* (London, Epworth Press, 1996).

Taitz, Emily, 'Jewish–Christian Relations in the Middle Ages: The Underside of a Shared Culture', in Ginor, Zvia (ed.), *Yakar Le'Mordecai: Jubilee Volume in Honour of Rabbi Mordecai Waxman* (Hoboken, NJ, Ktav, 1998), 189–201.

Talmage, Frank, *David Kimhi: The Man and the Commentaries* (Cambridge, MA, Harvard University Press, 1975).

'R. David Kimhi as Polemicist', *Hebrew Union College Annual* 38 (1967), 213–35.

Talmage, Frank (ed.), *From Disputation to Dialogue* (New York, Ktav, 1975).

Tierney, Brian, *Origins of Papal Infallibility, 1150–1350: A Study of the Concepts of Infallibility, Sovereignty and Tradition in the Middle Ages* (Leiden, Brill, 1997).

Toaff, Ariel, *Love, Work and Death: Jewish Life in Medieval Umbria* (London, Littman Library of Jewish Civilization, 1998).

Trachtenberg, Joshua, *The Devil and the Jews* (New Haven, Yale University Press, 1943).

Ware, K., 'Christian Theology in the East 600–1453', in Cunliffe-Jones, H. (ed.), *History of Christian Doctrine* (Edinburgh, T&T Clark, 1978).

Watts, Michael R., *The Dissenters*, 2 vols (Oxford, Clarendon Press, 1978 and 1995).

Weinberg, J., 'The Quest for Philo in Sixteenth-Century Jewish Historiography', in Rapaport-Albert, A. and Zipperstein, Steven J. (eds), *Jewish History: Essays in Honour of Chimen Abramsky* (London, P. Halban, 1988), 163–87.

Williams, L., *Adversus Judaeos: A Bird's-Eye View of Christian Apology until the Renaissance* (Cambridge, Cambridge University Press, 1935).

Wirszubski, Chaim, *Pico della Mirandola's Encounter with Jewish Mysticism* (Cambridge, MA, Harvard University Press, 1989).

Wolfson, Elliot R., 'The Tree that Is All: Jewish–Christian Roots of a Kabbalistic Symbol in Sefer ha-Bahir', *Jewish Thought and Philosophy* 3 (1993), 31–76.

Modern

Adenauer, K., *Memoirs: 1945–1953*, trans. von Oppen, Beate Ruhm (London, Weidenfeld & Nicolson, 1966).

Aitken, James K. and Kessler, Edward (eds), 'Christianity in Jewish Terms: Dabru Emet and its Significance', in *Challenges in Jewish–Christian Relations* (New York, Paulist Press, 2006).

Alberigo, Giuseppe (ed.), *History of Vatican II*, vol. 3 (English version ed. Komonchak, Joseph A.) (Maryknoll, NY, Orbis, 2000).

Almond, Gabriel A., Appleby, R. Scott and Sivan, Emmanuel, *Strong Religion: The Rise of Fundamentalism around the World* (Chicago, The University of Chicago Press, 2003).

Andrews, James F. (ed.), *Paul VI: Critical Appraisals* (New York, Bruce Publishing Company, 1970).

Arkush, Allan, *Moses Mendelssohn and the Enlightenment* (Albany, SUNY Press, 1994).

Aronsfeld, C. C., 'Jews and Christians in England', *Midstream* 39.8 (November 1993), 16–18.

Avineri, Shlomo, *The Making of Modern Zionism: The Intellectual Origins of the Jewish State* (New York, Basic Books, 1981).

Baldwin, James, 'Negroes Are Anti-Semitic because they are Anti-White', in *The Price of the Ticket: Collected Non-Fiction, 1948–1985* (New York, St Martins, 1985).

Balthasar, Hans Urs von, *Einsame Zwiesprache: Martin Buber und das Christentum* (Köln-Olten, Verlag Jakob Hegner, 1958; Einsiedeln, Johannesverlag, 1993).

Banki, Judith Hershcopf, 'The Church and the Jews: The Struggle at Vatican Council II', in Fine, M. and Himmelfarb, M. (eds), *American Jewish Yearbook* (New York, Jewish Publication Society, 1966).

Bar, Haviva and Eady, Elias (eds), *Interaction between Catholics and Protestants from Northern Ireland at Neve Shalom* (Jerusalem, Israel Institute of Applied Social Research, 1987).

Barkun, Michael, 'From British-Israelism to Christian Identity: The Evolution of White Supremacist Doctrine', *Syzygy: Journal of Alternative Religion and Culture* 1 (1992), 55–61.

Barnett, Victoria J., *Bystanders: Conscience and Complicity during the Holocaust* (Westport, CT, Praeger Publishers, 1999).

Bartoszewski, W. T., *The Convent at Auschwitz* (London, The Bowerdean Press, 1989).

Bartov, O., *Murder in our Midst: The Holocaust, Industrial Killing, and Representation* (Oxford, Oxford University Press, 1996).

Bar-Yosef, Hamutal, 'Jewish–Christian Relations in Modern Hebrew and Yiddish Literature: A Preliminary Sketch', in Kessler, E. and Wright, M. (eds), *Themes in Jewish–Christian Relations* (Cambridge, Orchard Academic, 2004), 109–50.

'The Jewish Reception of Vladimir Solov'ëv', in van den Bercken, Vil, de Courten, Manon and van der Zweerde, Evert (eds), *Vladimir Solov'ëv: Reconciler and Polemicist* (Leuven, Peeters, 2000).

'Sophiology and the Concept of Femininity in Russian Symbolism and in modern Hebrew

Poetry', *Journal of Modern Jewish Studies* 2/1 (2003), 59–78.

Bauer, Yehudah (ed.), *Remembering for the Future*, 3 vols (Oxford, Pergamon Press, 1989).

Bauman, Zygmunt, *Modernity and the Holocaust* (Cambridge, Polity Press, 1991).

Bea, Augustin, *The Church and the Jewish People: A Commentary on the Second Vatican Council's Declaration on the Relation of the Church to Non-Christian Religions* (London, Geoffrey Chapman, 1966).

Begin, Menachem, *The Revolt* (London, W. H. Allen, 1979).

Bell, G. K. A., *Christianity and World Order* (Harmondsworth, Penguin, 1940).

Beller, Steven, *Vienna and the Jews 1867–1938: A Cultural History* (Cambridge, Cambridge University Press, 1989).

Bentley, J., *Secrets of Mount Sinai: The Story of the Finding of the World's Oldest Bible – Codex Sinaiticus* (London, Orbis, 1985).

Berdyaev, Nicholas, *Christianity and Anti-Semitism*, trans. Spears, A. A. and Kanter, V. B. (New York, Philosophical Library, 1954).

Berenbaum, Michael (ed.), *Witness to the Holocaust* (New York, HarperCollins, 1997).

Bergen, Doris L., *Twisted Cross: The German Christian Movement in the Third Reich* (Chapel Hill, University of North Carolina Press, 1996).

Berman, Paul (ed.), *Blacks and Jews: Alliances and Arguments* (New York, Delacorte Press, 1994).

Berry, Donald L., *Mutuality: The Vision of Martin Buber* (Albany, State University of New York Press, 1985).

Bethge, Eberhard, *Dietrich Bonhoeffer: A Biography*, (Minneapolis, Fortress Press, rev. edn, 2000).

Birnbaum, P. and Katznelson, I. (eds), *Paths of Emancipation: Jews, States and Citizenship* (Princeton, NJ, Princeton University Press, 1995).

Biser, Eugen, *Buber für Christen: Eine Herausforderung* (Freiburg, Herder Verlag, 1988).

Blaich, Roland, 'Selling Nazi Germany Abroad: The Case of Hulda Jost', *Journal of Church and State* 35/4 (Autumn 1993), 807–30.

Bleich, J. D., *Contemporary Halakhic Problems*, vol. 1 (New York, Ktav, 1977).

Blet, Pierre, *Pius XII and the Second World War According to the Archives of the Vatican* (Mahwah, NJ, Paulist Press, 1999).

Böckenförde, Ernts-Wolfgang and Shils, Edward, *Jews and Christians in a Pluralistic World* (London, Weidenfeld & Nicolson, 1991).

Boys, Mary C., 'The Sisters of Sion: From a Conversionist Stance to a Dialogical Way of Life', *Journal of Ecumenical Studies* 31/1–2 (1994), 27–48.

Bradshaw, Paul, F. and Hoffman, Lawrence, *The Changing Face of Jewish and Christian Worship in North America* (Notre Dame, University of Notre Dame Press, 1991).

Braybrooke, M., *Children of One God: A History of the Council of Christians and Jews* (London, Vallentine, Mitchell, 1991).

'The Impact of the Holocaust on the Church of England', in Roth, John K and Maxwell, Elisabeth (eds), *Remembering for the Future, The Holocaust in an Age of Genocide* (Basingstoke, Palgrave, 2001), vol. 2, 544–60.

Brenner, R. F., *Writing as Resistance: Four Women Confronting the Holocaust. Edith Stein, Simone Weil, Anne Frank, Etty Hillesum* (University Park, Pennsylvania State University Press, 1997).

Brenton Betts, R., *Christians in the Arab East* (Athens, Lycabettus Press, 1978).

Brockway, Allan, van Buren, Paul, Rendtorff, Rolf and Schoon, Simon, *The Theology of the Churches and the Jewish People: Statements by the World Council of Churches and its Member Churches* (Geneva, WCC, 1988).

Brodkin, Karen, *How Jews Became White Folks and What that Says about Race in America* (New Brunswick, Rutgers University Press, 1998).

Burns, M., *Dreyfus: A Family Affair 1789–1945* (New York, Harper Collins, 1991).

Busch, E., *Unter dem Bogen des einen Bundes: Karl Barth und die Juden 1933–1945* (Neukirchen-Vluyn, Neukirchener Verlag, 1996).

Cahm, Eric, *The Dreyfus Affair in French Society and Politics* (London, Longman, 1994).

Cargas, H. J. (ed.), *The Unnecessary Problem of Edith Stein* (Studies in the Shoah 4) (Lanham, MD, University Press of America, 1994).

Carmelle, M., NDS, *Alphonse Ratisbonne* (Rome, Pontifical Gregorian University, 1984).

Theodore Ratisbonne (Ars, St Julien Monastic Press, 1984).

Cesarani, David, 'Seizing the Day: Why Britain Will Benefit from Holocaust Memorial Day', *Patterns of Prejudice* 34/4 (October 2000), 61–6.

Chapman, G., *The Dreyfus Trials* (London, Batsford, 1972).

Cheyette, Bryan, *Constructions of 'the Jew' in English Literature and Society: Racial Representations, 1875–1945* (Cambridge, Cambridge University Press, 1993).

Cheyette, Bryan and Marcus, Laura (eds), *Modernity, Culture and 'The Jew'* (Cambridge, Polity Press, 1998).

Cohen, Derek, 'Shylock and the Idea of the Jew', in Cohen, D. and Heller, D. (eds), *Jewish Presences in English Literature* (Montreal, McGill-Queen's University Press, 1990), 25–39.

Cohen, Derek and Heller, Deborah (eds), *Jewish Presences in English Literature* (Montreal, McGill-Queen's University Press, 1990).

Cohen, Naomi (ed.), *Essential Papers on Jewish–Christian Relations in the United States: Imagery and Reality* (New York, New York University Press, 1990).

Cooke, S., 'Beth Shalom: Re-thinking History and Memory', *Journal of Holocaust Education* 8/1 (1999), 21–41.

Cornwell, John, *Hitler's Pope: The Secret History of Pius XII* (New York, Viking, 1999).

Croner, Helga (ed.), *More Stepping Stones to Jewish–Christian Relations: An Unabridged Collection of Christian Documents 1975–1983* (Mahwah, NJ, Paulist Press, 1985).

Stepping Stones to Further Jewish–Christian Relations: An Unabridged Collection of Christian Documents [1948–1975] (London, Stimulus Books, 1977).

Cunningham, Philip A., *Education for Shalom: Religion Textbooks and the Enhancement of the Catholic and Jewish Relationship* (Collegeville, MN, The Liturgical Press, 1995).

Davies, Alan and Nevsky, Marilyn, *How Silent Were the Churches? Canadian Protestantism and the Jewish Plight during the Nazi Era* (Waterloo, Ontario, Wilfred Laurier University Press, 1997).

Davies, A. T. (ed.), *Anti-Semitism and the Christian Mind: The Crisis of Conscience after Auschwitz* (New York, Herder and Herder, 1969).

De Costa, Denise, *Anne Frank and Etty Hillesum: Inscribing Spirituality and Sexuality* (New Brunswick, NJ, Rutgers University Press, 1998).

de Lubac, Henri, *Christian Resistance to Anti-Semitism: Memories from 1940–1944* (San Francisco, Ignatius Press, 1990).

Dietrich, Donald, J., *God and Humanity at Auschwtiz: Jewish–Christian Relations and Sanctioned Murder* (New Brunswick, NJ, Transaction Publishers, 1995).

Ditmanson, Harold H. (ed.), *Stepping Stones to Further Jewish–Lutheran Relationships: Key Lutheran Statements* (Minneapolis, Augsburg, 1990).

Doosry, Y. (ed.), *Representations of Auschwitz: 50 years of Photographs, Paintings and Graphics* (Oświęcim, Auschwitz-Birkenau State Museum [for] Department of European Studies, Jagellonian University, Kraków, 1995).

Dov Kulka, Otto and Mendes-Flohr, Paul R. (eds), *Judaism and Christianity under the Impact of National Socialism* (Jerusalem, The Historical Society of Israel and the Zalman Shuzar Center for Jewish History, 1987).

Eaglestone, Robert, *Postmodernism and Holocaust Denial* (Cambridge, Icon Books, 2001).

Edelstein, Alan, *An Unacknowledged Harmony: Philo-Semitism and the Survival of European Jewry* (Contributions in Ethnic Studies 4) (Westport, CT, Greenwood Press, 1982).

Ellis, Marc H., *Unholy Alliance: Religion and Atrocity in our Time* (London, SCM Press, 1997).

Endelman, Todd M. and Kushner, Tony (eds), *Disraeli's Jewishness* (London, Vallentine Mitchell, 2002).

Erb, Reiner and Schmidt, Michael (eds), *Antisemitimus und judische Geschichte* (Berlin, Wissenschaftlicher Autorenverlag 1987).

Ericksen, Robert P., *Theologians under Hitler: Gerhard Kittel, Paul Althaus and Emanuel Hirsch* (New Haven, Yale University Press, 1988).

Ericksen, R. P. and Heschel, S. (eds), *Betrayal: German Churches and the Holocaust* (Minneapolis, Augsburg Fortress Press, 1999).

Everett, R. A., *Christianity without Antisemitism: James Parkes and the Jewish–Christian Encounter* (Oxford, Pergamon, 1993).

Feuerverger, Grace, *Oasis of Dreams* (New York, Routledge Falmer, 2001).

Fisch, Harold, *The Dual Image: A Study of the Jew in English Literature* (London, World Jewish Library, 1959).

Fisher, Eugene and Klenicki, Leon (eds), *In our Time: The Flowering of Catholic–Jewish Dialogue* (Mahwah, NJ, Paulist Press, Stimulus Books, 1990).

Spiritual Pilgrimage: Pope John Paul II on Jews and Judaism 1979–1995 (New York, Crossroad, 1995).

Fisher, Eugene J. *et al.* (eds), *Twenty Years of Jewish–Catholic Relations, 1965–1985* (Mahwah, NJ, Paulist Press, 1987).

Flannery, Austin (ed.), *Vatican Council II: The Conciliar and Post Conciliar Documents* (Northport, NY, Costello Publishing, 1975; Study Edition, 1987).

Fleischner, Eva and Phayer, Michael (eds), *Cries in the Night: Women who Challenged the Holocaust* (Kansas City, Sheed & Ward, 1997).

Frank, Anne, Frank, Otto and Pressler, Mirjam (eds); trans. Massotty, Susan, *The Diary of a Young Girl* (London, Viking, 1997).

Fredricksen, P. (ed.), *Perspectives on the Passion of the Christ* (New York, Miramax, 2004).

Friedländer, Saul, *Nazi Germany and the Jews: The Years of Persecution, 1933–1939* (New York, HarperCollins, 1997).

Friedman, Maurice, *Martin Buber's Life and Work*, 3 vols (New York, E. P. Dutton, 1981–3).

Fuchs, Gotthard and Henrix, Hans Hermann (eds.), *Zeitgewinn: Messianisches Denken nach Franz Rosenzweig* (Frankfurt, Verlag Josef Knecht, 1987).

Gannon, Thomas M. (ed.), *World Catholicism in Transition* (New York, MacMillan, 1988).

Ganz, D., 'Sholem Asch and the Jewish–Christian Idea', *Mosaic* 17 (1995), 38–48.

Gardiner, H. C., *Catholic Viewpoint on Censorship* (Garden City, NY, Hanover House, 1958; rev. 1961).

Gavron, Daniel, *The Kibbutz: Awakening from Utopia* (Lanham, MD, Rowman & Littlefield, 2000).

Gilbert, Arthur, *The Vatican Council and the Jews* (Cleveland, The World Publishing Co., 1968).

Glock, Charles, Y. and Stark, Rodney, *Christian Beliefs and Anti-Semitism* (New York, Harper, 1966).

Gopin, Marc, *Holy War, Holy Peace: How Religion Can Bring Peace to the Middle East* (New York, Oxford University Press, 2002).

Gordon, Haim and Bloch, Jochanan (eds), *Martin Buber: A Century Volume* (New York, Ktav, 1984).

Gordon, Robert S. C., *Primo Levi's Ordinary Virtues: From Testimony to Ethics* (Oxford, Oxford University Press, 2001).

Greenberg, G., 'Wartime Orthodox Jewish Thought about the Holocaust: Christian Implications', *Journal of Ecumenical Studies* 35/3–4 (1998), 483–95.

Greenberg, I., 'Cloud of Smoke, Pillar of Fire: Judaism, Christianity, and Modernity after the Holocaust', in Fleischner, E. (ed.), *Auschwitz: Beginning of a New Era? Reflections on the Holocaust* (New York, Ktav, 1977), 7–55.

'Judaism, Christianity, and Partnership after the Twentieth Century', in Frymer-Kensky, T. et al. (eds), *Christianity in Jewish Terms* (Boulder, CO, Westview Press, 2000).

'The Third Great Cycle in Jewish History', in *Perspectives* 1 (New York, National Jewish Resource Center, 1981).

Gruber, R. E., *Virtually Jewish: Reinventing Jewish Culture in Europe* (Berkeley, University of California Press, 2002).

Grümme, B., 'Ein schwieriges Verhältnis: Karl Rahner und die Juden', *Zeitschrift für katholische Theologie* 119 (1997), 265–83.

Gushee, David P., *The Righteous Gentiles of the Holocaust* (Minneapolis, Fortress Press, 1994).

Gutierres, Gustavo, *The Theology of Liberation* (Maryknoll, NY, Orbis, 1973).

Gutman, Y. and Berenbaum, M. (eds), *Anatomy of the Auschwitz Death Camp* (Bloomington, Indiana University Press published in association with the United States Holocaust Memorial Museum, Washington, DC, 1994).

Haberman, Joshua O., *Philosopher of Revelation: The Life and Thought of S. L. Steinheim* (Philadelphia, Jewish Publication Society, 1989).

Hadda, Janet, 'Christian Imagery amd Dramatic Impulse in the Poetry of Itsik Manger', *Michigan Germanic Studies* 3/2 (1977), 1–12.

Hallie, Philip, *Lest Innocent Blood Be Shed: The Story of the Village of Le Chambon and How Goodness Happened there* (New York, HarperPerennial, new edn, 1994).

Halpérin, Jean, 'Vladimir Soloviev Listens to Israel: The Christian Question', *Immanuel* 26–7 (1994), 198–210.

Halpérin, Jean and Ucko, Hans, *Worlds of Memory and Wisdom: Encounters of Jews and African Christians* (Geneva, WCC, 2005).

Hamant, Y., *Alexander Men: A Witness for Contemporary Russia*, trans. Bingham, S. (Torrance, CA, Oakwood Publications, 1995).

Harder, G. and Niemöller, W. (eds), *Die Stunde der Versuchung: Gemeinden im Kirchenkampf* (Munich, Chr. Kaiser, 1963).

Hastings, Adrian (ed.), *Modern Catholicism: Vatican II and After* (Oxford, Oxford University Press, 1991).

Haynes, Stephen B., *Holocaust Education and the Church-Related Colleges: Restoring Ruptured Traditions* (Westport, CT, Greenwood Press, 1997).

Reluctant Witnesses: Jews and the Christian Imagination (Louisville, KY, Westminster John Knox Press, 1995).

Hebblethwaite, Peter, *Paul VI: The First Modern Pope* (New York, Paulist Press, 1993).

Heilman, S., *Defenders of the Faith: Inside Ultra-Orthodox Jewry* (New York, Schocken Books, 1992).

Heller, Celia S., *On the Edge of Destruction: Jews of Poland between the Two World Wars* (New York, Schocken Books, 1980).

Henderson, J. Frank, *Liturgies of Lament* (Chicago, Liturgy Training Publications, 1994).

Henrix, Hans Hermann and Kraus, Wolfgang (eds.), *Die Kirchen und das Judentum, vol. 2: Dokumente von 1986–2000* (Paderborn, Bonifatius Verlag; Gütersloh, Gütersloher Verlagshaus, 2001).

Herbstrith, W. (ed) *Never Forget: Christian and Jewish Perspectives on Edith Stein*, trans. Batzdorff, Suzanne) (Washington, DC, ICS Publications, 1998).

Herberg, Will, *Protestant-Catholic-Jew* (New York, Anchor Books, 1960).

Herzl, Theodor, *The Jewish State* (New York, American Zionist Emergency Council, 1946).

Heschel, Susannah, *Abraham Geiger and the Jewish Jesus* (Chicago, University of Chicago Press, 1998).

'The Challenge of Modernity and Postmodernity', in Bayfield, T., Brichto, S. and Fisher, E. (eds), *He Kissed him and they Wept* (London, SCM Press, 2001).

Hoffman, Mathew, 'Us and the Cross: Russian-Jewish Intellectuals Take a Stand on the Crucifix Question', *Journal of Jewish Studies* 53/2 (Autumn 2000), 354–70.

Homolka, W., *Jewish Identity in Modern Times: Leo Baeck and German Protestantism* (Oxford, Berghahn Books, 1995).

Huck, Gabe (ed.), *A Blessing to Each Other: Cardinal Joseph Bernardin and Jewish–Catholic Dialogue* (Chicago, Liturgy Training Publications, 1996).

Hundert, G. D. (ed.), *Essential Papers on Hasidism: Origins to the Present* (New York, New York University Press, 1991).

Hussar, Bruno, *When the Cloud Lifted*, trans. Megroz, A. (Dublin, Veritas Press, 1989).

In Pursuit of Justice: Examining the Evidence of the Holocaust (Washington, DC, United States Holocaust Memorial Museum, 1997).

Irwin, Jane, *George Eliot's Daniel Deronda Notebooks* (Cambridge, Cambridge University Press, 1996).

Jacob, Walter, *Christianity through Jewish Eyes: The Quest for Common Ground* (New York, Hebrew Union College Press, 1974).

Jasper, R. C. D., *George Bell: Bishop of Chichester* (Oxford, Oxford University Press, 1967).

Jelinek, Y. A. and Blasius, R. A., 'Ben-Gurion and Adenauer im Waldorf-Astoria: Gesprächsaufzeichnungen vom israelisch-deutschen Gipfeltreffen in New York am 14. März 1960', *Vierteljahreshefte für Zeitgeschichte* 45 (1997), 309–44.

Johnson, Frank J. and Leffler, William J., *Jews and Mormons: Two Houses of Israel* (Hoboken, NJ, Ktav, 2000).

Jones, S., Kushner, T. and Pearce, S. (eds), *Cultures of Ambivalence and Contempt: Studies in Jewish–non-Jewish Relations: Essays in Honour of the Centenary of the Birth of James Parkes* (London, Vallentine Mitchell, 1998).

Katz, J., *Exclusiveness and Tolerance: Studies in Jewish–Gentile Relations in Medieval and Modern Times* (London, Oxford University Press, 1961).

Katz, S. T. (ed.), *Interpreters of Judaism in the Late Twentieth Century* (Washington, DC, B'nai B'rith Books, 1993).

Kedourie, Elie, *Nationalism* (London, Hutchinson University Library, 3rd edn, 1966).

Kennedy, Eugene C., *Cardinal Bernardin: Easing Conflict – and Battling for the Soul of American Catholicism* (Chicago, Bonus Books, 1989).

My Brother Joseph: The Spirit of a Cardinal and the Story of a Friendship (New York, St Martin's Press, 1997).

Kenny, Anthony, *Catholics, Jews and the State of Israel* (Mahwah, NJ, Paulist Press, 1993).

Keogh, Dermot, *Jews in Twentieth-Century Ireland: Refugees, Anti-Semitism and the Holocaust* (Cork, Cork University Press, 1998).

Kepel, Gilles, *La revanche de Dieu: Chrétiens, juifs et musulmans à la reconquête du monde* (Paris, Editions du Seuil, 1991).

Kepnes, Steven, Ochs, Peter and Gibbs, Robert (eds), *Reasoning after Revelation: Dialogues in Postmodern Jewish Philosophy* (Boulder, CO, Westview Press, 1998).

Kertzer, David I., *The Kidnapping of Edgardo Mortara* (New York, Vintage Books, 1997, 1998).

Unholy War: The Vatican's Role in the Rise of Modern Anti-Semitism (New York, Alfred A. Knopf, 2001; London, Macmillan, 2002).

Kessler, E., *An English Jew: The Life and Writings of Claude Montefiore* (London, Vallentine Mitchell, 1989).

Kessler, E. and Goldberg, D. (eds), *Aspects of Liberal Judaism: Essays in Honour of John D. Rayner* (London: Vallentine Mitchell, 2004).

King, Christine E., *The Nazi State and the New Religions: Five Case Studies in Non-Conformity* (New York, Edwin Mellen Press, 1982).

King, Martin Luther, Jr, *A Call to Conscience: The Landmark Speeches of Dr Martin Luther King, Jr*, ed. Carson, Clayborne, *et al.* (New York: IPM in association with Warner Books, 2001).

Klappert, B., *Israel und die Kirche: Erwägungen zur Israellehre Karl Barths* (Theologische Existenz heute 207) (Munich, Chr. Kaiser, 1980).

Klappert, Bertold and Starck, Helmut (eds), *Umkehr und Erneuerung: Erläuterungen zum Synodalbeschluß der Rheinischen Landessynode 1980 'Zur Erneuerung des Verhältnisses von Christen und Juden'* (Neukirchen-Vluyn, Neukirchener Verlag, 1980).

Klein, E., *The Battle for Auschwitz: Catholic–Jewish Relations under Strain* (London, Vallentine Mitchell, 2001).

Kling, S., *Joseph Klausner* (New York, Yoseloff, 1970).

Kornblatt Deutsch, Judith, 'Vladimir Solov'ev on Spiritual Nationhood, Russia and the Jews', *Russian Review* 56 (April 1997), 157–77.

'Solovyov's Androgynous Sophia and the Jewish Kabbalah', *Slavic Review* 50/3 (1991), 489–96.

Krajewski, S., *Poland and the Jews: Reflections of a Polish Polish [sic] Jew* (Kraków, Austeria, 2005).

Kriener, Katja and Schmidt, Johann Michael (eds), *Gottes Treue – Hoffnung von Juden und Christen: Die Auseinandersetzung um die Ergänzung des Grundartikels der Kirchenordnung der Evangelischen Kirche im Rheinland* (Neukirchen-Vluyn, Neukirchener Verlag, 1998).

Krondorfer, B., *Remembrance and Reconciliation: Encounters between Young Jews and Germans* (New Haven, CT, Yale University Press, 1995).

Kulka, O. D. and Mendes-Flohr, P. R. (eds), *Judaism and Christianity under the Impact of National Socialism* (Jerusalem, The Historical Society of Israel/The Zalman Shazar Center for Jewish History, 1987).

Landau, D., *Piety and Power: The World of Jewish Fundamentalism* (London, Secker & Warburg, 1993).

Langmuir, Gavin, *Toward a Definition of Anti-Semitism* (Berkeley, University of California Press, 1990).

Langton, D., *The Life and Thought of Claude Montefiore* (London, Vallentine Mitchell, 2001).

Lapide, P., '"Wieviel wir einander zu geben haben": Karl Rahner zum jüdisch-christlichen Dialog', *KNA Ökumenische Information* 15 (1984), 12–13.

Lapide, Pinchas E., *Three Popes and the Jews* (New York, Hawthorne Books, 1967).

Larsen, Timothy, *Friends of Religious Equality: Nonconfirmist Politics in Mid-Victorian England* (Woodbridge, Boydell Press, 1999).

Laurentin, René, *L'église et les juifs à Vatican II* (Paris, Editions Casterman, 1967).

Lavender, Abraham D., *French Huguenots: From Mediterranean Catholics to White Anglo-Saxon Protestants* (New York, Peter Lang, 1990).

Lederhendler, E., *Jewish Responses to Modernity* (New York, New York University Press, 1994).

Lerner, Michael, *Jews and Blacks: Let the Healing Begin* (New York, G. P. Putnam's Sons, 1995).

Lerner, Michael and West, Cornel, *Jews and Blacks: A Dialogue on Race, Religion and Culture in America* (New York, Plume, 1995).

Levine, Deborah J., *Teaching Christian Children about Judaism* (Chicago, Liturgy Training Publications, 1995).

Librett, Jeffrey S., *The Rhetoric of Cultural Dialogue: Jews and Germans from Moses Mendelssohn to Richard Wagner and Beyond* (Stanford, CA, University of Stanford Press, 2000).

Liedtke, R. and Wendehorst, S. (eds), *The Emancipation of Catholics, Jews and Protestants: Minorities and the Nation State in Nineteenth Century Europe* (Manchester, Manchester University Press, 1999).

Lipman, V. D., *Sir Moses Montefiore: A Symposium* (Oxford, Oxford Centre for Postgraduate Hebrew Studies, 1982).

Lipstadt, Deborah, *Denying the Holocaust: The Growing Assault on Truth and Memory* (New York, The Free Press, 1993).

Littell, F. H. and Locke, H. G. (eds), *The German Church Struggle and the Holocaust* (Detroit, Wayne State University Press, 1974).

Littell, Marcia Sachs and Gutman, Sharon Weissman (eds), *Liturgies on the Holocaust: An Interfaith Anthology* (Valley Forge, PA, Trinity Press International, new and rev. edn, 1996).

Loewe, Louis (ed.), *Diaries of Sir Moses and Lady Montefiore* (London, Jewish Historical Society of England, 1983).

Loewenstein, Andrea Freud, *Loathsome Jews and Engulfing Women: Metaphors of Projection in the Works of Wyndham Lewis, Charles Williams and Graham Greene* (New York, New York University Press, 1993).

Luz, Ehud, *Parallels Meet: Religion and Nationalism in the Early Zionist Movement, 1882–1904*, trans. Schramm, Lenn (Philadelphia, Jewish Publication Society, 1988).

Manemann, J., *'Weil es nicht nur Geschichte ist': Die Begründung der Notwendigkeit einer fragmentarischen Historiographies des Nationalsozialismus aus politisch-theologischer Sicht, Religion – Geschichte – Gesellschaft* (Fundamentaltheologische Studien 2) (Münster, Lit. Verlag, 1995).

Marquardt, F.-W., *Die Entdeckung des Judentums für die christliche Theologie: Israel im Denken Karl Barths* (Abhandlungen zum christlich-jüdischen Dialog 1) (Munich, Chr. Kaiser, 1967).

Marrus, Michael, *The Holocaust in History* (London, Weidenfeld & Nicolson, 1987).

The Nuremberg War Crimes Trial 1945–46: A Documentary History (Boston, Bedford/St Martin's, 1997).

Meister, P. (ed.), *German Literature between Faiths: Jew and Christian at Odds and in Harmony* (Frankfurt, Peter Lang, 2004).

Mejìa, Jorge Marìa, 'An Appreciation of Cardinal Willebrands' Involvement in Catholic–Jewish Relations', *Information Service* (The Pontifical Council for Promoting Christian Unity) 101 (1999).

Melber, J., *Hermann Cohen's Philosophy of Judaism* (New York, J. David, 1968).

Mendelsohn, Ezra, *On Modern Jewish Politics* (New York, Oxford University Press, 1993).

Mendes-Flohr, Paul, *Divided Passions: Jewish Intellectuals and the Experience of Modernity* (Detroit, Wayne State University Press, 1991).

Mendes-Flohr, Paul, and Reinharz, Jehuda (eds.), *The Jew in the Modern World* (New York, Oxford University Press, 1980).

Merkley, Paul C., *The Politics of Christian Zionism 1891–1948* (London, Frank Cass, 1998).

Meyer, Michael, *Response to Modernity: A History of the Reform Movement in Judaism* (Oxford, Oxford University Press, 1988).

Morgenstern, Julian, 'The Foreskin of the Heart; Ecumenism in Sholem Asch's Christian Trilogy', *Prooftexts* 8/2 (1988), 205–36.

Morgan, Michael L., *Dilemmas in Modern Jewish Thought: The Dialectics of Revelation and History* (Indianapolis, Indiana University Press, 1992).

Morley, John, *Vatican Diplomacy and the Jews during the Holocaust 1939–1943* (New York, Ktav, 1980).

Myers, David N., *Re-inventing the Jewish Past: European Jewish Intellectuals and the Zionist Return to History* (Oxford, Oxford University Press, 1995).

Myers, David N. and Ruderman, D. B., *The Jewish Past Revisited: Reflections on Modern Jewish Historians* (New Haven, CT, Yale University Press, 1998).

Naman, Ann Aresty, *The Jew in the Victorian Novel: Some Relationships between Prejudice and Art* (New York, AMS Press, 1980).

Nespoli, Isabella (ed.), *Gerhart M. Riegner* (Brussels, World Jewish Congress, 2001).

Neudecker, Reinhard, 'The Catholic Church and the Jewish People', in Latourelle, René (ed.), *Vatican II: Assessment and Perspectives: Twenty-five Years After (1962–1987)*, vol. 3 (New York, Paulist Press, 1989), 282–323.

Niemöller, M., *From U-Boat to Pulpit* (London, W. Hodge, 1936).

Niemöller, Wilhelm, *Wort und Tat im Kirchenkampf: Beiträge zur neuesten Kirchengeschichte* (Theologische Bücherei 40) (Munich, Chr. Kaiser, 1969).

O'Brien, Darcy, *The Hidden Pope: The Personal Journey of John Paul II and Jerzy Kluger* (New York, Daybreak Books, 1998).

Oesterreicher, John M., *Auschwitz, the Christian and the Council* (Montreal, Palm Publisher, 1965).
The New Encounter between Christians and Jews (New York, Philosophical Library, 1986).
The Unfinished Dialogue: Martin Buber and the Christian Way (New York, Philosophical Library, 1986).

Opsahl, Paul D. and Tanenbaum, Marc H., *Speaking of God Today: Jews and Lutherans in Conversation* (Philadelphia, Fortress Press, 1974).

Oved, Yaacov, *Distant Brothers: History of the Relations between the Bruderhof and the Kibbutz* (Ramat Efal, Yad Tabenkin, 1993).

Patruno, Nicholas, *Understanding Primo Levi* (Columbia, University of South Carolina Press, 1995).

Pelt, R. J. van and Dwork, D., *Auschwitz: 1270 to the Present* (New York, W. W. Norton, 1996).

Perlemutter, Amos, *The Life and Times of Menachem Begin* (New York, Doubleday, 1987).

Perry, M. and Schweitzer F. (eds), *Jewish–Christian Encounters over the Centuries: Symbiosis, Prejudice, Holocaust, Dialogue* (New York, Peter Lang, 1994).

Petrie, J., 'The Secular Word HOLOCAUST: Scholarly Myths, History, and 20th Century Meanings', *Journal of Genocide Research* 2/1 (2000), 31–63.

Phayer, Michael, *The Catholic Church and the Holocaust, 1930–1965* (Bloomington, Indiana University Press, 2000).

Pierard, Richard V., 'The Contribution of British-Israelism to Antisemitism within Conservative Protestantism', in Locke, Hubert G. and Littell, Marcia Sachs (eds), *Holocaust and Church Struggle: Religion, Power and the Politics of Resistance* (Lanham, MD, University Press of America, 1996), 45–68.

Poliakov, L., *The History of Anti-Semitism* (London, Elek Books, 1965, 1966; London, Routledge & Kegan Paul, 1974–5).

Prior, M. and Taylor, W. (eds), *Christians in the Holy Land* (London, World of Islam Festival Trust, 1994).

Pulzer, P., *The Rise of Political Anti-Semitism in Germany and Austria* (London, Peter Halban, 1988).

Rajak, T., 'Jews and Greeks: The Invention and Exploitation of Polarities in the Nineteenth Century', in Biddiss, M. and Wyke, M. (eds), *The Uses and Abuses of Antiquity* (Bern, P. Lang, 1999).

Ramati, Alexander, *The Assisi Underground: Priests who Rescued Jews* (New York, Stein and Day, 1978).

Rapaport, L., *Jews in Germany after the Holocaust: Memory, Identity and Jewish–German Relations* (Cambridge, Cambridge University Press, 1997).

Reinharz, Jehuda, *Chaim Weizmann: The Making of a Zionist Leader* (Oxford, Oxford University Press, 1985).

Reinharz, Jehuda and Shapira, Anita (eds), *Essential Papers on Zionism* (London, Cassell, 1996).

Rendtorff, Rolf and Henrix, Hans Hermann (eds), *Die Kirchen und das Judentum, vol. 1: Dokumente von 1945–1985* (Paderborn, Bonifatius Verlag; Gütersloh, Gütersloher Verlagshaus, 2001).

Rhodes, Anthony, *The Vatican in the Age of the Dictators 1922–1945* (New York, Holt, Rinehart, Winston, 1973).

Riegner, Gerhart M., *Ne jamais désespérer* (Paris, Cerf, 1998).

Ritter, Immanuel, *History of the Jewish Reformation* (4 volumes, Berlin, 1858).

Rittner, C. and Roth, J. K. (eds), *Memory Offended: The Auschwitz Convent Controversy* (New York, Praeger Publishers, 1991).
Pope Pius XII and the Holocaust (London, Continuum, 2002).

Rittner, C., Smith, S., and Steinfeldt, I., *The Holocaust and the Christian World* (London, Kuperard, 2000).

Roffey, J. W. (ed.), *When Jews and Christians Meet: Australian Essays Commemorating Twenty Years of Nostra Aetate* (Melbourne, Victorian Council of Churches, 1985).

Rosenstock-Huessy, Eugen (ed.), *Judaism despite Christianity: The 'Letters on Christianity and Judaism' between Eugen Rosenstock-Huessy and Franz Rosenzweig* (University, University of Alabama Press, 1969).

Roth, John K. and Berenbaum, Michael (eds), *Holocaust: Religious and Philosophical Implications* (New York, Paragon House, 1989).

Rothschild, F. (ed.), *Jewish Perspectives on Christianity* (New York, Crossroad, 1990).

Rosmovitz, Linda, *Shakespeare and the Politics of Culture in Late Victorian England* (Baltimore, MD, Johns Hopkins University Press, 1998).

Rubenstein, Richard L. and Roth, John K., *Approaches to Auschwitz: The Holocaust and its Legacy* (Louisville, Westminster John Knox Press, rev. edn, 2003).

Rubinstein, William D. and Hilary L., *Philosemitism, Admiration and Support in the English-Speaking World for Jews 1840–1939* (London, Macmillan, 1999).

Rudin, A. James, *Israel for Christians: Understanding Modern Israel* (Philadelphia, Fortress Press, 1983).

Ruether, Rosemary Radford and Ruether, Herman, *The Wrath of Jonah: The Crisis of Religious Nationalism in the Israeli–Palestinian Conflict* (Minneapolis, Fortress Press, 2002).

Rychlak, Ronald, *Hitler, the War and the Pope* (Columbus, MS, 2000).

Rynne, Xavier [Francis X. Murphy], *Vatican Council II* (Maryknoll, NY, Orbis Books, 1999).

Salamon, H., *The Hyena People: Ethiopian Jews in Christian Ethiopia* (Berkeley, University of California Press, 1999).

Sánchez, José M., *Pius XII and the Holocaust: Understanding the Controversy* (Washington, DC, Catholic University of America Press, 2002).

Schilpp, Paul Arthur and Friedman, Maurice (eds), *The Philosophy of Martin Buber* (La Salle, IL, Open Court, 1967).

Schmidt, Stjepan, *Augustin Bea: Cardinal of Unity* (New York, New City Press, 1992).

Augustin Cardinal Bea: Spiritual Profile: Notes from the Cardinal's Diary with a Commentary (Dublin, Geoffrey Chapman, 1971).

Schmied-Kowarzik, Wolfdietrich (ed.), *Der Philosoph Franz Rosenzweig (1886–1929)*, vols. 1 und 2 (Freiburg, Verlag Karl Alber, 1988).

Schneier, Marc, *Shared Dreams: Martin Luther King, Jr and the Jewish Community* (Woodstock, VT, Jewish Light Publishing, 2003).

Scholder, K., *A Requiem for Hitler and Other New Perspectives on the German Church Struggle* (London, SCM Press; Philadelphia, Trinity Press International, 1989).

Schoon, S. and Kremers, H., *Nes Ammim, ein christliches Experiment* (Neukirchen-Vluyn, Neukirchener Verlag, 1978).

Schultz, Tad, *Pope John Paul II: The Biography* (New York, Scribner, 1995).

Schulz, Winfried, *Das neue Selig- und Heiligsprechungsverfahren* (Paderborn, Bonifatius Verlag, 1988).

Schwarz, H.-P., *Adenauer – Der Aufstieg: 1876–1952* (Stuttgart, Deutsche Verlagsanstalt, 1986).

Schwarzfuchs, Simon, *Napoleon, the Jews and the Sanhedrin* (Oxford, Oxford University Press, 1984).

Shalvi, Alice (ed.), *Daniel Deronda: A Centenary Symposium* (Jerusalem, Jerusalem Academic Press, 1976).

Sherwin, Byron L. and Kasimow, Harold K. (eds), *John Paul II and Interreligious Dialogue* (New York, Orbis Books, 1999).

Shimoni, Gideon, *The Zionist Ideology* (Hanover, MA, Brandeis University Press, 1995).

Siegele-Wenschkewitz, L., 'Auseinandersetzungen mit einem Stereotyp: Die Judenfrage im Leben Martin Niemöllers', in Büttner, U. (ed.), *Die Deutschen und die Judenverfolgung im Dritten Reich, Festschrift für Werner Jochmann zum 70. Geburtstag* (Hamburger Beiträge zur Sozialgeschichte 29) (Hamburg, Christians, 1992), 239–319.

Simpson, W. W. and Weyl, R., *The Story of the International Council of Christians and Jews* (Heppenheim, ICCJ, 3rd edn, 1995).

Smith, S. D., *Making Memory: Creating Britain's First Holocaust Centre* (Newark, Quill Press, 1999).

Snyder, L., *The Dreyfus Case* (New Brunswick, NJ, Rutgers University Press, 1973).

Solomon, Norman, 'Zionism and Religion: The Transformation of an Idea', in *Annual of Rabbinic Judaism* 3 (2000), 145–74.

Sonderegger, K., *That Jesus Christ Was Born a Jew: Karl Barth's 'Doctrine of Israel'* (University Park, Pennsylvania State University Press, 1992).

Sorkin, David, *Moses Mendelssohn and the Religious Enlightenment* (London, Peter Halban, 1996).

Steigmann-Gall, Richard, *The Holy Reich: Nazi Conceptions of Christianity, 1919–1945* (Cambridge, Cambridge University Press, 2003).

Stillman, Norman A., *Sephardi Religious Responses to Modernity* (London, Harwood Academic Publishers, 1995).

Stone, Dan, 'Day of Remembrance or Day of Forgetting? Or, Why Britain Does not Need a Holocaust Memorial Day', *Patterns of Prejudice* 34/4 (October 2000), 53–9.

Tal, U., *Christians and Jews in Germany: Religion, Politics and Ideology in the Second Reich, 1870–1914* (Ithaca, NY, Cornell University Press, 1975).

'On the Study of the Holocaust and Genocide', in Marrus, M. R. (ed.), *The Nazi Holocaust: Historical Articles on the Destruction of European Jewry, Volume 1. Perspectives on the Holocaust* (Westport, CT, Meckler, 1989), 179–224.

Telford, William R., '"His blood be upon us, and our children": The Treatment of Jews and Judaism in the Christ Film', in Christianson, Eric S., Francis, Peter and Telford, William R. (eds), *Cinéma Divinité: More Explorations in Theology and Film* (London, SCM, 2005).

Temkin, Sefton, *Creating American Reform Judaism: The Life and Times of Isaac Mayer Wise* (London, The Litman Library of Jewish Civilisation, 1998).

Ucko, Hans, *People of God, Peoples of God, a Jewish–Christian Conversation in Asia* (Geneva, WCC Publications, 1996).

The People and the People of God, Minjung and Dalit Theology in Interaction with Jewish–Christian Dialogue (Münster, LIT-Verlag, 2002).

Unsworth, Tim, *I am your Brother Joseph: Cardinal Bernardin of Chicago* (New York, Crossroad/Herder & Herder, 1997).

Van Elderen, Marlin, *Introducing the World Council of Churches* (Geneva, WCC Publications, 1990).

Vital, David, *A People Apart: The Jews in Europe, 1789–1939* (Oxford, Clarendon Press, 1999).

Wagner, Richard, *Judaism in Music and Other Essays*, (trans. Ashton Ellis, William) (Lincoln, University of Nebraska Press, 1995).

Waldman, N., 'Glimpses of Jesus in Yiddish and Hebrew Literature', *Jewish Book Annual* 50 (1992), 223–39.

Wasserstein, Bernard, *Divided Jerusalem: The Struggle for the Holy City* (London, Profile Books, 2001).

Watts, Michael R., *The Dissenters*, 2 vols (Oxford, Clarendon Press, 1978 and 1995).

Weigel, George, *Witness to Hope: The Biography of Pope John Paul II* (New York, HarperCollins, 1999).

Weitzman, Mark, '"The internet is our sword": Aspects of Online Anti-Semitism', in Roth, J. K. and Maxwell, E. (eds), *Remembering for the Future: The Holocaust in an Age of Genocide, volume 1 History* (London, Palgrave, 2001).

West, Cornel, *Prophesy Deliverance!: An Afro-American Revolutionary Christianity* (Louisville, KY, Westminster John Knox Press, 2002).

Wigoder, Geoffrey, *Jewish–Christian Relations since the Second World War* (Sherman Studies of Judaism in Modern Times) (Manchester, Manchester Univesity Press, 1988).

Willebrands, Johannes, *Church and Jewish People: New Considerations* (Mahwah, NJ, Paulist Press, 1992).

Wistrich, Robert S. *Antisemitism: The Longest Hatred* (London, Thames Methuen; New York, Schocken Books, 1991).

Wollaston, I., 'Auschwitz and the Politics of Commemoration', *Holocaust Educational Trust Research Papers* 1/5 (1999–2000).

Wright, Melanie J., '"Don't Touch My Holocaust": Responding to Life is Beautiful', *The Journal of Holocaust Education* 9.1 (2000), 19–32.

'The Nature and Significance of Relations between Historic Peace Churches and Jews during and after the Shoah', in Porter, Stanley E. and Pearson, Brook W. R. (eds), *Christian Jewish Relations through the Centuries* (Sheffield, Sheffield Academic Press, 2000), 400–25.

Yoder, John Howard, *The Jewish–Christian Schism Revisited* (London, SCM Press, 2002).

Young, J. E., *The Texture of Memory: Holocaust Memorials and Meaning* (New Haven, Yale University Press, 1993).

Writing and Rewriting the Holocaust: Narrative and the Consequences of Interpretation (Bloomington, Indiana University Press, 1988).

Zola, E., *The Dreyfus Affair: J'accuse and Other Writings*, ed. Pagès, Alain (New Haven, Yale University Press, 1996).

Zucotti, Susan, *The Italians and the Holocaust* (New York, Basic Books, 1987).

Under his Very Windows: The Vatican and the Holocaust in Italy (New Haven, Yale University Press, 2000).

Institutional documents on Jewish–Christian relations

Collections

Abbot, Walter M. (ed.), *The Documents of Vatican II* (New York, Guild Press, 1966).

Acta et Documenta Concilio Oecumenico Vaticano II Apparando, vols 1 and 2 (Rome, Vatican Polyglot Press, 1961).

Brockway, Allan, van Buren, Paul, Rendtorff, Rolf and Schoon, Simon, *The Theology of the Churches and the Jewish People: Statements by the World Council of Churches and its Member Churches* (Geneva, WCC, 1988).

Croner, Helga (ed.), *More Stepping Stones to Jewish–Christian Relations: An Unabridged Collection of Christian Documents 1975–1983* (Mahwah, NJ, Paulist Press, 1985).

Stepping Stones to Further Jewish–Christian Relations: An Unabridged Collection of Christian Documents [1948–1975] (London, Stimulus Books, 1977).

Ditmanson, Harold H. (ed.), *Stepping Stones to Further Jewish–Lutheran Relationships: Key Lutheran Statements* (Minneapolis, Augsburg, 1990).

Flannery, Austin (ed.), *Vatican Council II: The Conciliar and Post Conciliar Documents* (Northport, NY, Costello Publishing, 1975; Study Edition, 1987).

Henrix, Hans Hermann and Kraus, Wolfgang (eds), *Die Kirchen und das Judentum, vol. 2: Dokumente von 1986–2000* (Paderborn, Bonifatius Verlag; Gütersloh, Gütersloher Verlagshaus, 2001).

Rendtorff, Rolf and Henrix, Hans Hermann (eds), *Die Kirchen und das Judentum, vol. 1: Dokumente von 1945–1985* (Paderborn, Bonifatius Verlag; Gütersloh, Gütersloher Verlagshaus, 2001).

Major institutional statements since 1945

Alliance of Baptists, *Statement on Jewish–Christian Relations* (1995, revised 2003).

Anglican Communion, *Jews, Christians and Muslims: The Way of Dialogue* (Diennial Lambeth Conference, 1988).

Central Board of the Swiss Protestant Church Federation, *Reflections on the Problem of 'Church-Israel'* (1977).

Christian Scholars Group on Christian–Jewish Relations, *A Sacred Obligation: Rethinking Christian Faith in Relation to Judaism and the Jewish People* (2002).

Church of England, Inter Faith Consultative Group of the Archbishops' Council, *Sharing One Hope? The Church of England and Christian Jewish Relations. A Contribution to a Continuing Debate* (London, Church House Publishing, 2001).

Churches' Commission for Inter-Faith Relations of the Council of Churches for Britain and Ireland, *Christians and Jews: A New Way of Thinking* (1994).

Congregation for Sacred Doctrine, *Catechism of the Catholic Church* (1992).

Consultation of the National Council of Synagogues and the Bishops Committee for Ecumenical and Interreligious Affairs, *Reflections on Covenant and Mission* (2002).

Church of Sweden, *The Ways of God: Judaism and Christianity* (2001).

Episcopal Church (USA), *Christian–Jewish Dialogue* (1979).

European Lutheran Commission on the Church and the Jewish People, *Statement on Antisemitism* (2004).

European Lutheran Commission on the Church and the Jewish People, *Recommendations for the Liturgy* (2003).

Evangelical Church (Augsburg and Helvetian Confessions) in Austria, *Time to Turn: The Evangelical Churches in Austria and the Jews* (1998).

Evangelical Church in Germany, *Christians and Jews: A Manifesto 50 Years after the Weissensee Declaration* (2000).

Evangelical Church in Germany, Council of the, *Christians and Jews* (1975).

Evangelical Lutheran Church in America, *Guidelines for Lutheran–Jewish Relations* (1998).

International Catholic–Jewish Liaison Committee, *Recommendation on Education in Catholic and*

Jewish Seminaries and Schools of Theology (2001).

International Catholic–Jewish Historical Commission, *The Vatican and the Holocaust: A Preliminary Report* (2000).

International Council of Christians and Jews, *An Address to the Churches, Seelisberg (Switzerland): The 10 Points of Seelisburg* (1947).

John Paul II, *Universal Prayer: Confession of Sins and Asking for Forgiveness* (2000).

Joint Commission of the Chief Rabbinate of Israel's Delegation for Relations with the Catholic Church and the Holy See's Commission for Religious Relations with the Jews, *Declaration* (2003).

Leuenberg Church Fellowship, *Church and Israel: A Contribution from the Reformation Churches in Europe to the Relationship between Christians and Jews* (2001).

Lutheran Church of Bavaria, *Christians and Jews* (1998).

Lutheran World Federation, *Antisemitism and Anti-Judaism Today* (2001).

National Jewish Scholars Project, *Dabru Emet – A Jewish Statement on Christians and Christianity* (2000).

Netherlands Reformed Church, *Israel: People, Land and State* (1970).

Pontifical Biblical Commission, *The Jewish People and their Sacred Scriptures in the Christian Bible* (2001).

Pontifical Commission for Religious Relations with the Jews, *Guidelines and Suggestions for Implementing the Conciliar Declaration Nostra Aetate (n. 4)* (1975).

Pontifical Commission for Religious Relations with the Jews, *Notes on the Correct Way to Present the Jews and Judaism in Preaching and Catechesis* (1985).

Pontifical Commission for Religious Relations with the Jews, *We Remember: A Reflection on the Shoah* (1998).

Presbyterian Church (USA), *A Theological Understanding of the Relationship between Christians and Jews* (1987).

Religious Leaders of the Holy Land, *Alexandria Declaration* (2002).

Roman Catholic Bishops of Australia, Bishops' Committee for Ecumenical and Interfaith Relations, *The Faithfulness of the Lord Endures for Ever: Guidelines for Catholic–Jewish Relations* (1992).

Roman Catholic Bishops of France, *Declaration of Repentance* (1997).

Roman Catholic Bishops of Germany, *Statement on the 50th Anniversary of the Liberation of the Extermination Camp of Auschwitz 27 January 1945* (1995).

Roman Catholic Bishops of the Netherlands, *Supported by One Root: Our Relationship to Judaism* (1995).

Roman Catholic Bishops of Poland, *The Victims of Nazi Ideology* (1995).

Roman Catholic Bishops of the United States, Bishops' Committee for Ecumenical and Interreligious Affairs, *Criteria for the Evaluation of Dramatizations of the Passion* (1988).

Roman Catholic Bishops of the United States, Bishops' Committee for Ecumenical and Interreligious Affairs, *Guidelines for Catholic–Jewish Relations* (1967, revised 1985).

Roman Catholic Bishops of the United States, Bishops' Committee on the Liturgy, *God's Mercy Endures Forever: Guidelines on the Presentation of Jews and Judaism in Catholic Preaching* (Washington, DC, National Conference of Catholic Bishops, 1988).

Southern Baptist Convention, *Resolution on Jewish Evangelism* (1996).

Synod of the Evangelical Church of the Rhineland, Germany, *Statement on the Jewish Question* (1950).

Synod of the Evangelical Church of the Rhineland, Germany, *Towards Renovation of the Relationship of Christians and Jews* (1980).

Texas Conferences of Churches, *Dialogue: A Contemporary Alternative to Proselytisation* (1982).

United Church of Canada, *Bearing Faithful Witness: Statement on United Church–Jewish Relations Today* (2003).

United Methodist Church (USA), *Building New Bridges in Hope* (1996).

United Synagogue of Conservative Judaism, *Emet ve-Emunah* (Truth and Faith) (1988).

Vatican II, *Declaration on the Relation of the Church to Non-Christian Religions, Nostra Aetate* (1965).

World Council of Churches (WCC), *Ecumenical Considerations on Jewish–Christian Dialogue* (1979).

World Council of Churches (WCC), *Ecumenical Considerations for Dialogue and Relations with People of Other Religions: Taking Stock of 30 Years of Dialogue and Revisiting the 1979 Guidelines* (2004).

World Council of Churches, Commission on Faith and Order of the, *The Church and the Jewish people* (1967).

World Council of Churches, First Assembly of the, *The Christian Approach to the Jews* (1948).

World Council of Churches, Fifth Assembly of the, *The Middle East and Jerusalem* (1975).

World Council of Churches Sub-Committee: The Consultation on the Church and the Jewish People, *The Churches and the Jewish People: Towards a New Understanding* (1988).

Journals

Christian Jewish Relations (London, Institute of Jewish Affairs, 1980–91).

Current Dialogue (WCC)

Service International de Documentation Judéo-Chrétienne (SIDIC)

Studies in Jewish–Christian Relations (Center for Christian–Jewish Learning at Boston College)

Dictionaries

Cohn-Sherbok, Dan, *A Dictionary of Judaism and Christianity* (London, SPCK, 1991).

Klenicki, Leon and Wigoder, Geoffrey (eds), *A Dictionary of the Jewish–Christian Dialogue* (Expanded Edition) (Mahwah, NJ, Paulist Press, 1984).

Petuchowski, J. J. and Thoma, C., *Lexicon der jüdisch-christlichen Begegnung* (Freiburg, Herder, 1989).

Index of names

This index of persons named in the *Dictionary* excludes biblical authors and characters.